THE LEARNING COMPANION

Volume 5

H
World History

S̶W̶

Originally published in 1996 by Larousse

©1998 Larousse-Bordas
21 rue du Montparnasse
Paris 75006

First English Edition
©1999 by The Southwestern Company
P O Box 305140
Nashville, TN 37230

Second English Edition
©2000 by The Southwestern Company

Conception, direction and planning
Anne Tavard, François Demay

Associate publisher, London: Nicholas Bevan

Prepared and compiled for Larousse by
Market House Books Ltd, Aylesbury, England

General Editor: Dr Alan Isaacs

Volume Editor: Mark Salad

PAGE 351 CONSTITUTES AN EXTENSION OF THIS COPYRIGHT PAGE

All rights reserved under International and Pan-American
Copyright convention
No part of this publication may be reproduced, stored in a retrieval
system or transmitted in any form or by any means, electronic,
mechanical, photocopying, recording or otherwise, without prior
permission of the copyright holders.

ISBN 0-87197-477-0

Printed in the United States of America

Preface

THE LEARNING COMPANION, first published in 1999, is a completely new three-book (six-volume) reference for the family. It is published by Southwestern through agreement with Larousse, one of the largest and most respected publishing houses in the world, which created the majority of the content. Its contents have been carefully constructed around a universal core of knowledge that Larousse is able to identify after more than a century of experience in educational publishing.

The aim of THE LEARNING COMPANION is to help students make better grades. It makes accessible to family readership definitive information on the widest possible range of subjects. It is designed for students ranging from approximately age eleven through adult. The scope of THE LEARNING COMPANION is divided into six major topic areas, called volumes, with two volumes printed in each book. The content of each area is organized in chapters that clearly identify, define, and explain every subject. Within each chapter extensive use is made of colour illustrations and page design to represent the clearest possible explanations and examples.

Book 1		Book 2		Book 3	
Vol. 1	**Vol. 2**	**Vol. 3**	**Vol. 4**	**Vol. 5**	**Vol. 6**
W The World	**S** General Science	**B** Biological Science	**A** The Arts	**H** World History	**P** People/Society
CLIMATES, PEOPLES, AND LANGUAGES Climates and Vegetation, Peoples, and Languages	MATHEMATICS Numbers, Arithmetic, Algebra, Geometry, Calculus, Sequences and Series, Probability and Statistics	THE LIVING WORLD Cell Biology, Genetics, Biochemistry, Animal Anatomy, Plant Anatomy	THE VISUAL ARTS European Tradition, The Americas, 20th-Century Western Art, Visual Arts Worldwide	EUROPE AND THE MIDDLE EAST Early Civilizations, Medieval Europe, Early Modern Europe, The Industrial Age, Islamic World	SOCIAL IDEAS Social Sciences, Linguistics, Anthropology, Psychology, Philosophy, Metaphysics, Epistemology, Ethics, Religion, Mythology
CONTINENTS, REGIONS, AND COUNTRIES Europe, Asia, Africa, The Americas, Australia and Oceania, The Polar Regions, Statistics, Atlas	PHYSICS Mechanics, Heat, Thermodynamics, Optics, Acoustics, Electricity, Electro-magnetism, Relativity, Quantum Theory	THE CREATIONIST PERSPECTIVE Two Models of Origin, Entropy	MUSIC Europe and the Americas, 20th-Century Western Music, Music Worldwide	THE AMERICAS North America, Latin America	SOCIAL ORGANIZATION Politics and Government, Electoral Systems, Political Parties, Law, Legal Systems, Criminal and Civil Law, Economics, Business and Finance, Marketing, International Trade, Finance, and Investment, Communications and Media
EARTH SCIENCES AND ASTRONOMY Geology, Mineralogy, Hydrology, Oceanography, Meteorology, Observation, The Universe, Stars, Solar System, Space Exploration	CHEMISTRY Equilibrium, Acids and Bases, Oxidation, Kinetics, Inorganic and Organic Compounds APPLIED SCIENCE Technology, Computers	THE HUMAN FAMILY Child and Adult Development, Marriage and Family AGRICULTURE Crop Plants, Farm Animals, Fish Farming, Forestry BIOTECHNOLOGY Genetic Engineering	THE PERFORMING ARTS Western Theatre, Dance of Europe and the Americas, Theatre and Dance Worldwide, Cinema THE LITERARY ARTS Europe and the Americas, 20th-Century Western Literature, Literary Arts Worldwide	ASIA AND OCEANIA China, Japan, The Mongol Empires, Indian Subcontinent, Southeast Asia, Oceania SUB-SAHARAN AFRICA THE WORLD IN THE 20TH CENTURY CHRONOLOGY OF WORLD HISTORY	

What You Find in World History

WORLD HISTORY is classified into six **supersections**:
- Introduction to History
- Europe and the Middle East
- The Americas
- Asia and Oceania
- Sub-Saharan Africa
- The World in the 20th Century

Each of these covers the history of a whole area of the world. The supersections are divided into a total of 16 **sections**, which are split down further into 85 **chapters,** each of which contains numerous **subheadings**. Special self-contained **feature pages** follow some chapters.

REFERENCE TO SUPERSECTION

SECTION TITLE
Each of the six supersections in WORLD HISTORY is subdivided into sections. Each section title is followed by the first chapter in the section.

CHAPTER TITLE
Each chapter covers an important theme or period of history within the region of the world covered by each supersection.

CHAPTER SUMMARY
Chapter subheadings are listed in italic type beneath the chapter heading as a quick guide to the content.

SEE ALSO
The reader is referred to related chapters in WORLD HISTORY and other volumes of the encyclopedia for relevant additional reading.

KEY TERM
*Terms important in the context of the historical period and region being discussed are indicated in **bold italic type**.*

Europe and the Middle East

EARLY WESTERN CIVILIZATIONS

The Ancient Near East

Mesopotamian city-states • The empires of Akkad and Ur • The rise of Assyria and Babylon • The Near East in chaos • The Assyrian Empire • Egyptian unification and the Old Kingdom • Egypt reunited and the Middle Kingdom • The New Kingdom • Egypt, Babylonia, and Persia

SEE ALSO
Introduction:
- The Beginnings of History

This section:
- Greece and the Hellenistic World
- Persia

Sub-Saharan Africa:
- Early Africa

The European Tradition (vol. 4):
- Ancient Art

European and American Literature (vol. 4):
- The Earliest Literature

Religion (vol. 6):
- Mythology

The world's first civilization developed in **Mesopotamia**, a word used by the ancient Greeks meaning 'between the rivers' (Tigris and Euphrates). It was the diversity of the region that attracted the earliest settlers in the 6th millennium BC. Undulating grasslands in the north give way to a barren featureless plain in the south, bordered by lagoons and reed marshes rich in wildlife. The southern plain is outside the area of rain-fed agriculture: over the millennia, however, the rivers laid down thick deposits of very fertile silt and, once water was brought to this soil via ditches and canals, it proved a very attractive area to farmers. For materials, such as wood, stone, and metals, however, people had to look to the mountains in the north and east, where the first settlers had originated.

Mesopotamian City-states
By c. 3000 BC, southern Mesopotamia (Sumer) had been settled by farmers and fishermen, and excavations have revealed a coherent sophisticated culture based in cities. The people living beside the rivers Tigris and Euphrates built imposing temples of mud brick, ornamented with mosaic and fresco, for their gods; they also achieved considerable mastery in stonecutting, metallurgy, and pottery. The most remarkable evidence for this urban civilization comes from the site of ancient Uruk (biblical name Erech), which was probably the largest city in the world at this time. One of the greatest advances in human history took place at Uruk at the end of the 4th millennium BC: the invention of a system of writing. Using a reed stylus to draw on tablets of clay, administrators kept an account of agricultural produce. Initially the records took the form of pictures of objects being counted together, with signs representing numerals. Eventually these pictographs became more stylized and wedgelike, or **cuneiform** (from the Latin *cuneus*, wedge), and adapted to write the local language, Sumerian. As the writing system evolved, abstract ideas could be expressed, allowing the Sumerians to record not only lists, but also events happening around them.

Uruk was not the only large settlement in Sumer. The wealth of another of these city-states is demonstrated by the so-called 'Royal

The Standard of Ur *Dating from c. 2600 BC, this mosaic shows scenes of everyday life in Sumer. This detail depicts a royal banquet, illustrating styles of dress and furniture. The standard is inlaid with shell, lapis lazuli, and red limestone.* ▼

Gilgamesh and the Flood
Gilgamesh is thought to have been the ruler of Uruk around 2700 BC. Later myths credit him with a journey to the edge of the world where he met Utnapishtim, the survivor of a flood that the gods of Mesopotamia had sent to destroy mankind because they made too much noise. Utnapishtim built a boat and loaded it with animals, plants, and his family. Having survived the flood, he offered a sacrifice to the gods who, realizing their mistake, repopulated the world with humans.

20

RUNNING HEAD
Running heads at the top of each page serve as an additional guide to sections and chapters.

MARGIN TEXT BOX
Tinted boxes contain additional information on a particular aspect or historical person of the period being covered.

REFERENCE WORD
Bold upright type *indicates that additional information is given in a marginal text box or in a tinted feature panel.*

CAPTION
Concise captions explain each map, photograph, and illustration, highlighting their relevance to the historical theme or period being covered.

iv

MAP
Fully annotated and keyed for easy reference, each map in WORLD HISTORY *clarifies the main themes of the period being covered.*

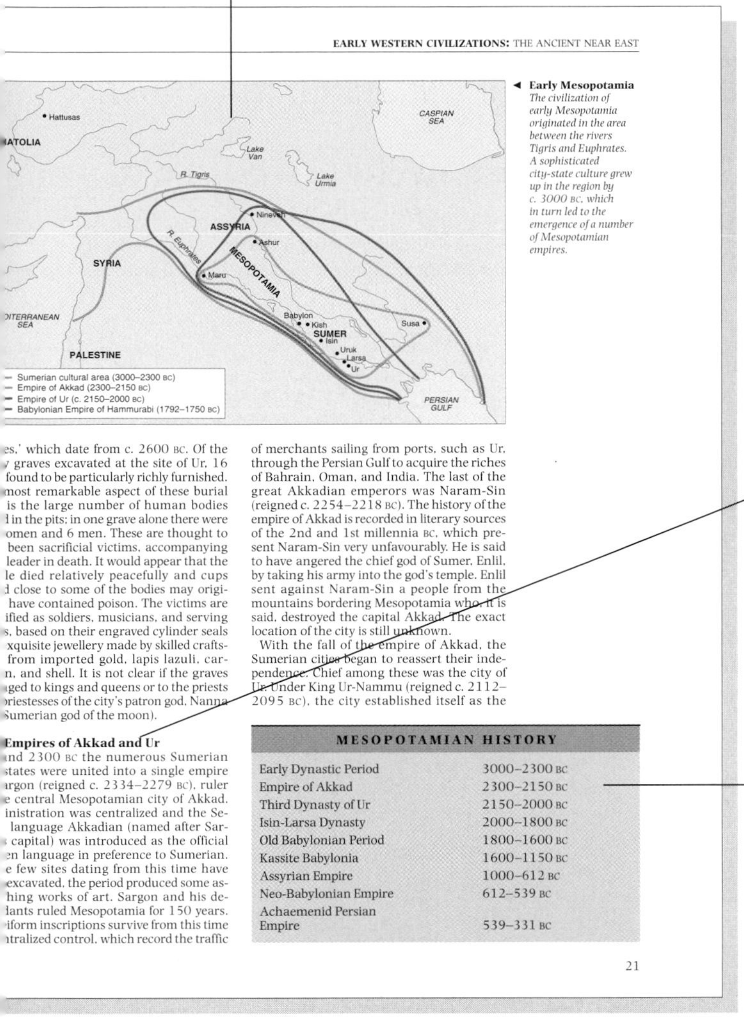

SUPERSECTION
WORLD HISTORY *is classified into six supersections, each providing coverage of the history of a whole region of the world.*

FEATURE PAGE
Special self-contained feature pages examine important historical and cultural topics in detail.

SUBHEADING
The main text within each chapter is divided both thematically and chronologically by subheadings in **bold type.**

TINTED PANEL
These contain more in-depth information or analysis on a particular aspect of the period examined in the chapter.

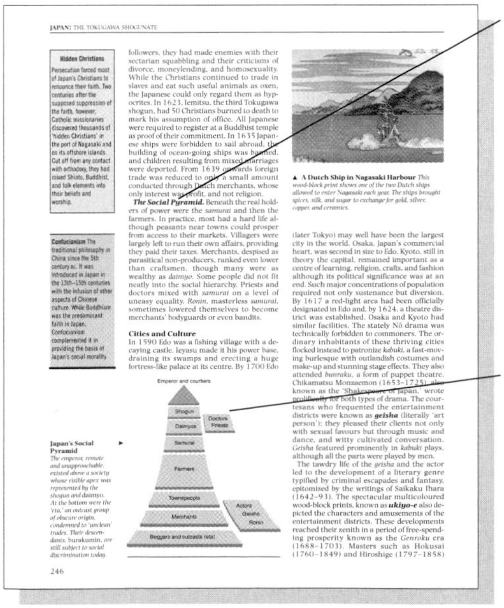

SUBSIDIARY HEADING
These introduce important aspects of the period being discussed.

QUOTATION
Extracts or quotations provide unique insights into the history of a particular period.

ARTWORK
Clearly labelled illustrations supplement important aspects of the historical period under discussion.

DEFINITION BOX
A blue tinted box between rules contains a formal definition of a term in the main text printed in **bold upright type.**

CROSS REFERENCE
References in the text direct the reader to other chapters in WORLD HISTORY, *or to other volumes in the set, in which further information can be found.*

ASIA AND OCEANIA

EARLY WESTERN CIVILIZATIONS: THE ANCIENT NEAR EAST

◄ **Early Mesopotamia**
The civilization of early Mesopotamia originated in the area between the rivers Tigris and Euphrates. A sophisticated city-state culture grew up in the region by c. 3000 BC, which in turn led to the emergence of a number of Mesopotamian empires.

- Sumerian cultural area (3000–2300 BC)
- Empire of Akkad (2300–2150 BC)
- Empire of Ur (c. 2150–2000 BC)
- Babylonian Empire of Hammurabi (1792–1750 BC)

es,' which date from c. 2600 BC. Of the y graves excavated at the site of Ur, 16 found to be particularly richly furnished. most remarkable aspect of these burial is the large number of human bodies d in the pits: in one grave alone there were omen and 6 men. These are thought to been sacrificial victims, accompanying leader in death. It would appear that the d close to some of the bodies may origi- have contained poison. The victims are ified as soldiers, musicians, and serving s, based on their engraved cylinder seals xquisite jewellery made by skilled crafts- from imported gold, lapis lazuli, car- n, and shell. It is not clear if the graves ged to kings and queens or to the priests riestesses of the city's patron god, Nanna Sumerian god of the moon).

Empires of Akkad and Ur
nd 2300 BC the numerous Sumerian states were united into a single empire argon (reigned c. 2334–2279 BC), ruler e central Mesopotamian city of Akkad. inistration was centralized and the Se- language Akkadian (named after Sar- capital) was introduced as the official en language in preference to Sumerian. e few sites dating from this time have excavated. the period produced some as- hing works of art. Sargon and his de- lants ruled Mesopotamia for 150 years. iform inscriptions survive from this time ntralized control, which record the traffic

of merchants sailing from ports, such as Ur, through the Persian Gulf to acquire the riches of Bahrain, Oman, and India. The last of the great Akkadian emperors was Naram-Sin (reigned c. 2254–2218 BC). The history of the empire of Akkad is recorded in literary sources of the 2nd and 1st millennia BC, which pre- sent Naram-Sin very unfavourably. He is said to have angered the chief god of Sumer, Enlil, by taking his army into the god's temple. Enlil sent against Naram-Sin a people from the mountains bordering Mesopotamia who, it is said, destroyed the capital Akkad. The exact location of the city is still unknown.

With the fall of the empire of Akkad, the Sumerian cities began to reassert their inde- pendence. Chief among these was the city of Ur Under King Ur-Nammu (reigned c. 2112– 2095 BC), the city established itself as the

MESOPOTAMIAN HISTORY	
Early Dynastic Period	3000–2300 BC
Empire of Akkad	2300–2150 BC
Third Dynasty of Ur	2150–2000 BC
Isin-Larsa Dynasty	2000–1800 BC
Old Babylonian Period	1800–1600 BC
Kassite Babylonia	1600–1150 BC
Assyrian Empire	1000–612 BC
Neo-Babylonian Empire	612–539 BC
Achaemenid Persian Empire	539–331 BC

21

MEDIEVAL WARFARE

62

JAPAN: THE TOKUGAWA SHOGUNATE

246

followers, they had made enemies with their sectarian squabbling and their criticisms of divorce, moneylending, and homosexuality. While the Christians continued to trade in slaves and eat such social animals as oxen, the Japanese could only regard them as hyp- ocrites. In 16-23, Iemitsu, the third Tokugawa shogun, had 50 Christians burned to death to mark his assumption of office. All Japanese were required to register at a Buddhist temple as proof of their commitment. In 1635 Japan- ese ships were forbidden to sail abroad, the building of ocean-going ships was banned, and children resulting from mixed marriages were deported. From 1639 onwards foreign trade was reduced to one small amount conducted through Dutch merchants, whose sole interest was profit, and not religion.

The Social Pyramid. Beneath the real hold- ers of power were the *samurai* and then the farmers. In practice, most had a hard life al- though peasants near towns could prosper from access to their markets. Villagers were largely left to run their own affairs, providing they paid their taxes. Merchants, despised as parasitical non-producers, ranked even lower than craftsmen, though many were as wealthy as *daimyo*. Some people did not fit neatly into the social hierarchy. Priests and doctors mixed with everyone on a level of uneasy equality. *Ronin*, masterless samurai, sometimes lowered themselves to become merchants' bodyguards or even bandits.

Cities and Culture
In 1590 Edo was a fishing village with a de- caying castle. Ieyasu made it his power base, draining its swamps and erecting a huge fortress-like palace at its centre. By 1700 Edo

▲ **A Dutch Ship in Nagasaki Harbour** *This mock-block print shows one of the two Dutch ships allowed to enter Nagasaki each year. The ships brought spices, silk, and sugar to exchange for gold, silver, copper, and ceramics.*

(later Tokyo) may well have been the largest city in the world. Osaka, Japan's commercial heart, was second in size to Edo. Kyoto, still in theory the capital, remained important as a centre of learning, religion, crafts, and fashion although its political significance was at an end. Such major concentrations of population required not only sustenance but diversion. By 1617 a red-light area had been officially designated in Edo and, by 1624, a theatre dis- trict was established. Osaka and Kyoto had similar facilities. The stately No dramas was technically forbidden to commoners. The or- dinary inhabitants of these thriving cities flocked instead to patronise *kabuki*, a fast-mov- ing burlesque with outlandish costumes and make-up and stunning stage effects. They also attended *bunraku*, a form of puppet theatre. Chikamatsu Monzaemon (1653–1725), known as the 'Shakespeare of Japan', wrote for the both types of drama. The cour- tesans who frequented the entertainment districts were known as *geisha* (literally 'art person'); they pleased their clients not only with sexual favours but through music and dance, and witty cultivated conversation. *Geisha* featured prominently in *kabuki* plays, although all the parts were played by men.

The tawdry life of the *geisha* and the actor led to the development of a literary genre typified by criminal escapades and fantasy, epitomised by the writings of Saikaku Ihara (1642–93). The spectacular multicoloured wood-block prints, known as *ukiyo-e* also de- picted characters and amusements of the entertainment districts. These developments reached their zenith in a period of free-spend- ing prosperity known as the *Genroku* era (1688–1703). Masters such as Hokusai (1760–1849) and Hiroshige (1797–1858)

Japan's Social Pyramid
The emperor, remote and isolated, symbolic- ally ratified above a society whose visible apex was represented by the shogun and daimyo. At the bottom were the 'eta,' *an outcast group of obscure origin, condemned to 'unclean' trades. Their descen- dants, burakumin, are still subject to social discrimination today.*

Emperor and courtiers
Shogun — Daimyo Priests
Daimyo
Bushi/Samurai
Farmers
Townspeople
Actors Geisha Ronin
Beggars and outcasts (eta)

SUB-SAHARAN AFRICA: EARLY MODERN AFRICA

300

Nilotic Tall Negroid *pastoral people who inhabit eastern Africa (the southern Sudan, parts of Kenya and Uganda, and neighbouring countries).*

after Alonso and his successors became clients of the Portuguese, their armies required to raid further into the interior to provide captives for the slave trade. Further south, Portuguese slave traders set up a port at Luanda and es- tablished similar trading connections with the Ngola of Ndongo. Subsequent Portuguese in- terventions caused conflict in the Luandan hinterland, which provided the Portuguese with a major source of slaves for their Brazilian colonies up until the 19th century.

Further inland the Lunda empire of Mwata Yamvo used a system of tribute collection and redistribution to become the major trading terminus of the central African interior to the 17th and 18th centuries. An important off- shoot of Lunda was Kasembe to the east. This kingdom was well placed to draw in a wide range of tribute, including copper from the nearby Shaba region, and to provide a wide range of transcontinental trading networks. To the southeast the Kalonga dynasty founded a Maravi empire, which derived its power from the ivory trade between the lower Zambezi River and the Swahili coast at Mozambique. To the south of the Zambezi, meanwhile, the Changamire Rozvi built an empire on the Zim- babwe plateau to rival that of Mutapa, a suc- cessor state to Great Zimbabwe. New goldfields were opened up and Portuguese traders in the Zambezi valley recognized Rozvi suzerainty with payments of tribute.

The demand [for slaves] is so great that we cannot count its size: since Portuguese traders are every day taking our people, sons of the land and sons of our noblemen and vassals and our relatives because [local] thieves and men of evil conscience seize them... and sell them... and, Sire, so great is the corruption and licentiousness that our country is being completely depopulated.
Afonso I, King of Kongo to the Portuguese King of Portugal (1526)

Peoples and States of Eastern Africa
By the 14th century, Bunyoro had become the major power of the lakeland region of east Africa, its peoples raiding for cattle and tribute as far south as Rwanda. The clans of Buganda, to the north of Lake Victoria, organized them- selves into a centralized state in the 17th cen- tury, surpassing Bunyoro in strength and importance by the 19th century.

East of Lake Victoria the Masai and other **Nilotic** cattle herdsmen pushed southwards through the Great Rift Valley. The Masai traded with Bantu-speaking farmers of cen- tral Kenya. In the Tanzanian region the Nyamwezi became important professional trad- ers between the interior ivory fields and the coast. On the east African coast the Portuguese built fortresses and used naval force to domi- nate Swahili trade. However, Portuguese vio- lence disrupted much of the trade they sought to control. By 1700, rival Arabs had confined the Portuguese to southern Mozambique.

During the 16th century Oromo pastoralists penetrated the southern Ethiopian highlands to become a permanent element of the south- ern Ethiopian population. Ethiopian kings, meanwhile, concentrated their power in the north, around the new capital of Gondar. They established trading links with the Ottoman Turks, who had seized the Eritrean port of Massawa in the 1550s. Many Somali nomads of the Horn, meanwhile, converted to Islam.

EUROPEAN CONTACT AND THE ATLANTIC SLAVE TRADE (1470–1800)	

Towards the end of the 15th century Portuguese ships ventured southwards along the coast of west Africa. Aim- ing to outflank Muslim North Africa and gain access to the gold of west Africa, and thence the spice trade of India and the Far East, they started trading at Elmina on the 'Gold Coast' of modern Ghana) in the 1480s. From 1532, however, the main demand of European traders was for slave labour to work the mines and plantations of the Americas. The Portuguese were joined by Dutch, French, Danish, and English slavers as the transatlantic

slave trade expanded from 20 000 a year in the early 17th century to between 50 000 and 100 000 a year in the 18th century, most of which were carried in English ships. See SOCIAL SCIENCES (VOL. 6): SOCIAL DIVISIONS.

European traders relied upon local African agents, rulers, and merchants to provide the captives and run the African side of the trade. Slavery was not unknown in African society before this time. Indeed, the states south of the Sahara had for centuries sold a certain number of captives into slavery across the desert. In most of west Africa, however, war captives had traditionally been put to work in the society of the victor and, in due course, were often ransomed back to their own country. Now the scale of the Atlantic trade dwarfed all other trading ac- tivity; the loss of between 10 and 20 million Africans over a period of 300 years was permanent. In exchange, Africans received liquor, guns, and other luxury goods. The exchange was unequal and caused an increasing amount of warfare in the interior.

Slave Capture *Africans captured in the interior were transported as slaves to European trading forts on the west African coast. From there captives were packed into ships for the transatlantic voyage. Many died of exhaustion or disease in the appalling conditions below deck.*

Contents

INTRODUCTION
TO HISTORY

INTRODUCTION

The Study of History

The writing of history • Modern historical method • The historian's tools • Archaeology • Schools of history

SEE ALSO

This section:
- The Beginnings of History

Early Western Civilizations:
- Greece and the Hellenistic World
- The Ages of Pericles
- The Growth of Rome
- The Roman Empire

Islamic World

China

Earth Sciences (vol. 1):
- Historical Geology

European and American Literature (vol. 4):
- Renaissance Literature
- The Age of Reason

Social Sciences (vol. 6):
- Human Societies and Sociological Perspectives
- Physical Anthropology

Most societies display a preoccupation with their past, whether through ancestor worship, the chronicles of holy men, the sagas of minstrels, or the performing of national ceremonies. Though the major developments in historical writing have taken place in the West, there are important schools originating in China and the Islamic world.

The Writing of History

The practice of recording historical events is an ancient one. Examples survive from early Egyptian civilizations, and the chronicles of the early Jewish kingdoms survive among the books of the Old Testament. The writing of analytical history, however, began with Herodotus (c. 484 BC–c. 425 BC) and Thucydides (c. 460 BC–c. 395 BC), who wrote towards the end of the classical age in ancient Greece; Polybius (c. 205 BC–123 BC), who wrote when Greece was falling under the dominion of Rome; and Livy (59 BC–17 AD), Tacitus (c. 55–120 AD), and Plutarch (c. 46–120 AD), the famous historians of imperial Rome. Both Greek and Roman writers aimed to provide 'exemplar history,' the study of which was a preparation for public life, preserving the memory of glorious deeds, and identifying past errors.

In the postclassical period writing about the past, like all scholarly activity, was left almost exclusively to clerics, who wrote straightforward accounts generally lacking in explanation and analysis. Examples include the *Anglo-Saxon Chronicle* and the *Ecclesiastical History* of St Bede (c. 673–735). Such writers as Otto of Freising (1111–58), and the Burgundian historian of the Hundred Years' War, Jean Froissart (c. 1333–c. 1400), provided fairly reliable accounts of their own times. They were, however, heavily influenced by St Augustine's *City of God* (426), a work of Christian apologetics that portrayed the history of the world as the long unfolding of God's will.

The Analysis of Sources. A tradition gradually developed of scrutinizing the authenticity of charters and other documents to establish the accuracy of sources; for example, the technical basis of historical study was advanced when Lorenzo Valla (1407–57) demonstrated that the Donation of Constantine, upon which many of the claims of the Church were based, was a forgery. Renaissance writers, particularly Leonardo Bruni (c. 1370–1444), Niccoló Machiavelli (1469–1527), and Francesco Guicciardini (1483–1540), turned again to the historical style of the classical authors in carefully analysing their sources and in seeking to teach political lessons. Stimulated by the French Wars of Religion (1562–98), the publication of great collections of primary texts started to appear (for example, those by the French Benedictines at St Maur). Textual criticism was further developed by Jean Mabillon (1632–1707), whose *De Re Diplomatica* was published in 1681; this work established the basis for 'erudite' history.

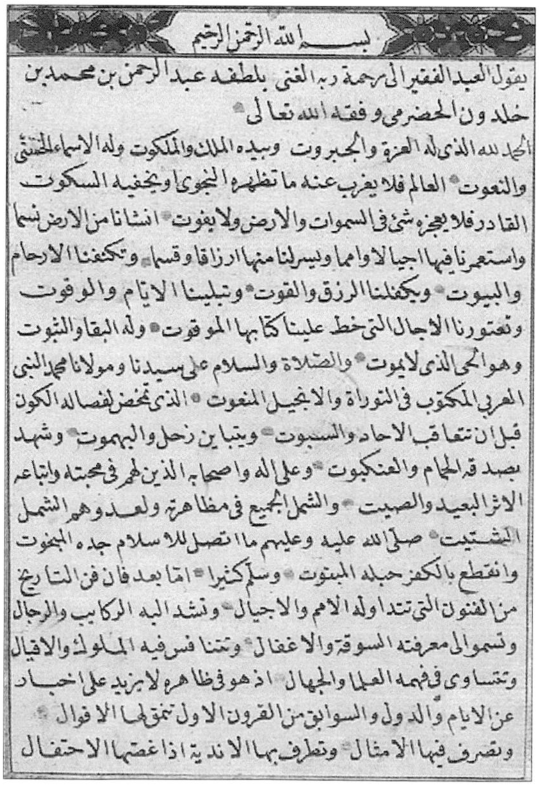

The historians of the Enlightenment completed the departure from the theological basis

بسم الله الرحمن الرحيم
يقول العبد الفقير الى رحمة ربه الغنى بلطفه عبد الرحمن بن محمد بن
خلدون الحضرمى وفقه الله تعالى
الحمد لله الذى له العزة والجبروت وبيده الملك والملكوت وله الاسماء الحسنى
والنعوت العالم فلا يعزب عنه ما تظهره النجوى او يخفيه السكوت
القادر فلا يعجزه شئ فى السموات والارض ولا يفوت انشانا من الارض نسما
واستعمرنا فيها اجيالا وامما ويسر لنا منها ارزاقا وقسما وتكنفنا الارحام
والبيوت ويكفلنا الرزق والقوت وتبلينا الايام والوقوت
وتعتورنا الاجال التى خط علينا كتابها الموقوت وله البقا والثبوت
وهو الحى الذى لا يموت والصلاة والسلام على سيدنا ومولانا محمد النبى
العربى المكتوب فى التوراة والانجيل المنعوت الذى تمخض لفصاله الكون
قبل ان تتعاقب الاحاد والسبوت ويتباين زحل والبهموت وشهد
بصدقه الحمام والعنكبوت وعلى اله واصحابه الذين لهم فى محبته واتباعه
الاثر البعيد والصيت والشمل الجميع فى مظاهرته ولعدوهم الشمل
الشتيت صلى الله عليه وعليهم ما اتصل للاسلام جده المبخوت
وانقطع بالكفر حبله المبتوت وسلم كثيرا اما بعد فان فن التاريخ
من الفنون التى تتداوله الامم والاجيال وتشد اليه الركايب والرحال
وتسمو الى معرفته السوقة والاغفال وتتنافس فيه الملوك والاقيال
وتتساوى فى فهمه العلما والجهال اذ هو فى ظاهره لا يزيد على اخبار
عن الايام والدول والسوابق من القرون الاول تنمق لها الاقوال
وتضرب فيها الامثال وتطرف بها الاندية اذا غصها الاحتفال

al-Muqaddimah ►
The first page of Ibn Khaldun's history, from an edition produced in 1805, is shown here. Ibn Khaldun's history is highly regarded today as a great historiographic work, demonstrating its author's skill in reconstructing the important historical trends over centuries, formulating general laws that affect societies, and analysing sources.

of historical writing, by extending it into the realms of society and culture. This trend can be seen most clearly in *Essay on the Manners and Character of the Nations* (1756) by Voltaire (1794–1778), in the works of scholars based at Göttingen, such as Johann Gatterer (1727–99), and in Scotland in the writings of David Hume (1711–76) and William Robertson (1721–93). Much of the former political emphasis, however, was maintained in such works as *The Decline and Fall of the Roman Empire* (1776–88) by Edward Gibbon (1737–94).

The aims of the Enlightenment historians were often as much literary as historical. It was only in the 19th century that the true foundations of modern academic history were laid. Historians of the 19th century were the first to appreciate the importance of studying past peoples in the context of their own time and cultures. This approach was derived in part from the hitherto neglected works of Giovanni Battista Vico (1668–1744) and J. G. von Herder (1744–1803).

Empirical History. The need to substantiate every statement from reliable historical sources was also developed in this period. The leading writer of empirical source-based history was the Prussian Leopold von Ranke (1795–1886). The founding, in 1821, of the *École des Chartes* in Paris was an early sign of the coming professionalization of history, which accelerated in the late 19th and early 20th centuries, as learned societies with their own journals were founded and systematic history courses established in the universities. Instead of broad surveys, which covered several centuries, historians now produced detailed highly focused works, typically in the form of monographs or articles.

While empirical professional history predominated, there were challenges from two directions, both of which continue. T. B. Macaulay (1800–59), in England, sought to write history in a form that would rival novels in popular appeal. On the other hand, the work of Karl Marx (1818–83) and the development of the social sciences led to support for a form of history that would, like the natural sciences, be 'law-based.'

China. Historical events began to be recorded in China as early as 1000 BC. The first real histories appeared after China was unified under one ruler (221 BC). The earliest such work to survive is Si-ma Qian's *Shi ji* ('Historical Records'; c. 85 BC), which greatly influenced later Chinese official histories, written up until the end of the last Chinese imperial dynasty in 1911. History played an important part in Chinese scholarly life; Confucius stressed the moral content of the lessons to be learned from history. One of the main functions of Chinese government thus became

◀ **Leopold von Ranke**
The Berlin historian placed a new scholarly emphasis on the study of history, the use of primary sources, and the identification of these for the benefit of the reader.

the recording and preservation of records, which resulted in the creation of a vast body of historical writings. These became more subtle and critical with time. One of the greatest historical writers was Liu Zhi-ji (661–721), who wrote *Shi tong*, the first history of Chinese historiography. The tradition of historical narrative in China is unmatched in any other country before modern times. It became increasingly sophisticated and in the 20th century adopted some elements of modern Western historiography.

Islam. Since the birth of Islam, in the 7th century, the strong Muslim historiographic tradition has produced works on Muslim conquests, world histories, dynastic histories, court annals, and biographical accounts. Following in this tradition, Ibn Khaldun (died 1406) attempted to compile a comprehensive view of history. In the *al-Muqaddimah*, the introduction to his *Kitab al-ibar* (a projected general history), Ibn Khaldun sought to explain the historical development of Islamic countries, based partly on his own experiences gained on numerous political missions. He created the first 'sociological' unbiased study of history; some of Ibn Khaldun's analyses are still highly respected. In a number of countries, particularly India, historical works appeared only after Muslim conquest or conversion to Islam.

Modern Historical Method

All scholars are the product of their own society, with their basic assumptions and preoccupations determined by that culture. The task of professional historians is to study past cultures and the people belonging to them; they must, therefore, put aside their own

Chinese Historians

One of the most notable contributors to the tradition of Chinese historical narrative is Ban Gu (32–92 AD). His prime achievement, the vast *Han shu* (The History of the Former Han Dynasty), has provided a model on which later Chinese historians have based their work. Zhu Xi (1130–1200), a philosopher and civil servant, produced a work, in 1172, that served as the basis for the first comprehensive history of China to be published in Europe – *Histoire Générale de la Chine* (1777–85) by J. A. M. Moyriac de Mailla.

▲ A Flat Earth
This map, produced in 1459, illustrates the belief, held by Europeans in the 15th century, that the earth was flat; it is, therefore, a most valuable primary source.

cultural conditioning in order to understand the societies of the past in their own context. Historians must examine the relics and traces left by the past (***primary sources***), which are often fragmentary, imperfect, and difficult to interpret.

If experience has taught historians to be cautious about the possibilities of objectivity, it has also taught them to be sceptical about grand theories of historical development governed by general laws. However, since the sources themselves do not present simple and unbiased accounts, historians cannot dispense with their own concepts and theories in order to bring together and make sense of disparate pieces of information; there is always scope for differences of interpretation.

In discussing historical methodology, it has to be made clear that 'history' is not a synonym for 'the past'; history is rather the collections of bodies of knowledge about the past, which have been produced by historians as a result of a careful analysis of primary sources. Since historians investigate many eras and many cultures, there is no single unified body of knowledge, let alone one universal explanatory framework.

Without a knowledge of the past, societies would be completely without identity; they would lack important resources for tackling the problems of the present. History, therefore, assumes as important a role as science in the existence of societies; both are required to be as accurate as possible. Modern historical methodology is designed to cope with all the difficulties and contradictory pressures inherent in the subject; its aim is to produce accurate and objective accounts of specific and clearly defined areas of the human past.

The first step a historian must take is to devise a strategy; this will involve selecting from the existing accounts of other historians (***secondary sources***) a gap, or unresolved problem, in the current body of knowledge on a given subject, or an area that can profitably be re-examined. The initial sets of primary sources to be examined must then be identified; as the work proceeds, it will become clear that further sets of sources will need to be drawn upon.

Primary Sources. Primary sources are documents or objects created by people in the past, for their own purposes, during the course of their everyday lives (see panel). The information they convey can be fairly direct, such as the record of an event or a decision. More often, however, the information that the historian seeks has to be derived indirectly, from a whole range of sources in which nuances and contradictions have to be balanced. Attitudes towards spouses, for instance, may be derived from wills; towards crime, not from the law itself, but from the detail of its enforcement. The nature of social hierarchy can come from a wide range of sources, which may include wage records or novels. The historian is usually searching, not for single facts, but for evidence of material conditions, states of mind, values, interconnections, balances between intention and outcome, and other matters of considerable complexity.

There are seven preliminary questions that must be asked of every source before any reliable evidence can be extracted:
1. Is the source authentic? An authentic 12th-century charter can tell its reader something about government in the 12th century, while a 16th-century forgery of a 12th-century charter can only reveal something about the 16th century. For example, the famous 'Peasant's Charter,' apparently originating in the Torreban rebellion in 17th-century Brittany, is available only in two later, and slightly discrepant, copies. The document offers rare insights into peasant mentalities only if it is genuine, which most scholars now believe it to be. Even a forgery, once it is recognized as such, and the circumstances of its fabrication known, can be of great intrinsic interest.
2. What is its place of origin? Sources are often consulted in the archives or museum that has collected them. For physical artefacts, however, it may be crucially important to know where the source actually originated.
3. When exactly was the source produced? Dating a source can be a difficult task in itself;

TYPES OF PRIMARY SOURCES

Records Central government (e.g. laws, charters, parliamentary records); local (e.g. electoral records, parish registers); other formal records (e.g. those of political parties, trade unions, etc.).

Private business (e.g. contracts, accounts, wage rates).

Surveys and reports Censuses, reports of commissions.

Chronicles and histories Monastic chronicles, town chronicles, civic histories.

Personal sources Letters, diaries, photographs.

Media and polemical sources Newspapers, cartoons, films, radio and television recordings, pamphlets, treatises, etc.

Archaeology Buildings, inscriptions, pots, artefacts, coins, machin-ery, furniture, etc.

Artistic sources Novels, plays, poetry, paintings, sculp-ture, architecture, films.

Other Maps, place names, aerial photography, oral accounts, advertisements, blood groups, statistics.

once it has been dated, the historian still has to establish the date's significance in terms of its relevance to the research being undertaken.

4. What is the exact nature of the source? Whether it is a private letter, an official report, or a public document or record will usually be obvious. This will determine the type of information contained in the source and, therefore, the techniques required to analyse it.

5. Who created the source? The author of the source would have been subject to the attitudes and prejudices of his sex, class, religion, occupation, and political views, which would have influenced his writing. Historians must take these factors into account, and also consider how, for what purpose and for whom the source was produced. Only when these matters have been determined, can the historian begin to make use of the information contained in the source.

6. To what extent does the source actually provide first-hand information on the topic under investigation? It may comprise a digest of other people's reports or be merely hearsay or conjecture. Historians cannot be satisfied with any source that merely happens to mention the issue they are researching; they must always seek out the most direct, most relevant, and often the most inaccessible sources.

7. What precisely was the source intended to convey? How was it understood by people of the time? Certain branches of historical investigation are specifically concerned with the illumination of meaning or with deciphering unfamiliar languages. The historian, however, must also be conversant with technical terms, contemporary allusions, and archaic usages.

The most important task, of course, is extracting the relevant information: both that which is directly communicated as well as the 'unwitting testimony.' The latter would consist of the many nuances, assumptions, and values indirectly conveyed by the source, which, for the historian, may be the most valuable elements in the source.

Carrying out and recording research are not entirely separate activities. It is only in producing written drafts that historians can begin to work out the sequences, structures, and interconnections indicated by the sources. Historical methodology entails an iterative process; as writing proceeds, gaps become apparent, and a return to the sources is required. The final written product of the research – an article or a book – requires a coherent structure; the purpose of the historical method is to ensure that this structure genuinely relates to the past and is not an arbitrary imposition on the part of the historian.

The Historian's Tools

The need for societies to study their history is testified by the fact that all modern societies have a highly organized historical profession, national archives, and a central library housing historic books and documents. A great range of bibliographical aids is now readily accessible to historians by computer, which can inform them of works already published on the subject of their research. Many of the cataloguing systems used in libraries and archives are now computerized. Modern technology, in the form of photocopiers and word processors, also aids the historian in recording exactly the primary sources on which all historical research must be based.

For the study of all pre-modern documentary sources, whether on parchment or paper,

To history has been assigned the office of judging the past, of instructing the present for the benefit of future ages. To such high offices this work does not aspire: it wants only to show what actually happened.

Leopold von Ranke, in the preface to his first book, *History of the Latin and German Nations from 1494–1514* (1824)

National Archives, Washington DC
Inscribed on the front of this building are the legends 'What is Past is Prologue' and 'Study the Past.' ▼

stratigraphy A vertical section through the earth showing the relative positions of the human artefacts and, therefore, the chronology of successive levels of occupation.

Historical Guns

In the USA there is still a business in manufacturing handguns, which are individually handcrafted as they were in the late 18th and early 19th centuries, before the introduction of the mass production of interchangeable parts. For both economic and military historians, the study of contemporary craftsmen at work in the old manner provides a unique type of historical source.

---

the related techniques of diplomatics, palaeography, and philology are essential.

Diplomatics. This discipline originated from the practical need to distinguish between genuine charters and forged ones; from the 17th century it became the primary tool of erudite history. Diplomatics concerns the formal qualities that distinguish one type of document from another, originals from drafts, and drafts from copies. It involves specialist knowledge of the characteristics of the offices issuing documents, such as royal households or chanceries, and the signatures and seals intended to confirm authenticity. For the analysis of seals, the techniques of ***sigillography***, which specializes in identifying the distinctive iconographies associated with royal seals, official seals, religious seals, town seals, commercial seals, and personal seals, are employed.

Palaeography. Concerned with the more physical aspects of documents, palaeography focuses on the ink and implements used, the style of writing, elucidation of abbreviations, the significance of decorative elements, and the type of binding used. The primary purpose of palaeography is to ensure that the historian is reading the document he believes he is reading, as well as understanding what the document was originally intended to convey. Diplomatics and palaeography together assist in establishing dates and place of origin of documents, and in distinguishing the authentic from the forgery.

Philology. As the basic discipline of many of the pioneering scholarly historians at the time of Ranke, philology is concerned with linguistics and exact translation. Historians are often confronted with obscure languages or hieroglyphics. Deciphering ancient inscriptions in stone is the specialist province of ***epigraphy***. Linguistic skills continue to be of great importance to historians, especially with the development of comparative and global history.

Archaeology

The discipline of archaeology represents historical methodology in its most potent form. There would be no knowledge at all of vast areas of the remote human past without the sources discovered and analysed by archaeological techniques. Archaeological investigations can be categorized into many types; for example, some are closely coordinated with written sources, while others open up hitherto unknown areas for investigation.

Most potential sites are discovered through systematic and informed reconnaissance work, though occasionally they are uncovered by accident; for example, the first cache of Dead Sea Scrolls was discovered, in 1947, by a Bedouin looking for a stray animal. In more recent years, sites have frequently been unearthed during road and building construction. Traditionally reconnaissance work has depended upon hints from written records, old place names, and the surfacing of the odd suggestive artefact. A vital tool is the design of specialist archaeological maps, onto which all existing information is systematically collated, thus pointing to areas where excavation might be fruitful. Aerial photography has served to highlight variations in soil colour and in density of crops, not apparent at ground level, which can suggest the existence of a site. Methods such as simply tapping the ground can indicate the existence of substructures, while electrical prospecting, based on the degree of electrical conductivity present in the soil, has been in use since the 1940s. Since 1957 deep probes combined with the use of photographic periscopes have been employed to reveal underground walls and chambers as, for example, in the case of the Estruscan tomb at Monte Abbatone in Italy. Various electromagnetic methods were developed in the late 1950s, one notable result being the discovery of the site of Sybaris, also in Italy.

Excavation. Two main methods of excavation are now in use: ***trenching***, which opens up only certain sections of the site, and ***open stripping***, which exposes the entire site. There are various types of archaeological site (see panel), which require different methods of excavation.

On most sites the fundamental activity is digging. While preliminary opening of the site may be done mechanically, the actual work is extremely delicate, often likened to that of a surgeon. Deep trial trenches, or sondages, may

---

DATING TECHNIQUES

Fluorine analysis of bones This was developed in the 1950s. The level of fluorine content in bones can indicate the period from which they date (the Piltdown Man hoax was exposed in this way).

Clay-varve counting A method used to estimate the age of glacial deposits formed during the ice ages.

Dendochronology The study of the annual growth rings of trees is used to date historical events.

Radiocarbon dating This technique is used to estimate the age of organic materials containing carbon atoms, such as wood, bone, or ash, up to 40 000 years old.

Potassium-argon dating This form of radioactive dating is used to date certain minerals. It has shown that the remains of humans and their artefacts that have been found in East Africa date back to at least two million years ago.

Thermoluminescence This technique is based on the fact that certain clay materials absorb and store energy through exposure to radiation, the amount stored increasing with time. When pottery finds are heated, the energy appears as light (thermoluminescence), which can be measured.

See EARTH SCIENCES (VOL. 1): HISTORICAL GEOLOGY.

TYPES OF ARCHAEOLOGICAL SITES

Tells are huge mounds, caused by the accumulation of matter on sites of human habitation over a period of centuries. Smaller tells are often exhaustively excavated, while larger ones are not. Famous examples are Troy (Turkey) and Ur (Iraq).

Closed sites can be pyramids, chambered tombs, barrows, or sealed caves. They are usually exhaustively excavated.

Sites without surface traces (identified by reconnaissance methods). Trenching is the usual method of excavation on such sites.

Cliffs or gravel beds have proved particularly rich in early Stone Age finds.

Underwater sites were made more accessible by the pioneering underwater work of Jacques Yves Cousteau (1910–   ), near Marseille, who developed the technique of scuba diving.

first be cut for inspecting **stratigraphy**. Trowels and brushes are then used for meticulous excavation work. Careful written records are compiled, including diagrams and photographs, as the excavation proceeds. However, as with all historical sources, little direct use can be made of the various discoveries until they have been analysed and classified.

Methods of Analysis. More than any other source, archaeological artefacts lend themselves to analysis by advanced scientific techniques in determining two fundamental facts: place of origin and date. However, the major dating strategies, stratigraphy and relative dating, far predate the wonders of contemporary science. More complex sites, when excavated thoroughly, reveal a series of layers superimposed on each other, the lowest layers being the oldest, the top layer the most recent. Each layer can be related chronologically to another. More accurate dating depends upon finding objects within particular layers, which can be more precisely dated, such as pottery of a known style or coins featuring a known king. Archaeologists can also date objects or remains from sites where there is little or no contextual knowledge (as provided by written records, for example); early European sites can be dated by comparison and correlation with better-documented sites, such as those of ancient Egypt and the ancient Near East; this technique is known as *cross-dating*.

However, traditional dating methods, ultimately dependent on lists of monarchs, coins, records, etc., can only be used for sources no older than 5000 years; stratigraphy is also far

from infallible. Archaeologists must, therefore, take advantage of current scientific dating techniques (see panel).

The disciplines of geology, petrology (analysis of rocks), and metallurgy have been central in determining the place of origin of materials and objects. For example, petrological analysis of Neolithic polished stone axes has made it possible to establish the location of prehistoric axe factories and trade routes.

The final outcome of an archaeological dig is a full printed report, which is usually considered to have the status of a primary source, as it is still open to future researchers for alternative interpretation. The fundamental primary sources are the site itself (if preserved), its components (walls, etc.), and the artefacts discovered there (which, if in reasonable condition, would be stored in an archaeological museum).

Other Tools. Both archaeologists and historians make use of epigraphy (the study of inscriptions), *numismatics* (the study of coins), *palaeobotany* (the study of fossil plants from peat bog and lake sediments, which provides evidence of vegetational and cultivational change), and *serology* (which analyses the distribution of blood groups in modern societies to indicate early settlement patterns).

There are a number of other processes used by historians and archaeologists:
• Aerial photography can be used to reveal, for

Underwater Discoveries
In 1958 the American Peter Throckmorton, a pioneer of underwater archaeology, discovered a number of ancient ships off the coast of southern Turkey; he then discovered a 14th-century BC shipwreck, the oldest ever recorded, at Cape Gelidonya. George Bass, developed the mapping of wrecks using stereophotographs while investigating a Byzantine wreck in the same area from 1961; he used the first two-man submarine built for archaeological work.

Underwater Archaeology *A scuba diver measures the line of an underwater site – the wreck of a boat off the coast of Bermuda – prior to its thorough investigation.* ▼

example, the contours of a medieval village or former field plans.

- Place names can be used to plot earlier settlement patterns.
- Data processing. The development of much cheaper, yet increasingly sophisticated, computers has allowed historians to manipulate and correlate hitherto unmanageable amounts of information. At the same time, since computers tend to generate work before they reduce it, the data input for analysis often has to be confined to limited populations (for example, studies of class are restricted to single towns, rather than a whole country). In spite of this the gain in accuracy of research results remains of inestimable value. Important historical documents, such as the Domesday Book, which provide a wealth of information on the society of a certain period, are now being transferred onto computer disk by new computerized laser-reading techniques. The result is that users can: search for words or phrases in specific contexts; display on the screen the pieces of text in which these words and phrases appear; sort information to predefined criteria; and abstract statistical values for analysis, displaying the results in tables, graphs, or maps as required. The feeding into electronic data banks of whole texts, or classes of texts, is having far-reaching implications in terms of the scope of historical research. Computer graphics have also enabled historians to reconstruct events (such as battles), historical sites, buildings, and artefacts, by using data from traditional sources, particularly archaeological finds.

The direct observation of surviving customs and practices, technical processes, and agricultural methods can also provide valuable historical information. Historians of medieval Europe study the practices still current in developing countries, in the hope that they will provide information on the agricultural techniques in Europe in earlier times.

Another area of historical research involves the study of surviving streets and buildings. The discipline of industrial archaeology falls into this category; it involves the study of relics of the industrial age, including buildings, the remains of buildings, machinery, and fragments of machines. Artefacts, furniture, and utensils are also valuable clues as to the way life was lived in the past.

Artistic Sources. Finally, historians are able to draw on the arts as historical sources. However, while such media as novels, poems, plays, films, television programmes, sculptures, paintings, operas, etc., provide rich evidence of the attitudes and assumptions of the period in which they were produced, as artistic works they are primarily works of the imagination, intended to entertain. This is not, of course, true of news media (e.g. newspapers, film news reels, television footage, radio recordings, and, more recently, video tapes); these must be treated differently, though the entertainment element inherent in all mass media should never be forgotten. For data on such matters as wage rates and material conditions, the historian would not look first to a novel of the period, but to sources that are much more direct and authoritative. Historians studying artistic sources must be familiar with the artistic conventions of the period being researched.

Schools of History

The many different kinds of historical accounts produced by historians can be categorized in various ways: by content, or by the theory and methods espoused. By the end of the 19th century, the writing of history was divided into two main branches: political, constitutional, and diplomatic history on one side, and economic, social, and cultural studies on the other. Historians may also be divided into those favouring a ***nomothetic*** approach, who seek to discover patterns and advance theories of history, and those favouring an ***idiographic***, or empiricist, approach. Those who continue to see history as a branch of literature have been less influential, although this approach was revived in the 1980s, in the USA, by two British historians, David Cannadine and Simon Schama. It may also be noted that the 'new' schools with which historians sometimes identify themselves are often very similar to each other. While many historians do deny belonging to any particular school of history, a small number of schools and theories have been extremely influential.

Marxism. The Marxist school has been the most important within the nomothetic group,

Aerial Photography
This aerial shot, taken over central England, shows the outline of what is thought to be a lane settlement with surrounding field patterns, dating from post-Roman times (from the early 5th century on). The circle in the bottom right-hand corner indicates the possible former presence of an Iron Age farmstead, thus locating a potential archaeological site. ▼

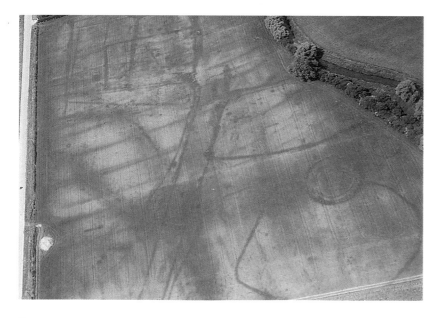

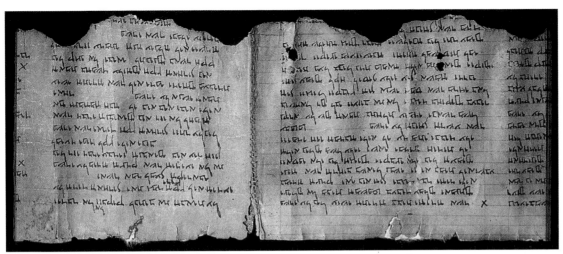

◄ **Dead Sea Scrolls**
First discovered in Israel in 1947, the scrolls date from 250 BC to 70 AD. Over 500 in number, they include many Old Testament texts, psalms, and prayers. Written in Hebrew and Aramaic scripts of the period, the scrolls provide historians with an insight into life in a Jewish community at the time of early Christianity.

affecting even those who are non-Marxists. Marxists claim that there is a clear pattern in the way that the past unfolds into the present, and on the basis of this they predict a pattern for the future. According to Marxist theory the great revolutions in Europe (1642 in England and 1789 in France) embodied the triumph of the bourgeoisie in their struggle against the aristocracy; now the struggle is between the working class and the bourgeoisie. The fact that the working class has so far failed is attributed to 'ideology,' the values and beliefs of the bourgeoisie, which the workers have been tricked into accepting. Perhaps the most influential Marxist historian of recent times was Georges Lefebvre (1874–1959), whose meticulous work actually helped prepare the way for the discrediting of the Marxist interpretation of the French Revolution.

Post-structuralism. This may properly be defined as a metaphysical school, since it was devised not by historians but by philosophers, psychologists, and literary critics in and around the École Normale Supérieure in Paris, in the later 1960s. Post-structuralism derives its fundamental ideas about social and historical development from Marxism; most of its adherents are committed to the notion of destroying 'bourgeois humanism'; they dismiss the history of traditional historians as mere ideology. However, the most celebrated figure of the post-structuralist school, Michel Foucault (1926–84), has written important historical studies of hospitals, crime and punishment, madness, and sex, which it is impossible for historians to ignore.

Economic and Econometric History. This fundamentally empiricist approach to history is mainly defined by its content, but also by its emphasis on statistics and on empirical economic theory. The major 20th-century advocates of this school are Sir John Clapham (1873–1946), effectively the founder of the British school of economic history, Ernest Labrousse who, in the 1930s and 1940s, published influential studies of economic crisis at the time of the French Revolution, and, in the USA, R.W. Fogel (1926–).

Women's History and Feminist History. One of the results of the feminist movement of the late 20th century has been a new interest in the roles and status of women in past societies. Many thoroughly empiricist accounts of the history of women's roles and experiences have been produced; these have been eclipsed, however, by feminist history, written from a committed feminist viewpoint and often employing the modes of post-structuralism. *Becoming Visible, Women in Europen History* (1977), by Americans Renata Bridenthal and Claudia Koonz, was a major work of this type and addresses such issues as the role of women in the Renaissance.

The Annales School. The most influential and prestigious historical school of the later 20th century takes its name from a journal with which it is associated. Founded in 1929 by Lucien Febvre (1878–1956) and Marc Bloch (1886–1944), *Annales* aimed at an 'integral history,' which would reunite all the subhistories, and above all, make full use of the resources of the natural and social sciences. Following World War II, the dominant figure of this movement was Fernand Braudel (1902–85), who incorporated in his sweeping, but brilliantly detailed, studies some of the concepts of structuralism. The third phase has been dominated by Le Roy Ladurie (1929–), who is celebrated for his work on the 'mental worlds' of past societies.

Decolonized History. As a reaction against traditional White 'colonialist' history, this movement was launched at an international congress of African historians at Dar es Salaam, Tanzania, in 1965. A leading figure is Oumar Kane, a founder of *Afrika Zamami*, an African historical review aiming to 'decolonize' approaches to history.

Oral History

Oral history is being used increasingly to study recent and contemporary history. A transcript of a tape-recorded interview (the primary source) may be consulted and reinterpreted by other historians. Oral history is particularly valuable with groups who do not normally generate written records; it has been much used in studies of undeveloped countries. Tape recordings of oral traditions, folk songs, and sayings still in use today offer insights into the customs and attitudes of quite remote periods in the past.

ARCHAEOLOGY IN PRACTICE

Archaeology (from Greek *arkhaiologia*, study of what is ancient) can be defined as the study of the human past by scientific analysis of the material remains of human cultures. The development of this discipline, with the aid of increasingly sophisticated scientific techniques, has allowed us to discover how humans have lived in different areas of the world in the relatively recent past, as well as how and when our species actually originated. Basic archaeological methods, types of sites, and dating techniques are discusssed in the opening chapter of this volume (see INTRODUCTION: THE STUDY OF HISTORY). In order to show archaeological methods in practice, this case study of a well-known site in southern Africa demonstrates how archaeologists have been able to derive knowledge of the former inhabitants of this particular site from the various techniques employed and artefacts analysed.

THE GREAT ZIMBABWE RUINS

Great Zimbabwe is the largest of the stone wall enclosures to be found on the Zimbabwe plateau, between the Zambezi and Limpopo rivers, in modern Zimbabwe (see SUB-SAHARAN AFRICA: AFRICAN STATES). Built by ancestors of the contemporary Shona people, the enclosures have been dated by radiocarbon techniques and by artefacts found within them to a period from the 10th to 15th centuries AD. The main structure, the

so-called 'Great Enclosure,' was the focus of the settlement and probably housed the chief's family. Its outer wall was 244 m long, 5.2 m thick, and 9.8 m high, making it the largest medieval stone structure known in sub-Saharan Africa. The Shona called sites of this type *zimbabwe*, which derives from the Shona word *dzimbahwe*, meaning 'stone dwelling' or 'court or grave of a chief.'

Monumental Architecture *The ruins of Great Zimbabwe demonstrate a highly skilled use of carefully selected granite blocks, laid in courses, to form these impressive structures: the Hill Ruin (top) shows where the walls (9 m high) were topped with turrets and monoliths; the parallel passage (bottom), showing the inner face of the outer wall of the Great Enclosure, is one of the finest examples of stonework at the site.*

Sculpture *(c. 1.2 m high) Carved from soapstone, available locally, several sculptures of this type have been found at Great Zimbabwe. They are thought to have been sacred in character.*

ARTEFACTS AS EVIDENCE FOR TRADE

Metals were mined at a number of locations on the Zimbabwe plateau during this period, and iron, copper, gold, and tin objects were produced at Great Zimbabwe. Trade was conducted, particularly in gold, with the African Islamic settlements on the east coast; finds at the site include Chinese and Persian 13th–14th-century ceramics, demonstrating that the Zimbabwe plateau was linked to a very extensive trading network. Trade also took place with other more distant societies in the African interior. Trade with the east coast undoubtedly helped to support the wealth and status of the Great Zimbabwe elite. The decline of the settlement in the 15th century coincided with the decline of the Islamic coastal trading centre at Kilwa.

Artefacts *These objects, found at the Great Zimbabwe site, provide evidence of the settlement's far-flung trading contacts. The glassware (left; largest piece 6.5 cm long), dated to the 14th century, is Near Eastern in origin; the iron gong (right; height 31 cm) is unlike any other metalwork found at Great Zimbabwe, although similar artefacts have been discovered in Zambia, the Congo basin, and West Africa, indicating long-distance interior trade links.*

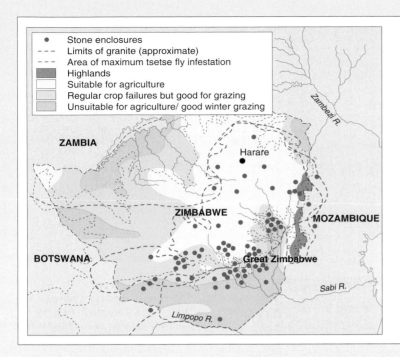

Legend:
- Stone enclosures
- Limits of granite (approximate)
- Area of maximum tsetse fly infestation
- Highlands
- Suitable for agriculture
- Regular crop failures but good for grazing
- Unsuitable for agriculture/ good winter grazing

ZAMBIA

Harare

ZIMBABWE

MOZAMBIQUE

BOTSWANA

Great Zimbabwe

Zambezi R.

Sabi R.

Limpopo R.

REGIONAL ANALYSIS

Human beings have always been mobile across land, whether they are foraging, conducting trade or warfare, or building alliances. Single sites (such as settlements) must, therefore, be located in relation to other sites and to natural resources in the region if we are to understand the pattern of social and economic life of which such sites form a part. The stone enclosures at Great Zimbabwe are only the most massive of a number of sites of this type, which are scattered across the Zimbabwe plateau. The hills around Great Zimbabwe are formed of granite, which can be broken into regular-shaped pieces with parallel surfaces, making it an ideal material for the building techniques employed at Great Zimbabwe.

The distribution of the stone enclosures on the Zimbabwe plateau suggests that they were located in an area in which tsetse fly infestation — a major threat both to human health and to livestock — was at a minimum. The stone wall enclosures are clustered on the areas of the plateau that have the greatest potential for cattle grazing. The map (left) shows the sites on the Zimbabwe plateau in relation to natural resources in the region.

EXCAVATION AREA

In the early 20th century, it was the usual practice of archaeologists to focus their excavation efforts on dating a site, or recovering artefacts that might indicate the ethnic affinity of the inhabitants. Modern archaeology involves extensive excavation of large areas of settlement sites, to recover information about the scale of occupation and the spatial organization as it relates to social relationships and economic activities. At Great Zimbabwe, the excavation of 1200 square metres around the stone wall enclosures has revealed the foundations of large numbers of densely packed 'commoners' huts; it is now estimated that the settlement had a total population of about 11 000 people.

ECONOMIC RECONSTRUCTION

The construction of such monumental architecture implies the existence of a social elite. The semi-urban population of the whole Great Zimbabwe settlement, depended on intensive food production and trade with distant centres. Excavation at the site has yielded substantial quantities of animal bone from food remains, almost exclusively from cattle butchered there. This, and the concentration of stone wall enclosure sites in good grazing, tsetse-free areas indicates an economy of intensive cattle herding. Some scholars believe that the ultimate abandonment of Great Zimbabwe was due to the depletion of natural resources as a result of the intensive activities of a highly populated settlement.

Conical Tower *Built between the old and new outer walls of the Great Enclosure, the tower (5.4 m in diameter and 9 m high) is the architectural focus of the enclosure. The decorated doorway leading to the tower and the high stepped platform beside it indicate that it was a centre of ritual.*

THE GREAT ENCLOSURE

As the most impressive area of the Great Zimbabwe site, the Great Enclosure (or Elliptical Building) is a symbol of the political power of the Shona rulers who inhabited it. Starting as a small circular enclosure (left), possibly as early as the 14th century, the area around it was enclosed with another larger wall. The great outer wall — built in the early 15th century, when the settlement reached the zenith of its power and prosperity — increased in size and sophistication as it was constructed. At its most complete it is thought to have been topped by decorated monoliths — many of which have been found at the site. The Great Enclosure has been found to contain the floors of *daga* (clay and gravel) huts, which would have housed the chief and his court, making the enclosure the political and ritual centre of the settlement. Stratigraphy techniques have revealed series of *daga* layers beneath the top floors, enabling archaeologists to date the huts and the successive walls of the enclosure.

The Beginnings of History

*This section presents a theoretical point of view based upon belief in Evolution
A Creationist viewpoint is in Volume 3, pages 119–134*

Scientists who support theories of Evolution believe that humans have evolved from primate ancestors. This school of thought states that mankind's primate heritage was preceded by ancestry with the whole animal kingdom. They believe the primate heritage, however, most accounts for our distinctive history.

Evolutionists believe humans' closest living 'relatives' are the great apes, although there are clear distinctions between species of apes or monkeys and the human species,

Homosapiens. Modern chimpanzees do have large social communities, use simple tools, are mobile over ground as well as in trees, and forage for high-quality food (mostly fruit with some animal protein). Early humans shared some of these traits; others were distinctly human.

Scientists have found fossils of ancient **Hominids,** which is the term they use to include human and ape primate species.

A Theory: Climate and Hominid Evolution

Adaptation to climate has been an important factor both in hominid evolution and in the way modern human populations have evolved in different regions. The fossil records of other adaptive forms reveal that the evolutionary expansion of the human brain and of human intelligence has no parallel. This depended on the evolution of a pattern of blood circulation to and from the brain, conducting heat away from the brain tissue, which is extremely sensitive to overheating. Such a pattern of blood supply evolved in early *Homo.*

In hot dry environments body heat can be dissipated most effectively by increasing the ratio of body surface area to body mass. This can be achieved by increasing stature without increasing body breadth, and by increasing the length of the extremities, such as limbs and ears. The fossil skeleton of an adult female hominid, *Australopithecus afarensis* (known as 'Lucy'), found at Hadar, Ethiopia, and dating from c. 3 million years ago, had a body mass of about 30 kg and a height of about 1.05 metres, with body proportions adapted to the temperature characteristics of both closed wet and open dry environments. The nearly complete skeleton of an 11–12-year-old *Homo erectus* male, found at West Turkana, Kenya, and dating from c. 1.6 million years ago (body mass c. 68 kg and height c. 1.80 metres), shows the increase in stature and body mass without a corresponding increase in body breadth. It seems, therefore, that African *Homo erectus* was inhabiting semiarid or arid

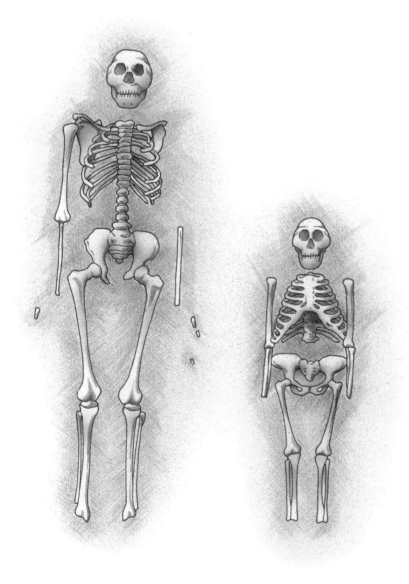

◄ **Climate and Evolution** *Skeletons of a male* Homo erectus *(left), dating from c. 1.6 million years ago, and a female* Australopithecus afarensis *(right), dating from c. 3 million years ago, show their different body sizes. These may demonstrate how stature and body size evolved to adapt to existence in changing climates.*

▲ Stone Tools *An early pebble chopping tool from Olduvai Gorge, Tanzania, dating from 2–1.5 million years ago, and an Acheulean hand-axe (side view to the left) from Swanscombe, England, dating from 450 000–250 000 years ago, are shown.*

logical temperature regulation for human survival. Modern Inuit peoples living in Arctic North America have low ratios of body surface area to body mass, while modern Nilotic peoples in Africa show the opposite pattern; pygmy peoples, whether from Africa or elsewhere, also have high ratios of body surface to body mass by virtue of their small size.

Culture, Stone Tools, and Food

Human beings are distinguished from other primates by the extent of our dependence on cultural traditions in learning how to orient ourselves in our environment. This increased dependence on learning the accumulated knowledge of the tribe enabled our ancestors to expand into new habitats and new continents. *Homo erectus* was the first hominid to spread out of Africa c. 1.2–1.4 million years ago; modern humans originate from a subsequent movement out of southern Africa 50 000–100 000 years ago. For cultural learning to have evolved into the dominant strategy by which our ancestors understood the world, there must have been regular supplies of readily available food over long

open country environments to which this body type was suited. **Bipedalism** is also an adaptation that reduces heat stress in open environments; upright posture minimizes the surface area exposed to direct sunlight and exposes the upper body surfaces to a greater flow of the cooling air that is found a few feet above ground level in savannah environments.

The various species of *Homo* adapted to overcome a number of physiological constraints created by the risks of heat stress and dehydration. This enabled successful colonization of hot dry open country habitats. Coping with the varying temperatures of different areas and habitat types remained, however, an important component of human survival strategies. Clothing and the use of fire for warmth must have been essential for the archaic humans who first colonized areas of higher latitudes. The Neanderthals, who may have evolved in the higher latitudes of Europe, seem to have had unusually broad bodies (adapting to cold environments by decreasing the ratio of body surface area to body mass). In modern human populations, most of the regional variation in body shape seems to have arisen during the last 10 000–15 000 years and shows the continuing importance of physio-

Fact or Theory? These theories of human development are taught in many schools, but are unproveable. Any student of humankind should also consider the alternative, or Creationist, viewpoint in Volume 3.

CULTURAL LEARNING

Cultural learning – the way in which knowledge and social customs are reproduced in traditional societies – is a distinctive universal human trait, by which individuals acquire the behaviour patterns of others; by imagining the actions of another person to produce a visible effect, a person then reproduces these actions, often with guidance from a more experienced person. This capacity for taking another person's mental perspective is central to human learning; it probably depends largely on the power of the human brain (which is more powerful than those of other primates).

The use of notation systems and artistic representation to record experiences also has a long prehistory. Engraved bone has been excavated from hunter-gatherer camps, dating to the end of the last glacial period in Europe (c. 13 000 years ago), with rows of notches made with different tools, suggesting some form of a 'tallying' system. The painted caves of France and northern Spain, dating from the later part of the last glacial period, may also have served as a kind of 'classroom,' where adolescents were exposed to images of the animals that they would hunt, which were such an important source of food and raw materials. These are just fragments of early systems of cultural learning.

Bipedalism

Humans are the only primates to move bipedally (by exclusive use of the legs and feet). Human anatomy reflects this adaptation in the form of long lower limbs and stiffened foot structures (which lack the grasping abilities of other primates). Bipedalism has freed the hands for the more complex manipulative actions and gestures that characterize human technology and social communication.

Early Pottery

The earliest pottery dates back to the early Holocene period (c. 10 500 BC); it was found in Japan and China. The craft appeared in northern Africa and the Near East by 7000–8000 BC; it had spread through most of Europe by 4000 BC. The production of pottery demonstrates the controlled use of heat by early cultures to modify raw materials.

the world, there must have been regular supplies of readily available food over long periods of time; hominids would, otherwise, have been better served by relying on individual observational learning to search for food. The stone tools that survive as a record of hominid technology vary little across regions or over long time spans, suggesting that the lifestyles of *Homo habilis* and *Homo erectus* were stable and well adapted to available resources.

The earliest stone tools date from c. 2.5 million years ago in east Africa; they were made by removing a few flakes of stone from a pebble core. By c. 1.6 million years ago, tools that demanded finer manipulative ability and more complex mental planning were being produced in Africa by hominids of the species *Homo erectus*. The symmetrical, ovoid, or teardrop-shaped handaxes of the Acheulean tradition (named after the site of St Acheul in

France, where they were first discovered) first appeared in east Africa at that time; they demonstrate the capacity of their makers to sustain a conventional way of working raw materials, which persisted over a wide area of Africa, Europe, and western Asia for about a million years. In east Asia, meanwhile, which was probably first colonized by hominids c. 1.3 million years ago, *Homo erectus* was using stone in a less elaborate way to make chopping tools. It is possible that bamboo was also being utilized for cutting tasks; tools made from organic remains, however, rarely survive for archaeologists to find.

The stone tools of these early species were used for chopping, cutting, scraping, and grinding; they would certainly have played a part in preparing meat and other animal products, such as hide and bone marrow. It was not until the time of early *Homo sapiens* that

THE DEVELOPMENT OF TOOLS AND METALS

Approximately 70% of humans use their right hand preferentially in fine manipulative tasks; this trait appears to have been established with the appearance of *Homo habilis* two million years ago. It reflects the pattern of evolution of the hominid brain, which has favoured areas located in the left side of the brain (which regulate the right side of the body), controlling skills in both manipulative actions and speech.

The ability to carry out fine manipulative actions is essential for the production and use of tools; the ability to generate innovative new solutions to technological problems is equally important. These abilities continued to evolve until the appearance of modern humans. *Homo erectus* had a larger brain than *Homo habilis* and manufactured stone tools that required more skill and mental planning to produce. However, the dimensions of the vertebral canals of fossils of this species suggest that the nerves supplying the hands and the chest wall (involved in regulating breathing in speech) had not yet reached their present level of complexity.

The controlled use of fire associated with *Homo erectus* has been detected archaeologically at a site in Kenya dating from 1.6 million years ago. It was subsequently developed from the time of early *Homo sapiens*, who produce more sophisticated stone tools. The pattern of use of controlled heat sources to modify the properties of raw materials is a recurrent element in human technologies. Pottery and metalworking both depend on it; whereas in pottery the raw material is shaped before firing, in metalworking the artefact is cast after smelting has been completed. However, the temperatures required for these processes are considerably higher than those needed for heat treatment of rocks. Pottery is completely fired at temperatures of 1000°C or more; a similar temperature is required to smelt copper and iron. Metalworking began with cold working of unsmelted copper by c. 7000 BC; the working of smelted copper,

▲ **Metalworking** *An early example of integrally cast metalwork is shown by this copper chariot model (height 7.2 cm) from Mesopotamia; it dates from c. 2700 BC.*

however, dates from 7000–6000 BC in western Asia and southeastern Europe, and from 2000–3000 BC in China. By 2000–3000 BC, knowledge of bronzeworking was widespread in Eurasia, while ironworking dates from 2000–1500 BC in western Asia; it had spread through Europe into southern Africa by the end of the first millennium BC. While the products of these processes tend to be hard and durable and thus survive as archaeological evidence, human technology has also involved long traditions of working with organic materials, such as wood, bone, and antler. The importance of these technological traditions can occasionally be gauged from preserved organic artefacts found in waterlogged or dehydrated sites, such as the fragment of a decorated wooden paddle recovered from a camp of fisher-foragers at Tybrind Vig, in Denmark, dated to between 5500 and 4000 BC.

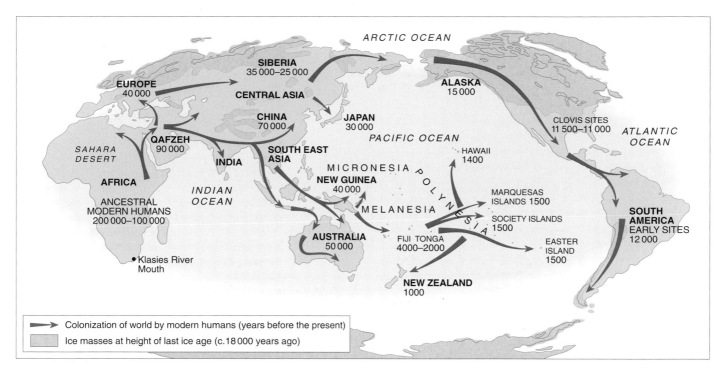

ARCTIC OCEAN

SIBERIA
35 000–25 000

EUROPE
40 000

CENTRAL ASIA

ALASKA
15 000

CHINA
70 000

JAPAN
30 000

CLOVIS SITES
11 500–11 000

ATLANTIC
OCEAN

PACIFIC OCEAN

QAFZEH
90 000

SAHARA
DESERT

INDIA

SOUTH EAST
ASIA

MICRONESIA

HAWAII
1400

AFRICA

ANCESTRAL
MODERN HUMANS
200 000–100 000

INDIAN
OCEAN

NEW GUINEA
40 000

MELANESIA

P
O
L
Y
N
E
S
I
A

MARQUESAS
ISLANDS 1500

SOCIETY ISLANDS
1500

SOUTH
AMERICA
EARLY SITES
12 000

• Klasies River
Mouth

AUSTRALIA
50 000

FIJI TONGA
4000–2000

EASTER
ISLAND
1500

NEW ZEALAND
1000

→ Colonization of world by modern humans (years before the present)

Ice masses at height of last ice age (c.18 000 years ago)

ing of rocks to temperatures of around 275°C drives the water out, making them more brittle and liable to fracture along more predictable planes relative to the point at which they are struck. Tools manufactured from heat-treated stone have been found at sites in Siberia, the Americas, and Australia, all with dates more recent than 50 000 years ago.

There is little clear evidence of the systematic hunting of large mammals before the appearance of archaic *Homo sapiens*. Where bones of large animals have been found, associated with hominid tools, the possibility remains that the meat was scavenged after the animal had been killed by another carnivore; in many cases, animal bone from such sites has cutmarks from hominid stone tools superimposed on carnivore tooth marks, indicating that they had been scavenged rather than hunted by the hominids. It seems likely that hominids in Africa lived off a broad spectrum of plant and animal foods. The movement of *Homo erectus* out of Africa, and the later appearance of Neanderthals in higher latitudes, where plant growth is more seasonal, may have necessitated a greater dependence on animal protein.

Colonization of the World

Whether due to biological advances, such as a full capacity for language, or to cultural advances, such as a new pattern of family organization, it is clear that the cultural behaviour of the earliest modern humans in many parts of the world was more inventive than that of their archaic predecessors. Scholars still disagree about the extent to which modern humans replaced archaic forms in Europe

and Asia. One view is that in the major regions of the Old World there was regional continuity between later *Homo erectus* or archaic *Homo sapiens* and the peoples of the present day. The weight of evidence, however, suggests that modern *Homo sapiens* colonized the world in a new phase of expansion.

The diversity of human **mitochondrial DNA** existing in the populations of the world today suggests that all humans are descended from a founding population of anatomically modern *Home sapiens*, which dispersed out of southern Africa between 90 000 and 140 000 years ago. These dates are speculative, based on estimated rates of genetic divergence rather than dated archaeological remains. However, the earliest known human skeletal remains of transitional modern form were found in Africa (Border Cave and the Klasies River mouth in South Africa and Omo in Ethiopia), with approximately contemporaneous or later modern forms found in Israel. These remains date from as early as c. 100 000 years ago. Archaeology also confirms the theory that the initial colonization of some of the most distant continents by modern humans took place during the last ice age (between 70 000 and c. 13 000 years ago).

The arrival of the modern form of *Homo sapiens* in ice-age Europe was relatively late, c. 40 000 years ago, by which time humans were also dispersing through Australia and were probably beginning to move into east Asia. The archaeological remains of their cultural behaviour in Europe, however, are most indicative of this new cultural inventiveness. Artefacts of bone, antler, and ivory appear for

▲ **Human Colonization**
Modern humans are thought to have spread out of southern Africa between c. 90 000 and 140 000 years ago. Approximate routes and dates of the earliest modern human colonists of the world are shown.

Mitochondrial DNA

The DNA molecule is responsible for the transmission of hereditary characteristics. Mitochondrial DNA is transmitted from the mother; it is a useful marker of relatedness between members of different populations within a single species. Recent studies of variation in human mitochondrial DNA have enabled the history of the earliest human colonization of the different regions of the world to be reconstructed.

Cave Art *Cave paintings, such as those (shown here) found in the caves at Niaux, in the Pyrenees , demonstrate artistic representation by early modern humans at the end of the last ice age (17 000– 14 000 years ago).* ▶

The Holocene Epoch

Climatic change has been characterized for at least the last 60 million years by a cycle of alternating cooler and warmer periods. These cycles were amplified when permanent ice sheets began to form on land masses in the high latitudes of the two hemispheres, beginning some five million years ago. For the last 12 000–13 000 years we have been living in a warm period within this cycle, referred to by geologists as the Holocene interglacial. At some future time the Holocene interglacial will end, initiating another ice age; however, the effects of human environmental pollution on global temperature and circulation patterns may alter its severity.

the first time; a greater range of stone tools, which were made using a technique that produced more cutting edges from a given mass of raw material, also appeared. Variation in traditions across regions and periods increases, implying greater social differentiation into ethnic groupings. The appearance of paintings on the walls of caves and engraved portable artefacts, the elaborate burial of the dead, the more controlled use of fire, and the construction of solid shelters all demonstrate the behaviour of modern humans in Europe. These were among the cultural innovations that enabled humans to colonize the harsher glacial environments of eastern Europe and northern Asia, where there was no previous history of hominid occupation.

The dispersal of modern humans into the habitable continents of the world was essentially complete by the early phases of the present interglacial period (or **Holocene** epoch), which began c. 13 000 years ago. This spread was assisted by an increased dependence on the hunting of large animals for their meat and hides. In the continents of Australia and the Americas, as in the islands of the Pacific,

animals would have been unaware of the threat of humans.

The period beginning towards the end of the last ice age (c. 13 000 years ago) is characterized by the loss of many large mammal and bird species around the world. In Europe and Asia extinct species include mammoth, cave bear, and giant elk. In Australia 19 genera, including over 50 species, disappeared towards the end of the last ice age; these included 13 genera of giant marsupials of which only the kangaroo survives today. In the Americas 33 genera of large mammals disappeared during

Domestication of Animals and Plants

The distribution of the wild primogenitors of the world's major domesticated livestock at the end of the last ice age (c. 13 000 years ago) is shown; the domestication of plant crops in Peru may date back to c. 8500 BC, while domesticated cultivation in other regions followed later. ▼

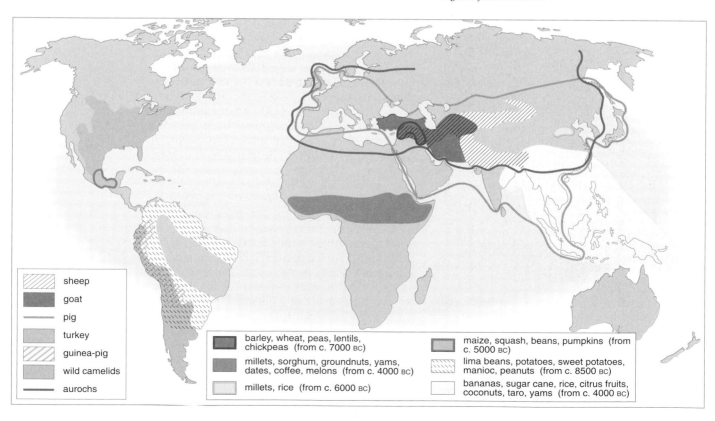

Legend:
- sheep
- goat
- pig
- turkey
- guinea-pig
- wild camelids
- aurochs

- barley, wheat, peas, lentils, chickpeas (from c. 7000 BC)
- millets, sorghum, groundnuts, yams, dates, coffee, melons (from c. 4000 BC)
- millets, rice (from c. 6000 BC)
- maize, squash, beans, pumpkins (from c. 5000 BC)
- lima beans, potatoes, sweet potatoes, manioc, peanuts (from c. 8500 BC)
- bananas, sugar cane, rice, citrus fruits, coconuts, taro, yams (from c. 4000 BC)

the few centuries c. 11 000 years ago, when archaeological evidence of human hunters first appears; these included mammoth, mastodons, giant sloths, and numerous other species including large carnivores, horses, and camelids.

The same pattern has been repeated in more recent times with the first colonization of such islands as New Zealand and Hawaii. While climatic change is not sufficient to explain this pattern, nor is human hunting alone; rather, it was a combination of hunting and natural climatic change and other natural and cultural factors (disturbance of the vegetation pattern and the introduction of exotic species into new habitats), which marked the emergence of humans as a major disruptive influence on the world's ecological structure.

Holocene Transitions to Agriculture

By c. 14 000–13 000 years ago, the glaciers of the polar and mountain regions were receding as global temperatures began to rise; this marked the transition from the last ice age to the present warm interglacial period. As the ice melted, sea levels rose, new weather patterns emerged, and vegetation zones changed with the expansion of temperate forest and grassland into high latitudes, and further into hilly and mountainous areas. A consequence of this was a change in the distribution of grazing animals, and of the carnivores that preyed on them. Humans appear to have

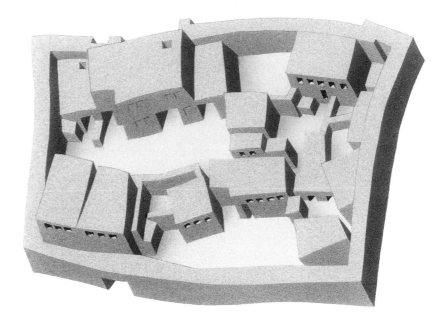

adapted to these changes by foraging for a broader spectrum of plant and animal foods.

By the early Holocene epoch (12 000–9000 years ago), people occupying small areas of most of the inhabited continents of the world had begun to switch from collecting wild plants (**foraging**) to actively cultivating them. The active management of animals, leading to their domestication, also emerged during this period. Domestication of plant species occurred in a wide range of habitats; the choice of species usually involved human selection, depending upon size, flavour, and ease of processing. Domestication of animals is successful almost exclusively with social species; it often involves selective breeding of smaller animals with more docile behavioural traits.

Between 9000 and 6000 BC cultivation of wheat and barley spread throughout the Near East, accompanied by the domestication of pigs, sheep, and goats. In parts of southern Asia cereal cultivation had begun by c. 7000 BC with herding of sheep, goats, and cattle. By c. 6000 BC, millet cultivation was being practised in northern China, as was management of domesticated pigs. Wet-rice cultivation in the Yangzi River basin dates from at least 2000 BC. In Africa domestic cattle were being kept in northern parts of the continent from c. 6000 BC (including parts of the Sahara, which was periodically wetter than it is today and supported areas of dry grassland). In Central America maize was domesticated by c. 5000 BC, while plant cultivation may have been practised in Peru from as early as 8500 BC. Relatively few species of social mammal remained undomesticated in the Americas following the extinction of species during the

▲ **Early Agricultural Settlement** *Small farming villages, such as that shown in this reconstruction from a site at Haçilar, Turkey (5000–4500 BC), developed as a result of the transition to an agricultural lifestyle. It is not known whether the surrounding wall was a high defensive structure or a low fence.*

▲ **Early Pottery** *This glazed pottery vase from China, dating from the 16th–15th century BC, is one of the earliest known glazed vessels. The cord marks on the body of the vase are typical of the Neolithic and later pottery of central and southeast China. The use of glaze at this early date is incredible, given that this technique was not developed in Europe until the 18th century AD.*

foraging The hunting and collecting of wild plant and animal foods to live. The lifestyle of foragers (also known as hunter-gatherers) can be contrasted with that of farming peoples, who cultivated land and reared livestock.

very early Holocene epoch; of those domesticated, the guinea pig was, by c. 7500 BC, providing almost half of the animal protein consumed by humans in the northern Andes.

Forming Lifestyles

The consequences of these agricultural developments were fundamental. The greater productivity of storable foods enabled larger settlements to develop, with the potential for social status and roles to become more differentiated, based on the ownership and distribution of produce. As agricultural work provided a greater incentive for a settled lifestyle, specialized crafts and trade in raw materials and finished artefacts became increasingly important. Life in early farming villages must have necessitated new forms of religious observance and new ways of regulating transactions based on property rights, evidence of which has sometimes appeared in archaeological finds.

These initial transitions from a way of life dependent on collecting wild resources to one based on their active cultivation and management occurred at roughly the same time across the various regions of the world; they also reflect the pressure that expanding human populations exerted on the old lifestyles during the early millennia of the present interglacial period. Developments in agricultural techniques continued into more recent times, including the exploitation of secondary animal products, such as milk and wool, and the development of crop rotation and fallowing cycles, which enable soils to be replenished with nutrients without whole settlements shifting to new locations. Ultimately, however, it was these first gradual agricultural transitions that facilitated developments in political organization and economic specialization, with associated population expansion and increased cultural diversity, which have characterized the subsequent millennia of human history.

THE ORIGINS OF WRITING

▲ **Early Writing** *This stone tablet, found at Kish in southern Mesopotamia, is one of the earliest examples of picture-writing, from which modern scripts developed. It has been dated to c. 3500 BC.*

Human history is conventionally thought to begin with the earliest written records. Archaeology and oral tradition are the principal sources of information for both the history of preliterate peoples, before their existence was first recorded by a literate outsider, and for the prehistory of those societies in which the use of writing has been longer established. By contrast, a full conventional writing system is a means of encoding information in a form that is transferable between people who are at some distance from one another, whether in space or in time. It also provides a durable record of transactions; it enables accounts to be kept of transfers of goods and services within a society, when these become too complex to be regulated by memory. As a system of notation, writing uses conventional symbols to represent objects, quantities, or (as with alphabetic script) the sounds of speech. The direct precedents of the first true writing systems in early farming societies are hard to discern from archaeological evidence. More than 200 examples of pottery engraved with marks, some of them complex motifs, were found at Tordos in Romania (c. 4500 BC); these marks appear to have been related to religious rituals rather than reflecting any form of economic book-keeping. Pots from early farming communities in western Iran carried distinguishing marks identifying the potter, before 4000 BC; they thus show the use of conventional notation to convey information, although these were almost certainly not the direct precedents of the true writing systems that developed 1000 years later in that region.

True writing systems were invented independently in Mesopotamia (c. 3500 BC), in Mesoamerica (c. 600 BC), and perhaps in China (c. 1400 BC). The pictographic scripts originating from Mesopotamia have had the most widespread influence on modern writing systems, having given rise first to cuneiform (wedge-shaped characters) and, secondly, to Egyptian hieroglyphics (pictures or symbols); the later alphabetic scripts of the Latin, Greek, Slavonic, and Brahmi systems also developed from the Mesopotamian scripts. True writing systems of this kind are characteristic of early urban civilizations; they reflect the need for a system to keep a record of the complex economic transactions that such civilizations involved. The origins of writing thus lie in the necessity for a record-keeping system, which accompanied the evolution of early civilizations.

EUROPE
AND THE
MIDDLE EAST

The Ancient Near East

Mesopotamian city-states • The empires of Akkad and Ur •
The rise of Assyria and Babylon • The Near East in chaos • The Assyrian Empire •
Egyptian unification and the Old Kingdom • Egypt reunited and the Middle Kingdom •
The New Kingdom • Egypt, Babylonia, and Persia

Gilgamesh and the Flood

Gilgamesh is thought to have been the ruler of Uruk around 2700 BC. Later myths credit him with a journey to the edge of the world where he met Utnapishtim, the survivor of a flood that the gods of Mesopotamia had sent to destroy mankind because they made too much noise. Utnapishtim built a boat and loaded it with animals, plants, and his family. Having survived the flood, he offered a sacrifice to the gods who, realizing their mistake, repopulated the world with humans.

The world's first civilization developed in **Mesopotamia**, a word used by the ancient Greeks meaning 'between the rivers' (Tigris and Euphrates). It was the diversity of the region that attracted the earliest settlers in the 6th millennium BC. Undulating grasslands in the north give way to a barren featureless plain in the south, bordered by lagoons and reed marshes rich in wildlife. The southern plain is outside the area of rain-fed agriculture; over the millennia, however, the rivers laid down thick deposits of very fertile silt and, once water was brought to this soil via ditches and canals, it proved a very attractive area to farmers. For materials, such as wood, stone, and metals, however, people had to look to the mountains in the north and east, where the first settlers had originated.

Mesopotamian City-states

By c. 3000 BC, southern Mesopotamia (Sumer) had been settled by farmers and fishermen, and excavations have revealed a coherent sophisticated culture based in cities. The people living beside the rivers Tigris and Euphrates built imposing temples of mud brick, ornamented with mosaic and fresco, for their gods; they also achieved considerable mastery in stonecutting, metallurgy, and pottery. The

most remarkable evidence for this urban civilization comes from the site of ancient Uruk (biblical name Erech), which was probably the largest city in the world at this time. One of the greatest advances in human history took place at Uruk at the end of the 4th millennium BC: the invention of a system of writing. Using a reed stylus to draw on tablets of clay, administrators kept an account of agricultural produce. Initially the records took the form of pictures of objects being counted together, with signs representing numerals. Eventually these pictographs became more stylized and wedgelike, or **cuneiform** (from the Latin *cuneus*, wedge), and adapted to write the local language, Sumerian. As the writing system evolved, abstract ideas could be expressed, allowing the Sumerians to record not only lists, but also events happening around them.

Uruk was not the only large settlement in Sumer. The wealth of another of these city-states is demonstrated by the so-called 'Royal

The Standard of Ur *Dating from c. 2600 BC, this mosaic shows scenes of everyday life in Sumer. This detail depicts a royal banquet, illustrating styles of dress and furniture. The standard is inlaid with shell, lapis lazuli, and red limestone.* ▼

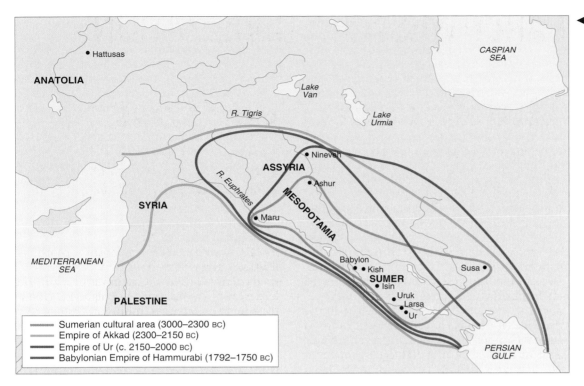

◄ Early Mesopotamia
The civilization of early Mesopotamia originated in the area between the rivers Tigris and Euphrates. A sophisticated city-state culture grew up in the region by c. 3000 BC, which in turn led to the emergence of a number of Mesopotamian empires.

Map legend:
- Sumerian cultural area (3000–2300 BC)
- Empire of Akkad (2300–2150 BC)
- Empire of Ur (c. 2150–2000 BC)
- Babylonian Empire of Hammurabi (1792–1750 BC)

Graves,' which date from c. 2600 BC. Of the many graves excavated at the site of Ur, 16 were found to be particularly richly furnished. The most remarkable aspect of these burial sites is the large number of human bodies found in the pits; in one grave alone there were 68 women and 6 men. These are thought to have been sacrificial victims, accompanying their leader in death. It would appear that the people died relatively peacefully and cups found close to some of the bodies may originally have contained poison. The victims are identified as soldiers, musicians, and serving ladies, based on their engraved cylinder seals and exquisite jewellery made by skilled craftsmen from imported gold, lapis lazuli, carnelian, and shell. It is not clear if the graves belonged to kings and queens or to the priests and priestesses of the city's patron god, Nanna (the Sumerian god of the moon).

The Empires of Akkad and Ur
Around 2300 BC the numerous Sumerian city-states were united into a single empire by Sargon (reigned c. 2334–2279 BC), ruler of the central Mesopotamian city of Akkad. Administration was centralized and the Semitic language Akkadian (named after Sargon's capital) was introduced as the official written language in preference to Sumerian. While few sites dating from this time have been excavated, the period produced some astonishing works of art. Sargon and his descendants ruled Mesopotamia for 150 years. Cuneiform inscriptions survive from this time of centralized control, which record the traffic

of merchants sailing from ports, such as Ur, through the Persian Gulf to acquire the riches of Bahrain, Oman, and India. The last of the great Akkadian emperors was Naram-Sin (reigned c. 2254–2218 BC). The history of the empire of Akkad is recorded in literary sources of the 2nd and 1st millennia BC, which present Naram-Sin very unfavourably. He is said to have angered the chief god of Sumer, Enlil, by taking his army into the god's temple. Enlil sent against Naram-Sin a people from the mountains bordering Mesopotamia who, it is said, destroyed the capital Akkad. The exact location of the city is still unknown.

With the fall of the empire of Akkad, the Sumerian cities began to reassert their independence. Chief among these was the city of Ur. Under King Ur-Nammu (reigned c. 2112–2095 BC), the city established itself as the

MESOPOTAMIAN HISTORY	
Early Dynastic Period	3000–2300 BC
Empire of Akkad	2300–2150 BC
Third Dynasty of Ur	2150–2000 BC
Isin-Larsa Dynasty	2000–1800 BC
Old Babylonian Period	1800–1600 BC
Kassite Babylonia	1600–1150 BC
Assyrian Empire	1000–612 BC
Neo-Babylonian Empire	612–539 BC
Achaemenid Persian Empire	539–331 BC

▲ Impression of Seal from Ur
(c. 2050 BC) This high-quality post-Akkadian cylinder seal possibly depicts the deified Ur-Nammu, king of Ur.

The Code of Hammurabi

Hammurabi is best remembered for his code of laws which, though presenting an idealized view of Babylonian society, dealt with many aspects, including witchcraft, property, slaves, and wages. The laws have survived in the Akkadian language and appear on the stele (shown below), which was found at Susa in 1901.

capital of an empire that rivalled that of the Akkadian rulers. Sumerian was reintroduced as the official written language of the dynasty, which is known to historians as the Third Dynasty of Ur. Like the earlier kings of Akkad, the rulers of Ur had to defend their kingdom against groups of people moving into Mesopotamia from the surrounding mountains and deserts, attracted by the wealth of the country. Under Ur-Nammu's great-grandson, Ibbi-Sin (reigned c. 2028–2004 BC), the empire collapsed as Amorite and Hurrian tribes established themselves throughout Mesopotamia. At the same time the Akkadian language largely replaced Sumerian, which – though no longer a living language – continued to be used by scribes for monumental inscriptions and religious texts. For the next 300 years the cities of lower Mesopotamia, chiefly Isin and Larsa, vied for control of the region.

The Rise of Assyria and Babylon

In northern Mesopotamia lay the country of Assyria, centred on the city of Ashur. Built high up on a rocky promontory, overlooking an important crossing of the River Tigris, the city dominated the caravans of donkeys carrying metals and rare materials from east and west, and the boats moving to and from the cities of Sumer in the south. As an important trading centre, Ashur had, by 1900 BC, established commercial colonies in Anatolia (modern Turkey). Cloth and Iranian tin were exchanged for Anatolian silver and records of these activities, inscribed on clay tablets, have been found at a number of sites in Turkey.

In the late 19th century BC an ambitious soldier, Shamshi-Adad (reigned 1813–1781 BC),

brought Ashur under his control. He established an empire that stretched across northern Mesopotamia. Following Shamshi-Adad's death the empire collapsed, as his sons lacked their father's military and political skills. Ashur and the north were now open to attack and when an assault came, it was from the southern town of Babylon.

As king of Babylon, Hammurabi (reigned 1792–1750 BC) united southern Mesopotamia into a single empire. During the second half of his reign he marched north and received the submission of kings, including the ruler of Ashur. However, as with his predecessor, Shamshi-Adad, Hammurabi's death led to his empire's break-up. The city of Babylon nevertheless remained the capital of a southern kingdom, Babylonia. In 1595 BC the dynasty of Hammurabi ended. Fragmentary written sources suggest that people from Anatolia, known as the **Hittites**, made a lightning raid down the Euphrates. They sacked Babylon and carried the statue of the city's patron god, Marduk, back to the Hittite capital, Hattusas.

Kassite Babylonians and Hurrian Mitannians. From c. 1600 to c. 1450 BC Mesopotamia passed through a period of cultural darkness. When written evidence became available again, during the 15th century BC, it is clear that Mesopotamia was dominated by two major powers: the Kassites ruling Babylonia and the Hurrian kingdom of Mitanni in the north. Much of the archaeological and historical evidence relating to these empires comes from their links with areas beyond Mesopotamia, such as New Kingdom Egypt and Hittite Anatolia. In c. 1350 BC the northern Mesopotamian kingdom of Mitanni collapsed under increasing pressure from the Hittite Empire in Anatolia. With the fall of Mitanni, Assyria reasserted its independence and began a process of consolidation that would lead the country to create a vast empire during the 1st millennium BC.

The Near East in Chaos

From c. 1200 BC the Near East faced conflict and devastation. The empire of the Hittites collapsed as a result of a general movement of people around the Mediterranean coast looking for areas to settle; these so-called 'Sea Peoples' were a mixture of dispossessed, brigands, and mercenaries. During these disturbed times several unsuccessful raids were made by the Sea Peoples against Egypt under the Pharaohs Merneptah (reigned 1213–c. 1203 BC) and Ramses III (reigned 1184–1153 BC). Tribes of Aramaeans were, meanwhile, moving into Mesopotamia from the west, pushing Assyrian boundaries back to Ashur.

By the 1st millennium BC the Near East had undergone marked political change. The

Stele of Hammurabi ▶
(18th century BC) This relief detail from the stele shows the Babylonian king receiving the symbols of kingship from the sun god, Shamash. Hammurabi's code is also inscribed on the stele, which is 2.2 m high and carved from basalt.

Mediterranean coast, north of Egypt, was now settled by Philistines. Further inland, Hebrew tribes were settling in the hill country. To the north (in modern Syria), traditions of the now vanished Hittite Empire were maintained by the so-called Neo-Hittites. In Mesopotamia various Aramaean and Chaldaean tribal groups competed for supremacy in Babylonia, while the Assyrians maintained a firm hold on their homeland, slowly moving against the groups that had settled in the region.

The Assyrian Empire

In the early 9th century BC Assyrian kings started sending military expeditions westwards in an attempt to control important trade routes and obtain tribute from less powerful states. An important Assyrian monarch of this period was Ashurnasirpal II (reigned 883–859 BC), who moved away from Ashur and built himself a new capital city at Kalhu (biblical name Calah, modern Nimrud). The raids of the Assyrian army against the Mediterranean continued under Ashurnasirpal's successors. However, when Tiglath-pileser III (reigned 744–727 BC) came to the throne he initiated changes in the administration of Assyria, including the annexation of countries into an empire.

Subsequent rulers of Assyria, such as Sargon (reigned 721–705 BC), Sennacherib (reigned 705–681 BC), and Esarhaddon (reigned 680–669 BC), not only built new capitals (Khorsabad and Nineveh) but expanded the Assyrian Empire until it extended from Persia (modern Iran) to Egypt. King Esarhaddon died while travelling to Egypt to re-establish control of the country after a rebellion by the Nubian Pharaoh Taharqo

(reigned 689–664 BC) of the 25th dynasty. The Assyrian king was succeeded by his son, Ashurbanipal (reigned 669–627 BC), who campaigned southwards as far as Thebes and placed Psamtek I (reigned 664–610 BC) on the Egyptian throne as the first ruler of the 26th dynasty, based at Sais in the Nile delta. In spite of a planned rebellion against his rule in Babylonia, Ashurbanipal boasts in his inscriptions of a peaceful and prosperous reign.

Egyptian Unification and the Old Kingdom

Civilization in Egypt was based on the River Nile. Swollen with flood waters each year between May and October, the river deposited a rich layer of soil over the floor of the valley. The agricultural potential created by this natural event attracted groups of early farmers and would ultimately make Egypt the granary of the ancient world.

▲ **Ashurbanipal**
The last of the great Assyrian kings, Ashurbanipal assembled at his capital at Nineveh the first systematically organized library in the ancient Middle East. He also decorated his palaces at Nineveh with epic bas-relief sculptures, depicting the key events of his reign. The relief above shows Ashurbanipal on a lion hunt.

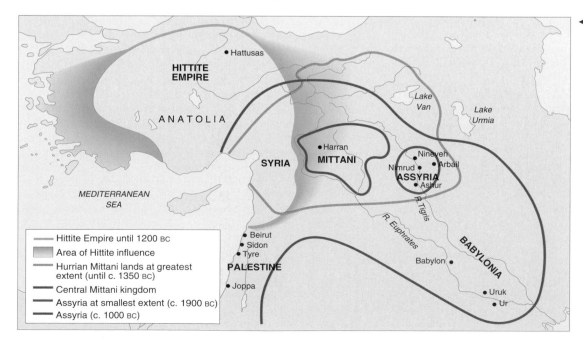

◄ **Empires in Conflict**
During the period 1500–1000 BC, several empires came into conflict over control of Syria and the east Mediterranean coast. After conflicts with Egypt, Mitanni eventually collapsed under increasing pressure from the Hittites (c. 1350 BC). Egypt, the Hittite Empire, and Assyria subsequently clashed before the Hittite Empire collapsed in c. 1200 BC.

HITTITE EMPIRE
• Hattusas
ANATOLIA
Lake Van
Lake Urmia
• Harran
SYRIA
MITTANI
Nineveh
Nimrud • • Arbail
ASSYRIA
Ashur •
MEDITERRANEAN SEA
R. Tigris
R. Euphrates
BABYLONIA
• Beirut
• Sidon
• Tyre
PALESTINE
Babylon •
• Joppa
• Uruk
• Ur

Hittite Empire until 1200 BC
Area of Hittite influence
Hurrian Mittani lands at greatest extent (until c. 1350 BC)
Central Mittani kingdom
Assyria at smallest extent (c. 1900 BC)
Assyria (c. 1000 BC)

▲ The Pyramids at El Gîza (Egypt)
Nearly 50 pyramids of various shapes and sizes were built as royal tombs at El Gîza, on the west bank of the Nile, during the Old Kingdom period (2613–2494 BC).

Later written sources suggest that Egypt was united as a country by kings before c. 3000 BC and that they succeeded earlier **dynasties** of rulers of the two lands of Upper and Lower Egypt. While it is likely that there was a gradual process of political unification over several centuries, by the start of the 3rd millennium BC the 1st dynasty of kings was established with the foundation of a capital at Memphis and a spread in the use of writing. Traditionally this was accomplished by King Menes. While the identification and existence of Menes are disputed, he may be the same as King Narmer or King Aha (c. 3100 BC).

The kings of the first three dynasties are known principally from their tombs. The contents of storage chambers within these structures have been preserved and reveal a remarkable quantity and quality of copper and stone objects. The most spectacular tomb belongs to King Djoser (reigned c. 2630–2611 BC), the second ruler of the 3rd dynasty (2686–2613 BC). Located at Saqqara, close to the capital at Memphis, the Step **Pyramid** is the oldest stone building of its size in the world. The period of Djoser's reign was considered by later Egyptians as a golden age; Imhotep, the probable architect of the Step Pyramid, came to be venerated as a god.

A major factor in the history of dynasties Four (2613–2494 BC) and Five (2494–2345 BC) was the worship of the sun god Re, of which the true pyramid was a symbol. The largest of these tombs were built by the kings Khufu (reigned c. 2590–2565 BC) and Khephren (reigned c. 2560–2530 BC) on the west bank of the Nile as part of a great cemetery complex, which included temples and rows of tombs belonging to Egypt's nobles. Unlike Mesopotamia, where the rulers of city-states were believed to be mortals chosen by the gods, the king of Egypt was himself regarded as a deity; when he died he was believed to join the sun god, crossing the sky by boat.

From the time of the unification of the country Egyptian kings had directed military campaigns against the inhabitants of Palestine and Libya, and south beyond the First Cataract of the Nile – an area of rapids and shallow water and the traditional border of Egypt – into Nubia. Such expeditions were undertaken to collect booty and maintain trading links. The port of Byblos, on the eastern coast of the Mediterranean, was the focus of contact with the East, while to the south the Egyptians sought the exotic products of Africa. Over the course of time relations with Nubia deteriorated, reflecting Egypt's declining power during the 6th dynasty (2345–2181 BC).

EGYPTIAN DYNASTIES

In the 3rd century BC an historian called Manetho divided the kings of Egypt before Alexander the Great into 30 groups known as dynasties (from the Greek word *dunamis*, 'power'). This system is still used by Egyptologists, who assemble the dynasties into the following kingdoms and periods:

Early Dynastic Period	Dynasties 1–3	c. 3100–2613 BC
Old Kingdom	Dynasties 4–8	2613–2125 BC
First Intermediate Period	Dynasties 9–11	2125–2055 BC
Middle Kingdom	Dynasties 11–12	2055–1795 BC
Second Intermediate Period	Dynasties 13–17	1795–1550 BC
New Kingdom	Dynasties 18–20	1550–1069 BC
Third Intermediate Period	Dynasties 21–25	1069–716 BC
Late Period	Dynasties 25–30	716–343 BC
Persian Period		343–332 BC

Provincial officials had by this time become hereditary holders of their posts and often defended their interests by the use of force. Royal power was eclipsed as the country declined. While numerous kings over the next 50 years (7th and 8th dynasties) were nominally accepted by the whole country, real central control had ceased to exist. During the First Intermediate Period that followed, Egypt was divided between the rulers of the 9th and 10th dynasties based at Herakleopolis, and the contemporary 11th dynasty based at Thebes.

Ancient Egypt *Founded on the fertile flood plains of the River Nile, the kingdom of Egypt gradually became politically unified (c. 3000 BC). Throughout subsequent periods of Egyptian history, dynasties of rulers relocated the capital of the kingdom. At its greatest extent Egypt's empire extended far into Nubia to the south, and into Palestine to the north. ▼*

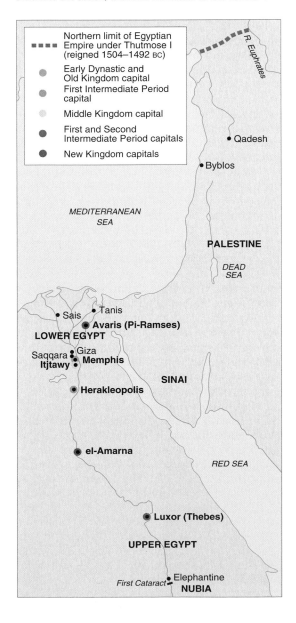

- ---- Northern limit of Egyptian Empire under Thutmose I (reigned 1504–1492 BC)
- ● Early Dynastic and Old Kingdom capital
- ● First Intermediate Period capital
- ● Middle Kingdom capital
- ● First and Second Intermediate Period capitals
- ● New Kingdom capitals

Egypt Reunited and the Middle Kingdom

The political division of Egypt ended when Nebhepetra Mentuhotep (reigned 2055–2004 BC) defeated the rulers of Herakleopolis, reunited the country, and ushered in the Middle Kingdom. Although Egypt was strong enough to send armies to Nubia and revive trade with the East, the 11th dynasty of kings ended when the vizier Amenemhat (reigned 1985–1955 BC) came to the throne as the first ruler of the 12th dynasty. The new monarch moved from Thebes to near Memphis, where he established the city of Itjtawy as his capital. This was part of a return to Old Kingdom traditions, which included a revival of the arts. Amenemhat shared the rule of Egypt for ten years with his son Senusret I (reigned 1965–1920 BC); during their reigns Nubia was conquered as far as the Second Cataract of the Nile, where the building of a series of great forts was begun. At the same time a number of literary works were composed. These intellectual achievements, together with the extraordinary quality of masonry and metalwork, made the Middle Kingdom a classical age for later Egyptians.

Under Senusret III (reigned 1874–1855 BC) Egypt's control of Nubia was strengthened with the aid of a standing army, and campaigns into Palestine ensured a considerable Egyptian influence north of the Nile delta. The king reduced the power of provincial governors and divided the country into four administrative regions.

For the next century Egypt remained powerful both at home and abroad. However, the ruling family of the 12th dynasty died out in c. 1795 BC and ushered in the 13th dynasty. Although there was a rapid succession of kings, the country remained stable as real power was now held by the country's highest officials, the viziers.

The Second Intermediate Period. Towards the end of the 13th dynasty (1795–1605 BC), many Asiatic immigrants, probably from Palestine, entered Egypt and settled in the eastern delta, where they were, apparently peacefully, absorbed into Egyptian society. During the unsettled times of the succeeding 14th dynasty, these foreign groups usurped the Egyptian throne. They are known as the **Hyksos**, a Greek name derived from an Egyptian phrase meaning 'ruler of foreign lands'; two contemporary lines of their kings represent the 15th and 16th Egyptian dynasties. In southern Egypt, meanwhile, a line of native Egyptians ruled from Thebes as the 17th dynasty. By the mid-16th century BC, the kings ruling from Thebes began a struggle to expel the Hyksos. King Kamose (reigned 1555–1550 BC) initiated the war against the

▲ **Senusret III**
A powerful king, Senusret radically restructured the government of Egypt and strengthened its control over Nubia to its south. This statue of Senusret illustrates the high-quality Middle Kingdom sculpture.

Pyramids and Ziggurats

Egyptian kings were buried in stone tombs in the form of pyramids during the period c. 2686–1650 BC (Dynasties 3–13). The largest pyramid is the Great Pyramid of King Khufa at El Gîza (230 m² by 146 m high). Ziggurats are Mesopotamian solid mud-brick stepped towers with temples built on the summit. The best preserved of these towers was built at Ur by King Ur-Nammu and measures at its base 61 m by 46 m. One of the most famous ziggurats was built in the city of Babylon and gave rise to the biblical story of the Tower of Babel.

Map labels:
R. Euphrates
● Qadesh
● Byblos
MEDITERRANEAN SEA
PALESTINE
DEAD SEA
● Sais ● Tanis
● Avaris (Pi-Ramses)
LOWER EGYPT
Saqqara ● Giza
Itjtawy ● Memphis
SINAI
● Herakleopolis
● el-Amarna
RED SEA
● Luxor (Thebes)
UPPER EGYPT
First Cataract ● Elephantine
NUBIA

◄ **The Colossi of Memnon** *Under the Pharaohs of the New Kingdom period in Egypt, major building works were undertaken. The monumental statues of Amenhotep III (reigned 1390–1352) shown here are prime examples of these works; they originally guarded the entrance to his mortuary temple.*

Pharaoh Royal title derived from the ancient Egyptian term *per aa,* 'the great house,' referring to the palace of the ruler. During the New Kingdom it became the polite way to refer to the Egyptian monarch.

Hyksos; it was his successor, Ahmose (reigned 1550–1525 BC), who reached the Hyksos capital at Avaris and finally drove the foreign rulers out of the reunified country.

The New Kingdom

As the founder of the 18th dynasty, Ahmose left Egypt unified and strong on his death (1525 BC). His son, Amenhotep I (reigned 1525–1504 BC), extended Egyptian control in Nubia; however, it was the military exploits of Thutmose I (reigned 1504–1492 BC) that exceeded earlier achievements. During the early years of his reign Thutmose led his armies to the River Euphrates, where he clashed with forces of the Mitanni Empire. The small states

along the coast of the Mediterranean Sea were bound to the **Pharaoh** by oaths of allegiance; Nubia, as far as the Fourth Cataract of the Nile, was ruled directly by a viceroy.

The Egyptian Empire produced much of the country's wealth, especially the important gold reserves of Nubia. Thutmose I was succeeded by Thutmose II (reigned 1492–1479 BC) whose son, Thutmose III (reigned 1479–1426 BC), ascended the throne while still a young boy. His mother, Hatshepsut acted initially as regent; in the boy's seventh year, however, she proclaimed herself 'king' (1503) and ruled as the dominant partner of a coregency.

After the death of Hatshepsut, Thutmose III launched a series of campaigns to re-establish Egyptian control of Palestine; however, the Mitannian Empire of northern Mesopotamia successfully resisted Egyptian expansion. During the last years of his reign, Thutmose III established a coregency with his son Amenhotep II (reigned 1427–1400 BC). New campaigns were directed into Palestine to affirm the allegiance of the region's petty rulers and the three major powers of the time, the Hittites, Mitannians, and Kassite Babylonians, sent gifts to the Pharaoh. Although Egypt lost to Mitanni under Thutmose IV (reigned

◄ **Queen Nefertiti** *(c. 1355 BC) Loyal wife of the pharaoh Akhenaten, Nefertiti is thought to have fallen from favour and retired before she died. This portrait bust was painted on limestone and found at the royal capital of el-Amarna.*

THE PHOENICIANS

During Egypt's New Kingdom period the people of Palestine were known as **Canaanites**. However, after the upheavals of the 12th century BC their land was restricted by the arrival of the Sea Peoples to a narrow strip along the coast. No longer able to sustain a land-based economy, the inhabitants increasingly turned seawards and became great sailors and traders. They are known today as Phoenicians (Greek for 'Canaanites'); their culture was based in ports, such as Sidon, Tyre, Beirut, and Joppa. The trading nature of these sites, already important during the 2nd millennium BC, increased substantially during this time.

Renowned as metalworkers, weavers, dyers, carpenters, and masons, Phoenician craftsmen carried their trade throughout the Mediterranean. Commercial contacts were established through resident Phoenician merchants in Cyprus, from where ships penetrated the Aegean Sea and Greece. Further west Phoenician traders established many colonies, chief among them being Cadiz in Spain and Carthage in North Africa. The growing military power of Assyria saw the wealth of these trading cities as an obvious target; campaigns were thus directed by the Assyrian kings to ensure that trade passing through the cities flowed freely in order to claim tribute and booty from the wealthy Phoenician rulers.

◄ **Phoenician Amulet** *The Phoenicians, who traded throughout the Mediterranean, were great craftsmen. The glass amulet shown here is of the type widely traded by the Phoenicians.*

1400–1390 BC), peace was made between the two empires before his death.

Peace brought wealth to Egypt, reflected in the monumental buildings and high-quality sculpture produced under Amenhotep III (reigned 1390–1352 BC), who cemented international relations by marrying more than one Mitannian princess.

Under Amenhotep IV (reigned 1352–1336 BC) the cult of the sun god was developed, particularly the aspect of the sun disk (Aten). In the fifth year of his reign, the king changed his name to Akhenaten ('beneficial to the sun disk') and established a new capital city at el-Amarna. Temples to other gods were closed and their names erased from inscriptions. Akhenaten had six daughters by his wife Nefertiti, who – under the name Nefernefruaten (Smenkhare) – may have shared the throne of Egypt before the death of her husband. They were succeeded by Tutankhamen (reigned 1333–1323 BC), of uncertain parentage but belonging to the family of Akhenaten. While the young king restored the cult of the national god Amun, real power lay in the hands of the chief official Aya (reigned 1323–1319 BC) and the general Horemheb (reigned 1319–1292 BC), both of whom, in turn, succeeded Tutankhamen to the throne.

Campaigns against the Hittite Empire were resumed during the 19th dynasty under Sety I (reigned 1294–1279 BC). His son Ramses II (reigned 1279–1213 BC) confronted the Hittites at the Battle of Qadesh (1275 BC); although the result was indecisive, Ramses presented it as a great victory. A truce was eventually agreed, and the Pharaoh's achievements were glorified by numerous building works and monumental statues. He moved the capital from el-Amarna to a location in the delta called Pi-Ramses ('Domain of Ramses'), formerly the site of the Hyksos capital, Avaris.

Egypt, Babylonia, and Persia

Between the 7th and 4th centuries BC, the kingdom of Egypt came under the control of successive Mesopotamian empires, leading finally to its fall in the face of a Macedonian (Greek) invasion.

Following the death in 627 BC of the powerful Assyrian king, Ashurbanipal – who had brought Egypt under Assyrian control – Assyria was faced with internal strife and destruction. To the east of Mesopotamia lay the empire of the Medes. In 614 BC a Median army under Cyaxares (reigned c. 653–586 BC) invaded the Assyrian homeland, attacked Nineveh, and destroyed the ancient city of Ashur. Two years later the combined forces of Cyaxares and the king of Babylon, Nabopolassar (reigned 625–605 BC), captured Nineveh. The Assyrian court fled west to the town of

Harran, where they were finally defeated in 609 BC by Nabopolassar's son, **Nebuchadnezzar** (reigned 605–562 BC). While the Medes withdrew to consolidate their conquests in the east, the Assyrian Empire passed into the hands of the kings of Babylon.

Sixty years of Babylonian supremacy was threatened during the reign of Nabonidus (reigned 556–539 BC), when Mesopotamia was faced with the expansion of the Persians from the east. In 539 BC the armies of the Persian king, Cyrus (reigned c. 550–c. 529 BC), marched on Babylon, where the population opened the city gates to the conqueror. In effect, this event brought to an end 3000 years of self-rule in Mesopotamia. The Persian army moved on to Egypt, where Psamtek III (reigned 526–525 BC) was defeated by Cyrus' son and successor, Cambyses (reigned 529–522 BC), who established Persian rule as the 27th dynasty. During this time an impoverished Egypt launched a successful rebellion against the Persians in 404 BC, which led to a series of short reigns by the rulers of the 28th, 29th, and 30th dynasties (see PERSIA).

The destruction of the Persian armies at the battles of Issus, in 333 BC, and Gaugamela, in 331 BC, by the Macedonian king, Alexander the Great (reigned 336–323 BC), led to the establishment of Greek rule in Mesopotamia. Egypt thus became part of Alexander's growing empire; he was welcomed into the country as a liberator from harsh Persian rule in 332 BC (see GREECE AND THE HELLENISTIC WORLD).

▲ **Babylon**
Under Nebuchadnezzar (605–562 BC) great building works were undertaken at Babylon. A reconstruction of the Ishtar gate is shown here; it stood 10 m high, with towers of about 20 m, and was one of eight fortified gates in the city walls.

Nebuchadnezzar

The king of Babylon, Nebuchadnezzar, attacked the rebellious city of Jerusalem in 586 BC. He took the Jews into exile and settled some of them in Babylonia, where the Old Testament was compiled. The city of Babylon had been glorified by Nebuchadnezzar in a programme of building works, which included the city walls, a huge palace, and, according to classical sources, the Hanging Gardens.

Greece and the Hellenistic World

*Minoan Crete • Mycenaean Greece • The Dark Ages • The Persian menace •
Athenian Empire • The Peloponnesian War • Rivalries of the 4th century BC •
Philip of Macedon • Alexander the Great • The Hellenistic kingdoms*

Pioneers of Bronze Age Archaeology

The cities of Troy and Mycenae were first excavated by German businessman Heinrich Schliemann (1822–90). At Mycenae he opened tombs containing gold, and at Troy he found rich jewels. The great palace at Knossos, on Crete, was discovered by Sir Arthur Evans (1851–1941). Its maze of passages caused speculation that he had found the labyrinth of the legendary Minotaur.

Civilization in Europe began on the island of Crete. This early period of history on Crete is called 'Minoan' after the legendary King Minos, who is said to have ruled not only all Crete but much of the south Aegean.

Minoan Crete

The Greek Bronze Age (c. 3000–1100 BC) was initiated by settlers from the east who, during the 3rd millennium BC, brought to Crete knowledge of copperworking and pottery. During the 2nd millennium BC these settlers established towns and their rulers built palaces on the island. Archaeological investigations indicate that the palaces were substantial buildings with columned entrances, open courts, and grand staircases to upper floors. Skilled craftsmen produced delicate pottery, gold jewellery, and engraved sealstones. Finds show that they had contacts with Egypt, Cyprus, and the Near East. An earthquake (c. 1700 BC) destroyed the palaces, which were subsequently rebuilt and decorated with colourful wall-paintings. The Minoans knew how to write; inscribed tablets have been found at many sites, yet the script, known as Linear A, remains undeciphered.

The neighbouring island of Thera (or Santorini) is a volcano. In c. 1500 BC, it erupted and buried a town in lava, preserving many of its houses. A second eruption (c. 1450 BC) was even more destructive and coincided with the end of Minoan rule on Crete.

Mycenaean Greece

Civilization on the Greek mainland lagged behind that of the islands. By c. 1500 BC, however, several centres had emerged, mostly in southern Greece. They share a number of common features: architecture, pottery styles, burial practices, and, above all, writing. At all the sites archaeologists have discovered inscribed tablets similar to those found on Crete. It is thought that the earlier Linear A script was taken from the Minoans by invading Mycenaeans and used to write down their language. This script, known as Linear B, can be read and is an early form of Greek. The tablets tell us much about social aspects of this culture, named after the principal site, Mycenae.

Mycenaean rulers seem to have controlled only small areas of land; judging by their fortified citadels, they were familiar with warfare. When they died, they were buried with their riches. Several tombs have been found, yielding fine examples of gold jewellery, engraved gems, inlaid weapons, and ornate vessels. The Mycenaeans reached the height of their power in c. 1400 BC, by which time they controlled Crete and were trading throughout the Mediterranean. After 1200 BC their position seems to have been weakened by hostilities; by 1100 BC their culture had ended.

Homer and the Trojan War. The palaces of Mycenae and Argos, Tiryns, and Pylos are featured in the works of Homer and in Greek myths. Homer's epic masterpieces, the *Iliad* and the *Odyssey*, were probably composed in the 8th century BC, when Greeks first began to write literature.

▲ **Bronze Age Fresco** *(16th century BC) The sophistication of Bronze Age civilization on Minoan Crete is apparent from its colourful frescos, such as that shown here, from the partially restored palace at Knossos. This detail depicts a procession of gift-bearers.*

Troy, a city in northwestern Anatolia, had been inhabited throughout the Bronze Age and maintained close relations with the Greek cultures. According to archaeologists Troy was destroyed and rebuilt many times – at least twice during the 13th century BC, when it probably faced a Mycenaean attack. Homer's works may record a war between Mycenae and Troy, but this is open to question.

The Dark Ages

Between c. 1100 and c. 800 BC Greece passed through a period of cultural darkness. The collapse of the Mycenaean world was followed by a time of unrest, during which many people were displaced and many skills were lost.

Among the few things to survive was the language itself, and just as important were the legends recounted in it. Our understanding of life in the Bronze Age would be greatly diminished without the stories of Agamemnon and Clytemnestra, Menelaus and Helen, Priam and Hecuba, and other epics.

Another chief survival was Greek religion. Clearly the pantheon of Olympian gods was fully formed in the Bronze Age; indeed many are named in the Linear B tablets.

The Greeks Overseas. During the Dark Ages peoples known as Dorians entered Greece from the north. By the mid-8th century BC, when Greeks began again to establish cities, the rising population soon exhausted the available land. The demand for food and raw materials encouraged them to trade abroad and found colonies. Greek cities were soon to be found throughout the Mediterranean, mostly in the Black Sea region and southern Italy, but also in Spain, Libya, and Syria.

Greek culture was thus exported to its overseas colonies; in some places, such as Sicily and the Egyptian delta, it remained a powerful influence for many centuries. A mixture of cultural traditions and styles are, therefore, discernible in the art of the period.

The Persian Menace

The Greeks were not the only expanding power in the region. In the 6th century BC the Persians overthrew the Medes and advanced westwards, threatening the Aegean. In the 490s the Greek cities of western Anatolia revolted against their Persian overlords. Although the revolt was crushed, it incited retribution; in 490 BC the Persians, under Darius (reigned 522–486 BC), attacked Greece by sea. Landing at Marathon, only 42 km from Athens, they were driven out by much smaller Athenian forces and suffered heavy losses.

In 480 BC Darius's successor, Xerxes (reigned 486–465), renewed the attack by land and sea. After early successes at the pass of Thermopylae on land, despite heroic defence by the

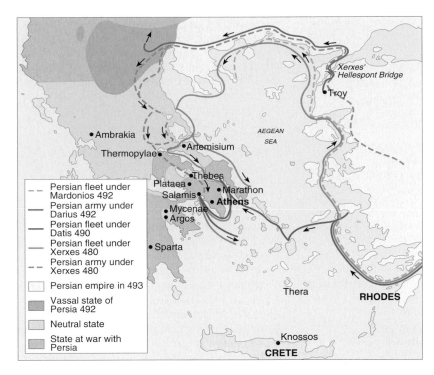

Spartans, and Cape Artemisium at sea, Xerxes advanced on Athens. The citizens fled leaving a small force to hold the Acropolis. After a two-week siege it fell, the defenders were slaughtered, and the temples destroyed. The Persian ships were then persuaded to sail into the narrow Salamis channel, where the Greeks lay in wait for them. A fierce battle ensued in which the Greeks were victorious.

The Persian fleet withdrew, ending the naval war, but the Persian army was still undefeated. The Athenians and Spartans chose this crucial time to join forces, and in 479 BC the Persians were defeated at Plataea, near Thebes. The survivors fled, leaving the victorious Greeks their freedom.

Athenian Empire

Greece comprised a collection of independent city-states rather than a single political unit. Any sense of unity sprang from the use of a common language and participation in religious festivals, especially the Olympic Games. The Greeks were also forced to cooperate to form a common defence against Persia. When Persia was finally defeated, Athens emerged as the natural leader of Greece.

In order to maintain this new political unity, the Greek states formed themselves into a confederacy, known as the Delian League, with Athens as its leader. Meetings of the assembly were held on the island of Delos, from which the league took its name. Members paid annual tribute, either in the form of ships or in money, which was used to maintain the fleet. Officers were appointed by Athens and commanders were Athenian generals.

▲ **The Persian Wars** *The Persians attempted to invade Greece twice, one in 490 BC under Darius and once in 480 BC under Xerxes. Both were ultimately unsuccessful. The routes taken by the Persian invaders, from 492 to 479 BC, are shown.*

Marathon runners

The modern marathon race commemorates the achievement of a Greek soldier who is said to have run 40 km, from Marathon to Athens, with news of the Athenian victory over the Persians in 490 BC. The distance run in the modern marathon is 42.195 km (26 miles and 385 yards), which is believed to be the distance between Athens and Marathon.

▲ Philip II of Macedon
As conqueror of Greece, the Macedonian king established a federal state with its own army, of which he was supreme commander.

Hellenistic period
The period of Greek history from the death of Alexander the Great (323 BC) to the end of the Ptolemaic dynasty in Egypt (31 BC).

Thucydides
The greatest Athenian historian of the 5th century BC, Thucydides (c. 460–400 BC) was principally concerned with the Peloponnesian War and the conflict between Athens and Sparta (431 and 404 BC). A great admirer of Pericles, Thucydides records the famous oration delivered by Pericles at the public funeral for the first casualties of the Peloponnesian War.

Initially the League existed to defend Greece against threats from Persia or other states. For 25 years this policy was pursued. In 454 BC the League's treasury was transferred to Athens and meetings of the assembly were discontinued; member states were clearly losing their independence, and the League gradually turned into an Athenian Empire based on command of the sea. It was under the rule of Pericles (495–429 BC) that the empire reached its height, both politically and culturally (see **THE AGE OF PERICLES**).

The Peloponnesian War
The spectacular success of Athens in the 5th century BC threatened the liberty of all other Greek states, particularly Sparta. The Spartans, who had been the heroes of the Persian Wars, were unwilling to cede their leadership of Greece to the Athenian imperialists.

The two cities represented Greek opposites. Athens was a democracy and leader of a seaborne empire; its inhabitants were ambitious and adventurous, culturally expressive, and fiercely proud of their liberty and free speech. Sparta, by contrast, was a land-based power with an oligarchical constitution; once a flourishing literary and musical centre, it had become a repressive and reactionary military state.

Sparta led a group of autonomous states in southern Greece – the Peloponnesian League. Provoked by Athenian interference in Corinthian alliances, the League invaded Attica, which bordered Corinth, in 431 BC. The ensuing war eventually involved nearly every state in the Greek world and lasted, intermittently, for 27 years.

As a result of the conflict Athens lost its economic and naval superiority. Particularly disastrous were a plague epidemic in 430 BC, the failure of an expedition to Sicily in 415–413 BC, and a Spartan alliance with Persia in 412–411 BC. The war ended in 404 BC with Athens being starved into submission. Both sides were permanently weakened and Greece never fully recovered its strength.

Rivalries of the 4th Century BC
The Peloponnesian War irretrievably weakened Athens, and Sparta's victory meant the return of Persia into Greek affairs. Sparta now attempted to impose oligarchic government on the cities of mainland Greece. In response Athens, Corinth, Argos, and Thebes formed a coalition to fight Sparta in the Corinthian War (395–387 BC). Spartan victory, assisted by Persia, restored Sparta's hold over Greece, but did not prevent the creation of a second Athenian Empire. It also failed to halt the rise of Thebes; in 371 BC the Spartans were defeated by the Thebans at the Battle of

Leuctra. Spartan power was now effectively at an end; the power vacuum created was temporarily filled by Thebes, yet it did not take full control of Greece, enabling most cities to regain their autonomy for a few more years.

Athenian imperialism was checked once more by the revolt of some of its allies. Athens fought the Social War (357–355 BC) in an attempt to recover them, but Persian threats forced Athens to back down. Persia, however, was not strong enough to mount a full-scale invasion of Greece. In the western Mediterranean, meanwhile, Carthaginian power was increasing.

Philip of Macedon
The city-state (or **polis**) remained the standard unit of political power in Greece until the rise of a centralized kingdom in Macedonia. Under Philip II (reigned 359–336 BC), Macedonia developed a new professional army, superior to any other. With this military force, Philip marched into Greece. By 346 BC he was master of northern Greece and, having made peace with Athens, was set to attack Persia.

The Athenians finally rallied their forces and Philip was subsequently forced to return to central Greece to face the combined forces of Athens and Thebes. Philip crushed the Greeks at the Battle of Chaeronea (338 BC) and established a federal state with its headquarters at Corinth. His eastern ambitions, however, were cut short by his assassination in 336 BC.

Alexander the Great
Alexander III (336–323 BC) inherited from his father, Philip II, the throne of Macedonia, control over the whole of Greece, and also an ambition to defeat Persia. He succeeded and, within five years, was hailed as king of Asia.

In fulfilling his ambition, Alexander fought three major battles. After crossing into Asia, with an army of about 40 000 men, he engaged the Persians at the Granicus River (334 BC). After victory there, he marched through Asia Minor and liberated Greek cities from Persian control. At Issus (333 BC), in northern Syria, he defeated the Persians again. Rather than accept peace terms, he marched south, capturing the port of Tyre and occupying Egypt. Still not satisfied, Alexander turned east to Babylonia and won his third and final victory over the Persians at Gaugamela in 331 BC. The Persian king, Darius III (reigned 336–330 BC), escaped, while Alexander occupied his capitals. The destruction of Persepolis symbolized the eclipse of Persia's empire.

Now an unstoppable force, Alexander swept through Bactria and Central Asia to northern India. On reaching the Indus River, however, his army mutinied and refused to continue. His reaction was to build a fleet and send half

Alexander the Great *A ruthless man, Alexander was, like his father, Philip II, a brilliant general. Although his conquests could not be maintained after his death, they made him a legendary figure. In this marble relief, by Pierre Pugot (1620–94), Alexander is shown adopting a characteristically heroic pose.* ▶

of his forces down to the Indian Ocean and up into the Persian Gulf. With his remaining forces, Alexander returned to Babylon, where he fell ill and died in 323 BC, aged 32.

The Hellenistic Kingdoms
Alexander died without naming a successor. For the next half-century his generals fought each other for possession of his empire. Antigonus (382–301 BC) was named supreme commander in Asia in 321 BC; however, jealousy united his rivals against him and he was defeated at the Battle of Ipsus, in Phrygia, in 301 BC by a coalition of Cassander, Lysimachus, Ptolemy, and Seleucus.

By 275 BC three dynasties had emerged: the Antigonids (named after Antigonus II), who ruled Macedonia (reigned 276–239 BC); the Ptolemies, who held Egypt, Cyprus, and parts of Syria and Asia Minor; and the Seleucids, who controlled the remainder of the empire in Asia. Greece itself was divided between two confederacies – the Achaean League in the Peloponnese and the Aetolian League in central Greece. Athens and Sparta, meanwhile, regained their liberty, but not their military strength.

The Seleucids were checked in the west by the Attalids, who established a new kingdom based on Pergamum, and in the east by the Parthians, whose capital was at Ecbatana. The new power of Rome, meanwhile, became involved in Greek affairs. First invited by Rhodes

and Pergamum to intervene against Macedonian aggression (200–196 BC), by 146 BC Rome had acquired all Greece as its territory.

Only the Ptolemies survived for another century. They had established a highly centralized state, governed by a purely Greek elite. Their rule resulted in both economic prosperity and cultural flowering and the cultural capital of the Greek world shifted to Alexandria. Hereditary rule continued until the death of Cleopatra VII (born 69 BC) in 30 BC.

The Campaigns of Alexander the Great (334–323 BC)
Having decimated the Persian Empire, Alexander conquered on through Central Asia to India, where an army mutiny finally forced him to turn back. ▼

THRACE
MACEDONIA
BLACK SEA
EPIRUS
Troy
Athens
Sparta
Ephesos
PHRYGIA
CRETE
CYPRUS
MEDITERRANEAN SEA
Issus
Tyre
Damascus
Alexandria
EGYPT
RED SEA
ARABIAN GULF
MESOPOTAMIA
Gaugamela
Ecbatana
Babylon
BABYLONIA
Persepolis
CARMANIA
ARMENIA
CASPIAN SEA
MEDIA
PARTHIA
Hekatompylos
ARIA
Herat
GEDROSIA
SOGDIANA
Marakanda
BACTRIA
KINGDOM OF POROS
Taxila
ARACHOSIA
INDIA

Route of Alexander
Empire of Alexander
Regions dependent on Alexander

THE AGE OF PERICLES

ACCORDING TO THE contemporary historian Thucydides (c. 460–c. 400 BC), Pericles (c. 495–429 BC) was Athens' greatest statesman. As a young man he opposed the aristocrat and general Cimon and, together with the democrat Ephialtes (died 461 BC), set about reforming the Athenian senate, the boule. After peace was agreed with Persia in 449 BC, Pericles emerged to dominate Athenian politics for the next two decades.

Rivals at home were removed; threats from other states (revolts in Euboea and Megara and a Spartan invasion of Attica) were suppressed; and in 445 BC Sparta and Athens concluded a 30-year peace treaty. Pericles was now free to secure the cultural and political pre-eminence of Athens.

On the domestic front, the temples on the Acropolis, sacked by the Persians in 480 BC, still lay in ruins. Pericles commissioned Phidias (active c. 490–430 BC), the most renowned sculptor in all Greece, to undertake reconstruction of the site. In 447 BC work began on the Parthenon, the temple of Athena Parthenos, the city's patron goddess. Since its completion, in 432 BC, the Parthenon has stood as the symbol of the golden age of Athens.

Pericles established a network of Athenian colonies, peopled by poorer citizens, to defend the weaker points of the empire, such as Chalcidice and the Hellespont, and to extend the influence of Athens, even as far as Italy and the Black Sea. A man of vision, integrity, and great oratorical skill, Pericles was totally committed to consolidating the power of the Athenian Empire. He foresaw conflict with Sparta and was confident that Athens would prevail. When war broke out in 431 BC, he was responsible for strategic planning; he died of plague two years later.

Pericles *Conducting the Peloponnesian War successfully until his death in 429 BC, Pericles helped Athens to achieve supremacy in Greece.*

The Parthenon
Commissioned by Pericles, this temple – with its colonnaded exterior of Doric columns – represents the zenith of classical Greek architecture. It originally contained Phidias' gold and ivory statue of Athena.

ATHENIAN DEMOCRACY

Pericles was a great imperialist, under whose rule the Athenian Empire reached its height. Yet in spite of his great influence, he ultimately derived his power from the democratic assembly. Many other states, especially those within the empire, used Athenian democracy as a basis for their own constitutions.

At the heart of the Athenian democratic process was the assembly to which all adult male Greek citizens belonged. It met once a month on a hill called the Pnyx, where there was space for 6000 people. The assembly – at which attendance was considered a duty rather than a privilege – debated and decided all matters relating to home and foreign affairs. Women, slaves, and foreigners, however, were all excluded; while comic playwrights, such as Aristophanes (c. 450–c. 388 BC), made political rights for women the subjects of their jokes, the enfranchisement of women was never a serious consideration.

The business of the assembly was prepared by the boule, a council of elders comprising 500 citizens chosen by lot to serve for a year. The boule, which met daily, was also responsible for supervising the magistrates (generals, such as Pericles, who were elected by the assembly), for controlling state expenditure, and for overseeing religious festivals.

In addition to their political democracy, the Athenians operated an effective judicial system. Justice was administered by the courts, whose jurors were chosen by lot from the citizen body. Like members of the boule, and most magistrates, they were paid, to ensure that civic duties could be performed by rich and poor alike.

Of all the cultural phenomena of Periclean Athens, perhaps the most sublime and intellectual was tragedy. It was performed in the context of a religious festival, the Great Dionysia, celebrated every spring in honour of Dionysus.

Like the great athletic events, the dramatic festival took the form of a competition. Each competing playwright produced four of his own plays (three tragedies and a lighter piece, or satyr play); he also had to write the music, direct the acting and the dancing, and, at first, even play some of the roles himself. Plays were performed in the open-air theatre of Dionysus on the south slope of the Acropolis, where there were seats for up to 14 000 spectators. Pericles introduced subsidies to enable poorer people to attend.

The subject-matter of the plays was usually mythological. There were, however, exceptions to this: the earliest play that survives by Aeschylus, *The Persians*, produced in 472 BC, is concerned with the recent victory at Salamis. Both the actors (who were all men) and the chorus (which was often central to the action) wore masks. Social, moral, and political issues were woven into the poet's treatment of the plot, while his principal purpose was dramatic: to challenge the audience's emotions, to create suspense, and to win the prize. Comedy was first given a place at the Great Dionysia in 486 BC. The surviving plays of Aristophanes, produced between 427 and 388 BC, focus on everyday life in contemporary Athens and provide us with a sparkling satirical commentary on post-Periclean society.

Theatre of Dionysus *Originally constructed in c. 330 BC, the theatre's flat circular area (the 'orchestra') was the scene of performances, processions, and sacrifices during the festival.*

THE CLASSICAL MOMENT

The period between the defeat of Persia in 479 BC and the start of the Peloponnesian War in 431 BC was one of the most creative in European history. For almost 50 years (known by the Greeks as the pentecontaëtia, 'the 50 years') there was relative peace as Persia, the common enemy of all the Greeks, had been defeated.

Greek Vase *This superb 5th-century BC painted vase, used for mixing wines, features a Dionysian scene depicting the ritual dismemberment of a wild animal.*

Frieze from the Parthenon *Sculptors of the day, such as Phidias, adorned the buildings of ancient Greece with friezes, which were impressive in their detail. This section from the Parthenon depicts the gods Apollo and Poseidon and the goddess Artemis.*

Athens was the focus of this cultural explosion. The sense of freedom, enhanced by the democratic system of government, and the economic stability, provided by imperial tribute and exploitation of the silver mines at Laurium, created a favourable climate for artistic and intellectual achievement.

In literature, the innovations were especially wide-ranging. Dramatists, such as Aeschylus (c. 525–c. 456 BC), Sophocles (c. 496–404 BC), and Euripides (c. 484–406 BC), developed a new public medium for the telling of (usually legendary) stories, while prose historians, such as Thucydides, set new standards in the chronicling and analysis of contemporary events. The themes of the lyric poets included celebrations of the victories of athletes in the games. It was orators, however, who moved the assembly with their rhetoric, emerging as the victors in the democratic arena.

The skill of rhetoric was taught by itinerant experts (called sophists), such as Gorgias (died c. 376 BC). Teachers of another sort, notably the philosopher Socrates (c. 470–399 BC), also began to expound new ethical and metaphysical ideas to audiences of young men with inquiring minds, eager to discover the nature of truth.

In the visual arts, architects made an elegant impact on the landscape with their defined orders of columns (Doric, Ionic, and now Corinthian). Painters and sculptors pursued new techniques of perspective and harmony with remarkable success, though few of their works survive. The sublime realism achieved by vase painters gives some indication of the lost masterpieces of the panel painters.

Persia

Medes and Persians • The Achaemenid Persian Empire •
Greece and Achaemenid decline • The Parthians • Sassanian Persia

The term 'Persia' was used by the ancient Greeks when referring to a province of the Achaemenid Empire, which was occupied by a people called the Persians during the 1st millennium BC. The province was the mountainous region of Fars, part of the dry rocky plateau that forms the modern country of Iran. As the Persians expanded beyond Fars the entire plateau came to be described as Persia. Situated between the Caspian Sea to the north and the Persian Gulf and Gulf of Oman to the south, the region had always been an important source of stone and metals for the people of the lowland plains of Mesopotamia to the west. Despite the often impenetrable mountain ranges surrounding Persia, trade routes had always crossed the region, linking the Mediterranean world with the Orient.

Medes and Persians

The early history of the Persians is inextricably linked with a people called the Medes. Mention of them first appears in Assyrian inscriptions of the 9th century BC as a loose confederation of tribes in western Persia. During the reign of the Assyrian King Esarhaddon (reigned 680–669 BC) treaties secured the support of the Medes, who by this time had united into a large kingdom based around their capital at Ecbatana (modern Hamadan). To the south, in the region of Fars, were based the Persians, who were their subjects. By 612 BC, the Medes, under King Cyaxares (reigned c. 653–586 BC), were a major military power, which, in alliance with the Babylonians, destroyed the city of Nineveh and overthrew the mighty empire of Assyria. While the king of Babylon, Nabopolassar (reigned 625–605 BC), inherited the bulk of the Assyrian Empire, the Medes consolidated their hold over western Iran and Anatolia, including the rich kingdom of **Lydia**.

In 550 BC, however, the Median King Astyges (reigned 585–550 BC) was deposed by Cyrus of Persia (reigned 550–c. 529 BC), who established himself as undisputed king of the Medes and the Persians. He claimed as his ancestor the legendary King Achaemenes, thus initiating the so-called Achaemenid period of Persian history.

The Achaemenid Persian Empire

Having established himself as the ruler of Persia, Cyrus turned his attention to Lydia. Croesus (reigned c. 560–?546 BC), king of Lydia, had taken advantage of the fall of the Median Empire to expand his own kingdom. Following an indecisive battle in 547 or 546 BC

**The Tomb of Cyrus
at Pasargadae** ▶
*Cyrus, the first and
greatest of Persia's
rulers, conquered
Lydia and Babylon,
thus establishing a
powerful empire.*

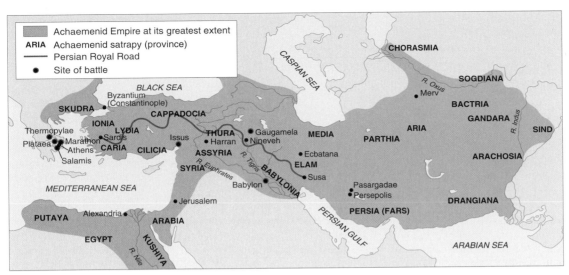

The Persian Achaemenid Empire was established by Cyrus the Great and stretched from the Aegean Sea to the Indus River. The empire subsequently flourished, reaching its greatest extent under Darius I, who divided it into satrapies (provinces) and had the Royal Road constructed.

Cyrus besieged Croesus in his capital, Sardis. The city soon fell to the Persian army; Croesus was either killed or, according to the Greek historian Herodotus (c. 484–420 BC), treated in a friendly manner by Cyrus. Western Anatolia thus passed into the hands of the Persians. Soon Lycia, Caria, and the Greek cities of Asia Minor were also incorporated into the growing empire.

At this time Cyrus built himself a capital at Pasargadae in Fars. The surviving palaces there have columned halls, which probably reproduce in stone the traditional form of houses built of mud brick and wood. The plan of Pasargadae suggests that alongside the royal buildings lay a park or garden. Building at the site continued under Cyrus' successors, and Pasargadae acted as a ceremonial and religious centre.

Cyrus now turned his attention to Babylon. In 539 BC the Babylonian King Nabonidus (reigned 556–539 BC) was deposed and Mesopotamia, Syria, and Palestine became the domains of the Persian ruler. In his inscriptions Cyrus now described himself with some justification as 'ruler of all the world.' He repatriated groups of captive peoples, including the Jews, who had been deported from Jerusalem by Nebuchadnezzar in 586 BC.

Cyrus was killed on campaign in 529 BC and succeeded by his eldest son, Cambyses (reigned 529–522 BC). The empire expanded as the Persian army invaded and subjugated Egypt. Though Cambyses is described as a vicious tyrant by Herodotus, evidence from Egypt shows that he followed the royal traditions of his newly acquired land. Towards the end of Cambyses' reign a revolt broke out led by two **magi**. Cambyses was killed while travelling on to Syria to deal with the revolt. The rebellion was eventually brought to an end by a group of seven conspirators, one of whom, Darius I (reigned 522–486 BC), became king.

Under Darius, the Achaemenid Empire reached its greatest extent, stretching from Egypt and Lydia in the west to the Indus River in the east. According to Herodotus the empire was divided into 20 provinces, each with its own governor, or **satrap**. Darius was the first Persian king to mint his own coins, and communications throughout the vast empire were maintained by the construction of a 'Royal Road,' which stretched from Susa to Sardis. Darius' main building work was at Persepolis, 30 km southwest of Pasargadae. This was continued by his two immediate successors, Xerxes (reigned 486–465 BC) and Artaxerxes (reigned 465–425 BC).

Greece and Achaemenid Decline

Towards the end of his reign, Darius was involved in a conflict with the Greeks. While Persian sources give no account of the event, classical accounts, especially the history of Herodotus, describe the attack in detail. In 490 BC a Persian force landed on the Greek mainland near the plain of Marathon. In the ensuing battle the Athenians gained the advantage, forcing the Persians to withdraw. Darius' successor Xerxes renewed the conflict in 480 BC: marching through northern Greece, the Persian army defeated the Greeks at the pass of Thermopylae and advanced to Athens, where the city was ravaged and the Acropolis temples looted and destroyed. The Athenians had retreated to Salamis, where Greek ships inflicted a decisive defeat on the Persian navy, many of whose ships were destroyed. Xerxes withdrew, leaving an army in northern Greece. In the following year (479 BC), however, the Persian forces were defeated on the plain of Plataea and expelled from Greece (see GREECE AND THE HELLENISTIC WORLD).

After Xerxes' assassination in his palace in 465 BC, there followed a long period of decline for the Achaemenid Empire. In 334 BC the

Lydia

The prosperity of the Lydians was based on the gold found in the region. This led to the proverbial wealth of Lydia's ruler, King Croesus. The Lydians have been credited with the invention of coinage. Indeed, the earliest coins stamped with a device to guarantee their weight were found at Ephesus; one carried an inscription in Lydian.

magi (from the Greek *magus* and Iranian *mobad*) A priestly class of the Medes. They acted as advisers and dream interpreters in the Median court and were involved with animal sacrifice, the exposure of the dead to be devoured by vultures, and tending the sacred fires that burned continuously on special altars. Many magi, active among the Persians as well as the Medes, were probably followers of the prophet Zoroaster.

Persepolis *The great dynastic centre of Persepolis served as a venue for annual festivities, rites, and banquets in honour of the royal house and its achievements, rather than as a regular residence of the Persian court. The city was a magnificent assembly of stone buildings with columned halls, gateways guarded by composite animals, and carved staircases. It was destroyed by Alexander the Great in 330 BC, following his conquest of the Persian Empire.* ▶

▲ **Gold Bracelet** *(5th century BC) Found on the Oxus River (Afghanistan), this bracelet is a fine example of Achaemenid Persian metalwork.*

Zoroastrianism

The prophet Zarathustra (Greek: Zoroaster) traditionally lived from c. 628 to 551 BC in eastern Persia, although he may have belonged to a remoter period. He reformed the religion of Persia, eliminating many lesser gods and leaving only a creator god, Ahura Mazda, the 'wise lord,' as the embodiment of goodness, wisdom, and truth. Zoroaster revealed the word of his god in hymns called the gathas in the sacred five books of the Avesta.

king of Macedon, Alexander the Great, entered Anatolia with his army. In the following year he defeated the armies of Darius III (reigned 336–330 BC) at Issus and again in 331 BC at Gaugamela (northern Iraq). Alexander marched across Iran to Susa, which his army looted, before moving on to Persepolis, which was burnt to the ground. Alexander left no successor and after his death in 323 BC his generals quarrelled and fought, splitting the empire between them. By 300 BC, the general Seleucus (c. 358–281 BC) emerged as the ruler of Persia, Mesopotamia, and northern Syria and founder of the Seleucid dynasty. For the next century and a half, Greek (Hellenistic) ideas influenced the main cities of Persia. Though there is little archaeological information from this period, it is clear that such cities as Susa contained typical Greek features, including gymnasiums and theatres.

The Parthians

The Seleucid dynasty was challenged towards the end of the 3rd century BC. Originally a nomadic Persian tribe, the Parthians under King Arsaces (reigned c. 250–c. 211 BC) seized the satrapy (province) of Parthia, east of the Caspian Sea. Arsaces' successors expanded their kingdom and by the death of Mithridates I (reigned 171–138 BC), often regarded as the founder of the Parthian Empire, the Parthians controlled much of Persia, Mesopotamia, and Central Asia. Indeed, by 113 BC Mithridates II (reigned 123–88 BC) had extended the empire to the River Euphrates. Parthia now dominated the Silk Road, controlling trade between China in the east and Rome in the west. Good

relations were enjoyed between Parthia and the Chinese Han dynasty (see CHINA: CLASSICAL CHINA), but expansion to the Euphrates brought them into conflict with Rome. The two powers clashed at Harran in 53 BC, which resulted in defeat for the Roman legions under Crassus (c. 115–53 BC) at the Battle of Carrhae. An attack by Mark Antony (83–30 BC) in 36 BC was equally disastrous for Rome.

Parthia was not challenged from the west again until 116 AD, when the Roman Emperor Trajan (reigned 98–117 AD) succeeded in marching his army into Mesopotamia as far as the Persian Gulf. Although Trajan had to

PALMYRA

The oasis of Tadmor (known to the classical world as Palmyra because of the area's extensive palm groves) was an important resting place on the caravan route across Syria. Linking the Mediterranean world of Rome and the empires of Parthia and later Sasanian Persia, Palmyra grew wealthy and powerful. In 264 and 267 AD the Arab ruler of Palmyra, Odaenathus (died c. 268), led successful campaigns against the Sassanians and reached their capital, Ctesiphon. He was, however, murdered and his wife Zenobia took over command of the Palmyran armies, leading them into Egypt and Anatolia. In 272 AD the Roman Emperor Aurelian (reigned 270–75 AD) captured Zenobia; in the following year he seized Palmyra.

withdraw soon after, Parthia was now in decline. Information about the Parthians comes largely from Greek and Latin authors, who are naturally biased. The Parthians themselves have left little written evidence apart from some inscriptions on coins.

Sassanian Persia

The last Parthian king, Artabanus V (reigned c. 213–24 AD), was overthrown by Ardashir (reigned 224–41 AD), a local ruler in Fars. As a descendant of a certain Sassan (active 1st century AD), Ardashir founded the Sassanian dynasty. The Sassanians, who viewed themselves as the natural successors of the Achaemenids, wished to restore the greatness of the first Persian dynasty. Their expansionist aims inevitably brought them into conflict with Rome and, later, Byzantium in the west. They contested control of the east–west trade route bringing silks, spices, and other luxury goods from the Orient.

As part of a process of centralizing government **Zoroastrianism** was made the state religion. Whether the Achaemenid kings of Persia were themselves devotees of the prophet Zoroaster is not certain; it is clear, however, that they followed the god Ahura Mazda. During the Seleucid and Parthian periods Zoroastrianism had been in decline. The Sassanian kings, however, reinvigorated the religion with the building of many fire temples; fire altars are often depicted on Sassanian coins.

Ardashir's successor Shapur I (reigned 241–72) defeated three Roman emperors: Gordian III (reigned 238–44), Philip the Arab (reigned 244–49), and Valerian (reigned 253–60). However, under Shapur's three successors, all called Bahram (reigned 273–76, 276–93, and 293), territory was lost. During these years Zoroastrian orthodoxy was imposed on the Sassanian Empire; all religious minorities were savagely persecuted, largely at the instigation of a powerful priest called Kartir (active 3rd century).

During the reign of Shapur II (reigned 309–79) the Sassanians moved successfully against the Roman army. To pay for his military activities Shapur imposed heavy taxes. Since the conversion to Christianity of Emperor Constantine I (reigned 324–37), Christianity now represented the official religion of the Roman Empire; Christians, therefore, bore the brunt of these tax demands. Shapur's reign also saw the Zoroastrian scripture, the Avesta, written down in Persian.

During the 5th century the Sassanians faced challenges from nomadic groups from the east; these were further exacerbated by drought and famine. Trouble was also created by a social and economic movement led by the prophet Mazdak (active late 5th century), who preached the need for a classless society. Sassanian society was rigidly hierarchical with four classes – priests, warriors, scribes, and common people – between which it was practically impossible to move. In c. 528 Mazdak and his followers were massacred by Crown Prince Chosroes Anushirvan (reigned 531–79). On ascending the throne, however, Chosroes Anushirvan revised the taxation system, following a detailed survey of the empire's resources. This allowed the king to maintain a standing army and produce an increase in the irrigation agriculture of Mesopotamia. He defeated the tribal groups to the north and east and was successful against the power of Byzantium to the west.

By 600 AD, the Sassanian King Chosroes II (reigned 590–628) ruled much of the Near East, having come to the throne with the aid of Byzantine troops. Internal conflicts in the Byzantine Empire allowed him to capture Jerusalem and Alexandria, and Sassanian troops even reached as far as the Byzantine capital, Constantinople (see EARLY AND MEDIEVAL EUROPE: THE BYZANTINE EMPIRE).

Within a few years, however, the Byzantine Emperor Heraclius (reigned 610–41) attacked eastward and defeated the Persians. The Persian generals revolted and Chosroes was killed. A rapid succession of Persian rulers was not able to stop the armies of the Arabs, which had now united under Islam. In 637 the Sassanians were defeated by an Arab army near their capital, Ctesiphon. A further defeat followed in 642 and the last Sassanian king, Yazdigird (reigned 632–51), fled from the battle and was assassinated at Merv. Sassanian rule in Persia thus came to an end, heralding the start of the Islamic era (see ISLAMIC WORLD: THE EMERGENCE OF A NEW EMPIRE).

▲ **Shapur II**
The silver plate shown here depicts the Persian king hunting; it is a typical Sassanian art form.

Sassanian Building

The splendour of the Sassanian monarchs is illustrated by their surviving palaces, such as those at the capital city of Ctesiphon in Mesopotamia. Domes and barrel-vaulted iwans (reception halls) were decorated with mosaics and stucco wall decoration that show a clear Roman influence.

Rock Relief of Shapur I *As victor against the Romans, Shapur I is shown here with Emperor Valerian kneeling before him.* ▼

The Growth of Rome

The kings • The early Republic • The growth of the Roman Empire •
The consequences of Empire • Civil wars • The fall of the Republic

**Plan of Rome
during the
Republic** *From a
small group of huts on
the Palatine hill in the
9th century BC, Rome
developed, between the
7th and 2nd centuries
BC, into a sophisticated
urban centre, protected
by impressive
fortifications and served
by several aqueducts.* ▼

According to legend, the city of Rome took its name from Romulus, a shepherd king who founded a settlement on the Palatine hill after killing his twin brother Remus, traditionally in 753 BC. Romulus was said to have been the first of seven kings who ruled until the end of the 6th century BC, when a republic was formed.

It is difficult to know how much truth there is in the legends of early Rome. Archaeologists have established that one or more villages existed on the hills of Rome, including the Palatine hill, from the end of the Bronze Age (c. 1000 BC). Other communities of a similar type have been identified at other hilltop sites in the same area, known in antiquity as Latium. In the 10th and 9th centuries BC the settlements were small isolated villages. During the 8th and 7th centuries BC they grew in size and sophistication with the development of external trade (including contacts with Greece), craft production, and the emergence of a wealthy aristocracy. At Rome, the Palatine settlement had expanded by 700 BC to include the Forum valley and possibly the Quirinal hill. Towards the end of the 7th century the Forum was laid out as a public meeting place with monumental buildings. At

this point Rome was transformed into an organized city-state.

Rome was situated on an important crossing of the River Tiber, which separated the Latins from their northern neighbours, the **Etruscans**. As a rapidly growing frontier town, Rome seems to have had a mixed population, including Sabines and Greeks as well as large numbers of Etruscans. Two of the kings were traditionally of Etruscan origin; it should not be assumed, however, that Rome was conquered by the Etruscans or that it became an Etruscan city. It did, however, share the same (Hellenizing) material culture as the cities of southern Etruria. Although heavily influenced by contacts with the outside world (including Greece and the Near East, as well as Etruria and Campania), Rome remained fundamentally a Latin city.

The Kings

The earliest written history of Rome at this time is recorded in literary sources of the classical period, such as the works of Livy (c. 59 BC–c. 17 AD). However, it is unlikely that they contain much reliable information about events that took place hundreds of years earlier. Claims that the city was originally ruled by kings are probably true, yet there can be no certainty about the traditional list of seven rulers: Romulus, Numa Pompilius, Tullus Hostilius, Ancus Marcius, Tarquinius Priscus, Servius Tullius, and Tarquinius Superbus. With the exception of Romulus these names may be those of genuine rulers, but the narratives of their reigns found in the works of Livy and others must be regarded as largely fictitious.

It is nevertheless possible that some elements of the traditional story are based, however loosely, on actual events. Tullus Hostilius is said to have conquered the region of the Alban Hills (to the south of Rome), an area that was almost certainly in Roman hands before the end of the 6th century BC. Similarly the organization of the calendar and the major priesthoods, traditionally the work of Numa, can be dated with some confidence to the 6th century BC or even earlier. The belief that the Roman monarchy was elective rather than hereditary is probably true; many institutions associated with the election process survived into the Republic. The **interrex**, an official who took charge of the Republic if

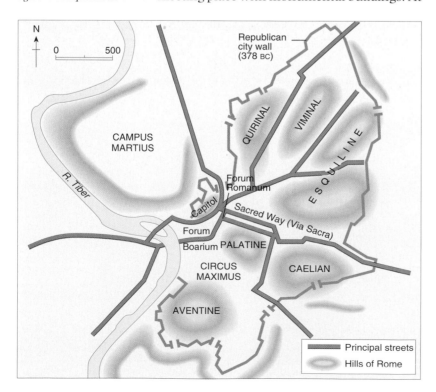

CAMPUS MARTIUS

Republican city wall (378 BC)

QUIRINAL

VIMINAL

ESQUILINE

R. Tiber

Forum Romanum

Capitol

Sacred Way (Via Sacra)

Forum Boarium

PALATINE

CIRCUS MAXIMUS

CAELIAN

AVENTINE

N

0   500

▬▬ Principal streets
◯ Hills of Rome

both consuls died in office, was probably a genuine relic of the time of the kings.

The last two kings are traditionally presented as tyrants, who adopted a populist style of rule similar to that of contemporary Greek tyrants. They pursued an ambitious foreign policy, patronized the arts, and embarked on grandiose building projects. Archaeological evidence confirms that Rome was a powerful, sophisticated, and cosmopolitan city at this time. Finally, Tarquinius Superbus (reigned 534–510 BC?) is said to have created a miniature empire in Latium, the existence of which is also presupposed in the first treaty between Rome and Carthage, a document quoted by the Greek historian Polybius (c. 200–c. 120 BC), and dated by him to 509 BC. This tends to confirm the authenticity of the account.

The Early Republic

The portrayal of the later kings as 'tyrants' (i.e. populist dictators) is consistent with the story that the last of them, Tarquinius Superbus, was expelled in an aristocratic coup and replaced by a republic governed by two annually elected **consuls**. These officials, who had equal powers, were assisted by a council of elders (the **Senate**) and, eventually, by boards of lesser officials, such as the **quaestors** (magistrates and administrators), who were also elected annually. In the event of an emergency, a single supreme ruler, the **dictator**, could be appointed for a maximum of six months.

The main outline of this traditional account is supported by the evidence of the **Fasti**, the list of consuls preserved in a number of sources, which is widely regarded as authentic. The *Fasti* lists the two consuls for each year from c. 500 BC. A late 6th-century BC date is estimated for the beginning of the Republic.

Sources for the Republic are in general more reliable than for the monarchical period. The sources from which the Roman historians obtained their information about the early Republic undoubtedly included the accounts of Greek historians, the traditions of the great noble families (partly preserved in written form), and public documents, such as laws and senatorial decrees. They also had access to archival documents in chronicle form, the most useful of which was a priestly chronicle, the *Annales Maximi*, which included lists of the magistrates for each year and other information about public events. The records for the 5th century BC were meagre and uncertain, while later literary narratives introduced much elaboration and perhaps even invention. However, there is no reason to doubt that a basic structure of documentary material underlies the accounts of our sources for the history of the Republic.

Patricians and Plebeians. During the early years of the Republic power was held by an aristocratic group known as the **patriciate**. Patricians were members of certain privileged clans (*gentes*), which had probably obtained special status under the monarchy. The patricians had an exclusive hold on all the chief religious offices; it was they who gave assent (known as *auctoritas patrum*) to decisions reached by the people's **assemblies** before they became binding. Although most consuls

A Latin Culture

Stone inscriptions found in the Roman Forum, which date from shortly after 600 BC, indicate that Rome was a Latin city and that its culture had been literate probably from before 600 BC.

consuls The two annually elected magistrates who jointly exercised the highest civil and military authority in the Republic. They were elected by assemblies of the Roman people and presided over the Senate. Under the empire they were nominated by the emperor and held office for only two to four months.

THE ETRUSCANS

The Etruscans were an ancient people who inhabited an area of northwestern Italy bounded by the River Tiber and the River Arno. Although their language was unlike all other Italian languages, their civilization was formed in Italy and developed from a preceding Iron-Age culture, evidence of which was discovered near Bologna in 1853. Etruscan civilization reached its cultural zenith in the archaic period (8th to 5th centuries BC), when powerful city-states emerged, including Veii, Caere, Tarquinii, Vetulonia, and Volsinii. Knowledge of these centres is based on archaeological evidence (particularly finds from their rich cemeteries), information in Greek and Roman histories, and Etruscan inscriptions, of which around 13 000 are now recorded. Although the language is not fully understood, the texts are written in the Greek alphabet, and the basic meaning of most of them can now be discerned.

▲ **Etruscan Culture** *This painting from the Tomb of the Leopards, at Tarquinii, dating from the 5th century BC, depicts a scene from an aristocratic banquet.*

THE FIRST SECESSION

At the 'First Secession' the plebs formed an assembly, elected their own officers (**tribunes** and **aediles**), and set up their own cult. For the next two centuries this remarkable plebeian organization fought to improve the lot of its members, by passing resolutions (**plebiscites**) and if necessary by secession. Their strongest weapons, however, were the tribunes, whom the plebs swore to protect. The tribunes thus became 'sacrosanct,' and were consequently able to frustrate the actions of magistrates by their personal intervention. This later became formalized as the famous tribunician **veto**.

▲ **The Roman Forum** *Situated at the heart of the city, the Forum was the focus of political and religious life. The Sacred Way, shown here, is the oldest street in Rome, which ran through the Forum.*

Assemblies

The Roman *comitia*, or popular assemblies, met frequently to elect consuls and other state officials, vote on major issues, such as war, pass laws, and try major cases. The voting units in plebeian assemblies were the local tribes, whereas consuls were elected by assemblies of 'centuries,' membership of which was determined by wealth. The system was organized so that the wealthy had a built-in majority and could always outvote the poor.

were patricians, it appears from the *Fasti* that the latter did not have a monopoly of political office until the middle of the 5th century BC.

The early 5th century BC was a period when Rome experienced military difficulties and economic recession. The poorer citizens suffered most, especially without the protection of the kings who had relied on their support. Debt, the need for land, and food shortages are recorded as the main grievances. Some of the poorer citizens, known as the ***plebeians*** (or plebs), are said to have taken matters into their own hands in 494 BC, when they withdrew – in the so-called **First Secession** – from the city to form their own alternative state.

The principal demands of the plebs were for debt relief and a more equitable distribution of economic resources, especially land. Tradition maintained that the codification of the law, in the form of the **Twelve Tables** (450 BC), was also a product of plebeian agitation. The plebeian organization was gradually recognized, obtaining a limited right to pass plebiscites binding on the whole population (in 449 BC, extended in 339 BC). Its membership seems to have increased and came to include growing numbers of wealthy and politically ambitious citizens. In the 4th century BC (and perhaps earlier) these richer plebeians began to use the organization to break down the exclusive privileges of the patricians. Thus the struggle became a direct conflict between patricians and plebeians.

In 367 BC the Licinio-Sextian laws made plebeians eligible for the consulship; in 342 BC the rule was established that one of the two consuls must be a plebeian. In 339 BC the *auctoritas patrum* was reduced to a formality; in 300 BC the major priestly colleges (of pontiffs and augurs) were divided between the two orders. By these and similar measures the plebeians were gradually reintegrated into the

state, a process that was completed in c. 287 BC, when plebiscites were made binding on the people and became equivalent to laws.

The Growth of the Roman Empire

After the fall of the monarchy the Romans were faced with a revolt by the Latins, whom they defeated in a great battle at Lake Regillus (496 BC). As a result Rome and the Latins formed a military alliance, which enabled them to defend Latium against the incursions of the Sabines, Aequi, and Volsci. By the later 5th century BC, regular raids by these peoples had ceased, and the Romans (with allied support) were able to take the offensive. They also gained an advantage against the Etruscan city of Veii, a long-standing rival, which they captured and destroyed in 396 BC. In 390 BC Rome itself was sacked by a Celtic war-band from northern Italy; this famous episode, however, was only a temporary setback. In the following decades Rome's power and influence steadily expanded. In 338 BC, after an abortive revolt, many of the Latins were incorporated into the Roman state, which also annexed northern Campania. Other defeated peoples were obliged to become allies and to fight alongside the Romans in subsequent wars. Part of their land was colonized by the poor (allies as well as Romans), who thus benefited from the process of conquest.

The fiercest resistance to Rome's advance came from the Samnites of central southern Italy; however, they were no match for Rome's efficient political organization and manpower resources. The fate of Italy was finally decided in 296 BC when a united force of Samnites, Gauls, Etruscans, and Umbrians met the Romans at the Battle of Sentinum. The Romans won a decisive victory and proceeded to defeat the remaining independent peoples of Italy. The last to succumb were the Greek cities of the south, particularly Tarentum, which, in 280 BC, summoned King Pyrrhus (319–272 BC) of Epirus (modern NW Greece and S Albania) to Italy to lead a war against Rome. This was ultimately unsuccessful and Tarentum surrendered a few years later; the Roman conquest of Italy was thus complete.

Shortly afterwards the Romans became involved in a major overseas war, when they challenged **Carthage** for control of Sicily in 264 BC. In spite of huge losses the Romans finally emerged as victors in 241 BC, in the so-called First Punic War (from *Punicus*, 'Carthaginian'); Sicily thus became the first Roman province. The Second Punic War began in 218 BC when Hannibal (247–c. 183 BC), the Carthaginian general in Spain, sought revenge by crossing the Alps and invading Italy with an army of 26 000 and several war elephants. After a heroic trek in which he lost some 10 000 men, he won spectacular victories at Trasimene and Cannae. However, Hannibal failed to win over Rome's Italian allies; he was gradually worn down by the tactics of Quintus Fabius Maximus (died 203 BC) and withdrew from Italy in 204 BC. Hannibal was finally defeated at Zama in Africa by Scipio Africanus (236–183 BC) in 202 BC.

As a result of these successes the Romans obtained further provinces from former Carthaginian possessions in Spain. They also resumed the conquest of Cisalpine Gaul (northern Italy), begun in 224 BC, which had been interrupted by Hannibal's invasion. By c. 173 BC, Roman armies had occupied the Po Valley, Liguria, and the Istrian peninsula. At the same time they were engaged in fierce fighting in Spain, which continued intermittently until 133 BC; this campaign led to the conquest of Lusitania and Celtiberia. Finally, campaigns in southern Gaul from 125 BC to 121 BC resulted in the conquest of Gallia Narbonensis (modern Provence).

At this time Rome became increasingly involved in the affairs of the eastern Mediterranean. The first Roman venture in this area, during the 220s BC, so alarmed the Macedonian king, Philip V (237–179 BC), that he made an alliance with Hannibal (215 BC), which provoked the First Macedonian War with Rome (214–205 BC). After the defeat of Hannibal, the Romans were free to concentrate on their ambitions in the east, and embarked on the Second Macedonian War in 200 BC. Roman troops invaded the Balkans and defeated Philip at Cynoscephalae (197 BC); however, these forces were withdrawn in 194 BC after the Roman commander Flamininus (c. 230–c. 174 BC) had confined Philip to Macedonia and pronounced the 'freedom of the Greeks.' Roman efforts to control events in the Greek world by diplomacy and threats were eventually unsuccessful and further military interventions occurred between 191 BC and 188 BC, when the Romans invaded Asia Minor and defeated Antiochus III (c. 292–187 BC) of Syria.

In the Third Macedonian War (171–167 BC) the kingdom of Macedonia was destroyed by the Roman victory at Pydna. Finally, in the 140s BC, Roman armies crushed revolts in Macedonia and Greece, which became Roman provinces. The Romans emphasized their dominance by ruthlessness, the most brutal example of which was the destruction of Corinth in 146 BC. In the same year Carthage was destroyed after a Third Punic War (149–146 BC), its territory becoming the Roman

---

The Twelve Tables

This document, produced in 451–450 BC by a board of ten men, formed a code of written laws. The Tables were subsequently regarded as the foundation of Roman law. Although the full text is lost, a sample of the contents is preserved in quotations. The Tables dealt systematically with legal procedures, obligations, property, inheritance, and personal injuries.

Carthage

Carthage was an ancient city in north Africa, near modern Tunis. The Punic name was *Kart Hadasht*, New City; it became the leading Phoenician trading centre in north Africa.

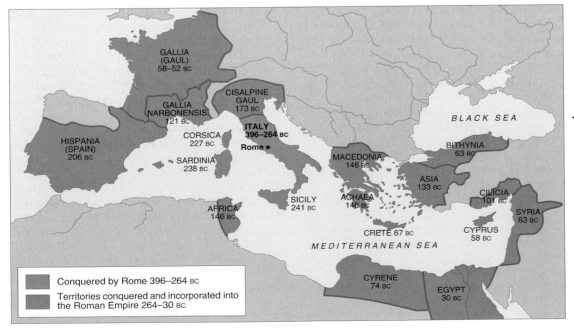

◄ **The Growth of the Roman Empire** (*showing dates of conquests*) *Roman domination of Italy was completed by 264 BC; a series of successful overseas campaigns meant that, by 30 BC, the Roman Empire included territories on every coast of the Mediterranean and far into northwestern Europe.*

Conquered by Rome 396–264 BC

Territories conquered and incorporated into the Roman Empire 264–30 BC

Slavery

The institution of slavery existed at Rome from the earliest times. During the age of imperial conquests the Romans enslaved hundreds of thousands of prisoners from Italy, Carthage, and other Mediterranean lands. By 44 BC, there were more than two million slaves in Italy. They had no rights and were treated as items of property. Many were employed in agriculture, working on the estates of rich landlords. Others were domestic servants in the city households. Romans often freed their slaves; in the later Republic freed slaves were a significant social group. Since they obtained Roman citizenship on release, they were quickly integrated with the free population.

The Greek Influence ▶

The Romans imitated all aspects of Hellenistic culture, as is illustrated by this Greek-style temple (dating from the 2nd century BC) in the Forum Boarium, Rome.

province of Africa. Further annexations occurred in Asia (133 BC), Cilicia (101 BC), and Cyrene (96 BC; it officially became a Roman province in 74 AD).

The Consequences of Empire

The Romans' successful overseas conquests had dramatic effects on all aspects of life in Rome and Italy. They consolidated the power of the noble elite, who dominated the Senate and virtually monopolized the senior offices of state. The plebs acquiesced in this provided that they benefited from the proceeds of military conquest; the tribunate became a means of advancing the careers of plebeian nobles.

The expansion of empire vastly increased the wealth of the upper classes, who invested in land. This led to the growth of large estates in Italy, worked by war captives imported as **slaves**. Slave labour on the estates replaced the small peasant farmers, who formed the backbone of the Roman army; however, they found that prolonged military service in distant locations made it increasingly difficult to maintain their farms. Roman and Italian peasants were thus driven off the land to a life of penury. The displacement of the peasant class also led to growing problems of military recruitment, since the law laid down a property qualification for service in the army. The rich, meanwhile, grew richer, enabling them to indulge their tastes for luxury and sophisticated pastimes. The influence of Greek culture became pervasive. Architecture, literature, and the visual arts flourished as the Romans imitated all aspects of Greek civilization.

The widening gulf between rich and poor eventually gave rise to social conflict and political breakdown. In 133 BC a tribune, Tiberius Gracchus (163–133 BC), introduced a land reform scheme that proposed to redistribute among the poor the state-owned land (*ager publicus*) that had been annexed by

the rich. This met with furious opposition; Gracchus was eventually murdered in an outbreak of political violence instigated by the nobles. Ten years later his brother, Gaius (153–121 BC), suffered the same fate, when he attempted to bring in more wide-ranging reforms. These embraced provincial administration and taxation, the urban grain supply, judicial reform, and the extension of Roman citizenship to Italian allies. Gaius' aim was to ensure that all citizens, not only the ruling class, should benefit from the proceeds of the empire, and that those who governed it should be made accountable for their actions. However, most of the measures that he passed as law were repealed after his murder (121 BC).

Civil Wars

In the following years Rome faced military difficulties in every part of the empire. These included a war in Africa, a slave revolt in Sicily (103–101 BC), and an invasion of Italy by migrating German tribes. The ruling oligarchy showed itself to be corrupt and incompetent in responding to these crises; the situation was only resolved when the able and ambitious Gaius Marius (c. 157–86 BC) was allowed to hold an unprecedented succession of consulships and to recruit a professional army from the proletariat.

While these measures solved the military problems, they had disastrous long-term consequences. Unscrupulous leaders were able to exploit their impoverished soldiers, while using armed force to obtain personal power. The situation was brought to a head by two events: first, the aftermath of the Social War (91–89 BC) – the revolt of the Italian allies who had taken up arms in order to obtain Roman citizenship, and secondly by an invasion of the eastern provinces by Mithridates VI (120–63 BC) of Pontus. These events created political chaos at Rome. Lucius Cornelius Sulla (c. 138–78 BC), the consul of 88 BC, was appointed by the Senate to lead an expedition against Mithridates; however, the plebeian assembly overturned this arrangement and gave the command to Marius. Sulla responded by marching on the city and driving Marius out. However, when Sulla and his army left for the east, Marius and his followers marched on the city, massacred opponents, and seized power (87 BC). When Sulla returned, having defeated Mithridates in 83 BC, full-scale civil war erupted between his forces and those of Marius's successors (Marius had died in 86 BC).

After a series of destructive encounters, Sulla emerged victorious and set himself up as dictator in 81 BC. He purged his opponents by means of the notorious ***proscriptions*** (lists of persons declared as outlaws with a reward for their capture); he also attempted to reform the

constitution, by strengthening the Senate and by reducing the powers of the tribunes. These efforts were ineffectual, however, since they addressed the symptoms rather than the cause of the problem. A fresh series of military crises in the 70s BC, including a major slave revolt led by **Spartacus,** brought the popular generals Pompey (106–48 BC) and Crassus (c. 115–53 BC) to power. As consuls in 70 BC they repealed most of Sulla's laws and restored the powers of the tribunes.

These events left the Senate with little power at a time when military difficulties and economic crises continued to afflict the empire. In 66 BC Pompey was appointed (by a tribunician plebiscite) the Senate's commander, in place of Lucius Lucullus (died c. 57 BC), to command a war in the east against Mithridates. He quickly ended the war and completely reorganized the eastern territories. In Italy, meanwhile, social unrest and discontent erupted in the conspiracy of Catiline (63 BC), which was quelled by the consul Cicero (106–43 BC).

In 62 BC Pompey returned, a conquering hero, to a magnificent welcome. The conservative nobles, led by Lucullus and Cato, frustrated his efforts to gain the land allotments he had promised as a reward for his veteran soldiers. The effect was to drive Pompey into an informal pact with Crassus and Gaius Julius Caesar (100–44 BC), sometimes called the First Triumvirate. Pompey's overwhelming popular support, Crassus' unlimited wealth, and Caesar's unscrupulousness and keen intelligence made the alliance irresistible. As consul in 59 BC, Caesar enacted all the measures his partners wanted and rewarded himself by leading a special command in Gaul, which he proceeded to conquer in a brilliant, though brutal, campaign (58–51 BC).

The Fall of the Republic

In Rome between 60 BC and 50 BC the Senate was powerless in the face of the dynasts, although the latter had less control over popular tribunes, such as Publius Clodius, whose agitations and radical policies caused embarrassment. Towards the end of the decade order threatened to break down completely. In 52 BC Pompey was appointed sole consul when riots prevented elections. By this time relations between Pompey and Caesar were becoming strained (Crassus had been killed in battle in 53 BC). Fear of Caesar's ambitions drove Pompey and the senators closer together, as they attempted to frustrate Caesar's aim of assuming a second consulship directly from his Gallic command. Caesar refused to lay down his arms; in 49 BC he invaded Italy (crossing the River Rubicon) at the head of an army and once again plunged the empire into civil war. Pompey, who presented himself as defender of the Republic, was eventually beaten at Pharsalus (48 BC) and murdered after fleeing to Egypt. Caesar proceeded to overcome the republicans in Africa and Spain before returning to Italy, where he became consul and dictator for life.

While Caesar embarked on a series of grandiose and visionary schemes, his monarchical tendencies went against republican tradition and offended the nobles. On 15 March 44 BC he was stabbed to death by a group of senators led by Brutus (c. 85–42 BC) and Cassius (d. 42 BC). The conspirators were unable to restore the Republic, however, as Caesar's chief aides, Mark Antony (c. 83–31 BC) and Marcus Aemilius Lepidus (died 13 BC), had the support of his armies; in 43 BC they joined Caesar's heir, the 19-year-old Octavian (63 BC–14 AD), to form a ruling Triumvirate, whereupon they divided the empire between them and purged their opponents. Lepidus was soon forced out of the alliance and the empire was uneasily divided between Octavian and Antony until 31 BC, when the issue was finally decided in Octavian's favour at the Battle of Actium. Mark Antony and his mistress Cleopatra, Queen of Egypt, committed suicide after their defeat, leaving Octavian in complete control of the Roman Empire.

▲ **Roman Leisure**
Seaside villas, of the type illustrated in this fresco from Pompeii, were used by wealthy Romans towards the end of the Republic as retreats from city life.

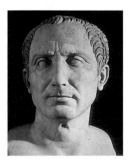

▲ **Gaius Julius Caesar** *Caesar's rise to power marked the end of the Roman Republic. He was a gifted administrator, orator, soldier, and politician.*

Spartacus

Spartacus was a Thracian gladiator who escaped in 73 BC and assembled a force of fugitive slaves on Mount Vesuvius. His army of tens of thousands of escapees roamed Italy for two years, defeating the Roman forces sent against them. Finally the slaves were conquered in southern Italy by an enormous army led by Marcus Crassus in 71 BC.

The Roman Empire

*Augustus • The succession • Government and administration • Expansion and decline •
The later empire: revival and reorganization • The army and military dispositions •
Pax Romana • Culture and religion • Architecture • Historiography*

▲ The Colosseum (Rome) *Built by the emperors Vespasian and Titus, the amphitheatre was opened in 80 AD. Able to seat up to 47 000, it was used mainly for gladiatorial and wild-beast fights.*

The defeat of Mark Antony (83–30 BC) and Cleopatra (69–30 BC) by Octavian at the Battle of Actium in 31 BC, followed by the latter's invasion of Egypt (30 BC), ended the civil war within the Roman Republic. These events mark the birth of the Roman Empire, which lasted in the west until 476 AD and in the east, as the Byzantine Empire, until 1453.

Augustus

Octavian (63 BC–14 AD) is known to history as Augustus. The name was conferred upon him, in 27 BC, after he had announced the 'restoration of the Republic.' The restoration was largely illusory, as it merely reinstated and preserved the trappings of the republican state as a cover for Augustus' personal rule. Thus he avoided such titles as '*dictator*' or *rex* (king), preferring instead ***princeps*** (leader). He gradually evolved a formula in which his power was based not upon a monopoly of the supreme office of consul (which he held annually until 23 BC), but upon a combination of constitutional powers and the possession of ***maius imperium*** (see panel). He gradually reduced the size of the army by half and handed over control of several provinces to the Roman Senate. He took care, however, to retain all those that contained an appreciable number of troops. Augustus' control of the military, combined with an immense weight of prestige and patronage, provided the real basis for his maintenance of power.

The Succession

One of the most problematic aspects of Augustus' reign was the search for a successor (and for a constitutional way of appointing a successor under a 'republic'). A smooth succession required the acquiescence of the senatorial and equestrian classes, the common people of Rome, the provincial armies, and the ***praetorian guard*** (the imperial bodyguard established by Augustus). The praetorian guard had considerable influence as the nearest military force to Rome. Augustus, as adoptive son of Julius Caesar, felt that a member of the popular Julian family was required. However, as all the obvious candidates had died before him, his eventual successor was his stepson Tiberius (reigned 14–37 AD), a Claudian, whom he adopted.

KEY ROMAN EMPERORS (31 BC–192 AD)	
Augustus	31 BC–14 AD
Tiberius	14–37
Gaius (Caligula)	37–41
Claudius I	41–54
Nero	54–68
(Year of the four emperors)	68–69
Vespasian	69–79
Titus	79–81
Domitian	81–96
Nerva	96–98
Trajan	98–117
Hadrian	117–38
Antoninus Pius	138–61
Marcus Aurelius	161–80
Commodus	180–92

AUGUSTUS AND THE IMPERIAL TITULATURE

Augustus' mother, Atia, was niece of Julius Caesar (100–44 BC). Introduced to public life by Caesar, whose adoptive son he became in 44 BC, he took the name Gaius Julius Caesar Octavianus (modern writers use Octavian). The Senate supported Octavian against Mark Antony; his victory in the civil wars left him master of Rome. The quasi-religious title 'Augustus' was granted to him by the Senate in 27 BC. All subsequent emperors (except Vitellius) took this title – as well as 'Caesar,' the family name of Julius Caesar – as part of their titulature ('Caesar' also came to designate the heir to the throne). Victorious republican military

commanders (holders of imperium, the supreme power to command and administer in military, judicial, and civil affairs), could be hailed as 'imperator' by their troops. Under the empire, this was the emperor's sole privilege, as his maius imperium outranked that of all others. Imperator also came to be used as a title that preceded the emperor's name, ultimately becoming the title 'emperor.'

◄ **Augustus** *Born Gaius Octavianus, the son of a Roman senator, Augustus became Rome's first emperor in 31 BC. Known to his contemporaries as Caesar, all subsequent emperors took this title.*

Adoption became a mechanism used to indicate a preferred successor; if an emperor had no son to succeed him, he adopted one.

Government and Administration

Augustus gradually overhauled every aspect of the government and administration of the Roman Empire. The length and relative peace of his reign led to an improved quality of life for the majority of the empire's inhabitants. Opposition to imperial rule was largely restricted to the senatorial class, now deprived of its former power. Subsequent emperors thus became more openly autocratic. Nonetheless, every emperor until Carus (reigned 282–83) was formally appointed by the Senate. Most emperors preserved at least the illusion of consultation; those who did not (for example, Domitian) were extremely unpopular with the old ruling class. The emperors are thus treated unfavourably by senatorial authors, such as Tacitus (c. 56–c. 120) and Pliny (c. 62–113).

Under the empire, control of the administration naturally passed from the Senate to the emperor. Claudius I (reigned 41–54) oversaw the expansion and centralization of the civil service, which gave many powerful posts to freedmen (liberated slaves) of ability. Hadrian (reigned 117–38) replaced the freedmen with equestrians, recognizing the need to establish a regular career structure for equestrians as well as for senators. The empire's provinces were administered by governors, while financial control was entrusted to an independent procurator (finance officer) as a check on the governor's power. Septimius Severus (reigned 193–211) further reduced the governors' power to rebel by subdividing provinces; the military functions of the praetorian prefect

(commander of the imperial bodyguard) were largely replaced with judicial and administrative duties.

Under reforms begun by Diocletian (reigned 285–313), and completed by Constantine I (reigned 324–37), each province was further subdivided: each governor (no longer the military commander) became responsible to the governor general of one of 13 *dioceses* (administrative areas) of the empire. Governors general reported to one of four praetorian prefects, who, instead of acting as the emperors' deputies, became the financial and judicial administrators of portions of the empire. Constantine also recognized the gradual territorial shift of the empire eastwards by establishing a second capital at Constantinople (begun 324; dedicated 11 May 330) in Byzantium.

Expansion and Decline

During the period of empire, the expansionist policy of the republican generals was initially continued. Egypt, realm of the Ptolemy dynasty, passed into Roman hands (30 BC). In the early years of Augustus' reign the conquest of Spain was completed, and Rhaetia and Noricum were also annexed (16–15 BC). A major revolt in Pannonia and Illyria (6–9 AD), and the annihilation of Varus' three legions in Germany (9 AD), caused Augustus to halt the empire's expansion. By this time, however, the general shape of the empire was established, encircling the Mediterranean and extending north to the rivers Rhine and Danube.

Thereafter expansion was intermittent. Claudius I began the conquest of Britain (43 AD), and organized the provinces of Mauretania Tingitana and Mauretania Caesariensis (44 AD), which extended Rome's hold on the

Roman Social Hierarchy *While Augustus improved the quality of life for most of the empire's inhabitants, great material inequality existed between the upper and lower classes of Roman society.* ▼

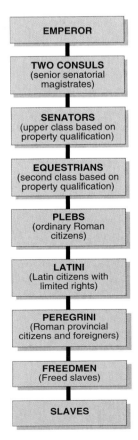

EMPEROR

TWO CONSULS
(senior senatorial magistrates)

SENATORS
(upper class based on property qualification)

EQUESTRIANS
(second class based on property qualification)

PLEBS
(ordinary Roman citizens)

LATINI
(Latin citizens with limited rights)

PEREGRINI
(Roman provincial citizens and foreigners)

FREEDMEN
(Freed slaves)

SLAVES

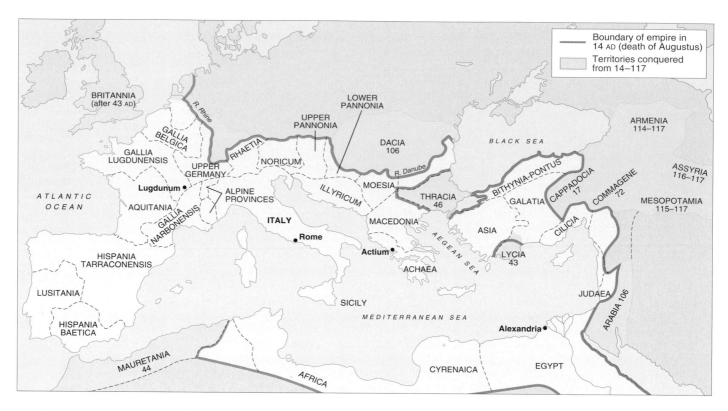

▲ **The Roman Empire** *The extent of the empire at the death of Augustus (14 AD) and subsequent conquests are shown. The empire finally reached its greatest extent under Septimius Severus (reigned 193–211).*

Year of the Four Emperors (69 AD)

Nero's suicide in 68 ended the Julio-Claudian dynasty. As there was no obvious Julian successor, a series of short-lived emperors followed as rival factions fought over the succession: Galba (June 68–January 69); Otho (January–April 69); and Vitellius (April–December 69). The eventual victor, backed by the legions of Syria, Egypt, and the Danube, was Vespasian (governor of Judaea in 68).

North African coast westwards. The African frontiers were also extended southwards, reaching their furthest extent under Septimus Severus and Caracalla (reigned 211–17).

The idea of indefinite northward expansion was gradually replaced by a more defensive outlook during the early period of the empire. It was the Flavian emperors (Vespasian, Titus, and Domitian) and their successors who implemented a more cautious policy; nevertheless territorial expansion continued when practical, particularly where it brought strategic advantages. Vespasian continued the advance north and west within Britain. He also conquered the *Agri Decumates*, the triangle of land between the headwaters of the rivers Rhine and Danube; the latter was a strategic advance that considerably shortened the empire's boundaries. Domitian was obliged, owing to lack of manpower, to halt the advance in Britain. The organization of semi-permanent frontier fortifications in vulnerable parts of the empire was also initiated: the *Agri Decumates* was enclosed by a system of earthen forts and wooden signal towers.

Under Hadrian, a 300-mile stretch of the German and Rhaetian frontiers was strengthened by the addition of a wooden palisade and ditch; much of the frontier system, however, seems to have relied on the protection of forts alone. In Britain, the road punctuated by forts spanning northern England was replaced by a wall (now known as Hadrian's Wall).

It is clear that these lines were not regarded as uncrossable boundaries; Roman forces did

patrol outside these limits as well as advance them. It is equally clear that Rome had not, at this time, abandoned all thoughts of conquests; under Trajan (reigned 98–117) a series of military victories allowed the establishment of the province of Dacia (106), north of the Danube; of Arabia (106), and, as a result of wars against the Parthians, of the short-lived provinces of Armenia, Mesopotamia, and Cappadocia (abandoned 117). Under Antoninus Pius (reigned 138–61), the British frontier was advanced northwards, for a time, from Hadrian's Wall to the Antonine Wall (Scotland). Further campaigning against Parthia under two warrior-emperors, Marcus Aurelius (reigned 161–80) and Septimius Severus, finally led to the more permanent annexation of Mesopotamia, bringing the empire's eastern boundary to the River Tigris; the empire had reached its greatest extent.

During the mid-3rd and 4th centuries the empire was forced onto the defensive. From c. 238 migrating Germanic tribes increasingly threatened the empire from the north, urged on both by further tribes behind them and by the attraction of the prosperous conditions within the boundaries of the empire. At the same time, the rise of the Sassanian Empire in Persia threatened the eastern frontiers. Effective Roman counteraction, meanwhile, was prevented by a succession of attempted usurpations, coupled with an increasingly fragile economy beset by rampant inflation. Gallienus (reigned 260–68) was forced to tolerate a breakaway Gallic Empire (259–73),

KEY ROMAN EMPERORS (193–305)

Septimius Severus	193–211
Caracalla	211–17
Elagabalus	218–22
Severus Alexander	222–35
Gordian III	238–44
Valerian	253–60
Gallienus	260–68
Claudius II	268–70
Aurelian	270–75
Probus	276–82
Diocletian	285–305

comprising the western provinces of Gaul, Spain, and Britain, under Postumus (from c. 258–68); in the east, Odaenathus, the Arab ruler of Palmyra (260–67), defeated the Sassanian King Shapur. While this action removed the Persian threat, it effectively detached the eastern provinces from central Roman rule (260–72). The abandonment of exposed territory north of the rivers Danube and Rhine was, therefore, perhaps inevitable: Dacia was relinquished in c. 270; the *Agri Decumates* some years earlier (c. 259–60).

The Later Empire: Revival and Reorganization

After Gallienus' assassination (268), a series of Illyrian warrior-emperors brought about a revival of Roman fortunes. Claudius II 'Gothicus' (reigned 268–70) inflicted a heavy defeat on the Goths in the Balkans; Aurelian (reigned 270–75) succeeded in reuniting the empire, retaking Palmyra in 272 and defeating Tetricus I (reigned 270–74), the last of the Gallic emperors, in 273. However, despite an excellent network of roads, designed primarily for military purposes, and a fast and efficient imperial postal service, an individual emperor administering such a vast empire from Rome faced an impossible task. Beset by various pressures, the form of government successful during the early empire began to break down; modifications were thus unavoidable. Gallienus and Aurelian began the process of reorganization of the frontiers, which included the abandonment of Dacia. It was Diocletian, however, who instituted the most radical reforms, devising a tetrarchic (four-part) system of government. He appointed a second emperor (or Augustus), Maximian (reigned 286–305), as his subordinate, to administer the western half of the empire; in 293, he appointed two deputies

(Caesars), Galerius (?250–311) in the east and Constantius I in the west.

This system was not a formal subdivision of the empire; while each ruler was allocated a particular area of responsibility, Diocletian reserved the right to intervene as he saw fit. He envisaged a self-perpetuating system, with the retirement of the Augusti after 20 years, and the automatic promotion of the two Caesars. Galerius and Constantius succeeded in 305; however, the system broke down in 306, after the death of Constantius. While the tetrarchic system failed, it became usual for an emperor to appoint at least one colleague; in 395, on the death of Theodosius I (reigned 379–95), the Roman Empire was finally divided: Arcadius, Theodosius' elder son, became Western Roman emperor (reigned 395–402), while his younger son, Honorius (reigned 395–423) was given the Eastern Empire.

The Army and Military Dispositions

The army of the early empire reflected current military thinking: a self-confident offensive policy was well served by the legions, heavily armed and disciplined infantry forces made up of citizen soldiers. These were reinforced by specialist non-citizen auxiliary troops, who carried lighter arms. As the aim of campaigns was to engage the enemy in an open infantry battle, forts and other military structures had relatively few defensive features. They were sited and constructed according to strategic needs and for ease of troop movement, rather than on the defensive merits of the position.

As the empire gradually moved onto the defensive and linear frontiers were developed, large numbers of troops were established in fixed positions, removing some of the armies' former mobility. Gallienus began far-reaching

Roman Imperial Coinage
From the 1st to the early 3rd century AD, the empire used a single currency comprising gold, silver, and bronze coins. The standard unit was the silver *denarius*, worth 1/25th of the gold *aureus*. During the 3rd century rapid inflation and debasement led to the collapse of the currency system; the government thereafter struggled to maintain a stable currency.

Hadrian's Wall
Begun in 122 AD, the wall stretched 120 km across northern England. Designed to control Scottish tribes, it comprised ditch, stone and turf wall, road system, and earthworks; it incorporated 16 forts. Although the wall was abandoned in 383 AD, substantial portions still stand. ▼

Tacitus

The most famous Roman historian studied with leading orators of the day. He became a senator, held the consulship in 97 AD, and was governor of Asia in 112–13. His early surviving works include the *Germania*, a geography and study of the Germanic tribes. His principal works were the *Histories*, documenting life in imperial Rome from 68–96 AD, and the *Annals*, (covering the period 14–68 AD (some 40 years survive).

▲ Roman Glassware
The material culture of the Roman Empire was highly sophisticated, as its fine surviving glassware demonstrates. This example is from Pompeii.

Later Roman Emperors (324–95)	
Constantine I	324–37
Constantine II	337–40
Constans	337–50
Constantius II	337–61
Julian	361–63
Valentinian I	364–75
Valens	364–78
Gratian	367–83
Valentinian II	375–92
Theodosius I	379–95

organizational changes, which placed greater emphasis on military mobility, particularly through the use of cavalry. Under Diocletian, the size of the army was greatly increased; a large mobile field force was assigned to each of the four rulers under the tetrarchy, each force designed to act swiftly as required in support of the static frontier troops. Constantine I completed the reforms initiated by Diocletian; he began the incorporation of large numbers of Germanic tribesmen into the new mobile field armies, a process that helped provide the manpower to repel further Germanic invasions.

Forts of the later empire reflect these changes: a defensive fixed-frontier policy required forts in more readily defensible positions; thicker walls, both to resist attack and to provide platforms for artillery; projecting towers and fortified gateways to allow enfilading fire (i.e. fire along the length of the wall); and external earthworks and moats to prevent enemy approach. These forts were designed to resist attack until a relief force arrived.

Pax Romana

The relative peace brought to the provinces by Roman rule provided substantial benefits. Towns and provinces were allowed a considerable degree of local autonomy. A general increase in their prosperity is observable up to the middle of the 3rd century. Most provinces became substantially Romanized, with the spread of Roman-style urban settlements and, in many places, of Roman-style *villas* (farms, country estates) around them. Well-constructed roads encouraged the growth of trade and industry, with foodstuffs (particularly grain, wine, and olive oil) and industrial output (particularly metals, pottery, and glass) being traded over long distances.

The empire's unity, provided by, for example, a single currency, was further enhanced by the eventual abolition of the distinction between Roman and provincial (a distinction largely of taxable status); in 212 AD Caracalla extended Roman citizenship to virtually all free citizens of the empire. Up to that time, certain provincial settlements had enjoyed improved status: in a *colonia* (colony), often founded through the settlement of legionary veterans, all the residents were Roman citizens and thus exempt from direct taxation (*tributum*); in a *municipium* (free town), only the leading citizens were Roman citizens, in order to strengthen the loyalty of the aristocracy of newly conquered regions to Rome.

Culture and Religion

In the east of the empire, **Hellenism** (Greek culture) remained pre-eminent. There, educated Romans spoke Greek as well as Latin; Greek and Etruscan influences can be seen in

CONSTANTINE AND CHRISTIANITY

The Battle of Milvian Bridge, outside Rome (312 AD), is famous for marking the conversion of Constantine I to Christianity and thus the birth of the Christian empire. Constantine credited his victory over Maxentius (reigned 306–12) to the intervention of the Christian God; Christian authors give several versions of the event: Eusebius (active 4th century) claims that Constantine was inspired by a vision of the cross inscribed 'by this conquer'; Lactantius asserts that Constantine caused the Christian chi-rho (XP) monogram to be displayed on the soldiers' shields. The Edict of Toleration (313) was followed by the active promotion of Christianity. Despite Constantine's reputation as the first Christian emperor, he was baptized only on his deathbed.

many aspects of Roman art and culture. The Romans achieved a high degree of material civilization: the houses of the rich were adorned with marble and bronze statuary, mosaics, and painted wall plaster; they also possessed gold, silver, and glass jewellery and tableware.

While Latin culture predominated over that of conquered nations, with the spread of Etruscan-style planned towns and Roman buildings and institutions, in Italy and the western half of the empire many elements of native culture survived. This is particularly true of native religions: the pagan Roman empire worshipped many gods. Rather than suppressing the worship of native gods, however, the Romans assimilated them. Oriental mystery cults, such as Mithraism, appealed widely, spread by the movement of military personnel. Under the empire, the worship of the *genius* (spirit) of the ruler became firmly established, deliberately fostered to encourage loyalty to Rome. Adherents of monotheistic religions, such as Christianity, were occasionally persecuted for political reasons, most famously under Diocletian; their refusal to acknowledge the imperial gods condemned them as subversives. The Syrian imperial family oversaw, in the early 3rd century, the rapid spread of eastern cults, while Aurelian declared *Sol Invictus* (the unconquered sun) to be the supreme Roman deity. The most radical change occurred with the conversion of **Constantine I** to Christianity in 312. The Edict of Milan (313) established religious toleration throughout the empire. The 4th century saw the rapid promotion of Christianity: at the Council of Nicaea (325) it became, in

Estamos con la gente

◀ **Aqueduct at Segovia (Spain)**
A superb example of the Romans' mastery of running water, the aqueduct's 128 arches span the centre of the city for 800 m. The aqueduct, built between 100 and 110 AD, under Trajan, brought water from a source 16 km away to a distribution point that supplied the town. Equally fine examples of Roman engineering skills survive at Carthage (in North Africa) and Nîmes (in the south of France).

effect, the official religion of the empire; in 391 Theodosius declared it the empire's only religion, banning pagan worship.

Architecture
The Romans were great builders; substantial amounts of their monumental architecture still survive, not least in Rome itself. The Roman way of life was predominantly urban. An average city contained several public buildings, forum, basilica, temples, public baths, theatre, and amphitheatre, as well as one- and two-storey houses; where land was at a premium, tenement buildings had as many as five storeys. In the provinces, where such towns did not exist, they were established as part of the process of Romanization. The patronage of the Roman emperors can be seen in particular in the monumental architecture of Rome (for example, the Colosseum) and in Constantinople; other areas and cities, such as Achaea (in N Greece) under Nero (reigned 54–68) and Hadrian and Leptis Magna (in Libya) under Septimius Severus, also benefited.

Historiography
While the early empire is fairly well documented by narrative histories and biographies, their authors – such as **Tacitus**, Suetonius (c. 69–c. 150 AD), and Cassius Dio (c. 155–c. 230 AD) – provide a rather limited senatorial standpoint. These works are complemented by other writings, such as the letters of Pliny the Younger, as well as by epigraphic evidence (career inscriptions, coins, etc.) and by archaeology. Poets and satirists, such as Martial (c. 40–c. 103 AD) and Juvenal (c. 55–c. 127 AD), provide additional material, which

is, however, sometimes more entertaining than historically reliable.

The later empire is less well documented; the *Historia Augusta*, probably the work of a 4th-century author, is a substandard work, containing biographies of emperors and usurpers from 117 to 284 AD. The only rival to Tacitus is Ammianus Marcellinus (c. 330–95), whose surviving work covers a period of only 25-years (354–378).

◀ ▲ **Pompeii** *The town of Pompeii, near Naples, Italy, was buried by the eruption of Mount Vesuvius in 79 AD. Pompeii's buildings (left), as well as normally perishable objects – such as food, wooden furniture, paintings, and even some of Vesuvius' unfortunate victims (above) – were preserved by volcanic ash. These have provided unparalleled evidence of daily life in Roman times.*

EARLY AND MEDIEVAL EUROPE

Northern Europe

*The spread of farming • Ritual centres • Trade and the growth of towns •
The expansion of the Roman Empire*

Language

It is thought that Indo-European languages spread into northern Europe with the early farmers, while the hunter-gatherer languages survived only in isolated populations on the edges of cultivable areas. Modern Basque languages (northern Spain) may be a survival of this kind.

Between c. 6000 BC and 395 AD Europe developed from an area inhabited by hunter-gatherer communities to one in which large fortified towns, with political and social structures, thrived, trading with distant settlements. The spread of farming, the emergence of ritual centres, the development of metalworking, and the effects of Roman expansion were all vital factors in the way in which European societies evolved during this period.

The Spread of Farming

Farming developed in the Middle East with the domestication of native cereals, sheep, and goats between 9000 and 6000 BC, and spread into northern Europe from c. 5500 BC. The principal route led northwest from the Balkans into central Europe: farming peoples subsequently colonized the fertile river valleys and plains from Hungary to the Netherlands from c. 5400 BC. They domesticated cereals, pigs, and cattle, which suited the new environments. They lived in villages of long houses and made pottery and stonecutting tools.

The foraging (hunter-gatherer) communities of the western Mediterranean coastline were, meanwhile, turning to more controlled exploitation of crops and animals. Domesticated

sheep and pottery predated cereal cultivation in these cultures; evidence suggests that indigenous foragers gradually adopted an agricultural way of life. By c. 5000 BC farming villages were established in southern France.

People continued to live by hunting, gathering, and fishing at the margins of northern Europe, and in coastal and riverine locations, where large populations were sustained. In Scandinavia, west Scotland, and Ireland, fishing cultures survived until c. 3000 BC. By this time, farming was widely established in fertile areas of cleared forest across northern Europe.

Between 3500 BC and 2000 BC, as farming intensified, populations grew. More extensive areas of forest were cleared; settlement expanded into upland regions, and the increased area of open country led to more intensive stock herding. The adoption of the plough in northern Europe by c. 3500 BC produced greater crop yields, while herded animals were exploited for meat, milk, wool, and their ability to pull ploughs and carts. Settlements were either small villages or isolated farmsteads. Contact between local populations was maintained by trading, evidence for which is based on the shells, amber, metalwork, and pottery styles found far from their place of origin.

**Megalithic
Monuments** *These
stone rows at Carnac
in Brittany (northwest
France), possibly
associated with grave
rituals, date from the
3rd millennium. This
site is one of the most
famous surviving
open-air monuments
from this period.*

Ritual Centres

Despite the small scale of these early farming societies, their monuments testify to the existence of political structures, which could bring local groups together for building work and for the performance of rituals. The early farmers who colonized central Europe buried their dead in individual graves. Elsewhere, however, large stones (**megaliths**) were erected to mark communal graves. Megalithic tombs were built by farming communities from Iberia to Scandinavia. From c. 3200 BC, open-air monuments, based on the concentric ring ditch with standing stone arrangements, became the centres for ritual, establishing a pattern that survived until c. 1500 BC. The monuments were associated with observations of the passage of the seasons and of astronomical cycles. The separate burial of individuals, in tombs filled with copper and stone weaponry dating from this time, indicates the increasing differentiation of social status.

Metalworking. The skills of metalworking had begun to diffuse into northern Europe from the Balkans by 4000 BC. The earliest copper and gold items derive from the Balkans and later from Iberia; they include jewellery, axes, daggers, and tools. Bronze had appeared in the region by c. 2000 BC; its hardness made it more useful than pure copper for tools and weaponry. The growth of metalworking is associated with increasing competition and with clearer inequalities of social status within and between groups. This is reflected in the appearance of small fortified centres throughout northern Europe between 1800 and 1500 BC, and the spread of new bronze weapons throughout the region by c. 1250 BC. Between 1200 and 800 BC, the production and use of bronze objects increased markedly; trade became a significant means of communication across wide areas of northern Europe. Bronze tools, such as sickles and saws, also increased the efficiency of agricultural production.

Trade and the Growth of Towns

By c. 800 BC, larger centres began to develop around specialized industries, such as the salt mines at Hallstatt in the Alps, where about 250 people lived. By 600 BC, larger fortified communities were found north of the Alps, where such crafts as ornamental metalworking were developed; trading contacts were maintained with distant communities, such as the Greek cities of the western Mediterranean. Between c. 450 BC and c. 200 BC these centres declined, and classical authors report the movement of peoples known as **Celts** into southern and eastern Europe.

By 200 BC much larger enclosed centres were developing again, with populations of up to 5000. They manufactured mostly iron tools.

◄ **Bronze Ornaments from Western Europe** *Dating from the early 1st millennium BC, these items demonstrate metalworking skills and indicate the existence of different levels of social status.*

While iron had been available in northern Europe since before 1000 BC, it was only in the period 200–100 BC that its use became widespread. By this time, metal coins were in use as standard units for trading. While most people continued to live in small villages and farmsteads, centralized political structures emerged, sustained by control of trade and agricultural resources and by commercial contacts with the Roman world.

The Expansion of the Roman Empire

The expansion of the Roman Empire into northern Europe was mainly driven by the ambition of Roman political leaders. The incorporation of southern and eastern Spain into the empire had begun in the late 3rd century BC; over the next 400 years, Roman territories expanded to include all of France, southern Britain, the remainder of the Iberian peninsula, and parts of modern Germany as far north as the Rhine.

By the 3rd century AD, the empire had begun to disintegrate as a result of economic and political disorganization within its boundaries and from expanding populations outside its frontiers. The growth of piracy in the north caused instability in the provinces; it was not until the 5th century that the Western Empire suffered serious territorial losses.

In the eastern parts of modern Germany and in southern Scandinavia, which were outside the limits of the Roman Empire, societies maintained their continuity between 500 BC and 300 AD. From dispersed farming settlements, trading centres and small kingdoms emerged between 300 and 700 AD as the foundations of Viking society.

Celts A group of tribes inhabiting central or western Europe. From the works of Herodotus and from later classical writers, it is known that the Celts sacked Rome in 390 BC and Delphi in 279 BC. Celtic art was distinctive, as seen in surviving examples of ornamental metalwork. The Celtic languages survived only on the margins of or outside the Roman Empire; they include modern Gaelic, Welsh, Cornish, Manx, and Breton.

Romanization

Roman imperialism depended on the authority of local provincial elites and on the power of the army. The accommodation of the Roman imperial system in the provinces of the Roman Empire led to changes in their language, government, law, religion, and culture.

The Catholic Church

The missions • Papal reform and imperial conflict • The later Middle Ages

The Church survived the collapse of the Western Roman Empire in the late 5th century. In France, western Germany, and Italy, bishoprics remained intact. The end of Roman rule (410) and the Anglo-Saxon invasions (5th century) led to the disappearance of Christianity in England, while in Ireland it flourished as a result of St Patrick's (c. 390–460) evangelization. In Spain Christianity thrived until the Church organization was destroyed by the Muslim invasion (711). The pope, based in Rome, was regarded as the senior bishop, though he had little real authority over the rest of the Church. The period from c. 400 to c. 850, however, was marked by the expansion of Roman Christianity and the emergence of **monasticism**.

The Missions

The conversion of England to Christianity began with the mission of St Augustine (died c. 604) in 597. There was, however, conflict between St Augustine's mission, based on Roman evangelization, and the Celtic Christianity taken from Ireland to Scotland, and thence to Northumbria. The Synod of Whitby

(664) resolved the conflict in favour of the Roman Church. From 590 the Irish monk Columban (c. 543–615) was responsible for the spread of Christianity and monasticism in eastern France and Switzerland. The Anglo-Saxon St Boniface (?680–?755) continued his work, founding the bishopric of Regensburg (739). Under Charlemagne (reigned 768–814), the Church expanded as the Saxons in northern Germany were converted. Roman Christian missions renewed their efforts to convert eastern Europe during the 10th century; the Vikings of Scandinavia were converted by missions from northern Germany.

Monasticism. First developed in Egypt in the 4th century, Christian monasticism had spread to Italy and south Gaul by the 5th century. St Benedict of Nursia (?480–547), abbot of Monte Cassino in Italy, composed the Benedictine Rule, which regulated monastic practice. It became the standard monastic handbook when it was publicized in the *Dialogues* of Pope Gregory I (reigned 540–604).

The 7th and 8th centuries saw the foundation of major monasteries, such as Bobbio in

Christianity in Europe
The routes of missionaries, principal monasteries and bishoprics, and the distribution of denominations are shown.

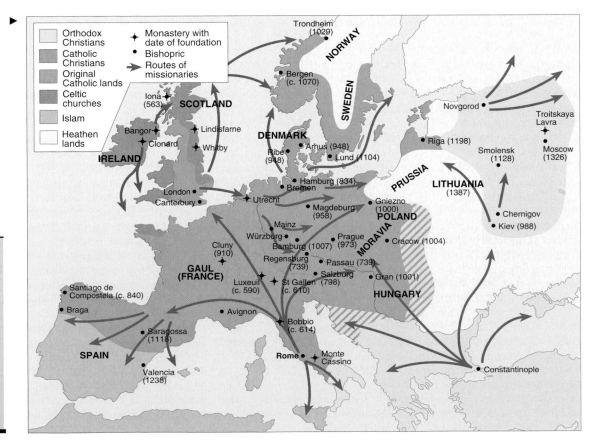

monasticism
A system under which men or women devote themselves to a religious life, either in solitude or in special communities removed from society. The first monks adhered to the three primary monastic principles of poverty, chastity, and obedience to the abbot.

northern Italy, Luxeuil in Burgundy, and St Gallen in Switzerland, which became important centres of cultural and religious life. Within the Carolingian Empire (at its height, France, western Germany, part of Spain, and much of Italy), monasticism was strengthened by royal patronage and reform.

Papal Reform and Imperial Conflict
During the 10th and early 11th centuries the papacy came to be dominated by rival Roman families, which jeopardized its moral authority over Western Christendom.

In 1046 Emperor Henry III (reigned 1046–56), ruler of the Holy Roman Empire (centred on Germany and northern Italy; see GERMANIC INVASIONS AND THE CAROLINGIAN EMPIRE), undertook to reform the papacy when he deposed three rival Italian popes at the Synod of Sutri. This began a long period of conflict between the empire and the papacy, which undermined the authority of both institutions.

Under Leo IX (reigned 1049–54) the influence of the papacy began to revive. Leo travelled extensively in Italy and France and launched campaigns against clerical marriage and **simony**. It was at this time that the cardinals (known collectively as the papal *curia* or court) came to form the elite of the Church administration, with their exclusive right to elect new popes.

The conflict between empire and papacy came to a climax when Pope Gregory VII (reigned 1073–85) excommunicated and deposed Emperor Henry IV (reigned 1084–1106), who wanted to retain control of Church appointments. Henry was forced to submit to the pope's authority when he was made to perform public penance at Canossa (1077). In 1095 Urban II (reigned 1088–99) assumed the moral leadership of western Europe when he proclaimed the First Crusade (see THE CRUSADES).

Throughout the 12th century successive popes sought to maintain and expand papal control over the Western Church. The papacy, meanwhile, developed an efficient financial administration and encouraged the development of canon (Church) law. However, the papal court was soon widely criticized for its greed and corruption.

In 1215 Innocent III (reigned 1198–1216), under whom the temporal power of the papacy reached its height, summoned the fourth Lateran Council, which proclaimed the Fifth Crusade to the Holy Land and greatly influenced formulation of doctrine and Church organization and law. Innocent III was also the real founder of the *Papal States* in central Italy, which were to survive until 1870. While successive popes had claimed extensive lands in central and northern Italy since the 8th

century, Innocent III was the first to rule them effectively (see THE MEDIEVAL ZENITH).

During the 13th century the papacy was challenged by Emperor Frederick II (reigned 1220–50), who sought to impose his power throughout Italy. With great difficulty Pope Gregory IX (reigned 1227–41) and, subsequently, Innocent IV (reigned 1243–54) were able to defeat the Empire and maintain the political independence of the papacy (see THE MEDIEVAL ZENITH). Pope Boniface VIII (reigned 1294–1303) tried to assert his power to tax and discipline French bishops, which brought him into conflict with Philip IV (reigned 1285–1314) of France. In 1303 Boniface was kidnapped by French royal agents and died soon after. With his death, effective papal claims to universal sovereignty ended.

Religious Orders. From its foundation in 909, the leading monastic house in western France was the Abbey of Cluny, which set new standards of elaboration and magnificence in the observance of the Benedictine Rule. During the early 12th century its influence was challenged by monks who wished to return to a simpler, more austere, form of monasticism. In 1098 a group of monks established a new *Cistercian* order (named after the original site at Citeaux, Burgundy); it determined to interpret St Benedict's rule as literally as possible. The order was soon joined by St Bernard of Clairvaux (1090–1153), who preached its message widely. By 1153 there were 300 Cistercian monasteries throughout Europe practising a regime of simple prayer and hard manual labour. Even more austere was the

◄ **Monastic Life**
Throughout the 7th and 8th centuries, monasteries were the primary, and sometimes the only, centres of literacy and learning. A monastic scribe is shown at work in this late 6th century illustration (probably from southern Italy).

simony In strict terms, the sin of buying or selling spiritual or ecclesiastical benefits. In the Middle Ages, it was most often applied to the use of money to secure appointment to an ecclesiastical office or benefice.

...standing before the castle gate, laying aside all royal insignia, barefooted and in coarse attire, he ceased not with many tears to beseech the apostolic help and comfort... All marvelled at our unwonted severity... At last, overcome by his persistent show of penitence... we released him from the bounds of anathema, and received him into the grace of the Holy Mother Church.

Gregory VII describes Emperor Henry IV's submission at Canossa (1077)

The East–West Schism

In 1054 there was a formal split between the Western Church of Rome and the Eastern Greek Church, based at Constantinople (see THE BYZANTINE EMPIRE). The Eastern Church refused to accept the authority of the papacy in deciding theological matters; the split has never been resolved.

THE INQUISITION

The Inquisition was an institution of the medieval Church designed to combat heresy and moral offences. Formally instituted by Pope Gregory IX in 1231, it attempted to place all control of heresy in papal hands. Papally appointed inquisitors, especially from the Dominican and Franciscan orders, had wide powers of arrest and interrogation. The use of torture was authorized in 1252 and secret trials were held. Fines and penances were imposed on those who confessed; dissenters were imprisoned or executed by burning. Confined to southern Europe, the Inquisition lapsed during the 14th and 15th centuries but was revived in Spain against Jews and Muslims.

The Avignon Papacy

Since the 12th century there had been opposition to papal rule in Rome. Disorder in Italy increased after the death of Boniface VIII in 1303. The French-born Pope Clement V (1264–1314) therefore removed the papal seat to Avignon in 1309. Clement relied on the protection of the French king, Philip IV (1268–1314), while avoiding his direct control (Avignon not being part of France at that time). The Avignon papacy lasted until 1377, during which time all six successive popes were French.

Carthusian order, founded by St Bruno (c. 1030–1101) at Chartreuse in 1085.

Heresy. From the 12th century the Church was challenged by heretics, who rejected the authority of the pope and Church hierarchy. The *Waldenses*, founded by Peter Waldes (died 1217), merely wanted the liberty to preach the message of simple faith in contrast to the wealth and power of many of the clergy. They were systematically persecuted by the church authorities. The *Cathars* (also known as the *Albigenses* of southern France) believed the material world was evil and only the spiritual was good. Although they enjoyed some support from powerful laymen, Innocent III proclaimed a crusade against them in 1208. Despite the military success of the papal forces, Catharism retained a strong hold over the population of southern France until it was finally crushed by the **Inquisition**.

The Mendicants. In response to the threat of heresy, new forms of orthodox religious life developed; most notable were the mendicant, or begging orders. St Francis of Assisi (?1181–1226), the son of a rich merchant, gave up his family life and career to live in poverty. He founded a new order of *Franciscan* friars, which, unlike previous religious

orders, travelled as itinerant preachers, begging for food. The movement tapped the same popular enthusiasm and discontent that inspired heresy and spread rapidly in the growing towns of northern Europe. The outwardly similar *Dominicans*, founded by St Dominic of Osma (1170–1221), emphasized preaching to combat heresy. They were always more firmly in the mainstream of Catholicism than the Franciscans, who came under attack for heresy later in the 13th century.

The Later Middle Ages (1300–1520)

In the 14th century the papacy lost much of the authority it had built up since 1046; national churches tended increasingly to develop their own identities. In 1309 the papacy moved from Rome to Avignon. The **Avignon papacy** became renowned for its corruption and greed. English and German criticism of French dominance over the papacy eventually forced its return to Rome under Gregory XI. Shortly afterwards there was a split in the Church (known as the *Great Schism*, 1378–1417), when some cardinals returned to Avignon to establish a rival papacy. The issue was resolved by the Council of Constance (1414–18), which enabled Pope Martin V (reigned 1417–31) to re-establish the papacy in Rome, its prestige having been severely damaged.

The New Heretics. In the later Middle Ages, the established Church faced renewed opposition. In England John Wycliffe (1330–84), an academic, questioned basic doctrines. He emphasized the importance of the Bible, supervising the first translation from Latin into English. After his death, Wycliffe's followers, known as *Lollards*, were persecuted and the movement soon died out. Wycliffe's doctrines, however, spread to Bohemia. In 1402 Jan Hus (?1372–1415) began preaching Wycliffe's ideas in Prague; in 1412 there were violent outbreaks against the sale of indulgences in the city to raise money for the papal armies. Although Hus was burned at the stake as a heretic in 1415, his ideas attracted widespread support. Though these movements were both ultimately suppressed, they anticipated many of the doctrines of 16th-century reformers, such as Martin Luther (1483–1546) and John Calvin (1509–64). Their revival of familiar issues, such as the sale of indulgences, sparked off the great European Reformation from 1517, which was to signal the end of the unity of Catholic Europe.

◄ **Confirmation of the Rule of St Francis of Assisi** *(Giotto, c. 1295)* In 1210 St Francis's preaching had attracted sufficient followers for Pope Innocent III to grant him permission to found the Franciscan order.

Germanic Invasions and the Carolingian Empire

Germanic invasions • The Carolingian Empire (751–888)

Europe between the late 5th and 9th centuries was dominated by invading Germanic tribes, which swept across the continent in the 5th and 6th centuries and established their own kingdoms. The invasion of these tribes heralded the collapse of the Western Roman Empire, plunging Europe into the 'Dark Ages,' a period of economic and cultural decline. The foundation of monasteries, however, provided centres of scholarship. Greater stability and a revival of learning followed during the 7th and 8th centuries.

Germanic Invasions

From the 3rd century, the Germanic tribes, of whom the Visigoths, Ostrogoths, Franks, Vandals, and Lombards were the most important, began to invade the Roman Empire. Increasing numbers of them, meanwhile, were incorporated into the Roman armies; by 400 AD, the bulk of Rome's western armies were recruited from "barbarians" (as the Romans referred to them). With the death of Emperor Theodosius (395) the Roman Empire was finally divided into two halves with a border running through the former Yugoslavia. The western half passed to Theodosius' weak son Honorius (reigned 395–423); real power, however, lay in the hands of Germanic military leaders, such as Flavius Stilicho (c. 365–408). Many areas of the Western Empire were subsequently conquered by Germanic tribes or simply abandoned.

Spain was invaded by the Vandals, Alans, and Suevi in 409, while Britain was left to Anglo-Saxon invaders in 410. Between 429 and 439 the Vandals took the whole of North Africa. Gaul (France) was settled by the Burgundians from 419 and by the Franks from 420. Rome was sacked by the Visigoths in 410 and by the Vandals, who sailed from Africa, in 455. The most destructive of these invaders were the Huns, a Turkic people from Central Asia, under the leadership of Attila (reigned 434–53); in 451, however, he was defeated near Troyes (France) by an alliance of the Romans under Flavius Aetius (died 454) and the Visigoths. When Attila died in 453, the power of the Huns collapsed.

However, this did not save the remnants of the Western Roman Empire. The final breakdown of imperial authority in the 5th century led to a mass migration of Germanic tribes into France, Spain, and Italy. In 476 the last emperor of the Western Empire, Romulus Augustulus (reigned 475–76), was deposed by the rebel Ostrogoth commander Odovacar (433–93), who became the first barbarian king of Italy.

The Ostrogoths in Italy (489–768).
The Germanic invaders did not destroy all Roman institutions; the Church, Romance languages (those derived from Latin), and some social structures survived. The invaders set up a number of kingdoms in their conquered lands. Northern Italy was ruled by the Ostrogoths; King Theodoric (reigned 471–526), who overthrew Odovacar, established an important kingdom, with its capital at the late Roman centre of Ravenna. In a series of wars (535–554) the kingdom was destroyed by Byzantine armies. From 568 Byzantine rule was itself overthrown by a new wave of Germanic invaders, the Lombards, from beyond the Alps, who established themselves in the north of the country.

The Merovingian Kingdom.
Increasing numbers of Franks, a Germanic tribe from east of the Rhine, settled in northern France,

====SEE ALSO====
This section:
- Northern Europe
- The Catholic Church
- The Byzantine Empire
- The Later Middle Ages

Islamic World:
- Muslim Spain

Invasions of the Germanic Tribes
Germanic tribes from northern, central, and eastern Europe had never been incorporated into the Roman Empire. These tribes, as well as others from as far away as Central Asia, began to invade the Roman Empire from the 3rd century. Weakened by the empire's division in 395, the Western Empire was increasingly vulnerable to conquest by the 'barbarian' tribes. ▼

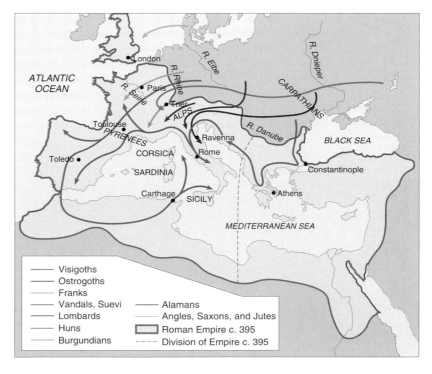

Legend:
- Visigoths
- Ostrogoths
- Franks
- Vandals, Suevi
- Lombards
- Huns
- Burgundians
- Alamans
- Angles, Saxons, and Jutes
- Roman Empire c. 395
- Division of Empire c. 395

▲ **Theodoric and his Mausoleum** ▶
An admirer of classical culture, Theodoric attracted many Romans to his court, among whom were the philosopher Boethius (?470–524) and the writer Cassiodorus (c. 490–c. 585).

At the court of Childebert [II]... Magnovald was slain by the king's orders... being in his palace at Metz, and looking at a sport in which a beast was being worried by a pack of dogs... summoned Magnovald to him. He came, and in ignorance of what was afoot, joined freely in the general laughter... Then a man who had received his orders... swung his axe and cleft his skull. He fell dead and was thrown out of a window... his own people buried him.

Gregory of Tours illustrates the arbitrary nature of royal power under the Merovingians *(History of the Franks)*

where a kingdom was founded by Clovis (reigned 496–511), the first great king of the Merovingian dynasty (ruled 476–751). In 500 Clovis destroyed the independence of the Burgundians and, in 507, drove the Visigoths to the south of the country, so becoming ruler of most of modern France and Germany as far as the Rhine. In c. 507 Clovis was converted to Catholic Christianity, in contrast to Arian Christianity from which most of the Germanic tribes were converted. After his death (511) the kingdom was constantly fought over and divided by members of Clovis's family. Dagobert (reigned 629–39) was the last Merovingian to wield real power.

The Merovingian kingdom set the pattern for later medieval monarchies. Its kings had no fixed capital, but moved between palaces in northern France, notably at Paris, Soissons, Reims, and Metz. The country was divided among counts, many of whom became independent dynasts. The central administration was simple, the most important figures being the principal domestic officials of the royal

household, such as the mayor of the palace (who oversaw the administration of the palace and was, in effect, a chief minister). The Franks usually cooperated with the bishops of each town, who were chosen from families of Roman origin. One such bishop, Gregory of Tours (bishop 573–94), wrote a *History of the Franks*, which is the main source of information on the period.

The Visigoths in Spain (507–711). The Visigoths had originally settled in the south of France; in the face of Frankish pressure, however, they began to move into Spain during the reign of Alaric II (484–507). After Alaric's defeat and death at the Battle of Vouillé (507) the Visigoths migrated to the Iberian peninsula. Under King Leovigild (568–86) a powerful kingdom was established with its capital at Toledo. In 589 King Reccared (died 601) was converted from Arianism to Catholic Christianity and the Visigoths integrated with the local population. The kingdom remained the strongest and most united of the Germanic kingdoms until its sudden collapse after the Arab Muslim invasion of 711. By 716, the Arabs had conquered almost the whole of the Iberian peninsula and established a strong state. From 756 Muslim Spain was ruled by emirs of the Umayyad family. Pockets of Christian resistance, however, survived in the mountains of Cantabria and the foothills of the Pyrenees.

Anglo-Saxon England. From the early 5th century England was settled by the pagan Angles, Saxons, and Jutes. As a result Roman culture disappeared almost completely. A number of small kingdoms were established. In 597 a mission sent by Pope Gregory the Great (reigned 590–604) and led by St Augustine (died c. 604) converted Ethelbert, king of Kent (in southeast England), to Christianity. At the Synod of Whitby, in 664, the allegiance of the English Church to Rome was established. In the 8th century the most important kingdom in England was Mercia, especially during the reign of Offa (757–96), who imitated Carolingian forms of government, including the minting of the first silver coins in England. Viking invasions from 793 onwards resulted in the collapse of Mercia in 874. Leadership passed to the kingdom of Wessex, where Alfred the Great (reigned 871–99) provided the only effective resistance against the invaders.

THE HOLY ROMAN EMPIRE

Regarded as the successor to the Western Roman Empire, the Holy Roman Empire has its origins in the Carolingian Empire. The decline of the Carolingian dynasty meant that the imperial title passed to the German kings. From the mid-10th century the empire was centred on modern Germany and Austria and linked with the German monarchy, with which it became synonymous. Successive emperors came into conflict with the papacy (11th–13th centuries) in their attempts to secure domination in Europe. Although this conflict greatly weakened the Holy Roman Empire, it survived, latterly under Hapsburg rule, from the mid-15th century until the beginning of the 19th century.

The Carolingian Empire (751–888)
The increasing powerlessness of the Merovingian kings after 639 meant that power passed to new families, notably the Carolingians, based in northern France. In 732 the Carolingian Charles Martel (c. 688–741) led the Franks to defeat an Arab invasion from Spain at the Battle of Poitiers, thus establishing

THE CAROLINGIAN RENAISSANCE

After the collapse of the Western Roman Empire in 476, classical learning became increasingly rare; there was a danger that the intellectual heritage of the ancient world would be lost. Apart from Rome itself, it was in Britain and Ireland that learning survived. Charlemagne, who had a genuine commitment to learning, established a palace school of intellectuals, and invited scholars from all over Europe to join. While the palace circle wrote poetry and prided themselves on their knowledge of the classics, little of their thought was original.

Charlemagne was also keen to spread literacy and ordered that

reading and writing should be taught in all religious houses. He encouraged the copying of books in a new clear form of writing that was developed, the Carolingian minuscule. Classical architecture was also encouraged, as Charlemagne's palace, at Aachen, illustrates. Elsewhere, buildings of a size and grandeur unknown since Roman times were built, such as the monasteries of St Ricquier (Picardy), and Corvey (Saxony).

◀ **Charlemagne** *Charlemagne conquered most of western Europe, centralized his empire's administration, and fostered a cultural revival.*

himself as military leader of the Franks, whose realm he reunited and ruled until his death (741). In 751 Pepin (c. 714–68), Charles's son and Carolingian mayor of the palace, deposed the Merovingian child-king Childeric III (reigned 743–51), causing the nobles to elect him as king. Pepin appealed to Pope Zacharias (reigned 741–52), claiming that he who held power had the right to be king. The pope agreed and Pepin was anointed as king at Soissons, thus establishing the new dynasty. Pepin was succeeded (768) by his son, known to history as Charles the Great, or Charlemagne (reigned 768–814). He ruled over an empire that came to include most of western Europe. In 800 Charlemagne was crowned emperor in Rome by Pope Leo III (reigned 795–816), thus inaugurating the **Holy Roman Empire**.

The Decline of the Carolingian Empire (814–88). Charlemagne was succeeded by his son Louis the Pious (reigned 814–40); Louis's death, however, led to a division of the empire, as his sons fought over the inheritance. In 843 the two younger sons, Charles and Louis, forced their elder brother, Lothair, to accept a formal division of the empire. The resulting Treaty of Verdun (843) established three kingdoms: one, including most of modern France, went to Charles the Bald (reigned

843–77); another, including the western part of Germany, was the share of Louis the German (reigned 843–76); and a third – the Middle Kingdom, including the Low Countries, Switzerland, and northern Italy – went, in addition to the title of emperor, to Lothair (reigned 843–55). In 855 the Middle Kingdom was partitioned between Lothair's sons, while the title of Holy Roman Emperor became increasingly meaningless. Political disintegration also occurred at a local level. The Carolingian monarchs were unable to mount an effective defence against Viking invasions; power gradually passed from the kings to local rulers. Many smaller landowners sought their protection and so became their feudal vassals.

▲ **Carolingian Coinage**
This 8th-century coin of the Emperor Charlemagne illustrates how techniques of coinage had improved under the Carolingians.

Charlemagne's Empire and its Divisions ▶
Charlemagne's empire included France, the Low Countries, and Germany west of the Rhine. From this base he expanded his power to include northern Italy, where the Lombard kingdom was annexed in 773, and Bavaria (788). Catalonia was added as the Spanish March in 786; from 772 to 804 the Saxons of northern Germany were defeated.

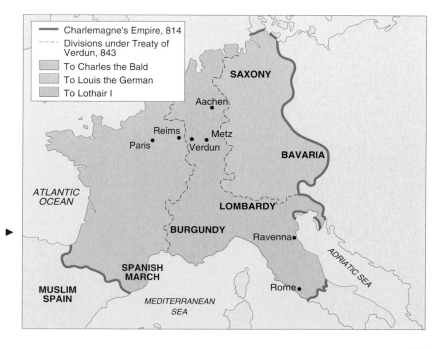

Charlemagne's Empire, 814
Divisions under Treaty of Verdun, 843
To Charles the Bald
To Louis the German
To Lothair I

SAXONY
Aachen
Reims
Paris
Verdun
Metz
BAVARIA
ATLANTIC OCEAN
LOMBARDY
BURGUNDY
Ravenna
ADRIATIC SEA
SPANISH MARCH
MUSLIM SPAIN
MEDITERRANEAN SEA
Rome

Invasions and Anarchy

Barbarian invasions • France (888–1100) • Germany • England •
Scandinavia • Europe in 1100

Vikings (from Old Norse *vik*, meaning creek or sea inlet) Immensely hardy pagan sea warriors from Denmark, Norway, and Sweden, who set out to raid and colonize surrounding lands from the late 8th to 11th centuries.

Despite the success of Charles the Fat, great-grandson of Charlemagne, in reuniting the Frankish kingdoms from 884–87, the Carolingian Empire had been irretrievably weakened by its subdivision, from 840, among members of the Carolingian family, and by **Viking** raids from the early 9th century. The fall of Charles the Fat in 887 marked the final disintegration of the empire, leaving western Europe was in a state of political disarray. In the following years the title of Holy Roman Emperor lost much of its prestige and, in the west, power once held by the monarchs was assumed by local counts and other dynasts, which led to the emergence of feudalism.

Barbarian Invasions

Of the new wave of barbarian invasions that hit Europe at this time, the most threatening were the Viking raids on Britain and western France. Europe was also attacked from the south by Muslim pirates from Tunisia and from Muslim Spain. Sicily was conquered (831) and settled by Arabs from Tunisia. They raided Rome in 841, burning down the Vatican. In southern France a group of pirates from Muslim Spain set up a base at Fraxinetum (Fréjus), from which they could raid

Provence; they were not dislodged until 972. From c. 890 **Magyars**, horse-riding nomads from eastern Europe, began to raid Germany and eastern France, causing massive destruction to towns and religious communities. The Magyars remained a menace to western Europe until their defeat by Otto the Great of Germany (reigned as king 936–61; as emperor 962–73); they subsequently settled and established the Kingdom of Hungary in c. 1000.

France (888–1100)

The later Carolingians had proved unable to defend the country from Viking and Magyar attacks; by 888 they had been replaced by Odo, count of Paris (reigned as king 888–98), who had defended the city against the Vikings. After Odo's death the old dynasty was restored and continued to rule as kings until the death of Louis V (reigned 979–87). In 987 the French nobles elected Hugh Capet (reigned 987–96). Although French royal power was now confined to a small area, the Île-de-France, which included Paris and Orléans, the king was supported by powerful churchmen.

The remainder of France was divided into feudal principalities, the most important being the county of Flanders, the duchy of

Barbarian Invasions *During the 9th and 10th centuries every area of Christian western Europe was subjected to attack from non-Christian invaders. While the Magyars and the Muslims were finally defeated in the 10th century, the Vikings settled, leaving a significant stamp on European history and culture.*

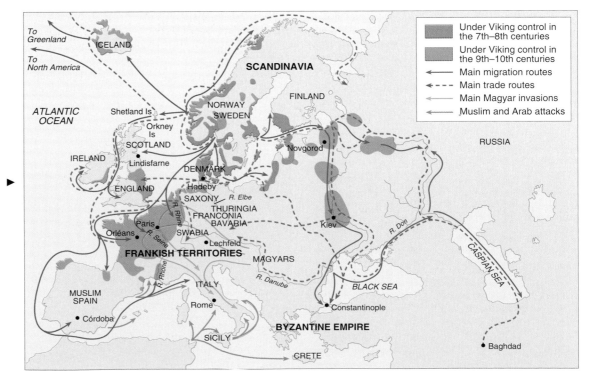

THE VIKINGS

The reasons for the great Viking expansion of the late 8th to the 11th centuries are not fully understood; however, a shortage of land to cultivate and the weakness of surrounding states are likely factors.

The first recorded Viking raid was on the northeastern coast of England in

▲ **A Viking Longboat** *Powered by oar and a single sail, longboats such as this carried the invading Vikings all around the continent of Europe and even across the Atlantic to North America. This Norwegian vessel was built in c. 850.*

794. In the 9th century Norwegians raided both England and France. By sailing up major river estuaries, they could penetrate far inland. In 865 they conquered the Anglo-Saxon kingdoms of East Anglia and Northumbria. Wessex resisted and, in 886, the Vikings were confined to the **Danelaw**. By 954, most of the Danelaw had been retaken by the kings of Wessex. Viking invasions of England began again in 980.

The Norwegian Vikings settled the Scottish islands of Orkney and Shetland in the early 9th century and established settlements in Ireland (836) and Iceland (from 860). From there they began to settle Greenland (c. 984), and then went on to North America, where there were short-lived attempts to establish permanent settlements on the east coast of modern Canada in c. 1000.

Vikings also raided Spain and Portugal in 844 and 860, but the Muslim opposition prevented any settlement. France suffered from Viking depredations from the early 9th century, speeding the break-up of the Carolingian Empire. In 885–86 an attack on Paris was repulsed. In 911 the Viking leader Rollo (c. 860–c. 932) agreed a treaty with Charles the Simple of France (reigned 893–922), which allowed his followers to settle in what became the duchy of Normandy.

More than just pirates, the Vikings had an interest in trade. Such settlements as Hedeby, in Denmark, became major commercial centres, recycling booty and slaves taken in raids. They were also skilled farmers, as demonstrated in their settlement of the English Danelaw, Orkney, Shetland, and Iceland.

Vikings also travelled east along the Russian river system. They sailed down the Rivers Don and Dnieper, reaching the Black Sea in 839 and threatening Constantinople in 860. The Russian Vikings traded with the Byzantine Empire, and established cities, such as Novgorod and Kiev, along trade routes, thus laying the foundations of medieval Russian civilization.

In the 11th century Viking expansion began to slow. Latin Christianity spread to Scandinavia and the Russian Vikings were converted to Greek Orthodox Christianity in c. 988. Colonies in Greenland and North America were abandoned and the Viking populations of the British Isles and Normandy integrated into the local populations. In Scandinavia itself, Denmark, Norway, and Sweden all developed conventional medieval states, which ultimately led to the decline of Viking power and the raiding way of life on which it had been established.

Normandy, the county of Anjou, the duchy of Aquitaine, the county of Toulouse, the duchy of Burgundy, and the county of Champagne. They were effectively independent, their rulers owing only nominal allegiance to the crown, which exercised no authority in their lands. The weakness of the monarchy was made obvious during the reign of Philip I (reigned 1060–1108). He was forced to look on helplessly while his nominal vassal, William, duke of Normandy (1028–87), conquered England in 1066, reigning as king of England from 1066 to 1087, thus becoming much more powerful than Philip himself.

Germany

In the eastern (German) lands of the Carolingian Empire, the impact of the barbarian invasions strengthened the monarchy. In 911 the last Carolingian, Louis the Child (reigned 900–11), died. By this time, real power lay

with the dukes of the great duchies of Bavaria, Swabia, Franconia, Saxony, and Lorraine; it was the duke of Saxony, Henry the Fowler (reigned 919–36), who was chosen as king. He mobilized Saxon forces and defeated the Magyars in 933, and the Danes in 934, so establishing himself as a powerful leader. On Henry's death, the German dukes accepted as successor his son Otto (the Great), who united the country after a series of civil wars and finally defeated the Magyars at the Battle of Lechfeld (955). Otto also initiated short-lived German expansion against the Slavs, east of the River Elbe, where he founded the archbishopric of Magdeburg (968). In 962 he invaded Italy and had himself crowned Holy Roman Emperor, thus beginning a long-lasting association between the German monarchy and the title of emperor.

Otto's reign heralded a period of a century during which Germany was the leading

Danelaw An area of eastern England that had come under Viking rule. There was extensive Viking settlement in the Danelaw, where Danish laws and customs prevailed from the late 9th to 12th centuries.

▲ **Falaise Castle**
(built 12th–13th century) As well as serving defensive purposes, the castle was the focus of the feudal unit. Stone structures began to replace wooden ones from the late 10th century. The castle shown here was formerly the seat of the dukes of Normandy.

political power in western Europe, controlling not only the German lands, but much of northern Italy. Successive emperors usually maintained good relations with the papacy, relying heavily on German churchmen for political support. This relationship was jeopardized in 1056, when Henry III (reigned 1039–56) died leaving Henry IV (reigned 1056–1106), aged only six, as his heir. Henry immediately faced opposition from the duchy of Saxony, the newly assertive papacy in Rome, and from the wealthy independent city-states

of Lombardy in northern Italy. Forced to submit to Pope Gregory VII (1077), Henry IV failed to make his power effective. When he died, in 1106, his own son, Henry V (reigned 1106–1125), had rebelled against him and Germany was in crisis.

England

Viking attacks in the 9th century destroyed many of the Anglo-Saxon kingdoms, notably Mercia in 874. However, Wessex under Alfred the Great (reigned 871–99) offered effective resistance, halting Danish expansion and recapturing London (886). Alfred was succeeded by Edward the Elder (reigned 899–924) and then by Athelstan (reigned 924–39), who succeeded in subduing the Danelaw; Athelstan also established a strong and effective government throughout the country. This period also saw a notable revival of monastic life and learning in England, under the leadership of St Dunstan (924–88).

Renewed Danish attacks during the reign of the incompetent Ethelred the Unready (978–1016) forced the English to pay tribute, known as **Danegeld,** to the Vikings. The ambitious Danish prince **Canute**, meanwhile, was determined to conquer the whole country. After Ethelred's death, Canute was vigorously opposed by Ethelred's son Edmund Ironside (c. 993–1016); however, the Danes won a

▲ **Otto the Great**
He united his German lands and was victorious over the invading Magyars (955), making the German Empire the leading political power in western Europe for the following century.

FEUDALISM

Feudalism was a social, political, economic, and legal system that developed in France during the 9th–11th centuries. Its main characteristics were:

• A landholder granted some of his land to another man; the two thereby became **lord** and **tenant**. This grant was in the form of a benefice or **fief**: ownership was not transferred, but the tenant enjoyed full powers over the land in return for some form of service (often military) and also personal loyalty. (Fiefs originated in the Carolingian Empire, when soldiers were granted lands by monarchs in exchange for military service, as there was no money to pay them.)

• A tenant's heirs had a claim on his fief, and by the 11th century fiefs were usually regarded as hereditary.

• A tenant would in turn grant parts of his fief, becoming the lord of a lower level of tenants. Thus, a hierarchy of land tenure was created.

• Within his fief, a tenant exercised many rights – in particular, the administration of justice and (until attempts to curb it in the 11th century) the right to make war on his

neighbours. The symbol, and guarantee, of a tenant's practical independence was the castle, which proliferated first in wood and later in stone.

Feudalism developed in the anarchy caused by the breakdown of the Carolingian Empire and the Viking invasions, and reflected the collapse of authority above a very local level. A 'grant' was often the legitimization of a seizure of land or rights by the tenant from the lord. As a result, the lord/tenant relationships in France were very complex and, until the 11th century, very fluid.

Over time feudalism became an accepted and orderly social system, which was carried to new areas. Thus, the feudal hierarchy that developed in England after the Norman Conquest (1066) was much simpler and the rights of the crown were not alienated.

Feudalism decayed from the 12th century as economic growth increased the importance of monetary ties rather than those of service and as rulers (whether kings or, as in Germany and Italy, the nobility or cities) consolidated their hold on governmental prerogatives.

great victory over Edmund at Ashingdon in Essex (1016). When Edmund died a few months later, the English accepted Canute as their king (reigned 1016–35).

After the death of Canute, England again became independent under the rule of the saintly Edward the Confessor (reigned 1042–66), after which the crown passed, not without opposition, to a leading noble, Harold Godwinson (reigned Jan.–Oct. 1066). Faced by threats of invasions from Scandinavia and Normandy, Harold defeated the Norwegian king, Harald Hardrada (reigned 1045–66), at the Battle of Stamford Bridge in 1066; three weeks later, however, he was himself defeated by William of Normandy, who rapidly conquered the whole of England and founded a new dynasty.

Scandinavia

In Scandinavia too, the 11th century saw a move away from the raiding of the Viking age to the establishment of settled states. Denmark was the most advanced of these; Canute the Great (reigned in Denmark 1018–35) was one of the most eminent monarchs of his age. He was succeeded by other members of his family, one of whom, Erik I (reigned 1095–1103), joined the First Crusade to the Holy Land.

Norway was slower to settle, despite the conversion of King Olaf I (995–c. 1000) to Christianity. Such kings as Harald Hardrada (reigned 1047–56) and Magnus Barelegs (reigned 1093–1103) maintained the seafaring lifestyle of Viking chiefs; it was not until the 12th century that Norway became more peaceful. The Swedish monarchy developed slowly and the country was politically divided until the 13th century.

Europe in 1100

Europe had developed significantly since 880; the strong monarchy in England contrasted with that in France, where the aristocracy enjoyed great autonomy, and in the German lands, where the monarchy confronted a major crisis, while maintaining its power. The frontiers of western Christendom were

KING CANUTE

▲ **King Canute** *As king of England, Denmark, and Norway, Canute was one of the most powerful rulers in Europe during the 11th century.*

King Canute created an Anglo-Scandinavian empire that came to include England, Denmark and much of Norway. He was a lawmaker, introducing both legal and military reforms, and a man of genuine Christian piety, which distinguished him from his Viking predecessors and made him acceptable to his English subjects. Canute prudently chose both Englishmen and Danes as his advisers, and while his reign was marked by internal peace and prosperity, he defended England from Viking attacks in 1017, 1026, and 1028. In 1027 he went on a pilgrimage to Rome to attend the coronation of Emperor Conrad II.

advancing into eastern Europe and the Iberian Peninsula (see ISLAMIC WORLD: MUSLIM SPAIN). There was rapid economic growth; forests were cleared and new villages established throughout the continent. One factor was a gradual improvement in the climate, which resulted in fewer very poor harvests. While mortality declined, population increased steadily. Technological progress may also have played a part; new types of plough, which could break up the heavy, but potentially rich, soils of northern Europe, were developed. Greater population, and the growing use of money, rather than barter, led to commercial expansion. Trading and manufacturing towns were emerging in northern Italy and in Flanders. Italian merchants also began to sail into the eastern Mediterranean in search of commercial opportunities. The stage was thus set for the zenith of European medieval civilization in the 12th and 13th centuries.

◄ **Agriculture and Economic Growth** *During the 11th century an increasing population and new agricultural methods led to the expansion of of Europe's cultivated regions. Forest clearance and increased agricultural activity produced greater yields, which in turn stimulated the growth of trade in Europe.*

MEDIEVAL WARFARE

MEDIEVAL WARFARE WAS characterized from the late 5th to the 15th centuries by a gradual change from the infantry of the Roman legions to heavily armoured cavalry. This in turn led, from the 10th century, to the development of castles – a central element of feudal society – and to methods of beseiging them.

This process was aided by the advent of the stirrup, which transformed the role of the horse in war. By the 8th century the use of the stirrup had spread to western Europe, greatly effecting the conduct of warfare by helping the warrior to remain in his seat on impact.

By the 11th century, wars, usually conducted for conquest or plunder, were dominated by the mounted knight, with his coat of mail (small metal rings linked together to form a flexible protective covering), spear (later a lance), and sword, riding a heavy horse. The mobility, strength, and skill of these highly trained and heavily protected knights enabled them to launch rapid surprise attacks, and intercept or evade offensives. However, as knights were expensive to equip and maintain, they generally formed only a small part of any army.

MOUNTED ARMIES

The effectiveness of mounted knights was demonstrated in the Norman conquest of England, in 1066, and in the military successes of the First Crusade (1095–99). Trained armies of knights were also effective against the Magyar attacks in Germany in the 10th century, while the development of such armies

was a factor in the declining success of Viking invasions in the 11th century. In the 14th century, chain mail was replaced by plate armour, which provided solid metal protection; straps and bolted joints allowed movement. Helmets now provided all-round protection for the head, which restricted vision to narrow holes in the visor.

The dominance of the knight was threatened from the 14th century by the development of archery, notably the longbow, which the English used to great effect at the Battle of Crécy (France) in 1346. The earliest guns were also introduced at about the same time, though they were not as effective as bows on the battlefield until the 16th century.

Mounted Knights (11th century) The basic medieval war tactic was a mass charge of knights, which could be devastating. It was used in the First Crusade (1095–99), as this manuscript shows.

War Machines A medieval machine with siege ramps and archers is shown. Such machines were used to attack castles.

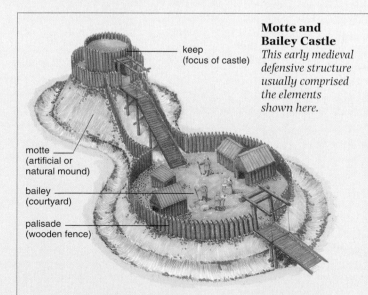

keep (focus of castle)

motte (artificial or natural mound)

bailey (courtyard)

palisade (wooden fence)

Motte and Bailey Castle This early medieval defensive structure usually comprised the elements shown here.

CASTLES

The building of castles as a form of defence developed in Europe from the 10th century. Most early castles comprised an earthen mound, or motte, often with a courtyard, or bailey, attached. From the early 11th century square stone keeps, or donjons, were built in the Loire valley (France) and these soon spread. After 1066 the Normans built large numbers of castles to maintain their control of England. Siege engines and the large swing-beam catapult were developed in the Middle East during the Crusades to attack stone castles. These developments meant that castles had to become more elaborate to provide active defence. Motte and bailey castles disappeared and stone keeps, supplemented by curtain walls with flanking towers, were built to enable archers to prevent attackers from reaching the castle walls. The finest examples of these castles are Crusader buildings, such as the Krak des Chevaliers (12th century; see THE CRUSADES) in Syria and others, such as those in north Wales, built by Edward I of England (reigned 1272–1307) to subdue the area. By the early 16th century gunpowder artillery rendered castles obsolete; thus lower, more massive styles of fortification were developed.

The Byzantine Empire

Government of the empire • Justinian the Great • Contraction and iconoclasm •
The great age of Byzantium • A Christian culture • Byzantium in decline •
The empire of Nicaea • The Palaeologan revival • From Constantinople to Istanbul

The Greek colony of Byzantium was founded on the Bosporus in c. 660 BC. Its strategic situation, at the entrance to the Black Sea, commended it to Emperor Constantine (reigned 324–37) as the site for his 'New Rome.' From 330 AD, when Constantine rebuilt the colony, it was a Christian city, known as Constantinople, 'the city of Constantine.'

Loss of territory in the west caused the Roman Empire to look east during the 3rd and 4th centuries. In 395 AD, the empire was formally divided. From the death of Theodosius I (reigned 379–95) the empire was divided between his sons: Honorius ruled the west from Italy (395–423) and Arcadius ruled the east from Constantinople (395–402).

The rulers of this eastern Roman Empire continued to speak Latin for several centuries, though their subjects spoke mostly Greek. It is now referred to as the Byzantine Empire, reflecting its Greek origins, although its people identified themselves as Romans. While the empire was associated with Orthodox Christianity, its culture was a mixture of Greek, Roman, and Christian elements.

Government of the Empire

Between 395 and 476 (when the Western Roman Empire finally fell), the Byzantine Empire, which still included Egypt and Syria, was prosperous and relatively untroubled, though it was heavily fortified against attack.

Government centred on the emperor, a remote figure, whose authority was confirmed only by the Church and the army. Below him a vast bureaucracy operated under the direction of a praetorian prefect. While salaries were low and corruption widespread, good education ensured effective government.

Power in the provinces was largely delegated to governors, who administered justice, financial affairs, and public works. Greedy and corrupt, they often initiated ambitious building programmes to obtain the goodwill of influencial senators and rich landowners. Much depended on city councils, responsible for maintaining roads and buildings, recruiting soldiers and labourers, and collecting taxes.

Within the Church, disputes between opposing parties over doctrinal issues were complex and bitter. A series of **ecumenical councils** failed to resolve these divisions.

Justinian the Great

The reign of Justinian (527–65) marks the high point of the early Byzantine period. Of humble origin, Justinian was a man of great energy and ambition. With his wife, Theodora (c. 500–48), generals Belisarius (c. 505–65) and Narses (c. 480–574), and administrators

===SEE ALSO===
This section:
• The Crusades
• Kiev-Rus and
  Eastern Europe
**Early Western
Civilizations:**
• The Roman Empire
Islamic World:
• The Emergence
  of a New Empire
• The Rise of the
  Ottoman Empire
**The European Tradition
(vol. 4):**
• Art of the Middle Ages
Religion (vol. 6):
• Christianity

ecumenical councils
Assemblies of bishops or other ecclesiastics representative of the Christian Church throughout the world. Before the 9th-century schism under Photius, seven councils met.

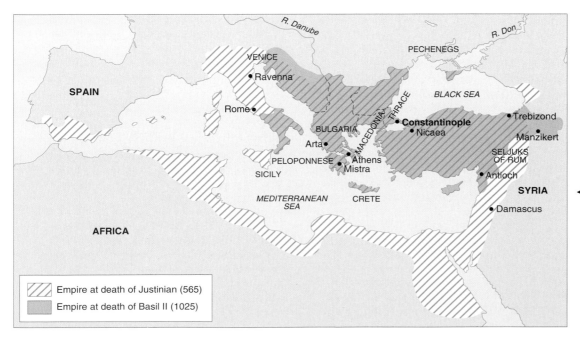

◀ **The Byzantine Empire** *Basil II died (1025) leaving the empire greater and stronger than at any time since the reign of Justinian (527–65). The empire subsequently declined, before the Palaeologan revival in the 14th century.*

63

The Great Church of St Sophia, Istanbul ▶

This impressive church still stands as a symbol of Justinian's achievements. When Justinian entered the completed church in 537, he exclaimed "Solomon, I have outdone thee!" In 1453 it became a mosque, and in 1935 a museum.

John of Cappadocia and Tribonian, he recruited loyal, talented, and ruthless advisers. Aiming to create a strong empire based on a single administrative system and a united church, he began reorganizing and codifying Roman law, one of Rome's greatest legacies. In an attempt to reduce corruption and increase efficiency, the old city councils were abolished, their responsibilities transferred to bishops and landowners.

Declining city populations were further reduced by plague. In 532 there were serious riots in Constantinople against the unpopular measures of Tribonian and John of Cappadocia. Order was restored by the generals. While Justinian himself was saved, one casualty was the old church of the Holy Wisdom, St Sophia, which Justinian subsequently had rebuilt.

Other churches were built throughout the empire. The emperor's hold over ecclesiastical affairs was strengthened by outlawing paganism and heresy and by closing the philosophical schools of Athens. His most remarkable achievement, however, was the reconquest of much of the Western Roman Empire. By the end of his reign, Sicily, Italy, North Africa, and southern Spain had been conquered, giving the empire control of the Mediterranean.

Contraction and Iconoclasm

The cost of Justinian's conquests had been enormous and they did not long survive him. Within a few years of his death, the Lombards had overrun northern Italy, the Moors had taken back most of Africa, the Avars were attacking the Balkans, and the Slavs had swept through Greece. Early in the 7th century Egypt and Syria were briefly occupied by the Persians. The empire was consequently left with Anatolia and pockets of North Africa, southern Italy, and the Balkans.

The 7th century saw the rise of a new power in the east. Within ten years of the death of the Prophet Mohammed (632), Arab Muslims had captured Damascus, Jerusalem, and Alexandria; by 700 they had conquered all of North Africa. As early as 673 they threatened to take Constantinople. The conquest of Byzantium was only abandoned when, in 747, the Muslims suffered a heavy defeat at sea and, in 754, the caliphate was moved from Damascus to the more distant Baghdad.

Within the empire urban civilization became confined to Constantinople and Thessalonica, while Byzantine culture was checked. By the end of the 7th century universities had closed and literary and artistic production had almost ceased. Civil authority was transferred to large military units (***themes***); the loss of such cities as Antioch and Alexandria emphasized the isolation of the capital.

Religious disputes also resurfaced in 726, when Emperor Leo III (reigned 717–41) condemned the worship of **icons**, which led to riots. However, destruction of icons (***iconoclasm***) was imposed to varying degrees by subsequent emperors until 843, when it was finally condemned by a council proclaiming the 'Triumph of Orthodoxy.'

The Great Age of Byzantium

The restoration of icon worship initiated a remarkable regeneration of cultural activity, which lasted until the 11th century. Greater emphasis was placed on education, notably by the patriarch (archbishop) of Constantinople, Photius (c. 820–?91), and universities were refounded. Serious attempts were also made to convert the Slavs to Orthodox Christianity (see KIEV-RUS AND EASTERN EUROPE).

Photius was elected to the office of patriarch twice (858–67 and 878–86); on the first occasion he was still a layman. His predecessor objected and appealed to Pope Nicholas I (died 867) for support. The pope, keen to promote Roman Catholicism at the expense of

icons Images of Christ, the Virgin Mary, or other saints that are fundamental to Orthodox Christian worship. They are believed to provide the pious worshipper with a direct relationship with the saint portrayed. The iconoclasts declared, in 754, that "the images of false and evil name have no foundation in the tradition of Christ, the apostles, and the Fathers." Icon worship was restored by Empress Theodora in 843.

Orthodoxy in Bulgaria, announced the deposition of Photius. Photius promptly summoned a council that excommunicated the pope and declared Catholicism heretical. The dispute was resolved and strained relations with Rome were resumed for another two centuries.

The empire also recovered its military strength during this period. The Byzantines fought against the Muslims in Anatolia, although Sicily was finally lost in 902. Crete (961) and Syria (969) were reconquered by John I (reigned 969–76), while Bulgaria remained a menace throughout the 10th century. It was not until the reign of Basil II ('the Bulgar-slayer'; c. 958–1025) that the whole area south of the River Danube was annexed.

A Christian Culture

Far from spurning their classical pre-Christian inheritance, the Byzantines took great pains to preserve it. The libraries of Constantinople contained all the principal literature of ancient Greece; its streets were lined with works of art from all over eastern Greece. Its systems of education, administration, and law, however, were established on Roman models; as late as the 12th century, aristocrats would boast that their ancestors had 'come over with Constantine.' Despite this pride in their past, the Byzantines chose to develop the Orthodox Church as an entirely different focus for their cultural expression.

In the visual arts, architects concentrated predominantly on churches and monasteries. Artists developed new techniques in mosaic, fresco, icon painting, and manuscript illumination in order to glorify God's house and His word. Writers, when not chronicling the history of the Church, were involved in complex theological controversy and exegesis.

◄ **The Monastery of Vatopedi on Mount Athos**
One of the greatest of the 10th-century foundations.

Monasteries were influential in the training of bishops and patriarchs. Monks were regarded as spiritually superior to human society. In order to pursue the contemplative life, they needed to be free from all worldly concerns. They consequently depended on the patronage of the rich. An emperor wishing to demonstrate his munificence would invariably bestow his gift on a monastery.

As the focus of considerable cultural attention, monasteries were granted substantial properties and treasures. Most important among them were the 20 monasteries of Mount Athos, several of which date from the 10th century. Their seclusion has enabled them to survive as the hub of Orthodox spirituality; many of them still demonstrate some of the splendour of middle Byzantine culture.

Byzantium in Decline

Basil II was succeeded by a series of ineffectual emperors, whose incompetence led to the loss of conquests of the previous century. The empire was threatened simultaneously on several fronts and, in 1071, the Normans captured southern Italy and the **Seljuks** defeated a large imperial army at Manzikert in Armenia. Anatolia, the source of the empire's food and soldiers, was now exposed. By 1080 much of this region was lost for ever.

The decline was halted by Alexius I Comnenus (reigned 1081–1118). With Venetian help he overcame the Normans and, with **Cuman** help, he defeated the **Pechenegs**, who had laid siege to Constantinople in 1090. An alliance with the First Crusade (1095; see THE CRUSADES) helped Alexius to recover western Anatolia. Recovery continued under Alexius's successors, John II (reigned 1118–1143) and Manuel I (reigned 1143–80). The latter, however, was heavily defeated by the Turks at Myriokephalon in 1176 and his death, in 1180, was followed by rapid disintegration of the empire.

The Venetians, as long-term allies of the Byzantines, had been granted special privileges by Constantinople, including their own quarters in the city, which they shared with the Genoese and other Latin peoples. These privileges enabled them to develop a highly profitable maritime empire of their own. As the Byzantine state weakened, it came to depend increasingly on the Venetians for aid.

In 1182, however, conflict between Greeks and Latins erupted in the capital. In the struggle for succession, a new emperor was swept to power on a tide of popular support, while the excited mob massacred the Latins in the city.

The Seljuks

The Seljuks were a Turkic tribe from Central Asia, who moved westwards in the 11th century. Having captured Persia and Baghdad, they attacked Anatolia, defeating the Byzantines at Manzikert in 1071. A branch known as the Seljuks of Rum established their capital at Konya (now in Turkey) and flourished until 1302.

Cumans A Turkic tribe that settled in the Ukraine in the 11th century, from where they were able to harass the Russians, the Bulgarians, and the Byzantines. Their regime was toppled by the Mongols in 1239.

Pechenegs A Turkic tribe from the south Russian steppe. They occupied the land between the River Danube and the River Don in the late 9th century, driving out the Magyars. The Byzantines used them as a diplomatic counter to the Bulgarians, the Russians, and the Magyars, although they often attacked the empire.

Relations with Rome

The division of the eastern and western halves of the Church was due to political, cultural, and, ultimately, doctrinal factors:
- The coronation of Charlemagne as Holy Roman Emperor in 800 caused great offence in Byzantium.
- The Eastern and Western Churches used different languages; by the 7th century they could not understand each other.
- The pope's claim to universal jurisdiction and the doctrinal issue of *filioque*.

The addition of the *filioque* to the Catholic Creed in the 11th century was the catalyst for relations being formally broken off in 1054.

▲ **The Interior Decoration of the Chora (Kariye Cami) in Istanbul** *Carried out in the late 14th century, it represents the artistic renaissance of the Palaeologan period.*

When the Fourth Crusade was diverted to Constantinople in 1204, the Venetians had their revenge. They devastated the city, stripping it of much of its ancient heritage and wealth. A Latin empire was established and the territories of the emperor were divided among the crusading states with the Venetians taking the greatest share.

The Empire of Nicaea

The collapse of centralized government resulted in the creation of a number of successor states within the former empire. In the west, the Angelos family established the despotate (realm) of Epirus, based at Arta. They drove the Latins out of Macedonia and proclaimed an empire in Thessalonica in 1225. By 1230, however, it had fallen to the Bulgarians.

In the east another 'empire' was set up around Trebizond, on the Black Sea, by a branch of the Comnenus family. Despite Turkish attacks, it survived until 1461.

The third state was at Nicaea in northwestern Anatolia, much closer to Constantinople. Here a small militarily effective regime was established by the Laskarid family. Gradually, they overcame the Latins, the Bulgarians, and the despots of Epirus, and by the 1250s they had recaptured Macedonia and Thrace. Finally, it was a usurper, Michael VIII Palaeologos (reigned 1261–82), who triumphantly re-entered Constantinople in 1261.

The Palaeologan Revival

Territorially, the restored 'empire' was only a few scattered fragments: the west coast of Anatolia, northern Greece, and the southeastern Peloponnese. It continued to shrink throughout the Palaeologan period (1261–1453). Epirus and Trebizond remained independent. By the 1360s the Ottoman Turks had taken most of Anatolia and Thrace, while the Serbs had occupied Epirus and most of Macedonia. Thessalonica fell in 1387 (and again in 1430 after a recovery). Epirus also fell to the Turks in 1430. Only the despotate of Mistra, in the Peloponnese, prospered, surviving until 1460.

Despite the empire's territorial decline, recurrent civil war at home, and attempts by various emperors to invoke a papal crusade by subjecting Orthodoxy to Roman jurisdiction, the last age of Byzantium was culturally rich. All the arts for which Byzantium is famous were flourishing – both in Constantinople and in Arta and Trebizond. Monasteries were founded at Meteora in Thessaly and on Athos. The fine city built at Mistra still stands.

From Constantinople to Istanbul

By the end of the 14th century the Byzantine Empire was reduced to the city of Constantinople. The population, protected by a circuit of walls, had shrunk from about one million in the 12th century to no more than 100 000. In 1394 it was besieged by the Turks. Emperor Manuel II (reigned 1391–1425) toured the capitals of western Europe in a vain attempt to enlist support. The siege was not lifted until 1402, when the Ottomans were defeated by the Mongol army of Timur (Tamerlane) at the Battle of Ankara.

Constantinople finally fell in April 1453 when Sultan Mehmed II besieged it with a force of about 80 000. The defending force was only about 7000. Despite a heroic effort, the city wall was breached. Emperor Constantine XI (reigned 1449–53) fell in battle, the city was sacked, and Mehmet became master of the eastern Roman Empire. The city, which had for so long symbolized Christian resistance to the spread of Islam, was renamed Istanbul and its churches were converted to mosques.

The Land Walls of Constantinople *Rebuilt during the reign of Theodosius II (401–50), they ran for 6 km from the Propontis to the Golden Horn. They remained unbreached for over 1000 years.* ▼

The Medieval Zenith

*The rise of France • England • Germany • Italy • The conflict of empire and papacy •
The reconquest of Spain*

The two centuries between 1100 and 1300 saw the expansion of every area of western European culture, in the development of political systems, in the arts, and, with the Crusades, the first European expansion into Asia. All this was made possible by a sustained period of economic growth. The population of Europe rose from about 42 million in the year 1000 to 70 million by 1300, the demographic high point of the Middle Ages. This increase was supported by greater agricultural production and new techniques, notably the heavy plough with a metal blade, which enabled new rich soils to be cultivated. This allowed villages to be established in forests, marshes, and deserts in all areas of Europe.

Towns also began to develop rapidly. Clothmaking towns, such as Bruges, Ghent, and Amiens in Flanders and northern France, emerged as industrial centres, while Florence became prosperous through the finishing of textiles. Italian cities, such as Venice, Genoa, and Pisa, became hugely wealthy with the development of Mediterranean trade. By the end of the 13th century, this growth had reached its limit; all surplus land had been absorbed and famines became increasingly common, a foretaste of the demographic decline and economic crises of the 14th century.

The Rise of France

France experienced the greatest growth in royal power. In 1100 France comprised several feudal principalities, of which the duchy of Normandy and the counties of Anjou, Flanders, and Champagne in the north, and the duchy of Aquitaine and the county of Toulouse in the south were the most important. The kings of the Capetian line, established in 987 by Hugh Capet (?938–96), controlled only a small area around Paris, known as the Île-de-France. During the 12th century, however, a sequence of successful monarchs transformed the power of the French crown.

France and the Angevin Empire *(1154–1314)* ▶
From the mid-12th century, when the Angevin Empire dwarfed the domains of the French king, the power of the French monarchy was dramatically increased by a series of rulers. By the late 13th century France had become a major European power, at the cost of the Angevins, now limited to England and Gascony.

Louis VI (also known as Louis the Fat; reigned 1108–37) established order in the Île-de-France with the aid of his adviser and biographer Suger (1081–1151), abbot of St Denis. His son, the pious Louis VII (reigned 1137–80), was faced by a new power. Between 1152 and 1154 Henry Plantagenet, count of Anjou (and king of England 1154–1189), brought Anjou, Normandy, Aquitaine, and England under his rule, thus establishing the **Angevin** Empire, which stretched from the borders of Scotland to the Pyrenees.

The French monarchy's security necessitated a policy of weakening the Angevin Empire wherever possible. Lacking military equality, Louis's main weapons were diplomacy, a judicious use of his position as Henry's feudal

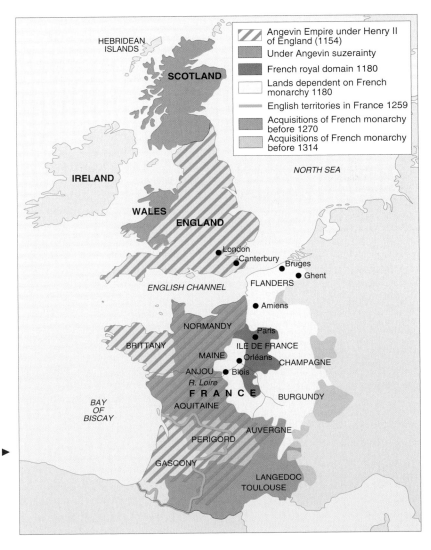

Angevin Empire under Henry II of England (1154)
Under Angevin suzerainty
French royal domain 1180
Lands dependent on French monarchy 1180
English territories in France 1259
Acquisitions of French monarchy before 1270
Acquisitions of French monarchy before 1314

HEBRIDEAN ISLANDS
SCOTLAND
IRELAND
NORTH SEA
WALES
ENGLAND
London
Canterbury
Bruges
Ghent
ENGLISH CHANNEL
FLANDERS
Amiens
NORMANDY
Paris
BRITTANY
ILE DE FRANCE
MAINE
Orléans
CHAMPAGNE
ANJOU
Blois
R. Loire
F R A N C E
BURGUNDY
BAY OF BISCAY
AQUITAINE
AUVERGNE
PERIGORD
GASCONY
LANGEDOC
TOULOUSE

THE ANGEVINS

The Angevins, now usually known as the Plantagenets (after the sprig of broom – *planta genista* – that was their emblem), were one of the most successful aristocratic families in medieval France. They had held the county of Anjou (from which the family name derives) on the lower River Loire since the 10th century. Geoffrey of Anjou (1131–51) married Matilda, daughter of Henry I, king of England and duke of Normandy. After Henry's death (1135) Geoffrey encouraged Matilda to pursue her claim to the English throne while he invaded Normandy, which he captured by 1144, becoming the most powerful ruler in western France. His son, Henry (II of England), succeeded to Anjou and Normandy on his father's death (1151). In 1152, Henry married Eleanor of Aquitaine, which gave him lordship over most of southwest France. By 1154, when Henry succeeded Stephen as king of England, he had built up an empire that easily overshadowed the domains of the French king. On Henry's death, in 1189, the empire passed to his son Richard. Under King John, Richard's brother and successor, Normandy and Anjou were lost to Philip II of France, in 1204, leaving only Gascony, in southwest France, and England in Angevin hands. The Angevins remained kings of England until the death of Richard II in 1399.

▲ **Henry II**
Founder of the Angevin Empire, Henry II initiated reforms that marked the beginnings of English common law.

overlord for his lands in France, and the exploitation of the Angevin Empire's internal divisions – either by encouraging rebellion against Henry's rule or, after 1173, by exploiting disputes within Henry's family. This policy was continued more ruthlessly by Louis's determined and able son, Philip II (also known as Augustus; reigned 1180–1223); it bore spectacular fruit in 1204 when he expelled the Angevins from Normandy and Anjou. These lands came under the French monarchy's direct control, making the king the most powerful figure in northern France. Philip's grandson, Louis IX (St Louis; reigned 1226–70), famous for his justice, piety, and his commitment to crusading, was a shrewd politician who presided over the extension of

French royal power to the south, especially to Languedoc in the wake of the Albigensian crusade. The 13th century also saw the growth of the machinery of royal government and – particularly during St Louis's long reign – its penetration into areas not directly controlled by the crown. By the accession of Philip IV (reigned 1285–1314), the French monarchy was the most powerful in Europe.

England

As with France, the power of the English monarchy grew in this period. Henry I (reigned 1100–35) was a firm ruler, under whom English royal government was the strongest in western Europe. His achievement was jeopardized in 1135, when he died without a male heir; the crown was seized by his nephew, Stephen of Blois (reigned 1135–54). However, Stephen's claim was challenged by Henry's daughter Matilda (1102–67). A civil war followed, causing Stephen's reign to degenerate into near anarchy.

In 1153 it was agreed that Stephen would be succeeded by Matilda's son Henry, who became King Henry II in 1154. During his long reign (1154–89) he restored order, revived the royal administration, and laid foundations for its future growth – notably the expansion and reorganization of royal justice that marked the beginning of English common law. Henry and his son and successor Richard I (known as the Lion Heart; reigned 1189–99) spent much of their reigns abroad, either in their French lands or, in Richard's case, on crusade.

England, as the most stable part of the Angevin Empire, demanded less attention from its ruler – which encouraged the development of bureaucratic royal administration. When King John (reigned 1199–1216) lost Normandy and Anjou to the French crown (1204), this changed: John took up near permanent residence in England and began to exploit his right to amass enough resources to recover his lands. His unscrupulous methods produced tensions with the barons that came to open revolt in 1215. John was obliged to issue the Magna Carta (Great Charter), in which various rights were confirmed.

The long reign (1216–72) of Henry III was a period of great prosperity and cultural activity. It saw the consolidation of royal government and the common law and the beginnings of parliament, spurred by the king's need for additional revenue in the form of new taxes. However, intermittant political crises came to a head in 1258 when a coalition of barons attempted to force Henry to accept restrictions on his government. Civil war followed (1264–65), in which the king was ultimately victorious. So strong was the English monarchy that, in 1272, Edward I succeeded unchallenged,

ENGLISH AND FRENCH MONARCHS (1100–1314)

House of Normandy		House of Capet	
Henry I	1100–35	Louis VI (the Fat)	1108–37
House of Blois		Louis VII	1137–80
Stephen	1135–54	Philip II (Augustus)	1180–1223
House of Plantagenet (Angevin Dynasty)		Louis VIII	1223–26
Henry II	1154–89	Louis IX (St Louis)	1226–70
Richard I	1189–99	Philip III (the Bold)	1270–85
John	1199–1216		
Henry III	1216–72	Philip IV (the Fair)	1285–1314
Edward I	1272–1307		

although he was on crusade and did not return to England until 1274.

Scotland maintained its independence despite the attempts of English kings, from Henry II on, to assert their overlordship. Under strong monarchs, such as William the Lion (reigned 1165–1214) and Alexander III (reigned 1249–86), royal power became firmly established in the south and east of Scotland. The defeat of the Norwegian king Haakon IV (reigned 1217–63) in 1263 allowed for the expansion of the kingdom into the Hebridean (Western) islands. When Alexander III died (1286) without an adult male heir, Scottish independence began to come under threat from England.

Germany

In contrast to France and England the power of the German monarchy declined during this period. The German kings were also Holy Roman Emperors, whose priorities were to pursue the wider obligations and ambitions associated with the imperial office, especially the maintenance of imperial power in northern Italy and resisting the claims of the papacy. During the 12th century the political structure of the kingdom of Germany was also undermined by population and commercial growth, which led to the clearance and settlement of forest areas. The eastward expansion of German peasant settlements was another result of these developments.

Germany had been the most powerful state in early medieval Europe. However, the power of Henry IV (reigned 1054–1106) had been undermined by his dispute with the papacy over control of Church appointments and, from 1073, by rebellions in Saxony against his attempts to establish the authority of the crown in northern Germany. His son, Henry V (reigned 1106–25), made peace with the papacy at the Concordat of Worms (1122), but failed to re-establish the power of the monarchy within Germany. Henry V died without an heir and the German nobles subsequently elected the duke of Saxony, who became Lothair III (reigned 1125–37).

Family rivalries and disputes over royal property gave rise to a feud between the noble dynasties of Welf and Hohenstaufen, which led to open warfare. In 1152 Frederick Barbarossa of Hohenstaufen (reigned 1152–90) was elected king in an effort to restore peace. He established order in Germany and, in 1180, succeeded in exiling his Welf rival, Henry, duke of Saxony (reigned 1142–80).

Frederick also tried to reassert imperial power in northern Italy but was strongly opposed by the Italian city-states and the papacy; at the Peace of Venice in 1177 he was forced to give up most of his claims south of the Alps.

GERMAN MONARCHS AND HOLY ROMAN EMPERORS (1054–1291)	
Henry IV	1054–1106 (Holy Roman Emperor from 1084)
Henry V	1106–25 (Holy Roman Emperor from 1111)
Lothair III	1125–37 (Holy Roman Emperor from 1133)
Conrad III	1138–52
Frederick I (Barbarossa)	1152–90
Henry VI	1169–97 (Holy Roman Emperor from 1191)
Frederick II	1212–50 (Holy Roman Emperor from 1220)
Rudolf I	1273–91

Germany and Italy *The German emperors faced opposition not only from princes within their own kingdom, but from the increasingly powerful city-states of northern Italy and from a strong papacy; both fell within the boundaries of an empire that stretched from the Baltic Sea to Sicily.* ▼

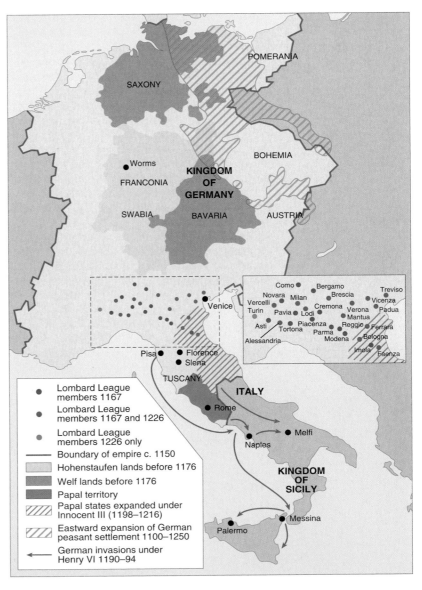

Lombard League members 1167
Lombard League members 1167 and 1226
Lombard League members 1226 only
Boundary of empire c. 1150
Hohenstaufen lands before 1176
Welf lands before 1176
Papal territory
Papal states expanded under Innocent III (1198–1216)
Eastward expansion of German peasant settlement 1100–1250
German invasions under Henry VI 1190–94

Their king, William, is admirable for his just conduct and... has great confidence in Muslims, relying on them for his affairs, and the most important matters... The king possesses splendid palaces and elegant gardens, particularly in the capital of his kingdom, Palermo... William is engrossed in the pleasures of his land, the arrangement of its laws, the laying down of procedure, the allocation of the functions of the chief officials... in a manner which resembles the Muslim kings.

Ibn Jubais (1145–1217), an Arab traveller, describes the court of William II of Sicily

Emperor Frederick I (Barbarossa)

(Venetian 14th-century codex) Having restored order in his own country, Frederick embarked on repeated expeditions into northern Italy in an attempt to impose his power there. His ambitions involved him in a prolonged dispute with the papacy. He is shown here receiving Venetian ambassadors. ▼

Frederick's successor, Henry VI (reigned 1169–97), had ambitious plans for a powerful monarchy and conquered the rich kingdom of Sicily (1194; he had claimed the Sicilian throne since 1189 through his wife, Constance). His early death precipitated a further period of Welf–Hohenstaufen feuding, before his son Frederick II (reigned 1212–50) established his rule in Sicily and Germany. However, Frederick concentrated on extending his power in Italy, allowing the German princes to become more independent. Frederick's death (1250) was followed by the Great Interregnum and a complete collapse of central authority in Germany. The election of Rudolf of Hapsburg as German king (reigned 1273–91) failed to restore unity as the German princes asserted their independence.

Italy

The development of Italy during the 12th and 13th centuries was very different in the north and the south of the peninsula.

Southern Italy. In the south, Normans from France, led by the Hauteville family, established a strong state in Sicily and southern Italy. Muslim-ruled Sicily had been conquered, between 1072 and 1093, by a force of Normans led by Roger I of Hauteville (died 1101). His son, Roger II (died 1154), succeeded in uniting Sicily with other Norman lands in southern Italy, and in 1130 was crowned king by the pope, thus establishing a monarchy.

After the death of the childless William II (Roger II's grandson; reigned 1166–1189) Emperor Henry VI eventually succeeded in his claim to the throne of the kingdom. His son Frederick II (king of Sicily 1197–1250) succeeded him. Despite Frederick's fondness for southern Italy, the kingdom's resources were increasingly used to fight wars against the papacy and the independent cities of northern Italy; his bureaucratic government thus became more repressive. In the later 13th century the **kingdom of Sicily** was fought over

by Frederick's heirs and a brother of Louis IX of France, Charles of Anjou (reigned 1266–85). In 1282 French rule on the island was overthrown by a popular uprising known as the ***Sicilian Vespers***, which led to a takeover by Aragon, while the mainland was held by Charles and his descendants.

Northern Italy. City life had never completely died out in northern Italy in the early Middle Ages, as it had in much of northwestern Europe. From the 11th century cities expanded into the rich and fertile lands of the Lombard plain. Their prosperity was increased by Mediterranean trade from c. 1100, and by the development of the textiles industry and the banking sector. As northern Italy was part of the Holy Roman Empire, its theoretical rulers were almost always absent beyond the Alps; cities thus came to be ruled by councils, or ***communes***, and by elected consuls.

There were social tensions within many communes between the upper classes, who dominated the councils, and the smaller traders, known as the ***popolo***, who formed associations to secure their interests. By 1300, the Italian communes saw the emergence of a large class of literate laymen, among whom the ideas of the Renaissance, which were to flourish fully over the next two centuries, had already begun to take root.

The Conflict of Empire and Papacy

The foundation of the Holy Roman Empire, marked by the coronation of Charlemagne by the pope, in 800, left the relationship between the head of the Latin Church and the senior ruler of western Christendom unclear. From 962, when King Otto I was crowned emperor, the imperial title was associated with the powerful German monarchy. During the 10th and early 11th centuries the emperors were able to dominate the enfeebled papacy.

In 1046 Emperor Henry III (reigned 1046–56) began the reform movement, which led to the revival of papal power. Under the forceful Pope Gregory VII (reigned 1073–85) the papacy challenged imperial control over the Church in Germany and northern Italy, especially over the right to make ecclesiastical appointments, or investitures. After a prolonged struggle, a compromise was agreed at the Concordat of Worms in 1122. Yet tension between emperors and popes remained, particularly during the reigns of the Hohenstaufen emperors Frederick I and Frederick II, both of whom tried to subjugate the papacy.

The communes that ruled the cities of northern Italy, meanwhile, became economically and politically powerful; they resisted, through the **Lombard League,** all attempts to assert imperial authority over their government. Propapal and proimperial parties grew up in

THE KINGDOM OF SICILY

Under the rule (1130–54) of Roger II, Sicily became the richest most centralized kingdom in Europe as well as the leading Mediterranean maritime power; it is said that Roger received more revenue from the city of Palermo alone, which had flourished initially under Muslim rule, than the king of England did from his entire country. His court, which enjoyed a great artistic reputation, was an intellectual centre for both Christian and Muslim scholars. Sicily was also remarkable for the way in which Latins, Greeks, and Muslim Arabs mixed on almost equal terms. Issuing a revised legal code in 1140, Roger headed one of the most sophisticated governments in western Europe. He was the last of the great Norman rulers in the south.

◄ **Roger II** *Having united the island of Sicily with mainland southern Italy, Roger was crowned king by the pope in 1130. He is shown here being crowned by Christ (12th century mosaic in the church of La Martorana, Palermo).*

The Lombard League

This alliance of Lombard towns was formed, with papal support, in 1167 to challenge Frederick I's ambitions in northern Italy. Following his defeat by the League at the Battle of Legnano (1176), he confirmed the League's communal liberties (1183). These were similarly threatened by Frederick II, whom the League also defeated. After his death (1250) the League was disbanded.

the cities; the propapal party were known as **Guelfs** (from Welf, the family name of the main German rivals of the Hohenstaufen) and the proimperial party as **Ghibellines** (from Waiblingen, a Hohenstaufen stronghold).

The struggle between pope and emperor intensified in the 13th century when Frederick II attempted to subdue northern Italy and the papacy. The alliances forged by Pope Innocent IV from 1245 and Frederick's death in 1250, which was followed by the Great Interregnum in Germany, finally broke imperial power. The Guelf and Ghibelline parties survived as factions disputing the control of Italian cities throughout the later Middle Ages.

The Reconquest of Spain

From 1008 the Muslim caliphate of Córdoba, which had ruled Spain since the 8th century, began to disintegrate into small *Taifa* kingdoms, often at war with each other. This provided the Christians in the mountainous northern areas of the peninsula with an opportunity to extend their lands southwards.

The Reconquest of Spain *In 1100 the Muslims still controlled much of Spain and Portugal. By the mid-13th century, however, the Christian kingdoms of Castile, Leon, Aragon, and Portugal had recovered almost all of the Arab Berber lands. Muslims nevertheless remained numerous in northeast and southern Spain.*

In 1085 they had taken Toledo; Valencia fell in 1094, though it was retaken by the Muslims in 1099. Saragossa in the northeast and Lisbon in the west were still Muslim strongholds. From the late 11th century, the Spanish Muslims were ruled by the puritanical Almoravide Berbers from North Africa, who were resented as uncultured foreigners.

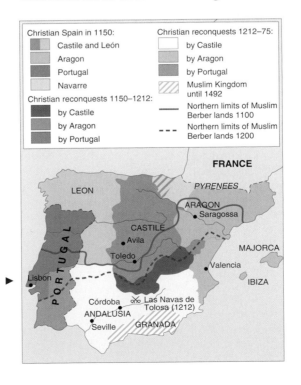

Christian Spain in 1150:
- Castile and León
- Aragon
- Portugal
- Navarre

Christian reconquests 1150–1212:
- by Castile
- by Aragon
- by Portugal

Christian reconquests 1212–75:
- by Castile
- by Aragon
- by Portugal
- Muslim Kingdom until 1492
- Northern limits of Muslim Berber lands 1100
- Northern limits of Muslim Berber lands 1200

FRANCE
PYRENEES
LEON
ARAGON
Saragossa
CASTILE
Avila
Toledo
PORTUGAL
Lisbon
MAJORCA
Valencia
IBIZA
Córdoba
Las Navas de Tolosa (1212)
ANDALUSIA
Seville
GRANADA

In the governing of their cities and in the conduct of public affairs they still imitate the wisdom of the ancient Romans. They are so desirous of liberty that... they are governed by the will of consuls rather than rulers. The consequence is that almost the entire land is divided among the cities... and scarcely any noble or great man can be found ... who does not acknowledge the authority of his city... From this it has resulted that they far surpass all other states of the world in riches and in power.

Otto of Freising (died 1158), a German bishop, on the Italian city-states

THE REVIVAL OF LEARNING

In 1100 literacy and learning were mainly confined to monasteries and Church schools. The 12th century saw a revival of learning centred on philosophy and its uses for understanding theology, the most important intellectual discipline.

The first major figure was St Anselm (c. 1033–1109), abbot of Bec in Normandy, and later Archbishop of Canterbury (in England). He employed question-and-answer techniques to debate the mysteries of Christianity for the first time since the end of the Roman Empire. Peter Abelard (1079–1142) was renowned for his spirited use of logic to question accepted truths and for his love affair with his pupil Héloïse – the daughter of a canon of Notre Dame cathedral – who hired thugs to castrate Abelard. After Abelard retired to a monastery and Héloïse became a nun, their correspondence became one of the most moving products of medieval Latin literature. Abelard also came into conflict with the austere St Bernard of Clairvaux (1090–1153), who advocated a simpler, more mystical view of religion.

At the end of the 12th century, the logic of Aristotle became available in translations from Arabic with the commentaries of the Spanish Muslim Averroës (1126–98). The 13th

▲ **Abelard and Héloïse** *The ill-fated medieval lovers are depicted in this 14th-century French manuscript.*

century saw attempts to reconcile logic and theology in a systematic way: St Bonaventure (c. 1217–74) demonstrated how logic could support religious faith. The great *Summa Theologica* of St Thomas Aquinas (c. 1224–74) was a systematic attempt to explain Christian belief in the terms of this new learning.

This learning, however, was not purely theoretical. By the end of the 12th century those who sought a good position in the administration of the Church or secular government

needed a higher education. In the early 12th century intellectual life was based in schools attached to cathedrals. The late 12th and early 13th centuries saw the development of universities, such as Paris and Bologna, which were licensed by the Church to offer teaching but were independent of cathedrals. Paris was given privileges by King Philip II in 1200 and in 1205 Pope Innocent III allowed the masters to elect their own officials, marking the beginning of the university of Paris as an independent institution. Others soon followed, notably at Oxford in England and Salamanca in Spain.

The university at Bologna in Italy developed a tradition of legal studies, where Irnerius (c. 1055–c. 1125) revived the study of Roman law and where Gratian (died c. 1140) codified the Canon law of the Church. Salerno (southern Italy) and Montpellier in France became centres of medical education, based on ancient Greek works translated into Arabic and then into Latin.

The 12th century also witnessed a golden age in Latin historical writing. The works of **Otto of Freising**, William of Tyre's (c. 1130–85) history of the Crusader states, and the chronicles of Matthew Paris (died 1259) are among the greatest.

Otto of Freising (c. 1111–58)

As well as his work on the deeds of his nephew, Frederick Barbarossa, Otto is known for his *Chronica sive historia de duabus civitatibus*, a history of the world until 1146, which is one of the most important historical-philosophical works of the Middle Ages.

In 1118 Alfonso I of Aragon (reigned 1104–34) captured Saragossa. By the 1140s the collapse of the Almoravide regime enabled the Christians to make further gains. In 1147 the Portuguese took Lisbon, a vital step in establishing Portugal as an independent kingdom under Alfonso I (reigned 1139–85).

The Almoravides were replaced by the Almohade Berbers, who controlled all of Muslim Spain by 1172. Between 1172 and 1212 the Almohades and the Christians fought fiercely for control of the Iberian Peninsula. The Almohades were hampered by tensions between the local population and Berbers, and by unrest in their North African empire.

The Christians were also divided. From 1157 to 1230 Castile and León were separate kingdoms. León preferred alliance with the Muslims to domination by Castile or Portugal. Yet Christian armies were strengthened by the armies of Toledo and other urban centres and by knights of military orders.

In 1195 the Almohade caliph al-Mansur (reigned 1184–99) defeated Alfonso VIII of Castile (reigned 1158–1214) and threatened to take Toledo. In 1212, however, Christian forces decisively defeated the Almohades at the Battle of Las Navas de Tolosa, opening most of southern Spain to Christian advances. In 1236 Fernando III of Castile (reigned 1217–52) captured the Muslim capital of Córdoba and in 1248 Seville also fell. In the east, James I of Aragon (reigned 1213–76) took Majorca (1229–30) and Valencia (1238), while the Portuguese completed the conquest of the Algarve with the capture of Faro in 1249–50.

The only remaining Muslim area was the mountainous southern kingdom of Granada. However, Muhammad I (1237–73) became the vassal of Fernando III of Castile and retained his kingdom. His descendants, the Nasrids, ruled Granada for a further 250 years until it fell to Castile and Aragon in 1492, so completing the reconquest of the peninsula.

The Crusades

Crusades to the Holy Land • Crusades in other areas

The term 'crusade' is applied primarily to the great military expeditions of the 12th and 13th centuries by western Europeans to recover and defend the Holy Land (Palestine) from the Muslims. The crusades are generally regarded as being eight in number.

Crusades to the Holy Land

In 1093 the Byzantine emperor, Alexius I, asked for military aid from western Europe against the Seljuk Turks. Pope Urban II took up and adapted this request: at the Council of Clermont (1095), he proclaimed a crusade.

The First Crusade (1095–99). The proclamation caught the popular imagination, and many ordinary people set off for Constantinople. Those that arrived, however, achieved nothing; with Byzantine aid they crossed the Bosporus and were massacred by the Turks (1096). Meanwhile the nobility (especially that of northern France) prepared for war; the main crusading armies arrived at Constantinople in 1096–97. The Turks were subsequently forced to retreat back across Anatolia and much former Byzantine territory was recovered; Alexius then withdrew from the campaign.

The crusaders besieged Antioch, which fell in 1098; Jerusalem itself was taken in 1099. The Muslim populations of both cities were massacred. While many crusaders returned home, others established the Kingdom of Jerusalem and other states. Subsequent conquests, such as Tripoli (1109) and Tyre (1124), consolidated their position. However,

Muslim disunity had been important to the crusade's success, and the crusader states' security now depended on it.

The Second Crusade (1145–48). In 1144 the fall of Edessa to Zangi, the Turkish emir of Mosul, alarmed the Christian world. Pope Eugenius III proclaimed the Second Crusade, which was energetically preached by St Bernard of Clairvaux. Unlike the First Crusade, its leaders were monarchs: Louis VII of France and Conrad III of Germany. The armies arrived at Jerusalem in 1148, but disagreed on the expedition's objective. Eventually, Damascus was attacked; but the siege was raised after five days (28 July 1148) and Conrad and Louis left for home.

The Third Crusade (1187–92). In 1154 Nureddin, the new emir of Mosul, acquired Damascus and in 1171 his nephew Saladin took control of Egypt. After Nureddin's death (1174), Saladin united these territories into a formidable empire. In 1187 he defeated the crusader states at the Battle of Hattin (4 July); Jerusalem fell on 2 October and by 1189 the crusader states had been reduced to a few coastal outposts.

Following the defeat at Hattin, Pope Gregory VIII proclaimed a crusade in 1187. The principal leaders, who arrived in Palestine in 1191, were Richard I of England and Philip II of France. Rivalry between the crusaders hampered the campaign. Acre, besieged since 1189, fell in 1191; but Philip then left for home. Richard, now in undisputed command, advanced on Jerusalem. He won the battle of

===SEE ALSO===
This section:
- The Catholic Church
- The Medieval Zenith

Islamic World:
- The Emergence of a New Empire
- Muslim Spain

Religion (vol. 6):
- Christianity
- Islam

O mighty soldier, O man of war, at last you have a cause for which you can fight without endangering your soul; a cause in which to win is glorious and for which to die is but gain. Are you a shrewd businessman, quick to see the profits of this world? If you are, I can offer you a bargain which you cannot afford to miss. Take the sign of the cross. At once you will have an indulgence for all the sins you confess with a contrite heart. The cross is cheap and if you wear it with humility you will find that you have obtained the Kingdom of Heaven.

St Bernard (1147)

◄ **Krak des Chevaliers** *('Castle of the Knights') Built by the Hospitallers in the early 12th century to defend the crusader state of the County of Tripoli (in what is now Syria), it is one of the foremost surviving medieval fortresses. It fell to Baybars I, sultan of Egypt, in 1271.*

The Fall of Jerusalem (1099)
This early crusader triumph is depicted in a mid-14th century edition of William of Tyre's Historia rerum in partibus transmarinis gestarum.

▶

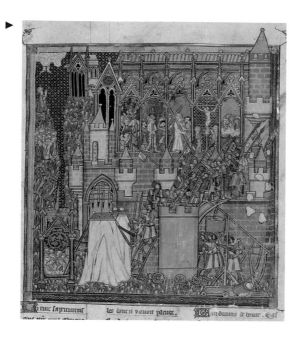

The Children's Crusade
In 1212 thousands of children from France and Germany set out to recover the Holy Land. Few reached their destination: many died on the journey, some settled in Italy, and others were said to have been sold as slaves. This event illustrates the fervour inspired by the crusades, and it encouraged Innocent III to proclaim the Fifth Crusade (1215).

Arsuf (1191) but then, considering that he could not take Jerusalem, made a truce with Saladin. It was agreed that the crusader states would hold the coast north from Jaffa. The crusade had failed in its main objective, but its territorial gains (including Cyprus, which Richard had conquered on his way to Palestine) allowed the crusader states to survive.

The Fourth Crusade (1198–1204). Saladin died in 1193, but his successors and the crusader states continued the truce. In Europe, however, Innocent III, who became pope in 1198, was anxious to promote a further crusade. An army led mainly by French nobles was assembled; Venice was to provide the shipping. The object was to capture Egypt as a bargaining counter for the return of Jerusalem. However, the army was diverted into aiding the ambitions of its leaders: it captured Zara (Hungary) for the Venetians (1202), and was then further waylaid to Constantinople to aid in a dispute over the Byzantine throne. On 13 April 1204 the crusaders captured and sacked Constantinople. They divided the spoils and the crusade went no further.

The Fifth Crusade (1215–21). Innocent III did not lose his enthusiasm for a crusade and proclaimed another in 1215. The objective was again Egypt, and Damietta was besieged (1218). A Muslim offer to cede Jerusalem was refused. Damietta was taken in 1219; but the crusade then stagnated and, after an abortive advance on Cairo (1221), a truce was agreed.

WHY WERE THERE CRUSADES?

When Alexius I sought help from the West, he had envisaged a conventional military force. Between this request and the First Crusade, as proclaimed at Clermont, lay a great imaginative leap, probably by Urban II himself. Underlying the crusades was the idea that lost Christian lands – especially Jerusalem – should be recovered; but other influences on Urban have been suggested:
• He wished to help Eastern Christians threatened by Islam.
• He saw a possibility of reuniting the Greek and Roman churches through a common struggle.
• Placing the papacy at the head of an important new movement would enhance its prestige and authority at a time when it was embroiled in the investiture controversy with the Holy Roman Empire.
• The Spanish Reconquista was beginning to show success against Islam, and influenced the crusades.
The idea of crusade caught the popular imagination of Latin Christendom. Religious fervour was a root cause, but other reasons have been suggested. These include:
• Previously in Latin Christian culture, warfare – the primary activity of the nobility – had been regarded as sinful or, at best, tolerated by God. The Church taught that warfare on a crusade was pleasing to God.
• Pilgrimages to Jerusalem had become increasingly popular in the 11th century; a crusade was seen as an opportunity to make such a pilgrimage in a fashion especially pleasing to God.
• The First Crusade saw the grant by the pope of the first ***plenary indulgence***, remitting all penalties for crusaders' confessed sins.
• The Church taught that those killed on crusade were equal to martyrs and would immediately enter heaven.
• Greater political stability, economic revival, and population growth in western Europe in the late 11th century encouraged an expansionist interest in the wider world.
• Those who 'took the cross' to become crusaders acquired a privileged status. Benefits included the suspension of legal proceedings involving them and the protection of their property while they were absent.

The success of the First Crusade added to the attractions of crusading; it was not uncommon in the 12th century for men to go to the Holy Land for a number of years, or to emigrate permanently. Disillusion grew after c. 1200. Jerusalem had been lost in 1187 and not retaken. The 13th-century crusades were less focused than previously and more closely enmeshed in European power-politics; they lost the simple appeal of an armed pilgrimage to Jerusalem. Plenary indulgences began to be granted to non-crusaders and then sold, and the papacy used crusades against its Christian enemies. Nevertheless, considerable idealism survived: crusading campaigns were occasionally undertaken in the late Middle Ages and the ideal of a further crusade endured until the 15th century. To go on crusade remained a knightly ideal until as late as the 16th century.

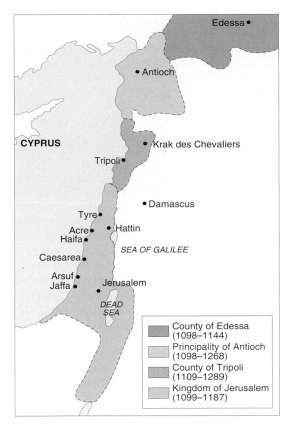

◀ **The Crusader States** *The states are shown at their greatest extent (before the Muslim reconquest of Edessa, 1144).*

CYPRUS

County of Edessa
(1098–1144)
Principality of Antioch
(1098–1268)
County of Tripoli
(1109–1289)
Kingdom of Jerusalem
(1099–1187)

The Sixth Crusade (1227–29). A notable, and much criticized, absentee from the Fifth Crusade had been Frederick II of Germany. His motives for finally going on crusade are unclear; an important factor was his claim to the throne of the Kingdom of Jerusalem. Many crusaders departed for Palestine in 1227 but Frederick was delayed by illness. The pope rejected this excuse and excommunicated him; many crusaders consequently refused to obey him when he arrived at Acre (1228). He turned to diplomacy and secured the return of Jerusalem and other territory by treaty (1229); he then crowned himself king of Jerusalem and returned to Europe. His treaty was denounced by his enemies and devout opinion, and his government of Jerusalem was ineffective in the face of local opposition.

The Seventh Crusade (1245–54). Jerusalem was recaptured by the Muslims in 1244. The main impetus for a new crusade came from Louis IX of France (St Louis), who arrived in Egypt in 1249 and took Damietta; but an advance on Cairo (1250) led to his capture, with his army, by the Muslims. Quickly ransomed, he spent the next four years negotiating the release of his soldiers and improving the defences of the Kingdom of Jerusalem.

The Eighth Crusade (1267–70). The final demise of the crusader states began in the 1260s: Caesarea, Haifa, and Arsuf were captured by Baybars I, sultan of Egypt, in 1265 and Antioch fell in 1268. St Louis began

preparations for a crusade in 1267; but, for reasons unknown, his expedition attacked Tunis (1270). It was undermined by disease, which killed Louis himself, and was evacuated without achieving anything. No further help was given to the crusader states. Acre, the last crusader outpost in the Holy Land, fell in 1291.

Crusades in Other Areas

Some crusades were directed at objectives unrelated to the recovery of the Holy Land. The Spanish Reconquista (see THE MEDIEVAL ZENITH) quickly acquired the same privileges as a crusade. In 1147 St Bernard permitted some German crusaders to campaign against Slavs east of the River Elbe, extending the idea of crusade beyond the recovery of formerly Christian lands to the acquisition of new ones. The Teutonic Knights, founded at Acre in 1190, expanded their operations to eastern Europe in 1211.

Crusades against heretics and schismatics were mooted in the 12th century. In 1208 Innocent III proclaimed the Albigensian crusade against the Cathars of southern France (see THE CATHOLIC CHURCH). A crusade against the papacy's lay enemies was proclaimed in 1240 by Pope Gregory IX against the Emperor Frederick II. Such crusades against Christian opponents became more common and their targets more trivial; in 1297 Pope Boniface VIII declared a crusade against his rivals in Roman politics, the Colonna family.

RESULTS OF THE CRUSADES

- The Church began to approve of some forms of warfare. This led directly to the monastic military orders, such as the **Templars** and **Hospitallers**, and greatly influenced the development of chivalry.
- Western European expansionism was channelled towards the Holy Land and (possibly) away from other areas.
- The growth of royal power in 12th-century Europe was probably helped by removing unruly elements on crusade.
- Trade between the Muslim Near East and western Europe expanded.
- The papacy's key position in the crusading movement enhanced its authority.
- The Byzantine Empire was permanently weakened by the Fourth Crusade's conquest of Constantinople (1204).

Templars (Poor Knights of Christ and of the Temple of Solomon) A religious military order founded c. 1120 to protect pilgrims to the Holy Land; its name derived from its first quarters in Jerusalem, near the site of the Temple. The order grew rapidly, becoming important to crusader states' defences, while gifts of land and property from Europe made it very wealthy. Yet the Templars made many enemies; by 1300 there were rumours of blasphemy and immorality. The order was suppressed by the pope in 1312. Speculation continues today concerning the Templars' beliefs and activities.

Hospitallers (Order of the Hospital of St John of Jerusalem) A religious military order that originated (c. 1070) as a hospital for sick pilgrims in Jerusalem. Enriched by gifts, it developed a military side dedicated to fighting the Muslims. After the fall of Acre (1291), the order moved to Cyprus, then successively to Rhodes (1309) and Malta (1530), where it remained until 1798. Based in Rome since 1834, the order now pursues humanitarian projects.

Kiev-Rus and Eastern Europe

*The period of the migrations • Conversion to Christianity •
Eastern Europe and the Balkans • Kiev-Rus*

Slavs Peoples of eastern Europe and parts of western Asia who speak a Slavonic language. The modern Slavonic languages are Russian, Ukrainian, Belorussian, Polish, Czech, Sorbian, Slovak, Bulgarian, Serbian, Croatian, Slovene, and Macedonian.

Most of the population of present-day Russia and eastern Europe consists of **Slavs**. The original home of the Slavs probably included the area between the Oder and Dnieper rivers with the Baltic Sea and the Carpathian Mountains forming, respectively, the northern and southern limits of settlement.

The Period of the Migrations

During the 6th and early 7th centuries, the Slav population began to disperse across a wide geographical area. As a result, three separate Slavic groups were formed: the Southern Slavs, who occupied the Balkans; the Eastern Slavs, who moved into Russia; and the Western Slavs, who inhabited the area of modern Poland, the Czech Republic, and Slovakia. In their new homelands, the Slavs interbred with Greeks, Celts, Germans, and Iranians.

The Slavic settlements were frequently overrun by invaders. In the 670s Turkic-speaking Bulgars, migrating from the steppe, conquered a large part of the Balkans and established the Bulgarian khanate (territory ruled by a khan). The so-called White Croats and White Serbs, who came originally from north of the Carpathian Mountains, occupied the northwestern part of the Balkan peninsula. In the 9th century Viking merchants (known to the Slavs as Varangians) settled the area of Russia from the Baltic to the Black Sea. The Vikings were known as **Rhos** or **Rus**, meaning 'seafarers'; it is from this word that 'Russia' is derived.

The Bulgars, White Croats and Serbs, and the Rus seafarers were swiftly absorbed by the larger Slavic populations over which they ruled. Other non-Slavic invaders, however, preserved their identity for a longer period. From the late 6th century until the end of the 8th century, the area of modern Hungary was ruled by the Avar nomads, who had fled from Central Asia. In 896, the Hungarians occupied the area of Avar settlement. First led by Turkic-speaking Onogur tribesmen, the Hungarians comprised mainly Magyars, whose original home was near the Ural Mountains. Magyars spoke a language related to Finnish.

Conversion to Christianity

The peoples who occupied the lands of eastern Europe and Russia practised a variety of religions. The majority of Slavs worshipped Perun, the god of thunder. During the 9th and 10th centuries, missionaries from Rome, Germany, and Byzantium converted the Slavs and Hungarians to Christianity. A leading role in the conversion of eastern Europe was played by the Greek monks, Saint Cyril (c. 827–69)

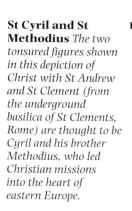
St Cyril and St Methodius *The two tonsured figures shown in this depiction of Christ with St Andrew and St Clement (from the underground basilica of St Clements, Rome) are thought to be Cyril and his brother Methodius, who led Christian missions into the heart of eastern Europe.*

and Saint Methodius (815–85). They translated religious works and service books from Greek and invented a new 'Glagolitic' alphabet for the use of Slavonic speakers. This was later reformed by the monks' pupils and is the basis of the Cyrillic alphabet, which is still used in Russia and parts of the Balkans.

In the 860s Cyril and Methodius completed the conversion of the Great Moravian Empire, which occupied part of the modern Czech Republic and Slovakia. In 865 the Bulgarian khan, Boris I (reigned 852–89), was baptized. The conversion of the Bulgarians was undertaken by Saint Clement and Saint Naum, who used the Greek missionaries' alphabet and translations. The Serbs were converted to Christianity during the 870s.

The Greek Orthodox Church, led by the Patriarch of Constantinople, was at this time in competition with the Roman Catholic Church led by the pope. Under pressure from the papacy and its allies, the kings and emperors of Germany, the rulers of the Great Moravian Empire replaced Cyril and Methodius's Slavonic texts with Latin service books. Hungary, several of whose chieftains had received baptism in Constantinople, was converted to Roman Catholicism by Prince Géza (reigned 972–97) and its first king, Stephen (reigned 997–1038). In 879, Croatia accepted Roman Catholicism, as did Poland in 966.

Eastern Europe and the Balkans

During the 11th and 12th centuries, several powerful states were established in eastern Europe and the Balkans. Under the ruling dynasties of Przemyślid and Arpád, Bohemia (successor to the Great Moravian Empire) and Hungary occupied a strategic central position in Europe. In 1102 Croatia became part of Hungary. The kingdom of Poland, however, founded by Mieszko I (reigned 963–92) in the late 10th century, disintegrated during the next two centuries into five separate warring principalities.

In the Balkans, an extensive Bulgarian empire survived until it was vanquished by Byzantine rulers in 1018. A second weaker Bulgarian empire was established in 1185. Serbia obtained its independence in the early 13th century, after which it became a leading power in the Balkans. At the end of the 14th century, however, both Serbia and Bulgaria were overrun by the Ottoman Turks.

Kiev-Rus

The Kiev-Rus state was founded by Viking seafarers. In 862, the Viking Roderick (or Rurik; died 879) seized the Slav town of Novgorod. By the end of the century, his successors had extended their rule as far south as Kiev, which became their capital.

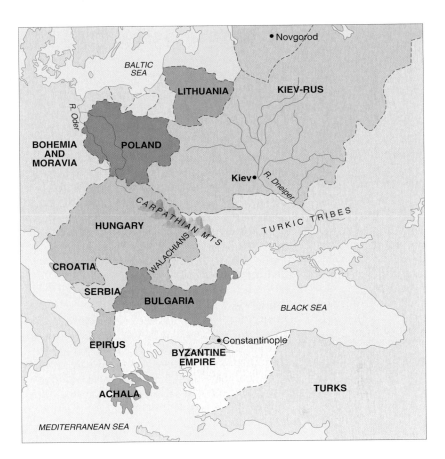

▲ **Eastern Europe in c. 1240** *After the period of migrations, eastern Europe comprised Slavs, Bulgars, Vikings, Avar nomads, and Magyars and was divided into several states.*

The Viking interest in the eastern Slav lands was initially commercial. During the 10th century, however, they established peaceful relations with neighbouring Slav tribes and intermarried with them. Gradually they adopted the Slav language now known as Russian and gave up their old Scandinavian names.

Missionaries from Constantinople were active in the Russian lands. In 957 Princess Olga, regent of Kiev-Rus (945–64), was converted to Christianity, but the new religion was not widely accepted. Olga's grandson, Vladimir (c. 956–1015), enticed by Byzantine offers of wealth, was baptized c. 988 and introduced Orthodox Christianity as the official religion.

In early medieval Russia the state was shared out among the ruler's relatives when he died. Gradually the unity of the Kiev-Rus lands was weakened as ever smaller portions of territory were created on the death of each ruler. During the 11th and 12th centuries, Russia disintegrated into several separate principalities over which rival descendants of the Viking Roderick fought for control.

Divided and enfeebled by civil strife, the Kiev-Rus lands were unable to resist the Mongol-Tatar armies, which attacked the region from the east in the early 13th century. In 1240 Kiev was sacked by the invaders. For the next 240 years the Russian lands formed a part of the Mongol-Tatar Empire and ceased to exist as independent states.

Walachians

Walachian, or Vlach, shepherds avoided absorption by the Slavs at the time of the migrations. Their language derives from Latin, and they were present in large numbers in the Balkans throughout the Middle Ages. The Vlachs contributed to the foundation of the second Bulgarian empire in 1185. In the 13th and 14th centuries, they migrated north and founded the Romanian principalities of Moldavia and Walachia.

The Later Middle Ages

England and France • Population fall • Social rebellion • Italian city-states • Germany and the Empire • Iberia • The revival of monarchy

The period from 1300 to 1520 in Europe was characterized by war, population reduction through disease, social ferment, interstate rivalry, disputes over succession, as well as cultural rebirth, a new impetus for exploration and discovery, and ultimately, the resurgence of monarchical power. See THE EUROPEAN TRADITION (VOL. 4): RENAISSANCE ART.

England and France

In 1300 England and France were both powerful monarchies with strong rulers – Edward I of England and Philip IV of France – who were followed by less able successors. The English kings ruled a united country with strong central institutions, augmented in this period by the development of parliament. First summoned by Edward I, by 1500 it had developed into a form still recognizable today. Its power depended upon the king's reliance on its grants of taxation. France was less unified; royal power was based upon the great extension in the 13th century of lands controlled by the crown. Its subsequent development was greatly influenced by the Hundred Years' War, which was fought entirely on its territory.

The Hundred Years' War. The king of England was also duke of Gascony, in southwest

ENGLISH AND FRENCH MONARCHS OF THE LATER MIDDLE AGES	
English	
Edward I	1272–1307
Edward II	1307–27
Edward III	1327–77
Richard II	1377–99
Henry IV	1399–1413
Henry V	1413–22
Henry VI	1422–61
French	
Philip IV (the Fair)	1285–1314
Louis X	1314–16
Philip V	1316–22
Charles IV	1322–28
Philip VI	1328–50
John II	1350–64
Charles V	1364–80
Charles VI	1380–1422
Charles VII	1422–61

The Battle of Agincourt ▶
(October 1415) One of the decisive English victories of the Hundred Years' War, it made possible Henry V's conquest of Normandy (1417–20).

John of Gaunt (1340–99)

As Duke of Lancaster and son of King Edward III, John was the most powerful English noble. Through his second wife, Constance, he unsuccessfully claimed the throne of Castile. In 1399 his son, Henry Bolingbroke, deposed Richard II and founded the Lancastrian dynasty.

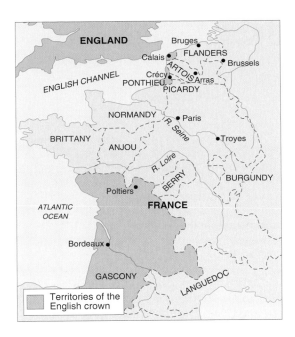

▲ France after the Treaty of Brétigny (1360)
*By 1360, during the first phase of the Hundred Years'
War, England had under its control a large part of
central and southwest France, as well as Calais.*

France; in this capacity he was a vassal of the
French king. This was the cause of considerable friction as the French monarchy wished
to establish complete control over Gascony,
while the English monarchy wished to
strengthen its independence. Another cause
of dispute was Edward III's claim to the throne
of France through his mother, Isabella, daughter of Philip the Fair of France. Edward's insistence on this claim resulted in the outbreak
in 1337 of a prolonged though intermittent
conflict, known as the Hundred Years' War
(1337–1453). During the first phase of the

BURGUNDY

Philip the Bold, duke of Burgundy and son
of King John II of France, married the
daughter of the last independent count of
Flanders and acquired control of the country after the count's death in 1381. The
powerful inheritance of Burgundy and
Flanders was enlarged further by Philip's
successors: John the Fearless (reigned
1404–19) and Philip the Good (reigned
1419–67). By the 1430s Burgundy had
become a major European power. Charles
the Bold (reigned 1467–77) tried unsuccessfully to extend its power by annexing
Lorraine, but when he died without an heir,
Burgundy's lands were divided between the
French Crown and the Hapsburgs.

war, prior to 1340, Edward tried to invade
France with the aid of allies in Flanders (in the
Low Countries). There followed a long period during which English troops carried out
sporadic large-scale raids into the heart of
France. The French were heavily defeated at
the Battle of Crécy in 1346; the town of Calais
was taken in 1347; and in 1356 John II
himself was captured at the Battle of Poitiers.
By the time of the Treaty of Brétigny (1360),
England controlled a large proportion of
French territory. Under Charles V the French
monarchy was revitalized. The English lands
were whittled away while pitched battle was
avoided. The war abated and a peace treaty
was concluded in 1396.

Full-scale war broke out again in 1415 between Henry V of England, an efficient ruler
and great general, and Charles VI of France, a
weak monarch, under whom France became
disastrously divided between the rival factions
of Burgundy and Armagnac. The French suffered a serious defeat by Henry V at the Battle
of Agincourt in 1415. This was followed by
the English conquest of Normandy (1417–19)
and by the Treaty of Troyes (1420), which recognized Henry V as regent of France and heir
to the throne. When Henry and Charles died
in 1422, France was effectively divided into
three parts ruled respectively by England, the
duke of Burgundy, and Charles VII, the disinherited son of Charles VI. For a time the English holding was extended, and in 1429 the
child-king Henry VI was crowned king of
France. But the tide was turning: Charles VII
gradually regained land and, after 1434,
ended his quarrel with the duke of Burgundy,
who recognized him as king at the Congress of
Arras in 1435. When the Hundred Years' War
ended (1453), England had lost all its French
territory except the **staple** town of Calais.

Population Fall
In 1300 Europe, largely composed of agricultural communities, was sufficiently heavily
populated for fertile land to have become
scarce. When bad weather caused poor harvests in 1315–17, there was widespread
famine. Although the population subsequently stabilized, the Black Death plague of
1348 had a devastating effect, reducing the
population by between one-third and a half
in most parts of Europe. This was followed by
other serious outbreaks of plague and then
by endemic plague, which lasted until the
17th century. The fall in population meant
that good land became more plentiful, food became cheaper, and average incomes among
the lower classes rose all over Europe. A subsequent effect was that more wealth was available for investment in industry and commerce.
As trade flourished in the period 1350–1500,

The Low Countries

Comprising modern
Belgium, Luxembourg,
and the Netherlands,
these lands were
divided, in the 14th
century, into several
duchies or counties.
Flanders, the most
important, relied on
English wool for its
textile industry. The
count of Flanders was,
however, a vassal of the
French king, resulting in
a conflict between the
region's English and
French interests.

staple A town specially
appointed to be the
exclusive market for one
or more major exports.
From 1363 the English
wool staple was usually
based at Calais, which
was held by the English
from 1347 to 1558.

Joan of Arc

A French peasant girl
moved by visions, Joan
(?1412–31) persuaded
Charles VII of France, in
1429, that she could
help him recover his
kingdom. She was
successful in relieving
the besieged city of
Orléans and assisted
the recovery of French
territory from the
English. Eventually
captured by the
Burgundians, she was
tried for heresy and
burned in 1431.

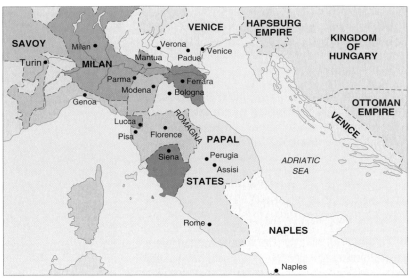

◄ The States of Italy *In the mid-15th century, following the Treaty of Lodi in 1454, Italy was dominated to the south of Rome by the kingdom of Naples; by the pope in central Italy; and by the states of Florence, Venice, and Milan in the north, whose land empires had been greatly extended since 1300.*

1378. Florence was the centre of a thriving woollen cloth industry, which was now in decline as the centres of cloth-making had moved to areas, such as England, where it could operate more cheaply.

Italian City-states

The large number of ***city-states*** – small states dominated by a single town or city that controlled the surrounding countryside – that had risen to prominence in northern Italy during the 11th and 12th centuries (see THE MEDIEVAL ZENITH) continued to flourish during the period 1300–1520.

In Tuscany the most important city-states were Florence, Siena, Pisa, and Lucca. Pisa, once the centre of a flourishing Mediterranean empire, was in decline; in 1405 it was taken over by Florence. The region of Lombardy encompassed many cities, of which Milan was the largest. On opposite edges of Lombardy were the two great commercial cities of Venice and Genoa. Venice retained its independence throughout this period, while Genoa, weakened by the conflict of noble families, was subjected to intermittent external control, either by Milan or France. In central Italy the pope administered the papal state from Rome; it included a number of independent or semi-independent cities, such as Perugia. As a consequence the papal state was an extremely unstable political unit, which several popes had to reconquer.

There were several important attempts by individual cities to build up an empire by extending their control over rival cities. This expansionism replaced the conflict between propapal and proimperial factions, which had dominated the area in the 13th century (the last serious invasions by German emperors were those of Henry VII in 1310–13 and Louis the Bavarian in 1328–29). Mastino della Scala, Lord of Verona, extended his domain as far as Parma and Lucca in 1335–37. The later 14th century was dominated by the ambitions of the Visconti family, rulers of Milan. Giangaleazzo Visconti (1351–1402) emerged as the most important force in Italy in the 1380s. He controlled most of Lombardy and tried to expand into Tuscany. Milan remained a threatening power in the early 15th century under Filippo Maria Visconti (1392–1447). After his death, his family was replaced by that of his son-in-law Francesco Sforza (1401–66).

such cities as Venice, Genoa, and Florence in the south and Bruges, Antwerp, and Cologne in the north became important centres.

Social Rebellion

The period 1370–1420 was a notable era of social rebellion. The economic effects of population decline led to serious social conflicts. In some cases these were caused by the breakdown of the manorial system of agriculture owing to shortage of tenants and labourers. Tenants wanted lower rents while labourers wanted higher wages. This was the main cause of the Peasants' Revolt of 1381 in England. It was probably also a factor in the Hussite rebellion, which erupted in Bohemia and Moravia, after the execution of the religious reformer Jan Hus in 1415. Social unrest in towns resulted from the relocation of industries, an example of which is the Revolt of the Ciompi, the wool carders, in Florence in

Italian Republicanism and Despotism

Some of the Italian city-states remained republican throughout this period, including Florence, Venice, and Siena. They were ruled according to constitutions, giving authority to officials and committees, which were elected by citizens. The men who possessed a franchise in any one of these cities numbered thousands. There was a tendency, however, for city government to be taken over by despots, such as the Visconti and Sforza, dukes of Milan, who assumed total power over foreign policy and the army. Disputes between states, particularly between Florence and Milan, were often seen as conflicts of republicanism versus despotism.

THE MEDICI

The Medici were originally a very wealthy merchant family in Florence, who came to dominate the city's government. Their primacy was established by Cosimo de' Medici (1389–1464), the wealthiest man in the city, who succeeded in exiling his rivals. From 1469 to 1492 the head of the family was Lorenzo the Magnificent (1449–92), banker, politician, poet, and patron of artists (including Michelangelo) and scholars. In 1494 the Medici were expelled from Florence following a revolt against corruption; however, they returned in 1512 and Giovanni de' Medici (1473–1521) became Pope Leo X in 1513. The family were eventually to rule Florence as dukes of Tuscany.

GERMAN MONARCHS AND HOLY ROMAN EMPERORS (1308–1519)	
Henry VII	1308–13; emperor from 1312
Louis IV of Bavaria	1314–47; emperor from 1328
Frederick of Austria	1314–26
Charles IV	1346–78; emperor from 1355
Wenceslas	1363–1419; emperor from 1376
Rupert of the Palatinate	1400–10
Sigismund	1411–37; emperor from 1433
Albert II of Austria	1438–39
Frederick III	1440–93; emperor from 1452
Maximilian I	1493–1519; emperor from 1508

Venice, meanwhile, began to expand into eastern Lombardy to counter the Milanese threat and, by the mid-15th century, had built up a substantial land empire, including such cities as Padua and Verona. There was a period of general peace following the Treaty of Lodi (agreed between Venice and Milan in 1454) until the beginning of the French invasions of 1494; Italy subsequently became an arena of conflict between the European powers of Valois France, Hapsburg Austria, and Spain.

Germany and the Empire

The Holy Roman Empire (see GERMANIC INVASIONS AND THE CAROLINGIAN EMPIRE) included modern Germany and Holland to the west and Bohemia, Silesia, Brandenburg, and Austria to the east. The king of Germany had come, in the late 13th century, to be chosen by seven electors: the archbishops of Mainz, Cologne, and Trier; the count palatine (of the Rhine Palatinate); the elector of Saxony; the margrave of Brandenburg; and the king of Bohemia. The position was confirmed by the Golden Bull of 1356. The empire became synonymous with the kingdom of Germany; the importance of coronation by the pope declined, and in 1508 Maximilian I began the practice of assuming the title without coronation. Under Frederick III, the the empire's final title emerged: Holy Roman Empire of the German Nation.

Power in central Europe was largely held by the rulers of individual states: many smaller states in the west, and fewer larger states, such as Bohemia and Austria, in the east. During the 14th and early 15th centuries the imperial title was held by members of the Luxembourg and Wittelsbach families; it subsequently became a de facto hereditary title of the Hapsburg family. The power of the emperor was, however, limited and depended mainly on support from family lands – the Luxembourgs' in Bohemia and the Hapsburgs' in Austria – which it enabled him to enlarge. Sigismund, of the House of Luxembourg, was an enterprising ruler, who played a major part in European affairs. He initiated the Council of Constance (1414–18), which ended the Great Schism within the Catholic Church. The reign of Frederick III, however, was to be the nadir of the empire, which thence became largely irrelevant to German politics.

The Hanse

This association of commercial towns was formed in north and west Germany in the 13th century to protect its economic interests overseas. The largest trading town was Cologne, while the most prominent politically were the northern seaports, such as Lübeck and Danzig. By the mid-14th century the Hanse, comprising some 100 towns, had established powerful trading monopolies in northeastern Europe. Danish and English opposition led to trade wars. Throughout the 15th century the Hanse remained important in German politics and in northern European trade.

◄ **Karlšteyn**
The impressive royal palace of Emperor Charles IV was built near Prague, c. 1350. Charles was king of Bohemia from 1346 as well as Holy Roman Emperor from 1355 until his death (1378). He was one of the most learned rulers and skilful diplomats of the time. During his reign Prague became the political, economic, and social centre of the empire.

NORTH SEA

BALTIC SEA

• Danzig

PRUSSIA

• Lübeck

BRANDENBURG

HOLLAND

SAXONY

POLAND

LUSATIA

COLOGNE

SILESIA

HAINAULT

LUXEMBOURG

Trier

• Mainz

PALATINATE

R. Rhine

• Prague

BOHEMIA

MORAVIA

BAVARIA

AUSTRIA

HUNGARY

• Zurich

STYRIA

SWISS
CONFEDERATION

TYROL

CARINTHIA

CARNIOLA

ADRIATIC
SEA

☐ Wittelsbach
☐ Luxembourg
☐ Hapsburg
- - - Boundary of empire

◄ **Germany and the Empire** *In the later 14th century the Wittelsbach family extended its rule to Brandenburg, while the Luxembourg family became the rulers of Bohemia.*

ultimately led to colonization and the establishment of vast empires by the Iberian powers.

Castile was a large wool-producing kingdom governed by nobles and parliaments. The death of Alfonso XI (reigned 1312–50) initiated a long succession dispute, which ended with the establishment of Henry II of Trastamara (1333–79) as king in 1369. It was the succession of one of the Trastramaran dynasty, Ferdinand I (reigned 1412–16), to the throne of Aragon that prepared the way for the eventual union of Castile and Aragon.

Aragon was a federation of three kingdoms – Catalonia, Aragon, and Valencia – dominated by Barcelona, an important commercial centre in the 14th century. Like Castile, Aragon suffered a serious succession dispute in the mid-14th century, when Peter IV (reigned 1336–87) resisted the claim to succession of his brother. Aragon and Castile were united by the marriage of Ferdinand of Aragon (reigned 1479–1516) and Isabella of Castile (reigned 1479–1504), who ruled the two kingdoms after 1479. They succeeded in reconquering the Islamic kingdom of Granada in the south, in 1492, thus completing the Christian reconquest of Iberia (see THE MEDIEVAL ZENITH).

Iberia

The majority of the Iberian peninsula was divided between the three Christian kingdoms of Portugal, Castile, and Aragon, which had consolidated their power during the Christian reconquest of the peninsula (late 11th–13th centuries). All three kingdoms played an important role in the maritime history of Europe. In the late 15th century both Castile and Portugal sent explorers to Asia and America (see **EXPLORATION AND DISCOVERY**), a process which

Ferdinand and Isabella *Columbus (left) departs from Palos in 1492 on his momentous journey of discovery. He had won the patronage of Ferdinand and Isabella (right) of Spain to fund the expedition.* ▼

THE ITALIAN WARS

When Charles VIII of France invaded Italy in 1494, to make his claim to the throne of Naples, he initiated a series of struggles between the families of Valois and Hapsburg, which continued well into the 16th century. His action provoked the formation of a Holy League by other powers in the area. Charles escaped back to France after the indecisive Battle of Fornova (1495). In 1496 Spanish troops occupied Naples. Louis XII invaded Italy in 1498 and occupied Milan. After 1503 Italian affairs were dominated by Pope Julius II (reigned 1503–13), who formed the League of Cambrai against Venice in 1508 and resisted France at the Battle of Ravenna in 1512. Emperor Maximilian now took a larger part in the affairs of Italy. The French, however, were successful at the Battle of Marignano in 1515 and when Charles V became emperor in 1519, the outcome of the Valois–Hapsburg conflict was still undecided.

Pope Julius II *(by Raphael) Pope Julius is best known* ▶ *as a patron of some of the finest artists of the Italian Renaissance, especially Michelangelo (1475–1564) and Raphael (1483–1520). He also commissioned the building of a new St Peter's basilica, in Rome.*

The Revival of Monarchy

By the mid-15th century the power of monarchy in Europe was relatively diminished. In England, the Wars of the Roses divided the kingdom from 1453 to 1485. Charles VII of France was, until 1461, recovering gradually from incursions by the English. Castile and Aragon were rent by divisions within their royal families, while the Holy Roman Empire was weak under Frederick III.

In the late 15th century, however, the situation changed: Louis XI of France was a strong leader, who was able to confront Charles the Bold, duke of Burgundy (reigned 1467–77), and the League of the Public Weal (an alliance of French nobles) in 1465. The death of Charles the Bold in 1477 ended all serious internal threats to the crown in France. In 1494 Louis' son, Charles VIII (reigned 1483–98), invaded Italy to assert a Valois claim to the throne of Naples, thus initiating the **Italian Wars**. Charles was succeeded by Louis XII (reigned 1498–1515), who conquered Milan, and by Francis I (reigned 1515–47). These monarchs were much more active in European affairs than their 15th-century predecessors. The power of the Hapsburg emperors was also revived as a result of the marriage

of Mary, daughter of Charles the Bold, to Maximilian I; the subsequent marriage of Maximilian's son, Philip, to the heiress to the kingdoms of Castile and Aragon maintained the Hapsburg influence. The result of these unions was that, after 1519, Maximilian's grandson, Charles V (king of Spain 1516–56; emperor 1519), ruled the Austrian lands, the Low Countries, and Spain, a European empire unprecedented in its size. The English monarchy, meanwhile, achieved a new vitality under the first two Tudor kings, Henry VII (reigned 1485–1509) and Henry VIII (reigned 1509–47). By the early 16th century Europe was divided between formidable monarchies.

The End of Byzantium and the Rise of Italian Humanism

The attempt to reunite the Eastern and Western Churches at the Council of Ferrara and Florence (1438–39) brought a large number of Greek scholars to Italy. These included Gemisthos Plethon (1353–1452), who is thought to have inspired Cosimo de' Medici to patronize the translation of the works of Plato by Ficino. The Council and the later capture of Constantinople by the Turks (1453) had the effect of producing a migration of Greeks to the west: John Bessarion (c. 1400–72), who became a cardinal and bequeathed his books to found the Marciana Library at Venice; George of Trebizond, and John Argyropoulos, who lectured in Florence.

◀ **The States of Europe in the Later Middle Ages** *By the early 15th century, Burgundy had become a major European power, while the influence of the Holy Roman Empire reached its lowest point under Frederick III (emperor 1452–93).*

EXPLORATION AND DISCOVERY

U NTIL THE LATE 15th century Europeans seldom sailed far from land. Thus, great cultures in distant parts of the world were isolated from Europe and Asia. While the Vikings had reached North America centuries before (c. 1000), their achievements were all but forgotten. Explorers of the 15th century were finally lured into the unknown in the hope of finding a new sea route to the East, thus breaking the Islamic World's monopoly on supplying Europe with spices, silk, porcelain, gems, and precious metals. The conquest of territory was not their prime motivation. Only later, as trade routes were regularized, did it seem desirable to seize and fortify strategic islands and harbours as anchorages or trading posts, thus laying the foundations for far-flung maritime empires, such as those of Portugal, Spain, the Netherlands, and England. These early explorers thus initiated a global trading system and the migration of peoples, plants, and disease between continents.

THE PORTUGUESE
The first phase of European expansion was dominated by Portugal. Prince Henry 'the Navigator' (1394–1460) established a school of seamanship at Sagres (SW Portugal), where captains were trained in navigation, astronomy, and cartography, thus putting exploration on a systematic basis. The Portuguese caravel (sailing ship) was also developed.

By annexing and cultivating the islands of Madeira and the Azores in the North Atlantic, the Portuguese established the first European-controlled tropical plantation economy. The importation of African slaves to Portugal in the mid-15th century also marked a turning-point in the evolution of a world economy, to which the slave trade made a huge contribution.

After more than half a century of gradual progress down the west coast of Africa, Bartholomeu Dias (c. 1450–1500) was

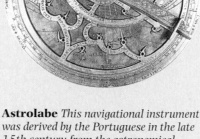

Astrolabe *This navigational instrument was derived by the Portuguese in the late 15th century from the astronomical astrolabe. By aligning it with the sun or certain stars, the time, longtitude, and latitude could be calculated.*

Circumnavigation *The expedition of Ferdinand Magellan, shown here passing through the strait named after him, was the first to circumnavigate the globe. Although Magellan himself was killed in the Philippines, he saw and named Tierra del Fuego and the Pacific Ocean.*

ordered by King John II to find the southern limit of Africa. Blown by storms around the Cape of Good Hope, he landed on the southeastern coast of Africa (Great Fish River) in 1488, thus proving that India could be reached via this route. It was Vasco da Gama (c. 1460–1524) who finally made the breakthrough to Asia in 1497. He rounded the Cape to reach Calicut in southern India in 1498, returning a year later laden with spices and gems. While commanding a second major expedition to India, in 1500, Pedro Alvarez Cabral (c. 1467–1520) made an accidental, yet momentous, discovery when he landed on the shores of Brazil, which he claimed for Portugal.

From the early 16th century the Portuguese extended their voyages from India to Southeast Asia (1509); for the remainder of the century they prospered from trade with Africa and Asia and fought to deny other Europeans access to it. Two Portuguese accidentally reached Japan, in 1543, further extending their trading empire into the Far East.

THE SPANISH
Spain's entry into the world of exploration was a result of the faith of its monarchs, Ferdinand and Isabella, in Christopher Columbus (1451–1506), an adventurer from Genoa, who proposed to reach the East by sailing westwards. By miscalculating the size of the earth, Columbus estimated that Asia was c. 6275 km west of the Canary Islands, i.e. approximately where America lies. Thus he discovered the West Indies, so named because Columbus believed he had reached islands off the east coast of the 'Indies' (Asia).

His discovery began an environmental revolution that eventually brought horses, sheep, wheat, and smallpox to the Americas, while potatoes, tomatoes, chocolate, the turkey, and syphilis were brought back to Europe. Columbus was followed by the Spanish *conquistadores*, who effectively enslaved the native peoples of South America and plundered the continent of its silver and gold, resulting in inflationary crises across Europe. See LATIN AMERICA: THE SPANISH AND PORTUGUESE EMPIRES.

FRENCH, DUTCH, AND ENGLISH EXPLORATION

From the late 16th century the Protestant Dutch and English were allies in politics and religion, against Catholic France, but rivals in trade. By 1600 all three nations were challenging Iberian supremacy from Asia to the Americas and seeking their own routes to the East by sailing north into Arctic waters. Ultimately the search for a Northeast or Northwest passage, by such navigators as Jacques Cartier (1491–1557) and Willem Barents (c. 1550–97), proved a costly failure; it did, however, lead to the establishment of direct trading links with Russia and the settlement of mainland North America from c. 1600, which created a new international trade in tobacco and furs. The labour needs of English sugar plantations in the West Indies made the transatlantic slave-trade a massive enterprise; see SOCIAL SCIENCES (VOL. 6): SLAVERY. The Dutch and English East India Companies emerged during the 17th century as the world's first multinational corporations. While the former exploited Indonesian spices and craft goods of Japan, the latter eventually came to rule the entire Indian subcontinent. By the 1640s Dutch navigators had touched Australia and New Zealand, yet their true size and shape was unknown until the expeditions of Captain James Cook (1728–79) in the late 18th century (see OCEANIA: AUSTRALIA, NEW ZEALAND, AND THE PACIFIC).

EFFECTS

By the 17th century, European statesmen were beginning to cherish trade and territory, as instruments of power. The strategic importance of maritime power stimulated major improvements in shipbuilding, cartography, navigation, and astronomy. European diets were diversified by the importation of tropical products, such as sugar and coffee, while the European imagination was stimulated by tales of strange lands and peoples across the seas. They became a vibrant theme in literature, inspiring the epic poem *Os lusíadas* (1572) by the Portuguese poet Luís Vaz de Camões, Thomas More's *Utopia* (1516), William Shakespeare's *The Tempest* (c. 1611), and Daniel Defoe's *Robinson Crusoe* (1719–22). Exploration thus enlarged not only people's knowledge of the world, but also their understanding of their place in it.

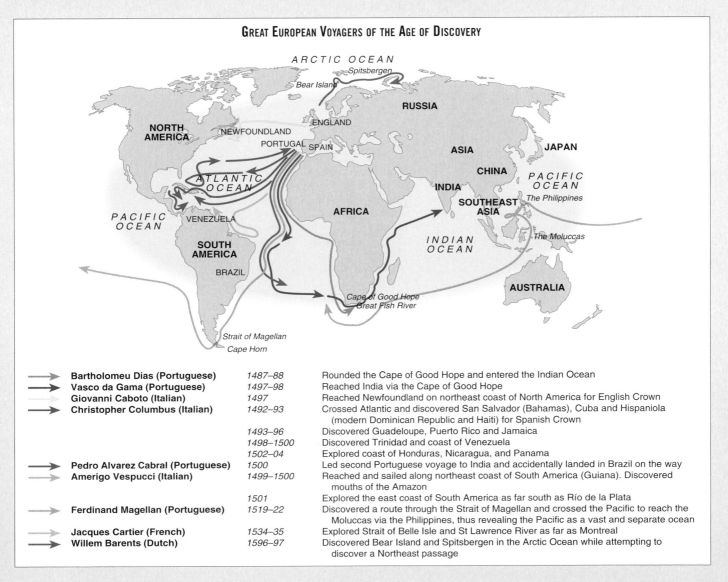

GREAT EUROPEAN VOYAGERS OF THE AGE OF DISCOVERY

→	**Bartholomeu Dias (Portuguese)**	1487–88	Rounded the Cape of Good Hope and entered the Indian Ocean
→	**Vasco da Gama (Portuguese)**	1497–98	Reached India via the Cape of Good Hope
→	**Giovanni Caboto (Italian)**	1497	Reached Newfoundland on northeast coast of North America for English Crown
→	**Christopher Columbus (Italian)**	1492–93	Crossed Atlantic and discovered San Salvador (Bahamas), Cuba and Hispaniola (modern Dominican Republic and Haiti) for Spanish Crown
		1493–96	Discovered Guadeloupe, Puerto Rico and Jamaica
		1498–1500	Discovered Trinidad and coast of Venezuela
		1502–04	Explored coast of Honduras, Nicaragua, and Panama
→	**Pedro Alvarez Cabral (Portuguese)**	1500	Led second Portuguese voyage to India and accidentally landed in Brazil on the way
→	**Amerigo Vespucci (Italian)**	1499–1500	Reached and sailed along northeast coast of South America (Guiana). Discovered mouths of the Amazon
		1501	Explored the east coast of South America as far south as Río de la Plata
→	**Ferdinand Magellan (Portuguese)**	1519–22	Discovered a route through the Strait of Magellan and crossed the Pacific to reach the Moluccas via the Philippines, thus revealing the Pacific as a vast and separate ocean
→	**Jacques Cartier (French)**	1534–35	Explored Strait of Belle Isle and St Lawrence River as far as Montreal
→	**Willem Barents (Dutch)**	1596–97	Discovered Bear Island and Spitsbergen in the Arctic Ocean while attempting to discover a Northeast passage

THE VOYAGES OF COLUMBUS

COLUMBUS, THE FIRST EUROPEAN since the Vikings to land in the Americas, commanded four voyages that led, ultimately, to the European colonization of the New World.

When Ferdinand and Isabella of Spain finally agreed to fund Columbus's expedition, they also agreed to make him admiral and viceroy, and to his receipt of 10% of the revenue from his admiralty.

THE FIRST TWO VOYAGES

The first expedition, which left Spain in August 1492, comprised three ships – the *Santa Maria*, the *Pinta*, and the *Nina*. When Columbus and his fellow voyagers finally landed on San Salvador, Columbus believed that he had reached the Orient. He promptly took possession of the island for Ferdinand and Isabella. On Cuba, which Columbus believed to be Japan, the voyagers hoped to discover the source of gold; instead they discovered a far more valuable commodity, tobacco. On Española, the *Santa Maria* ran aground, forcing Columbus to leave behind men and supplies. The remaining ships arrived back in Spain in March 1493. Fearing rivalry from Portugal, the king and queen were keen to send another expedition soon and obtained a papal bull granting Spain the territories discovered.

Columbus's second, much larger, expedition was planned to populate and develop the 'Indies.' On returning to Española, he found that the men he had left there had been killed.

Columbus's conduct as viceroy of the new Spanish lands was not exemplary, treating those who doubted him very harshly. Discontent grew when his brother was appointed governor, and in March 1495 Columbus had 500 native slaves shipped back to Spain. Complaints against him prompted Ferdinand and Isabella to send out an official to report on Columbus's activities. Deeply humiliated, Columbus left the Indies in April 1496; on his return to Spain he managed to sway opposition against him, and the king and queen subsequently confirmed his privileges and authorized him to populate Española with convicts.

COLUMBUS'S DOWNFALL

Columbus began his third voyage in May 1498. On arriving in Española, he faced a rebellion: Ferdinand and Isabella responded by appointing a new governor. Columbus refused to acknowledge their appointee, who confiscated his property, and had Columbus arrested and shipped back to Spain in chains. Realizing that Columbus was not a fit governor, the

Christopher Columbus *An imaginative, intelligent, yet obsessive man, Columbus believed that he was fulfilling a prophecy in embarking on his westward journey to the 'Indies' (i.e. Asia), an expedition from which he sought great honour and wealth.*

king and queen, to placate him, agreed to a final voyage to search for a route through the Indies to other seas beyond.

On returning from this voyage in November 1504, he requested that the government of the Indies be restored to him. His requests refused, Columbus died a humiliated, frustrated, and forgotten man in May 1506.

COLUMBUS'S VOYAGES IN THE NEW WORLD

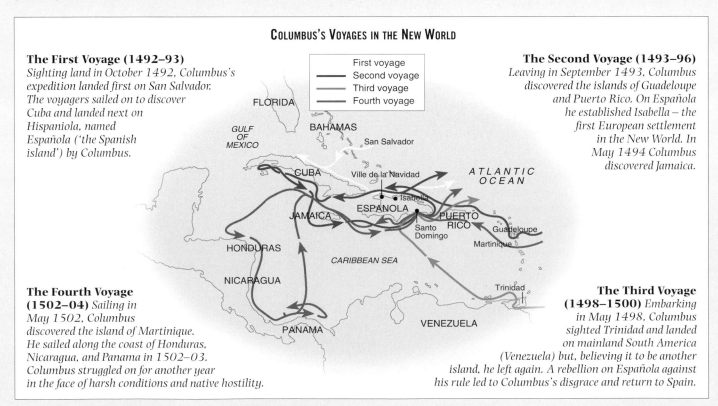

The First Voyage (1492–93)
Sighting land in October 1492, Columbus's expedition landed first on San Salvador. The voyagers sailed on to discover Cuba and landed next on Hispaniola, named Española ('the Spanish island') by Columbus.

The Second Voyage (1493–96)
Leaving in September 1493, Columbus discovered the islands of Guadeloupe and Puerto Rico. On Española he established Isabella – the first European settlement in the New World. In May 1494 Columbus discovered Jamaica.

First voyage
Second voyage
Third voyage
Fourth voyage

FLORIDA
GULF OF MEXICO
BAHAMAS
San Salvador
CUBA
Ville de la Navidad
ATLANTIC OCEAN
JAMAICA
Isabella
ESPAÑOLA
PUERTO RICO
Santo Domingo
Guadeloupe
Martinique
HONDURAS
CARIBBEAN SEA
NICARAGUA
Trinidad
PANAMA
VENEZUELA

The Fourth Voyage (1502–04) *Sailing in May 1502, Columbus discovered the island of Martinique. He sailed along the coast of Honduras, Nicaragua, and Panama in 1502–03. Columbus struggled on for another year in the face of harsh conditions and native hostility.*

The Third Voyage (1498–1500) *Embarking in May 1498, Columbus sighted Trinidad and landed on mainland South America (Venezuela) but, believing it to be another island, he left again. A rebellion on Española against his rule led to Columbus's disgrace and return to Spain.*

The Reformation and Hapsburg Dominance

The Reformation • New monarchies • The end of the Hapsburg–Valois wars •
The rise of Calvinism • The French Wars of Religion • The Dutch Revolt •
Philip II of Spain

The 16th century was a period of new horizons and new ideas, during which European explorers first revealed the potential of the unknown continents of America and the East. In Europe a confident new generation of rulers emerged, together with a new secular culture, which thrived on the wider availability of books made possible by the invention of printing. These changes were reflected in the world of ideas. The rising movement of **humanism** questioned some of the most valued medieval assumptions, inspired by the rediscovered classical civilizations of Greece and Rome. Among the first to be affected by these developments were the clergy; lay people, led by such men as the Dutch humanist Desiderius Erasmus (1469–1536), became critical of low standards and abuses in the Church hierarchy.

The Reformation

Criticism of the Church ultimately provoked the Protestant Reformation – a great movement for Christian renewal, which transformed the political and religious landscape of Europe. The crisis of the Reformation was initiated in 1517 by Martin Luther (1483–1546), a distinguished and successful Augustinian monk, who developed views critical of traditional doctrine. Deciding to initiate a debate on the conduct of Church affairs, in October 1517, he nailed to the door of All Saints Church, in the German town of Wittenberg, 95 propositions ('theses') for public debate. The initial point at issue was the established papal practice of selling indulgences – certificates granted by the pope, which assured pious purchasers of a reduction in their

time in purgatory – to raise funds. However, Luther soon broadened his attack to cover a wide range of abuses and Church practices.

Inspired by Luther's writings (written mostly in German, rather than Latin – the usual language of learned debate), the German public responded to the appeal of Luther's call for 'pure' Gospel preaching, which spread rapidly throughout Germany. The forces that might have checked Luther were slow to react. Only in 1520 did the pope finally excommunicate him; in 1521 the new emperor and king of Spain, Charles V (reigned 1516–56; Holy Roman Emperor from 1519), granted Luther a personal hearing at the Imperial Diet (Assembly) of Worms, at which Luther made a brave and highly public declaration of

══════SEE ALSO══════
This section:
• Absolute Monarchy and
  Bourbon Dominance
Early and Medieval Europe:
• The Catholic Church
• The Later Middle Ages
Islamic World:
• The Decline of the
  Ottoman Empire
The European Tradition (vol. 4):
• Renaissance Art
European and American Literature (vol. 4):
• Renaissance Literature
═══════════════════

Martin Luther in 1520 *This famous woodcut by Lucas Cranach (1472–1553) captures the intensity of the young monk, who challenged papal authority and initiated the crisis from which the Protestant Reformation emerged.* ▶

▲ The Hapsburg Empire in 1535

The vast empire inherited by Charles V condemned him to a life of ceaseless travel as he attended to the problems of his empire, defending it from the territorial aspirations of Europe's other rulers.

Here I stand; I can do no other. So help me God.

Martin Luther at the Diet of Worms, 1521

The Hapsburg–Valois Conflict

This conflict, involving the Valois kings of France and the powerful Hapsburg dynasty, lasted for two generations (1494–1559). The principal area of the conflict was Italy, where both ruling dynasties had territorial claims and aspired to domination. (See EARLY AND MEDIEVAL EUROPE: THE LATER MIDDLE AGES.) The Treaty of Cateau-Cambrésis (1559) concluded the struggle.

defiance. Over the next decade, his movement spread rapidly, as independent Protestant churches were established in the cities and states of Germany.

The Reformation in Difficulties. The forces unleashed by Luther's call for reform proved hard to control. Inevitably Luther was soon challenged by those who sought more radical change. In 1525 large numbers of German peasants rose in protest against the harsh conditions in which they lived. The subsequent German Peasants' War was a traumatic event in the history of the Reformation; Luther was persuaded to denounce the rebels and the peasants were suppressed with great brutality. By 1529 Luther had also separated himself from the radical supporters of the Peasants' War, the Anabaptists, and from the Swiss branch of the Protestant movement, led by the reformer Ulrich Zwingli (1484–1531). The division proved to be a permanent one and a major source of weakness in the Protestant religion.

New Monarchies

Changes in the intellectual and religious climate of Europe were followed by significant changes in the political order. The gradual disintegration of feudalism in medieval society facilitated the emergence of a new generation of rulers, who exercised much closer control over the lives of their subjects. The stimuli for these developments were changes in military technology – particularly the generalized use of artillery – and the advent of more sophisticated defensive fortifications (the ***Military Revolution***). These changes necessitated larger armies to fight the continuing dynastic and territorial wars of the early 16th century. States were, therefore, forced to improve their

administrative structures and tax collection capacity to cope. The new class of educated laymen provided civil servants in the new state. The enhanced political strength of the new 16th-century rulers, who made increasingly unrestrained claims to absolute power, was reflected in an opulent court culture.

Charles V. Foremost among the new-style monarchs was the young Hapsburg emperor Charles V. As heir to the empires of both his maternal grandparents, Ferdinand (reigned 1479–1516) and Isabella (reigned 1479–1504) of Spain, and of his paternal grandfather, Emperor Maximilian I (reigned 1493–1519), Charles had, by the age of 18, inherited vast lands. These included the kingdoms of Spain and Naples, the Burgundian inheritance in the Netherlands, and Spain's potentially vast New World possessions. His election as Holy Roman Emperor in 1519 completed an unprecedented concentration of lands and power, which was difficult to accommodate in Europe's fragile power system.

Francis I. Charles's most inveterate foe was the Valois monarch, Francis I of France (reigned 1515–47). Francis was also an exponent of the new-style monarchy; personal rivalry added a bitter edge to the struggle between them. In the initial stages of the conflict Charles won a decisive victory at the Battle of Pavia in 1525, when Francis led his army into Italy. In spite of Francis's defeat and capture, Charles was not able to make this temporary superiority the basis of a lasting peace. Immediately following his release, Francis repudiated the peace terms agreed under duress in captivity; subsequent wars gradually restored the balance of power between the two rivals.

FRENCH AND ENGLISH MONARCHS OF THE 16TH CENTURY	
French	
Francis I	1515–47
Henry II	1547–59
Francis II	1559–60
Charles IX	1560–74
Henry III	1574–89
Henry IV	1589–1610
English	
Henry VII	1485–1509
Henry VIII	1509–47
Edward VI	1547–53
Mary I (Tudor)	1553–58
Elizabeth I	1558–1603

The **Hapsburg–Valois conflict** proved to be immensely costly and destructive; while Charles freely spent the new wealth gathered in the Americas, Francis was forced to levy ever greater taxes from his subjects. Nevertheless, this was in some respects a golden age for the French monarchy. Francis's creation of a court that combined a domineering assumption of monarchical power and a careful cultivation of the best of the new Renaissance arts helped France to banish comparatively recent memories of English occupation during the Hundred Years' War. France thus began to emerge as a great European power.

England. Royal power also developed significantly in England in the early 16th century. The reign of Henry VII (1485–1509) was a period of recovery after the divisive Wars of the Roses in the 15th century. Henry's efficient management of royal finances provided a basis for the re-establishment of royal authority. The benefits of this were seen mostly after the accession of his ambitious and flamboyant son, Henry VIII (reigned 1509–47).

Henry immediately set about creating the cultured court life pioneered by continental monarchies; he embarked on an active foreign policy designed to enhance England's European prestige. The tone was set by a diplomatic conference between Henry VIII and Francis I outside Calais at the so-called ***Field of the Cloth of Gold*** (1520). The elaborate hospitality displayed there could not conceal the rivalry between the two monarchs. The meeting was fruitless, doing little to improve relations between England and France. Henry returned from the meeting to sign a treaty of alliance with Charles V. However, the collapse of Henry's first marriage to Catherine of Aragon (1485–1536), the aunt of Charles V, put this alliance under almost intolerable pressure. When Catherine failed to provide Henry with a male heir, the king began to petition for a divorce, meeting with determined opposition from Charles V. The pope ultimately refused to grant the divorce. By 1532 Henry's patience was exhausted; by marrying his pregnant mistress, Anne Boleyn (1507–36), he set in train the parliamentary steps that would sever England's allegiance to the Catholic Church.

While Henry remained personally loyal to Catholicism, he nevertheless made use of

Francis I *Often called 'the Renaissance prince' because of his ability, keen intelligence, and patronage of learning and the arts, Francis fought a series of expensive foreign wars against his great rival, Charles V. In the later years of his reign, Francis suppressed the Protestant movement in France; in 1545 he ordered an attack on the Waldenses of southern France, a religious group who rejected many Catholic doctrines.*

VARIETIES OF PROTESTANTISM

While Luther initially aimed to reform the whole Church, the new Protestant movement, which had grown from the crisis he initiated in 1517, quickly split into competing groups:
• **Lutherans** Followers of Martin Luther, who took a conservative position on Church ceremonies but rejected the Catholic sacraments.
• **Zwinglians** Followers of Ulrich Zwingli, the reformer from Zürich. They took a more radical position on the central doctrine of the Eucharist.
• **Calvinists** Followers of John Calvin (1509–64), leader of the Swiss Reformation from 1555, who adopted a middle position between Zwingli and Luther on doctrine. The clarity of his writings and his organizational skills gave the Reformation new impetus.
• **Anabaptists** Radicals who rejected the mainstream Reformation by abandoning infant baptism and advocating complete withdrawal from normal society. Their supporters were primarily the poor and dispossessed; they were persecuted by rich and poor alike. Prominent leaders were the German Thomas Müntzer (c. 1490–1525) and the Dutch John of Leiden (died 1535).

Church property to finance his expensive wars: four years after the break with Rome, the English parliament implemented the **dissolution of the monasteries**. The trend towards Protestantism continued during the reign of Henry's young son, Edward VI (reigned 1547–53). By this time royal power in England was unchallenged; although Mary Tudor (reigned 1553–58) effected a temporary restoration of Catholicism, the damage to the old Church was not easily repaired. The

Dissolution of the Monasteries

The closing down of the monasteries in England and the seizure of their property was one of the most dramatic acts of the Tudor state. The dissolution struck a fatal blow against the central pillar of medieval religion; it transferred large quantities of valuable land to new lay owners.
Its architect was the brilliant administrator Thomas Cromwell (c. 1485–1540).

The Huguenots

The Huguenots (from the German *Eidgenosse*, confederate) were French Protestants. Chiefly followers of John Calvin, they soon became an influential national minority. Rivalry between their leaders, especially the Condé, a French princely family, and the prominent Catholic Guise family, gave rise to the French Wars of Religion (1562–94). The Edict of Nantes (1598) guaranteed the Huguenots freedom of worship, but in the 17th century they were increasingly persecuted, leading to their mass migration after 1685. Persecution continued until 1789.

reign of Elizabeth I (reigned 1558–1603), Mary's successor and half-sister, was a long and successful one, which both confirmed England's destiny as a Protestant country and consolidated the success of the Tudor dynasty as rulers.

The End of the Hapsburg–Valois Wars

Mary Tudor's death also brought a significant shift in Europe's strategic balance of power. Since 1556 the empire of Charles V had been under the rule of his son, Philip II (reigned 1556–98), who had consolidated his position in northern Europe by marrying Mary Tudor. With this tie now broken, Philip was persuaded to bring the long Hapsburg–Valois conflict to an end. The Treaty of Cateau–Cambrésis (1559) confirmed that 40 years of warfare had not significantly altered the strategic balance between Europe's two major powers. The treaty confirmed Hapsburg supremacy in Italy and left the Netherlands intact; it was unable, however, to recover the Hapsburg ancestral lands in Burgundy, now successfully integrated into the French kingdom. The settlement was one with which both powers could be reasonably content.

The Rise of Calvinism

By the 1540s Protestantism was in need of a new source of inspiration. By the time of Luther's death (1546), the German evangelical movement appeared to have reached the limits of its possible expansion, mostly in the

German princely states and in Scandinavia; other active evangelical movements, such as those in France and the Netherlands, had been stifled by determined persecution. However, Protestantism now found a new leader in John Calvin, a French refugee scholar resident in the small Swiss city of Geneva. Exceptionally gifted as both a writer and a preacher, Calvin established, in Geneva, a community that became a model of a godly society and a prototype for similar movements elsewhere. By 1555 he was the dominant figure of the Swiss Reformation; his writings were beginning to find a ready audience elsewhere in Europe.

The French Wars of Religion

The growth of Calvinism made its first significant impact in France, Calvin's homeland. Under the rule of the fiercely anti-Protestant Henry II (reigned 1547–59) its growth was contained. Henry's sudden death, however, set off a dual political and religious crisis. The short reign of Francis II (1559–60) was marked by an increased level of confrontation between an emerging Protestant (soon called **Huguenot**) faction at court and the ultra-Catholic Duke of Guise (1519–63); the latter was the maternal uncle of the young king and the dominant force in government. When Francis in turn died, to be succeeded by his nine-year-old brother, Charles IX (reigned 1560–74), confrontation could not long be delayed. Fighting broke out in 1562, the first of a series of wars that left France exhausted

THE ST BARTHOLOMEW'S DAY MASSACRE

The massacre was sparked off by a failed attempt to assassinate the Huguenot leader, Admiral Coligny (1519–72). When it became clear that Coligny had survived, the court, fearing a Huguenot backlash, ordered a pre-emptive strike against the Huguenot nobles gathered in Paris. The murder of Coligny on 24 August (1572) was followed by the deaths of over 4000 Protestants, as the population of Paris turned on the hated religious minority.

The massacre was celebrated by Catholics across Europe as a decisive blow against heresy. In contrast, the event left Protestants devastated. "I write without collecting my wits, stricken in spirit, and with a sense of tragic foreboding" was how Théodore Beza (1519–1605), Calvin's successor, reported the massacre. The atrocity permanently poisoned relations between the two faiths and was regarded throughout Protestant Europe as an act of Catholic bad faith and perfidy.

◄ **St Bartholomew's Day Massacre**
As the corpse of Coligny is thrown from an upper window (right), elsewhere the massacre begins.

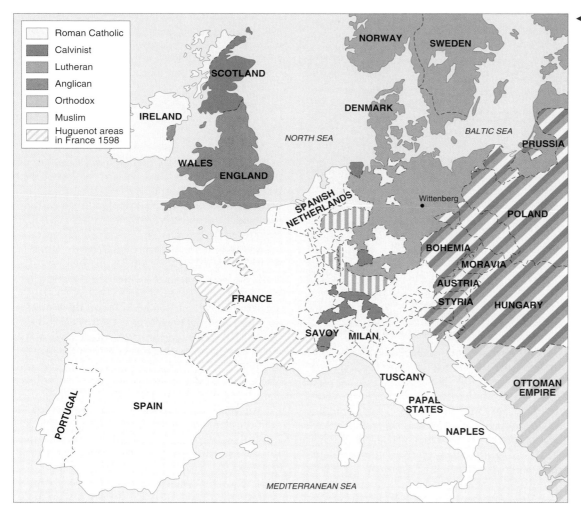

Roman Catholic
Calvinist
Lutheran
Anglican
Orthodox
Muslim
Huguenot areas
in France 1598

◄ **Distribution of Religions in Europe** *(mid-16th century) By 1560, the Protestant Reformation had spread across Europe, owing largely to the proliferation of printed works, produced by the recently invented process of printing with movable type. Though several Catholic states, particularly France and Poland, were affected, Italy, Spain, and Portugal remained wholly Catholic.*

▲ **William (the Silent), Prince of Orange** *Recognized as the father of the Dutch nation, William guided the rebel Dutch forces towards independence.*

and effectively neutralized as a political force for a generation.

The first decade of the wars was characterized by sharp bursts of fighting interspersed with prolonged attempts to agree a settlement. These attempts were led by Catherine de' Medici (1519–89), the mother and regent of the young king. In 1572, however, her peace initiatives were rendered futile by the **St Bartholomew's Day Massacre**.

In the wake of the bloody massacre the Huguenot leadership established what was, in effect, an independent state in southern France; neither Charles nor his equally ineffective brother, Henry III (reigned 1574–89), were able to make any impression on the Huguenot strongholds as royal authority deteriorated. The situation was resolved only when the assassination of Henry III brought his cousin, Henry of Navarre (Henry IV; reigned 1589–1610), to the throne. As leader of the Huguenot party, Henry inevitably faced determined opposition from the powerful Catholic League, an association of ultra-Catholic French nobles. In 1594, however, he effectively disarmed moderate opposition by announcing his own conversion to Catholi-

cism. A settlement with his former Protestant allies in the Edict of Nantes (1598), guaranteeing them limited rights of worship, finally brought the long wars to an end.

The Dutch Revolt

In the Netherlands the rise of Calvinism led to a similar crisis of authority, which plunged this humane and prosperous part of Europe into a long and terrible conflict.

Dutch religious dissidents linked their call for freedom of religion with the grievances of the powerful local nobility, who resented their exclusion from power by the provinces' absentee ruler, Philip II of Spain (reigned 1556–98). When Philip refused to concede on either issue, the provinces erupted, in 1568, in a demonstration of petitioning and disobedience, during which the Calvinist ministers quickly emerged as the leading force. Their radicalism, however, soon alienated their former noble allies; the royal government was able to restore control even before the arrival of a force, sent by Philip, to quell the rebellion.

Consigned to exile, the Calvinists now joined forces with the remnants of noble opposition, led by William, Prince of Orange (reigned

The Imperial Succession

Charles V had originally intended all his lands to go to his son, Philip. However, his brother, Ferdinand (king of Bohemia and Hungary 1526–64), who had administered the German lands for Charles since 1530, as king of the Romans, was not easily disinherited. In 1551, therefore, Charles reluctantly agreed to the division of the Hapsburg Empire between the two branches of the family.

◄ **The Spanish Armada** *Of the 130 ships sent by Philip II to invade England in 1588, only 86 returned to Spain. The rest were destroyed, either in engagements with English ships in the English Channel, or in storms as they tried to escape around Scotland and Ireland. The failure of Philip's 'Great Expedition' dealt a fatal blow to his plans to destroy the Protestant powers of northern Europe.*

The Battle of Lepanto

The greatest naval battle of the 16th century took place off Lepanto, Greece, on 7 October 1571. The combined fleets of Spain, Venice, and the papacy overwhelmingly defeated the Ottoman navy, which was threatening to dominate the Mediterranean. Of the Christian force of about 30 000 fighting men, over 7000 died. Some 15 000 Turks were killed or captured and 10 000 Christian galley slaves were freed.

▲ **Philip II** *This portrait by Sofonisba Anguissola captures the cold intensity that Philip brought to the pursuit of his political objectives.*

1533–84), who soon emerged as the hero of the revolt. In 1572 the rebels succeeded in establishing a secure defensive position in the Netherlands, in the northern province of Holland; this became the base for a gradual expansion of territory held by the rebel forces. Despite vast expenditure on military resources, the Spanish regime was unable to break the rebel resolve. The new governor of the Netherlands, the Duke of Parma (governed 1578–92), did succeed, by 1585, in securing the southern provinces; the final outcome of the conflict, however, was decided by Spain's failure to break the emerging alliance between the Dutch and their principal Protestant protector, England. Spain was, nevertheless, slow to acknowledge Dutch success: it was only in 1609 that fighting was brought to an end by the Twelve Years' Truce; only in 1648 did Spain finally acknowledge the independence of the free United Provinces.

Philip II of Spain

In the face of the spread of Protestantism, Philip II of Spain stood out as the defender of the Catholic cause. A dour and orthodox Catholic, he regarded the defence of his inheritance (the vast empire of Charles V, with the exception of the German lands) as a sacred trust. His refusal to contemplate compromise with 'heresy' made the wars of the later 16th century inevitable.

In the early years of his reign, however, the problems of northern Europe took second place to the more immediate threat posed to Spain by the Ottoman Turks, who challenged Spanish power in the Mediterranean. The seriousness of this challenge was emphasized by the disaster at Djerba (1560), when a Spanish

expeditionary force to Tripoli was destroyed by the Turkish war fleet. In 1569 Philip faced a crisis closer to home, when the Moorish inhabitants of the southern province of Granada rebelled. It was only with the victory at the **Battle of Lepanto** (1571) that Philip succeeded in restoring some equilibrium between the two great Mediterranean empires; by this time, however, his absolute priority had become the security of Spain.

After 1572 Philip turned his attention to the problems of northern Europe. The rebellion in the Netherlands was only one aspect of a complexity of problems with Protestant 'heresy' at its core: the Huguenot struggle in France and the increasingly overt intervention by Elizabeth I of England on the side of Spain's enemies. By 1580 Philip had devised a strategy to deal with all these difficulties at once: a great amphibious expedition to drive England out of the war, permitting him to deal freely with the rebels in the Netherlands.

The Spanish Armada (1588) thus represented the climax of the religious wars of the later 16th century. The Armada was destroyed by a combination of the English fleet and gales in the North Sea, which made England and the Dutch rebels virtually immune to defeat. Its failure doomed Philip II's attempts to reassert Catholic orthodoxy by military means. The final resolution of these conflicts at the end of the century confirmed Spain's waning power. From this time Hapsburg influence in European affairs would be gradually eroded by the rising powers of France and the new Dutch Republic (United Provinces of the Netherlands). Philip II died in 1598, a defeated and disappointed man.

Philip's death marked the beginning of Spain's decline as a great European power. The recovery of France under Henry IV restored the traditional rivalry between Europe's two great continental powers; the Hapsburg rulers faced increasing difficulties defending both their European interests and their overseas possessions from the incursions of eager rivals. The treaties that ended the 16th-century wars left several issues unsettled. Germany, in particular, remained troubled by religious divisions, which would shortly erupt in one of the most destructive conflicts in Europe's history: the Thirty Years' War.

Absolute Monarchy and Bourbon Dominance

Economic crisis, war, and rebellion • The decline of Spain • Richelieu's rule in France •
Civil war and revolution in England • Louis XIV and French expansionism •
A new power in the north • The Hapsburg Empire under Leopold I

The 17th century in Europe was an age of stark contrasts. While war was almost constantly being waged, the period was marked by considerable splendour and courtly display, with the elegant baroque style dominating art and architecture. Monarchs built magnificent palaces, such as El Escorial (Madrid), Versailles (Paris), and, on a lesser scale, the Hofberg (Vienna) for their courts, while the common people suffered poverty and hardship.

Economic Crisis, War, and Rebellion

Economic recession, which began in the 1630s, deepened and continued into the next century. It was accompanied by a gradual shift in the balance of Europe's economy away from the Mediterranean basin to the Atlantic coasts and the Baltic, as colonial trade and grain supply from eastern Europe grew in importance. The prominence of Venice and the central German towns declined, thus setting the scene for the rise of the northern seafaring peoples of Britain and the Netherlands. Spain, unable to support the costs of empire, was eventually replaced as the foremost European power by France under the Bourbon monarch, Louis XIV (reigned 1643–1715).

The need to finance large standing armies obliged monarchs to develop stronger state bureaucracies and to erode the traditional privileges of provinces, institutions, and the nobility. Many new direct and indirect taxes were raised; at the same time sovereigns were forced to sell crown lands, titles of nobility, and offices in the administration. Currencies were debased, loans raised, and tax collection contracted out to private financiers, all in order to generate ready money. The pressure of these measures on society provoked riots and rebellions in many states, from the peasant revolts of the *nu-pieds* in Normandy in 1639, to the Revolt of the Catalans and the secession of Portugal from Spain in 1640, the English Civil War (1642–46), and the **Fronde** in France (1648–53). Marauding armies during the **Thirty Years' War** (1618–48) devastated large parts of central Europe, while the weight of taxes left the peasantry of Castile and France in dire poverty.

Absolute Monarchy. In most states, the power of the ruler developed at the expense of representative institutions. Drawing on such notions as the divine right of kings and on imperial imagery, monarchs tried to avoid

===SEE ALSO===
This section:
- The Reformation and Hapsburg Dominance
- The Growth of the Russian Empire
- The Enlightened Despots

North America:
- Colonial North America

Islamic World:
- The Decline of the Ottoman Empire

Physics (vol. 2):
- The History of Physics

The European Tradition (vol. 4):
- Baroque and Rococo Art

European and American Literature (vol. 4):
- The Age of Reason

Religion (vol. 6):
- Christianity

The Fronde

These civil conflicts comprised two rebellions against the ministry of Cardinal Mazarin. The first was led by the Paris parlement (1648–49) and the second by the princes (1650–53).

◄ **The Palace of Louis XIV at Versailles**
The magnificent royal residence at Versailles, near Paris, was built between 1662 and 1682 for Louis XIV. Versailles encapsulates the opulence of Louis's reign.

Venality of Office

It was a widespread European practice for judicial and administrative offices to be sold by the monarchy to their incumbents, in order to raise money. The result was that offices became hereditary property. The system existed in England, Spain, Italy, and Germany, but reached its height in France, where there were over 65 000 such offices in the 1660s; many more were created during the reign of Louis XIV. Venal offices became both an investment and a channel of social mobility for those who purchased them.

restrictions on their power, by developing the concept of ***absolute monarchy***. However, the demands of warfare meant that these monarchs were unable to do more than tilt the internal balance of power in their favour. They were unable to crush completely the opposition of the powerful nobility. Only in Britain and the United Provinces of the Netherlands did the representative institutions defeat the claims of absolute monarchy.

Religious Division. In the wake of the 16th-century Protestant Reformation, 17th-century Europe was dominated by religious strife. In the first half of the century religious divisions fuelled bitter clashes, perpetuated by the continuing **Counter-Reformation** championed by Emperor Ferdinand II (king of Bohemia 1617–19 and 1620–27; Holy Roman Emperor 1619–37). Where toleration did eventually emerge, it was more the result of expediency than principle. Although often in conflict, both the Protestant and Catholic churches were able to extend their influence.

At the same time, however, scientific and philosophical advances were beginning to undermine the classical and religious views of the world. In 1633 the Inquisition suppressed the unacceptable theories of Italian scientist,

Galileo Galilei (1564–1642), which asserted that the earth was not at the centre of the universe. However, the works of René Descartes (1596–1650) and Isaac Newton (1642–1727) amounted to a scientific revolution, which laid the foundations for a new view of the world. By the end of the century, rigorous application of reason and, increasingly, scientific experimentation were accepted as the basis for intellectual activity.

The Decline of Spain

Philip IV of Spain (reigned 1621–65), a devout Catholic, was determined to defend his religion and empire. In 1621, with the ending of the Twelve Years' Truce (1609–21), he sought to reconquer the United Provinces of the Netherlands – which had revolted against Spanish rule in the previous century – encouraged by the recent Hapsburg victory over Protestant forces in Germany. The Dutch conflict, combined with war against France (now pursuing an anti-Hapsburg line in the Thirty Years' War) and a fall in the supply of American silver, caused economic crises and severely stretched the resources of Philip's empire.

The reforms of Philip's chief minister, Count Olivares (1587–1645), were intended to

THE THIRTY YEARS' WAR (1618–48)

This was not a single episode but a series of conflicts, some of which were directly related while others merely interacted. Religion was an important factor in the wars, but so too were dynastic policies and diplomatic manoeuvring to retain a balance of power.

In 1618 the Protestant nobles of Bohemia, part of the Holy Roman Empire, revolted against their Hapsburg Catholic ruler, Ferdinand II, who was trying to undermine their religion. Ferdinand was deposed (1619) and Frederick, the Protestant elector of the Palatinate, was elected king of Bohemia. In 1620, however, Ferdinand II, now Holy Roman Emperor, defeated Frederick's Protestant forces at the Battle of the White Mountain. In 1625

The Thirty Years' War Ravages Europe *In this contemporary woodcut, the war is shown as a voracious monster wreaking widespread havoc in Europe. Germany's commerce and industry were ruined, while its population and agriculture were devastated. Civilian losses were as high as 50% in places.*

the king of Denmark, Christian IV (reigned 1588–1648), attacked Ferdinand, encouraged by the Protestant Dutch, who were faring badly in their renewed war with Spain. Yet by 1629, Ferdinand's forces, under generals Johan von Tilly (1559–1632) and Albrecht von Wallenstein (1583–1634), had conquered most of Germany; Ferdinand intended to enforce Catholicism throughout its lands by the Edict of Restitution (1629).

At this point Sweden, under King Gustavus Adolphus (reigned 1611–32), entered the war to defend the oppressed Protestant German princes. He won important victories over the Catholic armies at Breitenfeld (1631) and Lützen (1632), where he was killed in action. In 1634 Swedish forces were defeated at Nordlingen; in 1635 the Protestant princes made peace with the emperor at Prague. However, since early 1631, fearing encirclement by the Spanish and Austrian Hapsburgs, France had been subsidizing Protestant efforts against Ferdinand. Now, in 1635, its allies defeated, France had no alternative but to enter the conflict. France and Sweden allied to make gains in Germany in the 1640s.

By 1648, extensive territorial devastation and the war weariness of the German princes combined with the defeats of the emperor (now Ferdinand III; reigned 1637–57) to end the wars by the negotiated Peace of Westphalia. Religious coexistence was recognized and the way opened for the emergence of absolutist rule by the princes, who now enjoyed greater freedoms from the authority of the Hapsburg-dominated Holy Roman Empire.

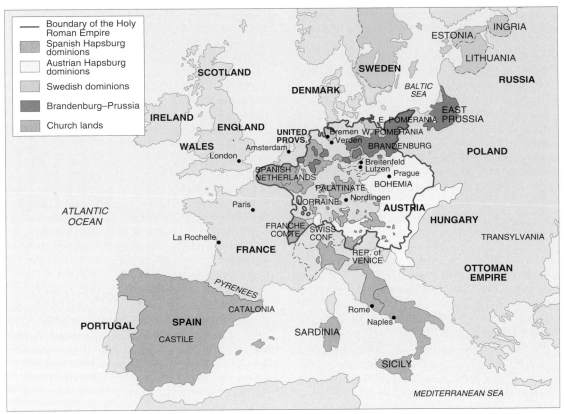

◄ **Europe at the Peace of Westphalia**
(1648) The Peace of Westphalia, which ended the Thirty Years' War, strengthened the sovereignty of Germany's 300 separate states and the Swiss Confederation, confirmed Dutch independence, and gave areas on the northern coast of Germany (West Pomerania and the bishoprics of Bremen and Verden) to Sweden.

increase contributions of arms and money towards the war. Instead they provoked rebellion in Catalonia in 1640 and the secession of Portugal. In 1648 Spain finally recognized the independence of the United Provinces and their right to trade freely in the East and West Indies; however, the war against France over territories in the Spanish Netherlands and southern France continued until 1659.

Although Spain managed to raise sufficient funds for a campaign against rebellious Portugal, Spanish forces were defeated by the Portuguese in 1665. Portugal's independence was formally recognized by Spain in 1668.

Charles II (reigned 1665–1700) succeeded to the throne aged four, yet his personal rule did not begin until 1675. The weakness of his rule led to severe internal decline in Spain, exacerbated by crop failures and disease. Further wars with France in the last quarter of the century left Spain with much of the Spanish Netherlands and its Italian lands intact, yet these conflicts contributed to Spain's now irreversible decline as a great imperial power.

Richelieu's rule in France

Louis XIII (reigned 1610–43) appointed **Cardinal Richelieu** as an adviser in 1624, when France was still rent by factional conflict. He determined to reduce the power of the Protestants and laid siege to the Huguenot stronghold of La Rochelle in 1627–28 (see THE REFORMATION AND HAPSBURG DOMINANCE),

afterwards reducing the privileges granted to them by the Edict of Nantes (1598).

In 1630 the Catholic party of the queen mother and several princes, whom Richelieu had alienated, failed to have him dismissed. Assured of the confidence of his king, Richelieu was now free to pursue his anti-Hapsburg policy in alliance with the Protestant princes of northern Europe. The subsequent wars against Spain and the imperial forces of the Holy Roman Empire necessitated a better organization of the state. New administrative officials (intendants) were appointed, who observed and coerced local officials in order to increase monetary receipts. Taxes trebled and provincial liberties were restricted. These harsh policies provoked popular revolts, often covertly supported by the provincial elites.

By 1642, when Richelieu died, his foreign policy had succeeded, although discontent

---

The Counter-Reformation

Between the mid-16th and mid-17th centuries, this movement within the Catholic Church attempted to counter the effects of the Protestant Reformation by reforming abuses, propagating the faith, and suppressing heresy. Many new religious orders, such as the Jesuits, were founded, seminaries were set up, and missionary work was conducted with renewed fervour.

CARDINAL RICHELIEU (1585–1642)

Armand Jean du Plessis, cardinal de Richelieu, came from a prominent French family, who held the seigneury (lordship) of Richelieu in Poitou. He became an adviser to the queen mother, Maria de' Medici, in c. 1616. As the king's first minister, from 1629 to 1642, he was hated for his centralization of royal authority (especially through his extensive civil service), heavy taxes, and ruthless repression of the Huguenots. Richelieu was a brilliant statesman, whose chief aim was to counter Hapsburg dominance in Europe.

▲ **William III**
As Prince of Orange, stadholder of the United Provinces, and king of England, William was the main opponent of Louis XIV. He was invited to invade England in November 1688 to save it from Catholicism.

Port of Amsterdam
(17th century) The significant commercial power of the Dutch in this period enabled them to use wealth from international trade to fight a successful war against Spanish control and encourage the flowering of Dutch culture. ▼

was widespread. Richelieu's policies continued to be pursued during the regency of Anne of Austria, mother of Louis XIV (who succeeded his father in 1643 at the age of five) and the rule of Jules Mazarin as first minister (1643–61). Thus, when war with Spain continued, even after the Peace of Westphalia (1648), the Paris parlement and several noble families rebelled. For nearly five years civil wars, known as the Fronde, increased France's woes. Royal victory over the rebels in 1653 was followed by victory over Spain, confirmed by the Peace of the Pyrenees in 1659.

Civil War and Revolution in England
In Britain, too, the problems of foreign war highlighted the deficiencies of existing institutions. Religion caused serious divisions as Puritans were deeply suspicious of what they saw as support for Catholicism by Charles I (reigned 1625–49).

War with Spain and France in the 1620s led to a dispute between Charles I and parliament over taxes and religious issues. Charles tried to rule without parliament during the so-called Eleven Years Tyranny (1629–40), collecting taxes and forced loans illegally. When Scotland rebelled against Charles's religious policies in 1640, he was forced to call the Short Parliament, which refused him subsidies for a campaign against the Scots. Subsequent Scottish military successes led Charles to summon the Long Parliament (1640–60); relations between Charles and parliament soon broke down and the crisis erupted in civil war (1642–46). Royalist 'Cavaliers' fought Parliamentarian 'Roundheads,' the latter winning a decisive victory at Naseby in 1645. In 1649 the king was tried for treason and executed. With parliament victorious, England became a republic, known as the Commonwealth.

By 1653, Oliver Cromwell (1599–1658), an effective leader of the Parliamentary army

during the Civil War, had quelled the royalists in Scotland and Ireland and emerged as Lord Protector of the Commonwealth; he ruled the country in the interests of Puritanism and commerce. Rivalry with the United Provinces led to a series of **Anglo-Dutch wars**, between 1652 and 1674, which foreshadowed the trade wars of the next century.

Two years after Cromwell's death the protectorate gave way to the restoration of Charles II (reigned 1660–85) as king of England, Scotland, and Ireland. Though the issue of sovereignty was still inconclusive, parliament continued to assert its authority (1678–79). However, the attempts of James II (reigned 1685–88) to promote a Catholic revival and a more absolutist monarchy led his opponents to invite the staunchly Protestant William of Orange, **stadholder** (chief magistrate) of the United Provinces of the Netherlands and husband of Mary, daughter of James II and heiress apparent to the English throne, to intervene. William invaded in 1688, causing James II to flee, and ruled England, Scotland, and Ireland from 1689 jointly with Mary until her death in 1694, and subsequently alone until 1702. These events, known as the 'Glorious Revolution,' were almost bloodless, taking the form of a compromise between the crown and parliament that was to endure throughout the 18th century. The immediate impact on foreign affairs was to involve Britain more closely in the coalitions against Louis XIV.

Louis XIV and French Expansionism
The death of Mazarin, in 1661, heralded the beginning of Louis XIV's personal rule. His determination to rule alone, based on his deep-seated belief in the divine right of kings, was symbolized by the arrest (1661) and trial of his talented finance minister Nicolas Foucquet (1615–80). Aided by such able administrators as Jean-Baptiste Colbert (1619–83), Michel Le Tellier (1603–85), and the marquis de Louvois (1639–91), rather than the high nobles of the court, he attempted to restore the power of the state and pursue his *gloire* (reputation for glorious deeds) in foreign wars.

State finances, the army, and the bureaucracy were all reformed; commerce was encouraged, manufacturing concerns established, the arts patronized, and the immense palace of Versailles constructed (1662–82). Louis invited potentially rebellious nobles to court, where he could observe their intrigues. Court festivities, ballets, the patronage of art and architecture, and a succession of mistresses created around the king a compelling aura of princely magnificence and authority.

Louis's ambition involved him in a war against the Dutch (supported by Spain) from 1672 to 1678, from which he acquired the

territories of Lorraine, Franche-Comté, and some towns in the Spanish Netherlands. From 1680 to 1684 he claimed territories along his borders, including Strasbourg, which provoked Spain, the Holy Roman Emperor, and German princes to form a coalition against him. The War of the Grand Alliance (1689–97), in which France fought an anti-French alliance of England, the Netherlands, the Austrian Hapsburgs and Spain, deprived Louis of many of his gains.

While the zenith of Louis's reign came in the 1680s, his persecution of Huguenots culminated in his revocation of the Edict of Nantes in 1685, and led to the emigration of 200 000 Protestants to Geneva, Brandenburg-Prussia, and England. Their fate fuelled images of Louis as a tyrant, easing William of Orange's efforts to create anti-French coalitions against him.

Older and wiser, Louis now desired peace, yet the problem of the succession to the Spanish Empire, which followed the death of Charles II, in 1700, proved insoluble without another major European war. The War of the Spanish Succession (1701–14), between France and the anti-French alliance, left France with its territory intact but its power severely diminished. The demands of war had undermined Louis's reforms and led his ministers to revert to most of the expedients that had characterized the state of France in the 1650s.

A New Power in the North

Sweden, a poor country in relation to other European states, experienced a brief period of greatness during the 17th century. The reign of Gustavus Adolphus saw sweeping internal reforms enacted, together with the suspension of the long-standing struggle between the monarchy and the nobility, allowing the king to raise funds to pursue his expansionist aims.

The claim of the Catholic Polish king, Sigismund (reigned 1587–1632), to the Swedish throne forced Gustavus to invade Polish Livonia (modern Latvia and Estonia) in 1621 and Prussia in 1626. Internal dissension within the weak state of Poland left it unable to defend its huge territories, while Brandenburg-Prussia was not yet strong enough to defy Sweden. The 1630s saw Sweden expand into Germany, and in 1644 it acquired some territory from Denmark. West Pomerania became Swedish territory at the Peace of Westphalia.

Under Charles X (reigned 1654–60), Sweden attacked Poland in 1655, which led to the First Northern War, involving Russia, Denmark, and Austria. The conflict was concluded with Sweden gaining Danish possessions north of the Baltic by the Treaty of Roskilde (1658). Charles XI (reigned 1660–97) gradually increased his control over the government of Sweden; by the 1690s he had reduced

◀ **Louis XIV** *Louis XIV – known as* Le roi soleil *from the sun emblem he adopted as his personal motif – expanded the borders of his kingdom and created an enduring monarchy that dominated his age. Yet despite the pomp and grandeur of his reign, the wars he undertook ruined France, leaving it with debts of 2000 million livres in 1715.*

L'état c'est moi.
(I am the state)

Attributed to **Louis XIV**

the power of the nobility and the estates to become an absolute monarch. He was succeeded by the enormously talented Charles XII (reigned 1697–1718).

The Hapsburg Empire under Leopold I

The extent of the Hapsburg dominions meant that the Hapsburg ruler, Leopold I (reigned 1658–1705), was able to exert influence in Germany, northern Italy, and towards the Ottoman (Turkish) Empire. The three crowns of Austria, Bohemia, and Hungary brought under one ruler peoples of many creeds, governed by regional elites with different institutions and languages. Nevertheless, governing institutions were reformed and finances improved during the 17th century.

Leopold's main aim was to restore Catholicism to his domains. Transylvania had been autonomous, but under Turkish suzerainty, since the 1560s; while defending the remaining strip of Hungary, Leopold took the opportunity to impose Catholicism upon formerly Protestant areas. In 1683, however, the Turks attempted to besiege Vienna itself. An army under the Polish king, John Sobieski (reigned 1674–96), with whom Leopold had agreed a treaty of mutual support (1683), defeated them. By 1699, Hapsburg forces, aided by Saxony, Poland, Savoy, and Russia, who had formed into a Holy League, had recaptured Hungary, Transylvania, and much of Serbia.

In the 1690s, Leopold's attention became focused on his ambition of acquiring part of the Spanish Empire. Indeed, in 1714 his empire was to be the principal territorial beneficiary of the long War of the Spanish Succession.

The Anglo-Dutch Wars

The emerging commercial powers of England and the Netherlands clashed three times in the second half of the 17th century, each conflict arising from trade rivalry. The first war (1652–54), which followed English attempts to eliminate Dutch involvement in its trade, led to English victory. The second conflict (1665–67) resulted in Dutch victory, when the entire English fleet was destroyed at anchor by the Dutch in 1667. The third war (1672–74) formed part of the more general conflict between France and the Netherlands (1672–78), in which England sided with France.

The Growth of the Russian Empire

Gathering of Russian lands • Opening to the east • The Time of Troubles (1598–1613) • Expansion under the Romanov dynasty • State and society

The Expansion of Muscovy
The unification and conquest of lands around the principality of Moscow was begun by Ivan III and continued until 1598; it laid a sound foundation for the expansion of the Russian Empire under the Romanovs from 1613. ▼

The first Russian state, Kiev-Rus, fragmented into numerous principalities during the 11th and 12th centuries; it was overrun by Mongol (or Tatar) invaders in the 13th century. By the mid-15th century, however, partial reunification had begun; by the late 17th century a vast Russian state, with its capital in Moscow, had been established. Russian society was steeply hierarchical and formidable power came to be concentrated in the hands of its ruler, the ***Tsar of all the Russias***.

Gathering of Russian Lands
Reunification, which began during the reign of Grand Duke Ivan III (1462–1505), took place around the principality of Moscow. By various means, Ivan absorbed both the lands within Muscovy and many weaker Russian principalities outside Moscow, the most important being the wealthy republic of Novgorod. By 1480 Ivan's position was strong enough to enable him to renounce Mongol authority over Russia. He also began to assert a claim to the Ukraine, the western lands that

had once belonged to Kiev and had come under Polish-Lithuanian rule. During the reign of Vasily III (1505–33), Muscovy absorbed the remaining independent Russian principalities.

Opening to the East
Ivan IV (known as 'the Terrible'; reigned 1533–84) opened the way to eastern expansion by destroying two of the khanates into which the Mongol Empire had fragmented – Kazan and Astrakhan – during the 1550s. Over the following decades the vast new territory claimed by Russia was gradually colonized. By 1600 the tsar's lands extended far beyond the Urals, where native tribes could offer little resistance.

To the northwest, however, Ivan made a fateful attempt to gain access to the Baltic by attacking Livonia. He thus initiated a war, which continued for 25 years (1558–83). Muscovy proved to be an inferior force to the Polish-Lithuanian-Scandinavian alliance that Ivan had provoked. In 1571 the Tatars of the Crimean khanate attacked from the south, devastating the capital. The war also caused sustained disruption and depopulation in the central and western regions of the country.

The Time of Troubles (1598–1613)
When Ivan IV's son, Fedor I (reigned 1584–98), died without an heir, Muscovy experienced a period of acute political, social, and economic instability. The crown passed to Fedor's brother-in-law, Boris Godunov (reigned 1598–1605); his efforts to stabilize the country, however, were blighted by famines (1601 and 1603). Thereafter Poland and Sweden sought to take advantage of Russia's political and military weakness. By 1610, however, the desire to restore order was sufficiently strong among the population for a triumphant Russian army to be raised. In 1613 Mikhail Romanov, a Russian nobleman, was chosen as tsar, thus restoring political stability.

Expansion Under the Romanov Dynasty
During the Romanov period, Muscovy's expansion resumed. Russian settlers established small towns across the expanses of Siberia, reaching the Pacific by the mid-17th century.

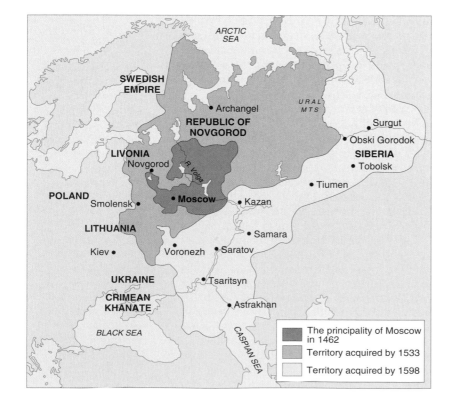

The principality of Moscow in 1462
Territory acquired by 1533
Territory acquired by 1598

◄ **The Russian Elite**
*A 16th-century
procession of boyars
followed by merchants,
the latter carrying furs
for trade, is shown in
this woodcut print by
Michael Peterle.*

To the west, Muscovy made use of new military techniques against Poland, while in the Ukraine it found invaluable allies among the **Cossacks**, whose loyalty to the Orthodox Church intensified their resistance to rule by Catholic Poland. In 1654 Tsar Alexis (reigned 1645–76) agreed to Cossack requests that he incorporate the Ukraine into the Muscovite state; thus by the Treaty of Andrusovo (1667) Poland finally ceded the eastern Ukraine.

During the reign of Fedor III (1676–82) and the regency of Sophia (1682–89) the military balance began to move against the Crimean Tatars. By 1696, when Peter the Great (reigned 1682–1725), who initially ruled jointly with his sickly half-brother, Ivan V (reigned 1682–96), took sole charge of government, a vast empire was taking shape.

State and Society

The Russian imperial state was characterized by a strict social hierarchy, a centralized administration, and the pervasive influence of the Church, which made itself felt in every aspect of Russia's political and social life.

The Monarchy. Unification under the rule of Moscow was accompanied by the creation of a powerful monarchy. Executive, legislative, and judicial authority lay with the tsar, who controlled all military and civil appointments. Muscovite ceremony also endowed the Grand Duke with a semidivine status.

The power of the monarch, however, was limited by the difficulty of creating a stable army responsive to his will, collecting sufficient taxes to pay his soldiers, and supervising the ill-trained officials charged with the government's business. There were, nevertheless, few institutional checks on his authority.

In 1549 Ivan IV summoned the first ***zemsky sobor*** (Assembly of the Land), a consultative body, dominated by the nobility and clergy, which successive tsars convened periodically to debate proposed reforms. The assembly was responsible for electing Mikhail Romanov as tsar in 1613, although it ceased to exist in the later 17th century.

A more constant source of influence was the ***Boyars' Duma***, comprising members of the Muscovite aristocracy, large landowners whose families had long served Moscow (the ***boyars***), and the descendants of formerly independent princes. The tsar legislated and acted in consultation with the Duma, yet its limited authority was demonstrated in the 1560s by the **oprichnina**, a bizarre experiment in despotism. During the 17th century, the Duma grew in numbers to around 180; under Peter the Great it declined and eventually ceased to exist.

The Nobility. The political power of the Russian elite was limited by the fragile nature of their landed wealth. They did not practise primogeniture and noblemen's fortunes were very quickly dissipated among a multitude of descendants. To restore family fortunes,

▲ **Ivan the Terrible**
Known for his cruelty, Ivan killed his gifted son and heir in a fit of rage. This action provoked political turmoil in Russia; while Ivan was succeeded by another son, Fedor, power soon fell to his favourite, Boris Godunov.

Cossacks Free warriors of chiefly east Slavonic descent, whose independent communities emerged during the 15th and 16th centuries. Most were originally discontented peasants who fled to the south, southwest, and southeast to escape serfdom and religious oppression in both Poland-Lithuania and Muscovy. Cossack communities, known for their horsemanship, were given special privileges by Russian rulers in return for military service.

THE RULERS OF MOSCOW	
Ivan III	1462–1505
Vasily III	1505–33
Ivan IV (the Terrible)	1533–84
Fedor I	1584–98
Boris Godunov	1598–1605
(Time of Troubles	1598–1613)
Mikhail	1613–45
Alexis	1645–76
Fedor III	1676–82
Regent Sophia	1682–89
Ivan V	1682–96
Peter I (the Great)	1682–1725

◀ **Russian Serfs** *Serfs endured severe hardship and poor living conditions in 17th-century Russia. Their attempts to flee from their lords led to government repression, which in turn resulted in peasant uprisings.*

noblemen sought service with the tsar. Leading families were thus more concerned to compete for political and military positions, and to benefit from royal grants of land, than to check the arbitrary authority of the tsar.

Serfdom. From the 16th century, the nobility grew rapidly, while the peasantry were gradually made serfs (unfree peasants who were bound to the land they worked. See THE ENLIGHTENED DESPOTS). The process began under Ivan III, who made conditional grants of land in return for military service.

Under Ivan IV the number of service noblemen, ***pomeshchiks***, swelled. Many were dependent for their livelihood upon the income from the peasants who worked on their farms. The peasants, therefore, tended to flee to newly colonized lands to escape the harsh conditions imposed on them; the *pomeshchiks* thus urged the government to use the repressive power of the State to retain their peasants. In 1649, peasants were forbidden to leave their lords without permission. Peasant resistance to these restrictions was poorly organized; there were, nevertheless, serious uprisings throughout the 17th century.

Serfdom reflected and perpetuated Russia's social and economic backwardness. Although there was a gradual expansion in foreign and domestic trade, agricultural methods remained primitive, urban life developed slowly, and the occupants of towns held a humble position in the political and social hierarchy.

The Church. During the 15th and 16th centuries, the Church was enormously influential; Moscow became the seat of the metropolitan (head of the ecclesiastical province) in the early 14th century, which contributed significantly to the rise of the principality. The Church played a pervasive role in the everyday life of the population. It benefited from the regular bequests of noblemen and was immune from various taxes. Its political power was considerable. During the Time of Troubles the patriarchate (established in 1589) became a vital focus of authority; the Church rallied the forces that drove out the Poles and established the Romanovs on the throne.

During the 17th century, however, the position of the Church became more defensive. Both the government and the *pomeshchiks* coveted its great landed wealth; repeated steps were taken to raise the Church's contribution to the state budget and to prevent more land coming under clerical control. The Church's spiritual hegemony was threatened following the absorption into Russia of the eastern Ukraine, where Orthodoxy had adopted some of the methods and ideas of the Counter-Reformation. A series of liturgical reforms were introduced partly to forestall foreign influences. Resistance to these reforms led, in the 1660s, to a major schism. The Church's reliance upon secular power, fines, torture, and execution made it increasingly dependent on, and subordinate to, the state.

The gradual decline in the influence of the Church, together with growing diplomatic, military, and commercial exchanges with western Europe, encouraged a measure of secularization and westernization in Russian culture. By 1700, this process had made little impact on the majority of Russian people, although its influences did affect the lifestyle of a small proportion of the elite.

The Oprichnina

In 1565 Ivan IV designated one-third of the country as his personal domain. He created a ruthless army of *oprichniks* to impose his will directly. They carried out a bloody assault upon leading boyars (many of them members of the Duma), churchmen, monasteries, and peasants to remove then from their land. Novgorod, which opposed Muscovite dominance, was also sacked.

A THIRD ROME

The notion of Moscow as the 'Third Rome,' heir to ancient Rome and Constantinople and the centre of true Christianity, became an important element in tsarist rhetoric and ideology. The image of the twin-headed eagle, inherited from Byzantium, was adopted as the royal emblem. Monarchical pretensions were enhanced when, from the reign of Ivan IV, the grand dukes were also crowned tsar (derived from the title 'Caesar'). This imperial ideology is expressed in a letter of 1510 from Abbot Philotheus of Pskov to Vasily III:

"Two Romes have fallen, the third (Moscow) stands, and a fourth there shall not be."

The Enlightened Despots

The Ancien Régime • Reforms • Prussia • Austria • Russia •
The end of the enlightened despots

From 1697 to 1789 Europe enjoyed relative stability, despite the threats posed by dynastic intrigues – such as the War of the Spanish Succession (1701–14) – commercial rivalries, and the intense intellectual ferment created by the Enlightenment. Culturally, Europe was dominated by France. French art, literature, and diplomacy influenced many European courts, while the Treaty of Utrecht (1713–14) had secured French frontiers, ending France's attempts at European expansion.

The sociopolitical order that dominated 17th- and early 18th-century Europe was characterized by absolutist rule and aristocratic privilege. This system anticipated the emergence, in the 1740s, of the 'enlightened despots' – a term coined in 1767 by the French writer Mercier de la Rivière (1720–94). These new absolutist rulers championed the ideas of the Enlightenment, introducing significant reforms to their countries. However, despite their promotion of advancement in the arts and sciences, their actions often failed to reflect their high-minded ideals; consequently the fundamental elements of the old order – the ***Ancien Régime*** – survived for a further half-century.

The Ancien Régime

The term 'Ancien Régime' was used by the French Revolutionaries to describe the established social and political system that they had overthrown in 1789. Inequality lay at the very heart of this system: a small minority owned the land; taxation laws and the penal code disadvantaged the poor in favour of the aristocracy and the clergy; and peasants were still subjected to many feudal obligations. In many countries, serfdom remained the chief mode of social organization, as the ruling elite regarded the masses as an ignorant and potentially disruptive force to be kept under strict control. Even in nations that were more socially advanced, public opinion was only just beginning to emerge as an influential element in the affairs of state.

Monarchical rule was absolute; according to the concept of the 'natural order' that had existed since the Middle Ages, monarchs were held to derive their authority directly from God and to rule by 'divine right.' There were strong practical bonds between Church and state, with many ministers being members of the ecclesiastical hierarchy. As the nature of God, or at least of established religion, came to be

===== SEE ALSO =====
This section:
● Absolute Monarchy
  and Bourbon Dominance
● The French Revolution
  and Napoleonic Europe
North America:
● The United States
  of America
**European and American
Literature (vol. 4):**
● The Age of Reason
Philosophy (vol. 6):
● Ethics
**Politics and Government
(vol. 6):**
● Introduction

◄ ▲ **Catherine the Great of Russia and Moscow during her Reign** *Catherine II (above) epitomized the enlightened despots of the age, combining absolute rule with Enlightenment ideas. Although the Russian capital was transferred to St Petersburg in 1712, industry and the arts flourished in Moscow (left) throughout her reign (1762–96).*

> Graft a prince onto...a philosopher and you will have the perfect ruler.
>
> Denis Diderot,
> *L'Encyclopédie* (1751)

THE ENLIGHTENMENT

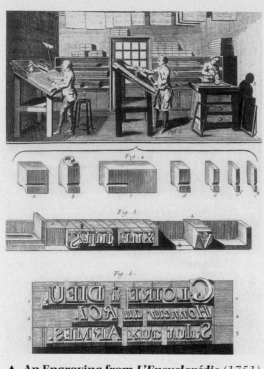

▲ **An Engraving from *L'Encyclopédie* (1751)**
This work, edited by Diderot, was a key text of the Enlightenment.

The origins of the Enlightenment, or ***Age of Reason***, lie in the scientific advances of the 17th century, which challenged the traditional Christian view of both the physical and the metaphysical world.

According to the philosopher Immanuel Kant (1724–1804), "Enlightenment is man's release from his self-incurred tutelage. Tutelage is man's inability to make use of his understanding without direction from another." This formed a common theme of the Enlightenment. Other recurrent ideas were equality, liberty, and natural law.

Reliance on reason undermined many religious orthodoxies and gave rise to ***Deism*** – the belief that God is a rational creator, a 'celestial watchmaker.' Many philosophers regarded the established Church as perpetuating superstitious beliefs.

The Enlightenment was not a unified movement; its philosophies varied among different countries and individual writers. Leading figures of the Enlightenment include the Baron de la Brède et de Montesquieu (1689-1755), René Descartes (1596–1650), Isaac Newton (1642–1727), Voltaire (1694–1778), and Denis Diderot (1713–84).

The Philosophes

A group of French 18th-century thinkers, whose belief in the supremacy of reason was expressed in their commitment to social and political reform. Among them were the writers Voltaire and Diderot, the mathematician the Marquis de Condorcet (1743–94), and the philosopher Jean Jacques Rousseau (1712–78). Philosophe economists, such as François Quesnay (1649–1774), were known as the ***physiocrats***; they argued that agriculture should take precedence over industry and mercantile interests.

questioned, so the divine right of kings was also doubted. During the 18th century, such questions provoked a debate on the nature of sovereignty, and whether it resided with a nation's monarch or its people.

Under the enlightened despots, varying degrees of social and political reform were instituted in the powerful nation-states of Prussia, Austria, and Russia. Reforming monarchs also reigned during this period in Sweden, Spain, and some Italian states (e.g. Tuscany). Despite the fact that France was the birthplace of so many of the leading Enlightenment figures – notably the **philosophes** – the absolutist regime of Louis XV (1715–74) cannot in itself be regarded as enlightened.

Reforms

Apart from their obvious liberalizing effect, Enlightenment ideas were also used by absolutist rulers to strengthen their power and to protect the state from both internal and foreign adversaries. In some cases, monarchs adapted programmes of reform already inaugurated by their predecessors to the new philosophies.

The reform programmes of the various absolute rulers in Europe had common themes; the monarchs believed that certain basic ideas could facilitate more efficient government of their countries. These included the concepts of natural law, equality before the law, reduction of the privileges of the nobility, education, religious toleration, and secularization of moral and physical welfare. Often priority was given to unifying and codifying the law, a powerful tool of state supremacy. While uniformity of laws within a kingdom and equality before the law can help to reduce privilege, legal reform was intended to counter the local autonomy that existed in such large and diverse kingdoms as that of the Hapsburgs, which comprised several countries with distinct laws and customs. Concern for the economy motivated fiscal reform; a fairer tax system not only alleviated the burden on the peasantry but also created more revenue for the government.

The importance of education at all levels was recognized by Enlightenment writers. Education of the masses was a complex issue that aroused diverse opinions. For the enlightened despots, an educated populace meant improved methods of agriculture and more efficient industrial workers and army recruits. Monarchs who were eager to free their governments from the influence of the Church favoured secular schools and universities as a source of civil servants.

Religious tolerance and anticlericalism were also prevalent; one of the objectives of the enlightened despots was to make the Church answerable to the state. The attempt to reduce ecclesiastical influence on everyday life reflected the Enlightenment's search for a new form of social morality, based on the mutual dependence of individuals, sociability, and compassion. The three secular virtues of humanity, toleration, and philanthropy (in place of Christian charity) were advocated by opponents of the old religious order. These were constant themes of the reforms, although each ruler had different problems to address.

Prussia

Frederick II (reigned 1740–86), king of Prussia, is often regarded as the epitome of the philosopher king, an image he was concerned to cultivate. In his youth he suffered great brutality from his soldier-king father, Frederick William I, because of his preference for the arts over the supposedly more fitting pursuits of statecraft and warfare. As king, he invited Voltaire to his palace of Sans Souci in Potsdam, where he remained for four years. During his reign he introduced a free press, abolished legal torture, restored the Academy of Science, and promoted elementary education. However, as a result of the vital role played by the army in the Seven Years' War – which marked Prussia's emergence as leader of the German states – Prussia continued to be dominated by the military; Frederick spent over half the country's revenue on maintaining an army of 160 000 men. He maintained

▲ **Frederick the Great** *Frederick II – who built Prussia into a formidable military and industrial power – is shown in this portrait (c. 1745) by Antoine Pesne.*

his father's direct personal 'cabinet' rule, increasingly circumventing the General Directory, the chief administrative body. Regarding himself as the first servant of the state, rather than an embodiment of it, he looked to his ministers for information rather than advice, and decentralized the bureaucracy.

Austria

Joseph II of Austria, Holy Roman Emperor (reigned 1765–90), lacked a broad education but showed an intelligent interest in statecraft. Although he was co-regent with his mother, Maria Theresa (archduchess 1740–80) from 1765, his lack of any genuine power led to frustrated ambition. He disliked any form of autonomous body, including the Church, believing that the army, clergy, and judiciary should be state servants. He wanted to combine universities, intermediate schools, and primary schools into one educational system under government control.

After gaining sole power in 1780, he began a major policy of centralization, reorganizing the army in order to secure Austria's status as a major European power. Joseph ordered the abolition of **serfdom** and, by the Edict of Toleration (1781), established religious equality in law and granted freedom of the press. His legal code, the *Josephina*, was opposed in various parts of the empire. He established a census with the intention of introducing a more equitable tax system, but his reforms were not completed. Joseph's reforms often foundered on provincial opposition, as he underestimated the cultural independence of his diverse subjects.

Russia

Under Peter the Great (reigned 1682–1725), Russia began to look westward and its policies became less isolationist. His reforms, including those of the tax system, were devised to increase industrial performance. The army and the civil service were reformed to ensure that promotion was by merit alone.

When Peter the Great's grandson, Peter III (reigned Jan.–July 1762), succeeded to the throne it became clear that he was incompetent. He alienated the people and lost the army's loyalty by supporting Prussia in the Seven Years' War. By contrast, his wife Catherine (reigned 1762–96) was intelligent and ambitious. With the support of the army, she seized power in 1762 and proclaimed herself empress. Peter died eight days later in suspicious circumstances, leaving Catherine vulnerable to the ambitions of the nobility.

Catherine was, nevertheless, supported by enlightened elements of the aristocracy. She was well-read and proud of her associations with such luminaries of the Enlightenment as

> The splendour of the royal city, its life and order and abundance... would be nothing without the tens of thousands of human beings ready to be sacrificed. Men, horses, wagons, guns, ammunition: the streets are full of them. If only I could adequately describe the monstrous piece of clockwork spread out here before one's eyes!
>
> **Johann Wolfgang von Goethe**, describing Berlin under Frederick the Great

Serfdom

Serfs were unfree peasants. Unlike slaves, they had certain rights and rented land for their own use. In the 18th century, serfdom was still common in Bohemia, Austria, Silesia, Galicia, Moravia, Hungary, and Russia. In Russia there were gentry-owned and state-owned serfs. Gentry-owned serfs, who comprised half the country's population, had no rights in law.

Pragmatic Sanction
A royal edict, usually relating to matters of succession, issued as a fundamental law. In 1713 the Hapsburg Emperor Charles VI (1711–40) proclaimed a Pragmatic Sanction, settling the succession to all Austrian lands on his daughter Maria Theresa. His purpose was to keep these lands intact in perpetuity.

Diderot, who visited the Russian court. She began work on reforming the legal code, which had not been revised since 1649, producing the *Nakaz*, a 20-volume book of instructions for the Legislative Commission that covered all aspects of society. One of the principles it expressed was that "the people do not exist for the ruler but the ruler for the people." However, it was considered too liberal and was heavily modified by her ministers.

Catherine was more successful in reorganizing local than central government. However, the result did not promote local autonomy but rather instead the task of applying the will of the sovereign in remote areas.

The End of the Enlightened Despots
Religious contention was a common cause of both internal and international discord. In Prussia, Frederick's predecessors, who had been Calvinist in a predominantly Lutheran country, showed that toleration was not only enlightened but politically expedient as well. In Roman Catholic countries, ecclesiastical reform and the expulsion of the Jesuits contributed to a reduction of papal power and influence. However, despite a more lenient attitude to Protestants in Portugal, Spain, and France by the end of the 18th century, only in Austria were they granted formal toleration.

In matters of equality of opportunity and equity in law and taxation, the intention of the enlightened despots was not always to benefit their poorer subjects. Frederick's legislation protecting peasant land from encroachment by the nobility also sustained peasant recruitment for the army. He emancipated serfs on royal land but did little to persuade his noble landowners to do so. He fostered the Prussian nobility; the vast majority of higher civil servants and army officers were aristocrats. In Russia, Catherine also courted the aristocracy, chiefly by means of her 'Charter of the Nobility' (1785), which relieved them of all military obligation and exempted them from direct taxation. At the other end of the social scale, serfs had their right of petition against cruel masters repudiated. In Austria, Joseph II's insensitivity towards local wishes (e.g. his proposal, in 1784, to exchange Bavaria for the Austrian Netherlands) provoked growing opposition.

Although the legacy of Joseph's reforms lasted into the 19th century, it was in Austria that the decline of enlightened despotism was most apparent. By 1788 the emperor's health was failing, the Austrian Netherlands were in revolt, and his subjects in the Tyrol and Hungary also became restless. On 30 January 1790 he withdrew most of his reforms; this withdrawal coincided with a series of events that heralded a dramatic and violent conclusion to the age of the enlightened despots – the French Revolution.

18TH-CENTURY EUROPE: KEY EVENTS AND RULERS

1701–14	War of the Spanish Succession; the last of Louis XIV's wars of expansion
1711–40	Charles VI reigned as emperor of Austria
1714	Treaty of Utrecht ended the War of the Spanish Succession
1715	Death of Louis XIV of France; Louis XV ascended the French throne
1725	Death of Peter the Great, emperor of Russia; succeeeded by Catherine I (reigned 1725–27)
1733–35	War of the Polish Succession: Spain and France opposed Russia and Austria in support of rival claimants to the Polish throne
1738	Third Treaty of Vienna; Hapsburg dominance in northern Italy confirmed
1740–80	Maria Theresa became empress of Austria
1740–86	Frederick II reigned as king of Prussia
1740–48	War of the Austrian Succession, fought by Austria and Great Britain against Prussia, France, and Spain
1748	Silesia came under Prussian control after Peace of Aix-la Chapelle; Charles VI's **Pragmatic Sanction** confirmed
1756–63	Seven Years' War: its underlying causes were Anglo-French colonial rivalry and the struggle between Austria and Prussia for control of Germany
1762–96	Catherine II (Catherine the Great) reigned as empress of Russia
1763	Treaty of Hubertusburg and Peace of Paris; Silesia confirmed as Prussian territory
1765–90	Joseph II reigned as emperor of Austria
1772	First partition of Poland; a third of Polish territory ceded to Russia, Prussia, and Austria
1773	Suppression of Jesuits by Pope Clement XIV (reigned 1769–74)
1774–92	Louis XVI reigned as king of France
1778	France began to aided US rebels in the American Revolution (1775–83)
1789	Beginning of the French Revolution

The French Revolution and Napoleonic Europe

*The 'Great Fear' and economic unrest • The end of the monarchy •
Counter-revolution and the Terror • The Directory •
The rise of Napoleon • Napoleon's zenith and decline*

The French Revolution – events in France at the end of the 18th century that led to the overthrow of the Bourbon monarchy and the creation of the First French Republic – aimed to destroy feudalism and privilege. Its consequences for the whole of western Europe were momentous. However, it also resulted in the Reign of Terror in 1793–94 and the military dictatorship of Napoleon from 1799.

The chain of events that led to the Revolution began with the rejection by an Assembly of Notables and by the Paris **Parlement** (the highest judicial court in France) of a fiscal reform proposal (1787). In the following year, the 'Revolt of the Nobility' took place, as the Parlement of Paris, provincial parlements, the Assembly of Notables, and the court all refused to accept tax reform. King Louis XVI (reigned 1774–92) was thus forced to agree to a summoning of the **Estates-General**.

When the Estates-General met at Versailles on 5 May 1789, a crucial issue was whether voting should be by 'head' or by 'order.' By separate order, the nobility and clergy could always combine to outvote the professional classes; by head, however, the third estate would dominate the two privileged orders. After much fruitless debate, the third estate declared itself to be the 'National Assembly' on 17 June. Barred from its meeting place, the Assembly met on 20 June in a tennis court, where it took the 'Tennis Court Oath' not to disband until a constitution was agreed. Louis rejected the Assembly's demands, summoned troops to Paris, and dismissed his popular finance minister, Jacques Necker (1732–1804).

Outraged citizens took up arms to defend the Assembly. On 14 July 1789 they stormed the Bastille prison, a hated symbol of the established order. The next day the electors of Paris organized themselves into the Commune as the city authority. The king responded by recalling Necker to office. The Estates General, now all meeting together, proceeded with reforms. On the night of 4 August a series of decrees effectively ended the structure of the old regime, abolishing feudal rights and privileges. On 27 August, the Declaration of the Rights of Man and the Citizen was proclaimed, which became the manifesto of the Revolution.

The 'Great Fear' and Economic Unrest

These events occurred against a backdrop of popular unrest, both in Paris and in the provinces. In late July and early August 1789 a widespread sense of alarm, known as the 'Great Fear,' arose, prompted by popular fear of brigands and of famine. Local uprisings resulted in the destruction of records of feudal dues and the burning of chateaux, the ancestral homes of the landowning classes.

On 6 October 1789 a mob marched from Paris to Versailles, seized the king and his family, and imprisoned them in Paris. Meanwhile the Constituent Assembly, as the National Assembly was now called, approved a number of reforms; for example, in February 1790 the country was divided into 83 departments, and Paris into 48 sections, each with its own local government. These changes were intended to herald a new style of government, based around a constitutional monarchy. Although Louis XVI appeared to accept these reforms, neither he nor his queen, Marie Antoinette (1755–93), were reconciled to the changes. As a sister of the Austrian Emperor Leopold II (reigned 1790–92), the autocratic Marie Antoinette continued to intrigue with foreign courts to reverse developments in France.

===SEE ALSO===
This section:
• Absolute Monarchy and Bourbon Dominance
• The Enlightened Despots
European and American Literature (vol.4):
• Romanticism and Reaction

Estates-General
The national assembly representing the three orders ('estates') of French society: the clergy, the nobility, and the third estate of professional classes.

Storming the Bastille *The infamous Parisian fortress was taken by revolutionary forces in July 1789.*▼

▲ **The Guillotine**
*An instrument of
capital punishment
used to decapitate
people, the guillotine
became a famous
symbol of the French
Revolution. It was
invented by the
Parisian surgeon
Joseph-Ignace Guillotin
(1738–1814).*

▲ **Georges-Jacques
Danton** *Danton, who
was minister of justice
from 1792, advocated
moderation of the
Terror. He was tried for
conspiracy to overthrow
the state and guillotined
in April 1794.*

The End of the Monarchy

A major turning point of the Revolution came
in June 1790 with the ***Civil Constitution of
the Clergy***. This gave the secular authorities
control over the administration of the Church.
The clergy were required to take an oath of
allegiance to the Constitution. When this act
was denounced by the pope in April 1791, it
became impossible to be loyal to both the state
and to the Roman Catholic Church. A royalist
counter-revolution in June 1791, during
which the king attempted to flee the country
with his family, failed when they were recognized and arrested. The royal family was thus
seen to have broken trust with the Revolution.

On 20 July 1791, in the Champs de Mars,
the National Guard fired on a crowd petitioning for a republic. The crisis deepened on 27
August 1791, when the Austrian emperor
and the king of Prussia jointly issued the
Declaration of Pillnitz, which raised the possibility of intervening to protect Louis. The king
accepted a slightly modified constitution on
13 September.

On 1 October 1791 the Legislative Assembly, which replaced the Constituent Assembly,
met for the first time. Legislation to consolidate the Revolution was agreed; for example,
the property of nobles who had fled the country was to be seized and uncooperative clerics
brought into line. The Revolution, however,
remained insecure, owing to problems of finance, a real or imagined threat of foreign
intervention, and factional politics. Populist
radicalism was in the ascendant in Paris; the
Paris Commune now emerged as a force to
rival the Legislative Assembly. The ***Girondins***
(moderates from the Gironde area of southwest France), then dominant in the Assembly,
thought that a foreign war would be the best
means of sustaining the Revolution. On 20
April 1792 they persuaded the Legislative Assembly to declare war on Austria. France was
to remain almost constantly at war during the
revolutionary period.

Louis's vetoing of certain pieces of legislation, and a radical government proposal to
garrison 20 000 revolutionary troops in Paris,
were signs of the continuing rift between state
and crown. This growing tension, particularly
in Paris, was reflected in the government's
declaration, on 11 July 1792, of a state of
emergency, to which fresh urgency was added
by the Declaration of Brunswick, on behalf of
the allied powers (Austria and Prussia). This
threatened an attack on Paris if the royal family was harmed. On 10 August the Tuileries (a
royal residence in Paris) was attacked by the
National Guard, revolutionary troops, and
sans-culottes ('without breeches'), radicals
from the poorer classes. The fate of Louis, who
had taken refuge in the Assembly, was sealed.

The power struggle in the Assembly continued. The majority were opposed to the republicanism favoured by the Paris Commune. By
intrigue and intimidation, orchestrated by
Georges-Jacques Danton (1759–94), the
Commune's power grew. With the threat of
invasion, 'enemies of the Revolution' were imprisoned; many of them were murdered later
that year in the September Massacres.

On 20 September the revolutionary army
beat the combined forces of Austria and Prussia at Valmy. On the same day the new legislature, the National Convention, met for the first
time. On 21 September, France was declared a
republic. The king was tried, found guilty of
treason, and executed on 21 January 1793.
This act further provoked the hostility of foreign powers; by mid-1793, France was at war
with most western European powers, including Austria, Britain, Prussia, and Spain.

Counter-revolution and the Terror

War brought conscription, provoking great
hostility and leading to a major uprising
against the Revolution in the Vendée area
of western France. This spontaneous insurrection of ordinary people in support of the
traditional clergy against revolutionary interference was backed by royalist elements. The
counter-revolutionaries defeated republican
forces sent to quell them and threatened to
march on Paris through northern France.
Their failure to capture Nantes in June,
however, signalled their downfall, although
bitter fighting continued for several months.
Reprisals claimed some 15 000 victims. Pockets of resistance remained in Brittany until an
amnesty was declared in December 1794.

By the autumn of 1793, the Revolution was
becoming increasingly radical. An uneasy
alliance between various radical groups led to
the purge of the Girondins. By the law of 14
Frimaire (4 December) 1793, according to the
new revolutionary calendar, the victorious
Jacobins tightened their centralizing hold
on government. Internal conflict continued
throughout the winter of 1793–94. With the
fall of rival factions, notably the Dantonists,
Maximilien Robespierre (1758–94) and his
followers held supreme power. Their law of 22
Prairial (10 June) 1794, which reformed the
Revolutionary Tribunal in order to gain more
convictions, resulted in a bloody climax to the
Reign of Terror, during which thousands were
executed. However, many members of the
Convention were either so appalled at these
excesses or fearful for their own safety that,
when Robespierre denounced continued corruption in the Convention, they turned on him
in the coup of 9 Thermidor (27 July) 1794.
Robespierre and more than 100 of his supporters were guillotined by the end of July.

The Thermidorian Convention. The Convention began to dismantle much of the previous legislation. On 1 August 1794 the law of 22 Prairial was repealed (thus limiting the power of the Revolutionary Tribunal, which was eventually abolished in May 1795), and the Jacobin Club was closed. These measures met with popular opposition; the Paris sections rose in revolt in April 1795, but were suppressed. The return of the monarchy had been virtually ruled out when, on 24 June 1795, Louis XVIII, brother of the executed king, issued the Declaration of Verona, threatening revenge on revolutionaries in the event of his return.

The Directory
By the autumn of 1795, the Convention had completed the drafting of a new constitution intended to ensure the continuance of a republican form of government. It established a legislature consisting of a Council of Elders and a Council of Five Hundred, with the executive entrusted to five Directors (the Directory). An attempt was made to oppose the new constitution on 13 Vendémiaire (5 October) 1795 by a crowd consisting of bourgeois from the more prosperous Paris sections, National Guards, royalists, and aristocrats. The crowd was dispersed by fire from artillery under the command of Napoleon Bonaparte (1769–1821), then a prominent young officer. The people were no longer strong enough to impose their will on the Convention by direct action.

The new constitution under the Directory was inaugurated on 27 October 1795. However, instability continued. Defeats by Austrian and Austro-Russian forces in early 1799 discredited the government. Napoleon's arrival in Paris in October sparked a new wave of political intrigue. His military prowess had won

---

REVOLUTIONARY REFORMS

The ***revolutionary calendar*** was devised as a replacement for the Gregorian calendar, which was associated with the Church. 'Year 1' of the new era, which was dated from the proclamation of the republic, began on 22 September 1792. The 12 months of the revolutionary calendar were given names derived from nature (e.g. *Brumaire*, the 'fog month'), while periods of ten days ('decades') replaced the seven-day week; each month consisted of three decades. The five days left at the end of the year were known as the ***sans-culottides***, feast days in honour of the sans-culottes. The calendar was introduced in October 1793, and was abolished by Napoleon on 31 December 1806.

Metrication was initiated by the National Assembly in March 1791 to replace a great variety of units of weights and measures. In the new system, the common unit of length – the metre – was one ten-millionth part of the quadrant of the earth's meridian through Paris.

▲ **Maximilien Robespierre**
This contemporary portrait shows the austere and 'incorruptible' advocate of a 'Republic of Virtue,' who held supreme power from March to July 1794.

---

him widespread popular support. The tide of public opinion had turned against radical revolution. In a coup staged on 18 Brumaire (9 November) 1799, Napoleon established the Consulate in place of the ousted Directory. The new constitution of December 1799 declared the Revolution completed. A general amnesty of October 1800 for all those who had taken up arms against the Republic confirmed that the radical Jacobins were now in the political wilderness. They had, nevertheless, played a crucial role in a revolution that had repercussions far beyond France's frontiers.

Jacobins
The Jacobins, a radical republican club, were the most prominent of the revolutionary organizations. The group was named after its meeting place, a former Dominican monastery of St James (St Jacques), in Paris .

◀ **A Prison Tribunal**
(1792) Trials of imprisoned aristocrats were conducted by revolutionary tribunals. The revolutionaries are wearing the so-called 'Phrygian bonnet,' a red cap that imitated those worn by freed slaves in ancient Rome and which, from 1792, became an official emblem of state in revolutionary France.

▲ **The *Légion d'Honneur*** *In 1802, Napoleon inaugurated the Legion d'Honneur as a means of rewarding service to the state. This and other forms of patronage made many fear the introduction of new forms of social hierarchy in France.*

The Rise of Napoleon

Napoleon Bonaparte is regarded as one of the greatest of all military leaders. He was also an outstanding ruler and has been described as the last 'enlightened despot.' Napoleon was born in Ajaccio, Corsica, to Charles-Marie (1746–85) and Letizia (c. 1750–1836) Buonaparte (Napoleon later changed the name to Bonaparte). He was sent to military school in France at the age of nine and in 1785 was commissioned into an artillery regiment.

After the French had stemmed the tide of invasion at the Battle of Valmy in September 1792, the Revolutionary army went on to the offensive. The principal objective was now to secure the 'natural frontiers' of France: the Pyrenees, the Alps, and the Rhine. Within months, the army had occupied Nice and Savoy and driven the Austrian garrison from the Austrian Netherlands (modern Belgium), seizing Antwerp. These gains precipitated war with Britain and the formation of the First Coalition between Austria, Prussia, and Britain. French successes continued with the final defeat of the Austrian Netherlands at the Battle of Fleurus (26 June 1794).

Napoleon first came to prominence in 1793 as a colonel in command of artillery at Toulon, then under siege from an Anglo-Spanish naval force. He was not only imbued with a revolutionary fervour, but also benefited from the decline of the culture of privilege that had characterized the Ancien Régime. His close association with the Jacobins caused his fall from favour after Robespierre's execution, but his quelling of the royalist uprising in October 1795 restored his standing.

Early in the rule of the Directory, French armies began to suffer setbacks. Napoleon restored French fortunes in Italy by defeating the Austrians at Rivoli (14 January 1797) and then advancing on Vienna. Austria sued for peace in the Treaty of Campo Formio (17 October 1797), accepting the terms that Napoleon imposed on his own authority. By this treaty, Austria ceded to France her possessions on the west bank of the Rhine and recognized the Cisalpine Republic, created by France in Lombardy – territory that had formerly belonged to Austria.

Egypt and the Coup d'Etat. In 1798 Napoleon embarked on an expedition to Egypt in an attempt to challenge Britain's trade and colonial supremacy. He defeated the rulers of Egypt – the Mamelukes – at the Battle of the Pyramids (21 July), but shortly afterwards his fleet was destroyed by the British navy, commanded by Admiral Horatio Nelson (1758–1805), at the Battle of the Nile (1 August 1798). Napoleon's subsequent attempt to invade Syria was thwarted by a successful defence of Acre. Abandoning his army in Egypt, he returned to France, where he was received with great acclaim. With the help of his brother Lucien (1775–1840), president of the council ruling France, he overthrew the Directory in the coup of 18 Brumaire (9 November) 1799. Three consuls were appointed to rule France, with Napoleon himself wielding virtually sole authority as First Consul.

A military campaign was then mounted against Austria, ending with Napoleon's defeat of Austria at the Battle of Marengo (14 June 1800) and the Treaty of Lunéville

The Napoleonic Empire in 1812 ▶

At its height, the Napoleonic Empire incorporated most of western Europe. Napoleon's ambition was to create a united Europe under French control. States controlled by, or allied with, the French Empire under Napoleon are shown here. Major engagements in the Napoleonic Wars are also indicated.

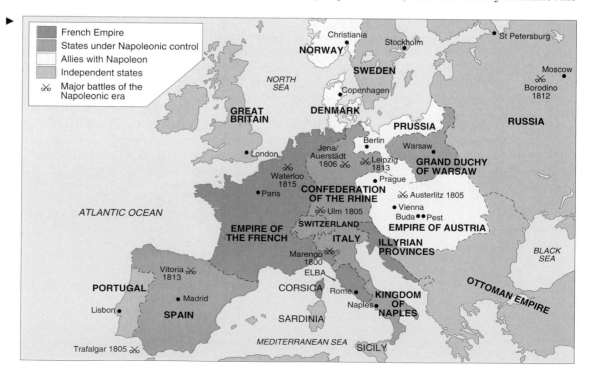

French Empire
States under Napoleonic control
Allies with Napoleon
Independent states
✂ Major battles of the Napoleonic era

Christiania · Stockholm · St Petersburg
NORWAY
SWEDEN · Moscow
NORTH SEA · Copenhagen · Borodino 1812
GREAT BRITAIN · DENMARK
· London · Berlin · Warsaw
Jena/Auerstädt 1806 · Leipzig 1813 · GRAND DUCHY OF WARSAW
Waterloo 1815 · Prague
· Paris · CONFEDERATION OF THE RHINE · Austerlitz 1805
ATLANTIC OCEAN · Vienna
· Ulm 1805 · Buda · Pest
EMPIRE OF THE FRENCH · SWITZERLAND · EMPIRE OF AUSTRIA
ITALY · ILLYRIAN PROVINCES
Marengo 1800 · BLACK SEA
Vitoria 1813 · ELBA
PORTUGAL · CORSICA · Rome · KINGDOM OF NAPLES · OTTOMAN EMPIRE
· Madrid · Naples
Lisbon · SPAIN · SARDINIA
MEDITERRANEAN SEA · SICILY
Trafalgar 1805
PRUSSIA · RUSSIA

(9 February 1801). Unwilling to continue the war unaided, Britain signed a peace treaty at Amiens (27 March 1802).

Napoleon's Zenith and Decline

In May 1803, Britain annulled the peace with France (followed by Austria in August 1805), in reaction to acts of aggression by Napoleon and the French desire for hegemony in Europe. This was epitomized by Napoleon's own personal ascendancy, culminating in 1804 when he declared himself emperor. A quick succession of French military victories saw Napoleon attain the pinnacle of his power. In 1805, the Austrians were defeated first at Ulm (17 October) and then at Austerlitz (2 December), where Napoleon achieved a conclusive victory over a combined Austrian and Russian army. Prussia, in turn, suffered a severe defeat at Jena and Auerstädt (14 October 1806). In 1807 Napoleon defeated combined Russian and Prussian armies at Eylau (7–8 February) and Friedland (14 June).

Only Britain remained undefeated, thanks to her command of the sea. Napoleon had assembled a vast army at Boulogne for the invasion of England, but after the French fleet was again destroyed by Nelson at the Battle of Trafalgar (21 October 1805) he abandoned this project in favour of economic warfare. In a campaign known as the **Continental System** (inaugurated 1806), he tried to use his control of the coastline from the Baltic to the Adriatic to impose a trade blockade on Britain and so force peace on his terms. However, this system proved impossible to enforce.

The First Reverse. In 1807 Napoleon sent an army to Portugal to enforce the Continental System. The subsequent Peninsular War (1807–14) became a constant drain on French resources. In 1808 Napoleon forced the king of Spain to abdicate in favour of his own brother Joseph Bonaparte (1768–1844). This led to a national uprising in Spain and provided the opportunity for British forces to attack the Napoleonic Empire.

The Russian Campaign. By 1812 relations between France and Russia had broken down as a result of the adverse effect on Russia of the Continental System. Napoleon raised an army of some 450 000 troops and invaded Russia on 24 June 1812. After indecisive engagements at Smolensk (16–18 August) and Borodino (7 September), Napoleon reached Moscow on 14 September, having already lost half his men. Finding the city in flames, he waited in vain for the tsar to sue for peace. On 19 October, as winter approached, he began a disastrous retreat. Fewer than 50 000 men survived Russian attacks, starvation, and freezing temperatures. This disaster marked the beginning of Napoleon's downfall.

▲ *Bonaparte Crossing the Alps* (1821) *This painting, by the French artist Jacques-Louis David (1748–1825), captures the pomp and glory of the Napoleonic era.*

Exile to Elba and the 'Hundred Days.' In 1813, after having suffered defeat at the hands of a combined Austrian, Prussian, and Russian army at the Battle of Leipzig (16–19 October), Napoleon surrendered and was exiled to the island of Elba. His empire was dismantled by the allies at the Congress of Vienna (October 1814–June 1815). The Bourbon monarchy under Louis XVIII (reigned 1814–24) was restored, yet proved unpopular. Napoleon escaped from Elba and returned to France on 1 March 1815 to resume power for the so-called 'Hundred Days' (20 March–29 June). An allied force comprising the Prussian army under General Gebhard von Blücher (1742–1819) and British, Dutch, and German troops commanded by the Duke of Wellington (1769–1852) defeated Napoleon at the Battle of Waterloo, south of Brussels, on 18 June 1815. Napoleon fled to Paris and abdicated. He was exiled to the island of St Helena in the South Atlantic Ocean, where he died on 5 May 1821.

Napoleonic Reforms

Napoleon enacted a programme of reform based on Enlightenment ideas of equality before the law, curtailment of privilege and feudal rights, and liberty of conscience. A new emphasis was placed instead on property rights. Napoleon continued classification of the judicial system and codification of laws. The civil code issued between 1804 and 1810 (named the 'Code Napoléon' in 1807) remains the basis of the French legal system. Napoleon also instituted other important reforms, such as a revised educational system and a Bank of France.

THE INDUSTRIAL AGE IN EUROPE

Industrial Revolution

The process of industrialization • The origins of the Industrial Revolution •
Effects of industrialization • Steam power • The growth of industrial societies

One of the greatest changes to occur in the history of Europe was **industrialization**. It was the process by which, between the mid-18th and the early 20th centuries, Europe was transformed from a society with an agricultural base to one in which the majority of people worked in industry or commerce and lived in towns. It dramatically affected population, standards of living, education, the environment, politics, and other facets of society. While industrialization began in Europe, it spread in varying forms throughout the world, facilitating the development of a world economy, which was to undergo continual technological evolution and growth.

The Process of Industrialization

A fundamental characteristic of industrialization was **mechanization**: the increased use of machines to perform manufacturing processes more efficiently than by manual labour. Others were the application of science to increase efficiency, the greatly increased use of minerals (coal and oil) as fuels and as raw materials, and geographical integration through improved communications and transport. These changes led to rapid growth in the output of goods and materials as well as to reductions in production and retail costs.

Several organizational changes occurred in industry, notably **centralization** of production into large units and **specialization**, in which communities made one product for a widespread market, rather than a variety of goods for local needs. Mechanization and centralization reduced the importance of labour and increased the importance of capital (buildings and equipment), which created new relations between the owners and their employees.

The most immediate change that accompanied industrialization was **urbanization**, as large sections of populations migrated into towns. In most European countries before industrialization, approximately 70% of populations lived in rural areas; by 1914 the figure was 5–10%. Higher levels of industrial employment boosted expanding populations. Higher incomes and altered standards of living helped to create a more consumerist society.

Industrialization was not a planned process, but the result of many developments in different spheres. A culture of rapid technological development and economic change evolved, replacing the gradual pace of earlier societies. The process began with the **Industrial Revolution**: the first breakthrough, by a series of economic and technological developments, in the shift from an agricultural economy to an

Railway Steam Locomotives
► *(Early 19th century) The first modern railway, built for locomotives, passenger services, and public traffic, was opened in Britain in 1830. By 1840 there were over 3200 km of railway in Britain. At this time, no other country had more than a few hundred kilometres, though most had developed extensive networks by the 1880s.*

THE INDUSTRIALIZATION OF COAL MINING

Coal mining was one of the most important industries of the mid-18th to early 20th centuries; it thus provides an example of the ways in which industries changed and developed in Europe during industrialization. While coal had always been mined on a small scale, demand increased rapidly from the early 18th century, owing in particular to the supply required by ironworks and steam engines. Coal output soared dramatically, boosted by improved transportation, new mining technology, and greater investment. In Germany, for example, output increased from less than 1 million tons in 1760 to around 250 million tons by 1914.

Increased coal production meant that a number of technical mining problems needed to be addressed, such as coal cutting, transportation, ventilation, drainage, lighting, and power supply. Natural ventilation, for example, was not adequate for deeper mines; a forced draught had to be created – by furnaces or, later, by mechanical fans. The excess water that collected in mines was removed by pumps: the first were powered by horses or waterwheels. The advent of steam engines from the early 18th century, however, was a breakthrough; engine-driven pumps were widely used by the early 19th century. Similar developments occurred in methods of raising coal to the surface, for which steam engines were used from the 1780s. Coal cutting began to be mechanized from the late 19th century. Electricity for lighting and machinery was used widely before World War I. Improved mining techniques, scientific prospecting, and new transport routes allowed new coal reserves to be exploited.

In the early 18th century coal mines were mostly very small and mined coal only superficially by means of simple tools. By the early 20th century, however, most coal was produced from deep collieries employing several hundred workers, which used fully mechanized equipment. The owners of coal mines amassed vast wealth, while the industry employed millions of miners across Europe. Abundant cheap coal provided the foundation for industrialization.

Two Collieries in c. 1800 and c. 1910 *At the earlier mine (top), coal was carried by cart and wound up a thatch-lined shaft by a horse gin. The later mine (bottom) was served by railway. Steam engines powered fans, aerial ropeways, pumps, and winding devices; coal was sorted and cleaned in a large washery. These types of mines could employ up to 3000 miners.*

industrial one. The Industrial Revolution began in Britain in the later 18th century, spreading into western Europe and North America in the early 19th century.

The Origins of the Industrial Revolution
The Industrial Revolution was not a sudden event. Between the 16th and 18th centuries Europe developed complex patterns of trade, especially for textiles and metals, which prepared the way for increased centralization and specialization of production by establishing widespread markets and accumulating capital. There were improvements in commercial organization and in transport facilities, with more efficient shipping, wooden railways, better roads, and navigation of inland waterways. Colonization of the New World from the 16th

century provided new export markets and import trade. Population growth met new labour needs and expanded markets further.

Many industries evolved gradually throughout the 17th and 18th centuries. Important technological advances diffused through Europe, including the blast furnace for smelting iron, better mining techniques, and the industrial use of coal. New industries were also created, such as the manufacture of cotton textiles and tin-plating. A better understanding of scientific principles laid the foundations for the development of industrial technology.

Britain was well placed to be the first country to industrialize. By the mid-18th century it had highly developed internal and colonial trade networks, improved transportation systems, a growing population with rising

**Richard Arkwright
(1732–92)**
As an important entrepreneur of his time, Arkwright contributed to industrialization through technical invention, organizational innovation, and business growth. By 1769 he had developed the *water frame*, a machine powered by water for spinning cotton. He built the first water-powered cotton factory at Cromford in 1771, and later opened numerous others. These established many of the subsequent characteristics of factories, such as mass employment on a single site, powered machinery, shift work, and the provision of company housing.

puddling A process for converting pig (or crude) iron into wrought iron by heating it with iron oxide in a furnace to oxidize the carbon.

incomes, and industries already adopting new technologies. Britain also had the advantages of mineral wealth, an open social structure, and extended periods of relative peace.

Effects of Industrialization

While the Industrial Revolution (c. 1760–c. 1830) affected many industries in many countries, its effects were initially concentrated in Britain. The centralization of mines and textile workshops became common in this period, resulting in larger operations. Integrated ironworks were established from the 1750s. Influential factories were also built, such as the Birmingham metalwares factory of Matthew Boulton (1728–1809), which opened in 1769. Their enterprises established such industrial practices as worker discipline, shift work, specialization of duties, and integration of processes on one site. They provided economies of scale and improved control over production.

Mechanization was introduced into many processes, such as pumping and winding in mines and rolling in ironworks. Its greatest impact was probably in the labour-intensive textile industries. While the production of cotton was the first to mechanize, the mechanization of other fabrics was gradual; power spinning for wool was not practical until the 1820s. The power loom was introduced by Edmund Cartwright (1743–1823) in c. 1785, though it was many years before it was used to manufacture all fabrics.

Steam Power

Artificial power sources facilitated the use of larger machines. Waterwheels provided the primary source of power until the mid-19th century; although they were common earlier than this, they were applied to new purposes and improved with scientific knowledge. The real breakthrough of the Industrial Revolution

was advent of the steam engine, invented by Thomas Savery (?1650–1715) in 1698, and developed by Thomas Newcomen (1663–1729) in 1712. These engines were applied quickly to pumping in mines; however, it was not until they provided rotary motion, introduced by James Watt (1736–1819), from the late 18th century, that they were used in such processes as cotton spinning, flour milling, and iron rolling. Steam engines thereafter became faster and more powerful. Up to 3000 were installed in Britain by 1800.

The substitution of minerals for organic resources aided the growth of productivity. Coal was vital, especially in ironmaking; however, it could not fuel iron smelting until 1709, when Abraham Darby (1677–1717) discovered that it could be used if *coked* to remove its impurities. This process facilitated a huge expansion in output from the 1750s. The invention of **puddling** by Henry Cort (1740–1800) in 1784 enabled the use of coal to manufacture wrought iron.

Centralization, specialization, and use of mineral resources were dependent upon efficient transportation. From the mid-18th century in Britain, ports and vessels continued to develop, many new roads were built and others improved, and a network of canals (covering 6400 km) was constructed, which traversed the country, linking ports, coalfields, and towns. Horse-drawn railways linked canals to mines and factories. The first steam-driven railway locomotives were introduced by Richard Trevithick (1771–1833) in 1802; by the 1820s they were being widely used.

These changes resulted in a huge growth in output in Britain, from about the 1780s. New industries flourished: for example, engineering evolved to supply machinery; chemicals manufacturing, and gas supply developed to deal with by-products or supply materials.

The enormous industrial changes of the period caused most people, including children, to become wage-labourers. Working conditions, which, by modern standards, could be terrible, came to the attention and concern of legislators and labour organizations. Populations shifted towards towns, where industries and expanding services were based. Most towns had, at this stage, appalling sanitation and housing owing to their rapid growth. Britain's total population grew from 7.4 to 16.3 million between 1750 and 1830.

◀ **Power-Loom Weaving** (*Late 18th century*)
Cotton manufacturing led the way with the mechanization of carding in 1738 and the introduction of water-powered spinning by Arkwright's 'waterframe' in 1769. The speed of weaving was greatly increased by the 'flying shuttle' after 1733.

By c. 1830 Britain was home to the most advanced industries in Europe; it served a vast percentage of the world's markets in such commodities as coal, copper, cotton, tin plate, and iron. Centralized and mechanized factories or integrated ironworks had also been established in France, Belgium, Switzerland, Germany, and the USA by the 1790s, directly following British models. By the 1830s these countries had achieved a high level of industrialization; they, too, witnessed rapid growth in their output, urbanization, and population.

The Growth of Industrial Societies

The period c. 1830–c. 1914 saw the spread of industrialization across Europe and the continuing evolution of industry and of industrial societies. The first countries after Britain to industrialize were those with mineral resources or developing textile trades. Belgium, Germany, and the USA, in particular, had begun, by the mid-19th century, to compete with Britain in international markets. Areas surrounding coalfields tended to industrialize earlier than others. The exploitation of these areas, however, depended on cheap transport: coalfields near navigable waterways developed first, while others awaited the advent of railways in the mid-19th century. By 1850 industrialization was also progressing in Austria, Italy, Spain, Sweden, Russia, Japan, and other regions. By 1914 most European countries were industrialized.

Mechanization was applied more effectively and to a greater number of processes. Industrial-style methods were adopted in agricultural production in some areas. Centralization of production increased and the trend towards very large enterprises accelerated.

New Methods and Materials. Steam engines had become the major source of industrial power by the late 19th century, when new forms of power were introduced. Internal-combustion engines were developed from the 1860s. The use of electricity also became significant after the first power stations were built in the 1880s. The cheap production of high quality mild steel was made possible by the ***Bessemer process***, invented in 1855 by Sir Henry Bessemer (1813–98), facilitating more sophisticated applications of iron. The development of plastics began in the early 20th century. Mass production, using interchangeable components, increased manufacturing efficiency before World War I. Large industrial corporations flourished; many companies developed international interests, especially in overseas colonies. The demand for oil for internal-combustion engines stimulated foreign investment, which enforced a transformation in political relations between oil-importing and oil-exporting regions.

▲ **Berlin in 1896**
Rapid urban growth resulting from industrialization is illustrated in this view of Berlin, showing a landscape of factories and houses, through which runs a railway, providing a marked contrast to rural life.

Communications were improved dramatically between c. 1830 and 1914. Railways and steamships allowed the speedy transportation of people, information, and products, including perishable goods. In such countries as Russia, railways were crucial to industrialization as they provided a quickly assembled transportation network, which covered huge distances: Russia had approximately 107 000 km of railway by 1910. The use of steamships was widespread by 1870. Motor vehicles were developed and used from the 1890s. The communication of information was transformed by the advent of the electric telegraph, first successfully promoted in the USA (1837–39). The first transatlantic link was made in 1866. Practical radio transmission was first achieved by Guglielmo Marconi (1874–1937) in 1897.

Industrial Societies. Social change continued to intensify with population growth and urbanization. By 1914 there were 140 cities of over 100 000 people in Europe. Public authorities began to tackle problems of urban growth through building regulations, slum clearances, and sanitation measures. Disposable incomes continued to increase, accompanied by material improvements in standards of living much greater than those recorded during the Industrial Revolution. Poor working conditions prompted governments to introduce measures regulating child labour, working hours, and safety. Such problems stimulated the growth of labour movements; by World War I trades unions had become established in many countries. As education became more accessible to greater numbers of people, the proportion of skilled workers increased. This, together with the development of more fluid social structures in Europe, enhanced pressures for more democratic government and social reform.

> **Gottlieb Daimler (1834–1900)**
>
> A leading inventor in late 19th-century Germany, Daimler set up his own engineering company, in Stuttgart, to develop internal-combustion engines. His engine was based on the four-stroke engine patented by Nikolaus Otto (1832–91) in 1876. In 1889 he developed the first purpose-built four-wheel motor car. In 1890 he built 350 cars. Daimler combined with Karl Benz (1844–1929); in 1926, they formed the Daimler–Benz company.

Liberalism and Reaction

The Congress of Vienna • Liberal and national movements • The July Monarchy • Two new nations: Belgium and Greece • The German confederation • The growth of democracy in Britain • 1848: the year of revolutions

Europe in 1815 ▶
At the Congress of Vienna, the territories of the former Napoleonic Empire were restored to their former status. In northern Italy, Austria regained Lombardy and Venetia; Belgium and Holland were merged into the Kingdom of the Netherlands as a buffer state against France; Prussia acquired half of Saxony, Westphalia, and part of Poland; the remainder of Poland became part of the Russian Empire. A confederation of 39 German states was also created, the most powerful being Austria.

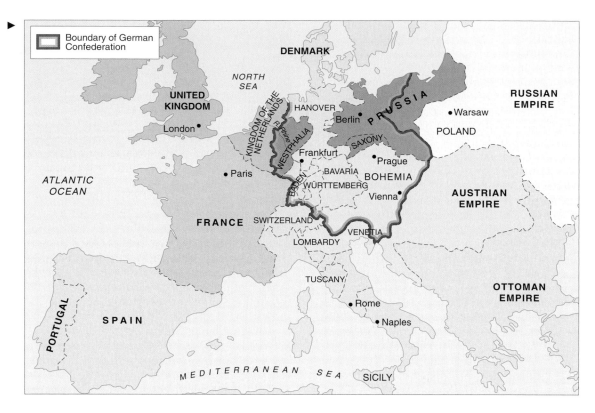

Prince Metternich

Klemens Metternich, Austrian foreign minister (1809 to 1848) and chancellor from 1812, was autocratic in outlook. He was the architect of the Congress System, created at the Congress of Vienna, which allied the four great powers against all revolutionary movements.

════SEE ALSO════
This section:
• Industrial Revolution
• Nationalism
 and Imperialism
Early Modern Europe:
• The French Revolution
 and Napoleonic Europe

The allied powers (Austria, Prussia, Russia, and Britain) that had defeated Napoleon at Waterloo (June 1815) were anxious to prevent any further spread of the revolutionary ideas that his occupying armies had been carrying to most of Europe since 1792. The Congress of Vienna, orchestrated by Austrian foreign minister, **Prince Metternich** (1773–1859), intended to restore the situation that had existed before the Napoleonic Wars and to use military force, if necessary, to maintain it.

The Congress of Vienna
The congress actually started before the Battle of Waterloo (October 1814), and continued until June 1815. Representatives of Austria, Prussia, Russia, and Britain negotiated over territories that Napoleon had liberated from monarchic rule in the creation of his European empire; as a result of the congress, these lands were restored to their former status.

In November 1815 the four powers signed the Quadruple Alliance for the "maintenance of the peace of Europe." The intention of Austria and Russia, in particular, was to return to traditional absolutist monarchy, as it existed

before the French Revolution. However, events had progressed too far to reverse the situation.

Liberal and National Movements
Almost immediately there were signs of discontent in several countries, mainly among young intellectuals, who had been exposed to liberal ideas, rather than the peasantry who, in most of Europe, were still largely illiterate. In Russia aristocratic, but anti-Tsarist, army officers formed secret societies (known as the **Decembrists**) from c. 1817 onward. They wanted to establish a constitutional monarchy, abolish serfdom, and liberalize the law. On the death of Alexander I (reigned 1801–25), they mounted an armed revolt and attempted to put their candidate, Count Constantine, on the throne. However, the revolt failed.

In Spain the peasantry had resisted French occupation. However, liberal ideas had taken root among the educated; in 1820 the army rebelled against the reactionary King Ferdinand VII (reigned 1808, 1814–33), demanding that he restore the Napoleonic constitution of 1812. A civil war was fought until 1823 when, ironically, a French army arrived and crushed the rebel forces. A similar conflict erupted in Portugal between monarchists and liberals; by 1828, however, absolutism had been re-established under Dom Miguel.

Italy was, at this time, divided into numerous kingdoms and principalities. In the kingdom of Naples and Sicily a rebellion broke out in 1820, demanding that the king's powers be limited by a constitution. It was not delivered and the rebellion continued until the Austrian army arrived and defeated the rebels (1821). In the same year there was a constitutionalist uprising in the north Italian kingdom of Piedmont. Although King Victor Emmanuel I (reigned 1802–21) abdicated, his successor called in Austrian troops to restore order. However, the movement for republicanism and unification could not be suppressed. **Giuseppe Mazzini** (1805–72) joined the secret Carbonari society, which had stimulated the revolts in Naples and Piedmont; in 1831 it sparked off further uprisings.

In France the exiled Napoleon had been replaced by a Bourbon king, Louis XVIII (reigned 1814–24). With British support, he ruled constitutionally, preserving many of the institutions of the Revolution; the electoral law of 1817, however, restricted the right to vote to only 80 000 wealthy citizens. France was deeply divided between conservative Catholic royalists and anticlerical constitutionalists; in 1820 outbreaks of violence led to the assassination of the Duc de Berry (1778–1820), the king's nephew and heir. This roused royalist fervour and Louis was forced to adopt repressive policies. On his death, in 1824, he was succeeded by his severely autocratic brother, Charles X (reigned 1824–30). It soon became clear that Charles intended to overthrow the constitution and institute absolutist rule.

The July Monarchy
In July 1830 the people of Paris manned the barricades; they deposed Charles X and replaced him with a constitutional monarch of their choice, Louis Philippe (reigned 1830–48). Though head of the Orléans branch of the French royal family, his father had been a revolutionary. Concerned with promoting domestic prosperity rather than waging costly wars, Louis was known as the 'Citizen King.' Although he encouraged the bourgeoisie to enrich themselves, the majority of the population remained exploited and voteless.

The deposition of Charles X had alarmed the reactionary Tsar Nicholas I of Russia (reigned 1825–55), who dispatched an army towards France. This was met by determined opposition in Warsaw, the capital of a much reduced Polish state. After a year-long struggle, the Poles were defeated and saw the vestiges of their nation swallowed up by Russia.

Two New Nations: Belgium and Greece
The French revolution of 1830 triggered an uprising in neighbouring Flanders, which had been incorporated into the Netherlands in 1815. The majority of the population were French-speaking Catholics, who resented Protestant Dutch rule. Although the new kingdom of Belgium declared its independence in 1830, it was not recognized by all of Europe until 1839.

On the other side of Europe, the Greeks, who had been ruled by the Ottoman Turks since 1453, rebelled in March 1821 and declared independence in January 1822. Turkey sent forces to quell the rebellion, which were initially successful. The Congress powers, however, were divided over the Greek question. Prussia and Austria refused to intervene in this liberal cause, while Russia, for strategic reasons, and Britain and France with idealistic motives, dispatched a fleet, which defeated the Turks off Navarino in 1827. In 1830 the rival powers found a compromise solution to the Greek question by inviting a Bavarian prince to be the first king of the Hellenes. However, the first serious crack had appeared in the Congress System.

The German Confederation
Although events in the German-speaking lands were less dramatic, they had greater long-term implications for Europe. During the Napoleonic Wars, the hundreds of German states that had existed previously were reduced to 39. In 1815 these were united into a

Giuseppe Mazzini

Having joined the secret Carbonari society, which aimed to overthrow Austrian rule in Italy, Giuseppe Mazzini was arrested and exiled in 1830; he returned in 1831 and founded the 'Young Italy' movement, which advocated the creation of a single Italian state. By 1833, the movement had 60 000 followers; however, subsequent uprisings were unsuccessful. From 1837 Mazzini spread his ideas of Italian nationhood by writing in exile. During 1848–49, with the assistance of his Italian compatriot, Giuseppe Garibaldi (1807–82), he created a short-lived Roman republic. Although Mazzini took little part in Garibaldi's campaign of 1859–60, he did live to see Italy unified.

CHRONOLOGY OF KEY EVENTS (1814–48)

1814–15	Congress of Vienna; Napoleon's final defeat at Waterloo (June 1815)
1817	Decembrists begin to form in Russia
1819	Murder of Kotzebue; Karlsbad Decrees
1820	Constitutional revolt in Cádiz, Spain
1821	Start of the Greek Revolt against Turkish rule
1824	Accession of Charles X to the French throne
1827	Britain and France destroy Turkish fleet at Navarino
1830	Revolution in Paris; Charles X abdicates; Louis Philippe chosen to become king
1831	Leopold I becomes constitutional monarch of Belgium; collapse of Warsaw revolt
1834	Zollverein formed; Austria excluded
1840	Frederick William IV crowned king of Prussia
1847	Frederick William calls a united German assembly
1848	Revolutions in Paris, Vienna, Berlin, Milan, the Italian states, Prague, and Budapest.

▲ **Louis Philippe**
The moderate conservative king, caricatured here by a contemporary artist, was seen to turn against the republicans and democrats who had brought him to power.

The Growth of Prussia

Prussia, a Lutheran (Protestant) kingdom, came to prominence under Frederick II (the Great; reigned 1740–86). He developed a highly trained army, officered by the landowning *Junkers*, who remained the ruling elite throughout the 19th century. By 1806, 70% of the Prussian economy was dedicated to the army; nevertheless, it was still heavily defeated by the French and Berlin was occupied. In 1812 Prussia cynically joined Napoleon's campaign against Russia, only to desert him during the retreat. Rejoining the allies in 1813, Prussia shared the spoils of victory, receiving half of Saxony, the Rhineland, and parts of Poland.

confederation of independent states, dominated by Austria and Prussia. The states sent delegates to an assembly (Diet) in Frankfurt. However, the Austrian chancellor, Metternich, alarmed by student unrest within the confederation, which culminated in the murder of conservative writer, August von Kotzebue (1761–1819), issued the Karlsbad Decrees in 1819. These reversed the more liberal provisions of the federal constitution, introduced press censorship, and set up secret police to investigate any 'revolutionary activity.'

In the states that had been occupied by Napoleon, such as Bavaria and Württemberg, parliamentary government was established, though few citizens were qualified to vote. In Prussia, however, the king refused to accept a liberal constitution. In 1828 Prussia established a customs union, or **Zollverein**, linking its eastern heartland with the Rhineland provinces. Neighbouring states also joined; by the mid-1830s, most of Germany was included in the union, greatly strengthening Prussia's claim to be the leading German state.

Political protest in Germany at this time was limited to a small university-based intelligentsia. While its aims were vague, most agreed that the language, culture, and moral virtues of the German people were being stifled by the petty states and their effete or autocratic rulers. While the Napoleonic Wars were still being fought, the patriotic orator Ernst Moritz Arndt (1769–1860) had formulated the mystical longings of the German people in aggressive racial terms. He was abetted by 'Father' Jahn (1778–1852), a fervent nationalist, who organized young men into patriotic gymnastic associations. Their influence led to the foundation, after 1815, of student associations, whose nationalist rallies and street violence had so alarmed Metternich.

In general, German political thought placed the nation state above individual rights, which provided intellectual justification for the illiberal, but effective, Prussian system of government. During the 1830s and 1840s, however, political unrest gradually mounted among peasants and workers suffering from the economic depression, and among nationalist liberals, who aspired to a united Germany.

The Growth of Democracy in Britain

Since 1688, the monarch's powers in Britain had been limited by a constitution, which provided a modest degree of parliamentary democracy. However, the French Revolution had provoked a conservative reaction; democratic movements were outlawed. The Industrial Revolution had created new centres of population, which lacked parliamentary representation, while the Napoleonic Wars had led to high taxation and the loss of foreign

markets; wages declined and food prices rose. In 1816 there were riots in London; radical leaders campaigned for universal voting rights, and spontaneous workers' uprisings took place in various towns. The government responded to more widespread support for reform with repression. In 1820 a group of extremists plotted to assassinate the entire cabinet, seize the Bank of England, and set up a provisional government; however, the conspiracy was revealed. This event was the closest that Britain came to revolution; most historians agree that the British simply wanted to reform existing institutions.

In 1830 there was further rioting in Britain; a general election voted the moderate liberal 'Whig' party into power. After much debating, the First Reform Act was passed (1832), giving greater parliamentary representation to Scotland, Ireland, and Wales and to industrialized cities in northern England. Nevertheless, voting rights were still restricted by a property qualification; the number of voters increased only from 500 000 to 800 000.

1848: The Year of Revolutions

Once again the first outbreak of revolution was in France. The growing conservatism of the July Monarchy was challenged by both liberal reformers and socialist revolutionaries. In February 1848 rioting broke out in Paris. Louis Philippe abdicated, a provisional government introduced the vote for all males over 21, and an assembly was summoned to draft a republican constitution. The socialist wing of the assembly, under Louis Blanc (1811–82), however, called for the setting up of National Workshops to provide work for all. While the new government complied, the result was the establishment of little more than a forced labour camp in Paris. It was here that renewed

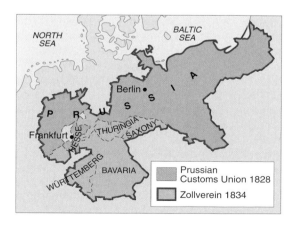

▲ **The Zollverein** *The customs union of 1828 linked Prussia's eastern and western territories. The single German Zollverein of 1834, which expanded as railways and industry developed, greatly enhanced Prussia's economic position.*

▲ **Prince Metternich** *His Congress System a failure, the arch-conservative Metternich was forced to flee from Vienna to London following the outbreak of revolution in 1848.*

fighting broke out, this time between the middle classes, supported by landowners and peasants nationwide, and the urban proletariat; the latter were defeated after several days of bloody fighting. The Second Republic was established and, in 1850, elected as its first president none other than Napoleon's nephew, Louis-Napoleon, who ruled as Emperor Napoleon III (1852–71).

Germany Attempts Unification. In March 1848 rioting broke out in Berlin and other German capitals. A number of German princes were deposed or forced to liberalize their governments. In Berlin, however, King Frederick William IV (reigned 1840–61), instead of crushing the rebellion, ordered his troops to withdraw and introduced a liberal constitution. However, when Denmark laid claim to the German territory of Schleswig-Holstein, Prussia's military instincts were revived; an army was sent to deal with Denmark and the liberal constitution was revoked. A group of academics in Heidelberg, who had been agitating for a united Germany, were, in the meantime, called upon to create one. They set up an elected National Assembly in Frankfurt to replace the non-elected Diet; in March 1849 the crown of a united Germany was offered to Frederick William of Prussia. When he refused the crown, many German states consequently withdrew their delegates from the Frankfurt assembly, which moved to Stuttgart. Prussian troops suppressed uprisings in Dresden and Baden and the assembly was dissolved in June.

The Austrian Empire. In virtually all the non-German speaking lands of the Austrian Empire there were uprisings and independence movements during 1848. Everywhere, peasants were leaving the land for the cities, only to find that there was no employment for them. Industrialization had not yet fully developed in these parts of Europe. In Hungary, the nationalist leader Lajos Kossuth (1802–94) harnessed popular unrest and achieved virtual independence within what became the Austro-Hungarian Empire. In Prague, Czech radicals tried to obtain similar status for Bohemia. Although the uprising was quelled by troops, the Czechs gained equal rights with the German-speaking minority.

In Austria's Italian lands a republic was declared in Venice, while Lombardy sought the protection of Piedmont. Despite Italian success against Austrian forces, Austria had re-established control by 1849. In Tuscany, Rome, and Naples-Sicily independence movements gathered strength, which was eventually to culminate in Italy's unification.

End of the Congress System. From March 1848, the people of Vienna were protesting in the streets; they included both the middle classes and workers. The Hapsburg royal family, fearing a French-style revolution, adopted a conciliatory approach. Emperor Ferdinand I (reigned 1835–48) moved his court to Innsbruck. Although the army eventually restored order and a new emperor ascended the throne, it was clear that Metternich's efforts to maintain stability in Europe had finally failed. Not only were democratic and nationalist movements too strong to resist, but Prussia, Russia, and France each had their own expansionist ambitions, which would ultimately conflict. Europe was, therefore, to provide the arena for regional and continental wars for the next hundred years.

The Young Karl Marx

Karl Marx (1818–83) was born in the Rhineland, where, owing to its occupation by revolutionary France for 20 years (until 1813), liberal ideas were current. Through discussions with his future father-in-law, a baron with progressive views, the teenage Karl learnt about the utopian socialism of French thinkers. In 1835 he attended the University of Berlin, where he was greatly influenced by the philosopher Hegel and his dialectic view of history. At 24, Marx was made editor of the liberal newspaper, *Rheinische Zeitung*. In 1844 he met Friedrich Engels, who had studied industrial conditions in England; in 1848 they published *The Communist Manifesto*.

The 1848 Revolutions
Armed protestors confront troops of Emperor Ferdinand I at the barricades on the streets of Vienna in October 1848. ▼

Nationalism and Imperialism

France's Second Empire • Russia, Turkey, and the Crimean War • Prussia and the unification of Germany • The Franco-Prussian War • Imperial rivalries and the arms race • The Balkans

The Crimean War *The fall of Sevastopol (September 1855) and an Austrian threat to intervene forced Russia to surrender and accept the Treaty of Paris. The war exposed the British army as poorly led and ill-equipped; the French contingent was four times larger than the British and better trained. In all, over 675 000 lives were lost, more from disease than gunfire, making it the most disastrous European war between 1815 and 1914.* ▼

The second half of the 19th century saw the culmination of various nationalist movements throughout Europe. The result was not only the birth of two new nations (Italy and Germany), but the eventual outbreak of a full-scale European war.

France's Second Empire

The most notable result of the 1848 revolutions was the election of Louis-Napoleon as president of France's Second Republic. While he established a powerful regime, Louis found the elected assembly a hindrance to his ambitions. In December 1851, when his four-year term was about to expire, he staged a coup d'état, dissolved the constitution, and declared himself Emperor Napoleon III. The advent of France's Second Empire heralded a period in which France once again felt able to wield power in Europe.

Russia, Turkey, and the Crimean War

The Ottoman (Turkish) Empire, having scarcely changed for 400 years, was believed to be on the verge of collapse. It included lands in Europe that now form modern Bosnia and Herzegovina, Albania, Macedonia, Bulgaria, and Romania. For Britain, France, and Austria, these territories were a useful barrier against Russian expansion. Constantinople, the empire's capital, controlled the strategically important Bosporus strait between the Black Sea and the Mediterranean; Britain and France were anxious that it should not fall under Russian control. The fact that 40% of Ottoman subjects were Orthodox Christians gave Russia an excuse to intervene in Turkish affairs; when, with Anglo-French support, Turkey resisted, Russia invaded the Turkish provinces of Moldavia and Walachia (modern Romania) in 1853. This action provoked a war (1853–56) in which Britain and France fought alongside Turkey; their combined forces eventually defeated Russia on the Crimean peninsula.

The treaty ending the Crimean War was drafted at the Congress of Paris (1856); unlike the earlier Congress of Vienna (1815), this merely confirmed that each European power would pursue its own national interests. One outcome was the insistence by France and Britain that both Russia and Austria should withdraw from the Balkans, thus encouraging nationalist movements there.

Prussia and the Unification of Germany

After 1848 the partnership between Prussia and Austria within the German Confederation became increasingly uneasy. In 1850 the new young Austrian emperor, Franz Josef I (reigned 1848–1916), and his chancellor, Felix Schwarzenberg (1800–52), with the support of Saxony, tried to regain the leadership of the Frankfurt confederation. However, by 1862 Prussia had a new king, William I (reigned 1861–88), a brilliant army chief of staff, Moltke (1800–91), and as minister-president, **Otto von Bismarck** (1815–98), who was to direct the destiny of Prussia and Germany for nearly 30 years.

Bismarck, a fervent royalist, exploited pan-German aspirations only to advance Prussia's interests. A shrewd opportunist, he saw that Austria's empire was beginning to crumble and decided to speed the process. In 1864 the Schleswig-Holstein dispute again flared up. Prussian and Austrian forces jointly invaded Denmark; after a swift victory, Bismarck deliberately picked a quarrel with Austria.

In 1866 the pro-Austrian diet voted for action against Prussia, which responded by invading the states of Hanover, Hesse, and

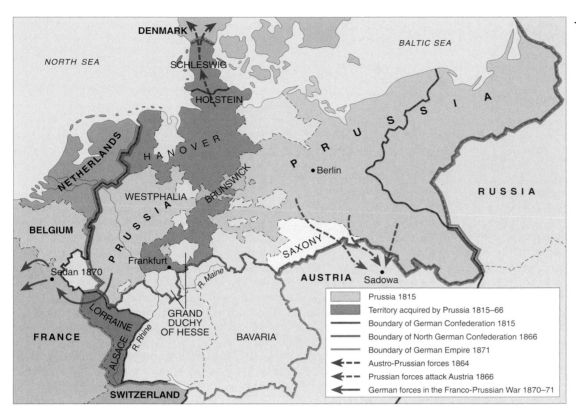

◄ Germany
War against Denmark, Austria, and France finally brought about the political unification of Germany. Austria was excluded from the confederation of north German states formed in 1867; the southern states joined in 1871 to create the German Empire, thus ending Austria's influence there.

Saxony. Prussia formed an alliance with the newly unified Italy, which declared war on Austria, while a large Prussian army marched into Bohemia and routed the Austrians at the Battle of Sadowa. Austria soon surrendered; by the Treaty of Prague (1866) Prussia's objectives were achieved: Austria was henceforth excluded from German affairs and the Confederation of 1815 was finally dissolved.

Prussia now formed the North German Confederation, comprising all the states north of the River Main. Though most states retained local autonomy, real power lay with the Federal Council and the **Reichstag** (or imperial diet) in Berlin. The Reichstag was a democratic body elected by universal male suffrage; however, its members had little control over foreign and military policy.

The Franco-Prussian War
France was now Prussia's only rival in continental Europe. Under Napoleon III, industry had flourished, while the French army had secured victories against both Russia and Austria. Most significant, however, was the fact that French territory included the partly German-speaking region of Alsace-Lorraine, where much of its coal and steel industry was situated.

France had already irritated Prussia by claiming German territory west of the Rhine and by securing the neutrality of Luxembourg. Bismarck, looking for an opportunity to provoke a war with France, was presented

with one in 1870. The Spanish throne had been disputed by two rival factions since the 1830s; when Queen Isabella II (reigned 1833–68) died, a revolutionary government decided to settle the dispute by inviting a German prince to take the crown. Bismarck encouraged the idea, knowing that it would provoke France; even though the prince's father renounced the candidacy, a French emissary demanded a personal guarantee of this from King William. While the king politely declined, his response was redrafted by Bismarck into a curt refusal (the 'Ems Dispatch'), which he subsequently circulated to the press of Europe. With France's honour at stake, war was declared on Prussia. Bismarck sprang his trap; massive Prussian and other German forces were soon sweeping through Alsace-Lorraine. The French were heavily defeated at Sedan in September 1870; by December Paris was under siege. While Napoleon III fell from power, the Reichstag voted to offer the crown of the German Empire to William I. In January 1871 peace talks were held at Versailles and William was proclaimed *Kaiser* (emperor) of Germany.

Imperial Rivalries and the Arms Race
Until the late 19th century, war in Europe had been a calculated use of force to secure particular objectives. As the century drew to a close, however, it seemed increasingly likely that a devastating conflict of races was inevitable. Shifting alliances were formed, which resulted in the emergence of two power blocs: the

Otto von Bismarck
Bismarck, one of the most important figures in 19th-century European history, combined a formidable intelligence with royalist instincts. As chief minister of Prussia from 1862, he regarded Prussia as being synonymous with Germany; he reorganized the army and devoted himself to furthering Prussia's interests by political and military means. Although he came into conflict with both the Catholic Church and with socialism, he was responsible for introducing universal suffrage and social insurance.

The Paris Commune (1871)

In the last days of the Franco-Prussian War, the German army besieged Paris. While a peace treaty was agreed on 1 March, the National Guard fought on in Paris, establishing a commune there. Germany allowed the republican government to send an army to crush the revolutionary commune. In May troops captured its strongholds, killing 20 000 people. Though it failed, Marx promoted the Paris Commune as a model for revolutionary organization.

empires of Britain, France, and Russia (the Triple Entente, 1907), and the major continental powers, Prussia and Austria-Hungary, together with Italy (the Triple Alliance, 1882).

Britain, confident of its superiority, had been willing to see France build its own empire in sub-Saharan Africa in the 1850s and in Indochina in the 1860s. Britain also took a major share in the French-built Suez Canal (1869).

When William II (reigned 1888–1918), who was envious of the British and French empires, became Kaiser, he demanded that Germany should have its own "place in the sun." However, to build an empire, Germany needed a navy to rival that of Britain. In 1907 and 1908 four battleships were built each year; Britain responded by building eight in 1909.

In western Europe the spread of literacy and the growth of a popular press enabled public opinion to become an important, yet easily manipulated, factor in politics. In the industrial nations, where international socialism was beginning to spread among the working class, governments found that patriotic warmongering served to counter this trend.

Germany alarmed Russia by befriending Turkey, while France and Germany twice nearly went to war over Morocco (1905, 1911), whose independence Germany supported. Britain, regarding itself as Germany's prime target, built a new North Sea naval base and strengthened its land forces.

Russian imperial prestige was severely damaged in 1904–05, when its fleet was destroyed and its army defeated by Japan; growing social unrest in Russia also led to uprisings and naval mutiny (1905). These events altered the balance of power in Europe in favour of Germany, who now made plans for an invasion of France. It seemed only a matter of time before an international conflagration would erupt.

The Balkans

In 1817 Serbia gained partial independence within the Ottoman Empire; subsequently Serbia claimed to speak for all Slav populations under Austro-Hungarian and Ottoman rule.

Russia's pan-Slav sympathies tended more towards Bulgaria than Serbia, which heightened Serbia's grievances. In 1875 the mainly

THE BIRTH OF THE ITALIAN NATION

Since the 1820s there had been periodic uprisings against Austrian rule in northern Italy, and against autocratic rulers elsewhere. In 1848 the republican Giuseppe Mazzini returned from exile to Italy; he was soon joined by his closest supporter, Giuseppe Garibaldi (1807–82); in 1849 they set up a republic in Rome. This provoked Austrian, French, Spanish, and Neapolitan armies to advance on Rome; the pope was reinstated and Mazzini and Garibaldi fled the country.

In the northern kingdom of Piedmont-Sardinia the ambitious Count Cavour (1810–61) became prime minister in 1852. A moderate conservative, he wanted to marginalize the republicans by creating a confederation of Italian states, led by Piedmont. Cavour had previously edited a newspaper, the title of which – *Il risorgimento* ('The Resurgence') – became the name given to the whole nationalist movement in Italy.

In 1858 Napoleon III met secretly with Cavour. They agreed that France would send an army to help Piedmont drive the Austrians out of Lombardy and Venetia and create the confederation. In return, France would receive the French-speaking territories of Nice and Savoy. The plan went ahead in 1859. The Austrian army was defeated, and Austria surrendered Lombardy, though not Venetia. Garibaldi now declared himself no longer a republican, but a champion of the king of Piedmont-Sardinia, Victor Emmanuel II (reigned 1849–78), who would rule a united Italy. In Tuscany and other central Italian states, plebiscites voted for union with Piedmont. In May 1860 Garibaldi, with his famous army of "A Thousand," landed in Sicily, where discontented peasants joined his ranks and defeated a large Neapolitan garrison. Cavour refused

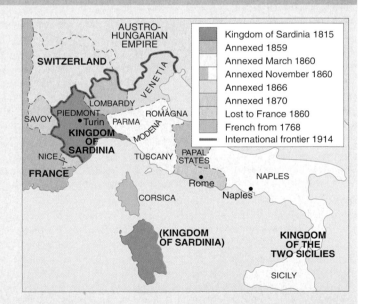

to send any assistance to Garibaldi, though it is believed that Victor Emmanuel secretly encouraged him. In August he crossed to the mainland, where again he met with great popular support. Within a few weeks he had taken Naples; the king fled and Naples-Sicily opted to join Piedmont. In October Garibaldi proclaimed Victor Emmanuel king of a united Italy (see map); in 1861 the first Italian parliament in Turin confirmed his rule.

In 1866 Austria finally ceded Venetia to Italy. The pope still nominally ruled Rome and the adjoining area. In 1870, however, Italian troops captured Rome; in 1871 Victor Emmanuel took up residence in the city.

KEY EVENTS (1848–1914)

1848	Louis-Napoleon elected president of France
1849	Short-lived Roman republic of Mazzini and Garibaldi
1851	Louis-Napoleon becomes Emperor Napoleon III
1854–56	Crimean War: Britain, France, and Turkey against Russia
1859	France invades northern Italy; Austrian army defeated
1860	Garibaldi lands in Sicily
1861	First all-Italian parliament
1862	Bismarck becomes chief minister of Prussia
1864	Second Schleswig-Holstein war
1866	Prussia defeats Austria
1870–71	Franco-Prussian War
1875	Bosnian revolt
1878	Independence of Serbia, Bulgaria, and Romania
1882	Triple Alliance between Germany, Austria-Hungary, and Italy
1907	Triple Entente between Britain, France, and Russia; second disarmament conference
1907–09	Battleship race between Britain and Germany
1912	Serbia and Bulgaria defeat Turkey
1913	War between Serbia and Bulgaria
1914	Assassination of Archduke Ferdinand at Sarajevo; Outbreak of World War I

▲ **Kaiser William II**
Having forced Bismarck to resign, Kaiser William began to direct foreign policy himself, with disastrous consequences. A vain and neurotic man, William pursued warlike policies and was determined that Germany should match Britain's naval power.

Serbian province of Bosnia and Herzegovina revolted against Ottoman misrule; Turkish retaliation resulted in Russia declaring war on Turkey. The subsequent peace treaty (1878) gave Bulgaria, Serbia, and Romania full independence, while Bosnia was to be administered by Austria under Turkish sovereignty.

In 1903 Serbian extremists, known as the Black Hand, murdered their king and queen and installed a figurehead. Croatia, a Slav province previously loyal to the Austrian Empire, now favoured an alliance with Serbia. In 1908 Austria annexed Bosnia. Serbia's protestations were backed by Russia against Austria and Germany. War was only avoided by a diversion created by a coup d'état in Turkey.

All the Slav states subsequently united in a Balkan league led by Serbia; in 1912 both Serbian and Bulgarian armies won victories against Turkey, forcing the Turks out of Europe. In the subsequent negotiations, Austria sought to deprive Serbia of access to the sea through Albania. Again Russia supported Serbia; war was averted when Albania was granted independence under a German king.

In 1913, while negotiations were still in progress, Bulgaria attacked Serbia but was crushed; Serbia, now undisputed master of the Balkans, posed a threat to Austria-Hungary. Austria considered creating a tripartite empire of Germans, Hungarians, and Slavs; Serbian nationalists, however, wanted total freedom. When the Austrian heir apparent, Archduke Franz Ferdinand (1863–1914), visited the Bosnian capital, Sarajevo, on 28 June 1914, he was shot dead by a Serb, Gavrilo Princip, acting for the Black Hand.

As a result Austria demanded that Serbia renounce its independence; Serbia's refusal prompted Austria to declare war. Interlocking treaties were invoked so that, within a period of weeks, Russia and France were at war with Germany and Austria. What became known as the 'Great War' (and later as World War I) had finally begun.

The Battleship Race *Despite disarmament conferences in 1899 and 1907, the arms build-up continued relentlessly, fuelled by Anglo-German naval rivalry. The strong British navy, shown here at the Spithead review of 1911, was perceived as a serious threat by Germany. The production of new battleships by Britain and Germany served to exacerbate political tensions in Europe.* ▼

Not by speech-making and the decisions of majorities will the questions of the day be settled... but by iron and blood.
Otto von Bismarck (1862)

World War I

The outbreak of war • Deadlock and attrition • Other offensives • Allied victory

World War I was the first fully mechanized war in history. As such, its geographical scope, the number of nations involved, and the sum total of casualties resulting from the conflict were quite unprecedented. The 'Great War,' as it justifiably became known, led to the collapse of four powerful empires, thus changing out of all recognition the political face of Europe.

The Outbreak of War

The assassination of the Archduke Franz Ferdinand (1863–1914), heir to the throne of Austria-Hungary, in Sarajevo in June 1914, sparked a European crisis, which rapidly degenerated into full-scale war. The Austrians, supported by the Germans, blamed Serbia for the assassination and threatened to invade. The Serbs subsequently appealed for help to the Russians, who began to mobilize their enormous army. This raised fears in Germany that Russia, with French support in the west, would attack, and triggered a German military strategy, known as the **Schlieffen Plan**, designed to defeat France before the Russians could advance westwards. On 4 August 1914 German troops, under the command of the German chief of general staff, Helmuth von Moltke (1848–1916), marched into Belgium, aiming to approach Paris from the north; a few hours later Britain (a guarantor of Belgian neutrality) declared war on Germany.

The Schlieffen Plan failed. Despite a German advance as far as the River Marne, east of Paris, French forces, under the command of General J.-C.-C. Joffre (1852–1931), and the British Expeditionary Force, under Sir John French (1852–1925), mounted a counter-attack, which forced the Germans to retreat. Both sides tried desperately to outflank the other, with little success. By October 1914, the rival armies had dug trenches, creating a line of defence, known as the **Western Front**, extending from the northern coast of France to the Swiss border. A Russian advance, under the command of Tsar Nicholas II (reigned 1894–1917), into East Prussia, meanwhile, had been halted by German forces, under General Erich von Ludendorff (1865–1937), in a series of battles around Tannenberg. A threat to Austrian positions from Russian troops in Galicia (Poland), however, had forced the Germans to divert resources to the east. The war thus became a stalemate.

Deadlock and Attrition

On the Western Front, the war was characterized by the **trench system**, which comprised elaborate defensive positions protected by machine guns, artillery, and barbed wire. Both sides were evenly matched; they launched offensives against each other that were damaging but not decisive. As the Germans, now commanded by Erich von Falkenhayn (1861–1922), occupied most of Belgium and parts of northern France, the **Allies** (Britain and France) had to initiate the offensive action.

Europe in 1914 ▶
The European crisis of 1914 quickly deteriorated into all-out war, involving all of the major powers on the continent. The Central powers of Germany and Austria-Hungary faced the Allied powers both to the east (Russia) and to the west (Britain and France).

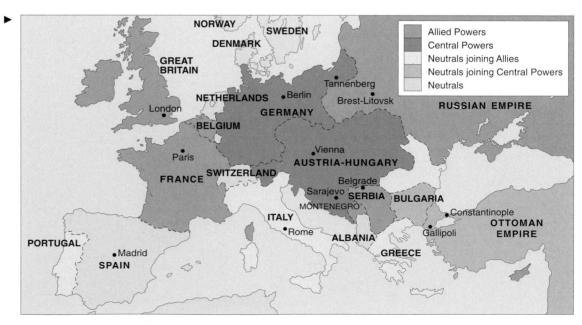

Allied Powers
Central Powers
Neutrals joining Allies
Neutrals joining Central Powers
Neutrals

NORWAY
SWEDEN
DENMARK
GREAT BRITAIN
NETHERLANDS
Berlin
Tannenberg
Brest-Litovsk
RUSSIAN EMPIRE
London
GERMANY
BELGIUM
Paris
Vienna
AUSTRIA-HUNGARY
FRANCE
SWITZERLAND
Belgrade
Sarajevo
SERBIA
BULGARIA
MONTENEGRO
Constantinople
ITALY
OTTOMAN EMPIRE
Rome
ALBANIA
Gallipoli
PORTUGAL
GREECE
Madrid
SPAIN

They sent their troops in waves across the area of shell-cratered ground between the two lines of trenches, known as ***no-man's-land***, into the fire of German guns. In 1915, offensives in Champagne (February), at Neuve Chapelle (March), and at Loos (September) cost the Allies thousands of men killed and wounded in return for little territorial gain. The situation in the east provided no more hope of a resolution; although the war was fought over a wider area, thus avoiding the trench deadlock of the west, neither side could achieve a decisive advantage. In mid-1915, the Germans managed to force the Russian armies to retreat back through Poland; Germany, however, then had to divert forces south to help the Austrian offensive in Serbia. By the end of 1915, Serbia had been invaded by Austrian and German forces, while Bulgaria had declared war on the Allies.

The war also escalated in other respects. As early as October 1914 the Turks joined Germany and Austria-Hungary to create the alliance of the ***Central Powers***. In May 1915 Italy joined the war on the side of the Allies. Both declarations opened up new battle fronts, requiring yet more men and munitions. The combatant nations could only cope with the demands of such a full-scale conflict by mobilizing their societies in support of the war; production of armaments increased and ***conscription*** (compulsory military service) was introduced or extended. Governments took control of production to ensure a steady supply of weapons; workers (including women) were directed into the arms industry, while men were forced to join the armed services.

The deadlock on the battlefields, however, continued. On the Western Front, there were horrific losses on both sides. In February 1916 the Germans initiated an attack on French fortresses around Verdun, on the River Meuse, which continued for most of the year; the result was nearly 700 000 casualties on each side. The British, now commanded by Douglas Haig (1861–1928), had, by then, also suffered crippling losses during an offensive in the Somme area of northern France; on 1 July 1916, the first day of the attack, nearly 57 000 British troops were killed or wounded; by November the figure had risen to 460 000.

In the east, a Russian attack near the Carpathian Mountains (the Brusilov Offensive) began in June 1916; after early gains, however, it soon degenerated into a disorderly retreat, resulting in nearly 1 million casualties. These losses, in addition to the enormous social and economic pressures inside Russia caused by the need to produce armaments, helped to trigger the **Russian Revolution** in March 1917. The revolution overthrew Tsar Nicholas II, facilitating the seizure of power by

▲ **Trench Warfare** *French soldiers prepare for battle in a trench on the Western Front (1916). The war on the Western Front was characterized by an elaborate system of trenches, which comprised a network of defensive positions. Smaller communication trenches, which ran perpendicular to the main trenches, were used to supply them with food, ammunition, fresh troops, and mail. Conditions in the trenches during World War I were appalling, as men lived in cramped, wet, and rat-infested surroundings.*

Vladimir Ilyich Lenin (1870–1924), leader of the Bolshevik faction of the Social Democratic Party.

Offensives on the Western Front sought to break the trench deadlock. Full-scale concentrated attacks, preceded by artillery barrages, attempted to open up breaches in the enemy defences for infantry and cavalry to exploit. As the number of casualties rose, the combatants found it increasingly difficult to find the manpower to replace them; it became clear that changes in techniques and in strategy were necessary. New weapons were introduced. In April 1915 the Germans used poison gas to asphyxiate Allied defenders near Ypres in western Belgium. Although soldiers

The Schlieffen Plan

Devised by the German chief of general staff, Alfred von Schlieffen (1833–1913) in 1905, the plan reflected Germany's fear of a simultaneous war against France in the west and Russia in the east. The plan was to concentrate forces against France, taking Paris after an advance through (neutral) Belgium, which would take six weeks to complete. German forces would then be sent by rail to the east to face the Russian army, which would need six weeks to mobilize. The plan did come close to success.

GALLIPOLI

On 25 April 1915, British troops and soldiers of the Australian and New Zealand Army Corps (ANZAC) landed from the sea on the Gallipoli peninsula, between the Aegean and Black Seas. The aim was to seize control of the peninsula from the Turks, allowing Allied ships to sail through the Bosporus strait to support the Russian armies. In the process it was planned that the Turkish capital, Istanbul, would be captured, thus forcing Turkey out of the war. Although the landings were opposed and the number of casualties grew, the British commander, General Sir Ian Hamilton (1853–1947), decided to continue with the attack. A second amphibious assault was launched on 6 August 1915, which was also met with fierce Turkish resistance. Allied forces were decimated and finally evacuated from the peninsula by 9 January 1916. This withdrawal without further losses marked the end of a disastrous operation.

were issued with gas masks to counter the effects, gas weapons rapidly became a feature of the war. Aircraft were also used to observe enemy positions and to drop bombs on ground targets. A new form of warfare developed, as both sides sent up fighter aircraft to protect their reconnaissance and bombing aircraft. Aerial 'dogfights,' in which rival airmen fought for command of the air, became a feature of 20th-century warfare. The British invented the **tank**, a lozenge-shaped tracked vehicle, designed to cross no-man's-land and trenches to destroy enemy machine gun positions, thus enabling the infantry to advance. As the tank was invulnerable to machine-gunfire, its advent marked the beginning of the end of trench warfare. New infantry weapons, such as mortars, flame-throwers, and grenades, also gave the soldiers increased firepower.

None of these individual developments greatly affected the progress of the war. Some success was enjoyed by tanks, when used in large numbers (as at Cambrai in November 1917); they proved, however, to be too slow and mechanically unreliable to exploit any tactical advantage. The Germans achieved more success by using their artillery to launch sudden 'hurricane' bombardments, which caught the enemy by surprise; they also effectively organized their infantry into small 'stormtrooper' units to infiltrate, rather than batter through, the trenches. The horrors of trench warfare, however, continued. After a failed French offensive in Champagne, in February 1917, elements of the French army, now under the command of General R.-G.

▲ **Tanks** *Introduced by the British during the Somme offensive, the tank was one of the key new weapons of World War I. Here the Germans are testing the capabilities of a captured British tank, redecorated with German insignia.*

THE RUSSIAN REVOLUTION

Pressure for social and political change existed in Russia long before the outbreak of war in Europe in 1914. Involvement in the war, however, fuelled opposition to the corruption and incompetence of the tsarist regime. As workers and peasants were forced to join the Russian army, leaving behind an industrial infrastructure that could not cope with the demands of the war, Russian society began to disintegrate. Enormous casualties, incurred in poorly managed campaigns, boosted popular unrest. By early 1917, large numbers of Russian soldiers were deserting the army.

In March 1917 food shortages led to riots in Petrograd (St Petersburg); local revolutionary committees, known as **soviets**, were subsequently formed by workers, soldiers, and sailors. A Provisional Government was established and, on 15 March, Tsar Nicholas abdicated. The change of government made little difference to the conduct of the war; when renewed offensives against the Central Powers led to yet more defeats, however, the soviets demanded yet further change. The situation was exploited by Lenin, who had just returned to Russia from exile; on 7–8 November 1917 he and his Bolshevik supporters seized the Winter Palace, in

▲ **Bolshevik Revolutionaries** *(Petrograd, November 1917) While the revolution itself took place with little loss of life, it was followed by four years of bloody civil war.*

Petrograd, the principal residence of the tsars for more than 150 years. Within 24 hours a special 'Congress of Soviets' had proposed peace negotiations with the Central Powers.

Nivelle (1856–1924), mutinied. This forced the British to accelerate plans for an attack around Passchendaele, near Ypres, beginning in July. Once again, the attack was a disaster, resulting in nearly 500 000 casualties, many of whom literally drowned in the sea of mud into which the battlefield degenerated. The war, which had already continued for much longer than expected, seemed set to continue indefinitely. Only in Italy, where the Germans, now commanded by Paul von Hindenburg (1847–1934), and the Austrians made a sudden advance at Caporetto, in November 1917, did a breakthrough seem likely; this was soon blocked, however, when the British and French sent troops to bolster up their ally.

Other Offensives

The war was not confined to Europe. As the stalemate became more intractable, alternative methods of attack were sought. Germany and Britain both sought to weaken the other by means of naval blockade, preventing the import of raw materials essential to the war effort. This led to a fight for control of the sea lanes; while full-scale naval battles were rare – the only major clash between the British and German fleets, at Jutland in May 1916, was indecisive – submarines were used to sink enemy merchant ships, principally in the North Atlantic. The German **U-boat** (submarine) offensive resulted in heavy British losses. When the German campaign was extended to attack any (even neutral) merchant ships carrying goods to Britain, it helped to trigger a declaration of war on the Central Powers by the United States of America (April 1917). German attempts to bomb British cities from the air, using **zeppelins** and bombers, caused significant damage, but not enough, however, to cause Britain to concede defeat.

An alternative strategy was to attack the enemy at weak positions away from the major land battles in Europe. The Allies embarked on this policy as soon as the war began, capturing German colonies in Africa. This was extended to include major offensives aimed specifically at the Turks, widely regarded as the weakest of the Central Powers. In April 1915 Allied troops mounted a seaborne attack on the **Gallipoli** peninsula (see panel). The attack was a fiasco, resulting in over 260 000 Allied casualties for no gain. In April 1916, a similar disaster befell British Indian troops in Mesopotamia (modern-day Iraq). While this campaign, together with another against the Turks in Palestine, eventually led to the capture of Baghdad, Jerusalem, and Damascus, the commitment of Allied forces required undoubtedly weakened the main effort on the Western Front, where the ultimate outcome of the war would be decided.

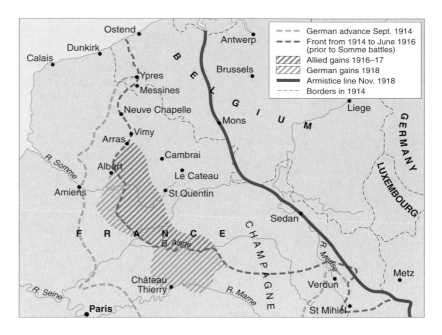

Allied Victory

By the beginning of 1918, Allied victory was far from assured. While the USA had promised to provide fresh manpower, which would probably tilt the balance in favour of the Allies, until these reinforcements arrived, the Germans had the advantage. In the aftermath of the Russian Revolution, the Bolshevik government made peace with the Central Powers at Brest-Litovsk in March 1918. This allowed Germany to concentrate its forces in the west.

▲ **The Western Front** *Once Germany had failed to knock France out of the war, and had forced Britain to join the conflict, a stalemate situation developed on the Western Front. Neither side could gain an advantage despite constant offensives, costing many lives. A final Allied counterattack, with US aid, in August 1918, finally led to the defeat of Germany.*

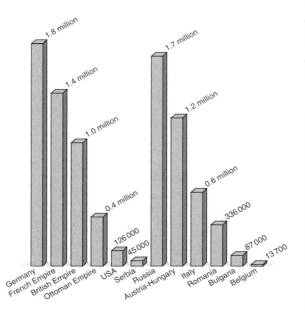

▲ **Casualties of War** *The 'Great War' of 1914–18 was the first 'global' war in history (thus it later became known as World War I). The combatants were able to utilize newly developed weapons of mass destruction, such as high explosives, machine guns, poison gas, and airborne bombs. The result was an unprecedented level of casualties and the decimation of the cream of European male youth.*

Zeppelins

Developed by Count Ferdinand von Zeppelin (1838–1917), these airships comprised an enormous fabric-covered aluminium frame, filled with hydrogen, powered by two 16-horsepower engines. During World War I, they were used in the first effective aerial bombardments. They ultimately proved to be too slow and explosive a target and too fragile in bad weather to be successful wartime machines.

Then I saw fellows drop lifeless while others began to stagger and limp; the fragments were getting us and in front was a belt of wire... I felt my feet sink and though I struggled to get on, I was dragged down to the waist in sticky clay... by yelling and firing my revolver into the air I attracted the attention of Sergeant Gunn, who returned and dragged me out... I was following Corporal Breeze when a shell burst at his feet. As I was blown backwards I saw him thrown into the air to land at my feet, a crumpled heap of torn flesh...

Edwin Campion Vaughan describes battle conditions at Passchendaele (Belgium), August 1917

CHRONOLOGY OF WORLD WAR I

1914	
1–4 August	Germany declared war on Russia and France and invaded Belgium; Britain declares war on Germany
26–29 August	Russian forces defeated at Tannenberg
5–9 September	German forces halted at Battle of the Marne
19 October	Turkey joined the conflict against Russia and Britain
1915	
22 April	First use of poison gas in combat
25 April	British and ANZAC landings at Gallipoli
24 May	Italy declared war on the Central Powers
1916	
21 February	German forces attacked Verdun
31 May	Naval battle of Jutland
1 July	British offensive on the Somme began
September	First use of tanks during Somme offensive
1917	
6 April	The USA declared war on the Central Powers
31 July	British offensive began at Passchendaele
7–8 November	Bolshevik Revolution in Russia
1918	
3 March	Treaty of Brest-Litovsk agreed between Russia and the Central Powers
21 March	German offensive on the Western Front
8 August	Allied counterattacked at Amiens
11 November	Armistice ended war

Gassed (John Singer Sargent) This painting depicts a dressing station on the Doullens–Arras road in 1918. It shows the arrival of soldiers, temporarily blinded by poisonous mustard gas, led by an orderly. Mustard gas was another new weapon first used by the Germans in 1917. ▼

On 21 March 1918, they attacked British positions using 'hurricane' artillery bombardments and stormtrooper units. While British forces had to retreat, the Germans soon lost impetus. In August 1918, the Allies counterattacked around Amiens, using tanks as well as ground-attack aircraft; the first of the US divisions, under the command of John J. Pershing (1860–1948), began a 100-day campaign, which created large gaps in the German defence lines. This counterattack coincided with the defeat of the Turks in Palestine and of the Austrians in Italy, leaving the Germans isolated. With food shortages leading to riots in German cities, fears of a spread of

Bolshevism to Germany from the east, combined with an Allied invasion from the west, Kaiser William II (1859–1941), the emperor of Germany, abdicated, leaving his generals to end the fighting. At 11 a.m. on 11 November 1918, an armistice was signed that reflected the exhaustion of the two sides. By that time, over 10 million people had died in the war and four empires – those of Germany, Austria-Hungary, Turkey, and Russia – had collapsed. While the Allied powers had won the war, the enormous cost of the victory made them determined to take revenge on the Central Powers once the peace treaties were imposed (see THE CAUSES AND COURSE OF WORLD WAR II).

The Causes and Course of World War II

The aftermath of World War I • The Depression • The rise of fascism •
The road to war • Campaigns in Europe and the Mediterranean, 1939–44 •
The Eastern Front, 1941–44 • War in the Far East, 1941–44 • Allied victory, 1944–45

The peace settlement of 1919–20 was flawed, containing within it the seeds of future conflict, made worse by the political and economic aftereffects of war. Fuelled by the worldwide economic depression of the 1930s, new ideologies, such as communism and fascism, spread. Territorial demands made by Germany, Italy, and Japan led to a new conflict that was to affect most of the globe. The victory that was finally secured by the ***Allied powers*** (the British Commonwealth, the USA, the Soviet Union, France, China, and Poland) was hard-won.

The Aftermath of World War I

In January 1919, two months after the end of World War I, the victorious powers met in Paris to discuss the peace settlement. Germany was not represented, and Russia, in the throes of civil war, did not attend. It remained for Britain, France, and the USA to decide the future shape of Europe. Their primary aim was to weaken Germany so that the perceived aggression of 1914 could never be repeated.

By the Treaty of Versailles, signed on 28 June 1919, Germany was held responsible for the war and forced to pay enormous amounts of money (***reparations***) to the Allies; the size of the German army was restricted to 100 000 men, conscription was forbidden, and Germany was banned from possessing tanks, military aircraft, and large naval vessels. In the east, the state of Poland was recreated to form a buffer between Germany and Russia; it was given a corridor of German territory through to the port of Danzig (Gdańsk); this 'Polish Corridor' split East Prussia from the rest of Germany. In the west, Germany lost northern Schleswig to Denmark, and Eupen and Malmédy (in the Ardennes) to Belgium, while Alsace and Lorraine were returned to France. All German overseas possessions were confiscated and passed to the Allies as mandates of the newly formed **League of Nations**.

The victorious powers also imposed terms on their other enemies. By the Treaty of St Germain (10 September 1919), Austria lost Bohemia and Moravia to the newly created state of Czechoslovakia, while Galicia went to Poland. Trieste, Istria, and the South Tyrol were given to Italy. The Treaty of Trianon (4 June 1920) stripped Hungary of two-thirds of its former territory to help form Yugoslavia; small areas also went to Czechoslovakia and Poland, while Romania received Transylvania. The Treaty of Neuilly (27 November 1919) forced Bulgaria to cede land to Greece. Outside Europe, the Ottoman Empire was dismantled by the Treaty of Sèvres in August 1920, as territories in the Middle East were transferred to British and French control as mandates of the League of Nations. An attempt was made to occupy parts of Turkey; however, a nationalist revolt, led by Mustapha Kemal (Kemal Atatürk; 1880–1938), forced the British, Italians, and Greeks to withdraw; in 1923 the Treaty of Lausanne gave the Turks more favourable terms.

These treaties, however, left many people dissatisfied: ethnic Germans, who had been arbitrarily transferred to Poland or Czechoslovakia; Italians, who felt that their role in the war had not been rewarded; and the French, who believed that Germany should have been more harshly treated. Many Germans also resented the Allied weakening of their state.

SEE ALSO

This section:
- World War I
- Postwar Europe

Islamic World:
- European Mandates

China:
- The Republic of China

Japan:
- The Meiji Restoration and Expansionism

North America:
- The United States of America

Southeast Asia:
- World War II and Independence

Business and Finance (vol. 6):
- International Finance and Investment

THE INTERWAR YEARS

1919		**1935**	
28 June	Treaty of Versailles signed	3 Oct.	Italy invaded Abyssinia (Ethiopia)
1922			
28 Oct.	Mussolini gained power in Italy	**1936**	
		17 July	Spanish Civil War began (ended 1 April 1939)
1929			
24 Oct.	New York Stock Exchange crashed	**1937**	
		8 Aug.	Japanese forces occupied Peking (Beijing), China
1931			
18 Sept.	Japan invaded Manchuria	**1938**	
		12 March	German troops entered Austria
1933			
30 Jan.	Hitler appointed German Chancellor	29 Sept.	Munich Agreement signed

The League of Nations

The Covenant of the League of Nations, outlined by US president Woodrow Wilson during the Versailles peace conference, enshrined two basic principles: that "no nation shall go to war…until every other possible means of settling the dispute shall have been fully and fairly tried," and that "under no circumstances shall any nation seek forcibly to disturb the territorial settlement arrived at as a consequence of this peace or to interfere with the political independence of any of the States of the world." The League, agreed to by 32 countries, was formed in January 1920. It was quickly undermined when the US Senate refused to ratify (accept) the Covenant, denying the League the authority it needed.

These problems were compounded by the apparent weakness of the Allies; the US Senate refused to ratify the Treaty of Versailles, insisting that the USA should withdraw from world politics. France and Britain, both weakened by the conflict, were thus left to police Europe alone. Although Germany was allowed to join the League of Nations by the Treaty of Locarno, in 1925, mistrust remained.

Russia. A further concern after 1918 was the spread of communism from Russia into the rest of Europe. The 1917 Revolution (see WORLD WAR I) led to civil war in Russia, in which the Bolsheviks ('Reds') fought a coalition of democrats, socialists, and reactionaries ('Whites'), the latter united only by their opposition to Lenin. The conflict continued until 1921, by which time the Red Army had not only defeated its enemies but also advanced into Transcaucasia (Armenia, Georgia, and Azerbaijan) and the Ukraine. In 1922 the Union of Soviet Socialist Republics (USSR) was created, presenting the rest of Europe with a new state of immense economic and military potential, run by men who were convinced that Western democracies were ripe for revolution. It would, however, take time for the USSR to recover from civil war and realize its potential. Lenin's death in 1924 led to a power struggle, which was not resolved until Joseph Stalin (1879–1953) took over in 1929. He then had to concentrate on economic reform and the suppression of internal enemies. This did nothing to lessen the threat of communism to the rest of Europe.

THE SPANISH CIVIL WAR

In July 1936 a right-wing Nationalist coalition, led by General José Sanjurjo, seized power in Spanish Morocco in protest against the policies of a left-wing Republican government in Madrid. On his death Sanjurjo was succeeded by General Francisco Franco (1892–1975), who used German aircraft to transport troops to mainland Spain, where they attacked Republican positions. By the end of July, the Nationalists controlled most of northern and western Spain; widespread popular support for the Republican cause opposed them elsewhere.

The Republicans sought aid from the USSR and raised International Brigades of foreign volunteers. Franco's Nationalist forces received support from both Italy and Germany, which gave them the advantage. The fighting was, nevertheless, bitter. In autumn 1936, Franco's forces took Madrid. In early 1937, however, they were defeated twice in battles around the city. This forced them to move north, into the Basque Provinces and Asturias. On 26 April 1937, the Basque town of Guernica was bombed by German aircraft. Subsequent ground offensives forced the Republicans to withdraw. Further indecisive battles in 1938 left the Republicans weakened. The Nationalists took Madrid and Barcelona in early 1939; on 1 April Franco proclaimed an end to the civil war. It had cost Spain an estimated 800 000 casualties.

The Depression

Economic weakness further undermined any attempt to police the peace settlement. The cost of the war had seriously disrupted the world economy, directing money that would have been used for trade and investment into the production of weapons. As European countries had diverted resources to armaments, their demand for imported commodities, especially food, increased. When peace was restored, demand declined, leading to lower prices as world markets were swamped; many countries resorted to international loans and the burden of enormous interest repayments. Rising inflation, in which money became worth less, was rapidly established, leading to further loans and larger repayments. Little money remained for investment or the production of profitable goods.

The situation was not helped by the deliberate weakening of the German economy by the Allies. Most of the money generated by German industry or agriculture was diverted to paying reparations. The new ***Weimar Republic*** (named after the town in which the postwar German government was set up) faced an impossible task as the German mark plummeted in value. At the Lausanne Conference (1932) reparations were finally cancelled. This action came too late. The world economy had virtually collapsed; ***Black Thursday*** (24 October 1929), when the New York Stock Exchange ceased to function, marked the beginning of the ***Depression*** – a period of global economic mismanagement. It lasted for most of the 1930s, creating mass unemployment and social unrest. Policies involving centralized regulation of prices and government-sponsored 'public works' projects for the unemployed – first introduced in the USA – were eventually adopted in Britain and France. By the late 1930s, the Depression had passed its worst point. Domestic crises, however, had diverted attention away from international events that were leading inexorably to a new war in Europe.

The Rise of Fascism

The conflict was to develop between those countries, such as Britain and France, that believed in democracy and those that were ruled by leaders who believed in ***fascism***, a strongly nationalistic and authoritarian system of government, which had emerged in Europe in opposition to the spread of communism. Fascism had its origins in Italy, where Benito Mussolini (1883–1945), leader of a right-wing group known as the Fasci di Combattimento, seized power as early as October 1922. It was in Germany, however, that the fascist philosophy developed fully. Humiliated by the Versailles treaty and economic hardship, the German

Hitler Comes to Power *On 30 January 1933 Hitler was appointed chancellor of Germany. He was quick to seize complete power, ordering the arrest of political opponents, banning trade unions, and passing laws that stripped German Jews of their civil rights.*

people proved susceptible to the rhetoric of Adolf Hitler (1889–1945), leader of the National Socialist German Workers' (or Nazi) Party. Imprisoned for taking part in an abortive coup in Bavaria in 1923, Hitler set out his ideas in a book entitled *Mein Kampf* ('My Struggle'): he believed that 'Aryan' Germanic peoples were superior to Slavs and to Jews (whom he blamed for Germany's current problems), and that the German 'Master Race' had to conquer territory in the east to create *Lebensraum* ('living space') for themselves. He used his oratorical skills, ruthless propaganda, and a force of 'Brownshirts,' from the Sturmabteilung (SA), to attack political opponents. By 1932 the Nazi Party was the largest in the German parliament; Hitler was appointed chancellor (head of government) in 1933.

Hitler had vast popular support in Germany during the 1930s. His policies to control prices and production quotas, together with his decision, in March 1935, to ignore the Versailles treaty and reintroduce military conscription, helped to reduce unemployment. In September 1935 Hitler began to implement anti-Jewish measures (the Nuremberg Laws). Over the next decade, Hitler's policies culminated in the murder of millions of Jews in German concentration camps in what is now known as the **Holocaust** or ***Shoah***. In Italy Mussolini also expanded the armed forces and introduced massive public works projects in an effort to reduce unemployment.

In the Far East, Japan was adopting policies that closely resembled European fascism. By 1936, Italy and Germany had united to form the Rome–Berlin Axis, while Germany and Japan signed an Anti-Comintern Pact against the USSR. These pacts created a bloc of anti-democratic expansionist states (the ***Axis powers***) that posed an unprecedented threat to world peace. Weakened by the Depression and domestic problems, neither Britain nor France could offer effective opposition.

The Road to War

International problems came to the fore in 1933, when the League of Nations proved incapable of dealing with a Japanese invasion of Manchuria (1931). In 1935, when Mussolini's forces invaded Abyssinia (Ethiopia), an attempt was made to impose economic sanctions on Italy; few countries carried out the threat. Similarly, between 1936 and 1939, the League tried to prevent the shipment of arms

to rival factions in the **Spanish Civil War**. By then, it was apparent that the League had little influence or power.

These events coincided with German policies of rearmament and expansion. After leaving the League in 1933, Hitler felt free to ignore the Versailles treaty. In 1936 he sent troops to occupy the demilitarized Rhineland. The lack of response from Britain and France, desperate to avoid another war, encouraged his belief that if he moved with caution, basing his territorial demands on the desire of ethnic Germans to return to the Reich (the German republic), the Western democracies would do little to stop him. By 1937, British and French politicians were following a policy of diplomatic negotiation known as 'appeasement.'

In these circumstances, it was inevitable that Hitler would move again. On 12 March 1938, he sent forces into Austria to impose an ***Anschluss*** (the incorporation of Austria into Germany), which was welcomed by Austria. While Britain and France protested, they took no action. Their response was similar when, six months later, Hitler turned his attention to Czechoslovakia, demanding the right of nearly three million ethnic Germans in Sudetenland to join the Reich. On 29 September 1938, Britain, France, Germany, and Italy signed the Munich Agreement, a peace treaty, which, without consulting the Czechs, handed the Sudeten region of Czechoslovakia over to Germany. It appeared that appeasement had been successful in avoiding war. Any hopes of lasting peace, however, were quickly shattered. In March 1939 Hitler's troops marched into the remainder of Czechoslovakia and the country ceased to exist. Less than a month later, Germany took over the district of Memel from Lithuania, while Mussolini, taking advantage of crises elsewhere, invaded Albania. On 22 May 1939 Hitler and Mussolini signed

The Holocaust

In January 1942 the Nazis decided to adopt a 'Final Solution' to the 'Jewish Question.' Jews from occupied countries were to be concentrated in the east and used as forced labour, through which many would 'fall through natural diminution.' In effect, the Jews were to be systematically exterminated. Death camps, such as Auschwitz, Treblinka, Sobibor, and Maidanek, were built specifically to carry out extermination. Jews from all over Europe were herded together and murdered, usually in gas chambers. Approximately 5.9 million European Jews (of a prewar population of 9 million) were exterminated by the Nazis. It was also Nazi policy to enslave 'inferior races,' such as the Slavs and the gypsies. Over 400 000 gypsies were exterminated through slave labour, together with great numbers of Slavs from Poland, Russia, and the Balkans.

CHRONOLOGY OF WORLD WAR II

1939

1 Sept.	Germany invaded Poland
3 Sept.	France and Britain declared war on Germany

1940

9 April	Germany invaded Denmark and Norway
10 May	Germany invaded France and the Low Countries
10 June	Italy declared war on France and Britain
22 June	France surrendered

1941

6–21 April	Germany overran Yugoslavia and Greece
22 June	Germany invaded the USSR
7 Dec.	Japan attacked the US Pacific Fleet at Pearl Harbor (Hawaii); the USA entered the war

1942

15 Feb.	Singapore surrendered to Japan
4–7 June	Battle of Midway (Pacific)

1942 (continued)

23 Oct.–4 Nov.	Battle of El Alamein (North Africa)
8 Nov.	Allied invasion of French northwest Africa
9 Nov	German forces landed in Tunisia

1943

2 Feb.	German forces surrendered at Stalingrad
9 Sept.	Allies invaded Italy
20 Nov.	US invaded Tarawa (Gilbert Islands)

1944

6 June	D-Day landings in Normandy
25 Aug.	Paris liberated
24–25 Oct.	Battle of Leyte Gulf (Philippines)

1945

1 April	US landing on Okinawa (Japan)
30 April	Hitler committed suicide in Berlin
8 May	Germany surrendered unconditionally
6 and 9 Aug.	Atomic bombs dropped on Hiroshima and Nagasaki (Japan)
2 Sept.	Japan surrendered

Secret Protocols

As part of the Nazi–Soviet nonaggression pact, agreed in August 1939, a number of secret protocols were negotiated, including arrangements for the partition of Poland between Germany and the Soviet Union, as well as German acceptance of an expansion of Soviet influence into the Baltic States of Estonia, Latvia, and Lithuania. One result was that, in the aftermath of the German–Soviet invasion of Poland, Stalin initiated a Soviet occupation of the Baltic States, which lasted (with the exception of the German occupation between 1941 and 1944) until the break-up of the Soviet Union in 1991.

an alliance (the 'Pact of Steel'). Finally, the Western democracies changed their policy, ordering rearmament and abandoning appeasement, while issuing guarantees to Poland, Greece, and Romania. These moves, however, came too late.

Hitler's next demand came in the summer of 1939, when he sought the return to Germany of the 'Polish Corridor.' Aware that this might provoke a reaction from the USSR, Hitler, in August 1939, surprised European powers by concluding a nonaggression pact with Stalin, which included a number of **secret protocols**. Now free from a Soviet threat, Hitler's forces invaded Poland on 1 September. Two days later, after a strongly worded ultimatum, Britain and France declared war on Germany.

Campaigns in Europe and the Mediterranean, 1939–44

In the face of a German blitzkrieg ('lightning war'), which rapidly reached Warsaw, and a Soviet attack, Poland collapsed. Meanwhile, the British had sent forces to France, expecting a repeat of the 1914 Schlieffen Plan (see WORLD WAR I). When this attack did not happen, the Allies took no action. The so-called 'Phoney War' lasted for eight months, giving Hitler time to prepare his next campaign.

His intention was to secure his western flank by defeating Britain and France in a surprise attack, so freeing his forces for an eastern assault against the USSR; despite the agreement

of August 1939, the USSR was seen as the main enemy of fascism. The German offensive began in April 1940 with attacks on Denmark and Norway. Anglo-French units deployed to help the Norwegians had little impact, particularly when, to divert Allied attention, on 10 May, the Germans suddenly invaded France and the Low Countries (Belgium, the Netherlands, and Luxembourg). The invasion was a great success; Allied armies were forced to retreat back across the Channel, having been trapped at Dunkirk. The French could not prevent a German advance on Paris and surrendered on 22 June, after which two-thirds of the country was occupied by German forces, while one-third remained unoccupied under a pro-German government, established at Vichy, by Marshal Pétain. General de Gaulle escaped to London, where he organized the Free French resistance fighters.

Britain now faced Germany alone. As German **U-boats** (submarines) and warships threatened to cut Atlantic supply lines, Hitler prepared for a seaborne invasion of England. In the Battle of Britain, fought over southern England in the summer of 1940, the German Luftwaffe (airforce) failed to gain air superiority over the British Royal Air Force (RAF). This was followed, however, by bombing attacks on London and other British cities (**the Blitz**), which continued until May 1941. These attacks produced horrific casualties but failed to give Hitler the superiority he needed to invade

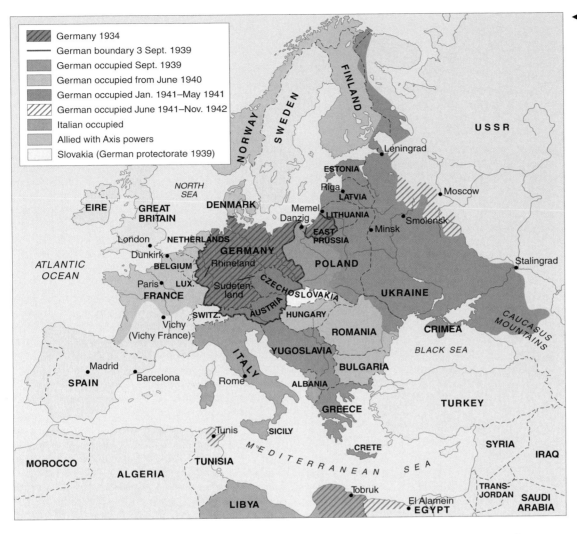

Germany 1934
German boundary 3 Sept. 1939
German occupied Sept. 1939
German occupied from June 1940
German occupied Jan. 1941–May 1941
German occupied June 1941–Nov. 1942
Italian occupied
Allied with Axis powers
Slovakia (German protectorate 1939)

◄ **The Expansion of Germany (1934–42)** *From 1935 until the outbreak of war in 1939, Hitler's contraventions of the Versailles treaty increased the size and power of Germany. Between 1939 and 1942 the blitzkrieg offensives of the German forces succeeded in extending German-occupied territory into Poland, Denmark, Norway, France, Yugoslavia, Greece, Russia, and North Africa. In November 1942, Germany's expansion reached its height when Russian forces counterattacked to prevent German armies from occupying Stalingrad.*

Britain. Instead, he decided, in spring 1941, to turn east to face the USSR, regardless of the lack of security on his western flank.

The war, meanwhile, had spread to the Mediterranean and Africa, following an Italian declaration of war on the Allies on 10 June 1940. Mussolini took immediate advantage of Allied weakness to seize British Somaliland and invade Egypt. Both attacks were repulsed. By August 1941 the Italians had been pushed out of Abyssinia. In February 1941 Hitler, desperate to prevent the complete defeat of his ally, sent forces to North Africa under General Erwin Rommel (1891–1944), who pushed British, British colonial, and Commonwealth forces back to the Egyptian border. Two months later, as Italian forces faced another defeat in Greece (which they had attacked in October 1940), the Germans invaded the Balkans, taking Yugoslavia and Greece in a swift campaign. By the end of May 1941, with the loss of the island of Crete, the British hold on the eastern Mediterranean was tenuous. The German invasion of the USSR in June eased the pressure, allowing British forces to counterattack in North Africa in November

(Operation Crusader). In early 1942, however, Rommel's forces struck back, forcing the British to retreat as far as Gazala.

A turning point had, however, already been reached. The Japanese attack on Pearl Harbor in December 1941 brought the USA into the conflict. The Battle of the Atlantic was the primary concern for the Allies; new radar aids to detect U-boats, and air cover for merchant ships in the Atlantic, gradually turned the tide of the battle. In May 1943 Germany withdrew its U-boats from the North Atlantic as a result of heavy losses. While this allowed the movement of US troops and supplies across the Atlantic, Germany had to be weakened before the Allies could risk a European campaign. In 1942 a combined RAF and US Army Air Force bombing campaign began against German cities and industry. Despite the devastating effects of these tactics, victory depended ultimately on the destruction of German armies.

In North Africa, despite the defeat of British, colonial, and Commonwealth, as well as French forces, at the Battle of Gazala and the loss of Tobruk (May–June 1942), the situation was transformed in October 1942: General

The Sino-Japanese War

In 1931 Japanese troops occupied the Chinese province of Manchuria. The Japanese launched a full-scale invasion in 1937, seizing Peking and Shanghai; by October 1938, they had occupied most of eastern China. Once World War II had spread to the Pacific and Far East (1941), the Chinese received Allied help. With the loss of Burma in 1942, however, China was isolated, enabling the Japanese to seize much of southern China. The Sino-Japanese War ended with the Japanese surrender in China (August 1945).

RESISTANCE AND COLLABORATION IN EUROPE

By mid-1942, most of Europe was in German hands. Wherever the Nazi conquerors went, resistance movements emerged, dedicated to attacking the occupying authorities. Some people, however, welcomed German occupation and collaborated with the Nazis. In France, for example, a collaborationist government was set up in June 1940 under Marshal Pétain to administer the 'unoccupied zone' centred on Vichy, while elsewhere small groups of people created resistance cells. In June 1944 French Resistance attacks on German lines of communication contributed to the success of Allied landings in Normandy.

Similar patterns of resistance occurred in the Netherlands, Belgium, Norway, and Denmark, while in the occupied parts of Russia and the Balkans, partisans (often organized by the communists) waged guerrilla warfare, forcing the Germans to divert troops from the front line to deal with them. For example, the activities of the Yugoslavian partisan forces under Marshal Tito, and those of the Greek resistance, forced the deployment of 30 German divisions in the Balkans. The war was not won by resistance movements, but their contribution to the weakening of German occupation was often significant. When the war ended, many collaborators were put on trial for treason (some were executed), while members of the resistance were, quite rightly, hailed as heroes.

Casualties

The global scale of World War II (1939–45) is reflected in the casualties suffered by the combatant nations. The figures given here show dead only (*military* and **civilian**).

USSR	*8 million*; **up to 40 million**
Poland	*300 000*; **5.8 million**
Germany	*4.5 million*; **593 000**
China	*3 million**
Japan	*1 million*; **600 000**
Yugoslavia	*500 000*; **1 million**
France	*200 000*; **400 000**
Britain	*300 000*; **97 000**
Italy	*150 000*; **150 000**
USA	*300 000*
European Jews	**5.9 million**

*No military/civilian distinction given

Bernard Montgomery (1887–1976) defeated Rommel at the Battle of El Alamein in western Egypt. This coincided with an Anglo-American invasion of northwest Africa (Operation Torch), threatening Rommel's forces from the rear. Despite heavy fighting, the campaign ended in Allied victory, in May 1943, clearing the North African coast. A Mediterranean campaign to defeat the Italians now seemed possible. Despite the USA's preference for a cross-Channel assault, Churchill persuaded Roosevelt to support an Italian operation. In July 1943 Sicily was seized; when Allied troops crossed to the mainland, the Italians, having ousted Mussolini, surrendered. Hitler hurriedly sent German units into Italy, forcing the Allies to fight a costly campaign northwards towards Rome. After bitter fighting, Rome finally fell to the Allies on 4 June 1944.

The Eastern Front, 1941–44

The gigantic German blitzkrieg against the USSR, code-named Operation Barbarossa, began on 22 June 1941. A three-pronged attack, comprising almost 3 million troops, took the Baltic States of Lithuania, Latvia, and Estonia in the north, before entering Russia southwest of Leningrad; the cities of Minsk and Smolensk were surrounded in the centre, trapping over 300 000 Soviet troops. Only in the south was Soviet resistance encountered, which destroyed the momentum of the attack. On 19 July Hitler diverted half the panzers (armoured units) of the central force to the

north, to help in the assault on Leningrad, and half to the south, to bolster the advance into the Ukraine. By the time these forces had returned north to attack Moscow in late September, however, the autumn rains had begun to fall, turning the ground to mud. Although some tanks came within 32 km of Moscow, winter snowfall and inadequate supplies forced the Germans to halt.

In 1942 Hitler shifted the emphasis of his attack to the south, where an advance into the Caucasus aimed to seize vital oilfields. After securing the Crimea, the bulk of German forces moved east towards Stalingrad (Volgograd). Once again, however, Hitler changed his mind, ordering his Sixth Army, under General Friedrich Paulus, to capture Stalingrad rather than support the main armoured advance. By September, Paulus was bogged down in urban fighting; in November, the Soviets counterattacked to surround the city, trapping nearly 200 000 German troops. On 2 February 1943, Paulus surrendered.

The Soviets pushed German forces out of the Caucasus and advanced westwards. German resistance, however, forced them to halt; a follow-up German attack in July 1943 achieved little. The resulting Battle of Kursk was the largest tank battle in history, in which the Germans lost over 2000 armoured vehicles.

The German loss of initiative enabled the Soviets to begin a series of crushing advances. Kiev, Leningrad, and the Crimea were all liberated; German forces retreated into the Baltic States. By May 1944 Soviet armies were close to the prewar Polish border; having entered Romania, they left the Germans overstretched.

War in the Far East, 1941–44

The war was not confined to Europe. The Sino-Japanese War, which had been fought since 1937, had led the USA to impose economic sanctions on Japan. This action resulted in a Japanese campaign of expansion into the Far East and western Pacific to seize resources. On 7 December 1941, Japanese aircraft bombed the US Pacific Fleet at Pearl Harbor in Hawaii. Simultaneous attacks on Wake Island, Hong Kong, the Philippines, and Malaya caught the Allies by surprise; in February 1942, the British surrendered Singapore to Japan; three months later, the USA lost the Philippines. By this time, Japanese troops had landed in New Britain and New Guinea, seized the Dutch East Indies (Indonesia), and were threatening Australia. British forces in Burma were also in full retreat.

The Allies were able gradually to reverse the position. In May 1942, a Japanese fleet, heading for New Guinea, was defeated at the Battle of the Coral Sea; a month later four

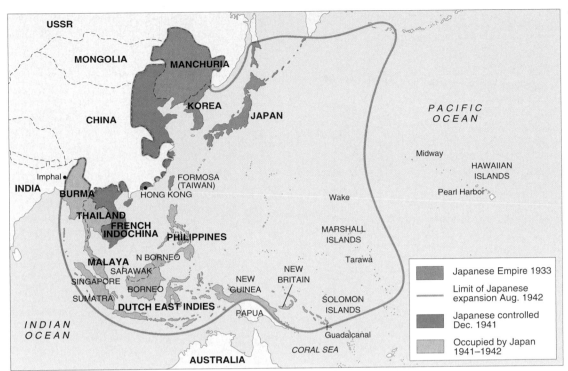

◄ **War in the Pacific (1941–42)**
From December 1941, when Japanese bombers launched a surprise attack on the US naval base at Pearl Harbor, thus bringing the USA into the war, Japan conducted a campaign of rapid expansion in the Pacific. This campaign reached its height in August 1942, by which time the Allies had begun to counterattack.

Legend:
- Japanese Empire 1933
- Limit of Japanese expansion Aug. 1942
- Japanese controlled Dec. 1941
- Occupied by Japan 1941–1942

Japanese aircraft carriers were sunk in the Battle of Midway. Action by Australian forces in New Guinea caused Japanese land forces to retreat; US General Douglas MacArthur (1880–1964) sent US marines to attack Guadalcanal (Solomon Islands) in August. After heavy fighting, the Japanese abandoned Guadalcanal in February 1943, enabling MacArthur to advance through the Solomons and New Guinea towards Rabaul (New Britain). Admiral Chester Nimitz (1885–1966), meanwhile, launched a counterattack in the central Pacific; Tarawa (Gilbert Islands) was assaulted in November 1943, followed by the Marshall Islands and then the Mariana Islands. The Japanese sent their fleet to oppose the landings on Saipan, only to be defeated in the Battle of the Philippine Sea (June 1944). A Japanese attack on Imphal and Kohima in eastern India, in March 1944, was blocked by British and Indian troops.

Allied Victory, 1944–45
By mid-1944 Germany and Japan were firmly on the defensive. Yet much had still to be achieved to ensure their defeat. In Europe, the Western Allies had to put forces ashore in a liberation campaign known as Operation Overlord. It began on 6 June 1944 (D-Day), when Allied troops under US General Dwight D. Eisenhower (1890–1969), and with help from the French Resistance, landed on the coast of Normandy (northern France). Paris was liberated on 25 August, after which the Allies conducted a swift campaign to liberate most of France, Belgium, Luxembourg, and the southern Netherlands, linking up with units that had landed in southern France on 15 August (Operation Dragoon). In September, Allied attempts to cross the Lower Rhine failed at Arnhem, stalling the advance. During the winter months the Allies could take little effective action owing to poor weather and a lack of supplies. Similar problems affected the advance to the north of Rome, in Italy.

ALLIED CONFERENCES

Even before the USA's entry into the war, President Franklin D. Roosevelt (1882–1945) and the British prime minister, Winston Churchill (1874–1965), met to discuss matters of mutual interest. In August 1941 they signed the Atlantic Charter, declaring that "All the nations of the world...must come to abandonment of the use of force," while their military staffs created the framework for later cooperation. Once the USA was involved in the war, regular meetings took place to discuss 'grand strategy.' At the Casablanca Conference, in January 1943, Roosevelt and Churchill agreed on a common war aim of the unconditional surrender of their enemies; at Quebec, in August 1943, and at Cairo, three months later, they devised the timetable for the invasion of Europe and discussed strategy in the Far East; the Chinese nationalist leader, Jiang Jie Shi (Chiang Kai-shek; 1887–1975) was also present at Cairo.

The most significant conferences were those that also involved the USSR. In November 1943 the 'Big Three' (Roosevelt, Churchill, and Stalin) met for the first time, in Tehran (Iran), to discuss the shape of postwar Europe. Talks continued at Yalta (the Crimea) in February 1945. Finally, at Potsdam (July–August 1945) the continuing war in the Far East and final details of postwar Europe were discussed. By this time, however, it was clear that the era of wartime cooperation was over; an East–West 'Cold War' was developing.

The Defeat of Germany *From 1942 to 1944 the Allies counterattacked, forcing a German retreat; notable Allied victories were at the Battle of Kursk (July 1943) on the Eastern Front and the Battle of El Alamein (October 1942) in Egypt. The final defeat of Germany was assured by the success of Operation Overlord, the Allied landings in northern France (June 1944), which initiated the campaign that liberated almost all of Europe from German occupation by May 1945.*

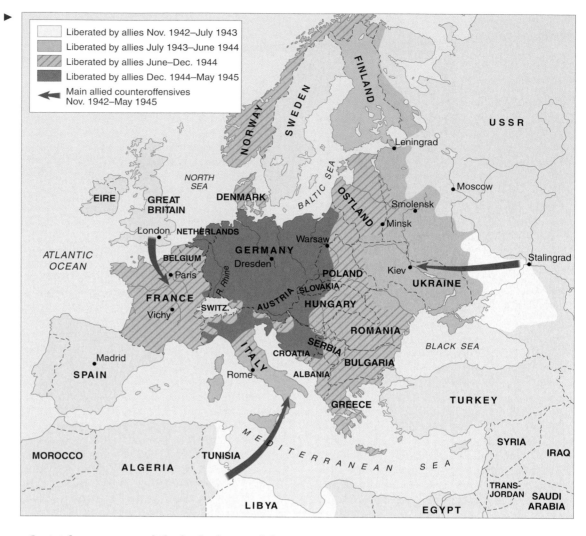

Legend:
- Liberated by allies Nov. 1942–July 1943
- Liberated by allies July 1943–June 1944
- Liberated by allies June–Dec. 1944
- Liberated by allies Dec. 1944–May 1945
- Main allied counteroffensives Nov. 1942–May 1945

Warsaw Uprisings

Two uprisings occurred during the German occupation of Warsaw. In January 1943 some 56 000 ghetto Jews staged an uprising, which was not quelled until 8 May. Between August and October 1944 the Polish Home Army also staged an uprising in an attempt to expel the German army from Warsaw before the advancing Soviet forces arrived. The uprising was crushed by the Germans owing to a lack of Soviet support. Poland thus became more vulnerable to political domination by the Soviet Union.

Soviet forces, meanwhile, had advanced, by early August 1944, as far as Warsaw. Further south, they thrust deep into the Balkans, defeating both Romania and Bulgaria and opening the way to the liberation of Greece, Yugoslavia, and Albania. Yugoslavia liberated itself with help from the Soviet army and guerrilla resistance forces, under the leadership of Marshal Tito (1892–1980). Albania liberated itself principally from the Italians, under the leadership of Enver Hoxha (1908–85).

Hitler mounted a counterattack on the Western Allies in December 1944 (the 'Battle of the Bulge'), hoping to defeat them in a surprise advance through northeastern France. As the Allies countered the attack, the Soviets took the opportunity, between 12 January and 4 February 1945, to advance over 500 miles eastwards, overwhelming German resistance and threatening Berlin.

Allied pressure on Germany increased. British and US aircraft destroyed German cities in a devastating bombing campaign: the firestorm on Hamburg (July–August 1943) killed 35 000 people, while 100 000 perished in an attack on Dresden (February 1945). Allied ground units advanced to the Rhine, crossing the river in March, before thrusting east to link up with Soviet forces. The Ruhr industrial area was taken in April. British and Canadian troops advanced into the Netherlands and southern Germany, carving out occupation zones that had been agreed between the Allies at the Yalta conference. On 16 April, the Soviet attack on Berlin began; despite bitter fighting, the city was surrounded within ten days and four days later, Hitler committed suicide. By this time, Soviet troops had met the Western Allies on the River Elbe, while US units had made contact with Allied forces from northern Italy, where a final offensive was launched in April. The Germans surrendered unconditionally on 8 May 1945.

In the Pacific, however, the war between Japan and the Allies continued. MacArthur invaded the Philippines on 20 October 1944, resulting in the Battle of Leyte Gulf (24–25 October); despite the use of kamikaze (suicide) pilots, the Japanese were defeated. MacArthur then attacked Luzon in January 1945. Heavy losses were sustained on both sides as US forces took Iwo Jima (February–March) and

▲ **The D-Day Landings** *The landings, which began on 6 June 1944, initiated the Allied liberation of Europe from Nazi rule. US forces are shown landing on the coast of northern France.*

Okinawa (April–June). An Allied campaign to liberate Burma by May 1945 was also costly.

An Allied submarine campaign had all but destroyed Japanese shipping by early 1945. US bombers, flying from China and the Mariana Islands, devastated Japan's cities. Still the Japanese showed no sign of surrender. US

President Harry Truman (1884–1972), who replaced Roosevelt in April, felt it necessary to deploy a new weapon – the atomic bomb – which had been developed by scientists working on the **Manhattan Project**. On 6 August 1945 the city of Hiroshima was destroyed by the bomb, leaving 78 000 people dead; three days later Nagasaki was also bombed, resulting in a further 35 000 deaths. Also facing a Soviet invasion of Manchuria, the Japanese surrendered on 15 August; the documents were signed on 2 September. Six years of war had cost an estimated 50 million lives.

The Manhattan Project

By 1939, scientists were already aware of the devastating potential of harnessing an atomic chain reaction. Fears that German scientists were working on such techniques led the Allies to pool resources in order to produce an atomic weapon. Research, which began in August 1942, was concentrated in the USA and code-named 'Manhattan Engineer District'; scientists throughout the free world were given unlimited resources for the research. The bombs were built in New Mexico and the first was successfully tested on 16 July 1945, producing a blast equivalent to 20 000 tons of conventional high explosive. The two remaining bombs were deployed against Japan in August 1945.

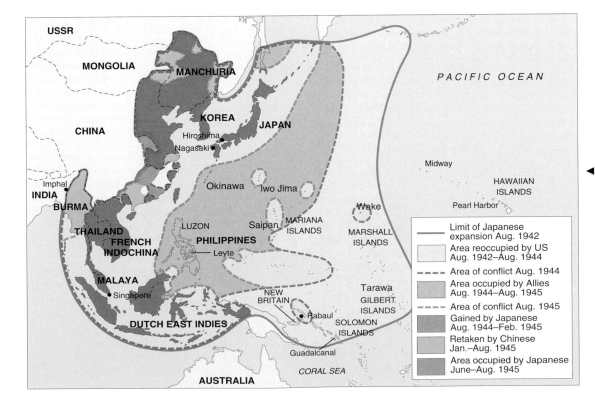

Limit of Japanese expansion Aug. 1942
Area reoccupied by US Aug. 1942–Aug. 1944
Area of conflict Aug. 1944
Area occupied by Allies Aug. 1944–Aug. 1945
Area of conflict Aug. 1945
Gained by Japanese Aug. 1944–Feb. 1945
Retaken by Chinese Jan.–Aug. 1945
Area occupied by Japanese June–Aug. 1945

◄ **The Defeat of Japan**
A concerted Allied counteroffensive from the east and southwest from mid-1942 began the reversal of Japan's fortunes. US, British, and Australian forces gradually liberated Japanese-occupied areas of the Pacific. Japan's final defeat was secured with the dropping of atomic bombs on Hiroshima and Nagasaki in August 1945.

Postwar Europe

The aftermath of war • The 'Iron Curtain' • The Cold War •
Eastern Europe (1968–89) • Western Europe • West European unity

From Stettin in the
Baltic to Trieste in the
Adriatic, an Iron
Curtain has descended
across the continent.

Winston Churchill, in a
speech delivered in the USA
(March 1946)

Negotiations between the Allied leaders
during the latter stages of World War II indicated that the division of postwar Europe was
likely to be a source of conflict. Churchill's
prediction that the majority of eastern Europe
and the Balkans would inevitably come under
Soviet domination was proved correct.

The Aftermath of War
By early 1945, the Red Army had advanced
through eastern Europe, conquering half of
Germany. However, the USSR did not annex
the territories it occupied; Stalin made it clear
that Russia wished to establish a ring of
friendly nations on its western borders to act
as buffer states against future aggression.

After their surrender, Germany and Austria
were split into US, Russian, British, and French
occupation zones. The former German capital,
Berlin, lay inside the Russian zone, but was
given special status under the four occupying
powers. The population of the US, British, and
French zones of Germany, swollen by millions
of refugees from the east, was close to starvation. In order to rebuild western Germany as a
bulwark against further Soviet expansion, the
Western Allies rapidly established democratic
institutions. In 1947 the **Marshall Plan** was
introduced to supply economic aid to Europe.

The 'Iron Curtain'
In the immediate postwar period, relations between the USA and the USSR were generally
good. However, experts within the US State
Department and Winston Churchill warned
of Stalin's intentions. Churchill popularized
the image of an 'Iron Curtain' across Europe,
dividing the free world from communism.

Apart from Yugoslavia, led by the anti-Stal-
inist communist Marshal Tito (1892–1980),

▲ **The Division of Central and Eastern
Europe After World War II** *Occupation zones
within Germany and Soviet satellite states are shown.*

and Greece, all of eastern Europe and the
Balkans was under Soviet control by 1950.

In Czechoslovakia the elected president, Ed-
vard Beneš (1884–1948), was forced to resign following a communist coup in 1948. In
the same year the popular Polish independent
communist leader Władisław Gomułka
(1905–82) was dismissed by Moscow. In 1949
the Soviet zone of Germany became the
German Democratic Republic, effectively a
one-party state controlled by the Socialist
Unity Party (SED) under its first secretary Walter Ulbricht (1893–1973). In Hungary the
communists assumed full control in 1949.

The Cold War
In June 1948, the Soviet authorities closed all
road and rail routes from West Germany to
Berlin. The USA and Britain responded with
an airlift of essential supplies of food and fuel
around the clock to the Western sectors of the
city, a lifeline that was to last for 11 months.

In April 1949 the North Atlantic Treaty,
which created the NATO military alliance, was

YALTA AND POTSDAM

The conferences held by the Allied leaders at the Black Sea resort of
Yalta in February 1945 and at Potsdam, near Berlin, in July shaped
the destiny of postwar Europe. At Yalta a treaty was signed calling
for the "establishment through free elections of governments responsive to the will of the people." However, Stalin's repression of
noncommunist partisans in eastern Europe indicated that the USSR
would not abide by this agreement. At Potsdam, the new borders of
Germany were set: the country was divided into four occupation
zones, with Berlin also under four-power control.

UPRISINGS

In 1953 riots erupted in several East German cities after the communist regime raised industrial targets without improving rates of pay. Party leader Walter Ulbricht enlisted Soviet military help to quell the disturbances.

Three years later, students and workers began an uprising in the Hungarian capital, Budapest. The Hungarian leader Imre Nagy (1896–1958) announced his country's neutrality and withdrawal from the Warsaw Pact. The USSR responded by invading Hungary with an army of 200 000 men and 2500 tanks. In bitter street fighting, over 3000 Hungarians were killed. Within days, the rebellion was crushed; Nagy was arrested and later executed, and a hard-line regime installed.

signed by the USA, Canada, and most western European nations. Shortly after, the Federal Republic of Germany was created from the three western zones of occupation. Its capital was Bonn, and its first chancellor Konrad Adenauer (1876–1967). Though West Germany did not join NATO until 1955, it was the main forward base for NATO forces from the outset.

The Cold War was characterized by mutual suspicion. In its most infamous episode, the German Democratic Republic built the Berlin Wall in 1961 to prevent emigration of skilled workers to the West; the wall became a symbol of the repressiveness of communism.

After Stalin's death in 1953, the Soviet Union took a more conciliatory line, withdrawing its troops from Czechoslovakia, Finland, and Austria. In 1955 the Warsaw Pact agreement between the USSR and its satellites created a military alliance to match NATO.

Eastern Europe (1968–89)

In 1968 Alexander Dubček (1921–92) became first secretary of the Czechoslovak Communist Party and began a programme of liberalization. The USSR, under Leonid Brezhnev (1906–82), sent Warsaw Pact troops into Prague in August. Dubček was removed from office and orthodox communism reimposed. Dissidents went underground or were imprisoned. In 1977 they publicly formed the pro-civil rights Charter 77 group.

From 1970 onwards there was sporadic unrest in Poland, where the liberal Gomułka was replaced by the conservative Edward Gierek (1913–   ). In 1980, following protests, Gierek was forced to resign; his successor signed an accord with workers' leader Lech Wałesa (1943–   ). Wałesa formed the National Confederation of Independent Trades Unions ('Solidarity'), with 10 million members. Despite imposing martial law and banning Solidarity in 1981, the movement had taken root.

In June 1985 Mikhail Gorbachov (1931–   ) was appointed first secretary of the Soviet Communist Party. His programme of reform heralded the demise of communism.

The Marshall Plan

General George C. Marshall (1880–1959), appointed US secretary of state in 1947, was the architect of the postwar programme of US economic aid to Europe. Stalin forbade all countries under Soviet occupation (including Finland) to accept Marshall aid. Between 1948 and 1952, about US $17 billion was distributed to the countries of western Europe and Turkey. The main beneficiaries were France, the United Kingdom, and West Germany. This aid enabled the war-shattered economies of these countries to recover within less than a decade.

◄ **The Berlin Airlift**
British and US aircraft had to bring in all supplies to the western sector of the city after the Soviets attempted to drive the Western Allies from Berlin with a total road and rail blockade that lasted almost a year (1948–49). At the height of the operation, an aircraft was landing in Berlin every minute. Here an American DC4 cargo plane is seen approaching Tempelhof airport, watched by an eager crowd; aircrews would sometimes drop sweets to children on their approach to the airfield.

▲ **General de Gaulle** *(1890–1970) When Germany occupied France in 1940, Charles de Gaulle escaped to London to head the Committee of National Liberation. After the liberation of France, he became president of the provisional government. Forming his own party – the RPF – in 1946, he was elected president of the Fifth Republic in 1959 and held office until 1969.*

A Solidarity Demonstration in Gdańsk, Poland *(1982) The powerful reforming trade union movement began in the shipyards of Gdańsk. ▼*

Western Europe

Great Britain. The Conservative wartime leader, Winston Churchill, was heavily defeated in 1945 by the Labour Party, which introduced the welfare state and large-scale nationalization. Years of austerity followed as Great Britain sought to rebuild its infrastructure and economy. This was accompanied by a loss of overseas possessions, as India and colonies in Africa were granted independence. The British economy suffered badly during the world recession of the 1970s. Politically, the country swung between Labour and Conservative administrations during the 1960s and 1970s. In 1979 the Conservative Margaret Thatcher (1925–   ) was elected on a ticket of privatization and reduced public spending. There followed a sustained period of right-wing government, which continued under her successor, John Major (1943–   ). As the country emerged from recession, the Labour Party, reformed under Tony Blair (1953–   ), won a huge victory in the 1997 general election.

France. From 1946 onwards, France was ruled by a succession of short-lived coalitions. Instability was exacerbated by France's involvement in the mid-1950s in wars against nationalist guerrillas in Algeria and Indochina. In 1958, de Gaulle was recalled from retirement to draft a new constitution. Elected president of the Fifth Republic in 1959, he granted independence to France's African colonies. In 1961–62, de Gaulle survived an attempted overthrow by French Algerians and army factions. In 1968, civil unrest by left-wing students and workers threatened the government. De Gaulle was succeeded by Georges Pompidou (1911–74); in 1981, the first socialist president for 35 years, François Mitterrand (1916–96), took office. In May 1995 the right-wing former prime minister, Jacques Chirac (1932–   ), was elected president.

Italy. Economic recovery in Italy after the war was slow. Lack of confidence in Christian Democrat administrations led to the growth of western Europe's largest communist party, which won considerable support in the 1970s. In the 1990s, trials of former politicians revealed widespread corruption. In 1993, electoral reform was endorsed by referendum; a new centre-left coalition was elected in 1996.

Spain and Portugal. Two nations in western Europe did not adopt democratic government after 1945. Portugal's dictator, António Salazar (1889–1970), had been in office continuously since 1933. His successor, Marcello Caetano (1906–80), was deposed by a military junta in 1974. Free elections were held in 1975, returning a socialist government that initiated land redistribution and granted independence to Portugal's African colonies. From 1989 industries were denationalized under a Social Democrat government. In 1995, the Socialist Party was returned to power, followed in 1996 by a socialist president.

The death in 1975 of the Spanish dictator Francisco Franco (1892–1975), who had ruled since 1939, led to the establishment of a constitutional monarchy and democratic government by his chosen successor, King Juan Carlos I (1938–   ). In June 1977 the first general election for 40 years was held. The socialist Felipe González (1942–   ) won elections in 1982 and 1986. Government corruption scandals in the early 1990s led to pressure for reform. In 1996 the conservative Popular Party, under José Maria Aznar, was narrowly elected to govern.

West European Unity

In 1948 the Organization for European Economic Cooperation was created to administer the Marshall Plan; it comprised every nation of western Europe, plus Turkey. In 1949 most members (except Spain and Portugal) formed the Council of Europe, with headquarters at Strasbourg, to foster political cooperation.

Belgium, the Netherlands, and Luxembourg formed the 'Benelux' customs union in 1948. Three years later, these countries, together with France, Italy, and West Germany, established the European Coal and Steel Community as a 'common market.'

With the signing of the Treaty of Rome in 1957, the ECSC became the European Economic Community, later known as the European Community (EC). In 1993 a single European market was established and the Maastricht Treaty made provision for further future integration. The designation of European Union (EU) was adopted and in 1995 the EU expanded to 15 members.

The End of Communism

The Soviet Union • Eastern Europe

The rapid collapse in 1989 of the state-socialist regimes of eastern Europe, followed by the disintegration of the Soviet Union by the end of 1991, signalled the collapse of communism. The reforms in domestic and foreign policy introduced by Mikhail Gorbachov (1931–   ), who was elected General Secretary of the Communist Party of the Soviet Union (CPSU) in 1985 and president in 1988, are of great importance in understanding how this came about. His objective of modernizing the Soviet Union in order to preserve its status as a great world power unintentionally hastened the demise of the communist system.

The Soviet Union

In April 1985, at a meeting of the Central Committee of the CPSU, Gorbachov announced plans to halt the increasing economic stagnation, evident since the latter years of the rule of Leonid I. Brezhnev (1906–82; CPSU General Secretary 1964–82). Gorbachov's economic policy of **perestroika** resembled that of his former patron, Yuri V. Andropov (1914–84; CPSU General Secretary 1982–84). At first Gorbachov did not envisage radical political reform. He believed that renewed economic growth could be secured by campaigns against corruption, waste, absenteeism, and alcoholism, and by restoring workplace discipline. These were combined with a programme of investment designed to modernize industry. The insufficiency of such measures prompted Gorbachov to initiate more radical reforms during 1986, which collectively came to be known as **glasnost**. Gorbachov mobilized support from intellectuals, the media, and ultimately the populace at large. In 1987 he called for more democratization within the party and state bureaucracy. By encouraging criticism of corruption and inefficiency, and permitting genuine (if limited) multicandidate elections of Communist Party and local officials, Gorbachov sought to promote his own supporters and overcome opposition to his reforms.

The June 1987 meeting of the Central Committee heralded more radical economic reforms. Following a law sanctioning individual family businesses on a limited scale, Gorbachov proposed legislation on state enterprises. Its aim was to replace the Stalinist system of central control with the cautious introduction of market mechanisms. Enterprises were now free to take their own decisions on production and were in theory responsible for financing

▲ **Dismantling a Statue of Lenin**
As communism collapsed throughout eastern Europe, symbols of the old regime were pulled down. Here, workmen prepare to remove a statue of Lenin, hero of the Russian Revolution, in Bucharest, Romania.

their own labour, materials, and capital costs. In May 1988, the Law on Cooperation in the USSR extended the scope of private enterprise, allowing newly formed cooperatives to provide consumer goods and services. Growing food shortages also made reforms in agriculture imperative. However, Gorbachov's support for increased production through the privatization of agriculture (i.e. decollectivization and the restoration of peasant family farming) was not fully translated into practice. In 1988 50-year leases of land were introduced, in the hope of stimulating an efficient agricultural sector. To increase the food supply, independent farmers were now permitted to sell privately produced food. Private property in the countryside, however, was not fully restored, despite the March 1990 law that allowed peasants to own, but not sell, their land.

This partial reform was mirrored elsewhere; inefficient enterprises continued to be financed by the state and punitive taxation limited the ability of the new cooperatives to increase production. The confusion caused by the failure to replace the Stalinist system with

═══SEE ALSO═══
This section:
• The Causes and Course of World War II
• Postwar Europe
The World in the 20th Century:
• The 'New World Order'
Europe (vol. 1)
Politics and Government (vol. 6):
• How Countries are Governed

perestroika
(reconstruction) The restructuring of the Soviet economy to incorporate the introduction of market mechanisms. *Perestroika* later came to embrace the concept of radical political reform.

glasnost (openness) The organization of popular opinion in support of Gorbachov's reform programme against bureaucratic obstructiveness. *Glasnost* is now regarded as a critical element in the democratization of the Soviet Union.

Mikhail S. Gorbachov

Mikhail Sergeevich Gorbachov was born into a peasant family in the Stavropol region of the USSR on 2 March 1931. Having graduated in law from Moscow State University in 1955, he later studied agronomy. He joined the Communist Party in 1952, and rose through the ranks in his native region. In 1978 he was appointed to the Central Committee of the CPSU, as Secretary for Agriculture; seven years later he became its youngest leader since Stalin. For his support of reform in eastern Europe, he was awarded the Nobel Peace Prize in 1990. Following a reduction of his powers after the unsuccessful coup against him in August 1991, Gorbachov resigned as president later the same year.

◄ **Gorbachov Addressing the UN General Assembly (1988)** *Although he won praise and popular acclaim abroad, Mikhail Gorbachov was reviled by many in the Soviet Union for his attempts to reform the economy.*

effective market mechanisms contributed to a dramatic economic decline; by 1990 the population faced growing shortages and the standard of living plummeted, causing dissatisfaction across the Soviet Union. Attempts to resolve the situation by a rapid transition to the market system foundered in the face of opposition from the conservative Congress of People's Deputies in December 1989.

Ironically, Gorbachov's political reforms succeeded all too well. Openness began to prevail in a number of areas: public discussion was tolerated of formerly unmentionable subjects, such as crime, drugs, and prostitution; suppressed material was published; open criticism emerged of the bureaucratic obstruction of economic reforms; and the mass murders perpetrated during Stalin's purges of the 1930s came to light. At the 19th Conference of the CPSU in June 1988 Gorbachov responded to pressures for political change, proposing a fundamental reform of Soviet government. A new Congress of People's Deputies was proposed, with two-thirds of its members democratically elected and the rest nominated by the CPSU and the trade unions. The Congress would elect a Supreme Soviet from its ranks to act as a new legislative parliament. On 26 March 1989 multicandidate elections to the Congress took place; leading communists suffered heavy defeats in such major cities as Moscow – where Boris Yeltsin (1931–   ) was elected – Leningrad (later St Petersburg), and Kiev. Gorbachov, who had replaced Andrei Gromyko (1909–89) as president of the Soviet Union on 1 October 1988, was re-elected in May 1989.

The scale of the political change wrought by Gorbachov was revealed by a series of popular

▲ **Nicolae Ceauşescu**
Ceauşescu's regime was one of the most hardline in eastern Europe; his 'Securitate' secret police were feared for their brutality. After extensive demonstrations and streetfighting in December 1989, Ceauşescu was overthrown and, together with his wife, executed by firing squad.

THE COLLAPSE OF COMMUNISM

Apr.–Jun. 1989	In Poland, Solidarity legalized; semi-free elections held
Sept.–Nov. 1989	Mass protests in East German cities follow attempts to halt emigration of citizens to the West; Berlin Wall breached; collapse of Honecker regime
Nov.–Dec.1989	Noncommunist coalition government formed in Czechoslovakia; Václav Havel (1936–) elected president
December 1989	In Romania, crushing of protests in western city of Timişoara leads to mass demonstrations in the capital, Bucharest; downfall and execution of Nicolae Ceauşescu (1918–89) and his wife
Dec. 1989–May 1990	Baltic States proclaim sovereignty (and later independence) from Soviet Union
March–April 1990	Noncommunist government formed in Hungary
October 1990	Reunification of Germany
June 1991	Reformer Boris Yeltsin popularly elected president of Russian Republic
June 1991	Communist government in Albania resigns
August 1991	Independence declared by former Soviet republics of Ukraine, Belarus, Moldova, Azerbaijan, Kyrgyzstan, and Uzbekistan
October 1991	Democratic forces win power in popular vote in Bulgaria
December 1991	Formal dissolution of the Soviet Union

actions in 1989. In July, over 300 000 miners went on strike to secure long-promised improvements in conditions, in food supply, and in pensions. They also advocated further political and economic reforms, including an end to the Communist Party's monopoly of political power, the direct election of the Soviet president, and workers' control of the mines.

More significantly for the future of the Soviet Union, a series of nationalist challenges emerged. In February 1988 the Christian Armenian majority in the Nagorno-Karabakh region of the predominantly Muslim Soviet Republic of Azerbaijan had begun mass demonstrations in favour of incorporation within the Armenian Soviet Republic; a bloody civil war ensued. In April 1989 a demonstration in Tbilisi, Georgia, demanding its independence from the Soviet Union, was crushed by Soviet forces. The major challenge to the unity of the Soviet Union came from Estonia, Latvia, and Lithuania, which had been ceded to the Soviet Union under the Nazi-Soviet pact of 1939. Protests escalated by August 1989 into a mass independence movement.

The subsequent history of the Soviet Union was characterized by conflict between conservatives and pro-democratic forces. Gorbachov failed to use his increased presidential powers to provide consistent leadership. On the one hand he introduced democratic reforms, legalizing competing political parties and restructuring the state by drafting a new treaty (the **Novo-Ogarev Agreement**) that devolved substantial economic and political power to the republics. On the other hand he appeased the conservatives, rejecting rapid transition to a market system and condoning attempts to crush the nationalist uprisings.

The threat to centralized power within the Soviet Union posed by the Novo-Ogarev Agreement precipitated a coup against Gorbachov by some of his own appointees in August 1991. The president of the Russian Republic, Boris Yeltsin, rallied popular opposition to the coup, which quickly failed due to bad planning and lack of significant military support. However, this violent challenge to emerging democracy finally discredited communism in the eyes of most Soviet people. Gorbachov's efforts in the autumn to create a new Union of Sovereign States failed and the Soviet Union disintegrated as many republics declared independence.

Democratic government remained fragile in post-Soviet Russia as Yeltsin's government faced opposition to political and socio-economic reform. Hardline parliamentary opposition during the early 1990s culminated, in 1993, in political crisis, which was only resolved by military intervention. A more centrist government put an end to radical economic reform, while a new constitution re-

placed the Congress of People's Deputies with a Federal Assembly. In 1994, Russian troops invaded the breakaway republic of Chechenya, beginning a two-year conflict that resulted in Russian withdrawal and humiliation. Meanwhile, Yeltsin struggled against ill health as the Communists gained strength in the State Dumas (parliament) in 1995. Yeltsin's victory over the Communist Party leader in the presidential elections of 1996. Following a power struggle in the Kremlin (1997) and an attempt to remove Yeltsin from office, he regained authority and in March and again in August 1998 replaced the entire government, apparently in order to increase the pace of reforms.

Eastern Europe

With the exception of Yugoslavia and Albania, communist regimes in eastern Europe were created by the Soviet Union after World War II. Attempts to overthrow the Stalinist system imposed on the satellite countries (e.g.

▲ **Protestors on the Berlin Wall**
The Berlin Wall, built in 1961, allegedly to "defend socialism," but actually to prevent mass emigration, was breached by East German protestors on 10 November 1989.

The hungry hare has no frontiers and doesn't follow ideologies. The hungry hare goes where it finds the food. And the other hares don't block its passage with the tanks.

Lech Walesa, Polish founder of the Solidarity trade union

141

The Sinatra Doctrine

The Brezhnev Doctrine was elaborated in 1968 to justify the Soviet military intervention that halted the reforms initiated by the Communist Party in Czechoslovakia. This doctrine claimed that the Soviet Union was justified in using military force to defend 'socialism' (as defined by the Soviet government) wherever it was threatened. By contrast, the 'Sinatra Doctrine' mockingly alludes to the song *My Way* performed by Frank Sinatra; it implied that the peoples of former Soviet satellite states in eastern Europe had the right to pursue their own destiny. The term was coined by Russian foreign ministry spokesman Gennady Gerasimov.

in Hungary in 1956 and in Czechoslovakia in 1968) were suppressed by Soviet military force. In Poland in 1982, martial law was imposed to try to crush the trade union Solidarity and forestall Soviet intervention. While this ensured the survival of largely unpopular communist governments, it did not eliminate opposition. In the 1980s, declining standards of living, growing foreign debt, and widespread corruption in the party fuelled discontent.

The emergence of democratic forces in the Soviet Union encouraged reformist movements in eastern Europe, as did Gorbachov's assurances that Soviet forces would not intervene to prevent reform. His renunciation of the Brezhnev Doctrine with regard to eastern Europe became popularly known as the **Sinatra Doctrine**. Realizing that it was no longer possible to maintain the system by force, some communist regimes instituted reform. In Hungary the replacement of hardliner János Kádár (1912–89) as party leader by Karoly Grosz in 1988 was followed by a multiparty system and legalization of private enterprise. In Poland, in August 1988, the government began negotiations with Solidarity to end a wave of strikes; in 1989 Solidarity regained legal status and free elections were held for 35% of the seats in parliament. Yet these attempts by communist parties to retain power ultimately failed.

In Czechoslovakia, East Germany, and Romania, hardline communist regimes made no attempts at reform. In late 1989, mass demon-

strations took place in many East German cities. These were sparked off by Gorbachov's visit to East Berlin in October, during which he unsuccessfully tried to persuade Erich Honecker (1912–94), leader of the ruling Socialist Unity Party, to institute reform. A critical factor in the success of eastern European revolutions was the failure of various national armies to suppress popular protest; Honecker's attempt to have demonstrators shot was overruled, while in Romania the army even supported the overthrow of the Ceaușescu regime.

Although 1989 marked the end of one-party communist regimes in eastern Europe, many former communist parties capitalized on the disillusion that followed adoption of the new free-market system. During the 1990s, countries such as Poland, Lithuania, and Hungary returned former communists to power, while in others (e.g. Ukraine) they formed the largest single parliamentary grouping. The transition in eastern Europe has not been smooth; Bulgaria and the Czech Republic (which separated from Slovakia in 1993) suffered political and economic crises in 1997 and civil unrest broke out in Albania in 1997 and 1998.

The Independent States of Eastern Europe, the Baltic, and Central Asia *The collapse of communism in the Soviet Union in 1991 brought liberation and independence to former Soviet republics and satellite states.* ▼

Former Soviet republics

Soviet satellite states of eastern Europe prior to the end of communism

ISLAMIC WORLD

The Emergence of a New Empire

Caliphate and counterattack • Continuing conquests • Administering an empire • The rise of the Umayyads • The Umayyad Caliphate • The fall of the dynasty • Towards a new culture

Before the rise of Islam (see RELIGION (vol. 6): ISLAM), Arabia was divided into numerous kingdoms, which fought each other for supremacy in different regions of the peninsula. The south (now Yemen) was inhabited by predominantly agricultural peoples. They were also trading peoples, who had developed a long and profitable trade route from East Africa and from India; further north their lifestyle was characterized by trade caravans. Central and northern Arabia was occupied mainly by migratory Bedouin tribes. The collapse of several powerful Arabian kingdoms in the late 6th and early 7th centuries led to the rise of the mercantile Quraysh tribe, which worshipped Allah and established control of the sacred enclave of Mecca. The Quraysh set up trading agreements with northern and southern tribes, which opened Arabia to widespread commerce.

The century following the sudden death of the Prophet Mohammed (born 570) in 632 saw the creation of an empire that spread his influence and the Arabic language from the borders of France to those of India and China. During this period a sovereign leader (the caliph) emerged. Under the authority of a succession of caliphs, a distinctive 'Islamic' culture began to appear in such fields as architecture, literature, and legal theory. Economic development was assisted by the imposition of order, the benefits of Arabic as a lingua franca, and the stimulus of pilgrimage to more extensive international contacts.

Caliphate and Counterattack

The death of Mohammed stunned the Muslim community. The acceptance of Abu Bakr (c. 573–634), whom the Prophet had authorized to lead prayers during his illness, avoided a conflict over succession. As **khalifah** (caliph), or 'successor' to Mohammed, Abu Bakr stressed that he was assuming the headship of the **ummah** (community of believers) without making any claim to inherit Mohammed's prophetic powers.

For many Arab tribes who had sworn allegiance to Mohammed, his death terminated their obligations. They ceased to pay taxes; as a result, Abu Bakr sent 11 separate punitive expeditions to enforce renewed obedience among those henceforth labelled 'apostates.'

Even before the Arabian peninsula was fully subdued, conquests were made in surrounding territories within the Byzantine and Sassanian (Persian) empires. Foremost among the Muslim generals was Khalid ibn al-Walid, the 'Sword of Islam.' Having already inflicted several shattering defeats on the Sassanians, he intervened in the campaign to seize the rich province of Syria from Byzantium.

Continuing Conquests

Abu Bakr's death, after a two-year reign, did not interrupt the victories of the Muslim armies. He had nominated Omar (died 644), another former companion of the Prophet, as his successor; in turn, Omar nominated a council to choose his successor. When Omar was assassinated, the council chose Uthman (died 656). When Uthman's death threatened

SEE ALSO
The Literary Arts
Worldwide (vol. 4):
• Islamic Literature
Religion (vol. 6):
• Islam
Law (vol. 6):
• Legal Systems and their Origins

◀ **Mohammed's First Followers**
(16th-century Turkish manuscript) Mohammed gave daily recitations of messages he believed were conveyed to him by God. Later recorded as hadith ('tradition'); they were to become a fundamental element of Islamic legal theory; evaluation of their authenticity became a major branch of scholarship.

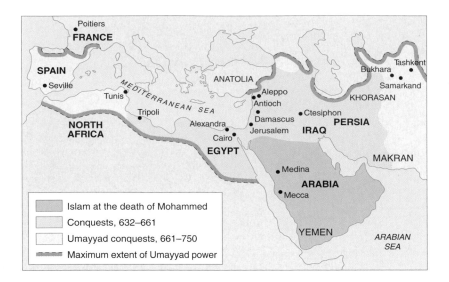

▲ The Expansion of the Muslim Empire *From 632 to 750 the Muslim Empire spread to incorporate lands stretching from western Europe to the Far East.*

Umayyads The first Muslim dynasty to hold the title of caliph. The Umayyads were mainly a merchant family of the Quraysh tribe. Initially resisting Islam, they eventually converted in 627 and became prominent administrators under Mohammed and his immediate successors. Mu'awiyah, the first Umayyad caliph, was Uthman's nephew.

to split the *ummah,* the process of territorial expansion came to a temporary halt.

In 636 a counteroffensive by a Byzantine army of 140 000 was annihilated by a Muslim force of 36 000 on the Yarmuk River, confirming the Arab hold on Syria. Arab forces turned north against Armenia and south into Egypt, and then westwards along the coast of North Africa. Acquiring naval capability, the Muslims seized Cyprus in 649. In the east, the Sassanian Empire had been overrun after a decisive victory at Qadisiyyah in 637. The Persian capital at Ctesiphon was also captured.

Administering an Empire
Omar confronted the problem of administering his expanding territories by appointing a governor for each province. Competent officials of the previous regime were left in office, while Greek and Pahlavi remained the languages of government. Little effort was made to convert local peoples to Islam once they had submitted to Arab rule. The armies of occupation remained in garrison towns – such as Kufa in Iraq – on the fringe of the desert.

The Rise of the Umayyads
Uthman's appointment of fellow **Umayyads** to top positions created grievances among those who remembered them as persecutors of the Prophet. Others were upset by the autocratic manner in which he determined to establish a single canonical text for the Koran. Mu'awiyah (c. 602–80) achieved a tight hold on the province of Syria, making it a bastion of Umayyad power. Discontent, however, began to unite around Ali (c. 600–67), the son-in-law of Mohammed himself.

Uthman's assassination was followed by Ali's accession to the caliphate. This was challenged by Aisha (c. 613–78), Ali's stepmother. Ali, moving the capital from Medina to Kufa, crushed this challenge near Basra. He then

turned to deal with Mu'awiyah, who still held Syria. At Siffin, on the Euphrates River, however, Mu'awiyah turned the tide of battle and Ali conceded. A group known as the **Kharijites** ('seceders') withdrew their allegiance to Ali and were responsible for his assassination (661). His death ended the line of four caliphs, dubbed **Rashidin** ('rightly guided'), all of whom had known Mohammed in person. Mu'awiyah, having added Egypt to his domains, bought off the claims of Ali's son, Hasan (624–680), to the caliphate. Those who accepted the legitimacy of Mu'awiyah's 'election' became known as **Sunnites** (followers of the *Sunna,* meaning tradition) while the rejectionist minority became known as **Shiites** (*Shi'at Ali,* or party of Ali). These remain the two irreconcilable factions of Islam.

The Umayyad Caliphate
Mu'awiyah's assumption of power resulted in another relocation of the capital to the ancient metropolis of Damascus. This change resulted in a new emphasis on luxury and grandeur, setting the caliph far above his fellow Muslims. Government became increasingly bureaucratic and less personal. Syrian Arabs, or even Christian ones, had a preferential place in the new social order. Succession to the caliphate continued, in theory, through 'election.' In practice, Mu'awiyah secured it for his son, Yazid (645–683), long before his own death.

An adept statesman, Mu'awiyah kept a firm grip on his inheritance. He enlarged it by renewing the thrust along the North African coast, establishing a major base at Kairouan in Tunisia in 670. Sustained campaigns to take Constantinople were, however, thwarted.

CHRONOLOGY OF MUSLIM RULERS (630–750)	
632	Mohammed dies
632–34	Abu Bakr
634–44	Omar
644–56	Uthman
656–61	Ali
661–80	Mu'awiyah (first Umayyad caliph)
680–83	Yazid
683–84	Mu'awiyah II
684–85	Marwan
685–705	Abd al-Malik
717–20	Umar II
724–43	Hisham
744–50	Marwan II (last Umayyad caliph)

THE EXPANSION OF ISLAM

Many factors contributed to the rapid expansion of the Islamic Empire. Among the primary ones were:
• a new zeal for warfare among the Muslim peoples, combined with a knowledge of ancient battle skills, produced novel military techniques;
• the new military techniques proved effective against opponents in neighbouring kingdoms, who were divided and exhausted by wars with each other;
• the fighting and riding skills of desert-dwelling Arabs – developed by years of feuding between rival clans and of raiding caravans and settled commmunities – became disciplined and unified by the Islamic faith; the conviction that death in battle was a direct route to paradise made the Muslims a formidable force in the field;
• the once great empires of Byzantium and Persia – exhausted by 25 years of war with each other – were unable to meet the new external Muslim challenge;
• the inhabitants of the cities and provinces of these crumbling empires had gradually been alienated by oppressive taxation and religious persecution; they, therefore, welcomed their new Muslim overlords as liberators;
• as the Muslims conquered more territory, they learned from their defeated enemies: from the Persians they learned seige tactics and from the Byzantines they acquired the art of naval warfare.

Mu'awiyah's death in 680 gave Ali's second son, Husain (626–680), an opportunity to rouse his father's old supporters and press his claim to the caliphate. They were easily overwhelmed at Karbala, near Kufa, and Husain's martyrdom henceforth became an occasion for major ritual mourning in the Shiite devotional calendar. The Umayyad hold on power was nearly lost when the sudden death of Yazid, in 682, was followed almost at once by that of his teenage son. However, another Umayyad, Marwan (623–685), was able to reassert control over Syria and Egypt, leaving his successor, Abd al-Malik (c. 646–705), to complete the work of reunification. This was achieved by crushing further revolts, establishing an efficient courier service, issuing an Islamic currency, and Arabizing the bureaucracy. The campaign of territorial conquest was again renewed, sweeping westward to the Atlantic and up to Spain. To the east it reached the borders of India and those of the Chinese Empire itself.

The Fall of the Dynasty

Iraq remained a troublesome area. Nurturing the cult of Ali, it provided a focus for anti-Syrian resentment. Members of the ***Abbasid*** line – descendants of Mohammed's uncle, Abbas (566–652) – began a secret campaign, denouncing Umayyad oppression and advancing their own claim to the caliphate.

The death of Caliph Hisham (born 691) in 743 led to widespread uprisings, from North Africa to Iran. His successor, the able Marwan II (c. 684–750), proved powerless to crush the Abbasid movement. Under the leadership of the Persian ex-slave, Abu Muslim (died 755), it was able to overcome the mutual antipathy between the Arab and Persian peoples to create an irresistible force against Umayyad rule. The rebels took Kufa in 749, while Damascus itself fell in 750. The Umayyads (with one significant exception) were hunted down and exterminated. Even the graves of their predecessors were systematically desecrated.

Towards a New Culture

The military creation of an Islamic empire was accompanied by the gradual emergence of a distinct Islamic culture. As a blend of Arab traditions and those of conquered peoples, it centred around the mosque. The increasing sophistication of mosques (see THE VISUAL ARTS WORLDWIDE (vol. 4): ISLAMIC ART) was accompanied by a cultural escalation as they began to house activities other than prayer, serving as schools, colleges, and libraries. While the Arab tradition of poetry continued, a prose literature also began to flourish (see THE LITERARY ARTS WORLDWIDE (vol.4): ISLAMIC LITERATURE). Of enduring significance were the compilations of *hadith*. Islamic law (see LAW (vol.6): LEGAL SYSTEMS AND THEIR ORIGINS) was still in its embryonic phase; Muslim judges continued to rely, to a large extent, on the prevailing codes and customs of the local province.

Kairouan
Founded on the site of a Byzantine fortress, this city served as a base for the further conquest of North Africa. It became the capital of the region in c. 800.

In the name of God, the Merciful, the Compassionate. Become Muslims and be saved. If not, accept our protection and pay a poll tax. Or else I shall come against you with men who love death as you love to drink wine.

Khalid ibn al-Walid's (died 642) challenge to Persian border chiefs

The Great Mosque at Kairouan *Enclosed within the ramparted citadel of the city, the mosque dates from the 7th century; its vast courtyard and multicolumned arcades and prayer hall exemplify the austere simplicity of early Islamic architecture.* ▼

The Abbasid Caliphate

*The new regime • The rise of the Mamelukes • The break-up of the empire •
The Seljuks • Muslim Sicily • Muslim recovery • Decline and destruction*

Between 750 and 1250 the Islamic Empire expanded to its greatest extent. This was accompanied by the elaboration of Islamic culture in its most distinctive aspects, notably architecture, law, and theology. The first century of Abbasid rule, until the death of Mutawakkil (822–61), is especially remembered as Islam's 'Golden Age.' The city of Baghdad during the rule of Harun ar-Rashid ('Aaron the Wise'; ?766–809) has become synonymous with romance, mystery, and sophistication, even for non-Muslims influenced by the charm of the tales of the ***Arabian Nights***.

The New Regime
The Abbasid caliphs were probably no more personally devout than their predecessors. They made particular efforts, however, to give their governments a self-consciously Islamic aura, invoking a reassertion of righteousness and orthodoxy to legitimize their bloody seizure of power. At the same time the empire's centre of gravity made a decisive move to the east as Damascus was abandoned in favour of a purpose-built capital at Baghdad. This resulted in Persians and other non-Arabs being integrated into the ruling elite. An elite guard recruited in the Iranian province of Khurasan became the core of the army, while the Barmakids, a talented Khurasani family, briefly dominated the key administrative posts. Persian fashions and foods similarly pervaded

the lifestyle of the court. The acquisition from Chinese prisoners of war of the secret of paper-making facilitated a further intensification of bureaucratic control.

Baghdad. The circular 'City of Peace' was built on a well-irrigated plain where the Tigris and Euphrates rivers run close to each other, providing the new capital with water, transportation, and defences. The site also overshadowed Kufa, the traditional centre of Shiite opposition to the previous regime. With a population of perhaps one million, Baghdad was one of the largest cities on earth. It certainly far surpassed anything to its west. Graced with hospitals, academies, libraries, and even a scholarly translation bureau, Baghdad become the warehouse of the world. It was a focal point for the exchange of spices, silks, and porcelain arriving by camel train and a trading centre for more essential items, such as dates, hides, and grain conveyed by river. A complex commerce developed, involving the use of extensive credit and even the 'cheque.'

Islamic Law. The Abbasid claim to righteous rule encouraged the elaboration of the corpus of law known as ***sharia*** ('path'). This was achieved through the critical evaluation of four elements: the Koran, *hadith*, analogy (*qiyas*), and consensus of learned opinion (*ijma*). The ultimate objective of the Muslim jurists (*ulema*) came to be the assignment of any human act to one of five categories:

The Muslim Empire
Under Abbasid rule the empire reached its greatest extent in the early 9th century. ▼

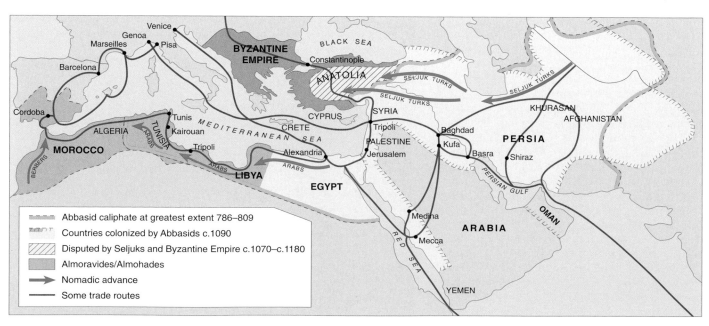

Key:
- ▩ Abbasid caliphate at greatest extent 786–809
- ▩ Countries colonized by Abbasids c.1090
- ▨ Disputed by Seljuks and Byzantine Empire c.1070–c.1180
- ▩ Almoravides/Almohades
- → Nomadic advance
- — Some trade routes

◀ **The Minaret al-Malwiyah** *Built in the 9th century, the helicoidal minaret stands next to the Great Friday Mosque at Samarra. The mosque is 1 km long, designed so that thousands of troops could worship there together.*

Rumi, who is claimed by the Mevlevi ('whirling dervish') order as their founder. To the guardians of orthodoxy and public order, such wayward manifestations of spirituality were a threat. It was **Abu Hamid al-Ghazali** (1058–1111), who brought reconciliation between the orthodox and the mystical paths.

Medicine and Mathematics. Muslim scholars drew on the heritage of both classical Greece and Rome and of ancient India in the field of science. Such basic scientific terms as alcohol, alkali, amalgam, and drug, and the basic mathematical concepts of average and zero have all come into Western languages through Arabic. The Muslims, however, were more than mere transmitters of information and techniques. Inhibited from dissection and surgery by religious prohibitions, Muslim physicians became expert pharmacists, drawing on the role of dietary, environmental, and scientific factors in the causation and treatment of disease. Mathematical studies went far beyond the practical needs of bureaucrats and architects, stimulated by the need to determine the hours and direction of prayer and to calculate the movement of heavenly bodies. Outstanding among Muslim mathematicians were al-Khwarizmi (c. 780– c. 850) – who originated the word 'algebra' and whose corrupted name has given us 'algorithm' – and the astronomer-poet Omar Khayyam (died c. 1123), who reformed the Muslim calendar.

The Rise of the Mamelukes

As the legal superstructure of Islamic rule became ever more abstruse and imposing, its actual influence began to crumble from within. In the capital itself effective power passed to army commanders, while beyond its defences local dynasties acquired hereditary authority in the provinces. The Khurasanian guard was replaced by Turkish-speaking tribesmen from the Eurasian steppes, *mamelukes* ('those who are owned' or slaves). Bought as boys, converted to Islam, trained in the arts of war, and divested of kin who might distract them from loyalty, they were bound solely to serve their commanders and became a self-perpetuating military oligarchy. It was Mu'tasim (794–842) who initiated their dominance by raising their number to 60 000. He ruled, with their protection, from the luxurious splendour of his palace complex at Samarra, 100 km north of Baghdad. Within half a century the deposition and murder of

forbidden, discouraged, neutral, recommended, and compulsory. Legal speculation thus came to embrace the entire range of human behaviour from ritual aspects of worship to personal and social conduct. Sunnite tradition eventually became grouped into four schools (*madhhab*) of law – Maliki, Hanbali, Shafii, and Hanafi – that afforded each other mutual recognition while each tended to prevail in different regions. The practical application of legal theory varied widely. Forceful caliphs were rarely restrained by constitutional details. In peripheral areas of the Muslim world, such as sub-Saharan Africa, considerable compromise was made with the customs of local peoples. However, in matters of family and property law, such as marriage, inheritance, charitable endowments, etc., the standards of Islam were generally observed.

Sufism. The institutionalization of orthodoxy by learned jurists was offset by a resilient strain of mysticism whose adherents became known as *Sufis*, from the rough woollen garment (*suf*) they often wore as a symbol of their unworldliness and poverty. Rejecting theological quibbles and ritualized worship in favour of ecstatic poetry and meditation, rhythmic dancing, and chanting, they turned away from the notion of a stern, remote, and abstract deity. Instead they proclaimed their desire for personal communion with a loving and merciful god. The female Sufi, Rabiyah, was popularly hailed as a saint by the time of her death in 901. Sufi devotion found outstanding poetic expression in the writings of the 13th-century Persian poet, Jalal al-Din

Abu Hamid al-Ghazali

After a brilliant judicial and academic career, al-Ghazali (1058–1111) became one of the outstanding intellects of the age. He underwent a crisis of faith so profound that he was prevented from teaching by a speech defect. A decade of pilgrimage, meditation, and solitude finally enabled him to articulate the compatibility of Sunnism with Sufism in *The Revival of the Religious Sciences* and other works, which have become classics of Islamic theology.

Arabian Nights

Set within the framework of a main story, this famous collection of tales includes those of Aladdin, Ali Baba, and Sinbad the Sailor. Originally transmitted orally, the tales have diverse origins, such as India, Iran, Iraq, Egypt, Turkey, and possibly Greece. The stories were added to in the 9th and 13th centuries and were first translated into a European language, and published, in the early 18th century. Providing a wealth of information on life in the medieval Arab world, the tales have almost become a part of Western folklore.

Samarra

Mu'tasim named his riverside retreat 'He Who Sees It, Rejoices,' adorning it with gardens, pavilions, pools, and racetracks. His successors extended its facilities until the town stretched along the Tigris for over 30 km. In 892 the capital was transferred back to Baghdad and by 1300 most of Samarra was in ruins.

caliphs by their own so-called 'bodyguard' had become routine. From 936 onwards Mameluke generals even put their own names on the coinage, alongside that of the nominal caliph.

The Break-up of the Empire

Spain, conquered in the early 8th century, was effectively independent of Abbasid rule from the start (see MUSLIM SPAIN). Morocco came under the control of a Shiite dynasty in 789 and around 800 Ifriqiyyah (Africa), the region between Morocco and Egypt, became autonomous under the Aghlabids. This followed the decision of the dynasty's founder to promote himself from a newly arrived representative of the Abbasids to independent ruler. By the same date a Kharijite (see THE EMERGENCE OF A NEW EMPIRE) dynasty had been established in Oman. Fratricidal conflict within the Abbasid family itself led to the emergence of independent rulers in eastern Iran from 821 onwards. Egypt also withdrew its allegiance between 868 and 905 and between 935 and 969, when it fell to the expanding power of the Shiite Fatimids, who claimed descent from Fatima, wife of Ali and daughter of Mohammed. They established a separate caliphate based on a new city, al-Qahirah ('the victorious'), corrupted by Westerners to 'Cairo.' Between 870 and 883 southern Iraq was convulsed by a massive slave revolt led by African (*Zanj*) salt miners, who organized a dogged resistance from the marshes around Basra. In Yemen a Shiite regime (*Zaidi Imams*) was established in 897. In 945 a Persian Shiite dynasty, the Buyids, took Baghdad itself before retiring to rule the eastern remnants of the empire from Shiraz.

The Seljuks

In the middle of the 11th century the tide of disintegration was temporarily reversed by the Seljuks. They were fierce and zealous Turkish tribal converts to Islam, who reunited most of southwest Asia under the banner of Sunnism and the Abbasids. In 1055 their *sultan* ('he with power'), Tughril Beg, entered Baghdad and released the caliph from Buyid servitude. In 1071 Tughril Beg's nephew (and successor), Alp Arslan, inflicted a huge defeat on a Byzantine army at Manzikert. This action inadvertently precipitated the appeal for Western aid, which resulted in the First Crusade. It also opened up the Anatolian plateau to large-scale Turkish settlement. After the death of Malikshah, however, in 1092, the Seljuk territories were divided among rival members of his house. This gravely weakened resistance to Crusader incursions and thus facilitated the establishment of four Christian-ruled states along the coast of the eastern Mediterranean.

▲ **Seljuk Brick Tower** *Built in the 11th century, this tower is a striking tribute to the ability of Muslim builders to appropriate varied techniques and materials to common religious purposes.*

▲ **Al-Azhar University** *Meaning 'the brilliant,' the city of Al-Azhar remains the greatest single centre of Islamic scholarship in the Muslim world. Founded in 972 by the Fatimids, it originally served as a mosque and a training centre for Shiite missionaries. It subsequently became a training centre for religious judges and teachers and a bastion of Sunnite orthodoxy.*

Muslim Sicily

After a century and a half of intermittent raiding the Muslim conquest of Sicily began in earnest in 827. It met with fierce resistance and was not completed until 966. Muslim hegemony was brief and by 1091 the entire island had fallen to Norman conquerors. However, such had been the enlightened nature of Muslim rule that the island retained this culture until the intolerance of the Crusaders eliminated the Muslim population by exile and massacre and consigned its language and culture to oblivion. Roger II (1105–54) warred with his Arab neighbours but was a liberal patron of Muslim scholars. He attracted into his service such luminaries as al-Idrisi, whose *Book of Roger* summarized the entire corpus of existing geographical knowledge. During the Muslim and early Norman eras the medical schools of Salerno and Palermo enjoyed an unsurpassed reputation in Europe.

Muslim Recovery

The Muslim counteroffensive began with the capture of Edessa by Zangi in 1144, which provoked the Second Crusade. It continued with the destruction of a large Christian army at Hattin by Salah al-Din (Saladin) in 1187,

▲ **Saladin** *This portrait of the legendary Muslim warrior by Cristofano Altissimo encapsulates Saladin's reputation as a firm yet virtuous ruler.*

which led to the Third Crusade. Crusader rule in the eastern Mediterranean ended a century later with the fall of their last secure position at Acre. By that time, a powerful new state had emerged in Egypt under a Mameluke regime and Turkish settlement had developed rapidly in Anatolia. The fragmentation of the Abbasid Empire had the paradoxical effect of invigorating rather than weakening the region's cultural life. Ambitious new regimes sought to legitimize themselves and excel each other in their lavish patronage of scholars and artists. The rise of a Persian intelligentsia, for whom Arabic was a foreign language, greatly stimulated the study of grammar and lexicography, leading to the formalization of 'classical' (i.e. literary) Arabic. Persian, meanwhile, enjoyed a literary renaissance, symbolized by the poet Firdausi (?941–1020), who composed the *Shahnama.* Arts utilizing ceramics and textiles benefited from the imitation of Chinese porcelain and silks, mosaic, ivory carving, and inlaid metalwork from Byzantine models. Carpet-making techniques were also introduced from Central Asia by the Seljuks.

Decline and Destruction

Economic buoyancy was undermined by environmental degradation. Administrative negligence led to the deterioration of complex irrigation systems, often accompanied by problems of salinity and overgrazing. The flow of the Euphrates River may have been substantially affected by climatological changes, which severed vital water supplies for the empire's irrigation network. Falling tax revenues indicated an increasingly depleted population in the countryside and a decrease in the area under cultivation. An attempt to extract more revenue by harsher methods of tax collection simply accelerated the downward spiral. Such difficulties appeared to herald an era of protracted decline. The fatal blow, however, came suddenly and unexpectedly from the east. As the Christian intruders were forced back towards the sea, a new power was arising in the remote central Asian steppe. In 1219 Shah Mohammed, ruling the eastern outposts of the Muslim world, imprudently murdered Mongol emissaries who had sought an alliance in terms he deemed to be insulting. The result was the destruction by Mongol armies of such cities as Bukhara, Samarkand, and Nishapur with a ferocity from which they never fully recovered. In 1242 the Mongols defeated the Seljuks of Anatolia and raided far into the peninsula. In 1258 Baghdad itself was sacked and Syria plundered. Arabia – sacred but unappealingly barren – was spared. In 1260 a Mameluke expeditionary force from Egypt inflicted an unprecedented defeat on the remnants of the Mongol invaders at Ayn Jalut in Palestine. This forced their final withdrawal to territories east of the Euphrates River, which remained under Mongol overlordship. Baghdad had been so thoroughly devastated that Cairo, which remained unscathed, henceforth became the leading city of the Islamic world. Its Mameluke masters, meanwhile, extended their influence into Syria, Arabia, Sudan, and along the coast of North Africa.

◀ ***The Shahnama*** *('Book of Kings') Firdausi recounts in the 'book,' in no less than 60 000 couplets, the achievements of the pre-Islamic heroes of Iran. The work, illustrated in this 16th-century Persian manuscript, remains Iran's national epic.*

The Great Warrior

Saladin (?1137–93), the most famous of Muslim heroes, became sultan of Egypt, Syria, Yemen, and Palestine. His skilful diplomacy and decisive military force earned him the reputation as a firm, yet virtuous, ruler. Driven by the concept of 'holy war' (*jihad*), Saladin inspired Muslim armies to a physical and spiritual strength equal to that of the Christian Crusaders, against whom he led his forces. Saladin's greatest achievement – the capture of the Kingdom of Jerusalem – followed a great victory over the Crusaders at the Battle of Hattin (1187). The fall of Jerusalem was a shock to the West. It provoked the Third Crusade, during which Saladin earned his legendary reputation as a chivalrous warrior.

Muslim Spain

The conquest • The founding of the amirate • Splendour and rebellion •
Disorder and decline • Granada • Economy and culture

Córdoba

Córdoba flourished under the Romans but fell into decline under the Visigoths; it was largely destroyed by the Muslims (711). Its renaissance began when Abd ar-Rahman I sited his capital there in 756.

The Great Mosque at Córdoba ▶

(interior) Abd ar-Rahman I began the mosque in 784. Its deep sanctuary of 19 aisles has 850 marble columns supporting double-tiered horseshoe arches. When the city fell to Christian forces, in 1236, the mosque was converted into a cathedral. However, it is still known as La Mezquita.

The Muslim occupation of the Iberian peninsula lasted for more than seven centuries. It left behind an enduring legacy that has affected almost every aspect of life: language, architecture, and music. At its peak the self-confident Muslim civilization of Andalusia greatly contrasted with the disarray of post-Roman Christendom. However, it was the contact, rather than the contrast, between the two cultures that was ultimately to prove significant; through Muslim Spain, Europe received both the practical benefits of new crops, such as citrus fruit and spinach, and the stimulus of Greek wisdom, preserved and transmitted through Arabic translations.

The Conquest

By the early 8th century Muslim conquerors held all of North Africa except the Christian outpost of Ceuta (Sabtah), which received supplies from Visigothic Spain. The death of Witiza, king of the Visigoths, in 709 provoked civil war; this gave the Muslims their chance to invade Spain in 711. The invasion force of 7000 men was commanded by Tariq Ibn Zayid (died c. 720), from whom Gibraltar takes its name (*Jebel Tariq*, or Tariq's Mountain). The Hispano-Roman inhabitants and their Visigothic rulers offered little resistance, even though the terrain favoured a guerrilla campaign. Tariq marched on Toledo, drawn by the legend that King Solomon's treasure was hid-

den there, and took the city with ease. The invaders were subsequently reinforced by a second army under the command of the governor of North Africa, Musa Ibn Nusayr.

The Muslims had overrun the entire Iberian peninsula by 714, except for some minor Christian states in the northwest. This they achieved with a force that never exceeded 20 000 men: mostly Berbers led by Arabs. They named their conquered territory *al-Andalus* (Land of the Vandals), referring to the predecessors of the Visigoths.

The momentum of conquest initially took the invaders beyond the Pyrenees and into the plain of Toulouse, but their thrust northward was checked by the Franks under Charles Martel at the Battle of Poitiers in 732. After 759 the Muslims prudently retired behind the natural barrier of the Pyrenees.

The Founding of the Amirate

For many, Muslim rule was welcomed as less oppressive than the system it replaced. Jews suffered less persecution, and serfs could become free men by converting to Islam. Even Christians who would not renounce their faith benefited from lighter taxes. The reasons for this tolerance were twofold: first, the invaders were too few in number to enforce harsh rule, despite a constant flow of migrants from North Africa. The immigrants numbered perhaps 50 000, the indigenous population an estimated 4 000 000. Second, a series of governors appointed and dismissed from Damascus in rapid succession made oppressive rule less likely.

In 756 Abd ar-Rahman I (died 788), an Umayyad prince, who had escaped the slaughter of his dynasty by the Abbasids, arrived in Córdoba and established an autonomous amirate (or princedom). Energetic and ruthless, he suppressed all opposition to his rule; he even forced Charlemagne to lift his siege of Saragossa and inflicted on him a humiliating defeat in the Pyrenees, at Roncesvalles (778). This event inspired the famous French epic poem *La Chanson de Roland*. Abd ar-Rahman's successors, Hisham I (788–96) and al-Hakam I (796–822), used Berber and even Slavonic mercenaries to crush rebellions among the Arab nobility. They also gave the teachings of the Maliki school of Islamic law official status; thus Spain became a bastion of conservative orthodoxy.

Splendour and Rebellion

Courtly life under Abd ar-Rahman II (822–52) was highly sophisticated, attracting such talents as the Persian musician and aesthete Ziryab and the poet al-Ghazal. An energetic diplomat, who exchanged ambassadors with the Byzantine and Frankish courts, Abd ar-Rahman II also vigorously defended the amirate against Viking intrusions. He repelled an incursion near Seville and established a naval base and arsenal there to ward off further attacks. He was an efficient administrator, organizing a generous distribution of wheat to ease major famines in 822–23 and 846. For 75 years after the death of Abd ar-Rahman II, his successors were beset by protracted rebellions; under Abd ar-Rahman III (reigned 912–16), however, these were finally crushed.

When the North African Fatimid dynasty assumed the title of caliph, thereby disrupting the religious unity of Islam under nominal Abbasid suzerainty, Abd ar-Rahman III likewise assumed this title himself, secure in the knowledge that he ruled Europe's most prestigious and wealthy state.

The reign of the cultured al-Hakam II (961–76) was a peaceful one; it is noted for the formation of a great library. As his appointed successor was a minor, effective power passed to the brilliant general, al-Mansur ('the Victorious One'; c. 938–1002), who destroyed the temporal power of the caliphs and ruled as a military dictator from 978 to 1002. Reducing Morocco to a dependent state, he also raided constantly into the Christian north, sacking virtually every princely capital.

Disorder and Decline

The early death of al-Mansur's son, al-Muzaffar (1002–08), initiated a quarter of a century of anarchy that saw the emergence of many petty states, controlled by contending elites of Arabs, Berbers, or former slaves. Their

▲ **The Court of the Myrtles at the Alhambra Palace, Granada** *The palace dates from the period of the Nasrid dynasty (1238–1492).*

continual rivalries allowed the Christian kingdoms of the north to expand gradually. Only the loss of Toledo in 1085 galvanized the disunited Muslims into summoning assistance from the Almoravides of North Africa. As their efforts to hold the shifting frontier against the Christian *reconquista* (see EARLY AND MEDIEVAL EUROPE: THE MEDIEVAL ZENITH) finally weakened, the Almoravides were succeeded by the Almohades, who had successfully challenged their hold on North Africa. By the second half of the 12th century, the Muslims held only the southern half of the Iberian peninsula. Although their counteroffensives met with occasional success, they could not reverse the tide of reconquest. Defeat at Las Navas de Tolosa in 1212 proved a decisive turning point, resulting in a series of important Christian victories during the next half-century. The city of Badajoz fell in 1228, Córdoba in 1236, Seville in 1248, and Cádiz in 1262.

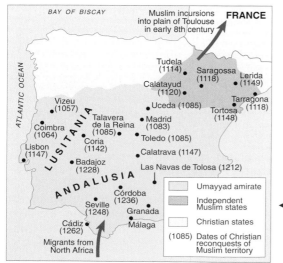

BAY OF BISCAY
Muslim incursions into plain of Toulouse in early 8th century
FRANCE

ATLANTIC OCEAN

Tudela (1114)
Saragossa (1118)
Lerida (1149)
Calatayud (1120)
Tarragona (1118)
Vizeu (1057)
Uceda (1085)
Tortosa (1148)
Talavera de la Reina (1085)
Madrid (1083)
Coimbra (1064)
Coria (1142)
Toledo (1085)
Lisbon (1147)
Calatrava (1147)
Badajoz (1228)
Las Navas de Tolosa (1212)

LUSITANIA
ANDALUSIA

Córdoba (1236)
Seville (1248)
Granada
Cádiz (1262)
Málaga
Migrants from North Africa

Umayyad amirate
Independent Muslim states
Christian states
(1085) Dates of Christian reconquests of Muslim territory

◄ **Muslim Spain** *By 714, the Muslims controlled almost all of the Iberian peninsula. This territory was reduced by half by the later 12th century. In 1262 Cádiz was finally taken by Christian forces, leaving Granada as the last outpost of Muslim power in Spain.*

Our Christian young men... are famed for the learning of the gentiles; intoxicated with Arab eloquence they greedily handle, eagerly devour, and zealously discuss their books... knowing nothing of the beauty of the Church's literature and looking down with contempt on the streams of the Church that flow forth from Paradise.

Criticism by a Christian writer (854) of the vogue for Arabic learning

A 13th-century Manuscript of the *Torah*, Systematized by Rabbi Moses Maimonides ▶

(1135–1204) Born in Córdoba, Maimonides was the outstanding thinker of medieval Judaism. After writing a treatise on logic at 16, he was later caught up in the persecution of Jews instigated by the Almohad rulers of Córdoba and fled to Egypt. His major work was a brilliant systematization of the whole body of Jewish law (the Torah*); he also became personal physician to Saladin and wrote a philosophical work in Arabic,* The Guide of the Perplexed.*

Granada

One outpost of Muslim power still remained in Spain – the mountain stronghold of Granada. Ruled by the Nasrid dynasty, it was sustained by three factors: volunteer reinforcements from North Africa; shrewd diplomacy between Christians and North Africans; and the ravages of the Black Death, which weakened the potential aggressors.

The regime in Granada reached its peak under Muhammad V (1354–59, 1362–91), who overcame intrigue to regain his throne. He maintained a cultured court that attracted the services of eminent men, such as the

historian Ibn Khaldun (d. 1406). Yet signs of terminal decline were apparent as renewed Christian pressure led to increased xenophobia and religious intolerance that fatally weakened the cohesion of the state. Its ultimate collapse resulted from mutual treachery among the Nasrids in the face of a final Christian onslaught. Muslim occupation of the Iberian peninsula ended, after almost eight centuries, in January 1492.

Economy and Culture

The vigour and sophistication of Muslim Spain is attested by the revival of urban life on a scale not seen since Roman times. By the reign of al-Mansur, Córdoba (Qurtubah) had a population of around 250 000, making it by far the largest city in western Europe. Toledo, the second largest city, had only 37 000 occupants. Other significant towns were Almeria and Granada, with populations about one-tenth of the size of Córdoba, and Saragossa, Valencia, and Malaga, each with a population of about 15 000. These cities boasted not only mosques and markets but also public baths, parks, libraries, and even paving and street lighting. Such amenities were not to be found elsewhere in Europe, except in the proximity of royal residences, for another 1000 years.

Innovations under Muslim rule included irrigation, the raising of thoroughbred horses, cultivation of citrus fruit and sugar cane, and state protection for plants that had medical properties or were used for the manufacture of textiles, such as flax, cotton, and esparto grass. Córdoban leather achieved an international reputation and the carving of rock crystal and ivory attained new levels of excellence. The manufacture of silk was jealously guarded as a state monopoly. Muslim scholars, returning from pilgrimage to the Arab heartland, brought with them Arabic manuscripts, including translations and commentaries on Greek classic writings on science, philosophy, and medicine. In Toledo and other centres of scholarship, these works were translated into Latin. Their further dissemination to northern Europe was a crucial stimulus to the revival of Christian scholarship from the 12th century onwards. Gerard of Cremona (1114–87) came to Toledo specifically to seek out a copy of Ptolemy's *Almagest*, which summarized the astronomical knowledge of the classical world. Gerard's translation remained the standard work on astronomy in European universities until the publication of the revolutionary theories of Copernicus in 1543. He also played a leading role in introducing to Europe the Indian symbols (including zero) used by Muslims for mathematical calculations, which thereafter became known as 'Arabic numerals.'

FOOD REGULATIONS IN 12TH-CENTURY SEVILLE

- There must be no sellers of olive oil around the mosque, nor of dirty products, nor of anything from which an indelible stain can be feared.
- Truffles should not be sold around the mosque, for this is a delicacy of the dissolute.
- Cheese should only be sold in small leather bottles, which can be washed daily.
- Sausages and rissoles should... not be made with meat from a sick animal, bought for cheapness.
- Cooks and fryers are forbidden to sell leftovers after a day's trading.
- Copper frying vats should be lined with tin, since copper with oil is poisonous.
- Flour should not be mixed with the cheese used for fritters. This is fraud.
- Large quantities of grapes should not be sold to someone likely to press them for wine.

The Rise of the Ottoman Empire

The context of expansion • The house of Osman • From Constantinople to Istanbul •
Institutions of empire • The reign of Suleiman • The onset of decline •
Reform and renewal

The Ottoman Empire was the largest and most enduring of all the Islamic states. At its zenith in the 16th century, it embraced the Middle East, North Africa, and much of the Balkans. While retaining its military traditions, the Ottoman regime patronized outstanding achievements in the arts. Its failure to capture Vienna in 1683 marked the end of almost four centuries of territorial expansion.

The Context of Expansion

After the Mongol incursions of the early to mid-13th century the central Middle East was roughly divided between the Mamelukes in the west; tribal confederations, under Mongol suzerainty, in the east; and, to the north, minor Turkish principalities. Bubonic plague devastated the entire region in the mid-14th century, killing perhaps one-third of the population and severely disrupting trade and agriculture. The process of restoring some hegemonic power over the region was retarded by political fragmentation and economic contraction. The 13th and 14th centuries were not, however, devoid of cultural achievements. In Iran, Rashid ad-Din (1247–1318) produced a world history regarded as the greatest work of classical Persian prose.

The House of Osman

The Anatolian plateau was the origin of *ghazi* ('fighters for the faith'), who undertook to extend Islamic territory. The Ottoman state has traditionally been traced back to a Turkmen chief, Ertugrul, but takes its name from his son, Osman (1258–1326), who succeeded to his small territory in northwestern Anatolia in 1280. Osman's victory over a Byzantine army at Bapheon in 1301 attracted many fighters to his cause. In 1326 Osman captured Bursa, which henceforth became the Ottoman capital. Osman's son, Orhan (1288–1359), continued the expansion, crossing the Dardanelles strait to establish a position in Europe at Gallipoli, thus initiating the conquest of Greece. Murad I (?1326–89) assumed the titles of 'sultan' and 'emperor' and absorbed the Balkans into his empire. Meanwhile, his forces extended the eastern frontier in Anatolia. In 1389 Murad inflicted a major defeat on

a massive Christian army at Kosovo but died on the battlefield. Most of the lands south of the River Danube subsequently came under Ottoman rule and the capital was relocated to Adrianople (now Edirne). Bayezid I (c. 1360–1403) made rapid conquests on both the Balkan and Anatolian frontiers of the Ottoman territories. In 1396 he confirmed his military reputation by besieging the city of Nicopolis but in 1402 suffered a crushing defeat by Timur (Tamerlane) at Ankara. He later died in captivity. Timur returned to his capital at Samarkand, while Bayezid's sons fought over their patrimony until Mehmed I (ruled 1413–21) emerged victorious. Suppressing revolts and reasserting control over former Ottoman provinces in the Balkans, Murad II (1404–51) defeated two great Christian armies at Varna (1444) and Kosovo (1448).

From Constantinople to Istanbul

Mehmed II (1432–81), Murad's son, became sultan in 1451. Determined to take Constantinople, his forces besieged the city for over two months. The last Byzantine emperor died fighting and the cathedral of Hagia Sophia was converted into a mosque. Renamed Istanbul, the city was restored and resettled by the Ottomans; in the century after its

▲ **The Mongols Besiege Baghdad** *(Persian manuscript) The Mongol Empire promoted the exchange of artisans and artists between the cultures of China and the Middle East, leading to an infusion of Chinese techniques into Islamic artistry, ceramics, and miniature painting.*

═══SEE ALSO═══
Early and Medieval Europe:
• The Byzantine Empire
The Mongol Empires:
• The Successor States
The Visual Arts Worldwide (vol. 4):
• Islamic Art
The Literary Arts Worldwide (vol. 4):
• Islamic Literature
Religion (vol. 6):
• Islam

The Fortress of Rumeli Hisar ►
Built in three months to blockade the Bosporous Straits, prior to the siege of Constantinople (1453), the fortress is still one of the principle landmarks of the straits.

The Janissaries

Taking their name from the Turkish *yeniçeri*, meaning 'new troops,' this elite guard played a powerful role in palace politics. Murad I created the guard, which came to be recruited through the *devshirme*; under Suleiman I they numbered 12 000. During the 17th and 18th centuries, the Janissaries engineered palace coups and murdered two sultans. After their insurrection in 1826, Sultan Mahmud II killed the entire corps.

---

conquest, the population rose from barely 50 000 to ten times that number.

Mehmed II reduced the Crimean Tatars to vassal status, strengthened the Ottoman hold on Greece and the Balkans, and built up the navy. Under Bayezid II (1447–1512) the Ottoman war-machine rolled on under the momentum of its success. However, a Persian-backed Shiite revolt in Anatolia and internal rivalry led to Bayezid's deposition by his ruthless son Selim I (c. 1470–1520). Crushing the Shiite rebels, Selim overwhelmed the Persians at Chalderan in 1514. This victory assured the absorption of eastern Anatolia and paved the way for expansion southwards to Syria and Egypt. The Mameluke regime, undermined by plague, famine, and inflation, was annihilated outside Cairo in 1517, resulting in the annexation of Mameluke territories, including the holy cities of Mecca and Medina. With the deposition of the last descendant of the house of Abbas, the Ottomans assumed the title of caliph (see THE ABBASID CALIPHATE).

Institutions of Empire

The Ottoman regime developed several distinctive institutions characteristic of its organization. **Devshirme**, meaning 'to collect,' was a unique procedure for recruiting candidates for the sultan's service. Special commissions toured rural areas of the Balkans, selecting the fittest and brightest Christian youths. 90% of these were hired out to landholders in Anatolia to be converted to Islam, learn Turkish, and have their stamina improved before returning to Istanbul for military training. The other 10% would enter the palace school for education in languages, mathematics, etiquette, and the arts of war. The reign of Mehmed II saw the consolidation of administrative power in the hands of this slave-elite at the expense of the old aristocracy. The breakdown of the *devshirme* and its training system in the late 17th century was symptomatic of the enfeeblement of the entire regime. Recruits unworthy of the palace school became the elite corps of the Ottoman infantry, known as the **Janissaries**.

The sultan's non-Muslim subjects had the status of **dhimmi** (protected peoples), who were taxed but exempted from military service. Dhimmi were organized into communities, according to sectarian affiliation.

The Reign of Suleiman I (reigned 1520–66)

Suleiman began his reign with two notable triumphs: the capture of the fortress of Belgrade in 1521 and of Rhodes in 1522, both objectives his predecessors had failed to secure. In

---

Map Legend:
- Ottomans 1300
- Acquisitions 1300–59
- Acquisitions 1359–1451
- Acquisitions 1451–81
- Acquisitions 1512–20
- Acquisitions 1520–66
- Acquisitions 1566–1683
- Ottoman Empire at its greatest extent

◄ **The Growth of the Ottoman Empire** *From 1300 to 1699 the empire grew to its greatest extent to include the Middle East, North Africa, and much of the Balkans.*

1526 he defeated the Hungarians at the Battle of Mohacs, occupied Buda and Pest, and installed an Ottoman vassal as ruler. The subsequent restoration of a Hapsburg candidate provoked Suleiman to return, in 1529, leading an army of 250 000. Part of this force raided deep into Germany, while the rest laid siege to Vienna, which was saved only by the onset of winter. By 1541, most of Hungary had been reduced to an Ottoman province. Intermittent war with Iran led to the acquisition of Iraq and parts of Armenia and Kurdistan. In the west Ottoman suzerainty was acknowledged along the North African coast. Suleiman's realm consequently stretched from the River Danube to the Yemen, from Algiers to the Crimea.

The Onset of Decline

Under Selim II (1524–74) the Ottomans captured Tunis in 1570 and invaded Cyprus, but a major naval defeat by the Hapsburg fleet off Lepanto, in 1571, tarnished the legend of Ottoman invincibility. Unlike his father, Suleiman, Selim did not lead his armies in person. After generations of able rulers the competence and dedication of the leadership declined. The sultan had always been the keystone of the Ottoman state; his weakness affected the whole structure. This was disguised in part by the abilities of ministers and generals, who increasingly undertook greater initiatives. Diffusion of authority resulted in corruption at court and in government.

Other corrosive factors, however, were at work. The influx of silver from the New World introduced the problem of inflation into the economy. Arbitrary price controls, confiscatory taxation, and currency devaluation were the ineffective responses. The incursions of the Portuguese and other Europeans into the Indian Ocean diverted the routes of the spice trade from land to sea, depriving Middle Eastern rulers of valuable profits. Overpopulation was also a problem for a technologically static economy. The unemployed often resorted to banditry, while many were absorbed into the army; the limits of territory open to conquest had effectively been reached. By 1600 the Ottoman army had exhausted its military capabilities as more distant campaigns could not be sustained. An empire whose vitality had been maintained by constant expansion would ultimately have to turn in upon itself.

Reform and Renewal

Reform was periodically attempted, notably by Osman II (1603–22); rumours of his plan to raise a Kurdish unit as a counterweight to the Janissaries, however, led to his death at their hands. Murad IV (1612–40) retained power, allegedly executing some 100 000 of his servants and subjects in a drive to restore the integrity and efficiency of Suleiman's 'golden age.' Murad's death was followed by an interlude of internal political squabbles. In 1648, Murad's mentally unstable brother, Ibrahim, was deposed in favour of his seven-year-old son, Mehmed IV (1642–93). A serious Venetian threat to Istanbul in 1656 led the young sultan's mother to entrust the fate of the empire to the apparently undistinguished Mehmed Köprülü (c. 1578–1661). With complete authority over policy and appointments, the new **grand vizier** waged war on the empire's enemies, both internal and external, rooting out corruption and incompetence. After his death in 1661 the crusade was continued by his son, Ahmed (died 1676), under whom Crete was taken in 1669. Ahmed was succeeded by his brother-in-law, Kara Mustafa Pasha (1634–83), who determined to take the prize that had eluded even Suleiman himself: Vienna. The catastrophic failure of this enterprise cost him his life, beheaded on the orders of Sultan Mehmed IV. With his death the Köprülü restoration ended.

◄ **Suleiman I**
(16th-century Turkish miniature) Known in the West as 'the Magnificent,' Suleiman's subjects called him Kanuni *('the Lawgiver'), in deference to the series of decrees issued by his able bureaucracy. The Ottoman Empire reached its political, cultural and military peak under Suleiman.*

---

grand vizier Chief minister to the sultan of the Ottoman Empire, from the Arabic *wazir,* meaning porter. The office is of Persian origin; it came to be used by the Muslims during the Abbasid period. The practical extent of the grand vizier's power depended largely on the willingness of sultans to devolve everyday responsibility to him.

Barbarossa

Khayr ad-Din (?1483–1546), or Barbarossa (Red Beard), was a renowned pirate, raiding Christian ships as well as the coasts of Spain and Italy. He entered the Ottomans' service to protect his possessions on the North African coast. As grand admiral of the Ottoman fleet in 1533, he secured Ottoman naval dominance in the eastern Mediterranean.

KEY OTTOMAN RULERS	
1288–1326	Osman
1326–1359	Orhan
1359–89	Murad I
1389–1402	Bayezid I
1413–21	Mehmed I
1421–51	Murad II
1451–81	Mehmed II
1481–1512	Bayezid II
1512–20	Selim I
1520–66	Suleiman I
1566–74	Selim II
1618–22	Osman II
1623–40	Murad IV

THE GREAT ARCHITECT SINAN

JOSEPH SINAN (1489–1588) is recognized as the most prolific architect in the history of Islam. His ideas, exemplified in the construction of mosques and other buildings, served as the basis for almost all later Turkish religious and civic architecture.

Sinan was drafted into the Janissary corps at the age of 23, thus beginning a lifelong service to the Ottoman royal house. During the reign of Suleiman the Magnificent (1520–66) the Ottoman Empire reached the zenith of its political power, and achieved a cultural brilliance to which Sinan very visibly contributed.

The future architect began his career as a skilled military engineer in the Ottoman army. Entering the field of civic architecture in 1539, he was to work for the rest of his life as the chief architect of the Ottoman Empire. During this time, Sinan undertook a prodigious number of projects, including 79 mosques, 34 palaces, 33 public baths, 19 tombs, 55 schools, 16 poorhouses, 7 religious schools, and 12 caravansaries. In addition, he designed and built granaries, fountains, aqueducts, and hospitals.

SINAN'S MOSQUES

Sinan's finest area of work, however, was in the design and construction of mosques. It is for three mosques in particular that he is best remembered: the Sehzade Mosque, the Mosque of Suleiman, and the Selim Mosque (above).

Selim Mosque (Edirne) *The dramatic exterior of the Selim Mosque, built between 1569 and 1575, exemplifies Sinan's mosque design. Considered by the architect to be his masterwork, it features a large central dome resting on eight huge piers, between which are recessed arcades. The whole impressive structure is framed by the four highest minarets in Turkey.*

Completed in 1548, the Sehzade Mosque, in Istanbul, was his first really important architectural commission. Its most notable features, namely its large central dome, which sits upon a square base, flanked by four half domes and numerous smaller ones, are common to many of his mosques.

Influenced by the architecture of the Byzantine Empire, which fell at the hands of the Ottomans in 1453, Sinan designed the Mosque of Suleiman, based upon the 6th-century Byzantine masterpiece, Hagia Sophia in Istanbul (see EARLY AND MEDIEVAL EUROPE: THE BYZANTINE EMPIRE). In designing the mosque, which was built between 1550 and 1557, its architect took full account of the wider social and cultural role that mosques had developed since the creation of the Islamic Empire in the 7th century. It provided not only a place of worship, but a whole social and commercial complex comprising religious schools, a hospital and medical school, a kitchen and refectory, baths, shops, and stables. The Mosque of Suleiman, constructed in the sultan's honour, has a huge central dome pierced by 32 openings, which serve to illuminate the interior of the largest mosque ever built in the Ottoman Empire.

Suleiman and Sinan *As the foremost Ottoman architect, Sinan attempted to reflect the empire's power, at its height under Suleiman, in all of his work. The sultan is shown in conference with Sinan in the Topkapi palace gardens (Istanbul) in this 16th-century manuscript.*

OTTOMAN GLORY

The military successes of Suleiman's reign were accompanied, on the domestic front, by his lawmaking and keen patronage of the arts. As Suleiman's chief architect, Sinan made an impressive contribution to the beautification of the Ottoman capital, Constantinople. He adapted the basic designs of the former occupants of the city, the Byzantines, to meet the needs of Muslim worship, incorporating into his mosques large open spaces for common prayer. The central dome became the focal point of the structure and Sinan pioneered the use of smaller domes, half domes, and buttresses to support the main dome. His use of minarets at each corner served to frame the structure. Sinan's ability to convey a sense of size and power in all of his larger buildings, in addition to the sheer number of projects he undertook, earned him the name of 'Great Architect Sinan.' His enduring legacy comprises some of the most striking architectural landmarks in the world.

The Decline of the Ottoman Empire

Ottoman losses • Arabian revival • Reform in Istanbul • Reform in Cairo •
Russian aggression • The Tanzimat • Democracy and despotism •
The collapse of the empire

The last two centuries of the empire's existence were dominated by its intermittent efforts to resist the encroachments of European powers. Efforts to strengthen its own military and administrative institutions in the face of rebellion by its subjects and resistance from a conservative ruling class were also major preoccupations. Conventionally portrayed as 'the sick man of Europe,' the Ottoman Empire became involved in a global conflict that led to its final destruction.

Ottoman Losses

The failure of the Ottomans to take Vienna in the siege of 1683 was followed by further defeats as the Hapsburgs regained territories north of the Danube. The refugee population created also placed a burden on the empire. Venice saw its chance to conquer part of the Adriatic coast and southern Greece. The Russians took Azov on the Black Sea, while Poland extended its power over the Ukraine.

The 1699 Treaty of Karlowitz confirmed, for the first time, losses of Ottoman territory. It thus symbolized a turning of the tide in the struggle between Islam and Christendom that dated back centuries. The line of confrontation, however, continued to fluctuate. In 1710–11 the Ottomans regained their losses to Russia and, in 1713, recaptured southern Greece from the Hapsburgs. Austrian intervention led to the loss of the remaining Hungarian lands and much of the Balkans. The Ottomans recovered many of these losses, however, between 1736 and 1739. The effects of these military conflicts on life within the empire included oppressive taxation, devaluation of the currency, popular uprisings, and the flight of peasants from the land. Egypt, Syria, and Iraq became effectively autonomous provinces. When a Russian offensive of 1768–70 threatened Istanbul itself, only Russia's internal difficulties and resistence from European powers prevented dissaster. The 1774 Treaty of Kuchuk Kaynarca left the Crimean **khanate** independent

===SEE ALSO===
Early Modern Europe:
- Absolute Monarchy and Bourbon Dominance
- The Growth of the Russian Empire
- The French Revolution and Napoleonic Europe

The Industrial Age in Europe:
- Liberalism and Reaction
- Nationalism and Imperialism
- World War I

◄ **The Ottoman Siege of Vienna**
In 1683 150 000 Ottoman troops led by the grand vizier laid seige to Vienna and the Holy Roman Emperor, Leopold I. After persuasion by Pope Innocent XI, John III Sobieski of Poland led a combined force to relieve the seige. This defeat of the Ottomans marked the beginning of the end of their domination of eastern Europe.

khanate The territory ruled by a khan, a title formerly held by Mongol and Turkic rulers.

157

▲ An Iznik Plate
The pottery and tiles made at Iznik in the 16th century were primarily used at court or to decorate great mosques. Influenced by Chinese styles and techniques, the Iznik potters produced brilliant multicoloured wares. By the mid-16th century, the industry had declined drastically.

The Decline of the Ottoman Empire *Between 1807 and 1924 the Ottoman Empire was gradually stripped of its remaining lands, having been subjected to attempts to seize its territories throughout the previous century.* ▼

of both Russia and the Ottomans. Nevertheless, Russia still gained several fortresses, Azov, the lands between the rivers Bug and Dnepr, maritime rights in the Black Sea, and limited power over the sultan's Christian subjects. In 1783 Russia annexed the Crimean khanate outright. A further war in 1787–91 led to Ottoman acceptance of the Russian position.

Arabian Revival
The region of Nejd, in central Arabia, had never been under effective Ottoman control. From 1745 onwards the Sa'ud family, inspired by the reformist piety of Muhammad ibn Abd al-Wahhab (1703–92), strove to expand its power in a campaign to purify Islam of deviant practices. Scarcely noticed outside the Arabian peninsula, this movement was the embryo of modern Saudi Arabia.

Reform in Istanbul
The efforts of vizier Halil Hamid Pasha to modernize the armed forces and to introduce French officers as advisers provoked Janissary resistance (see THE RISE OF THE OTTOMAN EMPIRE), leading to Hamid's execution in 1785. In 1792 Sultan Selim III (1761–1808) attempted to establish 'New Order' units, modelled on European forces, supported by a medical service and a Western-style officers' academy. In 1793 Selim established permanent diplomatic relations with several European states. Napoleon's invasion of Egypt in 1798 was aborted by British naval power, yet it exposed the military inadequacy of both Mameluke and Ottoman forces. Selim was deposed and the 'New Order' initiative cancelled. A countercoup cost Selim III his life; when his successor, Mahmud II (1784–1839), tried to revive the reforms he only saved himself by abandoning them for 20 years, when he was able to organize the final destruction of the Janissaries (1826). He subsequently set up a

road-building programme, ordered a census, and established a postal service. An official newspaper was also started and schools of engineering, medicine, and military science were founded. European books were translated to make knowledge accessible to a wider readership.

Reform in Cairo
Mahmud II's belated modernization lagged behind that of his nominal servant, Mohammed Ali Pasha (1769–1849), a Balkan opportunist and troop commander whom he had confirmed as governor of Egypt after the Napoleonic debacle. In 1811 Mohammed Ali secured his position by killing the Mameluke leadership. He then followed Selim III's example by founding a military academy and medical school. Irrigation was improved and cotton introduced as a cash crop for the European market. Mohammed Ali reimposed Ottoman suzerainty over Arabia in 1811–18 and helped to crush a Greek national rising in 1821–27. He then directed his forces at his former master and, in the 1830s, attempted to take the empire for himself. He was thwarted, however, by European intervention. In 1841 the sultan awarded Mohammed Ali the hereditary governorship of Egypt and the Sudan for his family as a means of assuaging him. His dynasty lasted until 1953.

Russian Aggression
During the later 19th century the European powers intervened to resist Russian pressure on the Ottoman regime and rewarded themselves at the Ottomans' expense. A Russian invasion in 1853 was neutralized by a counterinvasion of the Crimea by British, French, Sardinian, and Ottoman forces. Huge Russian gains in the war of 1877–78 were reduced by an international congress in Berlin. The Ottomans lost Cyprus to Britain and Bosnia-Herzegovina to Austria. Ottoman indebtedness to foreign creditors led to the humiliating establishment of an Ottoman Public Debt Administration, to ensure the repayment of outstanding loans. In 1881–82 British forces occupied Egypt, crushing a nationalist movement and reducing the ruling dynasty to the status of a puppet.

The Tanzimat (Reorganization)
The reform movement of Tanzimat continued under Abdülmecid (1823–61) and Abdülaziz (1830–76). The timing of such reforms as the Noble Rescript of Gulhane (1839) and the Imperial Rescript (1856), in the aftermath of major crises, implies that they were motivated by external as well as internal factors. A number of reforms, such as the granting of equal legal status to Muslims and non-Muslims,

	Losses 1807–29
	Losses 1830–78
	Losses 1879–1915
	Losses 1916–23
	Turkey 1924

were reversed or circumvented. There were, however, attempts to systematize provincial administration and establish municipal administrations. A Western-style commercial code was declared in 1850 and the telegraph was introduced in 1854.

Democracy and Despotism

Private newspapers began to appear in the 1840s, reflecting the gradual emergence of a reforming intellectual class. In 1865 a group founded what later became the Young Ottoman Society. Scorning slavish imitations of the West, they sought to reconcile the best Western practices, such as participatory government, with Islamic traditions. The financial ineptitude of Abdülaziz led to his deposition, in 1876, in favour of Abdülhamid II (1842–1918). Pledging to establish a parliamentary form of government, he issued a constitution. The first parliament, however, was dissolved in 1878 and a total autocracy, backed by armies of spies and informers, was instituted in its place. The Armenian minority in the empire, suspected of subversion, was subjected to horrific massacres during the 1890s. However, newspapers and schools continued to proliferate and a modern university was founded in Istanbul in 1900.

KEY OTTOMAN RULERS	
1789–1807	Selim III
1808–39	Mahmud II
1839–61	Abdülmecid I
1861–76	Abdülaziz
1876–1909	Abdülhamid II

Pressure to restore the constitution gradually united an opposition movement. In 1907 an Ottoman Committee of Union and Progress (CUP) was established to press openly for reform. Food shortages in 1908, which led to riots, strikes, and a military mutiny in Macedonia, forced the sultan to restore the constitution, making the CUP the most effective power in the land. It won a landslide victory in the 1912 parliamentary elections. Moves towards a genuine liberalism were, however, hampered by the need to tackle major external crises. Italy was invaded by Libya (1911) and Greece, Bulgaria, Serbia, and Montenegro launched an attack on their former overlord in 1912, resulting in the Balkan Wars. In 1913 the CUP welcomed a military mission from Germany that sought to ingratiate itself with the military-led regime; it proved to be a fateful alliance.

The Collapse of the Empire

Fundamentally it had been Britain's reluctance to see the Ottoman Empire undermined that had enabled it to survive. However, the Ottomans were tempted into an alliance with Germany and Austria in World War I against the old enemy, Russia, with the hope of regaining lost territories in the Balkans and Transcaucasia, in spite of retribution from Britain in the event of defeat. On the Transcaucasian front Turkish troops were responsible for the massacre of almost one million Armenians. Nevertheless, the collapse of the Central Powers (Germany and the Austro-Hungarian Empire) deprived the empire of vital supplies, making surrender unavoidable. National revival was now impossible and this event thus marked the end of the Ottoman Empire.

The Europeans have now put their hands on every part of the world. The English have reached Afghanistan; the French have seized Tunisia. In reality this usurpation, aggression, and conquest has not come from the French or the English. Rather it is science that everywhere manifests its greatness and power.

> Jamal al-Din al-Afghani (1838–97), Islamic revolutionary

▲ **Sultan Abdülhamid II**
Despite his efforts to modernize and democratize the empire, Abdülhamid created a harshly repressive regime.

Persia and Central Asia

The Safavids • Greatness and decay • The Qajar period • Central Asia

▲ **Calligrapher by
Reza Abbasi**
*(c. 1570–c. 1635)
Reza was the favourite
painter of Shah Abbas
the Great. He was the
last great Persian
painter of originality.*

Persia was restored to glory and converted to Shiism by the Safavid dynasty between 1502 and 1736; it was to endure two centuries of weak government and economic retardation after the Safavids' demise. Recurrent attempts by nomad leaders to re-establish the steppe-based empire of the Mongols petered out by the mid-18th century, after which their ignorance of modern firepower restricted them to a peripheral role in Asian politics.

The Safavids

This dynasty emerged from an order of Sufi devotees (see THE ABBASID CALIPHATE) founded in northwestern Iran, by Sheik Safi ad-Din (1253–1334). Sheik Junayd (died 1460) transformed the spiritual strength of the order into militant political power. While still no more than a boy Ismail I (1487–1524), founder of the Safavid dynasty, established his capital at Tabriz and assumed the title of **shah** (from the Persian, meaning 'king') in 1501, thus giving Persia its first native dynasty for more than eight centuries. By 1506 Ismail had conquered the entire Iranian plateau and by 1508 he had overcome most of Iraq. In 1510 he crushed the Uzbeks on his eastern frontier but was himself severely checked by the Ottomans at Chalderan in 1514 (see THE RISE OF THE OTTOMAN EMPIRE). Nevertheless, Ismail continued to support a vigorous campaign that permanently transformed Persia from a Sunnite country to the only Shiite one (see THE EMERGENCE OF A NEW EMPIRE). This sharpened

KEY SAFAVID RULERS	
Ismail I	1501–24
Tahmasp I	1524–76
Abbas I (the Great)	1588–1629
Abbas II	1642–66

Persia's sense of identity and distinctiveness from its neighbours: Turkish, Arabic, Uzbek, or Mogul. One important effect of this process of mass conversion was to strengthen the power and prestige of religious scholars and judges, who later came to exercise a check on arbitrary rule and provided national continuity through periods of weak government.

Greatness and Decay

The Safavid Empire reached its peak under Shah Abbas the Great (1571–1629), who equipped his standing army with 500 cannon and 6000 muskets. Like his Ottoman counterparts, he recruited a slave-elite of foreign converts to give his army a loyal and stable core. In 1598 Abbas decided to move the seat of government away from his contested western frontier to the more central position of Isfahan, a former Seljuk capital. The glories of this location are well attested by the accounts of European traders and diplomats. Under the rule of Abbas the city was renowned for its carpets, tiles, textiles, and school of miniature painting. A decade after the death of Abbas a

**The Meydan at
Isfahan** *This huge
rectangular plaza is
one of the outstanding
features of the city.*

▲ The Royal Mosque at Isfahan
Commissioned by Shah Abbas the Great, it was not completed until after his death (1629). The mosque boasts an impressive dome covered in colourful mosaic decoration.

lasting peace was finally concluded with the Ottomans. The later Safavids proved to be weak rulers. Husayn I (1668–1726) was ousted by a badly organized Afghan uprising, which, after a long siege, reduced Isfahan largely to rubble (it was not to be restored until two centuries later). The Afghan revolt was eventually crushed by the ruthless Nadir Shah (1688–1747). A brilliant soldier, he raided as far as Bokhara and Delhi, inflicting defeats on both the Afghans and the Ottomans before being assassinated by his own Afshar tribesmen. After Nadir's death the Afshars retained northeast Persia, while the bulk of the country was ruled from Shiraz by Karim Khan Zand (c. 1705–79), *vakil* (deputy) to a series of Safavid puppet rulers. Anarchy followed his death, in 1779, until the Qajar dynasty established their capital at Tehran in 1796.

The Qajar Period
For most of the 19th century the Qajar's nominal realm provided a ravaged backdrop to the imperial rivalries of the Russians, pressing from the north, and the British, attempting to counter their influence from the south. Only the feeblest efforts were made to emulate

Ottoman modernization and, as late as 1900, the country had only eight miles of railway, while one-quarter of the population still lived as tribal nomads. Popular discontent with the incursions of foreign powers and commercial interests resulted in a struggle to establish parliamentary government, which lasted from 1905 until 1911. Although a constitution was granted in 1907, the Qajars were able to disregard this and the *majlis* (parliament), thanks to their tsarist supporters, until the country was again turned into a fighting arena during World War I. It was the British who emerged as the dominant element in Persia and, after the collapse of an ill-fated attempt to establish a Soviet-style republic in the north, were content to accept, in 1921, the seizure of power by General Reza Khan (1878–1944). He commanded the 15 000-strong Cossack brigade, the only coherent military force left in the country. After crushing tribal opposition to his coup, General Khan deposed the last Qajar, in 1925, and assumed the title of shah in the following year.

Central Asia
The acquisition of firearms and artillery by the powers bordering central Asia effectively extinguished the threat that steppe nomad horsemen had posed against their settled neighbours for 1000 years. By the mid-18th century Russia and China were advancing steadily into the power vacuum, establishing forts and colonies. Travellers during the 19th century reported Mongol society to be stagnant and apathetic. Although its glory seemed to have faded in central Asia, it had flourished elsewhere, in the form of the Mogul and Manchu dynasties that had given India and China their last displays of greatness before they succumbed to Western intrusion.

A Crucial Resource
In 1901 William Knox D'Arcy, a British subject, obtained a concession to prospect for oil on behalf of the Anglo-Iranian Oil Company (AIOC), a creation of the British government. The first Middle Eastern commercial discovery of oil east of Abadan, in 1908, was a milestone in the history of the region.

The Smoking Boycott
In 1890 Naser ad-Din Shah (1848–96) granted a monopoly on Persia's tobacco trade to a British company, in return for a percentage of the profits. This outraged the bazaar merchants, who staged a smoking boycott until the concession was withdrawn.

◄ Reza Khan *He began his career as an Iranian army officer, who eventually rose through the ranks to become shah of Iran. He chose the dynastic name of Pahlavi to legitimize his regime, a name that harked back to pre-Islamic grandeur.*

European Mandates

The postwar settlement • Reforming regimes • The mandates

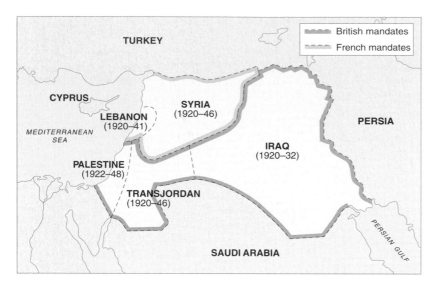

▲ **The Middle Eastern Mandated Territories** *While France received control of Syria and Lebanon, Britain were entrusted with Iraq, Transjordan, and Palestine.*

═══SEE ALSO═══
The Industrial Age in Europe:
• World War I
• The Causes and Course of World War II

Kemal Atatürk

Born in Salonika (now in Greece), Mustafa Kemal served with distinction in several Ottoman military campaigns before leading the nationalist revolt against the proposed partition of Turkey. He was determined to strengthen his country by rejecting traditions that he believed had caused its weakness.

During the course of World War I Britain, France, Italy, and Russia secretly agreed to divide between them what remained of the Ottoman Empire in the event of their victory (see THE DECLINE OF THE OTTOMAN EMPIRE). Britain also made potentially conflicting pledges to establish an independent Arab state under Husayn ibn Ali (c. 1854–1931), who led the 'Arab revolt' against Ottoman overlordship. However, Britain also supported "the establishment in Palestine of a National Home for the Jewish people."

The Postwar Settlement

The settlement that ultimately emerged did little to satisfy the aspirations of the central Middle Eastern inhabitants. Under the aegis of the League of Nations, Britain and France were entrusted with 'mandates' that legitimized the imposition of their quasi-colonial rule over Iraq, Transjordan, Palestine (British), Syria, and Lebanon (French) as an intermediary step towards full independence.

Meanwhile, the Saud family, having stayed on the periphery of the Arab revolt, began to extend its control over the Arabian peninsula. By 1934 the present boundaries of the Saudi state had been established.

Kemal Atatürk *In 1935 he encouraged his people to adopt Western-style surnames; he assumed the surname 'Atatürk,' 'Father of the Turks.' He remains, more than half a century after his death, a revered figure in Turkey. There are statues of him in virtually every Turkish city, town, and village.*

Reforming Regimes

The humiliating 1920 Treaty of Sèvres, accepted by the Ottoman government, demanded the demilitarization of the straits linking the Mediterranean and the Black Sea and the division of western Anatolia between Greece, Italy, and France. Led by an Ottoman general, Mustafa Kemal (later known as **Kemal Atatürk**; 1880–1938), a nationalist revolt ejected Greek occupying forces and secured a renegotiation of frontiers that was confirmed by the 1923 Treaty of Lausanne. In the same year Mustafa Kemal became president of the new secular Republic of Turkey and initiated a programme of westernizing reforms. The sultanate had been abolished in 1922 and the caliphate followed it in 1924. Emphasizing the ethnic rather than the dynastic nature of the new state, its capital was transferred from Istanbul to Ankara, in central Anatolia.

By the end of the decade, Turkey's educational and legal systems had been secularized, the Arabic script replaced by Roman characters, and the Gregorian calendar introduced. Commerce and industry were encouraged by the state and factories established to produce textiles, cement, sugar, and steel, all protected by tariffs. While Turkey was, in theory, a liberal parliamentary democracy, any dissent was suppressed. There were also limits to the

lifestyle revolution. The wearing of the veil was never banned and the Sufi dervish orders (see THE ABBASID CALIPHATE) were driven underground rather than destroyed. In practice it was a one-party state. A shrewd neutrality brought peace to the nation and the population rose from 12.5 million in 1923 to 17 million by 1938. After the death of Atatürk in 1938 the Turkish republic came under the control of his closest colleague, Ismet Inönü (1884–1973), who permitted the gradual emergence of a genuine political opposition. Inönü maintained Turkish neutrality during World War II until February 1945, when a formal declaration of war on Germany enabled Turkey to become a founding member of the United Nations.

In Iran Reza Shah Pahlavi (see PERSIA AND CENTRAL ASIA), supported by rising oil revenues, attempted to emulate the transformation of Turkey, establishing the basic framework of a modern state by creating a civil service as well as a standing army based on conscription. The nomadic lifestyle was curbed and a trans-Iranian railway connecting the north and south of the country was completed in 1936. Agriculture, however, remained underdeveloped and only a small minority benefited from the shah's revolution. Reza Shah's pro-Nazi sympathies led, in 1941, to his deposition, at the hands of the British and Russians, in favour of his son, Mohammad Reza Pahlavi (1919–80).

The Mandates

In Iraq the British established a regime so dependent upon their support that they made a formal withdrawal in 1932. Authentic Iraqi independence and republic status came with the overthrow of its monarchy in the bloody revolution of 1958.

In Transjordan a small but highly efficient, British-trained military became the backbone supporting the monarchy. Transjordan retained close ties with Britain, even after attaining formal independence and enlarging its territories in 1946 (see MIDDLE EAST (VOL.1): JORDAN).

In Palestine, immigration and a natural increase in the birth rate raised the Jewish proportion of the population from 11% in 1922 to 29% by 1936. This resulted in mounting tension with the indigenous Arab population and widespread disorder between 1936 and 1938. The 1937 Peel Commission proposed partition as a solution and the British also announced the imposition of an upper limit to Jewish immigration. These proposals proved unacceptable to both Arabs and Jews. The Jews, meanwhile, had built up a general labour organization, the **Histadrut**, under the guidance of David Ben-Gurion (1886–1973).

▲ **Unrest in Palestine** *Following a two-year period of disorder and friction between Arabs and Jews, British troops are shown searching Arabs in Jerusalem (October 1938).*

This began to function, in many ways, as a parallel state, sponsoring schools, hospitals, businesses, and a socialist-style type of settlement, the **kibbutz**, where inhabitants lived a communal life and took equal wages, while developing local resources through agriculture and crafts. Another crucial institution was the Jewish Agency, which promoted inward migration. By 1939 Jews in Palestine numbered nearly 500 000 and accounted for almost one-third of the population (see THE ARAB-ISRAELI QUESTION).

In their mandated territories the French were welcomed by the local Christian population and were able to establish a predominantly Christian Lebanese state, enlarging its territory at Syria's expense. The constitution of 1926 devised a system of power-sharing between different religious groups and, from 1937 onwards, a convention was established that the president would be a Maronite Christian and the prime minister a Sunni Muslim.

French rule in Syria provoked an armed uprising in 1925–27 that twice forced the French out of the capital, Damascus, before it was crushed. The election of a Popular Front government in France led to negotiations for independence in 1936. These were terminated, however, by the outbreak of World War II in 1939. In 1941 British and Free French troops invaded Syria to oust local supporters of the Vichy government (which controlled German-occupied France). Although Syrian independence was proclaimed in 1944, French reluctance to withdraw led to further fighting in May and June of 1945. The French finally evacuated Syria in 1946.

▲ **David Ben-Gurion** *Born in Poland, he emigrated to Palestine in 1906. Having led the socialist Mapai party from 1930, he served as Israel's first prime minister from 1948 to 1953; he held office again from 1955 until 1963.*

The Arab-Israeli Question

The birth of Israel • The Suez War • The Six Day War •
The Yom Kippur War • The path to peace

Changing Frontiers
The borders of the Jewish state of Israel, created in 1947, underwent several changes throughout the Arab-Israeli conflict. ▼

Exhausted by war, distracted by other imperial commitments, and harassed by the attacks of the Jewish underground movement and the 'illegal' immigration of some 30 000 Jews who had escaped the Holocaust, Britain referred the future of its Palestine mandate to the newly formed United Nations (UN) in 1947.

The Birth of Israel

The UN backed a plan for partitioning Palestine into independent Arab and Jewish states, with an international administration for Jerusalem. As British forces withdrew, in May 1948, the leaders of the Jewish Agency, Histadrut (see EUROPEAN MANDATES), proclaimed the independent State of Israel. Armed forces from Egypt, Jordan, Iraq, Syria, and Lebanon promptly invaded Israel. This conflict resulted in Israel retaining four-fifths of the former Palestine mandated territories, though not all of Jerusalem. Some 700 000 Palestinian Arabs fled, or were expelled, from their former homeland, creating a refugee problem. By 1949 a cease-fire and the recognition of frontiers – but no peace treaty – had been achieved.

The Suez War

The overthrow of the Egyptian monarchy by an officers' coup, in 1952, was followed by the emergence of Gamal Abdel Nasser (1918–70) as leader. This was accompanied by an increase in frontier tension with Israel. In 1956 Nasser's nationalization of the Suez Canal led to collusion between Israel, France, and Britain. The result was Israel's invasion of the Sinai peninsula and the intervention of a Franco-British expeditionary force in the Suez Canal zone; their aim was to reassert Western control over the Canal. Pressure from the USA and the UN forced the Western powers to withdraw. Israel withdrew to its borders, having shown its military capability. Disillusioned by the apparent impotence of Arab governments, the Palestinians established an armed resistance movement, al-Fatah, in 1959–62. This provoked the Arab states, avowed protectors of the Palestinians, to sponsor the creation of a Palestine Liberation Organization (PLO), acting as a quasi-government in exile, in 1964.

The Six Day War

Palestinian raids, Israeli reprisals, and armaments build-up by the Arab states renewed frontier tensions in the mid-1960s. Nasser, persuaded by other Arab regimes, secured the removal of a UN peacekeeping force positioned between Egypt and Israel. Anticipating an attack by its Arab neighbours, Israel made a successful pre-emptive strike on the Egyptian air force on 5 June 1967. After six days of fighting, Israeli forces had taken the Gaza Strip and Sinai from Egypt, the Golan Heights from Syria, and the West Bank and East Jerusalem from Jordan. Following the conflict, the UN adopted Resolution 242 calling for all states in the region to acknowledge each other's independence and territorial integrity, to withdraw from territories seized by force, and to achieve a just settlement of the refugee problem. This resolution remained the basis of repeated attempts by the UN and major powers to bring about a lasting settlement of the Arab-Israeli conflict.

The Yom Kippur War

The trauma of another Arab defeat strengthened the resolve of al-Fatah radicals and, in 1969, they took control of the PLO, with

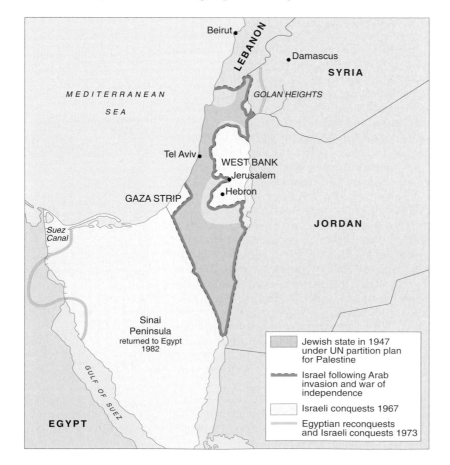

Beirut
LEBANON
Damascus
SYRIA
MEDITERRANEAN SEA
GOLAN HEIGHTS
Tel Aviv
WEST BANK
Jerusalem
Hebron
GAZA STRIP
Suez Canal
JORDAN
Sinai Peninsula returned to Egypt 1982
GULF OF SUEZ
EGYPT

Jewish state in 1947 under UN partition plan for Palestine

Israel following Arab invasion and war of independence

Israeli conquests 1967

Egyptian reconquests and Israeli conquests 1973

Yasser Arafat (1929–) as chairman. Israel, meanwhile, struggled to contain internal resistance, external harassment from Arab guerrillas, and an undeclared war of attrition with Egypt along its border. In October 1973, the Islamic fasting month of Ramadan and the Jewish fast of the Day of Atonement (Yom Kippur) coincided, highlighting the gulf between Arab and Jew. Egypt chose this time to launch an attack across the Suez Canal, breaking through the defensive Bar-Lev line, while Syria tried to recapture the Golan Heights. Taken by surprise on two fronts, Israel fought for 16 days to force a cease-fire. No major territorial revisions were achieved, but Israel's reputation for invincibility was sufficiently dented for the Egyptian president, Anwar El Sadat (1918–81), to negotiate a peace. He made a dramatic appeal to the **Knesset** (Israeli parliament) in November 1977. Negotiations culminated in the US-sponsored Camp David Agreements of March 1979, by which Egypt recognized Israel and regained Sinai in return. Pledges to achieve a form of self-government for Palestinian majority areas in Israeli-occupied territories were, however, unfulfilled by subsequent negotiations. The establishment of new Israeli communities in these areas further compromised the pledges. In 1980 the European Community – prompted by an increase in the price of Arab-controlled oil – added to existing international pressure on Israel by adopting the 'Venice Declaration,' recognizing the need for a Palestinian 'homeland.'

The Path to Peace

Having secured its frontier with Egypt, Israel, provoked by a decade of Palestinian raids across its northern borders, invaded Lebanon in June 1982. This action forced the PLO to relocate its headquarters to Tunisia. However, PLO forces remained in Lebanon until 1984. Israeli success was later tarnished by the massacre of Palestinian non-combatants in the Sabra and Shatila refugee camps at the hands of Maronite Christian militiamen fighting in collusion with Israeli forces. Unlike previous military actions, the invasion of Lebanon divided Israeli domestic opinion and, in 1985, Israel withdrew its forces, leaving a 'South Lebanon Army,' friendly to Israel's interests, as a buffer along the border.

In 1988 the PLO launched a strategy of widespread resistance (**intifada**) that brought continuing disorder to Israel. This presented the Israeli military with the politically challenging task of keeping public order in a civilian environment. The inevitable result was adverse publicity, in which Israeli forces were seen as brutally repressive. Persistent US and European efforts to promote a Middle East peace process through international negotia-

tions were hampered by the intransigence of Syria, by the continued encouragement of guerrilla activity by Iran, and by the internal deadlock of Israeli party rivalries. The latter was broken in 1992 by the election of a government headed by Itzhak Rabin (1922–95), architect of Israel's victory in the Six Day War and prime minister from 1974 to 1977. Rabin was prepared to risk this prestige in attempting to relieve Israel of its isolation and security burdens, without jeopardizing its national interests. Eagerly encouraged by US president Bill Clinton (1946–), Rabin and Arafat met in Washington, in 1993, to sign an historic accord that granted some self-government for Palestinians in return for Palestinian acceptance of Israeli nationhood. In 1994 peace was agreed between Israel and Jordan, Israeli troops withdrew from Gaza and Jericho, and interim Palestinian self-government began there. In September 1995, it was agreed that Palestinian self-rule would expand under an elected Palestinian Council, while progressive Israeli redeployment from the West Bank was scheduled for 1996. However, violent opposition to the peace process by extremists on both sides has hindered implementation. The assassination of Itzhak Rabin, in November 1995, cast doubts over the peace process. The election of Benjamin Netanyahu (1949–) – hard-line leader of the Likud Party – as prime minister, in May 1996, did little to ease the tension. US-hosted peace talks resumed after a further period of violence. Israeli troops withdrew from Hebron in early 1997. However, Israel's decision to start building new Jewish settlements in East Jerusalem, in the face of international and Arab opinion, led to the effective collapse of the peace process in March 1997. Concerted US efforts to effect reconciliation have yet to yield results.

▲ **An Historic Agreement** *President Clinton, Prime Minister Rabin, and Yasser Arafat meet in Washington, September 1993.*

The Nobel Peace Prize

In 1978 Israeli prime minister Menachem Begin (1913–92) and Egyptian president Anwar El Sadat were jointly awarded the Nobel Prize for Peace in recognition of their role in the achievement of the Camp David Agreements.

▲ **Anwar El Sadat** *As president of Egypt (1970–81), he was assassinated by Islamic extremists for initiating the 1979 peace agreement with Israel.*

Oil and the Middle East

The struggle for control • Iran • Iraq • Saudi Arabia • Libya • Algeria

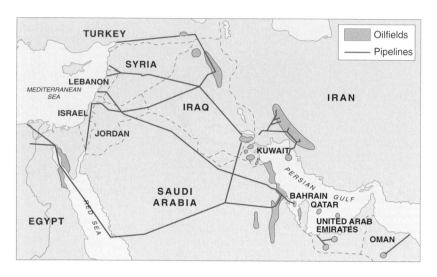

▲ Oilfields and Pipelines in the Middle East *The presence of oil in the Middle East has transformed political and economic life in the region.*

═══SEE ALSO═══
The Industrial Age in Europe:
• Postwar Europe
North America:
• The United States of America
Religion (vol. 6):
• Islam

▲ Sheikh Yamani *As oil minister for Saudi Arabia (1962–86), he sponsored OPEC, exercising a moderating influence on a number of its members.*

During the last half century oil has increasingly become a political issue, accompanied by major shifts in the balance between the interests of producers and consumers. The oil-producing states of the Middle East have used their immense revenues to fund armaments, welfare, and development projects, generating both benefits and discontent and provoking unprecedented political and social changes.

The Struggle for Control

For 30 years following World War II the economic history of the Middle East was dominated by the efforts of oil-producing states to renegotiate extraction rights conceded to Western-owned companies. In 1960 Venezuela joined Arab oil-producers and Iran to establish the Organization of Petroleum Exporting Countries (OPEC) to defend their interests.

In 1967 the Saudi Arabian oil minister, Sheikh Yamani (1930–), advocated that producer governments should share in the profits of international oil companies, both from selling crude oil and from refining, marketing, and derivatives production. In 1971 Algeria nationalized its oil industry outright; Iraq and Iran soon did the same.

Oil embargoes were used to advance Arab interests in 1973. Western states seen to support Israel in the Yom Kippur War (see THE ARAB-ISRAELI QUESTION) had their oil supplies withdrawn and there was a four-fold increase in the price of crude oil. By 1976 the major oil states controlled their own extraction operations.

A second 'oil shock' in 1979 tripled the price of oil by 1981. However, revolution in Iran and the outbreak of the Iran–Iraq War had weakened OPEC's influence. Energy-saving programmes, diversification into other energy sources, and international recession in the late 1980s further depressed demand for oil.

Iran

In 1963 Mohammad Reza Shah Pahlavi (see PERSIA AND CENTRAL ASIA) launched a 'White Revolution' that promised Iranians land reform, equal rights for women, and the secularization of law and education, all of which affronted traditional Islamic values. The shah also expanded his armed forces – intent upon becoming the leading power in the Middle East.

Iranian oil revenues quadrupled in the 1970s, but few Iranians benefited. The consumerism of the landowning elite offended both the poor and the pious. Hostility to the regime was strong enough to force the shah into exile in January 1979. This enabled the exiled Ayatollah Khomeini (1900–89) to return to lead an Islamic revolution and institute a fundamentalist regime. Khomeini was succeeded by Ali Akbar Rafsanjani (1934–); relations with the West slowly improved as Iran tried to rebuild its economy. Widespread discontent with economic conditions led to the decisive election, in 1997, of the more liberal

Iran–Iraq War *A fire rages after an Iranian oil rig is hit by Iraqi shells. The eight-year war destroyed 50 towns and cities, killed one million people, and ended in the mutual exhaustion of both nations.* ▼

▲ **The Gulf War** *The Allied Operation Desert Storm was highly successful against Iraq.*

'Ayatollah'

The title 'Ayatollah,' from the Arabic meaning sign from God, is conferred on leading Shiite theologians in recognition of outstanding piety, scholarship, and wisdom. The career of Ruholla Khomeini made the word familiar worldwide for the first time. He was exiled for opposing the shah's land reforms in 1963. In 1979 he returned to revolutionary Iran, where he was revered as a symbol of deliverance from the repressive reigns of the shahs. He used his remarkable charisma to back the war against Iraq, publicly condemning the final acceptance of the ceasefire. Khomeini's death was accompanied by scenes of mass-mourning.

Seyyed Mohammad Khatami as president; his victory seemed to herald a new era for Iran.

Iraq

The overthrow of the monarchy in 1958 was followed by a decade of coups until the Ba'athist party emerged supreme. The oil revenues of the 1970s funded economic diversification and a free health service, and the armed forces were built up to rival those of Iran. In 1980 Saddam Hussein (1935–   ), recently established as president, took advantage of Iran's revolutionary chaos to launch an attack to seize the Shatt al-Arab waterway, controlling Iraq's access to the Gulf. The resulting eight-year war badly damaged the oil-production facilities of both sides. Iraq finally conceded Iranian control over the waterway.

In 1990 Iraq sought to restore its depleted oil revenues by invading Kuwait. Under UN auspices, a US-led coalition drove Iraq out in February 1991 (Operation Desert Storm). Despite Iraq's defeat, Saddam Hussein retained power. His brutal suppression of Kurds and Shiites led to the setting up of UN safe havens and 'no-fly zones' in Iraq; a UN commission was set up to dismantle Iraq's weapons of mass destruction. Saddam was re-elected president in (uncontested) elections in 1995, since when sanctions against Iraq have been maintained and disputes with the UN have continued.

Saudi Arabia

With a quarter of the world's estimated oil reserves, a peak annual income of US$100 billion, and control of Islam's holiest cities, Saudi Arabia has a powerful influence in the Arab and Muslim worlds. With a population of only 10 million, it has attracted 2 million migrant workers, thus becoming a major source of wages income to Egypt, Jordan, and Yemen. When the Iran–Iraq War disrupted oil supplies, Saudi Arabia alternately boosted and cut production to stabilize prices. During the Gulf War it allied with Western forces for protection, in return for increased oil output and the funding of much of the US/UK Gulf forces. Despite the modernity of its urban life, Saudi Arabia still strictly observes Islamic law.

Libya

Led by Colonel Moamar al Gaddafi (1942–   ), who headed the coup that overthrew the monarchy in 1969, Libya did not start to export oil until 1961. During the 1970s Libyans experienced a transformation, enjoying access to Western goods but not to Western-style civil liberties. The state provided free education, medical care, and pensions while it controlled imports, retailing, urban property, and the legal system. An anti-imperialist, Gaddafi supported terrorism, increasing Libya's international isolation in the 1980s and provoking sanctions and an oil embargo in the 1990s.

Algeria

Algeria used its oil wealth to develop its gas reserves, establish Africa's largest oil-refining capacity, and build up other industries. Despite its economic modernization and commitment to 'progressive' policies, Algeria faced major civil strife 30 years after the end of French colonial rule. The seizure of power by a military junta in 1992 provoked violence by fundamentalists from 1993. Government offensives against the guerillas followed failed peace talks in 1994. Since the election of General Lamine Zeroual as president in 1995, violence between Islamic terrorists and security forces has escalated.

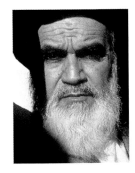

▲ **Ayatollah Khomeini** *One of his last public acts was to issue a death sentence (by **fatwa**) on the Indo-British author, Salman Rushdie, for his novel* The Satanic Verses.

THE DISCOVERY OF PETROLEUM

THE WORD PETROLEUM (from Latin *petra*, rock, and *oleum*, oil) is of paramount significance throughout the world – it was coined by a German mineralogist in 1556, although oil seeps in rock formations were known in the Middle East to the ancient Babylonians and Sumerians. Perhaps as a result of the Muslim Arab occupation of southern Spain from the early 8th century, the chemical process of distilling petroleum into light fractions suitable for illumination became known in Europe by the 12th century. However, in many countries, from the 16th to the 19th centuries, the main fuel used in oil lamps was an oil made from whale blubber.

Striking Oil *Petroleum flows up over the top of the derrick at one of the first wells to be drilled during the first decade of the 20th century – that at Masjed Soleyman in southwestern Iran.*

Saudi Arabia
In the early 1990s Saudi Arabia was the largest single producer of crude petroleum in the world. While its enormous oil wealth has enabled Saudi Arabia to modernize, some of its inhabitants still use traditional modes of transport.

By the middle of the 19th century whales were becoming difficult to find in sufficient numbers and some kerosene (or paraffin) made from coal was being used in Europe and North America. It was a combination of the demands of the

Industrial Revolution for lubricants and the growing use of oil as an illuminant that provided a spur to the development of the petroleum industry. Petroleum was first mined for these purposes in Pennsylvania (USA) in 1859, and by the end of the 19th century oil fields had been discovered in many parts of North America, in Europe, and in East Asia.

During the 20th century, following the development of the petrol engine, the demand for petroleum products escalated enormously. Refined oil now became the primary energy source for motor vehicles while its use as an illuminant decreased with the availability of domestic and industrial electricity. The discovery of petroleum has also led to the development of a vast petrochemical industry, which manufactures such products as detergents, plastics, fibres, fertilizers, and drugs.

While World War I (1914–18) has been called the last of the horse wars, it was also the first war in which the internal-combustion engine was used to take men into battle – on land, at sea, and, for the first time, in the air. By World War II (1939–45), petroleum had become the essential resource for conducting warfare, thus boosting its demand and supply. It was the discovery of petroleum in the Middle East, however, that contributed most dramatically to the growth of oil supplies. Of the 37 supergiant oil fields in the world 26 are to be found in the Arabian-Iranian

THE GROWTH OF WORLD OIL SUPPLIES

= 100 billion barrels

1859–1968   1859–1978   1859–1988

It took 109 years (1859–1968) to produce the first 200 billion barrels of oil throughout the world; the next two amounts of 200 billion barrels were produced in only 10 years each (1968–78; 1978–88).

sedimentary basin in the region of the Persian Gulf. Oil was discovered in Iran as early as 1908, yet it was the discovery of the first field in Bahrain, on the Arabian side of the basin, in 1932, that initiated the whole-scale search for oil in the Arabian interior. From the mid-1930s on these activities transformed the economy of the Middle East (SEE ISLAMIC WORLD: OIL AND THE MIDDLE EAST). Some 64% of known world petroleum reserves are now concentrated in this basin and since 1960 Saudi Arabia alone has been producing more petroleum than the USA.

THE AMERICAS

NORTH AMERICA

Early North America

North America's first inhabitants • The age of discovery

Amerindian Religion

Religion moulded the social organization, economy, art, and conceptions of warfare of Amerindians. While religious practices varied from tribe to tribe, all religions were based on a belief in the spirit world. According to Indian mythology, spirits were the powers that ruled the universe. They could be invoked through prayer, incantation, sacrifice. Special rituals celebrating rites of passage were associated with puberty, pregnancy, childbirth, and death. Religious leaders, known as medicine men or *shamans*, officiated at other group ceremonies designed to achieve specific ends, such as rainmaking.

For thousands of years the only inhabitants of North America were those peoples – misnamed 'Indians' by Columbus – whose ancestors had left Asia c. 35–40 000 years ago and had drifted across the Bering Strait to Alaska. From there they fanned out across the length and breadth of the Americas. By 1600 AD there were perhaps 1.5 million Amerindians in what are now Canada and the USA.

North America's First Inhabitants

The physical appearance of American Indians was uniform: straight black hair, high cheekbones, thin lips, broad faces, and copper-coloured skin. Their cultures, however, were extremely diverse: they spoke an estimated 600 different languages. While some tribes were nomadic, others were sedentary; some lived by hunting and fishing, others by agriculture; some were warlike, others peaceful. Amerindian dwellings ranged from birch bark wigwams, conical tepees made of hides, long dwellings built for many families, small wattle huts, and adobe or stone cliff-dwellings.

Compared with other Amerindians, such as the Mayas of Mexico and the Incas of Peru, North American Indians were primitive. No tribe before the arrival of the Europeans had devised a written language, though some had discovered pictographs (picture writing).

The Age of Discovery

While Christopher Columbus was certainly not the first European to set foot in the New World, the question of who preceded him, and when, remains controversial. Archaeological evidence confirms Norse legends of seafarers, from Iceland and Greenland, reaching Newfoundland and Labrador in the early 11th century. The Norsemen did not stay and no Europeans followed them for almost 500 years. Columbus's first voyage of discovery in 1492 marked the beginning of European colonization. The Treaty of Tordesillas (1494) divided the New World between the Portuguese and the Spaniards. Beginning in the 1520s, Spanish explorers pushed north from Mexico. They discovered, however, that the Mississippi Valley, the Great Plains, Texas, and Florida

▲ **Principal Amerindian Tribes** *By 1600 AD, Amerindians had settled every corner of North America and formed themselves into distinct tribes.*

contained neither the precious metals nor the docile Indian societies found in Central and South America. While the Spaniards turned their backs on the inhospitable north, they did not relinquish their claims to it.

In the 16th century England and France disputed these claims by sending expeditions to seek a Northwest Passage to Asia. Although none of them found such a route, these 'voyages of discovery' were of major geographical significance and an essential prelude to colonization. The first English expedition was that of Giovanni Caboto (1450–98) – an Italian – who reached the North American coast in 1497. In 1524 Giovanni de Verrazano (?1485–?1528) explored the Atlantic coastline from North Carolina to Maine. Further French voyages between 1534 and 1541 ranged over the Gulf of the St Lawrence. The 1570s and 1580s brought a new wave of English exploration. Martin Frobisher (?1535–94) and John Davis (1550–1605) ventured beyond the Arctic Circle, while, in the course of circumnavigating the globe (1577–80), Francis Drake (?1540–96) laid claim to California.

Colonial North America

Colonization begins • The first English colonies • The completion of English settlement • Population, immigration, and slavery • Mercantilism and the colonial economy • Indian wars and international rivalries

For most of the 16th century Spain's imperial dominance in America was unchallenged. The decline in Spain's power, however, allowed her European rivals – France, England, the Netherlands, and Sweden – to settle colonies in North America, defying Spain's claim of exclusive possession.

Colonization Begins

Colonization began in 1605, when France established a settlement at Port Royal (now Annapolis Royal, Nova Scotia). The real foundations of New France, however, were laid in 1608, when Samuel de Champlain (?1567–1635) founded Quebec. The fur trade and a missionary zeal to convert the Amerindians were the twin spurs to French expansion. By 1673 Louis Jolliet (1645–1700) and Jacques Marquette (1637–75) had explored much of the Mississippi; by 1682 Robert Cavelier de La Salle (1643–87) had followed the river to the Gulf of Mexico and had claimed Louisiana for Louis XIV (1638–1715). New France, however, attracted only a trickle of immigrants: in 1663, the population was a mere 3000; even in 1754 there were fewer than 80 000 French in North America. In 1609 the English explorer, Henry Hudson (died 1611), commissioned by the Dutch, sailed into what is now New York harbour and up the Hudson River (named after him). In 1624 the Dutch West India Company established a fur-trading post at Fort Orange (now Albany, New York); two years later it founded New Amsterdam (later New York City). The Dutch, however, were always more interested in furs than in colonization. Having been infiltrated by settlers from neighbouring English colonies, the Dutch outposts were overrun during the Second Anglo-Dutch War (1664–67); at the end of this war New Netherland was ceded to England.

The First English Colonies

The English were inspired to emigrate to the Americas by a combination of motives, both utopian and materialistic. The work of colonization was undertaken by trading companies and individual proprietors, who had received royal land grants. During a period of 150 years, these ventures planted a string of settlements along the Atlantic seaboard and in the Caribbean. They grew at widely different rates, evolved dissimilar economies and religious forms, and attracted populations of varying ethnic and racial strains. The London Company, which founded the first successful English colony at Jamestown, Virginia, in 1607, envisaged trading posts, such as those established in Asia, rather than agricultural settlements. A decade of disasters, however, brought the colony close to extinction; only the discovery that tobacco would grow successfully there enabled it to survive. Tobacco also sustained the economy of neighbouring Maryland, founded in 1633 as a **proprietary colony** of the Calvert family.

In contrast to such economic enterprises as Virginia and Maryland, the settlement of New England was primarily motivated by religion. The pioneers were a tiny group of English religious separatists, or *Pilgrims*, who sought refuge from the Church of England's hostility by sailing across the Atlantic from England in the *Mayflower* (1620). Aiming for the Hudson River, they landed instead at Cape Cod (Massachusetts). Their Plymouth colony grew only slowly; in 1691 it was absorbed by the larger colony of Massachusetts Bay. Though the Puritans (extreme English Protestants) who founded Massachusetts Bay, in 1630, left England for religious reasons, they were not religious refugees. They went to New England in order to establish a form of worship based on their own beliefs – and to stamp out every other form of worship. Intolerance in Massachusetts Bay spawned other New England colonies: Rhode Island (1636) and New

===SEE ALSO===
Early Modern Europe:
- Absolute Monarchy and Bourbon Dominance

Latin America:
- The Spanish and Portuguese Empires

proprietary colony
A colony in North America, granted by the British Crown in the 17th century to a person or group of people with full governing rights.

The Pilgrims Land at Plymouth, December 1620
Having arrived in the New World, the Pilgrims drew up the Mayflower Compact, which based their government on the colonists' will, not on that of the English Crown. ▼

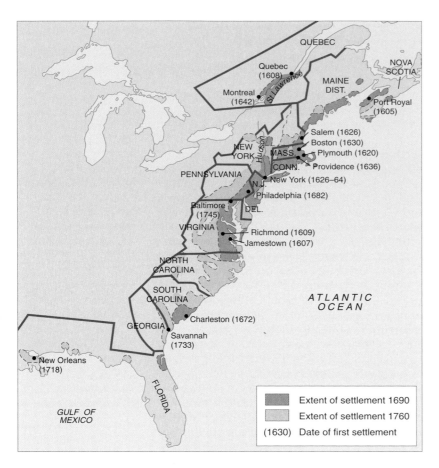

▲ **Colonial Settlement** *Between 1690 and 1760 colonies were established along the whole of the eastern seaboard and had begun to spread inland.*

John Winthrop (1588–1649)

A devout Puritan, Winthrop saw an opportunity to build an uncorrupted church and retrieve his personal fortunes in the Massachusetts colony. His departure for New England (March 1630) marked the beginning of the Puritan Great Migration. Winthrop was elected governor of the colony and was criticized by the clergy for leniency towards dissenters.

Hampshire (1638). New England's stony soil and harsh climate ruled out the production of staple crops; it developed instead a lucrative export trade in timber and fish.

The Completion of English Settlement

Colonization entered a new phase after 1660. New settlements gave England a continuous chain of seaboard outposts from French Canada almost to Spanish Florida. The first was Carolina, immediately south of Virginia, awarded to a group of prominent politicians in 1663. The northern half of the grant soon became differentiated from its southern half; by 1712 North and South Carolina had become separate colonies. The former Dutch colony of New Netherland, conferred by Charles II on his brother, James, Duke of York (1633–1701) was also divided into two. James kept the area he renamed New York; he gave the remainder to two friends, who called it New Jersey. Although English Quakers were among the earliest settlers of New Jersey, they encountered much hostility; in 1681 a prominent co-religionist, William Penn (1644–1718), decided to found a refuge of his own – Pennsylvania. Penn sold large tracts of his royal land grant to English, Welsh, and Irish Quakers; he attracted thousands of colonists from the British Isles, Holland, and the German Palatinate with the promise of political and

religious freedom. With the founding of Pennsylvania, the colonizing impulse was nearly exhausted. The only subsequent English settlement was Georgia in 1732.

Population, Immigration, and Slavery

Between 1700 and 1763, as the colonists advanced westward from the Atlantic coast, the settled area doubled. The population increased eightfold to reach two million, owing to a significantly lower death rate than in Europe and to the large volume of immigration. Initially, the great majority of immigrants were English. After 1660, however, when the English government came to believe that people were a vital national resource, emigration was officially discouraged. Vagrants, paupers, and political and military prisoners continued to be systematically shipped out to North America. Felons too were sent out, especially after 1717, when the English parliament created the legal punishment of transportation. Between 1717 and the American Revolution (1775–83), at least 30 000 British convicts were transported to the colonies.

From the late 17th century onwards, appreciable numbers of non-English immigrants arrived. Among them were French Huguenots, deprived of religious freedom by Louis XIV in 1685; small groups of Scots, Welsh, Dutch, and Sephardic Jews also arrived. By far the largest groups were Germans and Scots-Irish; they had been driven out either by religious persecution or by economic pressure. With the exception of New England, which remained predominantly English, immigration produced an increasingly cosmopolitan population in North America.

The majority of immigrants reached the colonies as indentured (contracted) servants, contracted to work for between four and seven years for colonial employers in return for a passage out. Servants were often harshly treated; when their terms expired, few had any choice but to become wage-labourers. Colonial masters found indentured servants expensive to keep as their service was relatively short; in addition, they frequently absconded and were hard to trace. Black slaves from Africa, however, presented neither of these disadvantages and thus constituted a more stable and economical labour force. Although the first Blacks from Africa to reach the colonies arrived, in Virginia, as early as 1619, their numbers grew slowly for some decades. Until c. 1660 the legal status of Black servants was unclear; legislation then differentiated them from White servants, declaring Blacks and their descendants to be slaves for life. As the African slave trade flourished, the importation of slaves rose rapidly. The colonial Black population soared from fewer than 20 000 in

1700 to around 350 000 in 1763. More than four-fifths of Black slaves lived in the Southern plantation colonies, where they were widely employed in gangs raising staple crops.

Mercantilism and the Colonial Economy

English colonial policy was inspired by ***mercantilism***, an economic philosophy common to all European countries from the 16th to the 18th centuries. Mercantilists wanted national economic self-sufficiency; colonies existed solely for the benefit of the mother country, to supply raw materials, buy manufactures, and provide employment for shipping. The Trade and Navigation Acts passed between 1651 and 1673, aimed at establishing an English monopoly of the colonial carrying trade, the colonial market, and certain valuable colonial products, such as sugar, cotton, indigo, and tobacco. Other legislation also sought to stifle competition from colonial manufacturing.

This legislation was never fully implemented. The weakness and inadequacy of royal colonial governors, the readiness of ill-paid customs officers to accept bribes to overlook infractions of the law, and the policy of 'salutary neglect' adopted during Robert Walpole's (1676–1745) long period in office as British prime minister rendered the legislation ineffective. Such burdens as it imposed were balanced by the benefits the colonists gained from the imperial system. Producers of colonial commodities received generous subsidies from the British parliament and enjoyed a protected market in England. Thus, while some mercantilist regulations damaged the colonies, they did not inhibit the development of a flourishing colonial economy.

Amerindian Wars and International Rivalries

Almost from the beginning of settlement, colonists were involved in conflicts with the Amerindians. As the Whites encroached upon traditional hunting grounds, friction, skirmishing, and, finally, open warfare developed. In New England the Pequot War (1637) resulted in the destruction of the Pequot nation; this was followed in 1675–76 by King Philip's War, in which the Wampanoags were annihilated. In Virginia conflict began with Opechancanough's slaughter of English settlers in 1622; it continued intermittently until the Shawnees were crushed in Lord Dunmore's War (1774). In the Carolinas, during the Tuscarora War (1711–12) and the Yamassee War (1715), similar bloodshed occured. Overshadowing these local conflicts was Pontiac's Rebellion of 1763: a powerful confederacy of western tribes ravaged 1000 miles of frontier, from Niagara to Virginia, before being subdued by British soldiers.

Warfare between colonists and Amerindians eventually merged with the larger international struggle for control of North America. Between 1689 and 1763 England was at war five times with either France or Spain. On each occasion, except the last, the conflict started in Europe; only later did it spread across the Atlantic. These conflicts gave rise to antagonism between colonists; in addition, English colonists resented the competition of French fur traders and fishermen; above all, they felt threatened by France's alliance with powerful Amerindian tribes. During the earlier Anglo-French wars there were French and Amerindian raids on outlying settlements in New England and New York. Later, Virginia, Maryland, and Pennsylvania were attacked. British colonial militia made retaliatory raids on the Amerindians and struck at French strongholds on the St Lawrence River. Britain, however, was long absorbed in European wars and apparently sufficiently indifferent to the fate of the colonists not to send them adequate help. It was not until the Seven Years' War (1756–63) (or the French and Indian War as it was known in America) – when Prime Minister William Pitt (1708–78) decided that the best way to defeat France was to strip her of her colonies – that a sizable British army was sent to the colonies. The capture of a succession of French strongholds, in 1758, by this expeditionary force was the prelude to the effective British destruction of French military power in Canada in 1759. By the Treaty of Paris (1763), which ended the war, Britain received Canada and all French possessions east of the Mississippi. While Britain was now the dominant power in North America, the completeness of Britain's victory paved the way for the American Revolution.

James Edward Oglethorpe (1696–1785)

An English general and member of the English parliament, Oglethorpe conceived the idea of enabling imprisoned debtors to make a fresh start in North America. In 1732 he and other philanthropists secured a royal charter to establish the colony of Georgia. The settlement attracted several hundred colonists; there were frequent clashes with Indian and Spanish raiders, however, and the settlers resented Oglethorpe's attempts to forbid rum and slavery.

The Seven Years' War *James Wolfe, commander of the British force that captured French Quebec, in 1759, is shown dying from wounds he received in battle in this painting by Benjamin West (1770).* ▼

The United States of America

Imperial restriction • Independence and revolution • Sectionalism and slavery • The road to disunion • Civil war • Reconstruction • Westward expansion • Industrial growth • Populism, imperialism, and progressivism • World War I • Reaction and prosperity • Roosevelt, the New Deal, and World War II • The Cold War • The new frontier and after • Vietnam to Watergate • Reaganomics • The end of the Cold War

The acquisition of the vast French possessions in North America, in 1763, presented Britain with complex problems: the alien French Canadian population needed to be governed; the conflicting demands of the Amerindians, the fur trade, and land settlement of the wilderness beyond the Allegheny Mountains had to be reconciled; renewed colonial defence was necessary. The new British colonial policy adopted to solve these problems was interpreted by the colonists as a tyrannical attempt to deprive them of liberties, which the imperial system had hitherto permitted and which they had come to regard as their rights. During a decade of controversy they questioned the constitutional basis of British demands and eventually opted for independence.

Imperial Restriction

The first British measure to provoke colonial opposition was the **Proclamation** of 1763, which banned settlement beyond the Allegheny Mountains, a region the colonists had long coveted. More unpopular still was the tightening of the laws regulating colonial trade, designed to yield more revenue. Equally unpopular were the unprecedented attempts – beginning with the Stamp Act of 1765 – to tax the colonists directly. Vehement colonial protest soon grew into open resistance. Although, on two occasions (1766 and 1770) the British government conceded, it resolved on coercion in 1773, when confronted with Boston's celebrated defiance of the Tea Act. It closed the port of Boston and reduced the powers of the Massachusetts assembly. These steps united the other colonies in defence of Massachusetts. In September 1774 delegates from 12 colonies attended the first Continental Congress, at Philadelphia, to plan concerted action. The majority, however, were reluctant to abandon the British; many remained so even after fighting had broken out between British and American forces at Lexington, Massachusetts, in April 1775. Only after a year of undeclared war did the Continental

▲ **George Washington** *The USA's first president was inaugurated at New York in 1789.*

Congress become convinced that there was no hope of accommodation within the British Empire. On 4 July 1776 it adopted the **Declaration of Independence**, drawn up mainly by Thomas Jefferson (1743–1826).

Independence and Revolution

It seemed that the colonists stood little chance of victory in a military conflict. Britain possessed a huge advantage in manpower and superior military and naval resources. The United States, by contrast, lacked not only an army and navy, but an effective central government. The **Articles of Confederation**, the constitution drawn up in 1777, conferred very limited powers upon it; in any case it was not ratified by the states until 1781, when the Revolutionary War was almost over. In addition, a sizable minority of Americans remained loyal to George III (1738–1820); some 30 000 took up arms for him. The Royal Navy, however, had been allowed to decay, British generalship proved ineffectual, and the task of subjugating so vast an area – especially from a distance of 3000 miles – was a formidable one. The ultimate success of the American cause owed much to George Washington (1732–99), commander-in-chief of the Continental Army. While he lost most of the battles he fought, he kept an army together during the eight-and-a-half year struggle. The decisive factor, however, was French intervention. A Franco-American alliance was signed in 1778; with the help of a French military and naval expedition, Washington was able to force the surrender of the British army at Yorktown, Virginia, in 1781. This persuaded the British government of the futility of the war; after protracted negotiations it concluded the Treaty of Versailles (3 September 1783), which formally recognized the independence of the United States of America.

Political and social changes during and immediately after the war, though limited, were nonetheless revolutionary in that they rejected the institutions and values of the Old World. The new state constitutions were based on popular consent; they introduced broader principles of representation, specifically limited the powers of government, and included **Bills of Rights** guaranteeing certain basic freedoms. Relics of feudalism, such as laws of primogeniture, were swept away; titles were forbidden; hereditary privilege rejected; the separation of Church and State was decreed; prisons and criminal codes were reformed; and, in the Northern states, slavery was abolished.

The Federal Constitution. For many Americans the most urgent problem of the 1780s was to strengthen the federal union. The Congress, charged with governing the USA, proved incapable either of sustaining public credit, suppressing disorder, or defending US rights against foreign powers. While the government's weakness was blamed on the Articles of Confederation, the states could not agree on how to amend them. A Federal Convention met at Philadelphia, in 1787, in response to a call for a stronger government; it took the unauthorized step of framing an entirely new Constitution. This gave the federal government power over taxation and trade; it created a federal executive and judiciary and sanctioned the enforcement of federal laws. While sovereignty was divided between state and federal governments, no attempt was made to define where ultimate power lay. Though ratification of the document was strongly opposed by those who regarded state rights as the only safeguard of US liberties, the Constitution won sufficient approval to come into force in 1789.

Federalists and Republicans. The Federalists, or proponents of the Constitution, achieved much during their 12 years in office

THE DECLARATION OF INDEPENDENCE

We hold these truths to be self-evident, that all men are created equal, that they are endowed by their Creator with certain unalienable rights, that among these are Life, Liberty and the pursuit of Happiness. That to secure these rights Governments are instituted among Men, deriving their just powers from the consent of the governed. That whenever any Form of Government becomes destructive of these ends, it is the Right of the People to alter or abolish it, and to institute new Government, laying its foundation on such principles and organizing its powers in such form, as to them shall seem most likely to effect their Safety and Happiness.

PREAMBLE TO THE DECLARATION, 4 JULY 1776

(1789–1801). George Washington, the first president (1789–97), clarified what the Constitution had left vague; Alexander Hamilton's (?1757–1804) financial programme restored public credit, ensuring the success of the new government; Britain and Spain were persuaded to fulfil their treaty obligations to evacuate US territory; neutrality was maintained when war with European belligerents threatened. Federalist policies, however, divided the country and rival political parties emerged. After Washington's retirement, in 1797, the Federalists declined rapidly. They lost to the Republicans in the presidential election of 1800, a defeat from which they never recovered; by 1824 they ceased to exist. Federalism nevertheless remained entrenched in the judiciary, owing to the long tenure of John Marshall (1755–1835) as Chief Justice of the USA (1801–35).

Thomas Jefferson, who assumed office in 1801, pledged himself to limited and economical government, strict construction of the Constitution, and reversal of the tendency, pronounced under Federalism, for the national government to gain power at the

American Victory
The British army, led by General Charles Cornwallis (1738–1805), surrender at Yorktown, Virginia, October 1781. This event signalled victory for the United States in their fight for independence. ▼

Territorial Expansion of the USA *(1783–1853)*
The Treaty that ended the war of the American Revolution in 1783 initiated the westward territorial expansion of the USA, when Britain ceded territory as far as the Mississippi. The great fortune of the Louisiana Purchase (1803) doubled the size of the USA, establishing US dominance in North America. The annexation of Texas (1845) and the outcome of the Mexican War (1846–48) finally fulfilled the aim of the US expansionist movement to extend the country's western boundary to the Pacific coast (1853).

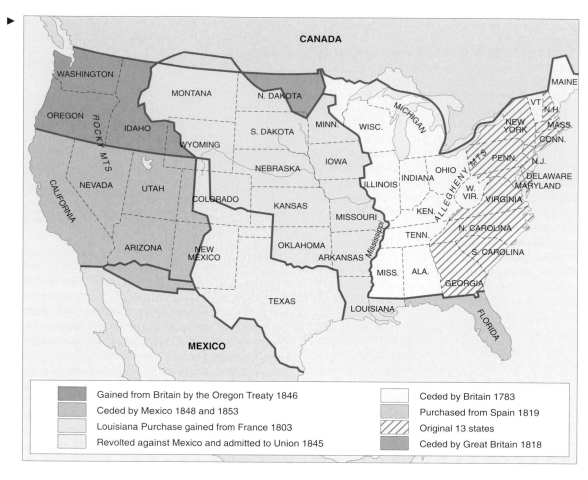

Gained from Britain by the Oregon Treaty 1846	Ceded by Britain 1783
Ceded by Mexico 1848 and 1853	Purchased from Spain 1819
Louisiana Purchase gained from France 1803	Original 13 states
Revolted against Mexico and admitted to Union 1845	Ceded by Great Britain 1818

Those for whose emancipation we are striving – constituting at the present time at least one-sixth part of our countrymen – are recognized by law, and treated by their fellowbeings, as brute beasts; are plundered daily of the fruits of their toil without redress; really enjoy no constitutional or legal protection from licentious and murderous outrages upon their persons; and are ruthlessly torn asunder... at the caprice or pleasure of irresponsible tyrants. For the crime of having a dark complexion, they suffer the pangs of hunger, the infliction of stripes, the ignominy of brutal servitude.

Declaration of Sentiments of the American Anti-Slavery Convention, 1833

expense of the states. Jefferson's presidency (1801–09), however, is best remembered for two events, which demonstrate that he compromised his principles. The Louisiana Purchase (1803), which extended US national territory to the Rocky Mountains, was a valuable gain for the USA; the $15 million it paid to France, however, was twice the annual national expenditure and contradicted the doctrine of strict construction. Similarly the Embargo Act (1807), in an attempt to compel respect for US maritime rights, virtually forbade US foreign trade; it extended, rather than reduced, federal power. Controversy over maritime rights culminated, in 1812, in renewed war with Britain. By 1814 there was pressure for secession from the United States from New England, whose commerce had been crippled by the war. The threat of disunion, however, vanished at the news that General Andrew Jackson (1767–1845) had overwhelmingly defeated the British at the Battle of New Orleans (8 January 1815); this led to the signing of a peace treaty at Ghent (24 December 1814). Jackson's great victory and other US successes in the War of 1812 served to revitalize national feeling.

The war also encouraged US manufacturing, especially in New England, while the defeat of Britain's Shawnee and Creek allies crippled Amerindian power east of the Mississippi River; this gave new momentum to westward migration and settlement. The establishment of a new agrarian West increased the number of states in the Union to 22 by 1820 and to 33 by 1860. By 1860, the population exceeded 31 million owing partly to the arrival, during the previous 40 years of some five million immigrants, mainly from Ireland and Germany.

Sectionalism and Slavery

From the 1830s the Southern slave states became more introspective and wary of federal power. Experiencing neither the industrialization nor the mass immigration that were transforming the North, they fell behind in population and thus in representation in the lower house of Congress. Southerners feared that the Northern Congressional majority would soon be large enough to override Southern wishes on the tariff and to attack slavery. In 1800 slavery, already abolished in the North, had also seemed moribund in the South. The rapid spread of cotton cultivation, based on slave labour, however, had revitalized it. Although Congress abolished the African slave trade in 1808, the number of slaves doubled every 30 years through natural increase, reaching nearly four million in 1860 (one-third of the Southern population).

Southern opinion, once inclined to be apologetic about slavery, came increasingly to defend it as a 'positive good,' integral to the plantation system and thus to Southern prosperity.

The South's defence of slavery intensified after 1830 in response to a militant abolitionist movement in the North, which condemned slaveholders and demanded immediate and uncompensated emancipation. Abolitionists established hundreds of antislavery societies. They failed, however, to convert the North to their cause. Most Northerners were prepared to abide by those provisions of the Constitution that protected slavery. At the same time, they became increasingly hostile to the extension of the institution beyond its existing limits.

Slavery in the Territories. The status of slavery in the unpopulated Western territories first became an issue in 1819, when the territory of Missouri sought admission to the Union as a slave state. While Missouri achieved statehood, slavery was prohibited in the rest of the Louisiana Purchase. The ***Missouri Compromise*** (1820) quelled the controversy over slavery in the territories for a quarter of a century; the Mexican War of 1846–48, however, revived it. Responding to 'manifest destiny,' the expansionist movement, which aimed to extend the US boundary to the Pacific, under President James K. Polk (1795–1849), tried to persuade Mexico to sell the provinces of New Mexico and California. When Mexico refused, he initiated a war (13 May 1846). For the USA the war was a success, culminating in the capture of Mexico City (14 September 1847). By the Treaty of Guadalupe Hidalgo (2 February 1848), Mexico ceded to the USA a substantial portion of its territory, including New Mexico and California.

In much of the North the war was highly unpopular; it was suspected that it stemmed from a slaveholders' plot to acquire more slave territory. Accordingly, opponents of slavery in Congress attempted to exclude slavery from any territory acquired from Mexico. This prompted a long sectional debate, which reached a climax early in 1850; California, its population suddenly multiplied by the **gold rush**, drafted a constitution excluding slavery and applied for statehood. Southerners were alarmed at the prospect of California becoming a state, because it would place the slave states in a minority in the Senate; some states consequently threatened secession. The danger of disunion was averted, however, when a series of compromise measures admitted California as a free state, strengthened the law to help Southerners recover fugitive slaves, and applied to the Mexican cession the principle of 'popular sovereignty,' which allowed the settlers of new territories to decide for themselves whether or not they wanted slavery.

The Gold Rush

Gold was first discovered in the USA, in California, in 1848. This led to the transcontinental migration of eastern profiteers to the region; some 80 000 arrived during the first year. Harsh conditions in the gold fields took many lives; only a few made a fortune.

JACKSONIAN DEMOCRACY

In 1828 the victor of New Orleans, Andrew Jackson, of Tennessee, became the first person from a Western state to be elected president (1829–37). Jackson was the hero of the common man; his election symbolized the rise of a new and vigorous democratic movement. ***Jacksonian democracy*** brought universal White male suffrage, which stimulated a greater popular interest in politics and trebled the electorate between 1824 and 1840. It also led to the growth of modern political parties (the Democrats and the Whigs), modern party organization, the replacement of secret caucuses with popularly elected nominating conventions, and the choice of presidential electors by direct popular vote, rather than by state legislatures; all of these developments tended to make government more responsive to the people's will. As president, Jackson clearly defined the key characteristics of the democratic movement. Casting himself as the champion of ordinary people, he greatly enlarged executive authority, while making the presidency a more effective and personal office. Believing that all citizens had the capacity to participate in public life, he developed and justified the spoils-system, in which political supporters were rewarded with public office. His hostility to privilege and monopoly was exemplified in the Bank War: in 1832, regarding the Second Bank of the United States, which acted as the repository for government funds, as an unconstitutional and undemocratic monopoly, he vetoed its recharter bill; he made the bank the main issue in his successful re-election campaign. While Jackson was considerate of state rights, he became an uncompromising nationalist when they threatened the Union; this was the case in the nullification controversy (1832–33). In this confrontation, South Carolina adopted an ordinance nullifying federal tariff acts, and threatened to secede if the federal government used force against it. Jackson's vigorous response showed that no state could, with impunity, defy the national authority.

▲ **Andrew Jackson** (1767–1845) As seventh president of the USA, Jackson came to symbolize the rise of the new democratic movement.

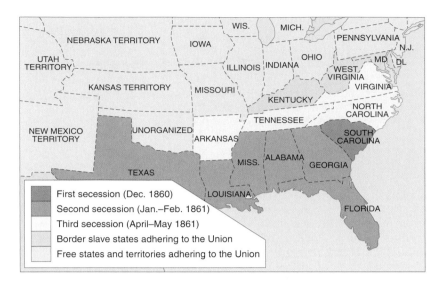

▲ The Secession of the Southern States
(1860–61) The Southern states, seeing their agricultural economy and entire way of life threatened by the abolition of slavery (by a Republican government), seceded from the North to protect slavery and state sovereignty. This act ultimately led to the outbreak of civil war.

Now, therefore, I, Abraham Lincoln, President of the United States, by virtue of the power in me vested as Commander-in-Chief of the Army and Navy of the United States in time of actual armed rebellion against the United States, and as a fit and necessary war measure for suppressing said rebellion...do order and declare that all persons held as slaves within... designated states and parts of states are, and henceforth shall be free...

The Emancipation Proclamation, 1 January 1863

The Road to Disunion

The Compromise of 1850 satisfied neither side. In 1854 the Kansas-Nebraska Act, which repealed the Missouri Compromise and applied 'popular sovereignty' to the northern half of the Louisiana Purchase, caused popular anger in the North as it appeared to open the region to slavery. In the political turmoil that followed, the party system was transformed. The Democrats fell increasingly under Southern domination, while a new Republican party, pledged to oppose the further spread of slavery, attracted widespread Northern support.

The violent struggle between Northern and Southern settlers for control of Kansas, the Supreme Court's decision in the Dred Scott case (1857), upholding the Southern position on slavery in the territories, and John Brown's (1800–59) attempt to incite a slave insurrection in Virginia (1859) exacerbated sectional feelings still further.

Civil War

While Republicans insisted that their object was to restrict, rather than abolish, slavery, the South refused to be reassured; when the Republican candidate, Abraham Lincoln (1809–65), was elected president, in 1860, seven Southern states seceded in order to protect slavery. In February 1861, they joined together as the Confederate States of America and drew up a Constitution modelled on that of the USA; the exception was that it protected slavery and acknowledged state sovereignty. Lincoln's attempt to reprovision the federal garrison at Fort Sumter, Charleston, provoked a Confederate bombardment (12 April 1861), which marked the beginning of the Civil War. Four more Southern states then seceded.

The American Civil War was one of the most bloody conflicts of the 19th century, causing the death of more than one million people. The Confederacy, which possessed a fraction of the North's manpower and economic resources, seemed invincible for the first two years of the war. Its armies, brilliantly led by Generals Robert E. Lee (1807–70) and Thomas J. (Stonewall) Jackson (1824–63), inflicted a succession of defeats on Union forces. The Confederacy's only chance of winning independence, however, lay either in outright military victory or in British intervention to break the Union blockade, which had cut off supplies of Southern cotton. Neither of these happened; after Lee's invasion of Pennsylvania had been repulsed at Gettysburg, in July 1863, the war began to turn in favour of the North. Nonetheless, it took two more years of fighting before the South surrendered (April 1865). Although Lincoln lived to see the end of the war, he was assassinated, on 14 April 1865.

The Civil War ended American slavery. Lincoln had long insisted that the war was being fought for the Union rather than for abolition. He eventually realized, however, that victory was unattainable as long as slavery survived. The Emancipation Proclamation he issued on 1 January 1863, applied only to areas under Confederate control; it dealt slavery a mortal blow. The ratification of the Thirteenth Amendment to the Constitution, in December 1865, removed the last vestiges of slavery.

Reconstruction

By that time Lincoln's successor, Andrew Johnson (1808–75), had initiated a lenient reconstruction plan, which would have enabled the seceded states to rejoin the Union without delay. Radical Republicans in Congress, however, were determined that they should not be allowed to do so without guarantees against renewed rebellion and the revival of slavery under other names. In March 1867, therefore, Johnson's plan was replaced with a harsher one that required the ex-Confederate states to frame new state constitutions, which gave the vote to Blacks and disfranchised those Whites who had helped the Confederacy. They had also to ratify the pending Fourteenth Amendment, which guaranteed Black civil rights. When Johnson tried to block the Radicals' plan, he was impeached; he was powerless for the rest of his term. By 1870 all the ex-Confederate states had fulfilled the conditions in the Radicals' plan, including the ratification of the Fifteenth Amendment (1870), which guaranteed Black suffrage; they were then readmitted to the Union. The Radical Republican state governments in the South relied heavily on Federal military support and on the Black vote. Public offices, however, were virtually monopolized by Whites. While Radical rule had substantial achievements to its credit, it was characterized by wholesale corruption and waste. Partly through legal methods, partly through terror, the South succeeded, by the early 1870s, in restoring White rule in many states. It was not until 1877, when Northern opinion had turned against coercion, that the experiment of Radical Reconstruction in the South was abandoned and the last federal troops withdrawn.

Most of the gains Blacks had made from Reconstruction were soon eroded. Supreme Court decisions deprived them of guaranteed civil rights, while the Southern states effectively disfranchised Blacks through elaborate suffrage qualifications, such as a literacy test. Racial segregation by statute, first introduced in the late 1880s, was thereafter systematically extended throughout the South to trains, hotels, schools, and residential districts. In the 1890s there were White mob attacks on Black neighbourhoods and a dramatic increase in lynchings of Blacks suspected of crime.

Westward Expansion

During the post-Civil War decades, westward-moving pioneers completed the settlement of the continent by occupying the vast expanses of the Great Plains, hitherto occupied only by Amerindian tribes and immense herds of buffalo. Miners, attracted by gold and silver discoveries, were the first Whites to invade the region. They were closely followed by cattlemen, who drove their herds northward on 1000-mile 'long drives' to railroad terminals. By the 1890s, the Great Plains had been opened up to settlement by the building of transcontinental railroads and the subjugation and removal of the nomadic and warlike Plains Amerindians. The development of agriculture on the arid Great Plains faced great difficulties. Barbed wire was used for fencing;

deep wells and steel windmills augmented the scanty water supply, while new farming techniques and improved machinery made agriculture viable. The White population of the Great Plains had, by 1890, increased sixfold within a generation; the settled area of the USA had doubled; and, for the first time, a continuous band of states stretched from the Atlantic coast to the Pacific.

Industrial Growth

US industry had, meanwhile, been making great progress. Its foundations had been laid earlier; the tariff, banking, and railroad legislation, passed in the postwar decades by a Congress sympathetic to business, and the protection the courts gave to corporations, created a climate in which industrial capitalism could flourish. Large amounts of capital was invested from abroad. Millions of immigrants, who provided an ample supply of cheap and tractable labour, flowed into the country. The railroads facilitated the exploitation of natural resources, while technological innovations – among them the telegraph, the telephone, the typewriter, the adding machine, electric light, overhead trolleys, the transatlantic cable – brought dramatic improvements in communication and enabled widely scattered organizations to operate on a national, and even an international, scale. Such industries as iron and steel, mining, oil production, flour-milling, and meat-packing enjoyed phenomenal expansion; by 1900 the USA had become the world's leading industrial nation. The characteristic feature of US industrialism was the consolidation of competing enterprises into giant industrial combinations, such as Standard Oil and United States Steel. Directed by gifted individuals,

> **Thomas Alva Edison (1847–1931)**
>
> The most well-known inventor of his day, Edison became a telegraph operator at 16. As a youth he was fascinated by electricity and devoted all his spare time to experiments. In 1876 he set up his 'invention factory' in New Jersey. Rejecting scientific theory in favour of trial and error, he and his team produced many new inventions; these included the phonograph, the storage battery, the motion picture projector, and the electric locomotive. His most notable achievement was the electric light bulb (1879), which introduced the wide-spread use of electric light.

◀ **Civil War**
The decisive rebuffal of the Confederate invasion of Pennsylvania, in July 1863, was the turning point of the American Civil War (1861–65). The eventual defeat of the Southern Confederate armies resulted in the final abolition of slavery throughout the USA.

▲ **The Railroads**
The building of railroads greatly accelerated the rate of settlement in the West. The Kansas–Pacific Railroad, illustrated here (1871), crossed the Great Plains, where buffalo were consequently slaughtered in great numbers.

Andrew Carnegie

Carnegie was taken to the USA by his parents in 1848, aged 13, where he became a telegraph operator. After the war he turned first to iron manufacturing and then to the newly developing steel industry. Quick to grasp the significance of new processes of steel manufacture, he founded the Carnegie Steel Company, which became the largest in the country. Having amassed an immense fortune, Carnegie retired in 1901 to devote himself to philanthropy.

such as John D. Rockefeller (1839–1937), **Andrew Carnegie** (1835–1919), and J. P. Morgan (1837–1913), the ***trusts*** – as they were known – were fervently defended by proponents of rugged individualism. Some felt the economic power of the trusts posed a threat to US democratic institutions, social unity, and industrial peace.

Populism, Imperialism, and Progessivism

The political stalemate that developed after Reconstruction was broken in the early 1890s by an explosion of agricultural discontent. After the Civil War, the price of staple crops fell drastically; farm indebtedness rose and many farmers sank into tenancy. Although the main cause was a worldwide crisis of overproduction, farmers blamed the government's railroad regulation, tariff, and currency policies. In 1892 farmers' organizations formed the Populist party, whose platform advocated, among other things, the unlimited coinage of silver to inflate the currency and increase commodity prices. The nationwide economic depression of 1893 gained the Populists support and, in the 1896 election, the Democrats endorsed the free silver proposal. The Democratic candidate, William Jennings Bryan (1860–1925), was, however, defeated; as farm prices rose at the end of the century, Populism disappeared as a political force.

The 1890s saw a revival of popular interest in the outside world; this led to a demand that the USA should assume a greater role in world affairs. These ambitions found an outlet when Spain refused to grant independence to Cuba. The USA thus intervened to secure it (11 April 1898). The Spanish-American War was brief and one-sided. In ten weeks, US forces overran Cuba and destroyed the Spanish navy. While

Cuba was freed, it remained under US political and economic control. The conflict led to the USA acquiring the Philippines, Puerto Rico, and Guam from Spain; Hawaii was also annexed. Thereafter, the USA showed more interest in both the Far East and Central America, one result being Theodore Roosevelt's (1858–1919) acquisition of the Panama Canal Zone in 1903.

Progressivism, the reform movement that swept over the USA between 1900 and 1917, was an attempt to tackle such evils as the excessive power of corporate wealth, political corruption, slums, unemployment, and child labour. Progressivism did not seek to rival existing parties; it operated within them. At the municipal level, its main target was the corruption of political leaders; in state politics, Progressive governors carried through programmes of reform and introduced devices to make government more responsive to the electorate. In the arena of national politics, the presidencies of Theodore Roosevelt, William Taft (1857–1930), and Woodrow Wilson (1856–1924) saw significant achievements in tariff revision, banking reforms, and government regulation of business. By 1917, however, the USA's entry into World War I diverted attention from domestic issues.

World War I

When President Wilson proclaimed US neutrality upon the outbreak of World War I (1914), virtually all Americans supported him. Wilson, however, was determined to defend US rights on the high seas; in April 1917, after Germany had resorted to unconditional submarine warfare against all vessels, neutral as well as belligerent, the USA reluctantly went to war. By March 1918, the US Expeditionary Force in France numbered 300 000; by Armistice Day it was two million. While their military role was relatively limited, the arrival of US troops heartened the Allies while it demoralized the Germans.

At the Paris Peace Conference, in 1919, Wilson failed to obtain the just peace he had wanted, though he did secure the adoption of a covenant establishing the League of Nations. On his return to the USA, he found growing opposition to the League as a threat to national sovereignty. As a result of Wilson's refusal to compromise, in March 1920, the Senate rejected both the Treaty of Versailles and US membership of the League.

Reaction and Prosperity

Disillusion with Wilsonian idealism was equally evident in the postwar period. A narrow nationalism characterized the 1920s. It was first manifested in the repression of radicals and supposed revolutionaries during the

Red Scare of 1919; subsequently, attempts were made to use the law to resist change and enforce moral, social, and intellectual conformity. The products of this movement were the immigration restriction laws of 1921–24; the revival of the **Ku Klux Klan**; the fundamentalist campaign against the teaching of evolution; and the Eighteenth Amendment (1920), which imposed a nationwide ban on the production and sale of alcohol.

For most of the 1920s, the USA enjoyed great prosperity. Aided by laissez faire policies, businesses made huge profits; unemployment decreased and wages rose. Prosperity, however, was built on insecure foundations; in October 1929, a stock market crash marked the start of the Great Depression, the worst in US history. For three years the economy spiralled downward. Factories shut, bankruptcies multiplied, families lost their homes; unemployment soared to between 12 and 15 million in 1932. Believing that the economy would recover spontaneously, President Herbert Hoover (1874–1964) used government powers sparingly to prop it up. The failure of his policies resulted in a defeat, in the 1932 presidential election, by the Democrat, Franklin D. Roosevelt (1882–1945) of New York.

Roosevelt, the New Deal, and World War II

The *New Deal*, Roosevelt's programme of policies for combating the Depression, was unprecedented in its scope. Its first phase (1933–35) consisted of industrial and agricultural regulation, banking and currency reform, massive public works, price stabilization, and unemployment relief. In 1935 it embarked on welfare legislation, imposed higher taxes on the rich, and granted workers the right of collective bargaining. The New Deal, however, succeeded in bringing about only a limited recovery: even in 1939, there were still 9.5 million unemployed. It did, nevertheless, restore national morale and lay the foundations of the welfare state; it also established the principle that government had primary responsibility for regulating the economy.

As the international scene became tense during the 1930s, the USA became increasingly pacific and isolationist. In the hope of avoiding involvement in another major war, Congress passed the Neutrality Acts (1935–37), which imposed an arms embargo against belligerents, prohibited loans to them, and forbade US citizens from travelling on belligerent ships. When World War II began, in September 1939, most Americans were in favour of non-intervention; in March 1941 Roosevelt persuaded Congress to pass the Lend-Lease Act, which authorized him to sell, lease, or lend arms, munitions, food, and other supplies, to

any country whose defence he deemed vital to that of the USA. This act led to an open, though undeclared, naval war with Germany. It was the USA's determination not to allow Japan to dominate Southeast Asia that drew it into the war. Roosevelt responded to Japanese aggression by increasing aid to China, thus denying Japan essential war-making materials. Attempts to reach a negotiated settlement failed; on 7 December 1941 Japan launched a devastating air attack on Pearl Harbor, Hawaii, crippling the bulk of the US Pacific fleet. Congress promptly passed a war resolution; on 11 December Japan's Axis partners, Germany and Italy, joined her in war against the USA.

The first necessity after Pearl Harbor was to stem the tide of Japanese conquest. This was achieved by decisive US naval victories in the Battles of the Coral Sea and of Midway (May–June 1942), after which Roosevelt felt free to give priority to the war with Germany. The USA pressed for an Allied cross-Channel invasion of occupied France. Launched in June 1944, it was wholly successful; Germany surrendered in May 1945.

The war in the Pacific was, by contrast, almost wholly a US affair. By 1945, US offensives had cleared the South Pacific. The Japanese had, however, resisted fanatically; Allied military experts believed that an invasion of Japan itself might cost more than a million US lives. Roosevelt's successor, Harry S. Truman (1884–1972), decided, therefore, to deploy the atomic bombs jointly developed with European scientists. Those dropped on Hiroshima and Nagasaki (6 and 9 August) caused great devastation, which ended Japan's resistance.

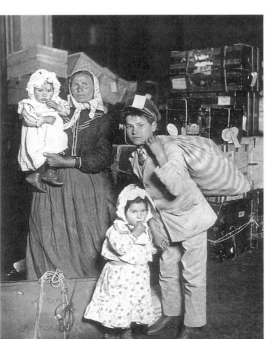

◀ **Newcomers** *The late 19th and early 20th centuries saw a huge influx of immigrants from Europe into the USA (almost 18 million people arrived between 1890 and 1910). Victims of poverty and persecution in their own countries, the immigrants, such as those shown here, saw the USA as a land of freedom and prosperity. Increasing restrictions were, however, put on the admission of immigrants; these included medical inspections and literacy tests.*

Ku Klux Klan A secret organization of White Protestant Americans, mainly in the Southern states, which used violence against Blacks, Jews, and other minority groups. The organization was formed by White Southerners after the Civil War to fight Black emancipation and Northern domination.

Immigration ▶

(1821–1990)
Immigration to the USA peaked at the turn of the century. The new arrivals dispersed into the vast western lands, boosting the growth of cities, and provided the labour upon which the USA's economic success has been built. While the immigrants, who came from all parts of Europe, Russia, Canada, Mexico, China, and Japan, have created problems of assimilation, they have also provided the USA with a hugely rich and diverse culture.

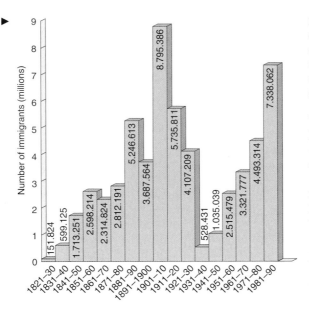

We conclude that in the field of public education the doctrine of 'separate but equal' has no place. Separate educational facilities are inherently unequal. Therefore, we hold that the plaintiffs and others similarly situated for whom the actions have been brought are, by reason of the segregation complained of, deprived of the equal protection of the laws guaranteed by the Fourteenth Amendment...

Chief Justice Earl Warren,
Brown v Board of Education
of Topeka (1954)

The Cold War

World War II left the USA in a position of world leadership. It took the lead in framing the United Nations Charter (June 1945). However, the mutual fears and suspicions of the USA and the USSR soon developed into a protracted **Cold War**. Alarmed that eastern Europe had fallen under Soviet domination, the Truman administration committed itself to resisting any further extension of communist power. The USA formulated and financed a postwar economic recovery programme for Europe – the Marshall Plan – and, in 1949, created a multi-nation defensive alliance, the North Atlantic Treaty Organization (NATO). In 1949, however, Mao Zedong's (1893–1976) communists gained control of mainland China. In June 1950 the Korean War began with a full-scale invasion by communist North Korea of the republic of South Korea. Truman promptly despatched US forces under General MacArthur (1880–1964) to help repel the invaders. Having checked and driven out the communists, US troops then crossed the 38th parallel to unify the Korean peninsula. This provoked Chinese intervention, which forced US troops to retreat in disarray. US citizens had now become alarmed by allegations of communist infiltration into government departments. This was fuelled by allegations of a communist conspiracy in high places made by Republican senator, Joseph R. McCarthy (1908–57). Popular discontent at the Korean War stalemate contributed to General Eisenhower's (1890–1969) election to the presidency in 1952. Eisenhower failed to end the war in Korea; it was not until July 1953 that the communists finally agreed to an armistice.

At home, there was mounting civil rights agitation, stimulated by the Supreme Court ruling (1954) that racial segregation in publicly funded schools was unconstitutional. However, Eisenhower did little to implement the decision. Led by Dr Martin Luther King (1929–68), Southern Blacks used demonstrations, boycotts, and 'sit-ins' to achieve desegregation in public places and on buses.

The New Frontier and After

Eisenhower's successor, John F. Kennedy (1917–63), began his presidency inauspiciously with the Bay of Pigs fiasco (April 1961); a US-trained expedition of Cuban exiles, aiming to overthrow Castro's communist regime, was overwhelmed. In October 1962 the Soviet leader, Nikita Khrushchev (1894–1971), challenged the USA by secretly installing medium-range missiles in Cuba. When this was discovered, Kennedy's firmness forced Khrushchev to remove the missiles, after which US-Soviet relations improved.

Kennedy outlined an ambitious domestic legislative reform programme, labelled the New Frontier. Most of its key measures, however, were blocked by Congress. Kennedy's murder in November 1963, in Dallas, Texas, stunned the country and created a legend from his modest achievements. His successor, Lyndon B. Johnson (1908–73), coaxed Congress into adopting nearly all the New Frontier proposals. A Civil Rights Act prohibited racial discrimination in public places, while an Economic Opportunity Act inaugurated a 'war on poverty.'

Despite greatly increased voting and office-holding by Southern Blacks, the Black unemployment rate remained twice the national average. Many Blacks turned away from the moderate civil rights movement to support militant organizations, such as the Black Muslims and the Black Panthers. Between 1965 and 1967, Black discontent erupted in major urban riots. The murder of Martin Luther King, in 1968, caused renewed rioting.

Vietnam to Watergate

By this time Johnson's attention had been diverted to Vietnam where, despite US aid to the Saigon government, the communist Vietcong (the revolutionary army of South Vietnam) had gained ground. Believing Vietnam to be vital to US security, the president, in August 1964, ordered air attacks on North Vietnam; he also committed more US ground forces. These proved ineffective in what was essentially a guerrilla war. In response to a strong antiwar movement, Johnson scaled down attacks on North Vietnam and proposed peace talks. In 1968 Richard M. Nixon (1913–94) became president; he sought to end US involvement by gradually withdrawing US troops and building up the South Vietnamese army. The slow pace of disengagement resulted in renewed antiwar agitation.

However, shortly after Nixon's re-election, in 1972, he reached a cease-fire agreement, which provided for the unilateral withdrawal of all remaining US forces from Vietnam. In April 1975 the Saigon government surrendered unconditionally to the communists.

In 1973 the Watergate affair began to unfold. Nixon and several political associates were implicated in an attempt, in June 1972, to bug the Democratic Party's headquarters. Nixon's refusal to disclose vital evidence persuaded many of his guilt. In July 1974, Nixon resigned under threat of impeachment.

Reaganomics

Ronald Reagan (1911–), elected president in 1980, was committed to reducing the role of government by lowering taxation, reducing federal spending, and minimizing business regulation. These policies, which became known as ***Reaganomics***, brought a drop in inflation and what many regard as the longest peacetime period of prosperity in US history.

The End of the Cold War

The presidency of Reagan's successor, George Bush (1924–), coincided with the collapse of Soviet communism and the end of the Cold War. These events enabled the USA and the USSR to reach an historic agreement in 1991 – the Strategic Arms Reduction Treaty (START). In 1989 Bush ordered the invasion of Panama to remove its dictator, General Manuel Noriega (1938–). Two years later he brought together an international coalition to liberate Kuwait, which had been invaded by Iraq. The resulting Gulf War ended in a swift Allied victory, which boosted Bush's standing at home. His popularity evaporated, however, when the US economy plunged into recession. In the 1992 presidential election he was defeated by Bill Clinton (1946–). His initial successes, such as the North American Free Trade Agreement (NAFTA), were overshadowed by Clinton's alleged involvement in irregular financial dealings. His health-care reforms were thwarted by Congress, which fell to the Republicans in 1994, seriously impeding further social reform. Abroad, Clinton supported the historic 1993 Arab–Israeli peace accord, sent peacekeeping troops to Somalia, and achieved a diplomatic coup in Haiti in 1994. Clinton was re-elected in 1996, but in 1998, amidst a sexual scandal he ordered the bombing of alleged terrorist targets in Sudan and Afghanistan in response to the destruction by terrorists of US embassies in Kenya and Tanzania.

The Apollo Moon Landing

In 1961 President Kennedy undertook that the USA would, by the end of the decade, land men on the moon. The Apollo programme, undertaken by the National Aeronautics and Space Administration (NASA), greatly expanded knowledge about rocket propulsion and manned spaceflight. On 20 July 1969 the goal Kennedy had envisaged was achieved, when Neil Armstrong (1930–) and Edwin 'Buzz' Aldrin (1930–), in Apollo 11, became the first men to walk on the moon.

PRESIDENTS OF THE USA (1789–1993)

President	Party	Term	President	Party	Term
George Washington		1789–97	Grover Cleveland	(Dem)	1885–89
John Adams	(Federalist)	1797–1801	Benjamin Harrison	(Rep)	1889–93
Thomas Jefferson	(Dem-Rep)	1801–09	Grover Cleveland	(Dem)	1893–97
James Madison	(Dem-Rep)	1809–17	William McKinley	(Rep)	1897–1901
James Monroe	(Dem-Rep)	1817–25	Theodore Roosevelt	(Rep)	1901–09
John Quincy Adams	(Dem-Rep)	1825–29	William H. Taft	(Rep)	1909–13
Andrew Jackson	(Dem)	1829–37	Woodrow Wilson	(Dem)	1913–21
Martin Van Buren	(Dem)	1837–41	Warren G. Harding	(Rep)	1921–23
William H. Harrison	(Whig)	1841	Calvin Coolidge	(Rep)	1923–29
John Tyler	(Whig)	1841–45	Herbert Hoover	(Rep)	1929–33
James K. Polk	(Dem)	1845–49	Franklin D. Roosevelt	(Dem)	1933–45
Zachary Taylor	(Whig)	1849–50	Harry S. Truman	(Dem)	1945–53
Millard Fillmore	(Whig)	1850–53	Dwight D. Eisenhower	(Rep)	1953–61
Franklin Pierce	(Dem)	1853–57	John F. Kennedy	(Dem)	1961–63
James Buchanan	(Dem)	1857–61	Lyndon B. Johnson	(Dem)	1963–69
Abraham Lincoln	(Rep)	1861–65	Richard M. Nixon	(Rep)	1969–74
Andrew Johnson	(Rep)	1865–69	Gerald S. Ford	(Rep)	1974–77
Ulysses S. Grant	(Rep)	1869–77	Jimmy Carter	(Dem)	1977–81
Rutherford B. Hayes	(Rep)	1877–81	Ronald W. Reagan	(Rep)	1981–89
James A. Garfield	(Rep)	1881	George Bush	(Rep)	1989–93
Chester A. Arthur	(Rep)	1881–85	Bill Clinton	(Dem)	1993–

Canada

Canada after the British conquest • From the Durham Report to confederation •
The expanding dominion, 1867–1914 • Canadian nationalism, 1914–50 •
Problems of Canadian identity

**Canadian
Territorial
Expansion** *Following
the creation, in 1867,
of the Dominion of
Canada (comprising
Ontario, Quebec, Nova
Scotia, and New
Brunswick), Canada's
boundaries gradually
extended west to
the Pacific and
north beyond the
Arctic Circle.* ▼

The conflict between Britain and France over the Canadian territories in the Seven Years' War, and Britain's acquisition of Canada in 1763, has determined the subsequent history of this vast area of North America. In Canada today the legacy of the former French and British interests in its territories clearly affects the lives of modern Canadians.

Canada after the British Conquest

The British government showed an enlightened approach in devising a permanent form of government for the French-speaking inhabitants of newly acquired Canada. The Quebec Act (1774) attempted to conciliate them by recognizing the privileged position of the Roman Catholic Church, preserving the land ownership system, and continuing the French legal system. The result of this was that French Canadians spurned the invitation of the Continental Congress, in 1775, to join in the independence struggle against Britain, and resisted the American invaders of Canada in 1775. The American attempt to storm the fortress of Quebec was repulsed (30 December 1775) and the invaders forced to retreat. During the peace negotiations that followed the American Revolution, the US commissioners vainly demanded the cession of Canada; the Treaty of Paris (1783), however, deprived Canada of the territory south of the Great Lakes, which the Quebec Act had assigned to

it, and embodied ambiguities regarding fishing rights and the border, which were to disrupt relations with the USA for decades.

The United Empire Loyalists. The American Revolution led to the arrival of some 50 000 refugees from the rebellious colonies, who had remained loyal to George III. Some of these *United Empire Loyalists* settled north of the Great Lakes. Others settled in a part of Nova Scotia, which became the separate colony of New Brunswick in 1784. Following the influx of United Empire Loyalists from the American colonies after 1763, the ensuing racial tension led the British government to divide Quebec into French-speaking Lower Canada (modern Quebec) and English-speaking Upper Canada (modern Ontario) in 1791.

The hostility of the Loyalist settlers towards the USA was rekindled by the US invasions of Canada during the War of 1812. With a tiny population and a practically undefended boundary 1000 miles long, Canada seemed incapable of resistance. However, two successive US incursions were repelled.

From the Durham Report to Confederation

The French character of Canada was further diluted, after 1815, by large-scale immigration from Britain. While the 1820s and 1830s saw economic growth, they were also a time of discontent. In Lower Canada French Canadians resented the pressures for anglicization and their exclusion from the mercantile life of Montreal. In Upper Canada new immigrants became disaffected with the ***Family Compact***, the wealthy tight-knit mainly Anglican clique that dominated the colony's political, economic, and religious life. The resulting rebellions of 1837 were easily suppressed; however, they prompted an inquiry by the Earl of Durham. Following his *Report on the Affairs of British North America* (1839), the two Canadas were once again merged, in 1841, into a single colony; in 1848 the colony achieved 'responsible government,' a system of self-rule in local affairs, with the executive responsible to an elected assembly.

By the late 1850s Anglo-French differences over representation in the legislature produced a succession of crises and short-lived governments. Canadian leaders came to feel that the only solution was the union of all the British

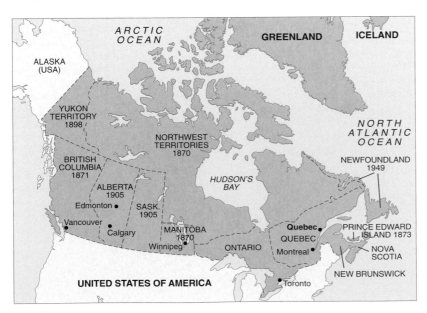

North American colonies. Fear that the USA would seek to annex Canada strengthened this sentiment. Under pressure from Canadian leaders, a project for uniting the Maritime Provinces was abandoned in favour of a plan for a larger confederation. This was created by the British North America Act of 1867; the new *Dominion of Canada* consisted of four provinces: Ontario, Quebec, Nova Scotia, and New Brunswick.

The Expanding Dominion, 1867–1914

Following confederation, the dominion's boundaries were extended west to the Pacific and north beyond the Arctic Circle. Five new provinces were created. In 1869 Canada bought the vast unsettled region known as Rupert's Land from the Hudson's Bay Company and other land from Britain. The provinces of Manitoba and the Northwest Territories were both created from these in 1870. British Columbia was persuaded to join the confederation, in 1871, by the promise of a transcontinental railroad link with the rest of Canada – the Canadian Pacific Railway (CPR), which reached Vancouver in 1885. Prince Edward Island, which had declined to join the confederation when it was formed, succumbed in 1873, when better terms were offered. Canada's fertile western prairies, opened up for settlement by the completion of the CPR, were the chief attraction for the 2.5 million immigrants who arrived, between 1896 and 1914, from central Europe and the Ukraine, as well as from Britain and the USA. The two new provinces of Alberta and Saskatchewan were created in 1905.

Expansion was punctuated by political upheaval. The Red River Rebellion, of 1869–70, was led by Louis Riel, whose followers – mainly **métis** (people of mixed White and Amerindian ancestry) – feared the loss of their lands to White settlers. The uprising was quelled and Riel fled the country. When he returned to lead a second métis revolt in Saskatchewan, in 1884, he was captured and hanged. In 1873, the Pacific Scandal, in which the ruling Conservative party was shown to have accepted a campaign contribution from a syndicate, which was then awarded a contract to build the CPR, resulted in the resignation of Prime Minister John A. Macdonald. During the depression of the 1880s, the resentment of the Maritime Provinces at federal fiscal policies caused intense anti-Ottawa feeling; Nova Scotia even threatened to secede. Manitoba was convulsed, in 1890, when the provincial legislature abolished Catholic schools and forbade teaching in French in the provincial school system. Western farm organizations engaged in protests when commodity prices fell

PRIME MINISTERS OF CANADA SINCE CONFEDERATION	
1867–73	Sir John A. Macdonald (Conservative)
1873–78	Alexander Mackenzie (Liberal)
1878–91	Sir John A. Macdonald (Conservative)
1891–92	Sir John J. C. Abbott (Conservative)
1892–94	Sir John S. D. Thompson (Conservative)
1894–96	Sir Mackenzie Bowell (Conservative)
1896	Sir Charles Tupper (Conservative)
1896–1911	Sir Wilfred Laurier (Liberal)
1911–20	Sir Robert L. Borden (Conservative/Unionist)
1920–21	Arthur Meighen (Conservative)
1921–26	W. L. Mackenzie King (Liberal)
1926	Arthur Meighen (Conservative)
1926–30	W. L. Mackenzie King (Liberal)
1930–35	Richard B. Bennett (Conservative)
1935–48	W. L. Mackenzie King (Liberal)
1948–57	Louis St. Laurent (Liberal)
1957–63	John G. Diefenbaker (Progressive/Conservative)
1963–68	Lester B. Pearson (Liberal)
1968–79	Pierre Elliott Trudeau (Liberal)
1979–80	Joseph Clark (Progressive/Conservative)
1980–84	Pierre Elliott Trudeau (Liberal)
1984	John Turner (Liberal)
1984–93	Brian Mulroney (Progressive/Conservative)
1993	Kim Campbell (Progressive/Conservative)
1993–	Jean Chrétien (Liberal)

between 1900 and 1910. Adopting the arguments of US Populists, they blamed eastern bankers and industrialists for their plight and resorted to political action. In 1911 Sir Wilfred Laurier's Liberal government negotiated a treaty with the USA providing for a reciprocal lowering of tariffs, but the agreement revived Canadian fears of US absorption and Laurier's heavy defeat in the 1911 election crushed the initiative. Despite cultural and regional antagonisms, Canada's economy grew prodigiously. The prairie wheatlands supplied Europe; the forests of British Columbia fed a growing paper industry; the development of hydroelectric power encouraged industrial growth; and the gold rush to the Klondike in the far northwest, in 1897, was followed by the discovery of gold, lead, and zinc in British Columbia and a variety of metals in northern Ontario. By 1914 Canada had a population of eight million.

Pierre Elliott Trudeau (1919–)

Canada's Liberal prime minister (1968–79 and 1980–84) was sympathetic to the aspirations of French Canadians, though he strongly opposed Francophone separatism. Believing that constitutional reform was necessary to preserve national unity, he succeeded in April 1982 in winning approval for a new Canadian constitution. This 'patriated' the British North America Act of 1867 (terminating the need to secure British Parliamentary approval of Canadian constitutional amendments) and also incorporated a bill of rights.

Quebec's Parliament House

The architecture of this impressive building (built between 1877 and 1886) is clearly influenced by both French and British styles. In 1992 Quebec celebrated its parliament's bicentennial. ▼

Canadian Nationalism, 1914–50

Canada contributed heavily to the Allied cause during World War I, sending 600 000 men to fight, 10 % of whom were killed in action. As well as boosting demand for farm produce and raw materials, the war stimulated Canadian industry. The introduction of conscription, in 1917, however, caused riots in French-speaking areas and bitter protests from farmers and organized labour.

Nationalists increasingly questioned Canada's colonial status. After the war, Prime Minister Sir Robert Borden and his successor, Mackenzie King, demanded greater independence in foreign and defence policy. Canada was separately represented at the Paris Peace Conference (1919) and became a founder member of the League of Nations. This independence was formally defined in the Statute of Westminster (1931), which ended imperial sovereignty over the autonomous dominions.

Canada's economic fortunes between the two World Wars followed those of the USA. In the 1920s most parts of the country prospered, although the Maritime Provinces were an exception; unemployment persisted in many cities. During the Great Depression of the 1930s, Canada was one of the areas worst affected. The Conservative government's solution was a programme of planning and social security; most of its provisions, however, were ruled to be unconstitutional in 1936.

Canada emerged from World War II with a flourishing agricultural sector, and as the world's fourth largest industrial power. Besides acting as a supply base for Britain, Canada's military contribution to victory in World War II was immense; one million Canadians served in the armed forces. This prominence led to more active involvement in international affairs. In 1945 Canada became a charter member of the United Nations Organization; in 1949 Canada was one of the 12 countries that set up the North Atlantic Treaty Organization (NATO). Newfoundland (including Labrador), formerly a dominion in its own right, became Canada's newest province in 1949.

Problems of Canadian Identity

The postwar decades were a period of growth. Between 1939 and 1967, the country's gross national product increased tenfold. Canada became the world's largest producer of nickel and newsprint; her steel and aluminium industries grew rapidly; uranium, iron, oil, and natural gas resources were discovered and developed; and atomic and hydroelectric power were utilized in industry. Canada's population grew from 11 million in 1941 to 27 million in 1991. Immigration exceeded three million; nearly one-third of the newcomers were British, while another third were Italian; in the 1980s numbers from Asia and the British West Indies grew. A sense of Canadian separateness was reflected in the adoption of a new flag and a new national anthem. In 1982 the Canada Act abolished the need for British Parliamentary approval of amendments to the Canadian constitution. The problem of avoiding economic and cultural domination by the USA persisted. From the 1960s, foreign capital derived mostly from the USA, which was the focal point of Canada's foreign trade; more than half of Canadian industry was US-owned. A free trade agreement with the USA was concluded in 1988. An even more worrying problem, from the 1960s onward, was the threat to national unity from the separatist movement in French-speaking Quebec. In 1976, the Parti Québecois, led by René Lévesque, won Quebec's provincial election. While independence was rejected in a provincial referendum (1980), the Parti Québecois continued to call for separation. The Meech Lake Accord, which attempted to satisfy French-Canadian aspirations, failed in 1987. In 1992 another attempt at compromise failed, when the Charlottetown agreement was rejected by six provinces, including Quebec. In the 1993 elections, the strong support given to two regional parties, the Bloc Québecois, which revived the demand for independence, and the western-based Reform Party, which opposed official bilingualism and special status for Quebec, raised again the question of the confederation's political survival. In 1995 Quebec narrowly voted by referendum not to leave the federation. Prime Minister Chrétien announced moves to recognize Quebec as a distinct society. The number of Québecois government appointments was increased in 1996. Taking advantage of economic recovery and Liberal Party popularity, Chrétien called a general election in 1997, which returned him and his party to power.

Early Latin America

First settlers • Early domestication

The colonization of the Americas is believed to have begun up to 35 000 years ago, during the ice age. At this time, Asian hunters crossed a land bridge that linked Siberia and Alaska across the Bering Strait. Those who settled Central America and western and southern South America were hunters of big game, such as mammoth and giant bison. Jungle settlers, on the other hand, lived on small mammals and fish. Both groups also gathered roots, nuts, and tubers. As pottery was unknown before 1200 BC, this era of early America is known as the ***Preceramic Period***.

First Settlers
Evidence from Peru suggests that by about 8500 BC, domestication of plants and animals had begun. Before this time, the inhabitants of the high Andean plateaus had eaten the ancestors of the modern potato and sweetcorn and hunted llama. Unlike most grazing animals, these Andean **camelids** were not migratory, which allowed their hunters to adopt a sedentary existence. These people therefore became adept at husbanding plants and animals; by 5000 BC, they had domesticated the potato (at least 200 variants are still grown in the Andes) and a variety of native tubers. Domestic animals included the llama and guinea pig. On the lower slopes, the amaranth plant was domesticated to produce maize – the staple food of Latin America.

Early Domestication
The earliest Americans fashioned tools from stone, wood, and bone. They used woven baskets in place of pottery and lived part of the year in caves. Evidence from Chile demonstrates, however, that at least some people lived in small villages, in houses made of animal skins tied over a wooden framework with wooden plank floors and foundations, at least for part of the year. Their food included wild potatoes and mastodon meat, and their hunting tools included slings and possibly bolas, as well as stone-tipped and wooden spears.

Coastal people depended heavily on the sea but also domesticated many plants (e.g. cotton, gourds, peppers, beans, and peanuts).

Their dwellings were houses made of mud bricks; Huaca Prieta, the oldest village site in Peru, contains small structures built partly beneath the ground. Cotton was used for making textiles, such as decorative netting and plain cloth, and for fishing nets. Highland people wove alpaca and other wool into fine clothing, decorated by a variety of processes including dyeing and painting. There was considerable interaction between the highland and coastal peoples, a pattern that continues to the present day.

Bering land
bridge

Sites older than
25 000 BC
25 000–15 000 BC

===SEE ALSO===
This section:
• Central American
  Civilizations
• Andean Civilizations
Art of the Americas (vol. 4):
• Pre-Columbian Central
  and South American Art
Social Sciences (vol. 6):
• Introduction to
  Anthropology

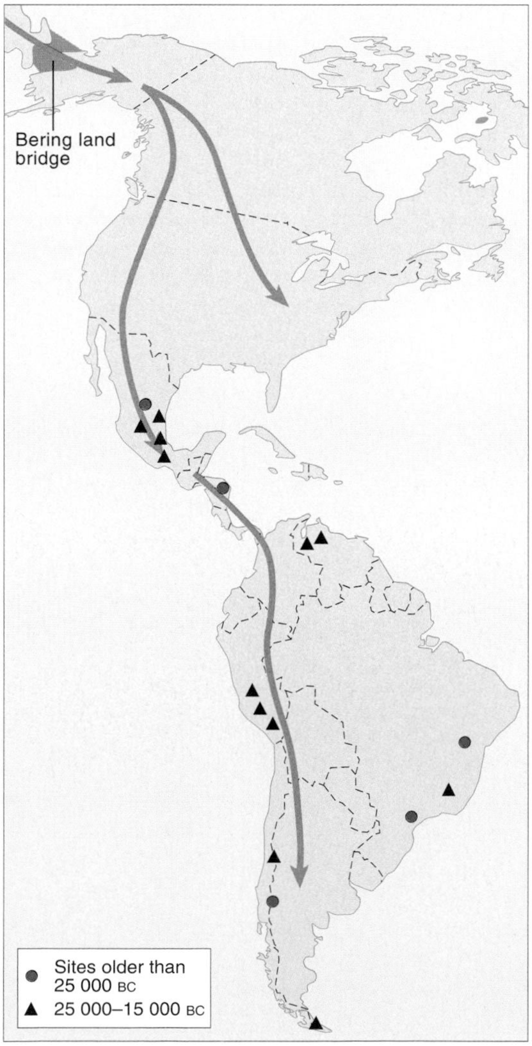

◀ **The Settlement of
the Americas**
*Sites of earliest
occupation by Asian
hunters from c.
35 000–15 000 BC
are shown.*

New World Camelids

There are four species of the camel family (camelids) in the Americas. The *vicuña* and the *guanaco* are the oldest species, thriving at high altitudes. Wild herds of these animals still roam the grassy plateaus of the Andes. The *llama* and the *alpaca* have been domesticated since earliest times; the latter is highly prized for its long fine hair. Unlike the sheep and cattle introduced by the Spanish, these native species do not harm the ecosystem, as their delicate hooves and mouths do not uproot upland grasses and cause soil erosion.

Central American Civilizations

The Olmec • The Toltec • The Maya • The Aztec

Main Sites of Mesoamerican Civilization *Sites of the various civilizations that occupied the Central American isthmus from 1200BC until the Spanish conquest are shown.* ▼

The Olmec civilization (1150–c. 400 BC) has traditionally been regarded as the mother culture of all the civilizations of **Mesoamerica**.The term 'Olmec,' from a native word (*ule*) for rubber, was first applied by the Spanish conquistadors and friars who came to the New World, due to the abundance of rubber trees in the region. The Olmec heartland, where the earliest and most important archaeological sites are to be found, is located on the southern Gulf coast of Mexico. From these early sites, artistic (and possibly also religious) influence soon spread to many other regions. It was once assumed that this was as a result of military expansion; however, a more recent theory advanced for the rapid spread of Olmec culture is that it arose through trade links.

The Olmec

The Olmec are renowned for their monumental architecture and especially for their 'colossal heads.' These impressive monuments, weighing up to 20 tonnes, were carved out of basalt and then transported, mainly by river and sea, for up to 70 km. They represent human heads often with child-like features, wide thick lips, and distinctive headgear. Since

no two heads are the same, they are thought to portray individual Olmec rulers. The Olmec also carved huge table-top altars or thrones. Their society was not egalitarian; evidence exists of an elite; for example, the differing quality of attire and ornamentation displayed by numerous sculptured figures.

San Lorenzo. This is the earliest site showing distinctive signs of Olmec culture. The Olmec settlement of San Lorenzo began in 1150 BC, although there is evidence of occupation of the site that predates them. San Lorenzo is located in a small semiartificial plateau set 50 m above the surrounding grassland. The construction of such a gigantic edifice implies the existence of a meticulous and ambitious leadership. Mounds and pyramids were built on top of the plateau and a complicated system of drains was created, linked to artificial ponds and fountains. Contacts with many parts of Central America were established and an extensive trade network was set up, which supplied the Olmec with a wide range of exotic goods, such as mica, serpentine, and iron ore to be used in rituals. In around 900 BC habitation of the San Lorenzo site came to an abrupt end. Monuments were

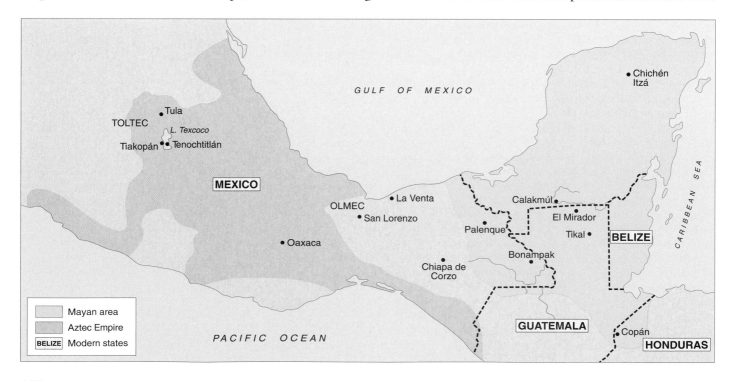

▲ **An Olmec 'Colossal Head'** *The tallest of these monumental sculptures, which are situated at San Lorenzo, is some 27 m high. The helmets of these figures are believed to represent headgear for the ritual ball games that were common to many Mesoamerican cultures.*

deliberately defaced, heads destroyed, and faces mutilated. The cause of this is unclear. At around the same time, however, another site was reaching its peak, at La Venta.

La Venta. Around 800 BC the site of La Venta emerged as the region's main social and political centre, which it remained for another 300 years. An elaborate ceremonial complex was constructed, including a large open court, many monumental structures, and an enormous platform measuring 325 m long by 260 m wide and 7 m high. Archaeological excavations have uncovered a serpentine mosaic pavement, together with buried corpses surrounded by funeral offerings, such as jade figurines, beads, and ear flares. These finds are unparalleled in Mesoamerica. Such sites as San Lorenzo and La Venta already give a hint of the heights of grandeur that Mesoamerica was to attain later in its history.

The Toltec

The Toltec derive their name from the Aztec word meaning 'skilled craftsperson' or 'artisan.' It may also originate from their capital Tollan (now called Tula) meaning 'place of rushes.' The Toltec people were composed of various ethnic groups, as a result of multicultural amalgamation. They introduced dramatic changes in public and religious architecture, as well as new styles of stone carving and ceramics. The Toltec and their capital

are inextricably linked with the mythical hero/god **Quetzalcóatl.** Tula was a vibrant city that was the leading power in Mesoamerica for the brief period from 900 to 1200 AD. The Toltec civilization never formed a homogeneous and compact territorial unit definable as an empire, since it was not an integrated territory with clearly defined boundaries. The Toltec nevertheless established far-flung trade networks throughout Mesoamerica. They were self-sufficient, importing only salt, obsidian, and freshwater products. Due to the prominent position of ritual in their society, they also imported exotic goods, such as *cacao* (chocolate), semiprecious stones, cotton, jewellery, and metal (which makes its first appearance in the area during this period). Metals probably arrived via long-distance trade with South or Central America.

Tula. Tula flourished for around 200 years. At its height, this metropolis may have housed between 30 000 and 60 000 people. The most remarkable structures in Tula are the so-called 'Atlantes.' These are huge stone figures, over 3.5 m high, depicting warriors in their full attire of feathered headdress, butterfly breastplate, necklace, bracelets, anklets, and sandals decorated with plumed serpents. Some artefacts from this site still show traces of the original paint. In 1200 AD, Tula was sacked and destroyed by unknown invaders. The details of its destruction remain a mystery; some sources describe how the remaining population began a long march, finally founding the new great city of Chichén Itzá on the Yucatán Peninsula. Despite the devastation of Tula, the Toltec lineage survived; among the later Aztecs, it was considered highly prestigious, even divine, to be of Toltec stock.

Mesoamerica A specific geographical area in Central America that shared a high degree of cultural unity at the time of the Spanish conquest. It comprises central and southern Mexico, Guatemala, Belize, and parts of El Salvador and Honduras. The people there had knowledge of hieroglyphic writing, stepped pyramids, the calendrical system, and the use of advanced farming techniques. The term is therefore more cultural than geographical.

QUETZALCOATL

According to legend, Quetzalcóatl became leader of the Toltec after the death of his father, a famous warrior. Under his rule, the arts and trade flourished. However, a rival who was envious of Quetzalcóatl's success caused him to get drunk. In disgrace, he was forced to leave his people and travelled to the Gulf of Mexico, where (depending on the source) he either set himself alight and ascended to the heavens to become Venus, or set sail on a raft of serpents, promising to return on the anniversary of his death. The figure of Quetzalcóatl was then incorporated into the mythology and religious observance of following civilizations, such as the Aztec, for whom he was the morning star and the god of fertility.

▲ **An Aztec Sculpture of Quetzalcóatl**
The name of the god means 'plumed serpent.'

Maya Observatory at Chichén Itzá ▶

From observatories such as this, the Maya determined the solar year with greater accuracy than the Julian calendar used in Europe until 1582. This observatory is known in Spanish as the caracol *(snail) from the shape of its interior spiral staircase.*

The Tenochtitlán Legend

The legend of the founding of Tenochtitlán recounts how the Aztec, on their arrival at Lake Texcoco, noticed an eagle sitting on a *tenochtli* cactus eating a snake, which they took to be a good omen for their enterprise. This image forms the modern state of Mexico's national emblem, appearing in the centre of the country's flag.

obsidian A black glassy volcanic rock formed by the rapid cooling of acid lava. Obsidian was an important material in Pre-Columbian Central America. One of its principal uses was for the blades of weapons; however, these were ineffective when the indigenous peoples fought the Spanish *conquistadores*, as they shattered against metal armour.

The Maya

Maya civilization flourished during the Classic Period (250–390 AD). The society of this period represented the culmination of over 1000 years of development. As early as 1000 BC, small Maya centres were producing advanced ceramics and exchanging such materials as **obsidian** and jade with distant peoples. The place of origin of these early Maya people is unclear, although Chiapas, Oaxaca, or the Gulf Coast of Mexico are the most likely areas. By the Late Preclassic Period, large Maya centres (e.g. El Mirador) were being constructed. During the Early Classic Period (300–600 AD), the site of Tikal emerged as one of the most powerful Maya centres. The central part of this city covered 16 sq km and included over 3000 architectural structures. Giant temple-pyramids together with courtyards, plazas, palaces, administrative buildings, ball courts, sweat baths, and causeways have been discovered. In around 600 AD, Tikal's development was interrupted after its conquest by its warlike neighbour Caracol. The Late Classic Period (600–900 AD) saw the climax of Maya cultural and artistic development. Having risen again to prominence, Tikal was forced to share the leadership with such sites as Palenque, Calakmúl, and Copán. Causeways, twin-temple complexes, and giant funerary temples were built. Stone carving and monumental art reached its zenith.

The Maya had a highly advanced civilization. Their calendrical cycle was a type of ritual almanac that had religious and divinatory purposes and was consulted by priests for guidance in many aspects of daily life: see MATHEMATICS (VOL. 2): NUMBERS. Hieroglyphic writing was highly developed, conveying information not only about calendrical matters but also about cycles of time, the role of the sun, moon, planets, religious practices, various aspects of daily ritualistic activities, and important historical information. Their mathematical system was unparalleled at that time: they devised place-system numerals and the concept of zero, neither of which existed in ancient Greece or Rome. At the end of the Late Classic Period the Maya experienced a decline in culture, population, and settlement. The reasons for such a drastic realignment are still unknown. Although several important political and religious centres existed throughout the Maya area, there was never a homogeneous state controlling the entire region.

More than 2 million Maya still inhabit large parts of Mexico, Belize, Guatemala, Honduras, and El Salvador. Maya-derived dialects are still spoken and many aspects of their religious and agricultural life can be traced back to their pre-Hispanic ancestors.

THE MAYA CALENDAR

The Maya calendar was based on a ritual cycle of 260 individually named days. This cycle, or *tzolkin*, was divided into 13 periods of 20 days and ran concurrently with the 365-day solar year. The Maya of the Classic Period kept a 'Long Count' calendar that marked time continuously from a base date that indicated the beginning of the Maya era (3113 BC). The later Yucatec Maya used a similar system, dividing longer periods of time into units of 20 years, 13 of which comprised a complete cycle, or *katun*. From the alternative name for this cycle – the *may* – the name of the race is derived.

The Aztec

The word 'Aztec' is a modern term derived from the name Aztlán ('the place of the seven legendary caves'), the mythical place of origin of the Aztec people. The Aztec called themselves 'Mexica' and originally came from the north of Mexico. Their level of civilization was very basic and they were considered barbarians by their neighbours. Their long march ended in the Basin of Mexico. Finding the land already overpopulated, they became nomadic.

From 1250 to 1298 AD the Aztec served as mercenaries for the Tepanecs of Azcapotzalco, then the greatest power in the region. According to legend, the Aztec war god Huitzilopochtli then led them to two vacant swampy islands in Lake Texcoco, where they founded the city of Tenochtitlán. This is believed to have taken place around 1345 AD. In alliance with the neighbouring cities of Texcoco and Tlacopán, they defeated their former masters, the Tepanecs, in 1428. This date marks the beginning of Aztec imperial expansion, which only ceased with the arrival of the Spanish in 1519. Thus, in a brief period, Tenochtitlán had come to dominate a great landmass that eventually stretched to the Gulf Coast in the east and as far south as Guatemala. However, the Aztec rarely subjugated other cultures with violence, preferring to demand tribute from a particular area rather than occupy it. If compliant, people in the conquered area were permitted to keep their customs, religious beliefs, and even their local ruler. Only if they refused to pay tribute would the Aztec use military force. Tribute and trade were therefore the basis of Aztec success.

The Aztec held sacrificial rituals, which usually involved extracting the victim's heart with an obsidian knife. They believed that the sun required an offering of human blood if it was to rise every day. Sacrifices were also performed on special occasions, such as the erection of a new building or to celebrate a military victory.

Tenochtitlán. The city of Tenochtitlán became the world's largest metropolis with between 250 000 and 300 000 inhabitants. An intricate grid system of canals was built, together with three causeways linking the city to the mainland. Dams controlled the water levels of the lake (to prevent flooding), prevented salt water from the northern part of the lake flowing into the fresh water of the southern lake, and aided crop irrigation. At the heart of the city lay the Great Temple of Tenochtitlán, which formed the centre of the Aztec cosmos, religion, and power. This comprised a twin pyramid with two staircases leading to two shrines or temples on top. One was dedicated to Huitzilopochtli, the war god. Next to it lay the shrine to Tlaloc, the rain god, symbol of fertility and life. Thousands of sacrifices took place here. Only the foundations and lowest levels of the pyramid remain, the rest having been destroyed by the Spanish *conquistadores*. The Aztec capital now lies beneath the modern metropolis of Mexico City.

▲ **A Mixtec Manuscript** *This manuscript, the Codex Fejervary-Mayer, depicts a creation myth, in which the god Tezcatlipoca tempts the earth monster to the surface of the 'Great Waters.'*

The Ceremonial Plaza in Tenochtitlán *The main building in this artist's impression is the Great Temple, with its two shrines, dedicated to the war god Huitzilopochtli and the rain god Tlaloc.* ▼

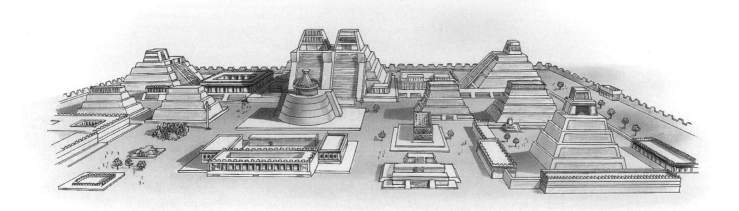

Andean Civilizations

The Chimu • The Inca Empire

The earliest highly developed Andean culture was that of the Chavín, which flourished in the period 900–200 BC. Based in the northern Andes and coastal area of present-day Peru, the culture takes its name from the highland site of Chavín de Huantar. The unifying force of Chavín culture was religious.

Between 400 and 800 AD, a period known to archaeologists as the Middle Horizon, a number of independent states arose in Peru. Prominent among these was Huari, which occupied the Ayacucho Valley in the southern highlands and had its capital at Wari. Although Wari covers some 700 hectares, not all of the site was occupied at the same time. The Huari also built regional administrative centres in the highlands and on the coast. It is thought that Huari society was a theocracy intent on converting the rest of Peru to its particular version of the common Andean religion, possibly in response to environmental instabilities, such as widespread prolonged drought and increased volcanic activity.

Inca The Quechua-speaking ethnic group from the Urubamba area that expanded outwards from Cuzco to conquer most of western South America. Inca was also the title of the ruler of the empire the Inca controlled, as well as the name given to the family of the ruler.

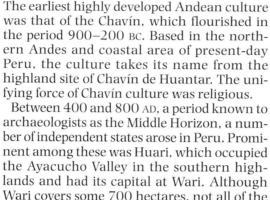

Andean Cultures ▶
Cultures of the Pre-Columbian period are shown. Cultures flourished in the Andes from the Middle Horizon period (c.400–800AD) up to the Inca Empire, which lasted for only a relatively brief period (1438–1532).

Key:
● Centres of pre-Inca civilization
□ Chimu Empire
□ Extent of Inca Empire under Huayna Capac

The Chimú

The Chimú occupied over 1000 km of the Pacific coast. They occupied an area extending from southern Ecuador to below the Chillon River (just north of the modern Peruvian capital Lima), and were second only to the Inca in size and power prior to the Spanish conquest. Their agricultural achievements were impressive; they cultivated areas without dependable water supplies by building large aqueduct systems to irrigate the desert.

The origins of the Chimú Empire lie in the Moche state. During the Middle Horizon, the Moche established a new capital at Pampa Grande in the Lambayeque Valley (near Chiclayo in the north of modern Peru), which itself was abandoned at the end of the Middle Horizon. The new dynasty dominant at this site thereafter was the Sican, which flourished between about 700 and 900.

Another branch of the former Moche state, which came to be known as the Chimú Empire, was established at a site further south called Chan Chan. Chan Chan was an imposing capital, covering almost 20 sq km. Its main features were the large palaces called *ciudadelas* (little cities). Their construction in pairs provides evidence that Chimú society was organized into a system of two parts called **moities**. Each Chimú was a member of one of these divisions, and each part had its own leader. The leader of the more important part was the paramount leader of the kingdom. On his death, the *ciudadela* became a shrine for his mummified body. There are at least nine *ciudadelas* at Chan Chan.

Much housing in Chan Chan was devoted to craftspeople, who had higher status than ordinary citizens. Metalworkers from Chan Chan were especially renowned; their work was highly prized by the Inca after their conquest of the Chimú in about 1470.

The Inca Empire

The **Inca** Empire was a relatively late phenomenon; occurring in a period known as the Late Horizon, it spans the years 1438–1532.

Much knowledge of Inca civilization comes from Felipe Wamán Puma de Ayala (1578–1621), a native writer, who chronicled the effects of the Spanish invasion of his land. In a letter to King Philip III of Spain, Wamán Puma relates the legend of the origins of the Inca: Four brothers and four sisters emerged from a tunnel at Pacari Tampu, which connected

▲ **Chimu Ceremonial Knife (*Tumi*)** *This fine example of Chimú worked gold is inlaid with turquoise.*

Tiwanaku, in Bolivia, to the Island of the Sun in Lake Titicaca. Their leader Manco Capac – who claimed to be the son of the Sun and the Moon – became the first Inca. He married his sister, founded the Inca dynasty at Cuzco, and established the Garden of the Sun (*Coricancha*), the most important Inca religious building.

The Inca are now thought to have originated in the 12th century AD. However, it is only with Pachacuti Inca Yupanqui (1438–71) – the ninth Inca, according to Wamán Puma – that firm evidence of **Tawantinsuyu**, the Inca Empire, emerges. Under Pachacuti, much of the southern highlands of Peru and northern Bolivia were added to the empire's territory. Conquest by the Inca was generally benign; Quechua, the language of the Inca, was made the official language, and new subjects were required to wear their distinctive regional dress wherever they travelled in the empire. Also, a portion of all the goods produced in any area were placed in state storehouses. These were used to maintain the army, and to provide emergency supplies during natural disasters. To fund these projects, a tax known as *mit'a* was levied on all subjects.

Pachacuti and his successor Topa Inca Yupanqui (1471–93) extended the empire into the highlands of Peru and parts of Ecuador. After he became Inca, Topa Inca Yupanqui completed the conquest of the south coast of Peru, southern Bolivia, northwestern Argentina and northern Chile. The last Inca before the arrival of the Spanish was Huayna Capac (1493–1525), who consolidated Inca control over Ecuador and established a second capital at Quito. Dispute over succession after Huayna Capac's death from smallpox plunged the empire into a bloody civil war between his sons Huáscar and Atahualpa.

The Inca emperor ruled absolutely and was considered divine. The empire had a hierarchical administrative structure. Below the Inca were the leaders of the Four Quarters, and various grades of leaders of the provinces. Local areas were organized into farming communities, or *ayllus*, an important administrative unit of the empire. Each *ayllu* controlled the land upon which the livelihood of the people depended, and its members were allotted fields for their own use.

The sophistication of Inca civilization is also evident from its material achievements. Inca architecture displays remarkable skill in design and construction. Close-fitting polygonal blocks and trapezoidal doorways and windows have allowed Inca buildings to survive devastating earthquakes. Textile weaving and metalworking were also highly advanced. Gold and silver – respectively known as the Sweat of the Sun and the Tears of the Moon – were sacred. These were not used for currency, but for decorating important buildings and for prestigious jewellery. The *Coricancha* had a garden containing life-size gold and silver replicas of animals and plants.

The Inkarí Myth

Inkarí was originally a hero of Pre-Columbian Inca culture, whose myth was combined with the story of later Inca leaders, particularly Tupa Amaru I (beheaded by the Spanish in 1572).The Inca believed that, in the underworld, the head of their leader would grow a new body, and that Inkarí would rise again to free them.

Tawantinsuyu (Quechua: The Land of the Four Quarters). The Inca thought of space in terms of four directions, each forming a *suyu*, or province. The Inca Empire's four quarters – Chinchasuyu in the north, Antisuyu in the east, Cuntisuyu in the west, and Collasuyu in the south – grouped around the centre, the capital Cuzco ('navel').

COTADOR·MAIOR·ITE3ORERO
TAVANTIN·SVIO.QVIPOC
CVRACA·CON DOR·CHAVA

con tador yiegonero — con ta dor

◄ **A *Quipucamayoc*** *Since the Inca had no written language, records were kept using an ingenious system of coloured cords knotted in specific ways, using a decimal system to record information. These were called* quipus, *and the record keepers* quipucamayocs. *This is one of many drawings from Wamán Puma's letter that depict officials in the Inca bureaucracy.*

The Spanish and Portuguese Empires

Spanish conquest • Portugal and Brazil • Consolidation of empire • Silver • Sugar and slaves • Colonial government and imperial reform • Decline

The foundations of the Spanish and Portuguese empires were laid at the end of the 15th century, in voyages designed to open a direct sea route to the rich spice and silk trades of Asia. The Portuguese led this quest with many voyages down the west coast of Africa; by 1488, Bartolomeu Dias (c. 1450–1500) reached the Cape of Good Hope, thereby opening a southeasterly route from Europe to the Indian Ocean. In 1492, Christopher Columbus (1451–1506), patronized by the 'Catholic monarchs' Isabella of Castile (1451–1504) and Ferdinand of Aragon (1452–1516), crossed the Atlantic, hoping to find a shorter route to India. On this voyage, he discovered the islands of the Caribbean, which he thought were the shores of Asia. His subsequent voyages and those of other explorers patronized by the Spanish monarchy led to expeditions of conquest and colonization.

Portugal came later to America. In 1497–99 Vasco da Gama (c. 1469–1524) made the first European voyage to India; his landing at Calicut in 1498 initiated Portugal's establishment of a rich trading empire in the Far East. Portugal's thrust towards Asia also opened a way to territorial expansion in the west. In 1500, a fleet commanded by Pedro Alvarez Cabral (1467–1520) embarked on a second Portuguese voyage to India. While sailing far to the west of Africa, Cabral's expedition discovered a land unknown to Europeans. Cabral called this territory 'The Land of the Holy Cross,' and claimed it for Portugal. Under the terms of the Treaty of Tordesillas (1494), Spain and Portugal had agreed to divide the world beyond Europe into two spheres, with new lands to the west reserved for Spain, while Africa and Asia were reserved for Portugal. Since Cabral's discovery lay east of the line of demarcation (drawn when the shape and size of the Americas were still unknown), Portugal's claim was upheld. This territory soon came to be known as 'Brasil,' after the many dyewood, or brazilwood, trees that grew there.

The Spanish and Portuguese presence in the Americas expanded and developed along separate lines for more than three centuries.

Spanish Conquest

Spaniards took the lead in American colonization. From the Caribbean colonies of Hispaniola and Cuba, they explored the mainland of the American continents in search of gold, slaves, and new territorial conquests. Colonization of the mainland started on the northern shores of South America in 1509–10, but the most significant conquests were in Mexico and Peru, where small groups of Spanish adventurers, through a mixture of good fortune and strategy, managed to subjugate established Amerindian civilizations. In 1519, Hernán Cortés (1485–1547) entered Mexico; by 1521, he had overthrown the Aztec state and, on the ruins of its capital Tenochtitlán, he

MEXICO · Cortés 1519 · AZTECS · 1492 Columbus 1493 · ATLANTIC OCEAN · Jiménez de Quesada 1536 · Tordesillas line dividing Spanish and Portuguese possessions · Cabral 1500 · CHIBCHAS · Pizarro 1531 · BRAZIL · PERU · INCAS · Vespucci · Valdivia 1540 · Garay 1580 · Mendoza 1535 · PACIFIC OCEAN · Magellan 1519

→ Principal expeditions
INCAS Indigenous peoples

◄ **Conquests and Early Colonization** *The names of the first Europeans to explore Latin America are given with the dates of their expeditions. Existing indigenous groups at the time of conquest are highlighted.*

◄ **The Murder of Montezuma** *The Aztec king Montezuma was held hostage by the Spaniards under Cortés and murdered during an uprising in 1520. After his death, his body and those of his chiefs were thrown into a canal.*

areas of conquest (i.e. Guatemala, **New Granada**, Chile) proved as rich in booty and resources as Mexico and Peru, but their acquisition did enable Spain eventually to establish imperial sovereignty in the vast territories traversed by the great continental mountain chain that runs the length of South and Central America.

Portugal and Brazil

Portugal was slow to colonize Brazil. After Cabral's discovery in 1500, the crown gave grants to private companies to trade in brazilwood, but the main focus for Portuguese expansion at this time was its eastern trade routes. In 1534–36, the lure of silver and the threat of French encroachment prompted King John III (reigned 1521–57) to encourage colonization of Brazil by dividing it into 15 regions, called **captaincies**, which he granted to individuals (*donatários*) who settled these regions at their own expense in return for economic and political privileges. Few were successful: by the late 1540s, only about 2000 settlers remained in Brazil, mostly concentrated in Pernambuco and São Vicente. To promote more effective colonization, the first governor-general was appointed in 1549, founding the town of Salvador (Brazil's first capital), and successfully stimulating settlement and exploitation of native resources. In 1567, a second royal captaincy was established at Rio de Janeiro.

New Granada A Spanish colony that encompassed much of the north of South America. It comprised modern Colombia, Ecuador, Panama, and Venezuela and became a viceroyalty in 1717. These territories were liberated by Simón Bolívar in 1819, with the new state thus created being known as Gran Colombia. After secession by Ecuador and Venezuela in 1830, the original name was revived for the remaining state – the Republic of New Granada – which lasted until 1858.

founded Mexico City, later the capital of the Viceroyalty of New Spain. In 1532, Francisco Pizarro (c. 1475–1541) penetrated into Peru; after capturing and killing the Inca king Atahualpa (c. 1500–33), he and his conquistadors entered the capital of the Inca Empire, Cuzco, in 1533, where they established a base.

By the mid-16th century, the Spanish had spread from their core areas of conquest into adjoining regions. None of the other main

AMERIGO VESPUCCI

The Italian navigator Amerigo Vespucci (1454–1512) is best remembered for the fact that the name 'America' derives from his first name. Vespucci was employed by both the Spanish and Portuguese courts. On a voyage for the Spanish king, in 1499–1500, he discovered the mouth of the River Amazon. Under Portuguese auspices, in 1501–02 he sailed down the east coast of South America and became the first European to sight the Rio de la Plata. This voyage convinced Vespucci that the lands he sighted were a New World, and not part of Asia, as others before him had supposed.

Vespucci's 1501 Expedition *Portuguese sailors engage an Indian coastal tribe in battle.* ►

His Catholic Majesty must know that we found these countries in such a condition that there were no thieves, no vicious men, no idlers.... We have transformed these natives, who had so much wisdom and committed so few crimes.... There was then no evil thing, but today there is no good.

Mancio Sierra, conquistador under Pizarro, 1589

Francisco Pizarro ▶

Pizarro was first attracted to the Inca Empire after seizing an Inca vessel carrying gold and silver ornaments. In the 1530s, after large deposits of silver were discovered at Potosí (in modern Bolivia), large-scale exploitation of the region's mineral deposits began.

After the Spaniards had left the city of Mexico, and before they had made any plans to attack us again, there came amongst us a great sickness, a general plague.... It raged amongst us, killing vast numbers of people. It covered many all over with sores.... Many died of the disease, and many others...starved to death because there was no one left alive to care for them.... Many had their faces ravaged; they were pockmarked, they were pitted for life. Others lost their sight, they became blind.

The Florentine Codex
(History of the conquest, written c. 1550 by Aztecs for Friar Bernardino de Sahagún)

The foundation of these royal captaincies marked a turning point in the development of Portuguese America. Settlers began to organize large-scale sugar production, drawing on previous experience in Madeira. They used Indian labour until, in 1559, the crown authorized trade in slaves from Africa to Brazil.

Consolidation of Empire

Spanish colonial settlement was concentrated on towns, which acted as bases for dominating the surrounding countryside. At first, Spanish colonists sustained themselves by living parasitically off the indigenous people. The primary mechanism for such exploitation was the *encomienda*, which gave individuals (known as *encomenderos*) the right to demand payments or services from the Indians. In this way, some settlers greatly enriched themselves, forming wealthy and powerful cliques that royal officials found difficult to control.

Indian peoples were relegated to subordinate positions within colonial society. The Spanish crown sought to justify its seizure of their lands by proclaiming a religious and civilizing mission. However, conversion did little to protect Indians from the dire effects of contact with Europeans, even when the missionaries sought to shield them from gross exploitation by settlers. Devastation of Indian communities started in the Caribbean, where, within two generations of Spanish colonization, native peoples had been all but annihilated.

When Spanish colonists moved to the mainland, they brought with them epidemics of smallpox, measles, diphtheria, influenza, and other Old World diseases against which Indians had little or no immunity. It is estimated that by the end of the 16th century the Amerindian population was only some 20% of that at the beginning of the century. A striking example of Indian population loss is found in central Mexico: this region may have had as many as 25 million inhabitants at the time of Spanish conquest in 1520–21; by 1568 the population was reduced to little more than 2.5 million, declining further to a low point of just over 1 million in the early 1600s.

Most Indian communities never fully recovered. Although highland areas of central and southern Mexico, Guatemala, and Peru had substantial Indian communities at the end of the colonial period, the Spanish American colonies generally became multiracial societies. In Spanish America as a whole, people of European descent were a minority; another minority group comprised Africans and their descendants, who worked as slaves. By far the largest elements of colonial populations were either Indians or people of mixed race, known as *mestizos*, *mulattos*, and *zambos*, who were born from unions between Whites, Indians, and Blacks. This mixture of peoples did not, however, produce integrated societies: Whites were regarded as socially superior simply by virtue of their ethnic origin, while Indians, *mestizos*, and Blacks were treated as inferiors.

In parallel with this demographic and social transformation, the introduction of European animals, crops, and agricultural practices changed the ecological face of the region. European livestock, such as cattle and pigs, multiplied rapidly in favourable environments, while European crops, such as wheat and barley, provided new sources of food to supplement or supplant the traditional Indian crops of maize, beans, and plantains. The Spanish also gradually developed their own economic enterprises with Indian labour, such as farms and ranches or mining industries. The wealth thus generated was invariably concentrated in the hands of a few; rich commercial families assumed the privileged positions previously held by *encomenderos*.

Silver

The discovery of immensely rich deposits of silver in Mexico and Peru was particularly important in shaping economic life in Spain's American empire. Mexican and Peruvian silver mines (and to a lesser extent, gold mines in New Granada) provided huge wealth for colonists and the crown. Taxes raised from mining and other economic activities supplied the Spanish crown with vast revenues, making Spain Europe's foremost power. Silver and gold also financed the importation of goods from Europe. This network of Spanish Atlantic commerce was supplemented by trade in the Pacific. In 1564, the Spanish established bases in Cebu and Luzon in the Philippines, so creating a thriving commerce in silk and silver between Mexico and Manila.

Sugar and Slaves

While Spain's American empire was built on silver, the Portuguese depended on sugar. By 1600, Brazil was the largest sugar-producing area in the Western world.

Social and economic life in Brazil revolved around the *engenho*, a unit comprising land and sugar mills. Brazil's Indian population fell victim to epidemic disease. African slaves became the largest single element of Brazil's colonial population; between 1550 and 1800, some 2.5 million Africans were sold into slavery on Brazilian plantations. A distinctive Afro-Brazilian culture began to develop.

In the second half of the 17th century, Brazil's economy was severely hit by competition from English and French Caribbean sugar plantations. However, towards the end of the century, a gold rush in the Minas Gerais region in the south created a new source of wealth. Rio de Janeiro, the port closest to the gold mines, became Brazil's capital in 1763.

Colonial Government and Imperial Reform

The Spanish crown created a formidable system of government for its American possessions. At its centre were the king and his Council of the Indies in Spain. In the colonies, the crown's chief representatives were the viceroys of Mexico and Peru and the judges of supreme colonial courts (known as *audiencias*) that were established in all the main colonial regions. Under them came the governors of provinces and the *corregidores*, who supervised district administration and the government of the Indians. Colonial towns and cities were run by municipal councils called *cabildos*.

In Brazil, effective royal government began with the creation of the first colonial capital in Salvador in 1549. By 1630, royal officials were in place in most of Brazil's captaincies, and the empire was divided into two colonies – the State of Brazil and the State of Maranhão. The two were reunited under the Viceroy of Brazil in 1774. Command of royal government lay with the king and his councils in Lisbon; its representatives in Brazil were a hierarchy of governors-general, governors, high court judges, and petty officials; towns were governed by councils, known as *senados da câmara*, usually dominated by rich planters, ranchers, and merchants.

In Spanish America, the missionary orders of the Roman Catholic Church, particularly the Franciscans, pioneered conversion of the Indians. Church influence increased from around the mid-16th century, when Spanish America's first five independent archdioceses were established. In Brazil, Jesuits were foremost in bringing Christianity to Indians and Blacks.

Between 1580 and 1640, Spain and Portugal were united under the monarchy of the Spanish Hapsburgs, and the two empires thus coalesced. Harassed by French, English, and Dutch enemies, Spain found itself unable to defend its sovereignty in the Americas. The ascendant powers founded their own colonies in the Caribbean and the east coast of North America, usually in areas that the Spanish had not colonized. However, during their protracted wars with the Spanish, the Dutch managed to seize part of northeast Brazil in 1630, where they remained until 1654.

> ### Jesuit Missions
>
> Early in the 17th century, members of the Jesuit order of the Roman Catholic Church established mission settlements (*reducciones*) in South America. The missions became sanctuaries of peace and industry in unsettled times. However, the suppression of the Jesuits, which began in Europe in the late 18th century, led to their expulsion from the Americas in 1767 and the closure of the missions.

◄ **Slaves on a Sugar Plantation** *The slave trade was vital to the economies of Spain and Portugal's American colonies. Millions of Africans died in the appalling conditions on sugar plantations.*

Despite these incursions, Spain and Portugal still had great overseas empires at the start of the 18th century, and during the following century both sought to exploit their American colonial resources to the full. Thus, the Bourbon monarchy (which came to the Spanish throne when Charles II, last of the Spanish Hapsburgs, died in 1700) reformed the systems of colonial trade and government, particularly during the reign (1759–88) of Charles III. Under the Marquis of Pombal (Portuguese chief minister 1755–77), efforts were made to consolidate control of Brazil by administrative and tax reform. By the end of the 18th century, Brazil had become Portugal's leading colony in economic terms.

Decline

The Bourbon and Pombaline colonial reforms upset the political equilibrium of both Spanish and Portuguese empires. In some Spanish American regions, resistance to reform triggered major rebellions, notably in Peru and New Granada in 1780 and 1781; in Brazil, royal authority was also briefly threatened, in 1789, by an abortive conspiracy to establish an independent republic in Minas Gerais. Such colonial rebellions were suppressed, but threats to imperial authority resumed after the French Revolutionary and Napoleonic Wars.

Latin America c. 1700

The system of colonial government was highly developed in both the Spanish and Portuguese American empires by the beginning of the 18th century. This map shows all the various administrative regions and their larger subdivisions in these empires. ▼

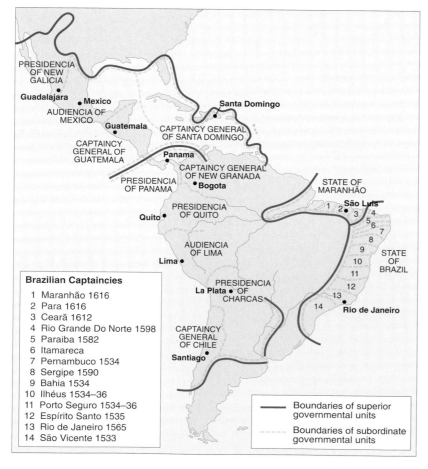

Brazilian Captaincies

1 Maranhão 1616
2 Para 1616
3 Ceará 1612
4 Rio Grande Do Norte 1598
5 Paraiba 1582
6 Itamareca
7 Pernambuco 1534
8 Sergipe 1590
9 Bahia 1534
10 Ilhéus 1534–36
11 Porto Seguro 1534–36
12 Espírito Santo 1535
13 Rio de Janeiro 1565
14 São Vicente 1533

——— Boundaries of superior governmental units

- - - - Boundaries of subordinate governmental units

INCA REVOLT

In 1780, a serious challenge to Spanish rule in South America broke out in the highlands of Peru; its leader was the educated and prosperous trader José Gabriel Kunturkanki Tupa Amaru (c. 1742–81), a direct descendant of the Inca leader, Tupa Amaru I, executed by the Spanish in 1572. After attempting to redress injustices against Indians by legal means, Tupa Amaru II (as he styled himself) hanged the *corregidor* of his native province of Tinta and began an uprising that lasted three years and cost 200 000 lives. The rebellion attracted wide support; from Black slaves (whom Tupa Amaru II freed) and mestizos, as well as Amerindians. However, delay and factionalism lost Tupa Amaru the initiative; he was captured and killed in May 1781.

Conflicts in Europe provided the catalyst to the ultimate demise of both the Spanish and Portuguese American empires. When Napoleon invaded Portugal in 1807, the prince regent and royal court fled to Brazil under British protection. Brazil became the centre of the Portuguese empire. Dom João presided over the imperial court in Rio de Janeiro and, in 1815, formally created a monarchy consisting of two kingdoms, Portugal and Brazil. He became king in 1816, but his unified monarchy did not last. In 1820, he returned to Lisbon, leaving his son Pedro as regent. When the Portuguese constitutional government tried to reassert its control over Brazil, Prince Pedro assumed the leadership of Brazilian opposition and declared Brazilian independence. In 1822, Pedro was crowned 'Constitutional Emperor and Perpetual Defender of Brazil.' Portugal's American empire was finally at an end.

Crisis in Europe also destroyed Spain's hold on its empire. In 1808, Napoleon seized control of government in Spain, forced the Bourbons to abdicate, and placed his brother Joseph on the Spanish throne. This provoked war in Spain, and in the ensuing imperial crisis the Spanish American empire began to break up. In 1810, several colonies in South America renounced rule from Spain, thus instigating a movement towards independence which, by 1825, was to result in the replacement of imperial government by independent republics throughout the mainland territories of Spanish America. Thereafter, Spain was left with only remnants of its former American empire, in the islands of Cuba and Puerto Rico, which remained under Spanish control until the close of the 19th century.

Independent Latin America

Independence movements • New nation-states • Caudillos •
Liberal dictatorships • Economic growth

The independence movements in Brazil and Spanish America were hesitant reactions to distant European events rather than the unfolding of any preconceived **Creole** design. The political disintegration of the Iberian empires began with the French invasion of Portugal in 1807, during which the prince regent (later King John VI) and the entire Portuguese court were compelled to flee to Brazil aboard British warships. This one event promptly reversed the normal subordination of colony to mother country. In 1808 Napoleon captured the Spanish king, Charles IV, and his son Ferdinand, and placed his brother, Joseph Bonaparte, on the Spanish throne.

Independence Movements

Appalled at the prospect of becoming subjects of Bonaparte, Spaniards and Spanish Americans everywhere formed provincial *juntas* to exercise political authority, in anticipation of the return of Ferdinand from captivity in France to assume the Spanish throne. Meanwhile, a supreme junta in Seville, claiming regency powers, convened a *cortes constituyentes* (constituent assembly) in the port of Cádiz which, in 1812, decreed a constitution to apply to all Spanish citizens, based upon liberal principles of representation. American deputies participated in the *cortes* but were grossly under-represented. However, the constitution guaranteed certain rights – e.g. equality before the law and the abolition of discriminatory taxes, such as the Indian tribute – which proved attractive to Indians and those of mixed race in Spanish America, who had suffered discrimination throughout the colonial period.

The suppression of information about political developments in Spain by the authorities there increased Creole uncertainty in America. In 1810, Creoles in Rio de la Plata, Chile, and New Granada went further than simply professing loyalty to Ferdinand VII, and established their own governments. In Buenos Aires and Caracas, republican Creoles even declared their independence from Spain. In Mexico, harsh Spanish repression following the first Creole junta in 1808 drove provincial Creoles to rebel, in September 1810, under the leadership of a parish priest, Miguel

Hidalgo y Costilla. Within days, 80 000 poor peasants and Indians had joined the rebellion. By 1811 Hidalgo's revolt and the other Creole governments in Caracas and Buenos Aires had been crushed, although popular insurgency continued throughout southern Mexico, which culminated in a formal declaration of Mexican independence at the congress of Chilpancingo in 1813. By 1815, this revolt was at an end and Spanish armies, with Creole support, had regained control over all of Spanish America except Rio de la Plata.

The legitimacy of Spanish government in America, however, had been irreparably damaged. After so much bloodshed, particularly during the Mexican uprising when hundreds of *Peninsulares* (Spaniards born on the Iberian peninsular) and thousands of Creoles and Indians lost their lives, it was impossible to revert to the tranquil period of royal absolutism. Independence was now only a matter of time.

When Ferdinand VII was restored to the Spanish throne in 1814, his immediate suspension of the constitution of 1812, closure of congress, and restoration of royal absolutism confirmed the determination of many Creoles to break with the mother country. However,

◄ **Miguel Hidalgo y Costilla** *Hidalgo's revolt of 1810, in which he led an Indian army against the colonial rulers of Mexico, combined nationalism with religious fervour. Although it was crushed within a year, this uprising was the first major challenge in the modern era to Spanish control of Latin America; it ushered in a century of violent struggle for independence throughout the continent.*

Creole A person of Spanish (White) descent, born in Latin America.

=====SEE ALSO=====
This section:
- Andean Civilizations
- The Spanish and Portuguese Empires
- Modern Latin America

Early Modern Europe:
- The French Revolution and Napoleonic Europe

The Industrial Age in Europe:
- Liberalism and Reaction
- Nationalism and Imperialism

The Americas (vol. 1):
- Central America
- South America

SIMON BOLIVAR

▲ **Simón Bolívar** *In this contemporary print, Bolivar is shown being feted as the liberator of the South American continent.*

The South American soldier and statesman Simón Bolívar, known as the 'Liberator,' was the major figure in the movements of liberation from Spanish hegemony that swept across the north of the continent from 1810 to 1825.

Bolívar was the son of a wealthy landowning family in Venezuela. After travels in Europe, during which he studied the philosophy of Rousseau and Adam Smith, he became imbued with the vision of emancipation of his homeland from the colonial power. This he achieved in 1813, but was soon driven from Venezuela into exile by opposition forces. After returning to that part of the Spanish colony of New Granada occupied by present-day Colombia, Bolívar led an army into the High Andes and won a decisive victory against royalist forces at the Battle of Boyacá on 7 August 1819. This vital engagement allowed him to capture Bogotá; in December, the new republic of Gran Colombia (which was to unite Venezuela, Colombia, and Ecuador) was proclaimed with Bolívar as president. Venezuela was finally liberated at the Battle of Carabobo in June 1821.

Bolívar conducted another arduous campaign, over the period 1823–25, to free Peru, the final South American colony under Spanish rule. This task, which had been begun by the liberator of Argentina and Chile, José de San Martín, was completed under the military command of Bolívar's most gifted general, Antonio José de Sucre (1795–1830). In honour of Bolívar's exploits, Upper Peru adopted the name Bolívia on its independence.

Declining health and the failure to realize his ambition of creating a unified Andean republic brought about Bolívar's disillusioned resignation as president of Gran Colombia in 1830; he died in December of that year.

Bernardo O'Higgins

The illegitimate son of an Irish-born soldier, who became governor of Chile, Bernardo O'Higgins led the Chilean independence movement. After initial setbacks, he joined with José de San Martín to defeat the Spanish at the Battle of Chacabuco in 1817. Appointed supreme dictator of Chile, O'Higgins's proposed reforms met with opposition and he was forced to resign in 1823.

Spain would not give up its American colonies without a struggle. The mother country could still count upon considerable loyalist sentiment among elite Creoles, who feared the masses more than they desired independence. In Mexico, wealthy Creoles recoiled from the violence of the Hidalgo revolt. In Peru, Creoles still dreaded the repetition of the bloody Inca revolt of 1780. In Venezuela, the arming of slaves and mulattos raised popular expectations and brought demands for equality and an end to slavery. Throughout Latin America, rebel bands targeted the property of the rich, regardless of whether it belonged to Spaniards or Creoles. Creole reluctance to form coalitions with Indians or castes and their enthusiasm for organizing counterinsurgency ensured that the revolutions acquired none of the democratizing zeal of the (North) American Revolution.

Independence was eventually achieved through the military prowess and sheer determination of two great 'liberators': Simón Bolívar (1783–1830), a brilliant general and constitutional thinker (see panel), and José de San Martín (1778–1850), a professional soldier and adventurer from Buenos Aires, who had resisted the French invasion of Andalusia in 1809. With the help of José Antonio Páez (1790–1873), leader of the *llaneros* (Venezuelan herdsman from the Orinoco basin, who formed formidable mounted units), Bolívar drove the Spanish out of northern South America and eventually liberated both Lower and Upper Peru, though his dream of a unified Andean state remained unfulfilled.

Meanwhile, in 1817, José de San Martín led an army across the Andes to aid the Chilean patriot **Bernardo O'Higgins** (?1778–1842) in defeating the Spanish at the Battle of Maipó in April 1818, which was decisive in the liberation of Chile. San Martín and O'Higgins organized a navy which, with British help, successfully took Lima in 1821. Holding the isolated coastal capital, however, did not provide a key to the liberation of the rest of Peru. San Martín and Bolívar met at Guayaquil in 1822, after which San Martín withdrew to Buenos Aires, leaving Bolívar and his generals to spread the campaign to the highlands. They defeated the last Spanish army on the American mainland at the Battles of Junín in August and Ayacucho in December 1824, effectively bringing to a close the Spanish American Wars of Independence. The islands of Cuba and Puerto Rico, however, were not liberated until after the Spanish-American War of 1898.

The reluctant Creoles of Mexico and Central America, for their part, eventually opted for independence in September 1821 under Agustín de Itúrbide (1783–1824), who had until 1820 been a loyal counterinsurgent. His revolt addressed conservative fears at the proposal by Spanish liberal deputies to take special privileges away from the Mexican Church and army. However, he also attracted former insurgents by invoking the 1812 constitution. Independence was achieved bloodlessly in September 1821, in an atmosphere of patriotic fervour. However, this euphoria was swiftly dispelled in 1822 when, having proclaimed himself emperor, Itúrbide promptly dissolved the constituent assembly upon which provincial Creoles throughout Central America had pinned their hopes for effective representation.

In contrast to the violence of Spanish-American independence, Brazil enjoyed a peaceful period under the exiled Braganza dynasty. In 1816 John VI returned to Portugal to reassume the crown, leaving his son Pedro in Brazil as prince regent. In 1821 a liberal constitutional assembly in Lisbon recalled Dom Pedro. However, encouraged by his adviser, José Bonifácio de Andrada e Silva, Dom Pedro declined the invitation, preferring to become the first emperor of Brazil. Independence was declared on 7 September 1822.

New Nation-states
Of the 18 independent states that eventually emerged from the larger confederations by 1839, only Chile and Paraguay had succeeded in forming governments that compared in effectiveness or legitimacy with the institutions of Spanish or Portuguese absolutism. Elsewhere – even in Brazil, which retained its monarchy until 1889 – rebellions and civil wars became customary political practice.

All the fledgling Latin American nation-states, even the Brazilian monarchy, rejected absolutism, preferring a liberal constitutional model of government, based upon principles of individual equality before the law, common rights of citizenship, varying degrees of popular sovereignty, and the separation of powers. These new constitutions, ranging from the most liberal in the Colombian province of Vélez (which went as far as enfranchising women), to the most authoritarian in imperial Brazil and Mexico, were largely modelled on those of European democracies. Yet however extensively it was adapted to local needs, liberal constitutionalism often clashed with political traditions and sat uneasily in many societies for a variety of reasons. Within two decades of independence, most of the early, more idealistic, liberal constitutions had either been suspended by supreme dictators or replaced with more conservative charters.

The gulf between modern liberal constitutional principles and entrenched traditions might not have been so unbridgeable had Latin America's economic prospects been better. However, in contrast to the economic expansion that followed North American independence, early nationhood in Latin America was marked everywhere by economic depression or crisis. This was especially true of the formerly prosperous mining countries – Mexico, Colombia, Peru, and Bolivia – where the industry was allowed to fall into neglect during the wars of independence. Of the numerous mining companies formed in Europe during the mid-1820s, very few survived the decade; the mineral extraction industry only revived with the construction of railways during the 1870s. Early European loans to the new states helped little, with most governments foreclosing on their debts by the late 1820s. As foreign credit and business confidence declined, so the ambitious regional confederations collapsed. The smaller fiscally weak states that arose as a result were themselves beset by conflicts between liberals and conservatives, rebellious regions, poorly disciplined and underpaid armies, meddlesome foreign merchants, and internal conflict.

Paraguay under Francia
Under the dictatorship of Dr José Gaspar Rodríguez de Francia (1776–1840), who was known as *El Supremo*, Paraguay's constitution was suspended, the legislature was closed indefinitely, and liberals were exiled. With this deliberate policy of isolation, Francia's regime (1814–40) and those following it brought Paraguay stability and relative prosperity.

Latin America in 1830 *The continent's new nation-states; Gran Colombia is shown prior to its division into three separate states.* ▼

Independent States
- Paraguay 1811
- United Provinces of La Plata 1816
- Chile 1818
- Gran Colombia 1819–1830
- Mexico 1821
- Peru 1821
- Brazil 1822
- United Provinces of Central America 1823
- Bolivia 1825
- Uruguay 1828

Peruvian Guano

Guano – seabird droppings that had accumulated on islands off the coast of Peru – formed a major element of the country's economy following its independence. Deposited by the numerous cormorants, pelicans, and other seabirds of the region over centuries, guano was found to be rich in nitrogen and potash, making it an ideal fertilizer. Its commercial exploitation is a classic example of mismanagement of a precious resource by early capitalism. Slave Amerindian and Chinese labour dug guano in massive quantities for export to Europe and North America; within decades, the resource was exhausted, without any benefit to Peru's own agriculture.

The Church, far from performing its traditional role as peacemaker and joint arm of government, contributed to political instability. The papacy refused to allow the power of ecclesiastical patronage, previously held by the Spanish crown, to devolve to the new, often anticlerical, states. Difference in attitudes towards the role of the Church in politics lay at the root of the liberal–conservative rivalry that characterized party politics throughout Latin America by the 1830s. Liberals favoured the separation of Church and state and promoted religious toleration in order to attract immigrants from Protestant countries. Conservatives, however, regarded the Roman Catholic Church as the sole guarantor of social order and as an important source of national identity.

Caudillos

The first states to emerge from the instability of the independence period were those with an Atlantic seaboard: these were best placed to respond to the growth of European demand for imported goods. Stability in this period also owed much to the **caudillos**, political strongmen who were able to enlist the support of rural followers organized into informal militias. The caudillos courted conservative landowners, as well as foreign merchants and diplomats who were keen to see the stability and prosperity of the colonial period restored.

Renowned caudillos of this period were José Antonio Páez in Venezuela, Juan Manuel de Rosas (1793–1877) in Argentina, and Diego Portales (1793–1837) in Chile. Uniquely in South America, Chile enjoyed five decades of stability under Portales' conservative presidential constitution of 1833, deriving steady prosperity from exporting wheat and wine along the Pacific seaboard, complemented from the 1850s onwards by minerals, especially copper and nitrates.

With a monarchy, Brazil needed no caudillo. Nevertheless, republican challenges from the northeast and south, suppressed with much bloodshed, delayed stability. Only with the recovery of sugar production in the northeast, the expansion of cattle grazing in the south and, most importantly, the first coffee boom around the capital, Rio de Janeiro, did the Brazilian empire acquire stability during the 1840s and 1850s under Pedro II (1812–91).

On its own, *caudillismo* could not resolve the social and economic divisions existing in the depressed societies of Colombia, Mexico, Peru, and Bolivia. By the 1830s, such countries had become bywords for civil unrest. To resolve the situation, these four countries (together with Paraguay and Ecuador) attempted to encourage domestic industry by adopting protectionist policies. However, these measures were undermined by cheap contraband imports from Europe, technological difficulties, lack of domestic demand, and above all, the political instability that was brought about by antiliberal legislation.

In Colombia, after three decades of conflict, liberals established an anticlerical federal state in 1863, without even a national army. This reform robbed the conservatives of their traditional power base. Helped by export revenues and bolstered by fraudulent electoral practice, liberals from the highland province of Santander ruled Colombia peacefully during the 1860s and 1870s. However, exclusion of the conservatives led to rebellions throughout the 1870s, culminating in 1898 in the

Steam Locomotives in Brazil *The late 19th and early 20th centuries witnessed a rapid growth of transportation networks in Latin America, chief among them railways to bring raw materials from the interior to the ports.*

War of a Thousand Days and the loss of the northern state of Panama, which gained independence in 1903.

Mexico was beset throughout the middle years of the 19th century by liberal–conservative conflicts. The return of the incompetent conservative General Antonio López de Santa Ana (1794–1876) to the presidency on no less than 11 occasions between 1835 and 1853 was a measure of the lack of political direction in this country. In its war with the USA (1846–48) Mexico lost a large part of its territory to the USA. This national humiliation was soon followed by Latin America's first major religious war, *La Guerra de la Reforma* (1857–61), in which Mexican conservatives rebelled against the anticlerical liberals. In defeat, conservatives turned to Europe for support, persuading Emperor Napoleon III of France (1808–73) to embark on a disastrous colonial adventure in 1862, which installed Prince Maximilian of Hapsburg (1832–67) as Emperor of Mexico in 1863. Five years of patriotic resistance by liberals forced the Europeans to withdraw from Mexico in 1867, abandoning Maximilian to his fate. Even with the disgraced conservatives removed from politics, stability proved elusive. For a further decade, Mexican liberals fought each other. Mexico also faced endemic banditry, rural unrest, and major Indian rebellions from the late 1830s until the late 1880s.

Liberal Dictatorships

During the 1860s and 1870s, many Latin American countries experienced further violent upheaval. These new conflicts accompanied the rise of an autocratic style of liberal leadership that emphasized the primacy of political stability and economic progress over liberty and equality. Venezuela's bloody 'federal wars' (1863–70) gave way to the regime of the modernizing General Antonio Guzmán Blanco (1829–99). In Brazil, the short military dictatorship that followed the collapse of the monarchy inaugurated the stable and prosperous Old Republic (1889–1930), during which Brazil became the world's principal coffee producer and most dynamic export economy. In Mexico, General Porfirio Díaz (1830–1915), who led resistance to French intervention and organized the forces of liberal regeneration, finally took power in 1876, ending 60 years of strife. Díaz ruled, almost unchallenged, until the outbreak of the Revolution in 1910.

Elsewhere, international wars and revolutions of liberal regeneration also led, paradoxically, to greater order. The War of the Pacific resulted in prolonged political stability both in Chile and the defeated nations. In Guatemala and Ecuador, dictatorship gave way, after a

▲ **The Execution of Emperor Maximilian** *Edouard Manet's painting depicts the death by firing squad of the ill-fated Hapsburg emperor of Mexico at Querétaro in September 1867.*

period of intensified liberal–conservative conflict, to stable, liberal, and anticlerical regimes (whose principal concern was to raise export revenue). The radical liberal Colombia of the Río Negro constitution was supplanted during the late 1870s by a centralizing regime that took a more conciliatory attitude towards the Church.

The consolidation of the Argentine nation was also a turbulent process that lasted almost 30 years. After the loose confederation of autonomous caudillo fiefdoms that had existed under Rosas, a series of liberal nation-builders succeeded in concentrating power in Buenos Aires. Tragically, this rationalizing process brought with it persecution of the Araucanian and Patagonian Indian tribes of the Pampas, who were largely exterminated in the War of the Desert (1879–80), which cleared huge areas of grassland for the expansion of great estates and immigrant settlement. A similar ethnocidal clearance campaign was undertaken by Chile during the 1880s.

Economic Growth

Behind these conflicts and political adjustments lay a remarkable economic dynamism that, by the 1880s, was beginning to yield extraordinary results. A continent chiefly noted for its revolutions had, almost overnight, become an attractive prospect for foreign investors and entrepreneurs. From the 1870s until the Wall Street Crash of 1929, which led to the downfall of governments throughout the region, most countries experienced sustained economic growth, political stability, and widespread social peace (with the exception of Mexico, torn by revolution after

---

War of the Triple Alliance (1864–70)

Also called the Paraguayan War, this devastating conflict was fought by Paraguay against an alliance of Argentina, Uruguay, and Brazil. The war arose as a result of Paraguayan territorial ambitions; at its close, it had cost this country more than half of its entire population (and some 90% of its adult males), together with considerable loss of territory. One positive outcome of the war was in Brazil: the heavy sacrifice of Black Brazilians led to the abolition of slavery in that country in 1888.

▲ **Porfirio Díaz**

Díaz governed Mexico between 1876 and 1910 (except for the years 1880–84). Under his harsh dictatorial rule, the country embarked on an extensive programme of modernization. However, discontent arising from Díaz's dispossession of the poorest sections of the population led to the outbreak of the Mexican Revolution in 1910.

INDEPENDENCE AND SOVEREIGNTY OF LATIN AMERICAN COUNTRIES

Country	Date of independence	Separate nation status
Argentina	1816	1816
Bolivia	1825	1839
Brazil	1822	1822
Colombia	1821†	1830
Costa Rica	1821‡	1838
Cuba	1898	1899
Chile	1818	1818
Ecuador	1821†	1830
El Salvador	1821‡	1838
Guatemala	1821‡	1838
Honduras	1821‡	1838
Mexico	1821	1821
Nicaragua	1821‡	1838
Panama	1821*	1903
Paraguay	1811	1811
Peru	1821	1821
Puerto Rico	1898**	—
Dominican Republic	1822	1822
Uruguay	1828	1828
Venezuela	1821†	1830

† Part of Gran Colombia until its break-up in 1830.
* Part of Gran Colombia 1821–30; part of Colombia 1830–1903.
‡ Part of the United Provinces of Central America from 1823–38.
** Ceded by Spain to the USA.

1910). From being at the periphery of world trade, Latin American economies assumed a more central position as suppliers of precious and industrial metals, raw materials, and an increasing variety of foodstuffs to Europe and the USA. Latin America also emerged as a principal market for European and American manufactured products and investment.

Improvements in transport and technology and social advances produced an economic revolution in Latin America. However, only a relatively small elite benefited, while the majority of the population remained unaffected by this period of rapid expansion.

The introduction of regular steamship services and the telegraph, the building of modern ports and railways, the establishment of banking and insurance services, and, most importantly, the advent of stable government transformed Latin America's commercial life. Mass immigration of labourers ensued from Europe and Asia. During the 1850s, slavery was abolished in Venezuela, Argentina, Peru, and Colombia; this was followed in the 1880s by Cuba and Brazil. In countries with large native populations, such as Mexico, Guatemala, and Peru, Indian forced labour was used on plantations.

Internal security and external influence grew. Not only could armies be regularly paid and better equipped but foreign states were also able to ensure the re-election of friendly regimes committed to export growth. Government by liberal constitutions, once a recipe for conflict, now became symbols of progress. As in the USA during this period, merchants and landowners dominated local politics through a system of patronage. During this period, grandiose development projects transformed such cities as Mexico City, Rio de Janeiro, and Buenos Aires.

The Mexican Revolution (1910), the first political movement in Latin America to involve the masses, exposed the essential fragility of the liberal development model. The revolution, which overthrew the dictatorial rule of Porfirio Díaz, raised many issues that affected the whole continent at the outset of the 20th century. Chief among these were governments' shortsightedness in servicing the needs of foreign entrepreneurs and investors to the detriment of their own populace; the danger of allowing urban elites to rule the rural masses; the tension between wholesale adoption of European culture by the ruling class and indigenous peoples' continued adherence to folk culture and native languages; and finally, the arrogant and pessimistic belief of the small White elite in the innate racial inferiority of the mass of the population. In its championing of many popular causes, such as political reform, economic and cultural nationalism, and mass education, the Mexican Revolution heralded the development of many Latin American states towards nationhood during the 20th century.

Modern Latin America

From the centenary to the Great Depression • Crisis, recovery, and revolution • Contemporary Latin America

In 1910 Latin America celebrated the centenary of the beginning of the independence movement. Since Cuba had gained its freedom from Spain (1899) and Panama had seceded from Colombia (1903), Latin America now comprised 20 different independent states, with a combined population estimated at 73 million. In addition, some European colonies remained, both on the mainland and in the Caribbean, where the growing influence of the USA was making itself felt. Political life in most Latin American countries was highly volatile, most strikingly demonstrated in the devastating revolution that began in Mexico in 1910.

From the Centenary to the Great Depression

Political Progress. As Latin America entered the 20th century, promising signs of economic development and social progress were evident. Civil wars were gradually giving way to stability throughout the region. Although representative forms of government and electoral politics were still very limited, democracy did flourish in several countries (e.g. Uruguay, Chile, Costa Rica, Colombia, Brazil, and Argentina). In Uruguay, President José Batlle y Ordóñez twice put an end to civil strife and encouraged social and political reforms. In Colombia, the conciliatory administration (1910–14) of Carlos E. Restrepo (1867–1937) instituted constitutional changes that guaranteed the increased participation of the opposition in Congress. Finally, in Argentina, where universal male suffrage had existed since 1853, the ruling Partido Autonomista Nacional (PAN) introduced substantial electoral reforms in 1912.

Dictators and Instability. In other countries, political stability was achieved at the cost

THE MEXICAN REVOLUTION

▲ **Emiliano Zapata** *The Mexican revolutionary leader is seen here in a wooden door carving by the artist Diego Rivera.*

In 1910, Francisco I. Madero (1873–1913), a member of a wealthy Mexican family from the northern state of Cohahuila, called on his compatriots to take up arms against the regime of Porfirio Díaz. Despite earlier promises to relinquish power, Díaz had again entered the presidential election of 1910. Madero initially campaigned against Díaz's re-election, but was soon imprisoned. After escaping to the USA, he launched a revolutionary uprising, crossing the frontier with 100 armed men in February 1911. By this time, a general insurrection was already under way in Mexico. In May, Díaz was forced to resign and fled into exile. In June, Madero entered Mexico City.

The revolutionary process did not end with the fall of Díaz. Madero's conciliatory position towards the old regime alienated some of his revolutionary allies, among them Emiliano Zapata (1877–1919), leader of a peasant movement in the state of Morelos. Madero fell victim to a coup led by General Victoriano Huerta (1854–1916) in 1913. Madero's death opened a second phase of the revolutionary process, characterized initially by a general rebellion against Huerta's rule. The insurgents' victory over Huerta in 1914 was followed by a struggle for power among the various revolutionary factions, marked by prolonged social unrest. In 1917 a new constitution drafted by President Venustiano Carranza (1859–1920) was adopted, incorporating land reform and separation of Church and state. However, many of its radical measures were only implemented much later. Restoration of state authority was an arduous process. Like Madero, many other leaders met a violent end. It has been estimated that about a million Mexicans died during the revolutionary period. The founding of the National Revolutionary Party in 1929 signalled the advent of stability. This party, which after 1946 became the Institutional Revolutionary Party (PRI), has governed Mexico ever since.

◀ **US Marines off Veracruz, Mexico**
US intervention in Latin America and the Caribbean has a long history. In the upheaval that followed the outbreak of the Mexican Revolution, the USA briefly occupied the coastal town of Veracruz in 1914 and, in 1916, sent an expeditionary force against the revolutionary-turned-bandit, Pancho Villa.

of liberty. In Venezuela, Juan Vicente Gómez (1857–1935) ruled without any serious challenge from 1909 to 1935. In Guatemala, the dictatorship of Manuel Estrada Cabrera (1857–1924) lasted from 1898 to 1920. Mexico, having suffered the most prolonged period of social and political unrest of any country on the continent, had been subjected to over three decades of authoritarian rule. In some countries attempts to develop constitutional regimes were curtailed by political turmoil or simply suppressed by dictatorial rule.

After the lynching of the once popular liberal President Eloy Alfaro (1864–1912), Ecuadorian politics entered a phase of instability, which was only ended when the military took power in 1925. In Peru, the constitutional regime that had developed since the turn of the century was interrupted first by a military coup in 1914 and finally replaced by the eleven-year dictatorship (1919–30) of Augusto B. Leguía (1863–1932). In Cuba, political turmoil, often accompanied by corruption and US intervention, was encouraged by the arbitrary rule (1925–33) of Gerardo Machado (1871–1934). Even the ruling regimes in those countries where constitutional and civilian government had developed were frequently beset with problems.

In the Brazilian First Republic (1889–1930) rebellion broke out in the regions of Paraná and Santa Catarina in 1912. More significantly, the Brazilian political order was threatened by a series of military uprisings in 1922, 1924, and 1925–27. In Chile, the progressive presidency of Arturo Alessandri (1868–1950), who won the 1920 elections, was interrupted by a military coup in 1924. Alessandri was recalled to govern in 1925, when he encouraged a major constitutional reform providing for the establishment of a welfare state. Yet Alessandri was again forced to resign; in 1927 his former Minister of War,

Carlos Ibáñez (1877–1960), took over the presidency, though he also pursued state interventionist policies to develop the economy.

New Parties. Latin American society during this period was far from static, and new political parties were constantly emerging. This tendency became increasingly evident with growing urbanization. Nevertheless, by 1910 Latin America was still predominantly rural. Significant sectors of traditional society were not fully integrated into the modern world that had been ushered in by independence. As the century progressed, further efforts were made to engage greater numbers of the populace in the political process.

Frequently, reformist aspirations were expressed in the organization of new political parties. The liberal–conservative dichotomy that had characterized much Latin American political life during the 19th century was gradually supplanted. In Colombia, however, the traditional partisan conflict between liberals and conservatives continued through the ballot box in the relatively tolerant atmosphere that developed after 1910. Uruguay was another country where 19th-century parties – *blancos* and *colorados* – remained the most important political institutions.

In most Latin American countries, however, the weakness of traditional parties became evident when faced with new challenges. Some new parties were established, but the general picture was one of political realignments and erosion of old loyalties. In Argentina, the radical party, founded in the 1890s, gained the presidency in 1916, partly as a result of electoral reforms. As the radicals consolidated their power, the hitherto dominant PAN disintegrated, leaving behind a fragmented opposition. In 1924, exiled Peruvians in Mexico founded the Alianza Popular Revolucionaria Americana (APPRA), with an anti-imperialist programme that included demands for agrar-

anarchosyndicalism
A working-class movement that arose at the end of the 19th century, arguing that trade unions should seek the destruction of the state, rather than political power within the existing system. The doctrine had an early impact in southern European countries; the Confederación Nacional del Trabajo was founded in Spain in 1910. Emigrants from Spain and from Italy, which also had a strong anarchosyndicalist movement, took the new doctrine to Argentina. By 1922, the Fedéracion Obrera Regional Argentina had 200 000 members.

ian reform and protection of the rights of indigenous peoples. In Mexico, the revolution erased any traces of earlier partisan politics.

Across the continent, but particularly in major ports and cities, socialist and communist doctrines were beginning to spread. **Anarchosyndicalism** found fertile ground in such cities as Buenos Aires, with its large proportion of Spanish and Italian immigrants. In 1912, Luis E. Recabarren (1876–1924) founded the Partido Obrero Socialista, later to become the Chilean Communist Party. Together with the Brazilian and Cuban communist parties, established in 1922 and 1925 respectively, these would become the strongest such organizations in Latin America; their appeal was generally restricted to small groups of intellectuals and workers. Moreover, political parties remained organized along vertical lines, cutting across class distinctions.

As social pressures became more acute, governments faced greater challenges beyond the traditional partisan oppositions. In 1918, student activism inspired a reform movement in the University of Córdoba in Argentina, which had a widespread influence across the continent. Urban riots broke out in Ecuador in 1922. More serious were the strikes in Buenos Aires in 1919, which undermined the authority of President Hipólito Yrigoyen (1852–1933). In the same year, unrest against the Chilean government broke out in mining areas. In 1928, the Colombian army used force against workers on banana plantations. Traditional institutions were also the source of social conflict; the Catholic Church inspired a peasant revolt (1927–29) against the Mexican President Plutarco Calles (1877–1945).

Independent Nations in World Affairs. In a period during which the expansion of colonialism reached new levels, the concern of

BUILDING THE PANAMA CANAL

The construction of the Panama Canal was a vast undertaking. Digging the channel, building the massive locks (especially those at Gatún, which raise ships over 25 metres), and damming two rivers to form the artificial Lakes Gatún and Miraflores all meant excavating and moving great quantities of rock and earth. One of the most remarkable feats of the engineers was to connect the lakes with a 13 km-long gorge – Culebra Cut – dug through the Continental Divide. Huge steam shovels and hundreds of locomotives were used in this task.

Malaria posed a constant threat in the swampy terrain of central Panama; special clinics were constructed by the US canal builders after the disease had taken a terrible toll of the original workforce.

Latin American countries to preserve their hard-won independence was not without foundation. However, the European powers showed little interest in establishing direct territorial control over Latin America. The intentions of the USA were the subject of greater fears in the region; victory in the Spanish-American War of 1898 had conferred a new imperial status on Latin America's powerful neighbour to the north.

The opening of the Panama Canal in 1914 symbolically confirmed the US presence in the region, although its influence over events in Central America and the Caribbean was not yet echoed elsewhere on the continent. There were direct US interventions in Honduras (1911 and 1924), Haiti (1915–34), the Do-

Excavating the Panama Canal
The Panama Canal, which links the Atlantic and Pacific Oceans across the Central American isthmus, was begun in 1880 by Ferdinand de Lesseps, French constructor of the Suez Canal. After he was declared bankrupt, a US company acquired the construction rights in 1904. The canal opened to commercial traffic in 1914. ▼

Railways

By 1914, a total of 60 000 miles of track had been laid in Central and South America, including 21 800 miles in Argentina, 15 800 miles in Mexico, and 15 445 miles in Brazil. Engineers often had to traverse difficult terrain; a prime example is the Central Railway in Peru, which rises into the Andes to a height of 4800 metres.

Prawn Fishing on the Brazilian Coast
Fishing is a vital element of many Central and South American economies. It is either conducted, as here, as a small-scale enterprise, or involves large fishing fleets (e.g. Peru). ▼

minican Republic (1915–24), Nicaragua (1912–33), and in Cuba, where, under the Platt Amendment (1901–33), the USA was given constitutional rights to intervene in the island's internal affairs.

The USA was able to count on the support of Central American and Caribbean republics when deciding to enter World War I in 1917. Brazil also declared war against Germany, in response to German naval aggression. A few Latin American countries severed relations with Germany (Peru, Ecuador, Uruguay, and Bolivia), yet a significant number remained neutral (Argentina, Mexico, Chile, Colombia, and Paraguay). Only two naval battles took place in South American waters; however, the war had a major economic impact in the region, besides opening the door for further US influence.

After the war Latin American diplomacy was conducted on an unprecedented scale on the European stage, largely as a result of the inauguration of the League of Nations. Some Latin American republics participated as founder members of this body. However, failure to get the Monroe Doctrine removed from the League's covenant was a cause of frustration; according to this doctrine, formulated in 1823, the USA reserved the right to intervene in South American affairs if it perceived a threat to its security. Argentina left the League in 1920 and did not rejoin until 1933. After being refused a permanent seat on the Council, Brazil withdrew in 1926. Attempts to achieve closer ties with Europe did not preclude Latin American republics from participating in the Pan American Conferences that were held in Buenos Aires (1910), Santiago (1923), and Havana (1928).

Economic Growth. From the mid-19th century onwards, Latin America had experienced rapid economic growth, which continued up to 1929, though its pace was often interrupted by conflicts and depression. This growth was mainly based on exports in response to demand from the expanding world economy: coffee from Brazil, Central America, and Colombia; meat from Argentina and Uruguay; sugar from Cuba and Peru; oil from Venezuela and Mexico; nitrates and copper from Chile; wheat and wool from Argentina; bananas from Guatemala, Colombia, Costa Rica, and Honduras. Export developments brought an influx of foreign capital, mostly from Great Britain and also from France and Germany, but increasingly from the USA, particularly in the years following World War I.

Export growth encouraged the development of a transport and urban infrastructure. Ports were modernized while some countries, such as Mexico and Argentina, built impressive railway networks. Air transport also developed rapidly during this period: in 1925, Scadta, a German–Colombian company, was the first commercial airline to run regular services from South to North America. More significantly, the process of industrialization that had begun in the 1870s was stimulated as exporters reinvested their profits in manufacture. Some emergent industries (e.g. leather goods manufacture, textile production, brewing, and soap manufacture) were directly linked to the availability of local raw materials. Activities around the ports and the production of some export commodities, such as coffee, stimulated the local manufacture of tools and machinery. Yet new industries depended mainly on imported machinery and industrial development remained limited.

Although exports grew mostly as a result of the adoption of the liberal principles of free trade, this period also saw states take a more active role in the economy. Government moved to maintain the price of coffee in Brazil, where policy-making was shaped by the foundation of the Coffee Institute of the State of São Paulo in 1924. Moreover, Brazilian intervention in the coffee market had repercussions for other coffee producers in the region. In Chile, state intervention was enacted through the revision of tariffs after 1914 and the establishment of various state agencies.

By 1930, Latin America had a population of 105 million. Buenos Aires, Rio de Janeiro, and Mexico City had become large metropolises. Population growth had been further stimulated by a massive influx of immigrants. Latin American economies had expanded hugely since the 19th century. Up to 1914, the economy of Argentina – then with a per-capita income comparable to most western European countries – had grown at an annual rate of 5%. Yet Argentina was exceptional in that it had managed to sustain and diversify its ex-

◄ **Scenes from Mexican History**
This mural by the artist Juan O'Gorman (1905–82), from the Chapultepec Palace in Mexico City, depicts various figures and episodes from the turbulent history of Mexico.

port sector. Most Latin American economies were heavily dependent on one or two commodities, for example: nitrates (Chile), sugar (Cuba), and coffee (Brazil and Colombia).

Crisis, Recovery, and Revolution

Most Latin American regimes were not robust enough to withstand the global economic crisis of 1929. Even those countries that had achieved some political progress faced considerable disruption. The governments of Bolivia, Argentina, the Dominican Republic, Peru, Guatemala, and Brazil had all been toppled by the end of 1930. Similar unrest occurred in Chile, Ecuador, Panama, and El Salvador in 1931. The experience of Colombia was unique: in 1930, a peaceful transition of power took place from the conservatives to the liberals.

Economic Nationalism. A trend already evident in previous decades developed into a wave of economic nationalism that swept Latin America in the 1930s, partly as a result of the Great Depression. This was reflected in the growth of state agencies, active government intervention in the economy, favouring of locally manufactured goods over imports, and hostility towards foreign capital. In 1937 all Standard Oil Company holdings in Bolivia were nationalized. More significantly, Dutch, British, and US oil companies were expropriated in 1938 by the Mexican president Lázaro Cárdenas (1895–1970), who also implemented drastic agrarian reform. However, being prone to recurrent financial crises, Latin American governments took an ambivalent attitude towards direct foreign investment. The general hostility towards foreign companies was sustained by the economic programme of President Juan D. Perón (1895–1974) in Argentina. Having launched his Declaration of Economic Independence in 1947, Perón nationalized the railways, river steamship lines, and public utilities. In 1952, the Bolivian government nationalized tin production, while the brief administration of Jacobo Arbenz (1913–71) in Guatemala attempted to dispossess multinationals.

Industrialization. The development of the industrial sector was mainly inspired by nationalism. The expansion of local manufacture in a growing export economy was stimulated by the Great Depression and World War II. By then the drive to industrialization was inextricably linked to economic independence. Industrialization became fully enshrined as a continent-wide policy with the establishment, in 1948, of the Economic Commission for Latin America (ECLA). Encouraged by state activism, the industrial sector grew rapidly. Light industries gradually gave way to the production of heavy goods. Brazilian President Getulio Vargas (1883–1954) managed to secure US financial assistance for the construction of a state-owned iron and steel plant at Volta Redonda in the early 1940s. Despite its achievements, state-driven industrialization also had its disadvantages: consumer prices rose, and regional development became more uneven. It also penalized the agricultural sector, discouraging exports. By 1960, the participation of Latin American countries in world trade showed a clear downward trend.

Unstable Politics. In the political confusion of the 1930s, a few personal tyrannies were

The Organization of American States (OAS)

Established in 1948 to promote peace and security and to foster collaboration among all the nations of the western hemisphere, the OAS had a distant precedent in the First Congress of American States, which took place at Panama City in 1826. Its immediate roots are in the Pan American movement that developed after the First Pan American Conference held in Washington DC in 1889. From its original 20 members, the organization has grown to 34 members.

209

Dictators

The right-wing populist leader Getulio Vargas came to power in Brazil in 1930 after a coup. He ruled until his suicide in 1954. In 1937 he launched the *Estado Novo* ('New State'), an authoritarian government styled on Mussolini's Italy. Vargas centralized the state, banned political parties, and enacted much social welfare legislation. Another enduring Latin American leader who seized power in 1930 was Rafael Trujillo, in the Dominican Republic. Trujillo's 30-year regime was highly repressive. After attempting to have the liberal Venezuelan statesman Rómulo Betancourt (1908–81) assassinated, Trujillo was himself murdered by army officers in 1961.

consolidated in Central America and the Caribbean. Between 1930 and 1961, the Dominican Republic suffered the dictatorship of Rafael Trujillo (1891–1961). In Nicaragua Anastasio Somoza (1896–1956), then the Commander of the National Guard, planned the assassination of the rebel César Augusto Sandino (1893–1934), thus inaugurating the long rule of the Somoza family in Nicaragua. Other dictatorships were established in Guatemala, El Salvador, and Honduras.

This was not, however, typical of the continent as a whole, where political instability became the rule rather than the exception. As in the past, there was no uniform political pattern; in some countries, politics alternated from dictatorial regimes to democratic inroads. In Venezuela the death of Juan Vicente Gómez, in 1934, opened up the system during a short period of intense electoral activity between 1945 and 1948. These democratic attempts could only regain impetus after the fall of Marcos Pérez Jiménez, who was in power from 1948 to 1958. The interruption of civilian government in Argentina in 1930 was followed by a decade of corrupt electoral politics. Colombia did not experience such frequent changes of regime, though the country did suffer a long period of partisan violence, which led to an interruption of constitutional government between 1953 and 1957.

Not all countries followed this unstable path. In Mexico the institutionalization of a corporate structure around a one-party system, and the implementation of a vast programme of social and economic reforms, under Lázaro Cárdenas, further legitimized the revolutionary regime under a civilian authority. However, Mexico only achieved stability at the cost of political rights and after a long period of internal conflict. The Chileans did not escape regime changes in the 1930s but there was a return to pluralistic partisan politics: by the 1950s, more than ten different political parties had seats in Congress. Electoral coalitions between right, centre, and left-wing forces were already a traditional component of Chilean politics. After some unrest in 1933, electoral politics returned to Uruguay, where a collegial system of government was adopted in 1954.

The Growth of the Electorate. Instability was, to some extent, the result of an uneasy accommodation of a growing electorate into weakly structured political systems. The expansion of cities and industrialization paved the way for the emergence of new social groups, whose demands challenged the existing order. Similarly, large human concentrations around mines and plantations contributed to the rise of militant unions. Political developments were also coloured by the polarized ideological atmosphere that prevailed elsewhere in the Western world. In a process fraught with tension and conflict, significant attempts were made to incorporate

ARGENTINA UNDER PERON

Juan Perón gained the Argentine presidency by constitutional means, first in 1946, for a second term in 1951, and finally in 1973. Following the 1946 election victory, however, his populist regime soon developed into arbitrary rule: unions were coerced into compliance, the press was censored, and the economy fell under state control. An initial rise in real incomes for the urban working classes was only achieved by artificially holding down prices and distorting the productive capacity of the Argentine economy. The transfer of resources from agriculture to develop domestic industry hit the export sector severely. Perón's reversal of these economic policies during his second administration in the 1950s could not prevent a crisis, exacerbated by political violence, corruption, and conflicts with the Church and the army. He was ousted from power in 1955. Ironically, Perón's own domineering personality – the basis of his appeal to the electorate – overshadowed his attempts to institutionalize his Justicialista party.

▲ **Juan and Eva Perón** *Perón and his wife are shown acknowledging the applause of the crowd at Government House in Buenos Aires in 1951.*

◄ **The Sinking of the *Admiral Graf von Spee*** *In one of the most famous naval engagements of World War II, the pride of the German fleet was scuttled by her own crew off the Río de la Plata estuary in December 1939.*

new social groups into electoral politics. In Argentina, the electorate had expanded greatly since the 1912 reforms. After 1955, Perón was forced into exile but Peronist voters repeatedly proved a force to be reckoned with. Universal male suffrage was finally introduced in Colombia in 1936, in Venezuela in 1947, and in Bolivia in 1952. In some countries, such as Brazil, Ecuador, and Chile, literacy remained a constitutional requirement to vote. Ecuador enfranchised women as early as 1928; they were later enfranchised elsewhere: in Argentina in 1947, in Costa Rica and Chile in 1949, and in Colombia in 1957.

This growing electorate was often channelled through the organization of new political parties. In 1931, Venezuelan exiles in Barranquilla, Colombia, established an organization that would later become the Acción Democrática (AD) in 1946. Together with the Christian Democrat Comité de Organización Electoral Independiente (Copei), these two parties formed the backbone of the democratization process that finally began in Venezuela after 1958. A Christian Democratic Party was also founded in Chile in the 1950s, though its origins could be traced back to the establishment of the National Falange in 1938. As a result of the **Chaco War**, old parties disappeared in Bolivia, where the Movimiento Nacional Revolucionario moved in to fill the political vacuum and, after taking over power in 1952, implemented a programme of nationalization and agrarian reforms, while attempting to bring the indigenous Amerindian peoples into mainstream politics. Social-democratic ideals figured prominently in the agenda of the National Liberation Party, established in Costa Rica in 1951.

World War II. Prior to the outbreak of war, fears of Nazi influence in the Latin American region were by no means groundless. German companies had made impressive inroads into Latin American markets: by 1938, through a series of barter negotiations, Germany had become the second largest trading partner of Latin America, behind the USA. Furthermore, in strategic sectors, such as air transport, the German presence was prominent in Brazil and in some Andean republics. Several governments, for example that of Eduardo Santos (1888–1974) in Colombia, readily joined the Allied cause. On the other hand, there were clear Axis sympathies within the Argentine government. Likewise, Chile hesitated and Vargas in Brazil actively contemplated forming an alliance with Germany. Ultimately, however, all 20 republics sided with the Allies. Although only a few republics committed military forces to active service, most were instrumental in providing vital strategic materials to the Allies. The war effort also brought the USA even closer to Latin America. The signing of the Inter-American Coffee Agreement on 28 November 1940, which included 15 American republics, was one of a number of measures that benefited Latin American economies through the war. After they had lost access to European markets in 1941, Latin American products found a guaranteed market in the USA.

Cold War Politics. At the end of the war Latin American expectations of direct assistance by the USA to promote economic growth were largely disappointed. The situation was made clear at the Inter-American Conference on Problems of War and Peace held at Mexico City in 1945; as priority was given to the reconstruction of Europe, policymakers and diplomats from Latin America and the USA were at variance over the best way to sponsor development. However, this did not prevent closer cooperation in other areas. The Inter-American Treaty of Reciprocal Assistance was signed in Rio de Janeiro in 1947. The following year, at a conference in Bogotá, the Organization of American States (OAS) was established. By this stage, it was ev-

> **The Chaco War (1932–35)**
>
> This war, devastating in its human and economic cost, was fought between Bolivia and Paraguay. The conflict's origins lay in a long-standing border dispute between the two countries over possession of the lowland Gran Chaco region. With a numerically inferior force, Paraguay emerged victorious. It is estimated that some 80 000 people perished, many of them highland Bolivian Indian conscripts.

BATISTA AND CASTRO

On 1 January 1959 a triumphant Cuban revolutionary army, led by Fidel Castro (1926–), entered Havana after the dictator Fulgencio Batista (1901–73) had fled the country. Batista had first come to power following the revolutionary events of 1933, when a coalition of students and middle-class organizations, backed by general strikes, overthrew the regime of Gerardo Machado (1871–1938). The short-lived collective that formed the revolutionary government introduced some important reforms, including extensive social legislation. The USA, however, did not recognize the government. Batista, who at around the same time had led a revolt of non-commissioned officers against the army hierarchy, emerged as the main power broker. The abortive revolution of 1933 left a legacy of bitterness and fostered instability. Attempts to institutionalize a constitutional regime after 1940 failed, while corruption and violence thrived.

In 1952, Batista assumed dictatorial powers. In an atmosphere of growing violence, political corruption, and nationalist frustration, Fidel Castro, the son of a wealthy sugar planter, came to prominence by leading an unsuccessful attack against military barracks in Santiago in 1953. Subsequently Castro spent time in prison, from where he publicized his cause. After his release, he launched a guerrilla campaign. Landing from exile in Mexico with 82 men, he established a base in the Eastern Sierra, from where he won growing support. The Cuban revolution was primarily nationalistic in character, but, faced with a US refusal to establish trade or diplomatic links, Castro was forced to seek support from the Soviet Union. While concerned to keep his country officially nonaligned, Castro's Marxism became increasingly orthodox; he labelled Mikhail Gorbachov's policy of *glasnost* as "counter-revolutionary."

Fidel Castro

Castro, seen here addressing a rally on the 30th anniversary of the Revolution in 1989, vehemently opposed the reforms that swept the Soviet Union and eastern Europe. After the collapse of the Soviet Union in 1991, Cuba was faced with a grave economic crisis. ▼

ident that security concerns had taken priority over economic relations. The growing influence of the Communist Party in the government of Jacobo Arbenz in Guatemala brought the Cold War to the forefront of debate in the hemisphere. A key military figure in the revolution that ended the Ubico dictatorship in 1944, Arbenz had been elected president in 1950, following the nationalist administration (1945–51) of Juan José Arévalo. His programme of land reform affected, among others, the interests of the US concern, the United Fruit Company, which had exerted

powerful economic and political pressure in the region since the turn of the century. Yet it was his accord with the communists that caused the overthrow of Arbenz by the army, in a coup engineered by the USA in 1954. In the aftermath of the revolution in Cuba, Cold War politics reached a new intensified pitch throughout the continent.

Contemporary Latin America

By the beginning of the 1960s, the region – with a population of almost 180 million – appeared once again to be moving towards liberal democracy. After the death of Vargas in Brazil, the presidency passed to elected civilian authorities. An agreement between liberals and conservatives to end partisan violence restored civilian government and electoral politics to Colombia in 1958, through a restricted system of power-sharing – the National Front. In Venezuela, the emergence of a two-party system (AD and Copei) went hand in hand with the consolidation of the democratic process. However, liberal democracy came under increasing attack not only from its traditional antagonists within the army but also from a militant revolutionary left wing, inspired by the Cuban revolution.

Revolutionary Violence. The success of Fidel Castro and his guerrilla movement encouraged the formation of revolutionary organizations elsewhere in the continent. Anti-imperialist feelings were further inflamed by the fiasco of the US-sponsored invasion of Cuban political exiles at the Bay of Pigs in

1961. Intellectual support for armed rebellion was further increased by the emergence of 'liberation theology,' a Catholic doctrine combining Christianity and Marxism, which developed after the Second Vatican Council in 1962. In 1961 the Frente Sandinista de Liberación Nacional (FSLN) was established in Nicaragua and the Movimiento de Izquierda Revolucionaria (MIR) in Venezuela. Urban terrorist groups were most active in Uruguay and in Argentina: the *tupamaros* and the *montoneros*, respectively. The links between all these movements and Castro, and the Soviet-inspired communist parties in the various Latin American countries were not always straightforward. In Colombia, where the movement had preceded the Cuban revolution, several organizations arose, with conflicting revolutionary views. Castro's support for revolutionary upheaval was evident in Venezuela, where the newly democratic regime of Rómulo Betancourt was threatened by a terrorist campaign in the early 1960s. Attempts to spread the Cuban revolutionary struggle to the continent became clearly evident in 1967, when Ernesto 'Che' Guevara (1928–67) set up a guerrilla group in Bolivia. After failing to attract the support of the local peasantry and having alienated his fellow communists in Bolivia, Guevara's adventure ended in disaster a few months later, when he was captured and executed by the army. The use of violence to attain socialist goals gained more justification among certain intellectual circles, after the Chilean army overthrew the Marxist-inspired government of Salvador Allende (1908–73) in 1973. In general, however, revolutionary violence was not a successful venture, except when employed in the struggle against some Central American

tyrannies, such as that of Anastasio Somoza in Nicaragua, where the FSLN took power in 1979. Elsewhere, violence merely served to undermine law and order, to polarize societies and to destabilize the democratic process.

Military Regimes. In 1961, Fidel Castro, leading an increasingly militarized regime, declared his adherence to Marxist-Leninism. A year later, after attempts to install Soviet missiles in Cuba, only 145 km from the coast of Florida, the world was close to a nuclear confrontation between the two superpowers (see THE WORLD IN THE 20TH CENTURY: THE GLOBAL COLD WAR). In order to prevent the spread of communism, President John Kennedy had launched his Alliance for Progress in 1961, a programme aimed at sponsoring development in Latin America within a democratic framework. Structural reforms were encouraged in Chile and Colombia, with uneven results. However, the polarized atmosphere frequently resulted in a succession of military takeovers, for example in Argentina, Brazil, Peru, and Ecuador. Coups even took place in Uruguay and Chile – countries with a long democratic tradition. Nevertheless, some countries, such as Mexico, Venezuela, Costa Rica, and Colombia, escaped military rule during this period.

Formerly, army officers had occasionally been instrumental in arbitrating conflict or in supporting individual ambitions in the struggles for power in Latin America. By contrast, the armed forces that displaced civilian politicians after the mid-1960s adopted a corporate approach towards the state, assuming the role of national saviour, and instituting an extreme and systematic repression of political and civil rights. In Brazil, the military promoted the process of industrialization, backed

▲ **Che Guevara**
An Argentinian who trained as a doctor, Guevara became an archetypal symbol of revolution for activists around the world. He was involved in revolutionary movements in Guatemala, Cuba, and Bolivia.

◄ **The Chilean Military Junta**
After overthrowing the democratically elected Marxist government of Salvador Allende in a violent CIA-backed coup in 1973, the regime of General Augusto Pinochet (third from right) introduced monetarist economic policies and moved to stifle internal dissent. Many liberal and left-wing Chileans went into exile during this period.

Petroleum Production in Latin America ▶

Lake Maracaibo (shown here) in northwestern Venezuela is the centre of the petroleum industry in Latin America. Thousands of derricks rise up from the lake as oil is now drilled in an area 40 km long and 12 km wide. Underwater pipelines carry the petroleum to storage tanks ashore. The industry was developed largely by foreign investment, yet, in 1975, it was nationalized.

The 1980s Depression

During the global economic depression of the 1980s, the real per capita expenditure of Latin American governments fell drastically. According to International Monetary Fund statistics, across the whole region, government spending fell by an average of 16.8%, while in some countries, this figure was much higher (20.2% in Chile, 29.3% in Argentina, and 30.6% in Uruguay).

by a technocracy that aspired to modernize the country. The Peruvian army that took power in 1968 attempted a revolution from above with disastrous consequences: agrarian reform decreased agricultural production and further impoverished the rural population, encouraging mass migration to the cities. In Argentina, the army finally came to terms with Perón, who was allowed to return from exile in 1973. Yet Perón's death in 1974 left the country in chaos, in the midst of an escalating campaign of terror from extremists on both sides. In 1976, exposed in its mishandling of the economy and beleaguered by accusations of gross abuses of human rights, the military establishment was discredited. In April 1982, the head of the military junta, General Leopoldo Galtieri (1926–   ), committed his forces to an invasion of the Falkland Islands/ Islas Malvinas, to which Argentina has laid a territorial claim since Great Britain took possession of the islands in 1833. After its defeat, the Argentine army began to surrender power at home. In Chile, the regime was identified with the personal rule of General Augusto Pinochet (1915–   ), around whom the army closed ranks after the overthrow of Salvador Allende. There followed 16 years of dictatorship, which ended in 1990 when Pinochet, internationally isolated and pressed at home to liberalize the system, decided to allow a return to electoral politics. Yet Pinochet managed to remain as the head of the armed forces and, as such, continued to play a significant role in the new phase of Chilean democracy.

The Lost Decade. Chile, Colombia, and Paraguay were the only Latin American economies that did not experience negative growth in the 1980s. For the rest of the conti-

nent, the 1980s were a period of serious economic crisis reflected in hyperinflation, diminishing trade and investment, unemployment, deteriorating living conditions, and mounting debt. In August 1982, the Mexican authorities announced their inability to repay foreign loans. Throughout the 1970s, a surplus of credit – mostly from Arab countries produced by a rise in oil prices, and channelled through banks in the USA, Europe, and Japan – led to a large influx of capital to Latin America. These loans were used to finance public projects, but were also directed towards military expenditure. By the early 1980s, it was evident that Latin American governments had borrowed far beyond their capacity to repay.

DEVELOPMENT IN AMAZONIA

The industrialization of unexploited areas surrounding the Amazon Basin has helped the repayment of foreign debt by some Latin American countries, but has caused social and environmental problems. The discovery of vast deposits of iron ore in the Guiana Highlands in the south of Venezuela and in the Carajás Mountains in the Pará region of Brazil has meant extensive deforestation and dispossession of indigenous Amerindian peoples. The Carajás project is a huge operation funded by European grants. In addition, ranching activities by settlers has further contributed to a displacement of traditional communities. In an attempt to stem indiscriminate development, the Brazilian government set aside a large area of wilderness as a protected zone.

The crisis was triggered by a rise in interest rates in the USA, followed by a recession in the world economy. The debt crisis was widespread in Latin America, although the bulk of the burden was shared by five countries: Brazil, Mexico, Argentina, Venezuela, and Chile. Since the early 1980s, significant efforts were made to alleviate the problem, involving international financial institutions, such as the International Monetary Fund and the World Bank. Yet in the early 1990s, only Mexico, Colombia, Chile, and Uruguay were fully meeting their obligations. Nevertheless, by then it was felt that the worst of the crisis was over, as a result of a combination of factors – the restructuring of Latin American economies, debt renegotiations, and a renewed impetus in world markets.

Return to Democracy. By the late 1970s the military were in retreat in Ecuador and Peru. Defeated in war in the South Atlantic and incapable of running a country devastated by economic problems, the Argentine military junta relinquished power: in 1983 the radical Raúl Alfonsín (1927–) was elected president after defeating the Peronist party at the polls. By the mid-1980s other military regimes, such as those of Brazil and Uruguay, had been supplanted by democratic regimes. In 1989, Patricio Aylwin (1918–), backed by a coalition of Christian Democrat and Socialist parties (La Concertación), won the presidential election in Chile. In Paraguay, the long-standing regime (1954–89) of Alfredo Stroessner (1912–) ended without military intervention. In Haiti in September 1994, the military junta that had ousted the democratically elected president, Jean-Bertrand Aristide (1953–) in 1991 was forced to accept a friendly occupation by the USA that restored the deposed president. Cuba, ideologically isolated after the collapse of the Soviet Union, was an exception to a clear democratic trend.

Countries that did not suffer military dictatorships (e.g. Mexico and Colombia) were also implementing reforms aimed at strengthening their political systems. In Mexico President Carlos Salinas de Gortari, who came to power tainted by electoral fraud in 1988, encouraged some electoral reforms. After years of frustrated attempts, Colombia incorporated some guerrilla groups into the political process, while a new constitution, approved in 1991, opened the way for new forms of political participation and secured greater human rights. Elsewhere in the continent, the re-emergent democracies showed some signs of vitality. In Argentina, President Alfonsín was defeated by the Peronist Carlos Menem (1931–), who was elected president in 1989. In Chile, Aylwin completed his mandate, presiding over an economy that continued to grow: his succes-

sor Eduardo Frei won the 1993 election. Charged with allegations of corruption, two heads of state – Fernando Collor de Mello (1949–) in Brazil and Carlos Andrés Pérez (1922–) in Venezuela – resigned without major constitutional disruption ensuing.

Problems and Prospects. In Peru, following his electoral victory in 1989, President Alberto Fujimori (1938–) dissolved Congress and assumed dictatorial powers with army support. Fujimori managed to stem violence by the Maoist terrorist group Sendero Luminoso and accepted a return to constitutional order. In 1995, Fujimori was re-elected. His popularity peaked following his forceful resolution of the protracted Japanese embassy hostage crisis in Lima in 1997. Despite nationwide protests against what Peruvians saw as Fujimori's increasingly authoritarian rule, the government in 1998 approved his bid to stand for election to a third term of office.

In Mexico, rebellions broke out, in 1994, in the poor southern state of Chiapas and, in 1996, in the state of Guerrero. Economic crisis and austerity measures provoked anti-government protests, while the domination of the ruling PRI was challenged by opposition parties. Negotiations with rebel groups failed to yield results; however, the PRI agreed an electoral reform pact with the main opposition parties and achieved a strong economic recovery by 1997. Ongoing conflicts between military and civilian authorities in Chile in the transition of power from the Pinochet regime had yet to be fully resolved. In Venezuela, economic crisis and social unrest posed serious challenges to the traditional parties. Political violence by guerrilla organizations and drugs cartels in Colombia began to be quelled by the

We are tired of discrimination. In Guatemala, we indigenous people are 65% of the total population; if we exist, it isn't because we have been wanted, but because we have known how to hold on to things, because we have known how to form our own organizations, to build that future which we so desire. And it has cost us dearly – so many dead – but in spite of it all we have an immense future. It is our hope that the conflict will end on the basis of justice, on the basis of equality, on the basis of significant change in the structures that have until now dominated us and imposed the conditions in which we live.

Rigoberta Menchu, Guatemalan civil rights campaigner, 1992

◀ **Alberto Fujimori**
The son of Japanese immigrants to Peru, Fujimori trained as an agronomist and only entered politics relatively late. During the 1989 presidential election campaign, he increased his support dramatically, finally securing victory over his rival with over 56% of the popular vote.

◄ **Mexico City** *With a population estimated at well over 20 million, Mexico City is one of the world's largest cities. In this huge conurbation, air pollution has become a serious problem.*

Population Growth in Mexico *Mexico provides a striking example of the rapid growth in population evident throughout Latin America. Feeding and housing this increased population are major challenges facing the continent. This graph indicates the growth in the Mexican population (in millions) from 1900 onwards.* ▼

strenuous efforts of the government, aided by US drug-enforcement agencies. However, allegations of presidential involvement in drugs cartels caused a political crisis in 1996. Relations with the USA deteriorated as Colombian government efforts to eradicate drugs crops met with guerrilla offensives, which continued in 1998 despite fresh peace initiatives by newly elected president Andrés

Pastrana. Protests against government privatization plans were staged in early 1997.

The prospects for sustained democracy and stability in Latin America nevertheless appear bright. By the mid-1990s, the results of an intense drive towards democracy were felt throughout the continent. Paraguay held its first multiparty elections in 1993 while Ecuador began to train its armed forces. However, both countries have suffered political instability as a result of attempts to implement privatization and free market policies. In Haiti, presidential and congressional elections were successfully held in 1995, but hostility to privatization plans and austerity measures led to strikes and violent protests. The ending of years of civil conflict in El Salvador, in 1992, and in Guatemala, in 1996, forced these countries to face the difficult transformation from revolutionary to constitutional politics. The Earth Summit, held in Rio de Janeiro in 1992, forced governments to address environmental issues of both domestic and international concern.

Political reform has gone hand in hand with economic reform. Most countries have implemented drastic measures to restructure their finances. These have not always been successful; both Brazil and Argentina experienced financial crises in 1995. However, far from the economic nationalism of the past, the renewed Latin American economies have aimed at strengthening their links with international markets. Both political and economic reforms have served to foster closer ties with Europe and the USA. In December 1993 the North American Free Trade Agreement (NAFTA) between Mexico, the USA, and Canada was finally approved by all parties; see BUSINESS AND FINANCE (VOL. 6): INTERNATIONAL TRADE/REGIONAL TRADING BLOCS. Elsewhere, in South and Central America, subregional organizations, such as Mercosur and the Andean Community, promoting economic integration have regained impetus. Real efforts have also been made to resolve long-standing border disputes, such as those between Ecuador and Peru, and Argentina and Chile.

It is still too early to judge the long-term impact of economic reforms, but newly elected governments have given priority to social policies with the aim of spreading more evenly the benefits of economic growth. Meanwhile, there has been growing concern about the need to strengthen state institutions, which could guarantee the durability of the new continental order.

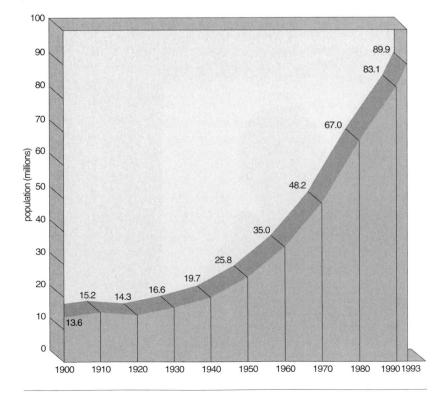

ASIA AND
OCEANIA

Early China

Legendary period • The rise of central authority • Age of the philosophers • Early Korea

Archaeological evidence indicates that early Chinese civilization developed on north China's Central Plains, along the River Wei and the southern bend of the Huang He (Yellow) River. Two distinct Neolithic cultures emerged here: the **Painted Pottery** (or *Yangshao*) culture (5000–3000 BC), and the **Black Pottery** (or *Longshan*) culture (3000–2200 BC). Painted pottery artefacts, typified by large storage vessels, have been unearthed primarily in the western Central Plains. The more advanced Black Pottery culture emerged at the same time in the eastern part of the plains, from where it spread. In addition, parallel contemporary Neolithic cultures have more recently been discovered at sites in the Lower Yangzi region and in southeast China. These finds indicate the existence of several distinct cultural regions in what was to become China.

Legendary Period
The peoples of the Neolithic cultures left no written records; subsequent traditional accounts, therefore, reveal a mythical history.

Fu Xi is known as the originator of fishing and inventor of pictographs, which developed into the Chinese written language. Shen Nong is said to have developed agriculture. The 'Yellow Emperor' is credited with inventing bricks for construction and with correcting the calendar.

Among the later legendary sage rulers, Yao and Shun are regarded as ideal emperors. Their successor, Yu the Great, is credited with draining off the flood waters, rendering the land habitable. The realm was inherited by his son, Qi. The dynasty thus founded (c. 2200) was the first of the Three Dynasties of Xia, Shang, and Zhou.

The Rise of Central Authority
Although traditional Chinese historical accounts show the Three Dynasties as succeeding one another, they seem to have coexisted in different parts of the Central Plains. While there is no solid evidence for the Xia, recent excavations at Erlitou, near Luoyang, may have unearthed its capital.

According to Chinese tradition, the last Xia ruler was so depraved that the people revolted. A new dynasty was founded, named Shang (c. 1600–c. 1050 BC), which has been proved to be fully historical by the excavation of inscribed oracle bones and bronze ritual vessels at its last capital, near Anyang.

Western Zhou. The Zhou people lived in the Wei Valley, west of the great bend of the Huang He (Yellow) River, close to the nomadic barbarians of the northwest. The Zhou were probably vassals of Shang; in c. 1050 BC they destroyed their overlords and succeeded in established their own rule over the expanding Chinese cultural area.

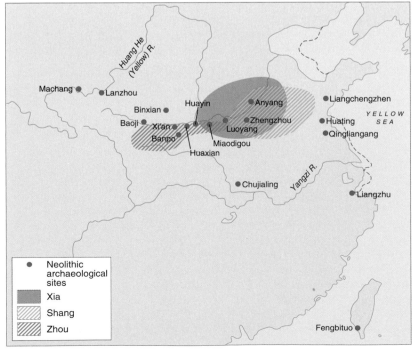

◄ **Early China** *Artefacts of the Yangshao (Painted Pottery) and the Longshan (Black Pottery) cultures, dating from 5000–3000 BC and 3000–2200 BC respectively, have been discovered at the sites shown. They identify the two main neolithic groups that occupied central and northwest China. The location of the first Three Dynasties of Xia, Shang, and Zhou are also shown.*

▲ **Shang Bronze Vessel** *Although the use of bronze during the Shang period (16th–11th centuries BC) was largely limited to ritual objects, three- and four-legged vessels, such as that shown here, were also used for practical purposes, and could be placed over a fire.*

Since the primitive communication methods of the time made it impossible to administer directly so large an area, the early rulers of Zhou set up a feudal system by delegating authority to a large number of vassals. Each relatively autonomous principality was in essence a small city-state, consisting of a walled town and its surrounding countryside.

The authority of the Zhou kings also derived from their important religious and ceremonial role. The chief Zhou deity was Tian, which came to mean 'Heaven'; as the deity was a human ancestor, the Zhou kings adopted the title 'Son of Heaven'; they justified their conquest of Shang on the grounds that they had received the 'Mandate of Heaven.'

Eastern Zhou. Over time the bonds of loyalty between the Zhou kings and their vassals weakened. In 771 BC the Zhou royal domain in the Xi'an area was conquered by an alliance of 'barbarians' and Chinese rebels. Although the royal line was re-established at Luoyang, in the east, the Zhou kings now held virtually no political or military power, retaining only certain religious and ceremonial functions. Real power was exercised by a number of emerging larger territorial states – such as Qi in the east, Yan in the north, Chu in the south, and Qin in the west – on the periphery of the Chinese cultural area. Engaged in perpetual struggles for supremacy, these independent states absorbed the smaller principalities.

Age of the Philosophers

While the late Zhou period (770 BC–256 BC) was characterized by constant warfare, it was also a time of great economic growth, social change, and intellectual ferment. In response to these challenges, attention was increasingly devoted to methods of government and political philosophy. Rulers wanting to preserve their position sought the advice of the scholar class – part of a new class of bureaucrats, produced by the spread of literacy and the needs of an increasingly complex political system. Thus the early Chinese philosophers were first of all practical politicians. Their disciples gradually formed themselves into schools of philosophy, which eventually produced the classical philosophical literature of late Zhou. Among the 'Hundred Schools of Thought' that flourished at this time, three are noteworthy.

Confucianism. Kong Zi, or Confucius (551–479 BC), was the founder of what was to become a remarkable ethical tradition. The disorder that reigned in his own time, he felt, could be corrected if there was a return to the political and social order created by the founders of the Zhou dynasty. He propounded the idea that good government was fundamentally a matter of morality, insisting that the ruler must set an example of proper ethical conduct.

Daoism. Next to Confucianism, the most important school of Chinese thought is Daoism. It was largely a philosophy of retreat and withdrawal by those who were appalled by perpetual warfare and, thus, did not strive to gain power, status, and wealth. The all-embracing mystical concept of the ***Dao*** (literally 'path' or 'way') was that a person's only concern should be to fit into the great pattern of nature. The Daoist sage would rule without effort and without benevolence, accomplishing everything by doing nothing (*wu wei*).

Legalism. The Legalists sought to secure and maintain a ruler's absolute power and strengthen the state. To this end they advocated a strict system of rewards and punishments, which would apply to all. The group of philosophers and politicians that developed these ideas were closely associated with the rising state of Qin (see CLASSICAL CHINA).

Early Korea

Outside the Chinese cultural area during the Neolithic period, the early Koreans were apparently tribal peoples who gradually adopted an agricultural lifestyle. Their ancestors had migrated to the peninsula from Siberia and Manchuria. Linguistically the Koreans are related to the Altaic peoples of north Asia. They probably lived under hereditary aristocratic chieftains, semi-religious in character. During the Bronze Age this communal clan-centred society gave way to walled town-states. The kingdom of Chosŏn, in the basins of the Liao and Taedong rivers, was among the most advanced.

▲ **Confucius** *(or Kong Zi, 'Master Kong') A native of the state of Lu (in central eastern China), he was China's first great moralist.*

▲ **Early Chinese Pictographs** *The earliest Chinese writing systems used pictures to represent objects and activities. Many archaic pictographs are clearly the ancestors of modern Chinese characters. The pictographs shown here, from the Shang period, depict common methods of carrying objects that are still employed in modern China.*

Classical China

Qin rule • The Han dynasty • The fall of Han

═══SEE ALSO═══
This section:
• Early China
• The Period of Disunity
**The Visual Arts Worldwide
(vol. 4):**
• Chinese Art
• Korean Art
Religion (vol. 6):
• Other Religions of
  India and the Far East

commandery
An administrative
unit of the central
government of early Han
China. Commanderies
(jun) were established
as distinct from the
principalities (guo),
which were autonomous
feudal entities.

Between 230 and 221 BC the state of Qin completed the unification of China by conquering its remaining rivals in rapid succession. King Zheng (c. 259 BC–?210 BC), the ambitious ruler of Qin, adopted the imperial title Shihuangdi ('first emperor'). In addition to the conquest of the Chinese cultural area, some of the 'barbarian' peoples south of the Yangzi River were brought under Qin control.

Qin Rule

To consolidate these conquests and boost the economy, King Zheng laid a radiating system of roads, unified weights and measures, and standardized the coinage. Legalist principles of government were also now extended to the entire empire: application of a centralized hierarchical system of administration; adoption of the Qin system of equal impersonal laws; and the concentration of the remaining hereditary nobles at Xianyang, the Qin capital of the Wei Valley. The destruction of books and the execution of scholars considered to be a threat to the ruler's interests were ordered.

The Failure of Qin. Zheng's dynasty survived his own death in 210 BC by only four years. His success had been too sudden and too severe; surviving scholars and noblemen were repelled by his brutal assault on the old order, while the common people were alienated by the harsh exaction of taxes and forced labour to build palaces, roads, canals, and China's first Great Wall, as well as for campaigns abroad. In the face of mounting opposition, the short-lived empire collapsed into rebellion.

The Han Dynasty

Having destroyed his rivals, Liu Bang (256–195 BC), one of the rebel generals, declared himself emperor in 206 BC, founding the lasting and glorious Han dynasty. He established his capital at Chang'an (modern Xi'an), near the old Qin capital. His descendants reigned for more than four centuries. Even today the Chinese refer to themselves as 'men of Han.'

Dynastic Consolidation. The success of the first Han emperor, best known by his posthumous title Gaozu ('High Progenitor'; reigned 206–195 BC), can be attributed to several factors. Although Legalism was discredited, Han Gaozu retained the practical aspects of Qin statecraft; he modified centralized rule by instituting a system combining bureaucratic and feudal administrators. Later emperors gradually reduced the power of the remaining hereditary princes, replacing them with men of talent, and learned to run the bureaucracy of central government.

As a man of humble origins, Han Gaozu was able to appreciate the concerns and needs of the common people. He lessened their tax burden and reduced the severity of punishments. In return, the people supported the new dynasty. Han Gaozu had, therefore, won the 'Mandate of Heaven.'

Expansion of Han. During the long reign (141 to 87 BC) of Han Wudi ('Martial Emperor') the empire expanded. The small states on the south coast, in Zhejiang and Fujian, were the first to come under Han control. In 111 BC the semi-Sinicized state of Nanyue (in modern Guangdong, Guangxi, and northern Vietnam) was annexed. These conquests

Map labels: XIONGNU TRIBES; Great Wall; GOBI DESERT; Conquered 109–106 BC; Huang He (Yellow) R.; YELLOW SEA; Luoyang; Huang He (Yellow) R.; Chang'an; QIN EMPIRE (221–206 BC); Yangzi R.; Xianyang; SOUTH CHINA SEA

Legend:
China in 206 BC
Boundary of former Han Empire
Territory added under former Han (106 BC–8 AD)
Territory added under later Han (25–220 AD)

◄ **The Han Empire** *Between 206 BC and 220 AD, the empire expanded into the south, the west, and the north. The greatest period of expansion was under Emperor Han Wudi (141–87 BC).*

The Great Wall *Situated in northern China, the wall* ▶
was begun in 214 BC as a defence against nomadic
tribes; it was largely rebuilt in the 15th and 16th
centuries. It is some 9 m high, with numerous
watchtowers along its length (c. 6400 km).

prepared the way for the southward expansion of the Chinese people in later centuries.

In the north, between 129 and 119 BC, Han Wudi dispatched several armies, some numbering as many as 150 000 men, against the perennial threat of the Xiongnu tribal confederation (later known in the West as Huns); these forces managed to destroy Xiongnu power south of the Gobi Desert.

Korea. In 108 BC Han Wudi overthrew the semi-Sinicized state of Chosŏn in northern Korea and southern Manchuria, setting up at modern Pyongyang the **commandery** of Lelang, which was to remain an outpost of the Chinese Empire until 313 AD. Only the area to the south of the Han River remained outside Chinese control during Wudi's reign.

Against the background of rising conflict with China, the formation and expansion of the confederated kingdom of Koguryŏ took place. Koguryŏ fought its most violent battle against the Xin dynasty of Wang Mang (45 BC–23 AD) in 12 AD.

Imperial Confucianism. During Han Wudi's reign Confucianism became the predominant philosophy of the court. However, it became a synthesis of ancient philosophies and current superstitions, rather than the pure ethical teachings of Confucius and Mencius (c. 371–289 BC). Nevertheless, the imperial Confucianism of Han became the philosophy of the bureaucrats and educated men who worked within what was formerly a purely Legalist type of government. This development marks the beginning of an efficient bureaucracy operated through a system of education based on Confucian texts. The cultural solidarity of China's elite resulting from this system assured the administration of a vast empire; it was a major factor in the lasting power of the Chinese imperial system, providing the forerunner to a modern civil service system based on merit.

The Fall of Han

Towards the end of the early Han period, weaknesses appeared in the empire, stemming from the greatly increased population, the consequent decline of per-capita acreage, and the flight of peasants, trying to avoid the greater burden of taxes, to the untaxed estates of local power holders. The remaining tax-paying peasants elsewhere were consequently left with a heavier tax burden on a smaller agricultural base. As state revenues declined,

the institutions of central government functioned less efficiently.

Wang Mang's Interregnum 9–23 AD. In 8 AD Wang Mang, who had sought to stem the tide of decline by vigorous reforms, usurped the throne and established his Xin ('new') dynasty. His daring attempt to 'nationalize' the private estates provoked great opposition from those with entrenched interests. Increasing hardship, aggravated by widespread famine, erupted into a popular uprising in 18 AD. The capital was sacked by rebel forces and Wang Mang was killed in 23 AD.

Later Han. One of the rebels, Liu Xiu, a descendent of the Han emperors, emerged victorious in the ensuing power struggle. Declaring himself emperor in 25 AD, he re-established the Han dynastic name and set up his capital at Luoyang.

Despite the cultural brilliance of the later Han period, the familiar economic and social problems that had beset the last years of the former Han soon re-emerged. Major challenges to a succession of ineffectual emperors were made by relatives of the imperial family; the perennial conflict between scholar-officials and powerful court eunuchs was also a factor in the decline of the Han. The dynasty was further weakened by two Daoist-inspired rebellions, which broke out in 184: the Yellow Turbans in eastern China, and the Five Pecks of Rice band in Sichuan. In 220 the later Han dynasty finally collapsed, the **dynastic cycle** having run its course.

The Dynastic Cycle

The Chinese have traditionally interpreted their past as a series of dynastic cycles, comprising a heroic founding, a period of great power, a long decline, and finally total collapse. The symptoms of dynastic decline were:
- reign by weak and depraved emperors;
- heavy taxation;
- administrative inefficiency, official corruption, and bureaucratic factionalism;
- the assumption of power by eunuchs;
- natural disasters; and
- the rise of rebellion.

CHINESE DYNASTIES

THE HISTORY OF ORGANIZED society in China stretches back over almost 4000 years, making it one of the oldest civilizations in the world. The development of a strictly hierarchical society (headed by a ruling dynasty) in China as early as the 2nd millenium BC, demonstrates how advanced Chinese civilization was in this early period. Early Chinese art and architecture also serve to confirm the sophistication of China's youngest cultures. See THE VISUAL ARTS WORLDWIDE (VOL. 4): CHINESE ART.

There has, however, been much debate among scholars worldwide over China's early history, owing to a lack of conclusive evidence and to the legendary histories that have survived through the millenia; the chart below represents an outline of the approach adopted for the section on China in this volume.

Tradition holds that the first Chinese emperor was Fu Xi, who is said to have been born in the 29th century BC, while China's first dynasty, the Xia, is regarded as legendary, as no evidence has yet been found to authenticate it. China's first historical ruling dynasty was the Shang, which came to control an area in the Huang He River valley in the 17th century BC. Although such early dynasties as the Shang and the Zhou did not control a unified Chinese state, their cultural influence was extensive. Unified rule, however, was established for the first time under the Qin dynasty, while under the Han the Chinese state was greatly expanded.

The chart shows each period or dynasty of Chinese history (first column) with its dates (second column); it also reflects the pattern of unity and partition that characterized the imperial era (third column), when the empire twice disintegrated and different areas were ruled by separate dynasties; the division of China's history into cultural periods (fourth column) is also shown, for example, the emergence of city-states during the Shang dynasty has been used to define that period of Chinese culture.

CHART OF CHINESE HISTORY

PERIOD/DYNASTY	DATES	UNITY/PARTITION OF EMPIRE	CULTURAL PERIODS
Painted Pottery (Yangshao) culture	c. 5000–c. 3000 BC		NEOLITHIC TRIBALISM
Black Pottery (Longshan) culture	c. 3000–c. 2200 BC		
Xia (legendary) dynasty	c. 2200–c. 1600 BC		
Shang dynasty	c. 1600–c. 1050 BC		CITY-STATES
Western Zhou dynasty	c. 1050–771 BC		
Eastern Zhou dynasty	770–256 BC		TERRITORIAL STATES
Qin dynasty	221–206 BC	Imperial Unity	
Han dynasty	206 BC–220 AD		
Wei dynasty	220–265	First Partition	
Shu Han dynasty	221–263		
Wu dynasty	222–280		
Jin dynasty	265–420		
Northern and Southern dynasties	420–589		
Sui dynasty	581–618	Imperial Unity	
Tang dynasty	618–907		EMPIRE
Ten Kingdoms Period	907–960	Second Partition	
Liao dynasty	907–1125		
Northern Song dynasty	960–1127		
Southern Song dynasty	1127–1279		
Yuan (Mongol) dynasty	1271–1368	Imperial Unity	
Ming dynasty	1368–1644		
Qing dynasty	1644–1912		
Republic of China	1912–1949		POSTIMPERIAL
People's Republic of China	1949–		

The Period of Disunity

Northern and southern dynasties • The coming of Buddhism •
Confederated kingdoms in Korea

After the outbreak of the popular revolts at the end of the Han dynasty (220), some of the imperial generals became virtually independent warlords. A three-way division of power gradually developed among the leading commanders, with Cao Cao (155–220) in the north, Liu Bei (162–223) in Sichuan, and Sun Quan (181–251) in the Lower Yangzi region and in the south. On Cao Cao's death, his son usurped the Han throne, naming his dynasty the Wei. In 221 Liu Bei established the Shu Han dynasty, and in 222 Sun Quan founded the Wu dynasty. The period of the Three Kingdoms (220–80) was one of incessant warfare. After a brief unification under the western Jin, between 280 and 304, the empire disintegrated once more.

Northern and Southern Dynasties

Non-Chinese Rule in the North. As a result of the disintegration of the imperial system, China was increasingly defenceless against the nomadic peoples of the north. From 304 to 439 north China was fought over and ruled by rival, partly Sinicized, 'barbarian' groups, known to history as the Sixteen Kingdoms. By 439, one tribe, the Toba from the northeast, had finally managed to establish a lasting government, which unified the north. In 386 the Toba founded the Northern Wei dynasty (386–535); in 494 they moved their capital to Luoyang. The process of cultural assimilation of the non-Chinese ruling class accelerated under this dynasty.

Succession States of the South. In 317 a Jin prince in south China declared himself emperor at Jiankang (modern Nanjing). His dynasty is known as the Eastern Jin, the first of a succession known as the Six Dynasties. Large numbers of Chinese fled the chaotic conditions of the north for the relative safety of the warmer more fertile area along and south of the Yangzi River.

The Coming of Buddhism

During this period of disunity (220–580), foreign peoples and influences seriously challenged Chinese civilization. One major stimulus was Buddhism, which Indian traders and travellers were carrying by sea to southern China. It also spread overland via the Silk Road to northern China, where the non-Chinese invaders were prepared to accept it, partly owing to the fact that, like themselves, it came from outside the old order over which they were now exercising control. For the Chinese upper class who had fled to the south, Buddhism offered solace and an intellectually satisfying explanation for the collapse of the old society. Emperors and commoners alike sought religious salvation in an age of social disintegration.

Confederated Kingdoms in Korea

Chinese control over much of Korea weakened with the fall of the Han dynasty. As the Chinese commanderies disappeared in the 4th century, three rival kingdoms reasserted Korean control of the peninsula: Koguryŏ in the north, Paekche in the southwest, and Silla in the southeast. From the late 4th century, Koguryŏ was the paramount power; during the course of the 6th century, however, Silla began to increase its influence.

▲ **Guan-yin**
The Buddhist deity of infinite compassion and mercy was worshipped in China from as early as the 1st century AD and had been introduced into all Buddhist temples by the 6th century.

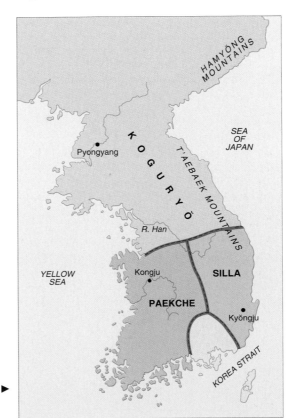

Korea (c. 400 AD) *The Three Kingdoms of Koguryŏ, Paekche, and Silla developed highly advanced cultures and accepted Buddhism.* ▶

The Sui-Tang Reunification

Sui rule • The Tang dynasty • Decline of Tang

Tang China
(618–907) At its height, Tang China was a highly centralized state, served by an effective transportation system (comprising roads and canals). This linked the provinces with Chang'an, the large and sophisticated capital of Tang. The Silk Road brought trade and foreign embassies from far afield, enriching the empire both materially and culturally. ▼

In 581 Yang Jian (died 604), a general of mixed Chinese and Xianbei blood, overthrew the last of the Sixteen Kingdoms in the north. He established the Sui dynasty, ruling as Emperor Wendi. The Sui, and its successors, the Tang, reinstated stable centralized government in China, which reunified the empire. The Sui-Tang period (580–907) was also one of cultural growth and sophistication, stimulated by international trade and the continued spread of Buddhism.

Sui Rule

In 589 Emperor Wendi conquered the Chen dynasty of the south, thus restoring the unified Chinese Empire. A strong centralized government was re-established for all of China, enabling the prosperity and prestige of the Chinese Empire to be fully restored. However, like their Qin predecessors, the Sui rulers were too ambitious.

Wendi was succeeded by his son who became the second Sui emperor, Yangdi ('Zealous Emperor'; reigned 604–18). He alienated his people by waging frequent foreign wars and by making great demands for labour for the construction of canals, walls, and palaces. The prestige of the dynasty was further damaged

KEY SUI-TANG RULERS	
Yang Jian (or Wendi)	581–604
Yangdi	604–18
Taizong	626–49
Gaozong	649–83
Empress Wu	690–705
Xuanzong (Minghuang)	712–56
Wuzong	840–46

by a disastrous campaign, in 612, against the Korean kingdom of Koguryŏ. When Sui forces were heavily defeated by the eastern Turks in 615, the empire started to disintegrate. Sui Yangdi was assassinated in 618.

The Tang Dynasty

The man who emerged victorious from the scramble that followed the collapse of Sui was Li Shimin (600–49), who was of mixed blood and came from the north. He captured the capital, Chang'an, in 617; in the following year he founded the Tang dynasty, and placed his father on the throne. Having eliminated his brothers and forced his father to abdicate in 626, he ruled in his own name

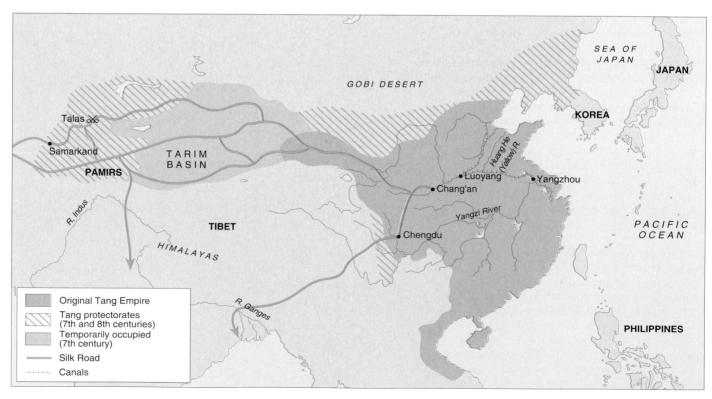

Original Tang Empire
Tang protectorates (7th and 8th centuries)
Temporarily occupied (7th century)
Silk Road
Canals

◀ **Emperor Taizong** *Taizong was the second Tang emperor, under whose reign (626–49) the empire reached its first high point.*

imperial patronage of the early Tang, but especially under Empress Wu. While the Chinese were modifying Buddhist ideas, they were also remoulding its institutions to facilitate their assimilation into Chinese society.

Gradually the great Buddhist monasteries, with their rich estates, came to be seen as a fiscal menace to the state, since land and men were removed from the tax registers. Thus there were intermittent persecutions, the most significant of which took place in 841–45 under Emperor Wuzong (reigned 840–46), who had become an ardent Daoist. The politically inspired persecutions severely weakened the institutional power of Buddhism in China.

Social Change. Tang China witnessed remarkable growth and a refinement of Chinese culture. Significant economic changes contributed to a great shift in the balance of society, as the ruling class gradually came to be more broadly based. The power of aristocratic families declined considerably with the appearance of a fully developed civil service **examination system**.

Tang Cosmopolitanism. During the early Tang period, China was pervaded by a spirit of cultural tolerance. Buddhism continued to be a vehicle for, and stimulus to, close contact with distant areas. A growing international trade by sea and by land brought the Chinese

Examination System

As part of the Tang drive to open the channels of bureaucratic mobility, several regular examinations, which tested classical scholarship, law, calligraphy, mathematics, and literary skills, were introduced. The latter eventually became the chief, and most prestigious, route to high government office.

until 649. Known to history as Taizong ('Great Ancestor'), his reign is considered the first high point of the Tang era.

However, the Tang dynasty was almost terminated by the Empress Wu (625–705); she dominated the later years of the reign of Emperor Gaozong ('High Ancestor'; 649–83) and, after his death, ruled through puppet emperors. In 690 she assumed the title of empress for herself and changed the dynastic name to Zhou. Although she has been condemned as a usurper by Chinese historians, she was in fact a strong and able ruler, greatly furthering the supremacy of the merit bureaucracy over the aristocracy. Her reign came to an end after a palace coup in 705.

The next able Tang ruler to ascend the throne was Xuanzong ('Mysterious Ancestor'), also known as Minghuang ('Enlightened Emperor'). His long reign (712–56) represents the second high point of the dynasty.

Buddhism and the State. Just as the Chinese incorporated the 'barbarians' into the expanding empire, they also gradually absorbed Buddhism. It continued to flourish, both economically and intellectually, under the

◀ **Tang Pottery Figure** *(8th century) The merchants who carried goods along the Silk Road to China were usually nomadic peoples of central and western Asia. This glazed pottery figure illustrates the amusement with which the Tang Chinese regarded such traders.*

Yang Guifei

Tang emperor Xuanzong (reigned 712–56) had a famous romance with the consort Yang Guifei (died 756), considered to be one of the four most beautiful women in China at the time. Intrigues at court and the An Lushan Rebellion (755), which marked the beginning of the end of the Tang dynasty, caused the emperor to flee to Sichuan. On the journey his soldiers mutinied and forced him to have his beloved Yang Guifei strangled as they blamed her for his downfall.

Emperor Minghuang's Journey to Shu *The scroll from which this detail is taken is probably a Song dynasty copy of an 8th-century original.*

various kingdoms in southeast, southern, and western Asia, recognized a moderate Chinese suzerainty by occasionally presenting tribute.

Tibet. Tibet, which had been unified for the first time in 607, initially accepted a degree of Chinese overlordship. As the Tibetan Empire grew stronger, however, relations with China became more hostile. In 763 the Tibetans sacked Chang'an, the Tang capital; their victory over Tang and Uighur forces near Beshbaliq, in 791, ended Chinese control over the protectorates in Inner Asia. The Tibetan threat ceased with the collapse of dynastic rule in 842, after which the country disintegrated into petty states.

Korea. Taizong's armies were twice repulsed by the Korean state of Koguryŏ; in 668, however, his successor Gaozong succeeded, with the help of the southeastern Korean kingdom of Silla, in crushing a coalition of Koguryŏ, Paekche, and Japanese elements. Thereafter Silla remained a loyal vassal of Tang. Towards the end of the 9th century, the central authority of Silla weakened, as the country was overrun by peasant uprisings. In the late 7th century, meanwhile, the rival state of Parhae had been established as successor to Koguryŏ in the northern part of the peninsula and what was later called Manchuria.

Decline of Tang

During Xuanzong's reign (712–56), Tang China was a far more populous and wealthy empire than it had been under Emperor Taizong. However, towards the end of his long reign signs of decay became apparent. Financial problems increased, and foreign military campaigns ended in disaster. The defeat of the Chinese armies, in 751, by the Arabs at the Battle of the Talas River, in Central Asia, was a turning point in east Asian history.

An Lushan Rebellion (755). Not long after the defeat at Talas, internal problems seriously weakened the dynasty. In 755 one of the powerful military governors of the border regions, An Lushan (703–57), rebelled. Although Emperor Xuanzong was restored to power, the revolt had dealt a serious blow to centralized government. As the system of regional commanders became established throughout the whole country, many of them exercised semi-independent control over their regions. The final break-up of the Tang Empire began with great uprisings in the north in 874. Finally, in 907, one of the regional commanders usurped the throne, bringing the dynasty to a formal end.

Chinese Buddhism
Buddhism continued to flourish under the patronage of the early Tang Empire. This imposing representation of Buddha was carved from rock at Leshan in Sichuan in the 8th century. It is some 70 m high, dwarfing those who stand at its base. ▼

into direct contact with the great centres of civilization in India and western Asia. Foreign exchanges brought to China many new agricultural products and some inventions. Tea, for example, was introduced from southeast Asia. Trade and foreign embassies brought thousands of foreigners to the Tang capital; with them came their many religions, such as Nestorian Christianity, Judaism, and Islam. At the same time, Chinese culture and statecraft continued to be adopted far afield.

Foreign Relations. In 630 Taizong subjugated the eastern Turks; in great campaigns in 639–40 and 647–48 he took the Tarim Basin from the western Turks. Chinese suzerainty was gradually extended beyond the Pamirs. Other states, such as Japan and

China's Middle Ages

The Song dynasty • China under Mongol rule • Koryŏ Korea

During the brief disintegration of centralized rule at the end of the Tang period (907), central and southern China were divided among various contending former regional commanders. There was a total of 14 such kingdoms, though official histories have grouped them together as the 'Ten Kingdoms.'

In northern China there were five successive and short-lived dynasties. New tribal 'barbarians' were, meanwhile, threatening China's borders. The Khitan (Qidan in Chinese) Mongols secured 16 border prefectures around Yanjing (modern Beijing), making them part of their Liao dynasty (907–1125).

The Song Dynasty

In 960 general Zhao Kuangyin overthrew the reigning later Zhou dynasty (951–60) in the north and founded the Song dynasty, which was to last until 1279. Known to history as Taizu ('Grand Progenitor'; reigned 960–76), the first Song emperor re-established centralized rule over much of China. However, northern Vietnam (Annam) was not reincorporated into the empire, nor did Song control extend over any part of Central Asia or the northern steppe. In the northwest the Song was pressurized by the Tangut kingdom known as Xi-Xia (western Xia), and was ultimately forced to pay tribute to both Liao and Xi-Xia.

Southern Song (1127–1279). In consequence of the Song's relative military weakness, the empire came under increasing pressure from internal uprisings and, more importantly, from external forces. Beyond the Liao, Tungusic tribes, known as the Jurchen (Ruzhen in Chinese), had gradually risen to power. They adopted the Chinese dynastic name of Jin ('Golden'; 1115–1234). In 1126 the Jurchen captured the Song capital Bianliang (modern Kaifeng) and pushed the Song southwards. The new capital of the southern Song Empire was set up at Lin'an (modern Hang-zhou) in Zheijiang.

The Medieval Economic Revolution. Although the southern Song Empire controlled only southern China, this area had become the economic heartland of China. As migrations of Han Chinese occupied the most productive parts of the south, rapid economic growth ensued, which supported significant scientific and technological advancement.

The reasons for this spectacular economic development include population growth and a considerable increase in agricultural productivity, including the double-cropping of rice. Technological advances included the abacus, gunpowder for weapons, further development of printing, and the beginnings of standardized mass production. Improvements in the techniques of shipbuilding (watertight bulkheads) and navigation (use of the magnetic compass) facilitated a flourishing maritime trade with India and the Middle East. China's imports consisted largely of horses from the steppes and luxury goods from the tropics. China exported printed books and art objects to Korea and Japan. Chinese copper disks, used

Urbanization and Prosperity *The detail from this scroll by Zhang Zeduan (thought to represent the northern Song capital of Kaifeng at the end of the 11th century) illustrates the urban commercial culture that thrived under Song rule.* ▼

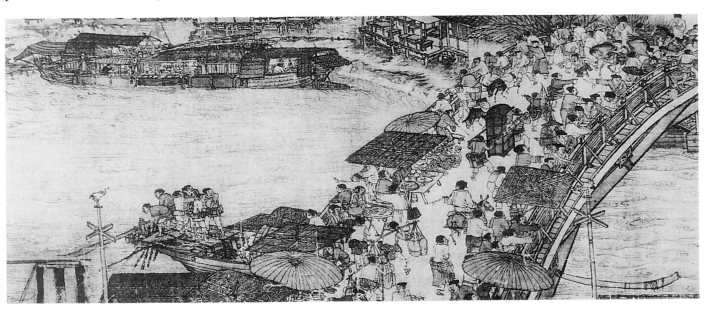

Marco Polo (1254–1324)

Marco Polo set out from Venice in 1271 for 'Cathay' (the name derived from 'Khitai,' referring specifically to north China.) After reaching Shangdu ('Xanadu,' in what is now Inner Mongolia) and Dadu ('Cambaluc;' modern Beijing), Marco spent 17 years in Qubilai's service (1275–92), returning to Venice in 1295. His experiences in China were published as *Description of the World.*

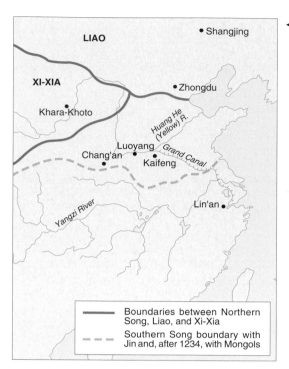

Boundaries between Northern Song, Liao, and Xi-Xia

Southern Song boundary with Jin and, after 1234, with Mongols

gentry The dominant social class of late imperial China, formally defined as holders of official degrees earned by passing the civil service examinations. They provided the pool of highly literate talent from which most Chinese bureaucrats were drawn.

Zhu Xi *Zhu Xi's philosophical synthesis of Neo-Confucian thought long dominated Chinese intellectual life; it was also highly influential in Korea and Japan.* ▼

as currency, were shipped to east and southeast Asia, while silk textiles and porcelains were in demand throughout the Old World.

There were also significant developments in the complexity of the currency system, such as the introduction of paper currency, rapid expansion of credit facilities, and a corresponding rise in the role of money in trade and government. In many respects, Song China was centuries ahead of Europe in its economic development.

Society and Culture. Economic growth was accompanied by significant changes in society and culture. The resulting developments were to remain characteristic of China until the 19th century. The rising **gentry** class depended much less on agricultural wealth than had the old aristocracy. It invested its wealth – often acquired through trade – in education. The perfection of the examination system brought new talent into an efficient civil service system. Social mobility, which had become justified by a greater acceptance of egalitarian principles, greatly increased in a more economically diversified society.

Another feature of the new society was its growing urbanization. Elite culture became more urbanized, sophisticated, and diversified. The greater subjugation of women may also have been associated with Song urbanization. The institution of concubinage, stricter social rules against the remarriage of widows, and the binding of women's feet are indicative of the decline of the status of Chinese women.

Neo-Confucianism. In terms of intellectual attitudes and formal philosophy, the Song period saw the appearance of patterns that

◄ **China during the Song Dynasty (960–1279)**
Although the Song were forced into the south of China by the Jin, in 1126, the southern Song Empire became the economic heartland of China. It was the focus of a medieval economic revolution, the effects of which were to survive in China until the 19th century.

were to remain characteristic until the very end of China's imperial age. The philosophical synthesis, known in the West as **Neo-Confucianism**, was partly a reassertion of ancient Confucian principles and partly a new creative movement. Its thinkers were strongly influenced by some of the Buddhist and Daoist concepts that had been so important in China in previous centuries. Neo-Confucianism was also influenced by a growing resentment and fear of outsiders. The principal synthesizer and organizer of this school was Zhu Xi (1130–1200). His synthesis gradually became established orthodoxy, reinforcing the growing rigidity of the attitudes of later Chinese society. Neo-Confucian indoctrination helped create a highly organized bureaucratic and efficient empire, as well as a stable traditionalist society.

China under Mongol Rule

It took the Mongols more than a generation to complete the conquest of China. Qubilai (or Kublai), who had become Great Khan in 1260 and adopted the Chinese dynastic name of Yuan in 1271, finally destroyed the southern Song dynasty in 1279. He subsequently set up his winter capital at Dadu (modern Beijing). In China the Yuan retained the administrative structure of the Song, although civil service examinations were suspended. This contributed to the lasting hostility of Confucian scholar-officials, causing the Mongols to employ many foreigners in China. They established a hierarchy of social classes, which comprised the Mongol overlords; their non-Chinese collaborators, mostly Muslims from Central and western Asia; northern Chinese and Sinicized Jurchen and Khitans who had capitulated earlier; and, at the bottom, the southern Chinese. The humiliation of inferior status provoked strong and lasting Chinese anti-Mongol feeling.

Koryŏ Korea

In 918 the Koryŏ dynasty was established in the southwest of Korea as a challenge to declining Silla. By 935, Koryŏ had annexed Silla and taken control of the entire peninsula. Although the new dynasty freed itself from Chinese domination, Chinese cultural influences and political patterns remained strong. Between 1231 and 1364, Koryŏ was a dependent kingdom of the Mongol Empire.

The Ming Dynasty

*Chinese rule re-established • China turns inward • The end of Ming rule •
Early western contacts • Yi dynasty Korea*

The Ming dynasty (1368–1644) was a period characterized by stable government, during which institutional foundations were laid that lasted throughout this period and into the subsequent Qing dynasty. Under the Ming, China's administrative system was improved and great public works undertaken, while the country shut itself off from foreign contact.

KEY MING RULERS	
Hongwu	1368–98
Yongle	1402–24
Ying Tsung	1435–49; 1457–64
Wanli	1573–1620
Chongzhen	1627–44

===SEE ALSO===
This section:
• China's Middle Ages
Japan:
• The Daimyos
The Mongol Empires
The Visual Arts Worldwide (vol. 4):
• Chinese Art
• Korean Art
Religion (vol. 6):
• Other Religions of India and the Far East

Chinese Rule Re-established

Fratricidal rivalry within the Mongolian (Yuan) imperial clan, frequent famines in north China after 1333, and severe flooding of the Huang He (Yellow) River contributed to the outbreak of rebellions against the alien Mongol rulers. The eventual victor among the Chinese rebels was Zhu Yuanzhang (1328–98), a man of peasant origin. In 1356 his rebel band seized Nanjing; by 1367, they controlled the entire Yangzi valley. In the following year Zhu took the Yuan capital, but continued to use Nanjing as his capital. He established the Ming (brilliant) dynasty, adopting the imperial title of Hongwu ('vast military power'). During his reign (1368–98) the autocratic tendencies of the former Yuan dynasty intensified.

After a devastating civil war against his nephew, who had inherited the throne at Nanjing, Emperor Yongle (reigned 1402–24) became the second strong ruler of the dynasty. In 1421 he moved the Ming capital to Beijing and rebuilt the city.

China Turns Inward

Upon gaining the throne, Hongwu immediately tried to re-establish the grand design of the Chinese state in his foreign relations. He sent envoys to the peripheral states – Korea, Japan, Annam, Champa, Tibet, and others – announcing his accession. Tribute missions soon came from these states. The suzerain–vassal relationship between the ruler of China and rulers of other countries expressed the traditional attitude that China was assumed to be their parent culture. Foreign rulers, if they wished for contact with China, had to accept its terms and acknowledge the supremacy of its emperor. Tribute relations involved, among other things, the regulation of trade.

Yet despite the spectacular **maritime expeditions** of Zheng He into the Indian Ocean (c. 1371–1435), Ming China failed to become a naval power. The state remained uninterested in commercial and colonial expansion overseas, having been an agrarian society since the earliest times. The revival of classical neo-Confucian values reinforced a strong anticommercialism. The Ming rulers actually placed restrictions on foreign trade, converting it into purely tributary exchange with those foreign nations that accepted China's suzerainty. Chinese subjects, meanwhile, were forbidden to travel overseas, which gave rise to smuggling and pirate raids on coastal China. The prohibition of maritime trade reflected the court's agrarian land-based orientation,

Ming China
Despite Ming China's desire to shut itself off from foreign influence, it was subjected to numerous incursions from the Mongols, the Japanese, and the Europeans.▼

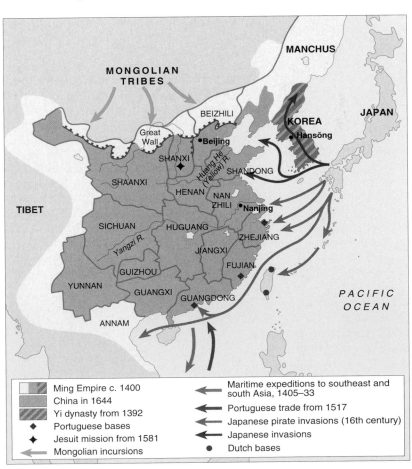

▨ Ming Empire c. 1400	⬅	Maritime expeditions to southeast and south Asia, 1405–33
China in 1644	⬅	Portuguese trade from 1517
▨ Yi dynasty from 1392	⬅	Japanese pirate invasions (16th century)
◆ Portuguese bases	⬅	Japanese invasions
✦ Jesuit mission from 1581	●	Dutch bases
⬅ Mongolian incursions		

◄ **The Forbidden City** *The vast complex of buildings that make up the imperial palace in Beijing, one of which is shown here, was built during the Ming dynasty. It housed the entire imperial court and was surrounded by a wall 11 m high and 4 km long. It was named 'the Forbidden City' as access by commoners or foreigners was allowed only with special permission.*

Eunuchs

Eunuchs served the emperor, his officials, and his harem in the extensive palace complex of the Forbidden City. They were organized into a hierarchy of offices, the most powerful being responsible for attending all the emperor's needs, and managing the other eunuchs in the palace. This chief eunuch could, if the emperor allowed it, virtually rule the empire. A series of eunuch dictators dominated government during the Ming era, while many others were honoured for their expert work in government.

Hongwu *As founder of the Ming dynasty, Hongwu was a shrewd statesman. Yet he was suspicious of scholar-officials in high-level government posts; in 1380 and 1393 he purged tens of thousands of them.* ▼

which encouraged economic self-sufficiency. The general disregard for foreign trade also reflected the rise of xenophobic tendencies in Ming China.

The early Ming emperors were much preoccupied with containing the persisting Mongol threat along China's inner Asian frontiers. In one of the many battles, in 1449, the emperor Ying Tsung (reigned 1435–49; 1457–64) was captured and held for ransom.

The End of Ming Rule

During the long reign of Emperor Wanli (1573–1620), the unmistakable features of dynastic decline began to appear. Under the rule of his 15-year-old successor, an imperial adviser, the **eunuch** Wei Zhongxian (1568–1627), assumed the powers of government. The problem of power abuse by scheming eunuch ministers thus reached its highest point. Wei purged his enemies in government and levied extortionate new taxes in the provinces.

Factional Politics. Confucian resistance to such corrupt government was carried on mainly by a group of scholars, known as the Donglin (Eastern Forest) party. Led by a dozen scholarly ex-officials, its members launched a moral crusade among scholars and civil servants to reassert the traditional principles of Confucian conduct. They became dominant in the factional struggle between 1620 and 1623, shortly before Wei Zhongxian achieved complete power. However, when a Donglin leader accused Wei of 24 serious crimes, the eunuch mobilized the enemies of the reform-

MARITIME EXPEDITIONS

Seven great maritime expeditions to southeast and south Asia began in 1405, by the order of Emperor Yongle, and continued until 1433. They were mostly led by a Muslim court eunuch, Zheng He. The first fleet of 62 vessels reached India, as did the second and third. The fourth voyage in 1413–25 reached Aden and Hormuz.

ers and retaliated violently. By the time Wei fell from power, in 1627, the Donglin party had been virtually eliminated.

The Ming court had gradually grown weaker; it was finally destroyed by endemic internal rebellion. One major rebel force was led by Zhang Xianzhong (1606–47), who had been raiding widely throughout northern China from 1630; he finally set up a government in Sichuan in 1644. His chief rival was Li Zicheng (?1605–45) who, by 1643, held much of Hubei, Henan, and Shaanxi. Early in 1644 he captured Beijing, just as the last Ming emperor, Chongzhen (reigned 1627–44), hanged himself on Prospect (or Coal) Hill, outside the Forbidden City.

Early Western Contacts

Portuguese adventurers were the first Europeans to reach China by sea in 1514, followed by Spanish, Dutch, and British traders. Christian missionary contact with the Ming during the early 17th century brought some new scientific, technological, and religious knowledge to China; however, this had little effect on the character of Ming intellectual life, nor did these contacts affect Chinese political, social, and economic institutions. The Jesuits were able to win a number of high-level converts and even to achieve some position of responsibility within the Ming bureaucracy. They adopted a policy of 'accommodation,' condoning certain Chinese cultural practices, such as ancestor worship.

Yi Dynasty Korea

In an almost bloodless coup, the military commander Yi Sŏng-gye overthrew the pro-Mongol King U of Koryŏ in 1388. In 1392 Yi established his own dynasty, Chŏson (better known as Yi), with Hansŏng (modern Seoul) as the capital. He subsequently carried out sweeping land reforms, which destroyed the old aristocratic order. The new social and political order was dominated by the Confucian literati class, which led to the development of the flourishing Yangban bureaucratic state. As a faithful tributary state, Yi Korea received Chinese military protection, which enabled the Koreans to repel two major Japanese invasions in 1592 and 1597. However, the country emerged much weakened from these exhausting conflicts.

The Qing Dynasty

Manchu conquest of China • The height of Qing power •
Qing decline and foreign aggression • China's republican revolution

The conquest of Beijing (1644) by Manchu forces from the northeast ushered in Qing rule (1644–1912), a period of 268 years, during which China flourished commercially and culturally, but suffered a series of defeats by foreign powers as well as internal rebellion. Bureaucratic conservatism, corruption, and opposition to modernization finally led to the fall of the Qing, China's last imperial dynasty.

Manchu Conquest of China

On the northeastern fringe of the Chinese cultural area the Manchus rose to power. Nurhaci (1559–1626), the founder of the Manchu state, united the Jurchen tribes and acquired sufficient power to challenge Ming China. His greatest achievement was to develop new administrative institutions with Chinese help. Under the so-called **banner** system, all tribesmen were enrolled under eight banners (military units) for administration and taxation purposes. Thus the transition was made from tribal to bureaucratic organization. As the Manchus expanded, eight Chinese and eight Mongol banners were added. In 1616 Nurhaci assumed the title of emperor. In 1636 his son Abahai (1592–1643) named the dynasty Qing (Pure).

The subsequent conquest of Ming China was a joint venture of Manchus, Mongols, and Chinese collaborators. The key figure was a Ming general, Wu Sangui (1612–78), who, instead of defending the last Ming emperor against Li Sicheng's attack (see THE MING DYNASTY), welcomed the advancing Manchus in 1644. The Manchu forces defeated Li, seized the throne, and proceeded to conquer the rest of China.

The Height of Qing Power

It took several decades of fighting before Qing rule was consolidated. By the late 1680s, however, the Manchus had established a strong stable regime. The new dynasty largely retained the administrative institutions inherited from the Ming. Seeking to legitimize themselves as the protectors of China's cultural heritage, the Qing soon became accepted by their Chinese subjects. They nevertheless forced all Chinese males to shave their foreheads and grow the Manchu-style pigtail as a sign of submission. Furthermore, in an effort to preserve their ethnic purity, the numerically insignificant Manchus forbade intermarriage and closed their Manchurian homeland to Chinese migration. In China itself Manchu military predominance was maintained by establishing banner garrisons at strategic points.

The reigns of emperors Kangxi (1661–1722), Yongzheng (1722–35), and Qianlong (1735–96) mark the high point of Manchu rule in China. Contemporary accounts of the 18th century suggest a prosperous society with abundant natural resources and a huge but largely contented population.

In 1696 a Manchu army led by Emperor Kangxi destroyed the Zungars, one of the tribes of the western Mongols. The final settlement came in the 1750s. After a long series of Mongol tribal rebellions, Qing bannermen not only destroyed the Zungars between 1755 and 1757, but in 1757–59 they also subjugated the Muslims of Kashgaria and established control over the oasis towns along the Silk Road. Similarly, Tibet became a protectorate of Qing at this time. During the 18th century the traditional Chinese state had attained its highest point of development. The population and the colonial territories of the Manchu-Chinese Empire were the largest they have ever been.

Qing Decline and Foreign Aggression

Towards the end of the long reign of Emperor Qianlong, the signs of dynastic decline began to appear. Prolonged domestic peace and relative prosperity had greatly increased the

SEE ALSO
This section:
• The Ming Dynasty
Japan:
• The Meiji Restoration and Expansionism
The Visual Arts Worldwide (vol. 4):
• Chinese Art
• Korean Art
The Literary Arts Worldwide (vol. 4):
• East Asian Literature

Qing China
Manchu expansion both before and after the establishment of the Qing dynasty (1644) created an empire that was the largest in Chinese history. The Manchu-Chinese Empire, which lasted for two-and-a-half centuries under Qing rule, extended to incorporate Outer Mongolia, the Tarim Basin, and Tibet. ▼

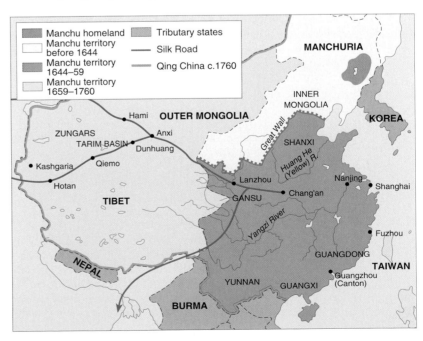

Manchu homeland		Tributary states	
Manchu territory before 1644		Silk Road	
Manchu territory 1644–59		Qing China c.1760	
Manchu territory 1659–1760			

◄
Opium Wars *The first Opium War (1839–42) was precipitated by the confiscation by the Chinese government of British opium stores in Guangzhou (Canton). This action led to the outbreak of hostilities in 1839. English ships are shown here bombarding Guangzhou.*

The Triads

The Triad organization originated as a Buddhist cult in China in 36 AD. It later became a political force, active against the Qing, and in support of the nationalist leader, Sun Yixian. Modern Triad societies are known for their criminal activities (especially drug dealing) outside China.

▲ **Empress Cixi**
Cixi ruled China ruthlessly between 1862 and 1908 (as regent for her son and then her nephew). Although politically astute, this former imperial concubine was responsible for the failure of dynastic regeneration and modernization.

population, creating difficulties of livelihood. Colonial conquests drained resources, while the decline of the banner forces and increasing corruption among officials undermined the state's efficiency. Combined with the effects of natural disasters, these developments led to famine, banditry, and rebellion.

Opium Wars. By the second quarter of the 19th century, China's internal weakness was aggravated by the challenge from industrializing Europe. Earlier Western attempts to gain greater access to the Chinese market had failed, as the Chinese continued to regard them as 'barbarian'; strictly regulated foreign trade was confined to the southern city of Guangzhou (Canton). However, by the 1830s a massive trade in illegal opium from British India to China was draining large amounts of silver from China, thus aggravating the growing agrarian crisis. When the Chinese authorities sought to stop the smuggling of the drug, hostilities broke out between Britain and China (1839). In several armed confrontations along the coast of China, British technological and military superiority forced the Qing government to conclude the Treaty of Nanjing (1842), later referred to as the first of the 'unequal treaties,' which gave Westerners greater access to and privileges in the empire via five designated ports. In addition, the island of Hong Kong was ceded to Britain. The second Opium War, fought between 1856 and 1860, culminated in an Anglo-French victory and further substantial concessions by China.

Mid-19th Century Rebellions. The internal and external pressures contributed to the outbreak of several major rebellions, which nearly destroyed the Qing dynasty. The Taiping Rebellion (1850–64) was the largest civil war in human history, in which some 20 million people lost their lives. Its leader, Hong Xiuquan (1814–64), was a failed scholar from Guangdong province, who, in 1843, declared

himself to be the younger brother of Christ. After his God-Worshipper Society had initiated an open rebellion in Guangxi province in 1850, Hong proclaimed the Heavenly Kingdom of Great Peace (*Taiping Tianguo*). Upon its capture in 1853, the Taiping rebels made Nanjing their 'Heavenly Capital.'

Whereas the Taiping rebels developed a comprehensive revolutionary ideology and an elaborate administrative structure, the Nian Rebellion (1851–68) had no particular ideology; its participants engaged primarily in mounted looting expeditions across much of northern China. Other contemporaneous rebellions include separate Muslim risings in Yunnan, Gansu, and Shaanxi, as well as a host of smaller insurrections by minority peoples, **Triad** secret societies, and sectarians.

Restoration. The Qing survived this period of insurrection through the policy and leadership changes known as the ***Tongzhi Restoration*** (Emperor Tongzhi reigned 1861–75), alluding to a return to the strength and power of the earlier years of the dynasty. The rebels were defeated by combined regional forces organized by staunch Confucian officials and local gentry, who opposed Taiping heterodoxy. By supporting the conservative Chinese scholar-generals in the provinces, the Manchu court, under the regency of the young Empress Dowager Cixi (1835–1908), achieved the restitution of central power.

Early Modernization. Some of the leading provincial authorities, who had been instrumental in suppressing the rebellions, were prepared to introduce changes that went beyond restoration. Their limited programmes, usually referred to as 'self-strengthening,' were initially confined to military modernization. In 1865 the Jiangnan arsenal was founded near Shanghai to supply modern arms; in 1866 the Fuzhou shipyard was opened to build steamships. In an effort to strengthen China against the West and to rival Japan's modernization, those statesmen who were reform-minded promoted the translation of Western textbooks and created a prototype foreign office. Subsequently, other modern economic enterprises were set up, such as Li Hongzhang's (1823–1901) China Merchants' Steam Navigation Company and his Kaiping Coal Mines. However, these early provincial attempts at modernization were largely uncoordinated, did not receive court backing, and were obstructed by the ignorant prejudice of the tradition-bound Confucian scholars.

The Zenith of Imperialism. The results of self-strengthening were found to be wanting during the Sino-Japanese War of 1894–95, which erupted over conflicting interests in Korea. The Japanese routed the north China army and sank a Chinese fleet off the Yalu River. Japan's victory over China initiated a decade of imperialist rivalries in the Far East. In order to pay the hefty indemnity to European bondholders, China went into debt. In 1898 Russia, Germany, Britain, Japan, and France all occupied or claimed spheres of influence in China, which usually consisted of a major port as a naval base. Foreign penetration into China was advanced by the rapid expansion of Christian missions. Their aggressive and essentially subversive activities were often supported by foreign gunboats. The response was increasing antimissionary riots, culminating in the **Boxer Uprising** (1900).

The Opening of Korea. For centuries the foreign relations of Korea had been limited to the sending of regular tribute missions to China and some other missions to Japan. The Korean rulers had resisted all Western attempts at opening the 'Hermit Kingdom'; however, it finally succumbed in the early 1880s. Treaties were signed with the USA (1882), Germany and the UK (1883), Italy and Russia (1884), and France (1886). The growth of foreign contact had violent repercussions within Korea; China, as Korea's traditional protector, was soon obliged to play

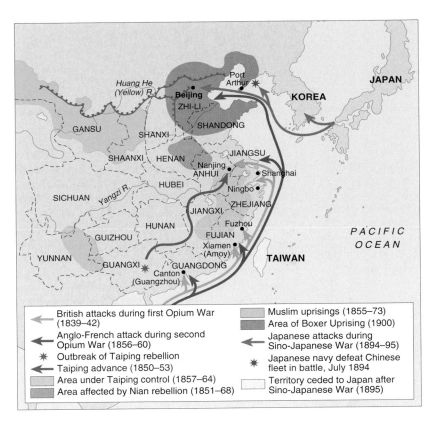

a more active role in Korea's government and politics, which brought China into conflict with Japan. Although serious conflict was avoided in the 1880s, full-scale war did break out between the two countries over Korea in 1894. Japan's victory culminated in the annexation of Korea in 1910.

China's Republican Revolution

In the wake of the Boxer fiasco, the first signs of a growing anti-Manchu Chinese nationalism became apparent, accompanied by insurrectionary activity. The Qing made a final attempt to preserve their dynastic rule by introducing reforms, which included plans for constitutional government. These centralizing reforms, however, came too late and provoked resistance among local elites, who had developed their own power bases and innovative programmes since the late 19th century. The common people reacted violently, faced with increased taxes to finance the reforms.

Meanwhile, since the 1890s, revolutionary activities had been organized (mainly from outside China) by Sun Yixian (Sun Yat-sen; 1866–1925), founding leader of the Chinese Nationalist Party. The revolution began with the accidental detonation of a bomb in a military camp on 10 October 1911. In February 1912 the boy emperor Puyi (reigned 1908–12) abdicated, thus bringing the Qing dynasty and the imperial system to an end. It was not, however, a revolutionary deposition, but a negotiated accommodation.

▲ **Conflict and Rebellion** *During the mid-19th century China was involved in disastrous conflicts with Britain, France, and Japan. China was also severely weakened by massive internal rebellions, which caused great destruction, contributing to the empire's decline.*

The Boxer Uprising

An uprising in which the rebels belonged to a secret society named the Fists of Righteous Harmony. Supported by the Empress Cixi, they violently opposed the Western presence in China, especially foreign missionaries and Chinese Christians. They marched on Beijing in June 1900, killing and pillaging in the process. The uprising was brutally suppressed by foreign forces in August.

▲ **Li Hongzhang** *As China's leading statesman of the 19th century, Li Hongzhang made great efforts to modernize his country. Between 1870 and 1895 he was involved in several major projects, including a railroad, a commercial steam ship line, and a military academy. Many of Li's programmes, however, were ultimately thwarted by the dynastic Confucian system of government. He is shown here with British prime minister William Gladstone (1809–98).*

The Republic of China

Warlords and the early republic • Rise of new forces • Anti-Japanese war (1937–45) •
The civil war (1946–49) • Colonial Korea

▲ **Sun Yixian**
(Sun Yat-sen; 1912)
*As a revolutionary
leader Sun Yixian
became the first
provisional president
of the new republic
(1912) and founder
of the Guomindang
(Nationalist Party).*

Following the end of imperial rule in 1911 revolutionary success was short-lived in China; actual power had fallen to the military and anti-imperial conservative forces in the provinces. Yuan Shikai (1859–1916), leader of the powerful Beiyang Army and first president of the new republic, had political opponents assassinated, purged parliament, and attempted to establish a new dynasty.

Warlords and the Early Republic

Following Yuan Shikai's death in 1916, the central power of China disintegrated. Outer Mongolia, Tibet, and to a lesser extent Xinjiang had already broken away in 1912. During the years between 1916 and 1928, and in some places long after that, China was ruled by numerous competing militarists, known as **warlords**. With few exceptions their regimes were harsh and their frequent wars highly destructive.

Rise of New Forces

From c. 1915 a strong iconoclastic ferment gripped China's young urban intellectuals. Initially known as the anti-Confucian New Culture Movement, its members sought to adopt the use of vernacular Chinese in literature and to explore different forms of Western cultural and political models. However, the movement's pro-Western orientation changed

dramatically when the terms of the Treaty of Versailles (which concluded World War I) became known in China. On 4 May 1919 student demonstrations took place in Tiananmen Square in Beijing, in protest against the decision to award Japan the former German concessions in Shandong province. After the May Fourth Incident, and influenced by events in Russia, many members of the movement (which henceforth became known as the May Fourth Movement) became politically active, developing a keen interest in Marxism and a strong anti-imperialist stance.

The Rise of Nationalist China. The Guomindang (Nationalist Party) of Sun Yixian (1866–1925) had led a precarious existence since the failed 'Second Revolution' of 1913. In 1917 Sun had established his headquarters at Guangzhou (Canton), as a base from which to unify the country. The party's image improved as a result of the formation of the First United Front (1924–27) with the fledgling Chinese Communist Party (founded in 1921), an alliance supported by the Soviet Union. During the years of cooperation in the mid-1920s, some great mass movements were established, such as revolutionary industrial labour organizations, women's movements, and peasant associations.

In the summer of 1926 allied Guomindang and communist forces launched the 'Northern Expedition' from Guangzhou, under the leadership of Jiang Jie Shi (Chiang Kaishek; 1887–1975), to free China from warlord rule and to unify the country under one government. By 1928, virtually all of China was under nominal Guomindang control; Nanjing became the capital of the new military-bureaucratic regime. Jiang Jie Shi, meanwhile, had ended his alliance with the communists.

Anti-Japanese War (1937–45)

During the years of Japanese encroachment on China, starting with the occupation of Manchuria in 1931, Jiang Jie Shi concentrated on internal unity, rather than resistance

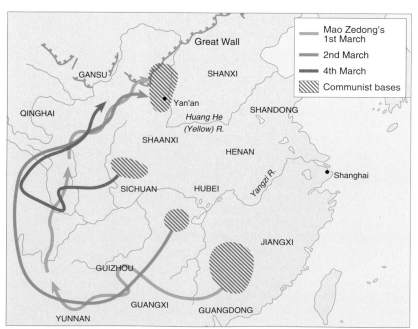

◄ **The Long March** *In October 1934 Mao Zedong, leading his First Front Army, embarked on a now legendary march from Jiangxi province to northwest China, to escape nationalist forces. Covering some 9656 km, and subjected to constant nationalist attacks, only some 8000 of Mao's 100 000 strong force finally reached Yan'an in October 1935.*

to the external threat. When Japan launched a full-scale attack on China on 7 July 1937, the Guomindang government withdrew to Chongqing in the southwest, enabling the Japanese to occupy the main cities and communications routes in eastern China.

The Rise of Communism. Having been defeated by the nationalists in the cities in 1927, remnants of the Communist Party, under the leadership of Mao Zedong (1893–1976), retreated to rural central China. However, Jiang Jie Shi's 'encirclement campaigns' forced the communists to abandon their bases, most notably the Jiangxi Soviet, in 1934 and embark on the epic Long March. Eventually a new base was established at Yan'an, Shaanxi province, in remote northwestern China.

When Jiang Jie Shi was kidnapped by mutinous troops in Xi'an in December 1936, communist intervention saved his life. Another alliance between Chinese nationalists and communists was formed to resist the external threat. Although this Second United Front ended in January 1941, it enabled the communists to move into areas behind Japanese lines, organize the rural inhabitants, and mobilize them for guerrilla warfare. They did this with particular effectiveness from 1943, when a comprehensive series of agrarian reform programmes and mass campaigns began to win over large numbers of the population.

The Civil War (1946–49)

Having defeated Japan in August 1945, ending World War II, the USA sought to mediate between the nationalists and communists in China. However, civil war broke out again in 1946. Whereas the communists had gained in strength and support during the Anti-Japanese War, the Guomindang had deteriorated. After 1945 Jiang's regime proved unable to deal with the problems of inflation, corruption, and factionalism. Commanding more and better equipped troops than the communists, Jiang's initial successes were quickly reversed when he overextended supply lines, sacrificing his best forces in the disastrous Manchurian campaign. By 1948, the nationalists were in full retreat. Jiang Jie Shi and his followers fled to the island of Taiwan a year later.

Colonial Korea

In 1910 Japan established a military administration in Korea and proceeded to rule the Koreans as an inferior subject people. All political activity by Koreans was prohibited. Although the Japanese modernized the country, most of the Korean population became increasingly impoverished.

The rapid spread of modern education methods and the practice of Christianity in Korea nourished increasing patriotic discontent among Koreans. These feelings culminated in a nationwide demonstration against Japanese rule in 1919. Known as the March First Movement, the demonstration was brutally suppressed by Japanese forces. The failure of this movement resulted in increasing support for communism as an effective weapon for anti-Japanese patriots in Korea during the 1920s.

▲ **Jiang Jie Shi**
On the death of Sun Yixian (1925), Jiang Jie Shi became leader of the Guomindang (Nationalist Party). He led nationalist forces against the communists in China's civil wars.

Shanghai Massacre

On 12 April 1927 Jiang Jie Shi's forces, supported by local underworld elements, started a campaign of terror against the Communist Party organization and labour movement in Shanghai. This marked the end of the first 'united front' (1923–27), a period of tenuous cooperation between communists and nationalists.

◄ **Communist Victory**
In pursuit of fleeing nationalist armies, communist forces advanced on Shanghai in April 1949. After a month-long siege, China's largest city fell suddenly with few shots being fired. Troops of Mao Zedong's Peoples' Liberation Army are shown here patrolling the streets of the city. By the end of 1949, the nationalists had been driven off the Chinese mainland.

235

Communist China

Creating the new state • The Great Leap Forward • The Cultural Revolution • Deng Xiaoping's reforms • Taiwan • Korea since World War II

The People's Republic of China *China, the largest country in Asia, has the world's greatest population.* ▼

The defeat of the nationalists by the communists in 1949 resulted in the creation of a one-party state. The ever-tightening grip of the communist regime on the Chinese people culminated in campaigns that attempted to transform completely the economic, social, and cultural nature of the country.

Creating the New State

Upon 'liberation' from the nationalists in 1949, the Chinese Communist Party (CCP) set out to consolidate its power and re-integrate most of the outer territories into the newly proclaimed People's Republic of China. At the same time, it embarked on the huge task of economic reconstruction. In addition, a Treaty of 'Friendship, Alliance, and Mutual Assistance' with the Soviet Union brought technical assistance and equipment, enabling China to launch a programme of heavy industrialization.

To secure total political control, the communists set up highly centralized administrative and public security systems. Those who challenged the CCP were destroyed. In an effort to break down the traditional values of family and religion and other aspects of Chinese culture that interfered with the regime's purposes, the CCP launched several large-scale campaigns in the early 1950s, involving propaganda and mass indoctrination. In the cities, civil servants, industrialists, and businessmen were brought under party control. In the countryside the land reforms of 1950–52 eliminated the landlord class.

The Great Leap Forward

Growing economic, political, and ideological differences between radicals and pragmatists inside the CCP leadership, led Mao Zedong (1893–1976) to launch the 'Great Leap Forward' in 1958. His aim was to achieve communism through rapid economic development by the mobilization of labour. Huge **Peoples' Communes** were thus set up in the country-

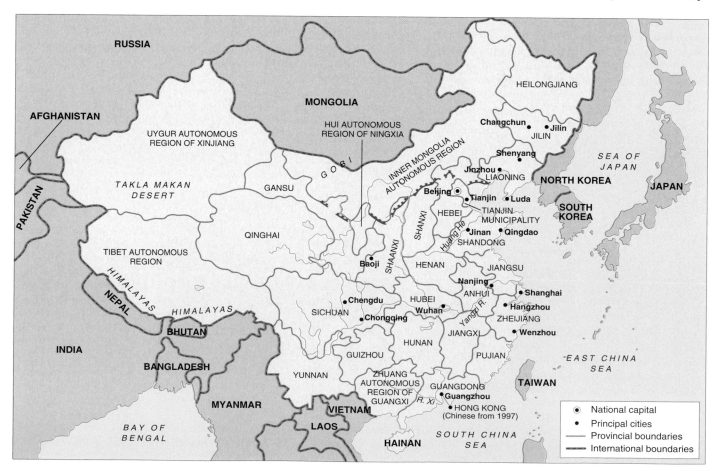

▲ **Mao Zedong** *Having proclaimed the People's Republic of China in 1949, Mao was its leader for the next 27 years. His political writings formed the ideological basis of the Republic's government, and in 1966 Mao initiated the Cultural Revolution.*

side. This campaign caused such disorder and hardship that it was abandoned in 1960. It also provoked a Sino-Soviet divergence in ideology, which led to the withdrawal of Soviet aid.

The Cultural Revolution

In 1966 the ageing Mao Zedong launched another mass campaign to silence his critics inside the CCP, revive the revolutionary spirit, and combat revisionism and the 'bourgeois mentality' of the bureaucracy. To carry out the directives of this 'Great Proletarian Cultural Revolution,' Mao and his supporters relied on the fanatical **Red Guards**. The period of Maoist radicalism (the Ten Bad Years) finally ended with Mao's death in 1976. Many of his most ardent disciples were purged.

Deng Xiaoping's Reforms

Soon after Mao's death his radical policies were abandoned and China embarked on a course of rapid development of industry, agriculture, science and technology, and national defence. Deng Xiaoping (1904–97), a strong new leader, was instrumental in implementing the decollectivization of agriculture, free markets, the growth of the private sector, and an open-door policy towards the outside world. In spite of a burgeoning population of more than one billion people (forcing the introduction of stringent population controls), economic reforms have brought spectacular results in advanced regions of China. The thriving free market economy of the former British colony of Hong Kong (Xianggang) had a stimulating effect, especially in southern China. Under a 1984 Sino-British agreement, the sovereignty of Hong Kong reverted to China in July 1997.

While China promised to retain a capitalist economy there, the abolition of Hong Kong's democratically elected legislature did not bode well for the civil rights of the region's people.

While economic liberalization has greatly benefited China, no political reforms have been contemplated. The bloody events in Tiananmen Square, Beijing, in 1989, when tanks crushed pro-democracy demonstrators, are a reminder of China's tradition of autocratic rule. Deng Xiaoping, who died in 1997, was succeeded by state president Jiang Zemin (1926–); he continued to implement Deng's economic policies, which were creating a widening prosperity gap between China's regions.

Taiwan

Integrated into the Manchu-Chinese Empire during the Qing dynasty, and then subjected to Japanese occupation between 1895 and 1945, Taiwan has been the sole base of Jiang Jie Shi's Republic of China since 1949 (his son, Jiang Jing Guo, was president from 1978 to 1988). With massive military and economic assistance from the USA, the nationalists have implemented effective reform policies. Under the rule of Chinese immigrants from the mainland, a minority in Taiwan, the island now has a large and modern army, a prosperous agricultural sector, a strong and expanding industrial base, and a high standard of living.

Korea since World War II

At the end of World War II the victors decided that US forces would accept the surrender of the Japanese in Korea south of the 38th parallel, and that Soviet troops would do the same in the northern portion. When the occupying powers failed to agree on a unified government, UN-authorized elections were held in southern Korea and the Republic of Korea was proclaimed in 1948. In September the communist Democratic People's Republic of Korea was established in the north.

In June 1950 North Korea, by invading South Korea, initiated the Korean War, during which US troops (nominally under UN control) and Chinese 'volunteers' became involved. Under the 1953 cease-fire, the peninsula remained divided. Despite political unrest and slow recovery, South Korea has experienced rapid economic growth in recent years, limited only by a regional financial crisis in 1997. The hostile North – under a rigid communist system and the long dictatorship of Kim Il Sung (1912–94) – has also seen rapid industrial growth, but little improvement in the standard of living. Floods and famine in 1995–96 forced the North to seek aid from the South. In 1997, an improvement in relations between them was evident when both nations entered into joint talks with the USA and China.

The Dalai Lama (1935–)

In 1950 Tenzin Gyatso acceded to power as the 14th Dalai Lama, the spiritual and political leader of the Tibetan Lamaist state. Shortly afterwards the Chinese People's Liberation Army invaded and annexed Tibet (the 'roof of the world'). Following unsuccessful uprisings by his people, the Dalai Lama fled to India in 1959.

Peoples' Communes

Central self-reliant units of rural administration (formed by the amalgamation of agricultural collectives), which combined industrial, agricultural, commercial, educational, and militia functions. The abolition of private plots, equality of the sexes, communal mess halls, and child-care facilities were designed to free more labour for productive purposes.

Red Guards

Organized by Mao's supporters to carry out the directives of the Cultural Revolution, these university and high-school students embarked on a reign of terror, abusing, humiliating, and even killing Mao's opponents in schools, universities, factories, and within the party. They destroyed places of worship, vandalized private homes, and disrupted the education system in the late 1960s.

JAPAN

The Early Empire

*Prehistoric Japan • The impact of Chinese culture •
Kyoto and court culture • The rise of the Samurai*

**Shotoku Taishi ('Prince
of Sagely Virtue';
574–622)**

The second son of
Emperor Yomei, Shotoku
acted as regent for the
Empress Suiko (reigned
593–628). He was an
influential patron of the
sinicization of Japanese
culture; he introduced
the '12 cap ranks' of
Chinese administration
and issued the famed
'17 Article Constitution,'
setting out principles of
government conduct and
imperial authority. He
ordered the compilation
of histories and initiated
direct diplomatic contact
with China. As a script-
ural scholar, Shotoku
vigorously promoted the
spread of Buddhism.

It is not known when Japan was first settled by
man. Paleolithic tools have only been discovered there since World War II; it is thought
that these were used by people who came to
Japan from the Asian continent.

Prehistoric Japan

Jomon Period (11 000 BC–c. 250 BC).
Japanese legend credits the first emperor,
Jimmu Tennu, with ascending the throne in
660 BC, and with being descended from the
sun goddess Amaterasu. At that time the inhabitants of Japan were making a type of pottery known from its decorative pattern as
Jomon ('cord-marked'), which gives its name
to this period. Jomon people also wove wicker
baskets, wore clothes made from skins or bark,
and filed their teeth, probably as an act to
mark attainment of adulthood. Jomon people
spoke an ancestral version of what is now
Japanese, a language that was distantly related to Korean and distinctly different from
Chinese.

Yayoi Period (c. 250 BC–c. 250 AD). This
new cultural phase began with the introduction of wet-rice cultivation, weaving, and metalworking in both bronze and iron. These
innovations came ultimately from China, the
world's most advanced state. For the next
millennium, China was to be Japan's great
mentor, though at this stage not a consciously
acknowledged one. *Yayoi* culture, also named
after a pottery type, developed extensive
irrigation systems and the beginnings of social distinctions of rank.

Kofun Period (c. 250 AD–c. 500 AD). This
period falls partly in the prehistoric period and
partly in the historic period. It takes its name
from the large burial mounds that were its
most notable achievement. The impressive size
of *kofun* tombs indicates the existence of a
highly organized aristocratic society. More
than 10 000 have been discovered, particularly in the **Yamato** region, to the south of
what is now the city of Kyoto. It is from this region that the royal house of Japan takes its
name, and it was here that imperial rule began
around 400 AD.

▲ **The *Kofun* of Emperor Nintoku** *The tomb,
at Sakai, in the Nara Prefecture, is 2718 metres in
circumference and 35 metres high. It is the largest
'keyhole' type tomb of the Kofun period; it is
surrounded by three moats. The labour required to
construct it would have been enormous.*

The Impact of Chinese Culture
Buddhism. Tradition holds that in 552 the
king of Paekche in Korea sent the Yamato
court a golden image of the Buddha and a collection of scriptures expounding his teachings.
The scriptures, first produced 1000 years previously, were recorded in Chinese. The task of
translation – and of rendering abstruse theological concepts in terms accessible and acceptable to the Japanese – was to preoccupy
the best minds of the nation for centuries.

The intrusion of Buddhism, coupled with the
advent of a system of writing, provoked the
guardians of Japan's native cult, Shinto, to articulate its traditions in two major works that
mark the beginnings of Japanese literature:
the *Kojiki* ('Record of Ancient Matters'), completed in 712, and the *Nihon Shoki* ('Chronicle
of Japan'), completed in 720. These compilations blended myth, history, and hagiography
to support the claims of the imperial line to divine ancestry and to an antiquity at least as
long and splendid as that of China itself.

This Shintoist fervour did not, however, prevent the spread of Buddhism from the courtly
elite to the population as a whole. Other-
worldly and speculative, the alien faith was

Cultural Influences on Japan *After the inundation brought by the land bridges between Asia and the Japanese archipelago, culture contacts, whether positive or hostile, accepted or challenged, did not pass unremarked or unrecorded.* ▶

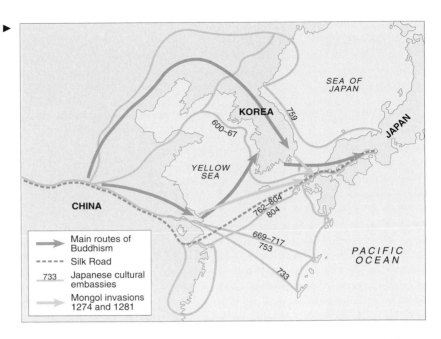

welcomed as a complement to, rather than a contradiction of, the indigenous rites that celebrated fertility and revered nature. Reassuring correspondences were identified between Shinto and Buddhist deities.

Emperor Shomu (reigned 724–49) ordered the establishment of a Buddhist monastery and a nunnery in every province and became the first emperor to renounce the throne to become a monk. In 752 he emerged from retirement to dedicate an immense (17 m high) Buddha statue, which still stands. The acceptance of Buddhism can also be seen in the increasing substitution of banishment for execution, of cremation for burial, and of vegetarianism for meat-eating.

Technology and Writing. From the mid- to late 6th century, Korea acted as a channel for the transmission of Chinese high culture to Japan. Medicine, mathematics and music, town planning and astrology, the secrets of making paper, silk, porcelain, and lacquer and, above all, the secret of writing, were among the many gifts showered on Japan and, under the patronage of Prince Shotoku, absorbed into the lifestyle of the elite. In 603 Chinese methods of bureaucratic rule were officially adopted, as was the Chinese calendar in 604. Government-sponsored missions were sent direct to China, ostensibly to exchange diplomatic courtesies but also to recruit scholars, priests, and craftsmen.

Later reformers incorporated further civic measures inspired by the Chinese: regularizing provincial administration, centralizing tax collection, building roads, and instituting land surveys, postal systems, and a census.

Kyoto and Court Culture

After a brief (694–710) false start at Fujiwara-kyo, a fixed capital was established at Nara in 710. Modelled on the Chinese capital of Chang'an (modern Xi'an), it may have grown to a population of 200 000 before being abandoned. After another false start at Nagaoka, a final move was made to Kyoto in 794. Initially known as Heian-kyo (capital of peace and tranquillity), it remained Japan's capital, in theory at least, until 1868.

The period 794–1185, prior to the establishment of warrior government at Kamakura in 1192, is known as the ***Heian*** period. The term Heian became, for subsequent generations, synonymous with the development of a courtly lifestyle of great aesthetic refinement.

The minutiae of palace preoccupations and pastimes were chronicled in two remarkable works, which are still widely read today: the *Pillow Book* of Sei Shonagon, a discursive diary, spiced with malice and snobbery, and the *Tale of Genji*, by Murasaki Shikibu, a meandering narrative of the life and loves of an ill-starred aristocrat.

During this period Kyoto also became the birthplace of the Tendai, Shingon, and Pure Land sects, which adapted Buddhism to Japanese needs and which, even today, command the widest followings.

The darker side of the Heian period was dark indeed. The peasant masses – more than 90% of the population, for there was little urbanization beyond the capital itself – endured terrible hardships. Apart from the usual hazards of medieval life, such as crop failures, epidemics, fires, and natural disasters, they were periodically ravaged by bandits and pirates. The response of the central government

Kobo Daishi Kukai (774–835)

One of Japan's favourite Buddhist saints, Kobo Daishi founded the Shingon ('True Word') sect; it has 12 000 temples, 12 million followers, and is divided into 47 subsects. A fine poet and calligrapher, and fluent speaker of Chinese, he is also credited with devising the hiragana phonetic syllabary used to supplement Chinese characters (*kanji*) in writing Japanese.

◀ **The Horyu-ji Temple (Nara)** *Founded in 607 as part of a monastic complex, by Prince Shotoku, Horyu-ji is an example of the imposing temples built in the Chinese style as Buddhism spread through Japan. Its ancient wooden structures have been preserved; it is the oldest wooden building in the world.*

239

Samurai *The elaborate* ▶ *armour of the samurai was not only protective, but a symbol of the warriors' social status. A samurai demonstrates his warrior prowess in this 19th century woodblock print.*

samurai (meaning 'one who serves') A class of warrior-bureaucrats that formed Japan's ruling elite from the 12th century until their abolition in 1873.

Sugawara no Michizane (845–903)

Japan's patron saint of scholarship, he was a fine poet and historian; his closeness to the emperor led the Fujiwara to exile him on false charges of treachery. After Sugawara's death, calamities at court were blamed on his wronged spirit and shrines were built to appease him. Students still invoke his aid before examinations.

shogun One of a line of military dictators who effectively controlled Japan while reducing the emperor to the role of nominal ruler. The title of *shogun* was hereditary, being held successively by three families from 1192 to 1868.

combined both indifference and impotence; political life revolved around place and precedence, rather than policy, and the armed force available to the central government consisted only of a palace bodyguard.

The Fujiwara. The most powerful faction at court surrounded the Fujiwara family, masters of intrigue. They emerged after a coup that displaced the previously dominant Soga family in 645. Henceforth they entrenched their position by marrying their daughters into the imperial line. In 858 a nine-year-old Fujiwara prince was enthroned as emperor, while his grandfather assumed the position of regent. Over the next two centuries no fewer than eight adult emperors were discreetly hustled into early retirement, leaving real power in Fujiwara hands. Fujiwara ascendancy reached its peak under Michinaga (966–1028), who could number two emperors among his nephews and three among his grandsons.

An imperial counterattack to the Fujiwara was masterminded by Emperor Go-Sanjo (1034–73), who devised an ingenious system of 'cloistered government,' which turned the intriguers' own trick of manipulating minors against them. This system loaded time-consuming ceremonial duties onto a minor, who nominally occupied the throne, while real power over appointments and expenditures was exercised from the seclusion of a monastery to which the previous adult occupant had 'retired.'

The Rise of the Samurai

The dilettantism of the Heian court created a power vacuum in the country that favoured the rise of warlord rule. The conscription of peasants for military service was abolished in 792. The last attempt at an official redistribution of land – theoretically the whole country was the property of the emperor – took place in 844. Positions of provincial authority became hereditary and their effectiveness came to rest, not on imperial commission, but on private armies of **samurai**, which enforced public order and collected taxes. On the frontier, these forces pushed Japan's aboriginals, the Ainu, into the backlands of northern Honshu. Inevitably, such conquered territories were added to the estates of the victors, rather than placed at the disposal of the emperor.

Taira and Minamoto. The terminal decline of courtly power began in 1156 with a wrangle over the succession between a cloistered emperor and a reigning emperor. The Fujiwara were divided and courtly in-fighting escalated into a decisive confrontation between the real powers in the land. Kiyomori (1118–81), head of the Taira, a warrior clan favoured by the imperial family, saw his opportunity to eliminate the Minamoto, a rival band who acted as the 'claws and teeth' of the Fujiwara. By massacring many Minamoto, as well as courtiers, the Taira were initially triumphant, awarding themselves titles and estates and marrying into the imperial line itself.

Meanwhile the Minamoto regrouped around a ruthless new leader, Yoritomo (1147–99). When, in 1180, the Taira put one of their own infants, Antoku, on the throne, Yoritomo struck back, although the actual fighting was led by his young half-brother, Yoshitsune (1159–89). The death of Kiyomori from a fever in 1181 was taken as a divine judgment on the arrogance of his clan. Their final destruction came in 1185 in a naval battle in the straits of Shimonoseki, between Kyushu and Honshu. Antoku was drowned and those Taira not slaughtered in the battle were hunted down and killed. Yoshitsune's success, however, so aroused Yoritomo's jealousy that the young warrior was driven to suicide, becoming one of Japan's great tragic heroes.

The First Shogun. Yoritomo established his seat of government at the coastal city of Kamakura. Surrounded by mountains, it was readily defensible and, having access to the sea, enabled him to move swiftly over long distances in an age when overland travel was slow and dangerous. In 1192 Yoritomo was awarded the title of *sei i tai* **shogun** ('great barbarian-subduing generalissimo'), thus inaugurating seven centuries of rule by military dictatorship, masked only by ritual obeisance to a powerless imperial figurehead.

The Early Shogunates

Strengthening the Shogunate • The Ashikaga Shogunate • The Japanese Renaissance

The Minamoto ascendancy was brief (see The EARLY EMPIRE). Although Yoritomo, the first shogun, was nominally succeeded by his sons, real power passed to his widow's family, the Hojo, who were of Taira descent. The assassination of shogun Sanetomo, in 1219, set the stage for an attempted coup by Emperor Go-Toba in 1221. When it was crushed, he and his son were exiled and 3000 estates were confiscated from his followers.

Strengthening the Shogunate

The confiscated lands were redistributed to maintain support for the shogunate among its 2000 vassals, who were bound to it by ties of economic advantage no less than by pledges of allegiance. By a further irony, the Taira-descended Hojo filled the office of shogun with candidates selected from the imperial and Fujiwara families, contenting themselves with the more modest title of 'regent' (shikken). At the same time their Kamakura-based regime developed a parallel administration to the bureaucratic structure, which was still nominally under imperial control but largely redundant in practice. A systematization of feudal custom, known as the Joei Code, was issued in 1232 and rigorous efforts were made to ensure that provincial appointees remained accountable for their office and carried out their duties to maintain public order and to foster economic expansion. Kamakura, meanwhile, expanded to a population of 50 000 but remained essentially a strategic and governmental headquarters, presenting no rival to the urban sophistication of Kyoto.

The Mongol Threat. Having seized most of China and Korea, the Mongol leader, Qubilai Khan, twice attempted to conquer Japan in 1274 and 1281. The Japanese mounted a ferocious and hugely expensive defence on both occasions; they owed their deliverance, however, to timely storms that twice wrecked the invasion fleets and were thus hailed as ***kamikaze*** ('divine winds'). Prudently avoiding reliance on such natural phenomena for their future security, the Hojo imprudently committed themselves to further burdensome defence expenditures that led them towards increasingly oppressive taxation and financial ruin.

The Imperial–Shogunate Power Struggle. Emperor Go-Daigo (1288–1339) repeatedly intrigued against the Hojo and, in 1333, managed to escape from offshore confinement and

▲ **The Great Buddha** *Situated at Kamakura, the bronze statue stands 11.4 m high and weighs 120 tonnes. Cast in 1252, it has been kept in the open air since the temple originally housing it was washed away by a tidal wave in 1495.*

raise support among Kyoto courtiers and western provincial magnates disgruntled by their exclusion from the Hojos' eastern power base. When an army was sent to crush the rising, its leader, Ashikaga Takauji (1305–58), defected to the emperor's side. When a second general also switched allegiance and marched on the Hojo headquarters, its occupants committed suicide *en masse* rather than suffer a worse fate at the hands of their former supporters.

Go-Daigo's restoration lasted barely three years. By showing exclusive favour to Kyoto sophisticates, he outraged the warrior allies who had put him back on his throne and he further compounded his error by raising a huge levy to pay for an extravagant royal residence. Ashikaga Takauji launched a countercoup, installing a puppet-emperor whose obedience could be guaranteed. Go-Daigo and his followers were driven into a mountain refuge at Yoshino, in the south, where he set up a rival court. Takauji installed his own candidate in Kyoto and assumed the title of shogun in 1338. It was not until 1392 that the two imperial lines were formally reunited.

The Ashikaga Shogunate

In 1378 the third shogun, Yoshimitsu (1358–1408), established his administrative headquarters at Muromachi, a district of Kyoto from which the imperial palace could conveniently be kept under close surveillance. Yoshimitsu went on to make a vast personal fortune by reopening, and monopolizing, official trade with China, which had been suspended since the Mongol invasions a century before. This wealth enabled him to become a

▲ The Mongol Invasions
The Japanese fiercely defended their islands against the Mongol threat, as shown in this late 13th-century scroll (detail).

---

tea ceremony (*chanoyu*)
A form of ritualized hospitality intended to stimulate aesthetic appreciation as well as psychological refreshment and calm. It was perfected by Senno-Rikyu in the 16th century.

Bushido

Bushido was the path or code of the warrior (*bushi*). It was only codified by *samurai* as it began to erode. It stressed courage, strength, honour, and contempt for gain. Bushido's stress on the supreme value of loyalty almost certainly highlighted its absence in an era of treacheries and betrayal.

---

lavish and discerning patron of the arts, sponsoring the work of the Nō master, Zeami, and constructing as his personal residence the Golden Pavilion (*Kinkakuji*), one of Japan's greatest architectural treasures.

The Breakdown of the Balance of Power.
The Ashikaga regime, also known as the Muromachi shogunate, established secure control of central Japan. Its authority, however, never extended over the whole country and the provinces of the east and south retained considerable autonomy. This balance of power endured for a century before disintegrating under the eighth shogun, Yoshimasa (1436–90). Preferring aesthetic pleasures to the increasingly grim realities of a state sliding out of control, he designated his brother as his successor in 1464. Shortly afterwards his wife gave birth to a son for whom she demanded the succession. The resulting dispute sparked the destructive Onin Wars (1467–77), during which Kyoto was incinerated; these wars also initiated a century of continuous warlord conflict and reduced Ashikaga authority to the limits of its devastated and largely irrelevant capital.

The Japanese Renaissance
Late medieval Japan has been compared to Renaissance Italy, where savage warfare coexisted with economic expansion and cultural innovation, branding it as an era of near-anarchy, but not of decay. The replacement of a barter system with cash (initially copper coinage imported from China) and the proliferation of markets and guilds attest to the former trend, while the emergence of significant new art forms – Nō drama, landscape gardening, the **tea ceremony**, and flower arranging – affirm the latter. While the development of literature languished, weighed down by the

conventions of Heian precedent, sword-making, sculpture, ceramics, and the painting of fine picture-scrolls attained new heights of technical excellence.

Religious Renewal.
The tendency of Buddhism (see THE EARLY EMPIRE) to develop distinctively Japanese forms followed two different paths in this period. First, there was the spread of Zen, especially among the warrior class, who relished its contempt for dogma and ceremony. The second path followed the rise of a populist sect, named after its charismatic and founder, Nichiren (1222–82). Both appeared to offer the believer a more direct and satisfying spiritual experience, the former through disciplined meditation, the latter through ecstatic ritual. Zen also had a great influence upon the arts, favouring the offbeat and the asymmetrical: the garden consisting entirely of rocks and gravel; the calligraphic scroll reduced to a few bold strokes.

The dogmatic Nichiren, with the fervour of an Old Testament prophet, condemned all rival sects and campaigned to have his nationalistic version of the faith propagated as the official religion of the state. He gained great prestige by prophesying the Mongol invasions, although the weakness of the late Kamakura and subsequent Ashikaga regimes prevented the enforcement of any doctrine as an orthodoxy. Nichiren's movement paralleled, in some ways, the later emergence of Protestantism in Europe, emphasizing salvation through faith rather than priestly intercession; focusing the believer's spiritual anxiety on the rewards of an afterlife in paradise; organizing worship around congregations rather than monasteries; translating scriptures into the vernacular; and merging religious and national allegiances so that they became synonymous.

The Daimyos

Civil strife • The fall of the Ashikaga • Southern barbarians

The period between the Onin Wars (1467–77) (see THE EARLY SHOGUNATES) and the reunification of the country under the Tokugawa (1600–15) has been called 'the era of warring states.' This is a classical reference to the period of Chinese history from 475 to 221 BC.

Civil Strife

For almost 150 years political life was dominated by the struggles of some 200 to 300 **daimyos** (literally 'great name') to achieve regional and, ultimately, national supremacy over their rivals. To qualify for *daimyo* status, a feudal warlord had to be able to command enough land to produce 10 000 *koku* of rice annually, one *koku* being the amount required to feed an adult for a year. The largest *daimyo* had estates capable of feeding millions.

Cutting across this period is a novel phase of 'culture contact,' known by Western historians as 'the Christian century.' Europeans first arrived in Japan in 1543. Traders came first and missionaries soon followed. In the absence of a strong central government, the alien intruders were soon able to establish themselves.

Guns and Castles. With the Europeans came guns. Within six months of seeing a gun, the Japanese had learned to make one themselves. Within 20 years, Japanese armies had a higher proportion of men armed with firearms than their European counterparts. Cavalry, fighting with sword and bow, increasingly gave way to infantry, armed with pike and gun. The use of artillery was a natural follow-on from the introduction of the handgun. This, in turn, led to the construction of castles, more than 180 of which were built in this period. The castles themselves led to the development of towns and many modern Japanese cities owe their origin to the warlords' stronghold on this turbulent age.

The Fall of the Ashikaga

From 1490 to 1558, what little remained of Ashikaga authority was exercised by their former dependants, the Hosokawa family. They were usurped by their retainers, the Miyoshi, and they, in turn, were ousted by their vassals, the Matsunaga. The abandonment of Kyoto

by the last Ashikaga in 1573 effectively marked the end of the dynasty. This classic example of **geko kujo** ('those beneath overthrow those above') underlined the sickness at the supposed heart of government. It was, however, largely irrelevant to the nation's destiny. This was to be directed by the ruthless drive of a succession of three warlords, determined to bring "all the country under one sword." A traditional story illustrates the differences in their characters: the three men sat watching a silent songbird in a cage. Nobunaga said that if it didn't sing, he would force it to. Hideyoshi said if it didn't sing, he would kill it. Ieyasu said if it didn't sing, he would wait until it did.

Oda Nobunaga (1534–82). As leader of a minor clan, Nobunaga quickly grasped the lethal potential of guns used on a large scale. He was also the first to use ironclad ships. Nobunaga established the last Ashikaga in power, only to discard him when he attempted to become more than just a puppet. When the warrior-monks of Enryakuji monastery tried to resist him, he burned down its 3000 buildings and massacred their defenders. Nobunaga finally fell victim to the treachery of one of his own generals, and disembowelled himself amid the resulting conflict. By the time of his death, he had brought more than half of Japan's provinces under his control.

Toyotomi Hideyoshi (1536–98). Nobunaga was swiftly avenged by a loyal lieutenant, the ugly undersized Hideyoshi, who felt entirely confident that he could continue his work. In 1588 he launched a 'sword hunt' to disarm the peasantry. By 1590 his supremacy was acknowledged throughout the land; in the same year, he also ordered a census as the

===SEE ALSO===
Early and Medieval Europe:
• The Exploration and Conquest of the Wider World
China:
• The Ming Dynasty
The Visual Arts Worldwide (vol. 4):
• Japanese Art
Literature Worldwide (vol. 4):
• East Asian Literature
Religion (vol. 6):
• Buddhism
• Christianity

The Master of Tea

Senno-Rikyu (1522–91), a merchant and Zen expert, is acknowledged as the aesthetic opinion leader of his age. An advocate of the natural and simple, he deplored the vulgar excesses displayed by the warlords of the time. He died by his own hand on the orders of Hideyoshi.

Himeji Castle *Built in the 16th century, the five-tiered castle provided a focus for the city's subsequent development. The castle was reconstructed in 1964.*

We bury our dead, the Japanese cremate most of theirs. People in Europe love baked and boiled fish; the Japanese much prefer it raw. Our paper is only of four or five types; the Japanese have more than fifty varieties. We consider precious stones and decorations of gold and silver to be valuable; the Japanese prize old kettles, ancient and racked porcelain...

Luis Frois, Spanish Jesuit, on Japanese customs

basis for a new taxation system. Farmers' rights to cultivate the land were confirmed, although this was on the condition that they were not to leave it. The decree of 1591 similarly obliged craftsmen and merchants to live in towns, forbidding them to reside in villages. Hideyoshi also destroyed many castles, issued new coinage, took over all gold and silver mines and foreign trade, and rationalized the system of weights and measures.

In 1592, having conquered his own country, unifying it under one rule, Hideyoshi set out to conquer China, and initially Korea. Whether this was motivated by his own personal power-seeking or a shrewd effort to divert the energies of redundant samurai, the result was disastrous for Japan's peaceful neighbour. Only Hideyoshi's sudden death led to the complete abandonment of the enterprise.

Tokugawa Ieyasu (1543–1616). Ieyasu was one of the five-strong council of regents established by Hideyoshi to guarantee that his legacy passed intact to his infant son, Hideyori. Ieyasu was a man of few scruples; by securing the backing of four other warlords, he sought supreme power for himself, bringing his rivals to a decisive confrontation at the Battle of Sekigahara on 21 October 1600. Victory enabled him to seize Kyoto and, with it, the emperor. Hideyoshi's peasant origins had disqualified him from a noble title, whereas Ieyasu claimed descent from the Minamoto, founders of the Kamakura shogunate (see THE EARLY SHOGUNATES). In 1603 he had himself proclaimed shogun. In 1605 he passed the title to his third son, Hidetada. This secured the succession to his line, while he kept the power for himself.

Tokugawa Ieyasu ▶
Founder of the Tokugawa shogunate, Ieyasu completed the re-establishment of central authority in feudal Japan. He is shown here tying on his helmet in preparation for battle.

▲ **A Japanese View of the Portuguese**
Portuguese missionaries used the trade from Portuguese ships to spread Christianity. Some merchant ships would not enter the ports of daimyos unless they displayed goodwill towards missionaries. The daimyos, *keen to profit from foreign trade and to acquire military equipment, therefore, progressively protected Christianity.*

Southern Barbarians

The first Europeans arrived by chance in 1543. They were Portuguese passengers on a storm-tossed Chinese boat. In 1549, however, St Francis Xavier spearheaded a series of Spanish Jesuit missions to Japan. Adopting saffron-coloured robes in imitation of Buddhist monks, they worked diligently to overcome the inherent barriers of culture and language. The first bilingual dictionary of Japanese and a European language was the fruit of their efforts. By the 1580s, the number of Christian converts numbered hundreds of thousands. Japanese interest in the Jesuit religion was exceeded, however, by an eager desire for clocks, carpets, tobacco, spectacles, and other Western novelties. While, in the long term, the novelties were accepted, the religion itself was rejected.

The Shogun's Englishman. Pilot William Adams (1564–1620) was the only foreigner ever to have become a *samurai*. Arriving aboard a Dutch ship, he was recognized by Tokugawa Ieyasu as an invaluable source of political and technical information. Forbidding Adams to return to England, Ieyasu also employed Adams as an interpreter and entrusted him with a commercial mission to the Philippines. Adams was additionally responsible for establishing trade relations between Japan and both the Dutch and the British East India Companies. He married a Japanese wife and died in his adopted country, where he is honoured as the symbolic founder of the Japanese navy.

The Tokugawa Shogunate

Securing the dynasty • Closing the country • Cities and culture •
Inevitable decline? • Civil war

Japan's final shogunate lasted from 1603 to 1867, longer than any of its predecessors. Under Tokugawa rule, Japan enjoyed peace, economic expansion, and cultural innovation, although this was at the expense of political repression and national isolation. The modernizers who eventually overthrew the Tokugawa (see THE MEIJI RESTORATION AND EXPANSIONISM) portrayed them as corrupt and uncivilized. The rapidity of Japan's modernization in the late 19th century, however, owed much to the increase in literacy and improvements in crafts, commerce, and agriculture that occurred during the previous two centuries. The stability that the Tokugawa imposed on an exhausted nation eventually secured their own downfall, but ultimately led to Japan's renewal.

Securing the Dynasty

The Battle of Sekigahara (1600; see THE DAIMYOS) was not conclusive in its outcome; Hideyori's supporters lived on to fight again. When a year-long siege of Osaka castle ended, in 1615, with Hideyori's suicide, the dynasty had, at last, vanquished all its challengers. In 1616 Ieyasu died, bequeathing a set of 'Laws for Military Households' as his political tribute. By encouraging *samurai* to cultivate the arts of both 'the sword and the brush' – to be literate warriors – Ieyasu looked to an elite of soldier-bureaucrats to safeguard the nation from further disturbance.

Divide and Rule. The Tokugawa regime, whose features Ieyasu had outlined, rested on a division of power between the shogunate and some 250 *daimyo* domains. The Tokugawa directly controlled about a quarter of the entire country, supporting their core holdings with buffer zones held by trusted vassals (***fudai***). Those 'outer' lords (***tozama***) who were defeated at Sekigahara and Osaka, were left to govern the peripheral regions. Unless peasant rebellion justified intervention, *daimyos* domains were allowed considerable autonomy. In spite of this, alliances through marriage and the building of fortifications were strictly controlled, and spies and informers were used widely to ensure compliance. All *daimyo* were also compelled to make 'alternate attendance' annually at the shogun's court. This was a time-consuming and costly procedure; upon departure, they were obliged to leave their wives and heirs behind for up to six months to

◀ **The Feudal Domains during Tokugawa Rule** *The system of government was complex during this period. It was characterized, however, by the military dominance of the shogun's government, which regulated the territories of the feudal lords.*

guarantee their loyalty, while they returned to govern their estates. Travel of all kinds was strictly supervised by a system of checkpoints set up by the shogunal authorities and the *fudai*. Pilgrimage, however, was regarded more leniently.

Closing the Country

Christians were persecuted intermittently under Hideyoshi. This practice intensified after the death of Ieyasu (1616), who had valued overseas contacts. His successors saw them as a potential threat to a hard-won peace. Although the Christians had won devoted

Hidden Christians

Persecution forced most of Japan's Christians to renounce their faith. Two centuries after the supposed suppression of the faith, however, Catholic missionaries discovered thousands of 'hidden Christians' in the port of Nagasaki and on its offshore islands. Cut off from any contact with orthodoxy, they had mixed Shinto, Buddhist, and folk elements into their beliefs and worship.

Confucianism The traditional philosophy in China since the 5th century BC. It was introduced in Japan in the 13th–15th centuries with the infusion of other aspects of Chinese culture. While Buddhism was the predominant faith in Japan, Confucianism complemented it in providing the basis of Japan's social morality.

Japan's Social Pyramid ▶
The emperor, remote and unapproachable, existed above a society whose visible apex was represented by the shogun and daimyo. *At the bottom were the 'eta,' an outcast group of obscure origin, condemned to 'unclean' trades. Their descendants,* burakumin, *are still subject to social discrimination today.*

followers, they had made enemies with their sectarian squabbling and their criticisms of divorce, moneylending, and homosexuality. While the Christians continued to trade in slaves and eat such useful animals as oxen, the Japanese could only regard them as hypocrites. In 1623, Iemitsu, the third Tokugawa shogun, had 50 Christians burned to death to mark his assumption of office. All Japanese were required to register at a Buddhist temple as proof of their commitment. In 1635 Japanese ships were forbidden to sail abroad, the building of ocean-going ships was banned, and children resulting from mixed marriages were deported. From 1639 onwards foreign trade was reduced to only a small amount conducted through Dutch merchants, whose only interest was profit, and not religion.

The Social Pyramid. Beneath the real holders of power were the *samurai* and then the farmers. In practice, most had a hard life although peasants near towns could prosper from access to their markets. Villagers were largely left to run their own affairs, providing they paid their taxes. Merchants, despised as parasitical non-producers, ranked even lower than craftsmen, though many were as wealthy as *daimyo*. Some people did not fit neatly into the social hierarchy. Priests and doctors mixed with *samurai* on a level of uneasy equality. *Ronin*, masterless *samurai*, sometimes lowered themselves to become merchants' bodyguards or even bandits.

Cities and Culture

In 1590 Edo was a fishing village with a decaying castle. Ieyasu made it his power base, draining its swamps and erecting a huge fortress-like palace at its centre. By 1700 Edo

▲ **A Dutch Ship in Nagasaki Harbour** *This wood-block print shows one of the two Dutch ships allowed to enter Nagasaki each year. The ships brought spices, silk, and sugar to exchange for gold, silver, copper, and ceramics.*

(later Tokyo) may well have been the largest city in the world. Osaka, Japan's commercial heart, was second in size to Edo. Kyoto, still in theory the capital, remained important as a centre of learning, religion, crafts, and fashion although its political significance was at an end. Such major concentrations of population required not only sustenance but diversion. By 1617 a red-light area had been officially designated in Edo and, by 1624, a theatre district was established. Osaka and Kyoto had similar facilities. The stately Nō drama was technically forbidden to commoners. The ordinary inhabitants of these thriving cities flocked instead to patronize *kabuki*, a fast-moving burlesque with outlandish costumes and make-up and stunning stage effects. They also attended *bunraku*, a form of puppet theatre. Chikamatsu Monzaemon (1653–1725), also known as the 'Shakespeare of Japan,' wrote prolifically for both types of drama. The courtesans who frequented the entertainment districts were known as ***geisha*** (literally 'art person'); they pleased their clients not only with sexual favours but through music and dance, and witty cultivated conversation. *Geisha* featured prominently in *kabuki* plays, although all the parts were played by men.

The tawdry life of the *geisha* and the actor led to the development of a literary genre typified by criminal escapades and fantasy, epitomized by the writings of Saikaku Ihara (1642–93). The spectacular multicoloured wood-block prints, known as ***ukiyo-e*** also depicted the characters and amusements of the entertainment districts. These developments reached their zenith in a period of free-spending prosperity known as the *Genroku* era (1688–1703). Masters such as Hokusai (1760–1849) and Hiroshige (1797–1858)

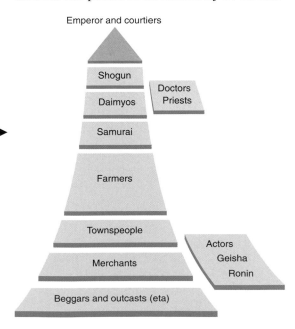

Emperor and courtiers

Shogun
Daimyos
Doctors Priests
Samurai
Farmers
Townspeople
Actors Geisha Ronin
Merchants
Beggars and outcasts (eta)

enlarged the scope of *ukiyo-e* to embrace landscape as well as more specific subjects.

Dutch Learning. Dutch traders, isolated on the island of Dejima, in Nagasaki harbour, provided the shogunate with a narrow view of the outside world. In 1722 the government relaxed its ban on the importation of books. 'Useful,' mainly pictorial, works on technical subjects, such as medicine, gunnery, and cartography, were eagerly studied by a small group of **rangaku** ('Dutch learning') scholars. Books on religion, politics, or history were still banned for fear that they would convey subversive ideas. The *rangaku* scholars were to provide an invaluable catalyst for the nation's intellectual rejuvenation a century later.

Inevitable Decline?

While the basic aim of the Tokugawa regime was to impose order in the interests of stability, the very peace they established eventually undermined their efforts. The official **Confucian** ideology of the regime affected to despise merchants while economic growth made them wealthy and, as *samurai* accrued debts to them, powerful too. The virtual nonexistence of foreign trade set absolute limits on the nation's food supply and, as Japan's population exceeded 30 million during the 18th century, peasants were driven to infanticide to reduce the number of mouths to feed. Overtaxation or a series of failed harvests sometimes pushed even the peasants too far; there were over 3000 rebellions during the 'Tokugawa peace.' Meanwhile the ruling elite attempted to cope with such challenges as fires, epidemics, and earthquakes, which were beyond its control, or inflation, which was beyond its comprehension. By the early years of the 19th

▲ **The USA's 'Black Ships'** *In an attempt to open trade relations with a reluctant Japan, it was implied by Captain Perry that dire consequences would be the result of Japan's failure to comply.*

century the Tokugawa regime was no longer stable, but dangerously rigid and increasingly floundering. A series of disastrous harvests in the 1830s culminated in a large-scale popular uprising in Osaka in 1837, led, ominously, by a former government official. That crisis was surmounted but there was soon to come an external challenge that could neither be ignored nor repulsed.

The Black Ships. In 1846 the USA went to war with Mexico. As a result, America acquired a Pacific coastline; with it came Pacific ambitions. Its commerce was henceforth directed at the immense market of China. Japan provided a useful point en route for safe anchorage, fresh food, and water. It remained, however, resolutely closed to outsiders. A US naval expedition, under the command of Commodore Matthew C. Perry, arrived in 1853 to 'request' the opening of trade relations. The Tokugawa realized the superior fire power which faced them. They were, therefore, forced to capitulate and sign a series of 'unequal treaties' that opened the country to trade and foreign settlement.

Civil War

The weakness of the shogunate in the face of foreign threats presented a long-awaited opportunity for the *tozama* lords, led by the Choshu and Satsuma clans, to take action. The result was a brief but bloody civil war (Boshin war); the rebels legitimized their action by invoking the name of the young new emperor, Mutsuhito, against the diminished authority of the shogun. The rebels were victorious and the capital was moved from Kyoto to Edo, subsequently renamed Tokyo. The emperor portentously adopted the name of **Meiji** ('Enlightened Rule') for his reign. The momentous events that brought down the Tokugawa are known as the 'Meiji Restoration.' This set Japan on a new course.

▲ **Kabuki actor** *Kabuki actors specializing in female roles often lived a virtually transvestite life, on and off stage; they became influential as leaders of fashion and manners.*

CHRONOLOGY OF THE LATER SHOGUNS	
1603–05	Tokugawa Ieyasu
1605–23	Hidetada
1623–51	Iemitsu
1651–80	Ietsuna
1680–1709	Tsunayoshi
1709–12	Ienobu
1713–16	Ietsugu
1716–45	Yoshimune
1745–60	Ieshige
1760–86	Ieharu
1837–53	Ieyoshi
1853–58	Iesada
1858–66	Iemochi
1867–68	Yoshinobu

The Meiji Restoration and Expansionism

*Meiji modernization • 'Civilization and enlightenment' • Reaction •
The road to empire • 'Taisho democracy' • The road to war •
Industrialization • From triumph to disaster*

▲ **Emperor Meiji**
*(1897) The new
emperor, who wore
Western clothes and ate
Western food,
epitomized the
imposition of Western
ideas and innovations
onto Japanese culture.*

For a century after the intrusion of the Perry expedition in 1853 (see THE TOKUGAWA SHOGUNATE), Japan's history was to be dominated by the country's responses to the challenge presented by the advanced nations of the West. This challenge was on four fronts: strategic, technological, cultural, and economic.

Meiji Modernization

In 1871 the new government of Japan, nominally headed by its young emperor, despatched a mission, under Iwakura Tomomi, to renegotiate the 'unequal treaties' imposed on its predecessor by the Western powers. These placed humiliating restrictions on Japan's sovereignty, binding it to impose tariffs no higher than 5% and to allow foreigners accused of crimes to be tried in their own consular courts, rather than under Japanese law. The reversal of the treaties was to remain a primary aim of Japanese foreign policy for the next 50 years.

The mission failed to gain significant concessions to the treaties. It did, however, directly expose its high-ranking members to the wealth and power of Western industrializing nations. Overwhelmed by railways, foundries, and armouries, they returned committed to the notion that rapid modernization offered Japan the only means by which outright colonization could be avoided. The first step was to replace the feudal structure of government with a Western-style administration, based on ministries and prefectures. This new administration led to investment in railways and port facilities, and promoted model enterprises, notably in silk manufacture, whose exports provided an invaluable source of foreign exchange. Agriculture benefited from the diffusion of good practice through advisers and exhibitions, while it bore the main burden of taxation required to finance modernization. All Japanese were also required to undertake public obligations previously required only of the *samurai* class, namely, school attendance and military service.

For many Japanese these changes seemed too great and too rapid. There were riots against conscription in 1873, *samurai* rebellions in 1874 and 1876, and a peasant revolt against taxes in the 1876. In 1877 the

▲ **The Modernization of Japan** *The building of a railway network irrevocably changed the face of life in Japan, allowing the transportation of goods and people at a speed never before experienced. This woodblock print contrasts the old modes of transport with the new.*

discontented rallied to support Saigo Takamori, a *samurai* who had played a prominent part in the Meiji Restoration. His rebellion was crushed by the new army of peasant conscripts, wearing Western-style uniforms. Saigo's defeat and suicide on the battlefield aptly symbolized the passing of the old order.

'Civilization and Enlightenment'

The craze for 'Western things' reached its height in the 1880s. It was epitomized by the opening in Tokyo of the *Rokumeiman* – 'The Pavilion of the Deer's Cry' – a government-sponsored cultural centre in which the new elite could mix socially with foreign residents and enjoy such novelties as musical concerts, billiards, and charity bazaars. Throughout the country, young highly paid *yatoi* (foreign experts) trained and supervised eager Japanese in establishing banks, shipyards, teaching hospitals, and other apparatus of a progressive state. Writers and artists also avidly studied the literary and aesthetic forms then current in Europe, turning away from native traditions, such as Noh drama and the tea ceremony (see THE EARLY SHOGUNATES), which declined for lack of aristocratic patronage.

Reaction

The Meiji Constitution, declared in 1889, and the Imperial Rescript on Education, issued in 1890, represented a reassertion of traditional authority. The constitution was based on the structure devised by Bismarck for the new Germany, which, like Japan, had recently been formed by uniting a number of petty princedoms. The constitution, which enshrined a strong executive and a weak legislature, proclaimed itself to be a gracious gift from the throne, rather than a concession to current demands for 'popular rights.' The 1890 Rescript similarly asserted that the Confucian virtues of loyalty and obedience to superiors applied equally to adults as to schoolchildren.

The Road to Empire

The humiliations endured at the hands of Perry and other Western intruders made Japan's military elite keenly aware of the nation's vulnerability. The northernmost island of the Japanese archipelago, Hokkaido, which now constitutes 22% of the national territory, was hastily annexed in 1868 to forestall possible occupation by a foreign power. The

▲ **A Victorious Japanese Army Flies its Flag**
The overseas victories of Japan's modernized forces against those of much larger nations became an immense source of national pride and a justification for further sacrifice.

proposal for a pre-emptive strike in Korea – described as 'a dagger pointed at the heart of Japan' – divided the government in 1874. This action was postponed while the nation gathered its strength. Control of the Korean peninsula eventually provided the motivation for Japan's wars with China in 1894–95 and with Russia in 1904–05. The first resulted in the annexation of Taiwan (Formosa) and the second in the takeover of Korea. In Taiwan, Japanese colonialism led to a rise in standards of health, education, and agricultural output, and thus encountered little opposition. In proud Korea, which had been an independent state for 1000 years, dogged resistance to Japan's presence provoked repression that endured until colonial rule ended in 1945, leaving behind it a legacy of bitterness.

The End of an Era. The successful acquisition of an overseas empire by force won for Japan the respect of the Western powers that had posed a threat half a century before. In 1900 Japanese troops took the leading role in rescuing foreign diplomatic envoys besieged by 'Boxer' rebels in Beijing. In 1902 Britain signed a treaty of alliance with Japan, allowing Japan to redeploy its fleet to home waters. The treaty also provided Japan with a guarantee against French intervention in the event of a Japanese war with France's ally, Russia. By 1911 the last of the unequal treaties had been revoked. In 1912 Emperor Meiji died after a reign of more than 40 years. The ritual suicide of war hero General Nogi on the evening of the emperor's funeral suggested to many, at home and abroad, that while Japan may have modernized, it had by no means westernized.

'Taisho Democracy'

The brief reign of the ineffectual Taisho emperor was characterized by further assertions of imperialist ambition, social tensions, and a modest extension of citizens' rights. In

The army of Japan is quite good for Asia but it could not stand up to European troops as its men lack the true military instinct.

Captain Grierson, of the British War Office (1886)

Fukuzawa Yukichi (1835–1901)

A prominent admirer of Western culture, he founded Keio University and introduced the art of public speaking. He accompanied the first Japanese mission to the USA in 1860, and the first to Europe in 1862. An influential author, and a pioneering advocate of women's rights, he became disillusioned with the hypocrisy of Western powers in their dealings with less advanced nations.

A DECADE OF INNOVATION

1868 First national paper currency issued

1869 Colonization of Hokkaido begins

1870 Telegraph links Tokyo and Yokohama; Commoners permitted to take surnames

1871 First Japanese-language newspaper published; Postal service established

1872 Tokyo–Yokohama railway opened; Modern school system established

1873 Gregorian calendar adopted; Conscription enforced

1875 Meteorological observatory established

1876 Wearing of swords banned

1877 Satsuma rebellion crushed

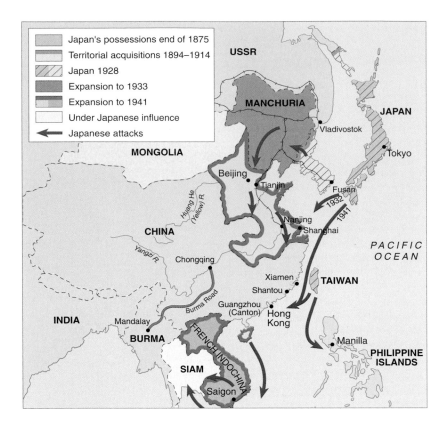

▲ Japan's Overseas Empire
The humiliations suffered at the hands of the US and other Western intruders led Japan towards the creation of its own empire between 1875 and 1941.

More than 200 000 troops on active service, more than 3 million in the veterans' organization, 500 000...middle and higher school students, and more than 800 000 trainees in local units, all of these will be controlled by the army, and their power will work as the central force aiding the Emperor in war and peace alike.

General Utagaki describes the militarization of Japanese society (diary entry, 1925)

1915 Japan attempted to take advantage of the distraction of the Western powers, involved in full-scale war in Europe, to present the weak government of the new Chinese republic with 'Twenty One Demands,' intended to strengthen Japan's economic presence in China. Procrastination and protests by the Chinese cut the list of demands to thirteen. These gave Japan little extra advantage; nevertheless, both Britain and the USA were alarmed. Although Japan was accepted as one of the 'Big Five' at the 1919 Paris Peace Conference, its efforts to add a racial equality clause to the charter of the new League of Nations were rebuffed. This insult was compounded by US restrictions on Japanese immigration in 1924. Japan did, however, accept a reduction in her naval strength as a result of the Washington Conference of 1921–22.

On the domestic front Japan was rocked by nationwide 'Rice Riots,' which were provoked by rampant wartime inflation. In 1923 national dislocation was further intensified by the devastating Kanto earthquake, which destroyed most of Yokohama and much of Tokyo, resulting in the deaths of approximately 140 000 people. The franchise was extended to include all adult males in 1925. This liberalization, however, was partly offset by the increase in police powers of surveillance over communists, students, trade unionists, and others who were deemed to be potentially subversive.

The Road to War
The instability of the Japanese economy was highlighted in 1927 by a financial crisis that caused the downfall of the government. The collapse of world trade between 1929 and 1931 virtually destroyed Japan's crucial export trade in silk, inflicting severe reductions in rural incomes. Sensing the rapidly diminishing appeal of internationalism, chauvinists among the military asserted the necessity for Japan to save itself by further expansion overseas to secure markets, obtain resources, and provide an outlet for emigrants. The result was the unauthorized invasion of Manchuria by Japanese forces in 1931. The puppet state of Manchukuo was established under the figurehead leadership of the last Qing (Manchu) emperor, Puyi. League of Nations censure of this aggression led to Japan's withdrawal from the League in 1933. In 1936 an attempted coup by junior officers was successfully crushed while, paradoxically, it strengthened the claim of senior officers that even more aggressive national policies were required to avoid revolution. In 1937 a full-scale invasion of China was launched and in the following year the domestic economy was put on a war footing. This was accompanied by a general militarization of public life, the effect of which was felt even in the school system.

Industrialization
Japan strove to modernize its economy in order to make the state powerful rather than to make its people affluent. War and exports, rather than domestic demand, provided strong stimuli for continued industrialization. By 1882 there were some 2000 factories in operation but most were small-scale enterprises, employing a total of 60 000 workers. It was the Sino-Japanese conflict that gave birth to

A DECADE OF TERROR

1928 Manchurian warlord, Zhang Zuolin, assassinated by Japanese army officers
1930 Prime Minister Hamaguchi mortally wounded by right-wing radical
1931 Two army coups aborted
1932 Prime Minister Inukai assassinated by naval officers
1933 Coup aborted
1936 Junior officers' coup crushed
1937 140 000 Chinese massacred in Nanjing
1938 National mobilization law passed

▲ **The Bombing of Pearl Harbor** *The magazine of the US destroyer* Shaw *explodes, having been hit during the raid.*

the giant government-funded Yawata steelworks and the production of Japan's first home-built locomotive. The Russo-Japanese War similarly boosted the heavy industry sector. The disruption of world trade that accompanied World War I enabled Japan to strengthen its position in those Asian markets that Britain was temporarily unable to supply. Despite the instability of the economy, the interwar period saw the emergence of significant new corporations, such as the car manufacturers Nissan, Toyota, and Mazda, Fuji in film, and Matsushita in electrical goods. The domestic market for the goods produced by such companies was, however, largely limited to the cities. In the countryside, dress, diet, and domestic interiors, with the exception of the occasional telephone or radio in more affluent households, had scarcely changed in half a century.

From Triumph to Disaster

Japan's decision to join Nazi Germany and Fascist Italy in an anti-communist alliance was motivated more by nationalistic ambitions than by any ideological affinity with these nations. It led to little effective cooperation in the conduct of a war in which Japan pursued its own objectives. Taking advantage of French weakness in 1940, Japanese forces advanced into Indochina. Pressure from the USA to force a Japanese withdrawal from its attempted conquest of China led to negotiations that ended in deadlock.

Japan's surprise attack on the US naval base at Pearl Harbor on 7 December 1941 anticipated its intended formal declaration of war. Despite inflicting considerable damage, the attack failed in its objectives to destroy vital aircraft carriers and repair facilities. It also served to unite the hesitant USA in favour of a major retaliation. Acknowledging the disparity

between the war potential of the two nations, Japan had intended to rob the USA of its naval striking power. This action would, in theory, have enabled Japan to complete its conquest of the resource-rich Asian mainland. It assumed that the USA could not conduct a campaign on the other side of the Pacific on the scale that would be required to dislodge Japan. The implications of this grave strategic miscalculation were temporarily masked by the brilliant successes of the Japanese army in seizing Hong Kong and Singapore, the bastion of British power in Asia, and in pressing on through Burma to threaten India itself.

The decisive damage to Japan's ambitions was, however, inflicted at sea. At the Battle of Midway (June 1942), Japan lost four aircraft carriers, a heavy cruiser, and 275 aircraft. With its long-range striking capacity shattered, Japan was forced on to the defensive. The 'island-hopping' strategy of the Allies enabled them to elude Japanese strongholds, while cutting off their supplies, until eventually they were able to establish bases from which Japan itself could be bombed. A three-day firebomb raid on Tokyo in March 1945 killed 150 000 people, providing an ominous portent of the fate of every other Japanese city except Kyoto. The destruction of the garrison of Okinawa, in addition to the killing of 100 000 civilians, demonstrated the scale of slaughter to be anticipated in the event of an actual invasion of Japan itself. Japan's surrender was finally secured by the dropping of atomic bombs on the cities of Hiroshima and Nagasaki (August 1945) and the simultaneous declaration of war by the previously neutral USSR. Rather than contemplate Soviet occupation, which might lead to the permanent division of the national homeland and abolition of the imperial throne, Japan's hasty surrender put its fate in the hands of the USA.

kamikaze Japanese pilots who deliberately crashed their own aircraft into enemy ships during World War II. Their name is taken from the 'divine winds' that had protected the nation from Mongol invasion in the 1280s (see THE EARLY SHOGUNATES). A tactic born of desperation, *kamikaze* attacks in the final stages of the war were carried out by novices guided to their targets by veteran flyers. Nevertheless, the 1465 *kamikaze* who died in action sank or crippled 129 ships and killed 3048 Allied seamen.

The Aftermath of the Atomic Bomb Dropped on Hiroshima *The city was largely destroyed and over 130 000 people were killed or injured. The city is now a major industrial centre and host to an annual conference opposing nuclear weapons.* ▼

Postwar Japan

Democratization • The road to recovery • Postwar politics •
The new Japanese • International relations

▲ **Electronics are One of Japan's Major Exports** *The industry has been an important vehicle for the nation's economic success.*

Tokyo Olympics

The 18th Olympiad, staged in Tokyo in October 1964, was a brilliant showcase for Japan's postwar recovery. The games were attended by 94 nations and widely praised for their efficiency.

=====SEE ALSO=====
The Industrial Age in Europe:
• Postwar Europe
China:
• Communist China
North America:
• The United States of America

Though nominally under Allied supervision, the postwar occupation of Japan was almost entirely a US operation, dominated by the personality of General Douglas A. MacArthur, Supreme Commander Allied Powers (SCAP).

Democratization

SCAP's first priority was to democratize Japan. Thousands of wartime politicians and generals were banned from public life, while left-wing dissidents were released from detention. These steps extended the authority of the civil service and strengthened the hold of the Left on the newly liberated trade union movement. 'War crimes' trials, of contested legality, led to the execution of ex-Prime Minister Tojo and other militarist leaders in 1948.

A new constitution came into force in 1947. Clearly proclaiming the sovereignty of the people and the purely symbolic role of the emperor, it enshrined the principle that all citizens have equal rights. This replaced the privileges previously accorded to men. Women were given the vote and civil rights were guaranteed. Article IX pledged Japan to renounce war as a method of settling disputes. The only armed forces would be for national self-defence.

Wide-ranging reforms in education and a redistribution of agricultural estates from landowners to farmers was a further means of reinforcing the commitment to democracy.

The Road to Recovery

Relief aid was generous in the early years of occupation, when Japan was on the verge of famine. Wartime destruction had reduced industrial output to 10% of its prewar peak, and the transport system was shattered. Raging inflation, racketeering, and violent labour disputes added to the nation's economic problems.

The rise of communism in China decisively altered SCAP's attitude towards Japan's recovery. Perceiving Japan less as a defeated enemy than as a bastion of freedom, SCAP abandoned its deconstruction of the prewar conglomerates, previously held responsible for Japan's aggressive expansionism. It also suppressed labour unrest and assisted financial authorities in imposing anti-inflationary measures. Out of this chaos emerged such companies as Honda and Sony, which set the pace of Japan's 'economic miracle.' By 1955 output had surpassed prewar levels. A period of almost 20 years of apparently unstoppable growth was brought to a brutal halt only by the 'oil shock' of 1973.

A lack of cheap energy forced Japanese industry to restructure away from steel, shipbuilding, and chemicals towards electronic and optical products. This involved more skilled labour, less energy and raw materials, and a shift of emphasis that both assisted the balance of payments and reduced pollution. Investment overseas also increased; the objectives were to relocate manufacturing facilities closer to their markets and to take advantage of lower labour costs in the declining industrial areas of Europe and North America, as well as in the emerging industrial zones of Southeast Asia.

Postwar Politics

Apart from a brief interlude of socialist rule in 1948, Japan was ruled by the same conservative parties until 1993. Funded by big business, they relied on rural votes, boosting support by using tax revenues to pay for public works that created jobs. Farmers also received subsidies. Lacking political cohesion, the conservatives initially fluctuated between Liberal and Democrat positions. They joined forces in 1955, however, in response to a reunited socialist movement. Forging strong links with the bureaucracy and major business organizations, the Liberal Democrats – despite periodic corruption scandals and factional infighting – enjoyed almost 40 years of uninterrupted power. Hesitant to undertake international initiatives, the Japanese ruling elite concentrated on fostering domestic economic growth, which gave voters ever-rising incomes, if not an ever-improving quality of life.

The New Japanese

Occupation and economic buoyancy resulted in far-reaching westernization of Japanese lifestyles. The gap in living standards between town and country was reduced. Longer school attendance and increased television ownership after 1953 sharpened ambitions for a better quality of life. An improved diet, modern medical care, and better working conditions gave the Japanese the longest life expectancy in the world. Housing standards, however, and the provision of public facilities, such as parks, fell short of those in Western countries.

Electrical appliances, precooked foods, ready-made clothes, and the rapid diminution of family size liberated the postwar housewife from the drudgery of previous generations. Spare time and money made traditional elite pastimes accessible to millions. From the

KOKUSAIKA

Kokusaika – internationalization – is a professed priority of official Japanese policy. It embraces a variety of activities, from the despatch of volunteers to developing nations to grudging 'market-opening' deregulation under pressure from GATT or disgruntled trading partners, such as the USA and the EU. Initial moves towards *kokusaika* were apparent with the establishment of the 'International House of Japan' in Tokyo in 1952; it pioneered exchange programmes and provided accommodation for visiting scholars and artists. In 1972 the Japan Foundation was established to promote a better appreciation of Japanese culture abroad. In the late 1970s, it initiated the JETS (Japan English Teaching Scheme) programme to recruit young English-speaking graduates from a range of countries to work as teaching assistants. During the 1980s local government structures, universities, and corporations were encouraged to develop their own *kokusaika* strategies; many saw the stimulus of overseas contacts as a valuable contribution to their institutional survival and development. By 1990 Japan had more than 500 clubs, associations, and foundations devoted to improving international understanding. As less than 10% of Japanese held a passport in 1990, the task of creating meaningful cultural links remained a formidable one.

▲ **A Modern Japanese Family** *The closeness of the Japanese family maintains an important continuity amid the hectic pace of modern Japanese society.*

1970s onwards the Japanese emerged as a great force in world tourism.

As memories of war faded, Western countries became as keen to import Japan's culture as its products. The national pride Japan felt in the global recognition of its cultural creativity was, however, tempered by an awareness that an unexpected by-product of economic success – a rapidly ageing population – would impose an increasing burden of support upon the labour force as Japan entered the 21st century.

International Relations

Japan recovered its sovereignty when Allied occupation ended in 1952. It immediately made a mutual security pact with the USA, which has remained the cornerstone of its foreign policy. Japan joined the United Nations in 1956, restored diplomatic links with Korea in 1965, and with China in 1972. Japan finally recovered control of Okinawa in the same year. It was not until 1992, however, that Japanese forces finally participated in a UN peacekeeping operation. In 1995, Japan formally apologized for its conduct during World War II.

In 1993, as Japan faced its worst postwar recession, domestic politics was transformed when the long Liberal Democrat ascendancy was superseded by a seven-party coalition. This heralded a return to preoccupation with domestic issues and a period of political uncertainty and electoral reform. However, following a brief interlude under a socialist premier, minority Liberal Democrat rule was restored in 1996. Financial deregulation measures were introduced in 1998, with the aims of enabling Tokyo to compete with the London and New York markets and sustaining Japan's global economic success.

Yoshida Shigeru (1878–1967)
Yoshida's diplomatic career included service in Korea, China, Rome and London; he was appointed ambassador to the UK in 1936. Retiring in 1939, he opposed Japan's alliance with the Axis powers (Germany and Italy) and, fearing the threat of communism, intrigued throughout the war for a compromise peace. Arrested and imprisoned in 1945, he became foreign minister later that year. As prime minister from 1946–47 and from 1948–54, he presided over the adoption of Japan's foreign policy and the establishment of the nation's self-defence forces in the face of bitter opposition. While his high-handedness clouded his final fall, he lived to be a respected statesman.

The High-Speed Bullet Train *Japan took the opportunity, at the 1964 Olympic Games in Tokyo, to unveil its latest service before the world's media.* ▼

The Genghis Khan Dynasty

The rise of Genghis • Genghis Khan's successors • The Mongol khanates

▲ **Genghis Khan**
(Persian manuscript)
Genghis founded one of
the largest land empires
in history, which he
ruled for 21 years.

The Mongol Empire, founded by Genghis Khan (c. 1167–1227), was created by his own military conquests and those of his successors. At its greatest extent (c. 1280) the empire stretched from Korea to eastern Europe.

The Rise of Genghis
Genghis was born into a nomadic tribal society in northeast Mongolia. He was able to attract followers and, by making alliances with leaders more powerful than himself, he gradually came to dominate the steppe grasslands; by 1206 he had become master of all the tribes of Mongolia; a *quriltai* (assembly of princes and notables) was held to acknowledge his supremacy. In order to cement the unity of the tribes, it was necessary to provide them with common enemies. Thus the conquest of much of the world began.

The Mongol army of Genghis Khan and his heirs largely comprised a cavalry force of archers. All adult male Mongols were liable for military service, providing variation on their nomadic existence. A substantial proportion of the population could, therefore, be mobilized, which accounts for the apparently very large size of the Mongol armies. Mongol soldiers were organized in small disciplined and manoeuvrable units.

Conquests of Genghis Khan. Genghis Khan's primary target for expansion was China, at that time divided into three states: Xi-Xia in the northwest, Jin in the north, and Song in the south. Xi-Xia was quickly brought

to submission (1207–10); however, the conquest of the Jin Empire was not completed until 1234. Genghis's campaigns began as predatory raids, which gradually became a process of permanent conquest. This process culminated in the fall, in 1215, of the Jin capital, near modern Beijing. Leaving an army in northern China, Genghis turned to the west. In 1218 the Mongols seized the Central Asian kingdom of Qara-Khitai. This extended Mongol-controlled territory to the borders of the kingdom of the Khwarazm-shah Ala al-Din Muhammad, who ruled much of what is now Uzbekistan, Afghanistan, and Iran. Provoked by the murder of Mongol merchants and an ambassador, Genghis invaded the kingdom in 1219. The ensuing four-year campaign caused enormous destruction and loss of life. Many of the great cities of the eastern Islamic world, such as Merv, Herat, and Nishapur, were devastated. Having returned to Mongolia in 1223, Genghis died in 1227 while on an expedition to China; he was succeeded by his third son, Ögödei (1185–1241), who was enthroned in 1229.

Genghis Khan's Successors
Under Ögödei (1229–41), the conquest of the Jin Empire was completed and further advances were made in the Middle East. The main expansion of Ögödei's reign was into Russia and eastern Europe. The Russian principalities were overwhelmed in a campaign that began in 1237; it was commanded by Batu (died c. 1255), Genghis Khan's senior grandson. Kiev fell in 1240; except for Novgorod, the Russian defeat was total. Batu continued to advance, in 1241, into Europe. While one army invaded Poland, the main force moved into Hungary. The Hungarian king was defeated on the River Sajó. Though the Mongols occupied Hungary, in early 1242

◄ **Mongol Conquests** *While the Mongol armies proved virtually invincible on the battlefield, they were not able to take fortified cities. For this purpose, equipment for attacking fortifications was acquired, manned by engineers from China and the Islamic lands.*

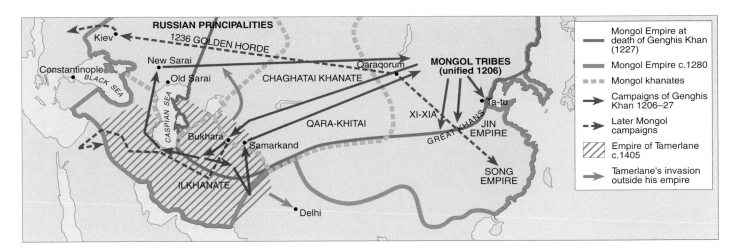

they withdrew to the south Russian steppes, probably on hearing news of the Great Khan Ögödei's death. An interregnum followed, until Ögödei's son, Güyük, was elected Great Khan in 1246. His relationship with Batu was extremely hostile, and only Güyük's sudden death, in 1248, averted civil war. In 1251 the sons of Genghis Khan's younger son, Tolui, mounted a coup d'état with the aid of Batu. The eldest brother, Möngke, became Great Khan (1251–59); the office of Great Khan henceforth remained in this branch of Genghis's family.

Under Möngke, the conquest of the southern Chinese Song Empire began in earnest. The principal commander was his brother (and successor) Qubilai. Another brother, Hülegü, was dispatched westwards to complete the conquest of the Middle East: he destroyed north Iranian strongholds in 1256, and, in 1258, he took Baghdad. In Syria, however, Hülegü's troops were defeated, in 1260, by the Mamelukes of Egypt. This marked the limit of Mongol expansion in the west.

The Mongol Khanates

By 1260 the vast territories of the Mongol Empire had been divided into four khanates, ruled by different branches of Genghis Khan's family. Mongolia and China were the domain of the Great Khan – Möngke, Qubilai, and their heirs. In Central Asia was the khanate of Chaghatai, Genghis's second son. Russia (known to westerners as the Golden Horde), was ruled by Batu and his descendants. In Iran and Iraq, and part of modern Turkey, the descendants of Hülegü established the Ilkhanate. All the khanates owed nominal allegiance to the Great Khan in China. Here, Qubilai (reigned 1260–94) completed the conquest of the Song in 1279. Qubilai's campaigns were not marked by the brutality of earlier Mongol warfare. He established a new capital for the empire at Beijing, declaring the Mongol royal house to be a Chinese imperial dynasty under the name Yuan (1272). His attempts at further expansion into Southeast Asia were unsuccessful; seaborne campaigns against Japan twice met with disaster (1274 and 1281).

▲ **The Mongol Empires** (1227–1405) *The Mongol Empire reached its greatest territorial extent in c. 1280, through the campaigns of Genghis and his successors. The empire had already been divided into four khanates since 1260. The subsequent decline of the khanates was followed by the creation of another empire under Tamerlane.*

CHRONOLOGY OF THE MONGOL EMPIRE (1206–94)

?1167	Birth of Genghis Khan	1246–48	Reign of Güyük, son of Ögödei
1206	Genghis Khan confirmed as supreme ruler of Mongolia	1251	Mongol throne seized by Möngke
		1256	Invasion of Iran by Hülegü
1207	First Mongol invasion of north China	1258	Hülegü sacks Baghdad; executes last Abbasid caliph
1215	Fall of Beijing to the Mongols		
1218	Mongols invade Qara-Khitai (Central Asia)	1260	Battle of Ayn Jalut; Mongols defeated in Syria by Egyptian Mamelukes
1219–23	Mongol campaigns against the Khwarazm-shah in Transoxania, eastern Iran, and Afghanistan	1260–94	Reign of Qubilai as Great Khan
		1272	Qubilai declares Mongols a Chinese imperial dynasty (the Yuan)
1227	Death of Genghis Khan		
1229–41	Reign of Ögödei, Genghis Khan's son	1274	First Mongol attack on Japan
1237–42	Mongols invade Russia and eastern Europe	1279	Fall of Song Empire to Qubilai
1241	Hungary occupied	1281	Second Mongol attack on Japan

The Successor States

*The decline of the Mongol khanates • Government of the Mongol Empire •
The empire of Tamerlane*

The eventual demise of the four Mongol khanates into which the vast empire of Genghis Khan had devolved led to the emergence a new Mongol power – the empire of Tamerlane, one of the most ruthless and irresistible conquerors in world history.

The Decline of the Mongol Khanates

Of the four Mongol khanates, the two based on sedentary civilization collapsed first. The Ilkhanate in Iran reached its zenith during the reign of Ghazan (1295–1304), who converted the Mongols within his kingdom to Islam; he also instituted reforms to repair the ravages of the 13th century. When his nephew Abu Sa'id, the last Ilkhan, died without an heir in 1335, however, the Ilkhanate suffered from factional struggles and collapsed. In China, too, the Mongols had adopted a form of one of the native religions, Buddhism. After 1323 there were long periods of internal conflict, pestilence, and natural disasters. From the 1340s there were large-scale revolts against Mongol rule in southern China. In 1368, the last Yuan emperor, Toghon Temür, was driven from China by rebel forces.

The two other khanates, Chaghatai and the Golden Horde, maintaining the traditional nomadic lifestyle of the Mongols, survived for much longer. Little is known of the history of the Chaghatai khanate. In the mid-14th century it split into two halves; the eastern half, called Mughulistan, remained traditionally

Mongol, nomadic, and pagan. The western half, Transoxania (modern Uzbekistan), was Muslim and largely sedentary, with several great cities (notably Bukhara and Samarkand). This was to become the base of the future conqueror Tamerlane (?1336–1405). The Golden Horde tended to rule the Russian principalities of the north indirectly. Mongol settlement was confined to the southern steppe grasslands, where they remained largely nomadic; there were, however, flourishing capitals at Old and New Sarai on the River Volga. These Mongols also adopted Islam, under their khan, Özbeg (1313–41). The Horde's decline, paralleled by the rise of Lithuania and Moscow, began in the later 14th century. In 1438 the Golden Horde was divided into two and further divisions followed. The traditional end of the Horde is marked by the victory of Mengli Girai, Mongol ruler of the Crimea, over the 'Great Horde' in 1502. However, Mengli took over rather than destroyed the Horde; its real extinction came when Catherine the Great (1729–96) of Russia annexed the Crimea in 1783.

Government of the Mongol Empire

The Mongol Empire, at its height, was the largest continuous land empire that has ever existed. The conquest and by no means short-lived rule of so vast an area by an originally illiterate nomadic people is a remarkable phenomenon. Much of the credit for the empire's success is due to Genghis Khan himself, who laid strong state foundations as well as initiating the long series of conquests. While the Mongols' military success was due primarily to the Mongols' own efforts, their skill in government owed much to others. The Mongols were pragmatists, willing to learn from those with experience that they themselves lacked. When vast sedentary territories in the east and west were conquered, the Mongols retained variant forms of the indigenous administrations: in Iran, the Iranian Islamic system was employed and, in China, the traditional Chinese bureaucrats continued in office at the lower levels. Mongol elements were added to these systems; in particular, Mongol taxes were added to those already existing. One necessary aspect of Mongol government of so large a land mass was the establishment of a postal courier network, a kind of pony express, across the length and breadth of Asia; this enabled

---

Khitans and Uighurs

In order to govern their empire in the early years of conquest, the Mongols employed Khitans (founders of Qara-Khitai in Central Asia). They also employed Uighurs, a Turkish people who had once ruled Mongolia and whose script was adopted by Genghis Khan for first writing down the Mongolian language.

Tamerlane (Timur) ▶
The court of Tamerlane equalled that of earlier Mongol emperors in its riches and splendour. This depiction of the court gives an indication of its magnificence.

◄ **Tamerlane's Tomb at Samarkand**
The last 35 years of Tamerlane's life were one long expedition of conquest and plunder. Much of the world was looted to glorify Samarkand, Tamerlane's capital. His tomb, shown here, was completed in 1234.

communications to be efficiently maintained. In addition, Genghis Khan was widely believed to have laid down a code of laws, the 'Great Yasa,' binding on his descendants; it is not certain, however, how effective this was.

The Empire of Tamerlane

Timur the Lame – known as Tamerlane in Europe – was born c. 1336 near Shahr-i Sabz in modern Uzbekistan. Though Turkish was his language, he was a nomad of Mongol descent. While he was not actually descended from Genghis, Timur later married into Genghis's family to gain prestige. Like Genghis, he was a successful robber chief, who attracted followers because of his success; he made alliances with those more powerful than himself and was able, gradually, by 1370, to become the dominant figure in the western half of the Chaghatai khanate. From then, however, his career differed from his predecessor's: while Genghis had conquered the sedentary world from the steppe, Timur, though a nomad, did the opposite. Iran, the former Ilkhanate, was constantly invaded from 1381. The nomads of Mughulistan to the east and of the Golden Horde to the north were defeated and neutralized; no attempt, however, was made to annex their territories. India was invaded in 1398 and Delhi sacked. In 1402 Timur captured the Ottoman Sultan Bayezid at Ankara. Finally, Timur assembled an expeditionary force to invade Ming China; as it set off in 1405, however, he fell ill and died.

Timur was a conqueror whose cruelty and ruthlessness far exceeded that of Genghis Khan; nor did he possess Genghis's constructive qualities. Timur's empire did not, as a whole, survive him, though his descendants

retained the eastern parts of his conquests for another century (until 1506), ruling from Samarkand in Uzbekistan and Herat in Afghanistan. This was a period of cultural revival during which Timur's descendants attempted to repair their ancestor's ravages. Finally, one of Timur's descendants, Baber (died 1530), mounted an expedition into India, where he founded the last and most durable of the Timurid kingdoms: the Mogul Empire.

CHRONOLOGY OF THE MONGOL EMPIRE (1295–1783)	
1295–1304	Reign of Ghazan, greatest Mongol ruler of the Ilkhanate in Iran
1313–41	Reign of Khan Özbeg of the Golden Horde
1335	Death of Abu Sa'id precipitates collapse of Mongol rule in Iran
?1336	Birth of Timur (Tamerlane)
1368	Toghon Temür, last Yuan emperor, expelled from China; establishment of Ming dynasty
1370	Timur dominant ruler in Transoxania (Uzbekistan)
1381	Timur invades Iran
1398	Timur invades India and sacks Delhi
1402	Timur defeats and captures Ottoman Sultan Bayezid at Ankara
1405	Death of Timur
1438	Division of the Golden Horde into two khanates
1502	Mengli Girai, Mongol ruler of Crimea, defeats and annexes 'Great Horde'
1530	Death of Baber, founder of Mogul Empire in India
1783	Annexation of Crimea to Russia by Catherine the Great

Early India

The Indus valley and the Aryans • Religious revolutions •
Magadha • Alexander the Great

Excavations at Mohenjo-Daro *These remains in the province of Sind (Pakistan) were first excavated in 1922. The name means 'the mound of the dead.'* ▼

As in other civilizations, the earliest peoples to inhabit the Indian subcontinent were hunter-gatherers and shifting cultivators.

The Indus Valley and the Aryans
Archaeological excavations have revealed that by c. 2500 BC a sophisticated civilization was thriving in the northwest of the subcontinent. It is known as the Indus Civilization because the largest cities excavated so far are on the Indus River in modern-day Pakistan. Two large cities emerged there, 560 km apart: Harappa in the north and Mohenjo-Daro in the south. Each was built of brick, laid out on a grid-plan with a raised citadel, an efficient drainage system, huge granaries, and residential quarters, which differentiated high from low. The inhabitants of these cities had domesticated livestock, poultry, and beasts of burden, worked copper, and wore cotton. They traded with the Middle East by land and sea and developed a system of writing that has yet to be deciphered. The absence of palaces and

numerous finds of seals, figurines, and imported goods suggest a society of priests, merchants, and farmers. This Indus Civilization covered a vast area: one of its southern-most cities, Lothal, is in the modern Indian state of Gujarat. It lasted, with little change, for around 1000 years, then disappeared around 1500 BC, possibly as a result of environmental disaster, perhaps compounded by either an epidemic, or an external attack.

As the Indus Civilization declined, India received the first of many subsequent waves of invaders from the northwest. They came literally riding out of Central Asia, and their chariots played a key part in the conquest. These light-skinned sharp-featured newcomers called themselves Aryan, meaning 'noble.' Their culture has been reconstructed less from material remains than from the anthology of 1028 Sanskrit hymns known as Rig-Veda, which celebrates their elemental deities – the rain god Indra, banisher of drought and 'destroyer of cities,' and the gods of fire, the sun,

and dawn. Hinduism, which integrates gods, man, and nature in a system of thought that is theological, sociological, and cosmological, emerged from the interaction of this Vedic pantheon with local cults. Events of the period c. 1000 BC can be gleaned from India's two great epics, though these books were written down much later. The *Mahabharata* ('Great Epic of the Bharatas'), some 100 000 couplets long, creates a world of gods and heroes, while dimly reflecting the tribal rivalries of the area between the upper Ganges River and the Jumna around 1000 BC. At the time that this immortal epic began to take shape, mastery of iron-working provided keener weapons with which to wage warfare and stronger tools with which to accelerate the clearance of the forests of the Gangetic plain. The subsequent southward expansion of the Aryans is implied in the *Ramayana*, India's other great epic, in which the heroine is carried away, far beyond the lands of forest-dwelling non-Aryans, to the island of (Sri) Lanka.

By the 6th century BC, the north Indian plain was divided between more than a dozen states, ranging from Gandhara, in the extreme northwest, to Magadha and Anga along the lower Ganges. The rise of Achaemenid power in Persia renewed the threat to the vulnerable northwest and, during the reign of Cyrus (558–528 BC), the gold-rich state of Gandhara became a province of the Persian empire. Cyrus's successor, Darius (c. 558–486 BC), briefly extended Persian power across the Indus itself. Taxila, capital of Gandhara, became a significant intellectual centre and home to the botanist Atreya and the Sanskrit grammarian Panini (active 350 BC).

Some of the states of the north Indian plain were kingdoms, others tribal oligarchies, but all used writing, coinage, systemized weights and measures, and commonly recognized hierarchical distinctions of rank between Brahmans (priests), Kshatriyas (warriors), Vaishyas (merchants), and Shudras (farmers). In these distinctions lie the origins of the caste system. Another Aryan practice was the cremation of the dead, to rid the world of pollution and decay. Both of these legacies remain fundamental to Hinduism.

Religious Revolutions

These societies produced, in c. 800 BC, the philosophical texts called *Upanishads*, which explore the nature of knowledge and moral action, and, in the 6th century BC, two founders of new faiths: Vardhamana (c. 599–527 BC), known as Mahavira ('Great Hero'), and the Buddha. Mahavira preached an unyielding asceticism as the path of escape from the endless cycle of rebirth. Jainism, which he taught, also upholds absolute non-violence,

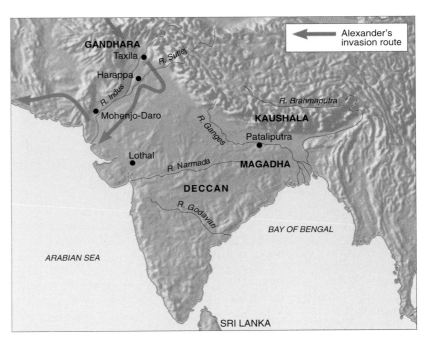

extending the principle even to respect for the lives of insects. Gautama Siddhartha (c. 563–483 BC), a contemporary of Mahavira, also renounced wealth and family to follow the ascetic path but ultimately forswore that too, in favour of a 'middle way.' Hailed as a Buddha ('Enlightened One'), he created a monastic elite, which spread his teachings. In time they travelled eastward and southward, far beyond India to Tibet, China, and Japan.

Magadha

The iron-rich state of Magadha came to dominate the area. A contemporary of Buddha, Bimbisara (died c. 554 BC) annexed neighbouring Anga, bolstered by the novel weapon of a standing army. In this way he gained trading access to the Ganges delta and to the sea, and further extended his territories by a programme of dynastic marriages. His successor, Ajatasatru, overcame the strongest remaining rival state, Kaushala, to extend his commerce southwards towards the Deccan. Around 413 BC, however, Ajatasatru's son lost his throne to a dynasty known as the Nandas.

Alexander the Great

The incursion of Alexander the Great (356–323 BC) was more than a raid, but it fell short of being a full-scale invasion. Although the city of Taxila had welcomed him, an Indian ruler known to Greek historians as Porus (died c. 321–315 BC) gathered a vast army and forced him into battle. Although Macedonian discipline and skill triumphed, Alexander's army refused to follow him further and he turned back to the west and met with an early death. His entire career remained unrecorded by the Indian chroniclers of the time.

▲ **Early India** *From the rise of the Indus Civilization in the northwest in the 3rd millenium BC, the north Indian plain, by the 6th century BC, had developed into more than a dozen states, from Gandhara in the northwest to Magadha on the lower Ganges. While the incursion of Alexander the Great into Gandhara in 327 BC and his subsequent campaign across the Punjab had no political or historical impact on India, some of his Greek companions did record their impressions of India.*

There is a Spirit which is pure and which is beyond old age and death; and beyond hunger and thirst and sorrow. This is Atman, the Spirit in man. All the desires of this Spirit are Truth. It is this Spirit that we must find and know: Man must find his own Soul. He who has found and knows his Soul has found all the worlds, has achieved all his desires.

Chandogya Upanishad

Empires and Rivalries

*India's first (Mauryan) empire • The empire of Ashoka •
After Ashoka • A second empire*

===SEE ALSO===
Religion (vol. 6):
• Hinduism
• Buddhism

The uncertainty and disorder following the withdrawal of Alexander's army (see EARLY INDIA) favoured bold and decisive action. Chandragupta Maurya (reigned c. 321–c. 297 BC) exploited revolts in the northwest to oust Porus from Taxila. He also seized the throne of Magadha.

India's First (Mauryan) Empire

In 303 BC Chandragupta confronted Seleucus Nicator (c. 358–281 BC), Alexander's legatee for the lands west of the Indus, and annexed them, including a large part of Afghanistan. By the end of the 4th century BC an Indian empire stretched from the Hindu Kush to the Bay of Bengal, with its fortified capital at Pataliputra on the Ganges.

The Empire of Ashoka

The conquests of Chandragupta Maurya were continued by his son Bindusura (died 273 BC) and, initially, by his successor, Ashoka (reigned c. 272–231 BC). However, Ashoka's campaign of 261 BC against the Kalingas, occupiers of today's Orissa on the Bay of Bengal, provoked in him a traumatic reaction against slaughter and destruction. Ashoka became a fervent convert to the doctrine of compassion taught by the Buddha and devoted the rest of

▲ **Empires of India** *Between 321 BC–535 AD the subcontinent was dominated successively by the vast empires of Ashoka and Chandra Gupta II.*

his reign to good works. Although he did not enforce his own vegetarianism on his subjects, he did ban animal sacrifices. His benefactions included free hospitals, veterinary clinics, baths, wells, shade trees, and rest houses for travellers. Nor did he neglect administration; he assiduously studied reports and instructed his senior officials to make regular regional tours of inspection. Under Ashoka's patronage, missionaries spread the knowledge of Buddhist doctrines far and wide, to the kingdoms under Greek rule in the northwest and to Sri Lanka in the south. Despite his endorsement of Buddhism, Ashoka contrived to remain on equable terms with Hindus and Jains.

After Ashoka

Ashoka's death (231 BC) was swiftly followed by the disintegration of his vast domains. Under the usurping Shunga line, the former empire dwindled to its ancient core, Magadha. For half a millennium no Indian dynasty was capable of uniting again so vast an area of the peninsula. The chronology of this period is complex, but certain trends and outstanding personalities can be discerned. One was a change in the nature of Buddhism. Abstract symbols of the Buddha's teachings were superseded by sculptural representations of him

THE EDICTS OF ASHOKA

▲ **Column of Ashoka, Delhi**

Throughout his realm, Ashoka ordered his edicts to be carved upon standing rocks or stone pillars. The pledge that he made to his people is shown by this example.

"I consider it my only duty to promote the welfare of all men. But exertion and prompt dispatch of business lie at the root of that... whatever effort I make is made in order that I may discharge the debt that I owe to all living beings, that I may make them happy in this world and that they may attain heaven in the next world. Therefore this record relating to *dharma* ['duty'] has been caused to be written by me on stone for the following purpose, namely, that it may last for a long time and that my sons, grandsons, and great-grandsons may conform to it for the welfare of all men. This, however, is difficult to accomplish without the utmost exertion."

(Map labels: Probable extent of Ashoka's Empire; Probable extent under Chandra Gupta II; GANDHARA; MAGADHA; Pataliputra; SAURASHTRA; DECCAN PLATEAU; KALINGA; ARABIAN SEA; ANDHRA; BAY OF BENGAL)

INDIAN DYNASTIES (4 BC–6 AD)

Date (in centuries)	Location	Dynasty
4 BC	Magadha	Nanda
4–2 BC	India except Mysore	Maurya
2–1 BC	North India	Indo-Greeks
2–1 BC	Ganges valley and central India	Shunga
c. 1 BC–3 AD	North Deccan	Satavahana
1 BC–4 AD	Western India	Saka
1–3 AD	North India and Central Asia	Kushan
4–6 AD	North India	Gupta

between 100 BC and 100 AD. Hinduism responded by exalting the gods Vishnu and Shiva. Another trend was the expansion of trade in pearls, ivory, pepper, and other spices. Trading partners ranged from the Middle East and Rome to Indonesia and Southeast Asia.

Among the significant personalities of this turbulent era were the rulers Menander and Kanishka. Menander ruled (115–90 BC) a Hellenized state in the northwest. He is known through a Buddhist treatise, which records his conversion to Buddhism; he continued, however, to fight bloody battles, in one of which he met his death. Kanishka was the ruler (c. 120–62 AD) of a sprawling realm that the Central Asian Kushans focused on Purushupura (Peshawar) and extended down the Ganges as far as Banares. Since his domains straddled the caravan routes linking China to the Mediterranean, Kanishka prospered from commerce. He gave generous patronage to Buddhist scholarship; he also convened the momentous Kashmir conference, which promulgated the *Mahayana* ('Great Vehicle') tradition of Buddhism, thus accommodating popular demands for a saintly pantheon; it became the dominant mode of faith in China, Korea, and Japan.

A Second Empire

The origins of the Gupta family are obscure, but – probably through a judicious marriage alliance – the family controlled Magadha by 319 AD. The founder of the new dynasty, Chandra Gupta I (reigned 320–c. 330 AD), adopted the significant title of 'King of Kings.' His aggressively expansionist son, Samudra, called himself 'Exterminator of Kings.' Under Chandra Gupta II (reigned c. 380–c. 415 AD), the Gupta Empire was at its height, stretching across northern India. Although some northern mountain states were among its tributaries, it included neither Gandhara in the far west nor the Deccan in the south. A programme of land clearance and village settlement increased agricultural output and state revenues. Brahmans became involved in this process, contributing their expertise with

regard to the calendar rituals. Buddhism meanwhile became isolated from the masses as its priesthood became preoccupied with doctrinal elaboration and life in wealthy urban monasteries. Metallurgical skills, astronomy, and mathematics flourished; Aryabhata (born 476 AD) speculated that the earth was a sphere rotating on its axis as it moved around the sun. During the second half of the 5th century AD, the western part of the Gupta realm was overrun by Huns from Central Asia, despite the heroic efforts of Skanda Gupta (455–70 AD). While this influx was later reversed, the financial strains and urban devastation it caused resulted in the demise of the Gupta Empire, although the dynasty survived in smaller kingships for another century.

The Ajanta Caves *The Buddhist rock-cave temples and monasteries, near Ajanta (western India), are famous for their wall paintings. While the paintings depict Buddhist stories (the adoration of Buddha is shown here), they also give some insight into court life around the time of the Gupta period.* ▼

The Contest for Dominance

Harsha • An age of warring states • From raiding to conquest • The Delhi sultanate

A rough unity was briefly restored to northern India, from Gujarat to east Bengal, by Harsha (c. 590–c. 647 AD). He shifted the focus of power from Pataliputra westwards to Kanauj, at the heart of the Gangetic Plain, which henceforth became the symbolic prize in the contest for dominance.

Harsha

Harsha's patronage of culture is attested by the dramas attributed to him and by the presence of 4000 students at the Buddhist monastery-university of Nalanda. Harsha eventually became the victim of a conspiracy against his life. As there was no adequate heir to succeed him, his empire died with him.

A CHINESE OBSERVER

Xuan-zang (602–64 AD), a Chinese pilgrim, journeyed extensively through India between 630 and 643 AD. He was particularly struck by the practices of exclusion and avoidance that resulted from the caste system and from an awareness of pollution: "Butchers, fishers, dancers, executioners, scavengers, and so on, have their abodes outside the city. In coming and going, these people are obliged to keep on the left side of the road until they arrive at their homes." He considered the ordinary people to be honest and law-abiding. Petty offences were punished with fines. As a Buddhist scholar, Xuan-zang noted the special status accorded to the priestly vocation. Having mastered the ancient languages of the Buddhist scriptures, he returned to China with an immense collection of manuscripts and images.

An Age of Warring States

From the 8th to the 10th centuries, northern India was the scene of rivalries among the Rashtakutras (based in the northern Deccan), the Gurja-Pratiharas (ancestors of the Rajputs, originating in Rajasthan), and the Palas (from whose Bengal base trading and diplomatic contacts were extended as far as Southeast Asia). In the 7th century Arabs following the new faith of Islam had penetrated Afghanistan and Baluchistan; in the 8th century they advanced as far as Sind, establishing the kingdoms of Multan and Mansura.

Southern India. Geographically isolated from northern struggles, this area was largely unaffected by them. It was instead dominated by the successive emergence of two powerful dynasties.

The Pallava dynasty (2nd–9th century) reached the height of its power under Mahendravarman I (c. 600–30), a contemporary of

◀ **Rock-cut Temples** *Excavated near the town of Ellora in western India, these impressive temples, dating from the 6th–8th centuries, are cut from rock cliffs. They are of Buddhist, Hindu, and Jain origins.*

The Southern Kingdoms and the Realm of Tughluq *While the south was dominated by the powerful Pallava and Chola kingdoms from the 6th to the 12th centuries, the Delhi sultanate reached its greatest extent in the early 14th century.*

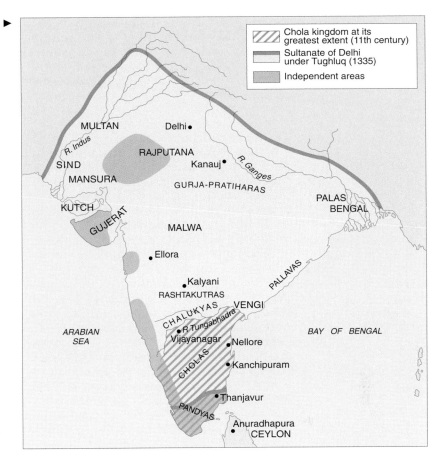

Harsha. Originating in the Deccan, the Pallavas eventually ruled from Kanchipuram (in modern Tamil Nadu state). Their rule was marked by colonization in Southeast Asia; their naval interests led to the development of port facilities, which laid the foundations for the extensive use of the navy by their successors, the Cholas. The Pallavas supported Buddhism and Jainism and they were keen patrons of the arts; they are also known for their great temples, which were built from granite. They fought an extended war against the Chalukyas (a dynasty that dominated the Deccan from the 6th to 8th centuries) over the Vengi region (on the west coast). In the late 8th century, the Gangas and Pandyas joined coalitions against the Pallavas, who could not finally withstand additional military pressure from the Western Chalukyas. Pallava power gradually fell to the Cholas; their territories passed to Chola rulers in c. 880.

The Chola dynasty was the most important in the subcontinent during this period, though their activities mainly affected the peninsula and Southeast Asia. The centre of Chola power was Thanjavur (in Tamil Nadu) during the reign of Vijayalaya. Parantaka I (907–53) laid the foundation of the kingdom, extending its boundaries as far north as Nellore (Andhra Pradesh). While he defeated the Pandyas in the south, his attack on Ceylon (modern Sri Lanka) failed. The reigns of Rajaraja I (985–1014) and his son, Rajendra (1014–44), are notable for ensuring the Chola kingdom's supremacy. Rajaraja reduced northern Ceylon to a Chola province, while a campaign against the Chalukyas extended northern boundaries to the Tungabhadra River. A naval campaign took the Maldive Islands, which, like Ceylon, were important to Chola control over trade with Southeast Asia, Arabia, and East Africa. Rajendra succeeded in conquering the heart of Chalukya territory, sacking its capital, Kalyani, as well as taking southern Ceylon. In 1021–22 a huge northern campaign was launched, which struck up the east coast to Bengal and then north to the River Ganges. An ambitious naval campaign was also launched against the Southeast Asian kingdom of Srivijaya, to protect trading interests with southern China. In the 12th and 13th centuries, Chola power gradually declined, while the Hoysalas in the west and the Pandyas in the south gained power. The latter became the dominant power in the

south; their supremecy, however, ended in the 14th century with the attack of Turkish armies. Much of Chola history has been reconstructed from huge numbers of inscriptions issued by the royal family and by temple authorities, village councils, and trade guilds.

From Raiding to Conquest

In the 11th century the Muslim Mahmud of Ghazna (971–1030) conquered an area stretching from the Caspian Sea to the Punjab and is said to have mounted annual raids deep into Indian territory. As a man of culture, however, he attracted to his court Firdausi (c. 935–c. 1020), the Persian poet, famous for his *Shahnama* (Book of Kings), and the Arab polymath al-Biruni, who compiled an encyclopedic account of the geography and population of India. Although Mahmud's empire was essentially a personal creation, which disintegrated after his death, he had exposed the weakness of a fragmented India and had paved the way for a more systematic conquest by Turkish-speaking invaders from Central Asia in the following century.

In 1186 Mohammed Ghuri (died 1206) seized the Punjab; in 1192 he defeated the Rajput princes. As his forces drove eastwards they sacked Nalanda, the last great stronghold of Buddhist learning. Muslim destruction, however, was to be offset in part by the

Bastion of Hinduism

Vijayanagar – 'City of Victory' – was founded in 1336 and became the capital of an empire that for the next two centuries served as a barrier against Muslim incursion and provided a haven for Hindu culture and art. The empire was at its height under Krishna Deva Raya (reigned 1509–29). His successors, however, were beset by enemies; in 1565, after a decisive defeat by a Muslim alliance, Vijayanagar was destroyed. Vestiges of the empire lasted for another half century. The city that once covered 33 sq km, and was reputed to have a population of half a million, is now a village called Hampi, with 1500 inhabitants.

introduction of such innovations as paper, porcelain, gunpowder, tea, and – in architecture – the minaret, the dome, and the pointed arch. In 1206 the leading general Qutb-uddin Aybak (died 1210) took Delhi and, following the assassination of his master, established a Turko-Afghan dynasty there.

The Delhi Sultanate

Although the Delhi sultanate never controlled all of northern India, it remained the dominant power in the region for three centuries. Qutb-ud-din was succeeded by his son-in-law Iltutmish (ruled 1211–36), who extended his control into Bengal, Multan, and Rajputana; this expansion was halted when the throne passed to his daughter Raziyya, who was assassinated four years later. After a period of anarchy, central authority was eventually restored by the general Balban (ruled 1266–87), but there was no competent ruler until the accession of Ala-ud-din (died 1316) in 1296.

The Delhi sultanate reached its maximum extent under the eccentric Mohammed ibn Tughluq (c. 1290–1351). Tughluq experimented with introducing a token coinage stamped on leather. He bought off the Mongols, but a great army that he sent to fight the Persians broke up for want of pay. Bengal broke away from his control in 1341, and in 1347 the Deccan provinces seceded to form the Bahmani kingdom, which itself broke into separate states in 1489.

Tughluq was succeeded by his cousin Firuz (reigned 1351–88). During his reign the martial Hindu state of Vijayanagar consolidated its hold on the area south of the Tungabhadra River. The western provinces of Malwa, Gujarat, and Kutch withdrew their allegiance, as did Jaunpur to the east.

Firuz was succeeded by six consecutive rulers within ten years. When the state was at its weakest, the Mongols, this time led by the great conqueror Timur (known as Tamerlane in Europe; ?1336–1405), marched on Delhi. By December 1398 the city was devastated. For half a century Delhi was ruled by Timur's viceroy Khizr Khan and his descendants; the throne was then taken by Bahlul (reigned 1451–89), an Afghan of the Lodi tribe, who reconquered Jaunpur. His son Sikandar (reigned 1489–1517) ruled from the Indus River to the frontier of Bengal. A conflict between Sikandar's son, Ibrahim (reigned 1517–26), and Afghan nobles of the Lodi line led to an appeal for help by the Lodis to Baber (1483–1530), king of Kabul. His response was to have momentous consequences.

> Above all men (he) delights most in giving presents and shedding blood. At his door is always seen some pauper on the way to wealth or some corpse that has been executed.
>
> **Ibn Battuta**, an Arab traveller, describes Tughluq

SRI LANKA

▲ **Buddhism in Sri Lanka** *Between c. 200 BC and 1200 AD, all of the Sinhalese kings were Buddhists. As a result, many Buddhist shrines and monasteries were built and impressive temples, such as that shown here at Anuradhapura, often with finely carved sculptures, flourished.*

According to tradition, an Indian prince, Vijaya, conquered the inhabitants of Sri Lanka in c. 6th century BC to become the first king of the Sinhalese. Some evidence of the indigenous people does survive in the interior of the island. The Sinhalese capital, Anuradhapura, became a major centre of Buddhist worship and study, supported by the productivity of a complex irrigation system. Between the 4th and 6th centuries AD, it witnessed a significant flowering of the arts under Buddhist inspiration. Sri Lanka came under Hindu Chola rule from 993 to 1070. Sinhalese rule was re-established thereafter, notably under the formidable Parakramabahu I (1153–86). From the 12th century a profitable spice trade was developed with the Arab world, which added a Muslim 'Moorish' minority to the population. The island's spices and gemstones, however, also attracted incursions from India, China, and Malaya in the 13th and 15th centuries. Spices also lured the Portuguese, who, from 1505 onwards, gradually extended their control over the whole island, except for the mountainous kingdom of Kandy. The island passed to the Dutch in the mid-17th century and then to the British in 1796.

The Great Moguls

An empire won • An empire enlarged • Reconciliation and toleration •
After Akbar • Servitude and stagnation • An Islamic reaction

Baber (1483–1530) was a descendant of Timur (Tamerlane; see THE MONGOL EMPIRES: THE SUCCESSOR STATES) on his father's side and Genghis Khan on his mother's. While his Mongol heritage was a source of inspiration for him, Baber never thought of himself as a Mongol, for he spoke a Turkic dialect and was a great admirer of Persian culture. He was schooled from an early age in the art of warfare, and at the age of 14 led an army that captured Samarkand, only to lose control of it almost immediately. Much of his remaining youth was spent in unsuccessful attempts to recapture this city, if only because it was a symbol of Tamerlane's vanished empire. By the age of 30 he held sovereignty over a small kingdom, which he ruled from Kabul.

An Empire Won

In 1526 Baber seized the opportunity provided by a quarrel between the Lodi sultan in India and his vassals to invade this rich and fertile region. Baber's Turkish artillery and superior generalship at the Battle of Panipat enabled him to advance on Delhi. The following year he destroyed a Rajput army at Khanua and in 1529 crushed the last organized resistance to his rule in a battle at the confluence of the Ganges and the Ghagra rivers.

Baber's autobiography reveals his disenchantment with his conquest: "Hindustan has few pleasures to recommend it. The people are not handsome. They have no idea of the charms of polite society." As a cavalryman, he was disappointed by the lack of good horses; as a mountain-dweller, he was appalled at the absence of ice and chilled drinking water. He also disliked Indian food. Moreover, he despised Hindu architecture and found the climate oppressive and dusty. Indeed, Baber could find only one aspect of India to like: "The chief excellency of Hindustan is that it is a large country and has abundance of gold and silver."

While Baber brought the vision of empire to India, he died, aged 47, before he could make it a reality.

An Empire Almost Lost. Baber's son, Humayun (1508–56), was an able and courageous ruler, in spite of being beset by ill fortune. A bibliophile and keen astrologer, Humayun placed too great a faith in the influence of the stars. A decade after his accession he was overthrown by his own vassal,

CHRONOLOGY OF MOGUL AND SURI EMPERORS (1526–1707)	
Mogul dynasty	
1526–30	Baber
1530–40	Humayun
Suri dynasty	
1540–45	Sher Shah Suri
1545–53	Islam Shah
1553–55	Muhammad Adil
1555	Ibrahim III
1555	Sikander III
Mogul dynasty	
1555–56	Humayun
1556–1605	Akbar I
1605–27	Jahangir
1628–58	Shah Jahan I
1658–1707	Aurangzeb

Baber *The first Mogul emperor (1526–30).* ▼

Mongols and Moguls

A *Mongol* is a person who comes from Mongolia, part of which is now a large republic in Central Asia. In the 13th century it was a vast empire ruled by Genghis Khan.

A *Mogul* is a member of an Indian dynasty of emperors, established in the 16th century, by Baber, a descendant of Genghis Khan. The word 'Mogul' is the European spelling of the Persian *mughal*, a Mongol.

The Mogul Empire (1530–1707) *While the empire was at its strongest under Akbar, it reached its greatest territorial extent under Aurangzeb.* ▼

Sher Shah Suri (?1486–1545), ruler of Bihar, and was compelled to take refuge with Tahmasp (1524–76), the Safavid shah of Persia. Sher Shah, founder of the Suri dynasty, created an efficient bureaucracy to administer his restructured system of land revenue. This system was developed further under the Moguls; consequently, although himself not a Mogul, Sher Shah laid the administrative foundations on which the empire's later greatness was built. He was killed in action after only five years in power, leaving his son to struggle to retain power. When he, in turn, was succeeded by his 12-year-old son, conflict broke out within the dynasty, enabling Humayun, with Safavid backing, to regain his realm in 1555. Within six months he was killed in an accident.

An Empire Enlarged

Humayun's son, Akbar (1542–1605), succeeded to the throne when he was 13 years old. Akbar combined his father's sophistication with his grandfather's martial vigour. Within a decade he had begun to annex the petty states that bordered on his empire. By 1569 all Rajputana was subdued, except Mewar. Gujarat was annexed by 1572. When, in the following year, this region rebelled, Akbar led 3000 horsemen over 600 miles in 9 days and defeated the astonished insurgents, returning to his capital 32 days later. This

A NEW RELIGION

Sikhism was founded by Guru Nanak (1469–1538) and consolidated by his nine successor gurus. Nanak, born a Hindu under Muslim rule, sought to transcend the exclusive nature of each faith and rejected idolatry and the caste system. His teachings, delivered in the form of hymns, soon attracted a devoted following. The fourth guru, Ram Das (guru 1574–81) founded the sacred city of Amritsar and the fifth, Arjan Mal (guru 1581–1606) compiled the *Adi Granth* (First Book), a collection of the 6000 hymns composed by his predecessors and others, which became the main scripture of the sect. Arjan Mal died in Mogul custody; the persecution of Sikhs that followed drove them towards greater militancy. The execution of the ninth guru, Tegh Bahadur (guru 1664–75) led to open warfare under his successor, the last guru, Gobind Rai (guru 1675–1708) and the establishment, in 1699, of an armed brotherhood, the *Khalsa* ('pure'), to defend the faith against persecution. Although the *Khalsa's* leader and 700 followers were executed in Delhi, in 1716, Sikh military power reemerged in the 18th century to achieve mastery of the Punjab.

Extent of Mogul empire 1530
Extent of Mogul empire 1605
Extent of Mogul empire 1707
Baber's Afghan kingdom
Suri empire
Attempted Mogul expansion
Emergent Maratha power by 1700
Safavid empire

AFGHANISTAN • Kabul
KASHMIR
PUNJAB
• Panipat
• Delhi
AWADH
BALUCHISTAN
MARWAR
BIHAR
SIND
BUNDELKHAND
MEWAR
BENGAL
GUJARAT
KHANDESH
GONDWANA
ORISSA
BERAR
AHMADNAGAR
BIDAR   DECCAN
GOLKONDA
BIJAPUR
ARABIAN SEA
BAY OF BENGAL
MALABAR

remarkable feat of arms secured the control of Gujarat, a fertile and wealthy trading province, for almost two centuries. Akbar conquered Bengal, the richest province in northern India, in 1576. Kashmir was taken in 1586, Orissa in 1592, and Baluchistan in 1595. The Deccan kingdom of Berar fell in the following year and the neighbouring province of Khandesh in 1600. At the time of his death, Akbar's territories stretched from Afghanistan to the borders of Burma, from the Himalayas to the heart of the Deccan plateau.

Aided by his highly skilled Hindu finance minister, Todar Mal, Akbar developed the bureaucratic structure he had inherited from the Suris. Todar Mal's accurate assessment of the revenue potential of each village secured a reliable income for the regime. Peasants were encouraged to extend the area they cultivated, bringing benefits to both government and cultivator; sound currency also provided a stimulus to commerce. Persian was promoted as the official language of public affairs. The governmental machine was organized along military lines, with 33 grades of officer, and all officers were answerable to the emperor alone. A combination of personal ability and imperial favour secured an individual's advancement. Neither power nor wealth were regarded as hereditary: both had to be earned. A Mogul nobleman's wealth was returned to the emperor on his death. Thus, as they were unable to bequeath money and possessions to their families, the aristocracy imitated their rulers by spending generously on buildings, benefactions, and tombs.

Reconciliation and Toleration

Although only one-third of his officials were native Indians, Akbar was content to employ and promote Hindus among them. In reconciling the Hindu majority to Muslim rule, he led by example, marrying a Hindu princess and making the offspring of their union, Jahangir (1569–1627), his heir. Rajput chieftains were given important military commands, and warriors from his region were appointed to guard the imperial residence. Early in his reign Akbar abolished the tax that previous Muslim rulers had imposed on Hindu pilgrims; he also abolished the poll tax (*jizya*) that was customarily levied on non-Muslims who lived under Islamic rule. Muslims were likewise forbidden to kill and eat cows, considered sacred by Hindus, and the Islamic lunar calendar was replaced by a solar calendar. The law that decreed capital punishment for renouncing Islam was suspended, and subsidies were given for the building of temples as well as mosques. Polygamy, slavery, and suttee were discouraged. Akbar's original religious policy was matched by his unconventional personal beliefs. He staged debates between exponents of different faiths, including not only Muslims and Hindus, Sufis and Parsis (Zoroastrians), but also Jains, Jews, and Jesuits. In 1582 Akbar announced the establishment of a new *Din-i-Ilahi* ('Divine faith'). Akbar, however, made no attempt to propagate this philosophy, preferring to surround himself with an intimate group of like-minded individuals. Far more importantly, Akbar was the first Muslim ruler of India who was able to win the voluntary allegiance and genuine loyalty of his Hindu subjects.

After Akbar

The strength of Akbar's empire is attested by its ability to survive his successors. Akbar's son, Jahangir, was more interested in artistic connoisseurship than in conquest. However, he finally subdued the rebellious province of Mewar, captured the hill state of Kangra, and extended his frontiers in the Deccan. Jahangir lost Kandahar to Shah Abbas of Persia.

Before acceding to the throne, Jahangir's third son, Shah Jahan (1592–1666), led a rebellion against his father that lasted for three years. Although he successfully crushed rebellions against his rule and stabilized the Deccan frontier, his efforts to

retake Kandahar and conquer Samarkand proved costly failures, which, combined with the expense of his lavish court and ambitious building programme, resulted in a heavy increase in taxation. Shah Jahan suffered serious illness in 1657, which sparked off a war of succession among his four sons. Aurangzeb (1618–1707), who emerged victorious, deposed and imprisoned his father.

Servitude and Stagnation

European traders were attracted to Mogul India not only as a source of valuable natural products, such as spices, pearls, gemstones, and indigo, but also as a producer of high-quality textiles. However, these European entrepreneurs were amazed to see how craftsmen and merchants – the producers of wealth – were reviled by their own compatriots. Unlike Europe, India had no middle class between the aristocracy and the peasantry. The French physician Bernier, who travelled widely in India between 1656 and 1668, noted that, except in cases in which local tradesmen were

---

The Buildings of Shah Jahan

The Mogul emperor, Shah Jahan, had a passion for fine architecture. His buildings at Delhi, notably the Red Fort, and those at Agra, mark the zenith of Indo-Muslim architecture. The world-famous Taj Mahal was built as a mausoleum for his favourite wife.

Akbar *(red saddle cover) While giving his continual attention to affairs of state, Akbar enjoyed rigorous outdoor pursuits, such as elephant hunting.* ▼

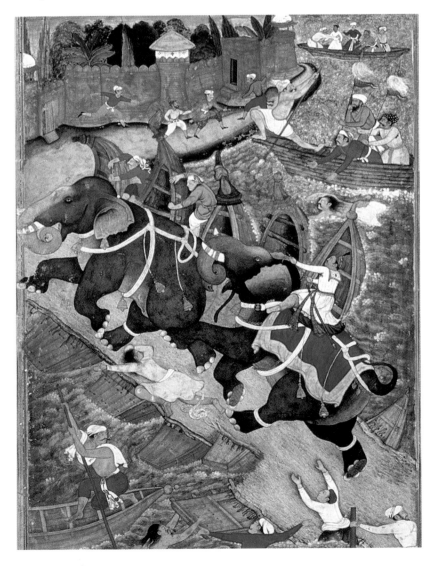

allowed to lodge complaints with the ruler himself, there was no independent judiciary to whom they could appeal for protection against abuses of power. When Mogul order broke down in the following century, the increased insecurity of property that resulted created even more disincentives to effort and enterprise.

An Islamic Reaction

As a self-appointed champion of Islamic orthodoxy, Aurangzeb made strenuous efforts to eradicate drinking, gambling, immorality, blasphemy, and heresy. He ordered the demolition of Hindu temples, reimposed the discriminatory poll tax on non-Muslims, and offered incentives to those who would convert to Islam. Shiites and Sufis were also subjected to persecution. Much of his reign was spent in suppressing rebellions provoked by his intolerance. In addition, he launched costly campaigns against Mewar, Jodhpur, Assam, and in the Deccan, where he finally succeeded in annexing the former tributary states of Bijapur and Golkonda, thereby enlarging the Mogul empire to its greatest territorial extent. Despite Aurangzeb's many virtues, his unbending piety made him ill-equipped to rule an empire, the majority of whose population did not share his faith.

THE EAST INDIA COMPANY

The English East India Company was formed in imitation of a similar Dutch trading company, but with only one-tenth of the capital. By pooling investments from a number of subscribers, it aimed to spread the risks inherent in the long voyages needed to reach the 'Spice Islands' of Southeast Asia. Frustrated by the Dutch in their efforts to secure a foothold in that region, the English eventually turned to India. The Portuguese had already established trading centres there, but had been trading in items, such as textiles, sugar, and saltpetre, that were far less valuable in proportion to their bulk than spices. In 1612 the English defeated the Portuguese off Surat; as a result, Jahangir granted them trading privileges in return for protecting Indian maritime commerce and pilgrim traffic from the Portuguese. Thus, the Company tacitly assumed the role of a Mogul navy. In 1640 a second 'factory' (trading post) was established at Madras. In 1674 the Company's headquarters were transferred from Surat to Bombay – which had originally been acquired by the English as part of the marriage settlement between King Charles II and his Portuguese bride, Catherine of Braganza. In 1690 Calcutta was founded; although it was situated in a malarial swamp, the location was chosen for its deep-water anchorage. These three strongholds were to become the bases from which the Company would eventually conquer the entire subcontinent.

The East India Company *Company ships are shown docked at a port in Kerala state (southern India), (George Lambert and Samuel Scott, c. 1731).* ▼

Second-class Citizens

Bernier, a French physician, who travelled widely in India (1656–68), said of the status of India's craftsman and merchants: "this debasing state of slavery obstructs the progress of trade… There can be little encouragement to engage in commercial pursuits, when the success with which they may be attended … provokes the cupidity of a neighbouring tyrant… When wealth is acquired… the possessor, so far from living with increased comfort… studies the means by which he may appear impoverished; his dress, lodging, and furniture continue to be mean and he is careful … never to indulge in the pleasures of the table. In the mean time his gold and silver remain buried at a great depth in the ground…"

The Era of the Raj

The decline of the Moguls • Anglo-French rivalry • The conquest of India •
Reform and revolt • The height of the Raj • Productivity and poverty •
The nationalist movement • The impact of war

The period 1707–1919 saw unprecedented changes in the way the Indian subcontinent was governed. The decline of Mogul power left Britain and France, who had both established profitable trading bases there, to vie for ascendancy. The subsequent emergence of Britain as the dominant power ushered in the British Raj, which brought both benefits and strife to the subcontinent.

The Decline of the Moguls

The tenacity of the Mogul emperor Aurangzeb (1618–1707) in his conquest of the Deccan depleted his treasury as well as his armed forces. Aurangzeb's long reign also weakened his dynasty. His son, Bahadur Shah (1643–1712), succeeded him at the age of 63, only to die five years later. He was followed by eight successive emperors in 50 years. Of these, one was deposed and three were murdered. In 1724 the Mogul governor of the Deccan proclaimed the region's unilateral independence, becoming the Nizam (ruler) of Hyderabad, a princely state that survived until 1948. In the southwest the Marathas, united as a Hindu nation by their leader, Sivaji (1627–80), posed a continuing threat. In 1739 the empire lost Kabul to Persia while Nadir Shah (1688–1747), a Persian adventurer, invaded the Punjab, dispersing the Muslim army. After terrorizing the inhabitants of the capital, Nadir Shah returned to Persia with a vast booty. By 1750 the regions of Sind and Gujarat had broken away, as had Awadh and the Punjab by 1754. When Delhi was sacked by Afghans in 1757, the Marathas answered the summons of the enfeebled Mogul to drive them out. The Marathas were heavily defeated at Panipat. Internal disputes led to the Afghans' withdrawal, leaving a political vacuum.

Anglo-French Rivalry

Seventy years after its foundation, the East India Company base at Bombay was still surrounded by Maratha power. Fort St George at Madras had grown large, but its occupants were wary of the neighbouring French base at Pondicherry. The British base at Calcutta also feared its French counterpart at Chandernagar. Fighting between the two rival nations broke out after 1744 as a result of war in Europe. It involved not only direct conflict: each side also supported rival princes who were contending for local power. Further fighting followed the outbreak of the Seven Years' War in Europe in 1756. Thanks to the skill of Robert Clive (1725–74; see panel) the British gained Bengal, Bihar, and Orissa.

===SEE ALSO===
Early Modern Europe:
• The French Revolution and Napoleonic Europe
The Industrial Age in Europe:
• Nationalism and Imperialism
• World War I
Islamic World:
• Persia and Central Asia
Religion (vol. 6):
• Hinduism
• Other Religions of India and the Far East

British Raj British rule in India. *Raj* is a Hindi word, meaning 'rule.' British rule was imposed on India in 1858 and ended in 1947, when the last viceroy, Lord Mountbatten, granted independence to India.

◄ **Conquest Begins**
Robert Clive, first governor of Bengal, receives a grant from Emperor Shah Alam conferring the administration of the revenues of Bengal, Bihar, and Orissa on the English East India Company.

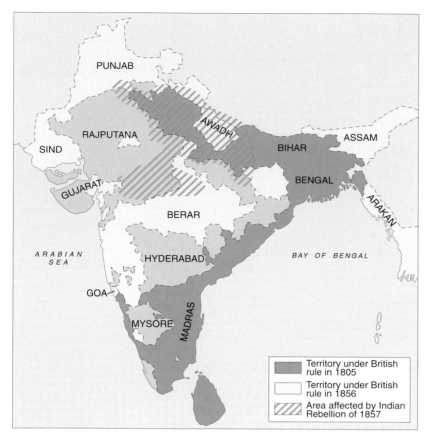

Territory under British rule in 1805

Territory under British rule in 1856

Area affected by Indian Rebellion of 1857

▲ **The British Empire in India** *In just over half a century, the British had subordinated almost all of the subcontinent.*

The Conquest of India

The East India Company's transition from trading corporation to conquering government was difficult and confused. Until 1772 the administration of government in the conquered provinces was managed by officials of the local ***nawab*** (ruling prince). Meanwhile the Company's servants returned to England laden with plunder and the Company itself came near to bankruptcy as a result of maladministration. Having been refused a loan by financiers of the City of London, it turned to the British government for aid. The outcome was parliamentary involvement in Company affairs and the beginnings of a conscious, yet largely negative, imperial policy. The India Act of 1784, negotiated by the British prime minister William Pitt (1759–1806), declared that territorial expansion was "repugnant to the wish, honour, and policy of this nation." In practice, the result was the extension of British authority in India. This was due less to the expansionism of the government than to the initiatives of those posted in India, who were drawn into dangerous local rivalries. Attempts to stabilize frontiers resulted in successive annexations of territory as a recently subdued area was protected by the addition of a neighbouring one. French involvement remained a factor. From the 1790s Anglo-French conflicts in India became an aspect of the global struggle between Britain and France that continued until 1815. With the removal of French opposition, the British were free to extend their influence and negotiated treaties with subordinated princes until, by 1818, the East India Company was the paramount power in India. For reasons of economy the alien administration was content to leave almost half of the territory, particularly the less fertile areas, under native rule, providing the rulers were willing to pay tribute and accept supervision. Split into more than 360, and eventually over 560, separate states, the princes were too isolated from each other and divided by their own rivalries to unite against their foreign overlords. The Hindu Marathas ultimately found the British less offensive than Muslim Moguls, while their neighbour, the Nizam, preferred them to the Marathas. The Sikh-dominated Punjab was conquered in two bloody wars, as was Lower (coastal) Burma. Military reverses led to Nepal being treated as an ally and Afghanistan as a buffer state.

Reform and Revolt

Corruption among British officials was largely eradicated simply by greatly increasing their salaries. The tolerant attitudes of the 18th century, when Europeans were receptive to Indian culture, began to change in the 19th century. The arrival of increasing numbers of missionaries, who saw Indian beliefs and customs as inherently inferior and threatening, exacerbated this rift. The rise of evangelical and rationalist philosophies in Britain encouraged administrators to enforce European modes of law and commerce in India, which greatly disrupted traditional systems of landholding and exposed handworkers to the competition of machine industry. Under the reforming administration of Lord William Bentinck (1774–1839; governor general

---

FOUNDER OF THE RAJ

As a clerk with the East India Company, Robert Clive displayed military flair, political guile, and administrative capacity. Having distinguished himself at the siege of Arcot in 1751, he became effective governor of Bengal at the age of 30. In recapturing Calcutta from the Nawab of Bengal, he massacred the nawab's army at Plassey in 1757, installing in his place a compliant prince, Mir Ja'far. By accepting huge rewards for his services, however, Clive initiated a wave of corruption that nearly ruined Bengal and the Company. On returning home he was knighted, while his attempt at a political career failed. Meanwhile, the overthrow of Mir Ja'far threatened the Company's position in Bengal and Clive was dispatched for a second term (1764–67), during which he stabilized the Company's territories, restored employee discipline, curbed corruption, and quelled an army mutiny, almost single-handed. On returning to England, he faced renewed corruption charges. Although he was vindicated, he subsequently committed suicide.

◄ **Indian Mutiny (1857)** *The rebellion and its suppression involved terrible atrocities on both sides. The passivity of most of the princes and the loyalty of the Madras and Bombay armies, as well as that of the recently defeated Sikhs, were crucial to the reassertion of British authority. However, the rebels' lack of planning and leadership were equally important factors.*

1828–35) suttee was suppressed, Western-style education was promoted, and English replaced Persian as the official language of government. Under Dalhousie (1812–60; governor general 1848–56) westernization proceeded at a vigorous pace: railways, postal services, and the telegraph were extended into rural areas. Despite these severe affronts to traditionalists, revolt, when it came, occurred within the ranks of one of the East India Company's own instruments of power, the Bengal army. In 1857 a new rifle was introduced that required that its paper cartridges be bitten before loading. Rumours spread that they were greased with the fat of cows (sacred to Hindus) or pigs (offensive to Muslims). An uprising in the state of Awadh, arising out of a variety of other grievances, turned into an advance on Delhi, where Bahadur Shah II (1775–1862), the aged Mogul emperor (who received a pension from the British), was seized as a figurehead of revolt. The most significant casualty of the rebellion was the East India Company. Having long since lost its monopoly of Indian trade, it now lost its governmental role; the British parliament transferred its authority to the Crown in 1858.

The Height of the Raj
After the upheaval of 1857–58 British security was strengthened by increasing the ratio of British to Indian troops from 1:5 to 1:2 and by giving British troops exclusive access to artillery. Noninterference in religious affairs and the existence of the princely states was reaffirmed, thus guaranteeing protected areas of cultural continuity. Entrance to the elite Indian Civil Service (ICS) was proclaimed to be

open to all; however, as the examinations were held only in London, Indians were effectively excluded. These measures actually reinforced the gulf between British and Indian. In 1883 Lord Ripon (1827–1909; **viceroy** 1880–84) supported legislation that would enable Indian judges to preside in cases involving White defendants. His initiative, however, was overthrown by a racist campaign, which inadvertently demonstrated to the emerging Indian national movement some of the techniques of political organization and agitation.

Productivity and Poverty
The half century following 1857 was marked by the increasing commercialization of agriculture. Plantations growing tea, coffee, and indigo were created; large-scale modern coal, jute, and cotton textile industries established; and the railway network was extended from 200 miles in 1858 to 35 000 by 1914. The influx of cheap European goods, however, devastated the traditional handicrafts sector, increasing pressure to live from the land. The result was continued widespread famine and a severe fall in population.

The Nationalist Movement
As the British Empire in India attained its greatest territorial extent with the annexation of Upper Burma in 1885, the first meeting of the Indian National Congress (INC) was held in Bombay. All members spoke English, two-thirds were Hindu, and over half were lawyers. Rather than advocating independence for India, they argued for greater opportunities for Indians to participate in the government of their own country, as both officials and elected

viceroy A governor of a colony, country, or province, who rules in the name of his sovereign or government. During British rule in India the viceroy governed with the help of an executive council, which oversaw the home, revenue, military, finance, and law departments. The viceroy, empowered to over-rule his councillors if necessary, took charge of the foreign department, occupied mainly with relations with princely states and bordering foreign powers. From the mid-19th century, additional nonofficial members were added to the viceroy's executive council, including some of the Indian nobility and loyal landowners. The council, therefore, began to serve as a very crude indicator of public opinion, enabling the viceroy to forestall any unrest or opposition. The viceroy in India was also known as the 'governor general.'

▲ **Gopal Krishna Gokhale** *Leader of the moderate wing of the INC.*

durbar A formal audience granted by an Indian ruler to his subjects. The term derives from a Hindi word meaning 'court.' During the British Raj in India, *durbar* was used to describe the elaborate ceremonies that were arranged to honour British monarchs, notably Queen Victoria's investiture as Empress of India in 1876 and the visit of King George V and Queen Mary in 1911 (the Delhi Durbar).

representatives. Accusing Britain of draining India of its natural wealth through taxation and unfair exploitation of its resources, the INC called for reductions in the military budget and the reimposition of tariffs to protect Indian manufactures. By 1888 the annual meeting of the INC attracted over 1200 delegates. The overbearing style of Lord Curzon (1859–1925; viceroy 1898–1905) made the INC even more popular and energetic. His decision to partition Bengal in the interests of administrative efficiency was seen as a policy to ensure that Bengali-speaking Hindus were a minority in both the Muslim east and the Bihari- or Oriya-speaking west. This brought the region to the brink of revolt and broadened the national movement into one of mass protest. When petitions failed to reverse the partition, the protesters resorted to boycotting British cloth in favour of its Indian equivalent (*swadeshi*). The movement soon spread to other Indian-made products and from Calcutta to Bombay and Madras. In 1906 'self-rule' (**swaraj**) was openly demanded by the INC. In the same year a Muslim League was established by Muslims anxious to protect the special interests of their community. In return for viceregal pledges of entrenched constitutional rights, the League proclaimed its loyalty to British rule and condemned the INC boycott. The election of a reforming Liberal government in Britain in 1906 led to new efforts to promote Indians in the ICS and to advisory positions, as well as the establishment of elected legislative councils at provincial level with greater powers of debate. The INC,

meanwhile, split into two factions. The moderate faction, led by Gopal Krishna Gokhale (1866–1915), wished to exploit the opportunities afforded by constitutional concessions. The radical wing, inspired by Bal Gangadhar Tilak (1856–1920), favoured more extreme tactics and was accused of fostering terrorism. In 1911 George V (1865–1936), the only reigning British monarch ever to visit India, used the occasion of his coronation **durbar** to announce the relocation of the capital from Calcutta to Delhi (a gesture to acknowledge its historic significance to Muslims); he also proclaimed the reunification of Bengal, minus Bihar and Orissa (as a gesture of conciliation to Hindus).

The Impact of War

The outbreak of World War I in Europe surprisingly brought widespread support for the British cause, even from Tilak, released after six years' detention. Nationalists reasoned that loyalty would be rewarded by political concessions. Muslims, however, were inhibited by their sympathies for the Ottoman Empire. The death of Gokhale removed a moderating influence, and when the INC reunited in 1916, it gained the support of the Muslim League for national freedom by offering greatly enhanced representation on future legislative bodies. The British responded by announcing plans to devolve all departments of government to the control of elected representatives, except for those responsible for foreign policy, finance, and security. Despite contributing one million troops to the British war effort, huge quantities of food and raw materials, and a gift of £100,000,000, postwar India was to be bitterly disenchanted by its reward. This was the extension, through the 1919 Rowlatt Acts, of wartime emergency curbs on political life. Led by Mohandas Karamchand (known as Mahatma) Gandhi (1869–1948), a pioneer of civil disobedience in South Africa and initially an enthusiastic supporter of the war, nationalists embarked on a nationwide protest campaign demanding their repeal. Support was strongest in the Punjab which, with 7% of the population, had supplied 50% of overseas troops and was now flooded with discharged ex-servicemen. Disorder led to repression, culminating in the massacre in April 1919 of some 400 unarmed civilians at Amritsar. Although General Dyer (1864–1927), who was responsible for the massacre, was relieved of his command, he was presented with money and a ceremonial sword by his British admirers. The many concessions contained in the Government of India Act, passed in December 1919, could do little to assuage the anger and distrust that Amritsar had created.

A MAKER OF MODERN INDIA

Rammohan Roy (1772–1833), born to a prosperous Bengali Brahman family, adopted unorthodox opinions from his youth. He was employed by the East India Company, where he experienced Western literature and ideas. Study prompted him to return to serious reexamination of the Hindu scriptures, producing summaries and translations of them in Bengali and Hindi. These vernacular publications violated Brahmanic tradition but gained him European recognition. He also came to advocate a reformed monotheistic Hinduism. Cooperation with Baptist missionaries on a Bengali version of the New Testament led him to publish his own account of Christian ethics. In 1823, having founded a progressive school and two weekly newspapers, he campaigned against British press censorship and plans to support a traditional Sanskrit college. He also denounced suttee, supporting British efforts for its suppression. In 1828 he founded the Brahmo Samaj ('Society of God'), which became a leading force in the reform of Hinduism. In 1829 Roy visited England to petition for reforms in Indian government and was received with respect. He extended his visit but died before he could return home. In seeking to learn from the West without discarding traditional learning, he indicated the path to a Hindu renaissance, which was initially cultural, but ultimately political.

Unrest, Partition, and Independence

*Diarchy and disobedience • World War II • The transfer of power •
Nehru's India • Indira Gandhi • The search for stability • East and West Pakistan*

The period from 1919 was characterized by the continued struggle of the Indian peoples for self-government and by conflict between Muslims and Hindus, which culminated in the birth of a separate nation – Pakistan. The partition of the subcontinent was attended by further civil strife and political instability.

Diarchy and Disobedience

In 1920 Gandhi (see THE ERA OF THE RAJ) won control of the Indian National Congress (INC) and launched a massive campaign of 'non-cooperation' to defy British rule. In the same year Mohammed Ali Jinnah (1876–1948), president of the Muslim League, left the INC, an ominous sign of divergent ambitions.

Civil disobedience reached its peak in 1921. The tense atmosphere led to peasant attacks on Hindu landlords, which provoked sectarian riots; these events further widened the gulf between the largely Hindu INC and the Muslim League. Having been imprisoned in 1922, Gandhi was released in 1924 owing to fears for his health. The INC demanded, in 1928, complete independence for India within a year. In 1930 Gandhi launched a high-profile civil disobedience campaign focused against the salt tax; the result, inevitably, was his arrest. Britain's attempt to move the debate forward by calling a 'Round Table' conference in London was thwarted by an INC boycott. While Gandhi did attend a second conference in 1931, the outcome was unsuccessful. By 1932 Gandhi was under arrest again.

In 1935 the complex Government of India Act was passed by the British Parliament. This not only provided for self-government at provincial level, but also for a national federal government; only foreign policy and defence matters were to remain the viceroy's responsibility. In 1937 elections were held for provincial assemblies under the terms of the 1935 Act. The INC formed ministries in 8 of the 11 provinces. The proposed federation, however, was delayed by the failure of the princely states to join and by the opposition of the Muslim League, which feared Hindu domination.

World War II

The outbreak of war in 1939 delayed the introduction of the federation apparently

▲ **Passive Resistance** *Gandhi leads protesters in a march against the salt tax (1930) as part of his campaign of civil disobedience. Using passive resistance, through which he sought to achieve his political ends, he led the movement that culminated in the end of British rule in India.*

indefinitely. In 1940 the Muslim League demanded the partition of India to create 'Pakistan' ('Land of the Pure'), a separate homeland of Muslim-dominated areas in the northwest and northeast.

In 1942, as Japanese troops advanced towards India through Burma, Britain made proposals that would rally Indian loyalty to the war effort: independence at the end of the war was offered, with new constitutional

═══SEE ALSO═══
**The Industrial Age
in Europe:**
● The Causes and Course
of World War II
● Postwar Europe
Religion (vol. 6):
● Islam
● Hinduism
═══════════════

I do not claim to have originated any new principle or doctrine. I have simply tried in my own way to apply the eternal truths to our daily life and problems. ... I have nothing new to teach the world.

Mahatma Gandhi

Maker of the Republic

Jawaharlal Nehru's active involvement in the Indian National Congress led him, with Gandhi's support, to become the chief tactician of the struggle for independence. As prime minister he pursued a foreign policy that encouraged other newly independent states to stand back from superpower rivalries. However, he mediated in Korea (1951) and Vietnam (1954), as well as sending Indian troops to support UN peace-keeping efforts in the Middle East, the Congo, and Cyprus.

arrangements that would enable Muslims and the princely states to form separate federations outside the projected Indian union. The offer was rejected by both the Muslim League and the INC; the latter carried their actions further by launching a 'Quit India' movement, which the British defused with mass arrests, including that of Gandhi. In 1945 the new Labour Government in Britain pledged itself to "an early realization of self-government in India."

The Transfer of Power

Following a deadlock in negotiations, the Muslim League proclaimed a 'Direct Action Day' in August 1946 to press for an independent state for Muslims. The result was massive communal rioting. In February 1947 the British government announced June 1948 as a deadline for the transfer of power. Following further rioting in anticipation of partition, the last viceroy, Lord Louis Mountbatten (1900–79), advanced the deadline to 15 August 1947. The event itself was accompanied by the migration of some 15 million people and the massacre of at least 250 000 people. Pakistan came into being as two entirely separate territories: a dominant Urdu-speaking west and an impoverished Bengali-speaking east. Between them lay 1000 miles of Indian territory.

The princely states were left to choose their own affiliations. Kashmir opted to join India, creating a conflict that left this state two-thirds under Indian control and the remainder with Pakistan, a UN truce-line between them. Half a century later Kashmir remained divided and

Jawaharlal Nehru (left) and Mohammed Ali Jinnah *The two leaders, representing Hindu and Muslim interests respectively, met in May 1946 to discuss the future of Hindu and Muslim communities.*

a continuing source of friction between the two states.

In January 1948 Gandhi, having repeatedly risked his life to calm communal rioting, was assassinated by a Hindu extremist. Mohammed Ali Jinnah, the founding father of Pakistan, died shortly afterwards.

Nehru's India

Having led the nation's mourning for Gandhi, Jawaharlal Nehru (1889–1964) assumed power as India's first prime minister, a position he retained until his death. The early establishment of an Atomic Energy Commission was an indication of his rejection of Gandhi's vision of an India of self-sufficient villages. Industrial output doubled in the first decade of independence. Subnational boundaries were reorganized to correspond more closely to linguistic groupings. Nehru also showed a willingness to use force in compelling Hyderabad to join India, in annexing the Portuguese enclave of Goa, and in fighting a border war with China.

Nehru's successor, Lal Bahadur Shastri (1904–66), fought a brief war, in 1965, with Pakistan, ostensibly over a disputed desert border area, the Rann of Kutch; in reality it was also about the contested area of Kashmir. Shastri died shortly after accepting mediation from the USSR to terminate the conflict.

Indira Gandhi

Nehru probably had no ambitions to found a dynasty. However, his daughter Indira Gandhi (1917–84) became prime minister in 1966. Whereas Nehru had established a reputation for moderation, Mrs Gandhi's style was more autocratic. In 1971 she backed the armed uprising that separated Bangladesh from Pakistan. By 1975 she was ruling by decree amid allegations of corruption and resentment of the birth-control campaign with which she sought to curb population growth. Her unpopularity led, in 1977, to the Indian National Congress Party's first defeat since independence and the formation of a Janata Party government under Morarji Desai (1896–1995). Divided and feeble, it failed to stifle rampant inflation and was swept aside by a landslide victory for Mrs Gandhi in 1980. Inflation continued to rise while the political scene was increasingly dominated by violent campaigns to achieve greater autonomy in such provinces as Assam and the Punjab. In 1983 emergency rule was invoked in the Punjab to suppress the terrorism of Sikh separatists. Counterinsurgency operations culminated, in June 1984, in the storming of the sacred Golden Temple in Amritsar, a stronghold of armed Sikh fundamentalists. The fighting that ensued left 400 dead. In October 1984 Mrs Gandhi was assassinated by Sikh members of her own body-

▲ **Sectarian Tensions** *Hindu militant demonstrations broke down into riots at the Babri mosque in Ayodhya, Uttar Pradesh, in 1992.*

guard. She was succeeded as prime minister by her son Rajiv (1942–91). In 1985 the boundaries of the Punjab were revised, making the Sikhs the majority population in that state.

The Search for Stability

Rajiv Gandhi served a five-year term, moderating but not resolving the situation in the troubled provinces. In December 1989 V. P. Singh (1931–) formed a Janata-led minority 'National Front' government. In November 1990 this gave way to a new Janata administration, headed by Chandra Shekar, but dependent on Congress Party support. With insurgencies still taking place in Assam, Jammu, Kashmir, and the Punjab, the election of May/June 1991 was accompanied by widespread violence and the assassination of Rajiv Gandhi. The election led to the formation of a Congress minority government under P. V. Narasimha Rao (1921–). In 1992 Hindu extremists demolished an ancient mosque in Ayodhya. The resultant rioting led to the death of 1200 people, most of them Muslims. In 1993 sectarian clashes in Bombay left 500 dead. During 1994–95 the Congress Party faired badly in state elections, a reflection of the impact of the government's economic liberalization programme. Rao's government was weakened by charges of corruption. Following the Congress Party's heavy electoral defeat in 1996, a broad coalition government, led by the National Front-Left Front (NF-LF)

alliance, was formed. Separatist violence in northern India continued, following state elections there in 1996. Congress withdrew its support from the government in 1997 and following a general election in 1998 a Janata-led coalition took office. Despite sectarian troubles, India experienced social and economic progress, but the international community was alarmed when India joined the nuclear arms race, carrying out five controlled nuclear explosions in May 1998.

East and West Pakistan

Pakistan was founded as a nation for Muslims rather than as an Islamic state. Its original purpose was more to remove the fear of Hindu domination than to restore the former glories of Islam.

The two provinces of West Pakistan and East Pakistan failed to integrate. The domination of the armed forces and civil service by Urdu-speaking westerners bred resentment in the Bengali-speaking east. Internal dissensions and external frictions with India led to support for autonomy; in 1958 General Ayub Khan revoked the constitution to rule by martial law. Strikes and riots forced him to hand over power to commander-in-chief General Yahya Khan (1917–80) in 1969. Pakistan's first fully free election, in 1973, brought to power a civilian government under Zulfikar Ali Bhutto (1928–79), leader of the Pakistan People's Party. Despite the armed uprising that led (with Indian help) to East Pakistan becoming independent as Bangladesh in 1971–72, Bhutto clung to power until unrest led to a coup in 1977, which restored military rule under General Zia ul Haq (1924–88). Bhutto was hanged in 1979 for conspiring to murder a political opponent. Under Zia, Islamic fundamentalism spread rapidly until his assassination. In the following elections Bhutto's daughter, Benazir (1953–), was victo-

It is extremely difficult to appreciate why our Hindu friends fail to understand the real nature of Islam and Hinduism. They are not religions in the strict sense of the word, but are, in fact, different and distinct social orders, and it is a dream that the Hindus and Muslims can ever evolve a common nationality... They neither intermarry nor dine together and, indeed, they belong to two different civilizations, which are based mainly on conflicting ideas and conceptions... To yoke together two such nations under a single state, one as a numerical minority and the other as a majority, must lead to growing discontent and the final destruction of any fabric that may be so built up...

Mohammed Ali Jinnah

East and West Pakistan *The two provinces of West Pakistan and East Pakistan failed to integrate as a single nation. East Pakistan became independent as Bangladesh in 1971.* ▼

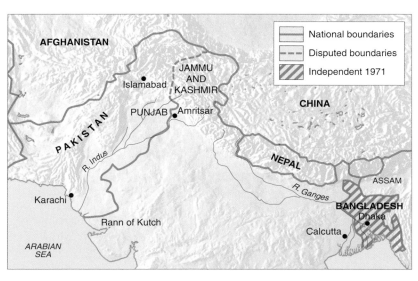

I shall work for an India in which the poorest shall feel that it is their country, in whose making they have an effective voice, an India in which there shall be no high class and low class of people, an India in which all communities shall live in perfect harmony. There can be no room in such an India for the curse of untouchability or the curse of intoxicating drinks and drugs... Women will enjoy the same rights as men... This is the India of my dreams.

Mahatma Gandhi

rious. She was overthrown by a coup in 1990 and replaced by the government of the newly formed Islamic Democratic Alliance, which lasted until 1993, when Bhutto was again elected as prime minister. Corruption allegations and escalating factional violence dogged Bhutto's premiership. Opposition peaked in 1996 when President Farooq Lehari dismissed her. In the 1997 elections the Pakistan Muslim League, led by Nawaz Sharif, was victorious. With the influence of the military increasing, the low turnout of voters reflected a severe lack of faith in the political process. In 1998 Pakistan carried out six nuclear weapons tests, becoming the world's seventh nuclear nation.

Bangladesh has yet to attain stability. Attempts to establish a socialist parliamentary democracy have been hampered by a cycle of floods and famine that claimed the lives of five million people in the period from 1971 to 1988. In 1975 Prime Minister Mujibur Rahman (1921–75), who had led the struggle for independence, assumed dictatorial powers to cope with mounting chaos. His murder during a military coup led to two years of nonparty government. From 1977 Bangladesh was governed by the presidency of Major-General Zia Rahman. While he made some progress in moving towards democracy, he was murdered in an army mutiny in 1981. His successor, General Ershad (1930–), survived, owing largely to massive foreign aid, until his deposition in 1990. The 1991 elections, the first for 12 years, were contested by 70 parties. The widow of President Zia emerged victorious. Shortly afterwards a cyclone killed 139 000 people and left 10 million homeless. Despite opposition to the government, Mrs Zia clung to power until 1996. Subsequent elections returned a government led by the Awami League leader, Shaikh Hasina Wajed.

SRI LANKA IN THE 20TH CENTURY

Sri Lanka ('Resplendent Island') has lived in India's shadow throughout its history, while developing its own distinctive culture. Its Buddhist and Hindu traditions have bequeathed a tragic legacy of violent ethnic conflict. Although it was under British rule from 1796, Sinhalese and Tamil groups united as the Ceylon National Congress in 1919 to press for self-government. While this was partially achieved, the island remained a crown colony until 1948, when it became a dominion within the British Commonwealth.

Forming a government led by Don Senanayake (1884–1952), the United National Party (UNP) remained in power until it was displaced, in 1956, by the Sri Lanka Freedom Party (SLFP), a strong advocate of Buddhist Sinhalese interests. Interethnic rioting in 1958 was accompanied by Tamil demands for a separate Tamil state. In 1959 Prime Minister Solomon Bandaranaike (1899–1959) was assassinated by a Buddhist and the leadership passed to his widow, Sirimavo (1916–), who, in 1960, became the world's first woman prime minister. The UNP was re-elected to govern from 1965 to 1970, when it lost power to the SLFP. In 1971 a Marxist rebellion was quelled after significant fighting. In 1972 a new constitution proclaimed the Republic of Sri Lanka. When the UNP returned to office in 1977, the constitution was radically revised to establish a presidential system of government. The country was subsequently renamed the Democratic Socialist Republic of Sri Lanka.

Continuing interethnic tension between the Tamil and Sinhalese communities erupted into major violence in 1977. Demands for a separate Tamil homeland (*Tamil Eelam*) were renewed, and the nation slid towards civil war as the 'Tamil Tigers' waged a guerrilla campaign for separatism. Although the security forces exercised severe repression, the Tamil Tigers established a stronghold for themselves in the Jaffna peninsula. India attempted to arbitrate in 1984 and undertook a large-scale armed intervention in 1987–89. In the 1989 general election, the first held for 12 years, the UNP won a majority. Tamil and Marxist terrorism, however, continued. In 1991 the army killed over 2500 guerrillas. Although peace talks began in 1992, they made little progress. In 1993 President Premadasa (1924–93) became a victim of a war that had already cost over 20 000 lives. The Sri Lankan economy, meanwhile, rapidly declined. The SLFP-led People's Alliance was elected in 1994. Prime Minister Chandrika Kumaratunga (1945–) was elected president in the same year, yet hopes for peace under the new government were short-lived as fighting resumed in 1995. The Tamils rejected peace talks in 1996 and violence continued to escalate.

▲ **The 1989 Election** *In the run-up to the first general election to be held in Sri Lanka for 12 years, supporters rally for Sirimavo Bandaranaike.*

SOUTHEAST ASIA

Early Southeast Asia

The spread of farming • Chinese influences • Indian influences

By 6000 BC, the peoples of Southeast Asia were well established in tribal societies, sustained by hunting, gathering, fishing, and – in some parts – by early tropical cultivation. In more favoured areas, particularly near rivers or seas, small village-like communities existed, whose inhabitants were producing pottery.

The Spread of Farming
More developed (rice growing) agriculture began to spread through the region from the northeast after 5000 BC, reaching parts of the south by 2000 BC. This spread was probably associated with the movement of peoples into the area from southern China. The first outlines of distinct Vietnamese, Thai, Khmer, and other linguistic groupings emerged during this period. At about the same time a separate migration led horticultural peoples, originally from Taiwan, to settle the eastern and southern islands and coastlines of the region, eventually forming the basis of Malay society.

Chinese Influences
Although the Neolithic cultures of Southeast Asia were long established and unique in character, the region's early agricultural societies were affected by cultural advances in China. Chinese influence had contributed to the development of bronze-working in Indochina by 1500 BC and iron-working by 500 BC. By this time, a fully developed metal-working civilization, known by archaeologists as the **Dong Son culture,** which grew irrigated wet rice as a staple crop, was established in the Red River delta of northern Vietnam. China eventually extended its political influence in this area; Chinese conquest in 111 BC was followed by the effective incorporation of the north of Vietnam into subsequent Chinese empires from 43 to c. 900 AD.

Early Southeast Asia *Neolithic and early Bronze Age sites, dating from c. 2000 BC, and later Bronze and Iron Age sites, dating from c. 300 BC, predate Chinese and Indian influences in the area. The sites of Dong Son drums (highly crafted bronze kettle drums) indicate a sophisticated Bronze Age civilization by 1 AD.* ▶

Indian Influences
In western Southeast Asia, influences from India took different forms. While Indian peoples did not settle there, from the 1st millennium BC Indian traders and pilgrims spread cultural and religious ideas down the western coast of the region, into Indochina, and through the islands to the south, particularly Java and Sumatra. Such contacts spread Indian concepts of society and the state among the formerly tribal societies of these areas.

The first recognizable state to evolve under this influence was Funan, in the lower Mekong basin, which reached its height between the 2nd and 6th centuries AD. It was succeeded in the 6th century by Chenla, which was further inland. These Khmer states controlled sea routes and the trade they carried around Southeast Asia was an important stimulus to political development in the region. In the same period, similar states influenced by Indian cultures began to appear on Sumatra and Java. The larger ones shared major characteristics with those on the mainland to the north; they were founded on wet rice cultivation and ruled by semidivine kings residing in temple-cities.

══SEE ALSO══
This section:
• The Temple States and their Successors
China
The Indian Subcontinent

▲ **Bronze Lamp Bearer** *This Dong Son tomb figure was found near Hau Loc, northern Vietnam; it dates from the 4th–2nd century BC.*

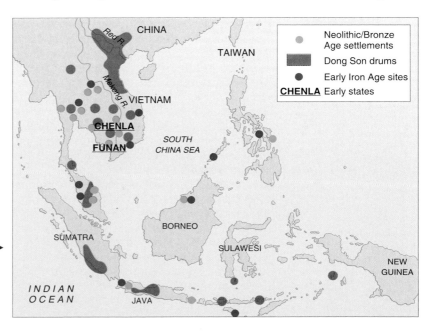

The Temple States and their Successors

*Vietnam • Cambodia: the rise of Angkor • Thailand: the Mons, Khmers, and Thais •
Burma and Pagan • Srivijaya • Java: from Sailendra to Majapahit*

Temples near Pagan *Many ancient temples, dating from the mid-11th to 13th centuries, cover the extensive plain of west Myanmar (formerly Burma). They are monuments to the predominance of Buddhism (which spread originally from India) in Southeast Asian culture.*

=====SEE ALSO=====
China:
• The Sui-Tang
  Reunification
• China's Middle Ages
• The Ming Dynasty
The Indian Subcontinent:
• Empires and Rivalries
• The Contest for
  Dominance
**The Visual Arts
Worldwide (vol. 4):**
• Southeast Asian Art
Religion (vol. 6):
• Hinduism
• Buddhism

As a result of its trade with India, from c. 400 BC, Southeast Asia began to be influenced by Indian socio-religious ideas. By 500 AD, many Hindu and Buddhist buildings had been constructed. Indigenous populations readily adopted the foreign gods; moreover, Hindu and Buddhist beliefs were often used by rulers to further their own political ambitions.

By 1000 AD, contact between mainland and insular ***polities*** (small city-states or kingdoms) had increased; this helped the spread of their particular form of Indianized culture.

Vietnam

During the 6th–9th centuries, the Chinese Tang dynasty controlled northern Vietnam. After its fall, the Vietnamese Ly clan established a Buddhist realm around Thang Long (near modern Hanoi); they built many monasteries on the plains of the Hong River.

By 1070, the Chinese Song and the Ly were at war. In 1225 the Tran dynasty assumed power. However, wars with the Mongols soon exhausted the leadership. An occupation by the Chinese Ming met with Viet resistance, led by a wealthy landowner, Le Loi (active 1426–43). The Le dynasty, under Le Thanh Ton (reigned 1460–97) established a government that was to provide a model for the next five centuries. After the dynasty fell, in the early 16th century, there were prolonged civil wars.

The Chams. The southern part of Vietnam was occupied by the Chams, who settled in coastal enclaves, such as Phan Rang near modern Panduranga. They existed as separate polities, constructing Hindu and Buddhist temple complexes in the river valleys, at such sites as Mi Son, Dong Duong, and Tra Kieu.

Having defended themselves against the Vietnamese in the 11th century, the Chams and the Viets joined forces against the Mongol-Yuan invasions. However, the Le kings of Vietnam began to expand into Cham territories from the late 14th century. They annexed all northern territories, though southern areas retained some independence.

Cambodia: the Rise of Angkor

To the west of southern Vietnam lay the Khmer lands. During the 7th century, Khmer rulers moved north, near the Tonle Sap lake. Rice growing provided the economic backbone of Angkor for the next six centuries.

Royal authority was expressed through a religious hierarchy. Shiva, Vishnu, and Buddha were the patronized cults. Jayavarman II (reigned 790–850) was the first to conquer the rice lands and establish himself near the future site of Angkor. A succession of kings followed Jayavarman, who built many temples and monasteries in the area. Suryavarman I (reigned 1002–50) extended the empire to include the Lopburi area of modern Thailand.

By the end of the 13th century, Theravada Buddhism had spread widely among the Khmers. The building of monuments ceased and Sanskrit inscriptions were replaced by Pali scriptures. Thai military aggression forced the Khmers, in the 15th century, to abandon Angkor and move south and east.

Thailand: the Mons, Khmers, and Thais
During the 6th century, Mon-speaking peoples dominated the Menam basin area. They were Theravada Buddhists and their temple remains extend as far north as Chiang Mai. Khmer influence gradually infiltrated from the northeast and remained a force until the 13th century. Thai peoples, meanwhile, had descended from the north to the plains to escape the Mongols. By the late 13th century the Thai King Mangrai (reigned 1296–1317) had conquered the northern Mon outpost of Haripunjaya (Lamphun), moving to Chiang Mai in 1296.

Sukhothai was the first Thai kingdom. Its second king, Ramkhamhaeng (reigned 1280–98), claimed to be the inventor of Thai script; he increased his realm tenfold from Luang Prabang in the east, through the central plains to the southern peninsula. The Mons in lower Burma also accepted his overlordship.

By the mid-13th century, Lopburi became independent of Angkor and Ayutthaya replaced it as a political centre.

Burma and Pagan
In the 9th century, the Pyu peoples had ruled northern Burma, while the Mons controlled the south, at Thaton. By the 11th century, the country was unified under the Burmans, who ruled from Pagan, an agrarian trading centre for the surrounding rice lands.

Pagan emerged as a major polity during the reign of Anawrahta (reigned 1044–77). His conquest of Thaton resulted in an infusion of Mon culture and Theravada Buddhism. By the 12th century, however, a shift had taken place from Mon to Burman culture, particularly under Kyanzittha (reigned 1084–1112).

By the late 12th century, loss of land to the monasteries created political disunity. The mid-13th century saw Pagan partitioned.

Like Angkor, Pagan was an inland agrarian polity, which controlled the coastal area. From the 11th to the 13th centuries, these states gave direction to the intellectual and material resources of mainland Southeast Asia.

Srivijaya
From the 4th century the Strait of Malacca became increasingly important as a maritime trade route. By the end of the 8th century, the state of Srivijaya, situated at modern Palembang, Sumatra, had become the main centre for maritime trade. Archaeological remains in Bengal and on the Thai peninsula also indicate Srivijaya's widespread influence. Its decline in the 11th century was due to military invasion by the Cholas from Tamil Nadu (southeast India) and, later, by the Javanese. Chinese shipping, meanwhile, had begun to move its trade to ports in Java and Thailand.

Java: from Sailendra to Majapahit
In the 7th century Java was dominated by the Sailendra dynasty. Little is known of the Sailendras; expelled from Java in the mid-9th century, they fled to Srivijaya. Their successors, the Sanjayan kings from Mataram (further south in Java), constructed the elaborate Hindu temple complex at Prambanan.

By the mid-10th century, the royal seat shifted eastwards to the Brantas River plain. This new site facilitated trade with Bali, Maluku, Sumatra, and the Thai peninsula.

A series of Hindu states emerged and declined until 1222, when the kingdom of Singosari was established. It culminated in the Majapahit Empire, which, at its peak in the mid-14th century, commanded Java, Bali, Madura, portions of south Borneo, Sulawesi, Sumbawa, and the Strait of Malacca. By the 16th century this empire was reduced to a local polity as sultanates on the north coast of Java seized power.

The Cult of the God-King
Jayavarman II, founder of the Khmer Empire, introduced a concept — the cult of god-king, or *devaraja* – that has dominated Khmer history for centuries. Jayavarman identified himself and all future kings with a god. This mystical association proved critical for guaranteeing the well-being of the realm. The building of temples reaffirmed the religious validity of the ruling dynasty. The *devaraja* concept was tempered by the tenets of Theravada Buddhism, in which the king was not divine, but was the protector and head of religion.

The Temple States
The Temple States, and those that succeeded them (indicated here), arose in Southeast Asia between the 10th and 16th centuries. ▼

Dynasties and Traders

The maritime world • Mainland Southeast Asia •
The new states of the 18th century • European trade empires

**Southeast Asia
c.1600–c.1800**
*Major political centres
that emerged in both
the mainland and
maritime areas
during this period
are shown.* ▼

In the early 16th century, the arrival of European traders in search of valuable spices marked the beginning of a new era for Southeast Asia. Old empires declined and new states emerged to capitalize on the opportunities presented by the growth in international trade. European influence was most pronounced in the maritime region, yet on the mainland as well European expansionism had an impact on the growth and consolidation of regimes.

The Maritime World

In 1511 the Portuguese seized Malacca, the centre of the Malay world. The Malay royal family fled and later re-established themselves at Johore-Riau, which became a major cultural centre but which lacked the political importance of Malacca. However, new regional states began to emerge, such as Banten on Java, and Aceh in north Sumatra. By the 1640s, the port of Macassar (modern name: Ujung Pandang) dominated the island of Sulawesi, and its Bugis soldiers terrorized the eastern seas. In the century following

Macassar's capture by the Dutch in 1699 many Bugis migrated westwards, usurping control of existing states and founding new ones, especially in the Malay peninsula. To consolidate their power, these maritime states often allied themselves with European powers, yet such alliances ultimately compromised their independence.

Java was dominated by the new kingdom of Mataram. Its first ruler, Sultan Agung (reigned 1613–45), launched wars of expansion only to be checked by the Dutch at Batavia (modern name: Jakarta), which he besieged in 1628–29. Mataram soon reached the limits of its power; by the middle of the 18th century the kingdom had divided and become a vassal of the Dutch.

Mainland Southeast Asia

The politics of mainland Southeast Asia were dominated by three dynasties in the area that now comprises Thailand (formerly Siam), Myanmar (formerly Burma), and Vietnam: respectively, the kingdom of Ayutthaya, the Toungoo dynasty, and the Le dynasty.

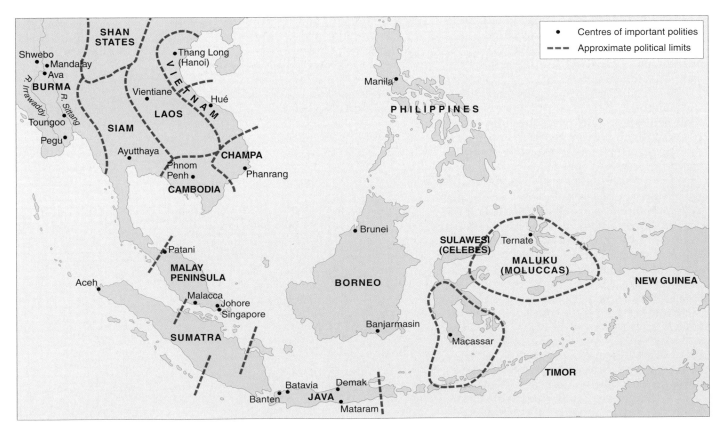

In Siam, the city of Ayutthaya became dominant from the mid-14th century. The country suffered repeated attacks from Burma, its chief rival in the region. Burmese occupation forces were expelled in 1584–87 and Ayutthaya took control of the Chao Praya River basin and Cambodia. King Narai (reigned 1656–88) undertook administrative reforms and spread the control of Ayutthaya to dominate the Muslim states of the south.

Burma achieved a degree of unity under the Toungoo dynasty. Tabinshwehti (1531–50) and his son Bayinnaung (reigned 1551–81) captured Pegu, capital of the Mon kingdom, subdued the Shan states in the north of Burma, and spread far to the east and south to defeat the cities of Ayutthaya in 1569 and Vientiane in 1574. However, this expansion ultimately overstretched the Toungoo and the power of the dynasty began to wane.

Early 16th-century Vietnam was characterized by warfare between rival clans, each claiming the right to uphold the Le dynasty (1428–1788): the Mac, dominant in the north; and the Nguyen, based in central Vietnam. The country remained divided throughout the 17th century, the challenge to the Nguyen coming this time from the Trinh. During this period Vietnam expanded southwards, crushing the old Cham state, and gaining control of the Mekong delta by the 1760s.

The New States of the 18th Century
By the 18th century the great dynasties of the mainland were in crisis. In 1740 the Mons of Pegu rebelled against the Toungoo; by 1752, they had captured the major political centre of Ava on the upper Irrawaddy, which had replaced the temple city of Pagan in importance in the region during the late 13th century. The Le dynasty in Vietnam succumbed in 1788 to a peasant uprising led by the Tayson brothers, who ruled the country until 1802. However, new dynasties arose out of disorder. The Konbaung dynasty (1752–1885) emerged at Shwebo, north of Mandalay, to reunify Burma and conquer Ayutthaya in 1767. In Siam the first of the Chakri dynasty, Rama I, established a new capital at Bangkok, near the ruins of Ayutthaya, in 1782. In Vietnam the Nguyen dynasty (1802–1945) defeated the Taysons and founded a new capital at Hué.

European Trade Empires
Portugal and Spain. In 1511 the Portuguese viceroy of Goa, Alfonso de Albuquerque (1453–1515), led an assault on Malacca and the eastern islands to impose a royal monopoly on the rich spice trade. A number of mercenary adventurers and traders followed his lead. The monopoly, however, never proved wholly effective and, by the early 17th century, Portuguese control of the area was challenged by Dutch and English traders.

Spanish involvement in Southeast Asia began with an expedition launched in 1542 from Mexico to the northern islands of the archipelago known as the Philippines (in honour of Crown Prince Felipe of Spain). They were occupied in 1564, and a capital was established at Manila in 1571. Though well positioned for trade to China, the colony did not provide the gold the Spanish had hoped for.

The Netherlands. The **Dutch East India Company** mounted expeditions against the Portuguese from the early 17th century onwards. Rapid expansion occurred under the governors Jan Pieterszoon Coen (1618–23; 1627–29) and Anthony van Diemen (1636–45). In 1619, the Dutch seized the settlement of Jakarta on Java and established a new capital there called Batavia. A wealthy creole society emerged, attracting many Chinese traders to the area. Dutch control over the Banda spice islands was secured in 1623, when the British were driven from Ambon. The Portuguese were expelled from Malacca in 1641.

British and Dutch Competition. In the 18th century the English East India Company expanded its interests in Southeast Asia to help finance its trade with China, thereby coming into conflict with the Dutch. In 1786 the company obtained the island of Penang from the Malay state of Kedah. Wars and alliances in Europe intensified colonial competition in Southeast Asia and led the British to seize Dutch possessions. They ruled Java from 1811 until 1819. In the same year, **Sir Thomas Stamford Raffles** (1781–1826) founded a new trading settlement at Singapore. The Anglo-Dutch Treaty of 1824 resolved the conflict. It drew a line south of Singapore, leaving the British dominant on the peninsula and the Dutch paramount in the islands, but permitted the British to trade there. The treaty remained in effect throughout the next century and marked the beginning of the era of formal colonial conquest.

> The King of the Portuguese has often commanded me to go to the Straits, because it seemed to His Highness that this was the best place to intercept the trade which the Muslims of Cairo and of Mecca and Jiddah carry on in these parts. So it was to do our Lord's service that we are brought here; by taking Malacca, we would close the Straits so that never again would the Muslims be able to bring their spices by this route.
>
> **Alfonso de Albuquerque**, addressing his men on the eve of the attack on Malacca, *Comentários de Grande Alfonso de Albuquerque* (1576)

Sir Thomas Stamford Raffles

Raffles was a principal architect of British expansion in Southeast Asia. Although remembered chiefly for his acquisition of Singapore for the East India Company, he was also a scholar, a founder of London's Zoological gardens, and served as lieutenant-governor of Java, where he introduced important land reforms.

THE DUTCH EAST INDIA COMPANY

Founded in 1598, the Vereenigde Oost-Indische Compagnie (VOC) was a major innovation in Asian trade. Unlike Portuguese commerce, which was a crown monopoly, the VOC was a joint-stock company, possessing a highly coordinated organizational structure and formidable military strength. VOC operations were centred on Batavia, from where it monopolized the export of spices and exotic goods to Europe. The VOC declined during the 18th century in the face of British competition, especially in the lucrative textile and opium trades. The company was wound up on 31 December 1799, when the Dutch East Indies came under the direct control of the Netherlands government.

European Conquest

The new colonial order • Economic and social change • The rise of nationalism

=====SEE ALSO=====
This section:
• Dynasties and Traders
• World War II and
  Independence
**The Industrial Age
in Europe:**
• Nationalism and
  Imperialism

The 19th century saw the consolidation of colonial rule and the establishment of the modern political boundaries of Southeast Asia, together with rapid economic expansion and social change. However, even at the height of European ascendancy, new forces were emerging to challenge foreign rule.

The New Colonial Order

Britain in Malaya and Burma. Throughout the 19th century Britain was the dominant power in the region. In 1826, Penang, Singapore, and Malacca combined to form the Straits Settlements. As their economies grew, so did British involvement in political affairs. Unrest in Perak led to British military intervention and the Pangkor Engagement of 1874, after which its Malay ruler accepted a British Resident (an official representative of the British government). This treaty of protection was extended to Selangor/Negri, Sembilan, and Pahang; the three states became the Federated Malay States in 1895. Between 1909 and 1914 the remaining peninsular states came under British control as the Unfederated Malay States. Britain's stake in Borneo was consolidated in 1888 when Brunei, Sarawak, and territories of the North Borneo Company became British protectorates.

Burma, vital to the British as a source of timber and as a gateway to India, was conquered in stages. The first Anglo-Burmese war of 1824–26 was fought to stabilize the frontier and led to the secession of Arakan and Temasserim to the British. The second war (1852) placed the territories of Lower Burma under British control. The Kingdom of Upper Burma under Mindon (1853–78) attempted to strengthen itself through reform but a third war (1885–86) ensured its decline and the annexation of Burma to British India.

French Indochina. France's commercial involvement in Indochina and its sponsorship of Catholic missions led to its political intervention in the region. Between 1858 and 1867, conflicts arose with the Nguyen over the persecution of Catholics; the south was absorbed to become the colony of Cochin China. Increased French involvement in the north led to a war with China in 1885. Thereafter Annam and Tonkin became French protectorates. These territories, together with the Kingdom of Cambodia (a protectorate since 1884) and the four principalities of Laos, were

Western Colonies in Southeast Asia

During the 19th century colonial rule was consolidated in Southeast Asia. The possessions of the European powers in the region during the 19th and 20th centuries are indicated. ▼

Chakri Reform in Siam

Siam was never formally under foreign rule. While political and economic change was instituted by the kings of the Chakri dynasty, economically the country was dominated by the British. King Chulalongkorn (reigned 1868–1910), a European-educated monarch, undertook many administrative and educational reforms. Demands for more democracy in the 20th century led to a bloodless coup in 1932, which installed a constitutional monarchy.

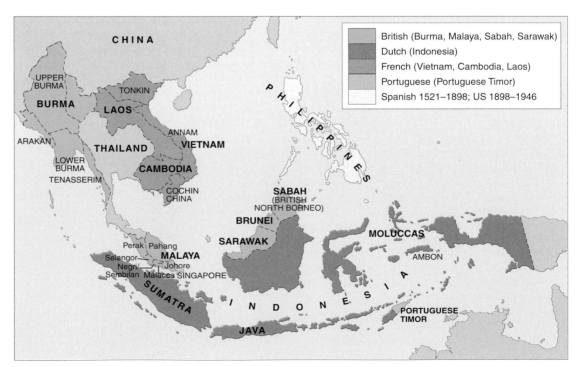

Key:
- British (Burma, Malaya, Sabah, Sarawak)
- Dutch (Indonesia)
- French (Vietnam, Cambodia, Laos)
- Portuguese (Portuguese Timor)
- Spanish 1521–1898; US 1898–1946

combined to form French Indochina in 1887. Initially, the impact of French rule was most evident in Cochin China, yet in the 1890s more interventionist policies were applied throughout Indochina.

The Dutch East Indies. The Dutch East India Company bequeathed a very diverse administrative system to the region. Outside the main areas of Dutch control, such as Java, Ambon, the Moluccas, and West Sumatra, Dutch influence was often exercised through a more general form of overlordship. The conquest of Indonesia continued throughout the century. Between 1898 and 1911, over 300 nominally independent states came under Dutch control, and a more uniform policy was applied throughout the islands. Ironically, this contributed to the rise of Indonesian nationalism in the 1930s by encouraging its people to regard the archipelago as a single entity.

Spain and the USA in the Philippines. During the 19th century, there was growing anticlericalism and resistance to Spanish rule. In 1896 the Philippines rose in rebellion. When the USA declared war on Spain in 1898 over control of Cuba, the Philippines resistance movement increased its activities. Although the islands were ceded to the USA by Spain in 1899, the independence struggle continued. The USA attempted to modernize the Philippines in readiness for self-government. By 1916 the USA had conceded Philippine independence in principle; in 1933 it was agreed that self-government would be implemented after a ten-year transitional period. The case of the Philippines gave great impetus to the ambitions of nationalists elsewhere.

Economic and Social Change

Under colonial rule, the economies of Southeast Asia expanded. Agricultural use of the land increased in Malaya, Indonesia, Burma, Siam (modern Thailand), and Indochina (Vietnam). The maritime region attracted large-scale European plantation enterprise, especially with the introduction of rubber to Malaya. Immigration increased vastly, as traders and labourers arrived from China and India. Such cities as Batavia, Singapore, and Saigon, became vibrant cultural melting pots.

By the end of the 19th century, colonial rule had transformed society in Southeast Asia. In southern Vietnam and Indonesia, in particular, new local elites emerged, many of whose members were European-educated. In the Philippines, the educated class, known as *illustrados,* led a resistance movement against Spanish rule. In Indonesia, during the early 20th century, the seeds of future nationalism were sown by indigenous reform movements promoting education, notably the Muslim *Sharikat Islam.*

The Rise of Nationalism

Many of the early movements of opposition to colonial rule were inspired by religion or revolved around traditional symbols of authority. One early movement that was opposed to French rule in Indochina was the *Can Vuong* ('loyalty to the king') revolt of 1885, which mobilized support around the old royal houses. In Indonesia the greatest challenge to the Dutch came from Islam. It was the inspiration behind the Java War (1825–30), the Padri wars in West Sumatra (1824–37), and a protracted struggle in Aceh (1873–1902), in which village religious teachers took the lead in resisting Dutch expansion. The USA also encountered Islamic resistance from the Moros in the southern Philippines (1902–13).

Although later nationalist movements often incorporated elements of earlier protest, by the early 20th century wholly new types of party-political organization were being created. A wide range of parties existed in Indonesia by the 1920s, including Southeast Asia's first communist party, which led a series of revolts against the Dutch colonial rulers in 1926. Communist parties emerged in Malaya and Vietnam. Nationalist struggles in India and China also helped raise the political awareness of Indian and Chinese immigrant communities in Southeast Asia. When economic conditions deteriorated during the Great Depression from 1929 onwards, a series of uprisings occurred. Communists attempted to capitalize on agrarian revolts in Tonkin and Annam. In 1930–31, the British were challenged by a rebellion in Burma, led by the messianic figure of Saya San (1876–1931).

Prince Diponegaro (1785–1855)

After a period of famine, a Javanese prince, Diponegaro, embarked on a bitter holy war against the Dutch in 1825. Many Javanese saw this uprising as fulfilling the prophesy of the coming of a 'just king,' which heralded a new age of righteousness. The revolt lasted until 1830, when Diponegaro was captured and exiled to Macassar, where he lived until his death. Diponegaro was later honoured as a hero of Indonesian nationalism.

◄ **Tapping a Rubber Tree on a Malayan Plantation** *Before the invention of synthetic rubber in the 1940s, natural rubber from Malaya was of vital importance in the development of modern industry and transportation. The precious natural resources in which the region abounded were heavily exploited by the colonial powers.*

283

World War II and Independence

Impact of the war • The struggle for independence •
The postindependence period • Southeast Asia in the 1990s

From the 1930s onwards Japan had regarded Southeast Asia as a source of raw materials and during World War II sought to annex the region. Japan formed an alliance with Thailand and, on the pretext of assisting the Vichy regime in France, had effectively occupied French Indochina by July 1941.

Japan's surprise attack on the US Pacific Fleet at Pearl Harbor on 7 December 1941 initiated Japan's rapid conquest of Southeast Asia. On 11 January 1942 Kuala Lumpur fell; on 15 February Singapore was captured. By the second week of March, Batavia, Rangoon, and the Philippines were in Japanese hands. However, at the height of Japanese supremacy, a series of Allied victories began to turn the tide. Burma was retaken by Allied forces. The USA advanced across the Pacific, while Japan itself came under aerial bombardment. Early in 1945 plans were made for Allied forces from India to recapture Malaya. However, this was never enacted; Emperor Hirohito announced Japan's unconditional surrender on 15 August 1945, after atomic bombs had been dropped on the cities of Hiroshima and Nagasaki.

Impact of the War

Nationalists and the Japanese. Although the Japanese established quasi-independent governments in Southeast Asia, their commitment to Asian independence was limited. Some nationalist leaders took the opportunity to advance the cause of independence by cooperating with the new rulers. Elsewhere resistance movements emerged: in Burma (now Myanmar), an Anti-Fascist People's Freedom League (AFPFL); in the Philippines, the Huk rebellion; in Vietnam, a national liberation front led by the Indochinese Communist Party; and in Malaya (modern Malaysia), the Communist Malayan People's Anti-Japanese Army.

The Struggle for Independence

Throughout Southeast Asia the returning European colonial rulers faced opposition from resistance movements, many of which controlled large areas and established independent governments after Japanese surrender.

Burma. In 1945 the British were forced to accept the principle of Burmese self-government and to include AFPFL leaders in the

**Japanese Conquests ▶
in Southeast Asia**
*This map indicates the
furthest extent of
Japanese military
domination in the
region, in August
1942. Japanese
aggression in the area
began with the air
attack on the US naval
base at Pearl Harbor on
Oahu Island in Hawaii
on 7 December 1941.*

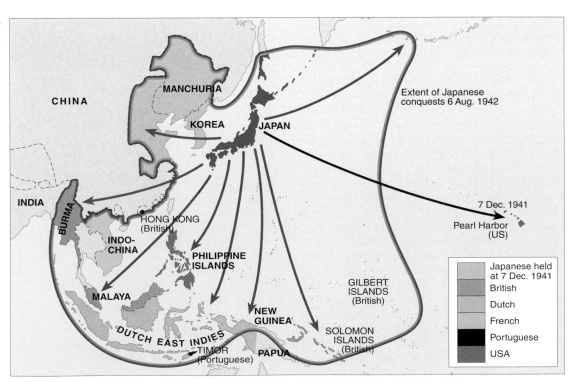

CHINA

MANCHURIA

KOREA

JAPAN

Extent of Japanese
conquests 6 Aug. 1942

INDIA

BURMA

HONG KONG
(British)

INDO-
CHINA

PHILIPPINE
ISLANDS

7 Dec. 1941

Pearl Harbor
(US)

MALAYA

NEW
GUINEA

GILBERT
ISLANDS
(British)

DUTCH EAST INDIES

TIMOR
(Portuguese)

PAPUA

SOLOMON
ISLANDS
(British)

	Japanese held at 7 Dec. 1941
	British
	Dutch
	French
	Portuguese
	USA

THE SECOND INDOCHINA WAR

After the partition of Vietnam (1954), a strong government failed to emerge in the south. Authoritarian regimes in the later 1950s and 1960s lacked popular support, leading to the formation of the National Liberation Front (NLF) in 1960, better known as the Vietcong. It soon controlled large parts of the countryside. The USA, alarmed that the fall of the south to communism would be repeated throughout the region – the so-called 'domino theory' – supplied large amounts of military aid to the south. After a US warship was attacked by North Vietnamese forces in August 1964, the US Congress authorized direct intervention. The first marine battalions arrived in March 1965; by 1967, US forces totalled around 525 000. US commander General William Westmoreland (1914–   ) deployed a large conscript army, yet failed to win the "hearts and minds" of the rural populace. In February 1968 the communist 'Tet offensive' was launched, which almost succeeded in capturing Saigon. US hopes for an early victory proved an illusion. As the bitter and costly war dragged on, a peace process began in Paris in 1968, which reached its conclusion in January 1973, when the USA began to withdraw. The last US combatants departed on 19 March 1973. The US objective was the removal of all external forces and a recognition of an independent government in the south.

▲ **US Troops in Vietnam** *A total of 2.5 million US troops were deployed in the course of the conflict.*

However, the north refused to accept the division of Vietnam. The USA continued to supply the army of South Vietnam, but in 1975 a new communist offensive finally overran Saigon.

administration. The AFPFL leader Aung San (c. 1914–47) became vice-chairman of the executive council, and the party won the 1947 elections. The Karen ethnic minority boycotted them and demanded their own government. On 19 July 1947 Aung San and seven associates were assassinated; the Union of Burma gained independence on 4 January 1948, under the leadership of U Nu (1907–95).

Indonesia. On 17 August 1945, two days after the Japanese surrender, **Sukarno** proclaimed Indonesian independence. The Dutch launched a reoccupation in July 1947, which had retaken Sumatra and most of Java by the end of 1948; Sukarno was taken prisoner. However, a new Indonesian republican army was assembled from World War II veterans. Dutch attempts to divide and rule Indonesia failed; the regions stayed loyal to the republic. International pressure and the need to keep the leadership in moderate hands compelled the Dutch to surrender formal Indonesian self-government on 27 December 1949.

Indochina. The Democratic Republic of Vietnam (DRV), headed by Ho Chi Minh, was established after the Japanese surrender on 2 September 1945. Chinese troops occupied North Vietnam down to the 16th parallel, and the British occupied the south. When the French resumed control of the south in March 1946, Ho persuaded them to recognize the north as a free state within a federal French

Indochina. The French refused to accept further independence, and in December 1946 tensions between the DRV and the south escalated into war. The conflict only ended in 1954 after France was defeated at Dien Bien Phu. Peace talks divided Vietnam at the 17th parallel between the communist DRV in the north, and the US-sponsored State of Vietnam, with its capital at Saigon. However, the peace did not last. In 1964 the **Second Indochina War** began, which ended in the reunification of Vietnam under communist rule in 1975.

Malaya and Singapore. When the British returned to Malaya in September 1945, they persuaded the communist guerrillas to surrender their arms. However, the communists began a campaign of unrest, which led to an armed insurrection, lasting until 1960. The British fought a successful counterinsurgency campaign and had largely quelled the uprising by 1951. Power was devolved to a multiethnic alliance between the main Malay nationalist party, the United Malay National Organization, and conservative Chinese and Indian parties. The alliance won the first federal elections in 1955 and led Malaya to independence on 30 August 1957. Singapore achieved self-government in 1959.

The Postindependence Period

Burma. The British left behind major political divisions in Burma. The Shan, Kachin, and

---

Sukarno (1901–70)

Sukarno, a gifted orator and charismatic leader, dominated Indonesian politics for nearly 40 years. Founder of the Indonesian National Party in 1927, he was imprisoned by the Dutch for much of the 1930s, but emerged to head the republic as president (1949–67).

▲ Ho Chi Minh
Ho Chi Minh ('he who enlightens') was the alias of Nguyen Ai Quoc (1890–1969). The son of a poor Confucian scholar, Ho spent many years abroad, only returning to Vietnam from the USSR in 1941 to lead the Viet Minh.

Workers in a Textile Factory in Jogjakarta, Indonesia *Many countries in Southeast Asia have experienced considerable economic growth in the final decades of the 20th century, as a result of high productivity and low labour costs.* ▼

Karen minorities demanded autonomy, and the Karen National Union began a protracted rebellion in 1948. The AFPFL under U Nu instituted a programme of Buddhist socialism. Following the AFPFL's poor performance in the elections of 1956, U Nu resigned. He returned to office in 1958, during a deepening crisis, in which he handed over power to a military caretaker government for 18 months. In March 1962 a military coup toppled U Nu, and brought General Ne Win (1911–   ) to power. The military sought to isolate the country from outside influence. Opposition was met with brutal repression; in 1988, many dissidents were arrested, including Aung San Suu Kyi (1945–   ), the daughter of Aung San, National League of Democracy (NLD) leader, and winner of the 1991 Nobel peace prize. Ne Win handed power to a State Law and Order Restoration Committee (SLORC). In 1989 Burma changed its name to Myanmar. The SLORC continued to suppress the pro-democracy movement, led by the NLD, and refused to accept the NLD's victory in the 1990 elections. Following the defeat of several ethnic guerrilla movements by government forces in 1995–96, Aung San Suu Kyi was released after six years under house arrest. In 1996 demonstrations calling for an end to human rights abuses erupted in Rangoon. In 1997 the USA imposed economic sanctions on Myanmar and the SLORC becamed the State Peace and Development Council (SPDC).

Thailand. After World War II Thailand's parliamentary government was disrupted by a series of military interventions. Between 1947 and 1957, under Phibun Songkhram, the military opposed communism and forged links with the West. His successor, Sarit Thanarat, promoted the values of 'king, religion, and nation' and encouraged King Bhumibol (reigned 1946–   ) to play a prominent political role.

From the late 1960s the government fought communist rural insurgency and supported US operations in Indochina. A new constitution was adopted in 1968, but the military resumed power in 1971. The military rulers fled the country in 1973 after pro-democracy uprisings. The military were again in power by 1976. Further coups throughout the 1980s and 1990s failed owing to lack of support by the king, who mediated between military and civilian interests. Since the mid-1980s Thailand has rapidly industrialized. Constitutional reforms in 1992 and 1995 strengthened its democratic system. However, the poor handling of the struggling economy by successive coalition governments has caused instability.

Indochina. In 1975 Vietnam, Cambodia, and Laos came under communist rule. Vietnam was formally reunited as the Socialist Republic of Vietnam, and Cambodia became Democratic Kampuchea. However, in 1979 the Cambodian capital, Phnom Penh, fell to a Vietnamese invasion, and in February China attacked northern Vietnam. The rival alliances forged in the Cold War – especially Vietnam's closeness to the USSR – gave new force to old rivalries. Cambodia had embarked on a disastrous course under **Pol Pot**, forcing the Vietnamese to intervene to establish a more moderate government. This led to resistance to the Vietnamese-sponsored regime by the Khmer Rouge and a coalition of parties led by the prerevolutionary ruler Prince Norodom Sihanouk (1922–   ). A ceasefire was negotiated in 1991; Sihanouk became King of Cambodia following elections in 1993. Khmer Rouge offensives resumed and fighting intensified. In 1996 there was large-scale Khmer Rouge defection to the government's side. Relations between the parties of the ruling coalition declined causing a crisis in government. In 1997, Pol Pot was captured and imprisoned by a Khmer Rouge faction and died in 1998. From the 1980s, Vietnam embarked on a course of liberal economic reform and openness; full diplomatic relations with the USA were restored in 1995. In 1997, the government publicly purged itself of corrupt elements.

Indonesia. From 1950 until 1957, Indonesian politics were unstable. The Communist Party of Indonesia (PKI) grew to over 160 000 members by 1954. Elections in 1955 exposed a rift between Java and the rest of Indonesia. The army helped to sustain unity, but was itself divided. Following the Sumatran rebellion of December 1956, the regional military took over government. In 1957 President Sukarno launched a new initiative called 'guided democracy' to dispense with party politics. Under martial law, he adopted an anti-Western stance, supported by the PKI. He annexed West Irian (1960–62) and opposed the formation of Malaysia (1963–65).

In September 1965 soldiers sympathetic to the PKI staged a coup. General Suharto (1921–) stepped in to restore order. Hundreds of thousands were murdered in reprisal. Suharto supplanted Sukarno as president in 1967 and established a 'new order,' stressing economic development and internal security. In 1975, Indonesia seized the island of East Timor, scene of severe human rights abuses. Detention of activists continued. Ethnic violence erupted in Irian Jaya and West Java in 1996 and repression of opposition parties sparked rioting in Jakarta. While ethnic violence continued, the 1997 general election returned Suharto's ruling Golkar alliance to power. Forest fires caused an environmental disaster (1997) and a financial crisis in 1998 provoked riots and protests demanding reform. Suharto was forced to resign in May 1998, but instability persisted.

The Philippines. The Japanese occupation divided Philippine society and discredited many collaborating politicians. Ramon Magsaysay (president 1953–57) attempted to bolster democratic institutions and end the Huk rebellion, but confidence in the old order was undermined. In 1965 Ferdinand Marcos (1917–89) became president and sought to govern by 'constitutional authoritarianism.' However, the Marcos regime faced revolts. Martial law, established in 1972, was lifted in 1981, but presidential powers remained in place. After opposition leader Benigno Aquino (1932–83) was assassinated, his widow Corazon Aquino (1933–) launched a protest movement known as 'people power.' Aquino won the election of February 1986. When Marcos claimed victory, mass demonstrations forced him into exile; Aquino was elected president. Fidel Ramos (1928–), Aquino's chosen successor, was elected president in 1992. He revived the economic reform process in 1996 and reached an agreement with Muslim secessionists in the southern Philippines, but financial problems shook the country in 1997. Joseph Estrada was elected president in 1998.

Malaysia and Singapore. In 1963 the Federation of Malaysia was created by the merger of Malaya, Singapore, Sarawak, and Sabah. It became apparent that the inclusion of Singapore in Malaysia would unsettle the racial balance of politics in the country; in 1965 Singapore was asked to leave the federation.

In Malaysia, government remained in the hands of an alliance of mainland parties and those from Sabah and Sarawak. All prime ministers have come from the United Malay National Organization (UMNO). The first, Tunku Abdul Rahman (1903–90), stepped down in 1970 after a poor electoral performance had provoked racial riots. The government of Dr Mathahir Mohamad (prime minis-

◄ **Corazon Aquino**
The former leader of the Philippines is pictured here during an election campaign. Her government survived a number of attempted military coups between 1986 and 1992.

Pol Pot (1925–98)

Born Saloth Sar, Pol Pot led the Khmer Rouge to power in 1975. One of his first acts was to order as many as 3.5 million city dwellers to work in the countryside. This ushered in a reign of terror, which peaked in 1976–78, when perhaps one million people died from disease or by execution.

ter 1981–) strove to modernize Malaysian society and its economy. By the mid-1990s, the country's economy was booming, but this was curtailed by an economic crisis in 1997.

Since secession from Malaysia, Singapore has been ruled by the People's Action Party. From 1959, its government was headed by Lee Kuan Yew (1923–), who modernized Singapore, which prospered. In 1990 Lee stepped down. Constitutional reforms were effected in 1991 and Ong Teng Cheong became Singapore's first directly elected president in 1993. The general election of 1997 once again returned the People's Action Party to power.

Southeast Asia in the 1990s

The end of empire in Southeast Asia coincided with a period of rapid change. By the 1990s, technological revolution and industrialization had created in the region some of the world's fastest growing economies. The end of the Cold War brought new prospects for regional integration, in which **ASEAN** took the lead. Society was also changing, notably with the rise of the educated middle classes. Governments attempted to change while fostering political stability. In the 1990s there were debates on how the new wealth might be distributed, on political institutions, and on the role of religion. Southeast Asia had entered a new era of political change. However, in 1997–98 the region suffered a serious economic collapse, triggered in part by currency speculation.

ASEAN (Association of Southeast Asian Nations)

ASEAN, founded in Bangkok in 1967 by Thailand, Malaysia, Singapore, Indonesia, and the Philippines, is a forum for collaboration on issues of mutual concern. After the Bali Summit of 1975, ASEAN took a more active role in regional integration. In the late 1980s, it succeeded in promoting peace in Cambodia. Brunei was admitted in 1984, Vietnam in 1994, and Myanmar, Cambodia, and Laos in 1997.

Oceania Before the Europeans

A world of islands • The first discoverers • Oceanic societies

===SEE ALSO===
The Visual Arts Worldwide (vol. 4):
• Art of Oceania and Australasia
Religion (vol. 6):
• Introduction

Maori Peoples living in New Zealand and the Cook Islands since before the arrival of European settlers. They are descended from Polynesian voyagers. Archaeological discoveries date Maori settlements at c. 800 AD and possibly earlier.

The Islands of Oceania *The area and pattern of the two waves of the great Oceanic migrations are shown, 6000 BC–800 AD.*

The term Oceania describes the thousands of islands of the central and South Pacific Ocean. They are divided into three regions: Melanesia ('black islands'), Micronesia ('small islands'), and Polynesia ('many islands'). The term also usually includes Australasia and the Malay Archipelago.

A World of Islands

The continental islands of Australia, New Guinea, and New Zealand were originally part of a prehistoric landmass. Most of the Pacific islands, however, were created by volcanic activity. Younger islands, such as Hawaii, still have active volcanoes and rich soil. Older islands consist of a build-up of coral on top of the crater of a sunken volcano. While these islands cannot support much vegetation, their coral reefs abound with fish and other marine life.

By the late 18th century, the Pacific islands (including New Zealand) had a total population of about 3 250 000; Australia was home to a further 300 000. Australian and Tasmanian Aborigines, together with some New Guinea islanders and others, were descended from the region's earliest **Australoid** ancestors. Other Pacific islanders are known as **Mongoloid**; these racial groups are of two general physical types: Melanesian in the west, and Polynesian in the east and north.

The comparative study of languages is a valuable way of tracing the movements of prehistoric peoples. The languages of Australoid peoples, known as **Papuan**, are still spoken in Australia, New Guinea, and islands close to it, such as Bougainville. All other Pacific islanders speak **Austronesian** languages, as do the people of Malaysia and the Philippines.

The First Discoverers

Australoid people first came to New Guinea and Australia from Southeast Asia about 50 000 years ago. Mongoloids, also from Southeast Asia, were colonizing the nearby

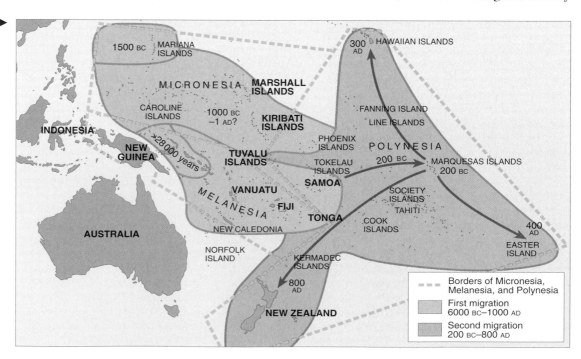

islands of Melanesia by 6000 BC. Using large sailing canoes, these migrants settled islands from New Caledonia and Bougainville to Fiji and the atolls of Micronesia. Different groups of travellers overlapped, especially in Melanesia, where a vast number of different languages and cultures developed. Other voyagers ventured much further, reaching Tonga and Samoa by about 1000 BC.

Later Migration (1000 BC–750 AD). It was from the island groups of Tonga and Samoa, from c. 1000 BC, that the distinctive Polynesian language and cultural base developed; it spread to other islands of the central and eastern Pacific and to New Zealand as a result of the great maritime voyages. Expeditions to the Marquesas group in about 200 BC, and subsequent journeys from the Marquesas to Hawaii, Easter Island, and New Zealand, between 400 and 800 AD, were voyages of up to 5600 km. Unlike Melanesia, Polynesia was settled within a relatively short period of time, 2000 years; its languages and cultures are clearly related.

Oceanic Societies

Although the Oceanic peoples kept no written records before European contact, oral history and early European observations indicate what their traditional societies were like. Australian Aborigines spoke hundreds of ancient languages and had a hunter-gatherer culture, which endures today. In their culture the physical and spirit worlds merged, in what present-day Aborigines call 'the dreamtime.'

Melanesians also spoke many languages and their cultures varied widely. A common feature, however, was the use of gift exchange

ISLAND VOYAGERS

There have been many theories about how the early voyagers discovered and colonized the islands, and much speculation about the islanders' origins. While it is not certain why islanders chose to migrate over such long distances, it is known that they originally came from Southeast Asia. They travelled deliberately, bringing livestock and plants, and used sophisticated navigational techniques. Sailing against the prevailing winds in long double-hulled 'canoes,' islanders needed to develop special sailing and direction-finding skills. Some islanders still practise traditional navigation, based on the observation of stars, wind and wave patterns, cloud formations, and birds. Scholars have used computer simulations to understand how such information allowed island navigators to 'read' the apparently empty ocean as if it were a map.

networks to define their 'countries,' rather than static territorial borders. Social organization could vary widely on a single island; generally individuals wielded power through birth, wealth, or military prowess and communities were relatively small (70 to 300 people). Melanesians cultivated plantations of yams and taro. They also fished and kept pigs.

Polynesians had a much younger culture and shared a common language base. Such concepts as *mana* (supernatural power, prestige) and *tapu* (taboo, sacred or restricted) existed throughout Polynesia. Most islands had hierarchical societies, varying from the overall island governments of Tonga to the numerous **Maori** chieftains of New Zealand. Their artwork was elaborate and decorative and included body ornamentation (**tatau**); they sometimes built in stone. Human sacrifice and cannibalism combined with hospitality in religions whose gods reflected all aspects of human nature. Most Polynesians cultivated root crops, while those living on coral atolls relied more on coconut and breadfruit trees; fishing was universal.

Micronesia, parts of which were colonized from Asia and Melanesia during the first Pacific migration, maintained greater contact with Asian culture than either Melanesia or Polynesia. The Marianas and Yap were settled mainly from the Philippines; they share a common language base and show developments in fishing methods from as far away as Japan. Other islands, such as Kiribati and Tuvalu, share Melanesian-based languages. Many Micronesian islands are coral atolls, whose soil could not support extensive agriculture. Although Micronesians grew hardy crops, including taro and pandanus, they also relied on coconut and breadfruit trees and developed an elaborate fishing technology.

▲ **Oceanic Canoes**
Inhabiting a world of islands made canoes essential to the peoples of the southern and central Pacific. Smaller vessels were used for fishing, transportation, and short-distance travel, while much larger canoes (with double masts) were used for voyaging, with the capacity to carry up to 60 people.

Tatau

Tatau was the art of making pictures or designs on the skin with indelible colours. It was practised on many Pacific islands, especially Tahiti. Tatau artists were revered figures whose work recorded the ancestry, religious affiliations, or achievements of their subject's life. Most designs were 'drawn' using charcoal and sharpened sticks, sometimes with colour. The practice of tatau has since been adopted in many countries.

Australia, New Zealand, and the Pacific

European exploration • Australia • New Zealand • Oceania • The Pacific way

===SEE ALSO===
The Industrial Age in Europe:
• World War I
North America:
• The United States of America
Latin America:
• The Spanish and Portuguese Empires
Southeast Asia:
• Dynasties and Traders

chronometer A timepiece designed to be accurate under varying conditions of temperature and pressure. It always showed British time and enabled navigators to determine the distance between them and Britain and thus calculate their longitude.

The Portuguese navigator Ferdinand Magellan discovered the Cape Horn sea route into the Pacific Ocean in 1520. It was not until the 17th century, however, that Europeans began exploring the Pacific in earnest.

European Exploration

The Dutch explorer, Willem Jansz, first sighted Australia in 1605; another Dutch expedition landed on the west coast in 1611. From the Dutch East Indies Abel Janszoon Tasman (1603–59) also went on an expedition to the South Pacific. In 1642–43 he discovered the island now called Tasmania, New Zealand, and the Tonga and Fiji Islands. Spanish ships, meanwhile, plied the Pacific between colonies in South America and the Philippines. However, without an accurate way of measuring longitude, European exploration of the Pacific Ocean was haphazard and dangerous.

Captain James Cook (1728–79). The British navigator, Captain Cook, undertook three voyages to the Pacific between 1769 and 1779, consolidating earlier European discoveries. Cook was able accurately to map many of the region's features for the first time, using the newly invented **chronometer**. In addition to his scientific motives, Cook had in-

structions to claim Australia and New Zealand for Britain; these acquisitions were to become the foundation of Britain's Pacific Empire. Although Cook was killed in Hawaii, his explorations encouraged further expeditions.

Australia

The British government exploited Cook's discoveries when the American Revolution (1775–83) forced it to find a new overseas gaol for prisoners. In 1788 a fleet carrying **convicts** sailed for Botany Bay, just south of present-day Sydney, to establish the British colony of New South Wales. They were soon followed by free settlers, attracted by opportunities in ranching or driven from Britain and Ireland by poverty and famine. By 1900, Britain had explored and colonized the whole continent, despite the protests of the Aborigines. In 1901 the colonies of New South Wales, Tasmania, Queensland, South Australia, Victoria, and Western Australia combined to form the ***Commonwealth of Australia***.

Australia's participation in World Wars I and II, as part of the British Empire, provoked nationalist sentiment at home; events at the Battle of **Gallipoli** in 1915, in particular, prompted the development of a unique Aus-

Cook's Voyages ▶
Cook's three voyages to the Pacific (1769–79) served to consolidate earlier European discoveries and dispel many myths about the Pacific. He claimed the east coast of Australia for Britain, circumnavigated and charted New Zealand, and discovered several Pacific islands.

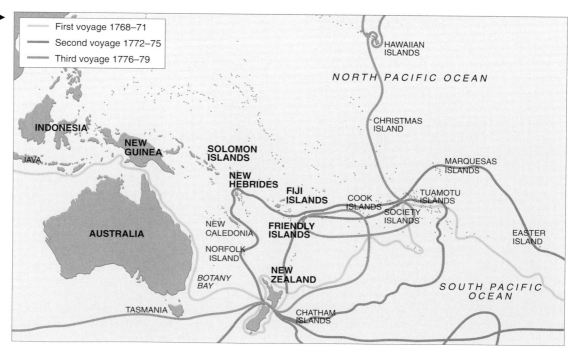

First voyage 1768–71
Second voyage 1772–75
Third voyage 1776–79

HAWAIIAN ISLANDS

NORTH PACIFIC OCEAN

CHRISTMAS ISLAND

INDONESIA

NEW GUINEA

JAVA

SOLOMON ISLANDS

MARQUESAS ISLANDS

NEW HEBRIDES

FIJI ISLANDS

COOK ISLANDS

TUAMOTU ISLANDS

SOCIETY ISLANDS

AUSTRALIA

NEW CALEDONIA

FRIENDLY ISLANDS

EASTER ISLAND

NORFOLK ISLAND

BOTANY BAY

NEW ZEALAND

SOUTH PACIFIC OCEAN

TASMANIA

CHATHAM ISLANDS

▲ **Convict Labour** *Convicted criminals were transported from Britain to Australia (and other British colonies) in large prison ships. Having endured the long voyage, in cramped conditions (shown here), the prisoners were put to hard labour.*

tralian identity and pride. Australia gained complete self-government status in 1941, but remained a member of the British Commonwealth. The USA began to play an important role in Australian affairs after World War II. During the 1950s and 1960s, the Cold War led Australia into an alliance with the USA against communist Asia. On the domestic front, successive governments emphasized full employment and social legislation.

During the 1970s Australia suffered from economic recession, high unemployment, and falling wool and mineral prices. Britain, now involved in European affairs, seemed less of a 'mother' country than ever, while Australian trade and diplomatic relations with Asia increased. By 1993, over half of Australia's exports were to East Asia. Australia's 150 000 Aborigines, discovering valuable minerals on their reserves, demanded resolution of their land claims. The High Court decision, in 1993, to recognize these claims was followed by a government programme of reconciliation. Changes to Australia's immigration policy have also created a more multicultural society. In 1996 the Liberal-National Coalition swept to power, ending 13 years of Labour government. Although many economic, social, and environmental concerns remained unresolved by the late 1990s, Australia was more confident about its national identity and its role in the Asia-Pacific region. In 1998 the government agreed to hold a referendum on Australia's becoming an independent republic.

New Zealand

After 1788 New Zealand's resources of timber and flax attracted traders from the Australian colonies, while whalers and sealers from Britain and the USA sought shelter and provisions from the Maori. Although trade de-

pended on peaceful cooperation, violent clashes with the Maori caused the British government concern about its inability to control the situation. Meanwhile, reports of New Zealand's fertile soil and temperate climate interested such colonial entrepreneurs as Edward Gibbon Wakefield (1796–1862). He advocated organized emigration to ease Britain's problems of over-population and unemployment. Concerned about Maori welfare, British missionaries in New Zealand petitioned their government to stop Wakefield's plans. A compromise was reached in which colonial rule was offered to New Zealand. This decision was confirmed by Maori chiefs, when they signed the **Treaty of Waitangi** (1840). The hastily prepared treaty has fuelled subsequent debates about Maori land rights in New Zealand.

Maori concerns about land sales and the erosion of traditional authority led to the Maori Wars of the 1860s. Subduing the Maori with difficulty, the government turned its attention to political reform. It became the world's first democracy to grant women the federal vote in 1893. In 1907, it attained dominion status within the British Empire. Refrigeration technology brought prosperity to New Zealand's farmers. Unlike Australia, New Zealand's connections with Britain remained strong after World Wars I and II and after independence in 1947. New Zealand also maintained a close relationship with Australia. This was reflected in a series of mutual defence agreements and in the migration between the two countries.

During the 1970s, New Zealand's antinuclear and environmental stance provoked Australia and, more seriously, the USA. Relations with France became strained in 1985,

WHO WERE THE CONVICTS?

The Industrial Revolution in Britain resulted in the mechanization of many traditional occupations and large-scale migration to new factory towns. Unemployment, and urban overcrowding led to an increase in the crime rate. British gaols overflowed; even the ships ('hulks'), used as transient prisons, became overcrowded. As prisoners could no longer be transported to the American colonies, the British government searched for an alternative destination. Botany Bay, the remote Australian harbour recently discovered by Cook, was its choice. Over 100 000 male and female convicts had been sent there by the time transportation to Australia was abolished in 1868. The convicts' labour helped establish the new colonies; their experience is an important part of Australian heritage.

Gallipoli
Under British command, soldiers of the Australian and New Zealand Army Corps (the '*Anzacs*') led an attack on Turkish-held Gallipoli on 25 April 1915. The operation was a disaster, resulting in the deaths of 36 000 Commonwealth troops. Gallipoli came to symbolize Australian courage and inspired Australia's desire for independence.

Australia
Boundary changes and new colonies (1825–1911). ▼

1825

1851

1863

1911

WA Western Australia
NSW New South Wales
SA South Australia
VIC Victoria
QLD Queensland
NT Northern Territory
VDL Van Dieman's Land
TAS Tasmania

▲ **Australian Aborigines**
The Aborigine peoples occupied Australia before European settlement. Threats to Aborigine lands and traditional lifestyle have come from mineral exploitation. A movement to protect Aborigines' rights thus emerged and gained support, and Aborigines and White Australians staged numerous protests (such as that shown here in Sydney); in 1993 Aborigines were granted permission to reclaim land formerly held under native title.

European custom is like a bird that settled, that has flown to our shores just now, but our custom has been here, like a banyan tree since the world broke up. It was here at the start.

Pentecost Island chief
(1970s)

after an attack by French agents on the Greenpeace ship *Rainbow Warrior* in Auckland harbour. New Zealand governments have also faced the challenge of Maori land claims. The Waitangi Tribunal, set up in 1975 to arbitrate in land disputes, had its mandate enlarged a decade later to include all disputes since 1840. While relations with the Maori improved, they regarded the compensation package offered to them in 1994 as insufficient. By the mid-1990s the economy faced serious problems; unable to rely on traditional products, New Zealand looked to the Asian-Pacific market to diversify its economy. Relations with France collapsed in 1995 with the resumption of French nuclear testing in the Pacific. A National Party–New Zealand First coalition government came to power under a new electoral system in 1996.

Oceania

During the late 19th century, the rival tropical empires of the great powers expanded until Britain, France, Germany, and the USA ruled all of the Pacific Islands between them. By 1990 most islanders were once again independent, with important exceptions.

New Caledonia and French Polynesia (including Tahiti) remain French territory, electing representatives to the National Assembly in Paris. Tahitians were less provoked than other Pacific islanders by France's decision to transfer nuclear testing from Algeria to Tahiti in 1963, since investment provided jobs. By 1995, however, when France resumed testing in the region, demonstrations and riots erupted in Tahiti, while the island's pro-independence movement began to attract increasing support. New Caledonians and Loyalty Islanders began actively resisting French rule during the 1960s; this unrest still continues.

World War II resulted in the unprecedented involvement of the USA in the affairs of the

Pacific region. It also led to greater European contact with the islanders, especially on such battlegrounds as Guadalcanal (Solomon Islands). Hawaii, which the USA had annexed in 1898, became the 50th US state in 1959. The Federated States of Micronesia (FSM), administered by the USA since 1947, became independent in 1986: the USA retains control of the FSM's foreign and defence policies. Similarly, Niue, Tokelau, and the Cook Islands rely on New Zealand in foreign affairs and defence.

The recent history of many other islands revolves around the retreat of the British Empire during the 1960s and 1970s. Of particular interest is Fiji, Britain's oldest Pacific island colony. In the 19th century, the British government authorized the immigration of Indian labourers to work on sugar plantations. By independence, in 1970, nearly half the population was Indo-Fijian. Elections became increasingly polarized along racial lines; in 1987 Fijian extremists carried out two military coups to ensure Fijian supremacy. Fiji left the Commonwealth in the same year. Civilian rule was restored in 1990. The Fijian constitution was amended in 1997 to eradicate its racist bias.

Other islands have had greater continuity. Tonga, in particular, whose government has always been independent, is the world's oldest direct-descent monarchy. By the 1990s, however, its absolute power was being challenged by an emerging pro-democracy movement.

The Pacific Way

Independent islanders, fearing that their tiny countries would be unable to influence international politics, saw regional cooperation as one way to deal with the political, social, and economic challenges facing them. The South Pacific Commission, set up in 1947 to represent the colonial powers, has expanded to include some of the new Pacific nations; in 1997 it was formally renamed the ***Pacific Islands Community***. More important is the ***South Pacific Forum***, established in 1971; it is attended only by Pacific countries: the island states, Australia, and New Zealand. Such issues as Asia–Pacific trade connections, long-distance communications, and environmental issues (the dumping of nuclear waste, for example) can be handled with greater impact by the Forum than by individual Pacific countries. Events, such as the 1987 Fijian coups, have challenged the Forum's attempts to combine democracy with indigenous methods of government. Islanders continue to hope, however, that the 'Pacific Way' of cooperation and negotiation will provide creative solutions. One such success was the Treaty of Rarotonga – drawn up by the Forum in 1985 to establish a South Pacific nuclear-free zone – which was signed by France, the UK, and the USA in 1996.

SUB-SAHARAN
AFRICA

SUB-SAHARAN AFRICA

Early Africa

Later African Stone Age • Early African Iron Age

The Sahara, the world's largest desert, has not always been so dry and desolate. Between c. 9000 and 4000 BC Africa's climate was considerably wetter than it is today. At the peak of the wet phase (c. 7000 BC) the Sahara consisted of grassy plains and flowing rivers. Lake Chad, in the southern part of the central Sahara, was many times its present size; it probably overflowed southwards into the Atlantic Ocean via the Benue and Niger rivers. Similarly, in eastern Africa the lakes of Kenya's Great Rift Valley were linked by rivers; the waters of Lake Turkana, bordering on modern Ethiopia, may have flowed northwards to connect with the upper Nile.

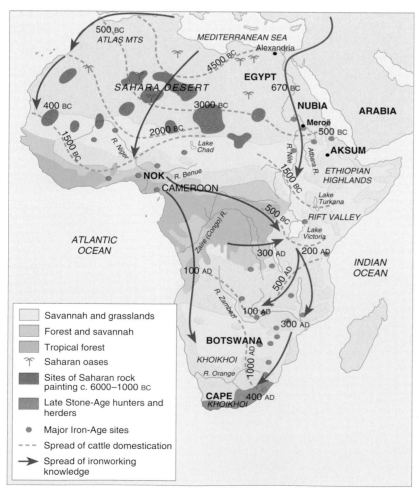

Savannah and grasslands

Forest and savannah

Tropical forest

Saharan oases

Sites of Saharan rock painting c. 6000–1000 BC

Late Stone-Age hunters and herders

● Major Iron-Age sites

--- Spread of cattle domestication

→ Spread of ironworking knowledge

Later African Stone Age

Archaeological evidence suggests that Africa's hunters and gatherers exploited the wetland areas of middle Africa; by 6000 BC, they had developed settled fishing communities along the banks of the extended rivers and lakes.

Origins of Tropical African Farming. It may have been the spread of desert conditions from the central Sahara (5000–3000 BC), ending the phase of wet climatic conditions, that prompted Africans of the former 'fishing belt' to domesticate and cultivate tropical cereals, such as sorghum and millet. Similarly, in the forest regions Neolithic farmers domesticated such crops as yams and oil palms. Between 3000 and 1000 BC crop cultivation became fairly widespread – while the traditional skills of hunting and gathering were also practised – across much of western and eastern Africa. In the drier grassland zones certain peoples developed the specialized skills of grazing livestock on grassland. It is thought that some of these earliest African pastoralists herded their cattle on the central Saharan grasslands before they became a desert. Rock paintings, dating from c. 6000–1000 BC, found in this region depict such activities.

South of the Zaïre (Congo) forest groups of specialized pastoralists, ***Khoikhoi***, herded sheep and cattle in the northern Botswana region from c. 1000 BC. By the 1st century AD, the Khoikhoi had extended their activities to the southwestern Cape. Elsewhere in southern Africa a hunter-gatherer way of life continued.

Early African Iron Age

To the south of ancient Egypt, in the final millennium BC, lay the Nubian kingdom of Kush. Kushite kings had briefly ruled Egypt as the 25th or 'Ethiopian' Dynasty (730–670 BC); however, following the Assyrian invasion of Egypt (c. 670 BC), they retreated to Nubia.

◀ **Early Africa** *(to 1000 AD) The spread of cattle and crop domestication and ironworking knowledge from northern into western, eastern, and southern Africa between c. 5000 BC and 1000 AD led to the gradual absorption of existing hunter-gatherer cultures and laid the foundations of African civilization.*

Kingdom of Meroë (500 BC–300 AD). Soon afterwards the Kushites moved their capital further south to Meroë, a fertile triangle of land between the Nile and Atbara rivers, where there existed a wealth of iron ore. The Kushites appear to have learned the techniques of iron smelting and manufacture from Egypt. The rulers of Meroë built a powerful kingdom based upon farming, iron manufacture, and trade between tropical Africa and Egypt, which they supplied with ivory, ebony, leopard skins, and gold. Although their culture was based, in many respects, upon that of ancient Egypt, the Meroites developed their own distinctive style of building, writing, and religious practice. It is possible that Meroë's decline in the 4th century AD was influenced by the rise of the neighbouring state of Aksum.

Kingdom of Aksum (100–800 AD). The origins of Aksum are to be found in a blend of immigrants from the Yemeni district of southwestern Arabia and local African farmers of northeastern Ethiopia. By 300 AD, Aksum had developed as a major trading state with a distinctive and sophisticated literate culture. Its craftsmen produced luxury goods of crystal, brass, and copper for the Roman market, while its stonemasons developed a unique style of architecture, building stone palaces, temples, and tombs for their rulers.

In c. 350 AD Ezana, king of Aksum (reigned c. 320–50 AD), was converted to Christianity by missionaries from Alexandria. This was the origin of the Ethiopian Orthodox Christian Church, which has survived to the present day. By 800 AD, Aksum had declined; its rulers subsequently removed their capital southwards into the Ethiopian highlands.

West Africa. Despite the Sahara's emergence as a desert from 3000 BC, there is evidence of continuing trade across it from very early times. Cloth, beads, and grain from the north were exchanged for salt at the desert oases; in turn salt was exchanged for ivory and gold from the south. It was probably along these trading routes that west Africans first learnt the skills of iron smelting and manufacture from the Phoenicians of North Africa, sometime during the final millennium BC.

Iron provided a superior material for making hoes, axes, spears, and arrowheads, which improved methods of farming and hunting. New smelting techniques also promoted the manufacture of baked-clay pottery, the remnants of which provide important information on life in early African Iron-Age societies.

By 500 BC, there were several communities of ironworking farmers in tropical west Africa, the best known being the peoples of the Nok culture of central Nigeria. By the 2nd century AD, ironworking had become fairly widespread through most of tropical west Africa.

The manufacture and use of iron enabled west Africans to develop larger and more technically advanced farming communities. The development of chieftaincy in this period laid the foundations for the later emergence of powerful states (see AFRICAN STATES).

Central, Eastern, and Southern Africa. The spread of ironworking and farming through the rest of central, eastern, and southern Africa is generally assumed to have been an extension of the west African Iron Age; as such, it is associated with the spread of **Bantu**-speaking peoples. Linguists have constructed an ancestral tree of the Bantu language family, which has been used to postulate that 'proto-Bantu' probably originated in the mountainous area of central Cameroon some 3000 years ago. It is thought that over the next 1500 years the original Bantu languages divided and spread east, south, and west to reach the southern coast of South Africa by the 5th century AD.

Archaeologists have, meanwhile, plotted the spread of Iron-Age farmers across the same region over a similar period. However, as none of these societies were literate, there is no clear proof that it was specifically Bantu-speakers who spread a farming culture through the region between 500 BC and 500 AD. Nevertheless, the correlation between linguistic and archaeological evidence is close enough for most historians to accept it as a fact.

The relatively rapid spread of Bantu-speaking farmers appears to have started with small-scale infiltration. As the first farmers to settle on hitherto uncultivated land, they were able to exploit the best sites before moving on in search of further virgin soil and sources of iron ore. As they went they intermarried with the pre-existing hunter-gatherer societies, thus absorbing them into the new farming society.

The only part of Africa to which ironworking farmers did not venture in this period was the far southwest: Namibia, the western Cape, and southwestern Botswana. As the climate was too dry for regular cultivation, the region was left to hunter-gatherers and Khoikhoi pastoralists.

◀ **Cattle Herding**
Pastoralist lifestyles existed in southern Africa from c. 1000 BC, notably among the Khoikhoi peoples. This early rock painting from Botswana depicts the herding of cattle.

Bantu

A linguistic term used to describe a family of some 450 related languages that stretch from Cameroon and eastern Nigeria, across central Africa, to the Kenyan coast of eastern Africa, and as far south as the southern coastline of South Africa. Linguists used the term 'proto-Bantu' to describe the ancestral language from which the Bantu family is descended.

Stelae of Aksum
(c. 300 AD) Built from single pieces of solid stone, these stelae were erected over the tombs of kings. The stele shown here is the largest still standing. ▼

African States

Empires of western Africa • Ethiopia, the Horn, and the coast of eastern Africa •
The later Iron Age in eastern, central, and southern Africa

Soninke and Malinke

Soninke and Malinke are
members of the related
group of languages and
peoples who inhabit
sub-Saharan west
Africa. This group (the
Mande) is a subgroup
of one of the main
African language
divisions, Niger-Congo.

The 1000 years following the spread of iron-working in Africa saw the further development of material cultures and craft skills, with regional specializations in farming and mining, and the expansion of long-distance trade. These in turn stimulated the emergence of powerful states, kingdoms, and empires across the continent.

Empires of Western Africa

Ancient Ghana (c. 500–c. 1200). By the 5th century AD a number of Soninke-speaking chiefdoms on the southern fringes of the Sahara grouped together in what may have been a defensive alliance against raids from Saharan nomads. The Soninke were well placed (on the borders of modern Mauritania and Mali) to develop both cereal cultivation and cattle grazing. They were also located between the Bambuk goldfields of the upper Senegal River and the salt pans of the central Sahara. The introduction of the Arabian camel from Egypt and north Africa during the 5th century made

possible regular caravans across the Sahara; the Soninke were thus able to expand their chiefdoms into the powerful trading empire of ancient Ghana.

The spread of Islamic states across north Africa from the 9th century increased the demand for gold coinage in the Muslim world. The wealth and power of Ghana's rulers increased accordingly, reaching their zenith in the 11th century. By the middle of the 12th century, however, Ghana had lost its trading monopoly and much of its former power to rival states to its east and west, who sought out alternative sources of gold and developed new routes across the desert.

The Empire of Mali (1235–c. 1450). Among those to take advantage of the trade from the new Buré goldfields to the south were the southern Soninke- and Malinke-speaking clans, who lived in the fertile plains of the upper Niger river. In 1235 Sundjata (died 1255), military leader of the Malinke Keita clan, brought together the Soninke- and Malinke-speaking clans to found a new empire known as Mali. At its height in the 14th century, Mali, with its capital at Niani on the upper Niger, took in both forest and desert, stretching from Atlantic to Gao on the middle Niger bend.

The rulers (*Mansa*) of Mali were Muslim; in 1324–25 Mansa Musa (reigned ?1307–?1332) brought international fame to his country when he went on a pilgrimage to Mecca with a huge caravan of courtiers, servants, and camels laden with gifts of gold.

In 1433 Tuareg nomads, raiding from the desert, seized Timbuktu, one of Mali's principal centres for trans-Saharan trade.

The Empire of Songhai (c. 1450–1591). By the mid-15th century, Mali's hegemony was being challenged by the rise of Songhai,

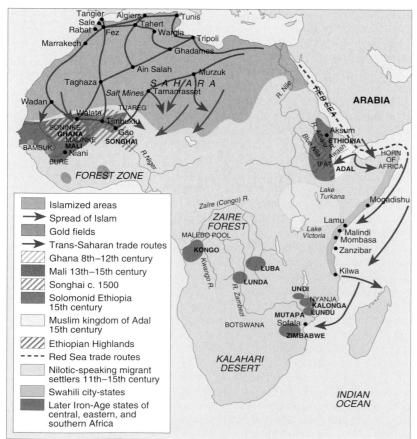

Islamized areas
Spread of Islam
Gold fields
Trans-Saharan trade routes
Ghana 8th–12th century
Mali 13th–15th century
Songhai c. 1500
Solomonid Ethiopia 15th century
Muslim kingdom of Adal 15th century
Ethiopian Highlands
Red Sea trade routes
Nilotic-speaking migrant settlers 11th–15th century
Swahili city-states
Later Iron-Age states of central, eastern, and southern Africa

◄ **Africa (900–1500)** *During this period powerful kingdoms, such as Ghana, Mali, and, later, Songhai in Western Africa flourished as a result of their exploitation of natural resources, such as gold, and expanding trans-Saharan trade. In eastern Africa the Christian kingdom of Ethiopia emerged and came into conflict with the Muslim states established in the Horn of Africa, while Muslim influence was also felt further down the east coast, where Swahili peoples and Muslim immigrants prospered from trade with Asia and established city-states. In the southern African interior sophisticated civilizations also developed; centralized states, such as Kongo and Zimbabwe, emerged.*

based at Gao. In 1468 the Songhai leader, Sonni Ali the Great (reigned c. 1464–92), recaptured Timbuktu from the Tuareg and built Songhai into an empire that totally eclipsed Mali. His successor, Askiya Muhammad Turé (reigned 1493–1528), extended the empire into the desert to capture the salt mines of Taghaza. Askiya Muhammad used the Islamic faith as a unifying factor to expand trade between Songhai and North Africa. He was recognized by the caliph of Cairo as the caliph of the whole *Sudan* ('the land of Blacks').

Ethiopia, the Horn, and the Coast of Eastern Africa

Ethiopia (850–1550). During the 11th century Ethiopia began to emerge from two centuries of isolation, as its rulers took advantage of a revival in Red Sea trade with Fatimid Egypt. In c. 1150 the Zagwe dynasty (1150–1270) initiated a new era of expansion southwards across the Ethiopian plateau. It was a time of great Christian revival, during which a series of remarkable churches were built.

In 1270 the Zagwe kings were succeeded by the Solomonid dynasty (1270–1550). This new line of kings claimed descent from the rulers of ancient Aksum and, through them, from the legendary union of King Solomon and the Queen of Sheba. The Solomonid period was one of further military expansion to the south, which brought them into conflict with rival Muslim states in the Horn.

Muslim States in the Horn of Africa. During the 10th and 11th centuries immigrant Muslim merchants from Arabia settled in the Awash valley to the east of Ethiopia. As they penetrated the highlands in the 12th century they grouped their settlements into the 'sultanate of Shoa.' This was succeeded by the kingdoms of Ifat and Adal in the 14th century.

Muslim-Christian Wars in Ethiopia (c. 1400–1550). By the early 15th century, Muslim Adal had come into conflict with expansionist Ethiopia. There followed more than a century of warfare between Christians and Muslims for control of the highlands. The Muslims of Adal eventually defeated the Ethiopians in 1529, which secured them control over the whole of southern Ethiopia. In desperation, the Ethiopian (Christian) king appealed to Christian Europe for assistance against 'the infidel.' In 1543 Portuguese mercenaries helped a revived Ethiopian army to inflict a harsh defeat on the Adalese. Over the next ten years the Ethiopians, under a new ruler, Galadewos (reigned 1540–59), recovered much of the southern plateau.

Swahili City-states of the East African Coast. The **Swahili** appear to have originated as Bantu-speaking farmers and fishermen, who traded with ships from the Red Sea and

▲ **Solid Rock Church of Lalibela, Ethiopia** *Carved by thousands of stonemasons during the reign of King Lalibela (c. 1200–50), and hewn out of solid rock, the eleven 'Lalibela churches' of Ethiopia, one of which is shown here, are a remarkable testament to the strength of Ethiopian Christianity. A number were named after the holy places of Jerusalem, such as Golgotha, the tomb of Christ.*

Persian Gulf from at least the early centuries AD. New trading opportunities with western Asia were opened up by the 8th century expansion of the Islamic Empire and by Muslim immigrants from Arabia.

By the 9th century, regular markets, dominated by Arabic-speaking Muslim merchants, were to be found all along the coastline, from Somalia to Mozambique. A principal early African export was ivory for the Indian and Chinese markets. The period 1050–1200 saw a strengthening of Asian trading links, with the arrival of further Muslim immigrants. From about 1250 the offshore island of Kilwa became one of the most powerful Swahili states, as it gained control over the rising trade in gold from the southern port of Sofala.

In 1498 Portuguese merchant venturers entered the Indian Ocean from the south and began a century of violent rivalry, which nearly destroyed the Swahili trade.

The Later Iron Age in Eastern, Central, and Southern Africa

Archaeological evidence indicates considerable development and change in African Iron-Age technology and culture between 800 and 1200 AD. For this reason the period after c. 1000 AD is referred to as the 'later Iron Age.' Some changes were clearly local developments, while others appear to have been initiated by small-scale immigration from neighbouring regions. There is evidence of more economic specialization: hunting, cattle keeping, and arable farming. Greater importance was attached to mining and metalwork, including craftsmanship in copper and gold. Archaeologists plot the development of later Iron-Age cultures through changes in pottery styles. Increasing specialization was accompanied by the development of regional and

Swahili Muslim east Africans, whose distinctive language and culture has been strongly influenced by Arabic and Islam. Owing to its long association with trading in the region, KiSwahili is today the lingua franca of much of eastern Africa; it is also the official language of at least one modern country, Tanzania.

Zimbabwe

The name *zimbabwe* (plural *madzimbabwe*) comes from the Shona (a Bantu language) *dzimba dzamabwe*, probably meaning 'stone dwellings,' many of which were built all over the central Zimbabwean plateau during the 14th and 15th centuries. The walls of these buildings were built from local granite. The style and methods of construction were evolved locally and used dry stone-walling techniques.

long-distance trade and the emergence of powerful states.

Eastern Africa. By c.1450, the state of Kitara had emerged from among the small chiefdoms of the lakeland region of Uganda. However, the most characteristic aspect of eastern Africa's later Iron-Age period was the spread of Nilotic-speaking immigrants from the north, who introduced new cattle-keeping skills. While in some areas they kept themselves aloof from the local population, they mostly married into the ruling class, grazed their cattle on the uplands, and established feudal-type relationships with local farmers. From these origins developed the Hima of Nkore and the Tutsi of Rwanda and Burundi.

Similarly, to the east of Lake Victoria, other Nilote immigrants moved into northern Kenya. Some retained their own distinctive language and culture, such as the Luo to the northeast of Lake Victoria. Others, combining cereal farming and cattle herding, absorbed pre-existing southern Cushite pastoralists to develop new communities of mixed cereal farmers and cattle-keepers, such as the Kalenjin of the western Kenyan highlands.

Central Africa. On the southern fringes of the Zaïre (Congo) forest the growth of the Luba and Lunda empires was based mainly upon well-developed iron and copper technologies, underpinned by plentiful agricultural surpluses. The rulers, who usually claimed some religious basis for their authority, taxed the miners, hunters, and farmers and used this wealth to promote and control regional and long-distance trade. From the 15th century small bands of migrants left Luba and Lunda and spread ideas of kingship and state formation across southern central Africa.

One of the most important states, which did not trace its origins to the Luba and Lunda heartland, was the kingdom of Kongo. The origins of Kongo are to be found in a grouping of prosperous Bakongo farming villages in the Malebo pool region of the Zaïre (Congo) River. On the margins of forest and savanna woodlands the Bakongo had ideal conditions for producing a wide variety of food surpluses; they were also located on a major natural trading crossroads. Bakongo arts and crafts were well developed, from metalwork to weaving; their products were much sought after in the region. By the 15th century, the authority of the Kongo king, the *Manikongo*, stretched from the Atlantic to the Kwango River.

Across the continent, to the east, the Chewa and Nyanja-speaking peoples of southern Malawi also developed states, which took advantage of the trade in ivory and other products with the Swahili on the coast. The peoples of these kingdoms of Kalonga, Lundu, and Undi were known collectively as *Maravi* ('peoples of the fire'), the name deriving from the important role of fire in their religious rituals.

Southern Africa. In the more open grasslands of southern Africa, the growth of cattle ownership as a source of social and political power underpinned the development of chieftaincy and early state formation from the 8th century. The earliest developments were in eastern Botswana, soon spreading across the Transvaal and the **Zimbabwe** plateau.

In Zimbabwe the origins of state power were also associated with the development of long-distance trade with the Swahili coast. Trade began in the 10th century with the development of gold mining by the people of the 'Leopard's Kopje' culture near modern Bulawayo. Settlements in the Limpopo valley provided the trading link with coastal Sofala. In the 13th century these settlements gave way to the rising Shona state of Great Zimbabwe on the eastern edge of the central plateau.

Great Zimbabwe was ideally placed between the western goldfields and east coast trade. It supported a wide range of upland and lowland grazing and wild animals to hunt for meat and ivory; it also yielded a plentiful supply of timber for charcoal and for building. Craftsmanship was developed in gold, copper, and iron, and in weaving in cotton; silks, cottons, and porcelain from India and China were also imported. At its height the capital housed an estimated 11 000 people, which must have put a considerable strain on local resources. In c. 1450 Great Zimbabwe was abandoned, possibly for environmental reasons, in favour of the Mutapa state in the Mazoe valley to the north. Great Zimbabwe is best known today for its massive stone walls, which surround the houses of the capital.

Nobles of the Kingdom of Kongo
Established south of the Zaïre (Congo) River, the prosperous kingdom of Kongo became one of the most powerful in the region by the 15th century. This contemporary engraving depicts members of the upper levels of Kongo society at leisure. ▼

Early Modern Africa

*States of west Africa • States of central Africa • Peoples and states of eastern Africa •
Southern Africa • The 19th century (1800–80)*

The dominant themes of early modern African history (1500–1880) were the growth of strong states, which reached their political and cultural zenith during this period and the direct and indirect effects of outside influence, particularly from Europe. Throughout the continent the demands and consequences of international trade increasingly affected economic development, political stability, and the rise and fall of states.

States of West Africa

Songhai. The great power of the Songhai Empire, which reached its peak in the early 16th century, gradually declined as it lost control of trans-Saharan trade; the gold trade, meanwhile, was diverted south to Europeans at the coast, who had begun trading there in the late 15th century. In 1591 the Moroccans invaded Songhai from across the Sahara, seizing control of the Niger region from Timbuktu to Gao and Jenne.

Borno-Kanem. The sultanate of Borno-Kanem emerged in the Lake Chad region as a trans-Saharan trading state. Its power increased in the 16th century with the importation of horses and firearms from North Africa, in exchange for captive slaves raided from the peasant societies to the south.

Hausa City-states. The Hausa originated from a combination of southern Saharan nomads and northern Nigerian farmers. The Hausa built stockaded towns and paid tribute to powerful neighbours, such as Songhai and Borno-Kanem. They developed considerable independent wealth from agriculture, manufacturing (in cloth, leather, and metal), and trade. While the towns became the nuclei of powerful trading states, rivalry and warfare between them left the Hausa city-states internally weak by the end of the 18th century.

Forest Kingdoms of Ife and Benin. The Yoruba and Bini (or Edo) kingdoms of Ife and Benin dated back to at least the 11th century. The peoples of the Nigerian forest had a long history of artistic sculpture; the Yoruba and Benin kingdoms of the 15th to 18th centuries are best known today for their bronze sculptures and plaques, and ivory carvings.

Savanna Kingdoms of Oyo and Dahomey. The Yoruba kingdom of Oyo, north of the Nigerian forest, developed as a powerful conquest state based upon a standing army of cavalry. In the late 17th century the people of

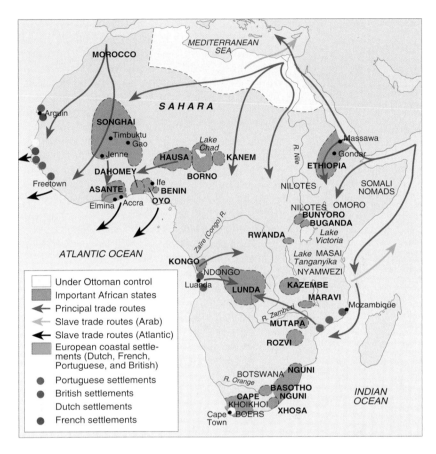

Oyo expanded southwards to make contact with European traders at the coast. Here they found a powerful rival in the Aja kingdom of Dahomey. Both Oyo and Dahomey remained important exporters of captives for the Atlantic slave trade throughout the 18th century, to the extent that Europeans referred to the region as the 'Slave Coast.'

Kingdom of Asante. The Akan kingdom of Asante was founded by Osei Tutu (died 1712) in the 1670s. The kingdom derived its power from control of the region's main goldfields; its territory was expanded by Opoku Ware (reigned *c.* 1720–50) to cover most of modern Ghana. During its wars of expansion Asante also supplied captives for the slave trade.

States of Central Africa

When the Portuguese first arrived near the mouth of the Zaïre (Congo) River they established diplomatic relations with the kingdom of Kongo. In 1506 they intervened to help a Christian convert seize the Kongo throne to become Afonso I (reigned 1506–43). There-

▲ **Africa (1500–1800)** *While kingdoms flourished in the interior of the continent – through more widespread cattle herding, economic diversification, and trade in copper and iron goods – coastal Africa was the scene of increasing trade activity and settlement by Europeans.*

═══ SEE ALSO ═══
This section:
• African States
• Colonial Africa
Latin America:
• The Spanish and Portuguese Empires
The Visual Arts Worldwide (vol. 4):
• African Art

Nilotic Tall Negroid pastoral people who inhabit eastern Africa (the southern Sudan, parts of Kenya and Uganda, and neighbouring countries).

The demand [for slaves] is so great that we cannot count its size, since Portuguese traders are every day taking our people, sons of the land and sons of our noblemen and vassals and our relatives because [local] thieves and men of evil conscience seize them... and sell them, and, Sire, so great is the corruption and licentiousness that our country is being completely depopulated.

Afonso I, King of Kongo, to his 'brother king' of Portugal (1525)

after Afonso and his successors became clients of the Portuguese, their armies required to raid further into the interior to provide captives for the slave trade. Further south, Portuguese slave traders set up a port at Luanda and established similar trading connections with the Ngola of Ndongo. Subsequent Portuguese interventions caused conflict in the Luandan hinterland, which provided the Portuguese with their main source of slaves for their Brazilian colonies up until the 19th century.

Further inland the Lunda empire of Mwata Yamvo used a system of tribute collection and redistribution to become the major trading terminus of the central African interior in the 17th and 18th centuries. An important offshoot of Lunda was Kazembe to the east. This kingdom was well placed to draw in a wide range of tribute, including copper from the nearby Shaba region, and to develop a wide range of transcontinental trading networks. To the southeast the Kalonga dynasty founded a Maravi empire, which derived its power from the ivory trade between the lower Zambezi River and the Swahili coast at Mozambique. To the south of the Zambezi, meanwhile, the Changamire Rozvi built an empire on the Zimbabwe plateau to rival that of Mutapa, a successor state to Great Zimbabwe. New goldfields were opened up and Portuguese traders in the Zambezi valley recognized Rozvi suzerainty with payments of tribute.

Peoples and States of Eastern Africa

By the 16th century, Bunyoro had become the major power of the lakeland region of east Africa, its peoples raiding for cattle and tribute as far south as Rwanda. The clans of Buganda, to the north of Lake Victoria, organized themselves into a centralized state in the 17th century, surpassing Bunyoro in strength and importance by the 19th century.

East of Lake Victoria the Masai and other **Nilotic** cattle herdsmen pushed southwards through the Great Rift Valley. The Masai traded with Bantu-speaking farmers of central Kenya. In the Tanzanian region the Nyamwezi became professional traders between the interior ivory fields and the coast.

On the east African coast the Portuguese built fortresses and used naval force to dominate Swahili trade. However, Portuguese violence disrupted much of the trade they sought to control. By 1700, rival Arabs had confined the Portuguese to southern Mozambique.

During the 16th century Oromo pastoralists penetrated the southern Ethiopian highlands to become a permanent element of the southern Ethiopian population. Ethiopian kings, meanwhile, concentrated their power in the north, around the new capital of Gondar. They established trading links with the Ottoman Turks, who had seized the Eritrean port of Massawa in the 1550s. Many Somali nomads of the Horn, meanwhile, converted to Islam.

EUROPEAN CONTACT AND THE ATLANTIC SLAVE TRADE (1470–1800)

Towards the end of the 15th century Portuguese ships ventured southwards along the coast of west Africa. Aiming to outflank Muslim North Africa and gain access to the gold of west Africa, and thence the spice trade of India and the Far East, they started trading at Elmina on the 'Gold Coast' (of modern Ghana) in the 1470s. From 1532, however, the main demand of European traders was for slave labour to work the mines and plantations of the Americas. The Portuguese were joined by Dutch, French, Danish, and English slavers as the transatlantic slave trade expanded from 20 000 a year in the early 17th century to between 50 000 and 100 000 a year in the 18th century, most of which were carried in English ships. See SOCIAL SCIENCES (VOL. 6): SOCIAL DIVISIONS.

European traders relied upon local African agents, rulers, and merchants to provide the captives and run the African side of the trade. Slavery was not unknown in African society before this time. Indeed, the states south of the Sahara had for centuries sold a certain number of captives into slavery across the desert. In most of west Africa, however, war captives had traditionally been put to work in the society of the victor and, in due course, were often ransomed back to their own country. Now the scale of the Atlantic trade dwarfed all other trading activity; the loss of between 10 and 20 million Africans over a period of 300 years was permanent. In exchange, Africans received liquor, guns, and other luxury goods. The exchange was unequal and caused an increasing amount of warfare in the interior.

◀ **Slave Capture** *Africans captured in the interior were transported as slaves to European trading forts on the west African coast. From there captives were packed into ships for the transatlantic voyage. Many died of exhaustion or disease in the appalling conditions below decks.*

Southern Africa

This period saw the emergence of Botswana and Basotho chiefdoms on the highveld (elevated open grassland) of southern Africa, while in the southeastern lowveld competition for resources prompted the formation of powerful Nguni states, out of which was to emerge the Zulu kingdom in the early 1800s. In the far southwest the Dutch East India Company established a refuelling station at the Cape; this was to develop into a colony of Dutch pastoralists (known as **Boers**), who seized land and cattle from the Khoikhoi (see EARLY AFRICA). Boer expansion eastwards brought them into conflict with Xhosa chiefdoms in the 1770s, which initiated a century of struggle for control of this fertile 'frontier' zone.

The 19th Century (1800–1880)

West Africa. In the early 19th century a series of Muslim holy wars swept away many of the old corrupted states of sub-Saharan west Africa and replaced them with powerful Islamic empires; these extended from Futa Toro and Futa Jalon in the west to Mandinka and Tukulor on the upper Niger and the Sokoto caliphate in northern Nigeria. They were to provide a focus for African resistance to European conquest at the end of the 19th century. European merchants, meanwhile, began to view west Africa as a source of raw materials. Africans responded by supplying products, such as dyes and gum arabic for textile production, groundnuts and palm oil for food, and soap for industrial uses. European competition and attempts to bypass African middlemen prompted the establishment of coastal European colonies from the 1870s.

A by-product of the movement for the abolition of slavery was the foundation of Sierra Leone by freed African slaves from England in 1787; added to these were those freed by the British antislavery squadron, which patrolled west African waters from 1807, when the British government banned the trading of slaves in British ships. Other European states soon did the same, although slavery itself and the transatlantic trade were not finally abolished until much later in the century. The colony of Liberia was also founded in 1822 by freed Blacks from the USA.

Central and Eastern Africa. Emergent states in central Africa were set up by the Chokwe, ivory hunters of the Angolan interior, and the Lozi, who developed a powerful kingdom, based on farming, on the upper Zambezi floodplain. Eastern central Africa suffered Ngoni invasions from the south in the 1830s and 1840s, as offshoots from the expanding Zulu kingdom strove to establish small new raiding states in eastern Zambia and Malawi.

◄ **Zulu Warrior**
The Zulus were traditionally cattle herders. Under their great warrior king, Shaka, they conquered an extensive empire from their homeland of Natal during the early 19th century. Utimuni, the nephew of Shaka, is depicted in this illustration by George French Angas.

As the Atlantic slave trade declined Brazilian traders sought an alternative supply from the east African coast where, from the 1770s, a trade in captives had already developed to supply the French sugar planters of Réunion and Mauritius. Zanzibar became a thriving market centre as Swahili-Arab caravans raided the east African interior for ivory and slaves.

Southern Africa. The nature and degree of disruption and depopulation in this region, known as the **Mfecane**, associated with the expansion of the Zulu kingdom in the early 19th century, has been debated by historians. Other factors, such as slave raids from the Cape Colony, may also have provoked conflict. Zulu offshoots, such as the Ndebele, established a state on the highveld in the 1820s before moving on to western Zimbabwe in c. 1840.

British seizure of the Cape Colony in 1806, their attempts to reform its land and labour policies, and the abolition of slavery there (1833), prompted thousands of Boers to trek northwards. They fought with Ndebele and Zulu before establishing a permanent presence in the interior. The British annexed the Boer colony of Natal in 1843, but left the Boers with their emerging republics on the highveld.

In 1869–71 diamonds were discovered at Kimberley, north of the Orange River; the British promptly annexed the territory. Control of diamond mining from the 1870s was kept firmly in the hands of Whites, while Africans were attracted to the mines as migrant labourers by a desire to buy firearms to protect their lands from further encroachment. Although wars of conquest were waged against powerful African states, such as the Zulu and the Xhosa, attempts to unite the British colonies and Boer republics of south Africa were not at this stage successful.

They spoke for a long time about our taking ... for our own use more of the land which had belonged to them from all ages, and on which they were accustomed to pasture their cattle. They also asked whether, if they were to come to Holland, they would be permitted to act in a similar manner, saying, 'It would not matter if you stayed at the Fort, but you come into the interior, selecting the best land for yourselves, and never once asking ... whether it will put us to any inconvenience...' ... we told them they had now lost that land in war, and therefore could not expect to get it back.

Diary record of Dutch Commander, **Jan van Riebeck**, of a meeting with Cape Khoikhoi (1659)

Colonial Africa

Conquest and resistance • Early colonial rule • Interwar consolidation • World War II • The road to independence

European Possessions in Africa in 1914
Only Ethiopia and the west African state of Liberia – which was founded by freed American slaves in 1822 and gained independence in 1847 – withstood the tide of colonization. ▼

From as early as the 1860s, European interest in the economic potential of Africa had been growing. For over a century Africa had supplied vegetable oils and other raw materials to European industry. West Africa was already well known as a major source of gold, while the discovery of diamonds and gold in southern Africa in the 1870s alerted Europeans to Africa's potential mineral wealth. Explorers had charted the course of all the continent's major rivers, which were seen as commercial highways into the heart of Africa. By the 1880s, the so-called 'scramble for Africa' had begun, creating another potential flashpoint in the rivalry among European states that was to lead to war in 1914. Following the British occupation of Egypt in 1882, French and British coastal colonies in Senegal, the Gold Coast, and Nigeria were poised to penetrate the west African interior.

At the Berlin Conference of 1884, European states agreed basic principles for their strategic division of Africa.

Conquest and Resistance

Military Power. During four centuries of contact Africans had managed to confine Europeans to coastal enclaves. Between 1885 and 1900, however, a number of European powers succeeded in gaining control of most of the continent. They were able to exploit long-standing rivalries between neighbouring African states. Moreover, European armies had a distinct military advantage. Although Africans had long owned guns, they were mostly obsolete. By the late 1880s, Europeans had two new weapons not available to Africans: artillery pieces that fired explosive shells and mobile machine guns.

Both Britain and France, the main contenders in the 'scramble,' deployed largely African armies with European officers. They recruited among former slaves and in states that had traditionally been oppressed and raided by the kingdoms and empires that the colonists wished to conquer. The main resistance to the French in west Africa came from the new Muslim empires of Tukulor and Mandinka. Tukulor held out for ten years, while Mandinka, under the leadership of Samori Touré (1865–98), resisted until 1898. The French conquest of Borno (1897–1900) was so fiercely opposed that it required the intervention of three armies. The main opponents of the British were Asante and Sokoto in west Africa and Ndebele and Zulu in southern Africa. In many cases it was the small loosely organized societies that held out most tenaciously against colonization. Some areas of Mozambique were not pacified by the Portuguese until after 1912. The one notable exception to the European conquest of Africa was Ethiopia, where a modernized army, under Menelik II (1889–1913), expanded into the southern Sudan and repelled an Italian army of invasion from Eritrea in 1896.

Treaties and Alliances. Some African nations preferred to reach an accommodation and signed treaties of alliance with European powers. A common belief was that this would protect them from their traditional enemies; however, many later discovered that they retained little power under the treaties. Yet in some instances, such as Bangwato (Botswana) under Khama III (1875–1923), or Lozi (western Zambia) under Lewanika I (1878–1916), treaties did save African territories from annexation by White settlers. Elsewhere Europeans ignored the treaties when it suited them, as with Tukulor and Mandinka, both of which had initially formed alliances with the French. Similarly, King Mwanga (1884–97)

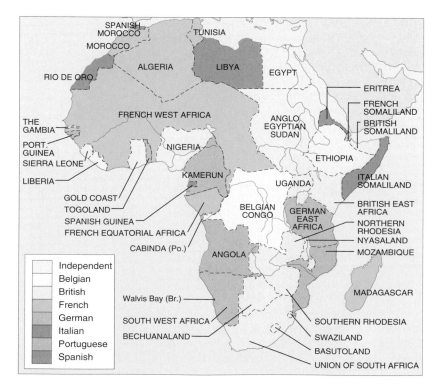

SPANISH MOROCCO
MOROCCO
TUNISIA
ALGERIA
LIBYA
EGYPT
RIO DE ORO
ERITREA
FRENCH SOMALILAND
FRENCH WEST AFRICA
ANGLO EGYPTIAN SUDAN
BRITISH SOMALILAND
THE GAMBIA
PORT. GUINEA
SIERRA LEONE
LIBERIA
NIGERIA
ETHIOPIA
KAMERUN
UGANDA
ITALIAN SOMALILAND
GOLD COAST
TOGOLAND
SPANISH GUINEA
FRENCH EQUATORIAL AFRICA
CABINDA (Po.)
BELGIAN CONGO
GERMAN EAST AFRICA
BRITISH EAST AFRICA
NORTHERN RHODESIA
NYASALAND
MOZAMBIQUE
ANGOLA
MADAGASCAR
Walvis Bay (Br.)
SOUTH WEST AFRICA
SOUTHERN RHODESIA
BECHUANALAND
SWAZILAND
BASUTOLAND
UNION OF SOUTH AFRICA

Independent
Belgian
British
French
German
Italian
Portuguese
Spanish

THE ZULU AND ANGLO-BOER WARS

In their colonization of southern Africa, the British came into conflict with both the indigenous population and established White settlers.

The Zulu War (1879) began when Britain attempted to annex Zululand, an area in Natal, on the southeast coast of Africa. Despite suffering an early defeat at Isandhlwana, the British succeeded in overcoming Zulu resistance by September 1879. The Anglo-Boer wars were sparked by tensions between the British and the **Afrikaner** settler community. The first war (1880–81) arose from

British annexation of the independent Boer republic of the Transvaal. War broke out again in 1899, when the demand of the Transvaal and Orange Free State for a guarantee of independence was refused. The Boers' guerrilla tactics initially brought success, but they were finally defeated. Many Afrikaner civilians died in concentration camps set up by the British to break Boer resistance.

◀ **The Battle of Isandhlwana** *In January 1879, Zulus under their chief, Cetshwayo, killed 1600 British troops at this battle.*

of Buganda had refused a British treaty and signed one with Germany before an Anglo-German Agreement of 1890 overruled Mwanga's preference and gave the headwaters of the Nile (modern Uganda) to the British.

Although the French offered a nominal challenge to the British at Fashoda on the White Nile in 1898, the only major intercolonial conflict to arise from European expansion was the second **Anglo-Boer War** of 1899–1902. British victory in this war led to the creation of the Union of South Africa in 1910.

Early Colonial Rule

Railways and Cash Crops. To gain access to the interior beyond the Niger and Congo rivers, railways were built, usually by African forced labour. European construction companies made huge profits. Yet, once the railways were built, Africans exploited the new economic opportunities: the production for export of groundnuts, palm oil, and cocoa in west Africa and cotton in Uganda was largely a result of African initiative. However, in the 'Congo Free State,' the personal fiefdom of the Belgian King Leopold II (1865–1909), royal agents were allowed to coerce local Africans into collecting wild rubber. The indiscriminate violence that resulted from this policy was widely condemned in Europe and in 1908 Leopold was forced to cede sovereignty of the territory to the Belgian government.

Mining and White Settlement. Control of mining concerns remained firmly in European hands, with Africans providing the unskilled labour, often on a seasonal or migratory basis. Colonial taxation, in cash, of all adult males was an almost universal policy that not only helped finance colonial administration, but also forced many formerly self-sufficient communities to send their young men to work in mines or on European-owned plantations.

White settlement was vigorously promoted by the British in Kenya and Rhodesia (Zimbabwe) and by the Germans in Tanganyika (Tanzania) and South West Africa (Namibia). As in South Africa, Africans were forced from the land or allowed to remain only on payment of rent or labour services.

World War I. During World War I (1914–18) locally recruited French, British, and Belgian armies invaded the German colonies of Togo, Kamerun (Cameroon), Rwanda, Burundi, and Tanganyika, while the Union of South Africa invaded South West Africa. Africans suffered badly in these conflicts as their food and labour were requisitioned by both sides. Of the one million conscripts who fought in the east Africa campaign some 10% died of disease, malnutrition, or exhaustion. Such losses were compounded by an influenza pandemic (1918–19). After the war the former German colonies were allocated to France and Britain on League of Nations mandates.

Interwar Consolidation

Economy. In the interwar years White settlement increased in Kenya and Rhodesia where, to curb the threat of African competition, restrictions were placed upon African farming and marketing opportunities. Elsewhere European-run plantations were expanded, while in parts of French west Africa peasants were forced to grow cotton for the state. Mining remained the most profitable European capital investment, from gold and tin in west Africa to copper, coal, gold, and diamonds in central and southern Africa. By the 1930s large-scale labour migration had become a characteristic feature of colonial policies and African economic life.

Social Conditions. Colonies were administered by a minimum of European personnel; African chiefs were employed to implement

Afrikaners Descendants of the original Dutch and Huguenot (French Calvinist) settlers of the 17th and 18th centuries. Formerly known as *Boers* ('farmers'), they began to refer to themselves as 'Afrikaners' from the 1870s onwards, to emphasize their permanence in Africa and to distinguish themselves from British settlers.

▲ **Satire on Colonialism in Africa** *A late 19th-century US cartoon shows Britain as a man grown overweight from the riches of his vast colonial possessions.*

▲ Haile Selassie
After his country was occupied by Italy in 1936, Ethiopia's emperor was forced into exile. Restored to power in 1941, Haile Selassie ruled Ethiopia until 1974, when he was deposed by a military coup.

colonial decrees, provide labour as required, and assist in collecting taxes. Colonial authority was backed up by the threat of armed force, which could be summoned from elsewhere if a local conflict threatened to escalate.

Mission schools in the 1920s and 1930s provided some Africans with new skills, while a few were sent abroad for higher education. Workers in the mining towns and ports organized informal unions and welfare societies, which often formed the basis for the later development of African nationalist politics.

South Africa. After independence from Britain in 1910, the Whites of South Africa – Afrikaners and British settlers, who comprised barely 20% of the population – enacted segregationist legislation to ensure that they retained permanent political and economic control. Africans, deprived of political rights, were confined to 13% of the land, unless they could prove they were employed by Whites.

World War II
For Africans the war against fascism began in 1935 with the Italian invasion of Ethiopia. The Italians' use of aerial bombardment and poison gas brought them a swift victory in 1936. The League of Nations took no effective action; it was not until war broke out in Europe that the Allies intervened to help Ethiopia. In 1941 Allied forces, with large contingents from east, west, and southern Africa, liberated the country and restored the emperor Haile Selassie I (1892–1975).

African troops were active in the war in north Africa and in the Burma campaign of 1944–45. In the face of resistance by many pro-Nazi Afrikaners, the South African leader, General Jan Smuts (1870–1950) committed troops to the Allied cause. Throughout Africa, colonial administrators urged farmers to provide raw materials and food for the Allies.

The Road to Independence
The war forced colonial governments to reappraise their attitudes towards Africa. They now considered African colonies as worthy of development in their own right. Even so, at this stage few Europeans seriously considered relinquishing control of African colonies.

Africans who had fought alongside Europeans in the war understandably took a very different view. Inspired by the liberation of Ethiopia and Indian independence in 1947, Africans began to work for independence.

Political Change. African nationalist political parties were usually led by small elites of teachers and lawyers. They had the knowledge, or even direct experience, of European and North American democratic principles and they demanded that these be applied in Africa. The British were the first to accede to their demands: first for reform, and then for political independence. Constitutions were revised and, as the franchise was extended, power gradually shifted to African politicians. The Gold Coast under Kwame Nkrumah (1909–72) led the way, gaining independence as Ghana in 1957. Once France accepted the principle of independence for sub-Saharan Africa, the pace of change quickened and 17 countries gained their independence in 1960.

White Settler Resistance. The British government took an ambivalent attitude to African aspirations in the two main settler colonies of Kenya and Rhodesia. After initially supporting settlers' demands for a curb on African political rights, the Mau Mau rebellion in Kenya (1952–57) finally convinced Britain that it should overrule settler opposition and come to terms with moderate African nationalism. Kenya gained its independence under Jomo Kenyatta (1892–1978) in 1963.

In Southern Rhodesia the power of White settlers was more firmly entrenched. In 1965 local colonists made a Unilateral Declaration of Independence (UDI) to forestall the movement to majority rule. It took a decade of guerrilla warfare before Africans won majority rule and independence as Zimbabwe in 1980.

South Africa. The Afrikaner National Party won the Whites-only 1948 general election. Their programme of *apartheid* (Afrikaans: 'separateness') was designed to consolidate White power and reverse the urbanization of Blacks, which had helped break down racial barriers during the war. Repressive legislation in the 1950s was met with African passive resistance until 1960, when police killed 67 demonstrators at Sharpeville. Thereafter the government banned all African political parties, including the African National Congress (ANC). Among the Black leaders imprisoned was the ANC activist and future president Nelson Mandela (1918–   ).

The Sharpeville Massacre *In March 1960, South African police shot dead over 60 unarmed Africans in a crowd protesting against discriminatory apartheid laws.* ▼

Postcolonial Africa

Economic background • The political inheritance • Changing political systems •
Secession, civil war, and conflict • The liberation of southern Africa •
The road to democracy

Most sub-Saharan Africans had gained their freedom from colonial rule by the end of 1968. Only the Portuguese colonies of Guinea-Bissau, Cape Verde, Angola, and Mozambique, the rebel settler colony of Rhodesia (Zimbabwe), Namibia, and South Africa remained under White minority control.

The new African nations of the 1960s began their 'independence decade' optimistically, with the hope that rapid expansion of education and health care would bring a new era of social and economic progress for the benefit of the African people. These early high expectations, however, were soon disappointed.

By the late 1980s, the predominant image of Africa was one of poverty and instability. Although this does not give the full picture – a number of countries experienced real social and economic advancement – nowhere were the high hopes of the early 1960s fulfilled.

Economic Background

The Colonial Inheritance. Seventy-five years of colonial rule had left the economies of the emerging states of Africa distorted. All tropical African economies exported raw materials to supply the developed industrial nations of Europe. At the same time, mass-produced European imports were able to underprice indigenous African goods, so that by the late colonial period even basic essentials (tools, clothing, domestic utensils) were imported.

Colonial policies deliberately obstructed the accumulation of indigenous capital upon which Africa's own industrial development might have been based. Profits from the export of valuable commodities and raw materials were not re-invested in the colonies, which also provided a captive market for manufactured goods, often of poor quality. This unequal exchange concentrated both investment capital and terms of trade in European hands.

Emerging Crisis. In the late 1950s and early 1960s the commodity markets for African exports experienced a boom that temporarily disguised this structural inequity. Africa's new leaders raised foreign loans for investing in a rapid expansion of education and health services, public housing, and transport infrastructure. By the mid-1960s the inherent weakness of Africa's economic position became apparent, as commodity prices for agricultural exports – cocoa, coffee, groundnuts, palm oil,

and cotton – began to fall. Economic crisis led to political instability, as politicians were unable to fulfil promises made at independence.

The international oil crisis of 1973 had a severe effect on Africa. Recession in the West prompted not only a collapse in commodity prices, but also inflation in the cost of manufactured goods. Thus Africa was receiving less for its exports, while having to pay more for its imports. Widespread drought in the periods 1974–75 and 1981–86 further weakened African economies and chronic indebtedness became endemic. By the mid-1980s sub-Saharan Africa was spending more on servicing foreign debts than it received in foreign aid.

The Political Inheritance

Two important aspects of the colonial political legacy – nationality and democracy – undermined the chances for African governments to achieve lasting political stability.

The Nation-state. The new nation-states of Africa were artificial entities, founded on the boundaries set by arbitrary parameters devised

===SEE ALSO===
This section:
• Colonial Africa
Politics and Government (vol. 6):
• Democracy and Electoral Systems
• Political Parties

The Decolonization of Africa *Countries are shown with their current names (mostly taken directly upon gaining independence) and their dates of independence.* ▼

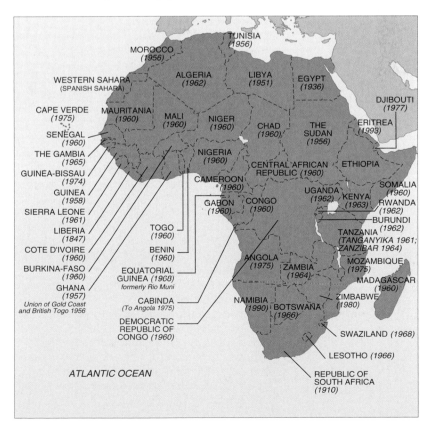

TUNISIA (1956)
MOROCCO (1956)
WESTERN SAHARA (SPANISH SAHARA)
ALGERIA (1962)
LIBYA (1951)
EGYPT (1936)
DJIBOUTI (1977)
CAPE VERDE (1975)
MAURITANIA (1960)
MALI (1960)
NIGER (1960)
CHAD (1960)
THE SUDAN (1956)
ERITREA (1993)
SENEGAL (1960)
THE GAMBIA (1965)
GUINEA-BISSAU (1974)
GUINEA (1958)
SIERRA LEONE (1961)
LIBERIA (1847)
COTE D'IVOIRE (1960)
BURKINA-FASO (1960)
GHANA (1957)
Union of Gold Coast and British Togo 1956
TOGO (1960)
BENIN (1960)
EQUATORIAL GUINEA (1968)
formerly Rio Muni
CABINDA (To Angola 1975)
DEMOCRATIC REPUBLIC OF CONGO (1960)
NIGERIA (1960)
CAMEROON (1960)
GABON (1960)
CONGO (1960)
CENTRAL AFRICAN REPUBLIC (1960)
ETHIOPIA
SOMALIA (1960)
UGANDA (1962)
KENYA (1963)
RWANDA (1962)
BURUNDI (1962)
TANZANIA (TANGANYIKA 1961; ZANZIBAR 1964)
ANGOLA (1975)
ZAMBIA (1964)
MOZAMBIQUE (1975)
MADAGASCAR (1960)
ZIMBABWE (1980)
NAMIBIA (1990)
BOTSWANA (1966)
SWAZILAND (1968)
LESOTHO (1966)
REPUBLIC OF SOUTH AFRICA (1910)
ATLANTIC OCEAN

305

It may interest you to know that to this day unhulled coffee is known in Uganda as *kiboko*. The word *kiboko* means 'whip.' This name derives from the fact that prior to the 1930s, if a farmer disobeyed a colonial order to grow coffee, he would be whipped.... We were conditioned to produce goods we did not consume, and to consume those we did not produce.

Yoweri Museveni, President of Uganda; speech on the structural distortions of the colonial economic inheritance, 1989

◄ **Kenya at Independence** *(1963) Kenyans erect a street sign in the country's capital, Nairobi, in honour of Jomo Kenyatta, who had opposed British rule and became president of the newly independent nation.*

was lost during the colonial period. Multiparty democratic constitutions were conceded late and reluctantly by the imperial powers. Ghana, untypically, had two universal franchise elections in the three years before independence in 1957. Mostly, incoming African politicians had less than a year before independence in which to implement new democratic constitutions. In the case of the Belgian Congo (now Democratic Republic of the Congo) the first, and only, democratic election was held just one month before Belgian withdrawal in June 1960.

Lacking a democratic heritage, African political parties sought to establish their power bases around precolonial nationalities or tribal affiliations. Divisive tribal politics threatened to destabilize the new nation-states and have bedevilled most African countries ever since.

Changing Political Systems

The One-party State. The strongest argument in favour of the one-party state in Africa in the 1960s was that tribally based multiparty politics threatened to weaken national unity, encourage secessionist movements, and foment civil war. Proponents of the one-party state argued that an official parliamentary opposition was a luxury that the new states of Africa could ill afford. Africa needed strong and stable government for the huge transformations that lay ahead and this, according to many African political theorists, could best be achieved through the one-party state.

Most states of former French West Africa – Senegal, Mauritania, Guinea, Côte d'Ivoire, Mali, Niger, Upper Volta (renamed Burkina-Faso in 1984), Togo, and Dahomey (renamed Benin in 1975) – became de facto one-party states on achieving independence. In Cameroon, which became independent in 1961, all opposition parties were absorbed into the ruling party in 1966.

In former British territories the issue was debated more openly and the transition, when it came, was more deliberate. Thus, although Kenya became a de facto one-party state when the Kenya African National Union (KANU) under President Jomo Kenyatta (?1891–1978) absorbed the parliamentary opposition by persuasion in 1964, it was not until 1982 that Daniel Arap Moi (1924–) declared Kenya a de jure one-party state. Moi's suppression of all legal opposition was cited as one of the principal reasons for the attempted coup in 1982.

In Tanganyika (renamed Tanzania in 1964 after union with Zanzibar) TANU (Tanganyika

by the colonizing powers. As a result, many countries' borders enclosed a disparate collection of ethnic groups, many with long histories of rivalry. Indeed, some colonial authorities are said to have encouraged 'tribal' antagonisms in order to weaken unified opposition.

Democracy. Multiparty democracy was a novelty to Africa. Where democratic practices existed in precolonial times, they took the form of consensus politics, often on a village basis. Yet even this level of democratic accountability

SIERRA LEONE

Sierra Leone's first postindependence multiparty elections in 1967 were won by Siaka Stevens, but the incumbent Albert Margai, supported by the military, refused to stand down. Civilian rule was restored under Stevens in 1968, but subsequent elections won by Stevens were considered dubious. In 1977 he declared a one-party state and in 1985 his unelected successor, General Joseph Momoh, took over. Despite promising democratic reform, Momoh was overthrown by the military in 1992, sparking off a conflict with armed rebels. A civilian government elected in 1996 was ousted by the military in 1997 but restored in 1998, despite continued conflict with the rebels.

African National Union) was overwhelmingly the dominant political party and President Julius Nyerere (1922–99) encountered no opposition in making it the only legal party on the mainland in 1965. In Zambia, President Kenneth Kaunda (1924–   ) attained a large measure of consensus before declaring a one-party republic in 1972. In Malawi, however, Dr Hastings Kamuzu Banda (1905–97) suppressed all opposition after independence in 1964. Banda officially established a one-party state in 1966 and declared himself president for life in 1971; see POLITICS AND GOVERNMENT (VOL. 6): POLITICAL PARTIES. In Uganda, President Milton Obote (1925–   ) suppressed opposition and suspended the constitution before declaring a 'one-party socialist republic' in 1969.

Ghana had been virtually a de facto one-party state since independence in 1957. Ghana had suffered ethnically based violent opposition since before independence, which Prime Minister (later President) Kwame Nkrumah (1909–72) was determined to suppress. Although he declared Ghana a 'one-party socialist republic' in 1964, he was ousted by a military coup in 1966.

Zimbabwe, which gained independence in 1980, began to move towards one-party rule under President Robert Mugabe (1925–   ) in 1987. Mugabe's failure to tackle Zimbabwe's economic problems and to deal with the effects of the 1991–92 drought made him unpopular. However, he was re-elected in 1996.

Military Coups. The emerging economic crisis of the postindependence decade, the intolerance of criticism in one-party states, and corruption among politicians combined to create circumstances favourable to military intervention. The spate of military takeovers between 1963 and 1969 were often initially welcomed by the populace. Only later was it realized that military rulers were often more autocratic and less competent than civilians.

The succession of African coups started in 1963 in the west African states of Togo and Benin (then Dahomey). In Benin Major Kérékou set up a 'revolutionary dictatorship,' in 1972, providing at least a measure of political stability for the next two decades. In Togo a second coup in 1967 brought General Eyadèma (1937–   ) to power. He suppressed all opposition over the next 25 years.

The example of Togo and Benin was followed by Central African Republic and Zaïre (1965), Burkina-Faso, Nigeria, Ghana, and Burundi (1966), Sierra Leone (1967), Mali and Congo (1968), and Somalia and the Sudan (1969). Military coups remained the most frequent means of achieving a change of government in Africa throughout the 1970s and 1980s.

The military regime in Ghana was the first to transfer to multiparty civilian rule, in 1969, though the military returned in 1972. After a period of corrupt and incompetent military rule, an uprising of the ranks brought Flight-Lieutenant Jerry Rawlings (1942–   ) to power in 1979. His 'revolutionary council' executed three former military heads of state before handing over power to an elected civilian president. The civilian politicians, however, failed to satisfy Rawlings's expectations and he seized power again in 1981.

▲ **Kenneth Kaunda**
Kaunda was one of the longest serving presidents in sub-Saharan Africa, governing Zambia from independence in 1964 until his electoral defeat in 1991. Kaunda was a staunch opponent of the apartheid system in South Africa.

◄ **Supporters of the African National Congress (ANC)**
ANC activists in the township of Soweto in South Africa campaign for the election of their party's leader, Nelson Mandela, in the country's first multiracial election, held in 1994. The ANC won the election with an overwhelming majority, and Mandela became president.

During my lifetime I have dedicated myself to this struggle of the African people. I have fought against White domination and I have fought against Black domination. I have cherished the ideal of a democratic and free society in which all persons live together in harmony, and with equal opportunities. It is an ideal which I hope to live for and to achieve. But, if needs be, it is an ideal for which I am prepared to die.

Nelson Mandela, in a speech delivered at his trial for treason, 20 April 1964

Soldiers in the Biafran War
(1967–70)
The secession of Biafra from Nigeria grew from tribal conflict, when the Ibo people attempted to protect themselves against Hausa dominance. The bloody conflict that eventually led to the defeat of the rebellious province cost many thousands of lives. ▼

Secession, Civil War, and Conflict

Zaïre. The former Belgian Congo was perhaps the most ill-prepared of all the countries that gained independence in the 1960s. There were no African officers in the armed forces, no state funding existed for secondary or higher education, and political activity of any kind was banned until 1957.

120 political parties contested the country's first elections, all but one of which were ethnically based. Within days of independence Prime Minister Patrice Lumumba (1925–61) faced a mutiny in the army and the secession of the copper-rich province of Katanga (modern Shaba). The country quickly degenerated into chaos – cynically manipulated by Cold War superpower rivalry – and Lumumba was murdered. A United Nations force eventually ended Katangan secession in 1963. However, relative stability was not established until the coup led by General Joseph-Désiré Mobutu (1930–97) in 1965. Yet Mobutu's human rights abuses and personal corruption brought his regime into disrepute and, combined with the collapse of copper prices in the mid-1970s, took his country to the verge of bankruptcy during the 1980s. In 1997 Mobutu was overthrown by opponents who renamed the country the Democratic Republic of the Congo.

Nigeria. Ethnic tensions in Nigeria, Africa's most populous state, were exacerbated by two coups in 1966. The massacre of 20 000 Ibo people in the northern Hausa-speaking region led to the secession of the Ibo area of the southeast as Biafra in 1967. Three years of civil war and horrific civilian casualties resulted before Nigeria's General Yakubu Gowon (1934–) brought the 'Biafran War' to an end.

Since 1970 Nigeria has been ruled by a succession of military regimes, apart from a brief civilian administration in the early 1980s. The country has been divided into 30 federal states in an attempt to curb ethnic rivalry. Despite this expedient, Nigeria has remained politically and economically unstable.

The Sudan. In the Sudan the unity of the nation-state has proved even harder to achieve. The south had a long precolonial history of oppression from the Arabic and Egyptian north. The British strengthened existing hostility by administering the Arab Muslim north separately from the African Christian and Animist south until shortly before independence in 1956. Since then, the south has fought an almost continuous civil war against northern domination. Following a brief respite in the 1970s, war resumed in the 1980s when the Khartoum administration revived its programme of Arabization and Islamization in the south. War and the displacement of civilians combined with drought caused famine in the Sudan in 1984–85, 1992, and 1998.

Chad. Ethnic divisions laid the foundations for almost perpetual civil war in Chad from 1966 onwards. Libya intervened, seizing the mineral-rich Aouzou strip in 1975. Coups, changes of government, and French intervention to curb Libyan expansionism failed to halt the conflict. Libya suffered defeat in Chad in 1987, and has since surrendered the Aouzou strip. The wide distribution of arms among rival groups perpetuated the civil war. However, a ceasefire was agreed between the government and rebel groups in 1996.

Uganda. Ethnic and religious division were exacerbated in Uganda by major linguistic differences between Nilotic and Sudanic-speaking northerners and Bantu-speaking southerners. Uganda's first generation of politicians compounded the problem by manipulating tribal animosity for political gain. President Milton Obote's one-party state was overthrown by General Idi Amin (1925–) in 1971. There followed one of the most brutal and destructive dictatorships in Africa, as thousands were massacred, while the country's economy and infrastructure collapsed.

When Amin's activities threatened the stability of the region, Tanzania invaded Uganda in 1979. Within six months the Tanzanians had expelled Amin and his forces. However, the subsequent civilian regime re-established divisiveness and institutionalized corruption. Disillusioned patriots under Yoweri Museveni (1944–) waged a five-year guerrilla war that brought them to power in 1986. Museveni pledged to reconstruct Uganda by establishing good governance on nontribal lines. Museveni was re-elected president in 1996, an endorsement of his non-party system and of his economic success in achieving one of the highest growth rates in Africa.

Ethiopia. Africa's most successful war of secession was that waged by **Eritrea**. After a 30-year guerrilla struggle, which brought down Ethiopia's Marxist military dictator Mengistu Haile Mariam (1937–   ), Eritrea wrested independence from Ethiopia in 1993.

Elsewhere in sub-Saharan Africa, despite further civil conflict in the 1990s (in Liberia, Rwanda, Somalia, Sierra Leone, Burundi, and Guinea-Bissau), Africa's political leaders, both military and civilian, have achieved a remarkable degree of success in holding their ethnically diverse nation-states together since independence.

The Liberation of Southern Africa

The Portuguese Colonies. Portugal was the only European power that refused to accept the process of African decolonization in the 1950s and 1960s. Independence for Portugal's colonies was won only after prolonged guerrilla wars. By the early 1970s, the strain of combating insurgency was beginning to tell on the Portuguese economy. In 1974 a military coup was staged in Portugal to end the futile colonial wars in Africa. Portugal withdrew from Guinea-Bissau and Cape Verde in 1974 and from Angola and Mozambique in 1975.

In Mozambique power was transferred to the guerrilla army FRELIMO (Frente de Libertação de Moçambique), under Samora Machel (1933–86). One-party rule was replaced in 1990 with a multiparty system. In 1994, 18 years of civil war between the FRELIMO government and the rebel Mozambique National Resistance (MNR) ended when FRELIMO won the presidential and legislative elections.

In Angola, guerrilla movements competed for dominance. This situation was complicated when South Africa and Zaïre (with US backing) intervened to try and prevent the Marxist MPLA (Movimento Popular de Libertação de Angola) from taking power. After Portuguese withdrawal, the MPLA proclaimed the People's Republic of Angola and then used Cuban and Soviet military aid to repel a South African invasion in 1975–76. South African and US backing for UNITA (União Nacional para a Independência Total de Angola), under the leadership of Jonas Savimbi (1934–   ), sustained civil war in Angola for the next 16 years. Multiparty elections were held in 1992; UNITA spurned the result and continued fighting. A ceasefire agreed in 1994 eventually led to the formation of a Government of Unity and National Reconciliation in 1997, which brought together the ruling MPLA and UNITA.

South Africa. As in Angola, South Africa sustained a rebel movement in Mozambique in order to destabilize its Marxist neighbour. South African propaganda claimed that opposition to its discriminatory and oppressive racial policies was orchestrated by an external communist conspiracy. Nevertheless, the South African government faced growing internal resistance to its policy of apartheid. Opponents within South Africa drew inspiration from the liberation of the Portuguese colonies in 1974–75. When police opened fire on a crowd of protesting schoolchildren in the Johannesburg suburb of Soweto in 1976, it provoked a violent uprising. This event destroyed the White regime's complacent faith in its own long-term security. Subsequent government efforts at limited reform failed to stem the rising tide of Black protest. Even the state of emergency imposed in 1985 failed to dissuade foreign investors from withdrawing.

With its army coming under severe pressure in southern Angola in 1988, South Africa agreed to stop supporting UNITA and to grant free elections and independence to neighbouring Namibia in 1989–90. At the same time, the South African government (formed exclusively by the National Party since 1948) began to accept that reform of White supremacy was inevitable. The final legal pillars of apartheid were removed, African political parties were unbanned, and political prisoners were released. On 11 February 1990 South Africa's most famous political prisoner, the African National Congress (ANC) vice-president Nelson Mandela (1918–   ), was freed after 27 years in gaol. There followed four years during which Mandela and the South African president, F. W. de Klerk (1936–   ), worked together to reduce tension and violence between the Black and White communities. Black enfranchisement was achieved peacefully in 1994, with a sweeping victory for the ANC; Mandela became president and head of a multiracial coalition government. The new government has since attempted to tackle the legacy of apartheid. However, frus-

▲ **Famine in Somalia** *(1992)*
Famine is a constant threat, especially in the Horn of Africa, where poverty has been exacerbated by war and misgovernment.

Eritrea

Eritrea is sandwiched between the Red Sea and landlocked Ethiopia. Part of Ethiopia in ancient times, Eritrea was seized by the Turks in the 16th century and remained an outpost of the Ottoman Empire until captured by the Italians in 1890. During World War II, it was occupied by the British (1941), who handed it over to Ethiopia as a self-governing state within an Ethiopian federation in 1952. In 1962 Ethiopia annexed Eritrea as a province. From that time Eritrean nationalists fought a prolonged guerrilla war against Ethiopian domination, finally winning their independence in 1993.

▲ **Namibian Independence**
(1990) Namibia gained its independence from South Africa after a long guerrilla campaign by the South West Africa People's Organization (SWAPO). SWAPO leader Sam Nujoma (1929–), pictured above with South African President F.W. de Klerk, was elected president.

Democracy in Africa: Two Success Stories

By the mid-1990s only two African countries — Botswana and Mauritius — had enjoyed constant multiparty democracy since independence in the 1960s, despite great handicaps. Until 1994, Botswana was under threat from South Africa, while Mauritius was overpopulated and disunited. Stability came through economic success, in the form of Botswana's diamond resources, and industrial diversification in Mauritius.

---

tration at the slow pace of reform manifested itself, while tensions between ANC and Zulu Inkatha Freedom Party members continued. A Land Rights Act addressed claims by those dispossessed by White land confiscation. In 1996, a new constitution was finally approved. The National Party withdrew from the coalition government into opposition.

The Road to Democracy

Elsewhere in Africa between 1990 and 1998, military dictatorships and one-party states were replaced by multiparty democracies.

External Factors. The end of the Cold War meant that Africa was no longer subject to strategic manipulation by the superpowers. Western democracies began to make receipt of aid dependent upon evidence of good governance and multiparty democracy. This policy forced two reluctant democrats, Daniel arap Moi in Kenya and Hastings Banda in Malawi, to subject their rule to scrutiny by popular mandate. Moi managed to retain power in 1992, albeit in suspect elections, while Banda was ousted by the electorate in 1994. Popular opposition within Kenya to Moi's government and external pressure from aid donors grew over the slow pace of economic and political reform. The dramatic events in Zaïre in 1997 only served to intensify calls for change.

Internal Factors. Between 1990 and 1998 several African governments were forced by internal pressure to discuss constitutional reform. In some countries, such as Zambia, a change of government was achieved through the ballot box. In others (e.g. Benin, Mali, Ethiopia) constitutional conferences assumed the authority of government, driving the incumbent head of state from office and hastening constitutional reform. President Mobutu

of Zaïre halted this process, provoking full-scale civil conflict in 1996, as his opponents united under rebel leader Laurent Kabila. The presence in Zaïre of one million Hutu refugees from the 1994 Rwandan civil war threatened to turn an internal conflict into a regional one. After sweeping gains by rebel forces, the Mobutu regime collapsed in 1997, when Kabila proclaimed the new Democratic Republic of Congo. All party political activity was suspended as Kabila assumed full presidential powers.

In Ghana and the Seychelles, heads of state who had gained power through coups effected a peaceful transition to multiparty politics. The Sudan and Chad have both made slow progress towards multiparty democracy. The continuing Islamist-Christian civil conflict has hampered the process in The Sudan, while in Chad multiparty presidential and legislative elections took place in 1996 and 1997 respectively.

Some countries have defied the democratic trend. In The Gambia in 1994 the military suspended a long-standing multiparty constitution shortly after peaceful elections. In Nigeria the military, having established a two-party system, declared the election of 1993 void. A further coup that year saw the abolition of all democratic institutions and the onset of political and social crisis. Nigeria's international isolation culminated, in 1995, in its suspension from the Commonwealth, following the execution of Ogoni human rights activists. External pressure on the military regime resulted in multiparty local elections in 1997 and the promise of a transfer of power to an elected civilian president in 1998.

AFRICAN INTERNATIONAL COOPERATION

The Organization of African Unity (OAU) was founded in 1963. It was hoped that it would usher in a political and economic 'United States of Africa.' However, the organization's effectiveness has been hampered by a constitution that prevents interference in the internal affairs of fellow member states. In 1991, OAU heads of government initiated moves towards an African Economic Community.

A scheme for East African economic integration failed to survive political rivalries in the region and collapsed in the 1970s. Since then, the Economic Community of West African States (ECOWAS, established in 1975) and the Southern African Development Community (SADC, founded in 1980–92) have shown the greatest potential for long-term regional integration.

THE WORLD
IN THE
20TH CENTURY

The Global Cold War

The first phase • Improved relations • Dangerous antagonisms • Détente •
Renewal of the Cold War • The end of the Cold War

The term 'Cold War,' coined in 1947, caught the popular imagination as an apt description of the tense standoff that developed between the USSR and its former allies after their victory over Germany (1945). The partitions that epitomized the ideological confrontations of the Cold War – e.g. in Germany, Korea, and Vietnam – testified that no clear victor had emerged from this conflict. This picture was dramatically altered by the collapse of the Soviet Union, in 1991, under the economic strain of maintaining superpower status. The last president of the USSR, Mikhail Gorbachov (1931–   ), realizing that the financial burden was too great, had already taken steps to terminate the Cold War in the late 1980s, through his policy of *glasnost* ('openness').

The First Phase
Some scholars regard the Cold War as having originated in 1917, when the Bolsheviks established the first communist state in Russia.

As early as 1918, V. I. Lenin (1870–1924) sought an accommodation with the capitalist world, believing that the preservation of the Soviet revolution was the key element in promoting world revolution. Soviet foreign policy until the outbreak of World War II was defensive. However, Lenin's successor as leader of the Soviet Union, Joseph Stalin (1879–1953), believed that war between capitalism and communism was inevitable and that the Soviet Union needed overwhelming military superiority to win. Consequently, Soviet military strategists, envisaging that wars would be fought on foreign territory, adopted an offensive doctrine.

World War II transformed the USSR into the leading European military power, rivalled only by the USA. Managing the relationship with the US government assumed vital significance for Moscow. In 1945 a partnership for peace seemed possible. The Soviet Union was an active participant in the formation of the Inter-

Let us not be deceived – we are today in the midst of a cold war.

Bernard Baruch
(1870–1965), in a speech delivered at Columbia, South Carolina, April 1947

The Yalta Conference ▶
In February 1945, the Allied leaders (from left to right: Churchill, Roosevelt, and Stalin) met at the Black Sea resort of Yalta to discuss the political future of Europe after the defeat of Hitler's fascist Third Reich.

McCARTHYISM

Joseph McCarthy (1908–57), a US Republican senator, instigated an anticommunist witch-hunt in the early 1950s that led to the unjust persecution and denunciation of many public officials and prominent citizens. McCarthy began his campaign in 1950, alleging widespread infiltration of the State Department by "card-carrying communists." Although this was refuted by a Senate investigation, McCarthy continued his unsubstantiated accusations of communist conspiracies, even in the US Army. His unscrupulous methods of questioning in televised hearings discredited him and brought him censure from the Senate.

◀ **Joseph McCarthy** *McCarthy at the Army–McCarthy hearings of 1954.*

national Monetary Fund (IMF) and the World Bank, and positive analyses of the benefits of membership were being forwarded to Stalin as late as December 1945. However, the IMF's demands that its employees should have access to sensitive economic data, including gold reserves, before any loan could be extended was at variance with Stalin's wish to conceal from the West the pitiably weak state of the Soviet Union's economy.

Stalin aimed to avoid a conflict with the USA and instructed communist parties in Europe to participate in the democratic process – and the business of government wherever possible, for example in France and Italy – and not to attempt to seize power. Both the US State Department and the British Foreign Office, under the leadership of the staunch anticommunist Ernest Bevin (1881–1951), became alarmed at the growth of communist influence in Europe. The consolidation of communist power in eastern and southeastern Europe in 1946 and the possibility that the communists would win the civil war in Greece eventually led the USA to formulate the **Truman Doctrine**. At the same time, the ***Marshall Plan***, an extensive programme of aid to Europe, was launched to help alleviate poverty, stimulate economic growth, and forestall the rise of communism (see POSTWAR EUROPE). The communist takeover in Czechoslovakia, which came about more as a result of miscalculations by local politicians than through Moscow's intervention, convinced many observers that communism was moving inexorably westwards.

The Soviet blockade of West Berlin began in June 1948 following currency reform in the western sector of the city. This further exacerbated the situation and precipitated the establishment of two German states – the Federal Republic in the west and the Democratic Republic (GDR) in the east.

Developments around the world contributed to increasing tension. With the founding of the People's Republic of China in October 1949, a second potential communist giant appeared on the world stage. The North Atlantic Treaty Organization (NATO) was instituted at the request of alarmed western European nations. In June 1950 North Korea, backed by China, invaded South Korea; and in Vietnam communist forces finally defeated the French at the siege of Dien Bien Phu in 1954.

This first phase of the Cold War was characterized by a military build-up, the division of Europe – and thereafter the world – into two distinct spheres of influence, and a total absence of meaningful negotiations between East and West (the Soviet Union even boycotted the United Nations for a time). As the conflict widened, increasing concern among the Western powers led them to misjudge both the intent and the military strength of the Soviet Union. For example, Stalin favoured a unified nonaligned Germany; however, the USA, strongly supported by the Federal German chancellor Konrad Adenauer (1876–1967), opposed the plan, fearing that such a state would be too readily influenced by the Soviet Union. The USA moved from a position of perceiving Moscow as posing no threat to its security to one of regarding it with fear. Anti-Soviet hysteria in the USA peaked in the early 1950s in the phenomenon of **McCarthyism**. Even after this had abated, deep suspicion of Soviet intentions continued to influence the debate.

The Truman Doctrine

The Truman Doctrine, formulated by President Harry S. Truman (1884–1972), remained a fundamental principle of US foreign policy until the end of communism in the Soviet Union. It was aimed at containing communist expansion. In March 1947, in response to communist insurgency in Greece and Soviet pressure on Turkey, Truman sent a message to Congress, which stated "that it must be the policy of the United States to support free peoples who are resisting attempted subjugation by armed minorities or by outside pressures."

A Soviet Propaganda Cartoon *Throughout the Cold War, each side attempted to influence domestic and world opinion by portraying its antagonist as the aggressor. This 1960s cartoon, from the Soviet satirical magazine* Krokodil, *shows the wolf of Western imperialism being driven from Africa by the continent's newly independent states.*

> Every year humanity takes a step towards communism. Maybe not you, but at all events your grandson will surely be a communist.
>
> **Nikita Khrushchev,**
> June 1956

Improved Relations

The death of Stalin in March 1953 and the election of US President Dwight D. Eisenhower (1890–1969), who was committed to ending the Korean War, signalled a period of negotiation between East and West and the end of the initial phase of the Cold War. As a result of acquiring a nuclear capability in 1952, Moscow had launched the doctrine of peaceful co-existence, feeling that the destructive power of the atomic bomb made obsolete the idea that war was inevitable. An armistice was signed in Korea in July 1953 and a ceasefire in Indochina in 1954. Wide-ranging negotiations between East and West, suspended since

1947, resumed in 1954, covering Austria, Germany, Korea, and Indochina. The USSR agreed to support the treaty that recognized a neutral Austria. Arguments over a united neutral Germany continued until 1958, when the Soviet premier, Nikita Khrushchev (1894–1971), declared that the achievements of the socialist GDR could not be negotiated away. Korea and Vietnam were divided.

Dangerous Antagonisms

The years 1953–69 saw the rise of dangerous antagonisms that made East–West relations extremely volatile. However, the period began optimistically: in 1955 the Geneva summit brought together Soviet and Western leaders for the first time since Potsdam in 1945. Nevertheless, two events in 1956 revived tension: an uprising against Soviet domination in Hungary was brutally repressed, and an Anglo-French invasion of Egypt to secure the Suez Canal was strongly opposed by the Soviet Union. Khrushchev's visit to the USA in 1959 heralded another period of negotiations and willingness to cooperate. However, this ended abruptly in 1960 when the Paris summit ended in discord following the shooting down of a US U2 reconnaissance aircraft that had violated Soviet airspace. Relations further deteriorated in 1961, when the GDR erected the Berlin Wall in an attempt to halt mass emigration of its populace to the West.

As a result of Khrushchev's unrealistic attitudes and mercurial temperament, Soviet foreign policy became far more unpredictable. During his term of office, cracks began to appear in the communist monolith for the first time as a result of growing tension between the Soviet Union and China. Khrushchev also widened the scope of Soviet diplomacy by visiting Asia (especially India) and the Middle East and offering ostensibly attractive trade and technical assistance deals to developing nations. The Cuban revolution of 1959 was not communist in origin but its leader, Fidel Castro (1926–   ), was forced by US intransigence to seek aid from the Soviet Union.

Khrushchev's brinkmanship, shown in his wish to use the Soviet nuclear arsenal as a bargaining counter, was evident in the most critical incident of the entire Cold War – the **Cuban missile crisis**. In the aftermath of the crisis, summits between the two countries continued until 1967. During this period, relations between the Soviet Union and China deteriorated still further.

In 1965, the USA took the fateful decision to intervene in the conflict in Vietnam (the Second Indochina War) and also sent troops into the Dominican Republic. The third Arab–Israeli war erupted in 1967 with the Soviet Union and the USA supporting opposing sides.

THE CUBAN MISSILE CRISIS

The Cuban missile crisis of September and October 1962, which brought the world close to nuclear war, resulted from Khrushchev's attempt to counter US dominance in intercontinental ballistic missiles by siting Soviet missiles on the island of Cuba, only some 150 km off the US mainland. President John F. Kennedy (1917–63) ordered US warships to blockade the island. Confrontation seemed inevitable as Soviet freighters carrying missile parts approached Cuba; however, Khrushchev relented, ordering the ships to turn back and existing sites to be dismantled.

The extreme danger of this crisis later became clear, when it emerged that Soviet commanders had been authorized to launch a nuclear strike on the USA if they believed they were under nuclear attack. In the USA, aircraft of the strategic bomber force had been kept constantly armed and airborne, ready to retaliate.

The crisis had a sobering effect in both camps; a nuclear test ban treaty was signed in 1963 and a hot line between the two presidents in Moscow and Washington was established.

NUCLEAR DISARMAMENT TREATIES

Several rounds of talks were held by the superpowers on nuclear weapons. In 1974 Strategic Arms Limitation Talks (SALT I), outlawed construction of antiballistic missile systems. SALT II (1979) was never ratified by the US Senate, due to the Soviet invasion of Afghanistan. START (Strategic Arms Reduction Talks) began in 1982, but were suspended. In 1987 the INF (Intermediate Nuclear Forces) treaty eliminated medium- and short-range weapons.

The 1968 Warsaw Pact invasion of Czechoslovakia, following the introduction of liberal policies (the so-called 'Prague Spring'), spread fear of an invasion in West Germany and raised tension elsewhere. It also split Western communist parties. The inauguration of Richard Nixon (1913–94) as US president in 1969 marked the beginning of a sustained period of negotiations, referred to as 'détente.'

Détente
This phase of reduced international tension produced many accords. In addition to major arms control agreements, the Conference on Security and Cooperation in Europe (CSCE) in 1975 resulted in the signing of the Helsinki Final Act. The Soviets won an important recognition of the inviolability of the post-1945 frontiers in Europe, but conceded that human rights were of international concern. A treaty signed in Paris in January 1973 agreed US withdrawal from Vietnam.

Détente marked the high point of Soviet power. It is ironic that at the very moment the USA conceded nuclear parity, the Soviet Union began to decline economically. Under the growing influence of the Soviet military, the Soviet Union and its client states became embroiled in conflicts in the developing world, such as the civil wars in Angola, Ethiopia, and Mozambique.

The Soviet invasion of Afghanistan in 1979 brought an abrupt end to the process of détente. This intervention was based on the erroneous belief that the operation would only take a few weeks and that the USA would not raise any major objections. The invasion was seized upon by those in the West who had been warning of Soviet expansionism to demand greater defence preparedness.

Renewal of the Cold War
This phase covers the period from the Afghan invasion, in 1979, to the appointment of Mikhail Gorbachov as Soviet leader in March

Global Cold War
Major conflicts and interventions – e.g. the Vietnam War (1955–75) – are shown from the start of the Cold War (c. 1947) to the demise of communism in the Soviet Union (1991). Less significant interventions – to maintain superpower spheres of influence – are also indicated (e.g. Grenada 1983). ▼

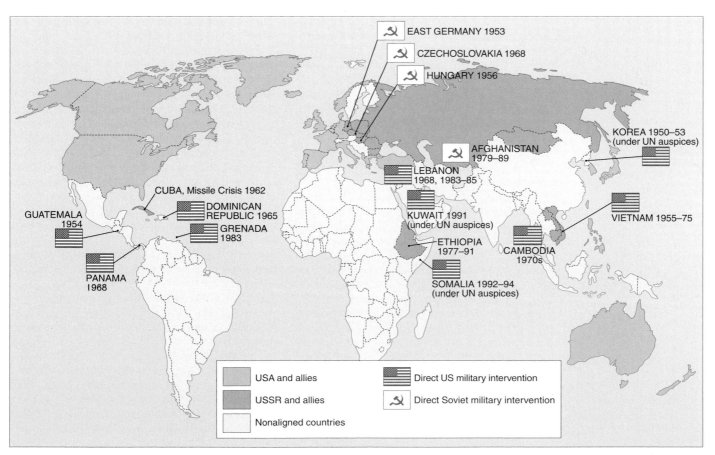

315

▲ **The Strategic Defence Initiative (SDI)** *In the 1980s the SDI project was instigated by President Ronald Reagan. This programme – popularly known as 'Star Wars' – was intended to intercept and destroy an incoming Soviet missile attack with lasers, as shown in this artist's impression. SDI never became operational; in 1993 it was admitted that test results had been falsified to make the USSR believe that SDI would work.*

President Reagan described the Soviet Union as the "evil empire." Moreover, it was accused by the US of supporting international terrorism throughout the world. One of the reasons for this was alarm about the number of communist states that had come into existence in and after 1974 in the Middle East, Africa, and Central America. The USA and its allies determined to redress the balance by imposing trade boycotts and pulling out of the 1980 Olympics in Moscow. The Soviets responded by withdrawing from the 1984 Olympics in Los Angeles.

The death of Soviet leader Leonid Brezhnev (1906–82) brought little change in Soviet attitudes. East–West talks continued in Geneva on intermediate-range nuclear weapons and strategic arms reductions; in Madrid on CSCE; and in Vienna on Mutual and Balance Force Reductions in Europe.

The End of the Cold War
The election of Mikhail Gorbachov as Soviet leader in March 1985 marked a change in international relations. Convinced that the arms race was crippling his country, Gorbachov gave priority to foreign policy and spoke of the "new political thinking." This pragmatic approach to international relations acknowledged that security could not be achieved by military means alone, that all states were interdependent, and that nuclear weapons should be abolished by the year 2000. Together with Foreign Minister Eduard Shevardnadze (1928–   ), he launched a highly successful popularity campaign in the West. His first meeting with President Reagan, in Geneva in November 1985, led to a joint statement proposing a reduction of 50% in the superpowers' nuclear arsenals. The next summit, held in Reykjavik, Iceland, in October 1986, foundered on disagreement over the US Strategic Defence Initiative (SDI). The third summit, in Washington DC in December 1987, achieved a historic breakthrough in the Intermediate Range Nuclear Forces agreement to eliminate an entire category of nuclear weapons.

One of the agreements reached at Geneva had been on the withdrawal of Soviet troops from Afghanistan, a process that was completed by February 1989. Good relations between President George Bush (1924–   ) and Gorbachov produced two important agreements: the Conventional Forces in Europe (CFE) Treaty of November 1990, and the START treaty, signed in July 1991. However, opposition from the Soviet General Staff undermined the CFE treaty and the disintegration of the Soviet Union halted progress on the START treaty. With the USSR now in the position of a supplicant, the Cold War was over.

1985; it was marked by a rapid rise in military expenditure by both sides. During the first Cold War (c. 1947–53) the USA had been the dominant economic power and had, albeit briefly, enjoyed a nuclear monopoly. By the early 1980s, the USSR believed that it was catching up and hoped to surpass the USA in nuclear capability. President Ronald Reagan (1911–   ) promised to restore US military superiority. The USA emphasized that it was ready to undertake military intervention in Third World states, such as Libya, Cuba, and Nicaragua, to promote pro-Western values. New intermediate nuclear missiles were deployed in Europe by both powers.

This new stage of the Cold War differed from its initial phase in that, by 1979, the West no longer feared communism as an ideology. Instead, the USSR had become a military and security threat. The violent suppression of the 'Prague Spring' brought an end to the popular appeal of Marxism. Virulent propaganda campaigns and debates ensued, one of the most vigorous of which concerned the state of the Soviet economy. It has since emerged that it was by then in a state of terminal decline, yet advocates of increased US defence spending were naturally unwilling to acknowledge this. Indeed, some US strategists even argued the necessity of a crippling arms race as a way of bankrupting the Soviet economy. A long-term side-effect of US defence expenditure of this period has been an enormous budget deficit.

Polemics ruled this period; when, in 1983, a Soviet interceptor shot down a South Korean airliner that had strayed into its airspace,

The New Economic Powers

Japan: role model for the Third World • The Tiger economies •
Development in Brazil and Mexico

In the years following the end of World War II (in 1945), the world was commonly viewed as being divided into three distinct segments. The term 'First World' was used to denote the liberal, democratic, and capitalist nations of the Western world. The term 'Second World' referred to the Soviet Union and its eastern European allies. The countries of Latin America, Africa, and Asia, many of which had once been colonies of the First World states, made up the so-called 'Third World.' The latter group are now referred to as 'developing countries.'

One of the main features of the world economic system since the 1950s, however, has been the growth in the economic power and importance of several Third World nations. The countries that had most success in modernizing their economies were those on the Pacific Rim of East Asia, such as Taiwan and South Korea. Such countries as Brazil and Mexico also experienced a large degree of success in industrializing and in improving their economic position. However, the most striking example of successful economic growth since the 1950s was that experienced by Japan. Japan not only provided a role model for the **newly industrializing countries (NICs)**, but it greatly influenced economic practice on a worldwide scale.

Japan: role Model for the Third World

By 1955 Japan had recovered from its status as a defeated nation. It was, however, only just ahead of the other major Asian countries in terms of economic performance. By 1975 Japan's position had been transformed; it had become the world's third largest economy (behind the USA and the USSR). During this period Japan experienced growth rates in its economy of around 11%; it had become a nation of well-educated and highly skilled urban workers, who enjoyed increasing standards of living. By the 1980s growth rates had slowed to an annual level of approximately 4%. However, Japan increased its exports to other countries; its often high-quality

====SEE ALSO====
Japan:
• Postwar Japan
Latin America:
• Modern Latin America
Southeast Asia:
• World War II
  and Independence
Technology (vol. 2)
Computers (vol. 2)
Economics (vol. 6)

◄ **The Growth of Seoul** *(South Korea) Seoul in 1910 (left) was a town of one-storey dwellings; by the 1980s South Korea's capital city (below left) had become a rapidly developing industrial, commercial, and administrative centre, reflecting the swift economic growth of South Korea itself.*

Newly Industrializing Countries (NICs)

An NIC is defined by the degree to which its industry relies on its exported goods and by what percentage of its GDP is manufacturing. Countries now usually considered to be NICs are: Hong Kong, Singapore, South Korea, Taiwan, Brazil, Mexico, Argentina, India, Egypt, Turkey, Malaysia, the Philippines, Thailand, and Indonesia. Those of Southeast Asia began to industrialize rapidly in the 1960s and 1970s.

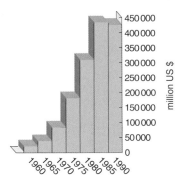

450 000
400 000
350 000
300 000
250 000
200 000
150 000
100 000
50 000
0

million US $

1960 1965 1970 1975 1980 1985 1990

▲ **Japanese Exports**
*(1960–90) The
1980s saw an easing
of Japan's protectionist
policies and a dramatic
increase in its exports.
As a leading world
economy, however,
Japan suffered the
effects of the global
economic recession
of the early 1990s.
Nevertheless, its
success still provides
an example of rapid
economic growth to
newly developing
countries around
the world.*

consumer goods were increasingly in demand, at home and abroad. Japan's success in the field of exports was such that the USA, in particular, became increasingly alarmed by their growing trade deficit with Japan.

One major factor in Japan's economic success was the cultural attitudes of its people towards work. For most Japanese, success in life and success in the workplace were inseparable. Great value was placed upon competition, industry, and effort. This attitude was largely instilled at school, where children – encouraged to take their studies very seriously from an early age – competed in a system that placed great emphasis on examinations. Universities in Japan had a clear hierarchy and students were aware that obtaining a place at a prestigious university would greatly increase their career opportunities. In the workplace, Japanese management practice involved a relatively high level of cooperation between the labour force and management. Workers were encouraged to identify themselves strongly with the company that employed them. This was reinforced by high levels of job security and the organization of unions within companies, rather than trade sectors.

Another factor in Japan's success was its relatively small defence budget. After World War II Japan relied largely on the USA to provide it with security; this gave it an economic advantage over many of its competitors.

A third factor was Japan's exclusion of foreign capital. It relied on a combination of large Japanese companies, such as Yamaha, and on a high level of state planning. A large and con-

centrated population provided sustainable domestic demand for Japanese products. Government measures guided and encouraged economic expansion. The initial growth of Japan's multinational companies depended on government protection, which reduced foreign competition. While this protectionism receded in the 1980s, it gave Japan's industry a lead in the world marketplace.

Japan's neighbours in East Asia, in particular, drew heavily on Japan's experience of economic success. The so-called 'Tiger economies' (South Korea, Taiwan, Hong Kong, and Singapore) were the most notable examples.

The Tiger Economies
In many respects the rapid growth of South Korea, Taiwan, Hong Kong, and Singapore matched the performance of Japan. However, in 1997–98 the region was shaken by a financial crisis.

South Korea. In some areas, the achievements of South Korea have actually rivalled those of Japan. Following the Korean War (1950–53) the South Korean economy grew at an average rate of 8%. This success had a beneficial effect on living standards and life expectancy. South Korea's growth was mostly due to its transformation from a largely agricultural economy to one more reliant upon industry. The Korean War had devastated the country and reduced the value of industrial output to approximately one-third of its level in 1940; by the 1980s, however, it had become one of the world's leading exporters of electronic goods.

**The Serra dos
Carajas Project,
Brazil** *Opencast
mining of the vast iron
ore reserves found in
the Carajas region
is shown. It was
projected that the
region would generate
US$17 billion per
year in export earnings
in the 1990s.*

▶

WOMEN AND ECONOMIC GROWTH

The industrial growth of NICs based on the export of consumer goods, such as textiles, clothes, footwear, electrical and electronic goods, and components, has been underpinned by a largely female workforce. The percentage of women in the industrial labour force of NICs is, in some cases, double that in most other countries. This is due primarily to the fact that women can be paid lower wages than men in similar occupations; women were also targeted as labour in NICs because

▲ **A Female Workforce** *Women employees work on microchip manufacture and design in a Singapore factory.*

of their assumed natural manual dexterity and willingness to take on tedious repetitive work, which would result in higher productivity levels. Much longer working hours than those in industrialized countries and piecework rates and bonuses have also helped achieve productivity levels far higher than those in industrialized countries. Limited alternative employment and state suppression of labour organizations, however, leave women workers vulnerable to exploitation.

South Korea's success can be attributed to many factors; of crucial importance, however, were very low labour costs and long working hours. Political repression also reduced disruptions to production. As in Japan, South Korea's economy was aided by state involvement. In 1973 the Heavy Industry and Chemicals Plan was instigated to force the pace of growth in large manufacturing industries, helping them to increase their share of the world market. In the 1950s South Korea relied on exporting such products as food, textiles, and beverages; in the 1980s the success of manufacturing industry allowed it to move increasingly towards machinery, transport, and electronics. More recently, as labour costs have grown, South Korean industry has begun to move its labour-intensive processes to less developed countries, such as Malaysia and Thailand, where wage costs are lower.

Taiwan. Taiwan's success has also been based on exports; by the 1980s it had become increasingly important as a manufacturer of electronic goods. In 1960 electronic products made up 1% of Taiwan's total exports; by the early 1980s this figure had increased to 18%. Taiwan's economic development has also involved substantial state intervention. Most of Taiwan's banking system had been under state control; in the 1960s, as foreign aid decreased, the government encouraged large-scale foreign investment. Much of Taiwan's ability to undercut competitors, and to attract investment from multinational companies based in countries overseas, was dependent on the government's ability to suppress trades unions and maintain low wage rates.

Hong Kong. Hong Kong relied more on external markets than on state intervention for its economic growth; it thus had to be flexible in responding to the changing demands of the global market. The service sectors, particularly financial services, were more central to

Hong Kong's success than to that of other Asian countries. However, the reversion of Hong Kong to the rule of communist China in 1997 leaves the future of its economy uncertain.

Singapore. Singapore also experienced high growth rates after the 1950s. By the 1980s, income per capita was approaching European levels. Between 1965 and 1980 growth rates were approximately 9%; foreign capital was vital in encouraging growth. By 1980, 13% of manufacturing industry was foreign-owned.

From the late 1950s the Tiger economies became important industrial powers; they progressed from exporting such goods as textiles to exporting sophisticated electrical equipment. By the 1990s, this trend seemed set to continue well beyond the end of the century.

Development in Brazil and Mexico

In the early 1980s the economies of Brazil and Mexico had a much greater gross national product (GNP) than those of the Tiger economies; for example, in 1982, Brazil's GNP was 55% greater than those of the four Asian countries combined. The pattern of development in the Latin American countries was also different. Both Brazil and Mexico pursued industrialization through a policy known as ***import substitution***; this involved restricting imports into the economy in an attempt to force the pace of domestic growth, which contrasted with the Asian approach of using the world market to force growth by concentrating on specialized exports. Both the Brazilian and Mexican economies experienced high growth rates in the period after the 1950s. Both countries also experienced shorter periods of exceptional growth. Between 1977 and 1981 Mexico had a growth rate of 8%; in Brazil growth was approximately 7% between 1974 and the early 1980s. Industrial output also increased rapidly at certain periods; for

The Carajas Project

In the late 1960s, a huge deposit of high-grade iron ore was discovered on the Serra dos Carajas in Brazil. It has become one of the country's largest development projects, which includes mining, logging, iron and aluminium smelting, and agro-industrial plantations. Some 800 000 sq km of Amazonion forest are being cleared; farming communities have lost their houses and crops to make way for steel plants, fuel terminals, and property development. In 1987 35 million tonnes of iron ore were exported; even at this rate of extraction, the Carajas reserves are estimated to last 350–400 years. While the project has dispossessed thousands of people, immigrants from other parts of Brazil are arriving in the hope of finding work.

example, between 1964 and 1980, steel production in Brazil tripled. The development of the Latin American countries did share some similarities with the NICs of Asia. Although industrialization was less rapid, the state played a significant role. In Brazil, the government of the 1950s followed a strategy that combined state investment in infrastructure, the imposition of import controls, and the encouragement of foreign investment. The state also helped to repress the trades union movement; in both Mexico and Brazil low wage costs encouraged investment from Western and Japanese multinational companies. During the 1980s and 1990s, Mexico and Brazil came under pressure from the increasingly interdependent world economy; they responded by increasing exports and lowering import barriers. While such actions have allowed continued growth and development, one of the major prices of industrialization, in both countries, has been very high levels of inflation and income inequality.

The rapid expansion of the economies of the newly industrializing countries, especially South Korea, since the 1950s has called into question the validity of the term 'Third World' when referring to such countries. The countries described here have led the way in reducing the dominance of the USA and western Europe in the world economy. Central to these developments was the **information technology revolution**, which was led by Japan. By the mid-1990s, however, it was clear that the Japanese economy did overstretch itself in the 1980s; in 1993 its economy contracted for the first time since the mid-1970s. The nations of the Pacific Rim of East Asia saw their economic growth continue into the 1990s; they have been joined by China, which began to modernize its economy in the 1980s by introducing market reform. In the early 1990s China's economy saw growth rates of 10%; with its huge potential domestic market, this trend will certainly continue into the 21st century.

THE INFORMATION TECHNOLOGY REVOLUTION

During the 1980s and 1990s, the manufacture of goods related to the so-called 'information revolution' became increasingly important to the economic growth of developing countries. However, the impact of information technology (IT) went far beyond such development issues.
The term IT is used to describe the compilation, storage, processing, and transmitting of information. It also applies to the technologies relating to electronics, computer systems, and telecommunications.
The speed of the IT revolution has been astonishing. With technological developments, the cost of manufacturing IT fell dramatically in the 1980s, allowing its widespread

usage. It has greatly affected many aspects of life, altering the way people work, shop, and enjoy their leisure time. A vast number of new jobs have been created, which relate to the processing and manipulation of information. In the manufacturing industry, IT has enabled the restructuring of work and management practice. Microchip technology has allowed much greater flexibility in production processes; companies are able to respond much faster to shifting patterns of demand. Such changes have resulted in production being based more on range of product and flexibility than on standardization and quantity. For some workers, these changes have led to more satisfying and skilled jobs, while others have experienced deskilling, highly repetitive work, and unemployment.
IT has also affected domestic life: microchips drive various domestic appliances and consumer goods. Personal computers have become a feature in homes in the USA and western Europe, while Japan has been the leader in diversifying the uses of information technology. IT has also affected the way in which people spend their money. Plastic payment cards have reduced the need for paper money, while the computerization of money has tranformed the conduct of international business. The development of telecommunications, such as electronic mail (e-mail) and the internet or world wide web, and satellite technology has effectively made the world a smaller place in which to live. Multinational companies have used these developments to globalize their production processes.
The advent of IT has, in general, been regarded as a positive development. Some commentators, however, have pointed to its negative effects, such as the use of microelectronics to construct more powerful weapons systems. IT has also allowed for the storing of personal information on databases, which has implications for civil liberties.

▲ **Data Processing** *The IT revolution has transformed the way in which data is stored and processed. This has resulted in huge benefits both for commercial organizations and government departments. Governments have thus invested in the necessary equipment, such as that shown here in the data-processing service of the federal senate in Brazil, in order to maximize the time and cost-saving advantages of using information technology.*

The 'New World Order'

The end of the Cold War • World problems

The collapse of communism in the Soviet Union, and the unprecedented international cooperation against Iraqi aggression in the 1990–91 Gulf War, led many commentators to talk of a turning point in world history. President George Bush (1924–) claimed that a "New World Order" had begun, characterized by a new approach to aggression in international politics. The United Nations (UN) was freed from the ideological factionalism that had characterized it during the Cold War; it was hoped that the organization would, at last, fulfil the international peacekeeping role that its founders had envisaged for it. In this new political environment, consensus would replace conflict in world affairs.

The End of the Cold War

The concept of a New World Order was founded on the success of the capitalist liberal democracies, which triumphed over the state-socialist systems in the Cold War. Such institutions as the International Monetary Fund encourage developing countries to open their economies to the free market. Political pluralism has flourished with the fall of one-party states in eastern Europe. Indeed the UN greatly extended its role following the collapse of the Soviet Union; it began to intervene in the internal affairs of states that violate the human rights of their citizens. The UN also became involved in countries, such as the former Yugoslavia, Somalia, Rwanda, and Haiti, where order broke down, although intervention has often produced considerably less successful results than were hoped for.

Another feature of the New World Order has been the reduction in the threat of a major nuclear war. A series of treaties, agreed in the early 1990s, relieved East–West tensions. In 1991 the US–Soviet Intermediate-range Nuclear Force Treaty obliged both sides to destroy all medium-range ground-to-ground missiles. Other important treaties included the START II Treaty, which reduced the numbers of long-range missiles by two-thirds, and the Open Skies Treaty (March 1992), signed by the 51 members of the Conference on Security and Cooperation in Europe. The end of the Cold War also led to a reduction in regional conflicts, for example in southern Africa, where the superpowers fuelled conflicts as a way of indirectly attacking each other. While it seems that, in a short period, the nature of international relations has been transformed, it is clearly too early to assume that a permanent new order in world politics has been achieved.

World Problems

Arms. The build-up of vast arms stores by many nations had long been a major problem. The break-up of the Soviet Union meant that control of the former Soviet nuclear arsenal became contentious. It was feared that there would be less control over access to the technology involved in nuclear production and that former Soviet scientists might sell their expertise in the international marketplace. In

═══SEE ALSO═══
This section:
• The Global Cold War
The Industrial Age in Europe:
• Postwar Europe
• The End of Communism
North America:
• The United States of America
China:
• Communist China
Religion (vol. 6):
• Islam
Politics and Government (vol. 6):
• International Politics

Russian Demilitarization
Following the end of the Cold War and the break-up of the Soviet Union, heavy arms and weaponry were destroyed. Thousands of Soviet tanks, such as those shown here (1993), were dismantled and scrapped. ▼

The Earth Summit

The United Nations Conference on Environment and Development (UNCED) — known as the Earth Summit — was convened in Rio de Janeiro, Brazil in June 1992. Attended by more than 100 heads of state, the summit's achievements included a comprehensive plan for global action in all areas of sustainable development, including climatic change, depletion of the ozone layer, deforestation, toxic wastes, and depletion of marine resources. The summit also addressed poverty and external debt in developing countries, as well as unsustainable production and consumption in industrializing countries.

Population ▶

The overcrowded streets of China's major cities, such as Shanghai (shown here), are a constant reminder of the country's burgeoning population. As China's population approaches 1.2 billion, the government has been forced to impose a strict policy of birth control, limiting each family to one child only. However, poorer countries, such as those in Africa, are without the mechanisms or resources to implement such measures.

the early 1990s many countries in politically unstable areas possessed, or were attempting to develop, nuclear capabilities. In 1998 India and Pakistan both tested nuclear weapons and such countries as Israel, Brazil, Iran, Iraq, and North Korea are also aspiring nuclear powers. It is feared that the threat to use nuclear arms could become a feature of future regional conflicts.

The arms trade in conventional weapons continues to grow, particularly in Asian countries where the potential for conflicts is great.

Instability. The end of the Cold War also ended the global stability of the balance of power between the USA and the USSR. The two superpowers had prevented their client states from engaging in full-scale conflict, for fear of sparking a major war. Without this restraint, conflicts in newly independent countries threatened to become more severe.

The role of the USA in the aftermath of the Cold War is also unclear. Some have argued that the new international situation will lead to US dominance of world politics. With Soviet opposition gone, the USA could assert its military power to protect its interests. Others have argued that the USA, rather than becoming too interventionist, will become more isolationist. Some prominent politicians in the USA have argued that their government should curtail its foreign operations, allowing other nations to assume more of the burden. In his 1991 election campaign, Bill Clinton (1946–) concentrated on domestic and economic issues; on his election as US president, he showed reluctance in committing US troops to UN operations, such as that in Bosnia. However, President Clinton was instrumental in the *rapprochement* between Israel and the PLO and between Israel and Jordan. The USA played a key role in the peace negotiations that finally ended the civil war in Bosnia in 1995. It has also responded forcefully to terrorism; in 1998 President Clinton ordered the bombing of targets in Sudan and Afghanistan, countries thought to support terrorists.

Ethnic Fragmentation. In such states as South Africa and the former Yugoslavia, ethnic tension resulted in conflict and potential or actual civil war. South Africa, however, managed to achieve a relatively peaceful transition to universal suffrage in 1994. In Bosnia, UN peacekeeping forces, humanitarian aid, and the concerted efforts of western European nations finally led to a peace settlement in 1995, though deep ethnic divisions remain.

The Environment. A host of environmental problems still plague the world. Such issues as the need for clean cheap renewable energy sources, global warming, and toxic dumping continue unresolved with only limited international cooperation.

Population growth presents a constant problem. Resources are heavily exploited in an attempt to feed, house, and clothe the people of the world, yet they are unable to provide a reasonable standard of living for a rapidly expanding population. In the poorer countries, where population is likely to grow fastest, people face starvation and misery, a problem that threatens to widen the gap between developed and developing nations. The associated problem of disease, particularly AIDS, is a reality for millions of people.

Russia and China. The situation in Russia and in China, in the late 1990s, remains unstable. In Russia, the transition from a centrally planned economy to a free market system has proved highly problematic, and a return to authoritarian rule cannot be ruled out. China also presented a potential threat to the New World Order. With communism retreating elsewhere during the late 1980s, the Chinese Communist Party remained determined to retain power at any cost. As China continues to modernize and reform its economy, it remains unclear to what extent such change will alter the political nature of the country.

Given the many and varied problems that beset the world at the turn of the millenium, talk of a new and lasting world order still has to be cautious.

Chronology

EUROPE AND THE MIDDLE EAST	THE AMERICAS	ASIA AND OCEANIA	SUB-SAHARAN AFRICA
c. 30 000 BC Earliest signs of human ritual activity	**30 000–10 000 BC** Hunters from Asia migrated to North America and spread south through Americas **c. 10 000–8000** Clovis culture flourished in midwest and southwest N America		
c. 9000–8000 Domestication of animals and crops; permanent Neolithic settlements in the Middle East	**c. 9000–8000** Domestication of plants and animals began in Peru	**c. 8500 BC** Pottery developed in Japan **Before 7000** Foragers settled in Indochina	
c. 6500 First farming in Greece and Aegean; dispersed throughout Europe by c. 4000	**c. 6000** Beginning of maize cultivation in Central America	**c. 6000** Melanesia and Micronesia settled by Australoid and Mongoloid peoples; rice cultivation (Thailand)	**c. 6000 BC** Fishing communities established on lakes and rivers of middle Africa; pastoralist communities herded cattle in central Saharan region
c. 5000 Farming settlements in Egypt		**c. 5000** Neolithic farming established in the Indus valley; horticultural Malay-speaking peoples moved from Taiwan into Indonesia **c. 5000–3000** Neolithic cultures established in the Huang He (Yellow) River Basin (China)	**c. 5000–3000** Desiccation of Saharan region began
c. 4000 Bronze casting began in Near East; first use of plough **c. 4000–3000** Development of first cities in Mesopotamia **c. 3300** Pictographic writing invented in Sumer, Mesopotamia **c. 3200** Construction of megalithic tombs and circles in W Europe **c. 3100** King Menes united Egypt; dynastic period began **c. 3000** Development of major cities in Sumer; spread of copper-working in Europe; Neolithic settlements in Crete **c. 2613–2125** Old Kingdom period in Egypt; great pyramids built **c. 2055–1795** Middle Kingdom period in Egypt; expansion into Nubia **c. 2000** Hittites invaded Anatolia and founded empire (1650); Indo-European speakers settled Peloponnese; Minoan civilization began on Crete **c. 1600** Beginnings of Mycenaean civilization (Greece) **c. 1550–1069** New Kingdom period in Egypt **c. 1500** 'Linear B' script in Greece **c. 1450** Destruction of Minoan Crete **c. 1200** Collapse of Hittite Empire; Jewish exodus from Egypt to Palestine **c. 1100** Mycenaean civilization collapsed; spread of Phoenicians in Mediterranean region (to 700 BC) **c. 1000–962** Reign of King David, who united all the Israelite tribes **c. 800** Rise of Etruscan civilization in Italy **753** Traditional date for foundation of Rome **721–705** Height of kingdom of Assyria (Mesopotamia) **c. 700–450** Late Bronze Age (Hallstatt) culture in central Europe **671** Assyrian conquest of Egypt **612** Collapse of Assyrian power **586–538** Babylonian captivity of Jews **c. 550** Cyrus (the Great) defeated Medes and founded Persian Empire **522** Persia under Darius I stretched from the Nile to the Indus	**c. 4000–3000** First pottery in Americas (Amazon region, Ecuador, and Colombia) **c. 2000** First metalworking in Peru; Great Plains tribes of N America began to hunt bison **c. 1200** Beginning of Olmec civilization (Mexico) **c. 1150** Olmec settlement at San Lorenzo (Mexico) established **c. 900–200** Chavín culture flourished in Andean region **c. 900–800** La Venta (Mexico) emerged as main Olmec centre, following abandonment of San Lorenzo (c. 900)	**c. 2750** Growth of civilization in Indus valley **c. 2000** Settlement of Melanesia by immigrants from Indonesia began; use of bronze in Southeast Asia **c. 1600** Shang dynasty founded in China; first urban Bronze Age culture **c. 1500** Aryan invasion of India; fall of Indus civilization; emergence of Hinduism; Bronze Age culture in Ganges basin; rice farming in Indochina **c. 1050** Shang dynasty in China overthrown by Zhou; Aryans expanded eastwards down Ganges valley **c. 1000** Development of Polynesian culture by migrant settlers began **c. 800** Aryans expanded southwards in India **771** Collapse of Western Zhou feudal order in China **c. 660** Jimmu Tennu, legendary first emperor of Japan **c. 566–463** Gautama Siddhartha, the Buddha; emergence of Buddhism **551–479** Kong Zi (Confucius), Chinese philosopher, developed his system of ethics	**c. 3000** Arable farming techniques spread to central Africa; first Nubian culture flourished in upper Nile valley **c. 2000** Rise of second Nubian culture **c. 1000** Khoikhoi pastoralists herded cattle in southern Africa **c. 900** Foundation of kingdom of Kush (Nubia, East Africa)

EUROPE AND THE MIDDLE EAST

c. 509 Roman Republic founded

490 Persian attack on Greece repulsed at Battle of Marathon
480 Persian invasion of Greece repulsed at Salamis and Plataea (479)
478 Foundation of League of Delos (later became the Athenian Empire)
431–404 Peloponnesian War between Sparta and Athens
338 Battle of Chaeronea: Macedon gained control of Greece
334 Alexander the Great invaded Asia Minor; conquered Egypt (332), Persia (330), reached India (327)
323 Alexander died; his empire divided between Macedon, Egypt, Syria, and Pergamum
312 Foundation of Seleucid Empire
304 Ptolemaic dynasty founded in Egypt (to 30 BC)

264 Rome completed conquest of Italy
264–241 First Punic War between Carthage and Rome
c. 250 Arsaces founded Parthian dynasty in Central Asia

218–201 Second Punic War
206 Rome gained control of Spain

168 Rome defeated Macedonia
149–146 Third Punic War: Rome destroyed Carthage
146 Rome sacked Corinth; Greece under Roman domination

88 Height of Parthian Empire
81 Sulla dictator of Rome (to 79 BC)
64 Pompey the Great conquered Syria, ending Seleucid Empire
58–51 Julius Caesar conquered Gaul
49 Julius Caesar invaded Italy; began civil war against Pompey
48 Pompey defeated; Julius Caesar became consul and dictator of Rome
44 Julius Caesar assassinated
43 Roman lands divided between Octavian and Mark Antony
31 Battle of Actium: Octavian defeated Mark Antony; birth of Roman Empire

27–30 AD Ministry of Jesus
43 AD Roman conquest of Britain began
44 AD Mauretania (N Africa) annexed by Rome

193–211 Roman Empire reached its greatest extent
224 Foundation of Sassanian dynasty in Persia
238 Incursions of Germanic tribes into Roman Empire began

THE AMERICAS

c. 500 First hieroglyphic writing in Mexico (Monte Albán)

c. 250 First Maya cities built

c. 100 AD Anasazi (Pueblo) Indian culture began in southwest N America

c. 300 AD Maya civilization flourished

ASIA AND OCEANIA

475–221 'Warring states' period (China)
c. 400 Indian traders established links with Southeast Asia

322 Chandragupta Maurya founded Mauryan Empire at Magadha, India

c. 300 Dong Son culture flourished in Indochina
272–231 Empire of Ashoka in India

c. 250 Yayoi culture in Japan: use of bronze and iron (to c. 250 AD)
221 Shihuangdi, Qin emperor, united China (until 206)
206 Han dynasty reunited China
c. 200 Settlement of eastern Polynesia began

141–87 Han Empire expanded under Emperor Han Wudi
111 Northern Vietnam conquered by Chinese Empire

9 AD Wang Mang deposed Han dynasty in China
25 AD Restoration of Han dynasty

c. 57 AD Emergence of three kingdoms on Korean peninsula: Koguryŏ, Paekche, and Silla
c. 60 AD Rise of Kushan Empire (controlled the northern Indian subcontinent, Afghanistan, and Central Asia until the 3rd century AD)
c. 100 Early Cambodian (Khmer) state of Funan established
220 Collapse of Han dynasty; China split into three states

c. 250 Rise of Kofun culture in Japan

303 Non-Chinese nomadic peoples invaded China from the north; China

SUB-SAHARAN AFRICA

500 BC–200 AD Period of Nok culture in northern Nigeria; spread of ironworking through West Africa
500 BC–300 AD Nubian kingdom of Meroë established in The Sudan; ironworking knowledge from Egypt
c. 500 BC–c. 500 AD Bantu and other Iron-Age farmers spread east and south from western central Africa

c. 100 AD Expansion of kingdom of Aksum (Ethiopia) began

EUROPE AND THE MIDDLE EAST

313 Constantine I issued Edict of Milan endorsing Christianity

330 New capital of Roman Empire established at Constantinople
395 Roman Empire divided into eastern and western halves

406 Vandals invaded Gaul and Spain (409)
410 Visigoths sacked Rome
429–39 Vandals took North Africa
429 Angles, Saxons, and Jutes began conquest of Britain
433–53 Huns invaded central Europe

476 Fall of western Roman Empire
486 Merovingian kingdom founded by Franks in northern France
488–93 Ostrogoths conquered Italy

507 Visigoths defeated by Franks and migrated to Spain
527–65 Emperor Justinian the Great ruled eastern Roman (Byzantine) Empire and reconquered Sicily, Italy, N Africa, and southern Spain

568 Lombard conquest of north Italy
579 Sassanian Empire at its greatest extent

611 Persian armies captured Alexandria and Jerusalem
616 Mohammed began to expound Islam
628 Byzantine Emperor Heraclius defeated Persians
632 Death of Mohammed; Arab (Islamic) expansion began
636–50 Arabs conquered Syria, Palestine, Egypt, and N Africa
642 Fall of Sassanian Persia

661 Umayyad caliphate established as rulers of Islamic Empire
670s Bulgars established Bulgarian khanate in Balkans
711 Muslim invasion of Spain
732 Battle of Poitiers: Franks repelled Arab invasion from Spain
750 Abbasid caliphate established as rulers of Islamic Empire
751 Carolingian dynasty established in France
756 Abd ar-Rahman established Umayyad amirate in Spain

774 Charlemagne conquered N Italy
793 Viking raids on Britain began
800 Charlemagne crowned emperor in Rome; beginning of new Western (later Holy Roman) Empire
c. 842 Rise of Mameluke power within Abbasid caliphate began
843 Treaty of Verdun: Carolingian Empire divided into three kingdoms

862 Novgorod seized by Rurik the Viking, founding Kiev-Rus state
887 Break-up of Carolingian Empire
c. 890 Magyars began to raid Germany and France

THE AMERICAS

c. 600–800 Huari culture flourished in Peru
c. 600–900 Maya civilization reached its peak

c. 900 Toltec civilization flourished

ASIA AND OCEANIA

ruled by separate dynasties in north and south until 581
320 Chandra Gupta I founded Gupta Empire in northern India

c. 400 Imperial rule began in Japan
400–800 Furthest reaches of Polynesia (including New Zealand) were settled

c. 450 Huns from Central Asia invaded northwestern India, leading to fall of Gupta Empire

543–757 Chalukya dynasty dominated Deccan (central India)
540 Gupta dynasty ended
c. 550 Transmission of Chinese culture to Japan (via Korea) began
552 Buddhism introduced to Japan

589 China reunified by Sui dynasty
598 Cambodian (Khmer) state of Chenla superseded Funan
c. 600 Pallava dynasty reached height of its power (southern India)

c. 606–647 Buddhist empire of Harsha in northern India

618 Tang dynasty assumed power in China following collapse of Sui

c. 645 Centralized Chinese-style government established in Japan
668 Korea reunited under Silla as a vassal of China
710 Japanese court established at Nara
c. 711 Muslim Arabs conquered Sind (modern Pakistan)

c. 750 Sailendra dynasty flourished on Java
751 Battle of Talas River: Arabs defeated Chinese armies
755 An Lushan's rebellion in China
c. 755–975 Rashtrakutra kingdom in Deccan

794 Heian period began in Japan
c. 800 Jayavarman II established Khmer Empire (Cambodia); state of Srivijaya flourished on Sumatra
842 Tibetan Empire disintegrated

c. 850 Burmese kingdom of Pagan established
858 Rise of Fujiwara family in Japan

c. 880 Rise of Chola kingdom in southern India

907 Fall of Tang dynasty; Khitans

SUB-SAHARAN AFRICA

c. 320 Kingdom of Meroë declined

c. 350 King of Aksum converted to Christianity (origin of Ethiopian Orthodox Christian Church)

c. 500 Rise of ancient Ghana (west Africa) began

c. 800 Decline of kingdom of Aksum; trading centres established along east African coast dominated by Arabic-speaking merchants from Islamic World; Arabs established trans-Saharan trading links with West Africa

EUROPE AND THE MIDDLE EAST	THE AMERICAS	ASIA AND OCEANIA	SUB-SAHARAN AFRICA
911 Vikings allowed to settle in N France, creating duchy of Normandy	at Tula (Mexico); decline of Mayan culture	(Mongols) established Liao dynasty in northern China **918** Koryŏ dynasty founded in Korea	
936 Abbasid caliphs lost effective power to Mamelukes **955** Otto I of Germany defeated Magyars at Lechfeld **962** Otto I invaded Italy **963** Mieszko I founded Polish kingdom **969** Fatimid dynasty conquered Egypt **987** Accession of Capetians to French throne **c. 1000** Kingdom of Hungary established by Magyars	**c. 1000** Viking settlements in Greenland and North America (Vinland); rise of Chimú state in Peru	**960** Song dynasty reunited China **993–1070** Sri Lanka under Chola rule **c. 1000** Rise of Japanese Samurai **c. 1001–26** Mahmud of Ghazna conquered Central Asia **c. 1009** Ly dynasty established Buddhist realm in northern Vietnam	**c. 1000** Zenith of ancient Ghana; beginning of later Iron Age (eastern, central, and southern Africa); greater economic specialization (hunting, herding, and cultivation); mining and metalworking became more important; greater craftsmanship; development of regional and long-distance trade; emergence of empire of Great Zimbabwe
1016 Danes defeated English; Canute ruled England, Denmark, and Norway (to 1035) **1031** Caliphate of Córdoba collapsed in Spain		**1038** Tangut tribes formed state of Xi-Xia in northwest China **1044** Burmese conquered Mon state at Thaton, unifying Burma **c. 1050** Height of Chola power	**c. 1050–1200** East African trading links with Asia strengthened; increased Muslim immigration
1054 Schism between Eastern Greek and Western Christian churches **1055** Seljuk Turks took Baghdad **1056** Almoravides conquered North Africa and southern Spain **1066** Norman conquest of England **1071** Battle of Manzikert: Byzantine forces defeated by Seljuk Turks; Normans conquered southern Italy **1073** Gregory VII elected pope: conflict of Empire and papacy began **1085** Start of Christian *Reconquista* against Muslim Spain **1095–99** First Crusade: Jerusalem captured; crusader states founded **c. 1100** German eastward expansion; emergence of early city-states in northern Italy **c. 1135** Almohades became rulers in NW Africa and Muslim Spain **1152** Hohenstaufen dynasty established in Germany **1154** Henry II established Angevin Empire in England and France **1170** Saladin defeated Fatimids and conquered Egypt		**1126** Jin (Jurchen) overran northern China; Song rule restricted to south	**c. 1096** Ghana attacked by Almoravides, ending its effective power **c. 1150** Zagwe dynasty established in Ethiopia; initiated expansion southwards; great Christian revival
1187 Jerusalem recaptured by Muslims under Saladin		**c. 1180** Khmer Empire (Cambodia) reached greatest extent **1185** Minamoto warlords dominated Japan **c. 1186** Mohammed Ghuri attacked India from Afghanistan and seized Punjab **1192** Shogunate established at Kamakura (Japan)	
1204 Fourth Crusade: Crusaders captured Constantinople	**1200** Tula destroyed by invaders **c. 1200** Foundation of Inca dynasty		**c. 1200** Emergence of Hausa city-states (west Africa); Yoruba forest kingdom of Ife flourished
1212 Battle of Las Navas de Tolosa (Spain): Christians defeated Almohades **1215** Magna Carta: King John made concessions to English barons		**1206** Islamic sultanate of Delhi established (northern India) **1207** Mongols under Genghis Khan began conquest of Asia	
1237 Mongols invaded and conquered Russia (1239) **1241** Mongols invaded Poland, Hungary, and Bohemia **1242** Mongols defeated Seljuk Turks **1250** Collapse of imperial power in Germany and Italy; Mamelukes established power in Egypt		**1215** Beijing fell to Mongols **1218–23** Mongol campaigns in Central Asia **c. 1220** Emergence of first Thai kingdom at Sukhothai **1234** Mongols conquered Jin Empire	**c. 1235** Foundation of Empire of Mali (west Africa)
		1256 Mongols invaded Iran and sacked Baghdad (1258)	**c. 1250** Kilwa emerged as one of most powerful Swahili states on the east coast; Shona state of Great Zimbabwe flourished in southern

EUROPE AND THE MIDDLE EAST

1258 Baghdad sacked by Mongols; end of Abbasid caliphate
1260 Mamelukes defeated Mongols at Ayn Jalut; spread of Mameluke influence in Middle East and N Africa
1261 Byzantine Empire restored under Palaeologan dynasty
1266–82 Angevin rule in Sicily

c. 1300 Cultural Renaissance began in Italy; Ottoman Turks founded state in Anatolia and began expansion
1309 Papacy moved to Avignon

1337 Hundred Years' War between France and England began

1348 Black Death from Asia swept across Europe

1360 Peace of Brétigny ended first phase of Hundred Years' War

1381 Burgundy acquired Flanders; rise of Burgundy as major power
1386 Union of Poland and Lithuania
1389 Battle of Kosovo: Ottomans gained control of Balkans

1402 Battle of Ankara: Timur defeated Ottomans in Anatolia

1415 Battle of Agincourt: Henry V of England resumed attack on France and conquered Normandy (1417–19)

1451–81 Ottoman Empire expanded further into Balkans and eastern Anatolia
1453 Hundred Years' War ended: England lost all French possessions (except Calais); Ottoman Turks captured Constantinople: fall of Byzantine Empire

1478 Ivan III, first Russian tsar, subdued Novgorod and repudiated Mongol authority (1480)
1479 Union of Castile and Aragon
1492 Fall of Granada to Castile and Aragon ended Muslim rule in Spain; Jews expelled from Spain
1494 Italian Wars began: Franco-Hapsburg power struggle

1501 Shah Ismail founded Safavid dynasty in Persia

THE AMERICAS

1345 Migration of Aztecs in Mexico to new capital at Tenochtitlán

1428 Aztec imperial expansion began
1438 Major expansion of Inca Empire began

c. 1470 Incas conquered Chimú Empire

1492 Columbus reached West Indies; first Europeans since the Vikings landed in the New World
1494 Treaty of Tordesillas divided New World between Portugal and Spain
1497 Giovanni Caboto reached Newfoundland
1498 Columbus landed in mainland South America
1500 Cabral claimed Brazil for Portugal

ASIA AND OCEANIA

c. 1260 Vast Mongol Empire divided into four khanates

1271 Qubilai Khan founded Yuan dynasty in China
1274–81 Mongols unsuccessfully attempted to conquer Japan
1279 Mongols conquered Song China
1296 Thai kingdom of Chiang Mai established

1313–41 Özbeg ruled Mongol khanate in Russia (the Golden Horde)
1333 Fall of Kamakura shogunate: rival courts ruled N and S Japan
1335 Collapse of Mongol rule in Iran
1336 City and empire of Vijayanagar (southern India) founded
1338 Ashikaga shogunate established in Japan
1347–1489 Bahmani kingdom in Deccan
c. 1350 Chaghatai khanate divided
1350 Height of Majapahit Empire in Java; Thai kingdom of Ayutthaya emerged
1368 Mongol rule overthrown in China; Ming dynasty founded
1370 Tamerlane (Timur) became ruler of western Chaghatai khanate
1381 Tamerlane invaded Iran

1392 Yi dynasty established in Korea
1398 Tamerlane invaded India and sacked Delhi
1402 Tamerlane captured Ottoman sultan at Ankara
1405 Tamerlane died
1405–33 Chinese maritime expeditions to Southeast and southern Asia
1438 Golden Horde khanate divided into two
1444 Khmers abandoned Angkor to Thais; Khmer court to Phnom Penh
1451 Rise of Lodi kingdom in the Punjab

1460 Le dynasty established rule in northern Vietnam
1467–77 Onin Wars initiated century of warlord conflict in Japan
1471 Vietnamese southward expansion: Champa annexed

1498 Vasco da Gama reached southern India from Portugal

1502 Mengli Girai annexed Golden Horde

SUB-SAHARAN AFRICA

Africa; forest kingdom of Benin flourished in west Africa (to 19th century)

c. 1270 Solomonid dynasty succeeded in Ethiopia and continued southward expansion

c. 1300s Zenith of empire of Mali; foundation of kingdom of Kongo

c. 1400–1550 Wars fought between Christian and Muslim states for control of Ethiopia

c. 1450 Power of Mali began to be challenged by rising empire of Songhai; Great Zimbabwe abandoned

1468 Songhai gained control of great trading centre of Timbuktu
1470s Portuguese began trading from 'Gold Coast' (modern Ghana)

c. 1480 Maravi empire founded by Kalonga dynasty in central Africa

1494 First encounter by Portuguese with kingdom of Kongo

1498 Portuguese began to threaten Swahili trade in Indian Ocean
c. 1500 Kingdom of Bunyoro flourished in east Africa; Mutapa empire flourished in central/southern Africa; Luba and Lunda empires

EUROPE AND THE MIDDLE EAST

1517 Crisis of the Reformation initiated by Martin Luther; Ottomans conquered Mameluke Egypt
1519 Charles V, king of Spain, inherited vast Hapsburg Empire
1526 Battle of Mohacs: Ottoman Turks annexed Hungary

1533 Henry VIII of England broke with Roman Church; Ivan the Terrible became tsar of Russia
1541 John Calvin founded reformed (Protestant) church at Geneva
1545 Council of Trent initiated Counter-Reformation

1550s Expansion of Russian lands under Ivan IV
1559 Treaty of Cateau-Cambrésis ended Franco-Hapsburg conflict
1562–68 Wars of Religion in France

1568 Dutch Revolt against Spain began
1571 Battle of Lepanto: Turkish sea power in Mediterranean curtailed

1588 Spanish Armada defeated by English
1588–1629 Safavid Empire reached its height under Shah Abbas the Great

1598 Time of Troubles began in Russia; Edict of Nantes granted liberties to Huguenots in France
1600 Foundation of English and Dutch (1602) East India Companies

1609 Twelve Years' Truce declared between Dutch and Spanish
1613 Romanov dynasty established in Russia; Russian expansion resumed
1618 Outbreak of Thirty Years' War

1630 Sweden joined Thirty Years' War

1635 France joined Thirty Years' War against Hapsburgs
1640 Portugal seceded from Spain

1642–46 English Civil War

1648 Peace of Westphalia ended Thirty Years' War; Spain recognized Dutch independence
1649 Execution of Charles I of England; republic declared

THE AMERICAS

1519 Spanish conquest of Aztec Empire began

1532 Spanish conquest of Inca Empire began
1534–41 French exploration of Gulf of St Lawrence

1549 First colonial capital of Brazil founded at Salvador
1550s Sugar cultivation began in Brazil; first African slaves imported

1567 Foundation of Portuguese royal captaincy at Rio de Janeiro

1580s Unsuccessful attempts to found English colonies in N America

1600s British, French, and Dutch established colonies in the Caribbean
1605 First French settlement in N America (Nova Scotia)
1607 First enduring English settlement in N America (Virginia)
1608 Quebec founded by French
1609 Hudson River navigated by English

1619 First African slaves arrived in N American colonies

1620 English Puritans initiated European settlement of New England
1626 Dutch traders established New Amsterdam
1630 Portuguese Brazil divided into two colonies; Dutch seized part of northeast Brazil (to 1654)
1630s Great Puritan Migration from England to New England
1637 Pequot War between New England settlers and Amerindians

ASIA AND OCEANIA

1511 Portuguese seized Malacca for spice trade
1517 European traders and missionaries gained access to China

1526 Baber of Kabul established Mogul Empire
1531 Toungoo dynasty established rule in Burma

1540s First European traders and missionaries arrived in Japan; introduction of firearms

1556–1605 Mogul Empire expanded to include most of northern and central India under Akbar

1564 Spanish occupied the Philippines and established Manila (1571)

1573 Fall of Ashikaga dynasty in Japan; Oda Nobunaga chief warlord
1584–87 Thais liberated their kingdom from Burmese occupation

1592 Japan reunified under one rule by Toyotomi Hideyoshi
1592 and 1597 Korea repelled two Japanese invasions

1600 Battle of Sekigahara; Tokugawa Ieyasu defeated rivals and established Tokugawa shogunate (1603)

1611 Dutch landed in W Australia
1612 English East India Company granted trading privileges in India
1619 Dutch established Batavia (Jakarta) on Java: start of Dutch colonial empire in East Indies
1620 Vietnam divided into rival states

1630s Japan adopted policy of isolation from foreign influences; Edo (later Tokyo) flourished as Japan's cultural and artistic centre
1641 Dutch expelled Portuguese from Malacca
1642–43 Dutch expedition discovered Tasmania, New Zealand, and the Tonga and Fiji islands
1644 Manchu forces conquered Beijing; collapse of Ming dynasty; foundation of Qing dynasty

SUB-SAHARAN AFRICA

flourished in central Africa (to early 19th century)
1506 Afonso I, a Christian convert, seized throne of Kongo with Portuguese help

1530s European traders began exporting slaves from Africa to the Americas

c. 1570 Kongo began to decline

1591 Moroccans invaded Songhai, causing its final collapse

1650 Yoruba kingdom of Oyo flourished and expanded southwards (to 1750)

EUROPE AND THE MIDDLE EAST

1652–54 First Anglo-Dutch War
1656 Köprülü dynasty ruled Ottoman Empire (to 1683)
1658 Treaty of Roskilde: Swedish Empire at height
1659 Peace of the Pyrenees between France and Spain
1660 Restoration of English monarchy
1661 Absolute monarchy of Louis XIV began in France; beginning of French expansion
1667 Poland ceded Ukraine to Russia

1683 Turkish siege of Vienna repulsed
1685 Edict of Nantes revoked: mass emigration of Protestants from France
1688 'Glorious Revolution' in England; constitutional monarchy established
1689 War of the Grand Alliance (to 1697) against Louis XIV

1699 Treaty of Karlowitz: Hapsburgs recovered Hungary from Turks; start of Ottoman decline
1700 Great Northern War between Russia and Sweden (to 1721)
1701 War of the Spanish Succession began
1709 Battle of Poltava: Peter the Great of Russia defeated Swedes

1713 Treaty of Utrecht ended War of Spanish Succession

1736 Safavid dynasty deposed by Nadir Shah
1740 War of Austrian Succession (to 1748): Prussia annexed Silesia
c. 1750 Beginning of Industrial Revolution

1756 Seven Years' War began

1762–96 Reign of Catherine the Great of Russia: reforms in Russia and expansion against Ottoman Turks
1763 Treaty of Paris ended Seven Years' War and confirmed Prussia as a major power

1772 First partition of Poland (2nd and 3rd partitions 1793, 1795)

1783 Russia annexed the Crimea

THE AMERICAS

1663 English settled in Carolina
1664 Dutch New Amsterdam taken by British (and renamed New York)

1673 French exploration of Mississippi River
1675–76 King Philip's War against White settlers in New England
1681 Foundation of Pennsylvania by English Quakers
1682 Louisiana claimed by France

1689 Anglo-French rivalry and conflict in Europe spread to N American colonies (to 1763)

c. 1700 N American colonies began to expand westwards; migration from Europe increased; importation of African slaves increased rapidly

1711–15 Conflict between Amerindians and colonials in Carolina
1712 Carolina divided into two separate colonies (North and South)

1732 English settlement in Georgia established

1756–63 French and Indian War between Britain and France for control of N American colonies
1759 Britain captured Quebec and Montreal (1760) from French

1763 Treaty of Paris: Britain gained Canada and all French possessions east of the Mississippi; Pontiac's Rebellion: Amerindian tribes retaliated against White settlers
1765 British Stamp Act imposed unpopular taxation directly on N American colonies
1773 Boston Tea Party: N American colonials resisted British taxes
1774 Two Portuguese colonies of Brazil reunited under a viceroy
1775 American Revolution against British colonial rule began in N America
1776 N American colonies made Declaration of Independence
1780 Inca revolt challenged Spanish rule in Peru (to 1783)
1781 British forces surrendered to Washington at Yorktown, Virginia
1783 Treaty of Versailles: Britain

ASIA AND OCEANIA

1658–1707 Mogul Empire expanded into S India and reached its greatest extent under Aurangzeb

1690 English East India Company founded Calcutta
1696 Chinese conquered Outer Mongolia

1724–57 Disintegration of Mogul Empire

1740 Mons rebelled against Toungoo rule in Burma
1750s China subjugated Tibet, Kashgaria, and Tarim Basin
1752 Mons of Burma captured Ava; Konbaung dynasty established and began reunification of Burma
1757 Battle of Plassey: British gained Bengal and established rule in India

1769 Captain James Cook began exploration of Pacific for Britain: charted New Zealand and E coast of Australia and claimed them for Britain

1782 Chakri dynasty founded in Thailand; established capital at Bangkok

SUB-SAHARAN AFRICA

1652 Dutch established colony at the Cape of Good Hope

1665 Disintegration of Kongo began

1670s Kingdom of Asante established in west Africa

1690s Foundation of empire of Rozvi on Zimbabwe plateau

c. 1700 Kingdom of Dahomey flourished and expanded in west Africa

c. 1720–50 Kingdom of Asante expanded to cover most of modern Ghana
1720s Muslim theocracy of Futa Jalon established in Guinea

1770s Westward expansion by Boers led to conflict with Xhosa chiefdoms

EUROPE AND THE MIDDLE EAST

1789 French Revolution began; abolition of feudal system

1792 French Republic proclaimed; beginning of revolutionary wars
1793 Louis XVI executed; Reign of Terror began in France (to 1794)
1796 Qajar dynasty established capital at Tehran
1798 Napoleonic invasion of Egypt
1799 Napoleon became First Consul of France, later becoming Emperor (1804)

1805 Napoleon defeated Austria and (1806) Prussia; Britain defeated French and Spanish fleets at Trafalgar
1807–14 Peninsular War fought in Spain between Britain and France

1811 Mohammed Ali assumed control in Egypt
1812 Napoleon invaded Russia
1814–15 Congress of Vienna; Napoleonic Empire dismantled; Bourbon monarchy restored in France
1815 Napoleon defeated at Waterloo and exiled to St Helena
c. 1817 Liberal movement began in Russia

1820 Liberal revolts in Spain and Italy
1821 Greeks revolted against Turkish rule

1827 Turkish rule in Greece ended with defeat at Battle of Navarino

1830 'July Revolution' overthrew French Bourbon monarchy; Polish revolt against Russian rule; Belgium declared independence from Netherlands
c. 1830 Reforms and westernization began in Ottoman Empire
1834 Formation of German customs union (*Zollverein*)

1841 Mohammed Ali recognized as hereditary ruler of Egypt

1848 Revolutions throughout Europe; proclamation of Second Republic in France; attempt to unite Germany failed

THE AMERICAS

recognized independence of the Thirteen Colonies; Canada lost territory south of Great Lakes
1789 US Federal Constitution came into force; George Washington became first president of the USA
1791 Division of Canada into (French-speaking) Lower Canada and (English-speaking) Upper Canada

1803 Louisiana Purchase from France almost doubled the size of US territory

1807 Portuguese court established in Brazil following Napoleonic invasion of Portugal
1808 US Congress abolished African slave trade
1810 Revolts against Spanish rule in Colombia, Chile, and Mexico (to 1815)
1811 Paraguay gained independence from Spain
1812 War between Britain and US over maritime rights (to 1814)

1816 Argentina gained independence from Spain
1818 Chile gained independence from Spain
1819 Bolívar gained independence for Gran Colombia (Colombia, Venezuela, Ecuador, and Panama)
1820 Missouri Compromise on slavery in USA
1821 Mexico and Peru gained independence from Spain
1822 Brazil gained independence from Portugal
1824–37 Presidency of Andrew Jackson in USA: electoral reform

1825 Bolivia gained independence from Spain
1828 Uruguay gained independence from Spain
1830s *Caudillos* brought political stability to Venezuela, Argentina, and Chile

1837 Rebellions in Upper Canada led to Durham Report (1839)

1841 Canadian provinces reunited as one colony of British Empire
1846 Treaty of Oregon settled US-Canada boundary
1846–48 US-Mexican War: Mexico ceded New Mexico and California to USA
1848 Gold rush began in California: thousands migrated west; system of local self-rule introduced in Canada
1850s Slavery abolished in Venezuela, Argentina, Peru, and Colombia
1850 US compromise on slavery; Indian Wars fought on western plains (to 1890)

ASIA AND OCEANIA

1788 Le dynasty overthrown by peasant uprising in Vietnam; first British colony established in Australia

1790–1815 English East India Company became dominant power in Indian subcontinent

1796 British conquered Sri Lanka

1802 Nguyen dynasty reunited Vietnam

1818 Indian subcontinent divided into British-ruled and protected states
1819 British founded trading settlement at Singapore

1824 Anglo-Dutch Treaty divided areas of dominance in Southeast Asia; British began conquest of Burma
1825–30 Java war: Indonesians rebelled against Dutch

1839–42 First Opium War: Britain annexed Hong Kong; westerners given greater access to China via designated ports
1840 Treaty of Waitangi: New Zealand became a British colony

1845–49 Sikh Wars: British conquest of Punjab

1850 Taiping rebellion in China (to 1864) caused immense loss of life

SUB-SAHARAN AFRICA

1787 Foundation of Sierra Leone by freed African slaves from England

c. 1795 Muslim state of Tukulor founded

c. 1800 Height of Lunda kingdom of Kazembe in central Africa; centralized state of Buganda began to surpass power of Bunyoro in eastern Africa
1806 British seized Cape Colony from Dutch
1807 Britain abolished slave trade

1809 Muslim caliphate of Sokoto established (in west Africa) by Fulani peoples following war against Hausa rulers

1820s Creation of expanding Zulu Empire under Shaka

1822 Liberia founded by freed African slaves from the USA

1835 Boer colonists from Cape began 'Great Trek' to establish settlements in south African interior

1843 Britain annexed Boer colony of Natal

c. 1850 Expansion of Tukulor in west Africa began

EUROPE AND THE MIDDLE EAST	THE AMERICAS	ASIA AND OCEANIA	SUB-SAHARAN AFRICA
1852 Fall of French republic; Louis Napoleon (Napoleon III) became French emperor **1853** Crimean War (to 1856)	**1854** Kansas-Nebraska Act repealed Missouri Compromise; US Republican Party formed **1857–61** Religious conflict in Mexico	**1851** Nian rebellion in northern China (to 1868) **1854** US naval expedition forced Japan to open trade with US **1855** Muslim uprisings in western China (to 1873) **1856–60** Second Opium War; Anglo-French victory **1857–58** Indian Mutiny; Britain assumed direct control of India **1858** French intervention in Indochina began **1860s** Maori Wars in New Zealand against European settlement	
1859 Piedmont-Sardinia and France attacked Austria; Piedmont acquired Lombardy (1860) **1861** Emancipation of Russian serfs **1862** Bismarck became chancellor of Prussia	**1861** Southern Confederate States of America seceded from the US Union; American Civil War began **1863** Confederate invasion of Pennsylvania repulsed; emancipation of slaves in US proclaimed; Liberals established federal state in Colombia; France invaded Mexico and installed Maximilian of Hapsburg as emperor **1863–70** 'Federal Wars' in Venezuela		
1864 Prussia defeated Denmark and annexed Schleswig-Holstein (1866); Polish revolt against Russian rule suppressed **1866** Prussia defeated Austria in Austro-Prussian War	**1864–70** War of the Triple Alliance: Paraguay fought an alliance of Argentina, Uruguay, and Brazil **1865** Confederate surrender ended American Civil War **1865–90** Settlement of Great Plains by migrants from eastern USA: subjugation and removal of Plains Amerindians; railroads built		
1867 Establishment of North German confederation and of Austro-Hungarian Empire	**1867** France withdrew from Mexico: Maximilian executed; Radical Reconstruction in southern US initiated (to 1877); Dominion of Canada established **1869–70** Red River Rebellion in Canada against White settlers **1870** Canadian provinces of Manitoba and Northwest Territories created	**1867** End of Tokugawa shogunate; Meiji Restoration (1868) in Japan initiated period of westernization **1868** Japan annexed island of Hokkaido	**1869–71** Discovery of diamonds at Kimberley in South Africa led to British annexation of the territory
1870 Franco-Prussian war: Napoleon III overthrown; Paris besieged; Italy unified **1871** German Empire proclaimed; beginning of Third French Republic	**1871** British Columbia joined the Canadian confederation **1873** Prince Edward Island joined the Canadian confederation **1876** Rise of General Díaz to power in Mexico ended 60 years of strife **1879–80** War of the Desert in Argentina: extermination of Araucanian and Patagonian tribes	**1873** Aceh War against Dutch expansion in East Indies	
1878 Treaty of Berlin: Romania, Montenegro, and Serbia became independent of Ottoman Empire; Bulgaria autonomous	**1879–83** War of the Pacific: Chile fought alliance of Peru and Bolivia		**1879** The Zulu War between British and Zulus led to Zulu defeat **c. 1880** 'Scramble for Africa' began – European powers divided the continent between them (to 1900) **1880–81** First Anglo-Boer War in South Africa
1882 Triple alliance between Germany, Austria-Hungary, and Italy		**1885** Indian National Congress founded **1887** French established union of Indochinese territories	
1890 Dismissal of Bismarck: Kaiser William II began to direct German foreign policy **1890s** Turkish massacre of Armenians **1894** Franco-Russian alliance	**1888** Slavery abolished in Brazil **1889** Monarchy overthrown in Brazil, inaugurating period of stability under First Republic (to 1930)		
1898 Arms race between Britain and Germany began	**1898** Spanish-American War: USA acquired Cuba, Philippines, Puerto Rico, and Guam; US annexation of Hawaiian Islands **1900–17** Political Progressivism swept the USA; immigration from Europe to the USA peaked	**1894–95** Sino-Japanese War; Japan annexed Taiwan **1896** Philippines rebelled against Spanish rule; ceded to USA (1899) **1898** Hawaiian Islands annexed by USA **1900** Boxer uprising in China **1901** Australian colonies combined to form Commonwealth of Australia	**1896** Ethiopia resisted Italian invasion **1898** Fashoda crisis between Britain and France **1899** Second Anglo-Boer War (to 1902)

EUROPE AND THE MIDDLE EAST

1904 Anglo-French entente

1905 Revolution in Russia; Duma (parliament) established; Norway independent of Sweden
1907 Anglo-Russian entente
1908 Austria annexed Bosnia and Herzegovina

1912–13 Balkan Wars: Ottomans lost most of their European territory
1914 Outbreak of World War I: the assassination of Archduke Franz Ferdinand, heir to the throne of Austria-Hungary, sparked a European crisis that led to the German invasion of Belgium with the aim of defeating France. Britain then declared war on Germany. A full-scale war rapidly developed involving all the major European powers. The Central powers of Germany and Austria-Hungary faced the Allied powers of Britain, France, and Russia.
1917 Revolutions in Russia: Tsar abdicated, Bolsheviks (communists), led by Lenin, took power; 'Balfour Declaration' supported National Home in Palestine for Jews
1918 Armistice ended World War I; civil war in Russia (to 1921)
1919 Versailles Peace Treaty redrew map of Europe
1920 League of Nations established; Syria and Lebanon became French mandates; Palestine, Transjordan, and Iraq mandated to Britain

1921–22 Nationalist revolt, led by Mustafa Kemal, expelled Greeks from Turkey; last Ottoman sultan deposed; Turkish republic proclaimed (1923)
1921–27 Arabia united under Saudis
1922 Fascists led by Mussolini took power in Italy; USSR created
1924 Death of Lenin; Stalin emerged as Soviet leader (1929)

1926 Reza Khan ousted Qajars and became shah of Persia

1929 Collapse of Wall Street Stock Exchange; start of Great Depression
1930s Collectivization and purges in USSR; increased Jewish settlement in Palestine

1932 British mandate in Iraq withdrawn
1933 Hitler became chancellor of Germany; beginning of Nazi rule

THE AMERICAS

1902 Cuba gained independence
1903 Panama gained independence from Colombia; Panama Canal Zone acquired by the USA

1905 Canadian provinces of Alberta and Saskatchewan created

1910 Mexican Revolution began
1910–14 Conciliatory government in Colombia under Restrepo
1911 Díaz resigned and fled Mexico
1911–34 Series of US interventions in Central America and the Caribbean
1912 Electoral reform under Partido Autonomista Nacional in Argentina
1914–18 Peru, Ecuador, Uruguay, and Bolivia severed relations with Germany during World War I; Argentina, Mexico, Chile, Colombia, and Paraguay remained neutral
1914 Military coup in Peru; US troops occupied Veracruz (Mexico); Canada entered World War I against Germany; Panama Canal completed
1916–17 US expeditionary force sent into Mexico against revolutionary bandit Pancho Villa; Brazil declared war on Germany
1917 USA entered World War I against Germany

1920 US Senate refused to ratify Treaty of Versailles and US membership of League of Nations; start of US isolationism
1920s Socialist and communist doctrines began to affect South American politics
1921–24 US imposed restrictions on immigration

1922–27 Military uprisings in Brazil

1924–30 Persecution of the Church in Mexico
1925 Military coup in Ecuador

1929 Crash of New York stock exchange; start of Great Depression
1930 Global economic crisis led to fall of governments in Bolivia, Argentina, the Dominican Republic, Peru, Guatemala, and Brazil; liberal government came to power in Colombia
1930–45 Dictatorship of Getulio Vargas in Brazil
1930–61 Dictatorship of Rafael Trujillo in the Dominican Republic
1931 Canada became independent from Britain; political unrest in Chile, Ecuador, Panama, and El Salvador
1932–35 Chaco War between Bolivia and Paraguay
1933 Military coup in Cuba eventually brought Fulgencio Batista to power (1940)
1933–45 US presidency of Franklin

ASIA AND OCEANIA

c. 1904 Nationalist agitation in India
1904–05 Russo-Japanese War; Japanese success stimulated Asian nationalism

1907 New Zealand became a dominion within British Empire
1910 Japan annexed Korea

1911 Military rebellion in China overthrew Qing dynasty; warlords rose to power

1914 Australia and New Zealand joined Allies in World War I against Central Powers

1915 Battle of Gallipoli: thousands of Allied troops killed by Turkish forces

1919 Amritsar massacre boosted Indian nationalism
1920 Gandhi launched campaign of non-cooperation to defy British rule

1926 Nationalist forces under Jiang Jei Shi (Chiang Kai-shek) began reunification of China; nationalist–communist alliance began to fail
1927–28 Civil war between Chinese nationalists and communists
1930 Mahatma Gandhi led civil disobedience campaign against salt tax

1931 Japanese occupied Manchuria

SUB-SAHARAN AFRICA

1910 Union of South Africa created as an independent dominion

1914–18 South Africa fought on side of Allied powers in World War I; German Togo invaded by Allied forces; German Southwest Africa occupied by South Africa; German Kamerun (Cameroon) and East Africa occupied by Allied forces

1919 Former German colonies became League of Nations mandates

1930s Growth of Afrikaner (Boer) nationalism in South Africa

EUROPE AND THE MIDDLE EAST

1935 Nuremburg Laws deprived German Jews of rights
1936 Anglo-Egyptian alliance; British retained control of Suez Canal Zone; Arab-Israeli unrest in Palestine; German reoccupation of Rhineland; Spanish Civil War began (to 1939)
1938 Germany annexed Austria; Munich Agreement allowed Germany to annex part of Czechoslovakia
1939 German-Soviet non-aggression pact; Germany invaded Poland; Britain and France declared war on Germany; Nationalist victory in Spanish Civil War: dictatorship under General Franco established
1940 Germany invaded Norway, Denmark, Belgium, Netherlands, and France; Italian invasion of Greece repulsed; Battle of Britain
1941 Germany invaded Russia; the USA entered the war

1942 Battle of Stalingrad; Battle of El-Alamein; German defeat and retreat; Anglo-American landings in Morocco and Algeria; systematic extermination of Jews began
1943 Germans surrendered at Stalingrad; Italian defeat
1944 Allied liberation of Europe began; Syria gained independence
1945 Yalta Conference; defeat of Germany; suicide of Hitler; Potsdam Conference; Germany and Austria divided into Allied occupation zones
1946 Transjordan became independent

1947 Development of Cold War; Marshall Plan for economic reconstruction in Europe introduced

1948 Communist takeover in Czechoslovakia; Berlin Airlift began; proclamation of State of Israel led to first Arab-Israeli War
1949 Formation of NATO alliance and of COMECON; German Democratic Republic established; communist takeover in Hungary

1952 Egyptian monarchy overthrown
1953 Death of Stalin; Khrushchev came to power in USSR
1955 Warsaw Pact signed
1956 Hungarian revolt crushed by Russians; Suez War caused by Israeli invasion of Sinai
1957 Treaty of Rome created European Economic Community (EEC)
1958 Fifth Republic in France established under de Gaulle; Iraqi revolution overthrew monarchy
1961 Construction of Berlin Wall by East Germans

1964 Formation of Palestine Liberation Organization (PLO)

THE AMERICAS

D. Roosevelt: introduced New Deal policies to combat the Depression
1934–40 Presidency of Lázaro Cárdenas in Mexico

1941 US Lend-Lease Act authorized supply of arms and supplies to Allied powers in World War II; Japanese attacked Pearl Harbor, and USA entered war on Allied side
1942 US troops deployed to fronts in Europe, North Africa, and the Pacific

1945 US took lead in framing United Nations (UN) Charter

1946–55 Presidency of Juan Perón in Argentina

1947 Cold War between USA and USSR began

1949 Creation of the North Atlantic Treaty Organization (NATO) by USA; Newfoundland became a province of Canada
1950–53 US involvement in the Korean War; McCarthy's witchhunt against alleged communists in USA

1954–56 Mounting Black civil rights agitation under leadership of Martin Luther King

1957 Nationwide Black civil rights campaign launched in USA
1959 Fidel Castro seized power in Cuba; Marxist regime imposed

1961 Bay of Pigs fiasco: US attempt to overthrow Castro's regime in Cuba

1962 Cuban Missile Crisis
1963 US President John F. Kennedy assassinated
1964 US involvement in Vietnam War began

ASIA AND OCEANIA

1934–35 'Long March' of Chinese communists
1935 Government of India Act granted partial self-government
1936 Japan signed anti-Comintern pact with Germany
1937 Full-scale war between Japan and China began; militarization of Japanese society

1940 Japanese forces invaded Indochina

1941 Japan attacked US base at Pearl Harbor, bringing USA into World War II; Chinese nationalists and communists formed another alliance
1942 Japan invaded Southeast Asia; Battle of Midway; USA halted Japanese expansion

1945 USA dropped atomic bombs on Japanese cities of Hiroshima and Nagasaki, forcing Japan's surrender

1946 Creation of Philippine Republic
1946–49 Civil war in China
1946–54 Indochinese struggle against France
1947 India granted independence and partitioned to create East and West Pakistan; New Zealand gained independence
1948 Gandhi assassinated; Burma gained independence

1949 Communist victory in China; People's Republic of China proclaimed by Mao Zedong; Indonesia gained independence from Dutch
1950–53 Korean War began
1951 China invaded Tibet
1952 US occupation of Japan ended; birth of Japan's 'economic miracle'

1954 French defeated by Vietnamese; Vietnam divided into north and south

1958–60 'Great Leap Forward' in China

1962 Sino-Indian war
1963 Federation of Malaysia created

1964–75 South Vietnam at war with communist North Vietnam
1965 Indo-Pakistan war

SUB-SAHARAN AFRICA

1935 Italy invaded and annexed (1936) Ethiopia

1940–42 Most of French West Africa controlled by Vichy France; Cameroon and French Equatorial Africa held by the Free French (to 1945)
1941 Ethiopia liberated by Allies from Italian occupation

1942 French West Africa held by Free French

1948 Afrikaner National Party elected to power in South Africa; apartheid introduced

1956 Morocco, Tunisia, and The Sudan gained independence

1957 Gold Coast gained independence as Ghana

1960 Sharpeville massacre in S Africa
1960–61 Belgian Congo gained independence; Katanga attempted secession (to 1963)
1960s Most of French and British colonies in Africa gained independence

1965 Independence declared by

333

EUROPE AND THE MIDDLE EAST

1967 Military junta established in Greece; Arab-Israeli Six Day War

1968 Czech liberalization quelled by Russian invasion; student unrest in western Europe and USA
1969 Outbreak of violence in Northern Ireland; coup overthrew monarchy in Libya
1970 Riots in Poland

1973 Arab-Israeli Yom Kippur War; international oil crisis; Britain, Ireland, and Denmark joined EEC

1974 Turkish invasion of Cyprus; end of dictatorship in Portugal
1975 Death of Franco; dictatorship in Spain ended; civil war in Lebanon

1977 Egypt–Israeli peace talks

1979 Leadership of Margaret Thatcher in UK (to 1990); fall of shah of Iran: Islamic Republic established under Ayatollah Khomeini; Camp David Agreements between Egypt and Israel
1980 Formation of Solidarity in Poland; Iran–Iraq War began (to 1988)
1981 Greece joined EC (formerly EEC); martial law imposed in Poland and Solidarity banned
1982 Israel invaded Lebanon

1985 M. Gorbachev became leader of USSR (to 1991) and began reforms
1986 Spain and Portugal joined EC

1988 Palestinian uprisings began in Israeli-occupied territories
1989 Democratic elections held in USSR: Boris Yeltsin elected President of Russia; collapse of communism in eastern Europe and establishment of multi-party democracies
1990 Unification of Germany; Iraq invaded Kuwait
1990–91 Secession of Baltic republics from USSR; disintegration of Soviet Union
1991 Gulf War: UN coalition forces led by USA defeated Iraq and liberated Kuwait; Middle East peace talks began
1991–92 Disintegration of Yugoslavia following outbreak of civil war
1992 Czech Republic and Slovakia became separate states; Treaty of Maastricht on European union signed
1993 War in former Yugoslavia escalated; Israeli-Palestinian peace accord signed
1994 Russian forces attempted to suppress secession of Chechnya; cease-fire in Northern Ireland

THE AMERICAS

1965–67 Black discontent erupted in major urban riots in USA
1967 Capture and execution of Argentine revolutionary guerilla leader, Che Guevara
1968–70 Public opposition to US involvement in Vietnam led to intensified antiwar agitation
1969 USA landed first man on moon

1972 USA agreed to unilateral withdrawal from Vietnam
1973 Chilean army overthrew Marxist-inspired government of Salvadore Allende
1973–74 Watergate affair led to resignation of President Nixon

1976 Separatist Parti Québecois won Quebec's provincial election

1979 Overthrow of Antonio Somoza by Sandinistas in Nicaragua led to civil war

1980s Multiparty democracies established in most of Latin America
1981–89 Right-wing Republican government under Ronald Reagan

1982 Argentina and Britain went to war over Falkland (Malvinas) Islands
1983 US-led forces invaded Grenada

1989–90 US intervention in Panama: fall of Manuel Noriega
1989–91 Collapse of communism in Europe signalled end of Cold War

1990 Sandinista rule ended with democratic election in Nicaragua

1991 USA and USSR agreed Strategic Arms Reduction Treaty

1992 Canadian national referendum rejected greater autonomy for Quebec; civil war in El Salvador ended
1993 Democrat Bill Clinton became US president

1994 US forces occupied Haiti under UN auspices to ensure transfer of power to civilian government; Chiapas rebellion in Mexico

ASIA AND OCEANIA

1966–67 Cultural Revolution in China
1967 Association of Southeast Asian Nations founded

1970 Fiji gained independence
1971 East Pakistan gained independence as Bangladesh; Pacific nations set up South Pacific Forum
1972 Sri Lanka declared itself a republic

1975 Communists took over South Vietnam, Laos, and Cambodia; Khmer Rouge government, under Pol Pot, took power and began purges
1976 Death of Mao Zedong; political reform and modernization under Deng Xiaoping began
1977 Military coup ended democratic rule in Pakistan
1979 Vietnam invaded Cambodia, expelling Khmer Rouge government

1981 Zia Rahman, president of Bangladesh, killed in army mutiny

1984 Indira Gandhi, prime minister of India, assassinated
1986 Fall of Ferdinand Marcos in the Philippines; Corazon Aquino elected president; Federated States of Micronesia gained independence
1987 Two military coups in Fiji
1988 Benazir Bhutto elected to rule Pakistan (to 1990)
1989 Student prodemocracy demonstration crushed in Beijing's Tiananmen Square

1991 Rajiv Gandhi, prime minister of India, assassinated; Mrs Zia elected president of Bangladesh

1993 Benazir Bhutto re-elected as prime minister of Pakistan; Aboriginal land claims recognized in Australia

SUB-SAHARAN AFRICA

White settlers in Rhodesia: outbreak of guerilla war
1967–70 Civil war fought in Nigeria following secession of Biafra

1974–75 Portugal withdrew from its colonies; Libyan intervention in Chad

1977 Suppression of anti-apartheid activity in South Africa

1980 Rhodesia gained independence as Zimbabwe

1984–85 Famine in Ethiopia and The Sudan

1989–90 Namibia granted free elections and independence by South Africa

1990 Reforms to dismantle apartheid in South Africa began; release of Nelson Mandela

Early 1990s Civil conflict in Liberia, Rwanda, Somalia, and Sierra Leone; famine in The Sudan (1992)

1993 Eritrea gained independence from Ethiopia

1994 First universal suffrage general election in South Africa: African National Congress (ANC) under Nelson Mandela gained power; civil war in Mozambique and Angola ended

EUROPE AND THE MIDDLE EAST

1995 Israeli prime minister, Itzhak Rabin, assassinated by Jewish extremist; Austria, Finland, and Sweden joined the EU; civil war in Bosnia ended
1996 War in Chechenya ended; Yeltsin re-elected Russian president; Binyamin Netanyahu elected prime minister of Israel
1997 Middle East peace process stalled over Jewish settlements issue; Labour government elected in UK; socialist government elected in France; Seyyed Mohammed Khatami elected president of Iran
1998 Yeltsin dismisses entire Russian government in March and again in August; Northern Irish peace terms agreed; unrest among ethnic Albanians in Kosovo, Serbia

THE AMERICAS

1995 Quebec opted to remain part of Canada

1996 Outbreak of rebellion in Guerrero, Mexico; Clinton re-elected president of USA; civil war in Guatemala ended

1998 USA responds to terrorist attacks on two US embassies by bombing targets in Afghanistan and Sudan

ASIA AND OCEANIA

1995 France resumed nuclear testing in the Pacific
1995–96 Taliban militia take over Afghanistan
1995–97 Famine in North Korea
1996 Benazir Bhutto dismissed as prime minister of Pakistan

1997 Death of Chinese leader, Deng Xiaoping; Jiang Zemin succeeded him; Hong Kong reverted from British to Chinese rule; Pol Pot captured and imprisoned by a Khmer Rouge faction in Cambodia; economic crisis as south Asian currencies collapse
1998 India and Pakistan carry out nuclear weapons test; riots in Indonesia lead to Suharto's resignation

SUB-SAHARAN AFRICA

1995 Nigeria suspended from the Commonwealth

1996 Civil war erupted in Zaïre

1997 Military coup in Sierra Leone; Mobutu regime ousted in Zaïre and country renamed Democratic Republic of Congo

1998 Civilian government restored in Sierra Leone; Sudan faces famine, is accused of harbouring terrorists, and is bombed by the USA

Index

Photograph Acknowledgements

All illustrations reproduced in this encyclopedia are protected by copyright. The publishers gratefully acknowledge permission to reproduce illustrations supplied by the bodies listed below.

Adrian Bentley, 162; Archiv für Kunst und Geschichte, 26 (bottom left), 45 (top), 84 (top), 103, 273; Archives de la Indias, Seville/MSI, 196; Ashmolean Museum, Oxford, 18, 26 (bottom right); Biblioteca Medicea Laurenziana, 53; Biblioteca Medicea Laurenziana/MSI, 195; Bridgeman Art Library, London, 30, 31, 33 (bottom right), 43 (bottom), 70, 72, 85 (top), 93, 96 (both), 97, 99 (right), 101 (right), 105, 106 (both), 107 (both), 109, 301; British Library, 2, 256, 268; British Museum, London, 37 (top), 160 (top); British Museum, London/MSI, 48; Cambridge University Collection of Air Photographs, 8; Comstock, Inc., 11 (right); Edinburgh University, 254 (bottom); E T Archive, 22 (bottom), 28, 32 (top), 37 (bottom), 60 (bottom), 61 (bottom), 62 (centre), 68, 78, 149 (both), 157, 158, 181, 219 (top left), 240, 244 (bottom), 247 (top), 248 (top), 271; Fitzroy Collection/MSI, 213; Werner Forman Archive, ix, 20, 22 (top), 23, 59, 145, 151, 189 (both), 190, 191 (top), 193 (bottom), 225 (bottom), 227, 239, 241, 243, 277, 295 (bottom); Sonia Halliday Photographs, 33 (bottom left), 61 (top), 62 (top), 66 (both), 73, 74, 142, 150, 153, 155, 156 (both), 254 (top); Hirmer Fotoarchiv, 14; Michael Holford, 25, 36 (bottom), 60 (top), 84 (bottom); Hulton Deutsch, 3, 76, 87, 89, 91, 102, 111 (bottom), 113, 116, 121 (bottom), 123, 124 (left), 129, 135, 159 (both), 161 (bottom), 163 (top), 168 (top), 174, 200, 204, 206, 210, 211, 219 (top right), 233, 234, 235 (top), 248 (bottom), 251 (both), 269, 272, 274, 283, 289, 291, 298, 304 (both), 312, 317 (top); Hungarian Academy of Sciences, Budapest/MSI, 152; Hutchison Library, 33 (top), 49 (top), 168, 186, 208, 258, 286 (bottom), 297, 317 (bottom), 319, 320; Imperial War Museum, London, 126; Krokodil Magazine/MSI, 314; Laurie Platt Winfrey, Inc., 242; Library of Congress/MSI, 175; Macdonald/MSI, 203, 207; Magnum/Abbas, 167; Magnum/Bruno Barbey, 24, 148, 264; Magnum/G. Beutter, 308; Magnum/Stuart Franklin, 193 (top), 253 (top); Magnum/Burt Glinn, 163 (bottom); Magnum/Hiroji Kubota, 252; Magnum/Costa Manos, 33 (top right); Magnum/Inge Morath, 26 (top); Magnum/Raghu Rai, 275; Magnum/Marc Riboud, 147; The Mansell Collection, 56 (left), 171; Mary Evans Picture Library, 57, 117 (bottom), 118, 168 (bottom), 300, 303 (top); MSI, 82, 100, 195 (bottom), 197, 223, 267; Museo del Prado, Madrid, 92 (bottom); Musée Cantonal des Beaux Arts, Lausanne, 90; National Gallery, London, 83; National Gallery of Canada, viii, 173; National Maritime Museum, Greenwich, 92 (top); National Museum Zimbabwe, 10 (bottom right); National Palace Museum, Taiwan, 225 (top), 226 (top), 228, 230 (bottom); PA News, 238; Panos Pictures, 10 (top, centre), 11 (left), 307 (bottom); Range Pictures, 121 (top), 137, 140 (bottom), 179, 180, 232 (both), 235 (bottom), 286 (top), 303 (bottom), 306, 309, 313; The Royal Collection, Her Majesty Queen Elizabeth II, 117 (top); Rex Features, 49 (bottom left), 141, 160 (bottom), 165 (both), 166 (both), 167 (top), 215, 292, 310, 321; Rex Features/Alfred, 139; Rex Features/Bocke, 140 (top); Rex Features/Paul Brown, 5; Rex Features/Gilles Caron, 138 (top); Rex Features/De Mulder, 27; Rex Features/Fotolandia/Prisma, 49 (bottom right); Rex Features/A. Gasson, 258; Rex Features/Bernard Gerard, 168 (centre); Rex Features/Images, 177; Rex Features/Laski, 138; Rex Features/Mayes/The Times, 307 (top); Rex Features/McNamee, 212; Rex Features/Tim Page, 285; Rex Features/Pena, 287; Rex Features/SIPA, 124 (right), 213 (bottom); Rex Features/SIPA/Hioglu, 237; Rex Features/Jacques Witt, 141; Robert Harding Picture Library, 17 (bottom), 34, 226 (top); South African Museum, Cape Town, 10 (bottom left, bottom centre); South American Pictures/Tony Morrison, 199, 205, 209, 214, 318; Scala/MSI, 4, 39; Scala, 42, 43 (top), 54, 56 (right), 71, 261; Science and Society Picture Library, 110, 111 (top), 112; Science Photo Library/US Dept of Defense, 316; Graham Speake, 65; Richard Tames, 148 (bottom), 244 (top), 246, 247 (bottom), 249, 253 (bottom); Telegraph Colour Library, 1, 19, 169, 217, 293, 311; Victoria and Albert Museum, London/MSI, 65; Zefa Pictures, vi, 7, 9, 16, 32 (bottom), 36 (top), 40, 44, 47, 50, 64, 81, 101 (left), 154, 161 (top), 202, 216, 121, 222, 230 (top), 260, 262, 278, 295 (top), 322.

Contributors

Professor Edward Acton; Richard Brickstock; Dr Peter Campbell; Paul Collins; Professor Tim Cornell; Dr Michael Czwarno; Keith Faulks; Dr Timothy Harper; Professor George Holmes; David Iguaz; Professor Maldwyn A. Jones; Richard Jones; Dr Hugh Kennedy; Dr Ronald Kowalski; Professor Arthur Marwick; Dr Martin McCauley; Angus McGeoch; Dr Anthony McFarlane; Dr David Morgan; Dr Andrew Pettegree; Dr John Pimlott; Eduardo Posada-Carbo; Dr Martin Rady; Sarah Roberts; Dr Jane Samson; Dr Kevin Shillington; Dr Graham Speake; Dr James Steele; Belinda Syme; Dr Richard Tames; Dr Guy Thomson; Dr Gary Tiedemann; Dr Peter Wakelin; Dr Edmund Wright

MANAGING EDITORS: John Daintith PhD, Elizabeth Martin MA
EDITORIAL ASSISTANTS: Jonathan Law, Fran Alexander, Giles Wilkes
DESIGN: Bob Gordon, Shelagh Ormiston
ARTWORK DIRECTION: Lynn Williams
ILLUSTRATORS: Helène Burrow, David Woodroff, Eugene Fleury, Evi Antoniou, Simon Tegg, Richard Tibbitts, Karen Hiscock, Kevin Maddison
COMPUTER GRAPHICS: Aitch Em Ltd, Hardlines Ltd, Micromap Ltd
PICTURE RESEARCH: Diana Phillips, Adrian Bentley, Linda Wells
PRODUCTION: Ann Furtado, Anne Stibbs
COMPUTERIZATION: Edmund Wright, Anne Owen

THE LEARNING COMPANION

Volume 6

P

People/Society

Originally published in 1996 by Larousse

©1998 Larousse-Bordas
21 rue du Montparnasse
Paris 75006

First English Edition
©1999 by The Southwestern Company
P O Box 305140
Nashville, TN 37230

Second English Edition
©2000 by The Southwestern Company

Conception, direction and planning
Anne Tavard, François Demay

Associate publisher, London: Nicholas Bevan

Prepared and compiled for Larousse by
Market House Books Ltd, Aylesbury, England

General Editor: Dr Alan Isaacs

Volume Editor: Mark Salad

Page 396 constitutes an extension of this copyright page

All rights reserved under International and Pan-American
Copyright convention
No part of this publication may be reproduced, stored in a retrieval
system or transmitted in any form or by any means, electronic,
mechanical, photocopying, recording or otherwise, without prior
permission of the copyright holders.

ISBN 0-87197-477-0

Printed in the United States of America

Preface

THE LEARNING COMPANION, first published in 1999, is a completely new three-book (six-volume) reference for the family. It is published by Southwestern through agreement with Larousse, one of the largest and most respected publishing houses in the world, which created the majority of the content. Its contents have been carefully constructed around a universal core of knowledge that Larousse is able to identify after more than a century of experience in educational publishing.

The aim of THE LEARNING COMPANION is to help students make better grades. It makes accessible to family readership definitive information on the widest possible range of subjects. It is designed for students ranging from approximately age eleven through adult. The scope of THE LEARNING COMPANION is divided into six major topic areas, called volumes, with two volumes printed in each book. The content of each area is organized in chapters that clearly identify, define, and explain every subject. Within each chapter extensive use is made of colour illustrations and page design to represent the clearest possible explanations and examples.

Book 1

Vol. 1

W
The World

CLIMATES, PEOPLES, AND LANGUAGES
Climates and Vegetation, Peoples, and Languages

CONTINENTS, REGIONS, AND COUNTRIES
Europe, Asia, Africa, The Americas, Australia and Oceania, The Polar Regions, Statistics, Atlas

EARTH SCIENCES AND ASTRONOMY
Geology, Mineralogy, Hydrology, Oceanography, Meteorology, Observation, The Universe, Stars, Solar System, Space Exploration

Vol. 2

S
General Science

MATHEMATICS
Numbers, Arithmetic, Algebra, Geometry, Calculus, Sequences and Series, Probability and Statistics

PHYSICS
Mechanics, Heat, Thermodynamics, Optics, Acoustics, Electricity, Electro-magnetism, Relativity, Quantum Theory

CHEMISTRY
Equilibrium, Acids and Bases, Oxidation, Kinetics, Inorganic and Organic Compounds

APPLIED SCIENCE
Technology, Computers

Book 2

Vol. 3

B
Biological Science

THE LIVING WORLD
Cell Biology, Genetics, Biochemistry, Animal Anatomy, Plant Anatomy

THE CREATIONIST PERSPECTIVE
Two Models of Origin, Entropy

THE HUMAN FAMILY
Child and Adult Development, Marriage and Family

AGRICULTURE
Crop Plants, Farm Animals, Fish Farming, Forestry

BIOTECHNOLOGY
Genetic Engineering

Vol. 4

A
The Arts

THE VISUAL ARTS
European Tradition, The Americas, 20th-Century Western Art, Visual Arts Worldwide

MUSIC
Europe and the Americas, 20th-Century Western Music, Music Worldwide

THE PERFORMING ARTS
Western Theatre, Dance of Europe and the Americas, Theatre and Dance Worldwide, Cinema

THE LITERARY ARTS
Europe and the Americas, 20th-Century Western Literature, Literary Arts Worldwide

Book 3

Vol. 5

H
World History

EUROPE AND THE MIDDLE EAST
Early Civilizations, Medieval Europe, Early Modern Europe, The Industrial Age, Islamic World

THE AMERICAS
North America, Latin America

ASIA AND OCEANIA
China, Japan, The Mongol Empires, Indian Subcontinent, Southeast Asia, Oceania

SUB-SAHARAN AFRICA

THE WORLD IN THE 20TH CENTURY

CHRONOLOGY OF WORLD HISTORY

Vol. 6

P
People/Society

SOCIAL IDEAS
Social Sciences, Linguistics, Anthropology, Psychology, Philosophy, Metaphysics, Epistemology, Ethics, Religion, Mythology

SOCIAL ORGANIZATION
Politics and Government, Electoral Systems, Political Parties, Law, Legal Systems, Criminal and Civil Law, Economics, Business and Finance, Marketing, International Trade, Finance, and Investment, Communications and Media

What You Find in People/Society

PEOPLE/SOCIETY is classified into two **supersections**:
• Social Ideas
• Social Organization
The first supersection covers the ideas and beliefs that have shaped human society.
The second supersection covers the institutions that characterize human society.
The supersections are divided into a total of 8 **sections**, which are split down further into 52 **chapters,** each of which contains numerous **subheadings**. Special self-contained **feature pages** follow some chapters.

REFERENCE TO SUPERSECTION

SECTION TITLE
Each supersection in HUMAN SOCIETY *is subdivided into sections. Each section title is followed by the first chapter in the section.*

CHAPTER TITLE
Each chapter explores an aspect of the subject area covered by the section title.

CHAPTER SUMMARY
Chapter subheadings are listed in italic type beneath the chapter heading as a quick guide to the content.

SEE ALSO
The reader is referred to related chapters in HUMAN SOCIETY *and other volumes of the encyclopedia for additional reading.*

DEFINITION BOX
A blue tinted box between rules contains a formal definition of a term shown in **bold upright type** *in the main text.*

Social Organization

POLITICS AND GOVERNMENT

Introduction

Ancient Greece • Medieval political thought • The Renaissance • The sovereign state and the social contract • Revolutions • Modern political ideologies

=SEE ALSO=
This section:
• Democracy and Electoral Systems
• How Countries are Governed
• International Politics
Early Civilizations of the Mediterranean (vol. 5):
• Greece and the Hellenistic World

Politics is a universal phenomenon, the root of which may be said to lie in the basic undeniable fact of human diversity, and the disagreements that arise from it. Human beings adopt a variety of strategies, both constructive and destructive, for dealing with disputes and conflicts. And, indeed, such features as discussion, campaigning, compromise, rebellion, and war are all integral to political life. However, there is one method of reacting to potential chaos that may be regarded as the true defining characteristic of politics, namely its imposition of rules, procedures, and laws by means of a supreme authority, or **government**. The order that government sustains ultimately depends on force, but some degree of consent and acceptance must nevertheless always be present, and this forms the principal element in free governmental systems. Modern governments have developed elaborate legal and constitutional systems alongside their armed forces, and in most countries in the 20th century, extensive provision is made for educational and social services.

All governments now operate within institutional structures known as **states**. The origins of states lie in the emergence of rulers or chiefs as customary authorities in villages or tribes. These forms of authority became more settled and organized in larger social units and were usually united, or at least loosely linked with religious and military institutions. These larger social units have varied in size from highly civilized cities to empires. History has shown that many state structures have disappeared or changed beyond recognition: the great majority of states existing in the modern world are creations of the past 200 years, many of them dating only from the turn of the 20th century.

The diverse conceptions of politics that have existed throughout history can be glimpsed by a brief chronological survey of different philosophies.

state A term used since the Renaissance to describe a self-governing group of people. The chief characteristics of a state are that it forms a territorial unit, and that it exercises sovereign power.

The Death of Socrates
This painting, by the French artist Charles-Alphonse Dufresnoy (1611–68), shows the Greek philosopher drinking the poison hemlock.

160

RUNNING HEAD
Running heads at the top of each page indicate the section and chapter.

The Ramayana
The Ramayana is an epic that illustrates ideals, such as loyalty and honour, as guides in all arenas of life. It tells the story of Rama, who, because of a promise made by his father to his stepmother, willingly goes into exile, followed by his wife Sita and his brother. While in the forest, Sita is abducted by the ten-headed demon king Ravana and held captive in his palace in Sri Lanka. Rama, with the help of an army of monkey-generals, defeats Ravana and rescues Sita, enabling the couple to return to their kingdom, Ayothya.

set transcendent at the same time. The term *Trimurti* refers to three different but complementary aspects of Brahman: as creator (**Brahma**), preserver (**Vishnu**), and destroyer of evil (**Shiva**). Although Brahma is the creator, his role in worship is less significant. Vishnu is the preserver of the universe and the world. He manifests himself on earth in various forms (animal, semihuman, and fully human) whenever peace and harmony are threatened. These manifestations are known as *avatars*, (from Sanskrit *avatara*, 'descent') and the tenth avatar of Vishnu is yet to come.

Krishna, the eighth avatar of Vishnu, is the most complete manifestation of Vishnu. He appears in many forms, including a divine child and a young cowherd playing the flute. The image of Krishna as the beloved is a central focus of devotion in the bhakti tradition.

Shiva, the third member of the Trimurti, has a complex nature, combining both male and female elements. As Lord of the Dance (**Nataraja**), Shiva symbolizes the cosmic energy that flows through the universe and the world.

There are other important deities, such as the elephant-headed Ganesha (remover of obstacles), and Hanuman, the monkey-god and devotee of the god Rama. There are also many village deities, known as *gramadevatas*.

The feminine dimension of the Divine is referred to as *Shakti*, meaning 'power' or 'energy'. The many goddesses of Hinduism are manifestations of this power. Saraswati, the consort of Brahma, is the goddess of wisdom and the arts. She is usually shown seated on a lotus flower, playing a stringed instrument and holding sacred texts. Lakshmi, the consort of Vishnu, is the goddess of wealth and prosperity and is pictured seated or standing on a lotus, dropping gold coins. Parvati (also known as Durga and Kali) appears as gracious

KEY TERM
Important terms relating to the topic under discussion are highlighted in **bold italic type**.

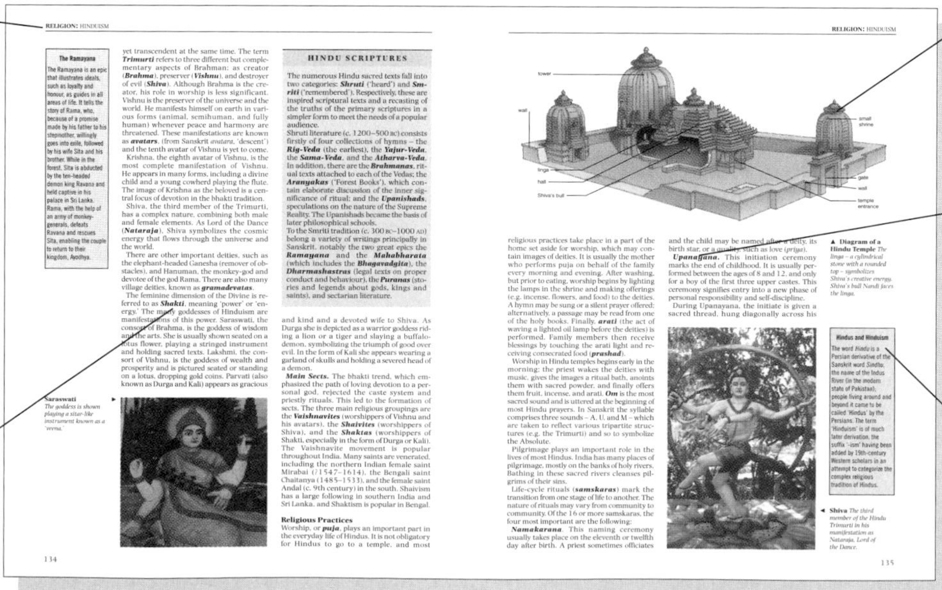

Saraswati
The goddess is shown playing a sitar-like instrument known as a 'veena.'

HINDU SCRIPTURES
The numerous Hindu sacred texts fall into two categories: *Shruti* ('heard') and *Smriti* ('remembered'). Respectively, these are inspired scriptural texts and a recasting of the truths of the primary scriptures in a simpler form to meet the needs of a popular audience.

Shruti literature (c. 1200–500 BC) consists firstly of four collections of hymns – the *Rig-Veda* (the earliest), the *Yajur-Veda*, the *Sama-Veda*, and the *Atharva-Veda*. In addition, there are the *Brahmanas*, ritual texts attached to each of the Vedas; the *Aranyakas* ('Forest Books'), which contain elaborate discussion of the inner significance of ritual; and the *Upanishads*, speculations on the nature of the Supreme Reality. The Upanishads became the basis of later philosophical schools.

To the Smriti tradition (c. 300 BC–1000 AD) belong a variety of writings principally in Sanskrit, notably the two great epics the *Ramayana* and the *Mahabharata* (which includes the *Bhagavadgita*), the *Dharmashastras* (legal texts on proper conduct and behaviour), the *Puranas* (stories and legends about gods, kings and saints), and sectarian literature.

and kind and a devoted wife to Shiva. As Durga she is depicted as a warrior goddess riding a lion or a tiger and slaying a buffalo-demon, symbolizing the triumph of good over evil. In the form of Kali she appears wearing a garland of skulls and holding a severed head of a demon.

Main Sects. The bhakti trend, which emphasized the path of loving devotion to a personal god, rejected the caste system and priestly rituals. This led to the formation of sects. The three main religious groupings are the *Vaishnavites* (worshippers of Vishnu and his avatars), the *Shaivites* (worshippers of Shiva), and the *Shaktas* (worshippers of Shakti, especially in the form of Durga or Kali). The Vaishnavite movement is popular throughout India. Many saints are venerated, including the northern Indian female saint Mirabai (?1547–1614), the Bengali saint Chaitanya (1485–1533), and the female saint Andal (c. 9th century) in the south. Shaivism has a large following in southern India and Sri Lanka, and Shaktism is popular in Bengal.

Religious Practices
Worship, or *puja*, plays an important part in the everyday life of Hindus. It is not obligatory for Hindus to go to a temple; and most

religious practices take place in a part of the home set aside for worship, which may contain images of deities. It is usually the mother who performs puja on behalf of the family every morning and evening. After washing, but prior to eating, worship begins by lighting the lamps in the shrine and making offerings (e.g. incense, flowers, and food) to the deities. A hymn may be sung or a silent prayer offered; alternatively, a passage may be read from one of the holy books. Finally, *arati* (the act of waving a lighted oil lamp before the deities) is performed. Family members then receive blessings by touching the arati light and receiving consecrated food (*prashad*).

Worship in Hindu temples begins early in the morning: the priest wakes the deities with music; displays the images a ritual bath, anoints them with sacred powder, and finally offers them fruit, incense, and arati. *Om* is the most sacred sound and is uttered at the beginning of most Hindu prayers. In Sanskrit the syllable comprises three sounds – A, U, and M – which are taken to reflect various tripartite structures (e.g. the Trimurti) and so to symbolize the Absolute.

Pilgrimage plays an important role in the lives of most Hindus. India has many places of pilgrimage, mostly on the banks of holy rivers. Bathing in these sacred rivers cleanses pilgrims of their sins.

Life-cycle rituals (*samskaras*) mark the transition from one stage of life to another. The most important are the following:

Namakarana. This naming ceremony usually takes place on the eleventh or twelfth day after birth. A priest sometimes officiates

and the child may be named after a deity, its birth star, or a quality such as love (*priya*).

Upanayana. This initiation ceremony marks the end of childhood. It is usually performed between the ages of 8 and 12, and only for a boy of the first three upper castes. This ceremony signifies entry into a new phase of personal responsibility and self-discipline. During Upanayana, the initiate is given a sacred thread, hung diagonally across his

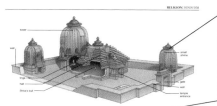

▲ **Diagram of a Hindu Temple** *The linga – a cylindrical stone with a rounded top – symbolizes Shiva's creative energy. Shiva's bull Nandi faces the linga.*

ARTWORK
Clearly labelled illustrations bring detailed aspects of the subject to life.

SUBSIDIARY HEADING
The text under some subheadings is further subdivided.

Hindus and Hinduism
The word Hindu is a Persian derivative of the Sanskrit word Sindhu, the name of the Indus River (in the modern state of Pakistan): people living around and beyond it came to be called 'Hindus' by the Persians. The term 'Hinduism' is of much later derivation, the suffix '-ism' having been added by 19th-century Western scholars in an attempt to categorize the complex religious tradition of Hindus.

▲ **Shiva** *The third member of the Hindu Trimurti in his manifestation as Nataraja, Lord of the Dance.*

MARGIN TEXT BOX
Tinted boxes contain additional information on an important concept, figure, or event.

134

135

iv

CAPTION
Explanatory captions accompany every illustration, indicating its relevance to the topic being covered.

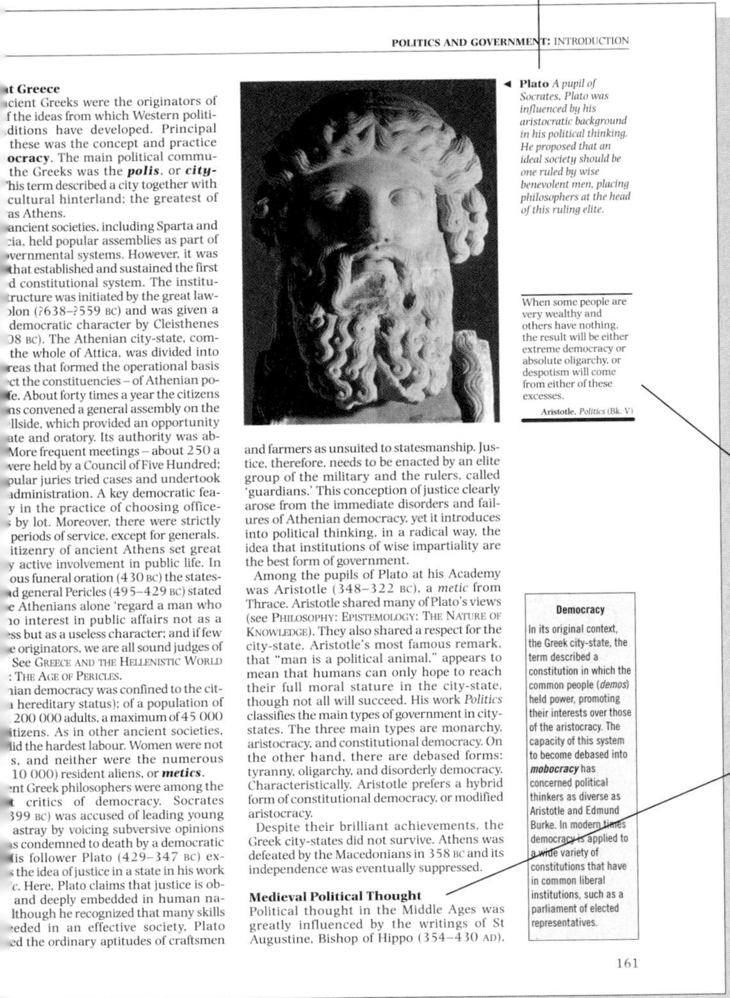

SUPERSECTION
HUMAN SOCIETY *is classified into two supersections, covering the ideas that have shaped society, and the organization of society.*

SOCIAL ORGANIZATION

FEATURE PAGE
Special self-contained feature pages focus in greater detail on selected topics.

▶ **Plato** *A pupil of Socrates, Plato was influenced by his aristocratic background in his political thinking. He proposed that an ideal society should be one ruled by wise benevolent men, placing philosophers at the head of this ruling elite.*

When some people are very wealthy and others have nothing, the result will be either extreme democracy or absolute oligarchy, or despotism will come from either of these excesses.

Aristotle, *Politics* (Bk. V)

t Greece
...ncient Greeks were the originators of f the ideas from which Western politi- ditions have developed. Principal these was the concept and practice ...ocracy. The main political commu- the Greeks was the **polis**, or city- his term described a city together with cultural hinterland; the greatest of ...as Athens.

...ancient societies, including Sparta and ...cia, held popular assemblies as part of ...vernmental systems. However, it was ...that established and sustained the first ...d constitutional system. The institu- ...tructure was initiated by the great law- ...olon (?638–?559 BC) and was given a ...democratic character by Cleisthenes ...08 BC). The Athenian city-state, com- ...the whole of Attica, was divided into ...reas that formed the operational basis ...ct the constituencies – of Athenian po- ...le. About forty times a year the citizens ...ns convened a general assembly on the ...llside, which provided an opportunity ...ate and oratory. Its authority was ab- ...More frequent meetings – about 250 a ...were held by a Council of Five Hundred; ...pular juries tried cases and undertook ...y in the practice of choosing office- ...s by lot. Moreover, there were strictly ...periods of service, except for generals. ...itizenry of ancient Athens set great ...y active involvement in public life. In ...ous funeral oration (430 BC) the states- ...d general Pericles (495–429 BC) stated ...e Athenians alone 'regard a man who ...o interest in public affairs not as a ...ss but as a useless character; and if few ...e originators, we are all sound judges of ...: See GREECE AND THE HELLENISTIC WORLD ...: THE AGE OF PERICLES.

...nian democracy was confined to the cit- ...hereditary status); of a population of ...200 000 adults, a maximum of 45 000 ...itizens. As in other ancient societies, ...lid the hardest labour. Women were not ...s, and neither were the numerous ...10 000) resident aliens, or **metics**.

...nt Greek philosophers were among the ...t critics of democracy. Socrates ...399 BC) was accused of leading young ...astray by voicing subversive opinions ...s condemned to death by a democratic ...is follower Plato (429–347 BC) ex- ...s the idea of justice in a state in his work ...c. Here, Plato claims that justice is ob- ...and deeply embedded in human na- ...lthough he recognized that many skills ...eeded in an effective society. Plato ...ed the ordinary aptitudes of craftsmen

and farmers as unsuited to statesmanship. Justice, therefore, needs to be enacted by an elite group of the military and the rulers, called 'guardians.' This conception of justice clearly arose from the immediate disorders and failures of Athenian democracy, yet it introduces into political thinking, in a radical way, the idea that institutions of wise impartiality are the best form of government.

Among the pupils of Plato at his Academy was Aristotle (348–322 BC), a *metic* from Thrace. Aristotle shared many of Plato's views (see PHILOSOPHY: EPISTEMOLOGY: THE NATURE OF KNOWLEDGE). They also shared a respect for the city-state. Aristotle's most famous remark, that "man is a political animal," appears to mean that humans can only hope to reach their full moral stature in the city-state, though not all will succeed. His work *Politics* classifies the main types of government in city-states. The three main types are monarchy, aristocracy, and constitutional democracy. On the other hand, there are debased forms: tyranny, oligarchy, and disorderly democracy. Characteristically, Aristotle prefers a hybrid form of constitutional democracy, or modified aristocracy.

Despite their brilliant achievements, the Greek city-states did not survive. Athens was defeated by the Macedonians in 358 BC and its independence was eventually suppressed.

Medieval Political Thought
Political thought in the Middle Ages was greatly influenced by the writings of St Augustine, Bishop of Hippo (354–430 AD),

QUOTATION
Extracts or quotations help place a particular idea or event in

Democracy
In its original context, the Greek city-state, the term described a constitution in which the common people (*demos*) held power, promoting their interests over those of the aristocracy. The capacity of this system to become debased into *mobocracy* has concerned political thinkers as diverse as Aristotle and Edmund Burke. In modern times democracy is applied to a wide variety of constitutions that have in common liberal institutions, such as a parliament of elected representatives.

SUBHEADING
The main text within each chapter is divided by subheadings in bold type. All subheadings appear in the chapter summary at the beginning.

161

SOLAR AND LUNAR MYTHS

158

PHILOSOPHY: METAPHYSICS

in his mind. Being imperfect himself, this idea must have a cause other than his own mind. Therefore the cause could only be an existing God. He also revised an argument first used by St Anselm (1033–1109), later known as the Ontological Argument. As God is, by definition, the supremely perfect being, He must exist, since existence is a necessary attribute of perfection. Both these arguments are highly controversial and remain a matter of debate.

From the existence of God, Descartes concluded that the world existed more or less as he encountered it, and that the world was divided into two substances, matter and mind. this doctrine is known as **metaphysical** or **Cartesian dualism** (see PHILOSOPHY OF MIND). He also argued that matter had no properties except extension in space and time. This led to his endorsement of the mechanistic model of the world that was emerging from the findings of 17th-century scientists. His views, in particular those related to geometry, remained influential for centuries, and combined with the work of Isaac Newton (1642–1727) to lay a solid foundation for modern science.

Although Descartes's system was never developed in any philosophical school, his rationalist approach was highly influential. Similar metaphysical systems were evolved by two major thinkers of the next generation, Baruch Spinoza (1632–77) and G. W. Leibniz (1646–1716). Spinoza disagreed with Descartes on the question of substance; in his view Descartes's matter and mind were merely two aspects of the same single substance, which he identified with both nature and God. Similarly, Aristotle's separate substances were treated as modes of the single universal substance. By contrast, Leibniz argued that there was an infinity of substances, called **monads**, which were incapable of interaction with one

another. However, God had ordained that the life of each monad should be in harmony with that of every other.

In opposition to these ambitious metaphysical systems, the empiricist tradition, which flourished especially in Britain, sought to discredit all attempts to gain knowledge that were not based on data from the senses. British empiricism was proposed by John Locke (1632–1704), was later elaborated by George Berkeley (1685–1753) and David Hume (1711–76). The metaphysical concepts of substance and an objective morality were attacked as meaningless. This undermined metaphysics itself. By the end of the 18th century, the philosophical traditions of rationalism and empiricism were starkly opposed in their metaphysical account of the world. It fell to the German philosopher Immanuel Kant (1724–1804) to achieve a synthesis of these two positions.

Transcendental Idealism
The basis of Kant's metaphysical system was that our knowledge of the world is inevitably limited by the categories under which we are able to conceive it (see EPISTEMOLOGY). These categories included the concepts of space, time, and causality and were imposed on our experience not by fundamental features of the world itself (as earlier metaphysicians had maintained) but by the nature of our own subjectivity. Kant accepted this subjectivity's fundamental role in the formation of the world. He held that there were things-in-themselves that caused our experiences, but that these were unknowable and that we could know the world only as it presented itself to us. Hence these aspects of the world that depend upon our awareness of them were not real. In this way that the things-in-themselves were real.

transcendental idealism
The view originated by Kant that the objects of our experience are merely appearances, with no independent existence. Transcendental idealists hold that no a priori knowledge of such concepts as space and time is transcendent – i.e. not derived from experience.

I have striven not to laugh at human actions, not to weep at them, not to hate them, but to understand them.

Baruch de Spinoza, Tractatus Philosophicus (1675), ch.1

CROSS REFERENCE
References in the text direct the reader to other chapters in HUMAN SOCIETY, or to other volumes in the set.

REFERENCE WORD
Bold upright type *indicates that the term is defined and elucidated in a margin text box or in a tinted feature panel.*

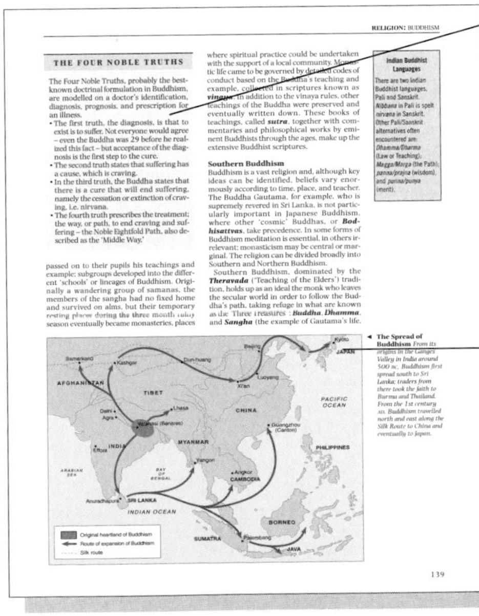

LEIBNIZ'S MONADS

Leibniz maintained that the world consisted of an infinite variety of independent things, each of which contained a life force. He called these basic indivisible units 'monads' (from Greek *monos*, meaning 'alone'). Every substance was composed of one or more monads. God was responsible for creating harmony between these entities. In this role God represented the "supreme substance," who acts according to a "principle of the best." It was this position, with its stress on the role of the individual within a rationally ordered universe, that was satirized by the French writer Voltaire in *Candide* (1759).

G. W. Leibniz *Leibniz's works include* Théodicée *(1710) and* Monadologie *(1714).*

76

THE FOUR NOBLE TRUTHS
The Four Noble Truths, probably the best-known doctrinal formulation in Buddhism, are modelled on a doctor's identification, diagnosis, prognosis, and prescription for an illness.
- The first truth, the diagnosis, is that to exist is to suffer. Not everyone would agree – even the Buddha was 29 before he realized this fact – but acceptance of the diagnosis is the first step to the cure.
- The second truth states that suffering has a cause, which is craving.
- In the third truth, the Buddha states that there is a cure that will end suffering, namely the cessation or extinction of craving, i.e. nirvana.
- The fourth truth prescribes the treatment; the way, or path, to end craving and suffering – the Noble Eightfold Path, also described as the 'Middle Way.'

passed on to their pupils his teachings and example; subgroups developed into the different 'schools' or lineages of Buddhism. Originally a wandering group of *samanas*, the members of the sangha had no fixed home and survived on alms, but their temporary resting places during the three month rainy season eventually became monasteries, places

where spiritual practice could be undertaken with the support of a local community. Monastic life came to be governed by detailed codes of conduct based on the Buddha's teaching and example, collected in scriptures known as *vinaya*. In addition to the vinaya rules, other teachings of the Buddha were preserved and eventually written down. These books of teachings, called *sutra*, together with commentaries and philosophical works by eminent Buddhists through the ages, make up the extensive Buddhist scriptures.

Southern Buddhism
Buddhism is a vast religion and, although key ideas can be identified, beliefs vary enormously according to time, place, and teacher. The Buddha Gautama, for example, who is supremely revered in Sri Lanka, is not particularly important in Japanese Buddhism, where other 'cosmic' Buddhas, or *Bodhisattvas*, take precedence. In some forms of Buddhist meditation is essential, in others irrelevant; monasticism may be central or marginal. The religion can be divided broadly into Southern and Northern Buddhism.

Southern Buddhism, dominated by the *Theravada* ('Teaching of the Elders') tradition, holds up as an ideal the monk who leaves the secular world in order to follow the Buddha's path, taking refuge in what are known as the 'Three Treasures': *Buddha*, *Dhamma*, and *Sangha* (the example of Gautama's life,

Indian Buddhist Languages
There are two Indian Buddhist languages, Pali and Sanskrit. Abhidana in Pali is spoken native in Sanskrit. Other Pali/Sanskrit alternatives often encountered are: *Dhamma/Dharma* (Law or Teaching), *Magga/Marga* (the Path), *panna/prajna* (wisdom), and *parina/purna* (merit).

TINTED PANEL
Feature panels contain a more detailed treatment of a subject examined in the chapter.

▶ **The Spread of Buddhism** *From its origins in the Ganges Valley in India around 500 BC, Buddhism first spread south to Sri Lanka, traders from there took the faith to Burma and Thailand. On Buddhism travelled north and east along the Silk Route to China and eventually to Japan.*

MAP
Each map in HUMAN SOCIETY, annotated and keyed for easy reference, helps the reader locate cities or regions discussed in the chapter.

139

V

Contents

SOCIAL IDEAS

SOCIAL SCIENCES

Origins of Sociology

*Major sociological concepts • Sociological activities • Specialized areas •
The influence of sociologists*

The development of sociology as a discipline may be attributed to five fundamental changes that took place in the Western world from the 16th century onwards. The intellectual and cultural tendency known as **humanism**, drawing on Greek and Roman culture, promoted a view of human beings as superior to any other life forms in nature because of their ability to reason; see EARLY AND MEDIEVAL EUROPE (VOL. 5). Eventually humanism became associated with opposition to orthodox religious beliefs, culminating in the **Reformation** and its refutation of the teaching of the established Church. The Reformation emphasized the individual's personal accountability to God and stressed that belief was based on a deep understanding of scripture. However, it diverged from humanism in regarding man as essentially sinful. In the 18th and 19th centuries, the economic system of **capitalism** emerged, with individual entrepreneurs establishing industrial enterprises and employing former agricultural labourers in return for a wage.

From this new organization of society arose the fourth fundamental change: the evolution of **democracy** and representative politics. Ordinary people now began to demand greater involvement in determining how their countries were governed. In consequence, revolutions occurred in England in the 17th century, in France and the USA in the 18th century, in various European and South American countries in the 19th century, and in Russia in the early decades of the 20th century. Furthermore, concurrent with these changes, **developments in science** enabled human beings to envisage the possibility of being able to exercise some control over nature. Scientific knowledge, based on verification by experiment, became the fundamental model for all forms of investigation, including those of a social nature.

In addition to these basic changes, other developments in the 18th and 19th centuries influenced the way in which human societies came to be viewed. The Enlightenment argued for the critical application of reason to the

Football Fans ▶
Dutch football supporters celebrate at the World Cup tournament in Italy in 1990. A football crowd consists of groups of people, each group having a powerful sense of identity. The groups manifest ritualized forms of behaviour that are common to such crowds throughout the world. These patterns of behaviour are of great interest to sociologists, much of whose work is concerned with the interaction between individuals and between groups.

THE PROTESTANT ETHIC

An early sociological work that set out as its aim the analysis of a particular social group was *The Protestant Ethic and the Spirit of Capitalism* (1905), by the German Max Weber (1864–1920). In this study, Weber argued that such qualities as hard work, abstinence, and reason characterized the Protestant attitude to personal salvation; in other words, financial and professional success came to be identified by Protestantism as an outward sign of God's favour to the individual. These same qualities, Weber maintained, were those that underlay the rise of capitalism in northern Europe from the late 16th century onwards. In particular, the shunning of expense on worldly pleasures, in favour of constant reinvestment of wealth, led to a steady accumulation of capital.

Early Calvinists *Weber claimed that modern capitalism arose during the Reformation in those areas most strongly influenced by Protestantism.* ▶

Man is a social animal.

Baruch de Spinoza
(1632–77), Dutch
philosopher

conduct of human affairs; this often went hand in hand with rejection of a divine explanation of the human condition. In philosophy, empiricism and positivism anticipated an ordered rational world that could be tested to establish universal laws. In the natural sciences, Charles Darwin's radical theory of evolution revealed that the human species had emerged over an enormous period through the process of natural selection. Perhaps most crucially, the emergence of urban industrial society that accompanied the rise of capitalism created a whole new stratification of society based on class (see SOCIAL DIVISIONS).

From the early 19th century a new perspective began to evolve, offering an explanation of the human condition that took account of the profound changes occurring in society.

Major Sociological Concepts

Social Groups. The concept of the group is a prominent one in sociology, since sociologists are interested in habitual, long-term, and institutionalized relationships between people. A group is defined as a number of individuals – however small or large – who interact with one another according to a set of common **norms** and differentiated roles. The members of a group are aware of their membership and of all the various rights and responsibilities that accompany it.

Groups are subdivided into ***primary groups*** and ***secondary groups***. A primary group is one whose members interact on a personal level (e.g. a family). A secondary group is more

diffuse, and as a result its members do not undertake direct interaction; an example of such a group is a political party.

A phenomenon that has always been deeply interesting to observers of human conduct is collective behaviour – the manner in which individuals can conduct themselves when gathered in a group. Often this bears no relationship to the way in which they behave when they are alone or together in small numbers. For example, extreme instances of crowd-induced behaviour may occur at football matches, at pop concerts, or among evangelical Christians in church. The total loss of inhibition, coupled with a frantic urge to conform with the behaviour of one's neighbours in the crowd, is the most disquieting aspect of collective behaviour. It is perhaps unsurprising that many of those who pioneered research in the area of collective behaviour were criminologists, concerned with the problem of individual responsibility for collective crimes.

In general, modern sociologists are concerned with identifying the particular ways in which collective behaviour differs from everyday behaviour, and under what conditions it is likely to arise.

Social Structure. Any pattern of social interaction that recurs and endures among individuals, who each perform a different role, can be regarded as a social structure. Thus all groups can be said to have an underlying social structure – from a relatively small unit, such as a teenage gang, to a large group, such as a whole society. The varying degrees of

norms Common expectations, rules, or standards that regulate behaviour; they are learned and internalized and any departure from them can result in sanctions (punishment).

CRIMINOLOGY

Criminology studies the nature and causes of crime, together with its prevention and correction. The early study *Delinquent Man* (1876) by the Italian criminologist Cesare Lombroso (1835–1909) attempted to show that certain physical attributes (e.g. a receding forehead) characterize the criminal. Although Lombroso's approach is no longer considered valid, it focused attention on the problem of criminality in society.

Modern criminologists now spend much of their time describing and classifying crimes or evaluating policies to contain it. There is no universal agreement as to what aspects of social experience predispose a person to criminal behaviour. While it is has been noted that many criminals come from broken homes and unsupportive families, clearly this background is not a sufficient cause for any individual to end up as a criminal. Similarly, while there appears to be strong evidence that a loving and supportive family is the best safeguard against crime, most people can readily think of everyday examples that run counter to this belief.

A Shanty Town
This shanty town, or favela, *is at Cubatao in Brazil. Many sociological studies of such 'informal housing,' especially in Latin American cities, have concluded that they offer the best means of housing the poor, in preference to large-scale public housing projects.* ▼

integration that occur between units in a social structure were classified at the end of the 19th century as *Gemeinschaft* ('community') and *Gesellschaft* ('association') by the German sociologist Ferdinand Tönnies (1855–1936). While *Gemeinschaft* describes a structure that is governed by personal emotional bonds of solidarity (for example, a village or a family), *Gesellschaft* denotes a structure in which relationships are more impersonal (e.g. a city).

Sociology has identified a struggle between social structures serving the purpose of imposing order on social interaction, and social interaction as typified by conflict, deception,

and the use of coercion. For example, in a society where interrelationships are constrained by a predetermined set of norms – for example, a system of institutionalized racial discrimination – social structure serves not as a means of avoiding conflict or ensuring cooperation, but rather as a way of shaping social interaction so as to perpetuate inequality.

Sociological Activities

Unlike the physical sciences, sociology does not have a generally accepted core of theoretical propositions to explain the vast quantity of sociological observations that have been collected, largely during the 20th century. Many of these observations have been made by sociologists in their own cultures and refer to their own times. Methods of research involve acquiring statistical data by observation, interview, or questionnaire, which is most easily achieved locally and in the present. Nevertheless, some studies have made comparisons between customs and social structures in different countries (***comparative sociology***), while others have investigated social conditions in the past (***historical sociology***).

However, the majority of working sociologists who carry out research are doing so in an attempt to understand, and by understanding to alleviate, social problems. The founder of sociology, Auguste Comte (1798–1857), himself justified the study for which he provided the name 'sociology' with the words *savoir pour prévoir pour pourvoir* ('to understand in order to foresee what needs to be done'). Thus, in order to understand the breakdown of

family life, sociologists need to go to the root of conflicts between husband and wife, or between children and their parents. In doing so, it is essential that sociology eschews any judgmental stance, especially where the emotionally charged subject of the family is concerned. Thus, the benefits that can be shown to derive from life within the family unit are considered by the sociologist in conjunction with an awareness that the family is also a potential source of harm and violence, such as mental illness, wife-beating, or child abuse.

The study of families can also encompass the particular social problems that are associated with the old and the young. The extended family is often regarded as an ideal group in which the aged can be cared for. However, in cultures that do not promote this form of family life other solutions have to be found for those too old to fend for themselves. The study of the role of families in preventing drug abuse and delinquency in young people is another sociological concern of great importance. Indeed the whole complex subject of the roots of criminality is widely studied by a branch of sociology called **criminology**.

All these aspects of sociology need to be examined within a specified social context, since different stresses are associated with different environments. For example, considerable stress may arise when a mother is the sole breadwinner in a household – an increasingly common occurrence as employment patterns shift more towards low-paid, part-time work for women. As well as earning, the working mother may still be expected to fulfil her traditional domestic role.

The evolution of this change in gender roles has been another major concern of sociology. Indeed, sociology has been a pioneering discipline in the field of women's studies; as long ago as 1892, the Department of Sociology at the University of Kansas in the USA offered a course on the role and status of women in society. Women, as mothers, have long been – and continue to be – a subject of social importance. A sociological concern for the role of women as achievers in their own right is a much more recent development, which largely arose as a result of the resurgence of feminism in the late 1960s and early 1970s. Since then it has been widely recognized that generalizations regarding male behaviour, obtained from studies on male subjects, cannot be extrapolated without qualification to females.

Apart from examining the social structures that exist within populations and the role of such social groups as the family, sociologists have many other concerns. These include attempts to analyse the causes and effects of poverty, homelessness, deprivation in inner cities, the growth of shanty towns, and the

provisions that governments need to make for social welfare. They are also concerned with relationships between the groups into which societies are divided; these include ethnic groups, social classes, religious congregations, and political parties. Understanding the many tensions, fears, and antagonisms that exist between the members of these different factions is a vital role for sociologists.

Specialized Areas

Sociology is subdivided into a number of specialized branches, many of which relate closely to other disciplines. In such cases, sociological research has enriched the core discipline by offering new insights from hitherto neglected perspectives. A few of the varied range of subfields are as follows.

Sociology of Education. The sociology of education is concerned with investigating the opportunities for education among different groups, as well as studying the administration of schools and colleges and the motivation and training of teachers.

Industrial Sociology. This subfield studies social relationships in the workplace. Industrial sociologists are interested in the social structures of work organizations and the forms and function of the division of labour (see ECONOMICS: ECONOMIC RESOURCES). The problem of management–worker conflict is at the root of many studies that have considered such matters as people's attitudes to and expectations of work, and the different attitude of white-collar workers and manual workers to trade-union representation. Marxist sociologists argue that conflict is inherent in the capitalist mode of production, in which workers are progressively deskilled by employers, who are concerned to lower labour costs.

▲ **Offenders in Prison (Latvia)**
Criminality and delinquency in all their forms have long been the subject of sociological study. The discipline of criminology arose as a specialized area analysing the causes of crime and advocating policies to contain it.

> The state is a power structure of men controlling men, a structure that is supported by means of 'legitimate' violence.
>
> **Max Weber.** *Collected Political Writings* (1921)

Military Sociology. This specialization, which grew after World War II, studies the cohesion and morale of armed forces, and the (often problematic) relationship between military and political institutions.

Medical Sociology. Medical sociology is one of the largest specialized areas of sociology. It has developed from a growing recognition that many of the problems of health care are social in nature. Social factors play an important role in determining people's susceptibility to particular diseases, or in triggering the onset of an illness. Ethical questions arising from the relationship between physician and patient have also been investigated by medical sociologists.

Sociology of the Arts. Sociologists working in this area have studied the role of publishers, critics, and gallery owners in mediating between the creative artist and the public. One particularly fruitful line of enquiry has been pursued by feminist researchers, who have analysed why so few women feature in the history or the production of art. See PHILOSOPHY: AESTHETICS.

Urban Sociology. Instigated by the Chicago School in the USA (see SOCIAL RESEARCH METHODS), the study of social interaction within an urban environment has developed from a generalizing approach to one that distinguishes between many types of city.

The Influence of Sociologists

From its very foundation, sociology has taken as the principal subject of its research the problems that afflict society, such as poverty, the dissolution of families, criminality, and discrimination in all its forms. In their writings, the founding fathers of sociology focus on groups that exist on the periphery of society, a subject that had been neglected by other disciplines. Moreover, these early sociologists, who began their studies in the early 19th century, clearly indicate that an agenda for change lies behind their attempts to give a systematic account of the laws governing social life. For example, Auguste Comte presents in his work a blueprint of a new social order, which he saw as being guided by a 'religion of humanity.' The intention of sociological theorists in the early phases of this social science was to try to overcome the deficiencies of existing society by alerting policymakers and legislators to their existence.

However, although many major sociologists have acknowledged such a reforming intention in their work, sociology has, since its inception as an academic discipline, striven primarily to present the facts in as scientific, objective, and dispassionate way as possible. As a result of this endeavour, sociological evidence and data may well then form the basis on which civil servants and politicians undertake improvements in society.

Thus, despite sociology's critical stance towards existing social order, much sociological research is now conducted at the instigation of governmental or commercial bodies, who expect its analysis of specific areas to be of practical use to them in formulating policy. One such application of the findings of sociology has been in the world of advertising.

Sociology's claim to academic impartiality has not prevented it from periodically becoming the focus of political disapproval, or even proscription. The subject has been especially maligned in countries governed by totalitarian regimes. This largely arises from the fact that sociology's investigation of the root causes of group behaviour and its analysis of social structure – both of which acknowledge diversity as an essential factor in society – run counter to such systems' rigid control of all social relationships. Thus, although sociology had become established in German universities by the end of World War I and had gained an international reputation, it was subject to hostility by the Nazi regime and was eventually banned. Similarly, during the Stalinist era in the former Soviet Union, sociology was long suppressed, except in so far as it supported the orthodox Marxist-Leninist analysis of society as being based exclusively on class exploitation in capitalist society.

Medical Care of the Elderly *The growth area of medical sociology has had a particularly strong impact on the fields of geriatrics, paediatrics, and psychiatry.* ▼

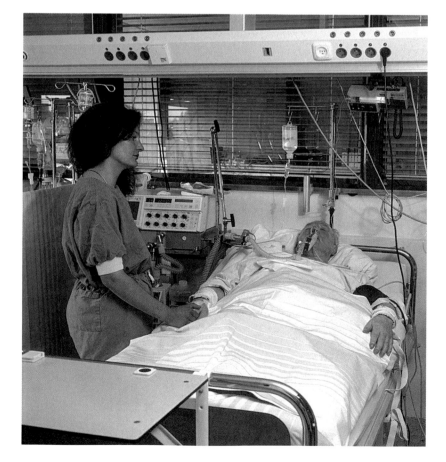

Social Research Methods

*Positivism • Interpretivism • Quantitative method • Qualitative method •
Secondary sources*

A method of research appropriate to the study of the social world first emerged in the early 17th century. The British thinker Francis Bacon (1561–1626) stressed the importance of observation and experience as the only source of human knowledge of the world. By the time of David Hume (1711–76), the Scottish philosopher of the Enlightenment, these essential requirements had been linked with the law of cause and effect – namely, that every effect has an antecedent cause. A further characteristic of this approach – now known as **empiricism** – is its reliance on **inductive** reasoning as a means of gathering evidence from a series of observations of the same occurrence, which enables a general law to be established. For example, persistent observations that people who eat certain mushrooms become ill, while those who eat different kinds of mushrooms do not, enables this empirical evidence to be used to suggest a rule that enables edible mushrooms to be identified.

Positivism

Closely allied to empiricism is positivism, an approach that has many variants. In general, positivism assumes that the natural world has an independent existence of its own governed by laws that can be discovered by the appropriate research methods. It proposes that an order exists in the world, whether or not people are aware of it, and that the research methods of the social sciences can be modelled on those of the natural sciences. From the outset, the proponents of positivism sought their evidence, using the experimental method pioneered by Bacon as the sole means for discovering the nature of the world. Indeed, positivism seemed to be vindicated by the successes of science in the 18th and 19th centuries. The French sociological pioneer Auguste **Comte** (1798–1857) not only coined the term 'sociology' (in 1838); he also introduced the term **positive philosophy** to indicate that the approach to acquiring knowledge used in natural science could be adapted to the new science of sociology.

It was Comte's terms of reference for the conduct of sociology that formed the basis of the work of John Stuart Mill (1806–73) and Herbert Spencer (1820–1903) in England and Emile Durkheim (1858–1917) in France. Durkheim, perhaps more than anyone else, made consistent use of the positivist method.

By his time, it had become clear that it was the impersonal forces of society, over and above the behaviour of individuals, that determined the nature of social life. Durkheim's view was supported by growing evidence that human life did conform to a predictable pattern and that individuals who were apparently acting in their own self-interest could produce a predictable and structured social life.

With the development of academic sociology during the 20th century, positivism, which made abundant use of the scientific method, advanced to utilizing surveys, questionnaires, statistics, accurate measurements, the testing of hypotheses, and the employment of the **hypothetico-deductive** method. In this method, a proposition is put forward asserting that something is the case: for example, that all footballers hate a penalty shoot-out. The method seeks to falsify the hypothesis, working on the assumption that a hypothesis cannot be ultimately proven. It was advocated by Karl Popper (1902–94), drawing on the work of Hume, who recognized that because all observed cases support a hypothesis does not prove that all future observations would do so.

========SEE ALSO========
This section:
• Origins of Sociology
• Social Divisions
• Introduction to Anthropology
• Cultural and Social Anthropology
• Linguistics
Philosophy:
• Applied Philosophy
Politics and Government:
• Introduction

Order and Progress.

Motto of **Auguste Comte**, later adopted by the Federative Republic of Brazil as its national motto

COMTE'S 'LAW OF THE THREE STAGES'

Auguste Comte maintained that society was like an organism, believing that there were laws governing human institutions similar to those that regulated nature. He therefore formulated a system of laws that would form the basis for society's reorganization, This **Law of the Three Stages**, as Comte called it, described the social and intellectual evolution of humanity in the following terms:

• a **theological** stage, in which human beings seek divine explanations for events;
• a **metaphysical** stage, in which answers are sought in nature;
• a **positive** stage, in which discoverable laws are relied upon as guiding principles.

▲ **Auguste Comte** *Comte regarded sociology as the principal science.*

Comte regarded this sequence of stages as indicating that society was progressing towards a better future.

▲ **Claude-Henri de Saint-Simon**
(1760–1825)
Saint-Simon – whose secretary, Auguste Comte, coined the term 'sociology' – was the first person to propose a science of social organization. Saint-Simon's theories envisaged an enlightened society governed for the good of all by an elite of scientists and industrialists.

One inconsistent observation in the future would cast doubt on *all* previously observed evidence. Popper turned this apparently damaging insight into a virtue by advocating that observers should actively seek evidence to falsify a hypothesis. Thus if a single footballer can be found who enjoys penalty shoot-outs, his existence will falsify the assertion that *all* footballers hate penalty shoot-outs; see PHILOSOPHY: APPLIED PHILOSOPHY.

Interpretivism

In a reaction to positivism, some later sociologists have indicated that there is a critical difference between the natural sciences and sociology. Because humans are conscious beings, capable of making choices, they clearly differ as objects of study from other entities of the natural world. Social life, it is claimed, is unique in that it involves understanding and the interpretation of meaning on the part of its participants. Indeed, this approach to sociological research is referred to as ***interpretivism***. In this perspective, each human situation is taken as a unique occurrence to which no general law applies. The problem of devising a method of research in these circumstances involves deciding how to gain access to any shared meanings in social life and how to discover the nature of these meanings to participants. In this respect, interpretivism makes use of the concept of ***verstehen*** (German: 'understanding') introduced by the German sociologist Max Weber (1864–1920). This concept asserts that as social life cannot be understood from the outside, researchers must establish an empathetic relationship with the people observed in order to understand their

motives and the meanings they attribute to their actions. Only by placing oneself in the position of the other person is the sociologist able to interpret subjective influences. Although there is another, more causal, side to Weber's sociology, many schools of thought draw on his interpretivist method.

Structuralism. A further theoretical school, structuralism, can be regarded as being responsible for a third research method, in addition to positivism and interpretivism. Structuralism is associated with the work of the French anthropologist Claude Lévi-Strauss (1908–), whose study of human cultures has been concerned with elucidating general laws of human behaviour. The basis of his method has been to uncover the patterns and structures that underlie people's thoughts. Structuralism, unlike positivism, is concerned with a level that is not directly observable to researchers or participants; moreover, unlike interpretivism, it is not concerned with the level of the individual and intersubjective meaning. Although some would claim that Marxism is to some extent positivistic, it has also been argued that Marxism involves a more structuralist approach.

Quantitative Method

In sociology, positivism is often referred to as a ***quantitative method***, while interpretivism is described as a ***qualitative method***. The difference between them lies in the kinds of questions asked and in what can be regarded as acceptable evidence. In quantitative methods attempts are made to quantify social phenomena by providing an accurate description or even by investigating suspected causes and effects. In this tradition, research designs are described as one of the following:
• descriptive;
• explanatory;
• experimental;
• investigative.
However, in practice, these designs are rarely found in their pure form, as there is a considerable degree of overlap between them. For example, descriptive designs are often to some extent explanatory, and vice versa; both are therefore often described as ***survey designs***.

Descriptive Designs. These are concerned with providing an accurate description of a situation or of an association between measurable variables. The priority is always to minimize bias and maximize the reliability of the evidence collected. Traditionally, this type of design has been concerned with the collection of factual information (for example, on the living standards of the poor) or, more recently, with attitudinal data (e.g. political views). Because the expense involved in surveying entire populations by census is far too

---

SUICIDE

An example of the way in which Durkheim saw society as having an overriding influence on individuals is his influential study of suicide (*Le Suicide*; 1897).

To demonstrate his contention that suicide was primarily a social and not an individual phenomenon, Durkheim identified different suicide rates among Protestants, Catholics, and Jews. He related these differences to the social bonds and levels of integration typical of each community. An overriding emphasis on individualism (as in Protestantism) led to high rates of suicide, whereas characteristically close communal ties (among Jews, for example) led to low rates of suicide. Durkheim also identified increased rates of suicide as being associated with disruptions to normal social expectations, for example during an economic or social crisis.

More recent research into suicide confirms some of Durkheim's conclusions. His belief that a community placing very heavy emphasis on integration and rigid expectations on how to behave could produce high suicide rates is corroborated by the case of modern Japan. Yet Durkheim's claims that suicide rates among Catholics are lower than among Protestants has not been borne out.

MARXIST SOCIOLOGY

A prime historical example of the use of the comparative method is Marxism. The basic belief of the German social scientist Karl Marx (1818–83) was that society should not simply be studied, but actively changed. He saw the history of society as being that of a series of struggles between two classes: between master and slave in ancient society, between lord and serf in feudalism, and between bourgeoisie and proletariat in capitalism. Only in the final stage, socialism (the classless society), would this pattern be broken. Marx saw the basic economic structure of society as having overriding legal, political, and spiritual 'superstructures' – it is these superstructures that bind people most strongly to the old order. Yet capitalism contains the seeds of its own destruction, relying as it does on the existence of a large body of exploited labour that would eventually join together to overthrow the existing order.

Karl Marx *The influence of Marx's thought grew after his death.* ▶

great, a sample is selected from a population, from the findings of which generalizations can be made. If sampling is used in this way, the accuracy with which the sample is selected is clearly of paramount importance. Once a representative sample has been selected, a questionnaire is devised and sent to the members of the sample by post. In some cases an interview with individual respondents is also arranged. In such descriptive designs, if resources allow, it is customary to carry out a pilot study – a small-scale preliminary version of the survey – in order to check the appropriateness of the questionnaire and the general procedures.

Explanatory Designs. These are usually devised to test causal hypotheses (for example, the assertion that poverty causes stress). However, causes in real life are exceptionally hard both to identify and to isolate; if Hume's beliefs are taken to their logical conclusions, cause is not a property of the social world but a psychological tendency, reinforced by custom, to expect one thing to follow from another.

Nevertheless, explanatory designs can produce useful results provided that there is great emphasis on what the concepts under examination (for example, 'poverty' or 'stress') will be taken to mean for the purposes of the research. If an attempt is being made to measure a parameter or to establish a cause it has to be recognized as such in the same way by all participants on every occasion.

Experimental Designs. These researches are undertaken in a laboratory or in the field (i.e. in a natural social setting). Laboratory experiments are rare in sociology; when they are used, they are concerned with the immediate effects of short-term treatments administered under tightly controlled conditions. Usually two randomly sampled matched groups are used, the ***experimental group*** and the ***control group***. The experimental group consists of people who are subjected to the experiment, while the control group comprises individuals who do not undergo the treatment, and who thus act as a comparison to the experimental group. Again, there is a problem of separating factors thought to be causal from extraneous factors. Even the impact of the experiment itself can have a considerable influence on the participants. In some cases it becomes apparent that the experimental group has responded more to being part of the event itself than to the treatment. In field experiments, on the other hand, it is often not revealed to those involved that an experiment is taking place. In such live situations, very few variables can be controlled. In addition, there is the moral issue of whether people should be involved in an experiment without their knowledge.

Investigative Designs. These substitutes for direct experimentation are of various kinds. One example, which is often used, is the longitudinal study. In this type, a sample is selected and referred to as a 'panel'. Members

It is not the consciousness of men that determines their being, but on the contrary their social being that determines their consciousness.

Karl Marx, *A Contribution to the Critique of Political Economy* (1859)

In the speed and complexity of its commercial, professional, and social life, the city forms... a profound contrast to a small town or the country, where all the sensory impressions and mental stimuli that life produces occur at a much slower, more regular and familiar pace.

Georg Simmel, German sociologist, *The City and Mental Life* (1902)

of the panel are contacted on a series of occasions, perhaps over a period of years, enabling the researcher to chart changes that occur during the period. Usually panels are large and members are contacted by interviews or by questionnaire. The drop-out rate is a major problem with this kind of design.

In addition to these four main types of quantitative methods, there is the ***comparative method***, which is not so much a type of research design as the harnessing of human judgment to the attempt to be scientific in social analysis. This amounts to collecting data about social situations with the intention of identifying causes by means of comparison. This comparison of differences and similarities between observed social phenomena enables various types of classification to be made and can potentially enable some causal associations to be isolated. The fundamental nature of the comparative method is indicated by its range and variety. It encompasses experiments or substitutes for direct experimentation (quasi experiments). The comparative method was the characteristic method employed by the founding fathers of sociology, who used it in comparing historical social systems and systems of belief; it is also the approach to social enquiry adopted in much more recent developments in sociology, such as comparative social policy, which is often engaged in cross-national comparisons.

In practice, some form of comparative process is an integral aspect of all research methods, including those characteristic of natural science, such as medicine. Clearly, criticisms from the tradition of interpretivism can be levelled at the comparative method. In interpretivism, all instances are regarded as unique and can be judged only on their own terms; this amounts to saying that the instances are not comparable by definition. The circumstances in which the comparative method can be regarded as acceptable are still a matter for debate.

Qualitative Method

In the interpretative tradition, several different methods are often described as qualitative. Some are also considered to be ethnographic, and ***ethnography*** – the study of human societies – is a characteristic tool of anthropology. The classic qualitative technique for gathering data, pioneered by the Chicago School in the early decades of the 20th century, is ***participant observation***. Here the researcher becomes a participant in a subculture of the society being investigated. The researcher, having gained access through initial contact with a key informant, becomes involved in a network of relationships, which are experienced as they would be by an insider. In some instances, participant observation is covert, i.e. the researcher's identity and motives are concealed; however, in some cases they are overt – at least some members of the subculture being aware of the real nature and purpose of the researcher's presence. In practice, there is a wide range of possibilities for the participant observer, ranging from complete participant at one extreme to complete observer at the other. The defining attribute of participant observation is that it sets out to explore uncharted territory, enabling the uninitiated to discover what it is like to become part of the activity being investigated,

Chicago in the 1920s *The large influx of immigrants into this bustling city in the northwest of the USA from the turn of the century onwards, to work in manufacturing industry or the stockyards, provided a rich environment for sociological study. The department of sociology at the University of Chicago was established in 1892. The Chicago School of sociology attempted to strike a balance between statistical techniques, case studies, and ethnography – although it has come to be particularly associated with the latter.*

without disturbing the balance of that activity. Participant observation is, however, a very time-consuming technique that makes great demands on the researcher's personality and social skills. It often works best when complemented by other methods.

The purpose of ethnography is to obtain insights into naturally occurring human behaviour and in events and the contexts in which they occur. The emphasis is placed upon everyday contexts, in which observation and informal conversation provide the data. This involves interpreting the meaning of much that is seen and heard, i.e. it is largely a process of discovery rather than the testing of hypotheses. The aim is to add to the mosaic of understanding human behaviour by adding fragments or stones of understanding of the subculture in question. The unit of analysis is invariably small, focused upon the subculture or even the individual. Ethnography's impact as a method can be seen in cultural anthropology, especially in the tradition of the case-study technique of the Chicago School.

Secondary Sources

Not all research involves the collection of data (primary data) at first hand by researchers; some methods concern the appraisal or reappraisal of existing data (secondary data) of various kinds. Examples of such data include:
- official statistics;
- archive material;
- documentary evidence;
- various repeated studies.

Official statistics will have been collected by government agencies, such as population censuses carried out at regular intervals, the collection of crime figures, or the registration of births, marriages, and deaths. Such statistics provide valuable data for sociologists; they should, however, be treated with caution and the sociologist should be aware of the purpose for which they were collected. A classic example of a sociological study in this area is Durkheim's *Suicide*. Agencies other than governments also collect statistics that may be used subsequently by sociologists. Schools, trade unions, charities, and businesses are examples of such agencies.

Archive material may consist of statistics or any other kind of data, often kept in one location as a permanent record of a specific individual, institution, or event. Archives may also consist of public or personal documents or texts. Public documents are all those that have provided a public record of a social encounter or rite of passage; these may include work, health, or educational records of individuals. While current, many of the documents will have been kept confidential, only later becoming available to researchers as a source of data.

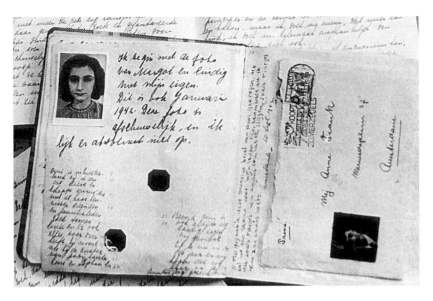

Personal documents may include diaries, journals, and letters. These constitute a first-hand account of individual experiences and often provide insight into both everyday life and great historical events.

An example that has provided enormous insight into both time and place is *The Diary of Anne Frank* (1947), a young German-Jewish teenager hiding from the Nazis in occupied Amsterdam (1942–43), while Thomas and Znaniecki's *The Polish Peasant in Europe and America* (1919) is a classic study of the letters exchanged by emigrants to the USA with friends and relatives in their country of origin. Although there are exceptions, most unsolicited diaries and letters are written spontaneously and unselfconsciously. However, sociology often actively seeks out people's accounts of their own lives, since autobiographies and diaries are comparatively rare. In the case of life histories, researchers encourage a subject to relate their experiences – perhaps on tape – which provides their own unique perspective on the world. With an oral history, on the other hand, people are encouraged to give their own account of a time, place, or event through which they have lived – again often on tape. Film and video now also play a role, in addition to still photography, in providing documentation of social life.

Undoubtedly the onus is on sociologists to proceed cautiously when working with secondary sources and documentary evidence. Sociologists now make use of specialized techniques, such as content analysis, in which meanings of the words that make up a text are systematically accounted for, and **hermeneutics**, in which attempts are made to recapture the intentions of original texts during translation (much as the translators of later versions of the Bible had to guess what was intended in earlier interpretations).

▲ **Correspondence of Anne Frank**
The diary and letters left by Anne Frank, a Jewish girl in hiding from the Nazis during World War II, form a first-hand documentary resource for sociologists and historians alike. Anne Frank was eventually discovered and imprisoned; she died in Bergen-Belsen concentration camp in 1945.

hermeneutics
The science of interpretation, especially of the scriptures. It is the branch of theology that deals with the explanation of biblical texts. Its meaning has been extended in philosophy and sociology to include the study of human behaviour and social institutions.

Populations and Families

Demographic change • Urbanization • Families and marriage • Rites of passage

There are marked differences in the life expectancies and population growth between economically advanced areas of the world and those areas that do not have the advantages of modern technology. On average, individuals in economically advanced countries (known as the 'developed world') can expect to live 75 years while for those in technologically simple societies (often referred to as 'developing countries') the life expectancy is 62 years. In Africa as a whole, it remains at 53 years. The age structure of the populations of the world is also not uniform. In developed countries the population is stable or declining (with the average age rising) in contrast to the young and growing populations of the developing world.

Demographic Change

The collection and analysis of information about populations is called **demography**. There are a number of ways by which demographers gather data about populations; chief among these is the census, which provides detailed information about individuals and groupings residing in a particular place on a specified date. Most countries collect demographic information by means of a census, though the information gathered varies from country to country according to their particular needs. In general, countries seek information about the age and sex of their populations; occupations; details of marital status; type of residence; and geographical distribution in the country. Sometimes information is sought about levels of education; place of birth; religion; and ethnic identity. The compulsory registration of births, marriages, and deaths – information that demographers call **vital statistics** – also provides valuable data in addition to that of the census. The reliability of all these figures, however, is variable as it depends on the efficiency of the bureaucratic system carrying out the registrations and on the population itself being sufficiently literate to understand what is being asked of them and to be able and willing to provide accurate answers. In most developed countries the registration of vital statistics and the census provide reliable information. Crude **birth rates** are calculated on the basis of the number of births per thousand women per year. Crude **death rates** are calculated from the number of deaths per thousand people in a year. The **infant mortality rate** is calculated by comparing the number of deaths of children under the age of one year for every thousand live

Scavenging Children in the Philippines
Scavenging on this refuse tip in Manila, known as 'Smoky Mountain,' has arisen as a result of a number of factors, including a chronic housing shortage and inadequate social welfare provisions. While the birth rate is increasing in developing countries, life expectancy there is shortened by deprivation and disease.

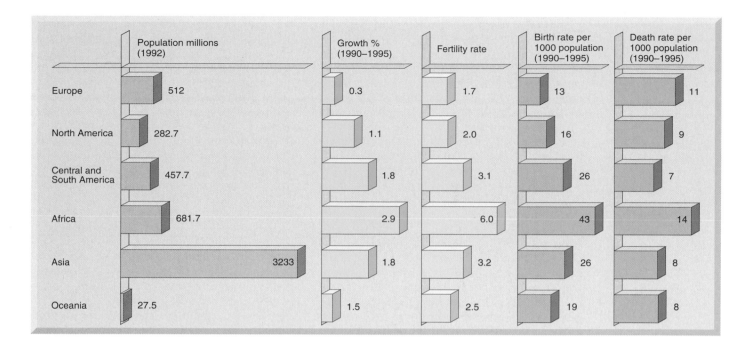

	Population millions (1992)	Growth % (1990–1995)	Fertility rate	Birth rate per 1000 population (1990–1995)	Death rate per 1000 population (1990–1995)
Europe	512	0.3	1.7	13	11
North America	282.7	1.1	2.0	16	9
Central and South America	457.7	1.8	3.1	26	7
Africa	681.7	2.9	6.0	43	14
Asia	3233	1.8	3.2	26	8
Oceania	27.5	1.5	2.5	19	8

births in that year. Census and registration systems are often supported by special investigations into aspects of population behaviour. Such studies, known as **cohort studies**, examine the behaviour during a specified period of a section of the population that has certain characteristics in common in relation to a particular issue of interest. An example of a cohort study might be an investigation of the employment patterns of unmarried males under the age of 25 years in a particular period. The comparison of population figures over a given period provides a dynamic view of population change and the basis for projects regarding population trends.

Populations grow by net increase, that is by an excess of births over deaths and also by an excess of immigration over emigration (more people move into an area than move out of it). Figures for Europe and the USA show that populations are not replacing themselves as a result of falling birth rates. Replacement of population is said to occur when there is an average birth rate of 2.1 live births per female of child-bearing age. The average number of children born to women has fallen considerably in Europe for most of the 20th century, with the exceptions of population rises in the years following World War I and World War II. Demographers point to a time of change in the 19th century, when European populations moved from high birth rates, high infant mortality, and high rates of morbidity (illness) to low birth rates, low infant mortality, and improved life expectancy. This change is referred to as the **demographic transition**. The precise cause of this change is uncertain but the factors likely to have been responsible include:

• improved public health measures (clean water and hygienic sewage disposal);
• medical advances (vaccination, antiseptic measures, etc.);
• improved provision of food (consequent on cheaper food supplies).

Since the 1920s, the low birth rate has been maintained by the growing use of family planning methods in the developed countries.

There is still some doubt about when and if the countries of the present-day developing world will achieve population structures and levels of population growth resembling those of the developed countries. The demographic transition took place in the context of specific historical, political, and economic conditions in the developed world, which are unlikely to be repeated in the developing world. However, whenever living conditions have improved for populations in developing countries, there has been a fall in the rate of population growth. As infant and child mortality decline, parents are more confident that their children will survive to adulthood and so fewer children are born.

Opportunities for women to be educated and earn a living have also had a considerable effect on women's fertility rates. A notable example of this is in Kerala state in India, where women's education and training are associated with lower birth rates. Yet it is doubtful if population growth rate in developing countries will fall rapidly to the levels of the developed world, as for many families in developing countries children are the best, or even the only, means for parents to achieve any security in their old age. Most developing countries lack social welfare schemes to support ageing people, who thus rely on their families.

▲ **Population Growth** *Growth is indicated by region in this diagram. Between 1990 and 1995 developed countries of the world grew at less than 2% per annum (less than replacement), while developing countries typically grew at 2% to 3% per annum; within the category of developing countries, African populations grew at more than 3% per annum.*

Sanitation

It is estimated that only some 2% of all urban sewage in developing countries is treated. This is caused by the failure of the infrastructure to keep pace with the massive increase in shanty towns around expanding cities.

13

Urban Growth

Between 1950 and 1990, the following conurbations in developing countries experienced huge increases in population:

- Mexico City's inhabitants increased from 3.1 to 20.2 million.
- Seoul in South Korea grew from 1 to 11 million.
- In Brazil, the city of São Paulo grew from 2.4 to 17.4 million, while Rio de Janeiro grew from 2.9 to 10.7 million.

Infant Mortality Rate *The rate of deaths among babies under one year of age is shown by region. Recent studies by UNICEF have indicated that there is no straightforward correlation between income of a country measured by GNP and level of immunization of young children against potentially threatening disease. For instance, inoculation is more prevalent in Bangladesh than in Kuwait.* ▼

Children in developing countries are not seen as mouths to be fed but as hands to work; indeed, from an early age children are expected to make a useful contribution to family income. Additionally, parents gain pleasure and prestige from having a large family.

The demographic analysis of population data is useful to governments in the planning of economic and social policies for countries. Birth rates can be used to project future availability of labour as well as to indicate the demand for schools and child healthcare facilities. The age structure of the population can be used in decision making by governments when allocating scarce resources to competing sectors of the population. For example, if a country has a high birth rate and a low level of life expectancy, there will be more young people than old in the society, which will affect the provision of goods and services by the government. In the developed world a growing proportion of the population is aged 65 years and over, causing apprehension to governments about the cost of supporting this increasing number of economically inactive persons, who may need specialized health and welfare.

In developing countries the main concerns are about the capacity of the economies to provide for the fast growing population caused by high birth rates. Unemployment and underemployment are features of many developing countries; fears therefore arise concerning the ability of populations to feed themselves. There are also disputes about the relationship between population growth and the availability of food. Some commentators argue that rapid population growth is a symptom of shortages and lack of opportunities, while others see it as a cause. Whatever the outcome of this

difference in interpretation, the general point remains that demographic data are significant factors in the formation of public policies. Without the data provided by censuses and vital statistics there could be no attempt to plan comprehensively for a nation's welfare and prosperity.

Urbanization

In the period of demographic transition in Europe, a marked feature of population change was the move towards urban living. In the 19th century the towns and cities of Europe grew very rapidly. People were attracted to urban areas by the prospect of employment in the new industrial, manufacturing, and service industries and by the lure of the modern amenities that cities can provide. The dense populations of towns and cities offered opportunities that rural life could not match. Although the relative percentages of rural and urban dwellers varies in the different countries of contemporary Europe there has been widespread urbanization throughout the continent.

There has been a similar rush to the towns and cities in the developing world in this century, for much the same reasons. New agricultural practices linked to commercial production have resulted in many smallholders losing their land, while others have found it hard to compete with large-scale modern farming. Often political issues are also involved; for example, agriculture may be seen by local politicians as a source of foreign currency by exporting produce, rather than merely as a source of subsistence for the rural population. These changes have forced many to abandon the rural areas and seek their living in towns. Moreover, for many young people, even in developing countries, towns offer job facilities and other attractions not available in the rural areas. For an unemployed person there are more chances of making a living in the town than in the rural area and, in addition, while one is searching for a job one is able to feel part of modern society, and all the facilities it has to offer.

Migration to the towns may take several forms; sometimes it is of a temporary nature, linked to seasonal production in the rural areas. In other cases, migrants may intend to spend only a brief sojourn in the town, perhaps to raise money for a specific purpose before returning home. However, in many cases migrants find that, whatever their original intentions, they are trapped in the town because they are unable to earn enough to save money for the journey home. Such migrants are often forced to live in poor housing with few, if any, facilities and have only intermittent paid employment. For many, the best

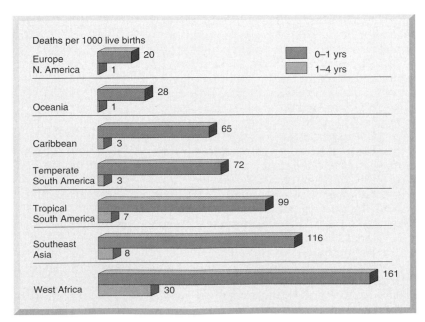

Deaths per 1000 live births

Region	0–1 yrs	1–4 yrs
Europe N. America	20	1
Oceania	28	1
Caribbean	65	3
Temperate South America	72	3
Tropical South America	99	7
Southeast Asia	116	8
West Africa	161	30

chance of making a living is to become self-employed in small-scale production or trading, which needs little or no capital or specialized skills. Many people who make their living in this way are petty traders or provide services for the urban population, such as dressmaking or hairdressing. Because it is easy to enter the so-called **informal economy**, many are attracted to it; however, competition between traders and providers of services is high, causing many ventures to fail. Women are often active in the informal sector, particularly in selling food – even where they do not play an active public role they are frequently involved in the preparing of goods within the household. Since the early 1960s, lack of opportunities in the rural areas, combined with the lure of modern life, have brought millions of people in the developing world into towns.

The rapid growth of informal housing in the form of shanty towns is a feature of the cities of the developing world. Urban dwellers erect their inadequate shelters out of whatever materials are readily and cheaply available. Often sewage disposal is not available, while the electricity and water supplies are usually uncertain and inadequate. Most spontaneous housing is illegal, and both city and national government are opposed to it. The authorities in many countries have even been known to raze areas of shanty towns to the ground. Urbanization has a great effect on populations, whether it involves those sufficiently fortunate to find employment or those who survive in the informal economy. Not only does it relocate people, it also leads to changes in their households and in their families. The analysis of demographic data provides a picture of such changes in populations that is essential to policy making.

Families and Marriage

States and governments take a keen interest in the functions of the family, for it is through families that individuals form part of a wider society. Demographic analysis in the developed countries has shown that over the last two or three decades there has been a considerable reduction in the number of large households and an increase in the number of one-person households and single-parent families. Households containing two or three generations of a family are declining rapidly both in the USA and in European countries. Divorce is increasing. However, many divorcees remarry, often creating new families in which children from previous marriages live together with half-siblings, born to the couple of the new marriage. These demographic trends are of great concern to governments because of the potentially far-reaching social and financial implications of widespread marriage break-up.

It has generally been assumed in most developed countries that the typical family unit is the **nuclear family** (or conjugal family), in which parents live together in a household with their dependent children. While this arrangement remains the norm in developed countries, many nonreligious couples dispense with marriage. Without a belief in the sacramental nature of the union and with new legislation treating cohabiting couples as if they were married, marriage as an institution may appear to be an unnecessary irrelevance. These developments have provoked concern about the stability of the family, with special emphasis on the fate of children from broken homes and the effects on society of these children.

Children are dependent upon their parents for a relatively long period compared to other animals, and the loss of the influence of one or the other parent when a nuclear family breaks up can create severe and lasting damage. It used to be a popular view among some social workers and psychologists that a 'clean break was better for children than a dirty marriage.' This view is no longer widely held.

Looked at more globally, however, it appears that the marriage and family forms of advanced industrial societies represent one pattern among many, with the contemporary changes producing families that are by no means unusual in other parts of the world.

In developed societies it is usual to think of marriage as a union between a male and a female, freely entered into and according to the wishes and the initiatives of the couple themselves – this is often called a **love marriage**. However, marriage may also be considered more than a union between two individuals, involving, as it does, large groups of people –

▲ **A Bangladeshi Extended Family**
An extended family is typically a household in which several generations live together as a single unit; the usual composition is grandparents, married child and her spouse, and grandchildren. This form of family is prevalent in many non-Western cultures.

informal economy
The sector of a country's economy that operates outside official legislation, in order to circumvent tax and labour laws. Because of its illegality, it is often referred to as the **black economy**. Many migrant workers in developing countries, who are willing to work for low wages and without any legal safeguards, work in the informal economy. The informal economy accounts for as much as 10% of all economic activity in industrialized countries, and up to 70% in developing nations.

A Traditional Hindu Marriage ▶

In a Hindu wedding ceremony, the bride and groom sit within a rope that symbolizes the joining together of man and woman. In Hindu communities in Western countries, children influenced by the concept of romantic love may rebel against a parentally arranged marriage with an unknown person.

The Nayars

The Nayars of Malabar in northern India are an example of the rare practice of polyandry. A woman may take many husbands but the man that she marries first is considered to be the father of all of her children. The Nayars also practise matriliny in matters of inheritance.

usually the kinsfolk of the couple. As marriage creates a relationship between these groups of kinsfolk, it is of interest to both parties that neither should be disadvantaged by an unfavourable or unworthy connection. For this reason marriage is too important to be left to the participants; with the honour of the family at stake, relatives may play a dominant role in the choice of marriage partner – this is the basis of an *arranged marriage*. Relatives are also involved in the collection of a dowry to enable one of their kin to marry. Dowries are common features of marriages all over the world and may be given to the families of either the bride or the groom. Since it is not unusual for a dowry to be beyond the means of the individual who plans to marry, it is necessary for kinsfolk to contribute.

INCEST

All societies have customary beliefs and practices that control sexual activity and marriage and hence the reproduction of children. Severe punishment is exacted for breaches of these customs that are regarded as *incest* – sexual relations between close relatives. However, what constitutes incest depends on the particular beliefs and practices of individual societies. In many cultures, only specified members of a person's close kin may be the subject of the incest taboo.

The biological reason for avoiding incest is that inbreeding would increase the risk of genetic defects in the resulting offspring. The taboo itself clearly predates such an explanation although it may have been arrived at on the basis of the observed results of these close unions. However, in some societies parents-in-law are included in the incest taboo, which confirms that observational evidence without a valid explanation is unlikely to provide a reliable basis for cultural conditioning.

In some ancient societies, a form of institutionalized incest among members of a ruling dynasty was permitted. In ancient Peru, Japan, and ancient Egypt, brother-sister marriages were encouraged in order to ensure continuance of the pure royal line.

In many African societies there are elaborate and complex customary procedures marking the contributions of kin, coupled with an obligation on the part of the person being so helped to make a reciprocal contribution to a future kinsman's marriage. Families are thus drawn into complicated networks of dependency; one marriage being dependent on other marriages. Marriage is considered a duty in many societies, making it rare to find spinsters or bachelors. Among some peoples, individuals are not deemed fully adult, and cannot enjoy the rights and privileges of adulthood, until they are married. For example, in some traditional African societies women's rights of land use are strictly marital – without a husband a woman has no right of access to land and without land she will starve.

Marriage preferences or requirements for groups are categorized by the terms **endogamy** and **exogamy**. Endogamy requires individuals to marry within their kin group while exogamy requires marriage outside the group. Endogamous marriage has the advantage of retaining property within the group. In traditional societies of the Middle East, the preferred marriage is with the father's brother's daughter; this is known as parallel cousin marriage. If there is no parallel cousin available, the next most preferred form is with the father's sister's daughter; this form of marriage is known as cross-cousin marriage.

Arranged marriages can take many other forms; these examples show that the love marriage prevalent in advanced societies is only one of many ways of selecting a partner.

Apart from the nuclear or extended family forms, there is also the *joint family*. Joint families have their own structure according to local custom and practice. The Hindu joint family is structured through relationships to land and inheritance practices. All males have equal rights in the property of their family by birth and all women of the family, whether as daughters or daughters-in-law, have the right to be looked after and have all their material needs met. In the joint family the senior male, who is usually the father or eldest brother, is the manager of the family property; all the married brothers, together with their wives and children, live on the property in a communal household eating food cooked on a common hearth. The brothers thus continue to live in their family of origin together with their family of procreation (the family they have created through marriage). The traditional African joint family consists of a man living in a compound with his wives and their children. Each wife has a separate hut, where she lives with her children; usually the wives take it in turns to cook for their husband and the food is taken to his hut. These two

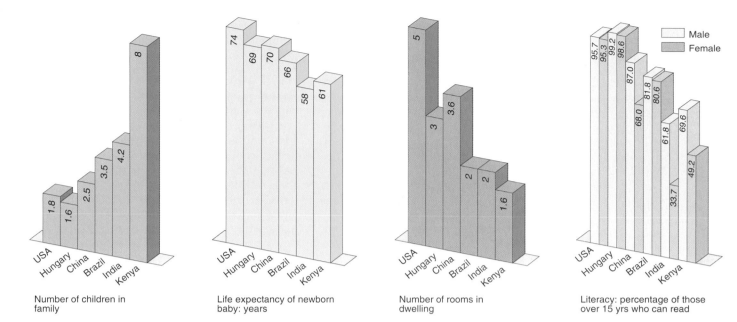

Number of children in family

Life expectancy of newborn baby: years

Number of rooms in dwelling

Literacy: percentage of those over 15 yrs who can read

examples illustrate the divergences in structure and organization that can exist within the category of a joint family.

Considerations of biology, residence, and inheritance are also important factors with regard to the family. In the nuclear family in developed societies it is usually assumed that the husband of a woman is the biological father of all children born to that woman. Terms drawn from Roman law are used to make the distinction between men who act as a social father to children although they are not their biological father (*pater*), and men who are the biological father of the children but not necessarily their social father (*genitor*).

Residence on marriage may be **neolocal** (a new residence set up for the couple), **patrilocal** (the couple live with the groom's family), or **matrilocal** (the couple live with the bride's mother).

Inheritance in families in developed societies proceeds according to a bilateral or **cognatic system**, in which heirs may inherit from both the male and female lines. In some societies, however, inheritance and descent is through the mother and not through the father; this system is called **matriliny** or **matrilineal descent**. Where descent and inheritance is through men it is called **patriliny** or **patrilineal descent**. Matriliny and patriliny have consequences for the recognition of family members; moreover, their different principles produce quite different family structures. For example, in a patrilineal system the children of a person's mother's sister are not recognized as kin.

The family and kinship systems of developing societies play a far more significant role in the lives of individuals and in social life than those of advanced Western economies. This is

reflected in the kinship terminologies of the two groups, with the more developed terminology of some non-Western societies distinguishing between maternal and paternal aunts.

Nevertheless, family and kinship are important in advanced Western societies. Despite cohabiting and the high divorce rate, marriage remains an important institution. The early socialization provided by the family is of great significance in children's lives. Families continue to provide support when its members are in need; this support is particularly strong between mothers and children. Indeed, one of the problems facing the family in developed societies is the clash between the mother's biological role in child care and her need to work to augment the family income.

Families also have an economic role, especially in setting up small businesses. In such cases the work of family members is usually found to be particularly valuable because they are flexible and willing to work long hours to ensure the success of a family enterprise.

▲ **Demographic Statistics** *These bar charts show four sets of statistics relating to people's living conditions and education, in selected countries in various regions of the world.*

HUSBANDS AND WIVES

The number of spouses is categorized in a number of ways:
- **Monogamy** – having only one spouse over a period of time – is the norm; **serial monogamy** describes the practice of having a succession of spouses, one at a time.
- **Polygamy** is having more than one spouse at any one time and may apply to either husbands or wives.
- **Polygyny** describes men having more than one wife; this is commonly allowed in Africa although in practice it is restricted to rich men, because a man must provide for all his wives equally.
- **Polyandry** is the unusual practice of women taking more than one husband at a time.

▲ **First Communion in Spain** *In Roman Catholic countries, children are prepared for this ceremony marking their full entry into the Church by being schooled in the catechism. Girls and boys traditionally wear white, which symbolizes purity, for this important rite.*

Despite the fears expressed about the decline of marriage, it appears that the family is resilient and adaptable. Although the form of the family does seem to be changing in advanced societies, these changes do not necessarily signal decay; the family is a product of a society and its culture – it is to be expected that it will reflect changes in society. The cycle of family life must change as family members play new roles in relation to one another. Indeed, change is a keynote of family life: when a married couple become parents their life changes, while the nature of the parent's role itself changes as children grow up. When the children leave their family the couple are again on their own and have to adapt to the changes this brings. Further changes occur if the children themselves become parents, making the original couple grandparents.

Rites of Passage

Rites of passage are ceremonies and rituals that celebrate the transition of individuals from one status in society to another. Because they involve the relationship between individuals and society, these rites are of public concern as well as being a private matter for the individual. The human life cycle is an inevitable and integral part of social life; human beings are born and human beings die. Society continues and society changes all the time because of changing personnel and because of the effect of changed relationships between people, itself a product of the changing personnel. The social reproduction of society, the means by which society renews and adapts itself to circumstances, is intimately linked to the life cycle and so to human birth, ageing, and death. It is customary to mark the major realignments for individuals and groups, which arise out of natural processes of maturation and ageing.

These are rites of passage. The French anthropologist Arnold van Gennep (1873–1957), who coined the term in 1909, identified three phases common to all rites of passage: the phase of *separation*, followed by the phase of *transition*, and concluded by the phase of *integration*. In the first phase individuals are separated from their current roles and positions in society in anticipation of the new ones they are to take; secondly, the individuals enter into a state of limbo or transition, during which they become detached from past relationships although they have not yet entered into new relationships with others. This intermediary stage is often thought of as very dangerous for those who are in transition, representing as it does a form of death in which one is separated from society without having achieved a new status.

In the last stage the transitional individuals move to their new status in society and emerge as new individuals. The fact that they have become different people means that all the other members of their society must readjust to the changed situation. It is in this way that the rituals and ceremonies, which often seem to focus on an individual, have a wider currency. Rites of passage are concerned with both individual and community adjustments to new and changed circumstances.

Circumcision as a Rite of Passage ▶
Masai tribesmen in Kenya, Africa, are prepared for the ritual circumcision that marks their transition from adolescence to full adulthood. Circumcision is a rite performed in many parts of the world, in cultures as diverse as Judaism and the Aboriginal peoples of Australia.

Traditional societies in which opportunities for individual achievement are more limited tend to give greater public emphasis to these rites than modern societies. Initiation rites are very significant because they enable children to become adult, marking a profound change in status and relationships. The period of transition is a considerable ordeal for the initiates, as they must prove themselves capable of adult behaviour, which in the case of young boys usually involves facing fear and pain. Having their bodies mutilated commonly provides an outward manifestation of the inward transformation that has occurred. Circumcision, the removal of teeth, tattooing, and facial scarring are all such signs of manhood.

In some societies there are similar initiations for girls, which take place around the time of puberty. These signal the move from an asexual world to one of sexual activity. Among East African pastoral people the initiation of young men is an important part of the political process. These societies are governed by elders, who are the senior **age grades** of the community. The lives of young men are highly structured into a hierarchy of age grades, each of which requires special action in relation to the community. Age grades are formed by the initiation of a cohort of young men every 10–15 years. Relationships within the age grade are egalitarian and free, and the young men form a corporate group, whereas those with adjacent age grades can be tense. Because cattle are the mainstay of such peoples, the **moran** ('warriors') are given the task of tending the cattle. This can involve long absences from home, which fosters the ties between the young men. After the moran have served their

term as herdsmen, they become elders and are integrated back into the community. Only then are they allowed to marry. The succeeding age grade then take their place as moran. The age grade and transition system allocates positions of authority in the community in a way that allows for individual mobility in a context of continuity in society.

Modern secular societies have few rites of passage for young people. However, for religious people, the rites persist; Christian baptism and confirmation, as well as circumcision and Bar Mitzvah in Judaism, are rites reflecting the entry of the candidates into the religious community and subsequently of acquiring the status of adulthood, allowing them full participation in religious duties.

In both traditional and modern societies the life cycle of birth, marriage, and death involves changes of status. On the birth of a first child there is a marked change of status for a couple who become parents. The presence of the child has to be recognized by society, and consequently there are ceremonies and rituals that incorporate the child into civil society as well as into a religious community, if desired. Weddings and funerals also involve altered statuses both for the central participants and for others close to them. Like marriage, bereavement requires that a new way of life be adopted. The funeral functions as an announcement to the community that, for the bereaved person, life without the departed has begun.

Communities vary in the extent and the range of the rites of passage that they observe. It is, however, a universal feature of human societies that individual change and transition is given public acknowledgment.

▲ The Mexican Day of the Dead
In Mexico, one night is set aside every year for people to keep vigil over the graves of their relatives. Prayers and songs are intoned to appease the souls of the deceased. The dead are honoured after their departure from life in many societies around the world.

Social Divisions

Societies with rigid divisions • Social differentiation • Class inequality •
Gender in society • Race in society • Religious divisions • Slavery

Human beings in almost all societies throughout history have tended to evaluate both themselves and the attributes of their world in different ways. However, in every human society people are expected to behave according to an inescapable set of norms. Because these norms are essential in the regulation of a society there is a need for sanctions (punishments) to be imposed on those who breach, or fail to conform to, the accepted standards.

Some sociologists claim that it is this tendency to evaluate combined with the imposition of sanctions on nonconformists that inevitably results in social divisions and inequality. According to this view, the division of society into layers begins when a minority evaluates the large majority for conformity and imposes sanctions on those who deviate from this norm. In some cases, social divisions will result from the attributes of the individuals themselves, while in others it will be a result of the position held by an individual independently of *who* holds that position.

In this context it is important to note that differences in sex, age, skin colour, or wealth, for example, do not in themselves result in

social divisions. It is the significance that these differences have for the social group and the meanings they give to them that cause the divisions. In other words, it is the social significance of the differences, not the differences themselves, that create social division. The perception of social difference is, it appears, a product of social definition rather than an inherent indication of human diversity. For example, children of different religions or of different ethnic origins play quite happily and unselfconsciously together – until they are told that persons of another faith or ethnic background are different and unacceptable in some way that is defined by the social groups to which their parents belong.

Nevertheless, this divisive process is enormously significant for individuals because it will directly affect their ***life chances*** (i.e. the likelihood of them achieving their goals). The underlying reality behind this description of the sources of social division is that power and power structures precede inequality. Social division is a secondary consequence of the social structure based on power. Those with power can deny others access to scarce resources and

Social Class ▶
This image of social inequality – showing British schoolchildren of the 1930s, from the upper and lower classes – provides a vivid example of the hierarchy of social divisions that exists in most societies.

THE ESTATES

Feudalism was characterized by the system of *estates* – different social groups within the community. The main estates were:
• the nobility (or 'lords temporal');
• the clergy (or 'lords spiritual');
• the commons (or vassals, peasantry).
The estate system existed in Europe from the Roman Empire onwards, reaching its peak in the Middle Ages. It began to decline in the 18th century as a result of the rise of the urban bourgeoisie. The system was retained longest in France, where it was swept away by the French Revolution in 1789; the Revolution's 'Declaration of the Rights of Man and the Citizen' asserted the equality of all men.
A rigid estate system also existed in pre-Tokugawa Japan; see JAPAN (VOL. 5).

can impose sanctions on those who fail to comply with the norms. This kind of analysis is associated with the work of the German sociologist Max Weber (1864–1920).

While not necessarily rejecting this view, some writers, including the French philosopher Jean Jacques Rousseau (1712–78) and the German economist Karl Marx (1818–83), have seen ownership and the nonownership of land, private property, and the means of production (e.g. factories) as the real sources of social division. This, however, fails to confront the question of how private property itself came into existence. To answer this question requires an analysis of the historical and economic factors behind the evolution of different societies and social systems.

Societies with Rigid Divisions
It is instructive to examine some societies in which rigid divisions were – and in some cases still are – adhered to by entire societies.

Slavery in Classical Societies. In ancient Greece and Rome, society was rigidly divided into masters and slaves. The master had the full social rights of citizenship, while the slave had none. In Greece individual mobility was not possible, although in Rome, a slave, or his master, could buy freedom. People became slaves as a consequence of conquest, as a punishment for a criminal offence, or by birth. The emergence of a slave economy depended on three basic factors: the private ownership of property, a shortage of labour, and a source of people to be enslaved. Classical slavery provided the model for this strict form of social division in the American slave trade and more recently for the use of slave labour in Nazi Germany (see **SLAVERY**).

European Feudalism. This system of social division was broadly applied throughout Europe in the Middle Ages. Society was rigidly divided into a number of different **estates**, with the majority in the third estate, as vassals. Vassals entered into a personal relationship with a lord to whom they paid homage and fealty (an oath of loyalty) in return for protection and often a fief (property or a fee). Mobility between estates was extremely infrequent, although not impossible. For example, a vassal could obtain his lord's permission to enter the Church.

The Caste System. This system of division groups people according to specific social rank. Membership of a particular caste is both hereditary and permanent. Systems of this kind have occurred in many parts of the world; the Hindu caste system that persists in India is regarded as being divinely ordained on the basis of the relative purity of its members (see RELIGION: HINDUISM). The divisions are supported by a considerable amount of ritual, and individual mobility is not allowed. Marriage within the caste is strictly practised; even in Hindu communities that have grown up outside India, arranged marriages to individuals of appropriate caste are still the rule.

In these examples of rigid demarcation, social mobility is rare; it occurs far more readily in more modern class-based societies.

Social Differentiation
Sociology tends to see social divisions in several different ways, depending on the basis and

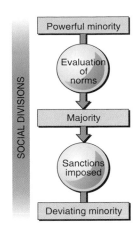

SOCIAL DIVISIONS

▲ **The Origins of Social Division**
This diagram illustrates one basic model of how social divisions arise, with a minority imposing norms on the rest of society and ostracizing those who fail to conform.

A King and his Vassals
This manuscript illustration shows the strict hierarchical organization that prevailed within the feudal system. ▼

I'm not interested in classes.... Far be it from me to foster inferiority complexes among the workers by trying to make them think that they belong to some special class. That has happened in Europe but it hasn't happened here yet.

John Llewellyn Lewis
(1880–1969), US labour
leader

Poverty in India
The dalits *('oppressed')
are the lowest caste in
India. Here,* dalits *are
pictured in a slum
dwelling in the city
of Jamshodpur.* ▼

nature of the social differentiation. Perhaps the most all-encompassing idea is that of social *stratification* – this term, with its image of a series of layers imposed upon each other, was borrowed from geography and geology. In this structure there is obviously a large layer at the bottom and a smaller one at the top, with ascending layers between them. Sociologists are interested in this structure because the strata in which people are located will directly affect their chances of fulfilment in life.

Closely related to the idea of stratification is the concept of a *hierarchy* with, again, its ranks arranged in ascending order. The clearest example of a hierarchy is provided by the institution in relation to which the term was first used. The ordained clergy of the Roman Catholic Church constitute a well-defined hierarchy (literally 'a gathering of high priests') that begins with the deacons and rises through the priesthood to bishops, archbishops, and cardinals, reaching its pinnacle with the pope.

Sociologists have concluded that there may also be ties that cut across any hierarchical division. Such ties link groups together – irrespective of individuals' positions in hierarchies – on the basis of a universally recognized criterion. This phenomenon, which is often called *pillarization*, occurs in a number of very diverse contexts, ranging from racial and ethnic allegiances to tribe and clan membership, with religion often playing a major role.

A further model, closely related to pillarization, suggests that individuals cluster together on the basis of how they define themselves. An example of such a grouping would be the gay community. Here the allegiances may be based on a community of interest, arising as a result of common motivations.

These models make it clear that an objective sociological definition of the nature of social divisions cannot be isolated from a subjective appraisal of the individual's own definition of the situation. An individual self-assessment may establish loyalties and ties that ignore any number of objective criteria, such as education, income, and occupation. Moreover, any model that reflects the nature of social divisions has to include the creation and maintenance of boundaries – between classes, religious groups, and political parties, for example – as a complex social phenomenon in its own right. There will always be those who are included and those who must be excluded, according to accepted criteria that form the basis of differentiation. According to these theories, the principal characteristic of social division is not simply acceptance or rejection on the basis of prejudice, but a real conflict for both legitimacy and access to scarce resources.

Class Inequality

The main social division in society has often been seen as being inequality based on class – particularly in the work of Karl Marx and Max Weber. Although Marx gave no complete or comprehensive formulation of class, he undoubtedly saw class as being the driving force of historical development. Marx contended that class did not exist in primitive tribal societies because they had a very simple division of labour. Class resulted from a more complex division of labour, which led to the creation of a surplus and allowed one section of society to live off the labour of another section.

In this view the division of labour is seen as identical to the possession or non-possession of productive private property. Thus, Marx defined class in relation to the ownership of the means of production, i.e. there were property owners (the bourgeoisie) and free labourers (the proletariat) forming the two hostile camps of capitalism. Although members of a capitalist society are born into a particular class,

SOCIAL MOBILITY

Social mobility describes the movement of individuals upwards or downwards between divisions in a social structure. In industrial and postindustrial societies, manual jobs are declining in comparison with those of a higher status; though in theory this should provide more opportunities for upward social mobility, it is offset by the dwindling job market as a whole and the rise in unemployment. Social mobility may occur on an **intragenerational** basis, i.e. within one generation, or an **intergenerational** basis, between generations.

As an example of intergenerational social mobility, many of the children of farmers or poor immigrants in the USA in the 19th century moved up into the middle class. This relatively high degree of upward movement may explain why socialism never achieved the success in the USA in the late 19th century that it did in Europe.

their future status may not be solely determined by the accident of birth. **Social mobility** in later capitalism is a real possibility: many political leaders are the sons and daughters of manual workers, who have managed to benefit from education, while many businesses are run by people from a similar background, whose entrepreneurial skills have enabled them to transcend traditional class barriers.

In *Das Kapital* (1867) Marx wrote that millions of families live under economic conditions that separate their way of life, interests, and education from other classes. Nevertheless, although these economic conditions were sufficient to define the position of an individual in a class, they were not enough in themselves, in Marx's view, to lead to an awareness of that position. That is, Marx drew a distinction between an objective class position and a subjective class consciousness, which he believed would emerge in the working class. In his later work, Marx produced a much more complex picture of the class structure than the initial two-class model. Even so, he was always concerned with capitalist class relations, rather than with relationships between individuals and static categories of stratification. For him, classes – and not individuals – were the basic actors on the historical stage.

Weber, on the other hand, stressed the role of individuals in relation to class and provided a subtle picture of the nature of class formation. For Weber, a class constitutes a number of individuals who are defined by their likelihood of acquiring goods, gaining a position in life, and

finding personal satisfaction. This likelihood is determined by the extent of their control over their own skills and the uses to which they put their ability to earn an income. Although Weber agreed that property and lack of property are the basic determinants of class structures, he insisted upon a link between the class situation and the market situation. In his view, the emphasis should be on the skills of the propertyless groups that can be sold on the market. These skills, which are often derived from education, lead directly to success or failure in life. On this basis there could be as many class divisions as there are minute gradations of economic position. With a potentially wide variety of economic classes, certain factors emerge to unify them into social classes.

Perhaps the most important factor is the extent to which an individual can move between economic classes. Nevertheless, social classes could never be considered as communities, with their own consciousness of a common prospect in life (individual consciousness of life's prospects is also limited). Market position, a multiplicity of classes, and a highly differentiated class structure for the propertied and unpropertied (based on the relative monopoly of marketable skills) summarizes Weber's view of class. However, to class Weber adds several related concepts that clarify his understanding of social divisions. Most significantly, Weber introduces the idea of **status groups** that, unlike classes in the world of production, are more concerned with a characteristic consumption of goods.

For Weber, status groups are normally communities whose members are usually conscious of their membership of the group. A characteristic style of life has to be exhibited by all those aspiring to belong to the circle. Status distinctions, which often involve social exclusiveness, are guaranteed by convention, by ritual, and in some cases by law. In their more extreme form, status groups can evolve into a closed caste.

Weber adds a further important concept to his analysis of social divisions – social closure. In social closure, certain groups (not necessarily status groups) monopolize access to scarce resources (e.g. fishing grounds) and deny access to outsiders, who often then organize themselves to challenge this arrangement. Indeed, conflict and the exercise of power underpin the whole of Weber's conception of social divisions. According to him, classes and status groups are by their very nature phenomena resulting from the distribution of power.

If social divisions based on class, status, and power are accepted as legitimate, there is a case for claiming that it is **authority**, rather than naked power, that is the critical concept.

▲ **Max Weber**
Unlike Karl Marx, Weber included the important element of social status in his analysis of class. Weber argued that this tended to produce peaceful competition, rather than class struggle.

The history of all hitherto existing society is the history of class struggle.

Karl Marx

The Underclass

The term 'underclass' has been created, with the rise in mass long-term unemployment, to describe those who live on the margins of society, either permanently unemployed or intermittently engaged in low-status occupations. The fear has been raised that a large underclass destabilizes society, through the involvement of its members in crime.

▲ **Working Women in a Developing Country** *Seamstresses make garments at a factory in the Philippines. In general, the workload of women is greater than that of men. However, because much of the work done by women is either low-paid or unpaid (in the home or community), women own a disproportionately small amount of the world's wealth.*

played by social mobility in shaping both the class structure and the individuals' perceptions of social divisions. Although conflicting data has come from various investigations of social mobility – often based on differing estimates of the scale and range of social mobility – it is undoubtedly true that changes have taken place. At the top of the structure a whole range of professional managers has emerged, with different backgrounds and interests from the owners of capital; in the middle ranges of the class structure, new middle-class office workers and shop assistants have appeared; while the formerly homogeneous working class has become internally differentiated.

There are differences in the actual class structures in different countries, the parameters of which have been largely determined by historical, climatic, or geographical features. Nevertheless, many of the changes that have occurred in capitalist societies since the end of World War II have taken place throughout the world. The collapse of communism in Europe has also encouraged a class structure to re-form in former communist countries, which reflects 20th-century changes in capitalist countries.

In some societies, the indisputable shift away from a rigid class structure that has taken place has helped to foster the widespread perception of the society as being open. Both this real change – and, more importantly, people's belief that there are virtually unlimited opportunities for social mobility, based on merit – have done much to alter earlier attitudes to wealth, poverty, inequality, and exploitation.

Indeed, some sociologists have claimed that social divisions have to be understood in terms of authority relationships, which would help to explain both the persistence and acceptance of inequality in society.

Other sociologists have suggested that some form of stratification is a necessary ingredient of a society. In this view, society has certain needs that have to be met and certain functions that have to be fulfilled. Individuals within that society are motivated to fill certain positions and to undertake the functions attached to them by the prospect of greater rewards. This can be justified by the greater contribution these individuals make to the welfare of society by undertaking these functions. Although this assumption has been much criticized, it does illustrate that social stratification systems need not be static and can involve considerable social mobility.

An important dimension of class inequality in advanced capitalist societies is the role

Gender in Society

The way people view evident differences in others in their community is the basis for most social divisions. This not only refers to divisions based on ethnic origins and religion – above all it applies to differences of gender. While there is an obvious physical basis to differences between the sexes, gender forms the social basis upon which acceptable behaviour patterns and codes of conduct are constructed for both men and for women. Quite often one of the sexes is seen to have its own innate characteristics: for example, gentleness in women or aggression in men. Although there may be limited evidence that this is actually the case, a belief in innate characteristics will have an effect on people's expectations or evaluations of others. Clearly, in the majority of societies in the world, throughout history, men have been dominant at the expense of women. Those societies in which men dominate women – socially, economically, politically, physically, and psychologically – are called *patriarchies*. The relatively rarer societies dominated by women are called *matriarchies*. As patriarchies have

---

OCCUPATIONAL STATUS

Because of the growing social and economic importance of work, many sociologists prefer to regard occupation as the most accurate measure of contemporary social stratification.

They have been aided in this by the development, by market research companies in the USA and western Europe, of a system of social grading by occupation. The main groups are:

Upper middle class (senior managers and professionals, e.g. lawyers, doctors)
Middle class (lower managers and professionals, e.g. teachers)
Lower middle class (routine white-collar workers, e.g. secretaries)
Skilled working class (skilled manual workers, e.g. carpenters)
Semiskilled/unskilled working class (manual workers, e.g. bus drivers, cashiers)
Residual class (casual workers or unemployed, e.g. labourers)

historically been seen as the norm, women may be unaware of the extent to which they have been oppressed and disadvantaged. However, during this century many women, through political organization and support, have come to see the inequity of their situation and have determined to redress the balance. In many developed urban industrial societies there is now substantial legislation to prevent discrimination against women in employment rights (e.g. equality of pay with men) as well as property and pension rights. There is, nevertheless, a constant struggle to overcome the prejudice that women cannot compete equally with men in virtually every area of life. There are still some men who are unable to accept that rewards and rights should be distributed equally between men and women.

Race in Society

A person's physical appearance as a human being has also come to be a source of social division. Race is a concept that attempts a strict categorization of people according to such objective criteria as skin colour. However, the concept has been misused, for example by making fallacious associations between skin colour and intelligence. In turn this encouraged the notion that some peoples could be considered superior or inferior to others. These judgments could be based purely on physical attributes or used in conjunction with social, cultural, and religious considerations.

Racism occurs when such social and superficial differences between human beings are used to the detriment of the group regarded as inferior. Usually, the group regarded as inferior would be a minority in a particular society. Racism has two distinct but related aspects: prejudice – a negative attitude formed prior to any adequate evidence or experience – and discrimination, a social disadvantaging of the minority. Human civilizations are at their worst when discrimination and prejudice are orchestrated by the state (e.g. in Nazi Germany) and at their best when ethnic distinctions are not treated hierarchically but as a source of richness and diversity in society.

A society that is characterized by sharp internal divisions between ethnic groups is referred to as a ***plural society***. This term is also used of societies that have pronounced religious or linguistic cleavages. The majority of countries in the world are pluralistic, to a varying extent. The USA, Russia, Nigeria, and India are examples of extremely pluralistic societies, due to their high degree of fragmentation into distinct groups. Whereas Marxist sociologists have tended to play down these divisions, preferring to focus instead on class, others treat pluralism as an inescapable fact within a mature democracy. Indeed, pluralism may become a source of peaceful competition and harmonious coexistence. All too frequently, however – especially where ethnic or religious divisions are concerned – pluralism may be a major contributory factor to bitter conflict, especially where there is a high degree of social or economic inequality between the constituent groups. In this century, examples of conflict between different ethnic groups within a society have occurred in Africa, the Middle East, and India with devastating results.

Eugenics

Eugenics is the study of the improvement of humans by selective breeding to enhance desirable physical or mental characteristics. This concept – pioneered in 1883 by the British scientist Francis Galton (1822–1911) – later fell into disrepute due to the misuse of its ideas by supremacists and racists. Eugenics flourished under the Nazi regime in Germany, which used it to further its policy of extermination of supposedly 'inferior' races, such as Jews and the Romany people, in order to promote a 'master race' (*Herrenvolk*).

◄ **Interracial Harmony** *Children of different ethnic backgrounds play together, unaware of the racial prejudice that is a fact of adult life and that constitutes a major social division.*

So many gods, so many creeds,
So many paths that wind and wind,
While just the art of being kind
Is all the sad world needs.

Ella Wheeler Wilcox
(1850–1919), US poet

CULTS

Originally a specific system of religious beliefs, a cult is now considered to be a quasi-religious organization that uses questionable psychological techniques to gain vulnerable young people as adherents.

The beliefs and practices of a cult usually depart radically from those of an orthodox religion; often a cult is seen as a threat to the religion itself. Cults, moreover, tend to be associated with a particular social arrangement:

- they tend to have an all-powerful figurehead (a 'guru'), whose word cannot be challenged and who is likely to be surrounded by trusted lieutenants;
- they usually have a broad mass of devotees whose faith in the cult is fanatical and exclusive;
- they are cut off from the wider society by a mutual process of rejection.

Cults are frequently associated with **messianic** beliefs (i.e. those that proclaim the coming of a chosen one or the end of the world). The failure of prophesies to materialize may trigger a desperate reaction. At its most extreme, this has resulted in the mass-suicide of cult members.

Cults have existed throughout history and most have remained peripheral to their parent religions. Nevertheless, some young people, particularly in urban industrial societies, are attracted to cults because they provide naive answers to their questions and a close community that offers an acceptable way of life, to replace the disagreeable society from which they have escaped.

Fundamentalism
Muslim girls from Malaysia are shown studying the Koran. In reaction against the failure of politics to solve pressing problems, fundamentalism has arisen in many faiths (e.g. Christianity, Islam, and Hinduism) in the late 20th century. It advocates a return to traditional doctrines and sees the authority of the religion's central text (e.g. Koran, Bible) as absolute. ▼

Religious Divisions

Religion has often been at the root of social divisions. Throughout the world, over thousands of years, religious beliefs have been misused as the justification for discrimination against nonbelievers and those who believe something different. Religious beliefs and rituals bind believers into a community with a clear range of rights, duties, and codes of conduct. Together, these constitute a **belief system**. This includes not only specific beliefs about specific deities and an afterlife (e.g. heaven and hell), it also incorporates what a person should think and do in this life. Indeed, most of the major world religions emphasize that *believers* should lead a 'good' life, treat others with consideration, and provide for those less fortunate than themselves. However, the extent to which these precepts are to

be extended to people of other faiths (or no faith) is often uncertain.

Historically, those who do not conform to a particular belief system have often been tolerated. Perhaps more often, they have either been persecuted or persuaded to convert to it. The reaction adopted has often been influenced by prevailing political circumstances.

It is sometimes difficult to tell where a particular belief system begins and ends in relation to the wider culture of a society. In certain societies (e.g. ancient Egypt), they are virtually the same thing; at other times a multireligious harmony has existed in a society. It is certainly true that children learn the religion of their parents in an unquestioning way and, in most cases, are not given a great deal of information about other religions. This can lead to intolerance unless the religion itself expressly forbids it. Even when a number of different religions coexist in a society there may be inequality of opportunity in that society as a result of religious prejudice.

Religious divisions are often at their most pronounced where religion and ethnicity reinforce each other. In many cases individuals do not have actively to proclaim their faith, as this is immediately disclosed by their appearance, their name, or their physical location. In this way, religion can furnish a person with both an individual and a social identity. Yet it is also increasingly the case that religion in many advanced societies does not provide such automatic group membership. Instead it fulfils a less well defined spiritual need for a sense of belonging and for an answer to the 'meaning of life'. In these circumstances, a person may consciously choose a religion rather than being born into it.

SLAVERY

SLAVERY HAS EXISTED in many different cultures throughout history. Even in the late 20th century, forms of slavery persist in some parts of the world, despite being outlawed by national governments and international bodies.

SLAVERY IN THE ANCIENT WORLD

Slavery was common in both ancient Greece and Rome. Roman military conquest in the 2nd and 3rd centuries BC brought huge numbers of slaves, who were forced into hard labour on estates and in mines and quarries. Slaves were also employed as domestic servants. Unique among slave societies of any period, Roman slaves could be educated, acquire property, and buy their freedom.

SLAVES FROM AFRICA

After slavery had declined in medieval Europe, it was lent a new impetus by the discovery and colonization of the New World by European powers from the late 15th century onwards. After the native population of the Americas had been devastated by diseases brought by the invaders, human labour was sought from a new source – Africa; see AFRICA(VOL. 1). Thus began the most protracted and large-scale exploitation of forced labour in the history of mankind.

Plantation Work *In this 18th-century engraving, slaves are seen preparing the land for a sugar plantation on the Caribbean island of Antigua.*

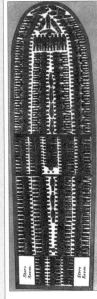

A Slave Ship *Disease caused by overcrowding killed many slaves.*

SHIPPING SLAVES
Throughout the 16th and 17th centuries, the enslavement and transportation of Black Africans to the New World was conducted on a massive scale. Altogether, some 15 million people were taken from their homelands in west and central Africa to work on plantations throughout the Americas and the Caribbean. On the voyage, human suffering was unimaginable; around one-fifth of all Black slaves died in transit.

ABOLITION

Moves to abolish slavery began in the 18th century. The US constitution, drafted in 1788, provided for the emancipation of slaves within 20 years. However, slavery persisted in southern states of the USA. In the early 19th century, Britain, France, and most of the newly independent nations of South and Central America outlawed slavery.

20TH-CENTURY SLAVERY

Slavery gained a new lease of life under totalitarianism. In the former Soviet Union, political opponents of Stalinism in the 1930s were forced to work in 'corrective labour' facilities. In Nazi Germany, millions of Jews and Slavs were literally worked to death in factories and mines.

Hunted Slaves *Slaves who tried to escape from enforced labour and ill-treatment were hunted down ruthlessly by plantation owners.*

Introduction to Anthropology

Fields of study • Social Darwinism • Modern anthropology

Anthropology is the general term for a collection of interrelated disciplines that have as their common denominator the systematic study of humankind, including its historical development, unity, and diversity. The scope of the general term, however, has evolved somewhat and is now understood differently in the USA and Europe. In the USA, it embraces four fields: physical anthropology, prehistoric archaeology, anthropological linguistics, and social and cultural anthropology; in most of Europe it is usually taken to mean only physical anthropology and social anthropology.

Fields of Study

Physical anthropology once studied the measurement and distribution of physical differences of the human species during the course of its development. Now called ***biological anthropology***, it is primarily concerned with the study of human evolution and the distribution of biological variables among human populations. Also, some modern physical anthropologists investigate those aspects of primate behaviour and social organization that they saay helped illuminate the transition that occurred in east Africa many millennia ago from the hominid to the human way of life.

Prehistoric archaeology is the study of ancient cultures. It used to be exclusively concerned with the study of classical civilizations (in Egypt, Greece, and Rome), but now includes past societies throughout the world; it is also more concerned with developing theories of social processes than with tracing the evolution of their material traditions. Because it relies heavily on the insights of social anthropology it is sometimes known as ***palaeoanthropology***.

Anthropological linguistics is the study of the languages spoken by non-Western peoples. Anthropological linguists study both the grammar and vocabulary of these languages and the ways in which they are used in different social and cultural contexts. They thus provide a broad range of examples, which enables Western linguists to test the universality of their general theories.

Social and cultural anthropology is the comparative study of the systems of ideas, beliefs, and traditions held by different peoples

People at a Travelling Shop in Tibet *One form of culture – the subject of all anthropological study – is that based on grazing animals and a nomadic existence, as in this traditional society.*

(cultural anthropology) and of their social behaviour (social anthropology). Until the mid-1960s, cultural anthropology was the characteristic approach of US anthropologists and social anthropology the characteristic approach of their British and French colleagues. Since the rise of structuralism under Claude Lévi-Strauss (1908–) in the 1960s the difference between the two approaches has disappeared, and the subject is referred to by its joint name.

Social Darwinism

Anthropology emerged as a separate academic pursuit in the middle of the 19th century. Its emergence was stimulated by the moral problems posed by the European domination and colonization of other parts of the world. What was the nature and status of these 'primitive' peoples? How should they be treated by their colonizers?

The aim of early anthropologists was then to produce a universal history of humankind. These pioneers of the discipline classified the peoples of the world hierarchically into 'races,' according to their physical characteristics, material culture, and social institutions. These hierarchies were thought to be the consequence of the evolution of *Homo sapiens* in different parts of the world. At that time it was believed that in some parts of the world, such as Australia, the original inhabitants had not evolved very far; in other parts, such as western Europe, they were thought to have evolved more than anywhere else.

According to this approach, the 'higher races' were those who valued scientific thought, promoted technological development, maintained a system of strong representative government, advocated the right to private property, practised monogamy, upheld a strict moral code, and believed in one god. Members of the 'lower races' were assumed to be unscientific, lacking in innovation, anarchic, promiscuous, amoral, and either irreligious or animistic.

Even though these theories were formulated at least a decade before the publication of Darwin's *Origin of Species*, this evolutionary approach to the study of anthropology became known as 'social Darwinism.' However, unlike Darwin's biological theory, which argued for a diversity of evolutionary paths, most anthropologists saw the development of the human species as a single uniform process. The optimists among them believed that although only some peoples had so far evolved to the level of the 'higher races,' all peoples had the potential to develop to that stage. Pessimists, however, regarded the 'lower races' as the degenerate survivors of earlier stages in human evolution:

certain peoples were thus 'naturally' inferior and incapable of further development.

It is now clear that early anthropologists categorized peoples according to the values of their own society, in an attempt to justify their own position as the most advanced (i.e. superior) culture. For example, in his *Ancient Society* (1877), the US anthropologist Lewis H. Morgan (1818–81) identified three stages of 'human progress': savagery, barbarism, and civilization. Characterizing each stage by various material, technological, and institutional criteria, he tried to place all known societies at one or other of these phases.

Morgan's account, and others like it, are based on the false premise that all societies should evolve in exactly the same manner. Yet just because 19th-century moralists regarded certain social practices as unevolved does not make them so. For instance, the Nyinba of Nepal practise polyandry not because they are degenerate but because it is an adaptive social mechanism preventing the repeated subdivision of the limited area of land exploited by each family: since all the sons of a family are married to the same woman, they do not produce offspring each of whom would have rights to a portion of their parents' land; instead they help to produce a single group of sons who inherit the family estate collectively.

Moreover, there is no historical evidence for any one primordial type of a social practice or even that any unique primordial type existed. How early humans governed themselves can never be known, since they left no records. It cannot be assumed that the first human populations all governed themselves identically.

Early accounts are too rigid in implying that certain sets of social practices always occur together. This was undermined by the discovery, at the turn of the century, that the Australian Aborigines, who still lived as hunter-gatherers and did not appear to have a fixed social organization, in fact had a highly developed set of religious beliefs and a complex kinship system.

Modern Anthropology

By the beginning of the 20th century many anthropologists were reacting against the speculative approach of the social Darwinists. Many of this new generation were sceptical of the notion of 'race,' pointing out that the differences between different types of humans were less than the degree of variation within each type. They therefore initiated the break between cultural and physical anthropology.

This break was subsequently maintained by both cultural and social anthropologists, who saw how antidemocratic politicians, such as the Nazis, could exploit physical anthropology for their own ends. Since the 1950s, most physical anthropologists have given up cate-

▲ **Claude Lévi-Strauss** *The French anthropologist Claude Lévi-Strauss became the leading exponent of structural anthropology. This approach reveals the underlying structures of cultures by examining their myths, belief systems, and rituals.*

Herbert Spencer and Social Darwinism

Herbert Spencer (1820–1903), who coined the term 'the survival of the fittest,' saw society as being like an organism. This is a central idea of social Darwinism. Politically, the doctrine is ultraconservative, holding social inequality to be natural, as it allows only the 'fitter' to thrive. This represents a basic misunderstanding of Darwin's evolutionary theory. At its most extreme, social Darwinism gave rise to abhorrent theories of racial superiority.

Physical Anthropology

*Genetic and environmental variation • Natural selection • Fossil hominids •
Bipedalism • Modern genetic distribution*

**This section presents theories of physical
anthropology maintained by Evolutionists. They
are not universally accepted.
Although this point of view is detailed here, the
Creationist viewpoint is presented in
Volume 3, pages 119-134.**

Physical, or biological, anthropology studies the origin, evolution, development, and causes and effects of human biological variation. No two people, even identical twins, are truly identical; similarly no two populations from different geographical locations or from different historical periods are ever the same; the differences pervade every aspect of our biology: genetics, biochemistry, physiology, morphology, and behaviour.

Genetic and Environmental Variation

Human genetic analysis has revealed ever more variation. Examining differences in the structure of body proteins, mainly enzymes, it has been estimated that at least 8000 of the coding genes must possess two or more alternative forms (alleles); see CELL BIOLOGY AND GENETICS (VOL. 3): GENETICS. In an approximately homogenous population of 50 million it was calculated some years ago that the likelihood of selecting at random two genetically identical individuals for just 15 of these genes is 1 in 6000. More recent molecular analysis of human DNA has indicated that even these calculations of variability levels were gross underestimates. Each individual, therefore, is genetically unique – except in the case of identical twins.

Variability in many characters from environmental causes is even greater. The environment of two individuals, even at any one moment in time, will never be totally the same, and what matters in human development is the sequence of environments experienced from conception to death. These sequences must differ for each individual, even identical twins. The characters most affected by environment differences are those in which development is furthest removed from the primary sites of gene action – those that gradually develop during growth and maturation. Examples of this are body size and shape, blood pressure, cognitive ability, and personality.

The interplay between genetic inheritance and environmental experience determines the development of all our biological attributes. To ask which is the more important is not valid with reference to an individual. Without either there can be no person. The question is only legitimate when applied to the *differences* between people; are these mainly of genetic or environmental origin or both? The answer always depends upon the particular circumstances in a particular place at a particular time; it will be determined by what genes are in the population and what environmental sequences are occurring. There is thus no absolute answer to the nature–nurture question. Variation in a particular character may be almost totally heritable in one circumstance and totally environmental in another. Recognizing this is of the utmost importance to practically every issue in biological anthropology.

Natural Selection

Environment has two important roles in anthropology – in development (as described above) and also in evolution. Biological evolution comes about through systematic changes in the frequency of genes and chromosomes in populations. A major force causing these evolutionary changes (though it may also produce evolutionary stability) is **natural selection**, as was first recognized by Charles Darwin in the 1850s. Natural selection occurs as a result of the survival and reproduction of the fittest individuals in a population. This differential survival, based on 'Darwinian fitness,' is often profoundly affected by the nature of environments. Genes that favour fitness in one particular environment may reduce it in another.

While other processes can alter gene frequencies, natural selection has been the major factor in determining the course of human evolution. The nature of this course can be traced directly from the fossil record but it can also be examined by comparing the DNA of modern humans with related species, especially the closest living relatives to modern humans: the two African apes – the gorilla and the chimpanzee. Molecular analysis of the similarities in the DNA of the African apes and humans suggests that their evolutionary separation occurred some 7–5 million years ago, with the chimpanzee somewhat more closely related to humans than the gorilla. In 1994 some fragmentary fossils – mainly teeth – were found in the Awash region of Ethiopia, which appear to date from between 4.5 and 4.3 million years ago. They have provisionally been attributed taxonomically to *Australopithecus ramidus*, which shows some clear human characteristics but also many primitive traits shared with the chimpanzee.

Fossil Hominids

More complete fossils from between 3 and 3.75 million years ago have been found in Ethiopia and Tanzania. They are attributed taxonomically by most authorities to *Australopithecus afarensis*. This species shows many similarities with present-day apes: small brain for its size, large jaws with projecting canine teeth, and an upper-limb anatomy well adapted to climbing in trees. However, more significant are some specifically human features of the teeth and especially of the hind limb, which show that *A. afarensis* was capable of walking upright on the ground.

The fossil evidence suggests that *A. afarensis* gave rise to a number of later australopithecines, which inhabited the eastern and southern African savannas from 3 to 1 million years ago. One form is referred to as *Australopithecus africanus*. This creature shows many

similarities with *A. afarensis*, including a small brain and large jaws; however, although it was larger it also had a slender physique. By contrast robust forms of australopithecines appear in the fossil record around 2 million years ago; they are referred to as *A. robustus* in southern Africa and *A. boisei* in East Africa. These fossils have particularly heavy skulls showing strong muscle markings and very large premolar and molar teeth. Both gracile (slender) and robust forms were, however, undoubtedly terrestrial bipeds. It is thought that the gracile australopithecines were essentially scavengers feeding largely on carcasses of the great herds of antelope and zebra, whose numbers had increased dramatically with expanding savannas. The robust australopithecines, on the other hand, were more likely to have been herbivores.

These hominids probably shaped wood, since chimpanzees do, and weapons of defence would have been invaluable to them against carnivores. There is, however, no evidence of stone tools in the archaeological record until about 2 million years ago. By that time there is fossil evidence for another species in Africa. This shows various advances over any australopithecines – particularly in brain size, which well exceeds that of both apes and australopithecines. Jaws and teeth are reduced and the postcranial skeleton resembles that of modern humans. The best preserved

> ### The Laetoli Footprints
>
> At Laetoli in Tanzania in 1976, a group of researchers discovered hominid footprints and the tracks of other animals dating from over 3 million years ago in a layer of volcanic ash. It is thought that rain falling shortly after the prints were made hardened the volcanic ash, thus ensuring their preservation. This remarkable find provided clear evidence of bipedalism in A. afarensis.

Skull Development
The skulls of Homo sapiens *and* Homo erectus *are shown in this diagram.* ▼

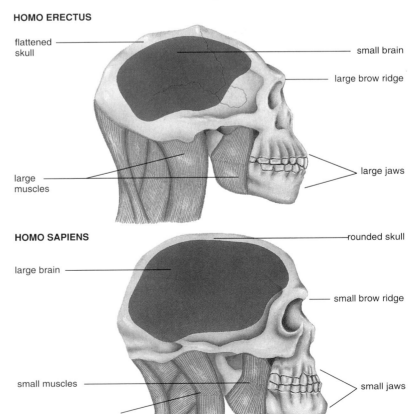

HOMO ERECTUS

flattened skull

small brain

large brow ridge

large muscles

large jaws

HOMO SAPIENS

rounded skull

large brain

small brow ridge

small muscles

small jaws

The Leakeys

A family of British descent long resident in Kenya, the Leakeys — Louis B. Leakey (1903–72), Mary Leakey (1913–96), and their son Richard Leakey (1944–) — have made major contributions to knowledge about human evolution. Louis and Mary Leakey made their first finds in Olduvai Gorge between 1931 and 1959. Mary Leakey discovered hominid remains and footprints at Laetoli in northern Tanzania, and Richard Leakey worked at Lake Turkana, where he found the oldest known fossils of Homo.

specimens come from Olduvai Gorge in Tanzania and from deposits around Lake Turkana in Kenya. They are assigned to the first species, *Homo habilis*, of our own genus. *H. habilis* was almost certainly the maker of the so-called Olduvai stone tools.

It is generally agreed that *H. habilis* was the ancestor of the next species to appear, *Homo erectus*. *H. erectus* was first discovered in Asia (Java and Peking man) but older versions have now been found at various African sites. The African specimens are dated at 1.5 million years or more old, whereas no remains originating elsewhere are older than 1 million years. *H. erectus* was, however, the first hominid species to occur outside Africa and probably became quite widespread in the Old World between 1 and 0.5 million years ago. This represented not only a geographical expansion but also an ecological change, with colonization for the first time in temperate regions. This change must have required the use of shelter, clothing, and fire; indeed, it is known from the stone-tool remains that the technology of *H. erectus* was much more advanced than that of *H. habilis* and that *H. erectus* had a larger brain. *H. erectus*, however,

retained several primitive skull features, such as lack of forehead and a heavy brow ridge above the eye orbits (***supraorbital torus***).

There is some controversy over the next phase of human evolution, with quite a number of fossils known from sites all over the Old World dating from 500 000 to 50 000 years ago; these fossils have varying morphology, intermediate between *Homo erectus* and modern humans. They tend to have larger brain cases than *H. erectus* and various modern features of the jaws and face. Typically, however, they have low foreheads and a supraorbital torus. One very well known group are the Neanderthals, who occupied Europe and neighbouring regions during the latter part of the ice age, from about 80 000 to 40 000 years ago. These people had particularly large brain cases, probably greater than modern humans, but they also had a number of unique features. They are the first known humans to inhabit really cold environments.

It has been customary to refer to all these groups as 'archaic *Homo sapiens*,' although there is now some doubt about whether most of them contributed to the descent of modern humans. Examination of the DNA of both the

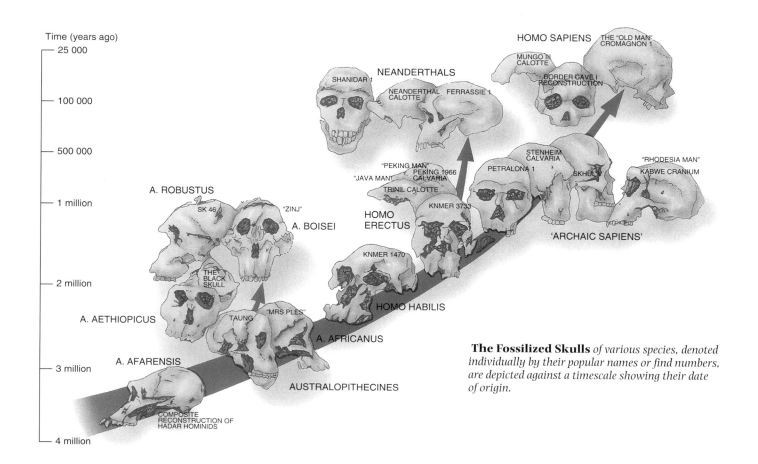

The Fossilized Skulls *of various species, denoted individually by their popular names or find numbers, are depicted against a timescale showing their date of origin.*

nucleus and mitochondria of cells from various present populations around the world suggests that we are all descended from a single small group of people, who lived in Africa about 200 000 years ago. There is also some fossil evidence of forms that are skeletally indistinguishable from our own in southern and eastern Africa at least 100 000 years ago. This is much earlier than anywhere else; modern-type remains are unknown elsewhere much before 40 000 years ago. It seems likely, then, that modern humans' ancestors were confined to Africa for around 150 000 years; this also explains the greater genetic heterogeneity of modern African populations. Some of these African populations then spread out over the rest of the world some 50 000 years ago, directly or indirectly causing the extinction of all the other groups inhabiting Europe and Asia. All the human fossils in Australasia and the Americas are of modern form, but none are definitely older than 40 000 years (in Australia) or 20 000 (in the New World). It follows that European Neanderthals were extinguished by competition with invading modern men from Africa at the end of the ice age.

The alternative explanation, known as the 'multi-regional hypothesis,' is that many of the populations of archaic *H. sapiens* in the Old World contributed to the descent of modern humans by evolving together under a common selection pressure and with an exchange of genes through continuous migration and intermixture. If some migration is long-range not much intermixture is required to maintain the integrity of a widely distributed species. This theory explains the persistence of various characteristics that distinguish early and late forms in the same geographical area, yet it cannot account for the molecular genetic distributions. What is beyond dispute is that all present-day human beings belong to a single biological species – *Homo sapiens*.

Bipedalism
Probably the most significant event in human evolutionary history was the erect posture and bipedal gait. This is not because bipedalism is a particularly effective form of movement but because it frees the forelimbs from being mere facilitators of locomotion, and enables the arms and hands to be used for making tools and weapons, and carrying the human infant, which is born very immature and needs lengthy nursing. These developments allowed early humans to build a home base. Why the earliest hominids became terrestrial and bipedal is not fully clear. At that time African forests were receding and the herds of game on expanding savannas pro-

vided new hunting opportunities for a variety of species. Early hominids probably took advantage of these changes to become daylight scavengers; day-time activity was aided by the erect posture, which substantially reduced the amount of heat absorbed from solar radiation. Free hands were also a great advantage, particularly for carrying when following migrating herds.

The long-term consequences of bipedalism were enormous. Increased manipulative skills involves not only evolutionary change in the hand but also in the sensory and motor areas of the brain. Availability of tools makes large jaws less necessary. Throughout human evolution there has been a progressive reduction in jaw size; this trend was reinforced by the discovery of fire and cooking, making meat easier to masticate. Teaching the use of tools and weapons would have favoured the progressive development of language; archaeological records also indicate the development of ever more complex social organizations, placing a premium on communication skills. Cognitive abilities must have increased in value, so explaining the growth of the brain. One crucial physiological change was the concealed ovulation of the female. Whereas other primates signal the time in the ovarian cycle at which they are most likely to conceive, human females are sexually receptive throughout their menstrual cycles – a strong basis for the pair bonding that created the human family.

Modern Genetic Distribution
Examining the genetic diversity of present-day populations reveals a number of important geographical patterns. For inherited characters populations tend to differ mainly in the frequency at which certain genes are present, rather than in their absolute presence or absence. Moreover, gene frequencies tend to change gradually with geographical distance and produce what are called ***clines***.

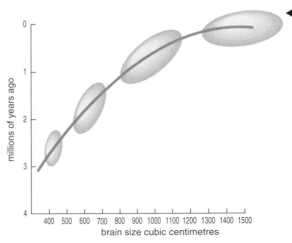

◄ **Human Brain Capacity** *The brain has enabled humans to become the dominant species. Brain power is related to its size; no other life form has a similar brain capacity. In 3 million years, the brain of the higher primates has quadrupled in size.*

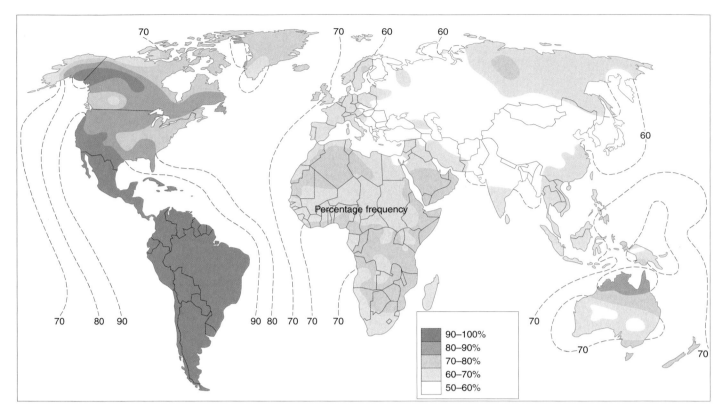

Percentage frequency

■	90–100%
■	80–90%
▨	70–80%
▨	60–70%
□	50–60%

▲ **World Distribution of the Blood Group O Gene** *In the ABO blood-grouping system most populations have both A and O genes and many also have B genes. However, the O gene ranges from around 100% to as low as 40% in different groups.*

However, there may be sharp changes in frequency, especially when two areas are separated by geographical barriers. Different genetic traits can also have different geographical distributions; thus, no similarity exists between the distribution of the genes of the ABO blood-group system and that of most other genetic systems.

These factors make classification of modern humans into distinct races arbitrary, if not wholly artificial. However, whether races exist and whether they can be neatly classified are two slightly different questions. The geographical origins of most groups of people can be identified solely from their biological characteristics. The classification system of caucasoid, mongoloid, negroid, and australopoid is also useful, although it has no absolute genetic validity. If race can be said to exist in human terms, it is a product of biological processes and not a cause for them.

Thus, some genetic differences between populations are due to the effects of natural selection. Various haemoglobin genes confer resistance to *falciparum* malaria in the early years of life and are thus found in peoples who live or have lived in places in which malaria is prevalent; see MEDICINE AND HEALTH CARE (VOL. 3): CONGENITAL DISEASES. Skin pigmentation is related to levels of ultraviolet radiation. Yet for many genetic systems no functional significance to the variety has been identified. While this may, in part, be attributed to the difficulty of detecting natural selection, many

geneticists believe that it is mainly due to the genes being neutral, i.e. to variety in the system having no effect on Darwinian fitness. When genes are neutral, their frequencies will change only through chance: a phenomenon known as **genetic drift**. Drift is particularly likely in small populations; throughout most of human evolution population sizes have been very small. On the neutralist view, geographical patterns of genetic variation are mainly the result of drift and intermixture; this means that they are more indicative of ancestry than if selection and the nature of the environment were the dominant influences.

Whatever the status of natural selection, other forms of adaptation certainly occur in humans. The individual organism is able to respond to environmental change in ways that facilitate survival and reproduction in the new environment. Thus, when lowlanders move to a high altitude, their heart and respiratory rates first increase. These responses are succeeded by more economical and effective changes in the lungs, blood, and tissue that improve oxygen uptake, transport, and usage. These changes are called **acclimatization**. Similar changes occur in relation to thermal, nutritional, and disease environments.

Almost every human physiological system demonstrates adaptability, but by far the most important is the neural adaptability that is reflected in behaviour. It is this that makes humans unique and has allowed them to colonize every kind of terrestrial environment.

Cultural and Social Anthropology

Durkheim and followers • Lévi-Strauss • Social behaviour •
Descent and kinship • Marriage • Myth and ritual • Race

Modern cultural and social anthropology arose at the turn of the century as a reaction to the evolutionist views of contemporary anthropologists. A new generation of anthropologists recognized the need for a more considered and critical approach to human history based on information gathered by direct observers.

In North America, the leader of this movement was the German-born Franz Boas (1858–1942). Unlike most former anthropologists, he did not rely on data collected by others but spent protracted periods first with the Inuit (formerly known as Eskimos) of Baffin Island and later with the Amerindians of the Northwest coast. Boas argued that anthropologists should live with the peoples they wished to study. Moreover, they should learn their language and write down everything that they observed or were told. Regarding cultures as integrated wholes, he urged fellow anthropologists to note even apparently unimportant information (such as recipes for blueberry pie) as well as native texts (myths, stories, and accounts of local events).

Although Boas wrote many volumes of ethnography, especially about the American Northwest coast, he never produced a single analytical account of an indigenous way of life: he preferred to collect and publish as much ethnographic data as possible, without using it to draw conclusions.

Durkheim and Followers

In western Europe, the French school headed by Emile Durkheim (1858–1917) and known as the *Année Sociologique* (after the journal they edited) was the main intellectual force in developing the subject. Durkheim argued that the study of society cannot be reduced to the study of the way individuals think. The social sciences are independent of psychology. Members of a society might have their own individual thoughts and opinions but collectively they maintain a certain social way of life in which particular rules of behaviour, standards of value, and expectations are observed.

In a technologically underdeveloped small-scale society, in which the majority of people carry out much the same tasks, the repeated

◄ **An Anthropologist Conducting Fieldwork** *The approach known as 'participant observation' involves lengthy participation in the daily life of the people being studied and detailed recording of information on kinship, marriage and other ritual activities, and the social organization of the group.*

Indians of the Northwest Coast ►
Amerindian societies were the subject of early anthropological research by the German scholar Franz Boas. This engraving shows members of the Nootka tribe.

Ethnographic Fieldwork

Fieldwork is the fundamental research method of cultural and social anthropology. Modern fieldwork methods were pioneered by Bronisław Malinowski, who conducted a two-year study of the inhabitants of the Trobriand Islands in New Guinea in the 1910s. Researchers in the field must live for a substantial period in close contact with the people whose culture they are studying, in order to identify patterns of behaviour and analyse them correctly. Proper introductions to the community through a person of high status are essential to this process if the researcher is not to become marginalized.

performance of communal rituals heightens the feelings of interdependence the members feel for one another. However, it is the fear of punishment, whether secular or supernatural, that ensures conformity to the common set of rules. Durkheim called this way of achieving social cohesion ***mechanical solidarity***, which he contrasted with the ***organic solidarity*** of more complex societies (see ORIGINS OF SOCIOLOGY). In these larger and technologically more developed societies, a sense of community is maintained not because people fear the consequences of breaking the rules but because different groups within it have to fulfil contractual obligations to one another. If, for instance, farmers stopped producing crops or artisans closed their workshops, society would disintegrate.

Durkheim pointed out that exchange is essential to the functioning of an organic society. It was, however, his nephew, Marcel Mauss (1872–1950), who realized its importance for all societies. People, he argued, exchange many other things besides goods and services. For instance, they may exchange objects of great value but little utilitarian use. Recipients of gifts are always socially obliged to make a countergift; moreover, the sort of gift one person gives to another symbolizes the relationship between them. For instance in Europe, a man would not normally give a male friend a bunch of roses.

The exchange of gifts and countergifts is one of the major mechanisms of social cohesion, serving both to establish and to maintain relationships between people. The social importance of exchange may be somewhat less in industrialized countries, where most transactions are conducted in an impersonal manner, but in small-scale societies where most people know one another they are crucial in the creation of a sense of solidarity.

Lévi-Strauss

The next major development in social anthropology was ushered in by Claude Lévi-Strauss (1908–), the creator of structuralism. Unlike Durkheim and Mauss, who were mainly interested in understanding forms of social organization, Lévi-Strauss has been primarily concerned with elucidating the structure of human thought. He argues that the fundamental patterns of the way people think and understand the world are structurally organized, like the sound systems of language. Languages are based on the significance given to arbitrary differences in sound. Precisely which differences are important depends on the individual language. In a conversation, the listener understands the utterances of the speaker by interpreting the stream of sounds being made. According to Lévi-Strauss, people organize their own experience in a structurally similar manner, by endowing with cultural significance arbitrary distinctions in their sensorial realm. The logic of this type of organization is especially evident in the more symbolically laden human activities, such as the recounting of myths and the performance of ritual.

Social Behaviour

Anthropology must be comparative if it is to rise above the level of studying the traditions of rules of behaviour of different societies. The important questions, however, are the way comparison is to be carried out and the precise aims of the procedure.

Bronisław Malinowski (1884–1942), the Polish-born British anthropologist, claimed that people only practise a custom or tradition if it has a function; if it had no use they would not bother to maintain it. Since individuals cannot exist without food and shelter, and since a community cannot survive unless its members reproduce, Malinowski argued that customs serve biological functions. Thus the purpose of comparative anthropology is to investigate which customs in different societies fulfilled the same biological needs.

Later anthropologists criticized Malinowski's functionalist approach for confusing biology and society. Just because an aspect of social life might serve a biological function did not mean that it did not also fulfil a social function. Malinowski's approach was also reductive, for by grouping together a wide variety of different customs in different societies that served the same end, he played down the strong possibility that they fulfil different social functions.

In the 1930s the British anthropologist Arthur Radcliffe-Brown (1881–1955), who was greatly influenced by the work of Durkheim, developed a more sophisticated version of functionalism. He argued that a society survives as a stable entity because of the integration of the social practices that constitute it. Thus, a social practice serves the social function of contributing to the maintenance of the social system. Radcliffe-Brown thought that by comparing the constitution of different social systems it would be possible to derive laws of social statics stating the needs essential for the survival of a society. However, the only laws that he derived were either platitudinous or hopelessly vague.

Edward Evans-Pritchard (1902–73), one of the most influential anthropologists of the 1940s and 1950s, criticized the apparently scientific approach of Radcliffe-Brown by arguing that societies were not natural systems but moral systems. According to this view, anthropologists were interested not in process but in design; therefore they should not seek scientific laws but patterns. Their aim should be to interpret rather than to explain. Anthropologists could not expect to compare societies in any mechanical way. Their preoccupation should be to make use of the analytical insights gained from the study of certain social aspects of one society when investigating similar aspects of different societies.

The structuralist approach of Lévi-Strauss, who dominated anthropology in both Europe and America in the 1960s and 1970s, had a different aim. Lévi-Strauss argued that since all peoples structure the way they perceive their own world, anthropologists are indeed able to carry out cross-cultural comparisons; however, they should not examine different social structures, as Radcliffe-Brown or Durkheim would have done, but different symbolic structures. This comparative work, Lévi-Strauss claimed, would enable anthropologists to deduce the fundamental structures of the human mind.

Some anthropologists have criticized structuralism as being too rigid and as not taking sufficient account of the ways in which societies change. They point out that people are not so much constrained by the symbolic structures of their societies; rather they creatively employ these structures for their own ends, and often modify them in the process. Moreover, since all communities are now experiencing increasing globalization, anthropologists should not think of societies as discrete bounded entities but should be comparing the ways in which different societies are resisting, or accommodating, the external forces of change.

Descent and Kinship

In a small-scale society almost every member will be related to all other members, either by blood or through marriage. An anthropologist who wishes to study a community of this type must investigate all these relationships, because the kinship system is one of the basic components of social organization. People know one another as either kin or *affines* (a relation by marriage) and they are morally obliged to perform services or to provide labour for their relations. The kinship system thus has a great effect on the organization of a society. It is also often of importance in the political organization of the society. Further, it may play a part in the organization of a local religion because relationships with kin may be used as models for relationships with gods.

The system of kinship in some societies may be very different from the common Western kinship system. For instance, among the Nuer of the southern Sudan, if a widow marries one of her late husband's brothers and they have children, these offspring are treated as children of his dead brother. Similarly, if she becomes pregnant by a lover, the child will not be known as his offspring but as that of her late husband. This example of socially assigned parentage suggests that the connections between kin may not be based on biological relations, although they are modelled on them; Nuer neighbours of the widow will treat all

▲ **Emile Durkheim**
This French sociologist made a major contribution to the discipline of social anthropology with his theories of archaic societies, in particular their forms of religious and social organization.

Potlatch

The giving of gifts has long been recognized by anthropologists — notably Mauss — as a basic method of creating and reinforcing social bonds. At the potlatch, which took the form of a ritual feast, claimants to rank and status would try to outdo one another in the distribution of lavish gifts, which would have to be returned with interest at subsequent potlatches. This practice was prevalent among the Kwakiutl people of British Columbia, where it was first recorded by Franz Boas.

Bridewealth

Bridewealth, common in Africa, is the money or property given by a bridegroom to his bride's family to establish his rights over the woman. Bridewealth normally consists of prestigious valuables (e.g. tusks, shells, and feathers), the supply of which is controlled by the male elders of the lineage. This enables the elders to exploit the labour of the male youths of the lineage, for if the young men do not work for their elders they will not be given the valuables required to obtain a wife.

Nuer Herdsmen *The Nuer of the southern Sudan are an example of a pastoralist society – a nomadic group that grazes its animals at different locations. Livestock is used by the Nuer as bridewealth.* ▼

her children, irrespective of who their fathers are, as the progeny of the same man.

In order to inherit such rights as ownership of land, access to pasture, or certain specialized bodies of knowledge, such as magical procedures, people in kin-based societies need to trace their descent from previous holders of these rights. The simplest form traces the descent through a line of men (patrilineal descent) or a line of women (matrilineal descent). If descent is traced matrilineally, it is not necessarily the women of the group who inherit the rights; rather a person, male or female, inherits rights on the basis of who their mother or mother's mother was.

Patrilineal descent systems are far more common than matrilineal systems. Since patrilineal systems occur in all types of society, whereas the majority of matrilineal systems are found in societies that rely on highly productive forms of agriculture (a mode of livelihood which only arose during the Neolithic period), it is thought probable that patrilineal systems are the older forms.

Few societies have exclusively one system or the other. In many cases one merely predominates over the other. For example, more important rights may be inherited patrilineally and subsidiary rights matrilineally.

Descent systems provide people with a form of continuity across space, through time, and over generations. For example, during most of the year, bands of the nomadic Wodaabe wander the arid grasslands just south of the Sahara. For a brief period every year, during the rainy season, they regroup into their lineages in order to stage their major festival. Descent systems are also a way of defining relations between the living on the basis of a common ancestor.

Marriage

In small-scale societies, marriage is best regarded as a contract between two parties concerned with the transfer of rights caused by the creation of a new domestic unit. In societies with patrilineal descent systems, the kin of the groom often pay **bridewealth** to the kin of the bride. This payment is usually seen by participants as a compensation to the bride's kin for the loss of her labour and of her reproductive potential. The children she bears will not be members of her original lineage but of the lineage into which she is marrying.

In many societies people marry outside their own immediate group. One social reason for this is to enable a small band to establish a network of alliances with other bands. In order to offset this loss of a woman, some groups do not demand bridewealth but require that a marriageable woman is eventually provided in return. Other groups practise a more circular form of exchange in which – to cite a straightforward example – a woman of group A marries into group B, a woman from which marries into group C, a woman from which marries into group A.

In western Europe and North America a marriage is usually established by the performance of a single ceremony. However, in many small-scale societies, a marriage ceremony is frequently a process lasting a long time and consisting of several exchanges between the two parties involved.

In some societies it is normal for a man to take several wives. A strong sense of solidarity may develop among co-wives, especially if, as happens among the Tiv of Nigeria, they choose who is to be their husband's next wife. Polyandry is less frequent. It is most common in areas of the Himalayas, where it serves to protect the integrity of a family's estate.

Myth and Ritual

A society's myths provide its explanations of the origin of the world and the evolution of its society; they also describe the way of life in the supernatural realm. They are often enacted in rituals, which are carefully prescribed routines repeatedly performed, often for religious ends but also for endowing culturally significant moments with further significance. Durkheim thought rituals reinforced a community's solidarity, but some are also a means by which subordinate groups (such as women) symbolically express their dissension from the accepted model of society.

BLACKS, COLOUREDS
& ASIANS

ANTSUNDU, KLEURLINGE
EN ASIËRS

◄ **Apartheid in South Africa** *The hated apartheid system – according to which the different races were supposed to 'develop' along separate lines – operated in South Africa from 1948 to 1994. This policy of discrimination against the Black majority was based on erroneous racial theories, which held that Whites were inherently superior.*

Myths express the attitudes and values of a society and provide a charter to legitimize the system of authority maintained by those in power. Lévi-Strauss argues that myths have a structure and a decipherable logic of their own; in his view they are used by their tellers to resolve enigmatic questions about the human condition by the use of symbols.

Race

In recent years anthropologists have spent an increasing proportion of their time working in modern Western societies, where they are able to use the findings of their studies to contribute to debates on such issues as nationalism, multiculturalism, urban migration, environmentalism, the effects of mass tourism, the nature of gender, and racism.

While most social anthropologists remain sceptical about the scientific value of the notion of 'race,' they are interested in examining the ways in which it is used by different groups. It is clear that a social definition of race may be very different from a biological anthropologist's definition. For instance, in Vanuatu in the southwest Pacific, both Melanesians (who are relatively short, dark-skinned, and frizzy-haired) and Polynesians (relatively tall, olive-skinned, and straight-haired) describe themselves as 'Blacks,' although some biological anthropologists would categorize them as different races.

In social settings, the concept of race is almost never used in a neutral way; invariably it is employed for political purposes. The supposed innate superiority of a dominant group is used to justify attempts to control, or to ignore the plight of, members of the race that is regarded as inferior. The most infamous example of the systematic adoption of theories of racial superiority for political ends was Nazism's concept of the 'Aryan superhuman,' used to justify the genocide of 'subhuman' groups, such as Jews and the Romany people.

The concept of race is one of several forms of social classification deployed within a society at any one time; it is important to examine the degree of overlap between these social classifications. In countries where the idea of class superiority is already well established, it is often easier to inculcate the notion of racial superiority. Race and class may also be compounded. In some Andean countries, for example, the lowest class predominantly consists of the indigenous inhabitants, the middle class are the descendants of mixed marriages, and the upper class are the descendants of the Spanish conquistadores.

In recent decades oppressed groups have begun to use racial classifications to increase the political cohesiveness of their own group and to emphasize and widen the gap between them and their oppressors. This strategy is often accompanied by a symbolic inversion, in which the oppressed stress as sources of pride the very characteristics that are derided by their oppressors. For instance, in parts of Papua New Guinea, the locals have accepted outsiders' classification of them as 'Blacks' and have revived many of the customs and rituals that were suppressed by generations of colonialist rule.

The anthropologist respects history, but he does not accord it a special value. He conceives it as a study complementary to his own: one of them unfurls the range of human societies in time, the other in space.

Claude Lévi-Strauss,
The Savage Mind (1962)

Linguistics

Origins • Comparative historical linguistics • Structural linguistics •
Psycholinguistics • Language acquisition • Chimp language •
Sociolinguistics • Bilingualism and multilingualism • Pragmatics

=====SEE ALSO=====
This section:
• Origins of Sociology
• Cultural and Social Anthropology
• Developmental Psychology
Philosophy:
• The Philosophy of Language
• Applied Philosophy
Languages of the World (vol. 1)

The Indo-European Family of Languages *Languages of this family subdivide into various groups, shown here in different colours. Indo-European languages are spoken by around half of the world's population.* ▼

Linguistics is defined as the scientific study of language. As this is a vast subject, **linguists** (those professionally trained in general linguistics) concentrate on specific aspects of the discipline. The most important subdivisions are **phonetics** (the study of human speech sounds), **phonology** (the study of the sound system of a particular language), **morphology** (the study of the words and word structures), **syntax** (the way that words are combined into larger units or constructions), and **semantics** (the study of meaning). Syntax and morphology, and sometimes also phonetics and semantics, make up the **grammar** of the language. There are also a number of subbranches of linguistics, for example **psycholinguistics** (the relationship between language and the mind), **sociolinguistics** (the link between language and society), and **pragmatics** (the study of the use of language).

Origins

In classical and medieval times, the study of language consisted of philosophical discussions about its relation to questions concerning truth, knowledge, nature, or the mind. The questions considered by scholars included: What was the origin of language? Was language God's creation, was it a natural development, or was it established by convention? What is the relationship between a word and its meaning?

As literacy became increasingly important, grammar was taught for the practical purpose of enabling people to learn and communicate by the written word. Foreign languages were learnt to facilitate trade. Language was not studied for its own sake as is often the case in the 20th century. There was little discussion of grammar until c. 500 AD, when the Latin grammarian Priscian defined the **eight parts of speech** (word classes) that are largely still in use. Linguistics has now achieved the status of an academic discipline in its own right, and grammar is recognized as a subdivision of linguistics.

Comparative Historical Linguistics

A major change in the study of language took place in 1786; this date is consequently now often seen as marking the beginning of linguistic science. Sir William Jones (1746–94), who was a judge in the British Court in India,

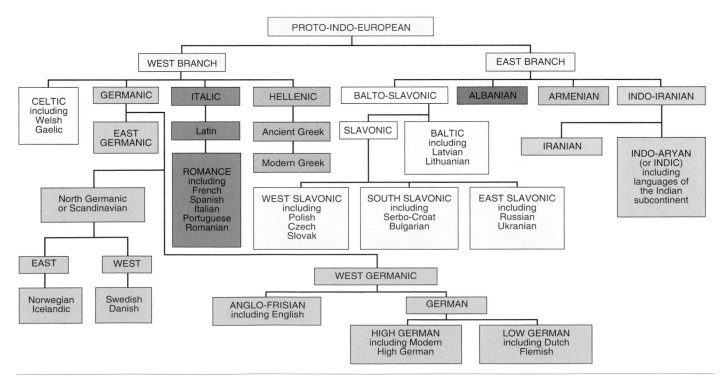

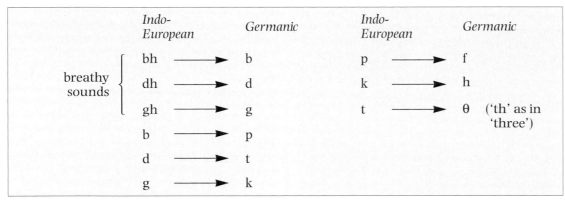

	Indo-European	Germanic		Indo-European	Germanic
breathy sounds	bh →	b		p →	f
	dh →	d		k →	h
	gh →	g		t →	θ ('th' as in 'three')
	b →	p			
	d →	t			
	g →	k			

◀ **Grimm's Law** *Jakob Grimm identified nine sets of correspondences between consonant sounds in related Indo-European languages. For example, words starting with 'p' in early Indo-European languages correspond to those with 'f' in Germanic languages (e.g. Latin* piscis; *English* fish).

discovered that **Sanskrit** (an early Indian language), Greek, Latin, the Celtic languages, and the Germanic languages all had certain structural similarities; he therefore concluded that they must have been derived from the same source, which perhaps no longer existed. For example, in words of similar meanings, where Sanskrit and Latin had a [p] at the start of the word, English had an [f], as is the case with Latin *pater* and English *father*. Linguists then became interested in comparing the characteristics of different languages. They wrote comparative grammars, attempting to reconstruct the hypothetical ancestor of these related languages, which they called **Proto-Indo-European (PIE)**; PIE is the presumed ancestor of such present-day languages as Greek, German, English, and Hindi. Thus the study of language became a tool in amassing historical knowledge. The word **philology** is often given to this type of comparative historical language study.

PRISCIAN'S PARTS OF SPEECH

nomen (noun) A word used to name a person, a place, or a thing, e.g. 'Priscian', 'Rome,' 'house.' It also included the class of word now called an 'adjective,' e.g. 'red.'

verbum (verb) A word indicating an action or event, e.g. 'go.'

participium (participle) A word formed from a verb, e.g. 'going.'

pronomen (pronoun) A word used to replace a noun, e.g. 'it' or 'they.'

adverbium (adverb) A word that qualifies a verb, e.g. 'quickly.'

praepositio (preposition) A word expressing a relation to another word, e.g. 'to.'

interiectio (interjection) An exclamation, e.g. 'oh!'

conjunctio (conjunction) A word used to connect words or phrases, e.g. 'and.'

19th-Century Linguistics. The rapid progress in the natural sciences during the 19th century, partly because of Charles Darwin (1809–82) and his evolutionary thesis *Origin of Species* (1859), resulted in the West in new attitudes towards scholarship. The natural sciences began to replace the Bible as the major source of wisdom, so that the only influential subjects were those that had a scientific basis.

Although language had been a topic of interest before this period, its study now came under the influence of scientific models. Thus the linguistic scholar Friedrich von Schlegel (1773–1829) likened his comparative grammar to comparative anatomy. Jakob Grimm (1785–1863), also remembered as a compiler of fairy tales, formulated a law (Grimm's Law; 1822) describing the progressive shifts in consonant values that occurred within the Indo-European group of languages (those descended from the hypothetical PIE), resulting in differences between the subgroups. Franz Bopp (1791–1867) devised a sound law (1824) that involved a mechanical explanation, relating the 'laws' of gravity to the relative weight of different syllables. Languages, as Bopp and Grimm conceived them, evolved according to laws, passed through phases of development, and finally perished.

Further developments in linguistics took place throughout the 19th century. Certain exceptions to Grimm's Law were unexplained until the Danish philologist Karl Verner (1846–96) recognized that a consonant can be affected by its position and by the position of the stress in the word. August Schleicher (1821–68) used a biological metaphor when he originated the 'Stammbaum' or family tree format for showing the evolution of language and the relationships between languages. In 1864, Max Muller (1834–98), the first Professor of Comparative Philology at Oxford University, claimed that language was by that time being studied for its own sake; his view was that languages can be classified, collected, and analysed much as an astronomer or a botanist treats stars or flowers, respectively.

Key Terms

vowel A voiced sound produced by the tongue without obstruction of the vocal passage.

consonant A sound in which the position of the tongue restricts the vocal passage. Consonants are identified by type, such as *stops* (e.g. 'b'), *fricatives* (e.g. 'f'), or *aspirates* (e.g. 'h'); and by position, such as *labials* (e.g. 'b'), *dentals* (e.g. 't'), *nasals* (e.g. 'n'), *palatals* (e.g. 'ch'), or *gutterals* (e.g. 'g').

stress Emphasis placed on a syllable by pronouncing it more loudly.

Ferdinand de Saussure *The work of this Swiss linguist was especially radical in regarding language as a social phenomenon.*

Neogrammarians

The Neogrammarians were based at the University of Leipzig, Germany, in the 1870s. They were the first scholars to make historical linguistics scientific by claiming that sound changes are subject to laws 'with no exceptions.'

Diachronic and Synchronic Studies

A diachronic study is concerned with the development of language over time rather than with the relationship between linguistic elements at any particular time. A synchronic study considers one language at a particular time and therefore does not reveal the changes that have occurred.

Towards the end of the 19th century, however, a group of scholars known as the **Neogrammarians** claimed that linguistic comparison was worthless and misleading when divorced from history. They thought that, because of the facts of human physiology, sound changes were completely regular, and would occur in all the relevant words of a given dialect simultaneously.

Structural Linguistics

The Swiss linguist Ferdinand de Saussure (1857–1913) was the originator of modern linguistics. Although originally a philologist of the Indo-European languages, he later rejected the historical analyses of the Neogrammarians, believing that language was too diverse a subject to be treated as a science, since it involved psychology, physiology, and sociology simultaneously. In his view it was necessary to abstract from language what was purely linguistic. He therefore defined as his object of study not language in general, but *a* or *the* language (such as French, Hindi, Russian, or Chinese) as a structured system, thus initiating *structuralism* (see PHILOSOPHY: APPLIED PHILOSOPHY). Saussure claimed that all the words (or, as he called them, 'signs') in a particular language are interlinked and can only be defined in relation to other words. For example, the meaning of the word 'chair' has to be defined in such a way that it cannot be mistaken for 'sofa,' 'couch,' or 'stool.' Similarly the names of colours can only be learnt if there is a recognition of the differences between the colours. In order to understand the meaning of red one has to be able to distinguish red from pink, orange, and other similar colours. According to Saussure, a language retains its identity irrespective of who writes or speaks it, in much the same way as the 08.25 train from Paris to Geneva is the same train even if different carriages are put on the tracks every day; what is important is that it must not be confused with the 08.20 or 08.30 train.

For Saussure, a language was a system of arbitrary signs: there is no essential reason why a cat is called a 'cat' – all that matters is that it is not mistaken for a dog or a lion. A sign is therefore identified only by contrast with other signs. Saussure later rejected the philological or historical approach to language study (**diachronic study**) on the grounds that it is possible to study only one language at one particular time (**synchronic study**) and that linguistic comparison is therefore fruitless. In Saussure's view, if one word changes or is added to the language system, a different system of relations, i.e. a different language, is the result. This led him to reject the philological or historical approach to language study.

Saussure believed that the system of signs that constitutes language exists incompletely in the brain of its users, and perfectly in the community of speakers as a whole. Saussure distinguishes between language and *speech*, which is the use of spoken language on any particular occasion. When one says, for example, that a person speaks a certain language, this does not necessarily imply that he or she is speaking it at all times, since people also speak foreign languages; on the other hand, a parrot could not be described as a 'speaker' of any language because it would have no knowledge of the language as a structured system. By referring to the speakers' knowledge of a language, Saussure turned linguistics into a branch of cognitive psychology (see EXPERIMENTAL PSYCHOLOGY).

Linguistics in the USA. In the USA between 1930 and 1960 linguistics was studied as an offshoot of anthropology (see CULTURAL AND SOCIAL ANTHROPOLOGY). Anthropologists were eager to describe the languages of the American Indian tribes, which were dying out, and so were not concerned with the issues of language in general. Edward Sapir (1884–1939), an American structuralist and successor of Saussure as an influential figure in the study of linguistics, was trained both as an anthropologist and a linguist. Influenced by the linguist and anthropologist Franz Boas (1858–1942), he was concerned with the relationship between language and culture, claiming that language did not exist independently of the culture to which it belonged. He showed how languages classify the world in

◀ **Lapplander and Reindeer** *To show the link between language and culture, Edward Sapir cited the example of Lapp languages, which have many terms for 'reindeer.' In general, Sapir found that the more significant a phenomenon in a particular culture, the greater the number of words that were used to describe it.*

different, culturally determined, ways. For example, Sapir discovered that the Inuit people of North America and Greenland have many 'snow' terms, while certain Arabic languages have various words for 'camel.'

Sapir's view, coupled with that of Benjamin Lee Whorf (1897–1941), was known as the **Sapir–Whorf hypothesis** (see PHILOSOPHY: THE PHILOSOPHY OF MIND AND LANGUAGE). Whorf was originally a fire-prevention inspector and learned from this profession that the way humans view the world is largely moulded by the language they speak. He noticed, for example, that people behaved carelessly in front of petrol drums labelled 'empty,' even though such drums often contained highly flammable fumes; in contrast, they were careful when surrounded by petrol drums they believed to be full. He concluded that the word 'empty' signalled 'harmless' to most people.

Whorf later became a pupil of Sapir, for whom he wrote articles on the links between language, culture, and thought. He became interested in American Indian languages, in particular Hopi, showing how the grammar of this language expresses a very non-European world view. In most Indo-European languages, verbs have a three-tense system – past, present, and future – but in Hopi there are no tenses; verbs instead have 'validity' forms that are dependent on whether the speaker is reporting the action or expects it, or whether the action has a general relevance. There is thus no formal way of distinguishing past and present, neither is time perceived as an entity. The importance of time in most European or 'Westernized' cultures may account for the fact that their languages have many ways of identifying periods of time. To the Hopi, however, time is merely an attribute of events and objects, which are seen as remaining the same

but simply getting later or older. Thus the Hopi cannot say when one day ends and the next begins. This is perhaps why rituals and repetition play such an important role in American Indian culture.

The Sapir–Whorf hypothesis is now applied to the view that language affects the way we think or the way we perceive the world. Sapir and Whorf both studied speech in its sociocultural setting and considered linguistics to be a social science. This shift of emphasis has parallels with the development of other social sciences, such as philosophy and psychology (see PHILOSOPHY: APPLIED PHILOSOPHY).

Leonard Bloomfield (1887–1949) perhaps exerted the greatest influence in making linguistics scientific. His book *Language* (1933), was principally about the scientific procedures for the description of any language. Unlike Saussure and Sapir, Bloomfield refused to

Hopi – one word (masa'ytaka) English – three words (aircraft, kite, bird)

◀ **Words and Concepts in Two Languages** *This illustration – based on an example cited by Whorf – demonstrates how English differentiates between various flying objects, while Hopi has only one word to cover all such objects. Conversely, while English refers indiscriminately to 'water,' Hopi distinguishes between flowing water in a natural setting and water that is contained in a vessel.*

Behaviourism

The behaviourist, or 'mechanist,' approach to language study was concerned with the directly observable. It has been opposed by the 'mentalist' approach, which deals with states of mind.

Computer Analysis of Language

Linguistics is increasingly finding an application in computer development, in a quest to devise fifth-generation systems that will recognize human voice patterns. ▼

incorporate any data relating to the mind into his linguistic theory, holding that only the observable or measurable was truly scientific. He was an advocate of **behaviourism** (see EXPERIMENTAL PSYCHOLOGY) and viewed semantic issues in terms of stimuli and responses.

Bloomfield used the following example to illustrate his radical theory of behaviourism. Jack and Jill are walking along a road when Jill, after seeing an apple, tells Jack that she is hungry. Jack climbs the tree to reach the apple, which he gives to Jill, who then eats it. Bloomfield explains the meaning of Jill's hunger in terms of the light waves being reflected from the apple onto Jill's eyes, her response to which causes muscular contractions in her stomach. She then makes an indirect response to these stimuli by means of her vocal organs to Jack, and this stimulates him to climb the tree. (A direct response would be for Jill to get the apple herself.) Behaviourists considered any discussion of mental events to be unscientific. Indeed anything untestable was regarded in the same light. Words describing concepts that had been explained by science were easily incorporated into Bloomfield's theory. An example of this is 'salt,' defined as NaCl. Such words as 'love' and 'hate,' however, had to be neglected

TRANSFORMATIONAL GENERATIVE GRAMMAR

This type of grammar, introduced by Chomsky, was an improvement on the constituent analyses typical of traditional school grammars. Instead of focusing merely on the distributional patterns of sentences, transformational generative grammar used a finite set of rules that had the ability to change sentences. For example, transformations could add, delete, and reorder sentence structures. 'I gave a doll to the baby' could be transformed into 'I gave the baby a doll' by reordering 'a doll' and 'the baby' and deleting 'to.' This process would reflect the intuition of native English speakers that these two sentences have the same meaning.

until science had made significant advances in this area.

Structuralist linguistics as conducted by Bloomfield's adherents therefore concentrated purely on the formal elements of language in order to arrive at a description of the language system. In order to break down sentences into their smallest component parts without any appeal to meaning, all that was needed was a knowledge of whether two utterances were the same or different. It would be necessary, for example, to establish whether the 'per-' in 'persist' is the same as the 'per-' in 'person.'

Psycholinguistics

Psycholinguistics is the study of the link between language and the mind. The mid-20th century saw the introduction of a form of linguistics that concentrated on the syntax of a language. This was initiated by Noam Chomsky (1928–   ), one of whose aims was to find a grammatical framework that would be applicable to all languages. Chomsky therefore proposed a **universal grammar** to account for a speaker's unconscious knowledge of language. This universal grammar described various elements, relating to language's sound patterns (phonology), meaning (semantics), and word patterns (syntax). Instead of taking the structuralist approach of analysing sentences as a body of data known as a **corpus**, Chomsky was more interested in accounting for the intuitive use of language by native speakers. Like Saussure, Chomsky distinguished between a speaker's *knowledge* of language (**competence**) and his or her actual *use* of language (**performance**), claiming that his universal grammar was a grammar of competence.

CONSTITUENT ANALYSIS

This method of analysis treats the elements that constitute a sentence as isolated entities. Sentences contain a number of recurring patterns, and this traditional technique of syntactic analysis identifies these patterns, using categories based on simple distributional, rather than semantic, criteria.

For example, the sentences 'She eats bananas,' or 'Dogs chase cats' could be substituted for the sentence 'The dogs may bite the postman' without disturbing the original syntactic pattern of the sentence. The tree diagram below shows how constituent analysis operates.

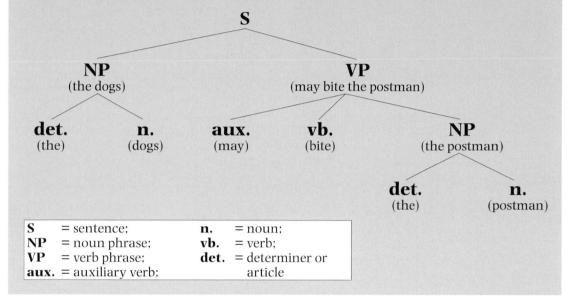

S	= sentence;	**n.**	= noun;
NP	= noun phrase;	**vb.**	= verb;
VP	= verb phrase;	**det.**	= determiner or
aux.	= auxiliary verb;		article

▲ **Noam Chomsky**
Chomsky, the leading figure of modern linguistic studies, is renowned not only for his scholarship but also for his outspoken views on human rights issues.

Chomsky is most famous for devising the concept of **transformational generative grammar**. This grammar accounted for a person's linguistic competence by describing the rules that 'generate' or predict all grammatical sentences of a language and preclude generation of ungrammatical sentences. In accounting for linguistic knowledge of the native speakers, transformational grammar rules demonstrated how speakers recognize that such sentences as 'The boy hit the ball' and 'The ball was hit by the boy' are semantically related, i.e. they have the same meaning.

Transformational rules show how one sentence can be transformed into another sentence, one forming the base, or **deep structure**, from which all others are derived. These deep or underlying structures are known intuitively by speakers, though they are not apparent on the surface. For example, the sentences 'the dog bit the postman,' 'did the dog bite the postman?,' 'bite the postman, dog' and the one-word sentence 'Bite!' are superficially different, but at a deeper level certain structural patterns emerge. For example the relationship between the words 'dog' and 'bite,' 'postman' and 'bite,' 'postman' and 'dog,' etc. is identical in every sentence. In addition, the **surface structure** (i.e. the word 'bite') does not contain all the information being conveyed, since who is doing the biting and who is

being bitten is not made clear. In this way, transformational grammar differs from traditional grammar. This latter form, or **constituent analysis**, simply analyses surface structures, such as the words on a page.

Language Acquisition
Because Chomsky concentrated on a native speaker's intuitive knowledge, linguistics reverted to the position it had occupied in Saussure's work, namely as a branch of cognitive psychology. Unlike Saussure, however, Chomsky was impressed by the speed with which children acquire language and attempted to account for this in his theory.

The first sound a newborn child makes is crying, an expression of distress and discomfort. The sounds of comfort occur later; these sounds are usually comprised of **back consonants** (consonants produced at the back of the mouth, such as [g]s and [k]s, unlike consonants produced at the front of the mouth such as [p]s and [b]s). After this, the babbling stage occurs, when a baby is about three or four months old. This is characterized by rising and falling intonation, which can often appear quite sentence-like: 'Goo goo CAH gaa.' However, a child at this stage is doing more than merely mimicking what he or she hears, since a child will often use sounds that do not occur in his or her

Deep and Surface Structure

The *deep structure* of a sentence is the underlying structure that contains all the relevant information for its interpretation. The *surface structure* is formed by the actual words spoken or written. Ambiguous sentences, therefore, have at least two deep structures corresponding to each meaning. For example, the sentence 'Flying planes can be dangerous' has two deep structures, namely 'To fly planes is dangerous' and 'Planes that fly are dangerous.' On the other hand, the two surface structures 'The boy kissed the girl' and 'The girl was kissed by the boy' have only one deep structure, one interpretation.

▲ **Sign Language**
Here, a teacher is shown using sign language to communicate with a deaf child. American Sign Language (ASL) is the most widespread of the manual linguistic systems.

morpheme A word, or part of a word, that has an independent meaning. It is sometimes defined as the smallest unit of meaning. For example, the prefix 'sub-' means 'below,' as in the adjective 'subhuman' or the noun 'submarine'.

Active and Passive

In an active sentence, the subject is usually the actor, whereas in a passive sentence, the subject is typically acted upon. Compare 'The boy (subject) hit the ball' and 'The ball (subject) was hit by the boy.'

particular language. Again, it is the back consonants that are most frequently heard.

The **holophrastic** (one word) stage generally occurs when the child is between 10 and 15 months old. At this stage individual words are formed, usually those that are most important to the child. The most frequent words heard by a child will be 'the,' 'to,' and 'it,' yet it will not say such words before the words 'mummy' and 'daddy.' Phenomena known as **overextension** and **underextension** are common at this stage. For example, a child will underextend the word 'dog' to refer to his own dog and not to dogs in general, or will overextend the word 'daddy' to all adult males.

Within a few months of one-word utterances, the child produces two-word utterances like 'mummy drink,' or 'car go.' Because the lack of grammar at this stage makes all utterances sound much like a telegram, it is known as the **telegraphic stage**.

The **joining stage** occurs when a child is about two years old. He or she will begin to show an awareness of grammar, observed chiefly in mistakes, such as 'hitted,' instead of 'hit,' 'holded' instead of 'held,' and 'sheeps' instead of 'sheep.' This demonstrates that a child is aware of the regular rules for segmenting **morphemes**: e.g. add 'ed' at the end of verbs to signify past tense; add 's' at the end of nouns to signify plurals; it is not, however, aware of the exceptions to these rules.

Children of around three or four years of age begin to develop an awareness of linguistic structure. They can often distinguish between the **active** and **passive** voices as well as producing utterances like 'give the baby the doll,' 'give the doll to the baby.'

It is not until children are around eight years old that they acquire an awareness of **metalanguage**, i.e. an insight into language

itself. Before this age they would probably deny that 'is' or 'the' is a word and would be unable to give a satisfactory definition of what constitutes a word. This awareness seems to be brought about by cultural factors, such as literacy and education.

The main problem with the subject of children's language acquisition lies in its **methodology** – i.e. what methods should be applied in studying this area? Testing a child's comprehension is more difficult than testing his or her production of speech, since a child cannot be questioned as to what he or she actually knows about his or her language. However, there are a number of tests that are specifically designed to find out about a child's comprehension. To ascertain whether a child understands particular grammatical features, such as tenses and plurals, the investigator can show a child a toy and describe it by using an invented term, e.g. 'Here is a wug.' Then the child is shown two more of the same objects and the researcher says 'Here are two...' to see whether the child can supply the missing plural form.

Similarly, the researcher might show the child a picture and say 'This man is jidding the ground, yesterday he ... the ground' in order to discover whether the child can form past tenses. The child can also be asked to carry out some actions to see whether he or she can distinguish between the commands 'Put the cup on the ball' and 'Put the ball in the cup.'

Chomsky was also responsible for contributing to the language acquisition debate – specifically to the 'nature–nurture' controversy. Some scholars, such as the behaviourist psychologist B. F. Skinner (1904–90; see EXPERIMENTAL PSYCHOLOGY), believe that language acquisition is merely the acquisition of a set of habits. In opposition to this theory, Chomsky and others take a nativist approach, holding that all humans have an innate, genetically programmed, knowledge of language. One argument Chomsky advanced for his nativist theory is that all children, irrespective of their native language, only hear a finite number of sentences yet are being able to produce an infinite number of novel ones. In addition, as has already been seen in the discussion of deep and surface structure, he claimed that everyone has an intuitive knowledge of the structure of their native language, without ever having been formally taught this structure as children. After all, Chomsky claimed, everyone has the ability to produce and understand utterances that have never previously been heard (e.g. 'The pink radiator ate a hedgehog'). Consequently, the only reasonable explanation of the way in which children acquire a language as complex as that of their parents is that they have all learnt a finite set of rules that enable them to produce an infinite number of new utterances. According to Chomsky, language develops along similar paths even in the different environments provided by dissimilar languages and social backgrounds. Language development must therefore have an innate component that is unique to humankind.

Chimp Language

Since the late 1960s, a number of psychologists have been attempting to disprove the Chomskyan theory that human language is unique to humans, by teaching chimpanzees to communicate in *sign language*. The first success in this field was achieved by a chimp called Washoe. Washoe was taught a form of American Sign Language (ASL) by a team of American researchers. They attempted to raise her in as 'natural' an environment as possible, by surrounding her with humans who only communicated with her and with each other in ASL. At first Washoe only used single signs for objects but later, like humans, began to demonstrate a limited amount of creativity in her use of signs, making individual signs and signs in sequences she had never seen or been taught before. The first time she saw a duck she used the sign WATERBIRD, and she spontaneously produced the sequence of signs ROGER WASHOE TICKLE, when she wanted to be tickled by her trainer. However, what Washoe seemed unable to do was to maintain a fixed order of signs. Children, on the other hand, do tend to preserve a fixed word order. More recently, other psychologists working with chimps have taught the chimps to communicate not only with ASL but also by other methods, such as plastic tokens and computers. In all these cases, the chimps have demonstrated not only that they are capable of learning certain elements of the human language system but also that they have a knowledge of the language's syntax. For example, they were able to distinguish between different commands, such as 'put the red square on top of the cup' and 'put the cup under the blue square.'

Sociolinguistics

Sociolinguistics is the study of the link between language and society. It is an important field of study because every language spoken varies from one region to another as well as from one speaker to another. As a result, this branch of linguistics covers a wide variety of subjects, treating many types of linguistic variation, such as dialects, accents, and **registers**. Sociolinguistics also studies some of the contributing factors for linguistic varieties, such as gender, age, class, ethnicity, and race.

When a person says 'I ain't got nothing,' for example, the assumption is made by hearers that he or she is of a lower social status than someone who says 'I do not have anything,' that someone who says 'apartment' and 'sidewalk' is speaking American English, while someone who says 'flat' or 'pavement' is speaking British English, or that someone who talks about ladies' fashions and jewellery is most likely to be either a woman or someone who works in the fashion industry. This type of knowledge is essential to a complete understanding of the nature of language and communication.

The field of sociolinguistics originated in the pioneering work of William Labov (1927–   ). Early in the 1960s, Labov became interested in linguistic variations, in particular those

metalanguage
The language used to describe language. This language varies from culture to culture and is influenced by literacy. Western culture often divides language up into segments referring to words, phrases, and sentences but in some societies in West Africa, the same term used for 'word' can be applied more widely to any segment of speech, such as a morpheme, line of a song, theme, etc.

The Chimpanzee 'Kanzi' *This chimp, trained by researchers in the USA, is shown performing vocabulary and syntax tests. Since experiments in teaching chimps to communicate began in the 1960s, several animals have acquired a vocabulary of signs, using a variety of learning methods.* ▼

register A form of language associated with a particular context or social situation. An example of a formal register might be: 'I beg to differ,' of an informal or colloquial register: 'get lost,' or of a register of scientific English: 'Galactose metabolism in yoghurt bacteria.' Register should not be confused with a **dialect** or **accent**, which varies according to its user.

DIALECT AND ACCENT

Dialect forms an important area of study within sociolinguistics: the term describes the language variant spoken in a particular geographical region. Dialects of the same language are, generally speaking, mutually comprehensible, though there may be extremely wide variation in such fundamental elements as vocabulary, syntax, and grammar. Whether a language variant constitutes a dialect or a separate language in its own right may be determined by criteria other than linguistic ones. For example, Dutch, Flemish, and Afrikaans (the language spoken by the Boers of South Africa, and once known as Cape Dutch) could, solely on the grounds of mutual intelligibility, reasonably be claimed to be dialectal variants of a single language, whereas they are deemed to be separate languages for political reasons.

Accent refers to a person's distinctive pronunciation. This is often conditioned by the dialect that they speak. Social factors exert a very strong influence on dialect development, especially with regard to accent. Thus, although sociolinguistics makes no value judgment about the 'correctness' of pronunciation, society in general may do so. The most socially prestigious accent comes to be regarded as the 'standard,' and regional accents are considered as deviations from this ideal norm. Those who speak with a regional accent may become the target of jokes, or may even be affected adversely in their career or their social life.

that occurred in the way that Americans pronounced [r] sounds after vowels (***postvocalic r***) in words such as 'car,' 'park,' and 'beard.' It was originally thought that such variations were not predictable but rather were in ***free variation***, i.e. random. However, in a survey conducted at Martha's Vineyard, an island near Boston, Labov revealed that such variations had a noticeable pattern. By analysing the inhabitants' speech, Labov noticed that the variations were conditioned by the different attitudes of the speakers. Whereas those who were committed to staying on the island

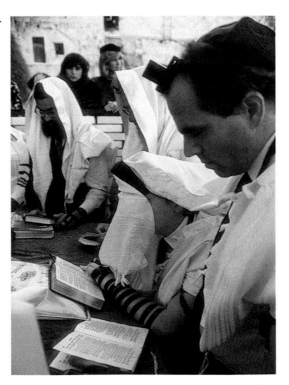

Jews Reciting Hebrew Hebrew is an example of the revival of a moribund language. When the state of Israel was founded in 1948, this ancient literary and religious language was chosen as the country's official language, as it was felt clearly to define the national identity of the Jewish state.

– generally the older inhabitants – pronounced the postvocalic r, those who intended to leave the island used the Boston pronunciation of dropping the [r] before a consonant.

Labov's next survey was to investigate the pronunciation of the postvocalic r in New York City. Here again he noticed that such speech was 'rule-governed' and guessed that the pronunciation would be correlated with social class. His method was to record covertly the speech of sales assistants in three department stores catering to people of different social status: upper class (Saks), middle class (Macy's), and lower class (Klein's). Labov found out which departments were on the fourth floor and then asked as many assistants as possible questions, such as 'excuse me, where are the women's shoes?' In the answer, which was 'Fourth floor,' Labov noticed that the pronunciation of the [r] was more prevalent in the speech of the assistants in the stores of higher social status. This survey concluded that the social stratification in New York is reflected in the speech of the individuals.

Bilingualism and Multilingualism

All languages are in contact with other languages and therefore are likely to be influenced by them. This is quite noticeably the case in bilingual and multilingual societies. Some people are ***monolingual*** (i.e. speaking just one language); others are ***bilingual*** (speaking two languages) or ***multilingual*** (speaking many languages). One interesting question for sociolinguists is which language is likely to be spoken in a particular situation in bilingual and multilingual societies. For example, the daughter of a mixed marriage may talk intimately to her mother in her mother's

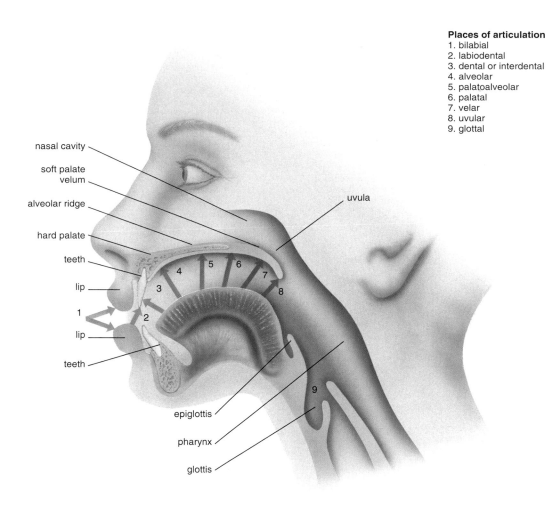

Places of articulation
1. bilabial
2. labiodental
3. dental or interdental
4. alveolar
5. palatoalveolar
6. palatal
7. velar
8. uvular
9. glottal

nasal cavity
soft palate
velum
alveolar ridge
hard palate
teeth
lip
1
lip
teeth
uvula
epiglottis
pharynx
glottis

◄ **The Vocal Tract and Places of Articulation** *This diagram shows the various parts of the mouth that are used to produce various sounds; the key gives the technical designation for each of these places of articulation. For example, **back consonants** are produced in the **velar** area (7), while sounds such as [p] and [b] are made by using both lips, which is referred to as the **bilabial** area (1).*

native tongue, but speak to her father about her job in his language. However fluent a speaker is in both languages, it is rare for them to be used equally in all situations. Normally, a great deal of **code switching** takes place, depending on, for example, the degree of formality or intimacy in the situation or on the content or topic of the conversation. In addition, one language is generally considered to be dominant, exerting influence on the less dominant ones.

In some cases, the dominant language may 'murder' the less prestigious one, by causing speakers to feel embarrassed about using it. ***Language death***, as this phenomenon is called, is usually triggered by social needs. When a language 'dies' (as happened with Cornish in Britain, with the demise of the last native speaker of this Celtic language in 1777), this does not mean that there is anything inherently wrong with the language itself. In extreme cases where a dominant culture irrupts suddenly and violently into the domain of a small linguistic community, the original language can die out within a generation; this was the fate of several languages of the Amazon Basin.

For example, in Sauris, a German-speaking enclave in northeast Italy, three linguistic varieties are spoken: a German dialect, Friulian, and Italian. Nearly all adults from this area speak all three languages equally well. There are, however, various situational factors determining the choice of language used. The German dialect spoken here does not resemble standard modern German, since it contains archaic Bavarian forms and other idiosyncratic features. Friulian is the common language and Italian the national language. Italian is the 'high variety' and is used in churches and schools. It is therefore a highly institutionalized variety and is used by people to signify that they are upwardly mobile. It is also used for conversing with outsiders who are known not to speak Friulian, with outsiders who prefer Italian, and with strangers who do not begin by speaking Friulian.

In addition, Saurians speak Italian to each other when in the presence of strangers, whether or not they are listening. Friulian is the 'mid variety' and characterizes informal conversation. It is used in bars, for example, or to attract someone's attention. The German variety, the 'low dialect', is used at home in

code switching The 'switch' speakers make in changing from one language, dialect, or register to another, depending on who they are talking to, or their topic of conversation.

Quechua-speaking Amerindians (Peru) ▶
Quechua – the official language of the Incas – is used by around 6 million people throughout the Andean highlands, from Colombia to Chile, and is an important lingua franca of this region. South America is one of the most linguistically diverse areas of the world; Quechua is just one of many indigenous Indian languages.

Lingua Franca

A lingua franca is a language that is used for communication between people with no common native language. English is the most widespread modern lingua franca. The term (from Italian: 'Frankish language') derives from a form of Provençal used as a common language between soldiers with different mother tongues during the Crusades (11th–14th centuries).

the company of the individual's own family. Its main characteristic is noninstitutionalized spontaneous conversation. Because of its low status, this variety virtually never influences the other two languages. German, then, is the language that is gradually being ousted. Some parents in Sauris no longer feel it necessary to communicate with their children in the language of low prestige. In this enclave, it is therefore common to find grandparents speaking to their children in German, and the children replying in Italian. Although German is still the mother tongue, schooling and television are now increasingly in Italian.

Pragmatics

Pragmatics is the study of language use. This area includes the speaker's and hearer's background knowledge as well as their understanding of the context in which a sentence is uttered. As with other branches of linguistics, pragmatics is regarded as rule-governed.

A simple example of pragmatics can be found in the ways in which people address others: there are certain rules about when to use a first name and when to use a surname, or when to use familiar or formal forms of address. Thus, a person would not usually call his or her doctor 'John' but would be expected to use the formal term of address 'Dr Smith,' and would not use a friend's surname when addressing him or her but rather would be expected to use the first name. Similarly, clearly defined conventions govern whether a person should use the familiar form of address in French or German ('tu' and 'Du,' respectively) or the formal form ('vous' and 'Sie').

A fluent speaker of English understands that the question 'Can you pass the salt?' does not require a yes/no answer but simply the non-verbal action of passing the salt. Similarly, a person who asks 'Have you got the time please?' does not expect a yes/no answer but to be told the time. On the other hand, a mother saying to her child 'How many times have I told you not to do that?' does not require any answer at all. This form of address is known as a ***rhetorical question***, since its form is conditioned by its intended effect rather than any questions of content or meaning.

These rules also apply to protracted periods of speech. Their function can be seen very clearly in various ***speech acts*** that people perform. This area of study is known as ***speech act theory*** and is associated with the work of such philosophers of language as J. L. Austin (1911–51), John Searle (1932–), and Ludwig Wittgenstein (1889–1951). (See PHILOSOPHY: THE PHILOSOPHY OF LANGUAGE.) Humans can do things with speech, such as make promises, warn people, and insult them. Sometimes, indeed, using words is the same as performing a nonlinguistic act. To *say* 'I bet you a pound it will snow tomorrow' is to *perform* an act of betting, and to say 'I promise I'll be there' is to perform an act of promising. The success of such speech acts usually depends on conventions or specific circumstances. Whether someone who says 'I name this ship *Queen Elizabeth*' has actually performed the act of naming a ship depends on whether he or she has the authority to do so; well-established conventions exist about who may name ships or conduct weddings.

Sometimes speech acts are ***implicit***, i.e. an act can be indirectly performed. For example, the single utterance 'There's a bull in that field' can be used to perform a wide variety of different speech acts. Depending on the context, it can be intended as a warning, a boast, a bet, or a promise. Practitioners of the academic discipline of pragmatics have therefore learned to take into account how context influences peoples' interpretation of utterances.

There are also rules (often unconscious) that govern who can talk at what point in everyday conversations. Talk is not a random sequence of utterances; it is a relatively structured phenomenon. There is usually a well-established opening (a greeting, such as 'Hello') and closing ('Goodbye'). Children's stories often begin with the words 'Once upon a time.'

In telephone conversation, there are set ways to make and answer calls. The opening and closing stages of conversations held on the telephone are especially distinctive; certain conventions govern sequences of acceptable and unacceptable utterances. It is usual for the person being called to speak first, by saying 'Hello,' or citing their telephone number, or, in the case of a company, stating the name of the firm. The caller then has the choice of either requesting to speak to a particular person, offering a greeting in return, or – in the case of a professional call – stating the nature of their business.

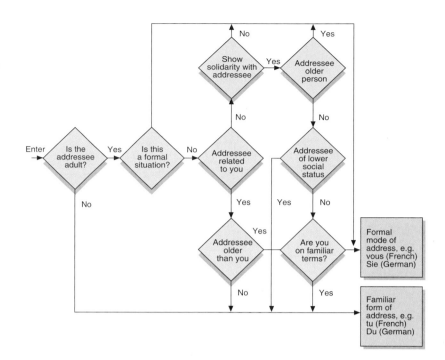

This particular area of language use is also conditioned by cultural conventions. The rules for talking on the telephone vary according to country. In Germany, for example, the telephone caller begins by announcing who he or she is before asking for the person they wish to speak to. In France, it is customary when calling someone to first apologize for troubling them. In addition, in France, it is usual for the caller to state the telephone number called and have it confirmed by the answerer, whereas in Britain it is more usual for the answerer to state their number.

Similarly, conventions exist concerning who can ask questions of whom. For example, a doctor generally asks questions of a patient but not vice versa, and a teacher asks questions of his or her pupils, even though he or she already knows the answer. The knowledge of these rules is often referred to as a person's ***communicative competence*** and this phenomenon is being incorporated into linguists' grammar. Communicative competence thus involves a knowledge of the speech acts of one's own native language but also where, when, by whom, and how such speech acts can be performed.

▲ **Simplified Diagram of Terms of Address**
This flow chart, the original of which was devised by the linguist Susan Ervin-Tripp (1927–   ), shows some of the considerations that condition a person's choice of address.

◄ **A Multilingual Sign in Switzerland** *Switzerland has four official languages: French, German, Italian, and Romansch (the latter spoken by less than 1% of the population). However, because there is territorial separation between the language groups, Switzerland has a lower proportion of people who speak more than one language than some officially monolingual countries.*

Psychology and the Individual

Attachment • Infant perception • Behavioural development • Temperament and personality

Maternal Bonding
Psychological research has shown that the relationship between a mother and her baby plays a vital role in forming the child's character. ▼

A learning process, which is known as ***social development***, operates on the individual from birth onwards. This lifelong process is the major determinant in shaping personality. Psychological and physiological studies have indicated that the social development occurring in the first few years of life is the most influential and persistent of all; ideas and beliefs inculcated into the child at this formative stage are likely to have an enduring influence.

Attachment

The importance of the relationship between the very young baby and its mother, or other closely associated person, has been emphasized by many psychologists. This relationship of physical and psychological bonding is referred to as ***attachment***. The main features of the attachment process were first described by the English psychiatrist Edward John Bowlby (1907–90). Bowlby was interested in juvenile delinquency but his most important work was concerned with the effects that a lack of close maternal association had on the child's mental and emotional health.

Bowlby believed that the mother's presence was essential for the formation of emotional bonds. These bonds were formed by physical contact, touching, stroking, caressing, maintaining eye-to-eye contact, and speaking in a high-pitched voice. He divided attachment behaviour into various stages, in which the baby initially interacted with anyone; interacted in a discriminating manner with one or more persons; formed a strong attachment to one or more people, usually at about seven months of age, but exhibited a marked fear of strangers or of unfamiliar situations; and finally a stage in which the baby was able to form reciprocal relationships with many people.

Later researchers have noted that a child that is securely bonded to its mother displays adventurous behaviour in the presence of its mother but ceases this and hurries to the mother in the presence of a stranger. By contrast, insecurely bonded babies avoid their mothers or behave ambiguously. Some psychologists have claimed that failure of proper attachment contributes to the later development of antisocial behaviour in children.

Infant Perception

Because an infant's central nervous system, especially the brain, has not yet reached the stage of full functional maturation, perception at birth, and for some time afterwards, is limited. Some of this neurological immaturity is due to the absence of insulating fatty sheaths on nerve fibres. The process of insulation is called ***myelinization*** and until it is complete, nerves cannot function properly. Nevertheless, the infant organism is avid for sensory input of all kinds. The desire for visual input, when the infant is awake, is especially strong. The most effective visual stimuli are from strongly patterned objects with sharp edges. A young baby will turn its eyes repeatedly towards objects that provide such stimuli. During the first six weeks or so of life the baby's power of selection and discrimination grows rapidly.

Extensive physiological research has ascertained that sensory input is essential for this neurological development to occur. Under the

PSYCHOLOGY AS A DISCIPLINE

Psychology is a scientific discipline that investigates the workings of the human or animal mind. Its subjects of study include: the mental faculties of memory, perception, and creativity; the ways in which children learn; how children acquire language; and how people behave in their working environment. Moreover, psychology encompasses a wide diversity of approaches, ranging from an interest in the workings of the brain (which has affinities with physiology) to research into the relationships between people (which is closely related to sociology and social anthropology). This broad discipline is perhaps best summarized in the words of one of its pioneers, William James (1842–1910), as 'the science of mental life.'

Psychology developed in the late 19th century as an attempt to provide answers to philosophical enquiries about the nature of sensory perception, memory, and emotion, The desire to establish the new subject as a science led to the rise of the rigorously 'objective' school of thought known as **behaviourism** from the 1920s onwards. This tendency to seek to measure behaviour, both normal and abnormal, dominated psychology until the 1960s. As a reaction against behaviourism's preoccupation with quantifiable patterns of behaviour, **cognitive psychology** arose at this time. This approach attempts to account for the mental states and emotional experiences of people, treating them not as objects of investigation but as sentient individuals.

Clinical psychology is concerned with the assessment and nonmedical treatment of emotional or behavioural problems. These include sexual or addictive problems, as well as unreasonable fears (phobias) and learning difficulties. Clinical psychology is distinct from **psychiatry**, a medical speciality concerned with the treatment by drugs of anxiety states (formerly called neuroses) and psychoses; see MEDICINE AND HEALTH CARE (VOL. 3): MENTAL HEALTH.

influence of such stimuli, more developmental changes take place in the cellular structure of the cortex of the brain – the 'higher' neurological regions – and in other parts of the brain, than at any other time. These changes involve the making of innumerable synaptic connections between nerve cells, providing the essential structural and functional basis for ever more refined sensory perception and increasingly refined motor control. The process of neurological maturation continues for several years. In the case of visual acuity, for instance, neurological plasticity, and the possibility of compensating for prior sensory deprivation by active intervention, is retained until about the age of seven. If no medical intervention is undertaken before that age, the damaging effects of the loss of sensory input, as from a drooping lid or a squint, become permanent. The connections between a 'lazy' (**amblyopic**) eye and the brain show a characteristic structural deficit in comparison with those for the normal eye.

Similar processes to those described for vision apply to all the other forms of sensory input, and deprivation of these has equally damaging effects. Children with early infections of the middle ear that diminish sound input may, unless promptly treated, suffer permanent loss of hearing. Global sensory deprivation is, of course, devastating in its effect and is associated with widespread structural abnormalities in the brain and severe general disability.

Behavioural Development

A highly influential exponent of social development is the Canadian psychologist Albert Bandura (1925–   ). Bandura has shown that children learn various modes of behaviour by watching other people in action. Imitative behaviour of this kind is more influential than verbal instruction, and children are conditioned in their behaviour more by observing the behaviour of their parents than by their parents' statements. The admonition 'Don't do what I do; do what I tell you' is unlikely to be effective if the child can observe the parents engaging in the proscribed behaviour.

The modes that children learn by observation from adults include aggression and its physical manifestations; various forms of social interaction, whether cooperative or not; selfishness; altruistic behaviour; patience; sharing of goods and advantages; and deferment of wanted gratification. Bandura has been especially interested in aggressive behaviour. He showed, for instance, that children who were able to observe punishment for aggressive behaviour in other children became less aggressive, while children who saw aggression being rewarded or treated with indifference tended to become more aggressive. This work had an important effect on the long-running debate on the influence on children of violence on television. As a result of Bandura's work, many psychologists concluded that the exposure of children to television violence has been one of the major factors

▲ **St Ignatius Loyola** *St Ignatius Loyola (1491–1556), Spanish founder of the Jesuit religious order (in 1533), recognized the crucial importance of early influences on children. He stated: "Give me the child until he is seven and I care not who has him afterwards." Jesuits became renowned as educators, establishing schools and universities throughout the world.*

> The separation of psychology from the premises of biology is purely artificial, because the human psyche lives in indissoluble union with the body.
>
> **Carl Jung** (1875–1961), Swiss psychoanalyst, *Factors Determining Human Behaviour*

contributing to the rise of violent crime and aggressive behaviour in Western societies (see COMMUNICATIONS AND MEDIA: ELECTRONIC MEDIA).

There are many other factors influencing behaviour and by no means all psychologists agree with this conclusion. It has been pointed out, for instance, that aggressive children are unpopular with their peers and may watch more violent television because their peer relationships are less rewarding. Such children may also justify their own aggressiveness in the high levels of television violence.

Temperament and Personality

The term 'personality' can be defined as the totality of all those mental and physical characteristics that contribute to a person's uniqueness as a human being. Personality encompasses intellectual and educational attributes, emotional disposition, behavioural tendencies, character, and temperament.

Personality results from the interaction between inherited characteristics and the total personal environment, especially that operating in early childhood. Psychologists now tend to discount the influence of heredity alone as relatively insignificant, but studies on twins have shown how strong genetic influences can be. Hereditary factors largely determine the bodily characteristics (the **somatotype**), the pattern of physical and mental development, and, to some extent, the way in which the endocrine (hormonal) system operates. These can affect the personality.

A more immediately obvious effect on the personality, however, is that of environmental factors. It is clear that the personality characteristics of parents or other family members can mould the personality of the growing child. Other important environmental factors

include educational and cultural influences, standards of nutrition, illnesses, and the individual's social environment. Among the family influences that make for a healthy and well-balanced personality are:
- confidence that physical and emotional support are readily available;
- uninhibited displays of love and affection;
- clear and consistent guidelines on acceptable and unacceptable forms of behaviour;
- freely expressed individuality within the constraints of the rules.

Although there have been many attempts to categorize personality within groups in accordance with behavioural patterns, these have not been particularly successful. The reason for this is that the large majority of people fall into an indefinable group in which none of the extremes of personality type is especially pronounced. The Swiss psychologist Carl Gustav Jung (1875–1961) identified two basic personality types: extrovert, or outgoing; and introvert, or inward-looking; see MEDICINE AND HEALTH CARE (VOL. 3): MENTAL HEALTH. Some people can be generally regarded as having extrovert or introvert personalities, while others possess some of the elements associated with these personality types. However, most cannot be realistically classified in this way at all

Vulnerable Personalities. In addition, a small number of people can be categorized as having obsessional, hysterical, or sociopathic personalities. The obsessional person is over-conscientious, meticulous, orderly and tidy, and excessively rigid in their habits. The hysterical person is demanding, histrionic, attention-seeking, manipulative, emotionally volatile and exaggerates consistently. The sociopath (also called **psychopath**) is conscienceless, overtly selfish, and behaves with no regard for the rights of others.

These people are, in general, mentally more vulnerable than average. The obsessional may develop a severe anxiety state, the hysteric a somatoform disorder (physical manifestations of mental upset), and the sociopath a psychopathic personality disorder. When the characteristics of these personality types develop to an exaggerated degree and become antisocial or disabling, they must then be regarded as disorders. None of these disorders is, however, an actual psychotic illness. Psychotic disorders usually take a form that appears to be determined by the personality (the ***prepsychotic personality***). Thus the introvert who becomes psychotic will usually suffer from schizophrenia, a disease in which the process of thinking and contact with reality disintegrate. On the other hand, the extrovert may develop a manic-depressive disorder, in which periods of deep depression alternate with brief feelings of excessive elation.

Identical Twins
Studies of personality have shown that identical twins who have been brought up apart retain close similarities in personality. Even allowing for coincidence, some cases of separated identical twins demonstrate this dramatically. ▼

Group and Social Psychology

Social grouping • Prosocial behaviour and aggression • Interpersonal communication •
Conformity issues • Group dynamics

The psychology of the group is not simply a multiplication of the psychology of the individual but has features of its own that differ from that of any single member of the group.

People gather in groups of many descriptions. Some groups have a brief life span and are then dissolved; others, such as the extended family, may last for many years or even centuries, as a result of the constant addition or recruitment of new members. The interaction of people in such diverse groups as families, associations at work, clubs, political parties, committees, athletic teams, adult education classes, and religious and other organizations possesses a number of common features. Groups are important for mutual protection, for psychological support, and for many other reasons. It is a natural human tendency to gather together and enjoy the company of others of a similar disposition.

Social Grouping

Social grouping and social divisions involve many cohesive factors, such as religion, race, profession, and recreational interests. All these factors have led to social stratification (see SOCIAL DIVISIONS). This is apparent even in the most egalitarian societies. In some cases the grouping is explicitly recognized and referred to; in others it is real but is left implicit.

Social grouping is readily recognizable in primates other than *Homo sapiens*, and can be assumed to have been a feature of human intercourse from the outset. In any population there will be marked individual differences in intelligence, physical strength, and the ability to acquire the symbols of status. Unless some form of equality is artifically imposed, individuals find their appropriate positions in the hierarchy. In so doing, they tend to associate with others with similar characteristics to form groups of like mind and ability.

In the past, social distinctions were openly acknowledged with little regard for the feelings of those whose inferior status was thus highlighted. The poor were conditioned to accept this unjust situation without demur.

Prosocial Behaviour and Aggression

Social stability can be seen as the mid-point between cohesive prosocial forces on the one hand and disruptive aggression on the other. While the reasons for the cohesive forces are clear, the roots of aggression are less obvious.

====SEE ALSO====
This section:
• Origins of Sociology
• Social Divisions
• Psychology and the
  Individual
• Developmental
  Psychology
Philosophy:
• Applied Philosophy
**Animal Anatomy and
Physiology (vol. 3):**
• Nervous Systems

◀ **Ritualized
Aggression** *Japanese
wrestlers compete at
sumo, a sport that has
many rituals and
ceremonies associated
with it. In highly
formalized encounters
such as this, aggression
is no longer a disruptive
force; properly
controlled, aggression
may help to foster a
sportsman's or
sportswoman's sense
of competitiveness.*

**Interpersonal ▶
Relations**
*This diagram shows a
group of nine girls
(yellow) and ten boys
(blue), composed of
three subgroups (ringed
in green). Each
subgroup has a leader
(A, B, and C) who is
popular and accepted.
Black lines between
individuals designate
mutual attraction,
while red lines designate
mutual antipathy.
Broken black and red
lines signify a one-way
relationship. While X
and Y are outsiders, W
has no positive
relationships, and Z
meets with almost
complete rejection.*

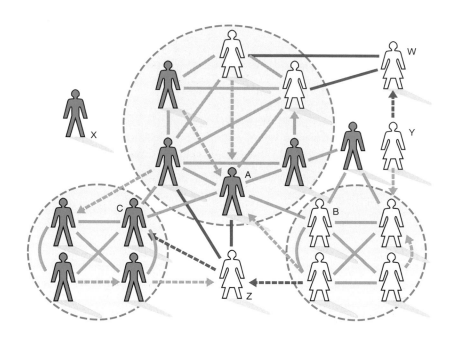

The first major studies into the causes of aggression were carried out by the Austrian ethologist Konrad Lorenz (1903–89). In his book *On Aggression*, published in 1963, Lorenz put forward the theory that aggression had an instinctive basis. However, for humans, unlike animals, aggression was not necessary for survival. With a proper understanding of human instinctual needs, Lorenz believed that aggression could be redirected into more useful behaviour.

The Austrian psychiatrist Sigmund Freud (1856–1939) believed that aggression was innate and that aggressive behaviour was partly the result of frustration but that it could also spring from the death instinct, for which he employed the Greek term (*thanatos*). Freud maintained that the repression of aggressive impulses had a major influence on human behaviour and mental health.

BEHAVIOURIST AND COGNITIVE PSYCHOLOGY

Behaviourist psychology is a school of inquiry pioneered by the US psychologists John B. Watson (1878–1958) and B. F. Skinner (1904–90). It rejects any 'introspective' data concerning such unquantifiable phenomena as thought, consciousness, and feeling, focusing instead on behaviour as a series of simple stimuli and responses. This process is known as ***conditioning***. See EXPERIMENTAL PSYCHOLOGY; THE ANIMAL KINGDOM (VOL. 3): ANIMAL BEHAVIOUR.
Cognitive psychology is concerned with internal mental processes, such as attention, memory, perception, and other higher faculties. This approach derives much hard information about the mind from physiological research, especially neurology. It rejects behaviourism's methods as inflexible, and regards the brain as a complex information-processing system.

Behaviourist psychology adopts the position that natural aggressive tendencies are reinforced by their successful use. Aggressive skills are acquired in practice and become recognized as being personally advantageous. Aggressive behaviour in successful people may also be used as a means of removing sources of frustration, disposing of threats, or even of earning respect. Few psychologists now believe, however, that frustration is the major cause of aggression. Frustration is unpleasant because it is associated with mental conflict and high physiological arousal. However, there are several available strategies for dealing with it, of which aggressive behaviour is only one and is not necessarily perceived as being the most effective.

Cognitive psychology maintains that human behaviour is influenced by personal values and by perceptions of situations. Thus, aggressive behaviour may often be seen to be justified if it is seen to be a proper retributive response to a wrong. The aggressive potential of almost a whole country can be mobilized if that country is threatened with invasion by an enemy. In such circumstances, aggressive behaviour is generally deemed to be justified. The small minority that considers that war is always wrong will not, however, necessarily be prompted into aggressive behaviour by this stimulus. Direct personal experience of an attack may, however, be sufficient to overcome previously held values.

Cognitive psychology also holds that aggressive retaliatory impulses may be activated by thoughts that amplify the stimulus or promote relevant anger, or inhibited by thoughts that analyse the situation and indicate that a more constructive response may be appropriate.

PARALINGUISTICS

An important aspect of the analysis of **nonverbal communication** is the study of how the meaning of human utterances may be altered by *how* something is said rather than by the actual words used. For example, hesitation in responding to a direct question normally indicates uncertainty. Similarly, the tone of voice used in the reply "Really?" to being given a piece of information may indicate surprise or scepticism. Context is highly significant in paralinguistics, and researchers take such factors as facial expressions and gestures into account.

All schools of psychology agree that aggression is also often motivated by feelings of personal inadequacy. An undersized or physically unattractive man, or a person aware of educational or intellectual inadequacies, may adopt aggressive behaviour in order to achieve desired dominance. This may be an almost unconscious process.

One important context in which the psychology of the group differs from that of the individuals is that of the mob. People in a disorderly crowd often behave more aggressively than they would as individuals. There are several reasons for this. Those who identify with the mob feel a reduced sense of personal responsibility; they can rationalize that it is impossible for so many people to be wrong, for so many people to be arrested, and for any individual to be held responsible for the damage and injury inflicted by the mob. Most will accept the leadership of others and conform to the obvious majority wish. Members of an excited mob experience heightened emotional arousal, partly because they observe the signs of emotion in others and partly because the normal controlling influences on their behaviour are reduced. In addition, many people harbour strong feelings of resentment that they would like to release in violence but are restrained from doing so because they fear the consequences. Membership of the mob confers a sense of anonymity and diminishes the sense of responsibility.

Mob violence is not necessarily directed at the real cause of the resentment but at any apparent symbol of it. Resentment over poverty may be vented by damaging or destroying any property that suggests affluence.

The effect of alcohol, in releasing inhibitions that might otherwise control aggressive impulses, is obvious. This is not to suggest that alcohol is an excuse for disorderly behaviour or that, on its own, it causes aggression.

Interpersonal Communication

Human communication involves far more than direct or indirect verbal interchange. Much of interpersonal communication is nonverbal, or even involuntary, and takes place through signs, which may or may not be designed to effect communication. Body language is a well-known example. Much information about the state of the emotions is conveyed by facial expression, gestures, and body movement, but the emotions are also revealed by particular body postures and by indications of muscle tension. Meaningful information of this kind is often transmitted in an almost subliminal way. Common observation has shown that specific meaning can be conveyed by certain physical actions or reactions. Eye contact is particularly eloquent and is one of the most common signals of a significant change in a human interaction. Pupil size, too, can signal interest or excitement, and perception of this is usually unconscious.

Body language is more effective than is generally appreciated. Communication begins whenever two people come within visual range of one another. The transmission of a mass of data occurs and this happens far more quickly than would be possible by verbal means. Information is conveyed by facial expression or lack of it; physical attitude or

Nonverbal Communication
This diagram shows four common gestures that convey clear information to the observer about a person's state of mind. In A, both arms folded and eyes downcast indicate a lack of self-confidence; in B, one finger to the cheek is a gesture signalling reflection; in C, both arms crossed high across the chest and a direct stare indicate arrogance and complacency; and in D, a speaker underlines a point with a wagging finger, an aggressive gesture to the listener. ▼

▲ **A Gang of Punk Rockers** *These youths base their lifestyle around loud discordant rock music, outlandish clothes and hairstyles, and antisocial behaviour. Although the teenagers that join such groups do so as a gesture of rebellion against society at large, there is intense pressure from their peers within the group to conform.*

Whoso would be a man must be a nonconformist.

Ralph Waldo Emerson
(1803–82), US poet and
essayist

posture; position of the arms; quality or state of the clothing; degree of proximity; tone of voice; accent; rapidity or otherwise of speech and response; presence and quality of body odour; and so on. While many people are highly conscious of the information they are passing in this way, others are unaware or indifferent. The most perceptive will be aware that information conveyed in this way is often more convincing than words.

Nonverbal communication is part of the stock-in-trade of many professionals who are concerned with influencing others. It is important for preachers, actors, salespeople, and teachers to use body language to good purpose. Politicians are increasingly being trained by personal image consultants in how to comport themselves to the best effect when in the public eye; this involves teaching the person concerned to underpin his or her speeches with positive hand gestures and facial expressions, and to use these sparingly, lest they become caricatured.

Body language invariably conveys much about the quality of the relationship of others. A man puts his arm around a woman's shoulder in public; she immediately stiffens and goes rigid. A couple sit ever closer together on a park bench. A child shyly puts her hand in that of her teacher. Solitary strangers repeatedly catch each other's eye in a restaurant. A police suspect under interrogation leans back casually and puts his hands in his pockets. Such nonverbal messages express emotions or desires or reveal attitudes. They may often radically qualify the words that a person is speaking. Body language can demonstrate a profound contradiction between what is said and a person's true feelings.

The question of human interaction has been closely studied by psychologists. One model proposes that three elements are involved. These can best be understood by representing the interactions as a triangle, the angles of which indicate the person, the behaviour, and the interactional situation. Each angle is joined to the other two by two-way arrows on the sides of the triangle. A person who behaves in a socially acceptable way will be positively affecting both the interaction and the subsequent behaviour. Unacceptable behaviour will have negative consequences both for the interaction and for the person.

Conformity Issues
The desire for conformity with the customs and conventions of a group, or the willingness to acquiesce in common patterns of behaviour, are powerful influences on human conduct. Such acquiescence is the result of the powerful pressures to conform that are imposed by a group on its members. These pressures are especially strong among socializing young people. While the reasons for particular patterns of behaviour, dress, accent, terminology, musical interest, way of walking, and so on are often far from apparent, the consequences of failing to conform are usually so obvious that few group members will have the mental resilience to rebel.

Conformity pressures can have adverse effects, as when an implicitly prescribed standard dress conflicts with weather conditions to the extent of causing severe discomfort. More seriously, such pressures can induce members of a group to behave in a seriously antisocial or criminal manner, even if such behaviour is contrary to the inclinations or convictions of individual members. Indeed, the majority of members of even the most delinquent gang do not engage in violent or criminal behaviour most of the time.

Many factors influence conformity. **Gender roles** are among the most prominent of these. Women who accept the feminine gender stereotype are more likely to conform than men. Indeed, male nonconformity arises partly as a consequence of individuality itself being a masculine stereotype. Therefore, males can sometimes be observed to conform in nonconformity.

Conformity is also affected by the size of the group and, particularly, by the absence of any one member with discordant behaviour. A group of eight is sufficient to apply maximal conformity pressure. If, however, a single member of the group shows willingness to resist conformity pressure, that pressure is greatly weakened. The effect of this, however, depends on the group status of the resisting individual.

The dissension of individual jurors at a trial provides an interesting context for studying conformity and nonconformity within small groups. A highly persuasive individual may emerge as an opinion leader within the group, and, by force of personal charisma and rhetoric, may succeed in progressively influencing the views of his or her co-jurors, even those who were originally inclined to reach a different verdict.

Group Dynamics

The psychological and social forces that operate when people associate together in groups are studied in the social science of group dynamics. This term was first used by the German psychologist Kurt Lewin (1890–1947) in the course of a study of group psychology that led to the development of his influential field theory. This has inspired a great deal of research in social psychology.

Lewin rejected the simple idea of a person motivated by instincts and desires and operating in an indifferent environment. Instead he proposed the concept of the 'life space.' The life space of a person is not simply the objective environment but the complex of the person and the environment, together with the way it is perceived and interpreted by that person. It also includes cultural pressures that determine when a particular form of behaviour is appropriate and when it is not. The interaction of the life spaces of the members of a group produces a field of force containing many different elements, some tending to drive the group in one direction of opinion, some pulling it in another. The combination of these forces determines the behaviour of the group.

A group might, for instance, contain some members who were strongly racially prejudiced and others who appreciated the necessity to respect the rights of others, regardless of race. If such a group were involved in a situation in which a threat was perceived as coming from a different racial group, tensions would arise and the outcome in terms of behaviour of the group would be determined by the relative strength of these. In any attempt to alter the outcome, little is likely to be achieved by attempts to change individual opinions. Since the life space of each member of the group is subjected to the pressures of the group field of force, it is this that must be altered if a change is to be achieved.

Lewin, who was trained in the physical sciences, was attracted by analogies between the dynamics of the group and physical fields of force, which he represented by topological and other mathematical models. However, this method – which may impress the nonmathematician – gave his arguments an unwarranted air of precision. Ultimately, the complex relations within a group cannot accurately be represented by mathematical models.

> **Occupational Psychology**
>
> This branch of psychology studies questions of management, career development, and problems arising from the relationship between individuals and their employers. One particular application of psychology has been in human resources departments of organizations, in the form of psychometric aptitude tests to aid personnel selection.

GENDER ISSUES IN PSYCHOLOGY

Psychology has increasingly come to recognize and account for fundamental differences in the psychology of men and women. Psychological gender differences have been investigated in the areas of mathematical, visuospatial, and verbal ability, as well as aggression. Some psychologists trace these differences to the different biological make-up of men and women. For example, men's different attitudes towards aggressiveness are thought to derive from the **androgens**, steroid hormones that determine male sexual characteristics; see ANIMAL ANATOMY AND PHYSIOLOGY (VOL. 3): REPRODUCTION.

Others explain them in terms of nurture (i.e. upbringing) rather than nature. Thus, the development of distinct gender-role stereotypes may be the result of a child seeking to imitate the behaviour exhibited by its parents.

Social psychology is concerned with sex differences as they relate to achievement. ***Attribution theory*** has been developed from studies relating to people's perceptions of their achievements. According to

▲ **Boys Playing with Toy Guns**
Psychology has investigated sex-role stereotypes. While some see sex roles as biologically determined, others stress the effect of upbringing.

this theory, women are more easily discouraged than men from becoming high achievers – both educationally and occupationally – because of the causes to which they attribute their successes and failures. It is claimed that women tend to attribute their successes to luck and their failures to an inherent lack of ability. Men, on the other hand, attribute their achievements to their skills and any failures they suffer to bad luck.

The fact that women tend to be more prone to depression than men has also been a focus of psychological investigation. The so-called ***learned helplessness theory*** accounts for this difference by claiming that women's greater passiveness and defeatism derives from the fact that their disadvantaged social position leaves them with very little control or influence over the sources of reward and reinforcement.

Experimental Psychology

Perception • Memory • Attention • Human performance • Learning • Reasoning

Experimental psychology is the study of psychological processes in a laboratory setting. The first psychological laboratory was established in Leipzig, Germany, in 1879 by Wilhelm Wundt (1832–1920) and for the next 50 years the field was dominated by German researchers. However, experimental psychology also developed vigorously in North America in the early 20th century, as a result of the rise of **behaviourism** (see GROUP AND SOCIAL PSYCHOLOGY). Experimental psychology has been influential but not dominant in Europe, where it has had to compete with ethology, psychoanalysis, and neuropsychology – represented most famously by Konrad Lorenz (1903–89), Sigmund Freud (1856–1939), and Alexander Luria (1902–90), respectively.

A typical situation in an experimental psychology laboratory is that a **subject** (usually a human, but possibly an animal) is required to carry out a task. This task often involves the presentation of stimuli (e.g. pictures or sounds) to which the subject must make a response. A response may be something straightforward – such as the press of a button – or something quite elaborate, such as an extended report of what the subject is currently thinking about. The strength of experimental psychology is the high degree of control that the psychologist is able to exert on the conditions surrounding the experiment: stimuli whose physical characteristics can be precisely described are presented to a subject for an exact time, and the subject's response is

precisely recorded. This procedure has enabled experimental psychologists to make detailed claims about the factors that influence a subject's performance.

The areas in which experimental psychologists have had most success are those dealing with perception, memory, attention, 'human performance,' learning, and reasoning.

Perception

Philosophers, physiologists, and psychologists have long been concerned with how we process information from the outside world. One of the central concerns of philosophy has been the validity of the information we collect from the outside world, while 19th-century physiologists made great strides in describing how information passes from the sense organs (e.g. the eye, the ear) along nerves pathways to the brain. However, it is the methods of experimental psychology that have enabled a precise record to be made of the factors affecting what a subject sees or hears.

Visual Perception. The sense organs are not passive recorders of external stimulation, like a camera or a tape recorder, but in conjunction with the brain they interpret outside stimulation in order to 'make sense' of it. A simple example of this is the phenomenon of **constancy**. For example, if a subject is shown a three-dimensional object from different angles, and illuminated in different ways, there will be enormous variation in the range of wavelengths and intensities that are reflected

Colour Perception ▶
*This illustration shows the results of an experiment in colour perception conducted by the psychologist William McDougall (1871–1938). A person with normal sight colours the parrot as in figure **A**; a person who can only differentiate between two adjacent colours makes a random choice of colours each time they identify such a difference (figures **B** and **C**); and a person who can see only red, green, and pink colours the bird as in figure **D**.*

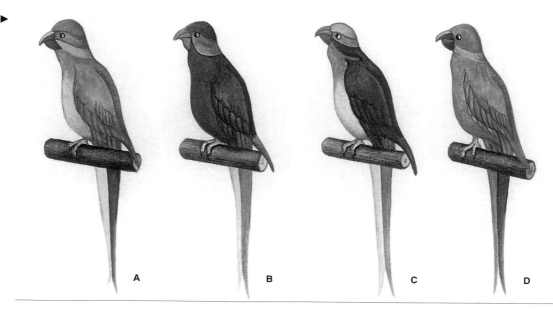

A   B   C   D

PSYCHOMETRICS

Psychometrics is the collective term for tests conducted by psychologists to measure aptitudes and personality characteristics, or to evaluate intelligence.

In ***projective tests***, a person's character is assessed from what they 'read into' ambiguous objects. For example, Rorschach tests, devised by the Swiss psychiatrist Hermann Rorschach (1884–1922), require the subject to describe what he or she sees in symmetrical shapes formed from inkblots. Such tests are typically used in clinical diagnoses of sociopathic traits.

Other projective tests (e.g. the Thematic Apperception Test, or TAT) ask the subject to tell a story about a series of pictures, each of which is open to several interpretations.

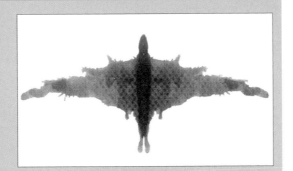

▲ **A Rorschach Inkblot** *In Rorschach tests, the interpretations that a subject projects on to a series of inkblots are used to form a profile of his or her personality. This is done by assigning certain scores to the subject's emphasis of particular elements of the blot, and comparing these with established norms.*

Gestalt Psychology

Gestalt psychology, developed by German psychologists in the early 20th century, claimed that human beings respond to their environment in a highly complex way. In contrast to behaviourism's stress on simple stimulus and response, this approach thought the human mind was characterized by a tendency to perceive affinities between the form (German: *Gestalt*) of things.

from the object and received by the eye. What a human or other organism would often wish to do is to ignore the incidental variations but record those properties that are intrinsic to the object. A red tomato should look red even if it is illuminated by coloured light; a black piece of coal should look dark, even if it is seen in bright sunlight; a round coin should look round, even if it is presented at a slant so that it objectively appears as an ellipse. Indeed, this is what the eye and the brain often manage to achieve: experimental methods have shown that subjects compensate for varying conditions, and report tomatoes as red (colour constancy), coal as black (brightness constancy), and coins as round (shape constancy), even when the objective information reaching the eye does not strictly justify this interpretation.

The peripheral sense organs are easier to study than central brain processes and a substantial amount is known about them. Careful experiments have charted the discriminative powers of the eye, in particular studying perceptual abilities as a function of the part of the retina that a beam of light falls on. (The retina is the light-sensitive area at the back of the eyeball.) Higher ***acuity*** (ability to make fine visual discriminations) is found at the centre of the retina (the fovea), while greater ability to detect movement is present at the periphery of the retina. This indicates that perceptual systems have evolved to serve several quite different functions, with high foveal acuity being used to make fine judgments about the stimuli we are concentrating on, while peripheral-movement sensitivity is useful for attracting attention to a prey or predator.

Eye movements themselves offer useful perspectives on the perceptual process. The eyes do not move smoothly over a stimulus, but dwell for short periods on particular areas of the stimulus (these are called ***fixations***); fixations are separated by rapid eye movements (***saccades***). Analysis of the factors governing the length and location of fixations can reveal facts about how the perceptual system works. For example, adults read a text by moving their eyes an average of about eight character spaces between successive fixations; they tend to avoid fixating on short predictable words such as 'the'; and reading is disrupted if the experimenter changes the length, or the first and last letters, of words that are up to 12 characters to the right of fixation. This suggests a process in which words are scanned so that they fall on the fovea, the region with the highest acuity in the eye, but information about the length and shape of words in the periphery of vision is used by the reader to decide where exactly to locate the next fixation. This 'stop-start' (fixation-saccade) pattern of eye movements poses particular problems for the brain, which needs to ensure that information from one fixation does not interfere with information from a subsequent one; some poor readers have difficulties because information from successive fixations runs together.

After retinal processing, visual information is transmitted in a series of pathways to the brain. Here separate elements of a stimulus, for example its colour and its orientation, are processed in different parts of the brain; see ANIMAL ANATOMY AND PHYSIOLOGY (VOL. 3): NERVOUS SYSTEMS. How such elements are reassembled so that the subject perceives a unitary object, and not a sea of unconnected features, is one of the functions of attention.

Auditory Perception. The auditory sense organ is the ear. Sound is transduced from mechanical vibrations in the outer ear to electric

▲ **Wilhelm Wundt** *Wundt laid the foundations of experimental psychology, by applying scientific principles of physiology to the study of sense perception.*

Déjà vu

Déjà vu (French: 'already seen') is an error of memory, in which a person believes that he or she is reliving a past experience. Most people suffer occasionally from this mild delusion. While people of a mystical or religious tendency regard déjà vu as proof of reincarnation, psychoanalysts believe that it arises from a partially forgotten (or suppressed) memory, fantasy, or dream.

Memory Types
Because a firm physiological understanding of the faculty of memory does not exist, the concept covers a number of diverse areas. Psychology distinguishes between many different types of memory; the most common designations are shown in this diagram. ▼

activity in the pathways leading to the brain in a series of steps involving, in particular, a vibrating strip, called the ***basilar membrane***, in the inner ear. The basilar membrane is intimately concerned with the perception of pitch; damage to particular parts of the basilar membrane leads to loss of sensitivity for particular pitches. Timing in the auditory system is extremely accurate; with the small difference in time it takes a sound in the environment to travel to one ear or the other enables the brain to determine the location of the sound; for example, a sound directly in front of a person will take the same time to reach each ear, whereas a sound coming from the right will reach the right ear shortly before the left.

The greatest triumph of the auditory system is ***speech perception***. Speech signals pose great problems for analysis, as scientists have found when working with machines that attempt to achieve the same discriminations as the ear and the brain. The problem is that speech is fast (a speaker may utter 20 different speech sounds per second, many of which run into each other). Listening to a native speaker of a language one does not understand makes one wonder how the brain can make these sounds intelligible. There are various theories about how the brain can do this; for example, speech may be treated in a special way by the brain – the same stimulus sounds different if it is interpreted as a speech sound or a non-speech sound.

Memory
The higher organisms are more able to adapt and survive because they have memories; i.e.

they do not respond only to the here-and-now, but can relate their performance to past experiences. For example, a bird remembers where its nest is, a baby recognizes its mother's face, and a hunter remembers that antelope come to the waterhole in the evening.

Length of Memory. There is considerable variation in the length of time that memories persist. Details of a jumble of letters flashed on a screen will not be remembered even one second later unless the subject takes deliberate steps to process them, and even then the subject can retain only a few items. Asked to retain an unfamiliar telephone number, a person can probably remember it for several seconds (several minutes if one repeats it to oneself several times) but the information is lost if distraction causes a person to stop rehearsing it. This type of memory is known as ***short-term memory***. A coherent piece of information can be retained for longer periods, though its vividness and reliability are far from perfect. The following generalizations can be made about length of retention in memory: initially we process a substantial amount of information from many sources; unless this information is attended to, memory of it will decay rapidly (less than a second for vision, a few seconds for audition). Information can be retained for longer with the help of a variety of processes: the most prominent is rehearsal, which maintains information on a temporary basis and can help to convert memories into a more permanent form, known as ***long-term memory***. A second set of processes influencing long-term retention is ***depth of processing***. If we process material paying attention to meaning and looking for associations we are more likely to remember it than if we process it on the basis of superficial physical characteristics.

Different Kinds of Memory. There are many different tasks involving memory. Subjects may be asked about particular events in their lives (***episodic memory***), or about general knowledge that is not linked to a specific experience (***semantic memory***). These form aspects of long-term memory.

Even deeper than long-term memory is ***genetic memory***, the hypothetical biological memory that organisms have, which is expressed in their innate fears and reflex actions. ***Unconscious memory*** is a store of memories derived from feelings and events that have been repressed.

At the opposite end of the scale is ***sensory memory***, an aspect of very short-term memory. This forms part of the process of perception and involves the very brief retention of information obtained by the senses. Brief visual experiences lasting for one or two seconds are called ***iconic memories***.

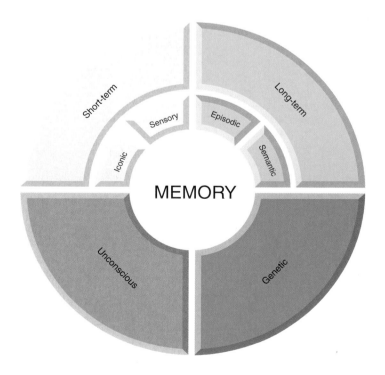

How far different memory tasks use different structures in the brain or merely different strategies applied to the same structure is still a matter for debate.

Attention

Perception and memory are not carried out passively: the subject often makes choices about what information to process, and these choices are the function of attention.

Selective attention was extensively studied in the 1950s and 1960s, and is best illustrated by the so-called 'cocktail party phenomenon': how can we attend to one speaker at a noisy party, when so many other conversations are going on around us? The use of the technique of ***shadowing***, in which a subject is required to repeat a message presented to one ear while the other ear hears irrelevant messages, led to the formulation of the ***filter theory***. This states that the brain is able to filter out unwanted messages, especially if they occur at locations or in voices that are different from those of the message that is to be attended to. Yet some unwanted information can slip through the filter, especially if it has relevance to the subject (as at a cocktail party when your name crops up in a conversation you were not previously attending to).

Focused attention deals with the problem of how the brain assembles the separate features that make up an object. This problem has been studied extensively by the British psychologist Anne Treisman. Treisman used several tasks that showed different patterns of performance, depending on whether the subject was able to exert focused attention. Without focused attention there is a risk of subjects reporting illusory conjunctions of features. In other words, in a scene where some objects are green and some objects are round, but no objects are both round and green, subjects will sometimes report erroneously seeing green round objects. Thus, the subject has assembled features from different objects. If subjects have an opportunity to focus their attention, the chances of error are greatly reduced. As with the distinction between foveal and peripheral vision, both focused and unfocused attention have their advantages: what unfocused attention lacks in accuracy it makes up for in terms of breadth.

Another important aspect of attention is related to the distinction between ***automatic*** and ***effortful*** processes. Automatic processes are outside our immediate control, do not require attention, and make little demand on our processing resources. Effortful processes are more under voluntary control; they require attention and make demands on resources. Practising a task helps to change it from one that requires attention to one that

◀ **Mouse in a Maze**
Experiments by cognitive psychologists have suggested that mice and rats are able to bring a mental process to bear on learning how to negotiate a maze successfully. This finding is at variance with those of behaviourists, who regard such behaviour solely in terms of conditioning.

can be carried out automatically. The novice car driver requires considerable attention to change gear, whereas the expert changes gear with so little thought that such manoeuvres have no noticeable effect on other activities, such as conversation with a passenger.

Human Performance

Analysis of stimuli is the province of perception, whereas the planning and execution of responses engages our ***motor*** skills. Some psychologists have noted that perception and motor skills have evolved together, i.e. perception collects the information enabling the animal to carry out suitable motor skills (such as reaching or jumping), and have concluded that perceptual and motor skills should always be studied together. This view is supported by observations that different brain mechanisms seem to be involved in perceiving those areas of space that are within reaching distance and those that are further away.

Human performance covers a wide range of tasks that have changed as technology has developed – for example, studies of performance on production lines, or of human interaction with computers and human control of complex systems (e.g. nuclear power stations). In many cases, the components of motor skill have become less prominent as technology develops, but the basic problem remains – how to fit actions to information received. This is true of straightforward perceptual-motor skills (e.g. catching a ball) and of situations in which the perceptual and motor components are slight (e.g. deciding when to press a button that will shut down a nuclear reactor).

The real question is not whether machines think but whether men do.

B. F. Skinner, US behaviourist psychologist, *Contingencies of Reinforcement* (1969)

THE WASON FOUR-CARD PROBLEM

There are four cards: each card has a letter on one side and a number on its other side. The four cards are placed on a table so that only one side of each is visible. The experimenter tells the subject that the following rule applies: "If a card has an A on one side it must have an even number on the other side." The four cards visible are A, B, 2, and 7. Which cards should the subject turn over in order to check whether the rule has been obeyed?

The answer is the card showing A and the card showing 7: the 'B' card is irrelevant because there is no

prediction for B; the '2' card is irrelevant since it could be paired with A or B without breaking the rule; the '7' card is crucial since if A is found on its other side the rule has been broken. This problem has proved difficult even for quite intelligent people, and is also sensitive to context: if the rule is reformulated in more everyday terms ('If you have drunk more than 1 pint of beer you must not drive a car') and label the cards 'driving,' 'not driving,' 'not more than 1 pint,' 'more than 1 pint,' the problem becomes easier. Exactly why this is so is still a matter for debate.

Learning

Learning and memory overlap, but learning tasks tend to be those in which the emphasis is on acquiring a skill (e.g. tying a shoelace, or solving a quadratic equation) without necessarily retaining memories of the events that led to its acquisition. Behaviourism exerted a major influence on the study of learning. This approach, which aimed to give psychology an objective foundation, by basing theories only on observable behaviour, excluded all introspective accounts of perceptions, thoughts, and feelings. Learning was thus left as the prime object for psychological study, which focused on a type of learning that fitted a *stimulus-response* (S-R) paradigm: the scientist gave the subject a stimulus and noted the response. If that response could be modified by such interventions as *reinforcement* (i.e. reward for appropriate behaviour) then learning could be said to have taken place.

Another attractive feature of behaviourism was that its methods could be applied to any organism. This made it possible to study general learning principles that extended throughout the animal kingdom. It emerged that certain very simple forms of learning (*conditioning*) were observable in most organisms. However it was also discovered that certain forms of learning were specific to a species. For example, it has never been demonstrated that human language can be learned by an organism with only basic types of learning ability.

By contrast, cognitive psychology takes a broader approach to the question of learning. Cognitive studies of animal behaviour indicate that many species may apply a form of consciousness or memory to successful completion of a task, and not simply respond in a conditioned way to stimuli.

Reasoning

A central concern for many psychologists is the nature of human thought. In general, thought does not lend itself to the methods of experimental psychology, since it is difficult to control by experimental means. However, some aspects of thought – primarily reasoning – have proved susceptible to experimental programmes. This is because many reasoning problems can be formulated in an S-R framework: the experimenter sets the problem (stimulus) and the subject has to reach a conclusion (response). Many problems can be formulated in deceptively simple ways and allow straightforward variations, so the experimenter can exert a substantial amount of control. The **Wason four-card problem** is one such problem.

The experimental framework required by experimental psychology is most easily achieved when subjects are amenable to instruction and can work in simple situations. Most social psychology, therefore, which involves complex interactions between people, is less easy to study experimentally, as are less pliant subjects, such as children and clinical populations. Experimental psychology has been criticized for being too restrictive, since humans and animals are not observed over a sufficiently wide range of environments, i.e. there are doubts about its *ecological validity*. In other words, its techniques are thought to be too remote from everyday experience. While it is true that no branch of psychology can afford to ignore the outside world (indeed, it is precisely phenomena in the outside world that have prompted some investigations by experimental psychology), the experimental method has great validity. One experiment can be worth a thousand anecdotes, since an experiment is controlled, while anecdotes are not.

Partial Reinforcement

One behaviourist research programme examined different sequences (or *schedules*) of reinforcement to see which produced most effective learning. It was found that partial reinforcement (intermittent reward) was more effective than constant reinforcement in promoting resistance to *extinction* (failure of the stimulus to elicit the appropriate response once reinforcement is withdrawn).

Developmental Psychology

Models of learning • Piaget's approaches • Vygotsky's approaches •
Intelligence and intelligence testing • Teaching for special needs

Developmental psychology is concerned both with the theories of learning and mental development and with the practical problems of teaching and learning. It deals with such matters as aptitude for various subjects, the factors that motivate both pupils and teachers, and the measurement of learning. It is thus partly theoretical, partly experimental, and partly practical.

The history of the subject, as a formal discipline, dates back to the beginning of the 19th century and was influenced by the writings of the French philosopher and social writer Jean Jacques Rousseau (1712–78). Other important workers in the field were the British scientist Francis Galton (1822–1911) and, especially, the US psychologist and educator Edward Lee Thorndike (1874–1949).

The closely related subject of educational psychology is concerned with improving teaching methods and with the special needs of children and others with learning difficulties. Educational psychologists also counsel older students about educational problems.

Developmental psychology, like many other branches of applied psychology, is still fragmented into several schools of thought and practice. For this reason, applied psychology is not always credited with the same scientific rigour as the hard sciences, such as physics.

Models of Learning

It is not easy to assess to what extent studies of the basic mechanisms of learning have been successful in improving practical education. This is partly because, at present, none of the theories put forward command universal acceptance and partly because of a failure to apply some of the principles that have been shown to be effective. In practice, developmental psychologists tend to be less concerned with these academic pursuits than with the effects on learning of such factors as ability, intelligence, aptitude, personality, social status, emotional development, and the environment in which learning occurs.

The Pavlovian school, based on the work of the Russian physiologist Ivan Petrovich Pavlov (1849–1936), held that all learning was a matter of conditioned responses to stimuli. This austere doctrine still carries some weight but is not now generally believed to represent the whole story.

Another school of learning theory was the 'trial and error' theory formulated by Edward Lee Thorndike, whose views dominated US psychological thought throughout the first decades of the 20th century. Thorndike postulated that learning occurred by random trials, some of which achieved accidental success and a reward of some kind. Actions that led to

====SEE ALSO====
This section:
• Psychology and the Individual
• Group and Social Psychology
• Experimental Psychology
Computers (vol. 2):
• Other Uses of Computers

Education is what survives when what has been learnt has been forgotten.

B. F. Skinner (1904–90), US psychologist (1964)

◄ **Computers and Learning** *Two boys are shown using a music package on a personal computer. The introduction of computers in the home and the classroom has revolutionized the way in which children learn. The latest technology has produced 'multimedia' learning materials for children, such as that shown in use here, which provide multiple stimuli in the form of text, pictures, speech, music, animated diagrams, and film or video clips.*

▲ **Jean Piaget**
Piaget was a leading figure in the research into the thought processes of children. His work had an enormous impact on children's education.

gratifying results were imprinted on the mind, while attempts that led to dissatisfaction were obliterated. Eventually, only actions bringing success remained, and learning had been accomplished. Thorndike also proposed an important principle concerning the transfer of mental abilities. This principle states: 'What is learned in one sphere of activity transfers to another sphere only when the two spheres contain common elements.' Thorndike's ideas were a key stage in the development of the behaviourist school of psychology.

In terms of development, behaviourist psychologists insist that progress takes place a small step at a time, under the influence of deliberately applied strong positive stimuli, with constant reinforcement. Some teachers follow these ideas without recognizing their formal origins; many hold that the ideas are simple 'common sense.'

Many developmental psychologists are influenced by the theories of the Swiss psychologist Jean Piaget (1896–1980), in particular adopting his theory that children pass through various stages of development (see panel) and construct their own concepts of reality by solving the problems encountered in real life.

Freudian psychologists, on the other hand, are concerned primarily with the role of the emotions and the exploration of feelings. To them, motivation is primarily a matter of the drive to achieve satisfaction of basic emotional needs. There is, however, now a movement away from Freudian concepts as a basis for a scientific study of educational or, indeed, any other mental processes.

Psychologists of other schools take a humanistic view, broadly basing their work on the assumption that children should be allowed to direct their own learning in a loving and supportive environment.

There is, therefore, no generally accepted historically based school of developmental psychology. The strongest emphasis is now on the school of cognitive psychology. Cognition is the process – whatever its nature – by which knowledge is acquired. Cognitive psychology, which claims to be the most scientific of the various schools, encompasses all human activities that relate to knowledge.

Certain facts are not at issue. It is generally accepted that knowledge is acquired by:
• perception, using all five senses (vision, hearing, smell, taste, touch);
• correlation of remembered data with recent acquisitions (what might be called acts of creativity);
• solving problems.

Many also hold that knowledge can be acquired by the process of intuition (i.e. by an instinctive process that is not directly ascribable to either perception or reason). As well as studying how knowledge is acquired, cognitive psychology is also concerned with how acquired knowledge is stored, correlated, and retrieved into consciousness. The subject is thus concerned with attention, with the processes of concept formation, with information processing, with memory, and with the mental processes underlying speech. The latter subject, known as ***psycholinguistics***, is represented most notably in the work of Noam Chomsky (1928– ; see LINGUISTICS), but owes much to the pioneering work of the Russian psychologist L. S. Vygotsky (1896–1934).

To cognitive psychologists, education is an information-processing system in which the brain accepts, operates on, and stores the data acquired by the senses. Much of this activity occurs without conscious awareness. To some extent, cognitive psychology is a reaction against the oversimplifications of stimulus–response psychology and the inflexibility of behaviourism, both of which it holds to be incomplete as theories of learning. Cognitive psychologists have little time for Freudian and other psychoanalytic theories; they do not believe that such approaches ever provide a plausible account of the processes of learning.

Piaget's Approaches

Jean Piaget was one of the outstanding figures in the history of research into child development and how children learn. Piaget, who became Professor of Child Psychology at the University of Geneva, set out to try to establish the biological basis of logic. To this end, and in the hope of throwing light on human thought

PIAGET'S FOUR STAGES OF DEVELOPMENT

Piaget defined four stages in development, for which he set specific age limits, and taught that each one had to be complete before the child could pass on to the next.
1. In its first year the child is in the ***sensorimotor*** stage, in which its experience of the world is limited purely to its senses and movements.
2. From 2 to 7 years the child enters the ***preoperational*** stage, in which it learns about the difference between fantasy and reality and, in particular, the relationship between cause and effect. As this happens the child may mistakenly believe that some major event in its life, such as the divorce of its parents, is a consequence of its own misbehaviour. At this stage a belief in magic is also common.
3. Between the ages of about 7 and 12 the child enters the ***concrete operations*** stage, in which it gradually acquires the capacity for logical thought about objects.
4. It is only from 12 years onwards that a child may enter the ***formal operations*** stage, in which logical manipulation of complex abstract concepts becomes possible. Many adults never reach this stage of cognitive development.

processes, he studied the development of thought in children. Because he was so fascinated by what he found, he devoted the rest of his life to this subject.

Piaget based his ideas on a close study of behaviour patterns and answers to questions of developing children. His early observations of consistent errors made by children of about the same age persuaded him that there were fundamental differences in the way children reasoned at different ages. This led him to a thorough investigation into the way children perceive the world at different stages in their development and hence into how they learn.

Piaget concluded that mental growth resulted from an interaction of environmental influences and an innate developing mental structure. The baby's inherent patterns of motor activity, such as grasping and sucking, allow it to interact with its environment, but, in so doing, are themselves changed and extended. A similar process occurs with knowledge. New information from the environment, Piaget claimed, challenged the child's concept of the world – its **paradigm** – so this had to be modified or expanded. This process, which occurred repeatedly, was either **assimilation** (taking in of new experiences) or **accommodation** (changing thought processes to adapt to new influences). Piaget held that this process implies the existence of an innate form of logic. The development of intelligence, which Piaget broke down into four stages, is essentially a progressive refinement of the logical system as a result of experience.

Piaget was an exceptionally prolific writer and published a large number of books and articles, some of which were written primarily as an aid to his own thought and inspiration. His most important works include *The Language and Thought of the Child* (1923), *The Child's Concept of the World* (1926), and *The Child's Concept of Physical Reality* (1926). Piaget remains one of the most influential figures in the study of the intellectual, logical, and perceptual development of children.

On the basis of Piaget's concepts of child development, effective teaching of young children requires that the teacher should be able to assess the level at which the child is functioning and should, ideally, be able to share in its concept of the world. It would then be necessary for the teacher to provide appropriate experiences for the child in order to stimulate mental progress.

Thus the teacher must recognize that, in its earliest years of education, the child's mental capacity is limited to simple concepts concerned with its physical interaction with the world. Later, as the child is able to reproduce and rehearse the physical operations it has experienced, instruction can be appropriately

broadened. The teacher must, however, recognize that at this stage there are severe limitations in logical thought. By junior-school age the child is capable of better coordination of thought, although this is still limited to objects rather than verbal concepts. There is no point, at that stage, in trying to introduce the child to formal logical propositions or to hypotheses and deductive reasoning. This must await early adolescence.

Vygotsky's Approaches

Lev Semyonovich Vygotsky, working at the Institute of Psychology in Moscow, evolved theories of the development of human consciousness and of the way in which knowledge is acquired (cognitive development). Vygotsky believed that the polarization of opinion in the debate about 'nature or nurture' (heredity or environment) was a mistake. He was also unhappy about the polarization of thought into the then fashionable physiological school of the German psychologist Wilhelm Wundt (1832–1920) and the introspective schools, which treated higher forms of mental activity as scientifically inexplicable.

Vygotsky saw the goal of scientific psychology as the breaking down of these divisions. He was therefore as willing to entertain cultural studies and intuitive ideas as he was to embrace more rigidly experimental work.

He was especially interested in the relationship between language and thinking, being remembered best for his work in **semiotics** (the theory of signs). He believed that language – the most universal system of signs – played a central part in the development of the mental life; he accordingly devoted himself to a study of the semantic structure of language. He held that words started as emotional exclamations, then developed into designations

▲ **Education in the USSR** *An elementary school in Petrograd in 1920. The regimented teaching methods employed in the former USSR, notably under the repressive regime of Joseph Stalin, focused on creating productive future workers for the state. The work of L.S. Vygotsky, with its emphasis on the role of language development in cognitive growth, was, therefore, very much at variance with Stalinist policies.*

INTELLIGENCE TESTS

The first formal tests of intelligence were devised in the early part of the 20th century by the French psychologist Alfred Binet (1857–1911) – and subsequently revised by psychologists at Stanford University (USA). These tests were designed to assess intelligence quotient (IQ), an age-related measure of intelligence level. The ratio of the child's 'mental age' (determined by its test score) to its actual age, multiplied by 100, gave the overall IQ of the child (the average score being 100).

The concept of mental age has since been discredited and many different tests – such as the Wechsler Intelligence Scale for Children – that examine a wide range of abilities are now used to measure intelligence and to recognize educational difficulties. Psychologists acknowledge that IQ is only one way of measuring intelligence. The narrow classifications produced by IQ tests (e.g. 'gifted,' 'retarded') have been superseded by the recognition that many factors, in addition to intelligence, determine the educational ability of a child.

of objects, and later acquired abstract meanings. This evolutionary process suggested that mental development has a social origin best understood in terms of sign-using, in which a sign (or word) can be used to achieve some goal. In this scheme, a stimulus does not directly evoke a response, but summons up a sign that leads to a response. Vygotsky used these ideas to explain the way that children make use of a private language in the course of their cultural development.

Vygotsky's place in developmental psychology is now unquestioned. The idea that mental development is intimately related to social factors has had a great influence on the practice of educational psychology. He pointed out, for instance, that in evaluating a child's mental development, it is not enough simply to assess its mental age. It is also necessary to assess its potential intellectual capabilities. This can be done by comparing the way a child solves particular problems by itself and the way it deals with the same problems when assisted by the teacher. This comparison reveals the child's ability to accept social prompting.

Vygotsky's most important work, *Thought and Language*, published posthumously in 1937 and translated into English in 1962, was ignored for many years, partly because it was said not to conform to Stalinist principles. It is now, however, acknowledged as a classic study in psycholinguistics. Other works of Vygotsky, translated into English, include collections of his papers under the titles of *Mind in Society* (1978) and *Psychology of Art* (1965, translated 1971).

Intelligence and Intelligence Testing

Vygotsky's stress on the role of social factors in children's mental development is echoed in contemporary views of intelligence.

Early researchers into intelligence, such as Francis Galton, founder of the discipline of **eugenics** (see SOCIAL SCIENCES: SOCIAL DIVISIONS), claimed that it was predominantly inborn and that educational and environmental factors played no part in its development. This approach is now discredited; although heredity does have some bearing on intelligence, it has been demonstrated that children born to intelligent parents themselves only acquire intelligence through being exposed to the right social and educational environment.

TALENTED CHILDREN

Also known as 'child prodigies,' talented children show exceptional ability at a very early age, but usually only in one specific activity, for example music. Others may excel in such areas as arithmetic or chess; child prodigies are far less common in the fields of writing or painting. Although these children manage to excel in a particular activity without help, owing to their exceptional memory capacity and mental ability to relate and organize experiences, many of the most famous child prodigies were the recipients of intensive training and instruction. Among the best-known musical child prodigies are Mozart, Schubert, and Mendelssohn, all of whom were composing before they reached their teens, while Frédéric Chopin and Yehudi Menuhin were performing in public by the age of 11.

The French mathematician, physicist, and philosopher Blaise Pascal (1623–62) studied in secret as a child after his father confiscated his mathematical books; as an adult he made many advances in mathematics and a number of discoveries in fluid mechanics.

Wolfgang Amadeus Mozart
(1756–91) Mozart's extraordinary musical talent was evident from a very early age. He began composing before the age of five, when he gave his first public performance. His father, a violinist and minor composer, controlled Mozart's early musical development.

Definitions of Intelligence. Psychologists now regard intelligence as a highly complex amalgam of different aptitudes and skills. The range of skills is extremely wide, and two people generally considered intelligent may have few aptitudes in common. There is still no clear consensus on which types of ability should be given precedence in determining a person's intelligence level. Definitions of intelligence have become confused with the techniques employed to measure it. Thus, successful completion of **intelligence tests** designed to evaluate reasoning power does not in itself provide conclusive proof of intelligence; rather, it demonstrates that the person concerned has been able to adapt their mental capacity to meet the requirements of this particular form of assessment.

However, it is precisely this ability to adapt that many psychologists consider to be the basic common denominator of all forms of intelligence. According to this view, a person's intelligence is not shown merely by the sum total of different mental tasks that they can successfully perform, but rather resides in an underlying factor, which has been defined as the capacity to abstract general principles from experience and apply them to new circumstances. The concept of a general ability factor (or '***g***') was first formulated by the British psychometrician Charles Spearman (1863–1945).

Cultural Factors. Another difficulty with assessing intelligence is that tests reflect the values and ideals of the culture in which they have been devised. Thus, the heavy emphasis in Western societies on scientific rationalism and technological progress means that tests tend to be slanted towards reasoning powers and numeracy. However, these skills may not be those that are most useful in the everyday life of other cultures; adaptability and flexibility, which enable a person to function successfully in a particular environment, are the key factors in intelligence.

Teaching for Special Needs
Teaching for special needs provides methods of instruction for those who derive little benefit from conventional methods.

Talented children, often with unusually high IQ scores, commonly have interests and a reading ability far ahead of their contemporaries; for them it is a serious disadvantage to be forced to conform to the normal level. It is important to provide them with special courses and activities. To some extent this can be achieved within conventional schools, by teaching gifted pupils with older children or by arranging individual tuition. Alternatively, they may be educated at an establishment catering specifically for their needs.

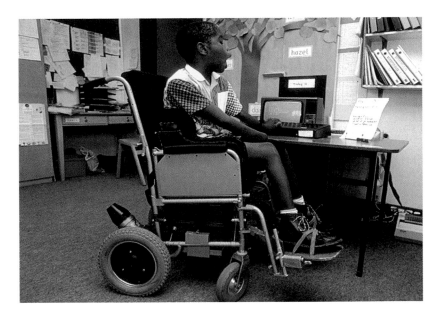

Children and others who, by reason of intellectual deficit or physical disability (or both), are unable to benefit from standard educational methods also require special education. This need arises for a variety of reasons.

Learning disabilities cover a spectrum ranging from the slightly disadvantaged but educable, to the wholly dependent and uneducable. The point below which little useful instruction is possible is not easy to determine; intelligence quotients are difficult to assess accurately in the low ranges. Generally, those with IQs between about 50 and 75 are educable and may attain, at best, the academic level of children between the ages of 9 to 11. Most children with IQs from 50 down to 25 can, with care and patience, be trained to dress themselves, attend properly to their excretory requirements, and undertake simple repetitive employment under supervision and in a protected environment.

Special teaching is also required for children and others who have impaired vision or hearing. In addition, many children of normal IQ are unable to benefit fully from conventional educational facilities because of physical disabilities, mainly of orthopaedic or neurological origin. Children with congenital skeletal abnormalities, various arthritic disorders, and especially cerebral palsy often require special education. However, cerebral palsy does not necessarily imply intellectual deficit. At least half of the children brain-damaged in this way do not have any such deficit. Poorly controlled major epilepsy can also require special arrangements. Less major absence attacks (formerly called petit mal) can lead to serious educational disadvantage because the child may be inaccessible for short periods hundreds of times each day. This must be recognized and compensatory arrangements made.

▲ **Special Needs Education**
A handicapped boy is shown using a computer. Special needs teaching accommodates children's needs at both ends of the scale – from the exceptionally gifted to those with very severe learning difficulties, often caused by physical or mental disabilities. Therefore, the teaching methods employed are very wide-ranging.

Motivation

Motivation– the force that impels an organism to activity – is a major factor in studying personal development. While strong motivation can never fully compensate for limited intelligence, weak motivation may hamper high intelligence. A vital role in motivating learning is played by emotional stimuli; arousing a person's enthusiasm greatly aids the learning process.

PHILOSOPHY

Origins of Philosophy

Eastern and Western philosophy • Origins of Western philosophy • The Socratic method

=SEE ALSO=
Religion:
• Hinduism
• Other Religions of India and the Far East
Politics and Government:
• Introduction

Eastern and Western Philosophy

Eastern philosophy debates the nature or ultimate purpose of existence, providing insights of a mystical or religious nature. Western philosophy is concerned with the clarification and analysis of concepts used in everyday life.

Philosophy (from Greek *philosophia*, 'love of wisdom') has taken an enormous variety of forms, but it has always been recognized as having important differences from other areas of inquiry, such as history and science. It is much harder to say what the positive characteristics of philosophy are than to point out its differences from other inquiries. However, central to most understandings of philosophy is the idea that it should seek to provide a *completely general* characterization of all aspects of the human condition and of the universe in which we find ourselves. It does this by seeking not so much to accumulate all the facts of the sciences as, by the purely reflective analysis of our thinking, to find the most fundamental features of the world that underlie all the generalizations of the sciences. This is an enterprise that is often thought to be best conducted without any specific method, but, on the other hand, many philosophers have sought a proper method for philosophy. Whether or not such a method could exist is itself a subject of philosophical inquiry.

Eastern and Western Philosophy

Many different conceptions of philosophy have developed in different cultures. Historically, the most important philosophical cultures have been classical India, China, ancient Greece, the Islamic world, medieval and modern Europe and the global culture of the 20th-century 'West.' 20th-century Western philosophy, however, has split into two distinct branches. In most of western Europe, the dominant schools have been phenomenology, existentialism, structuralism, and related approaches, known collectively as ***continental philosophy***. In Britain and the USA, ***analytical philosophy*** has been dominant; this holds that an understanding of language is fundamental to confronting philosophical problems in general. The approaches of these two traditions differ greatly both in substance and in style, and their understanding of the nature of philosophical thought is correspondingly diverse. Marxism, a key strand of 20th-century political thought, shares many characteristics with continental philosophy.

The School of Athens ▶ *(1508–11) In this fresco by Raphael (1483–1520), which is in the Vatican, two of the great classical philosophers – Plato (centre left) and Aristotle – are shown debating.*

Even more profound differences exist between Eastern and Western philosophy, with Islamic philosophy poised between the two (though closer to the thought of Europe, in whose development it played an important part). The chief characteristic of Eastern philosophy is the pursuit of wisdom, a state of mind that renders the thinker immune to the fluctuations of ordinary life.

The founding texts of Indian philosophy are the four collections of hymns known as the **Vedas**, which were composed around 1200 BC. Their content was explored and illustrated in the works of classical Indian philosophy, the most important of which are the **Upanishads**, written in c. 400 BC. The study (**mimamsa**) of these texts and the system of teaching that they gave rise to – known as **Vedanta** – helped to establish the basic philosophical tenets of Hinduism. These are: that the universe is inherently cyclical and that the cycle of creation and destruction is itself eternal; that there is no fundamental metaphysical difference between matter and mind; and that the good life consists in hedonistic escape from existence.

Chinese philosophy also has foundational texts. All Chinese thought originates from two sources, the teachings of Kong Zi (known in the West as Confucius; 551–479 BC) and the Dao. These two schools offer opposing views of the relation between man and the universe. Confucianism stresses that the good life consists in the attempt to bring the world into conformity with the self, while Daoism teaches that the object of existence is to achieve maximum conformity with, and integration into, nature. Both schools were influenced by the principles of *yin* (passivity) and *yang* (action).

By the end of the ancient period (c. 400–200 BC), these two schools had been synthesized into the **Yin-Yang School**, which continued to develop throughout the medieval period. Further diversity was added by the arrival of Buddhist ideas from India in the second half of the 1st millenium AD. This led to the development of a highly idealistic system of metaphysics, a significant aspect of which was the emergence of Zen Buddhism, with its stress on the importance of meditation as a key to understanding reality.

In the East, philosophical developments tended to accompany changes in religious belief. This is connected with the absence of a scientific tradition. This does not, however, mean that Eastern philosophers omitted to consider the fundamental problems, such as the nature of reality and appearance, that engaged Western philosophy. In the West, and especially in Greece, as there was a less well-developed tradition of religious dogma, many important questions were left open, in the post-mythological period, to free speculation.

▲ The Temple of Apollo at Delphi
Apollo was believed to speak through the medium of a priestess at Delphi. Above the temple entrance were the words 'Know thyself,' a key idea in Western philosophy.

It is primarily for this reason that the Greeks were the first to evolve a scientific method and the particular attitude to philosophy that this gives rise to.

Origins of Western Philosophy

The thinkers who first engaged in rational speculation about the world are collectively known as the **Pre-Socratics**, even though

---

PRE-SOCRATIC PHILOSOPHERS

Thales of Miletus (6th century BC) First of the Ionian thinkers. He held that the world was made of water.

Pythagoras (6th century BC) Southern Italian philosopher, who regarded numbers as more real than sensible objects. Pythagoras was the first thinker to use the term 'philosophy.'

Heraclitus (c. 540–c. 480 BC) Ionian thinker, who believed that all things were constantly changing, that opposite properties were the same and that the universe was made of fire.

Parmenides of Elea (c. 510–c.450 BC) Influential southern Italian philosopher, who concluded that reality is an indivisible phenomenon (since it is impossible for anything not to exist). This strictly logical position is known as **monism**.

Anaxagoras (c. 500–c. 428 BC) Ionian scientist-philosopher, who expounded the theory that the world began with a cosmic rotation caused by the Divine Mind and that there was a piece of everything in everything else.

Empedocles (c. 490–430 BC) Sicilian philosopher, who taught that the world was made of four elements – earth, water, air, and fire – in a constant state of exchange and that philosophy could lead to freedom from sin.

paradox An apparently absurd or self contradictory statement that nevertheless appears to be derived from other statements that are true.

KEY PHILOSOPHICAL TERMS

epistemology The study of knowledge.
ethics The study of right and wrong.
logic The study of argument and proof.
metaphysics The study of being.
aesthetics The study of the beautiful.
phenomenology A school of thought, founded by Edmund Husserl (1859–1938), that seeks to describe directly the contents of conscious experience.
indexicality The property of having a meaning that is only relative to a particular context.
essence The properties that something cannot lose without ceasing to be that thing.
sense-datum An immediate object of experience.
norm A standard of behaviour acceptable to rational persons.

The Paradoxes of Zeno

Zeno's paradoxes show motion and change to be apparently impossible. For example, the paradox of the 'flying arrow' argues that an arrow cannot travel from A to B, since at any given moment it is stationary and its supposed flight consists of a series of such moments.

many of them were contemporary with, or even younger than, Socrates. They fall into two main groups, those of Ionia (now western Turkey) and those of southern Italy. Although their views were strenuously refuted by later classical Greek philosophers, some of their ideas were not without resonance. For example, the earliest Ionian, Thales, bequeathed to his successors an interest in the nature of matter. His view that everything is made of water, though fallacious, has affinities with modern atomic theory, which proposes that all phenomena share a common material base. The later Ionians, notably Heraclitus and Anaxagoras, also investigated the principles by which matter was arranged.

By contrast, the ideas of the group of speculative philosophers from Elea are merely of historical interest. Their central doctrine, that reality is timeless, motionless, and changeless, is summarized in the **paradoxes of Zeno** (c. 490–c. 430 BC), Parmenides' pupil.

The Socratic Method

The interest in metaphysics (see METAPHYSICS) of the two greatest classical Greek philosophers, Plato (c. 428–c. 347 BC) and Aristotle (384–322 BC), is matched by their interest in moral philosophy. In this, they were influenced by Socrates of Athens (c. 470–399 BC). Socrates lived at a time when travelling thinkers known as **sophists** claimed to offer the key to a successful life in return for payment. Opposing them, Socrates claimed that the first step to adopting the right moral values and actions was to understand the basic terms in which morality was discussed, such as 'virtue,' 'courage,' and 'piety.'

Though unsuccessful, he anticipated the central task of Western philosophy, i.e. the analysis and investigation of fundamental concepts. Socrates thought that the best method for clarifying thought was a reflective process of cross-questioning known as *elenchus*, which was designed to reach clear definitions of difficult terms. The further development of this technique by Plato and Aristotle set the tone for Western philosophical debate thereafter.

Philosophy, then, is often referred to as **second-order** questioning, with **first-order** questioning – direct questions about the world and moral behaviour – being the domain of science or religion. Philosophy's practical use is thought to reside in its attempt to define the concepts by which we interpret our world.

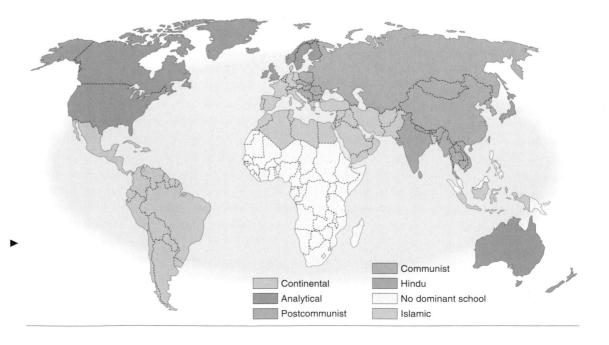

Schools of Philosophy ▶
The types of philosophy taught in the late 20th century in different parts of the world are shown.

Continental
Analytical
Postcommunist
Communist
Hindu
No dominant school
Islamic

Metaphysics

*Plato's theory of Forms • Aristotle • Neo-Platonism and scholasticism •
Rationalism and empiricism • Transcendental idealism • Modern metaphysics*

Metaphysics is at once the most fundamental and the most difficult of the branches of philosophy. Metaphysicians question the nature of being in a variety of ways: the different ways in which things can exist, the different kinds of things that exist, and the relationships between them. These matters appear similar to those studied by natural scientists. However, metaphysics differs from physics in that it asks questions that cannot be resolved by experimental evidence.

Over the centuries a great many different metaphysical systems have been expounded. They are often highly complex and obscure. Appraisal of a metaphysical system is made especially difficult because any criticism must be made from another distinct metaphysical standpoint. Hence, particularly in more recent times, there has often been no clear rationale for choosing one system over another. Therefore metaphysics is best presented as a history of the different frameworks that have been used for understanding reality, rather than as a debate over which system is likely to be closest to the truth.

The term 'metaphysics' derives from Greek, literally meaning 'after physics.' This is usually taken as referring to the position within the works of Aristotle of his great treatise, the *Metaphysics*, which comes after his equally important treatise *Physics*. However, metaphysics is equally concerned with questions of religious importance; many metaphysical systems place God at their centre, as the basis of all reality.

Plato's Theory of Forms

The Pre-Socratic thinkers, such as Parmenides, Heraclitus, and Zeno of Elea, who flourished in Greece during the 5th century BC, were interested in what constitutes reality and unreality, and how things come into and pass out of existence. Pythagoras and his followers were fascinated by numbers and mathematics and the way they can exist without referring directly to physical objects. Socrates was concerned with morality and how we understand moral concepts. Plato was influenced by these earlier thinkers, especially by Socrates.

When Socrates was forced to commit suicide in 399 BC, Plato left Athens for some ten years. On his return, he began to compose his dialogues, in which Socrates appears as a penetrating critic of the ignorance and pretensions of his contemporaries. The early dialogues are mostly *aporetic* – that is, they come to no firm conclusions. However, by the time of the great dialogues of the middle period (c. 380–370 BC) – the *Phaedo*, the *Republic*, the *Phaedrus*, and the *Symposium* – Plato, through the mask of Socrates, is beginning to advance his own

◄ **A Philosopher and his Disciples** *In this 4th-century fresco, from the Catacomb della Via Latina in Rome, a philosopher (thought by some to be Aristotle) is depicted with his disciples.*

Aristotle *Aristotle studied in Plato's Academy for 20 years before leaving to engage in empirical research and eventually to found his own school. He believed the changing world of experience to be real and that it therefore can, and must, be studied by science. He also portrayed the good life as a mixture of virtuous moderation and philosophical contemplation.*

▶

> Plato is dear to me, but dearer still is the truth.
>
> Aristotle, *The Nichomachean Ethics*, Bk.I, ch. 6

substance The entity that many philosophers took as being metaphysically fundamental. The essential property of substance is a matter of contention; it is that which has independent existence; it is that which remains constant through change (as, for example, a piece of wax remains the same wax while it melts into a different shape); it is what 'supports' physical attributes, such as extension, mass, and shape. Some philosophers claim that substance is a meaningless concept.

positive view. Plato reasoned that, for example, whereas square things (e.g. a table top, a shape in the sand, a window) may vary, the property of squareness remains the same. Hence 'squareness' is more real than things that are square. Plato therefore assigned the greatest degree of reality to the **Forms**, which embody similarly unchanging features of the world. For example, there is the Form of Man, the Form of Goodness, the Form of the Table, and so on. The Form is what gives something its individual properties (e.g. its 'squareness' is what makes a particular shape a square) and it is because we know what the Form is that we can recognize individual instances of it (e.g. because we know what 'squareness' is, we can recognize a particular shape as a square).

This system was criticized because it was unclear how the Forms, remote from humanity in their Platonic heaven, could possibly play the major role Plato envisaged for them. Eventually, criticism of the theory of Forms became overwhelming; there are signs that Plato recognized this in his dialogue the *Parmenides*, which contains a version of the famous **Third Man Argument** (later perfected by Aristotle) against the theory of Forms.

The central preoccupations of Plato's later work are with language, knowledge, and morality, although he does investigate the key metaphysical concepts of existence and nonexistence in two late dialogues, the *Sophist* and the *Statesman*. These dialogues also develop another major interest of Plato's, the nature of definition. Indeed, these two problems

are closely connected. The definition of a thing must contain the conditions under which that thing exists, and the particular way it exists (its **mode** of existence).

Aristotle

Aristotle, once a pupil at Plato's Academy, developed a markedly different metaphysical system from that of Plato. In the *Categories*, which was probably composed when he was still a member of the Academy (he left after Plato's death), he first devised a unified metaphysical system intended to embrace all the things that exist. Aristotle organized things into ten different metaphysical categories – not all, however, of equal importance. The fundamental category is that of **substance,** without which no other category could exist. To be a substance is to be the bearer of attributes; for example, being a horse, or a man, or a square is to be the bearer of the attributes of those things. He maintained that general properties were less fundamental than particular substances; whiteness is less real than those things that are white. In making this distinction Aristotle is much more down-to-earth than Plato. Things that really exist, and on which the existence of everything else depends, are the ordinary everyday objects of our experience, not remote entities accessible only to philosophically trained minds, such as Plato's Forms.

Aristotle's view of the contents of the world was further influenced by his scientific studies. His investigation of the changes that biological entities undergo drove him to refute the views

THE THIRD MAN ARGUMENT

Suppose that on first meeting Socrates, Plato wished to confirm that Socrates was a man. According to the Platonic theory of Forms, this could only be achieved by comparing Socrates with the Form of Man, which embodies all the essential attributes of Man.

However, how could Plato have known that the Form of Man used in this way was itself a man? Again, according to Platonic theory, this knowledge itself can only be obtained with a Form. It is therefore necessary that another Form exists (a Third Man), which is required to identify the Form of Man. From this argument it becomes clear that there needs to be an infinite number of Forms of Man, since each new Form requires another new Form to establish its identity. Because this is clearly absurd, Plato's theory of Forms must be wrong.

of certain Pre-Socratics, who claimed that nothing that existed could really change, and to show that change was possible. In the *Physics*, he argued that all entities, whether natural bodies, such as plants and animals, or artefacts, were composed of two different components, matter and form. (This notion of form is different from Plato's – thus, modern scholars spell it with a small 'f.') The possibility of change was explained in terms of replacing one form by another without changing the matter. For example, wax melting is the same matter changing its form. Although contradictions emerged in his metaphysical works, Aristotle's common-sense view of reality remained hugely influential for 2000 years.

Neo-Platonism and Scholasticism

The technical complexity of metaphysics and the disagreement between the two great classical thinkers led to a decline in interest in the subject during the Hellenistic era. During the 3rd century AD, however, Plato's ideas were revived and modified. This revival is known as **Neo-Platonism**; its most influential thinker was the Egyptian-born Plotinus (205–270 AD).

The central idea of Plotinus' system is that there is a single fundamental metaphysical Principle, which consists of the "One" of Plato's *Parmenides* (relating to existence) and the "Good" of the *Republic* (relating to value). The final goal of his philosophy was to achieve unification with the "One." Plotinus' system was a dominant school of Western philosophy for a thousand years and has much in common with the mysticism of Eastern philosophy.

Scholasticism is the name of the philosophy that predominated in the universities and religious institutions of medieval times. Greatly influenced by such early thinkers as St Augustine of Hippo (354–430 AD) and Boethius (c. 480–c. 524 AD), the greatest scholastics were Christian philosophers, such as Peter Abelard (1079–1142) and Peter Lombard (1100–1160). They sought to reconcile the conflicting demands that faith and reason made on Christian doctrine. The rediscovered works of Aristotle represented the side of reason, and provided much impetus for the work of St Thomas Aquinas (c. 1225–74). Aquinas set himself the task of making a clear distinction between Aristotle's position and that of Neo-Platonism, intending to restore Aristotle's common-sense approach. In some respects, Aquinas went beyond Aristotle, notably in his insistence that reason is a sufficient basis for a genuine knowledge of the world. Aquinas' importance is that by reinterpreting Aristotle he encouraged medieval philosophers to reconsider classical Greek ideas.

During the later scholastic period of the 14th century this reinterpretation of classical metaphysics had its greatest influence. Thereafter, humanism and the new understanding of the world revealed by the scientific discoveries of the 16th century required a complete reassessment of traditional metaphysics.

Rationalism and Empiricism

Against this background, the two main modern metaphysical schools of **rationalism** and **empiricism** emerged. Rationalism aimed to replace the medieval world-view with a metaphysics compatible with the recent discoveries of science. It held that the nature of reality could be discerned through deductive reasoning alone, without the aid of the senses.

The first rationalist system was that proposed by René Descartes (1596–1650). His starting point was that, since he was a thinking being, he must exist: he expressed this thought in a Latin phrase, *cogito ergo sum*, which is now famous. It means 'I think, therefore I am.' He deduced that God must also exist by observing that he had an idea of a supremely perfect God

> If you wish to understand nature, you should consult nature, not Aristotle.
>
> **Francis Bacon**
> (1561–1626), English philosopher

Averroës *Averroës is pictured reclining at the base of this lavishly illuminated manuscript. One of the great medieval Islamic scholars of Aristotle, Averroës took a Neo-Platonic approach in his 38 commentaries on the Greek classical philosopher's works.* ▼

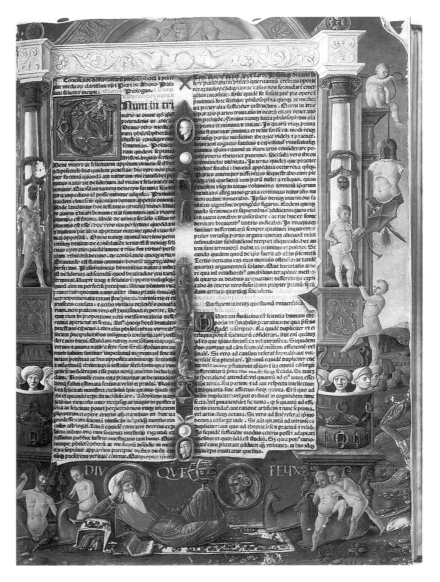

transcendental idealism
The view originated by Kant that the objects of our experience are merely appearances, with no independent existence. Transcendental idealists hold that our a priori knowledge of such concepts as space and time is transcendent – i.e. not derived from experience.

in his mind. Being imperfect himself, this idea must have a cause other than his own mind. Therefore the cause could only be an existing God. He also revived an argument first used by St Anselm (1033–1109), later known as the Ontological Argument. As God is, by definition, the supremely perfect being, He must exist, since existence is a necessary attribute of perfection. Both these arguments are highly controversial and remain a matter of debate.

From the existence of God, Descartes concluded that the world existed more or less as he encountered it, and that the world was divided into two substances, matter and mind; this doctrine is known as **metaphysical** or **Cartesian dualism** (see PHILOSOPHY OF MIND). He also argued that matter had no properties except extension in space and time. This led to his endorsement of the mechanistic model of the world that was emerging from the findings of 17th-century scientists. His views, in particular those related to geometry, remained influential for centuries, and combined with the work of Isaac Newton (1642–1727) to lay a solid foundation for modern science.

Although Descartes's system was never developed in any philosophical school, his rationalist approach was highly influential. Similar metaphysical systems were evolved by two major thinkers of the next generation, Baruch Spinoza (1632–77) and G. W. Leibniz (1646–1716). Spinoza disagreed with Descartes on the question of substance; in his view Descartes's matter and mind were merely two aspects of the same single substance, which he identified with both nature and God. Similarly, Aristotle's separate substances were treated as modes of the single universal substance. By contrast, Leibniz argued that there was an infinity of substances, called **monads**, which were incapable of interaction with one another. However, God had ordained that the life of each monad should be in harmony with that of every other.

In opposition to these ambitious metaphysical systems, the empiricist tradition, which flourished especially in Britain, sought to discredit all attempts to gain knowledge that were not based on data from the senses. British empiricism, first proposed by John Locke (1632–1704), was later elaborated by George Berkeley (1685–1753) and David Hume (1711–76). The metaphysical concepts of substance and an objective morality were attacked as meaningless. This undermined metaphysics itself. By the end of the 18th century, the philosophical traditions of rationalism and empiricism were starkly opposed in their metaphysical account of the world. It fell to the German philosopher Immanuel Kant (1724–1804) to achieve a synthesis of these two positions.

Transcendental Idealism
The basis of Kant's metaphysical system was that our knowledge of the world is inevitably limited by the categories under which we are able to conceive it (see EPISTEMOLOGY). These categories included the concepts of space, time, and causality and were imposed on our experience not by fundamental features of the world itself (as earlier metaphysicians had maintained) but by the nature of our own subjectivity. Kant accorded this subjectivity a fundamental role in the formation of the world. He held that there were 'things-in-themselves' that caused our experiences, but that these were unknowable and that we could know the world only as it presented itself to us. Hence those aspects of the world that depend upon our awareness of them were not real, in the way that the things-in-themselves were real.

I have striven not to laugh at human actions, not to weep at them, nor to hate them, but to understand them.

Baruch de Spinoza, *Tractatus Philosophicus* (1677), ch.1

LEIBNIZ'S MONADS

Leibniz maintained that the world consisted of an infinite variety of independent things, each of which contained a life force. He called these basic indivisible units 'monads' (from Greek *monos*, meaning 'alone'). Every substance was composed of one or more monads. God was responsible for creating harmony between these entities. In this role God represented the "supreme substance," who acts according to a "principle of the best." It was this position, with its stress on the role of the individual within a rationally ordered universe, that was satirized by the French writer Voltaire in *Candide* (1759).

G. W. Leibniz *Leibniz's works include* Théodicee *(1710) and* Monadologie *(1714).* ▶

His metaphysical position is thus known as a 'Two Realms Account,' or **transcendental idealism**. The 'two realms' are the knowable realm of experience, which we interpret through our innate concepts, such as space and time, and the unknowable realm of the things-in-themselves.

Kant's philosophy dominated metaphysical thinking throughout the 19th century, especially in Germany during the romantic age. It provoked a change in metaphysics, moving the emphasis onto how a self-conscious subject helps constitute the perceivable world. The chief philosophers to develop Kant's ideas were J. G. Fichte (1762–1814), F. W. J. von Schelling (1775–1854), and G. W. F. Hegel (1770–1831). The systems they expounded were vast and intricate – and some would say wilfully obscure. Hegel was the most influential of the German idealists after Kant. He introduced the notion of the Absolute, which operates in the world by a succession of oppositions. These oppositions do not happen at random but are governed by an elaborate pattern called the **Hegelian dialectic**. The aim of Hegel's philosophy was to reveal the pattern of this dialectic as it manifested itself in the history of the universe and of man. This approach exerted a strong influence on subsequent philosophy, in combining metaphysical speculation with the analysis of politics and history.

19th-Century Metaphysics. Hegel's approach contrasted sharply with the work of his contemporary Arthur Schopenhauer (1788–1860), who lectured at the same university. Schopenhauer also believed that the underlying force behind experience could be known; this, however, was not the Absolute but the blindly striving Will. Since our experience was wholly conditioned by this striving, our lot was inevitably tragic: the Will could never achieve its aim and our achievements would always fall short of our designs. The only escape from this cycle lay in the pursuit of something resembling the Hindu ideal of nirvana, to which the most direct route lay through the arts, especially through music.

Hegel's metaphysical analysis of the development of history was echoed in the works of Karl Marx (1813–1883), whose system went on to become a dominant theory of political economy. Marx held that the only metaphysically existent thing was matter; his view is known as *dialectical materialism*. Both Hegel and Marx were highly political philosophers. Hegel saw himself as the official philosopher of the Prussian state, and Marx's attitude was that the purpose of philosophy is to change the world. Another original approach was offered by the French philosopher Henri Bergson (1859–1941). Having the benefit of the insight provided by Darwin's

IMMANUEL KANT.

◀ **Immanuel Kant**
Kant's importance for metaphysics lies in his attempt to reconcile the rational and empirical views of the world. Kant demonstrated that a person's knowledge of the world depends both on the raw data supplied by the senses and the application of reason to this data.

evolutionary theory, he argued that the phenomena of life could not be reduced simply to matter; the development of life on earth could only be explained in terms of the operation of a general force, which he called the *élan vital*.

Modern Metaphysics

The common element of all these different metaphysical systems is that they are holistic, in the sense that they assume the world must form a coherent whole with a comprehensible underlying pattern. This perspective has remained influential in continental philosophy, especially in the work of such existentialist philosophers as Jean-Paul Sartre (1905–80) and Martin Heidegger (1889–1976).

Most analytical philosophers, however, especially **logical positivists**, regard the whole enterprise of philosophy as incompatible with metaphysics. There are some, though, who do allow the possibility of metaphysical models. This matter is still disputed, for example, by Willard Van Orman Quine (1908–   ) and Sir Peter Strawson (1919–   ). Quine argues that the notions of physical objects, minds, and meanings should be purged from our scientific concept of the world (in other words from our metaphysical scheme). Strawson, on the other hand, still maintains that one of the primary tasks of philosophy is to clarify such concepts as 'physical object,' 'the passage of time,' and 'mind,' as these form an important part of our understanding of the world; indeed, they are the basis of the common-sense metaphysics that we share as a species.

Hegelian dialectic
A process of logical argumentation, in which a proposition, or *thesis*, is contrasted by its opposite, the *antithesis*. Each position is insufficient for ascertaining the truth of the point at issue, but from their meeting emerges the *synthesis*, which resolves disputes at a higher level.

logical positivism
An extreme empirical approach to analytical philosophy, which was at its most popular in the 1920s and 1930s. Logical positivists held that the statements of metaphysics were neither true nor false but meaningless, since no experience could confirm or deny them.

Epistemology

*Scepticism • Descartes and rationalism • Empiricism • Foundationalism •
Phenomenalism • Coherence • Kant and epistemology •
Naturalized epistemology • Nietzsche • Other approaches*

Philosophy can be characterized as the study of humanity's place in the world. While metaphysics attempts to determine what the real nature of the world is, epistemology tries to explain our knowledge of that world. While the natural sciences increase the sum total of our knowledge about the world, they do not ask how such knowledge comes about. The problem that concerns epistemology, then, is the gap between appearance and reality. Optical illusions demonstrate the deceptiveness of our visual sense. Another well-known illusion concerns the sense of touch: if one puts one's right hand in hot water and one's left hand in cold water, and then plunges both hands into lukewarm water, it will feel simultaneously hot (to the left hand) and cold (to the right).

Epistemology is concerned with bridging the gulf between our beliefs about the world and the reality that underlies these beliefs. It attempts to set criteria for the possession of knowledge, and in so doing create a foundation for our understanding of the world.

Scepticism

Historically, the most important work in epistemology is *Meditations on First Philosophy* by René Descartes. Prior to this the followers of Pyrrhon of Elis (c. 360–c. 272 BC) had argued that, since there is no way of distinguishing between conflicting appearances, we are not able to say definitively what constitutes reality. Descartes, however, went further than this; he resolved to doubt anything of which he was not absolutely certain, thereby imposing conditions of the utmost stringency on the possession of true knowledge. Descartes imagined an evil demon who deceived him about

Scepticism

The sceptic argues for the conclusion that we know nothing, by attacking our grounds for what we know. An example of a sceptical argument is as follows: If our memory provides knowledge of the past, it must be reliable. To find out if it is reliable we must check what it tells us against what we know about the past. So memory can only give us knowledge of the past if we have some *other* source of knowledge. But every other source is checked for its reliability against memory. So there can be no knowledge of the past. Since epistemology tries to establish the possibility of knowledge, one of its key objectives must be to prove scepticism wrong.

PLATO'S CAVE

On the question of appearance and reality, Plato (in *The Republic*) likened human experience to lifelong prisoners chained in a dark cave. These prisoners can only see directly in front of them; their only experience of what is going on outside the cave is in the form of shadows cast on a wall by a fire behind them.

When one of the prisoners escapes from the cave and witnesses reality for the first time, his reports are disbelieved by the others. For Plato philosophy was the intellectual process of making this escape from the world of appearances into the world of the Forms that constitute reality.

ANTRVM PLATONICVM.

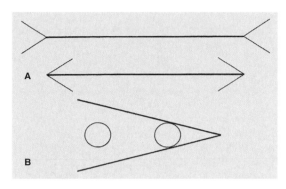

▲ **Optical Illusions** *Showing how appearance and reality can diverge, the lines in* **A** *are of equal length (though the top seems longer), and the circles in* **B** *are identical (though the right-hand one seems larger).*

everything, offering only a mass of fabricated experiences. The demon was even capable of deception about the very existence of the material world. Neither sense nor reason are able to defeat this great doubt, it was asserted. Hence Descartes vividly illustrated the gulf between the world of experiences and the real world. His subsequent attempt to 'defeat the demon' is taken by many to be the first major work of epistemology in modern philosophy.

Descartes and Rationalism

Descartes's solution to scepticism was that he knew that God existed and God would never allow him to be so deceived. He provided two arguments for God's existence, claiming that neither rested on premises vulnerable to the demon's deceptions. For Descartes, knowledge of the world is based on knowledge of God, which is in turn based on truths of reason.

Descartes's response to his own scepticism is a ***rationalist*** epistemology. Rationalist epistemology is modelled on Euclidean geometry: there are some intuitive first principles (axioms) that cannot be doubted and are thus known **a priori**. All true knowledge is ultimately based upon these axioms. Other rationalist philosophers were Baruch Spinoza and Gottfried Leibniz who both deduced that the world was very different from how it appeared.

Yet rationalist epistemology faces a dilemma. Either the facts yielded by rational enquiry are simply true by definition (e.g. every son has a father), in which case nothing substantial has been gained, or they are potentially false (e.g. John Smith has a son), in which case reason alone cannot ensure their truth, and one is forced to rely again upon experience.

Empiricism

Empiricist epistemology, the most influential proponent of which was the Englishman John Locke, starts with the claim that if we know

anything about the world we know it through the senses. In his *Essay Concerning Human Understanding* (1690) Locke argued against humans having any ***innate*** knowledge, i.e. knowledge with which one is born. Rationalist philosophers had taken the position that, although some knowledge is clearly based on the evidence of the senses, other ideas that are grasped by the human mind cannot have come from the source of sense data; numbers are an example of this. By contrast, Locke always relates knowledge to experience, calling it the "perception of the agreement or disagreement of two ideas." His arguments have only recently been challenged, for example by Noam Chomsky (1928– ; see LINGUISTICS), who has argued that all humans are born with some universal linguistic ability, which is then drawn upon in learning a specific language. This ability is hence a kind of innate knowledge. The rise of evolutionary biology has provided the means for reconciling the existence of innate knowledge with empiricism.

The Scottish philosopher David Hume distinguished "matters of fact" from "relations of ideas." Matters of fact are always contingent, that is, they depend on another occurrence

John Locke *Locke is regarded as the most influential English philosopher and the founder of the school of empiricism. His studies encompassed a wide variety of topics, including physics, politics, education, personal identity, language, and religion. Locke argued against the possibility of innate knowledge, claiming instead that all ideas are derived from experience.* ▼

▲ **Descartes's *Meditations*** *This work, one of the most significant texts in the history of philosophy, was published in Paris in 1641.*

A Priori and A Posteriori Knowledge

A priori (Latin: 'from what comes before') knowledge is knowable without reference to experience. A posteriori ('from what comes after') knowledge relies on experience, and can be refuted by it. For example, I know "All parrots are either blue or not blue" without having seen one; this is a priori knowledge. On the other hand, I cannot know "Jason's parrot is blue" without having seen it; this is a posteriori knowledge. Most of our knowledge is a posteriori.

Unsupported Sitting in a Circle
The coherentist thinks that a sufficient number of beliefs about the world that all confirm each other need no further support. This picture is an analogy of the coherentist position; if there are enough people, they can each remain seated without any of them requiring the external support of a chair.

(e.g. it might not have rained today; human beings might not have evolved). Therefore, there can be no a priori argument to a matter of fact. But **a posteriori** argument must begin with experiences, and all experiences may be composed of nothing but conflicting, possibly illusory, appearances. Somehow, it is necessary to discover which appearances correspond with reality.

The two main ways in which empiricists try to bridge the gap between knowledge of appearances and knowledge of reality are known as foundationalism and coherentism.

Foundationalism

Foundationalism holds that beliefs about the world correspond to an independent reality. Knowledge requires a certain foundation for these beliefs. Locke, Bertrand Russell

David Hume *In a passage that expresses his naturalistic approach to philosophy, the Scottish philosopher David Hume wrote: "The great subverter of ... the excessive principles of scepticism is action, and employment, and the occupations of common life. These principles may flourish and triumph in the schools [universities]; where it is, indeed, difficult, if not impossible, to refute them. But as soon as they leave the shade...they vanish like smoke."*

(1872–1970), Ludwig Wittgenstein (1889–1951), and Rudolf Carnap (1891–1970) were all foundationalists. There is some dispute as to which experiences can be treated as indubitable. For instance, it is possible to doubt that one is now seeing a page. Consider the two claims: (a) I now see a white rectangular page, and (b) it *looks* to me as if there is a white rectangular object. Only the second statement is not undermined by the possibility of my being asleep, but it differs from the first in not saying anything about the world outside of the individual. The indubitable foundations of knowledge must be descriptions of how things *appear*. How things *are* is another matter. Once this is recognized, the problem that then arises is how appearances can serve as evidence for claims about the world. One response is to deny that a reality independent of appearances is a meaningful concept, a position held by phenomenalists. Another is to claim that appearances being occasionally deceptive does not necessarily mean that they cannot be reliable most of the time.

Phenomenalism

If every statement about material objects could be translated into a statement or statements about experiences, then perhaps this would explain how knowledge of experiences, which is held to be indisputable, can provide knowledge of the world. The phenomenalist thinks that such a translation is necessary; this is a stance strongly associated with verificationism (see THE PHILOSOPHY OF LANGUAGE). For example, the statement 'there is a tree outside my house' might be translated as: if I were to go to the front window, I would have a visual experience of such-and-such a type. Obviously, it would be necessary to specify the experience of seeing a tree in terms of shapes and colours without mentioning trees. Also, it would be necessary to express in terms of pure experiences, without mentioning material objects, what it would be to walk to the front window. However, it is practically impossible to effect this translation in even the simplest of cases, though Rudolf Carnap made a sustained attempt to do so in his work *Der Logische Aufbau der Welt* (1928).

Coherence

Coherentists hold that no individual belief is rendered indubitable by its correspondence to an independent reality. Instead, the truth or falsity of a belief is determined by whether it is consistent with all our other beliefs. There is an inevitable circularity here; each belief depends for its truth on being consistent with other beliefs, which in turn depend on it. However, the coherentist claims that this circularity is benign. Beliefs are not tested piecemeal against the world, but examined as a set. If a large number of beliefs confirm each other, it makes sense to treat them as true. There is an analogy: three people cannot sit on each other's laps but 30 can. It is the coherence of a large enough number of beliefs that shows them to be true. Coherentist epistemologists include George Berkeley, Otto Neurath (1882–1945), Brand Blanshard (1892–1987) and W. V. O. Quine (1908–).

The main criticism of coherentism is that there could be more than one coherent set of beliefs, but there is only one true set. Thus a good historical novel is probably internally consistent and may perhaps not conflict with one's personal experiences, but these are not sufficient grounds for believing it to be true. In reply to this example the coherentist can point out that this coherence may provide *prima facie* reasons for belief, but that upon accepting the book to be a novel, a belief in the truth of what it describes would conflict with the distinction between history and fiction. The book merely provides a small subset of consistent statements, but not the largest set available.

Kant and Epistemology

Immanuel Kant claimed that by a "Copernican Revolution" he could resolve the conflict between rationalism and empiricism. Nicolaus Copernicus (1473–1543) was an astronomer who solved several problems concerned with eclipses by assuming that the earth moved round the sun rather than the established view that the earth was at the centre of the universe and consequently that the sun revolved around the earth. Kant thought that we should not try to answer epistemological questions by looking just at the sources of knowledge, but we should also consider the objects of knowledge. God knows everything without having to discover it through the senses, so he can know the world in itself – which Kant called the noumenal world. We,

VISUAL DEPTH

The British philosopher Bertrand Russell believed that the data presented by vision, which are the foundations of knowledge, are two-dimensional and that, as children, we have to *learn* to make judgments of distance in the third dimension. This kind of perception, which is essential to our existence in the world of phenomena, is known as ***veridical perception***.

Russell's opinion may well be confirmed by the apparent 'naivety' of children's art. In line with his theory, he regarded learning to draw as *un*learning to see in three dimensions; the two-dimensional nature of drawings by children may indicate that that they are closer to the original sense data than adults. Learning to replicate on paper the experience of depth in space through the use of perspective is a highly sophisticated technique.

however, can only know things through our senses, so we can only know the world as it is for us – which he called the phenomenal world. The phenomenal world is a product of the interaction of us and the noumenal world. The objects of knowledge, such as tables and trees, are made for us to know them.

Hence, by drawing a priori conclusions about our nature, we might gain a priori knowledge of the world. For example, instead of asking how we could know, on the basis of experience, that there are persistent objects in space (that is something the evil demon may have deceived us about), he asks whether we could have perceptual experience that is not of objects in space. If this is inconceivable, as Kant has suggested, then the limitations of our experience require that the phenomenal world contains objects persisting in space. This is called a ***transcendental argument***, and it mixes epistemological and metaphysical considerations.

Naturalized Epistemology

The epistemological project started by Descartes is ***normative***, in that it attempts to establish what one *ought* to believe about the

> Our knowledge can only be finite, while our ignorance must necessarily be infinite.
>
> **Karl Popper**, *Conjectures and Refutations*

We simply lack any organ for knowledge, for 'truth': we 'know' (or believe or imagine) just as much as may be *useful* in the interests of the human herd, the species: and even what is here called 'utility' is ultimately also a mere belief, something imaginary and perhaps precisely that most calamitous stupidity of which we shall perish some day.

Nietzsche, *The Gay Science*

world. W. V. O. Quine has proposed a non-normative naturalized epistemology. Its object is not to show what, given the evidence, it is rational to believe, but to take both the evidence and our beliefs as given and to show how they are related. According to Quine, philosophers should not stand outside science and judge, prior to any discoveries about the world, under what conditions it would be rational to form beliefs about the world. Rather they should, within science, discover how bold theories derive from scanty evidence and how new principles refute established positions.

Normative epistemology takes the perspective of the individual seeker after knowledge and asks how such a person can, from his own perspective, tell what ought or ought not to be believed on the basis of experience. Naturalized epistemology takes an impersonal perspective, considering the knower from outside and asking how the knower's beliefs were formed and whether these methods were reliable.

It might seem that if such a project in the study of knowledge could show that most of our perceptual beliefs were reliable it would answer the sceptic. However, to assess, say, whether a person's vision is reliable, we must know both how the world appears to him or her and also how it really is. Thus, this way of responding to the sceptic presupposes that we have knowledge of reality, which is precisely the premiss that the sceptic is questioning. The naturalized epistemologist must go further than this and demonstrate that scepticism itself involves an illicit attempt to stand outside science, imposing conditions upon the possession of knowledge that are neither useful nor correct.

Nietzsche

The normative approach to epistemology was also rejected by the German philosopher Friedrich Nietzsche (1844–1900). Nietzsche argued that we do not have a clear concept of reality as something distinct from the mass of conflicting appearances and our interpretations of them. It follows that while some beliefs may be better justified than others, no set of beliefs is the uniquely correct set; there is no ideal that epistemology can help us achieve. This inspired a tradition of criticism of both scepticism and epistemology on the grounds that both assume that there is some absolute criterion for coming to a definitive judgment on competing claims to the truth. When that assumption is rejected, the most pressing questions of epistemology are how the concepts of rationality, evidence, and justification are bound up with particular power structures and political institutions. The consequence of rejecting this central assumption is a slide towards metaphysical **relativism**, i.e. a position that holds that reality differs from person to person. This can be avoided if we distinguish the concept of rationality from the way in which it is exploited by a particular social group. If the concept of rationality did not incorporate the idea that there is only one standard of rationality, the criticism that someone is irrational would not carry any weight.

Other Approaches

In line with his materialist approach to the world, Karl Marx dismissed the attempt to produce an abstract intellectual refutation of scepticism as "purely scholastic." Whether we can ever attain objective truth is, according to him, a "practical question." However, there is a flourishing school of Marxist epistemology, the central debate in which is whether the best way to overcome alienation is to recognize the reality of the objective world of science, or to take reality as a human construct that can thus be modified.

Feminist epistemology – unlike the traditional concern with the *nature* of knowledge – considers the central question in epistemology to be 'Whose knowledge?' Instead of giving an account of knowledge that treats all knowers as equivalent, feminist epistemologists think that one cannot understand what it is rational for someone to believe unless one knows about the social and historical context and the gender of that person.

Finally, there exists an approach known as common-sense philosophy, which holds that there are certain propositions that are universally accepted as true (e.g. that the earth exists). This insight, represented chiefly by the British philosopher G. E. Moore (1873–1958), rejects idealism and scepticism.

G.E. Moore

Moore's common-sense philosophy derived from an empirical tradition, but emphatically rejected the scepticism that often arose from such an approach. ▼

Ethics

Greek ethics • Christianity • Early modern ethics • Kant • Utilitarianism •
Marx and Nietzsche • 20th-century ethics

Ethics, or moral philosophy, is the philosophical study of different kinds of ethic, or morality. The objects of ethical judgment include people, conduct, and states of the world; among the concepts characteristic of ethical judgment are good and evil, right and wrong, obligation, virtue, and wellbeing.

Philosophy is interested not only in particular moral dilemmas but in asking what is the status of moral beliefs. Some philosophers hold that morality is merely the name human beings give either to opinions that are widely accepted in society or to personal opinions. Others argue that morality constitutes an objective code of conduct – and some go so far as to claim that this is validated by God. Further philosophical enquiries of an ethical nature concern whether moral values should bind a person to action, and what the relationship is between a person's own interests and wider ethical interests.

The history of ethics reflects the diversity of its subject matter. The Greeks focused on the individual and what his ideal virtues might be. Medieval ethics paid more attention to the concepts of **duty** and obligation. Utilitarianism rendered ethics a more scientific study, its purpose being to maximize some quality, such as happiness or pleasure. In the 20th century, the concept of human **rights** has become a key issue in ethics – one can now talk of the rights of religious minorities or the rights of the unborn.

Greek Ethics

Moral philosophy in the Graeco-Roman world was primarily a Greek phenomenon. The most searching analyses of ethics were written between the 5th and 3rd centuries BC; they were the work of Socrates, Plato, Aristotle, Epicurus, and Stoic thinkers, such as Zeno.

What is the best kind of life that a human being can live? Greek ethical enquiry concentrated on the way in which the conflicting claims of pleasure, virtue, and philosophy can be reconciled by individuals. Greek philosophers tended to think that the 'best' life is the one that is most desirable for oneself. Despite this patently self-centred approach, there was also great emphasis placed on learning how to behave correctly. In this way Greek ethical thought had its practical side; it investigated not only what *is* good, but the process of *becoming* good; hence the question of individual motivation was central.

The first great moral philosopher in the West was Socrates. His influence on subsequent Greek ethical thought was vast, as much for his way of life as for his ethical views. He believed that political power and material belongings were worthless if one neglects the good of one's soul. Philosophical understanding is necessary to achieve this good; indeed, if this level of understanding could be achieved, nothing more would be needed.

In his most important ethical work, *The Republic*, Plato developed an analysis of virtue

▲ *The School of Plato In this somewhat fanciful depiction in the decadent style of the late 19th century – by the French painter Jean Delville (1867–1953) – Plato is shown teaching a group of his followers.*

═══SEE ALSO═══
This section:
• Origins of Philosophy
• Metaphysics
• Epistemology
• The Philosophy of Mind
• Applied Philosophy

Chrysippus ▶

The philosopher Chrysippus (c. 280–207 BC) was considered the greatest leader of the Stoics; his philosophy was subsequently treated as representative of Stoic philosophy.

I know not how I can conceive the good, if I withdraw the pleasures of taste and the pleasures of love and those of hearing and sight.

Epicurus

God and Good

If one grants that whatever God commands is good, then is it good because God commands it, or is it commanded by God because it is good? The former alternative implies that if God were to command, say, torture, that would necessarily make torture good; the latter suggests that goodness is independent of God's will, so that God is not really all-powerful. This dilemma demonstrates the difficulty in having the moral law dependent on some kind of external authority.

with similar implications. He drew an analogy between the soul and society. In the virtuous person, each part of the soul performs the role proper to it. In particular, reason should govern the emotions and appetites. This is the best state of the soul. Correspondingly the best-arranged society is governed by those in whom reason is most fully developed: in the ideal society, the rulers are philosophers.

Aristotle also thought that the best life is that of a virtuous person. However, he included amongst the virtues those of the intellect and the body as well as of the character. The virtues of character are 'mean values' between excess and deficiency in respect of both action and feeling. For example, a brave man feels the correct amount of fear and acts accordingly. This fear will lie between the excesses of rashness and cowardice. Discovering the mean requires intelligence and experience. The best life is "an active life of the rational part of the soul." This rational part includes the character; however, Aristotle also suggested that the very best life is purely philosophical, since philosophy is the highest activity.

Epicurus (341–270 BC) was the most important Greek advocate of the view that what makes the best life best is its pleasantness. Epicureans aimed at a life as free as possible of unnecessary desires and fears, and identified this as a virtuous life enhanced by the friendship of fellow Epicureans. The Stoics, by contrast, insisted that nothing else was needed to make a life good besides virtue. To live virtuously is to live in accordance with reason and with nature. Certain Stoic themes, such as the natural equality of all human beings, resemble later ideas prominent in Christianity.

Christianity

The second main ancient source of modern Western ethics is the Judaeo-Christian tradition. This tradition embodies a 'divine command' conception of moral obligation, i.e. the conviction that God's law determines what one ought to do. Central to this law is the so-called **Golden Rule**: do to others what you would wish others to do to you.

The Hebrew Bible (Old Testament) at times approaches ethical questions in a philosophical way, notably in the Book of Job, a profound reflection on the justice and wisdom of God. In the New Testament, a radical ethic of self-transformation is expounded in the teachings of Jesus (c. 4 BC–30 AD), who exhorted his followers to a childlike trust in God's care. None of the concerns of this world is as important as the need to prepare oneself for the coming Kingdom of God.

In subsequent Christian ethics, certain features are relatively constant, such as the recognition of faith, hope, and charity (love) as virtues. But many questions have been answered in different ways at different times. Is human nature entirely corrupt until redeemed by faith in Jesus? Can one person deserve salvation more than another? Is philosophical reasoning likely to help or hinder a person in their striving to lead an ethical life?

A common focus of debate among Christian philosophers is the question of how we can tell what God wants us to do. St Thomas Aquinas (c. 1225–74) argued that one source of such knowledge was "right reason," exercised in the use of conscience, whereas William of Ockham (c. 1285–1349) maintained that God's will is inscrutable to our unaided reason. Followers of St Augustine of Hippo (354–430) located the source of right conduct in the human will, assisted by divine grace.

Early Modern Ethics

In the 16th century, the religious wars that resulted from the conflict between the Roman Catholic Church and the reformers Martin Luther (1483–1546) and John Calvin (1509–64) made more urgent the search for grounds for ethical judgment that were independent of any ecclesiastical authority. This reinforced the appeal of the idea of **natural law**, prominent in Aquinas' thought: according to this principle, certain moral precepts are valid for all humans because they are in accord with universal human nature, thought of as essentially rational.

Similar ideas reoccur in the writings of Thomas Hobbes (1588–1679). Whether virtue and the capacity to be law-abiding and to honour agreements are morally required of a person depends on whether they are in the person's interests and thus depends upon the person's social circumstances. In the **state of nature**, i.e. in the absence of a political order, no such thing as injustice exists and everyone has a 'natural right' to everything. Another British philosopher, John Locke (1632–1704), assigned only a limited range of rights to individuals in the state of nature but opposed Hobbes in believing that these rights also belong to the citizens of a developed society.

The ideas of Hobbes and Locke continued to be influential in the 18th-century. Enlightenment thinkers were concerned with the ways in which people become happy and morally good and with the question of how far a concern for others' interests can be part of an enlightened individual's 'self-love.'

During this period the question arose of whether moral judgement is wholly rational. The Scottish philosopher David Hume (1711–76) believed it was not; he wrote "morality...is more properly felt than judged of." Hume raised a difficult question for traditional ethics. Moral arguments often proceed from premises concerning how the world is to conclusions about how people ought to act. But these two categories – 'is'-propositions and 'ought'-propositions – are so unlike one another that it is unclear how any conclusion of the latter type can be deduced from premises of the former type. Hume insisted that this deduction required the input of human feeling.

Kant

A similar objection to earlier theories is found in the moral philosophy of the German thinker Immanuel Kant (1724–1804), who held that the grounds of moral obligation must be independent of any empirical facts. He also saw a radical contrast between two kinds of human motivation: most of our actions are motivated by desire and by the pursuit of happiness, whereas genuinely moral action is free of such motives. Moral actions he saw as being guided by a **categorical imperative**.

However, Kant stands opposed to Hume in regarding the activity of moral judgment as a rational exercise. According to Kant, an act is morally prohibited if one cannot will that its "maxim" be a universal law. Suppose, for instance, that one contemplates telling a lie for one's own convenience. Can one will that everybody in similar circumstances should do the same? Surely not; therefore the act of lying is morally prohibited.

Utilitarianism

While Kant had tried to establish our duties independently of considerations about happiness, the utilitarians took an opposite course, maintaining that the sole criterion of the moral status of an action is its **utility** – how it affects the happiness of those concerned.

THE CATEGORICAL IMPERATIVE

Kant proposed the categorical imperative as the fundamental moral law. According to this law, an act can only be moral if the principle guiding it is universally applicable. Kant also formulated this imperative as a requirement of respect for others: "act in such a way that you always treat humanity...never simply as a means, but always at the same time as an end." The other, and more typical, type of motivation, known as the **hypothetical imperative**, is sustained by desire ('If you want X, do Y').

Kant's view of ethics was essentially anti-authoritarian, since it showed individual duty to be independent of all external influence.

This theory was first fully developed in the work of Jeremy Bentham (1748–1832), who intended it to govern both the acts of legislators and the actions of private individuals. Whether an act is right or wrong depends on the total amounts of pleasure and of pain that result from it, with allowance being made for the greater and lesser probability of such results. Bentham defended utilitarianism as the only reasonable approach to moral issues; the chief alternative, guidance by individual conscience, rendered disagreement insoluble.

Bentham's successor John Stuart Mill (1806–73) advocated a more complex version of the theory, muting its radically reformist tone. He admitted as relevant to the morality of actions not just the quantity but also the kind (or "quality") of pleasures likely to result from them. He argued that actually calculating all the likely effects of an act was best restricted to unusual occasions; ordinarily, the utility of people's choices will tend to be

> The greatest happiness of the greatest number is the foundation of morals and legislation.
>
> **Jeremy Bentham**

◀ **Jeremy Bentham**
In his philosophical writings, Bentham, a pioneer of utilitarianism, attempted to reduce ethical decisions to a set of scientific principles. He was a leading radical, who championed reform in many areas. After his death, Bentham's body was embalmed and surmounted with a wax replica of his head. It is still preserved in this condition at University College, London.

Determinism and Responsibility

Determinism is the view that every event, including every human choice and action, is caused by some other prior event. Philosophers differ on the ethical implications of determinism. *Incompatibilists* claim it would mean that a person had no choice in doing what they did and hence could never be held responsible for their actions. *Compatibilists* say that determinism is compatible with free will if a person's desires are the cause of his or her actions.

greater if they have the policy of following a number of simply applied rules rather than of working out the consequences of each possible action in the particular case.

A difficulty with utilitarianism is that it appears to sanction immoral acts if they produce great happiness. For example, it might allow the murder of one innocent man to save the lives of two others, an act we would not normally see as ethical. Utilitarianism is hence often starkly opposed to human rights, allowing the individual to be sacrificed for the greater good. It still has many adherents, however, but has grown more complex in response to the many objections that are made to it.

Marx and Nietzsche

Within philosophy, an ethic of historical progress had been espoused by G. W. F. Hegel, who advocated a form of freedom achieved through rational self-consciousness that owed much to Baruch de Spinoza. Hegel had a further indirect impact on ethical debates through the adaptation of a number of his central ideas by Karl Marx. For Marx, freedom was an essential element of human wellbeing; the poor state of freedom in existing societies was partly due to people's lack of self-understanding and partly to their enslavement to ideologies that sustained economic exploitation. Freedom from such ideologies, according to Marx, also meant liberation from attachment to certain entrenched moral notions, notably those of justice and rights.

Friedrich Nietzsche ▶

The German philosopher Nietzsche saw the basic motivation behind all human life and endeavour as being the will to power. He argued for a new set of values that would openly acknowledge this drive, in place of the self-deception of traditional value systems.

A similar rejection of central aspects of traditional morality in favour of other values marks the work of Friedrich Nietzsche (1844–1900); as with Marx, the rejection was based on an attempted unmasking of the hidden function of moral ideals. Nietzsche's chief targets were Christian and utilitarian ethics, whose spirituality and praise of humility Nietzsche regarded as driven by jealousy and hatred of true vitality. In place of these 'slave moralities' he urged strength, creativity, and a bold affirmation of life; all these qualities he envisaged as being embodied in the figure of the "superman" (*Übermensch*).

20th-Century Ethics

A common feature of various strands of 20th-century ethical thought is the conception of moral evaluation as virtually unconstrained by empirical knowledge: to find out how things *are* is not to determine how things *ought* to be. This view was shared by two schools of thought, which otherwise differ considerably in their origins and conclusions: existentialism and noncognitivism.

Existentialism. Among the ancestors of existentialism was the Danish thinker Søren Kierkegaard (1813–55); its best-known spokesman was the French philosopher Jean-Paul Sartre (1905–80). To be human, according to Sartre, is to be unavoidably free. How we decide to live is entirely up to us; any claim that our nature or our circumstances require us to act in a certain way is ultimately only self-deception. Existentialists thus tended to refrain from moral prescriptions, except at the level of insisting on individual responsibility and decrying its evasion as 'bad faith.'

Noncognitivism. This approach is similarly characterized by a deliberate neutrality regarding the substantial questions of how to live. The movement had a remote source in Hume's views about the relation of 'ought'-propositions to 'is'-propositions and a more immediate origin in the logical positivists' views on linguistic meaning, according to which ethical statements, being neither empirical nor a mere matter of definitions, cannot be meaningful statements at all. Noncognitivism, consistently with this, held that the function of ethical language is not cognitive: it is not to make rational statements but to express or prescribe attitudes of approval and disapproval. This implied a radical contrast between the domains of fact and of value. Hence noncognitivists believe that moral values are not objective; there are no moral 'facts.' Critics of this position claim it removes all ground for ethical argument. They state instead that although values are only felt, this does not mean that they are not real; feelings reflect a real part of the world.

Aesthetics

The definition of art • Aesthetic experience • The value of art • Art and society

Aesthetics – or the making of critical judgments about art – is a relatively new discipline. Although the questions it addresses have been asked since the time of the ancient Greeks, it is only since the 18th century that the issues have been brought together as a single discipline. The modern subject combines two interests. The first is with a class of objects, namely works of art. These give rise to such questions as: Can 'art' be defined? Why are these objects important? How do paintings represent the world? How does music express emotion? The second interest is in a specific experience, usually called 'aesthetic experience.' This experience is not confined to the appreciation of art. The enjoyment of a beautiful view, for example, is often said to constitute aesthetic experience. This gives rise to questions about how this kind of experience can be defined and how it differs from other categories of experience.

The Definition of Art

There have been many attempts to define the central features. In the 20th century the **expression theory** of art has been vigorously promoted, particularly by the British philosopher R. G. Collingwood (1889–1943) and the Italian Benedetto Croce (1866–1952). According to this theory, a work of art is the *expression* of feeling. A feeling is expressed, as opposed to indicated, when its nature is illustrated and explored within the artwork.

An advantage of this theory is that it links art to something which is humanly important. It also seeks to explain all of the arts under a single unified theory. What gives painting, poetry, sculpture, and dance their common identity as arts is that they all facilitate this development and exploration of emotion. However, there seem to have been periods when very fine work was done that does not fit this general account. For example, Byzantine mosaics and many portrait paintings do not seem to involve the expression of emotion. Yet these are generally agreed to be great works of art.

The question of whether art can be defined at all has been much debated in the 20th century. The immediate cause of this was the exhibition in art galleries of a number of objects that in previous periods would not have been designated as art; for example, in 1915, the French artist Marcel Duchamp (1887–1968) exhibited a snow shovel. Duchamp's snow shovel does not have any obvious features in common with traditional works of art. It does not display the skill of the artist, it does not represent anything, and it does not express anything. Whatever beauty it possesses has nothing to do with Duchamp. Thus, attempts have been made to find less obvious similarities. For example, the snow shovel was 'exhibited,' i.e. it was displayed for public viewing by someone called an 'artist.' It is also true of much art of the past that it was exhibited by people called artists, but that does not mean that this is its definition. 'Art' defined in such a narrow context would be unlikely to prove as important to human beings as it clearly is.

These disputes about the definition of 'art' are far from settled. Although, like many philosophical debates, it has not reached any definitive conclusions, the debate about the definition of art does help us see the problems and nature of art more clearly; the least we can expect is to learn why it is so difficult to define 'art.'

▲ *Madonna of the Harpies In this work, by Andrea del Sarto (1486–1530), the painter attempts not to copy the world but, through inspiration and selection, to present an ideal vision of beauty. This function of art contradicts Plato's view that painting is an intrinsically inferior copy of reality.*

=====SEE ALSO=====
This section:
• Origins of Philosophy
• Metaphysics
• Epistemology
• Applied Philosophy
The Visual Arts (vol. 4)

Performance Art ▶
Performance art, shown here being practised by the artist Yves Klein, is one of a number of modern art forms or movements that challenge traditional conceptions of what constitutes 'art.'

Aesthetics

This word is derived from the ancient Greek *aisthesis* meaning 'perception by means of the senses.' Seeing and hearing, for example, are examples of aisthesis. The term 'aesthetics' was coined by the German Alexander Baumgarten (1714–62) in 1750.
Aesthetics differs from art history in attempting to describe elements that are common to all aesthetic experience, rather than explaining the meaning of particular works of art.

Aesthetic Experience

Immanuel Kant's work was enormously influential in aesthetics. Central to his *Critique of Judgment* (1790) is the discussion of aesthetic experience. Kant put forward the idea that there is a special ***disinterested pleasure*** that constitutes the appreciation of beauty (whether in nature or in art), and which is distinct from other forms of pleasure that exist to gratify desires. His intention was to show that this response has a universal significance. According to this theory, if a person looks at a rose, or a painting, and has this special experience, he or she is right to call the rose or the painting beautiful, and is also right to expect that all others find it beautiful.

Kant eliminated alternative kinds of response from being relevant to the appreciation of beauty; for example, liking the object because it is useful, morally good, intellectually persuasive, or politically significant. Thus he came to define aesthetic contemplation as finding something satisfying to perceive (i.e. to look at or listen to) because of the perceptual experience it causes in us. He went on to describe this experience positively in terms of the free play of the imagination and the understanding. What he meant by this was that our capacities for perception were themselves excited and there was no need for a further goal (e.g. knowledge, practical use, goodness, etc.) to explain our satisfaction in the object of art. This made aesthetic experience distinct from other kinds of experience, which have a further end beyond themselves.

The writer Friedrich Schiller (1759–1805) regarded the disinterested nature of aesthetic experience as central to art's role of leading humanity towards a state of spiritual freedom and completeness. According to Schiller, moral regeneration could only be achieved by disengaging oneself from the immoral compulsions and ambiguities of real life and exercising judgment on a higher plane.

Individual Response and Public Claim. The tension between the individual (subjective) aspect of aesthetic response and the public (***intersubjective***) quality of the judgment is a long-standing point of contention.

When a person says that an object or a work is beautiful or artistically successful, they mean merely that it pleases them in a certain way. However, implicit in the statement is that others should agree and also find it beautiful. In other words, the judgments lay claim to ***objectivity***. Two points encourage this claim. First, in spite of the influence of fashion, many works are recognized as great from one century to the next. This point was made by the Greek writer Longinus (1st century AD) in his work *On the Sublime*: "For when men who differ in their habits, their lives, their enthusiasms, their ages, their dates, all agree together in holding one and the same view about the same writings [or works of art], then the unanimous verdict... of such discordant judges makes our faith in the admired passages [or works] strong and indisputable."

Secondly, intellectual reasoning can be used to support the claim that aesthetic judgments have intersubjective validity. Certain features of a painting can be highlighted as evidence that it is artistically successful. For example, the composition of a work may be shown to be balanced, in terms of the poses of the figures depicted or in its arrangement of landscape features. Although these features do not provide incontrovertible proof that a person's judgment of a painting is correct, they do give others objective reasons to agree.

No writer on aesthetics has demonstrated that either of these positions – the claim to objectivity and the personal basis of the judgment – can be shown to be false, but neither has it been shown definitively how they can be reconciled.

THEORIES OF PICTORIAL REPRESENTATION

Everyone would recognize the highly schematized figure below as depicting a person. However, aesthetics offers two competing explanations of the method by which we arrive at this conclusion:

Convention
We have to learn that this figure stands for a human being – for instance, by being repeatedly confronted with a similar figure and being told that it represents a man.

Natural Similarity
The figure shares many visual structural features with the real human body. As a result, we are naturally disposed to see the figure as resembling a human being.

Ville d'Avray (1835; Louvre) This work, by the French artist Camille Corot (1796–1875), depicts an ordinary rural scene. However, Corot's treatment of his subject allows the viewer to see it as the artist did, revealing an unexpected beauty. The artist has transfigured the scene in paint. This is one example of a work of art having intrinsic value.

The Value of Art

There are many ways in which paintings, pieces of music, and other art forms can be valuable. For example, they can communicate information, promote certain sorts of behaviour, or simply distract and entertain. Latterly they have even come to be regarded as useful financial investments. These are all ways in which works of art can have *functional value*. Many art works are valuable in such ways. For instance, many items of religious art or portraits perform functions of this sort. Yet works of art can also have *intrinsic value*; that is, they are valued simply because of the kind of perceptual experiences that they enable the viewer to have. These experiences are prized for their own sake, and not because of any higher purpose or further benefit that they might serve.

There is no necessary opposition between these two ways in which a work of art can be valuable. The fact that a certain painting is a portrait, which attempts to preserve a likeness of the sitter and to communicate information about that person – and thus has a functional value – does not prevent the painting being intrinsically valuable at the same time. Yet neither does the successful performance of that function alone make the painting intrinsically valuable.

KEY WORKS IN AESTHETICS

Plato:	*The Republic; Ion*
Aristotle:	*Poetics*
Hume:	*Of the Standard of Taste* (1757)
Kant:	*Critique of Judgment* (1790)
Schiller:	*On the Aesthetic Education of Man* (1795)
Hegel:	*Lectures on Fine Art* (1835–38)
Nietzsche:	*The Birth of Tragedy* (1872)
Santayana:	*The Sense of Beauty* (1896)
Tolstoy:	*What is Art?* (1898)
Croce:	*Breviary of Aesthetics* (1913)
Collingwood:	*The Principles of Art* (1938)

Art and Society

Works of art are created and appreciated within societies. Many philosophers of aesthetics argue that works of art should be examined primarily in this context. In other words, works of art are interpreted both in terms of what they reveal about the societies in which they were made and, conversely, in terms of what those societies tell us about the works themselves.

The esteem in which certain works are held may be considered a reflection of their social function. So, for example, some pictures are highly regarded because they celebrate the way of life or beliefs of the dominant social group. However, this explanation of the value of art cannot account for the fact that many works transcend the specific cultural and social conditions of their creation, and appeal to very different societies. Therefore, the social facts of the creation of art do not in any way compromise the view that the value of art is intrinsic.

Art: Superior or Inferior?

In Book 10 of *The Republic*, Plato claimed that painting is inferior to the real visual appearance of objects, since it merely *copies* reality. Plato even recommended banning painters and other artists from his ideal republic. By contrast, later philosophers have claimed that by inspiration and selection a painter presents an ideal vision of beauty that does not seek to copy the world but to transform it.

The Philosophy of Mind

Aristotle • Cartesian dualism • Behaviourism • The unconscious •
Contemporary materialism

Philosophy studies the nature of the world and our relationship to it. Philosophy of mind is central to this study, since the mind is the means by which the world is understood. It covers a great number of complex topics, including perception, rationality, memory, the use of language, and the nature of consciousness. As the secrets of the universe are slowly unravelled by the natural sciences, the mind and the mystery of how conscious existence comes about may be the last obstacle to a fully scientific understanding of everything.

Since the dawn of philosophy a great variety of views has been advanced to explain what it means to have a mind. Progress in understanding biology, computer intelligence, and

language have served to widen the debate. The mind remains a subject that is sufficiently enigmatic and mysterious to admit a wide spectrum of conflicting opinions, from the belief that we all have immaterial immortal souls, to the claim that anything, even a computer, has the capacity to think.

Aristotle

Aristotle's *De Anima* ('On the Soul') is the most influential work on the mind in Western philosophy. For Aristotle, all living things had an animating force (*psyche*, translated as 'anima' in Latin and usually as 'soul' in English) by virtue of which they are alive. He lists four properties of souls, corresponding to the four functions of living things: nutrition, movement, perception, and thought. According to Aristotle, humans have all four functions; animals have nutrition, movement, and perception; and plants only nutrition. Thought is, therefore, uniquely a function of man. To possess a soul, and thus to live, is simply to be capable of one or more of these functions.

Thus a soul is not a separate thing to the body; rather, it is the body's ability to live. Aristotle suggested that the relation between body and soul is similar to that between a piece of wax and its shape. The shape of a piece of wax is not a separate thing from the wax, but a particular property the wax has. Therefore, just as the shape cannot exist without the wax, so the soul cannot exist without the body.

Cartesian Dualism

By the 17th century, the mechanistic science of Robert Boyle (1627–91) and Isaac Newton had made it impossible to think of plants and animals in Aristotelian terms. Scientific advances led to the view that the natural world was composed of atoms in the void, their movements obeying simple mechanical laws. In such a world-view the most important question became whether or not the mind could be expected to obey the laws of physics. The view that it can, which is called ***materialism***, was advocated by Thomas Hobbes; the alternative view is that the mind is immaterial and not part of the natural world studied by

◀ **The Soul** *Traditional thinking sees the soul as a similar entity to the body, as portrayed in this painting,* The Last Judgment, *by Fra Angelico (c.1400–55).*

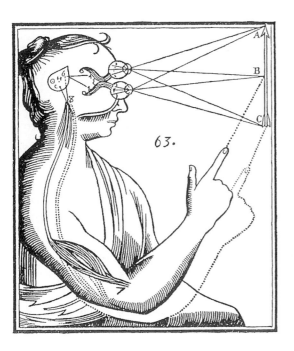

▲ **The Pineal Gland** *This gland, situated within the brain, was, for Descartes, the site of the interaction between body and soul. Although now widely discredited, this theory draws attention to the intuitive feeling that mental events occur in a definable location.*

the sciences. This latter view, known as **dualism,** holds that there are two kinds of substance, physical and mental. The idea that the mind is a distinct entity from the body finds its most dominant source in Descartes.

Descartes took a first-person approach to the mind, asserting that from this perspective he had complete and infallible knowledge of its contents. Whereas knowledge of the external world is subject to error and misperception, Descartes thought that, with respect to our minds and nothing else, we are immune to the twin failings of ignorance and error. This view is now widely discredited. Descartes's main argument for dualism turns upon the claim that the mind is a substance whose essential property is thought and the body is a substance whose essential property is the occupation of space. Descartes wrote that he had a clear conception of mind and of body as distinct substances, and that whatever is clearly conceivable, God in his infinite power could make actual. Therefore mind and body are distinct.

Some critics have claimed that Descartes committed the **Masked Man Fallacy**; the fact that one can doubt the existence of one's body but not one's mind does not show that they are not identical (they could be the same thing under different descriptions). Other critics argue that from a subjective viewpoint one cannot make valid assertions about the essential properties of matter.

Problems with Cartesian Dualism. Cartesian dualism creates as many problems as it solves. One is the problem of other minds, which was first posed by the Irish philosopher George Berkeley, who was an ***idealist***; he held that everything that existed was mental. If the mind and body are logically separate entities, then there can be no logical proof from physical premises that other people have minds at all. From Descartes's perspective, he might be the only thing in the world with a conscious mind! Another problem is that Cartesian dualism leaves an element of mystery about the interaction of mind and matter. Mental events (e.g. pains) cause and are caused by physical events (e.g. sitting on a pin). So physics ought to mention not only physical objects, such as atoms and electrons, but also mental events, such as pains and thoughts. But there appears to be no need to do this; every physical event seems to be totally accounted for by other physical events, without resorting to the use of mental concepts. So either mental events are not causally active (a view known as ***epiphenomenalism***) or they have both a physical and a mental aspect, contradicting Descartes's assertion that mind and body are distinct.

Cartesian dualism has also frequently been criticized for failing to put anything positive in the place of materialism. The soul is only defined in a negative way. For example, it is not physical, it does not occupy space, it does not die, and so on. We are left with no idea of how these souls *work*, and this divests the study of the mind of much of its explanatory power. Descartes postulated that the soul operated through the pineal gland. which is a pea-sized organ situated within the brain; see ANIMAL ANATOMY AND PHYSIOLOGY (VOL. 3): ENDOCRINE SYSTEMS. This theory illustrates how awkward it is to find a 'place' in which the soul resides.

The Masked Man Fallacy

It is sometimes claimed that Descartes commits the following fallacy in trying to prove that mind and body are distinct:
1. I am certain that I have a mind.
2. I am not certain that I have a body.
3. Therefore my mind is distinct from my body.

This argument can clearly be seen to be fallacious if one compares it with the following:
1. I know who my father is.
2. I do not know who this masked man is.
3. Therefore this masked man is not my father.

PROPERTIES OF THE MIND

There are several properties that could (but not necessarily do) distinguish the mind:

Consciousness Early philosophers believed that whatever one is directly aware of is a mental object (often termed an 'idea' by Cartesian philosophers). Some modern thinkers still maintain that consciousness is an essential attribute of thought.

Intentionality Thoughts are *about* something – they concern objects in the outside world and propositions about those objects.

Privacy What one is thinking cannot be known by other people.

Freewill How one thinks is never wholly determined by external events – it is a matter of one's own choice.

Infallibility One cannot be mistaken about the contents of one's mind. To feel a pain, for example, is to have that pain.

Rationality One's beliefs and desires develop within a rational framework – what one believes about a certain matter is rationally constrained by one's beliefs about other related matters.

The Mind-Body Problem

The mind and the body are intimately connected but strangely different. What is the relationship between the two? This question poses a great dilemma. Any solution that places emphasis on the physical aspect of the mind will be accused of ignoring what is characteristic of the *mental* – i.e. the subjective aspect of thought. On the other hand, if the mind is treated apart from the physical world, the mystery of mind-body interaction will remain unexplained. Some philosophers claim that the problem is inherently mysterious and insoluble by the human mind.

Behaviourism

In *The Concept of Mind* (1949) Gilbert Ryle (1900–76) launched a powerful attack on Cartesian dualism, accusing Descartes of making a huge 'category mistake' in treating the mind as an object or thing. He proposed instead the doctrine of behaviourism, which was also upheld in psychology by B. F. Skinner (1904–90). The behaviourist thinks that to be in a mental state means no more than to be disposed to behave in certain ways. For example, to believe that it will rain is to be disposed to take an umbrella, cancel your visit to the beach, and so on. The reason we are better judges of what we think than anyone else is simply that we observe more of our own behaviour. Much of the impetus for behaviourism comes from the hypothesis that the only observable data for psychological analysis is behaviour, and use of other concepts is therefore meaningless or at best pointless.

Behaviourism as a philosophical and practical theory has been discredited in several respects. First, it is impossible to deny that pain is a real experience, that there is not only pain behaviour but also a conscious experience of pain. This experience is eliminated in behavourial analysis. A belief in behaviourism led some doctors to use paralysing drugs as anaesthetics, with awful consequences. Since no pain behaviour was observed, the doctors did not believe the patients' reports that they were in pain during the operation.

Secondly, behaviourism underestimates the complexity of the relations between thoughts and behaviour. What is actually believed cannot be defined piecemeal, but only by taking into account the whole structure of the mind. Whether certain behaviour indicates a belief that it will rain, for example, also depends on other relevant beliefs and desires (e.g. whether the person in question cares about getting wet). This property of the mind is sometimes called the ***holism of the mental***.

The Unconscious

The view that we should identify the self with consciousness has been historically dominant in both Western and Indian philosophy. In the Hindu tradition, the conscious self is eternal and immutable but a passive spectator of the world. It is not involved in perception or the decision to act. In the Western tradition, the self is thought of as the agent that observes, reasons, and acts. The mind is accorded a central position in the explanation of a person's behaviour. Sigmund Freud (1856–1939) suggested that we could explain some of people's behaviour by their ***unconscious*** beliefs and desires. A belief or desire is unconscious if the person concerned is not aware of having it.

The possibility of unconscious mental states contradicts the Cartesian view that everything in the mind is known perfectly. It also undermines the ***privacy*** of the mental; the idea that what we are thinking cannot be determined by others. But recognition of the category of unconscious thoughts enables us to explain a great many actions; for example, being able to stop a friend from stepping into the street

PERSONAL IDENTITY AND THE SELF

A number of philosophical dilemmas have undermined our confidence in the unity of the self and its persistence through time. Imagine that your body was destroyed and replaced elsewhere by an exact replica. Would you survive this experiment, or would another person be suddenly created in your place? And what if your body was not destroyed but duplicated, so that an identical copy, with all the same memories and character traits, was created? Would this mean that you had become two people? Since the early 1970s, philosophical attention has focused on ***split-brain operations***, which cut the corpus callosum, separating the two hemispheres of the brain. The left hemisphere, which controls speech, is only able to describe stimuli occurring in the right visual field.

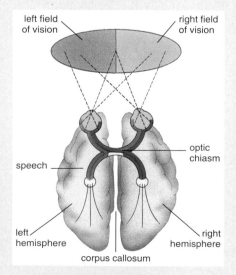

left field of vision

right field of vision

optic chiasm

speech

left hemisphere

right hemisphere

corpus callosum

▲ **Split-Brain Operations** *These operations, performed to alleviate epilepsy, separate the two hemispheres of the brain.*

The patient is able to react to stimuli in the other visual field, but in his speech he claims to know nothing of what he is doing. It appears that the patient becomes two persons within the same body, each aware of a half of the visual field.

Philosophical dilemmas such as these draw our attention to the intuition that we are only contingently related to our bodies, and that our *selves* are distinct and cannot be split as our bodies can. One response is to claim that the existence of a soul ensures the existence of a distinct self. Another is to deny that the concept of the self is meaningful – to claim that there is simply no determinate answer to the question 'Will that person be me?' However, this contravenes one of our most cherished beliefs about the mind.

A Phrenological Head *Phrenology, now regarded as a pseudoscience, was founded at the end of the 18th century by the German physician Franz Joseph Gall (1758–1828). Gall believed that the shape of the skull reflected that of the brain, and hence the development of various mental processes that were associated with different areas of the brain.*

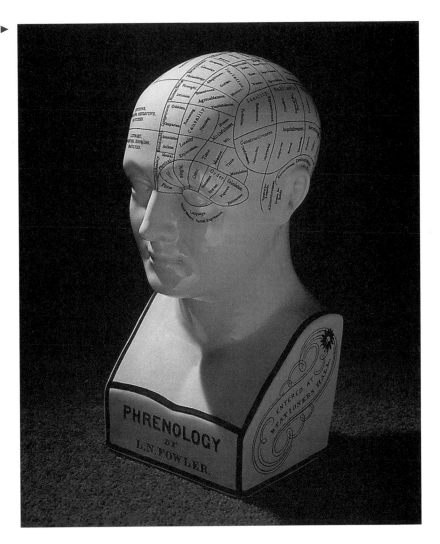

before one has realized that one has seen an oncoming lorry. It also allows us to accept that scientific investigation, as well as introspection, may play a part in determining the contents of the mind. On the other hand, the issue of personal identity becomes less clear – a familiar human response is to deny responsibility for actions that cannot be remembered; in these circumstances, a person may say 'That wasn't me,' as if the unconscious self were another person.

Contemporary Materialism

Since the widespread rejection of behaviourism, the study of the mind has begun to embrace a more diverse range of studies. Advances in computer technology have invited questions concerning the relationship between computation and thought. The doctrine of **functionalism** holds that anything embodying the right functional organization can think; this opens the possibility that not only animals, but a whole range of objects, are capable of consciousness. The **Turing Test** focuses attention upon the issue of intelligence in artificial objects.

WHAT IS IT LIKE TO BE A BAT?

The question of whether the mind could ever be the subject of a total scientific reduction has long divided the philosophy of mind. In asking 'What is it like to be a bat?' Thomas Nagel (1937–) was arguing that an objective science would never be able to answer questions like this – questions about the subjective 'feel' of mental states – and that hence a scientific reduction of everything mental could never be achieved. Nothing that is observed 'from the outside' could, for example, tell a deaf person what it is like to experience the sound of a trumpet. This provides a strong objection to behaviourism and other 'scientific' analyses of the mind, which attempt to explain mental events in terms of objective physical phenomena. Science will never be able to explain the subjective attributes of the mind; perhaps it is its subjective nature that makes the mind special.

Following new insights into evolutionary theory, a school of philosophy has emerged that treats the mind as a purely biological entity. Leading proponents of this **teleological** approach include Daniel Dennett (1942–). His work *Consciousness Explained* (1991) examines consciousness in terms of its evolutionary purpose, rejecting familiar premises of the philosophy of mind; for example, that there is a 'stream of consciousness,' or a self, or any mystery about what it is like to be a bat.

Philosophers of language, such as Donald Davidson (1917–), drawing on the close relationship between mind and language, have emphasized the logical structure of our beliefs and desires in order to show that physical laws could never determine the ascription of such mental states. The position Davidson advocates is called **anomalous monism** ('anomalous' means 'not obeying laws') and helps explain how freedom of the will can be compatible with materialism. Other issues related to language include the questions of how our thoughts manage to have content – how they can be *about* things in the world – and whether or not it is possible to think without words.

The Turing Test

In 1950, Alan Turing (1912–54) proposed a test for artificial intelligence. The tester communicates through a terminal with both the computer to be tested and another person in a different room. He has to guess with which he is communicating on the basis of the answers to his questions. A computer that fools the tester has intelligence. Critics claim that the Turing test merely demonstrates that, in passing the test, a computer *simulates* human rationality – it does not show anything about real minds.

The Philosophy of Language

Four theories of language • Sense and reference • Verificationism • Indeterminacy of translation • Poststructuralism

▲ *The Tower of Babel* Language has long been a subject of contention. This painting, by Pieter Brueghel the Elder (c. 1525–69) shows the biblical myth of the Tower of Babel. To punish its builders for daring to try to reach heaven, God caused confusion by making them all speak different languages.

Words are remarkable vehicles for communicating a huge variety of ideas, sometimes between people who have never met. Philosophers of language try to find out how such simple objects as words can have such power. The answer lies in their *meanings*. But what are meanings? They are not physical properties of words like shape or colour, so what are they and how do words acquire them?

Four Theories of Language

The first thing to notice is that there is an arbitrary element in the choice of a word: for example, there is nothing about the animals called mice and the word 'mice' that makes them specially suited to each other. The word could easily have denoted something different, and mice could have had another name (indeed they do, in other languages). Therefore, the meaning that a word imparts must be the result of some human involvement. There are four alternative views on the nature of this involvement.

> When they [my elders] named some object, and accordingly moved towards something, I saw this and grasped that the thing was called by the sound they uttered when they meant to point it out... Thus, as I heard words repeatedly used in their proper places in various sentences, I gradually learnt to understand what objects they signified....
>
> **St Augustine of Hippo,** *Confessions*

PLATO'S BEARD

Plato was clean-shaven, so Plato's beard did not exist. Here it has been said of something, namely Plato's beard, that it lacks a property, namely existence. Alexius von Meinong (1853–1920) argued that one cannot say of nothing that it does not exist, for that is nonsense. 'Plato's beard did not exist' is not nonsense, so Plato's beard must be something. Hence language appears to commit us to the existence of nonexistent objects, such as Plato's beard. Yet this is a paradoxical conclusion.

Augustinian theories (after St Augustine of Hippo) state that meaning is determined by a public convention associating words with objects. To understand a word one must know the convention, which is normally learnt as one grows up. ***Lockean*** views (after John Locke) hold that the meaning of a word is determined by the thoughts ('ideas') in the minds of the speaker and possibly also the hearer. Words are thus labels for our own private collection of ideas. ***Wittgensteinian*** theories – after Ludwig Wittgenstein (1889–1951) – claim that the meaning is simply determined by the use of the word. Understanding is a practical ability to use the word in the appropriate way. Finally, ***causal*** theorists think that words mean what they do because speakers are *caused* to utter them by the presence of the various objects. For example, it is because one would say 'Ah, Rome!' when in Rome that one's word refers to that city.

Sense and Reference

According to Lockean theories, there is no absolute fact about what a word means, there are only facts about what each individual person takes it to mean. Effectively each person has his or her own language, called an ***idiolect***, and we only mean the same when, for example, we both say 'Rome,' in so far as our idiolects overlap. Gottlob Frege (1848–1925) criticized this reduction of meaning to the psychological states of speakers. He argued that, while it is true that each person has private associations for each word, these should not be confused with the meaning of the word. If that were the case, communication would be impossible, since no two people are ever likely to mean precisely the same by a word, and if they did they would not know that they did. That communication does occur is evident, so there must be something more to meaning than our own private associations.

Frege introduced two technical notions, ***sense*** and ***reference***. The reference of a term is that thing in the world that the word refers to. So the reference of 'Rome' is the city and the reference of 'mouse' is a member of a species of small rodent. Each unambiguous word has a unique reference.

The sense is the way we think about the reference. Thus the senses of 'Rome' and 'The Eternal City' are different, although they are different names for the same thing. We must know the sense of a word to understand it. However, since there are different ways of thinking about the same thing, two words can have the same reference but different senses, as in the example above of 'Rome' and 'The Eternal City.' The senses of words combine to make meaningful sentences. Frege thought that if communication is to be possible, each word must have a single sense that anyone is capable of grasping. Unless you grasp the right

▲ **Gottlob Frege**
Frege thought of word meanings as being distinct from anything that goes on in an individual speaker's mind, in the same way that an optical image is distinct from a retinal image.

WITTGENSTEIN'S TWO THEORIES OF MEANING

Ludwig Wittgenstein was remarkable in having created two complete but incompatible philosophies in his life. Both were based around theories of meaning. In the *Tractatus Logico-Philosophicus* (1921) he held a picture theory of language. All meaningful sentences are analysable into compounds of names for simple objects. Each simple object has just one name. A fact is a complex relation of simple objects, and a sentence represents this fact by combining the names for the objects in a way that pictures their relation. Thus the only use for language is to state facts about objects in the world. Any attempt to use language for another purpose, such as value judgment or metaphysics, involves an incoherent effort to step outside the bounds of sense. Wittgenstein never specified what simple objects were, though they are clearly not everyday objects, such as cats and tables. Nor did he

▲ **Ludwig Wittgenstein** *Wittgenstein's theories of language were highly influential.*

perform the analysis of sentences that his theory demanded.

In the 1930s Wittgenstein constructed a new theory of meaning, published posthumously in his *Philosophical Investigations* (1953). Its central idea was that, in trying to understand the meaning of a word, we should not ask what it stands for, but how it is used. Each word and phrase only has life within a language-game with certain objectives, and it is an abuse of language to take it out of that language-game. For example, number words exist within the language-game of counting, as employed by a greengrocer counting apples. It is nonsense to take the word 'five' out of this context ('five apples') and ask what kind of mysterious nonphysical object it refers to. This leads to ***quietism***, which holds that there are no significant metaphysical questions. In both his books, Wittgenstein expresses the thought that studying philosophy is attempting to stretch language beyond its natural limits and enlightenment comes not from answering philosophical problems but seeing that we were mistaken in posing them.

▲ **Willard Van Orman Quine**

Quine believed that, on the basis of evidence, there was no way of discovering the meaning of words – and hence that no such meanings existed.

The paradoxical character of language lies in the fact that while its practice must be subject to standards of correctness, there is no ultimate authority to impose those standards from without.

Michael Dummett, *The Logical Basis of Metaphysics*

sense for each word, you do not understand that word: you do not know what it means and thus you lack competence with that part of the language.

The distinction between sense and reference also serves as a criticism of Augustinian and causal theories. Since these theories can only account for the objects in the world to which words refer, they cannot explain the difference in sense between two words that refer to the same object.

Other developments have encouraged a resurgence of Lockean theories. One is the suggestion by H. P. Grice (1913–88) that the meaning of a word or sentence is determined by the speaker's intentions successfully to communicate a particular thought to a particular audience. Hence each word is attached to a particular *intended* idea. The other is the work of Noam Chomsky on the idea that we have an innate body of linguistic knowledge.

Verificationism

The verificationist movement represented an extreme version of empiricism. Its philosophy is sometimes described as ***logical positivism***, and was primarily an attempt to impose conditions of meaningfulness on language. It was founded in the 1920s by a group of philosophers in Austria, known as the Vienna Circle, led by Moritz Schlick (1882–1936) and Rudolf Carnap (1891–1970). Verificationism holds that the meaning of a proposition is the experience with which it would be verified or falsified. For example, 'it is sunny' would be verified by certain experiences of warmth, the look of the sky, the brightness of the light, and so forth. Therefore, to say that it is sunny just means that these verification conditions are

in place. It follows that any sentence that has no verification conditions is meaningless. For example, if there can be no evidence in the form of particular experiences for or against the existence of God, then the sentence 'God exists' is literally nonsense.

Verificationism is a powerful tool in metaphysics and epistemology, allowing whole debates to be dismissed as meaningless (it was the verificationists who started using 'metaphysics' as a pejorative term). For example, it is possible to question whether this book really exists or whether it is merely an insubstantial idea in the mind. For the verificationist, either 'this book exists' is verified by experiences that one might have in certain situations, or it is meaningless. If a book *appears* to exist, then it does. Hence there is no debate.

Strong forms of verificationism can easily be shown to be false: the statement 'verificationism is true' is meaningless, which shows the theory to be self-defeating. However, there are weaker forms: the ***antirealism*** of Michael Dummett (1925–   ) and the ***internal realism*** of Hilary Putnam (1926–   ), which relate the truth of a sentence to the evidence for it. Thus sentences for which there can be no evidence cannot be either true or false, so they say nothing about the world.

Indeterminacy of Translation

All the views considered so far assume that there is a unique correct answer to the question of what a given word or sentence means. This has been challenged by W. V. O. Quine (1908–   ). He asks us to consider the project of ***radical translation***, when one has to interpret an unknown language; the paradigm case concerns an encounter with a previously undiscovered tribe and the task of translating what they say. Clearly, all there is to go on is their verbal behaviour. They assert certain sentences in certain situations and one has to work out what these sentences mean. Quine thinks that in such a situation it is necessary to make particular assumptions; most importantly, that most of their assertions are true. This assumption was named the ***Principle of Charity*** by Donald Davidson.

For example, suppose that whenever a tribesman is confronted by a rabbit he utters the word 'gavagai.' One would assume that he is saying something true (and hence not, for example, that he is confronting an octopus). The most natural translation of 'gavagai' would be 'rabbit'; however, how would one know that he does not mean 'undetached rabbit leg'? Quine contends that, although the first translation is more natural, one would be equally justified, on the basis of the available evidence, in choosing the second. Any attempt to clarify the issue by, for example, asking the

MEANING MORE THAN ONE SAYS

The philosopher H. P. Grice made a study of the way in which people use language to communicate more than what they say. He claimed that all conversations are governed by four maxims: (1) ***Quantity***: give neither too much nor too little information; (2) ***Quality***: do not say what is false or doubtful; (3) ***Relation***: keep to what is relevant; (4) ***Manner***: do not be obscure, ambiguous, or verbose. One can deliberately break these rules in four ways: (a) by violating a rule, for example by lying; (b) by opting out of a rule, for example by saying that one is not in a position to provide more information; (c) by facing a conflict between two rules, such as when one cannot say enough to be helpful without saying things of which one is unsure; (d) and by ostentatiously flouting a rule. A famous example of flouting a rule concerns a philosophy tutor asked to provide a reference for one of his students. He simply writes 'Jones has beautiful handwriting.' The employer will reason that the tutor was silent about Jones's intellectual abilities in order to avoid saying something derogatory; in this way the tutor can be derogatory without saying an unkind word.

tribesman how many 'gavagai' there were would necessitate further translations. In this case, one would need to understand their number system, which would introduce similar problems. This scenario indicates the **holism** of language.

Quine concludes that given the total possible evidence available under the conditions of radical translation, the correct translation is **indeterminate**. If there can be no evidence to choose between two translations, there can be no fact to distinguish between which is right and which wrong. There is thus no determinate fact about whether 'gavagai' means rabbit or undetached rabbit leg. This conclusion can be generalized to the whole of language, for Quine claims that we never have more evidence than the radical translator. Moreover, if a child learning a language is in a similar position to that of the radical translator, then there are no determinate meanings for him or her to learn. Quine is an **irrealist** about meaning; there are no real meanings.

In response to Quine one might say that everyone knows that one cannot verify that other people mean *exactly* the same thing in the use of a word as one does; indeed, the identity of meaning is not essential for communication. Alternatively one might try to find some other evidence that would determine the correct translation of 'gavagai.' Noam Chomsky argued that there is evidence in the structure of the mind or brain that determines the correct translation – evidence that amounts to an **innate language**.

Quine and Chomsky's positions are, respectively, empiricist and rationalist (see EPISTEMOLOGY). Chomsky stresses the underlying similarities in the structure of all human languages. He rejects the empirical approach of radical translation, which treats language learning as the discovery of underlying rules and patterns on the basis of evidence alone, without any prior linguistic ability. The presence of innate linguistic knowledge would explain how language can be **generative** – how we can use it to create and understand an infinite number of new sentences.

Poststructuralism

Poststructuralists, such as the French philosopher Jacques Derrida (1930–), reach a similar conclusion to that of Quine. They argue that if in a particular language one asks what a word means, all that emerges are more words from that language; what they mean, if they mean anything, remains open. Thus any objective fact that determines what words mean must lie outside language. But our only way of representing this fact would be through language itself, so it could not be outside language after all. Hence there are no metaphysical foundations for language.

Derrida believes in two possible positions: either there is a metaphysical foundation for language or there are no real facts about what words really mean. By accepting the second option, he is claiming that we are deluded in thinking that there are right and wrong ways to use a word. Philosophers such as Wittgenstein and Dummett attempt to provide a theory of meaning that rejects the choice Derrida wishes us to make. They try to show that there are facts about what a word means, but that these are not founded in some extralinguistic reality. These facts can be established within the language: a word's meaning lies in its correct usage within its proper context.

> **holism** The property of language implying that a word or sentence only has meaning in the context of the language taken as a whole. It is the interrelations between *all* the words or sentences of a language that determine what each of them mean. Introducing a new word changes the meanings of the whole language. This view is related to structuralism in linguistics.

CHOOSING WHAT ONE'S WORDS MEAN

◄ **Humpty Dumpty and Alice** *This illustration, by Sir John Tenniel (1820–1914), shows two of the characters from* Through the Looking Glass, *Lewis Carroll's famous children's book.*

'I don't know what you mean by "glory,"' Alice said.

Humpty Dumpty smiled contemptuously. 'Of course you don't – till I tell you. ... When I use a word,' Humpty Dumpty said in a rather scornful tone, 'it means just what I choose it to mean – neither more nor less.'

Lewis Carroll (1832–98) wrote children's stories that played with philosophical and mathematical ideas. In this episode, from *Through the Looking Glass* (1872), he ridicules the idea that we can make our words mean what we want them to. For a language to be used properly, the user must recognize that the words have their meanings partly or wholly determined by a publicly accepted convention. Wittgenstein also attacked the notion of a private language.

> **The Liar Paradox**
>
> Using language to talk about language generates paradoxes. For example:
> 'This sentence is not true.'
> If the sentence is true, then things are as it says they are, which means that it is not true. If it is not true, then things are not as it says they are, which means that it is not not true, i.e. it is true. This is called the Liar Paradox, because it also occurs if one says 'I always lie.'

Applied Philosophy

Method and proof • Positivist approaches • Popper • Lakatos, Kuhn, and Feyerabend •
The special sciences • The Frankfurt School • Structuralism • The philosophy of science

deduction A method of reasoning that moves from one general fact to another or to a particular fact via some other particular fact. Its opposite is *induction*, which moves from a series of particular facts to a general conclusion.

Philosophy is often regarded as an abstract activity with no immediate relevance to the real world. There are, however, some important practical areas in which progress appears impossible without some philosophical speculation; in these areas philosophy, like mathematics, has to be applied to the real world.

Method and Proof

The most important area of application for philosophy is that of science. Science is undeniably of crucial importance to our understanding of the world, and the technology derived from it is indispensable to the whole modern way of life. It is widely assumed that science delivers, in some sense, proven truths. Yet the status of the claims of science to do this can be disputed, and it is a philosophical task to assess these claims. Closely connected with this is the question of what distinguishes science from other disciplines that attempt to predict and explain phenomena, such as astrology or psychoanalysis.

The question of the **unity** of science is another philosophical matter. A study is unified if the same explanatory concepts are applied to all of its subject matter. So can the same method be used by scientists whether they are examining the structure of matter, the arrangement of the cosmos, the evolution of species, or the nature of human societies?

A simple definition of science would be 'any study conducted according to a certain kind of method.' However, this only defers the problem to the explanation of what that method is. Such an explanation has proved extremely elusive. Science appears to aim at achieving **generalizations** that can then be used in explanation of natural phenomena. There are, however, some doubts as to the existence of a reliable method for reaching such generalizations. In the purely abstract sciences, such as mathematics, it is possible to arrive at conclusions by logical **deduction**. This is because the abstract sciences only study the relations between general propositions; for example, the proposition that $2 + 3 = 5$. In the empirical sciences, the aim is to derive general laws from the **evidence** of particular cases. This cannot be achieved by deduction, but only by the less reliable method of **induction**.

Since the time of the Scottish empiricist philosopher David Hume, it has become generally accepted that induction is problematic. The problem is that it tries to achieve generalizations that apply to all instances of a certain sort. For example, 'cats have four legs' is meant to apply to all possible cats. However, one cannot observe all instances of a certain sort – and hence it is always possible for the conclusion to be proved wrong. The traditional philosophy of science has largely been concerned with attempts to defend the inductive method against this weakness. The method was first explicitly proposed by Francis Bacon (1561–1626) in the early 17th century, and was defended against Hume's criticisms by John Stuart Mill in the 19th century.

Positivist Approaches

The inductive method was also defended by the **positivist** movement, launched in France by the sociologist Auguste Comte (1798–1857). This held that all scientific claims must be backed by positive evidence, even the sciences of the mind and of society. The culmination of this tendency was the **logical positivism** of the Vienna Circle during the second and third decades of the 20th century

Francis Bacon ▶
More than any other thinker, Bacon pioneered the modern concepts of the scientific method and of scientific justification. In his Novum Organum, *he argued that all presuppositions must be abandoned in science and that people should rather respond to the evidence that they encounter. Later philosophers have come to consider this view naïve.*

Hon.ᵐᵒ Francisc° Bacon.° Baro de Veru-
lam. Vice-Comes Sᵗⁱ Albani. Mortuus 9 Aprilis,
Anno Dni. 1626. Annoq. Aetat 66.

(see THE PHILOSOPHY OF LANGUAGE). Logical positivism devised elaborate defences of the inductive method. One was to claim that induction made general propositions more probable, and thus increased the reasonableness of our believing them to be true. Another was the view that it was meaningless to criticize induction for not being rational, since it was by induction that the standards of rationality were set in the first place.

Other philosophers denied that the universal generalizations of the sciences aspired to being true. This approach – which holds that theories are useful tools rather than attempts to state general facts about the world – takes various forms, known as pragmatism, instrumentalism, and operationalism. It flourished in the USA under C. S. Peirce (1839–1914) and William James (1842–1910).

Popper

None of the defences of induction, for all their ingenuity, were completely convincing; however, a rival conception of the scientific method and of scientific justification was provided by the Austrian-born philosopher Karl Popper (1902–94). He noted that there was a logical asymmetry between the tasks of confirmation and refutation. It requires an infinity of instances to confirm a universal generalization but only one to refute it. Thus we can never hope to totally confirm a scientific hypothesis, but we can at least hope to dismiss it. Scientific hypotheses, according to Popper, are not mere instruments. They aspire to describe how the world is. By using their **refutability** we can at least avoid errors.

Moreover, we *can* come to some positive conclusions. If a hypothesis has been subjected to persistent and severe testing, and has still not been refuted, then it is rational for us to accept it. Even then, however, we cannot be said to know its truth for certain. Popper claimed that

such a hypothesis has been 'corroborated' rather than proven; he argued that genuine science seeks to produce hypotheses that are bold and thus relatively easy to refute, since, if they are then not refuted, we have genuinely gained in understanding of the world. Irrefutability, such as he saw in the "scientific superstitions" of Marxism and psychoanalysis, is a great weakness, not a strength, in a scientific theory.

Popper's account of science seems to avoid some, at least, of the objections to induction. However, it shares one very important property with the positivist conception, and this is closely connected with the objections that can in turn be made against Popper. The shared property is the belief that a genuine distinction can be drawn between the contents of a scientific theory and the immediate description of the evidence on which that theory is based. It is a fundamental tenet of both Popper and the positivists that the evidence for scientific theories can be presented in a way that is completely **neutral** as between those theories. Scientists then have the task of seeing which theory best fits the evidence. This view is still influential in the popular conception of science, although it has since come under heavy attack from philosophers. It has been forcefully argued that there can be no way of describing the evidence for scientific theories that is neutral to that theory. In other words, everybody's perception of the world is **theory-laden**. There can be no wholly unbiased confrontation with 'mere' experience.

In addition to this, scientists often have a tendency to regard their subject as a complete and mutually interdependent body of knowledge, a concept of science known as **holism** (see PHILOSOPHY OF LANGUAGE). This means that the terms used in a scientific theory only have meaning within the context of that theory. A holistic theory tends to change the meaning of

▲ **Karl Popper**
Popper was the first to argue that philosophers and scientists should abandon attempts to defend induction either as a means of discovery or as a means of confirmation. Instead, the scientist should deliberately put forward theories that are likely to be disproved.

---

evidence Data in the form of a measurement, event, or manifestation that serves to support a statement, conclusion, or proof.

POPPERIAN REFUTABILITY

The following analogy of the black and white crows may be used to illustrate Karl Popper's idea of the asymmetry that exists between the contrary processes of confirmation and refutation.

However many black crows one may observe, empirical observation would never be sufficient to establish the truth of the statement 'all crows are black.' This is because it would never be possible to observe *all* conceivable crows.

On the other hand, the observation of only one white crow enables the theory to be refuted incontrovertibly.

---

generalization
A principle or theory that applies not to one specific subject but to a wide range of subjects. For example, 'red apples taste good' is a generalization; 'this apple tastes good' is not, since it only applies to one particular apple.

The Life of Galileo
In this play, the German Marxist dramatist Bertolt Brecht (1898–1956) used the figure of the Italian Renaissance mathematician and astronomer Galileo Galilei (1564–1642) to investigate the role and responsibilities of the scientist in society. Many modern philosophers of science share Brecht's ambivalent attitude that scientific and technological advance, while bringing undoubted benefits, must never become an end in itself. ▶

1610 - PADUA - 1610

objective Existing independently of any particular point of view or bias. The physical sciences aim to establish objective facts.
A ***subjective*** view, on the other hand, is linked to a particular point of view; it can therefore change if the point of view changes.

Science is an essentially anarchistic enterprise: theoretical anarchism is more humanitarian and more likely to encourage progress than its law-and-order alternatives.

Paul K. Feyerabend, *Against Method* (1975)

its terms in the face of contrary evidence. Therefore, it cannot be refuted by having one of its statements proved wrong, since that statement cannot be treated apart from the other statements that make up the theory.

Holistic objections were raised against the positions of both Rudolf Carnap (1891–1970) and Popper. Carnap responded by maintaining that observation and evidence still played a part in science; however, it is necessary to assume certain theories to be true, on pragmatic grounds. Similar ideas were proposed by the Hungarian Imre Lakatos (1922–74) and the US philosopher Thomas Kuhn (1922–96).

Lakatos, Kuhn, and Feyerabend

Lakatos proposed that science organizes itself into what he called "research programmes," which involve assuming some postulates as facts. They form the "hard core" of the theory; they are surrounded by a "soft core," which can be modified in the light of experimental evidence. If these modifications are still unable to account for the contradictions, then it is always possible to abandon the programme by significantly altering a part of the hard core. Kuhn held a similar position; he called the basic unquestioned assumptions of a scientific theory a ***paradigm*** and offered a reinterpretation of the history of science, divided into two sorts of period; those in which a paradigm is generally agreed upon and those in which a paradigm is questioned. He called the first period 'normal' and the second 'revolutionary.' In normal science, scientific activity conforms to traditional accounts of science,

with scientists concentrating on solving problems rationally. However, in periods of revolution, the adoption of a different paradigm cannot be rationally defended in the same way. Indeed two paradigms cannot even be compared, since all their terms will be defined in the context of their role within the paradigm.

This view of scientific activity is controversial, since it suggests that science is only rational up to a point. The logical positivists hoped to show that science arrives at conclusions to which no rational person in full possession of the evidence could possibly object. The theories later offered by Carnap, Lakatos, and Kuhn, on the other hand, suggest that, while much scientific activity is rational, some very important parts of it are arbitrary. Some philosophers, especially the Austrian-born Paul K. Feyerabend (1924–94), have gone so far as to claim that science is always revolutionary. Feyerabend attacks the notion of a rational scientific method, claiming that any proposed methodological recommendations would be as likely to have the opposite effect as the one intended. Thus there is no reason to see science as different from other activities, such as religion. Feyerabend argues for science to be placed under democratic control.

The Special Sciences

The problems considered so far have concerned the philosophy of the so-called ***hard sciences*** and especially of physics. The scientific world-view tends to maintain that physics supplies the fundamental description of the world, providing laws to which there are no exceptions – there can be no loopholes in the laws of nature! It also describes nature at its simplest level – the level of its smallest parts – and thus it is to be distinguished from the *special sciences*, which study matter that is more highly organized or of greater complexity. A clear example of this is the study of living things by biological scientists. It is usually thought that the study of human phenomena, whether of the individual or of society, is still higher in level of complexity.

There is a traditional debate about the extent to which the methods and approaches that are appropriate in the hard sciences should also be thought appropriate to the special sciences. Thus, even if one concludes that the science of matter can be completely rational and **objective**, it does not follow that one can adopt a similar attitude to the examination of human culture and society. Many thinkers have argued that if the ideal of objectivity is unrealistic for the social sciences, then neither is it appropriate for them to aspire to the ideal of freedom from moral assumptions. It is impossible to analyse human society without adopting some sort of moral perspective.

The opposing view, that social science should seek to explain phenomena in the same way as hard science, is known as *scientism*. According to this view, human nature is continuous with the rest of the world and the primary business of the social sciences is to predict what human beings are likely to do and thus to be able to control them. This is done using the same method as in the hard sciences; by examining evidence and constructing general theories to explain it. When such generalizations have been found under which prediction can reliably occur, the role of the social sciences will have been fulfilled. Although the laws of the social sciences will always have exceptions, these will not affect their essential nature as scientific generalizations.

However, some regard it as a mistake to think that sociology, for example, could or should ever aspire to the kind of predictive explanation that is characteristic of hard science. They maintain that such explanations would be impossible to make with any reliability, but, more importantly, they would not be what we were seeking even if they were possible. When we study human affairs either in the past – through history – or in the present – through anthropology – we are seeking to see the world as the protagonists themselves see it. Only then are we in a position to understand the real meaning of experiences that are different from our own. The German thinkers Wilhelm Dilthey (1833–1911) and Max Weber (1864–1920) considered the aim of the social sciences to be that of *Verstehen* (empathetic insight), which they contrasted with the

Verständnis (rational knowledge) that is sought by physics and the other hard sciences.

A key matter related to the nature and purpose of social science is the question of whether we should seek to explain group phenomena in terms of the experience of individuals – or the experience of individuals in terms of the group phenomena. This question centres on the issue of **reductionism**. A reductionist believes that any complicated arrangement of matter can be explained entirely at the 'lower' level of its constituents; for example, such a standpoint in the social sciences argues that group effects can be analysed completely by examining the workings of the constituent members of the groups. This is an *individualist* position. By contrast, *collectivism* argues that the experience of the individual is meaningless in isolation from its wider context, without which the evidence is totally distorted.

A striking example of the tension between individualist and collectivist conceptions of social theory is provided by the history of 20th-century Spanish philosophy. This has been dominated by two great thinkers, Miguel de Unamuno (1864–1936) and José Ortega y Gasset (1883–1955). Unamuno favoured an individualistic interpretation of society, denying it an existence beyond that of the individuals of which it is composed. By contrast, Ortega argued that it is only in the context of the historical perspective that we can hope to make any sense of individual lives. His view is called *historicism* – the belief that the events

> **reductionism** The view that some entities can be fully explained in terms of simpler ones, of which they are supposed to be composed. So, for instance, a reductionist view of society would hold that all social facts could be explained in terms of the individuals that make up that society. According to this approach, the concept of society would only be retained for convenience rather than for serious explanation.

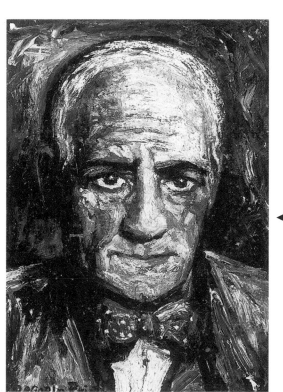

◄ **José Ortega y Gasset** *Ortega, shown in this portrait by Gregorio Prieto (1897–1992), argued that one must adopt the perspective of an era in order to understand it. All perspectives on the world are equally valid – the only false perspective is that which claims sole validity.*

The Invisible Hand

Adam Smith, in his work *An Inquiry into the Nature and Causes of the Wealth of Nations* (1776), claimed that the intrinsically selfish activities of individuals were channelled through the free-market system for the public good. He suggested that the individual was "led by an invisible hand to promote an end which was no part of his intention." In other words, in amassing personal wealth, an entrepreneur benefits society through the jobs that are created.

semiotics The study of signs and symbols. The 19th-century Swiss linguist Ferdinand de Saussure argued that linguistic interchange could be seen entirely as a rule-based exchange of signs, and other thinkers have claimed that all cultures depend upon subtle rules governing both linguistic and nonlinguistic signs.

GAME THEORY – THE AMERICAN INDIANS

Game theory is the study of problems (or games) in which the 'players' have certain specified objectives and behave in such a way as to achieve those objectives. The actions of all the players determine how well each player does. The solution of a game often requires analysing the actions that are in the interests of the other players in the game. This is illustrated in the following example.

Problem: An American Indian chief has five prisoners, A, B, C, D, and E, and he proposes a test by which they may win their freedom. He ties red feathers behind the heads of A and B, and white feathers behind the heads of the others. He then tells them that there is at least one red feather, and that the rest are white. Each day the prisoners are allowed, if they want, to guess the colour of the feather on their head. They see each other once a day, but cannot communicate. If they guess correctly, they are set free; if wrong, they are

executed. If they make no guess, they return to their cell for the night. How long does it take for A to guess the colour of his feather? *Solution*: Two days. On the first day, A will notice one red feather on B and three white feathers on the others. He will reason that if he, A, had a white feather, then B would immediately know that he, B, had the only red feather, since all B would see would be white feathers. Therefore, when A returns the next day and learns that B hasn't left, he realises that he, A, must have a red feather too.

Note that A assumed that B would not make a guess until he was certain, but that when he was certain, he would guess immediately. Such assumptions about the other players are a key part of game theory.

Game theory is of great importance in business, where the scenarios involve companies trying to calculate what actions their competitors are likely to take.

of any given era can only be understood in terms of the mentality of that era itself. There are no absolute cultural facts or values that can be transmitted from age to age. Hence all historical events are unique and one cannot make objective historical generalizations.

A view of social explanation that stands midway between individualism and collectivism is the doctrine of the **Invisible Hand**. An explanation of this kind was used by the Scottish economist Adam Smith (1723–90) to elucidate his theory of the free-market economy. This sort of explanation is now frequently invoked to explain how the sheer complexity of a system may lead to outcomes not planned by any of the participants. To avoid intolerable

complications, it is usually assumed that the participants are motivated solely by their own private ends, which they pursue by rational means. However, it may be that it is rational for one participant to consider what is rational for another, which can very quickly lead to convoluted circles of reasoning. Games often provide simplified environments in which these problems can occur; these problems of rationality have been explored by a branch of mathematics known as **game theory**. However, the processes by which decisions are reached cannot be assumed to be purely rational; thus there is also scope for a type of study that concentrates entirely on the decision-making process itself.

The Frankfurt School

The Frankfurt School was led by four thinkers: Max Horkheimer (1895–1973), Theodor Adorno (1903–69), Herbert Marcuse (1898–1979) and Jürgen Habermas (1929–   ). Their intention was to produce a social philosophy based on an updated form of Marxism. Horkheimer developed an approach to social issues known as *critical theory*, based on the writings of the young Marx, on the nature of consciousness and especially the theory of alienation. Adorno was prominent in the application of Marxist concepts to the interpretation and philosophy of music. Marcuse attempted to integrate the thinking of Marx

◄ **Herbert Marcuse** *Marcuse's radical critique of society influenced many on the Left in the 1960s.*

with that of Freud in order to bring about a revolution in industrial and social practices, notably in regard to sexual morality. Habermas elaborated a theory of history that saw revolution and crisis as being necessary ingredients. The Frankfurt School produced a highly influential critique of scientistic and individualistic conceptions of social theory, providing many of the central concepts for the current development of cultural studies.

There have also been two important subsidiary schools in current Western thought about society. The Marxist tradition was maintained in the Eastern-bloc countries, though it has been discredited since the fall of communism. The collectivist theories of the anthropologist Claude Lévi-Strauss (1908–) and the linguist Ferdinand de Saussure (1857–1913) have led to the attempt to explain culture in terms of signs (**semiotics**) or structures (**structuralism**). This approach has been particularly dominant in France, where it has been extended, and in some ways transformed, by the deconstructionist theories of Jacques Derrida.

Structuralism

The semiotic and structuralist traditions have been still more complex. The central idea behind both schools is that culture only achieves meaning by the use of a wide variety of codes and signs, by which its members are bound together. A true understanding of a culture must therefore identify these signs. This has been most clearly attempted in the writings of the anthropologist Claude Lévi-Strauss. It has been argued that this form of analysis is more suited to the discussion of a remote culture than a familiar one. The practice of analysing structures has, in any case, been transferred to literary criticism by Roland Barthes (1915–80) and his many successors, while Michel Foucault (1926–84) used a structuralist perspective to criticize the social treatment of minority groups, such as the mentally ill and homosexuals. In the mid-20th century purely structuralist ideas were cross-fertilized with *existentialism*, with the work of the German Martin Heidegger (1889–1976) and the Frenchman Jean-Paul Sartre playing an important role.

Structuralism led to the view that works of art and other social and cultural institutions cannot be properly understood until their underlying patterns and structures have been investigated. This is the project of *deconstruction* as practised by Derrida. To what extent this represents a strictly philosophical position is contentious. However, Derrida holds that one should concentrate on the surface phenomena of language and culture. This is similar to ordinary language philosophy in

the analytical tradition and especially that of Wittgenstein (see PHILOSOPHY OF LANGUAGE).

Another philosopher within this broad tradition is Louis Althusser (1918–90). In stark contrast to the Frankfurt School, Althusser sought to reinstate the scientific interpretation of Marxism and argued that Marx was right to hold that the contradictions of noncommunist societies would inevitably lead to their eventual collapse and revolutionary transition to communism. However, he thought that Marx was wrong to suppose that the only contradictions that could bring this about were those occurring at the level of economic relations. Other cultural and social contradictions could also precipitate revolution, which was why the only revolutions that had actually led to communism were in economically backward countries, contrary to the predictions of Marx. The most interesting feature of this view is that it seems to hold that social developments are to some extent independent of the economic and material base.

A great deal of the social theory that has been devised in continental Europe in the 20th century has been both antiscientistic and collectivist. It resists the impulse to examine society and culture in terms of the individuals who make up that society, or to search for general social laws (the scientific position). In both of these respects, it contrasts sharply with the dominant attitude towards psychological and sociological explanation in the English-speaking world. For example, researchers into psychological causation and language have developed theories that make psychological phenomena continuous with the rest of nature, as displayed most notably in the attempts to produce artificial intelligence (see PHILOSOPHY OF MIND). The implications of this approach for the development of mainstream social science are likely to become apparent over the next few decades.

▲ **A Citroën DS** *In his highly influential work* Mythologies *(1957), the French critic Roland Barthes examined the role of signs and symbols. He illustrated his theory with a wide variety of cultural icons, including wrestling, food, and cars. Of the latter, Barthes claimed "I think that cars today are almost the exact equivalent of the great Gothic cathedrals:... the supreme creation of an era, conceived with passion by unknown artists."*

structuralism The study of recurrent patterns in social artefacts, including both institutions and works of art, music, and literature. Structuralism is highly anti-reductionist, in that it holds that the life of a culture cannot be exhaustively explained in terms of the wishes and intentions of its participants.

THE PHILOSOPHY OF SCIENCE

SCIENCE IS THE study of nature and natural phenomena by the scientific method. The scientific method relies exclusively on observation and reproducible experiment, which involves accurate measurement and quantification. Belief, hearsay, and lore play no part in scientific discoveries. Science has enabled human beings to walk on the moon, harness the energy trapped in atoms, map and improve the structure of genes, and eradicate smallpox. The philosophy of science is about the way scientists think.

The traditional view of science as inductive and empirical identifies its origins in experience, from which general laws and principles are inferred. However, this simplistic view is clearly insufficient; it cannot form the basis for such complex abstract theories as Newtonian physics and Darwinian evolution.

An alternative model, first proposed in the 1930s, is the hypothetico-deductive method. This states that science begins not with observations but with problems. Hypotheses are proposed to solve them, and from these hypotheses various consequences are deduced and tested by experiment. Those hypotheses not verified by experiment are rejected.

TRUTH AND FALSIFICATION

This orthodox view was challenged by the Austrian-born philosopher Karl Popper (1902–94). In his major work

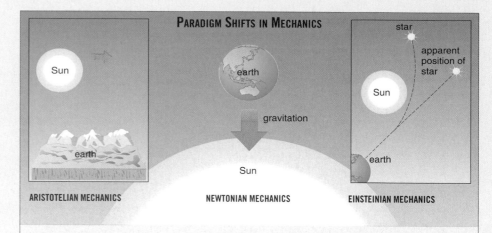

PARADIGM SHIFTS IN MECHANICS

ARISTOTELIAN MECHANICS   **NEWTONIAN MECHANICS**   **EINSTEINIAN MECHANICS**

In Aristotle's mechanics a force is required to create and maintain motion. The sun needed to be dragged across the flat earth, as in the Greek legend of the sun being pulled by a team of horses driven by the charioteer Helios. In Newton's mechanics all bodies continue in steady motion unless acted on by a force. Once moving, the earth orbits the

sun because no force slows it down. It is held in orbit by the gravitational force between massive bodies. In Einstein's mechanics gravitation results from the curvature of space-time caused by the presence of massive bodies. Light rays from a distant star passing close to the sun are also bent by gravitation.

Die Logik der Forschung (The Logic of Scientific Discovery; 1934), he argued that verification was less important in science than falsification. Scientists strive not to prove, but to disprove (or falsify) their theories. This, according to Popper, is what distinguishes science from other disciplines.

PARADIGMS

A differing view was offered by the US philosopher of science Thomas Kuhn in his book *The Structure of Scientific Revolutions* (1962). Kuhn claimed that an accepted theory is first developed. Scientists try neither to verify this nor falsify it; instead, during a period of 'normal science,' they work within what is essentially a value system, which Kuhn called a paradigm.

However, from time to time observations or experiments arise that contradict the established system. At first, the theories are modified in an attempt to 'save the system,' but eventually a 'scientific revolution' creates a paradigm shift – e.g. the shift in physics to relativistic and quantum mechanics that took place in the early 20th century. In the basic science of mechanics there have been three such paradigm shifts in the last 2300 years: Aristotelian mechanics, Newtonian mechanics, and Einsteinian mechanics.

A Philosopher Lecturing on the Orrery *(1766) This painting, by the English artist Joseph Wright of Derby, shows an early scientific lecturer using a model to demonstrate the workings of the solar system. Science was once referred to as 'natural philosophy.'*

RELIGION

Introduction

Characteristics of religion • Explanations of the origin of religion •
Primal religions • New religious movements

Although religion as a universal human phenomenon has been a subject of keen academic interest throughout the 20th century, no agreement has been reached on defining the term itself. Many scholars today prefer to use a working definition of religion that outlines the field of study without being too narrowly restrictive. In general, religions originate in a fundamental human urge to find an ultimate meaning to existence and have at their centre the concept of a supreme and mysterious authority. This authority is regarded as supernatural – that is, existing beyond space and time – and is thought of as ordaining certain beliefs, practices, and guidelines concerning our moral and social conduct.

Characteristics of Religion

Most religions involve a system of belief of one kind or another supported by rituals, characteristic myths, religious practitioners, moral teachings, religious texts, and sacred art.

Rituals. Rituals re-enact, either literally or symbolically, the content of sacred stories. They possess the characteristics of a drama, with members of the believing community assuming various roles that utilize the symbols defined in the shared myths. The dramatic repetition of rituals has the effect of bringing myths alive for the community of believers.

Rituals are of four types: calendrical, liturgical/calendrical, life-cycle-based, and crisis-based. *Calendrical* rituals are repeated regularly according to the season of the year (e.g. harvest time). *Liturgical/calendrical* rituals re-enact the actual events of the myth at specific times each year, such as at the new year in ancient Mesopotamian rituals or the Passover for Jewish communities. *Life-cycle-based* rituals occur at times of transition in the lives of people, such as birth, puberty, marriage, and death. *Crisis-based* rituals are performed when people experience major threats to their wellbeing, as in times of famine, drought, or war.

Myths. A myth is a story from an earlier age that relates how the world was given its form and orientation. This central characteristic of a myth – its presentation of a **teleology** – distinguishes it from other types of story, such as legends or fairytales. The characters of myths include divinities, superheroes, or great ancestors. Myths fall into three major categories. *Cosmogonic* myths tell of the origin of

===SEE ALSO===
This section:
• Mythology
Social Sciences:
• Cultural and Social
  Anthropology
Philosophy:
• Metaphysics

The Ancient of Days (1794) A watercolour by the English romantic artist William Blake (1757–1827) depicts God holding compasses, as the architect of the universe.

Easter at Danilov Monastery, Russia ▶
Ritual is a vital element of religion. Here, priests of the Russian Orthodox Church spread incense as part of the Mass.

teleology A belief that explains the existence of the universe in terms of the design or purpose of a higher existence.

Science without religion is lame, religion without science is blind.

Albert Einstein, (1877–1955) *Science, Religion, and Philosophy*

the universe and how the world came to have its present form. *Sociomoral* myths aim at reinforcing the traditional values of a society. *Historical* myths tell how a particular people came into existence (usually through an ancestral hero) and how they came to occupy the land that they now inhabit.

Religious Practitioners. A religious practitioner is one who mediates between the believing community and the gods or spirits. Types of religious practitioners include holy persons, prophets, shamans, priests, and religious teachers.

Holy persons are regarded by believers as sacred in themselves. For Christians, Jesus Christ is God, the second person of the Trinity. Many

followers of Gautama Siddhartha, the Buddha, elevated him from being one who saw into the meaning of existence to one who actually embodied that meaning. Some traditional African kings were said to have descended directly from the first ancestor and thus were regarded as divine.

Prophets receive direct instruction from the higher authority, which they convey to their people in order to save them from whatever threatens them. The prophets of Israel, for instance, announced a message of doom for those who failed to act justly and obey the God of the Israelites. In Islam, the prophet Mohammed received wisdom from God through His emissary, the angel Gabriel. Mohammed thereafter began to proclaim the divine truths revealed to him among the peoples of the Arabian peninsula.

Shamans traditionally were found in Arctic regions. They were distinguished by their capacity to enter into ecstatic trances, and could travel to remote spiritual worlds. The purpose of their visits to other worlds was to learn things that the community needed for its welfare, such as informing hunters which direction caribou herds were travelling or diagnosing and prescribing cures for illnesses. Shamans undertook a priestly role because they acted as intermediaries, bringing knowledge and goodness from spirits to humans.

In more formalized religions, priests act as intermediaries between the supreme authority and man and are responsible for administering the sacraments.

Religious teachers have no mystical relationship with the deity, but are scholarly authorities versed in the laws and practices of the religion. Their duties, like those of the priest, also extend to pastoral work among the community.

Moral Teachings. The authority of the absolute moral values of any religion rests on their supposed sacred origins. To disobey the moral imperative disrupts life, threatens well-being, compromises orderly existence, and ushers in the chaos characteristic of existence before the Sacred Being imposed its will on the world. Sacred authority is expressed clearly in the Hebrew scriptures, where the Commandments are delivered by God to Moses, but it also exists in such traditions as Chinese Confucianism. In this, although the moral teaching is often only given in the form of proverbs, this wisdom is considered vital to people's harmonious coexistence and obedience to the perfect design set by heaven.

Religious Texts (Scriptures). The term 'scripture' literally means an act of writing and thus generally refers to the written texts of literate religious traditions. However, all written texts have evolved from oral traditions.

BELIEF SYSTEMS

Systems of belief fall into a number of distinct categories, chief among which are:
- **monotheism**, belief in one God
- **polytheism**, belief in many gods
- **pantheism**, a belief that everything is God
- **deism**, an understanding developed during the European Enlightenment of the 17th and 18th centuries that the Supreme Being is a rational creator who does not contravene the laws of nature
- **henotheism**, belief in a particular god without denying the reality of the gods of others or their right to worship them

Some religions never develop written sources, but pass on their teachings, myths, rituals, and moral understandings in oral form from generation to generation. Teachings and events began to be recorded to preserve the stories accurately and to guard against their misinterpretation (as in Islam) or to present the sacred events in an organized and unified way (as in the case of the Christian Gospels).

Sacred Art. Religious art encompasses a wide variety of genres, including painting, music, architecture, drama, sculpture, and storytelling. It is ***presentational*** when it transports the believer directly into the presence of the sacred. For example, in Eastern Orthodox Christianity, paintings or wood carvings portraying Christ – known as icons – are objects of intense devotion. ***Representational*** art, on the other hand, tells a story, conveys a truth, or teaches a lesson. To an Alaskan Inuit, a half-raven half-human shaman's mask evokes the mythical creation stories of this culture that centre on the figure of the raven-man.

Explanations of the Origin of Religion

The study of religion as a Western academic discipline began in the 19th century as details of religious practices around the world were related by missionaries and explorers. Of particular interest to early anthropologists

▲ **An Inuit Shaman's Mask** *As a person who is thought to have access to the spirit world, the shaman plays a central role in many communities.*

AN AFRICAN COSMOGONIC MYTH

In the beginning Mwari (God) created the first man, Mwedzi (moon), and placed him in a pool. However, Mwedzi asked to be released into the world, as life in the pool was boring. Mwari allowed him to do so, but only after a bitter debate. Mwari had insisted that Mwedzi would regret it since the earth was a lonely and desolate place. After a few days of wandering, Mwedzi came back to Mwari and complained that he wanted a partner to stay with. He was given Massasi (evening star). The two departed to the earth. In the evening, they made a fire to warm their bodies. Mwedzi had a medicine horn. He grabbed it and, rubbing its oil on his index finger, touched Massasi. She became pregnant and gave birth to trees, grass, cattle, goats, and the forests. After two years, Mwari took Massasi back to the pools, leaving Mwedzi lonely. Mwedzi petitioned for another partner. He was given Murombo (morning star), who conceived and bore the first boys and girls and wild animals, such as the lion, the civet cat, and the snake.

influenced by Darwinian theories of biological evolution was the origin of religion. It was thought that the study of what were termed the 'primitive' religions of tribal societies would explain how religion evolved in more 'developed' societies.

The process of religious evolution was described late in the 19th century by the British anthropologist Sir James Frazer (1854–1941), who held that the first stage of religion is magic, which he defined as a primitive science. In his major work *The Golden Bough* (1890), Frazer argued that, through the use of charms, incantations, or spells, 'primitive' humans tried to manipulate forces greater than themselves in order to secure health or to ensure justice. When magic failed to achieve the desired results, primitive man believed that the forces had a will of their own and thus needed to be influenced by various means, such as sacrifice and prayer. These attempts to persuade the spirits came to characterize religion both in its crude lower polytheistic phases and in its higher forms of ethical monotheism. The final phase for Frazer was science, which understands that the real causes of misfortune and their cures are attributable neither to magical forces nor to supernatural beings but to natural laws.

The term 'animism' was coined to describe primitive man's perception of a living soul (Latin: *anima*) that resided in all forms of nature. Primal societies developed the notion of a life force that departed from the human body at the time of death. By extension, such objects as trees and stones were thought to possess souls. This in turn led to polytheism, which perceived souls not only within objects but also in powerful nonphysical spiritual forces that had to be appeased. Later, a hierarchy of divinities was conceived, giving

Religious Architecture

The highest aspirations of religious art are often realized in the architecture of buildings dedicated to worship. The Temples of the Israelites, the cathedrals of Christianity (especially medieval Gothic cathedrals), and the mosques of Islam provide magnificent examples of the homage humans have paid to their gods through art.

totem An animal – or sometimes a plant or vegetable – that represents or symbolizes the clan. The totem attains a sacred power when the clan assembles because it becomes the focus of ritual activities. The totem, however, is not itself sacred since it refers to the clan with its social rules, customs, practices, and beliefs.

Hindu Sacred Art *Art is especially important in Hinduism, which has numerous deities, each with very different characteristics. Here, offerings are laid before a statue of the elephant-headed deity Ganesha in a Hindu temple in Bombay.* ▼

rise to the idea of a sky god and eventually to monotheism.

Another view of early religion held that its original source was not animistic, but an impersonal force called **mana**. Mana operated invisibly, particularly in objects or persons regarded as powerful. Direct appeals could not be made to mana; a person either had it or did not have it. Because its power was considered dangerous, it could be withdrawn or even turned against others by the use of charms, amulets, or other magical means. Closely associated with mana is the idea of a **taboo** – an object that is considered mysterious or dangerous, either because it possesses mana or because it is impure and hence potentially contaminating. Anything that is taboo must either be dealt with only in clearly prescribed and understood ways or avoided altogether. This theory of the origin of religion is called **dynamism**.

In his studies of religion, the French sociologist Emile Durkheim (1858–1917) argued that its most basic form manifests itself in primitive social organizations called **clans** and their **totems**. Rather than consisting entirely of blood relations, the clan is united by its common totem, sharing the same taboos (such as never eating the totem) and following the same rituals and customs.

Primal Religions

The collective term 'primal religions,' used to designate indigenous or tribal religions, is preferred by many modern scholars to such earlier classifications as 'primitive' or 'preliterate.' Global adherents are estimated at over 100 million in 101 countries.

Primal religions take a hierarchical view of the spirit world, with family ancestors the most common object of ritual activity, followed by spirits representing a wider geographical region, all of which are ultimately overseen by a high God. The spiritual hierarchy corresponds to the social order in many primal societies, where the chief can be consulted only through properly appointed intermediaries.

In addition to the ancestral lineage, other spirits exist, both benign and malevolent. Some may become **alien spirits**, who settle on a person chosen to be a medium and generally act, like an ancestor, for the benefit of the community. Other spirits that have been wronged or harmed in life return as **avenging spirits**, who attack the offending party or his descendants. Those who have been born of practitioners of evil or persuaded to practise the craft (often called 'witches' or 'sorcerers') use supernatural forces to bring illness, misfortune, or death.

The ancestral hierarchy exists to protect the people and ensure their wellbeing. When the people neglect the ancestors or break their established traditions, the activities of malicious spirits or practitioners of evil are permitted. This may result in misfortune descending on a family or territory. To repair the situation, an animal is often sacrificed. The purpose of this is to offer the spirits something that is valuable to the community, as a sign of deference.

A common feature of primal religions is the widespread existence of a spirit medium who becomes possessed by the ancestral spirit. When in this state, the medium is regarded by believers as the deceased ancestor. The medium often assumes the voice and mannerisms of the ancestor in order to listen to the complaints of the people and to give advice.

Primal religions assume an original harmony between humans, society, nature, and the spirit world. Any misfortune indicates that the harmony has been disturbed. Explanations must be sought and measures taken to restore the equilibrium. In an ideal primal world, the spirits are honoured and respected, people live to an old age, the elders occupy their place of authority, the forms of subsistence are abundant, and people share with one another so that no families are unduly elevated materially above the others.

New Religious Movements

Missionary activity across many centuries, and instigated by many cultures, caused a number of indigenous people to lose faith in their original primal religion. At the same time, the religion of the invading culture (usually Christianity, but sometimes Islam or Buddhism) was still regarded as foreign and unnatural. As a result, new religious movements developed, discarding many of the elements of the original religion while retaining traditional emphases, such as those on healing, trances, possessions, and dreams.

MACUMBA

Macumba is a syncretic Afro-Brazilian religion consisting of a wide range of different elements. Despite attempts by the more mainstream Christian churches to combat its growth, its popularity continues to increase. Macumba has a number of sects, the two most important of which are Umbanda and Candomblé.

Umbanda is widely practised in urban areas, such as Rio de Janeiro and São Paulo. It incorporates elements of the Yoruba religion of Nigeria, from which it derives its name for the Supreme Being (*olôrun*: 'one who owns the sky'), and combines these with Hindu and Buddhist influences, indigenous Amerindian practices, and folk Catholicism. The estimated number of Umbanda adherents in 1980 was 33 million.

Candomblé, which is prevalent in the Bahía region, is regarded as the most distinctly African of the Macumba sects, involving frequent sacrifice, ecstatic dancing, and the leading of rites by a spirit medium in a trancelike state. Catholic saints are given African names.

▲ **Ritual Dance in a Macumba Ceremony**
A woman dancer in an ecstatic trance.

In sub-Saharan Africa, new religious movements are widespread. Recent estimates suggest that there are more than 10 000 separate movements involving between 10 and 12 million active participants. Similar movements have developed among indigenous peoples in many parts of the world, including North America, the Caribbean, parts of South America, New Zealand, and Melanesia. More recently, new religions have arisen in Asia, notably Korea, where over 200 have developed over the past century.

These movements are classified as follows: **neoprimal** – those that largely retain the original indigenous religion but borrow from the invading religion; **synthetist** – those that reject both the original and the foreign religions and build a new composite one; **Hebraist** – those that resemble the religion of Israel as presented in the Hebrew scriptures; and **independent churches** – those that incorporate some form of faith in Jesus Christ.

Independent churches are subdivided further into **orthodox separatists** (also called 'African' or 'Ethiopian' churches), which have broken away from the founding mission churches, such as the Baptists or Anglicans; **prayer-healing churches** (or 'Zionists'), which stress healing by prayer and faith and use dreams, visions, prophecies, and possession by the Holy Spirit; **syncretist churches**, which fuse Christian and traditional elements.

Most new religious movements have a founder who has received a revelation, often in the form of a dream or through a mystical experience. For example, Simon Kimbangu of Zaïre (then the Belgian Congo) experienced visions of healing; this led to life imprisonment in 1921 by the Belgian authorities. After his death in 1951, his youngest son organized the Kimbanguist Church, which merged traditional African features with Christianity. A current example of a religious founder is the Prophetess Juliana Chikoto of Zimbabwe, who claims to have been taken by a mermaid under the water in a pool for many years, where she was taught traditional morality and the Bible.

Voodoo. Voodoo, which developed among west African slaves, is an example of a synthetist movement that combines primal religious practices with a number of aspects of Roman Catholicism. Voodoo is most widespread on the island of Haiti, but it is also practised in other parts of the Caribbean, the southern states of the USA, and Brazil. Its central religious activity involves possession by African deities for the purposes of healing, protecting against evil forces, or bringing good or evil to individuals and communities. Voodoo rituals have incorporated Roman Catholic saints, follow the Catholic liturgical calendar, and relate to a hierarchy of spirits consistent with both traditional African and Catholic cosmologies.

The Unification Church

Unlike primal religions, new religious movements often become missionary, spreading beyond where they were founded. An example is the Unification Church, founded in 1954 in South Korea by Sun Myung Moon (1920–). Moon claimed that Jesus and other religious leaders had instructed him to unite the world into one family.

Judaism

*Early Jewish history • Rabbinic Judaism • The medieval period • Kabbalah •
Modern Judaism • Jewish beliefs and practices • The Principles of Faith •
Feasts and fasts*

covenant (Hebrew *berit*)
A form of contract made
between God and the
Israelites. In return for
obedience to the law
(Torah) as delivered to
Moses, the Israelites were
promised a privileged
relationship with God, as
His chosen people.

Judaism is the oldest of the monotheistic religions. It is at the same time either actually or nominally the faith of the Jewish people, who number between 14 and 15 million throughout the world.

Early Jewish History

The Biblical Period. Jews trace their origin and their religion to the patriarch Abraham. The story of Abraham's acceptance of God's call is recorded in the Old Testament (which Jews refer to as the Hebrew Bible). Abraham's grandson Jacob, whose name was changed by God to Israel, became the father of 12 sons, traditionally the ancestors of the 12 tribes of Israel. After centuries of slavery in Egypt, Jacob's descendants, now grown in size to a people, were led to freedom by Moses into the promised land, the Exodus from Egypt. At Mount Sinai in the wilderness, the people as a whole experienced a divine revelation and entered into a **covenant** with God – a relationship of mutual responsibility, loyalty, and love. This covenant included a promise by God to Moses to grant them a new land in which to create a new society under God.

The Old Testament records the conquest of the land of Palestine and the subsequent

THE DIASPORA

The term 'diaspora' (from Greek: 'scattering') denotes the dispersal of the Jewish people outside Israel. It began with the Babylonian exile, with small Jewish communities existing in Babylon and Egypt throughout antiquity. In the Middle Ages Jews spread to Spain and France and in later centuries to eastern Europe and North Africa. In the 19th century many Jews moved to the USA from Poland and Russia in order to escape persecution; after the Holocaust, which destroyed many old European Jewish communities, the two main centres for Jews became the new State of Israel (about 4 million) and the USA (about 5 million).

establishment of a kingdom under King David, in about 1000 BC. David's son Solomon built the Temple in Jerusalem as the central place for religious worship. The kingdom subsequently divided into two parts. The Northern Kingdom of Israel was destroyed by the Assyrians in 721 BC, and the population was deported, never to return, giving rise to the legend of the Ten Lost Tribes. The Southern Kingdom of Judah (from which the word 'Jew' is derived), with its capital in Jerusalem, was conquered by the Babylonians in 586 BC and King Solomon's Temple was destroyed. After the 70 years of the Babylonian exile, the Jewish people returned to re-establish their community. The biblical record ends shortly after this, but Jews continued to live in this territory under successive empires (Persian, Greek, and Roman). The Temple was rebuilt only to be destroyed again by the Romans in 70 AD, following a Jewish rebellion. Thereafter, Jews were banned from living in Jerusalem and were expelled from the land, though a small presence was maintained throughout later centuries.

◀ **Worshippers at the Western Wall in
Jerusalem** *The Western Wall forms the boundary of
the Temple Mount, site of both the First and the Second
Temples. It is a sacred place of prayer and pilgrimage for
Jews throughout the world.*

▲ **The First Temple** *This artist's impression shows the Temple built by King Solomon (c. 950 BC), and destroyed by the Babylonians in 586 BC.*

Rabbinic Judaism

The second period of Jewish life, or **Diaspora**, saw the origins of what were to become key elements in the subsequent Jewish religion.

With the destruction of the first Temple and its sacrificial cult, a fixed daily liturgy and private prayer became the new way of relating to God, both as a community and as individuals. The sacrificial altar was symbolically replaced by the family table, with the father of the household substituting for the priest as the prayer leader for domestic services and rituals.

Though Jewish fast days and liturgies continued to mourn the destruction of the Temple and pray for its restoration, a new centre of Jewish religious and community life was gradually established – the synagogue. Its three Hebrew titles indicate its nature: *Bet Tefillah*, the House of Prayer; *Bet Knesset*, House of Assembly, where all communal gatherings took place and wayfarers could stay; *Bet Hamidrash*, House of Study, where the traditional religious texts could be studied and interpreted.

During this same period the nature of religious leadership also changed. In the biblical period, the ritual life of the people was regulated by the hereditary priesthood. It was believed that the will of God was conveyed to the people by 'prophets,' ranging from visionaries and ecstatics to 'professionally trained' court prophets, traditionally employed to foresee the outcome of particular ventures. From their ranks unique individuals arose who sought to safeguard the religious integrity of their society and whose teachings are recorded in the named prophetic books of the Old Testament. In the post-biblical period, the rabbis emerged as the new spiritual leaders of the community, as interpreters of the tradition, and as teachers and judges. Their authority was not inherited but derived from their religious learning. The rabbinic movement, from its beginnings in about the 1st century BC, effectively created the pattern of post-biblical Judaism that still exists.

The Torah – Written and Oral. Central to rabbinic Judaism is the ***Torah***, the teaching given to Moses at Sinai. Beside this written Torah, contained in the first five books of the Old Testament (the Pentateuch), the rabbis taught that God gave to Moses an oral Torah, a complementary set of laws covering all aspects of life. These two essential parts of the one Torah constituted the eternally valid word of God, to be constantly studied and reinterpreted. This oral tradition was codified in writing in the **Mishnah** at the end of the 2nd century AD and subsequently debated and commented upon in the ***Talmud***, with its two versions: the Jerusalem Talmud, or *Yerushalmi*, completed about 400 AD, and the Babylonian Talmud, or *Bavli*, completed 100–300 years later. The latter is considered authoritative. The Talmud, covering both religious and civil matters, contains a mixture of laws, customs, religious debates, stories, and favourite sayings of the rabbis. Though apparently diffuse, it is constructed with its own logic and has been the central document for religious learning in the *Yeshivot*, the traditional Jewish study academies. In a parallel development, Jewish analysis and interpretation of the Old Testament created a series of collections of **Midrash**, which reflected attempts to understand the will of God in changing contemporary situations.

Mishnah (Learning) The codification of the oral Torah, consisting of rabbinic decisions and interpretations and forming the basis of the Talmud. It was compiled by Judah HaNasi in the 2nd century AD.

Midrash (Explanation) Rabbinic interpretation of either legal (Midrash Halachah) or homiletical (Midrash Haggadah) character, sometimes expressed in parables.

◄ **A Torah Scroll** *In Hebrew, Torah means 'teaching.' As a biblical term it came to mean the whole content of the word of God revealed to Moses at Mount Sinai. Readings are given from the Torah scroll in synagogue services.*

▲ **Theodor Herzl**
(1860–1904) A Hungarian-born journalist and writer, Herzl founded the movement known as **Zionism***, which campaigned for a Jewish homeland. In 1896, he wrote the work* Der Judenstaat *('The Jewish State'), which advocated the establishment of a world council for the foundation of a Jewish state. Herzl never saw his vision realized during his lifetime.*

Ushpizin Prayer ▶
This prayer forms part of the Kabbalistic tradition of mysticism in Judaism, and commemorates the seven biblical figures who are believed to visit the tabernacle erected during the autumnal festival of Sukkoth.

The Medieval Period

The Codification of Jewish Law. In the medieval period, the need to establish a standard Jewish practice for diverse Jewish communities that were widely scattered led to the creation of a series of comprehensive legal codes, culminating in the *Shulchan Aruch* (the Prepared Table), compiled by Joseph Caro (1488–1575), and published in Venice in 1565. Subsequent adaptations of the law to changing circumstances were decided by individual rabbis of recognized learning and authority, in *Teshuvot* (Responsa).

Judaism still has no central religious authority, each rabbi being independent. Orthodox communities operate a *Beth Din*, a Jewish law court, made up of three *dayanim*, 'judges,' rabbis with particular expertise in Jewish law, to deal with Jewish legal disputes. Larger orthodox communities may appoint a 'Chief Rabbi' for a particular region.

Ashkenazim and Sephardim. Following the destruction of the second Temple, Jews migrated throughout the Roman Empire. Under Roman law they were granted freedom of religion and permitted to deal with internal matters under their own Jewish law. Much of this freedom was lost, however, when the Empire became Christian. Jewish history and religious development until the 17th and 18th centuries were deeply influenced by the experience of living as a minority under both Christianity, frequently involving persecution and expulsion, and Islam, where a greater tolerance was experienced. During the Middle Ages, Jews in Germany and east European

countries, where the Judaeo-German vernacular, Yiddish, was spoken, became known as ***Ashkenazim*** (the word comes from Genesis 10:3 and was identified in the Middle Ages as Germany). Those living in Spain, Portugal, and Provence were known as ***Sephardim***. This name, also from the Bible (Obadiah 20), denoted an unknown place where Jewish exiles from Jerusalem had settled, and which medieval scholars identified as Spain. Sephardim speak Ladino, a mixture of Hebrew and Spanish. These two main branches of the Jewish world differ in their pronunciation of Hebrew and in details of liturgy and religious customs.

In addition, many other communities of Jews exist in various parts of the world, and have often been assimilated into the local population. For example, until this century there was a community of Chinese Jews in Kaifeng; the 'Falashas' are a black ethnic group in Ethiopia, who claim to be of Jewish origin, descended from King Solomon and the Queen of Sheba.

Kabbalah

Besides the intellectual and legal traditions of Judaism there has existed a mystical trend referred to generally as *Kabbalah* (Hebrew: tradition). In the early rabbinic period there are references to mystical teachings about the creation and the 'divine chariot' described in Ezekiel (Chapter 1). The best-known Kabbalistic work is the *Zohar* (Splendour), a commentary on the Pentateuch, traditionally ascribed to the 2nd-century Rabbi Simeon bar Yochai but more probably the work of Moses de Leon in the 13th century. As well as seeking an esoteric meaning to the biblical texts, it encompasses astrology, the transmigration of souls, angelology, and *gematria* (the adding of the numerical values of the Hebrew letters to create relationships between words and ideas). In the Middle Ages, in addition to mystical speculation, a practical Kabbalah appeared, which aimed at mastering the secret name of God to acquire wonder-working powers.

In the 16th century in Safed, Galilee, Kabbalistic thought was transformed by the teachings of Isaac Luria (1534–72) and his circle. Through *tzimtzum* (Hebrew: contract), God allows room for creation to take place. In this process the 'vessels' containing the divine light are shattered, enabling chaos and evil to enter the world; this depraved world requires a process of *tikkun*, 'repair,' which includes overcoming the exile of the Jewish people and also the mystic exile of the *shechinah*, the indwelling presence of God. This mystical speculation became messianic zeal for the physical return of the Jewish people to the land of Israel. Luria's ideas later reappeared in an internalized quietist form within the Chassidic movement.

Modern Judaism

Though Jews are scattered throughout the world, a Jewish identity was preserved until modern times by a shared belief in God, underpinned by common traditions. These traditions included a universally binding legal system, *Halachah*, as well as a common language (Hebrew) for prayer and a common liturgy. The central basis for this Jewish identity has undergone considerable change since the period of Jewish emancipation. As Jews have become citizens in increasingly more secular societies, the binding authority of the specifically Jewish law has weakened. Jews may now interpret their Jewishness in widely differing ways, ranging from the strictly Orthodox to the purely secular. Moreover, this sense of Jewish identity may change with circumstances within the lifetime of the individual. In addition to the various groupings that consider themselves Orthodox (as strict adherents of traditional Jewish law), non-Orthodox religious communities (variously designated as Conservative, Reconstructionist, Reform, Liberal, or Progressive) make a synthesis between classical Jewish tradition and contemporary values. The majority of these religious Jews, in spite of their differences of emphasis, share fundamental beliefs, such as the unity of God, the centrality of the covenant, the special calling of the Jewish people, and the significance of the land of Israel. In addition, however, there are many secular Jews, proud of their ethnic origins, who are unable to accept the tenets of the religion.

Anti-Semitism, the Holocaust (Shoah), and the State of Israel. Though the word 'anti-Semitism' was only coined in the 19th century, it has come to stand for the irrational hatred of Jews that has been manifest throughout two millennia. It has found its expression in different times and places in ways that range from prejudice and discrimination to anti-Jewish legislation, riots, and ***pogroms*** ('pogrom,' a Russian term for devastation, describes the organized attacks against Jews common in 19th-century Russia).

Ultimately, in the 20th century, this hatred turned to genocide. No survey of the Jewish religion can ignore the impact of the Holocaust, known to Jews by the Hebrew word *Shoah* (destruction). During the 12 years of the Third Reich, from 1933 to 1945, the Nazis murdered more than five million Jews, approximately one-third of the then world Jewish population. The trauma of the Holocaust continues to affect not only second- and third-generation offspring of survivors of the concentration camps but has also left the whole civilized world with an insoluble enigma. How could it have occurred? It is hardly surprising that since the Holocaust some Jews have lost

ANTI-SEMITISM

Hostility against Jews has a long history. It began with the Diaspora, and is experiencing a resurgence in the late 20th century. Such is the irrational nature of anti-Semitism that despite the Holocaust, it continues to recur, even in places where virtually no Jewish community exists. The hatred that is fomented is usually exploited for political ends.

Since medieval times, European Jews have been persecuted by expulsion (England 1290, France 1306, Spain 1492), massacres (Germany 1348, Spain 1391), Inquisition (Spain 1478), ghettos (15th-century Italy and 19th-century Poland), pogroms (19th-century Russia), and genocide (20th-century Germany and Nazi-occupied Europe).

◄ **Caricature of a Jew** *This 18th-century French engraving shows a Jewish stereotype – the figure of the 'Wandering Jew.' According to legend, he was condemned to wander the earth until Judgment Day for rebuking Christ on the way to his crucifixion, telling him to carry the cross faster. Anti-Semitic caricatures have a long history, being used since the Middle Ages to stir up hatred against Jews.*

their belief in a God who apparently abandoned them to destruction; contemporary Jewish theologians and those whose faith remains intact are left to wrestle with the question of ***theodicy***, the attempt to justify God's attributes and actions while at the same time recognizing the existence of evil in the world.

With the creation of the State of Israel in 1948, a new epoch of Jewish life began. The existence again of a national homeland, Jewish sovereignty, and the experience of taking responsibility for the running of a society present enormous challenges to a religious community used to being a powerless minority seeking to accommodate itself to external powers. Israel Independence Day is celebrated as a religious festival.

The creation of the State of Israel also represents the reversal of 2000 years of Jewish experience and history. As it continues to develop its own culture and identity, new kinds of relationship between the Jews of the Diaspora and the whole non-Jewish world will continue to evolve.

Jewish Beliefs and Practices

Central to Jewish belief is the covenant with God and the special task for which they see themselves as having been chosen. However, Judaism does not teach that it represents the *only* way to reach God; indeed, it insists that all peoples can have a relationship with God

Kosher

The Old Testament contains regulations about the animals that Jews may eat; those permitted, for example, both chew the cud and have a cloven hoof. The origins of these dietary laws are obscure but animals that have only one but not both of these characteristics are excluded, as are all kinds of animals that hunt or scavenge. Since it is forbidden to eat the blood of the animal, only a permitted animal that has been correctly ritually slaughtered is considered 'kosher' (Hebrew: clean). Only those fish having fins and scales may be eaten, which excludes all shellfish.

The Thirteen Principles of the Jewish Faith

These beliefs are the articles of faith of Orthodox Judaism.

 1 God exists
 2 God is one
 3 God is incorporeal
 4 God is eternal
 5 God alone is to be worshipped
 6 Prophecy exists
 7 Moses was the greatest prophet
 8 The Torah was given by God
 9 The Torah, both oral and written, is authentic
10 God knows all that human beings do
11 God will reward the just and punish transgressors
12 The Messiah will come
13 The dead will be resurrected

through their own religious paths. This plurality is expressed in the concept of the 'Seven Laws of the Sons of Noah,' seven universal religious duties given to the descendants of Noah prior to the election of Abraham. With minor variations they include: prohibition of idolatry, blasphemy, bloodshed, sexual sins, theft, and eating the flesh taken from a living animal, as well as the positive command to ensure justice for all by creating a just legal system.

A Jew is defined in Jewish law as someone born of a Jewish mother (matrilineal) or who becomes a Jew through a recognized process of conversion. Whereas in the early rabbinic period conversion to Judaism was common, under Christianity and Islam the life of the convert and the converting rabbi might be forfeited; thereafter, Jews became more cautious about accepting converts. Judaism is not a proselytizing religion. Nevertheless, it is possible to enter the Jewish community through a process (lasting from one to five years) that assesses the sincerity and Jewish knowledge of the would-be convert. Further requirements are **circumcision** for a man and immersion in a ritual bath (*Mikveh*) for men and women. Family life is extremely important to Jews, and traditional ceremonies mark the key stages of life. At the age of 13, Jewish boys pass through the ceremony of ***Bar Mitzvah*** (Hebrew: son of the commandment), after which they become responsible for their actions under Jewish law.

Marriage (often 'arranged' in strictly Orthodox communities) is another key ceremony. It consists of three elements: the reading of

circumcision On the eighth day following their birth, all Jewish boys are ritually circumcised as a sign of the covenant that God established with Abraham:
And God said to Abraham…this is my covenant, which you shall keep between you and your seed after you. Every man child among you shall be circumcised. (Genesis 17: 9–14).

Jewish Wedding under a *Chuppah* ▶
The canopy in this ceremony symbolizes the bridal bower.

the wedding contract (*ketubah*), the declaration ('Behold you are married to me with this ring, according to the Law of Moses and Israel.'), and the seven blessings recited over the couple by the rabbi. Blessing the home and mourning customs after a death are other family rituals that form an important part of Jewish life.

However, most Jews now make their own private 'anthology' of Jewish practices, depending on the community in which they live. The openness of society has also meant that some Jews marry non-Jews with a consequent erosion of Jewish customs in the next generation.

The non-Orthodox religious movements, in addition to maintaining Jewish tradition in modified ways, strive to treat men and women equally. Whereas in the traditional marriage ceremony it is the man alone who makes a declaration, a non-Orthodox ceremony will include a reciprocal declaration. Similarly most non-Orthodox movements have a **Bat Mitzvah** ceremony for girls and many have introduced a 'naming ceremony' as a way of marking the birth of a daughter. New ceremonies that relate more specifically to aspects of a woman's life cycle have been introduced.

The Principles of Faith

Judaism rarely expresses itself in terms of dogmas, beyond that of the unity of God. Instead, Jewish beliefs tend to be perceived through actual conduct and religious practice. The Ten Commandments are seen as a central part of the divine revelation at Sinai, and contain the key to Jewish values. Nevertheless, in the rabbinic view all parts of the Torah are of equal value as the word of God and rabbis resisted attempts to give the Ten Commandments any liturgical prominence, suggesting that they might represent either the whole or the essence of Judaism.

Moses Maimonides (1135–1204), the great Jewish philosopher and codifier of Jewish law, derived a codification known as the **Thirteen Principles of Faith**. Based on Muslim prototypes, they marked a first attempt at a Jewish statement of faith and became the source of much controversy. However, a version was eventually included in the liturgy and, in the form of a hymn, forms part of the closing section of the Sabbath evening service.

Messiah and the Messianic Age. The Old Testament contains two visions of the future: one includes the restoration of Jewish national sovereignty in the land of Israel under a leader, who will be a descendant of King David; the other prophesies that all nations will turn to Israel's God in Jerusalem and that this will bring about an era of universal justice and peace. These two visions are expressed in Rabbinic thought in the title 'Messiah' (from the

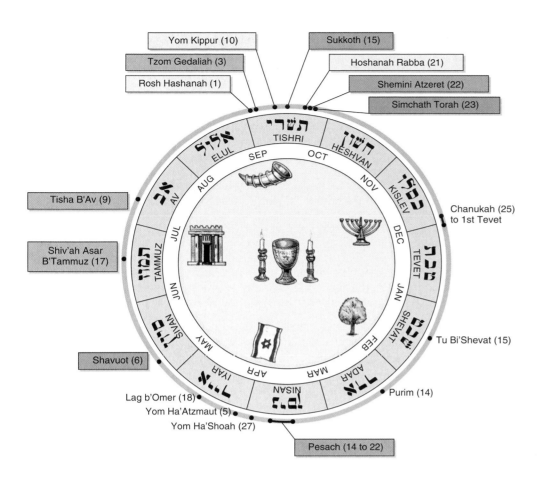

Yom Kippur (10)

Tzom Gedaliah (3)

Rosh Hashanah (1)

Sukkoth (15)

Hoshanah Rabba (21)

Shemini Atzeret (22)

Simchath Torah (23)

Tisha B'Av (9)

Shiv'ah Asar B'Tammuz (17)

Shavuot (6)

Lag b'Omer (18)

Yom Ha'Atzmaut (5)

Yom Ha'Shoah (27)

Pesach (14 to 22)

Chanukah (25) to 1st Tevet

Tu Bi'Shevat (15)

Purim (14)

ELUL · TISHRI · HESHVAN · KISLEV · TEVET · SHEVAT · ADAR · NISAN · IYAR · SIVAN · TAMMUZ · AV

SEP · OCT · NOV · DEC · JAN · FEB · MAR · APR · MAY · JUN · JUL · AUG

The Jewish Calendar *The relation of the months to those of the Gregorian calendar and the overlapping cycles of festivals are shown. Between the Jewish New Year and the Day of Atonement lie the* **Ten Days of Penitence**, *during which people are supposed to make amends with those they have wronged and generally restore proper human relationships. If this has been done, then the tenth day takes away the sins committed between individuals and God.*

Pilgrim festivals

Penitential season

Fast days

Torah cycle

Hebrew 'anointed with oil,' a ceremony used at the induction of biblical kings, priests, and prophets). The Messiah is seen as a human political leader through whom God will fulfil both of these visions. Throughout Jewish history there have been a number of claimants to this position. The most famous of these were Jesus of Nazareth, Bar Kochba (died 135 AD; he led an unsuccessful revolt against Roman rule), and Shabbatai Zevi (the 17th-century claimant whose conversion to Islam to save his life had catastrophic effects on large parts of the Jewish world).

There is currently a major debate about the messianic implications of the creation of the State of Israel. Some Orthodox groups reject the State as a human attempt to pre-empt God's work. The cautious position of the Israeli Chief Rabbinate is conveyed in the Prayer for the State, which includes the phrase 'the beginning of the sprouting of our redemption.'

Feasts and Fasts

The Sabbath and New Moon. The Jewish sense of time is largely conditioned by its Festival Calendar. A 'day' runs from sunset to sunset, so that all Sabbaths and festivals begin in the evening. The biblical pattern of six days of work followed by a day of rest, established in Genesis (Chapter 1), imposes a regular timescale upon human activity, irrespective of the season. The seventh day, the Sabbath (*Shabbat*), is considered the most important of the festivals – a day to stop all toil and labour and to seek spiritual renewal.

The Jewish calendar is lunisolar: the months are calculated according to the moon, and the years according to the sun. As there are 11 days left over after each 12 months, an extra month is added every four years to ensure that the annual cycle of festivals keep their original relationship to the harvest seasons.

The New Moon (*Rosh Chodesh*, literally 'the head of the month') is a minor festival, with special additions to the daily service.

The Pilgrim Festivals. The most obvious cycle consists of the three Pilgrim Festivals. These coincided with the end of the winter barley harvest, the late spring wheat harvest, and the autumn ingathering of fruit. From an early period these three festivals became linked with three key historical events of the biblical period: Passover (*Pesach*) with the Exodus from Egypt; Pentecost (*Shavuot*; 50 days later) with the Revelation at Sinai; and The Feast of Tabernacles (*Sukkoth*) with the wandering in the wilderness.

On the eve of Passover, a family meal with prayers (the *seder*) is held; the *Haggadah* (narration) recounting the story of the Exodus

Tu Bi'Shevat This minor festival is first mentioned in the Mishnah, in which it was designated as the beginning of the New Year for the purpose of collecting tithes. In modern Israel, the holiday is marked with the planting of saplings.

Orthodox and Non-Orthodox Jews

The most visible Orthodox Jewish groups belong to the *Chassidim*, a popular pietist and mystical movement that developed in eastern Europe in the 18th century. Their time and place of origin is often reflected in their clothing. Of these groups, the Lubavitch Chassidim, now based in New York, are the most zealous in encouraging Jews to return to traditional ways.
In contrast, various non-Orthodox movements have taken the lead in pioneering reform, such as the ordination of women.

The Traditional *Seder* Meal *This ritual meal commemorates the start of the festival of Passover. Some Jews lay an extra place for the prophet Elijah, who, should he appear at the meal, will signal the imminent coming of the Messiah.* ▼

from Egypt is read. Bitter herbs are eaten to symbolize the distress of slavery and *matzo*, unleavened bread, eaten throughout the eight days of the festival, is a reminder that the Israelites left in such haste that there was no time to bake proper bread. Thus each Jew is supposed to consider him or herself as having personally come out of Egypt, from slavery to freedom. The festival's liturgy includes the reading of the biblical Song of Songs, understood as expressing the love of God and Israel.

Pentecost occurs seven weeks after Passover. Dairy foods are eaten, symbolizing the sweetness of the Torah. Traditionally young children began their Jewish studies on this day. The biblical Book of Ruth is read, partly because the events it records take place at this harvest season, and partly because Ruth is an 'outsider' who chose to enter into the covenant with Israel's God. The festival anticipates the coming of the Messiah, descended from King David, who, in the traditional view, was born and died on this day.

In the autumn The Feast Of Tabernacles (*Sukkoth*) is celebrated in a temporary shelter (*sukkah*) attached to the side of the house. This recalls the makeshift shelter in the wilderness, protected from the elements only by divine providence. This *sukkah*, which is open to the sky, is decorated with fruit as a reminder of the harvest. The biblical book is Ecclesiastes, whose world-weary wisdom accords with the autumnal mood of the festival.

Rejoicing in the Law (Simchath Torah).

A second cycle overlaps with the autumn festival – the weekly Torah reading in the synagogue. In the Ashkenazi tradition the entire Pentateuch is read in the year. On *Simchath Torah*, the cycle is completed and the Book of Genesis is begun again. This celebration coincides with the end of *Sukkoth*, extending the festival by an extra day (two days in Diaspora). All the Torah scrolls in the synagogue are paraded to chanting and singing and particular members are honoured as Bridegroom (also Bride in non-Orthodox circles) of the Torah (who reads the closing of Deuteronomy) and of 'Bereshit' (who reads the opening of Genesis – *Bereshit*).

The Penitential Season.

A third cycle, which relates to the penitential season surrounding the autumn Festival of the New Year (*Rosh Hashanah*), is identified by rabbinic tradition as the 'birthday of the world,' when all creation is judged before God. The 'Book of Life' is opened and inspected. Those who are completely bad are written down for death, those completely good for life, but most are 'in-between.' This season, too, does not simply start on the first day of the New Year, but is prepared for by the month of 'Elul,' when a *shofar*, a ram's horn, is blown daily to call the people to repentance. Likewise the final sealing of one's fate only takes place on *hoshanah rabba*, which coincides with the end of *Sukkoth*.

Fast Days.

A cycle of fasts commemorates stages leading up to the capture of Jerusalem climaxing in the destruction of the First and Second Temples on the same day, the ninth day of the month of Av (*Tisha B'Av*). Many other disasters befell the Jewish people on that day, including their expulsion from Spain in 1492. The day is marked by reading the biblical Book of Lamentations. This sequence also impinges on the autumn festivals because the final fast day, commemorating the assassination of Gedaliah, the governor of Judah installed by the conquering Babylonian army, falls on the third day of the New Year.

Minor Festivals.

In the early spring comes *Purim* (lit. 'lots') which is based on the events recorded in the biblical Book of Esther. The central feature is the reading of the *megillat ester*, the 'scroll of Esther,' accompanied by pandemonium whenever Haman, the Persian courtier who wished to wipe out the Jews, is mentioned. A major feature of the festival is distribution of gifts to the poor.

Chanukah ('dedication'), which falls in the middle of winter, commemorates the victory of the Maccabean priests over the Greeks who had sought to impose their gods on them. The event is recorded in the First and Second Books of Maccabees, which do not form part of the Jewish biblical canon. The Talmud merely recounts a legend that when the Temple was rededicated, only enough sacred oil for one day remained. By a miracle, it lasted for eight days, hence the duration of this festival, during which a candle is lighted each day in a special eight-branched candlestick (*menorah*) to 'proclaim the miracle.'

Christianity

The life and teaching of Jesus • Jewish origins • The spread of Christianity •
Christian beliefs • Worship and prayer • Dissent and division • Modern Christianity

Christianity is the religious faith of about one-third of the world's population. It is based on the life and teachings of Jesus of Nazareth (c. 4 BC–30 AD), known as ***Jesus Christ***, as recorded in the New Testament of the **Holy Bible**. The term 'Christianity' does not describe a single unified entity but the beliefs and practices of a number of Christian churches (***denominations***) that have developed from the early Church. The main categories of denomination are the ***Roman Catholic Church***, the ***Orthodox Churches***, and the various ***Protestant Churches***. The unique feature of the Christian faith is the belief that the man Jesus was also the Son of God.

The Life and Teaching of Jesus

Knowledge of the life of Jesus comes from accounts written by his followers in the years following his death. Four of these accounts, traditionally attributed to saints Matthew, Mark, Luke, and John, are accepted as authoritative by Christians and known as the ***Gospels***. The four Gospels constitute the first four books of the New Testament. The earliest of the Gospels, the Gospel according to St Mark, is thought to have been compiled about 65–70 AD.

Although the Christian world dates the modern era from Jesus' supposed birthdate, more recent research has determined that he was in fact born between 6 and 4 BC. According to Matthew and Luke, he was born in the town of Bethlehem in Palestine (on the West Bank of the River Jordan) into a Jewish family. A census being held at the time by the Roman occupiers of Palestine required that all Jews register themselves in their ancestral home towns for the purposes of taxation. As a result, Joseph, a carpenter from Nazareth (in the

═══SEE ALSO═══
This section:
• Judaism
Early and Medieval Europe (vol. 5):
• The Catholic Church
• The Byzantine Empire
• The Crusades
Early Modern Europe (vol 5):
• The Reformation and Hapsburg Dominance

The Holy Bible

The Bible, the sacred book of Christianity, consists of the scriptures of the Old Testament (also the basis of Judaism) and those of the New Testament. Prophesies in the Old Testament are seen as foretelling the coming of Christ, as recounted in the New Testament.

◄ **The Isenheim Altarpiece**
(c.1510–15)
This work, by the German Renaissance painter Matthias Grünewald (c.1468–1528), shows the mocking inscription placed over the cross by Christ's Roman executioners. INRI stands for 'Iesus Nazarenus Rex Iudaeorum' ('Jesus of Nazareth, King of the Jews').

117

Symbols of the Four ▶ Evangelists *This illustration of the symbols is from the highly illuminated manuscript of the Gospels known as the 'Book of Kells,' which was produced in Ireland in the 8th–9th century. Ireland was one of the first strongholds of Christianity as the faith began to spread throughout western Europe.*

The 12 Apostles

The apostles (from Greek *apostolos*, meaning 'a person sent') were 12 of Jesus' chief disciples, chosen by him to preach his message. They included Lake Galilee fishermen and a tax collector. After Jesus' death, the Apostles spread his teaching throughout the Roman world. The doctrine of apostolic succession, in the Roman and Orthodox Churches, claims an unbroken line of succession in the Christian ministry from the original Apostles.

province of Galilee some 100 km north of Jerusalem) and his wife Mary travelled to Bethlehem (about 7 km south of Jerusalem), birthplace of Joseph's distant ancestor King David. During their stay, Mary gave birth to their child Jesus. Luke and Matthew state that the child was conceived not of man but of the Spirit of God, and that Mary was a virgin when she gave birth (the doctrine of the *Virgin Birth*). Matthew adds that after Jesus' birth the family fled into Egypt because King Herod, believing the long-awaited Jewish Messiah had been born and was a threat to him, had ordered all new-born boys in the province to be killed. The family later returned to Nazareth, where Jesus is presumed to have learned his father's trade. The Gospels say very little about his early life. Luke describes one incident in Jerusalem, where the 12-year-old Jesus, lost by his parents who had paid a visit to the capital, was eventually found debating lucidly with theological scholars in the temple.

When aged about 30, Jesus began his ministry of preaching and healing in Galilee, attracting huge crowds wherever he went. During this time, he selected 12 men to help him with his teaching; these men became known as the **Apostles**. Jesus' teaching was wholly concentrated on the purposes of God, the God whom the Jewish people had long worshipped as the sole creator of the universe. Jesus' acts of healing reinforced his message that God's power was at work, and his preaching posed challenging questions to people about their own choices and priorities in life. Most memorably, his teaching includes the collection of sayings known as the **Sermon on the Mount** and a series of parables about the

nature of God and His purposes towards humankind. Many of these deal with the coming of the **Kingdom of God**, a state of perfect harmony in the world that is spoken of both as a future promise and as a present possibility. It is a matter of controversy whether Jesus regarded himself as divine, although some of his recorded statements imply that he did. His teaching suggested, without ever making it explicit, that his own life and ministry represented a decisive turning-point for world history. When he eventually challenged his disciples to say how they regarded him (the crucial conversation recorded in Mark 8:27 ff.), he implicitly accepted the title 'Messiah' or **Christ** (from Greek *khristos*, meaning 'the anointed one'). However, he carefully repudiated the immediate political claim that Jews attached to the title of Messiah (see JUDAISM). He preferred to refer to himself as the 'Son of Man,' an enigmatic phrase taken from the prophecies of Daniel (7:13), where it apparently denoted the Jewish people as a whole.

Despite such caution, Jesus' ministry encountered opposition from the religious authorities, principally because it was considered seditious, and therefore likely to disrupt the delicate political accommodation that had been reached between Jewish leaders and the Roman occupying power. Jesus faced this

THE SERMON ON THE MOUNT

The Gospel of St Matthew (chapter 5) describes in detail a sermon preached by Jesus on an unidentified mountain in Galilee: this collection of sayings is usually seen as the central statement of Christ's ethical teaching. It opens with a series of proclamations known as the *Beatitudes*, listing the qualities required to enable a person to enter God's Kingdom. These include:

• Blessed are the poor in spirit: for theirs is the Kingdom of God.

• Blessed are the meek: for they shall inherit the earth.

The Beatitudes are followed by a number of exhortations that go beyond traditional Jewish teaching in their demand for moral improvement. Example of these are:

• You have heard it said, 'An eye for an eye, and a tooth for a tooth.' But I tell you this: do not resist evil, but when somebody strikes you on the right cheek, turn the other one.

• You have heard it said that you should love your neighbour and hate your enemy. But I tell you this: Love your enemies, bless those that curse you, and do good to those that hate you.

A River Baptism in Guatemala *Baptisms are performed to celebrate the acceptance of a new member into the Church. Most commonly, infants are baptized, by being marked in water with a sign of the cross on the forehead (rather than fully immersed). Throughout the world, the words spoken at the ceremony are "I baptize you in the name of the Father, and of the Son, and of the Holy Spirit."*

opposition directly by visiting the capital city, Jerusalem, for the week leading up to the important Jewish festival of Passover. He was welcomed into the city by an enthusiastic crowd and openly confronted the religious leadership by preaching in the Temple, the central holy place for the Jewish people. Aided by the treachery of one of his apostles – Judas Iscariot – a conspiracy was hatched to bring about Jesus' downfall. At a Passover meal, known as the **Last Supper**, Jesus foretold his death and exhorted his disciples to commemorate him by taking bread and wine; shortly thereafter, he was arrested, condemned by the ruling religious council, and handed over to the Roman governor, Pontius Pilate, for execution. Although reluctant to have this sentence carried out, Pilate was persuaded by pressure from the Jewish leaders, and especially by the accusation that Jesus had effectively claimed to be 'King of the Jews,' thereby defying Roman imperial authority. Jesus was crucified in the company of two thieves, at a place outside the city walls of Jerusalem, known in Hebrew as *Golgotha* ('the place of the skull').

According to the Gospels, two days after his death some of Jesus' followers visited the cave in which his body had been entombed and found that it had disappeared. Jesus then appeared to one of his followers, Mary Magdalene, and later to a group of his disciples, who had gone into hiding, and instructed them to continue his work. Christ's return from the dead is known as the **Resurrection**; the festival commemorating the event, **Easter Sunday**, is the most joyous and significant date in the Christian calendar. The Gospels state that, after making many appearances following the Resurrection, Christ ascended bodily into heaven, an event known as the **Ascension**. The news of Christ's life, death, and resurrection spread among the Jews of Judaea, among the peoples of the eastern Mediterranean (through the missionary work of St Paul), and later throughout the inhabited world.

Jewish Origins

The meaning and purpose of Jesus' ministry are bound up with the history and faith of the Jewish people of whom he was a member.

Jesus' ministry was probably inspired by that of his forerunner John the Baptist (died c. 28). In the tradition of the ascetic prophets of the desert, John appeared in the Judaean wilderness, warning of God's judgment on an unfaithful people and appealing for individuals to repent of their indifference to God and to be **baptized** (dipped under the surface of a river, to signify cleansing and rebirth to a new life). John regarded himself as the precursor of a still more important messenger of God, and saw this prophesy fulfilled when Jesus presented himself for baptism. The Gospels suggest that it was in that act that Jesus felt his vocation by the Holy Spirit confirmed – namely, to adopt, on behalf of the Jews and indeed of all humanity, the life of preaching and teaching that was to lead to his death.

The relationship with God that was so central to the life and work of Jesus can only be adequately understood within the long tradition of the patriarchs and prophets of Israel. To this, Jesus brought a new note of intimacy and immediacy by referring to God as his 'Father,' a practice that was profoundly shocking to many Jews, who saw the deity as a remote and

---

The Death of John the Baptist

Like Christ after him, John the Baptist was executed for spreading controversial views. He was imprisoned for criticizing the divorce and remarriage (to his own niece Herodias) of Herod Antipas (21 BC–39 AD), governor of Galilee and son of Herod the Great. At Herodias' urging, her daughter Salome requested from Herod, as a reward for her dancing at a feast, that John the Baptist's head be brought to her on a plate.

CHRISTIANITY'S MESSAGE OF LOVE

The concept of love is central both to the Christian understanding of God and to Christian ethics. Ideally, love towards God and towards one's fellow human being should be indivisible for the Christian. Christ himself encapsulated the ten Jewish commandments into two new ones – to love God; and to love one's neighbour:

And you shall love the Lord God with all your heart, and with all your soul, and with all your mind, and with all your strength: this is the first commandment.

And the second is similar, namely this: You shall love your neighbour as yourself. There is no other commandment greater than these.

(Mark 12: 30–31)

Similarly, St John's Gospel records Jesus's words to his disciples at the Last Supper:

A new commandment I give to you, that you love one another; even as I have loved you, that you love also one another.

St Paul, too, stressed love as the highest of all spiritual gifts, while St John penetrated to the heart of the Christian revelation:

Beloved, let us love one another: for love is of God; for everyone that loves is born of God, and knows God... for God is love.

(I John 4: 7–8)

forbidding entity. Jesus was thoroughly schooled in the Jewish scriptures, yet taught them from the perspective of direct knowledge and experience, rather than in the abstract and academic manner of the rabbis and scribes of the time. Since the earliest times, Christians have referred to the Hebrew Bible as the 'Old Testament.'

The Spread of Christianity

The message preached by the first followers of Jesus proved so attractive that they were soon having to struggle with the complexities of leading a quite new form of community – the Church (Acts 2–5). The Christian community was initially regarded as a dissident movement within Judaism. Despite tensions with the religious authorities, a definitive break did not occur until the Church began to admit Gentile converts without insisting on circumcision or adherence to Jewish ritual law.

A decisive factor in the emergence of Christianity as a world religion was the experience of a young Jew, Saul of Tarsus (c. 3–c. 64 AD), who had been commissioned to curb the spread of the new teaching into Syria. On his way to Damascus, Saul experienced a vision that persuaded him that in persecuting the Christians he was actually persecuting God's Son. As a result the most dangerous enemy of the new faith became its most ardent and successful missionary, changing his name to Paul and spreading the story of Jesus and Christianity throughout the Gentile world, even as far as Rome, to which he was eventually brought as a prisoner in chains. A key feature of Paul's teaching was the insistence that faith in Christ freed believers from slavish obedience to the Jewish law.

Before the end of the 1st century AD, the new faith had begun to spread in all directions: northwards through Syria, Mesopotamia, and Asia Minor to Armenia (whose people still consider themselves the first country to have become wholly Christian); eastwards into Arabia, Persia, and eventually throughout central Asia and into the China of the Tang dynasty in 635 AD; southwards into Egypt and Ethiopia, where the local ruler looked favourably on the faith of a shipwrecked Christian from Tyre, Frumentius, who in about 341

The Spread of Christianity up to 600 AD *The extent of the faith at the time of the First Council of Nicaea (325) and the sites of other ecumenical councils are shown.* ▼

▨	areas Christianized by 325
▢	areas Christianized by 600
○	ecumenical council
+	patriarchate

THE GROWTH OF CHRISTIANITY

Year	World population (millions)	Christians (millions)	Proportion (%)
30	169.7	0.0	0.0
100	181.5	1.0	0.6
500	193.4	43.4	22.4
1000	269.2	50.4	18.7
1500	425.3	81.0	19.0
1800	902.6	208.2	23.1
1900	1619.9	558.1	34.4
1980	4373.9	1432.7	32.8
1996	5804.1	1955.2	33.7

was made Bishop of Abyssinia by the great Patriarch Athanasius of Alexandria (c. 296–373); and westwards to Rome and throughout western Europe, as far as Ireland, most notably by St Patrick (c. 389–c. 461), who was first brought to the island from Britain as a slave. The arrival of Christianity had a lasting effect on the culture and identity of certain peoples, though this occurred in many different ways and to different extents. Often the Christian message was enacted in charitable ways: in medieval Europe religious foundations provided education, accommodation for the destitute, and care for the sick.

In later centuries the continued spread of Christianity was checked by such momentous events as the overthrow of the Western Roman Empire, the Mongol invasions, and the Muslim conquests in central Asia, North Africa, and Spain. With the Renaissance bringing new vigour in Europe, attention was turned westwards to the New World. Columbus' successful crossing of the Atlantic Ocean in 1492 led to Christianity quickly becoming widespread in the Americas. Unfortunately, as the faith at this time was inseparable from expansionist political forces, this discovery and conquest also led to racism and cruelty being perpetrated in the name of Christianity. Similarly, in conjunction with European imperialism, Christianity spread into Asia, making little impact on the great traditions of faith there, and into Africa, where it was generally received more favourably.

Christian Beliefs

Christianity has been subject to many permutations throughout the world, yet the core of the faith has remained firmly based on the doctrine of the **incarnation** – the belief that Jesus Christ was both God and Man. Belief in Christ's divinity led the early Church to formulate another distinctive doctrine, that of the **Trinity**.

Although Christianity is a religion believing in a single God, traditional (Trinitarian) Christian teaching maintains that this single God has the following three coequal aspects:

• **God the Father.** The creator of all, to whom humanity is accountable for its actions. The powers of death and **sin** (a general term for all the choices, attitudes, and actions by which human beings alienate themselves from God) will be overcome when God's kingdom comes.

• **God the Son.** The man Jesus of Nazareth, who sits at the right hand of the Father (the place of the advocate), and who represents and intercedes for humanity. Jesus is regarded as

The Trinity *The Three-in-One nature of God in Christianity is portrayed in this work (Abraham's Three Angels, c. 1411) by the Russian icon painter Andrei Rublev (c. 1360–1430).* ▼

▲ **The American Evangelist Billy Graham** *Evangelical preachers, such as Billy Graham, who spread the message of the Gospels, attract crowds as large as 250 000 to meetings throughout the world. Evangelists also use the electronic media to preach and raise funds, especially in the USA.*

Creeds

The three Christian creeds (statements of belief) are the **Apostles' Creed**, supposedly written by the Apostles; the **Nicene Creed**, compiled at the first Council of Nicaea (325 AD); and the **Athanasian Creed**, compiled by the patriarch St Athanasius (?296–373 AD)

the saviour of mankind, who won the decisive victory over the power of death by dying on the cross and rising again from the dead and who overcame human frailty by resisting sin and by remaining receptive to God even when on the cross he felt God had abandoned him. He is viewed by Christians as both wholly God and wholly man: the human being who was sent into the world to make God known in as full and definitive a way as humanity could accept. Christians believe that through Jesus they can enter into a personal relationship with God that can survive even death. Theologians sometimes speak of God the Son as existing prior to the birth of Jesus and of his having been active in the work of creation. In this context he is referred to as the **Word** or **Logos**. His incarnation in Christ is referred to as the **Word Made Flesh**.

• **God the Holy Spirit.** The invisible power of God, active from the beginning of creation. The Holy Spirit is believed to have spoken through the prophets of Israel, to have empowered Jesus at his baptism by John, and to have been shared with the Apostles after the Resurrection. According to the New Testament, the spirit descended on the Church on the day of the **Pentecost**, originally a Jewish feast held on the fiftieth day after Passover and now a major Christian festival. The Holy Spirit is considered by the Church to be its ultimate guide, inspiration, and guarantor.

Other points that are emphasized in almost all manifestations of the Christian faith include:

• **Repentance and Forgiveness.** God's forgiveness is always available, no matter how grave a person's sin. However, it is not effective until the sinner acknowledges the fault and repents. Once this has happened, a transforming renewal of life and relationships becomes possible.

• **Love.** The love of God, which received its fullest expression in Jesus, acts as the basis, inspiration, and model for human love. Love should be the most characteristic quality of the Christian and the distinctive direction in which Christians look for the purpose and fulfilment of all human life.

• **Worship and Mission.** The dual command to praise God and present to him all human cares and concerns and to devote one's time and gifts to the service of converting others.

• **The Bible.** Christians regard both testaments of the Bible as evidence of the actions of God in history and thus as the foundation for the teaching of the Church. Like many other matters of doctrine (i.e. right teaching) and of ethics (i.e. right behaviour), the Bible's authority is the subject of ongoing debate within the Church. Some Christians, known as **fundamentalists**, believe in the literal truth of everything in the Bible, while others accept that many passages must be read as poetry, fable, or symbol. **Evangelical** Christians believe that the Bible (especially the Gospels) contains God's revelation of himself in its entirety, while those belonging to the Catholic and Orthodox traditions stress the role of the Church in formulating and handing down teaching. **Liberal** Christians emphasize the role of reason and secular knowledge in interpreting the Bible, believing that however useful the definitions and **creeds** bequeathed from earlier ages, each new generation of Christians has to discover them anew.

Worship and Prayer

All Christians, and all churches, practise personal prayer and corporate worship, just as Jesus and his disciples did. Here, as in other areas, there is immense diversity. Among the many forms of Christian worship can be found the unprogrammed and largely silent waiting on God characteristic of the Society of Friends ('Quakers'); the richly colourful ceremonies of the Eastern Orthodox Churches; and the exuberantly informal services of many African churches, in which almost all the congregation participate in spontaneous worship.

Whatever the forms used, there are certain common elements of corporate worship: the praise of God for creation and thanksgiving for blessings; readings from the two testaments of the Bible; interpretation of God's word through scripture readings or sermons; prayer commending the congregation and others for whom they are concerned into God's care; and singing to heighten the emotional impact of the act of worship.

The central act of worship in most Christian churches is the **sacrament** of the **Eucharist** (from Greek *eucharista*, meaning 'thanksgiving,'), in which bread and wine are blessed and shared amongst the congregation. In this way the church remembers and re-enacts both Jesus' final meal with the disciples before his death and his triumphant meetings with them after his resurrection. This service is called the **Mass** by Roman Catholics, the **Holy Liturgy** by Orthodox Christians, and the **Lord's Supper** by Protestants.

Personal forms of worship by individual Christians are even more varied; they often involve reading from the Gospels followed by a reflective setting of the life of Jesus alongside the worshipper's own experience. Almost all Christians use the prayer that Jesus taught his disciples, known as the **Lord's Prayer** (or 'Our Father').

Dissent and Division

Division and dissent have all too often marked the history of the Christian Church. The first major cause of dispute among the early Christians concerned the extent to which Gentile converts were obliged to accept the Jewish ritual and dietary laws. In order to forestall damaging divisions, the first Church adopted the strategy of a council, in which these contentious issues could be openly discussed (Acts 15). The resulting directive was a compromise allowing for a more flexible internal discipline

▲ **Bishops of the Armenian Orthodox Church** *These are leaders of the Armenian Church, resplendent in their ornate robes. Armenia, whose Church was founded by St Gregory the Illuminator (c. 240–332), was the first nation to adopt Christianity as a state religion.*

SACRAMENTS

In Christian belief a sacrament is a ritual that acts as a visible sign of spiritual grace conferred on the believer. Two sacraments – those of the Eucharist and Baptism – are explicitly mentioned in the Gospels and are accepted by all mainstream denominations:

The Eucharist, in which bread and wine are blessed by the celebrant and shared among the congregation, is the principal sacrament of the Christian Churches. Christians believe that it was instituted at the Last Supper, when Christ used bread and wine to represent his sacrificial death and the new relationship between God and humankind that this would make possible. Most Christians believe that Christ himself is present in the sacrament, although this idea has been interpreted in many different ways. Roman Catholic teaching maintains that the substance of the bread and wine is changed into the body and blood of Christ at the moment of consecration – the doctrine of **transubstantiation**. By contrast, many Protestants hold that the bread and wine represent Christ in a purely symbolic or figurative sense. Most Orthodox Christians, Anglicans, and Lutherans believe in the **real presence** of Christ in the sacrament without accepting the language of transubstantiation.

Baptism is the sacrament in which new members of the Church are immersed in or sprinkled with water as a sign that they have been cleansed of sin and made part of the Church. While the Roman Catholic, Orthodox, Anglican, and Lutheran churches practise infant baptism, many

Protestant denominations believe that candidates for baptism should be old enough to understand the main elements of the faith.

In addition to the Eucharist and Baptism, five other sacraments are accepted by the Roman Catholic and Orthodox churches, and by many Anglicans:

Confirmation completes the initiation of a baptized Christian into the Church. In the Orthodox churches it is administered immediately after baptism, while in the Roman Catholic and Anglican churches it is reserved for those old enough to understand the faith.

Penance is the sacrament through which a Christian admits his or her sins and seeks forgiveness for them. In the Roman Catholic and Orthodox churches, the sacrament of penance involves spoken confession to a priest; this practice is also adopted in some Anglican and Lutheran churches.

Marriage is the sacrament by which a man and woman are joined in a Christian union.

Ordination is the sacrament by which men (and women in the Anglican Church) are admitted to Holy Orders, becoming a priest or deacon. The sacrament is thought to be indelible; Holy Orders remain valid even if the priest (or holder of another order) commits grave sins.

Anointing of the Sick (Extreme Unction) is a sacrament administered to the seriously ill or dying. A priest anoints the eyes, ears, nostrils, lips, hands, and feet of the person and grants absolution for his or her sins.

Pope John Paul II ▶
(1920–   )
As spiritual leader of the Roman Catholic Church (Christianity's most populous denomination) from 1978, Pope John Paul II travelled more widely than any previous pontiff. He is pictured here on a visit to Tanzania in East Africa in 1992.

The Seven Ecumenical Councils

Regarded by both the Eastern and the Western Churches as councils of the undivided Church:

325	Nicaea I
381	Constantinople I
431	Ephesus
451	Chalcedon
553	Constantinople II
680–	
81	Constantinople III
787	Nicaea II

than the Jewish law was able to offer, while remaining firm in its strictures about avoiding religious or sexual impurity.

As the Christian faith came into greater contact with the Hellenistic civilization of the Mediterranean, many other problems had to be confronted – principally new interpretations of the faith that were enthusiastically promoted by some Christian teachers but were considered heretical by others. From time to time it therefore became necessary for other councils to be held. The first of these councils brought the early bishops together at Nicaea (Iznik in modern Turkey) in 325 to decide on the opposing views of the Libyan theologian Arius (?250–?336) and the Alexandrian patriarch Athanasius. This dispute centred on the question of whether Jesus Christ was truly divine, which the Arians denied. The first Council of Nicaea drew up, as a summary of biblical and Christian teachings, the first text of what has come to be known as the **Nicene Creed**; this contained the statement that God the Son was "...of one substance with the Father..." A later council, held at Chalcedon in 451, established an agreed statement dealing with the 'two natures' of Christ. This was, however, not accepted by the majority of the bishops from beyond the borders of the Roman empire and so led to the first lasting split among Christian believers.

Despite the councils, the Eastern Church grew steadily apart from the Western Church, especially after Constantinople replaced Rome as the political capital of the Roman Empire. After the first seven councils, which both the Eastern and Western Churches consider **ecumenical** (coming to decisions authoritative for the whole Church; the word is derived from the Greek *oikumene*, meaning 'inhabited world'), it was no longer possible to bridge the gulf. In 1054 the final irreparable division of the Churches occurred in Constantinople, as a result of the addition of the so-called *filioque* clause (Latin, 'and the Son') to the Nicene Creed by the Roman Church. This stated that the Holy Spirit proceeded from both the Father *and the Son* and was never accepted by the Eastern (Orthodox) Church. The Greek patriarch and the legate of the Latin pope, Cardinal Humbert, pronounced each other excluded from recognition and thus from sharing in the sacrament of the Eucharist. This formal breach still exists. Recently, the Orthodox Churches that suffered persecution under communism have bitterly resented the reappearance of **Uniate** churches (i.e. churches that retain the forms of worship of the East while accepting the jurisdiction of the Roman pope and repudiating that of the Orthodox patriarchs).

Another fundamental division arose from the **Reformation** in Europe. This was triggered in 1517 by the quest of the German Augustinian monk, Martin Luther (1483–1546), for a deeper confidence in God's forgiving acceptance of sinners than he found in Roman Catholic teaching of the time. Convinced that salvation was open to the sinner solely through faith in Christ, Luther denied many accepted practices and institutions. Chief among these was the practice of selling

Christians in the World (1993; in millions)	
Africa	341
Asia	300
Europe	410
Latin America	443
North America	241
Oceania	23
Eurasia	112
Total	**1870**

indulgences (remissions of the temporal penalties imposed for sins that have been confessed to God). Luther, who believed passionately that scripture, and not doctrine, represented the final authority for all Christian belief, came to reject the whole notion of the Church's mediating role between God and the faithful. To make possible his ideal of a 'priesthood of all believers,' Luther produced a translation of the Latin New Testament into accessible contemporary German, so that it could be read by ordinary people. The popularity of Luther's Bible was immense and its effect far-reaching.

John Calvin (1509–64) led a comparable movement in France and Switzerland from 1533 onwards, which gained strength especially in the Netherlands, Scotland, Hungary, and Poland, while Lutheran ideas came to predominate throughout Scandinavia, in large parts of Germany, and in England. Soon 'wars of religion' were raging in much of Europe, diminishing only with the signing of such treaties as that of Westphalia in 1648 (at the conclusion of the Thirty Years' War), which decreed that each state should follow the religious allegiance of its ruler.

Each subsequent century has seen significant manifestations of the 'Protestant principle' (i.e. that people should be able to read the Bible in their own language and use their personal judgment in its interpretation and in shaping the life of their own Church). The most recent example of this is the great number of Pentecostal and African Instituted Churches that have sprung up in the course of the 20th century.

Modern Christianity

The 20th century has witnessed renewed attempts to rediscover Christ's original call to unity among his followers, by stressing that

Christianity in the Modern World
Countries that are predominantly Christian are shown coloured according to the largest denomination. The vast landmass of post-Soviet Russia is indicated as partially Orthodox in belief. ▼

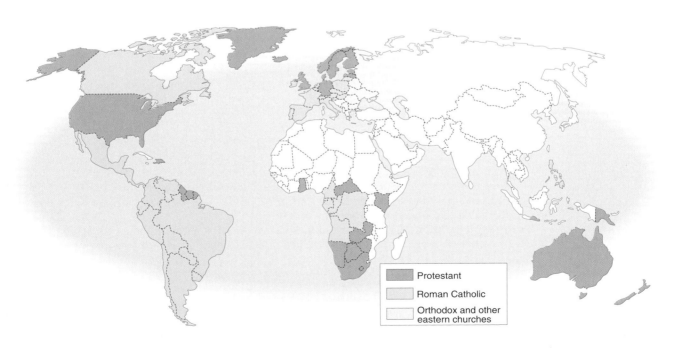

Protestant
Roman Catholic
Orthodox and other eastern churches

◀ **Religious Procession in Peru** *Believers are shown carrying a statue of Christ. Such processions are common throughout the Catholic world.*

movements inspired by the Edinburgh conference, such as 'Life and Work,' established at a Universal Conference in Stockholm in 1926, became the precursors of the World Council of Churches (WCC). The creation of such a global Christian body was agreed just before World War II but formally inaugurated only after the end of the conflict. Since then the WCC has developed a considerable programme, drawing long-separated Churches into common action and investigation of problems. In this it has been much strengthened by the reforming Second Vatican Council (1962–65) of the Roman Catholic Church.

Although Christianity is a truly worldwide religion, it is especially vibrant in Africa and in Latin America. This latter region has been responsible for new developments within the faith, such as **liberation theology**. Christianity owes its existence in these areas of the world to the influence of the missionary movement; however, the modern Christian world can no longer be divided into 'sending churches' and 'receiving churches,' as was the case when Europe was mainly responsible for the spread of the faith (roughly between the 16th and early 20th centuries). Christians of all cultures now intermingle and influence one another.

what binds Christians together is more important than any of the factors that divide them. The World Mission Conference held in Edinburgh in 1910 agreed to create an International Missionary Council, which began to give formal shape to the collaboration of Christians across denominational divides. Other

Liberation Theology

A controversial movement that arose in the Roman Catholic Church in the developing world in the 1960s and 1970s, particularly in Central and South America. Its exponents maintain that the Bible's promise of redemption must be worked out in material and social, as well as spiritual, terms. This means that the Church should actively support the poor in their struggle against political and economic oppression. Opponents argue that it substitutes a quasi-Marxist view of society for orthodox Christian teaching.

THE CHRISTIAN YEAR AND MAJOR FESTIVALS

Advent: Four weeks leading up to Christmas

Christmas (December 25): The birth of Jesus

Epiphany (January 6): Jesus is shown to the wise men; many churches also celebrate the baptism of Jesus on this day

Ash Wednesday (before the first of 6 Sundays before Easter): A day of penitence and self-denial, the first day of Lent

Lent: Six weeks of reflection, penitence, and often of fasting, preparing for Holy Week (which includes the next three festivals)

Palm Sunday (6th in Lent): Jesus enters into Jerusalem

Good Friday: Jesus dies on the cross

Easter Day (first Sunday after the full moon after the spring equinox of the northern hemisphere): Jesus rises to new life

Ascension Day (Thursday, 40 days after Easter): Jesus returns to the Father

Pentecost (Sunday after Ascension Day): The Holy Spirit empowers the Church

Additional feasts observed by the Catholic and Orthodox Churches and by some Anglican congregations include:

The Purification of the Virgin Mary (February 2; also referred to as **Candlemas** and the **Presentation of the Lord**): Commemoration of Mary's presentation of Jesus in the temple 40 days after his birth

The Annunciation (March 25): The angel's announcement to Mary that she would bear the Christ child

Corpus Christi (Thursday after Trinity Sunday): Celebrates the institution of the Eucharist

The Assumption (August 15): Mary's death and bodily assumption into Heaven

MAJOR CHRISTIAN DENOMINATIONS

Denomination	Membership (millions; 1995 est.)	Foundation	Authority	Organization and ministry	Characteristic beliefs and practices
Roman Catholics	1058	Traditionally, by Christ when he named St Peter the rock on which he would found his Church (Matthew 16:18–20). Imperial Rome was converted in the 4th century.	Tradition, as partly recorded in scripture and expressed in church councils. The pope has supreme authority when speaking in matters of faith and morals.	Episcopal with cardinals headed by the pope. Celibate male clergy.	Seven sacraments; transubstantiation; emphasis on the role of the Virgin Mary as intercessor.
Orthodox	174	Broke with Roman Church in 1054, after centuries of doctrinal disputes.	Scripture, tradition, and the church councils up to the second Nicaea Council (787). Bishops have authority in doctrine and policy.	Several autonomous episcopal churches; bishops elect a patriarch, archbishop, or metropolitan. Male clergy; priests may marry but bishops are celibate.	Seven sacraments; Holy Spirit proceeds from God the father only; veneration of icons.
Anglicans (Protestants)	78	Henry VIII separated English Catholic Church from Rome (1534). The US equivalent is the Protestant Episcopal Church (founded 1789).	Scripture as interpreted by tradition, especially the 39 *Articles* (1563).	Episcopal; male or female priests, who may marry.	Wide spectrum of belief from Catholic to Evangelical and liberal.
Lutherans (Protestants)	75	Martin Luther in Wittenberg, Germany, objected to Catholic sale of indulgences; break complete by 1519.	Scripture; Augsburg Confession (1530) and other creeds.	Varies from church to church but mainly congregational (i.e. each congregation is self-governing). Title of bishop retained in Sweden and Denmark.	Salvation by faith; infant baptism; Eucharist (Lord's Supper) retained but transubstantiation rejected.
Baptists (Protestants)	36	John Smyth led English separatists (1609) and Roger Williams (1639) led US movement.	Scripture; fundamentalist beliefs held by some.	Congregational. All believers regarded as equal.	No creeds. Adult baptism by immersion. Lord's Supper.
Methodists (Protestants)	20	John Wesley founded movement (1738) in England. First US church, Baltimore (1784).	Scripture; 25 Articles taken from Anglican 39.	No priests. Superior officers of the church are known as superintendents.	Lord's Supper. Baptism of infants or adults.
Presbyterians (Protestants)	2	16th-century Calvinist reformers differed with Lutherans over sacraments and church government. John Knox founded Scotch Presbyterian Church (1560).	Scripture.	Ministers and lay people known as presbyters.	Infant baptism; Christ's spiritual presence in the Lord's Supper symbolized by bread and wine.

Islam

The Prophet Mohammed • Muslim beliefs and practices • The expansion of Islam • Sunni and Shia • Islamic culture • Modern Islam

Islam Term deriving from the Arabic *'aslama*, meaning submitting (to the will of Allah and the message of his prophet, Mohammed).

Islam is the faith of around one-fifth of the world's population. It is a monotheistic religion, that is, one in which a single God is worshipped. The word for God is Allah; followers of Islam are called **Muslims**. Islam is the dominant faith in the Middle East but the countries that have the largest populations of Muslims are Indonesia, Bangladesh, Pakistan, India, and Nigeria.

The Prophet Mohammed

Mohammed was born in the wealthy Arabian trading city of Mecca around the year 570 AD. His father died before his birth, his mother died when he was six, and the grandfather who subsequently cared for him died two years later; thus, despite an aristocratic lineage, he had a harsh childhood. As a young man he travelled widely as a camel driver and later as a merchant, earning the name 'Al-Amin' ('The Trustworthy') for his fair dealing. After marrying his employer, a prosperous widow named Khadija, he had the option of a life of ease, but – unsettled by the exploitation,

corruption, and superstitions of the Arab life around him – he took to meditation and fasting in the mountains outside his native city.

In Islamic tradition, the angel Gabriel appeared to Mohammed as he lay shivering in a cave on Mount Hira. Fearing first that he might have lost his wits, he spontaneously recited, in poetry of great brilliance, what he later interpreted as messages from God; convinced by the power of his own verse, he realized that he had a mission to preach. It was, however, three years before he began to proclaim his revelations.

Mohammed's opposition to social injustices and his challenge to the traditional religion and hierarchy made him increasingly unpopular in Mecca; in 622 he led his band of devoted followers into exile at the oasis of Yathrib (modern Medina), whose feuding clans had invited him to be their arbitrator. This event, the **Hijra** (breaking of ties), is regarded by Muslims as the start of the Islamic calendar.

From Medina, Mohammed launched a campaign of armed conflict against the Meccans,

Dome of the Rock ▶
The octagonal mosque in Jerusalem erected in 691 by Abd al-Malik on the Temple Mount, around the rock from which Mohammed is traditionally believed to have ascended to heaven. It is one of the few remaining buildings of the Umayyad dynasty (630–750). The Temple Mount has been sacred to three religions: for the Jews, it was the site of the first and second Temples; and during the Crusades it became a Christian church, reverting to Islam after the Ottoman conquest (1517).

which ended in complete victory for the followers of the new religion. Returning to his native city in triumph, Mohammed purged the central shrine of Mecca (the **Ka'aba**) of its idols and eventually gained the allegiance of tribes throughout virtually the whole of the Arabian peninsula. By faith, struggle, and example he had established a new religion as well as a new pan-Arab state. He died quite suddenly, in 632, in Medina.

During the Prophet's lifetime his revelations were memorized by his followers, and after his death an official collection was compiled as the **Koran**.

Mohammed saw himself as the last of the great prophets, who included such figures as Abraham (Ibrahim), Moses (Musa), and Jesus (Isa). Muslims do not regard Mohammed as divine, which he never claimed to be, but as the model for all human action – the ideal statesman, soldier, citizen, businessman, father, husband, and neighbour.

Muslim Beliefs and Practices

Muslims share some central beliefs with Jews and Christians – that one God created the universe and judges mankind and that death is the door to an afterlife that will be enjoyed by the righteous and suffered by the wicked. However, Muslims differ from Jews in believing God's revelation to be for all peoples and not reserved for one chosen people; they differ from Christians in rejecting the concept of the Trinity, which they see as a contradiction of monotheism. Indeed, to deny the oneness and uniqueness of God is regarded as the worst possible heresy.

The secular law of Islam, known as **sharia** (the road to the watering place), contains the **Five Pillars**. For devout Muslims belief is empty unless it directs behaviour. The teachings of the Koran and Mohammed's example, enshrined in hundreds of **hadith** (traditions based on his sayings or deeds), prescribe detailed guidance for every aspect of living. Male Muslims are circumcised. Both sexes are bidden to dress modestly. Women are enjoined to cover their legs, arms, and hair. In highly orthodox countries, it is not uncommon for women to wear an all-concealing veil, or **chador**, though this practice is not prescribed in the Koran. Although Muslims are permitted to have up to four wives, polygamy has never been common except among the wealthy or in times of warfare, when widows and orphans had to be given the protection of surviving males. Divorce is regarded as 'the most hated of permitted things.' Like Jews, Muslims are forbidden to eat the flesh of the pig and should only eat **halal** (permitted) meat, which has been ritually slaughtered and drained of its blood. In some parts of the Muslim world, local

CHRONOLOGY OF MOHAMMED'S LIFE	
c. 570	Born in Mecca
595	Marries Khadija
610	Receives his first revelation
616	Reveals himself as a prophet
622	Moves to Yathrib (Medina)
623	Wins the Battle of Badr against the Meccans
628	Attempts his first pilgrimage to Mecca
	Makes Treaty of al-Hudaybujah in which Meccans recognize his authority
630	Enters Mecca as the recognized Prophet
632	Leads pilgrimage to Mecca
	Dies in Medina

Islamic calendar The Islamic year of twelve months, calculated on a lunar cycle. Dates are reckoned from the *hijra* (c. 16 July 622 AD) and are designated by the abbreviation AH, from Latin *anno hegirae*. Because, on lunar months, a year only contains between 345 and 355 days, the year 2000 AD will correspond to 1420 AH.

custom has exercised a strong influence on the framing of laws. Worship is undertaken at the following times of day: before sunrise, after midday, in the late afternoon, at sunset, and at night. Muslims are permitted to pray anywhere, though preferably in a mosque. The faithful are called to prayer by a **muezzin**, who chants from a raised place in the mosque, often a slim tower known as a **minaret**. Each prayer consists of two to four units, during which the worshipper adopts a prescribed attitude, such as bowing and touching the forehead to the prayer mat. With every change in posture, the statement 'God is great' is recited.

Particular practices are associated with the **hajj**, the pilgrimage to Mecca that is central to the life of every Muslim. When the pilgrim is ten kilometres from the Holy City, he puts on

The Koran
For Muslims, the Koran (from Arabic qur'an, *'recitation') is the word of Allah given to his prophet Mohammed by the angel Gabriel. The Koran is comprised of 114 chapters, or surahs. Among the many injunctions to good works that it contains are the following words (from Surah IV): "Be kind to parents and the near kinsman, and to orphans, and to the needy..."* ▼

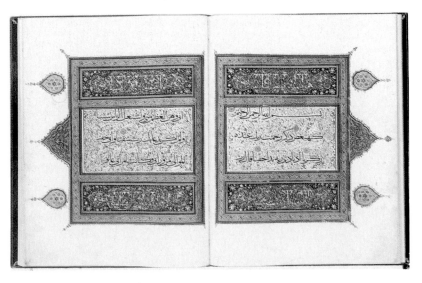

The Pillars of Islam
1 *Shahada*. The statement of faith 'I testify that there is no god but God and that Mohammed is his messenger.' All that is needed to become a Muslim is to make this statement in public in front of Muslim witnesses.
2 *Salat*. Prayer five times a day. Prayers are said in Arabic, whatever the native language of the believer. Prayer is preceded by the washing of hands, head, face, and feet and is said facing Mecca. On Fridays adult males are expected to offer their prayers in a mosque, where the *imam* (prayer-leader) will usually preach a sermon.
3 *Zakat*. Giving alms. These donations are used to support education and charities.
4 *Sawm*. Fasting during daylight hours throughout Ramadan, the month in which the Koran was first revealed to Mohammed.
5 *Hajj*. Pilgrimage to Mecca at least once in a lifetime – but only if the expense and absence caused by the journey do not endanger the believer's family. Some Muslims regard *jihad* (struggle) as a sixth pillar. It can mean both warfare in defence of Islam and the struggle inside each person to lead a better life.

two seamless garments and neither shaves nor cuts his hair and nails until the end of the ceremony. At the al-Haram mosque in Mecca, the pilgrim walks seven times around the *Ka'aba* sanctuary, which Muslims believe to be the place where divine power and bliss touches the earth. They kiss and touch the black stone set in the shrine, which tradition holds was given to Adam after his fall from grace with God and has turned black through absorbing the sins of all the pilgrims who have ever touched it.

At the end of the pilgrimage, **Id al-Adha**, one of the two major Islamic festivals, is celebrated. The other, **Id al-Fitr**, marks the end of Ramadan. In some Islamic countries the birthday of the Prophet is also an occasion for public celebration.

Among the many traditions of Islam is the belief that the Prophet ascended to Heaven from Jerusalem (*mi'rādj*, 'ascent'), rising to the last of the seven levels of heaven, the home of God and the angels. The event is known as the Night Journey and is sometimes interpreted as a mystical experience. The ninth caliph, Abd al-Malik ibn Marwan (reigned 685–705), erected a magnificent mosque, known as the Dome of the Rock (691), on the traditional site of the Prophet's departure from earth.

The Expansion of Islam

Bedouin Arabs had always excelled in desert skills, but they lacked discipline, unity, and a cause beyond personal gain and honour; all of these Islam supplied. The rhythm of daily prayer taught obedience to authority. Belief that death in battle would be followed by

admission to paradise enhanced their courage. After Mohammed's death a number of Arab tribes gave up Islam, believing their loyalty had been to the man rather than the faith. Mohammed's successor – the first caliph, Abu Bakr (c. 573–634), forced them back to obedience. Muslim victory in these campaigns launched a great tide of conquest. In neighbouring Byzantium and Persia, the Muslims faced empires reduced to exhaustion by decades of mutual conflict. In the Byzantine provinces of Egypt and Syria, the Muslims were welcomed as liberators from harsh taxation and religious persecution. The Muslims were willing to spare the lives and property of those who accepted their rule without resistance and allow them to worship in their own way as **dhimmi** (protected people). As 'peoples of the book' Jews and Christians were respected but they were forbidden to bear arms and forced to pay **jizya** (poll-tax).

In 635 Khalid ibn al-Walid (died 642), known as the 'Sword of Islam,' captured Damascus and in the following year, in the valley of the Yarmuk, routed a huge Byzantine army. As the conquests gathered pace the Arabs mastered the military methods of their former enemies, learning siege-craft from the Persians and naval warfare from the Byzantines. In just over a century after Mohammed's death his followers had conquered an empire stretching from southern Spain to the borders of India. For centuries after the military expansion of Islam, the spread of the religion continued into Africa and Southeast Asia, largely through Muslim traders and the preaching of the *sufis* (Muslim mystics).

The Muslim conquests are unusual in history as an instance of a nomadic people making significant changes to the way of life of the settled communities they conquered. For Muslim and non-Muslim alike, Islam provided a framework of law and government extending from the Sahara to the Indus Valley with Arabic becoming the language of culture, commerce, and administration.

Sunni and Shia

After Mohammed's death the leadership of the Muslim community passed to his close companions Abu Bakr (632–34), Omar (634–44), and Uthman (644–56). They took the title of **caliph**, a word deriving from the Arabic *khalifa* ('successor'). The title survived until the end of the Ottoman Empire in 1922.

The succession of Ali (656–61), Mohammed's adopted son and son-in-law, was

◄ **A Group of Muslims at Prayer** *A mass gathering of worshippers in Cairo, Egypt. They are shown in one of the ritual prayer positions.*

challenged by Mu'awiyah, governor of newly conquered Syria. Ali's death led to a split between those who believed the succession should only pass to descendants of Ali (**Shi'at Ali**, party of Ali) and those who believed it could be held by anyone who followed the correct beliefs and behaviour (**Sunna**) established by Mohammed. Sunni Islam has remained the mainstream religion ever since.

The Shiites have split into many different sects and developed their own distinctive, often mystical, beliefs. Today, Shiites are widely scattered throughout the Muslim world, forming a majority only in Iran. The orthodox majority of Shiites are known as 'Twelvers,' because of their recognition of 12 **imams** as infallible spiritual leaders. The last of these disappeared in 878, and Twelvers believe that he will return at the end of the world. Among Iranian Twelver Shiites, principal theologians are referred to as **ayatollahs**.

Islamic Culture

A minaret on a mosque in Spain clearly differs from one in India or Africa, but all are recognizable as minarets. The creation of a distinctive architecture is remarkable, considering Islam's origins in a nomadic culture. Drawing on the skills of conquered Byzantines and Persians, the Muslims learned to construct vast

◄ **Ritual Ablutions**
A Muslim worshipper is pictured at a fountain outside a mosque in the act of cleansing his hands and feet prior to prayer.

buildings and engineering projects. Mosques are built to detailed specifications – usually around a courtyard, surrounded on all four sides by arcades. The direction of Mecca, towards which all prayers are said, is indicated by a small niche, or *mihrab*. The Umayyad mosque in Damascus, Syria, and the Taj

Dervishes

Dervishes are ascetic followers of the mystical Sufi branch of Islam, living either as hermits or as members of religious communities. The Turkish order known as the *Mevlevi*, or 'whirling dervishes,' uses dance in order to induce a state of religious ecstasy.

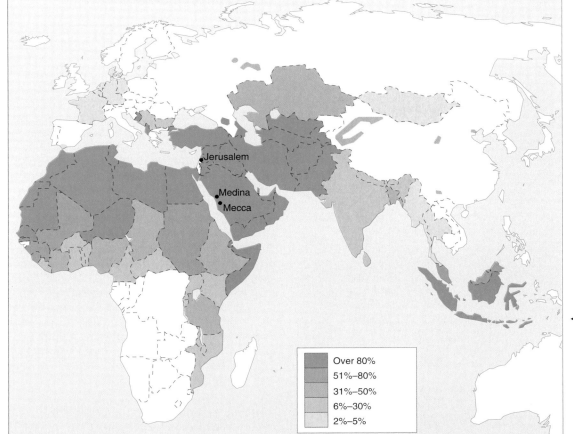

Jerusalem

Medina
Mecca

Over 80%
51%–80%
31%–50%
6%–30%
2%–5%

◄ **The Islamic World**
The distribution of followers of Islam is shown in percentages of populations. In addition to its traditional heartlands, there are significant Muslim communities in western Europe.

131

Muslims in the World (1996; in millions)	
Africa	307
Asia	778
Europe	32
Americas	7
Oceania	0.4
Total	**1124.4**

Mahal, a tomb of the Mogul period in Agra, India, are among the supreme achievements of Muslim architecture. One particular characteristic of Muslim art arises from the fact that it is forbidden to depict living beings (as such portrayal would be presumptuous imitation of God); from this prohibition arises the elaborate abstract decoration seen in Islamic design, most notably in examples of Koranic calligraphy and tilework.

In the two centuries after the death of the Prophet, a characteristically Islamic culture arose, making great advances in mathematics and medicine. Al-Khwarizmi (died 850) invented algebra (Arabic *al-jabr*, 'restoration') and helped to introduce Arabic numerals into European mathematics; these numerals originated in India and were brought to Europe by Arab travellers in the 10th century AD. Al-Kindi (died 870) was the first of a series of encyclopedists; his 270 works range from essays on astrology to practical handbooks on cookery and sword-making. Ibn Sina (980–1037), known in medieval Europe as Avicenna, compiled encyclopedias of philosophy and medicine; the latter remained a standard work of reference for five centuries after his death. Ibn Khaldun (died 1406) was one of the earliest historians to develop theories explaining the rise and decline of states and empires.

Classical texts were rediscovered and translated by Muslim scholars. Much of the Western classical heritage would never have survived had it not been preserved and transmitted through Spain and Sicily in the form of Arabic translations.

Modern Islam

Islam, as both a religion and a form of nationalism, remains a major force in the Arab world as well as in the central Asian republics of the former Soviet Union and in Southeast Asia. Even in European countries that have no historical link with the Arabic and Ottoman empires, Islam is exerting a cultural and political influence via Muslim communities that have developed there. For example, in France, postcolonial immigrants from the Maghreb (i.e. Algeria, Morocco, and Tunisia) and from West African Muslim nations, such as Senegal and Mali, now form 5% of the population.

Since the end of World War II, political events have contributed to a strong resurgence of Islamic fundamentalism, notably the creation of the State of Israel in the former Muslim land of Palestine and the overthrow in Iran of the pro-Western Shah Mohammed Reza Pahlavi (1918–80) by followers of Ayatollah Khomeini (1902–89). Since it advocates a strict adherence to **Shari'a** (the secular law of Islam), fundamentalism has raised considerable antipathy to Western values. In the 1990s, Islamic fundamentalism was on the rise in Turkey, Egypt, and North Africa.

Islam and Marriage

Islam strongly encourages marriage, which is performed in a civil ceremony. Arranged marriages are the norm, with a partner being chosen by the parents. Although polygamy is permitted, it is rare in modern times. Adultery is an extremely serious offence, punishable in ultra-orthodox countries by strokes of the lash or even death by stoning. Traditionally, a man could divorce his wife simply by pronouncing the formula 'I divorce thee' before witnesses. Reforms in some Islamic countries now give the woman a limited right to divorce.

PARADISE AS A GARDEN

Islamic culture exercised a profound influence on many aspects of Western life. One such area was ornamental gardening.

In the Koran, heaven is described as a lush garden with flowing streams and gushing fountains – an especially appealing image for the peoples of a region as arid and infertile as Arabia. The word 'paradise' is derived, via Greek, from the ancient Persian term for a walled garden, and the art of landscape gardening probably originated in Persia.

Islam favoured geometric, symmetrical gardens. These were seen as symbolic of divine order and harmony and were often based on four streams representing the four rivers of heaven listed in both the Koran and the Bible. Trees, water, shrubs, and roses created an aesthetic appeal to all five senses.

Islamic poetry and textiles abound with images and motifs that reflect the central importance of the garden.

◄ **A Mogul Miniature** *This scene (c. 1590; Mirza Abd al-Rahim) shows the Garden of Fidelity, laid out by the Indian Mogul emperor Babur (1483–1530).*

Hinduism

Key concepts of Hinduism • Gods and goddesses • Religious practices •
Festivals • Hindu social structure • Modern Hinduism

Hinduism encompasses a complex variety of traditions, religious practices and beliefs, philosophies, mythologies, and folklores. Hindu tradition does not rest on a founder, a centralized authority, or a body of beliefs or doctrines, but rather has been shaped by the insights of many spiritual teachers and saints. Hinduism posits a broad concept of the Truth or the Divine as the underlying principle of existence; the faith has more to do with acting in conformity with religious, social, ethical, and family norms than with doctrinal beliefs.

Hinduism is the major religion of India and of Nepal. It is also the main religion on the Indonesian island of Bali. Some 80% of India's almost 900 million inhabitants are Hindus. The religion has evolved gradually over a period of 4500 years. The roots of the tradition can be traced to the ancient civilization of the Indus valley (c. 2500–1500 BC). Later (around 1500 BC) the Aryans brought to India their beliefs and practices, together with the language of Sanskrit (in which Hinduism's earliest sacred literature, the **Veda** – meaning 'knowledge' – is written). Other significant influences within Hinduism include the **bhakti**, or devotional movements that emerged first in southern India (c. 7th century AD), and the various philosophical schools that arose partly through an encounter with Buddhism.

Key Concepts of Hinduism

Samsara. In the Hindu tradition, time is cyclical: an endless process with no beginning or end. The universe goes through a process of creation and destruction and all life is subject to the wheel of **samsara**, the cycle of birth, death, and rebirth. Hindus seek release from the wheel of samsara to be united with god. There are three main paths to **moksha** ('salvation'): **karma** ('action'), **bhakti** ('devotion'), and **jnana** ('knowledge').

Karma. This includes all the thoughts and actions that shape a person's destiny. The circumstances of one's present life are seen as the result of one's past karma. On death the soul casts off its worn-out body and enters into a new one to gain new experience. A person's karma may be worked out in a human or animal body, either in this world or in other worlds, before salvation is achieved. The idea of repeated births implies a progressive development of the individual towards perfection.

Dharma. This is one of the key concepts, and has several meanings, including 'eternal law,' 'truth,' 'the nature of things,' 'behaviour', 'morality,' 'righteousness,' and 'duty.' Dharma is one of the four aims of life, the others being **artha** (wealth), **kama** (pleasure), and **moksha**. Each person has a duty towards family, society, and the world. Adherence to dharma is seen as leading to good karma and finally to moksha.

Ahimsa. Meaning 'non-harming,' this is one of the highest ethical principles, although the use of violence in certain circumstances is justified. It has enormous significance in Jainism and Buddhism. Vegetarianism is widespread among Hindus, and pork and beef are universally forbidden, the cow symbolizing the sanctity of all creation.

Gods and Goddesses

Trimurti. Hindus believe in one Supreme Reality – **Brahman** – the sole eternal principle that is present in all aspects of creation and

====SEE ALSO====
This section:
• Islam
• Buddhism
• Other Religions of India and the Far East
The Visual Arts Worldwide (vol. 4):
• Art of the Indian Subcontinent
Music Worldwide (vol. 4):
• Music of the Indian Subcontinent
The Literary Arts Worldwide (vol. 4):
• Literature of the Indian Subcontinent
The Indian Subcontinent (vol. 5)

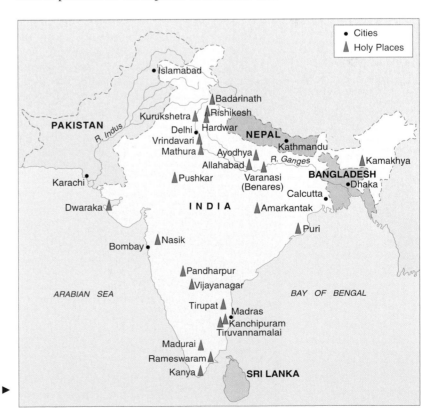

Hindu Religious Sites *Principal holy places (i.e. temple and pilgrimage sites) are shown.* ▶

The Ramayana

The Ramayana is an epic that illustrates ideals, such as loyalty and honour, as guides in all areas of life. It tells the story of Rama, who, because of a promise made by his father to his stepmother, willingly goes into exile, followed by his wife Sita and his brother. While in the forest, Sita is abducted by the ten-headed demon king Ravana and held captive in his palace in Sri Lanka. Rama, with the help of an army of monkey-generals, defeats Ravana and rescues Sita, enabling the couple to return to their kingdom, Ayodhya.

yet transcendent at the same time. The term **Trimurti** refers to three different but complementary aspects of Brahman: as creator (**Brahma**), preserver (**Vishnu**), and destroyer of evil (**Shiva**). Although Brahma is the creator, his role in worship is less significant. Vishnu is the preserver of the universe and the world. He manifests himself on earth in various forms (animal, semihuman, and fully human) whenever peace and harmony are threatened. These manifestations are known as **avatars**, (from Sanskrit *avatara*, 'descent') and the tenth avatar of Vishnu is yet to come.

Krishna, the eighth avatar of Vishnu, is the most complete manifestation of Vishnu. He appears in many forms, including a divine child and a young cowherd playing the flute. The image of Krishna as the beloved is a central focus of devotion in the bhakti tradition.

Shiva, the third member of the Trimurti, has a complex nature, combining both male and female elements. As Lord of the Dance (**Nataraja**), Shiva symbolizes the cosmic energy that flows through the universe and the world.

There are other important deities, such as the elephant-headed Ganesha (remover of obstacles), and Hanuman, the monkey-god and devotee of the god Rama. There are also many village deities, known as **gramadevatas**.

The feminine dimension of the Divine is referred to as **Shakti**, meaning 'power' or 'energy.' The many goddesses of Hinduism are manifestations of this power. Saraswati, the consort of Brahma, is the goddess of wisdom and the arts. She is usually shown seated on a lotus flower, playing a stringed instrument and holding sacred texts. Lakshmi, the consort of Vishnu, is the goddess of wealth and prosperity and is pictured seated or standing on a lotus, dropping gold coins. Parvati (also known as Durga and Kali) appears as gracious

HINDU SCRIPTURES

The numerous Hindu sacred texts fall into two categories: **Shruti** ('heard') and **Smriti** ('remembered'). Respectively, these are inspired scriptural texts and a recasting of the truths of the primary scriptures in a simpler form to meet the needs of a popular audience.

Shruti literature (c. 1200–500 BC) consists firstly of four collections of hymns – the **Rig-Veda** (the earliest), the **Yajur-Veda**, the **Sama-Veda**, and the **Atharva-Veda**. In addition, there are the **Brahmanas**, ritual texts attached to each of the Vedas; the **Aranyakas** ('Forest Books'), which contain elaborate discussion of the inner significance of ritual; and the **Upanishads**, speculations on the nature of the Supreme Reality. The Upanishads became the basis of later philosophical schools.

To the Smriti tradition (c. 300 BC–1000 AD) belong a variety of writings principally in Sanskrit, notably the two great epics the **Ramayana** and the **Mahabharata** (which includes the **Bhagavadgita**), the **Dharmashastras** (legal texts on proper conduct and behaviour), the **Puranas** (stories and legends about gods, kings and saints), and sectarian literature.

and kind and a devoted wife to Shiva. As Durga she is depicted as a warrior goddess riding a lion or a tiger and slaying a buffalo-demon, symbolizing the triumph of good over evil. In the form of Kali she appears wearing a garland of skulls and holding a severed head of a demon.

Main Sects. The bhakti trend, which emphasized the path of loving devotion to a personal god, rejected the caste system and priestly rituals. This led to the formation of sects. The three main religious groupings are the **Vaishnavites** (worshippers of Vishnu and his avatars), the **Shaivites** (worshippers of Shiva), and the **Shaktas** (worshippers of Shakti, especially in the form of Durga or Kali). The Vaishnavite movement is popular throughout India. Many saints are venerated, including the northern Indian female saint Mirabai (?1547–1614), the Bengali saint Chaitanya (1485–1533), and the female saint Andal (c. 9th century) in the south. Shaivism has a large following in southern India and Sri Lanka, and Shaktism is popular in Bengal.

Religious Practices

Worship, or **puja**, plays an important part in the everyday life of Hindus. It is not obligatory for Hindus to go to a temple, and most

Saraswati
The goddess is shown playing a sitar-like instrument known as a 'veena.'

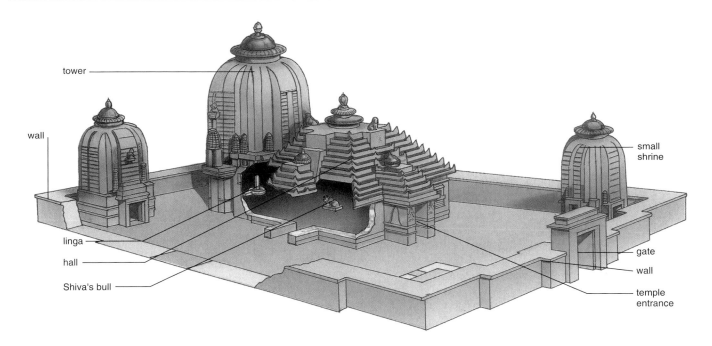

tower

wall

linga

hall

Shiva's bull

small shrine

gate

wall

temple entrance

religious practices take place in a part of the home set aside for worship, which may contain images of deities. It is usually the mother who performs puja on behalf of the family every morning and evening. After washing, but prior to eating, worship begins by lighting the lamps in the shrine and making offerings (e.g. incense, flowers, and food) to the deities. A hymn may be sung or a silent prayer offered; alternatively, a passage may be read from one of the holy books. Finally, *arati* (the act of waving a lighted oil lamp before the deities) is performed. Family members then receive blessings by touching the arati light and receiving consecrated food (**prashad**).

Worship in Hindu temples begins early in the morning; the priest wakes the deities with music, gives the images a ritual bath, anoints them with sacred powder, and finally offers them fruit, incense, and arati. **Om** is the most sacred sound and is uttered at the beginning of most Hindu prayers. In Sanskrit the syllable comprises three sounds – A, U, and M – which are taken to reflect various tripartite structures (e.g. the Trimurti) and so to symbolize the Absolute.

Pilgrimage plays an important role in the lives of most Hindus. India has many places of pilgrimage, mostly on the banks of holy rivers. Bathing in these sacred rivers cleanses pilgrims of their sins.

Life-cycle rituals (**samskaras**) mark the transition from one stage of life to another. The nature of rituals may vary from community to community. Of the 16 or more samskaras, the four most important are the following:

Namakarana. This naming ceremony usually takes place on the eleventh or twelfth day after birth. A priest sometimes officiates

and the child may be named after a deity, its birth star, or a quality, such as love (*priya*).

Upanayana. This initiation ceremony marks the end of childhood. It is usually performed between the ages of 8 and 12, and only for a boy of the first three upper castes. This ceremony signifies entry into a new phase of personal responsibility and self-discipline.

During Upanayana, the initiate is given a sacred thread, hung diagonally across his

▲ **Diagram of a Hindu Temple** *The linga – a cylindrical stone with a rounded top – symbolizes Shiva's creative energy. Shiva's bull Nandi faces the linga.*

Hindus and Hinduism

The word *Hindu* is a Persian derivative of the Sanskrit word *Sindhu*, the name of the Indus River (in the modern state of Pakistan); people living around and beyond it came to be called 'Hindus' by the Persians. The term 'Hinduism' is of much later derivation, the suffix '-ism' having been added by 19th-century Western scholars in an attempt to categorize the complex religious tradition of Hindus.

◀ **Shiva** *The third member of the Hindu Trimurti in his manifestation as Nataraja, Lord of the Dance.*

▲ **Pilgrims Bathing in the River Ganges at Varanasi (Benares)** *Varanasi is the most sacred place of pilgrimage for Hindus. Pilgrims bathe from steps, or ghats.*

The *Mahabharata*

The epic Mahabharata which contains about 100 000 verses, describes the dynastic rivalry between the Pandavas and the Kauravas, both descended from King Bharata. Included in the Mahabharata is the Bhagavadgita ('Song of the Lord'), the most popular sacred text since Indian independence. It is a dialogue between Arjuna (one of the Pandava brothers) and the Lord Krishna, who becomes his charioteer. Krishna urges Arjuna to fulfil his duty by fighting his opponents without hatred.

---

body from his left shoulder to the right waist. Traditionally the rite marked the beginning of a 12-year period of religious study under a *guru*, or spiritual teacher. The life of a Hindu is seen as progressing through four stages – student, householder, hermit, and renunciant – called *ashrmadharma*. Once initiated, a boy is required to recite the sacred verse called *gayatri mantra* to the Sun God: "We meditate on the lovely light of the god Savitri. May it inspire our thoughts" (Rig-Veda 3, 62, 10).

Vivaha. In the Hindu tradition, the sacrament of marriage links not only two individuals but two families. Although arranged marriages are the norm, marriages for love are not uncommon. The most important stage of the wedding ceremony is the symbolic act by the bride and groom of taking seven steps (*saptapadi*) together or walking around the fire seven times while Vedic mantras (sacred verses) are recited by the priest.

Antyesti. Hindus cremate their adult dead, but children are buried. Passages from the Bhagavadgita or devotional songs may be sung or sacred verses recited. The last rite is for a male relative, usually the eldest son, to light the funeral pyre. The ashes are collected on the third day and scattered in a sacred river. Neighbours provide hospitality for the bereaved family during the mourning period, which may last for five to twelve days. Relatives and friends are invited to a meal to mark the end of mourning and the resumption of normal life. Some Hindus perform an annual memorial ceremony known as *shraddha*.

Festivals

Hinduism has numerous festivals, universal or local, particular or general.

Diwali. Held in October or November, *Diwali* ('row of lights') is the most widely celebrated of the Hindu festivals and lasts for two to five days. It celebrates the triumph of good over evil and is associated with the goddess Lakshmi (wealth). Diwali is a time for feasting, giving presents, and family celebrations. In northern India Diwali is associated with the triumphal return of Rama and Sita to their kingdom. During the festival, lamps are lit to symbolize the couple's homecoming.

Raksha Bandhan. Meaning 'protection tie,' this one-day festival is celebrated in north and west India in July or August. It celebrates the bond between male and female siblings and is marked by sisters tying *rakhi* (amulets) onto the right wrists of their brothers and wishing them well.

Holi. Celebrated mainly in northern India in February or March, *Holi* marks the arrival of spring. Many stories, customs, and rituals are associated with this festival. Social norms and rules are relaxed, and Hindus of different social backgrounds mingle freely. A significant feature of Holi is the lighting of a bonfire.

Pongal. This is a southern Indian harvest festival lasting for two to three days in January. Thanks are offered for a good harvest; then comes the festival of *Mattu Pongal*, in which cows and buffaloes are festooned with garlands and their horns are painted.

Hindu Social Structure

The social dimension of Hinduism may be explained in terms of the four *varnas*, or groups, and of *jati*, or caste. The Rig-Veda records the division of society into four varnas: priests (*brahmans*), warriors (*kshatriyas*), merchants and cultivators (*vaishyas*), and serfs (*shudras*). Those in the fourth varna are assigned the task of serving the first three.

The castes are innumerable and the relationship between the concepts of caste and varna is complex. The caste system has little to do with the Western socioeconomic concept of 'class.' A caste is a group of people linked by birth, occupation, and specific dietary rules and religious customs. The ranking of castes is based on norms of purity and pollution. Certain occupations, such as butcher or cobbler, are considered impure because of their association with the flesh of animals. Marriage is usually among members of the same group; however, urbanization and other factors have led to a greater interaction between the various castes.

Brahmans head the caste hierarchy, although very few of them are actually priests. The bottom caste are the Untouchables, or *harijans* ('people of god,' a term coined by Mahatma Gandhi), who now prefer to call themselves *dalits* ('the oppressed'). The place of other castes in the social hierarchy varies from region to region. Although caste discrimination is against the law, the practice continues in one form or another.

The caste system has its critics and defenders. Some argue that it promotes a stable society in which everyone has a clearly defined role, while others think that it hinders individual initiative and leads to social stagnation.

Modern Hinduism

Hindu thinkers in 19th-century British India were concerned to reform Hinduism while defending it against Christian missionaries who attacked it as pagan. Rammohan Roy (1772–1833), a Bengali Brahman and founder of the reform movement Brahmo Samaj ('Society of God'), rejected image worship, stressing instead the idea of the one formless God. He and other progressive thinkers fought for women's rights, in particular the abolition of the socially oppressive custom of **sati** (self-immolation of widows on their husbands' funeral pyres). Swami Dayananda Saraswati (1824–83) founded the Arya Samaj ('Society of Aryans') in Bombay in 1875 in order to affirm Hindu identity. More recent Hindu organizations, such as Rashtriya Swamsevak Sangh (RSS) and Vishwa Hindu Parishad (VHP), are highly politicized minority groups that agitate for a Hindu nation, or **rashtra.** The rise of Hindu nationalism, which runs counter to India's secular constitutional provision of equal respect for all religions, became apparent in the violent conflict at Ayodhya in 1992. Claiming that Ayodhya was the birthplace of Rama, Hindu extremists destroyed a mosque on the alleged site.

▲ **A Hindu Wedding Ceremony**
In Hinduism, the marriage ritual marks one of the four most important transitions in life.

Swami Vivekananda (1863–1902), disciple of the 19th-century Bengali saint Ramakrishna Paramahamsa, brought to the West the nondualistic philosophy of **Advaita Vedanta**, which affirms the essential divinity of all human beings and places great stress on meditation. In 1897 he founded the Ramakrishna Mission in Calcutta, which combines religion with social service and has centres worldwide. Other famous Hindus include Sri Aurobindo Gosh (1872–1950), whose philosophy of integral yoga aims at transforming human consciousness; the Bengali mystical poet Rabindranath Tagore (1861–1941); Mohandas ('Mahatma') Gandhi (1869–1948), renowned for his nonviolent campaigns against British rule; and the southern Indian statesman and philosopher Sarvepalli Radhakrishnan (1888–1975), who tried to reconcile Eastern and Western systems of thought.

One of the most popular Hindu gurus of the 20th century is Sri Sathya Sai Baba (1926–), known simply as 'Baba.' Regarded by many as a god in human form, he is credited with performing miracles. Another well-known guru is Bhaktivedanta Swami (1896–1977), who founded the International Society for Krishna Consciousness (also known as the Hare Krishna movement) in New York in 1965. Through such agencies, Hinduism has spread far beyond India. Also instrumental in this development have been the Hindu migrant communities who have settled in different parts of Southeast Asia, the Far East, Africa, the Caribbean, and Europe.

◀ **The Festival of Diwali** *A priest in Sri Lanka lighting the lamps that are associated with Diwali. During this festival, people clean and decorate their houses, sweets are prepared, and fireworks are set off in the early hours of the morning. Diwali is also celebrated in the Sikh religion.*

The Hindu Diaspora

A Hindu diaspora has developed, initially through the migration of indentured labour to British colonies. The following countries have significant Hindu communities. The year when substantial migration began is given.

Guyana	1838
Trinidad	1845
Jamaica	1845
South Africa	1860
Fiji	1879
East Africa	1895
Singapore	1895
Burma	1852
Canada	1875
UK	1955
USA	1965
Australia	1973

Buddhism

Gautama Siddhartha • Southern Buddhism • Northern Buddhism • Other forms • Modern Buddhism

An Image of the Buddha *The Buddha Gautama, who is normally shown sitting in a meditative position, is also known as Shakyamuni. This representation is located in Thailand.* ▼

Buddhism originated about 2500 years ago in India with the teachings of a spiritual guide named Gautama Siddhartha, respectfully known as the Buddha, or 'awakened one.' Though almost extinguished in India by the 13th century through the effects of Muslim invasion and reabsorption of Buddhist ideas and practices into Hinduism (the Buddha came to be regarded as the ninth *avatara* or incarnation of Vishnu), Buddhism spread by contact rather than conquest to become, over a period of about 1000 years, the dominant religion of Southeast Asia and the Far East. Southern Buddhism spread southeast from India to Sri Lanka, Myanmar (formerly Burma), Thailand, Laos, and Cambodia while Northern Buddhism penetrated the Himalayan kingdoms, central Asia, China, Tibet, Mongolia, Korea, and Japan.

Gautama Siddhartha

Buddhism's founder, Gautama, is the subject of many legends, which are constantly retold because they convey key Buddhist teachings. Gautama probably lived during the 5th century BC (earliest date of birth 566 BC, latest death date 368 BC, according to modern scholars). As the son of a king, he was born into luxury. Moreover, he was already destined to become a great spiritual teacher, a **Buddha**, as a result of a vow he made in an incarnation countless aeons ago to a previous Buddha called Dipankara. Legend has it that Gautama's father tried to conceal from his son the suffering inherent in human life. Gautama married at 16 and had a son. At the age of 29, on a chariot ride around the city, Gautama saw on successive days an aged man, a sick man, and a corpse, and realized that he, too, would one day become sick, old, and die, simply as a consequence of being born into this world. He then caught sight of a serene and happy **samana**, a member of a monastic order, and immediately resolved to become a samana himself and seek liberation from suffering. Leaving the palace while his family slept, Gautama entered the forest. His renunciation of worldly life set the pattern for Buddhism's later development; a monastic life is the ideal in many forms of Buddhism.

The Buddha's Nirvana. Gautama sought out spiritual teachers and practised a variety of techniques of meditation, most of which found their way into later Buddhism. For a period he tried extreme asceticism, fasting almost to death in an effort to achieve enlightenment by force of will. Then taking some food he sat in meditation under a pipala tree and, at the age of 35, after an epic inner struggle with the evil tempter Mara, attained a spiritual state of liberation or enlightenment called **nirvana** or **nibbana**, literally 'extinction.' Nirvana does not mean self-destruction in a negative sense, but the final quenching of the 'fire' of craving or desire, which, according to Buddhist thought, is the cause of our continual rebirth in this world and hence of our suffering. Following his enlightenment, the Buddha was persuaded by the god Brahma to teach others the way to liberation, setting an example of wisdom combined with compassion for others that subsequent Buddhists have sought to emulate.

The Community. The Buddha wandered as a teacher in India for 40 years, attracting a large following of faithful disciples, supporters, and interested outsiders. Following his death at the age of 80, a group of his followers (the **sangha**, or community) maintained and

THE FOUR NOBLE TRUTHS

The Four Noble Truths, probably the best-known doctrinal formulation in Buddhism, are modelled on a doctor's identification, diagnosis, prognosis, and prescription for an illness.

- The first truth, the diagnosis, is that to exist is to suffer. Not everyone would agree – even the Buddha was 29 before he realized this fact – but acceptance of the diagnosis is the first step to the cure.
- The second truth states that suffering has a cause, which is craving.
- In the third truth, the Buddha states that there is a cure that will end suffering, namely the cessation or extinction of craving, i.e. nirvana.
- The fourth truth prescribes the treatment; the way, or path, to end craving and suffering – the Noble Eightfold Path, also described as the 'Middle Way.'

passed on to their pupils his teachings and example; subgroups developed into the different 'schools' or lineages of Buddhism. Originally a wandering group of samanas, the members of the sangha had no fixed home and survived on alms, but their temporary resting places during the three-month rainy season eventually became monasteries, places where spiritual practice could be undertaken with the support of a local community. Monastic life came to be governed by detailed codes of conduct based on the Buddha's teaching and example, collected in scriptures known as **vinaya**. In addition to the vinaya rules, other teachings of the Buddha were preserved and eventually written down. These books of teachings, called **sutra**, together with commentaries and philosophical works by eminent Buddhists through the ages, make up the extensive Buddhist scriptures.

Southern Buddhism

Buddhism is a vast religion and, although key ideas can be identified, beliefs vary enormously according to time, place, and teacher. The Buddha Gautama, for example, who is supremely revered in Sri Lanka, is not particularly important in Japanese Buddhism, where other 'cosmic' Buddhas, or **Bodhisattvas**, take precedence. In some forms of Buddhism meditation is essential, in others irrelevant; monasticism may be central or marginal. The religion can be divided broadly into Southern and Northern Buddhism.

Southern Buddhism, dominated by the **Theravada** ('Teaching of the Elders') tradition, holds up as an ideal the monk who leaves the secular world in order to follow the Buddha's path, taking refuge in what are known as the 'Three Treasures': **Buddha**, **Dhamma**, and **Sangha** (the example of Gautama's life,

> **Indian Buddhist Languages**
>
> There are two Indian Buddhist languages, Pali and Sanskrit. *Nibbana* in Pali is spelt *nirvana* in Sanskrit. Other Pali/Sanskrit alternatives often encountered are: *Dhamma/Dharma* (Law or Teaching); *Magga/Marga* (the Path); *panna/prajna* (wisdom), and *punna/punya* (merit).

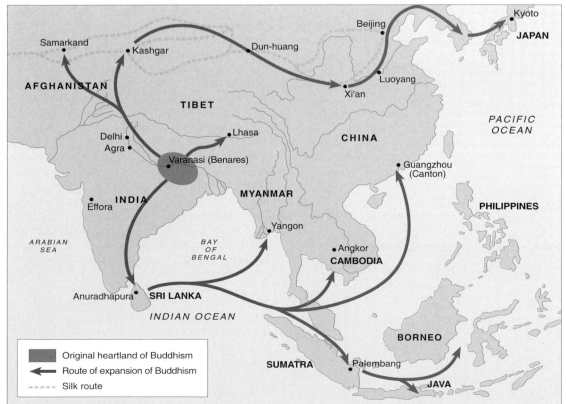

◀ **The Spread of Buddhism** *From its origins in the Ganges Valley in India around 500 BC, Buddhism first spread south to Sri Lanka; traders from there took the faith to Burma and Thailand. From the 1st century AD, Buddhism travelled north and east along the Silk Route to China and eventually to Japan.*

139

▲ **Buddhist Monks in Tibet** *Buddhism stresses pacifism, and Tibetan monks have been at the forefront of the peaceful protests – often brutally repressed – against the Chinese annexation of their country.*

his teachings, and the community of monks). Gautama is the role model for the Theravada tradition, revered as an exceptional man who by achieving liberation from samsara showed a path for others to follow. Though popular devotion is often directed towards the figure of the Buddha in Theravada countries, the Buddha is not thought of as a living deity but respected as the great teacher. There have been Buddhas in the past and will be in the distant future, but for now his teaching (Dhamma) is our guide. Buddhism coexists peacefully alongside beliefs in gods and spirits who will respond to prayers and are invoked in matters of 'communal religion,' such as marriage. Even the gods themselves are temporary, caught up in the cycle of rebirth, and must eventually seek salvation through Buddhism.

Lay people – those outside the monastic sangha – are not expected to practise meditation or adhere to all of the vinaya rules. Yet they may gain merit by generosity, leading a moral life, and respecting the Dhamma, in the expectation of becoming a monk in a future life. For most Southern Buddhists, therefore, Buddhism means supporting basic moral precepts (such as not stealing) and learning something of the Buddha's teachings through stories and occasional attendance at sermons. There are also pilgrimages to places connected with Buddhism and participation in Buddhist festivals, such as **Wesak** (or **Vesakha**), which takes place around May and commemorates the Buddha's birth, enlightenment, and death.

The Theravadin sangha is exclusively male; the Buddhist order of nuns died out nearly a thousand years ago, though some women live a cloistered life similar to that of monks. In the sangha monks encounter Theravada teachings, which share many of the key ideas of Hinduism. For example, the universe is thought of as limitless and largely illusory. Living beings are trapped by their desires and actions (**karma**) into an endless round of birth and death (**samsara**). Only rarely do they achieve the human state – birth as an animal or other lower form results from evil deeds. Similarly, temporary periods in different heavens are a reward for virtuous actions. Birth as a human (especially in a Buddhist country) is fortunate, since it offers an opportunity to escape from this vicious circle.

Complementing this world-view are distinctive Theravada teachings, which are ideas emphasized by the Buddha. Buddhist concepts often take the form of numbered lists, making them easy for monks to memorize. Key ideas include the Three Marks, the **Four Noble Truths**, and the **Noble Eightfold Path**.

The Three Marks. According to the Buddha everything in the world, including ourselves, is impermanent (**anicca**), suffering (**dukkha**), and **no-self** (**anatta**). These Three Marks are interrelated. We suffer because we attempt to deny that our body, thoughts, and emotions are always changing, and that we age and die.

Meditation and Monastic Discipline. Also studied by monks are techniques of meditation and the **patimokkha** code of monastic discipline, which is recited regularly with confession of any infringements. Theravadin monks are strictly celibate and may not work or handle money. They are completely dependent on daily offerings by the laity, who in turn expect monks to uphold the vinaya.

Northern Buddhism

Northern Buddhism shares many basic beliefs with Southern Buddhism but offers a greater variety of paths to enlightenment. Some of

THE NOBLE EIGHTFOLD PATH

The Noble Eightfold Path refers to eight aspects of our behaviour and personality that need to be developed more or less simultaneously and eventually perfected if we wish to achieve nirvana. The different aspects are grouped under three headings: wisdom, morality, and meditation.

panna (wisdom)	1. Perfect view or understanding 2. Perfect directed thought
sila (morality)	3. Perfect speech 4. Perfect action 5. Perfect livelihood
samadhi (meditation)	6. Perfect effort 7. Perfect mindfulness 8. Perfect concentration

NO-SELF (ANATTA)

The Buddha's teaching that we have no self is another way of describing the impermanent nature of all existence. Although it denies the existence of a permanent 'soul' or 'self,' Buddhism accounts for the fact that we nevertheless have a *sense* of personal continuity with the analogy of a row of candles. The first lights the second and the second the third. As the flame of the third candle comes from the flame of the first, it is the same, but as an individual flame, it is different. The delusion of self is a major cause of frustration and suffering, but it can be cured by following the Buddhist path.

these are monastic, while others are designed to facilitate spiritual progress within society. Most forms of Northern Buddhism are variants of **Mahayana** Buddhism.

The Bodhisattva. Mahayana Buddhists take as their role model the Bodhisattva, or 'enlightenment-being,' a near-Buddha whose spiritual development is guided by a vow to help all other living beings attain enlightenment. For Mahayanists, this replaces the ideal of the monk seeking his own liberation. The Bodhisattva ideal echoes the Buddha's own decision to teach. Mahayana Buddhists believe that spiritual liberation without compassion is not true enlightenment.

Emptiness. The idea of **shunyata**, or 'emptiness,' is central to Mahayana Buddhism. According to the great Buddhist teacher Nagarjuna (c. 150–250 AD), founder of the **Madhyamika** or 'Middle-ist' philosophy, humans become attached not only to illusory notions but also to orthodox Buddhist ideas. Nagarjuna argued that even correct concepts are only helpful when approached in the right way. He showed that all ideas depend on their opposites and are ultimately 'empty.' Through meditation the mind is freed of all conceptual attachments. The idea of emptiness recalls the Buddha's own image of his teaching as a raft: when the raft has taken us across the river we should leave it behind, and not carry it with us. In the same way, the student should use, but not become attached to, Buddhist teachings.

'Skilful Means.' According to the Lotus Sutra, probably the most widely read scripture of Mahayana Buddhism, the cosmic Buddhas are like wise and kind fathers who use many methods, such as well-meaning deceptions or 'skilful means,' to help living beings escape from the 'burning house' of samsara, the eternal cycle of rebirth. Gautama's appearance in the world, dispensing simple truths, is regarded as one such strategy.

'Mind-only.' Mind-only is the main doctrine of the **Yogachara** ('practice of yoga') school of Buddhist thought popular in China, Tibet, and Japan. It claims that what we see as real is only a product of the mind, like a dream. The purpose of Buddhism is to wake from this dream, just as the Buddha, the 'awakened one,' did. In Tibetan Buddhism this process is thought to take many lifetimes. The Tibetan tradition also stresses the importance of the guru–disciple relationship, regarding some spiritual teachers as incarnations of Bodhisattvas, continually reborn to lead disciples to enlightenment.

Other Forms
In **Zen Buddhism**, found in China, Korea, and Japan, mind-only means that we are already fully and perfectly awake but do not realize it. Consequently, complete enlightenment can be found here and now, given the right meditational technique and perhaps with the help of a Zen master. This tradition contains stories of

Mahayana A form of Buddhism meaning 'great vehicle,' referring to its grand scope, Mahayana is thought to have originated in visions of the Buddha by followers after his death. It criticizes other forms (such as Theravada), which regard the Buddha as merely a man. Mahayana *sutras* (scriptures) reveal that 'human' Buddhas, such as Gautama, are temporary forms of numerous eternal, inconceivable, and formless Buddhas. The best-known Buddhas are Amida, Buddha of the Western Pure Land, Maitreya, the Buddha-to-Be, Bhaisagyaguru, the Healing Buddha, and Gautama.

A Buddhist Mandala *The mandala (Sanskrit: 'circle') is a vital element of meditation in Tantric Buddhism. It takes the form of a highly complex geometric diagram.* ▶

mantra A sacred phrase, constantly repeated, which is believed to transform the one who recites it. Probably the best-known mantra in Buddhism is the Tibetan 'Om Mani Padme Hum.' Another, 'Namu-myoho-renge-kyo,' includes the title of the Lotus Sutra in Japanese and is used by the Nichiren sects of Japan. It is the transformational power, not the meaning, of these mantras that is important.

monks who, having spent years in apparently fruitless meditation, suddenly gain enlightenment by unexpected means, such as being hit by the master or falling into a puddle.

Esoteric Buddhism. Esoteric Buddhism (also known as the **Tantric, Mantrayana**, or **Vajrayana** tradition) is found throughout Northern Buddhism. Tantric Buddhism offers enlightenment in this life through mystical identification of the mind and body with a chosen Buddha. Intensive techniques to achieve this include recitation of **mantra**, the use of **mudra** (symbolic gestures), and meditation on a **mandala**, a graphic representation of a sacred reality. The esoteric tradition, particularly influential in Tibet and Japan, has produced much colourful Buddhist art.

Devotional Buddhism. Certain Buddhas, Bodhisattvas, sacred sites, and texts associated with Buddhism have attracted special devotion. Maitreya, the coming Buddha, has been a focus for messianic religiopolitical movements that claim to herald a new and better era. The largest Japanese devotional Buddhist denomination is **Jodo Shinshu** (the True Pure Land sect), founded by the medieval monk Shinran (1173–1263) and devoted solely to Amida Buddha. Shinran claimed that people no longer have the power to liberate themselves from samsara, so Amida has created – through his Bodhisattva vow – an easy path that anyone can follow. This involves reciting Amida's name in gratitude for having been saved. Simply uttering Amida's name is already evidence of Amida's power working through us and we are therefore assured of rebirth in his beautiful Pure Land. This sect is only one of many forms of Pure Land Buddhism found in China and Japan, where devotion to Amida has taken many forms, ranging from complex meditational techniques to the simple practice of chanting Amida's name.

Modern Buddhism

Buddhism has always played a key role in Asian history and politics, not least in anti- and postcolonial movements that aim to assert a national identity, e.g. in Vietnam, Sri Lanka, Myanmar, and Tibet. Buddhism is also reappearing in parts of the former USSR.

In some countries, such as Laos, Vietnam, and Cambodia, Buddhism has suffered heavily from war and political upheaval, while in Sri Lanka, it has become a source of ethnic identity for nationalist Sinhalese opposition to the Tamil population. In mainland China the practice of Buddhism has been politically circumscribed since the advent of communism. Buddhism in Tibet has suffered almost complete destruction by the Chinese over the last 30 years. On the other hand, the dispersal of Tibetan Buddhists following the Dalai Lama's escape from Tibet in 1959 has led to an unprecedented expansion of Tibetan Buddhism. Japanese Buddhism underwent drastic changes in the late 19th century from which it has hardly recovered. These included withdrawal of government funding for temples and encouragement for priests to marry. The most vigorous forms of Japanese Buddhism today are mass movements developed by and for lay people, with little involvement of priests and monks (who mainly provide funeral and memorial services).

In countries where Buddhism has flourished for many centuries, it has done so with the protection of the state or because the state regards itself as Buddhist. Modern secularism – the tendency to separate religion from politics, economics, and law – poses as much of a threat to traditional Buddhism as it does to other institutionalized religiopolitical systems. Buddhism's response, in order to retain its vitality, has been to institute reform, in either a progressive or fundamentalist way, depending on the circumstances.

As for its impact in the West, Buddhism has long been regarded as offering an ethical way of life, free of magic or theistic dogma. This idealized image of Buddhism as rational, tolerant, and sophisticated has been seen by some as the antithesis of revealed religions, such as Islam and Christianity. However, it is far too early to say whether real Buddhism will take root in the West as it has in so many Asian countries.

AVALOKITESHVARA

Avalokiteshvara ('Lord who looks compassionately down upon the world') is the ideal of the 'celestial' Bodhisattva. Avalokiteshvara is known throughout Northern (Mahayana) Buddhism and is regarded as equal to, or even greater than, the Buddha. In India, Avalokiteshvara is male and is described as the creator of the world and all the Hindu gods and goddesses. Tibetan Buddhists consider their spiritual leader, the Dalai Lama, as an emanation of the Bodhisattva, while in China (as Guan-yin) and in Japan (as Kannon) the Bodhisattva is female; she cools the burning fires of hell, saves people from shipwrecks, grants them children, and helps living beings in a wide variety of different guises.

▲ **The Goddess Guan-yin**
A sculpture of the Chinese manifestation of Avalokiteshvara.

Other Religions of India and the Far East

Confucianism • Daoism • Shinto • Sikhism • Jainism • Zoroastrianism

Although the world religions of Islam and Hinduism account for the majority of believers in the Indian subcontinent, and Buddhism in its various forms is widespread throughout the Far East, other religious traditions – some of which are older than any of the major faiths – are followed by many millions of the inhabitants of these regions.

Confucianism

The school of doctrines commonly referred to as 'Confucianism' represents a philosophical tradition that is primarily ethical and political rather than religious in its preoccupations.

Origins. Confucianism is conventionally held to derive from the teachings of Kong Zi (K'ung Fu-tse; 551–479 BC), an impoverished and self-educated wandering Chinese scholar of the Zhou (Chou) dynasty (c. 1050–256 BC), who is known in the West as Confucius. Having lived through a period of constant warfare and anarchy, Kong Zi desired above all the restoration of the hierarchical but harmonious society that he believed to have existed at the beginning of the Zhou dynasty. Since he thought that an enduring social order depended not on the enforcement of laws but on the personal qualities of those in power, he advocated the creation of a moral meritocracy. He regarded individual morality as being based on filial piety. This virtue was a key element in Kong Zi's beliefs, as it represented respect for authority and tradition and could be refined through the study of classical culture and the practice of moderation, loyalty, decorum and rectitude, tempered by benevolence. Veneration of ancestors, a central manifestation of filial piety, was therefore not a superstitious fear of ghosts but a dignified display of grief and a demonstration of moral continuity.

Kong Zi's thinking was therefore fundamentally rational and pragmatic, avoiding the metaphysical and regarding the mystical with distaste. It was also optimistic, for it assumed the basic goodness of all men and the perfectibility of at least an elite. A truly good man was deemed to be one who pursued and

practised virtue for its own sake rather than for profit or utility. According to Kong Zi, a gentleman was not born but made. Although Kong Zi claimed no originality as a thinker, he is credited with writing or editing works of divination, such as the *Yi jing/I Ching* ('Book of Changes'); history, such as the *Shu jing/Shu ching* ('Book of Documents'); and music, such as the *Shi jing/Shi ching* ('Book of Songs'). Sayings attributed to him and his disciples were collected as the *Analects* (*Lun yu*), as were a number of texts concerned with the correct performance of religious rituals. Mengzi (Mencius; c. 371– c. 289 BC), the 'second sage' of the Confucian tradition, stressed the intrinsic goodness of human nature and the

═══SEE ALSO═══
This section:
● Islam
● Hinduism
● Buddhism
China (vol. 5)
Japan (vol. 5)
The Indian Subcontinent (vol. 5)

Kong Zi (Confucius) *This rubbing depicting the founder of Confucianism is taken from a stone stele in the Forest of Stelae, Xi An, Shaanxi Province, China.* ►

143

A Confucian Rite ▶

This traditional rite is being performed in South Korea. Despite Confucianism's relatively small number of religious devotees, it continues to influence east Asian society in many ways. Confucian rationalism, pragmatism, respect for learning, diligence, and self-discipline are all major features in the dramatic economic progress in the late 20th century of many states of the region (e.g. Singapore, Hong Kong, Vietnam, South Korea, and Japan).

Thoughts of Confucius

Confucius is renowned for his wise aphorisms, which offer advice for many aspects of life. These are to be found in the *Analects* (*Lun yu*), which is thought to be the only work wholly by Confucius. Among the sayings are:

"Learning without thought is labour lost; thought without learning is perilous."

"To be able to practise five things everywhere under heaven constitutes perfect virtue...gravity, generosity of soul, sincerity, earnestness, and kindness."

"Our greatest glory is not in never falling, but in rising every time we fall."

endorsement of a ruler's moral authority by the 'mandate of heaven.' If this mandate were withdrawn from corrupt and self-seeking rulers, it would legitimize popular revolt. Mencius also identified five key social relationships: between ruler and ruled, parent and child, old and young, husband and wife, and friend and friend. Only the final relationship is equal, while all the others are hierarchical.

Development. Persecuted under the Qin (Ch'in) dynasty (221–206 BC), Confucianism survived to be adopted as the official ideology of the Han dynasty (206 BC–220 AD) and later dynasties up to the beginning of the 20th century. In 124 BC a state college for Confucian learning was established; bureaucratic selection by examination, testing knowledge of classic Confucian texts, was instituted at the same time and lasted until 1905. Under the Han, Kong Zi became the focus of a state-sponsored cult and historians attributed supernatural powers to him. Similarly alien to the rationalist spirit of Confucianism was the interpretation of the role of the ruler as exemplar and guarantor of Confucian rectitude. Divination and calendrical superstitions thus became absorbed into Confucianism.

Spread. By the 4th century AD, Confucianism had spread to Korea, whence it was transmitted to Japan. Both states adopted the Confucian mode of state organization and placed a knowledge of Confucian classic texts at the centre of higher learning. In Japan, however, pure educational merit never replaced hereditary social privilege as the basis of selection for government positions, nor did Confucianism ever challenge Buddhism as the dominant cultural influence.

Revival. Under the Southern Song (Sung) dynasty (960–1279) Confucian theory experienced a revival in China, partly because both Buddhism and Daoism were felt to be ethically inadequate. The Cheng-Zhu school of Neo-Confucianism focused on the universal opposition of 'principle' (*li*) – the permanent, rational, and benevolent essence underlying existence – and 'ether' (*qi/chi*), the physicality of the world. The task of philosophy was to enable a man to purify his 'ether' through study and introspection. Wang Yangming (1472–1529) subsequently opposed this dualism, claiming instead that subjective intuition was the basis for moral standards. The re-establishment of an authoritarian feudal order in Japan under the Tokugawa shogunate led to the adoption of Cheng-Zhu (known as Zhu Xi to the Japanese) as the official ideology of the regime. Confucian scholarship flourished, becoming a key to political advancement.

Endurance. Even after the fall of the Tokugawa, Confucian values of harmony, hierarchy, loyalty, diligence, and benevolence continued to underpin the modernized system of public education in Japan until the end of World War II. Also, such fundamental Confucian beliefs as the fear of anarchy, reverence of orthodoxy, and respect for state functionaries have continued in communist China, despite the rejection of Confucianism as a religion.

Daoism

Daoism is in many ways a mirror image of Confucianism, valuing intuition over study, spontaneity over self-discipline, freedom over order, and mysticism over rationality. Thus, in many respects Daoism complements the austere intellectualism of Confucianism, the ideology that for many centuries appealed to China's ruling male elites. Daoism consequently found its strongest devotees among peasants, women, and dissidents.

Origins. As a philosophical tradition, Daoism is credited to the sage Laozi (Lao-tzu; ?6th century BC), supposed author of the *Daodejing/Tao-te Ching* ('Classic of the Way and its Power'). Later Daoists claimed that he lived more than once and had travelled to India, where he became the Buddha. Dao ('Way,' hence 'path,' 'guide,' or 'course of action') is the central concept resident in all things, which can never be understood by reason or expressed in language but only learned instinctively through mystical ecstasy.

De is the manifestation of Dao, which when completely possessed by a person implies a perfect harmony with their essential nature and with the fundamental rhythms of the universe (i.e. night and day, the changing seasons, life and death). The rigour, rituals, and regulations so beloved of Confucianists are thus regarded as barriers rather than paths to self-realization. Wisdom is to be acquired not through knowledge but by discarding illusion and desire.

Development. By the 2nd century AD, Daoist teachings had become embodied in organized religious communities that employed a great variety of spiritual techniques in the pursuit of self-perfection and immortality. This might seem to contradict the Daoist injunction to accept death passively but the search for immortality appeared to many Daoists to be a way of attaining ultimate harmony between individual and cosmic existence. Accordingly, Laozi was given semi-legendary status, and was regarded as the first of the perfected Immortals (*xian*) of the Daoist pantheon. Among the skills attributed to the Immortals were flight, living for centuries on dewdrops alone, and eternal youth. Daoists embraced meditation, complex diets, controlled breathing, sexual disciplines (e.g. avoidance of ejaculation), gymnastics, alchemy, and the use of magical talismans (*fu*) to ward off demons, heal illnesses, and communicate with the Immortals.

Daoist-inspired popular movements, which often take the form of secret societies, have been persecuted by the Chinese authorities as threats to order, except during the Tang dynasty (618–907 AD), when Daoism was much favoured at court and emperors claimed descent from Laozi. On the Chinese mainland, the communist authorities have maintained this tradition of official disapproval of popular Daoism. Their attitude may also partly explain its acceptance as a valid expression of spirituality by the noncommunist government on the island of Taiwan (Republic of China).

Shinto

Japanese religion from the 6th century AD combined Buddhism, Daoism, and Confucianism (imported from China and Korea) with a variety of indigenous beliefs and practices focusing on divinities called **kami**. Sacred sites were marked by shrines to the kami and Buddhist temples, indicating that both Buddhist and native Japanese divinities were seen as part of the same spiritual entity. Some kami were ancestors of the land and its people, while others were protective deities, as were the buddhas and bodhisattvas. The Japanese revered both the kami and the buddhas.

State Shinto. The notion of a religion separate from Buddhism called Shinto ('the kami way') was a late development in Japanese religion. It had its roots in the Confucian-style 'national learning' movement of the 18th century. This set out to rediscover ancient mythologies about the founding of Japan. It took its modern shape in imitation of Western models of religion in the late 19th century when Japan – after more than two centuries of isolation – opened her doors to the West and embarked on the transition towards a modern industrialized state. Following the Meiji Restoration of 1868, when the feudal system was overturned, sacred sites were 'cleansed' of Buddhist elements and government support for Buddhist temples was withdrawn. The shrines were then incorporated into a new quasi-religious system known as 'state Shinto,' whose main purpose was to promote obedience to the emperor as a divinity, thereby identifying religious loyalty with a civic duty and providing a justification for suppressing dissent. State Shinto governed Japanese religious life until the end of World War II.

Japanese Religions since 1945. Under the US-style postwar constitution Shinto, Buddhism, Christianity, and the many new

▲ **Yin and Yang**
An early Chinese classic work on divination, the Yi Jing (12th century BC), influenced both Daoism and Confucianism. This contains the fundamental principles of yin and yang. The conventional symbol for these (above) shows the dark passive mode, thought of as feminine, interlinked with the light masculine active mode. In addition to the perfect balance between the principles, each contains a small part of the other.

A Daoist Funeral
Many of the participants in this funeral procession, at Gansu in China, are wearing white shrouds (the colour of mourning in China). ▼

Kami

While around 1 million kami exist in Japan, the precise identity of the kami of a shrine is not always certain. This elusiveness is part of their very nature. Apart from their principal manifestations as ancestral spirits or protective deities of a particular location or household, a kami may be a living person or a special place imbued with spiritual energy, such as a mountain, waterfall, or rock.

religions of Japan all coexist, and prewar state Shinto ideas, such as the divinity of the emperor, are no longer taught in schools. Most people attend Shinto shrines and Buddhist temples according to the occasion, regarding both as part of a single religious system. Broadly speaking, Shinto is associated with domestic affairs: the family, youth, growth, marriage, prosperity, good harvests or success in business, vitality, purification, and renewal. Buddhism on the other hand is associated with other-worldly matters, such as funerals, meditation, the afterlife, and memorial rites for the ancestors (see BUDDHISM). Shinto activities centre on the local shrine, whose kami protects the community and is the focus of many kinds of celebrations and festivals (*matsuri*). A protective *kamidana* (altar to the kami) can be found in most Japanese homes and amulets from shrines are popular. There are more than a 100 000 shrines in Japan, 80 000 belonging to the official Shrine Association. Each has its own local history and mythology. The most famous regional shrines attract millions of visitors, particularly at New Year, a time of renewal. Few Japanese people think of Shinto as a formal religion to believe in, but most take part in Shinto rites at some time in their lives.

Many of the successful **new religions of Japan** combine Shinto and Buddhist elements, promising a fulfilled and successful life to those who purify themselves and take proper care of ancestral spirits.

A Shinto Priest ▶

This priest is from the main Japanese island of Honshu. Shinto priests have performed rituals of purification and renewal from 100 BC onwards.

THE NEW RELIGIONS OF JAPAN

Many religious movements in Japan, even those that have their origins in the early 19th century, are classed as 'new religions.' They vary in size from a few hundred members to over 10 million, and together involve some 30% of the population.

Among the most successful new religions are Buddhist sects, such as the Sōka Gakkai ('Value-Creating Society') which has spread to Europe, Asia, and South America. By contrast, some of the earlier new religions are relatively small Shinto sects. These tend to focus on one kami as a 'parent' deity.

Many of the new religions that have arisen in the 20th century stress the role of magic, as a reaction against the growing rationalization of modern Japanese society.

Sikhism

Sikhism is one of the youngest of the world's religions, originating in the Punjab region of northwestern India in the late 15th century. The word 'Sikh' means 'learner' or 'disciple.' Sikhs are disciples of their founder, Guru ('religious teacher') Nanak, and his nine successors. Guru Nanak was born to Hindu parents in 1469 in the village of Talwandi (in modern Pakistan). Religion in 15th-century Punjab was influenced by Sufism (Islamic mysticism), and the Hindu *bhakti* (devotional) movements, which rejected caste distinctions. Both movements placed emphasis on a personal experience of God. These factors were to have a profound impact on Guru Nanak.

The *janam sakhis* (life stories of Sikh saints) portray Guru Nanak as devout but also critical of Hindu ritualism and the priesthood. Showing no interest in possessions, at the age of 30 he left his wife and children to become a wandering ascetic. While bathing in a river he underwent a profound religious experience, which led him on a journey of preaching, accompanied by his Muslim friend, Mardana. Finally he settled down with his family in Kartarpur in the Punjab. Before his death Guru Nanak appointed his disciple Lehna (later named Angad, meaning 'limb') to succeed him as guru. After the death of the final guru, Gobind Singh, the Sikh Holy Book became the vehicle of the divine revelation.

Sikh Beliefs. Sikhism is a monotheistic religion. Like Hindus, Sikhs believe in *karma* (deeds) and rebirth. It is not through the performance of rites, sacrifices, or offerings that a person can be released from the endless cycle of rebirth, but by *Nam Simran* – i.e. meditation on the *Nam* ('name') of God. However, final liberation can only be attained through the grace of God.

Scriptures. The Holy Book of the Sikhs is called the ***Guru Granth Sahib*** (also known as *Adi Granth*, 'the primal book'). This collection of teachings and hymns of Muslim and Hindu saints, was mostly compiled by the fifth guru, Arjan, in 1604 and completed by the tenth guru.

Worship. The Guru Granth Sahib plays a central role in Sikh worship. It is placed on a raised platform and covered with a canopy. Behind it sits the ***Granthi*** (reader), who waves over it a ***chauri*** (yak hairs bound into a silver or wooden handle). Since Sikhism has no priesthood, the scripture can be read by any person, male or female. Sikh men and women are required to remove their shoes before entering the temple, and to cover their heads during the service as a mark of respect. They bow or prostrate themselves before the Scripture. They receive ***karah prashad*** (a special ceremonial food of flour or semolina, sugar, and clarified butter).

Although worship may take place at any time, Sikhs tend to worship early in the morning or in the evening. Services begin with a recitation from the Guru Granth Sahib. The hymns of the gurus are sung to musical accompaniment. The service ends with a prayer called ***Ardas*** ('petition'). On special occasions Sikhs read the whole scripture for 48 hours. The Holy Granth is put away at night and brought into the main hall every morning.

Sikhs eat communal meals in their places of worship. This practice (known as ***langar***) was established by Guru Nanak as a rejection of caste distinctions.

Other ceremonies take place in the presence of the Guru Granth Sahib. Children are named by opening the Scripture at random; a name is chosen that begins with the first letter on the left-hand page. Sikh marriages are solemnized before the Scripture. The bride and bridegroom bow before the Holy Granth and walk around it four times while hymns are sung. Like Hindus, Sikhs cremate their dead. At the home of the bereaved family the Holy Granth is read continuously for ten days.

Festivals. Like Hindus, Sikhs celebrate Diwali but for a different reason. They commemorate the release from wrongful imprisonment of the sixth guru, Hargobind Singh.

▲ **The Golden Temple** *This marble and gold shrine, at Amritsar in the Punjab, India, is the centre of the Sikh faith. It stands in the middle of an artificial lake known as the 'Pool of Immortality.'*

THE FIVE 'K'S OF SIKHISM

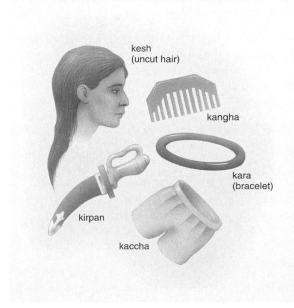

kesh (uncut hair)

kangha

kara (bracelet)

kirpan

kaccha

Guru Gobind Singh introduced the distinctive marks of Sikh identity – the five Ks (or ***Panj kakke***), which all initiates wear: ***kesh*** (uncut hair), ***kangha*** (comb), ***kirpan*** (sword), ***kara*** (steel wrist bangle), and ***kaccha*** (cotton shorts worn as underpants). Each item has a special significance. Hair, as a gift from God, should never be cut but washed regularly and combed twice a day. Although a turban is worn to keep the hair tidy, it is not one of the five Ks. The sword, symbolizing dignity, is only used in self-defence. The steel bangle worn on the right wrist is a symbol of equality and commitment. The cotton shorts (once part of a soldier's clothes) signify 'modesty, moral restraint, and continence.' Sikhs also abstain from tobacco, alcohol, meat slaughtered in the Muslim way, and adultery.

The Ten Sikh Gurus

1. Guru Nanak (1469–1539)
2. Guru Angad (1504–52)
3. Guru Amar Das (1479–1574)
4. Guru Ram Das (1534–81)
5. Guru Arjan (1563–1606)
6. Guru Hargobind (1595–44)
7. Guru Har Rai (1630–61)
8. Guru Har Krishan (1656–64)
9. Guru Tegh Bahadur (1621–75)
10. Guru Gobind Singh (1666–1708)

▲ A Sikh in a Gurdwara *Sikh places of worship are known as Gurdwaras ('abodes of the guru'). They contain no images but the Guru Granth Sahib, the holy book that is the focus of worship.*

Khalsa

Sikhs had suffered persecution under Mogul rule; the formation of the Khalsa marked the beginning of a distinct Sikh identity. The guru baptized five Sikhs, who offered up their lives for their faith, using *amrit* (nectar) made from water and sugar crystals and stirred with a double-edged sword. These initiates were called *Panj Pyare* ('the five beloved Sikhs'). Thereafter, all initiated males have been given the title *Singh* ('lion'), while women initiates are called *Kaur* ('princess').

During this festival, Sikhs light clay lamps and the Golden Temple in Amritsar is illuminated. Other celebrations in the year mark the births of Guru Nanak, and Guru Gobind Singh and the martyrdom of the fifth guru, Arjan.

The New Year festival for both Hindus and Sikhs is **Baisakhi** (which usually falls on April 13); it also marks the end of the spring harvest festival in the Punjab. The festival has a special significance for Sikhs because on this day in 1699 Guru Gobind Singh created the brotherhood of the **Khalsa** ('pure ones'). This is the occasion when Sikhs are initiated into the faith. On this day, Sikhs also commemorate the tragic events of 13 April 1919, when the British General Reginald Dyer (1864–1927) shot dead some 400 Sikh men, women, and children at Jallinwala Bagh (near the Golden Temple), whom he suspected of being agitators for independence.

Sikhs form nearly 2% of the population of India and live mostly in the Punjab. Sikh communities are now found worldwide – especially in North America, several European countries, and Australia.

Jainism

Jainism originated in Bihar in eastern India at about the same time as Buddhism (6th century BC). Its name derives from 24 saints called **jinas** ('conquerors'). The final saint, Vardhamana Mahavira ('Great Hero'; c. 599–527 BC), was a contemporary of the Buddha. Although the roots of Jainism may date from as far back as the civilization of the Indus Valley (c. 2500–1500 BC), Mahavira is regarded as its founder. Unlike Buddhism, Jainism is still practised in its land of origin; indeed, it has not spread beyond India. In total, there are about

4 million Jains in India, located mostly in the west and north of the country and in Mysore in the south.

Like the Buddha, Mahavira renounced a life of luxury and left his family to become an ascetic. He wandered for 12 years, subjecting himself to severe hardship. In order to avoid harming insects by treading on them, he swept them away with a broom. After gaining enlightenment, he discarded his clothes and spent the next 30 years spreading his teachings. Mahavira died at the age of 72 in Pava, a village near modern Patna, which has become an important place of Jain pilgrimage.

The sacred literature of the Jains was systematized during the 4th and 3rd centuries BC. The teachings of Mahavira are found in the scriptures of the two Jain sects known as **shevtambaras** ('white-clad') and **digambaras** ('space-clad,' i.e. naked). The canon of the shevtambara sect consists of 60 texts in three groups – the **Purvas** ('old texts'), the **Angas** ('limbs') and the **Angabahya** ('outside the limbs'). Digambaras follow their own canon.

Jains do not believe in a Creator God or Brahman. The universe is governed by an eternal law and goes through cycles of progress and decline. Since everything in the universe, whether animate or inanimate, is believed to possess a soul, it is important to avoid harming any living being. Jains place great emphasis on **ahimsa** (nonviolence); Jain monks even wear a muslin mask over their mouths to avoid killing insects by breathing them in. As strict vegetarians, Jains do not work in such occupations as agriculture that involve killing animals. They tend instead to work in commerce and industry. Mahatma Gandhi was greatly influenced by Jain ideas of renunciation and nonviolence.

Jains believe in karma and rebirth. The nature of a person's next life is determined by his or her karma. Actions that cause harm to living things lead to bad karma, which clings to the soul until it is worked out. Jainism places great emphasis on honesty and propriety in all matters, and on renunciation of material possessions. Good karma can be attained through following the path of the 'three jewels' (**triratnas**): right conduct, right faith, and right knowledge. Final liberation from rebirth is possible only when the soul is free of both good and bad karma.

Jain temples contain the images of saints, who are revered rather than worshipped as gods. These images are intended to help Jains in their contemplation and in implementing the saints' teachings. The Jain mode of worship is similar to that of Hindus and is performed by a priest. It involves washing the images, anointing them with sandalwood paste, and offering washed rice.

Jain festivals celebrate the lives of their saints. ***Mahavira-jayanti***, in April, is one of the most important of these, celebrating the birth of Mahavira. Both monks and lay people join in the festivities, chanting hymns and waving lamps in front of an image of Mahavira. Jains also celebrate ***Diwali***, which is associated with Mahavira's enlightenment ('nirvana'). The Jain festival of ***Paryusana*** is a time of fasting and repentance.

Zoroastrianism

Zoroastrianism is one of the oldest religions, dating from around 3000 years ago. Zoroastrianism retains some of the practices of early Hinduism (Vedic period), such as the use of fire and reverence for the forces of nature. The religion is named after its founder, Zarathustra (known to the Greeks as Zoroaster), who is believed by most scholars to have lived in Iran in the 6th century BC. Zoroastrianism was the national religion of the three pre-Islamic empires that existed in Iran (Persia) between 645 BC and 636 AD. With the Arab conquest of Iran in the 8th century AD, Zoroastrianism became a minority religion in its country of origin. Many Zoroastrians fled to India, where they are known as Parsees ('Persians'). The majority of the small Zoroastrian community is in India (chiefly Bombay) and Pakistan, though some adherents still live in Iran.

The prophet Zoroaster is said to have had a divine revelation that led him to proclaim his faith in one god – ***Ahura Mazda***, the Lord of Wisdom. Zoroastrianism is based around the struggle between two opposing forces, the 'hostile spirit' (***Angra Mainyu***, often called Ahriman) and the 'beneficent spirit' (***Spenta Mainyu***). The good or evil nature of the two spirits is not predetermined, but results from the choice they make between truth and falsehood. Evil is finally defeated by Ahura Mazda.

The Zoroastrian scriptures – the ***Avesta*** – contain many writings; the oldest are the ***gathas*** ('songs'), attributed to Zoroaster. The gathas affirm Ahura Mazda as the one God. Although hardly mentioned in the teachings of Zoroaster, rituals now play a major role.

Fire features prominently in Zoroastrianism but it is not worshipped in itself. Light in the form of a sacred fire is the symbol of Ahura Mazda. It symbolizes the presence of God in creation. In Zoroastrian places of worship the sacred fire (or ***Atar***) is kept burning continuously in an urn. Only ritually purified priests are allowed to enter the inner sanctuary.

At the initiation ceremony known as *naojot* ('new birth'), a child is given a sacred shirt (***sudrah***) and thread (***kusti***) to be worn around the waist to remind the wearer to follow the path of righteousness. Marriages usually take place within the Zoroastrian community. However, because Zoroastrianism does not seek to make converts, numbers are dwindling and marriage outside the community is becoming more common.

The Zoroastrian New Year's Day festival marks the coming of spring and symbolizes the annual resurgence of life and the defeat of evil. At the ***Farvardin*** festival special ceremonies are performed for the departed souls. The guardian spirits of the dead – ***Farvashis*** – are called upon in prayer.

Zoroastrians do not cremate or bury their dead, as both fire and the earth are considered pure and must not be defiled. The dead are left exposed in specially built large circular towers known as ***dakhmas*** ('Towers of Silence') where vultures eat the flesh.

Zoroastrians believe in a day of judgment, heaven and hell, a saviour (***saoshyant***) who will resurrect the dead, and in eternal life. It is highly likely that these beliefs influenced Judaism, Christianity, and Islam.

▲ **A Jain Statue**
This colossal effigy of Lord Bahubali, a Jain saint, stands at Sravana Belgola in the Karnataka province of southern India and is a place of pilgrimage for Jains. The nude effigy in meditative pose symbolizes the spirit of Jain renunciation and peace.

Mythology

Ancient Egypt • Ancient Near East • Greece • Rome • Celtic mythology •
Germanic mythology • The Americas • Africa • Solar and lunar myths

**Theseus and the
Minotaur**
*Mythology has long
been the subject of art.
This depiction of the
struggle between the
hero Theseus and the
half-man, half-bull
figure is from a 5th-
century* BC *Athenian
wall painting.* ▼

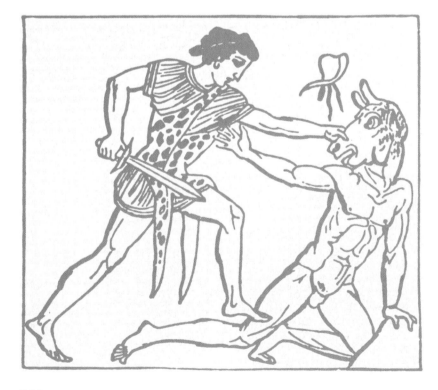

Mythology means literally the 'study of stories' (from the ancient Greek *mythos*, meaning 'tale' or 'fable'). Through myths, humanity has attempted to interpret momentous events. For instance, myths may concern the origin of the world, the actions of gods and goddesses, the purpose of life, or the meaning of death. Myths are deeply rooted in the early development of human societies and belong to an oral, rather than a literary, tradition (though they may later be disseminated and developed in written form). They may relate to actual events. Thus, the biblical story of the Flood and its antecedents in ancient Sumerian literature may derive from the periodic flooding of the River Euphrates, while the Greek myth of Theseus and the Cretan Minotaur relates to the Minoan sport of bull-dancing, in which boys leapt on to the backs of charging bulls.

Mythology is usually associated with the religious life of extinct cultures. Yet living religions have drawn on these primal accounts of man's relation to the world, while certain cultures still see myths as literally true. Thus in some American Indian traditions the creation myth is recited to newborn children to integrate them into the life cycle that is believed to have begun when the cosmos was made.

It would, then, be wrong to regard myths – as 19th-century scholars did – as 'primitive' forms of history, science, or theology. Myths are attempts to make sense of human experience, in addressing such questions as the purpose of life and the meaning of death. Even from a modern scientific viewpoint, mythologies continue to play a valid role.

Mythology also continues to be a rich source of material and images for writers, artists, and musicians. Often a literary version of a myth becomes its best-known form. The many myths retold by Ovid in *Metamorphoses* are examples of this; see EUROPEAN AND AMERICAN LITERATURE (VOL. 2): CLASSICAL LITERATURE. In general a distinction can be made between 'living myths' and mythological narratives that have been treated extensively in literature and art as **folk tales** – stories of magical or supernatural happenings that are recounted primarily on the level of fiction.

Ancient Egypt

Egyptian life was permeated by religious ritual and symbolism. The pharaoh himself, in his role as both secular ruler and head of the priesthood, was regarded as the divine 'son of the sun' and an incarnation of Horus, the sky god. The rhythm of life was set by the sun god Ra in the daily voyage of his ship across the sky, and by his deputy, the great magician and moon god Thoth.

Although the evidence for Egyptian mythology, in both art and literature, is vast, it is difficult to identify distinct coherent myths until a relatively late stage. Foreign writers, from Plutarch onwards, tried to devise 'classic' versions of Egyptian mythological narratives, using as a model the myths of ancient Greek literature, but Egyptian mythology is far more complex than these accounts suggest. The principal deities worshipped varied from one locality to another, and the pharaohs associated themselves at different times with a number of supreme gods. The essence of Egyptian religion lay not in a fixed belief system but in ritual and cult activities, for example the elaborate 'rites of passage' intended to ensure the safe journey of the dead into the underworld. There were some attempts by the priesthood to rationalize and codify religious beliefs, and in the 14th century BC the pharaoh Akhenaten (reigned 1379–1362 BC) introduced a monotheistic religion centred on the sun god Aten.

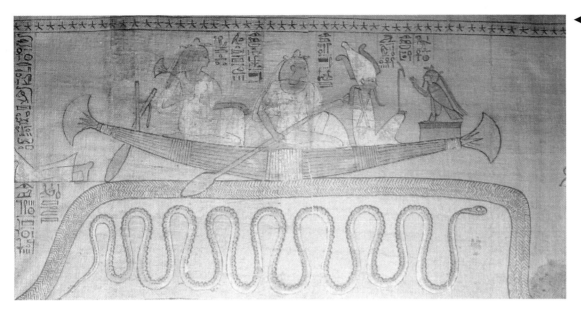

However, this was suppressed after his death and a polytheistic system, based around the rival wind god Amen, was reinstated.

Ancient Egyptian gods were identified with particular animals that were thought to embody the god's soul: the jackal was associated with Anubis, an early god of the dead; the hawk with the sky god Horus; the baboon or ibis with Thoth, god of the moon and of writing; and the cat with **Bastet**. Deities were often portrayed as human figures with an animal's or bird's head, and were further identified by special attributes indicative of their powers. Thus the headdress of Hathor – the disc of the sun between two curving horns – was later adopted by the great goddess Isis.

Deities were often worshipped as a trinity of father, mother, and child. At Heliopolis, centre of worship of Ra, belief centred on an ***ennead*** (a family group of nine deities): Ra (originally Aten), the creator and sun god, fertilized himself and gave birth to Shu, god of air, and Tefnut, goddess of moisture. These became lost in the primal abyss, where Ra sent his divine Eye to seek them; when they were reunited, the tears wept by Ra became the first humans. Shu and Tefnut bore the earth god Geb and the sky goddess Nut, who in turn produced two sets of twins: Isis and Osiris, and Set and Nephthys. One myth tells of Set's attempts to destroy his brother, Osiris, and how Isis rescues her husband/brother, and, by piecing together the fragments of his body, creates the first mummy. Set is finally defeated by the son of Isis and Osiris – Horus – who then succeeds Ra as chief of the gods (Ra and Horus are both shown with falcon heads). At Thebes the trinity of Amen, Mut, and Khons was worshipped; when, in the Middle Kingdom, Thebes became the royal seat, Amen was merged with the sun god to become Amen-Ra, king of the gods.

Ancient Near East

Mesopotamia. The earliest civilization (4000 – 3000 BC) to flourish in Mesopotamia (the region between the rivers Tigris and Euphrates) centred on the region of Sumer in what is now southern Iraq. It was here that writing was first developed, and Sumerian mythology and literature had an enormous influence on the later civilizations of Babylon and Assyria, in whose royal libraries much of the Sumerian tradition was preserved. Such works as the Epic of Gilgamesh or the poem of creation recited at the Babylonian New Year festival are Sumerian in origin; see EUROPEAN AND AMERICAN LITERATURE (VOL. 4): THE EARLIEST LITERATURE. Many Mesopotamian deities

---

Folk Tales

Folk tales often have mythical elements, but differ from myths in that they deal with stories of individual human (or animal) experience and do not have the religious connotations of myths. Examples of folk tales are the oral fairy tales collected by the German brothers Grimm in the early 19th century.

THE CAT GODDESS BASTET

The Egyptian fertility goddess Bastet (or Bast) was thought to protect grain – a highly important commodity – against vermin. In this role, she became identified with the cat and was depicted either as such or as a woman with a cat's head. Bastet's temple was located at Bubastis on the Nile Delta, site of a great annual festival. The feline nature of the goddess showed itself in contrasting qualities: the fierceness of a lion when roused on the one hand and the tenderness of a mother cat with kittens on the other. Real cats were venerated as sacred to Bastet; it was taboo to kill a cat, and owners mourned a dead animal by shaving their eyebrows. Bodies of mummified cats were buried in a vast cemetery at Bubastis.

An Egyptian Amulet ▶
This amulet is of a reclining cat with two kittens.

▲ Gilgamesh
Part of a seal impression illustrating the Sumerian Epic of Gilgamesh shows the hero figure fighting a lion.

can be identified in texts and art, but mythological accounts of their actions are less easy to interpret; different cities often worshipped rival deities or different forms of the major gods. One early cosmic image that occurs throughout Mesopotamian art was the 'tree of life,' nurtured by supernatural beings and reaching up from the watery abyss of uncreated matter (*apsu*) to join earth to the heavens.

A Sumerian creation myth tells how the primal goddess Nammu gave birth to the sky god An and the earth goddess Ki, who in turn engendered the 'great gods.' The air god Enlil, associated with breath or spirit, ordered the world and provided man with the materials for living. Enki (or Ea) played a similar role; he was associated with wisdom and the fertilizing properties of water, and with the creation of humans to serve the gods. Other major deities in the Mesopotamian pantheon include the mother goddess and earth goddess Ninhursag and her daughter Ninurta.

The goddess Ishtar (or Inanna) was the centre of a major cult. She was queen of heaven, presiding over both sexual love and warfare. Her father was Anu, a sky god later supplanted by Enlil in his role as chief of the gods, and her husband was the vegetation god Tammuz (or Dumuzi). One myth recounts Ishtar's descent into the underworld, from which she is released only on condition that she sends a substitute for herself. She names her husband Tammuz, who thereafter must spend half the year in the underworld, during which time (the period of the hot season) plants wither

Sacrificing to Bel (Baal) ▶ *This impression of a sacrifice to Baal is by the illustrator Evelyn Paul. Baal, the god of fertility, was worshipped throughout the ancient Near East, especially in Canaanite lands. The myth of Baal's conflict with Mot – god of death and sterility – symbolized the natural process of death and regrowth of the earth's vegetation.*

and vitality deserts the soil. Ishtar's mourning for Tammuz's seasonal 'death' was a focus for ritual lamentation throughout the Near East.

In southern Mesopotamia the control of water through irrigation systems had always been of paramount importance, and the gods were closely associated with the power of the waters. In the myth of the Flood, which occurs in the Epics of Atrahasis and Gilgamesh, Enlil decides to destroy human life by sending a deluge, but Enki warns a chosen survivor figure (known as Atrahasis in the former epic, and Utnapishtim in the latter), who builds a boat to save himself, his family, and animals.

The hero figure Gilgamesh was possibly based on an early Sumerian ruler. In the various versions of the Epic, he is a king of Uruk and semidivine son of the goddess Ninsun. Together with the wild man Enkidu he sets out on an adventure that culminates in the overthrow of the evil giant Humbaba, guardian of the great cedar forest on the edge of the world. After the death of Enkidu and further fantastic exploits, Gilgamesh meets with Utnapishtim, but fails to achieve immortality.

Syria and Palestine. While the Babylonians adapted Sumerian mythology, the inhabitants of Syria and Palestine (peoples of the Semitic group) developed a different mythological framework. In Phoenicia – a group of city states on the Syrian coast that flourished c. 1000–330 BC – worship centred on a goddess called Baalat ('mistress') and a god known as Baal ('master'). Baal was a storm god, 'rider of the clouds,' the son of El (the chief god of the Canaanites, inhabitants of Palestine before the Israelites) and rival of the sea god Yam. In their struggle for supremacy, Baal vanquishes Yam with the aid of two magical clubs. The Phoenicians' major goddess was Astarte, a fertility deity equivalent to the Mesopotamian Ishtar. Astarte also figures in the Egyptian myth of Osiris, in which she assists Isis in the search for her murdered husband.

Baal was perceived as the arch-rival of the Israelite god Yahweh, who in Hebrew scripture shares some of Baal's implacably vengeful nature, crushing his enemies and assuring victory to his followers. Yahweh is a primary creator god and, like the Phoenician El, a patriarchal figure. From a very early stage, however, Hebrew religion was monotheistic, lacking an extended pantheon or divine family, and its mythological component is mostly restricted to the Book of Genesis. Here Yahweh both creates the world and unlike other Near Eastern creator deities, remains closely involved in the fate of his human creation, with whom he communicates, delivering moral laws through the prophet Moses. Through the Psalms, Yahweh also emerges as a personal god, whose presence is directly felt by individual worshippers. This situation has comparatively few parallels in ancient mythologies. However, the Genesis story bears a striking resemblance to Sumerian myths, notably the episode of the Flood and the ark, and the Garden of Eden, which recalls the paradisial 'faraway land' where the immortalized Utnapishtim dwells after his salvation from the cataclysmic deluge.

Persia. Ancient Persian mythology centres on the opposition of Ahura Mazda, the god of wisdom, light, and fire, and the evil spirit Angra Mainyu (known earlier as Ohrmazd and Ahriman). Ahura Mazda spoke through a prophet, Zarathustra, and became the patron deity of the Persian royal house. The god of social order, but also of war, Mithra (his name means 'contract' or 'covenant') was an earlier supreme deity displaced by Ahura Mazda. Mithra's sunlike power was symbolized by his golden four-horse chariot. He was one of the principal foreign deities adopted by the Romans (as Mithras).

Greece

Ancient Greek mythology is the most widely known tradition, largely because it provided the subject matter of the greatest works of Greek art and literature, which later Western civilizations have drawn on extensively.

The stories of Greek mythology centre on the exploits of a large pantheon of gods and goddesses, who were imagined in human form, leading lives that paralleled those of their

PL. XVIII. Page 187.

Q·POMPONI. MVSA

THE TWELVE OLYMPIANS

The Greeks worshipped many deities and heroes, but chief among them were the gods whose home was Mount Olympus, the highest peak in Greece (on the borders of Macedonia and Thessaly). These 'high gods' were 12 in number; their Roman equivalents are given in brackets:

Aphrodite (Venus)	Goddess of love and fertility
Apollo (—)	Averter of evil and god of oracles
Ares (Mars)	God of war
Artemis (Diana)	Goddess of hunting and childbirth
Athena (Minerva)	Goddess of wisdom; patron of Athens
Demeter (Ceres)	Goddess of corn and crops
Hera (Juno)	Wife of Zeus; guardian of marriage
Hephaestus (Vulcan)	God of fire; patron of blacksmiths
Hermes (Mercury)	Messenger of the gods
Hestia (Vesta)	Goddess of the hearth
Poseidon (Neptune)	God of the sea and earthquakes
Zeus (Jupiter)	Supreme god; 'Father of gods and men'

human worshippers in many respects. Poets from Hesiod (8th century BC) and Homer (c. 800 BC) onwards created literary versions of these myths. However, it is not easy to determine the various regional and chronological differences in the beliefs and myths of ancient Greece. Certainly, from an early period Greek philosophers cast doubt on the literal truth of myth and began to interpret stories in allegorical terms, and by Plato's time educated Greeks regarded the myths of the Olympians as symbolic stories rather than as living religion. In the early 3rd century BC Euhemerus (fl. 300 BC) suggested that the Greek gods were in fact deified ancient kings and that their myths were merely a confused version of distant events.

The Greek pantheon is an intricate and extensive family tree, beginning with the first ruler of the universe, Uranus ('heaven'), and his wife Gaea ('earth'). Their six children are known as the ***Titans***, the pre-Olympian race of gods. One of the Titans, Chronos ('time'), fearing that he would be deposed by his own children, devoured them at birth. His son Zeus, however, was hidden and overthrew his father to found a dynasty of immortals. This group of major deities were known as the **Twelve Olympians**.

◄ **The Nine Muses** *The Muses – Clio, Thalia, Terpsichore, Euterpe, Polyhymnia, Calliope, Erato, Urania, and Melpomene – represented different branches of art, science, and learning. Many of the more minor deities in Greek mythology appear in groups: others include the Graces (three in number, personifying the virtues of beauty, charm, and grace) and the three Furies, who pursued and punished criminals.*

The Oedipus Myth

Oedipus, the son of the king of Thebes, was brought up separated from his parents after his father had been warned by the oracle of Apollo at Delphi that his son would kill him. On returning to his native land, Oedipus fulfilled the prophesy, unwittingly murdering his father and marrying his mother. On discovering the truth, in a frenzy of remorse, he blinds himself and goes into exile.

The founder of modern psychoanalysis, Sigmund Freud, saw this tragic story as an expression of every male child's unconscious desire to destroy his father, the arch-rival for his mother's love. Freud coined the term 'Oedipus complex' to describe this repressed hostility and mother-fixation.

Dionysus
The Greek god of wine is shown leaping from his chariot and followed by ecstatic revellers in this detail from the painting 'Bacchus and Ariadne' (1523) by the Italian artist Titian (c. 1490–1576). ▶

Lares and Penates

In Roman religion, the lares were thought of as the spirits of the dead. They were worshipped as gods of good fortune at crossroads and also as guardians of the home. While lares looked after the whole household, the storeroom or cupboard (*penus*) was guarded by the penates. Shrines to these deities have been found by archaeologists in Roman homes.

In addition to the high gods, many divine, semi-divine, or human heroes were venerated. Dionysus (Roman: Bacchus), a young god associated with fertility and especially wine, was the focus of a widespread cult. Heracles (Roman: Hercules) was Zeus' son by a Mycenaean princess, and his 'twelve labours,' involving superhuman feats of strength and endurance, became one of the most popular mythological story cycles. The exploits of the hero Theseus, son of King Aegeus of Athens, particularly his slaying of the Minotaur in the Cretan labyrinth, were also popular. In the later Greek world an important cult centred on the healing god Asclepius. He was the son of Apollo by a human princess, who possessed such great skill in medicine that, even as a mortal, he was able to bring the dead back to life, causing Hades, keeper of the dead, to object. Asclepius was struck down by Zeus but became an immortal.

Rome

The city of Rome was founded during the 8th century BC, and from earliest times Roman religion included the worship both of the major gods (whose head was Jupiter), and many minor deities, or *numina*, who presided over everyday activities and objects. Few of these minor gods were individualized;this aspect of Roman religion was later satirized by St Augustine of Hippo (354–430 AD), who pointed out that while the Romans required several gods to guard a door – one for the threshold, one for the hinges, one for the door itself – a single human porter could perform the task.

At first even the high gods had no associated mythology; the earliest form in which the sky god Jupiter was worshipped, for example, was a stone – Jupiter Lapis. Later, Roman religion borrowed elements from the Greeks, who had colonized much of southern Italy and Sicily. Thereafter many Roman gods became assimilated with their Greek equivalents, taking on their human forms and attributes. The Romans also adopted deities from other cultures; for example, Minerva was first based on a deity

ROMULUS AND REMUS

Romulus and his twin brother Remus were the sons of a priestess, Rhea Silvia, who had been raped by the god of war, Mars. When they were born, to hide the disgrace, the children were thrown into the River Tiber; however, they were saved, suckled by a she-wolf (above) and raised thereafter by a shepherd. Romulus is said to have founded Rome in 753 BC, but killed his brother shortly afterwards in a quarrel.

of the Etruscans of central Italy (though was later heavily influenced by the Greek Athena).

Roman religion centred on the festivals of the state cult, which, like the Roman Catholic saints' days in the Christian era, marked out the calendar and formed the framework of social, political, and economic life.

While Roman deities were seldom personalized, a more vigorous mythology developed in connection with Roman history. The Romans' legendary ancestor, Aeneas, was a Trojan prince, who escaped the fall of Troy to the Greeks and, after many adventures, founded a dynasty in Italy. His story forms the subject of Virgil's *Aeneid*, a work that came to be regarded as the Roman national epic.

Celtic Mythology

The term 'Celtic' is applied to the related languages, art, and culture of the European peoples who spread from Germany to settle areas as distant as Ireland and Asia Minor from the 9th to the 2nd centuries BC. Celtic peoples did not share a single belief system and left no religious texts. Foreign commentators (e.g. Julius Caesar in his *Commentaries on the Gallic War*) attempted to impose a classical structure on their mythology, which comprised a multitude of local cults and tribal deities. Later records, notably medieval Irish epics and the Arthurian literature of Britain and France, contain elements of pagan Celtic tradition, but are cast in an essentially Christianized medieval narrative mode. A broad distinction in mythology as in other cultural areas can be made between the 'continental' (i.e. mainland European) Celts and the 'insular' Celts of Britain and Ireland. Due to their longer resistance against Roman, and later Christian, culture, it is insular Celtic mythology that has been handed down in the most coherent form.

Throughout the Celtic lands, divine properties were associated with mountain summits, watercourses, woodlands, and animals. Oak and mistletoe had special significance; the Helvetii (a people living in an area that is modern Switzerland) worshipped the bear goddess Artio; while a great goddess Epona, associated with the horse, was widely venerated. The Romans named Mercury as the supreme Celtic god; in fact he is probably to be identified as Lugh (or Lug), after whom many European towns are named (e.g. Lyon in France and Leiden in the Netherlands). Lugh appears in Irish legend as the young hero of the Tuatha De Danann people, who came from 'northern islands of the world' to conquer Ireland in the battles at Magh Tulredh.

Other Celtic deities include the Great Father, Daghdha, god of plenty, and his daughter Brighid, a fertility goddess who was later transformed into the Christian St Bride, protectress of flocks and of women in childbirth, whose feast day on 1 February is the same as that of the pagan festival. The Gauls worshipped a thunder god – Taranis – whom the Romans equated with Jupiter. There are many images of an antlered god known as Cernunnos. He appears as Lord of the Animals and is often shown seated in a Buddha-like posture, as on the silver Gundestrup cauldron. Irish legends recount the exploits of various superhuman heroes, such as the ferocious warrior Cu Chulainn, hero of the 'Ulster cycle' of tales, and the hunter-poet Finn and his son Oisin, heroes of the 'Fenian cycle.'

Germanic Mythology

As the Roman Empire disintegrated between the 3rd and 5th centuries AD, the Germanic peoples migrated to lands throughout northern Europe. In Scandinavia, Christianity was not established until relatively late, and Germanic pagan mythology is clearly evident in the medieval literature of these regions. It is from the medieval Icelandic literature of the seafaring Vikings ('people of the inlets'), who settled as far west as Greenland and North America, that the most coherent account of Germanic mythology comes. The so-called *Prose Edda* (c. 1222–23) is a poetic compilation recording many ancient myths.

The Germanic creation myth tells of a primal abyss, the Ginnungagap, which stretched from the land of ice to the land of fire. Water flowing through the abyss was turned to ice, which was melted by winds, the first drops of meltwater forming the giant Ymir. From Ymir's body emerged both giants and the first humans. Ymir was fed by a cow, Andhumla, who licked the ice to engender Buri. His son, Bor, had three sons, Odin, Vili, and Ve, who slew Ymir and created the world – the sea came from his blood, the sky from his skull, and the earth from his body.

Asgard The dwelling place of the gods. Asgard was connected to the land of men –*Midgard* – by a rainbow bridge. Within Asgard stood *Valhalla*, a great hall where Odin hosted the souls of dead heroes.

◄ **The Gundestrup Cauldron** (detail) *This Iron Age vessel was found in a Danish peat bog. It is richly adorned with typically Celtic mythological motifs, such as the antlered god and war trumpets. Cauldrons themselves are a recurrent motif in Celtic myths, in which they have life-giving properties.*

The Swastika

Although in modern times the swastika has become identified with Nazism, the symbol has a long history that predates Germanic culture.

The swastika (from Sanskrit *svastika*: 'bringing good fortune') was used as a mark of good luck in almost every ancient culture throughout the world. It appears in ancient Mesopotamia, early Christian art, in Hinduism, and in pre-Columbian America.

A central motif in Germanic mythology is the struggle between the gods (who, from their home in **Asgard**, bring order) and monsters and giants (who bring destruction). The world is seen as an island on which stands the great World Tree, Yggdrasil, surrounded by an ocean where the World Serpent lives. The tree is a multiple symbol: it reaches down to the underworld and the source of all knowledge and up to the skies. Major deities include Odin, ruler of the gods and associated with magic and warfare; his consort Frigg and his son Balder; the fertility siblings Freyr and Freyja; the thunder god Thor; and the trickster Loki. In the myth of the cataclysmic Battle of Ragnarök, Loki, who has been punished for the death of Balder, escapes to lead the giants against the gods. In the conflict Odin is devoured by the wolf Fenrir, and Thor and the World Serpent destroy each other. The world is engulfed first by flames then by the ocean, but finally re-emerges cleansed and repopulated.

The Americas

North America. A wide variety of religious beliefs and practices characterizes the mythological traditions of the many Native North American peoples. Common features include a clear distinction between sacred living myths, which may only be divulged to initiates, and folk tales, which may be told for instruction or entertainment. Myths often convey a bond between humans and animals. Myths of creation and origin are especially important. The trickster figure features widely, sometimes in animal guise, e.g. the raven of the Northwest coast or the coyote of the Southwest and Plains regions; in Navajo mythology the coyote is a creator, giving seeds from the underground world to mankind.

Sigurd's Sword ▶
Tales of heroes, such as Sigurd (Siegfried) and Beowulf, abound in Germanic mythology. Sigurd slew the dragon Fafnir with a magic sword. This wood carving showing the reforging of the sword comes from a door panel of a 12th-century Norwegian church.

The distinction between sacred and secular is foreign to the Native American tradition, and so all aspects of life may have mythical significance. Direct contact with the spirit world is achieved through the 'vision quest,' in which a period of solitary fasting and prayer may be rewarded by the sight of an individual's guardian spirit, usually in animal or bird form. The guardian spirit may select an individual to become a shaman, a mediator between men and spirits who acts in a divinatory role.

The creation of the cosmos is often ascribed to a 'great spirit,' such as Gitchi Manitou in the Woodlands region and Wakan Tanka in the Plains. A frequent figure is the 'earth diver,' an animal – often a turtle – that brings mud from the sea bed to create the earth. The Inuit people of the Arctic traditionally worshipped three great spirits, the sea, moon, and air, who were both providers and punishers. The sea spirit was thought to be a girl, who had been consigned to the sea by her father after her forced marriage to a dog has failed. He first hacked off her fingers, which became seals and other sea beasts. Transformed into the sea spirit, the girl is joined by her dog-husband and her father, forming a group of feared and powerful deities. Belief in the immortality, transmigration, and rebirth of the soul is strong in Inuit culture, and artefacts depicting animal 'helpers' often include a tiny human face representing the animal's soul.

Mesoamerica. The earliest mythology of ancient Mexico belongs to the Olmec culture, which flourished on the Gulf coast in the first half of the 1st millennium BC. A powerful image in Olmec art is the jaguar-man and this symbolism remained strong in later Mesoamerican mythologies. Other Olmec gods who recur in later guises were a rain god, a fire god, a maize god, and the antecedent of the Aztec god Quetzalcóatl.

Unlike North America, where a nomadic or seminomadic lifestyle persisted in many regions into the modern era, pre-Columbian Mesoamerica was characterized by the early development of sophisticated urban societies. Despite widespread destruction during the Spanish conquest many remains of huge ceremonial centres survive; these comprise religious and governmental buildings dominated by massive stone pyramids that once supported altars or temples. Political and religious power were closely intertwined.

The Maya, a people inhabiting a region centred on the Yucatán peninsula from ancient times to the present day, traditionally worshipped a vast number of deities. Maya civilization was at its height between 250 and 390 AD. The supreme creator god was Itzamna ('lizard house'), to whom the invention of Maya hieroglyphic writing was ascribed.

The warlike Aztec empire, centred on Tenochtitlán (now Mexico City), dominated Mesoamerica in the century before the Spanish conquest. The supreme Aztec deity was Huitzilopochtli ('hummingbird of the south'), a war god and a storm god (later also a sun god), who was believed to have emerged fully armed from the womb of the earth goddess Coatlicue. Huitzilopochtli was worshipped with human sacrifice at the Great Temple at Tenochtitlán. Quetzalcóatl ('plumed serpent'), was the patron of priests and craftsmen and the inventor of the calendar.

South America. One of the earliest major cultures to flourish in the Andean region was the Chavín, between 900 and 200 BC. Chavín art indicates widespread worship of two powerful but mysterious deities, the so-called 'smiling god' and 'staff god.' Both have pronounced fanged mouths, recalling the awesome qualities ascribed to predatory creatures, especially the jaguar, throughout Pre-Columbian Mesoamerica and South America. Spiritually significant places, known as *huacas*, were important in Andean religion from the earliest times. *Huacas* might be features of the landscape, such as springs or rocks, but they might also be artificial objects. At Moche, centre of the Mochica culture that flourished in coastal Peru during the 1st millennium AD, the *Huaca del Sole* (Pyramid of the Sun) and *Huaca della Luna* (Pyramid of the Moon) were so vast that European observers thought that they were natural features.

Gold had a special spiritual significance, being associated with life-energy and the sun, and golden objects played a vital role in worship. The European conception of gold as a purely material substance was alien to indigenous peoples. European dreams of the riches of South America focused on the legend of El Dorado (Spanish: 'the golden one'), which derived from a ritual practised on Lake Guatavita in Colombia, in which a new ruler was covered with a film of gold dust.

The Inca empire, which flourished between c. 1438 and 1532, extended from northern Ecuador through Peru into Argentina and northern Chile. It was a highly organized centralized state; the ruler was worshipped as a deity, the 'son of the sun.' The great creator god Viracocha was a remote figure; in more immediate evidence were the sun god Inti, represented as a sun disc with a human face and thought to be the Incas' own ancestor; his sister and consort the moon goddess Mama Milya; and the thunder god Ilyap'a.

Africa

African mythology comprises many different traditions, although some features are widely shared, disseminated through the migration of peoples, trade, or conquest. Some mythologies (e.g. those of the non-Bantu-speaking peoples of the Niger-Congo region) are particularly rich, while others are relatively unknown. African cultural history has also often suffered from the imposition of Western viewpoints, which have affected the interpretation of African iconography. The celebration of sexuality is central to much African art and religion, which places great emphasis on fertility and procreation, and legendary lineages of venerated ancestor figures or 'culture heroes' (heroes responsible for establishing the norms of human society). One such hero is Lebe, venerated by the Dogon people of west Africa; after his death and rebirth he brought knowledge and social order to the human world. Kings are often thought to be of divine descent; thus the Zulu king derives his command of the rains from his heavenly ancestor, a god's son exiled for the theft of his father's white cow. Trickster figures are widespread, either in animal guise or in the person of Eshu (or Elegba). For the Yoruba of Nigeria, Eshu is a restless mischievous troublemaker but also a guardian figure; in the kingdom of Dahomey in west Africa he was seen as the gods' messenger, who was able to interpret every language. Eshu is a vigorous spirit of change and transformation, often depicted with a distinctly phallic headdress.

Many African creation myths share the concepts of the primal serpent, from whose body the earth itself and living creatures emerged, or the cosmic egg. In a Dogon myth the cosmic egg burst open to produce spirits called **Nommo**, who then created the world and mankind. Relations between the first humans and the gods are expressed in tower myths. In the tale of the Luba people of Zaïre, humankind, having irritated the gods, is exiled from heaven and sent down to earth, where life proves so unpleasant that a huge wooden tower is constructed in an attempt to return to the skies. To signal completion of their work, the tower builders sound a drum and flute, but this again disturbs the chief god, who destroys the tower.

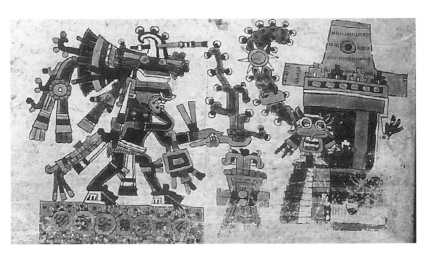

▲ **Aztec Mythology**
In this manuscript page, an offering is being made by the god of darkness. He stands before a temple inhabited by the rational owl, a symbol of destruction.

The Underworld

A main function of all myth is to describe an Underworld inhabited by the dead. In Egyptian and Etruscan culture, preparation for death was the centre of elaborate rituals. In Greek mythology the fearsome old man Charon ferries the dead to the Underworld across the Styx in return for payment. Thus the practice arose of putting a small coin, or obolus, in the mouth of a corpse.

SOLAR AND LUNAR MYTHS

EGYPTIAN SUN WORSHIP
Queen Nefertiti (died c. 1346 BC) is shown adoring the disc of the sun in this limestone carving. Worship of the sun was central to religion in Ancient Egypt. Solar religion was promoted by the state, and all pharaohs claimed to be incarnations of the supreme sun god Ra.

THE MAJOR CELESTIAL bodies – the moon and sun – are the subjects of many myths throughout the world, with many deities being identified with their powers. Both are revered as givers of light and markers of the passage of time, but they differ in attributes that are often related to gender.

MOON MYTHS AND GODDESSES

The moon, whose shape and movement through the sky clearly vary from day to day, is customarily regarded as female (not least because of the parallel between the lunar and the menstrual cycles). The moon's softer light creates a more mystical atmosphere, evoking imagination, and the creative and magical arts. Moon goddesses preside over the phases of a woman's life, especially sexuality, fertility, and childbirth. The moon's constant changes also link it to trickster figures. The sun and moon are sometimes portrayed as sexual partners.

SUN MYTHS AND GODS

The sun is typically seen as masculine. As a vital life force, it is associated with constancy, dominance, intellect, and social order. Solar myths often involve a god's travels and his combats with the powers of darkness. By day, the Egyptian sun god Ra sailed through the sky in a boat; each hour he passed through was thought of as a separate region. By night, Ra descended to the underworld to do battle

An Astrological Disc *This 16th-century Turkish illustration shows the seven stages of the sun (within the inner circles) surrounded by the twelve signs of the zodiac.*

with the serpent Apep. The Greek god Helios drove the flaming chariot of the sun through the skies; one day he allowed his son Phaeton to perform this task; unused to their new driver, the horses bolted, carrying Phaeton first past the constellations and then down past the earth, nearly incinerating it.

SOCIETIES AND MYTHS

Politically centralized societies, such as Ancient Egypt and the Inca Empire in the Andes, evolved a theology that associated the country's ruler with the sun god. In Mesoamerica it was widely believed that the sun god, especially as the Aztec war god Huitzilopochtli, needed constant nourishment in the form of human sacrifice. The symbols of solar mythology survive in Christian symbolism: the sun disc of Ra and other sun gods can be seen in the halo around saints' heads.

Some societies reverse gender roles in myths; an African myth tells how the female sun smashed the male moon to pieces in anger at his claim to be more beautiful than her. As a result, the moon now dares to appear in his full form only once a month. The Egyptian and Semitic moon deities, Thoth and Sin, were both male patrons of wisdom and writing. In Native American mythology, the Inuit moon spirit (Tarqeq) is masculine and is regarded as a sky-dwelling hunter who guarantees fertility and moral order.

INCA MONARCHS
These two portraits – from Lima in Peru – show monarchs of the Inca Empire with their celestial symbols.
On the left Manco Capac Inca I, who was known as 'the son of the sun' and ruled the empire just prior to the Spanish conquest in the 1530s, holds aloft an emblem of the sun, while on the right his sister Mama Occo, whom he married, carries an emblem of the moon.

SOCIAL ORGANIZATION

POLITICS AND GOVERNMENT

Introduction

Ancient Greece • Medieval political thought • The Renaissance •
The sovereign state and the social contract • Revolutions • Modern political ideologies

Politics is a universal phenomenon, the root of which may be said to lie in the basic undeniable fact of human diversity, and the disagreements that arise from it. Human beings adopt a variety of strategies, both constructive and destructive, for dealing with disputes and conflicts. And, indeed, such features as discussion, campaigning, compromise, rebellion, and war are all integral to political life. However, there is one method of reacting to potential chaos that may be regarded as the true defining characteristic of politics, namely its imposition of rules, procedures, and laws by means of a supreme authority, or ***government***. The order that government sustains ultimately depends on force, but some degree of consent and acceptance must nevertheless always be present, and this forms the principal element in free governmental systems. Modern governments have developed elaborate legal and constitutional systems alongside their armed forces, and in most countries in the 20th century,

extensive provision is made for educational and social services.

All governments now operate within institutional structures known as **states**. The origins of states lie in the emergence of rulers or chiefs as customary authorities in villages or tribes. These forms of authority became more settled and organized in larger social units and were usually united, or at least loosely linked, with religious and military institutions. These larger social units have varied in size from highly civilized cities to empires. History has shown that many state structures have disappeared or changed beyond recognition; the great majority of states existing in the modern world are creations of the past 200 years, many of them dating only from the turn of the 20th century.

The diverse conceptions of politics that have existed throughout history can be glimpsed by a brief chronological survey of different philosophies.

state A term used since the Renaissance to describe a self-governing group of people. The chief characteristics of a state are that it forms a territorial unit, and that it exercises sovereign power.

The Death of Socrates ▶
This painting, by the French artist Charles-Alphonse Dufresnoy (1611–68), shows the Greek philosopher drinking the poison hemlock.

Ancient Greece

The Ancient Greeks were the originators of many of the ideas from which Western political traditions have developed. Principal among these was the concept and practice of **democracy**. The main political community of the Greeks was the ***polis***, or ***city-state***. This term described a city together with its agricultural hinterland; the greatest of these was Athens.

Many ancient societies, including Sparta and Phoenicia, held popular assemblies as part of their governmental systems. However, it was Athens that established and sustained the first recorded constitutional system. The institutional structure was initiated by the great law-giver Solon (?638–?559 BC) and was given a clearly democratic character by Cleisthenes (died 508 BC). The Athenian city-state, comprising the whole of Attica, was divided into small areas that formed the operational basis – in effect the constituencies – of Athenian political life. About forty times a year the citizens of Athens convened a general assembly on the Pnyx hillside, which provided an opportunity for debate and oratory. Its authority was absolute. More frequent meetings – about 250 a year – were held by a Council of Five Hundred; and popular juries tried cases and undertook minor administration. A key democratic feature lay in the practice of choosing office-holders by lot. Moreover, there were strictly limited periods of service, except for generals.

The citizenry of ancient Athens set great store by active involvement in public life. In his famous funeral oration (430 BC) the statesman and general Pericles (495–429 BC) stated that the Athenians alone 'regard a man who takes no interest in public affairs not as a harmless but as a useless character; and if few of us are originators, we are all sound judges of policy.' See GREECE AND THE HELLENISTIC WORLD (VOL. 5): THE AGE OF PERICLES.

Athenian democracy was confined to the citizens (a hereditary status); of a population of around 200 000 adults, a maximum of 45 000 were citizens. As in other ancient societies, slaves did the hardest labour. Women were not citizens, and neither were the numerous (about 10 000) resident aliens, or ***metics***.

Ancient Greek philosophers were among the fiercest critics of democracy. Socrates (470–399 BC) was accused of leading young people astray by voicing subversive opinions and was condemned to death by a democratic jury. His follower Plato (429–347 BC) expounds the idea of justice in a state in his work *Republic*. Here, Plato claims that justice is objective and deeply embedded in human nature. Although he recognized that many skills are needed in an effective society, Plato regarded the ordinary aptitudes of craftsmen

◄ **Plato** *A pupil of Socrates, Plato was influenced by his aristocratic background in his political thinking. He proposed that an ideal society should be one ruled by wise benevolent men, placing philosophers at the head of this ruling elite.*

When some people are very wealthy and others have nothing, the result will be either extreme democracy or absolute oligarchy, or despotism will come from either of these excesses.

Aristotle, *Politics* (Bk. V)

and farmers as unsuited to statesmanship. Justice, therefore, needs to be enacted by an elite group of the military and the rulers, called 'guardians.' This conception of justice clearly arose from the immediate disorders and failures of Athenian democracy, yet it introduces into political thinking, in a radical way, the idea that institutions of wise impartiality are the best form of government.

Among the pupils of Plato at his Academy was Aristotle (348–322 BC), a *metic* from Thrace. Aristotle shared many of Plato's views (see PHILOSOPHY: EPISTEMOLOGY: THE NATURE OF KNOWLEDGE). They also shared a respect for the city-state. Aristotle's most famous remark, that "man is a political animal," appears to mean that humans can only hope to reach their full moral stature in the city-state, though not all will succeed. His work *Politics* classifies the main types of government in city-states. The three main types are monarchy, aristocracy, and constitutional democracy. On the other hand, there are debased forms: tyranny, oligarchy, and disorderly democracy. Characteristically, Aristotle prefers a hybrid form of constitutional democracy, or modified aristocracy.

Despite their brilliant achievements, the Greek city-states did not survive. Athens was defeated by the Macedonians in 358 BC and its independence was eventually suppressed.

Medieval Political Thought

Political thought in the Middle Ages was greatly influenced by the writings of St Augustine, Bishop of Hippo (354–430 AD),

Democracy

In its original context, the Greek city-state, the term described a constitution in which the common people (*demos*) held power, promoting their interests over those of the aristocracy. The capacity of this system to become debased into ***mobocracy*** has concerned political thinkers as diverse as Aristotle and Edmund Burke. In modern times democracy is applied to a wide variety of constitutions that have in common liberal institutions, such as a parliament of elected representatives.

particularly his book *The City of God* (413–25 AD). Augustine was writing during the decline of Roman power, and was concerned to dissociate Christianity from its demise. For Augustine, there was a major distinction between the necessities of the earthly life and the spiritual realm; and it was with the 'heavenly city' that humanity should ultimately be concerned. The worldly life, including politics, had its duties and should be lived in a Christian way, but supreme and eternal values were not temporal, but spiritual.

In the Middle Ages in Europe, a highly fragmented political system developed , for which **feudalism** provided a basis. Political authority and landholding were united: rights to land for cultivation or any purpose were dependent on obligations to service. Thus political units were small, communication was difficult, and administration hard to operate. In these circumstances the Christian religion provided the unifying link, both as a universal set of beliefs and morals, and – through the institution of the Catholic Church – an organization with authority, laws, property, and power that were independent of secular rulers. The distinction between religion and politics – often referred to as the **two swords** – was established.

A synthesis of medieval political theory can be found in the writings of St Thomas Aquinas (1227–74). The greatest Christian philosopher and theologian of the era, he was much influenced by Aristotle. Nevertheless, unlike Augustine and modern writers, Aquinas lived in an age in which Christianity was dominant and not open to question. Rulers were, for Aquinas, subject to the authority of God, and so were obliged to rule justly; similarly, it was the duty of subjects to obey. The concept of law pervaded all of Aquinas's writings, as it does all medieval thought. He distinguished four types of law: eternal, divine, natural, and human. Of these, natural law was crucial, for although it was God-given (like all natural things), humans had access to it through their powers of reason. Thus, human laws had to relate to natural law. Aquinas sought to unite faith and reason in a Christian philosophy. However, in later centuries the attempted union came under great strain.

The Renaissance

The politics of the modern age begins with the sense of new knowledge that arose in the Renaissance, the keynote of which was a

St Thomas Aquinas
One of the foremost theologians of medieval Christianity, Aquinas developed the principle of 'natural law' as a basis for the secular law of the state. ▼

FEUDALISM

Feudalism, a term only coined in the 19th century, was the characteristic system of social organization and land tenure in medieval western Europe, from the 9th century onwards. The word derives from the Latin *feodum*, meaning a 'fief' or property granted by a lord to his tenant, or **vassal**, in return for military service and a pledge of loyalty. Although the king was ultimately the supreme authority, the granting of hereditary fiefs meant that authority in practice devolved to a number of barons. Feudalism died out from the 12th century onwards, as a result of three principal factors: monarchs sought to curb the power of the barons; the shortage of labour after the Black Death; and the growth of towns.

renewed confidence in human competence. The achievements in the arts and sciences brought not unity, but rather the compartmentalization of knowledge into many diverse branches. One of these was politics, and a leading exponent in this realm was a Florentine diplomat, Niccolò Machiavelli (1469–1527). Machiavelli, who was exiled during the reign of the Medici in Florence (1512–27), wrote a number of important treatises. The shortest and most famous of these, *The Prince* (1513), scandalized Europe. In it, Machiavelli gave advice on how to achieve and retain power. For instance, it was better for a ruler to be feared, according to Machiavelli, as this gave a ruler more security. While not discounting benign rule in favourable circumstances, he advocated cruelty as a method of retaining power in adversity This pragmatism detached politics from religion, and so promoted the development of political authority, as distinct from ecclesiastical sanction. It also revived political philosophy as a branch of learning and instigated political argument as a distinctive mode of discourse. Machiavelli is accused of propounding the doctrine that 'the end justifies the means,' but the dictum applies only to the sphere of politics and should not be taken as an absolute judgment that sanctions amoral behaviour. Politics is a law unto itself, in that considerations of the state or of the community are paramount. The people most admired by Machiavelli were those who possessed the quality of *virtù*, meaning courage and public concern. His major work is the *Discourses on the First Ten Books of Livy* (1513–19). Here, Machiavelli emerges as a supporter of republican government, not arbitrary rule. Moreover, it contains advice on how this is to be secured; a body of citizens with *virtù* must establish a system that encourages patriotic concern with public affairs.

The Sovereign State and the Social Contract

The advent of renewed turmoil in Europe, in the shape of the Reformation, engendered a further critical development for the modern age; namely the arrival of the **sovereign state** (see INTERNATIONAL POLITICS). It was the belief of both Catholics and Protestants that in any state there should be uniformity of faith, and that it was the duty of rulers to enforce this principle. The multitude of small states in medieval and postmedieval Europe did not display such uniformity. However, in England and France, and thereafter in the Netherlands and Spain, more unified power began to develop. The creation of centralized power, referred to as **sovereignty** or **absolutism**, meant that in Catholic countries the papacy became dependent on secular rulers, while its

◄ **Niccolò Machiavelli**
Machiavelli is renowned for his exposition of the art of statesmanship. Despite a popular reputation for advocating ruthlessness and deception in political power struggles, Machiavelli's works in fact argue for a mixed republican constitution combining democratic and aristocratic features, and stressed the virtues of civic responsibility.

position in Protestant countries was even more precarious. The tension created spawned many wars of religion during the period. At the conclusion of the most extensive and destructive of these, the Thirty Years' War, the treaty of Westphalia (1648) endorsed many of the new principles.

The spirit of scientific discovery that pervaded this period provided further impetus for change. The common factor in many of the new political theories was the idea of a 'social contract,' namely an agreement made between ruler and subjects that defined the rights and responsibilities of each. The Civil War in England in the mid-17th century was sparked off after parliament challenged the monarch's claim to rule by 'divine right.' This doctrine descended from medieval notions of a 'great chain of being,' according to which the concept of hierarchy was implicit in all things (including social and political authority) and was ordained by God. Among the royalists was the philosopher Thomas Hobbes (1588–1679), yet Hobbes's legacy to the history of political thought was, paradoxically, his creation of a theory of political authority that made divine right superfluous. In *Leviathan* (1651) Hobbes began by expounding a theory of human nature: people are mechanical and driven by causation. Self-interest makes them seek power, but reason makes them fear violent death. Therefore they agree by a contract with their fellow citizens to obey a sovereign, or an assembly. The sovereign must have absolute power to provide order and security; otherwise, "a war of all against all" will ensue and – in Hobbes's most famous phrase – "the life of man will be solitary, poor, nasty, brutish

Since, then, a prince is necessitated to play the animal well, he chooses among the beasts the fox and the lion, because the lion does not protect himself from traps; the fox does not protect himself from wolves. The prince must be a fox, therefore, to recognize the traps and a lion to frighten the wolves.

It is necessary for him who lays out a state and arranges laws for it to presuppose that all men are evil and that they are always going to act according to the wickedness of their spirits whenever they have free scope.

Machiavelli, *The Prince* (ch. 18); *Discourses* (Bk. 1, ch. 3)

The Frontispiece of ▶
***Leviathan* (1651)**
*The body of the giant
in this illustration
accompanying Thomas
Hobbes's political
treatise is composed of
tiny human figures
representing the state.
The sword and the
bishop's crozier are
symbolic of secular
('civil') and spiritual
('ecclesiastical')
authority respectively,
as are the smaller
illustrations to the
right and left of the
title below.*

belief was not necessary if there was no likelihood of disorder, and persecution should
therefore cease. However, this toleration excluded atheists, who had no fear of God, and
English Roman Catholics, who were considered likely to support foreign powers, such as
France and Spain.

Revolutions

The fundamental ideas of limited government
and of toleration mark the beginnings of one of
the great political ideologies of the modern age
– *liberalism* (although the term itself did not
come into use until the 19th century). The period from the early modern era until the end of
the 18th century witnessed a consolidation of
centralized states, characterized by absolute
monarchy, in Europe. The next great developments in politics occurred with two revolutions of the late 18th century: the struggle for
American independence in 1776 and the
French Revolution of 1789.

The causes of these dramatic events are
highly complex, but much political thought
may be said to have anticipated them. In
France, the Baron de Montesquieu
(1689–1755) advanced his constitutional
doctrine that only 'power checks power' and
formulated the tripartite separation of governmental institutions into a legislature, an
executive, and a judiciary, in his work *Spirit of
the Laws* (1748). The famous *Encyclopédie* of
the 1750s was edited by Denis Diderot
(1713–84), and contributors included
Voltaire (1694–1778). This monumental
work expresses the confidence in knowledge
and reason as the keys to human progress, including the rebuilding of human government.

Most importantly, Jean Jacques Rousseau
(1712–78) challenged some of the most cherished notions of the Enlightenment. Far from
bringing better things, Rousseau believed that
the progress of the arts and sciences had distorted human life from its natural state of innocence, and that private property was the
prime cause of human inequality. In his most
famous political work *The Social Contract*
(1762), Rousseau claims that sovereignty
should belong to the 'general will' of a people.
This will is not the sum of their individual self-
centred wills; but rather describes a collective
desire for the well-being of all.

In North America, the upheaval took the
form of an independence struggle undertaken
by former colonies. In the process, a new
constitutional form of government was established, based on the principle of popular assent. The American constitution owed much
to the ideas of Locke and of Montesquieu. The
classic work of this period is *The Federalist*
(1787–88) by Alexander Hamilton, James
Madison, and John Jay. In the following

and short." The sovereign ruler is not a party
to the contract and rules by force. Rebellion is
thus an act of mutiny against one's fellow subjects, and is thus never justified, except when
a sovereign fails to provide security. Beyond
the establishment of peace and order, however,
Hobbes does not prescribe governmental responsibilities. Once security is attained, then
the arts, commerce, and industry can flourish.
In short, Hobbes's views appeared to have provided a secular basis for absolute rule. This
position pleased neither the supporters of parliamentary government nor the apologists of
the divine right of kings.

The most important exposition of the social
contract was given by Hobbes's compatriot,
John Locke (1632–1704). His version of the
social contract is found in the *Second Treatise
on Civil Government* (published in 1690). For
Locke, man's natural state included inviolable
rights to liberty and property. The duty of
rulers was to safeguard these rights by providing security, in the form of law, order, and
defence. Rule was thus legitimized by the *consent* of the people, which could be withdrawn
if the ruler endangered natural rights by
incompetence or oppression. Locke was not
advocating radical democracy, but in later circumstances his doctrine of consent was advanced in that cause.

Locke also promulgated the idea of toleration
in religious belief. In *Letters Concerning Toleration* (1689–92), he argued that uniformity of

ideology A term devised
(around 1796) by Destutt
de Tracy (1754–1836). It
now refers loosely to
clusters of ideas, more or
less interconnected.
These ideas rest on
fundamental
assumptions about
human nature or morals
and have broad
implications for action.

decades the USA developed a democratic form of government with a wide franchise (at first, like Athens, excluding slaves and women). Thus was created the first large-scale and enduring democracy of the modern era. The French Revolution had different effects. It was accompanied by a reign of terror (1793–94), with summary execution of real or imagined enemies of the revolution, and was succeeded first by the military rule of Napoleon Bonaparte, and thereafter by the restoration of the monarchy. Its effect was partly to encourage radical movements throughout the world, and yet there was also an understandable reaction of revulsion against it. Indeed, in the response of an Anglo-Irish writer, Edmund Burke (1729–97), lie the seeds of another modern ideology: *conservatism*. Like many intellectuals of the period, Burke had sympathized with the American Revolution, but was horrified by the degeneration of the French Revolution, with its high ideals, into the Terror. In *Reflections on the Revolution in France* (1790), he denounced the revolutionary leaders for their ambitions and their arrogance. Burke was sceptical of the idealistic notion that the individual has a highly developed capacity for reason, and therefore concluded that political change should be gradual and derived from past experience. In economic matters Burke favoured free trade over protectionism, yet the role of the state was not wholly disregarded: "it is a partnership in all science; a partnership in all art; a partnership in every virtue and in all perfection."

Modern Political Ideologies

Political ideas that have evolved over the last two centuries following the revolutions may be briefly explained in terms of *ideologies*.

The development of liberal ideas has been extremely broad and diverse. Most liberals are fundamentally optimistic – believing that enough freedom will ensure a positive outcome to all human endeavour. A great stimulus was provided to this current of thought by the Scottish economist Adam Smith (1723–90) in *Wealth of Nations* (1776). Smith rejected previous attempts by government to guide economic activity to the national advantage, advocating instead free trade between countries. Liberalism was supported by the philosophical doctrine of utilitarianism, whose chief exponent was Jeremy Bentham (1748–1832). This offered a straightforward explanation of human behaviour: mankind is driven by two motives, pain and pleasure; and the object of law and government should be to maximize pleasure (happiness). Obstacles to this ideal should be swept away; reform should be on rational grounds without regard to tradition, custom, or special interests. This doctrine was refined in the mid-19th century by John Stuart Mill (1806–73), who was concerned with the "improvement of mankind." Mill anticipated the later division within liberalism between those who emphasized market freedoms as the first essential, and those who believed that the development of people's potentials, even if promoted by state action, would maximize liberties.

We hold these Truths to be self-evident, that all Men are created equal, that they are endowed by their Creator with certain Unalienable Rights, that among these are Life, Liberty, and the Pursuit of Happiness. That to secure these Rights, Governments are instituted among Men, deriving their just Powers from the Consent of the Governed.

Declaration of Independence of the United States of America, 4 July 1776

The American Declaration of Independence *This 1794 painting by John Trumbull shows the American revolutionary leader Thomas Jefferson and his cosignatories presenting the Declaration of Independence to the Continental Congress.* ▼

Left and Right

The terms 'left-wing' and 'right-wing' derive from the pre-Revolutionary assembly in France – the States General – where the supporters of the king sat to his right, while the commoners (or 'third estate') sat on the left. This arrangement also operated in the revolutionary National Assembly, and the metaphor has been retained to this day.

Conservatism has often provided a counterpoint to other creeds, by stressing their weaknesses and follies and by distrusting liberal optimism. The highly complex theories of one of the major thinkers of the modern period, the German philosopher G. W. F. Hegel (1770–1831), have been claimed by both conservatives and liberals as supporting their views. Hegel's most pervasive idea was that history was an inexorably rational process, whereby the state was regarded as the supreme human achievement. For Hegel, therefore, the state was the embodiment of moral supremacy and the sole determinant of law and justice.

Both Hegel and Rousseau anticipate the most widespread ideology of modern times: **nationalism**. From the beginning of the 19th century, the conviction became widespread that every group of people who believed themselves to be a 'nation' should have the right to live in one united independent state. This doctrine rejected older dynastic systems. Many nations claim ethnicity as the basis of their unity, whereas others (such as the USA) rely on a shared history and culture. In practice, such claims are generally exaggerated, since there are always sizeable minorities within states or putative national territories. So attractive was the concept of nationalism that the nation-state has become a universal norm.

Socialism, the other great ideology of the 19th century, has had more varied fortunes. Its most cogent expression was in the form of **Marxism**. Since the collapse of the Soviet bloc in 1989–90, surviving governmental forms of a socialistic kind should properly be termed 'social democratic,' since they combine extensive provision for social welfare with democratic principles, such as a plurality of political parties. The current tendency is for both political poles to approach the centre: thus much conservatism is now merged with 'market liberalism,' and much socialism may now be termed 'welfare-oriented liberalism.'

UTOPIAS AND DYSTOPIAS

Sir Thomas More (1478–1535) derived the title of his work *Utopia* (1516) from the Greek words for 'good' and 'nowhere'. More's work depicts an ideal society and draws a satirical contrast with the mercantile societies of his age. Other fictional portrayals of such systems include Francis Bacon's *New Atlantis* (1627; a society run by scientists) and William Morris's *News from Nowhere* (1891; a paradise for craftsmen)

The term 'utopia' came in time to be applied outside literature to any any visionary system of political or social perfection. Several social reformers have attempted to set up real communities along utopian lines. Among these may be numbered some of the early colonial settlers in the New World, who hoped that self-sustaining villages would become the predominant social unit, and the **Owenites**, followers of the industrialist Robert Owen (1771–1858), who established model industrial communities in England and the USA. The French socialist Charles Fourier (1772–1837) designed ideal communities where the inhabitants could live in planned harmony. The distant future of full communism as envisaged by Marxism has a distinctly utopian character. Utopianism is criticized by conservatives, who claim that it disregards human weakness. They contend that real reform can only be cautious, and its ultimate consequences cannot be foreseen.

In contrast to the depiction of ideal worlds, there are dystopias – imaginary places of total misery. Like utopias, these have also been portrayed in fiction. Literary dystopias exaggerate particular negative traits of existing societies to expose their potential evil, but put no positive model in their place. Famous examples of the genre include Jonathan Swift's *Gulliver's Travels* (1726) and George Orwell's *Nineteen Eighty-Four* (1949).

VTOPIAE INSVLAE FIGVRA

Illustration from the First Edition of More's *Utopia* ▶

Democracy and Electoral Systems

Representative government • The extent of the franchise • Varieties of electoral systems •
Social cleavages and party systems • The 'best' voting system • Women's suffrage

Although the basic concept of democracy derives from the Ancient Greeks, who applied it in the administration of some of their city-states, the theory and practice of democracy was held in low regard for the following two millennia (see INTRODUCTION). It re-emerged in a different guise in Western Europe in the final quarter of the 19th century. Modern democracy consists of representative government.

Representative Government

The concept of a political democracy raises six basic questions:

Why is Government by the People Desirable? This is, historically, a pertinent question considering the profound distrust in which democracy was held for so long. Modern democracy rests on the notion of representational government; i.e. enfranchised citizens are able to vote for persons to represent them in the assemblies that decide how the state or country will be governed. It also rests on the existence of a competitive struggle for power in which those representatives are chosen on the basis of electoral support (i.e. the candidate with the most votes becomes the representative). In this arrangement, one system is considered more democratic than another if it extends the vote to more persons. Alternatively, it is considered more democratic if the level of competition between those seeking the support of the voters is greater. In modern democracy the values highlighted are usually liberty, political equality, and the closeness with which policy decisions follow the wishes of the electorate. Again, one system is regarded as more democratic than another if it goes further towards realizings these ideals. While it has to be accepted that no system will ever fully realize them, these are the considerations that make democracy a desirable form of government.

Direct or Indirect Democracy? In a direct democracy, those who have a vote use it to express an opinion about what the group of which they are a part should do. This was the practice in the Greek city-states. Advocates of direct democracy argue that a system in which citizens determine their own laws and policies collectively allows the fullest expression of political equality and the possibility of extensive political participation. Although there are considerable practical problems in realizing direct democracy in a large nation-state with millions of citizens, a number of devices have been proposed by which to approach it: the use of the **referendum**, an institutional structure that relies on small local decision-making units, and the extension of democracy to the workplace, are just some examples. Indirect democracy, by contrast, is a system in which voters choose some of their

===SEE ALSO===
This section:
• Introduction
• Political Parties
• How Countries
  are Governed
Communications and
Media:
• Print Media
• Electronic Media
The Industrial Age in
Europe (vol.5):
• Liberalism and Reaction

referendum A vote on a particular political question by the entire electorate of a country. Referendums are sometimes held in democracies when a fundamental change to the constitution is the subject of proposed legislation.

Direct and Indirect ▶
Democracy *The two*
diagrams show the
operation of these forms
of democracy.

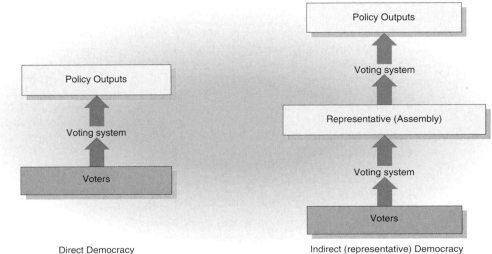

Direct Democracy

Indirect (representative) Democracy

▲ The Boston Tea Party (1773) *The dumping of tea from British merchant ships into Boston harbour, by American patriots dressed as Indians, was a famous incident in the campaign against attempts by the British government to raise revenue from the American colonies, which culminated in the American Revolution of 1776. A widespread slogan of the time was 'No taxation without representation.'*

That this nation, under God, shall have a new birth of freedom; and that government of the people, by the people, and for the people, shall not perish from the earth.

Abraham Lincoln
(1809–65), Dedication of the National Cemetery, Gettysburg ('The Gettysburg Address')

number to be responsible for making decisions about policy or legislation. Although in principle this choice could be made in many ways, the dominant version of the selection mechanism supposes that those chosen will in some way represent the electorate as a whole. Indirect democracy therefore adds an interim element in the relation between voters and collective decisions.

Does Democracy have a Continuous History? On the one hand, it can be argued that the ancient Greek concept of democracy is a valuable guide, in that it identifies specific institutions or ideals as indispensable elements of the system. On the other hand, it could be contended that the world of Ancient Greece is so remote and alien as to be worthless as an aid to understanding contemporary democratic practice. Critics point to the Greek acceptance of slavery, the exclusion of women from public life, and the restrictions on the extent of citizenship even among adult males, as reasons for discrediting the original model. Those who argue for some continuity maintain that there are many contexts (such as committee voting) in which direct democracy remains relevant, and that while indirect democracy may be necessary to take account of hugely increased electorates, it should, as far as possible, satisfy the basic requirements of the direct democracy from which it is derived.

Is Competition a Vital Element of a Democracy? The competitive liberal representative democracy that emerged in the 19th century may not be the best or only version of democracy in a large nation-state. Some political systems have called themselves 'one-party democracies'; in such cases the claim is that democracy is compatible with absence of competition between parties for the following reasons:

a) there is competition within the one party;

b) the one party produces policies in accordance with the wishes and interests of the people; or

c) the competitive element is not required in a democracy in which there is substantive equality between citizens.

Is Personal Independence and Equality Necessary in a Democracy? There is considerable disagreement about the preconditions for democracy, whether direct or indirect. In direct democracy, approximate economic equality, or at least independence, has been thought necessary. If people are to be able to express their own opinions, they must not be dependent on anyone else; otherwise, votes will be bought or economic leverage will be exerted and the process will be corrupted. In an indirect democracy, this issue has become identified with the defence of secret ballots. More general controversies concern the variety of economic systems with which democracy is compatible. Does democracy require, or at least work best in a free market? Or does it achieve its aims only if resources are owned collectively, rather than individually? What are the cultural requirements of a successful democracy, particularly with respect to the tolerance of competing views and accepting the legitimacy of the outcomes of the democratic process?

What is Fair Representation? Representative government relies on some understanding of the nature of representation and of the requirements of fair representation. The concept of representation is itself complex, but there are three important aspects in a political context. First, representation may be symbolic, in the way that a flag or head of state represents a nation. Secondly, one person may represent another by being authorized to act on that person's behalf, in the way that a lawyer represents a client. Thirdly, one person might be taken to represent other persons by possessing characteristics in some way typical of these others. These common features could include sharing a locality, class, or political attitudes with those represented. The problem of fair representation is to arrange the relationship between representatives, usually members of an assembly or parliament (typically containing between 65 and 700 individuals; see panel) in such a way that it is a fair reflection of the whole of the electorate. Although it is not essential that representation should involve a voting system, systems of representative government usually legitimize the process of selection of representatives by allowing citizens to cast votes to choose them. Hence the problem of fair representation becomes, in part, a problem of selecting the most appropriate voting system in a particular set of circumstances. However, the most fundamental

ELECTORATES AND REPRESENTATIVES

Country	Size of Electorate (millions)	Number of Members of Parliament	Voters per Representative
Argentina	20.0	257	77,821
Brazil	84.0	503	166,998
Canada	17.7	295	60,000
France	37.0	577	51,993
Guatemala	3.2	116	27,586
Israel	2.9	120	24,166
Malta	0.25	69	3,623
Mexico	38.0	500	76,000
Sweden	6.3	349	18,051
United Kingdom	43.1	659	65,402
United States	180.0	435	413,793

question in any consideration of the question of democracy and representation is who is to be an elector, in other words, the extent of the franchise.

The Extent of the Franchise

A casual view of democracy suggests that it is a political system resting on the principle of 'one person, one vote.' Nevertheless, even when this principle is fully enacted in practice, there will be marginal exceptions. Persons who suffer from serious mental illness, for example, are often excluded from voting as part of a denial of their legal capacities. Again, many systems make temporary or permanent exceptions of those found guilty of serious offences against the legal code. Apart from these marginal exceptions, however, the franchise has varied throughout history with respect to four considerations: age, gender, property ownership, and legal status.

All systems need to define some minimum age that must be reached before a person may vote. This is often linked to duties of citizenship, such as military service, or is tied to other tests of adulthood, such as the age at which a person is permitted to consent to sexual relations or to legally binding contracts. In general, the age at which individuals are recognized as having political competence has been reduced over the years, and in many countries stands at 18.

A second variable is gender. In many 'democracies,' women acquired the right to vote later than men – usually not until after World War I and in some countries not until after World War II (see **WOMEN'S SUFFRAGE**). This late enfranchisement of women was in part a consequence of the lingering effect of a distinction in classical political thought between 'the public' and 'the private.' This classical view separated the realm of public decision-making and concern for the common good from the world of household affairs and private pursuits, assigning a capacity to deal with the common

A Civil Rights March Civil rights leader Martin Luther King (1929–68) heads a group of protestors marching from Selma to Montgomery, Alabama, in 1965. Peaceful demonstrations such as this were influential in changing unfair legislation on the voting rights of Blacks in the USA. ▼

Voter Registration

Even in democracies, certain groups can still effectively be disenfranchised. For example, up to the early 1960s, high poll taxes and violence by White extremists kept large numbers of Black voters in the southern states of the USA away from the polls. After a vigorous registration campaign by civil rights activists, the Voting Rights Act was passed in 1965. The numbers of registered black voters rose from 1.5 to 2.5 million, an increase from 33 to 58 percent of all those eligible to vote.

good only to male heads of households. This view of the political naivety of women was also related to the whole problem of education.

A third variable is the property qualification. The long-standing distrust of democracy was based on two major fears: that allowing 'the people' to govern was necessarily to allow the least qualified to rule; and that enfranchising the relatively poor would undermine the security of private property, since their representatives would legalize dispossession. The notion that only persons with a certain amount of property should share in political power was (and is) defended by several arguments: that only those who possess property have a real stake in the affairs of the community because they have something substantial to lose; that only those who have taxable property should be allowed to participate in the process of setting government expenditure; that only those with a permanent residence are sufficiently responsible to be entrusted with the vote. Some arguments discriminate between property in land and other sorts of wealth, on the grounds that financial property is highly mobile and does not associate its owner as closely with a particular political society as landed property does. For national elections, most of the European countries abolished property qualifications in the late 19th century or early 20th century.

Finally, there is the issue of legal status, which depends on particular systems. Some political systems have a definition of citizenship that relies on qualifications of birth and/or residence. The status of citizen can be acquired by naturalization more readily in some systems than in others. Some migrant workers, for example, enjoy the right to vote in the host country, others do not. Historically slaves were, of course, not entitled to vote.

Apart from various forms of overt discrimination, political systems can also make it more or less easy for any particular person to secure a vote. For example, lengthy procedures of voter registration can indirectly discriminate against the less literate and the less leisured, as well as those who are highly mobile (such as seasonal agricultural workers). Again, the secrecy of the ballot affects the value of the franchise to those vulnerable to physical or economic intimidation.

The vote can be regarded both as a democratic right (in the sense that the people are entitled to cast a ballot) and a democratic duty (in the sense that the people ought to cast a ballot). Indeed, in some countries (e.g. Australia, Belgium, and Brazil) the electorate is required by law to vote. Clearly, any view of the proper extent of the electorate is bound up with how the whole purpose of representation and the voting system is conceived.

▲ **President Boris Yeltsin** *(1931–   ) Yeltsin casts his vote in the 1990 elections that were to secure him the presidency of the Russian Federation.*

Varieties of Electoral Systems

In a representative democracy there are two main ways in which elections may involve the people with their government.

First, some countries use a ***presidential system***. Such countries have two kinds of elections. They elect the members of an assembly that has responsibility for legislation; but the people also elect a president who is responsible for executing or administering these laws. Power is divided, therefore, between two branches of government.

Secondly, there are ***parliamentary systems*** in which the people elect the members of the parliament, and the government is then formed by some of the members of that parliament; usually, though not always, it is formed by the political party that controls a majority of seats in parliament or by several parties that between them control a majority of seats.

Presidents. Not all countries that have directly elected presidents are presidential democracies, because the office may be purely ceremonial (the presidency of the Republic of Ireland is one example). A presidential system operates in the United States and it has been common in many Latin American countries, but most political scientists regard it as a less stable form of democracy than those that have a parliamentary system. A few European countries (Finland, France, and Portugal) have elected presidents who have some independent executive powers, but not the full range; this form of government is known as a semi-presidential system.

A president may be elected in one of two ways, directly or indirectly. The simplest form of direct election is to count up the number of votes cast for each candidate and to declare the candidate with the most votes the winner. A problem with this arrangement arises when there are many candidates none of whom can attract a large share of the vote: the winner may then emerge as one supported by only a relatively small proportion of voters. To prevent this, some countries, including France, have a second, 'run off' election if the winning candidate in the first election fails to obtain an absolute majority of the votes; the run off election is contested between the first and second placed candidates in the original election. However, if none of the candidates in that election wins a large proportion of the votes, it is still possible that in the run off election neither candidate might be well supported among the electorate, even though one will have a majority of votes cast (failing a tie).

An indirect election for a president takes place by means of a system called the **electoral college** (see panel).

Parliaments and Assemblies. While the presidential system has been common in much of the Americas, the European democracies and former British colonies have favoured the parliamentary system. Both parliaments and the legislative assemblies in presidential systems vary in size. Countries with a small population often have correspondingly small assemblies, while the more populous countries tend to have larger parliaments . It is thought to be impractical to have a parliament with more than about 700 members because interaction between members would become difficult.

Elections are used not only to select the members of an assembly in the first place, but they can also be used to replace them before their term of office is over; this is the so-called ***recall election***. This device has not found favour in the European parliamentary regimes, but it is available to citizens in some American states (though rarely used). The state legislator can be made subject to a recall election providing the required number of registered voters sign the relevant petition; if the incumbent loses the recall election a special election is then held to fill the vacant seat.

There is considerable variation in the way parliaments and assemblies are elected. Electoral systems vary in three kinds of ways: ***ballot structure***, ***district magnitude***, and ***electoral formulae***.

Ballot structure. This refers to the electorate's choice of candidate and the methods by which it expresses its preference on the ballot paper.

The first variable is whether electors vote for a party on the ballot form (as in Israel), are only able to indicate support for a party by voting for a particular candidate of the party (UK), or can do both (Germany). Next comes the question of whether voters are restricted to voting for those parties (or candidates) whose names appear on the ballot paper or whether

Elections are won by men and women chiefly because most people vote against somebody rather than for somebody.

Franklin P. Adams
(1881–1960), US journalist

THE ELECTORAL COLLEGE

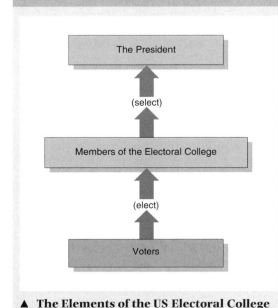

▲ **The Elements of the US Electoral College**

The electoral college system was introduced by the founding fathers of the United States in 1787 and laid down in the country's constitution. Its originators envisaged it as a device to decide on who would make the best president. Victory in a popular vote secures membership of the college; rather than being directly elected by the people, then, the president and vice-president are chosen by this body.

The system operates as follows: Each state has as many votes in the electoral college as it has senators (two) and members of the House of Representatives (at least one). This system gives most votes to the largest states: thus, while the smallest states, such as Delaware and Rhode Island have three votes, the largest (California) has 54. All the electors from any state pledge themselves to vote for the presidential candidate who wins the most widespread support in that state. As a result, the elected president usually gains a larger majority in the college than he would have had on the basis of a popular vote throughout the country. The college casts its votes by postal ballot.

The automatic nature of this selection process has negated the original purpose of the college; it rapidly ceased to be a genuine forum for discussion of the relative merits and shortcomings of presidential candidates.

first-past-the-post
Denoting electoral
systems in which a
candidate requires only a
simple majority (more
votes than anyone else)
to win, as against an
overall majority (more
than half the votes).

they can write in the name of another party or candidate. Some American states allow voters to write in the name of another candidate, although such candidates rarely win.

A third variable is whether or not the voters can show an order of preference between parties (or candidates). For example, Party A might be the first choice, Party B the second choice, etc. Some electoral systems do not accommodate a ranking of voter preferences, while others (such as the Single Transferable Vote, or STV, used in Ireland) require that the order of preference is given.

District magnitude. All members of a parliament could be elected in a single national constituency; indeed, this is the practice of Israel and the Netherlands. Most states, however, including all the larger democracies, divide the country into smaller territorial units, often called constituencies, in which separate electoral contests are organized. In the most extreme versions of this system (e.g. in the UK and Canada), each constituency elects only one member of parliament. Single member constituencies have several advantages:

• the smaller size of the constituencies enables representatives to maintain contact with their constituents;

• it is easier for a voter to know who their representative is and to make contact with him or her;

• it provides effective representation for those territories that are quite distinct from the rest of the country.

However, unless single-member constituencies are used in conjunction with some other

kind of electoral system (as in Germany) they have two related disadvantages: they do not allow for the use of proportional electoral formulae and, therefore, the number of seats won by a party in a general election may not be in proportion to the number of votes cast for it nationally. Secondly, the way in which the boundaries are drawn between the constituencies can have a major impact on the outcome of an election.

Electoral Formulae. Perhaps the most important difference between electoral systems is the formula they use for relating the votes cast by the electorate to the allocation of seats in the parliament (or assembly). The main distinction is between proportional and nonproportional formulae.

A ***proportional formula*** seeks to ensure that there is some correspondence between a party's share of the vote and its seats in parliament. This is achieved directly in ***party-list*** systems of voting – the most common form of electoral system in Europe. A mathematical formula is used to provide for the proportional representation (PR) of the parties. In fact, different formulae are used in different countries, some of which are more proportional in their operation than others. In general, two main factors promote disproportionality in PR systems:

• Some countries have electoral thresholds, i.e. they do not allocate parliamentary seats to parties that win less than a given percentage of the vote. (In Germany the threshold point is 5% of the total vote.)

• the smaller the number of representatives to parliament elected in each constituency, the more difficult it is to achieve a high degree of proportionality between votes and seats. (Spain and Greece provide examples of this effect.)

The *STV* form of PR provides for a fairly high degree of proportionality. However, the complexity of this voting system, which involves voters giving an order of preference for every candidate, means that there has to be a relatively small number of seats per constituency. This can create some disproportionality.

Nonproportional systems make no attempt to relate votes to seats. The best-known system of this kind is the **first-past-the-post system** (also called the ***plurality system***) used in the United Kingdom and the United States. It is entirely possible that the party that gains the largest share of the vote nationally may not receive the largest share of the seats in the legislature. Other forms of nonproportional formulae are the Second Ballot for the French National Assembly, the Alternative Vote (Australia) and the semi-proportional system that was in operation in Japan up to 1994.

**Posters for Parties
Contesting the
1992 General
Election in Israel**
*Although Israeli
governments are always
formed by the two
major parties – Labour
and Likud – to secure
power, they often have
to strike deals with one
or more of the many
minor parties that have
proliferated under the
country's particular
system of proportional
representation.*

Social Cleavages, Electoral Systems, and Party Systems

In practice, many people tend to vote for candidates and parties that represent interests in society with which they identify. This raises the question of which interests are politically relevant. Those special interests that generate conflict in a community can act as focal points in mobilizing voters at elections. This raises two important questions:

• which social cleavages have been at the centre of political conflict?
• what is the connection between the existence of a significant social cleavage and the formation of political parties?

Social Cleavages and Competition for Votes. The most overt lines of social cleavage have been class, wealth, locality, language, religion, and race. (Gender has always been a major source of advantage and disadvantage in societies, but until recently it has rarely been a central focus of competition for political power.) Candidates and parties have appealed to these sources of identity when seeking electoral support. The fact that some cleavages are more important in some countries than in others was the subject of investigation by two political sociologists, S. M. Lipset (1922–   ) and Stein Rokkan.

Lipset and Rokkan argued that support for political parties in the 20th century is the product of a series of social conflicts that arose during the preceding three or four centuries. In particular, they identified four lines of cleavage:

Centre-periphery This first source of division in European societies originated from the the Reformation and Counter-Reformation of the 16th and 17th centuries. Two issues that were to have a continuing impact on social identity arose from it – religion and language.

State-church This split emerged from the aftermath of the French Revolution, setting the claims of the state against those of the church.

Land-industry. This cleavage emanated from the Industrial Revolution and contrasted agricultural interests with those of industry.

Owner-worker. This, the second cleavage to emerge from the Industrial Revolution, put the owners of capital against those who had nothing to sell but their labour.

The outcome of the conflicts arising from these cleavages affected how the next conflict was played out. Eventually, in each country, distinctive patterns of social coalitions and antagonisms provided a basis for the different party systems that were formed during the first few decades of the 20th century.

The Interaction of Cleavages and Electoral Systems. The main thrust of the Lipset and Rokkan argument is that 20th-century party systems reflect patterns of social cleavage that differ from one European country to another and that reflect the development of social conflict over the preceding centuries. They gave relatively little weight to the role that electoral systems play in shaping the form that a party system took. In this respect they disagreed with a major tradition in political science – the argument that electoral systems were a key variable in shaping party systems.

A major proponent of this view has been the French political scientist Maurice Duverger (1917–   ), who argued that plurality electoral systems tended to produce two-party systems, while PR electoral systems produced multiparty systems. While Lipset and Rokkan held that party systems were caused by social factors, Duverger argued that the specific kind of political institution in a country was the chief determining factor.

Neither side can claim complete victory. Sociologists were correct in claiming that patterns of voting could survive changes in an electoral system, and that more usually it was changes in a party system that prompted a change in an electoral system, rather than the other way round. But the 'rules of the political game,' of which electoral systems are one type, help to shape the political environment, and make it possible for politicians to exploit particular types of cleavage. The institutionalists are right in insisting that a party system is not simply a reflection of a given pattern of conflict in a society; changes in the institutional environment can help to make some social cleavages more relevant than they otherwise would be, while others became less relevant.

Frozen Cleavages in the Electorate. One of Lipset and Rokkan's most famous arguments was that European party systems in the

▲ **The Owner-Worker Cleavage**
An English engraving of a textile workshop in the early years of the Industrial Revolution illustrates the division that arose between capitalist owners and the new mass of labourers recruited to work in industry. On the far right, the factory boss, stick in hand, creeps up to beat the exhausted worker who has fallen asleep at his loom (left).

> You won the elections,
> but I won the count.
>
> **Anastasio Somoza**
> (1925–80), Nicaraguan
> dictator, replying to political
> opponents' accusations of
> ballot rigging

mid-20th century reflected earlier patterns of social cleavage. Societies had changed in the intervening period, whereas party systems had not. Parties were still appealing to the same sectors of society as they had traditionally. There were two main reasons for this. On the one hand, allegiance to a particular party tended to be inherited within families and through other social networks, so that the best way to predict how someone would vote was how their parents voted. On the other hand, it is difficult and costly to start new parties, so that the older parties do not experience enough competition to make them shift from their old electoral coalitions. In this sense, politics had become frozen.

In the 1970s it was thought that this pattern might be breaking down, but despite evidence of growing electoral volatility in some countries (notably Denmark), there was no evidence of a general trend towards the break-up, and reformation, of European party systems. Nor was there much evidence of this happening in liberal democracies elsewhere in the world. However, in the early to mid-1990s, some re-evaluation of this conclusion was needed. In a few countries – notably Canada, Italy, and Japan – major electoral defeats for governing parties meant that new parties came to prominence, either sharing power or as the major party of opposition.

Significantly, in all three countries the political upheavals went hand-in-hand with reform of the electoral system or of electoral rules. In Italy and Japan major reforms of the electoral system occurred, while in Canada one of the major controversies concerned demands for making the upper chamber of the legislature (the Senate) an elected body. These examples illustrate the significance of the 'rules of the game.' Changing the rules can have an impact on who wins; for this reason

The Count *Counting ballot papers and announcing the result of a national election can be a lengthy procedure, especially if ballot boxes have to be collected from remote districts of a country (such as here, in the Philippines) or if voting in many constituencies is so close that recounts become necessary.* ▼

ELECTORAL FRAUD

Manipulating the electoral system to frustrate the wishes of the people can take a number of forms, such as ballot rigging (e.g. bribery or intimidation of voters), personation (multiple voting by one individual), misleading campaign propaganda, fraudulent counting procedures, or even false polling stations established in areas with a strongly anti-ruling party electorate (where all votes cast are taken away and destroyed).

Sometimes, governments simply defy the choice of the electorate and refuse to relinquish power. In June 1993 in Nigeria, the military junta – the National Defence and Security Council – declared void the result of the free and fair election, which had been won by the Social Democratic Party.

periods of electoral upheaval are always likely to be associated with efforts to change some of the political rules – including, in some cases, the electoral system.

The 'Best' Voting System

It is no simple task to determine whether one voting system has characteristics that make it superior to all others. Questions about the appropriateness of procedures in any one country arise only infrequently, when it becomes apparent that the existing system has particular disadvantages. This happened in the 1990s in Italy, for example, when moves were made to reduce highly proportional and fragmented representation in parliament. Conversely, in some other countries (e.g. the UK), concerns have been voiced over the lack of proportionality produced by the first-past-the-post system. Critics argue that geographically dispersed support is underrepresented and that the plurality system unduly favours two-party politics.

From these and other cases, it is apparent that the answer to the question of whether there is a 'best' system depends upon where it is to be used and what system it is to replace. For example, the plurality system employed in a society already bitterly divided between a permanent majority and minority on religious grounds is likely to produce undemocratic results; a proportional system that encourages the mobilization of a very large number of distinctive political attitudes may suffer frequent changes of coalition government if there is not a general acceptance of a need for accommodation (e.g. the French Fourth Republic, 1946–58).

WOMEN'S SUFFRAGE

THE ORGANIZED CAMPAIGN for the enfranchisement of women began in the mid-19th century and had won women the right to vote in many countries by the 1920s. At the end of the 20th century, women's suffrage is a near-universal reality, although other forms of discrimination persist in some parts of the world.

BEGINNINGS

The first assembly on women's rights took place in the USA. The Seneca Falls Convention of 1848 in New York State voiced the principle that 'all men and women are created equal.' 1869 saw two important developments; the NAWSA (National American Woman Suffrage Association) was established with the aim of securing the ballot for women by an amendment to the constitution, and Wyoming became the first legislative body to adopt women's suffrage.

NATIONAL RECOGNITION

In 1893, New Zealand became the first country to accord women the vote at a national level. Australia followed suit after the turn of the century. In western Europe, Nordic countries (i.e. Finland, Norway, and Denmark) pioneered votes for women between 1906 and 1915.

Force Feeding of a British Suffragette
While in prison, women hunger strikers were subjected to feeding by force. Even those who were released on medical grounds were later rearrested.

A great impetus to votes for women in western Europe was given by the outbreak of World War I. Women became indispensable to the war economy, acquiring new skills and responsibilities. At the end of the war, in the period from 1918 to 1920, many countries gave women the vote.

SUFFRAGETTE PARADE LEADER
Women in the USA were at the forefront of the campaign for voting rights. In 1920 the 19th Amendment to the constitution was proclaimed, giving women equal voting rights with men.

WOMEN LEADERS

Women's suffrage also enabled women with political ambitions to develop their talents.
Many women have had distinguished political careers. Their parliamentary representation is particularly strong in Nordic countries, and South Asian stateswomen have been prominent on the world political stage.

▲ **Indira Gandhi** *(1917–84)*

◀ **Golda Meir** *(1898–1978)*

Benazir Bhutto *(1953–)* ▲

In the United Kingdom, some limited reforms abolishing discrimination had been achieved by the end of the 19th century, but failure to secure the vote led to the formation of the most radical early women's organization in 1903. The members of the WSPU (Women's Social and Political Union) undertook militant actions, such as bombings and chaining themselves to railings. Restricted voting rights – for all women over 30 – were finally won in 1918; in 1928, the franchise was extended to women over 21, putting female voters on an equal footing with male voters.

In countries that had resisted the initial wave of female enfranchisement, World War II proved decisive, with Italy, France, and Japan extending suffrage to women in 1945. During the late 1940s and early 1950s, most South American countries gave the vote to women; in Argentina, Eva Perón was instrumental in securing this right.

Although most Muslim countries now allow women the vote, the absolute monarchies of Arabia (e.g. Saudi Arabia and Kuwait) still do not accord their female citizens this right.

Political Parties

*Parties, movements, and pressure groups • Party systems • Parties and nations •
Political orientations • Parties and the state • Origins • European parties •
US parties • African parties • Parties in former communist countries •
Asian parties • The future of political parties*

Many thinkers have attempted to define the concept of a political party. Perhaps a simple working definition would be: a group of men and women united together to promote the national interest by means of a clearly articulated and coherent set of policies agreed between them. However, it needs to be added that the national interest is open to a number of different, and often conflicting, interpretations.

Parties, Movements, and Pressure Groups

There is some difficulty in distinguishing between a political party and a political movement. In general, a movement is an association of people who share a common set of political beliefs, though these beliefs may be very loosely defined. For example, the socialist movement is international. In many countries there is a socialist party, organized in such a way that it aspires to form a government. Each national party, while adopting the broad principles of the movement, adapts them to local political and cultural conditions. The difference between a movement and a party may further be illustrated by the fact that a movement embraces a number of different bodies, all of which are affiliated to the central entity, the party. For example, in some countries the socialist movement embraces the trade unions and a number of organizations devoted to various aspects of the welfare of workers, as well as the narrowly political party.

Pressure groups are associations that seek to *influence* a government, whereas parties seek to *form* a government. Frequently, the members of pressure groups may have diverse political views, but come together to promote a single issue. One such grouping is CND (Campaign for Nuclear Disarmament), whose membership crosses traditional party lines.

**A Ballot Paper for the South African General
Election** *This election, held in April 1994, gave the
great majority of the South African people – the entire
Black populace – their first opportunity to participate
in the democratic process. However, as many of this
disadvantaged group are illiterate, posters displayed the
symbols of the many competing parties, together with
pictures of the party leaders, to help voters identify
their choice correctly.* ▶

Party Systems

According to the form of government operating within a particular country, which may have arisen through revolutionary change or evolved through tradition, party systems fall into various categories. **Multiparty democracy** is the most common of these; several parties compete for power, with one either winning outright or two or more governing in coalition. In countries in which elections are conducted by a first-past-the-post system (e.g. the USA and the United Kingdom; see DEMOCRACY AND ELECTORAL SYSTEMS), **two-party** systems have tended to develop. Although other

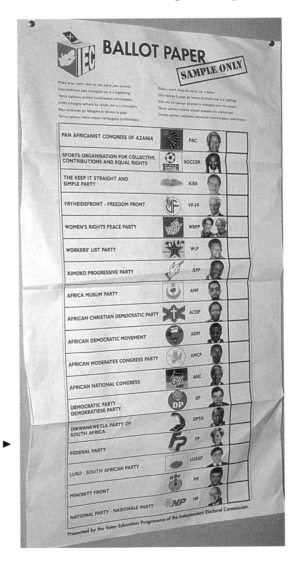

An elective
despotism was not
the government we
fought for.

Thomas Jefferson,
expressing his mistrust of
political parties

◀ **A National Convention of the US Republican Party** *Conventions – gatherings of party delegates – are organized by both major political parties in the USA to nominate a candidate for the presidential election.*

parties exist within such systems, only two parties ever stand a realistic chance of governing. In the ***one-party state***, government is conducted by a single organization, which justifies its monopoly of power by appeals to national unity. It remains in power until ousted.

Parties and Nations
Because they are strongly identified with the promotion of sectional interests, political parties have been condemned by some thinkers as being fundamentally hostile to the concept of a unified nation. One of the originators of the American constitution, Thomas Jefferson (1743–1826), was very concerned at the prospect of sectional interests being institutionalized in a party system. John Stuart Mill (1806–73), the influential English liberal thinker, argued in his essay *On Liberty* (1859) that an extension of the franchise to those not ready for complex political decisions would result in what he called the "tyranny of the majority." Others writers have gone even further in formulating their distrust of the development of political parties: the French philosopher, Jean Jacques Rousseau (1712–78), argued that the only way a democracy could operate was through direct participation; that is, citizens should involve themselves in political decisions without others representing their interests. His concept of an ideal democracy was the direct system of ancient Greece (see INTRODUCTION).

In the modern world, however, a direct system would not be viable. The practical difficulties of consulting all citizens on even the general direction of government legislation,

much less the details of policy, would be insuperable. Therefore, although some forms of direct democracy are occasionally attempted – e.g. plebiscites or referenda – the most common form of democracy in the 20th century is representative democracy, in which individuals are represented in parliament by members of the political party they support.

In times of crisis, such as war or major economic depression, political parties often agree that the national interest is best served if they cooperate in a government of national unity.

Political Orientations
A key element of a political party is the set of values that it collectively holds to and attempts to articulate to the electorate. These sets of beliefs and values are referred to as ***ideologies***; that is, systems of ideas describing the way in which a society is structured, and how the society might be changed for the better (see INTRODUCTION). Almost all political parties are – or claim to be – influenced by at least one ideology. A standard way to divide these ideologies in their relation to political parties is to describe them as either ***left-*** or ***right-wing***. These concepts are derived from the legislative body in pre-Revolutionary France known as the States General, or *Estates-General* (see INTRODUCTION). The term 'right-wing' denotes parties who favour the status quo and are broadly conservative, whereas 'left-wing' parties are more radical and favour making social and economic changes to achieve greater equality, especially in terms of income, security, and opportunity. ***Centre*** parties, as their name suggests, are those that fall somewhere

Party or Pressure Group?

An example of a single-issue pressure group becoming a significant political party is offered by the right-wing French protest movement of the 1950s known as *Poujadisme*. Founded by the shopkeeper Pierre Poujade (1920–) in order to form a lobby against high taxation, this movement drew support from peasants and small businessmen. In the 1956 General Assembly elections, Poujadiste candidates attracted over 2 million votes and won more than 50 seats. However, all these electoral gains were soon lost, and *Poujadisme* reverted to being a pressure group.

Lenin's method leads to this: the party organization at first substitutes itself for the party as a whole. Then the central committee substitutes itself for the party organization, and finally a single dictator substitutes himself for the central committee.

Leon Trotsky

COMMUNIST PARTIES

The origins of communist parties lie in the writings of the German thinkers Karl Marx (1818–83) and Friedrich Engels (1820–95). Central to Marx's theory was a conception of the progression of history: "the history of all hitherto existing society is the history of class struggles." (*The Communist Manifesto*, 1848.) Marx asserted that capitalism would be overthrown by the large exploited working class, or **proletariat**, on which it depended. A new phase would then begin, also of class rule (or 'dictatorship') by the proletariat, called **socialism**. Eventually, though, class rule becomes unnecessary and a final phase, known as **communism**, will emerge. The main variants of communism that have influenced the formation of parties are:

Marxism-Leninism. Lenin (1870–1924), leader of the Bolshevik Party that spearheaded the Russian Revolution of October 1917, espoused the theory of a 'vanguard' of revolutionaries to lead the proletariat. In effect this meant the Soviet Communist Party.

Trotskyism, named after the Russian revolutionary Leon Trotsky (1879–1940), supports world revolution, instead of the 'state capitalism' existing in the Soviet Union. Many revolutionary socialist parties and

movements, especially in western Europe, are Trotskyist in nature.

Maoism, promulgated by the Chinese communist leader Mao Zedong (1893–1976), differed from Marxism by basing its ideas on a revolutionary peasantry rather than an industrial proletariat. Maoism has had only limited influence beyond China. No mainstream political party follows this line, though the Peruvian guerrilla group *Sendero Luminoso* ('Shining Path') is Maoist.

Banners at A May Day Parade in the Former Soviet Union *A banner showing three of the founding fathers of communism. Left to right: Marx, Engels, and Lenin.* ▶

What is conservatism? Is it not adherence to the old and tried, against the new and untried?

Abraham Lincoln
(1809–65), US President, in a speech, 27 February 1860

in between these two positions. This form of analysis gives a rough guide to the attitudes and values of most parties, but not all. For instance, the ideology of fascism does not readily fit into this scheme: fascist parties are often regarded as being on the right wing of politics, yet they certainly do not wish to retain the existing structures of power. Instead they seek radically to transform society. The main tenets of the principal ideological traditions that have influenced political parties are summarized below, together with some examples of parties following these ideologies.

Conservative Parties. Political parties influenced by conservative doctrines stress gradual, rather than radical, change in society. Social order expressed in the principle of the 'rule of law' is a central conservative theme. Likewise, individual responsibility and individual freedom are important tenets of all conservative philosophies. In terms of policies, conservative parties attempt to free the individual to pursue private enterprise within a market system but not at the expense of social

harmony. The Christian Democratic parties of western Europe accept that the state needs to intervene in the economy to offset the social inequality that a free-market system engenders if left unregulated.

In the 1980s, some parties, such as the Republican Party in the USA and the British Conservative Party, attempted a radical departure from the tradition of state intervention espoused by the old-style conservative parties. This experiment is now largely discredited, but the attempt to 'roll back the state' led some to argue that such parties are no longer conservative but **neo-liberal**, in that their policies owe more to the classical liberal economics of Adam Smith. In Western democracies, conservative parties have consistently been the most successful in gaining office and retaining power, and their populist 'common-sense' approach has given them the flexibility to adapt their policies to the particular demands of the age.

Liberal Parties. Liberalism as a political philosophy has had a much wider influence than might be expected from the number of political parties that call themselves 'liberal' (in such diverse places as South Korea, the United Kingdom, and Colombia). It has also had considerable influence upon social democratic parties, and even conservative parties. Classical liberalism developed alongside such historical events as the French and American revolutions in the 18th century and the Industrial Revolution throughout western Europe in the 18th and 19th centuries. It originally emphasized the rights of man, with the English liberal thinker John Locke (1632–1704) stressing man's natural rights to "life, liberty, and property." Classical liberals envisaged a limited role for the state and maximum freedom for the individual in a 'laissez-faire' economic system (see ECONOMICS: THE PRICE MECHANISM).

Liberals have also argued that capitalism prevents many people from enjoying true liberty because of the vast inequalities it produces, and have consequently advocated limited state intervention to create a safety net for the sick or unemployed. In this form, liberalism was highly influential upon the development of social welfare systems throughout the Western world. Unlike socialists, however, liberals of all persuasions defend the market system as the most effective way of distributing wealth and resources throughout society, and they see private property as a key freedom that the state should defend.

Social Democrats, Socialists, and Communists.
Political parties in the social democratic tradition have been central to the politics of western Europe. Since their inception in the later 19th century, these parties, which operate under a variety of names, have as their central principle the defence of the interests of the growing working classes that industrialization had engendered. At the outset, social democratic parties were highly radical in their aims, opposing capitalism as an immoral and deeply flawed system. At this early stage, all were essentially socialist parties that wished to replace the divisive individualistic capitalist system with a communal and fraternal order. The central difference between social democratic parties and communist parties, therefore, lay not in the end they sought, which was the creation of socialism, but in the means of achieving this. The original social democratic parties in such countries as Germany aimed to transform society by electoral means rather than through the violent revolution advocated by communist parties. One of the key theoretical founders of social democracy was the German politician Eduard Bernstein (1850–1932). In his work *Evolutionary Socialism* (1899), he argued that through democracy the working class could make real and meaningful gains, both in economic and social terms. Bernstein advocated a blend of private initiative and social reform and rejected many of the predictions of Karl Marx, such as the seizure of power by the proletariat, pointing to rising wages among workers to counter Marx's forecast of increasing poverty among this class. During the 20th century parties of a social democratic nature have become much more moderate and have largely abandoned the aim of creating a socialist system. Such parties as the Labour Party in the United Kingdom and the SPD

Communist Parties in Crisis

In 1988 the general secretary of the Communist Party of the Soviet Union, Mikhail Gorbachov (1931–   ), was appointed president and instituted a programme of reform. Encouraged by the atmosphere of debate provoked by Gorbachov's policies of *glasnost* (openness) and *perestroika* (reconstruction), the forces for change became unstoppable. In 1989 the satellite states of eastern Europe rejected the one-party system. Following a failed coup by hardline communists against Gorbachov in 1991, the party was declared illegal by Gorbachov's successor Boris Yeltsin.

◄ **An Italian Neofascist Rally**
Supporters of the Movimento Sociale Italiano (MSI) *give the straight-armed fascist salute. The term 'fascism' comes from the Latin fasces, a bundle of rods and an axe that symbolized the authority and power of Roman magistrates. The Italian dictator Benito Mussolini (1883–1945) called his black-shirted followers* Fasci di Combattimento.

Green Parties

Green parties first arose in western Europe – most prominently in West Germany – in the 1970s in response to concerns about global pollution. They differ from traditional parties in having no single party leader and in setting as their main priority the preservation of natural resources. European Green parties enjoyed some electoral success in the late 1980s, winning a number of seats in the European Parliament.

(*Sozialdemokratische Partei Deutschlands*) in Germany have sought instead to manage capitalism more efficiently and fairly than their liberal and conservative opponents, creating a hybrid theory of the 'social-market economy.' Social democracy has had little impact on US parties, whose dominant traditions are conservative and liberal. In the Third World, socialist parties have tended to follow a more rigidly Marxist-Leninist approach rather than a social democratic path. An example of this is the Zimbabwe African National Union (ZANU) under Robert Mugabe (1925–). However, with the collapse of communist power in the Soviet bloc and the loss of sponsorship from this source, there is some evidence that social democracy is becoming more of a political force.

Fascist Parties. Fascism emerged as an ideology in Europe in the interwar years. Its principal influence was felt in Italy and Germany, where fascist parties dominated from 1922–43 and 1933–45 respectively. Although the regimes of these countries were defeated in World War II, some forms of fascism have survived or re-emerged. Parties with either an expressly or covertly fascist agenda operate in several European countries, including the United Kingdom, Norway, and Belgium. In Italy in 1994, a right-wing coalition that included fascists won seats in both national and European elections. Fascism, however, is not confined to Europe. In South Africa, the white supremacist Afrikaner Resistance Movement (AWB) is avowedly fascist. Fascism has also influenced groups in South and Central America (e.g. the Arena Party in El Salvador, associated with right-wing death

squads), and North American movements, such as the racist Ku Klux Klan. As a system of thought, fascism is hard to define, being based on highly irrational and ahistorical assumptions. At its heart, however, there tends to be a deeply entrenched racism against particular ethnic groups, notably Blacks and Jews. Fascist movements are always anti-communist and see politics as a way of mobilizing disaffected people and uniting them under a strong leader. Violence and terror are regarded as acceptable political tools.

Ecological Parties. Parties chiefly concerned with the world's ecology, or **green parties** as they are more commonly known, emerged as a minor political force in the 1970s. By the late 1980s green parties had gained either representation or a relatively sizeable vote in most western European democracies. The greens emphasize the interrelationship between humanity and the natural world and are highly critical of the damage that industrialization has inflicted on the environment. Their policies reflect these concerns, focusing upon the regulation and restriction of industry, conservation of energy supplies, and the protection through global legislation of such natural necessities as the rain forests of the Amazon Basin. They also tend to see social justice and local grassroots democracy as vital to fostering a more responsible attitude among people to the natural world. In many ways green parties have been more akin to pressure groups than to political parties in the function they perform. Though having little chance of gaining significant power or influence, the green movement

Green Party Conference

▶

A gathering of the West German Green Party during their heyday in the mid-1980s. In gaining over 5% of the popular vote, Die Grünen *won representation both in regional assemblies and at the federal parliament in Bonn, where their unorthodox dress and debating practices brought colour to an otherwise conventional establishment.*

PERONISM

Peronism is a nationalistic and populist movement in postwar Argentina, named after Juan Domingo Perón (1895–1974). Perón, who rose to prominence in the army and the labour movement, based his political appeal on a charismatic personality and a demagogic style of public oratory. Peronism envisaged a widespread national recovery for Argentina, which had witnessed a sharp decline in its economy since the Great Depression of the 1930s. Radical social measures during Perón's presidency included redistribution of wealth in favour of the urban working classes, or *descamisados* ('shirtless ones'), from whom he drew much of his support, and nationalization of utilities. Perón was elected president in 1946. His popularity was enhanced by his second wife Eva (1919–52), who played an active role in politics, securing the right to vote for Argentinian women. After her death his support waned and he was deposed in a coup in 1955. The Peronist movement continued to command support despite tension between its factions; as a populist movement, it transcended traditional demarcations, appealing both to left-wing trade unionists and right-wing nationalists. In one of the world's most astonishing political comebacks, Perón regained the presidency after almost 20 years, in 1973. He died in office in 1974. The Peronista Party survived, returning their candidate Carlos Menem (1931–) to the Argentinian presidency in 1989.

◄ **Carlos Menem Celebrating Election Victory in Buenos Aires**

has succeeded in putting ecological issues at the forefront of political debate. The manifestos of many mainstream political parties now include a specific commitment to prudent environmental management.

Populist Parties. Populism is not an ideology in the strict sense of the term, since it has no cogent body of thought informing it. Rather, it is a political tradition in which disaffection with mainstream politics is channelled into political action, often under the direction of a charismatic leader. The term has been applied to a variety of political movements, perhaps the most notable recent example occurred in the 1992 presidential elections in the USA, where a populist candidate emerged to challenge the nominees of the two major parties. H. Ross Perot (1931–), a Texan billionaire businessman, gained considerable support in the early stages of the campaign for his anti-establishment stance, an approach designed to appeal to an electorate that was disillusioned with traditional politics as represented by the Democratic and Republican parties.

In the event, however, he did not have sufficient persuasiveness as an international leader to take the voters with him. There are, however, times when a populist leader can emerge and carry his electorate with him.

Parties and the State

The functions of political parties within the state are to a large extent determined by the political culture and historical context of a particular country. For example, the aims of the Bolshevik Party in post-1917 Russia were very different from those of the modern Democratic Party in the USA. The representative party systems of the Western world have to a large extent provided the universal model for democracy. As a result of the popular uprisings in eastern Europe in 1989, and the collapse of the Soviet Union in 1990–91, eastern Europe has also turned to Western-style institutions to form their new democracies.

The liberal democratic system in a complex society seeks to provide regular constitutional opportunities for changing government officials as well as a social mechanism enabling people to influence major decisions by selecting the candidate of their choice. Thus, competition between political parties allows for the formation of a legitimate government and an effective opposition of one or more parties. This competition in liberal democracies both offers the people representation and provides a convenient focus for the often apathetic or ill-informed voter. Moreover, policies must reflect the views of the public since it is the public that holds the key to power; if a significant number of voters are not represented by the existing parties then new parties form to act for these unrepresented viewpoints. This can be illustrated by the creation of many social democratic parties in 19th- and 20th-century Europe, which were formed to represent the

If I had not been born Perón, I would have liked to be Perón.

Juan Perón

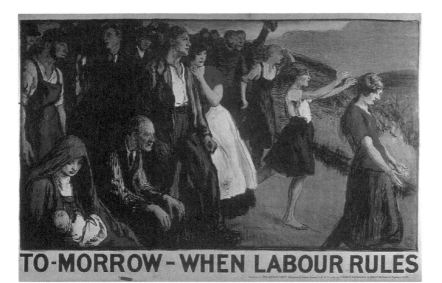

TO-MORROW – WHEN LABOUR RULES

▲ **An Early Political Poster** *A poster from the 1920s for the British Labour Party. Like many democratic socialist parties, the Labour Party was established at the end of the 19th century to represent the interests of working people, and had its origins in the trade-union movement.*

Coalition Governments

Coalitions are alliances between two or more separate parties for the purpose of gaining or retaining power. In recent history, the most enduring example of a country governed by coalitions is the Federal Republic of Germany. In 1966, the so-called 'Great Coalition' was formed between the Social Democrats (SPD) and Christian Democrats (CDU–CSU). Thereafter, the country has consistently elected coalition administrations.

newly enfranchised working classes. Contrary to the fears expressed by Thomas Jefferson, political parties in most states have to have a broad appeal and encompass many views if they are to attract a sizeable proportion of the huge electorate.

Another function that political parties perform is to provide ministers for government. In both first-past-the-post electoral systems and in **coalition governments**, party affiliation is crucial to the running of a country. For example, governments are more easily held accountable if they carry a readily identifiable overall label, or if individual members within coalitions are associated with a particular party's policies. Accountability would be much more difficult to achieve if governments were composed of private individuals. In terms of elections, too, the party label is a vital element in enabling the voter to identify his intended representative and, indeed, in enabling the candidate to identify his supporters. In most political systems, and particularly in Europe, people vote for parties and the policies or ideologies they represent, rather than the personality or skills of a particular candidate. Even in the USA, where the two major parties share many policies on several aspects of policy, the label 'Democrat' or 'Republican' is nevertheless invaluable for being elected to Congress. In summary, political parties help to maintain and stabilize a democratic political system by providing channels of representation and participation between people and their governments. This legitimizing function of parties is essential if a particular social system is to survive and prosper. The collapse of Communist Party rule in the one-party states of the Soviet Union and eastern Europe provides one recent example of the instability that is inherent within a system with no such legitimacy.

Origins

The first example of a rudimentary party system was that in ancient Rome at the end of the Republic (510–27 BC), which arose as a result of a division between progressive thinkers and conservative thinkers, who gathered together in loose coalitions. However, this embryonic development of political parties effectively died with the replacement of the Roman Republic by the imperial system and did not reappear as a feature of politics until the Renaissance in 14th-century Italy. Political parties in the modern sense did not begin to emerge until the 18th century; these forerunners of modern parties tended to centre on a powerful individual leader or family. These 'factions' first acted as advisors to the monarchies but gradually claimed more power for themselves, through their membership of legislative bodies. Their struggles for power, both with the monarchs and among themselves, increased both their self-confidence and their organizational efficiency.

The major factor in transforming factional groupings into representative political parties was the gradual extension of the franchise to the populations of Europe (see DEMOCRACY AND ELECTORAL SYSTEMS). At first representation was very limited, involving only property owners; moreover, corruption and manipulation were a major hindrance to the workings of democracy. As the franchise was extended, powerful families were still able to ensure support because most of the new voters were workers on their estates, who depended on them for their economic wellbeing. The relationship between the parties and the voters could therefore best be described as a patron–client relationship.

The strong relationship between voters and powerful factional parties was broken down largely by the processes of industrialization. In the UK – the first industrialized country in the world – the earliest of the modern party systems developed, driven by the mercantile classes, who were demanding more political influence to reflect their growing economic importance. The creation of huge factories also increased the opportunity for the masses to organize themselves politically. The emerging political parties had already demonstrated that they could be an effective source of political and social change; in the 19th century this encouraged the formation of the first mass parties throughout Europe. Effective organization for mass political parties was made even more necessary because they could not rely on personal wealth to fund political campaigns. Because each member could only afford to make a small contribution, parties needed to attract many new members to maintain funds. Parties could not afford to be merely legislative bodies; they now required extensive extra-parliamentary organizational structures.

A distinction can be drawn between those parties that developed through parliamentary factions and those that evolved from extra-parliamentary activity. The former are normally referred to as **cadre *parties***, examples of which include the various Conservative and Liberal parties that emerged throughout Europe in the 18th and 19th centuries. The latter group can be described as ***mass parties***; the socialist parties in Europe are examples of this type, as they grew from the perceived need for parliamentary representation for the trade union movement. While this distinction is useful in understanding the origins of political parties, it must be said that in the modern era of full adult suffrage, all parties are now regarded as mass parties, since they all need to attract millions of votes if they are to gain power. At the same time, it would also be misleading to describe all mass parties as class-based. Various social changes and conflicts other than class have been instrumental in the formation of modern parties. Nationalism, religion, and cultural differences have all played a role – for example, many of the smaller parties in Israel, such as the extreme right-wing Kach party, have arisen largely to promote ultra-Orthodox religious interests.

The type of electoral system in a country has also greatly influenced the degree to which parties focus their attention on a particular group. In general terms, in those countries that have first-past-the-post systems (e.g. the USA and the UK) the political parties have to attempt to attract as many supporters as possible in order to have a realistic chance of being elected to government. They therefore have to be wary of being associated too closely with one section of society. By contrast, in proportional representation systems, parties can afford to be more specialized in the interests they represent, as the chance of at least a share of political power is much greater.

European Parties

Political parties, especially in western Europe, play a vital role in giving political behaviour a coherent structure. Most parties tend to be broken down into smaller units often based on geographical location. These are normally referred to as ***branches*** or ***constituencies***. It is at this level that much important work is carried out; for example, canvassing voters and selecting candidates for election to the national legislative assembly. The local branches enable local members to participate in politics and facilitate communication between party headquarters and local communities. The local branch also sends delegates to the party's annual conference, which provides a forum for discussion of issues and policy formulation. It is often at such party conferences that officials are elected to run the party, usually in conjunction with the party's permanent paid staff at its head office. This head-office staff performs a similar role to that of the civil service within a government, ensuring the smooth and efficient running of the party machine. Representatives of a political party that have been elected to serve on the legislative body also tend to have their own organization,

cadre Originally a military term, in the political world, a cadre is a group of dedicated professional activists trained to mobilize and lead a party. The term is particularly associated with communist parties that are organized along military lines.

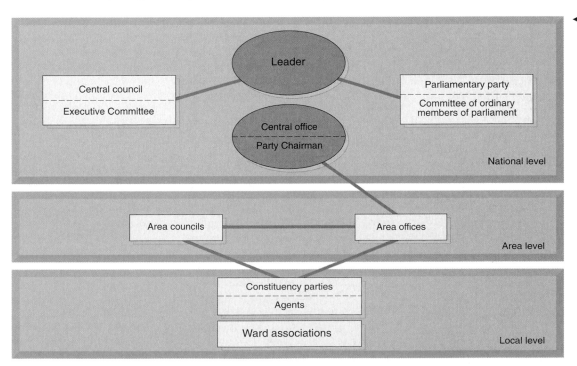

◄ **The Organizational Structure of a Party**
The organizational structure shown here is, in its basic elements, typical of many western European mass parties.

183

The Democratic Jackass

The US Democratic Party has as its symbol the jackass, or male donkey. The origins of this unheroic emblem lie in early American political history. The Democrat Andrew Jackson (1767–1845), seventh president of the USA, was mocked by his opponents for a supposed lack of sophistication, due to his frontier upbringing in Tennessee. In a pun on his name, they satirized him as a jackass. However, the Democrats gladly adopted this image as one of positive stubbornness and endurance.

The Administrative and Policymaking Subdivisions of US Political Parties *The structure illustrated applies to both of the major American parties.* ▼

from which members of a government are selected should the party gain total or partial governmental power. While there are notable variations and exceptions to this basic model (e.g. west European Communist parties), it does provide a useful starting point for an understanding of the operations of political parties.

The nature of a political party depends on whether a balance exists between its various elements or whether one group dominates decision making. The extent to which a party organization is democratic depends heavily upon the motivations of individual members, the strength of particular factions, and the wider political circumstances in any given period. An individual person may have joined a party in order to fulfil a personal ambition or to extract gain from the party, in terms of power and prestige. Alternatively, party members may derive their reward from their role in the formulation of policies in which they believe, or from the solidarity and sense of belonging that membership brings. The struggle within political parties for power between careerists, pragmatists, and idealists ensures that all political parties are dynamic and ever-changing organizations. However, a sceptic might regard all political parties as essentially undemocratic, in that an elite will always emerge to lead a party. This situation arises because there are bound to be occasions in which fast and effective decision making is required. In these circumstances there is a tendency for party members to rely increasingly upon egotistical and charismatic individuals to provide dynamic solutions. The presence of an elite in political parties has been referred to as the 'Iron Law of Oligarchy.'

US Parties

From the Declaration of Independence onwards, political parties in the USA have been regarded with much suspicion. However, although the American constitution makes no reference to political parties, by the end of the 18th century it became apparent that differences were emerging among the political elite over attitudes towards such issues as the economy and the French Revolution. By 1800 these differences had been institutionalized into the Federalist and Republican parties. These parties supported their own candidates for election to the legislative body (Congress) and the executive (i.e. the presidency), although the development of parties throughout the individual states was only a gradual process.

Several main reasons have been advanced for the growth of parties in the USA. First, the diversity of society was so great that rivalry and conflict were inevitable; in a country with democratic pretensions the development of parties was therefore necessary to ensure peaceful resolutions of these differences. Secondly, the constitution provided ex-colonial politicians with a national arena, which required a party structure to enable them to operate. Finally, the decline of political deference and the new confidence of the population after their successful insurrection against British rule also contributed to the growth of parties, as outlets for strong political sentiments.

During the 19th century the two parties developed into the modern Republican and Democratic parties, which dominate the presidency and Congress. The basic organization of these parties is very similar, each party having a national committee that draws officials from each state. These committees organize the party and coordinate communication between state and federal level. Every four years a national convention nominates the presidential candidate and determines, albeit loosely, a party policy. Each state has its own party organization, which is further broken down into congressional district committees, intermediate committees, ward committees, and local party committees. A major difference between US political parties and European political parties is that individual candidates are much more important in the former. The parties in the USA do not impose candidates in Congressional or other elections; instead, candidates compete for the party label through ***primary elections***, in which they often run their own election campaign separate from the party structure. The increasing need to make use of communications media, such as television, to get their message across has tended to undermine democracy, since the key to getting elected to many important positions (e.g. state senator) is having the

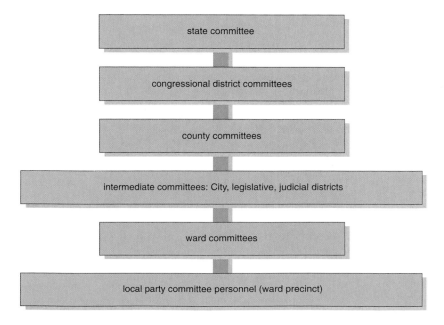

state committee

congressional district committees

county committees

intermediate committees: City, legislative, judicial districts

ward committees

local party committee personnel (ward precinct)

money to stand for office. As candidates become less dependent on party structures, the need for activists within parties has decreased. Many tasks, such as gathering information about the electorate and determining how it might influence policy, are now done by professional consultants and pollsters. The development of candidate domination has been seen as contributing to the decline of the political party in the USA.

African Parties

Not surprisingly, the formation of political parties in most of Africa is a much more recent occurrence than in Western nations. Although some exceptions can be found, such as the True Whig Party in Liberia (founded 1860), parties in these countries are largely a 20th-century development, and in many cases only emerged after World War II. While there are many differences between political parties throughout Africa, some general observations can be made. First, many African political parties are parties of the state. In other words, they do not compete for power with other parties but are instead parties of integration that work in conjunction with other powerful elites, such as the civil service or military, to provide a focus for loyalty to the state. Secondly, such parties often have their origins outside the electoral process, having been created by a powerful individual, and they tend towards instability. In Africa attempts to establish liberal democratic party systems have not met with great success.

The continuing struggle against poverty and famine in many African states has tended to monopolize the efforts of the state. However, some democratic structures have managed to

assert themselves. African states, such as Malawi and Ethiopia, that formerly had single-party regimes (either Marxist or non-Marxist) have now been superseded by multiparty systems. The peaceful transition to full democracy and majority rule in South Africa in 1994 may provide a role model for attempts to achieve real democratic states in other parts of the continent. The appointment of Nelson Mandela (1918–   ) as president after a free and fair election only marginally disrupted by violence from the extreme right wing was a triumphal end to more than 25 years of struggle by his party, the African National Congress (ANC). Some of the credit for the speed with which the oppressive politics of apartheid were dismantled must go to Mandela's predecessor F. W. de Klerk (1936–   ), with whom he shared the Nobel peace prize (1993).

▲ **Military Coup in Liberia** *Liberia, a West African country founded by freed American slaves in the 19th century, was the scene of a violent coup by indigenous Africans in 1980 that ended more than a century of rule by the True Whig Party.*

THE PRI IN MEXICO

It has been argued that long-term electoral domination by one party – preventing damaging factionalism – is more suited to the pressing economic and social needs of developing countries than frequent changes of administration. An example of this is the *Partido Revolucionario Institucional* (PRI), which has been in power in Mexico since 1929. This party arose in the turmoil that followed the revolution of 1910 and has presided over a period of political stability unprecedented in Central America; see LATIN AMERICA (VOL. 5): MODERN LATIN AMERICA. However, the party has been accused of retaining power through electoral fraud. The PRI influences all areas of public life, including professional associations, cultural organizations, and agrarian leagues.

Parties in Former Communist Countries

In the former USSR and former countries in the Soviet bloc, government was basically by a single party – the Communist Party. In some of those countries, other parties were permitted to exist in coalition, on terms laid down by the Communist Party. For example, in Poland, the Communist Party (the United Polish Workers Party) allowed peasant interests to be represented by the United Peasant Party, while the professions were permitted to form a small Democratic Party. However, by controlling the nominations for the leadership of these parties, the communists were able to ensure that there was no challenge to the single-party system. When communism collapsed in eastern Europe in the period 1990–92, government by multiparty systems emerged. Indeed, in Russia and several of the former states of the USSR, a proliferation of so-called socialist parties were formed to replace the banned

A Rally of the African National Congress (ANC)
The ANC was banned for many decades in South Africa and its leader, Nelson Mandela, was imprisoned for 28 years. Denied a constitutional voice, the party adopted a policy of armed struggle against the apartheid regime of the National Party until it was allowed to participate in the democratic process.

▲ **Dr Hastings Kamuzu Banda**
(1905–97) In 1971, Banda was proclaimed president for life of Malawi, a southeast African country. Under Banda, Malawi became a one-party state. After holding power for over 30 years, growing opposition forced Banda to hold a referendum, in which two-thirds of the people voted for multiparty democracy.

communist parties. In some of these countries with substantial Moslem populations, these socialist parties were opposed by Islamic parties.

Asian Parties

Political parties in Asia present a very varied picture. Stability has characterized the very different political systems of China and Japan. The Chinese Communist Party has governed the country since 1949; reformist movements calling for greater openness were ruthlessly suppressed by the party's ageing leadership in 1989. In Japan, the Liberal Democratic Party has dominated politics since 1955, though recent years have seen some weakening of its power. Indonesia has been ruled by military strongmen since its independence from the Netherlands in 1949.

Elsewhere in Asia, radical change has taken place. In the 1980s, the Philippines, governed for decades by the US-backed dictator Ferdinand Marcos (1917–89) saw the rise of the populist 'People Power' movement under Corazon Aquino (1933–   ), wife of a murdered political opponent of Marcos. After Aquino won the backing of the military, Marcos fled the country in 1986. In India, the rise of Hindu fundamentalism is challenging the traditional nonsecular political parties in this, the world's largest democracy.

The Future of Political Parties

Political parties are indispensable elements for organizing political behaviour. They have undoubtedly contributed to coherent democratic government, helping to stabilize societies in many countries, and have helped mobilize ordinary people to participate in the politics of their country. Under totalitarian systems of government, however, parties have been used as instruments of repression rather than representation.

Many new social conflicts, such as those based on gender or race, have grown in prominence. The rise of the phenomenon of 'post-materialism,' reflected in such groups as the ecology movements, has placed new issues on the political agenda; the inability of mass parties to accommodate such a world-view has led to the growth of special-interest and pressure groups, and a corresponding decline in the membership of traditional parties. Opinion polls reveal an increasing distrust of political parties among many electorates.

Another development that appears to be undermining the effectiveness and value of political parties is the explosion in communications technology, which has helped increase the importance of the individual candidate as opposed to the party he or she represents. Such factors as an individual's televisual appearance and their mode of delivery have become important in election campaigns. Consequently, the contemporary politician makes extensive use of public-relations consultants and advertising agencies. The use of professional campaigning staff has also reduced the role played by ordinary party members and therefore undermined the key function of participation.

How Countries are Governed

Parliamentary systems • Separation of powers • National constitutions •
The administration of government • Local and civic government

Government of a modern nation-state is a highly complex matter, involving various agencies with separate and clearly defined roles. By far the most common form of government is that which operates through the parliamentary system.

Parliamentary Systems

All democracies have parliaments or **legislatures**. Legislatures vary greatly in the ways in which they are elected, the elected members' term of office, and the part which they play in the government of their country. The US Congress is one of the most powerful legislatures in the world, but generally they have a limited influence on policy making. This arises from the fact that members of the legislature from the majority party pass the legislation of their government without objection, in order to keep it in office.

Despite the variation in their influence, legislatures usually have a role in the approval of the budget of their country, in raising taxes, and in decisions about how public funds are to be spent. By means of committees they examine the work of the executive branch of government, and seek to check the power of presidents or other leaders of the executive branch. In some countries, the chief executive is elected directly by the people, but in others he or she is a member of the legislature, and only holds office through the support of parliament, or at least of the members of the governing party in the legislature. The central importance of parliament as a symbol of democracy is demonstrated by the efforts made by leaders of coups d'état to seize the parliament building; this happened, for example, in Spain in 1981 when members were voting to elect the prime minister.

As international organizations, such as the European Union (EU), have acquired greater decision-making powers, it has been felt necessary for them to develop their own legislatures to provide a democratic force to counteract unelected bureaucracies, such as the European Commission. The European Parliament (based in Strasbourg, in France, and Brussels, in Belgium) is unique among such international bodies in being directly elected by the citizens of the countries of the European Union. Although its influence has grown since the late 1980s, it still lacks many of the powers of a conventional parliament. It has no formal power to initiate legislation, its legislative activities are focused on particular areas of the European Union's work, such as the internal market, and it can only block

=====SEE ALSO=====
This section:
• Introduction
• Democracy and Electoral Systems
• Political Parties
Law:
• Judicial Processes and Administration
• International Law
Continents, Regions, and Countries (vol. 1)

legislature A representative assembly that is elected by the citizens in a free and fair election, for a fixed term of office. Legislatures are empowered to make laws in ways that are, in most countries, laid down in the constitution.

◄ **The National Congress Building in Argentina** *The seat of government in the capital, Buenos Aires. As in the majority of countries, the Argentinian parliament consists of two chambers: the Senate and the Chamber of Deputies. In addition, each of the country's 22 provinces has its own government.*

A Unique State

Alone among the states of the USA, Nebraska has a one-chamber legislature. All other US states, like the national administration, have a bicameral system. In addition, all Nebraskan representatives are independents, elected without party-political affiliation.

POWERS OF THE EUROPEAN PARLIAMENT

The Single European Act adopted in 1987 gave the European Parliament the power to propose amendments to decisions reached by the Council of Ministers on the internal market. Of the 1724 amendments proposed by the Parliament between 1987 and 1990, 719 were subsequently accepted by the Council. The Maastricht Treaty of 1992 creates a new joint decision-making procedure between the Council and the Parliament over a wider area of European Union affairs. The new procedure includes the convening of a conciliation committee with equal membership from the Parliament and the Council in the event of disagreement. The Parliament can also reject the budget proposed by the Commission and has the final say on discretionary parts of the budget. It has to approve or reject any application by a country that wishes to join the European Union.

decisions taken by the Council of Ministers, drawn from the governments of the member states, after going through a lengthy decision-making procedure. However, its influence is expected to increase as a result of the powers vested in the Parliament by the treaties relating to the European Union. The attention given in documents, such as the Maastricht Treaty, to enlarging the powers of the European Parliament illustrates the way in which parliaments are regarded as giving a decision-making body democratic respectability.

One- and Two-Chamber Parliaments. Most parliaments are made up of two chambers and are described as **bicameral**. There are a few exceptions to this rule: most examples of **unicameral** parliaments (i.e. having

only one chamber) occur in smaller countries, such as New Zealand or Denmark. The preference for two-chamber legislatures reflects a concern that a single chamber might acquire too much power, which a second chamber can check and, if necessary, restrict. A second chamber may also be able to undertake tasks that the first chamber does not have time for.

Many countries of the world have ***federal systems of government***, according to which the country is split into a number of distinct territorial units, each with their own legislatures. In such countries one of the chambers is generally based on the representation of the federal units. For example, in Germany the lower chamber (Bundestag) is popularly elected, while the upper chamber (Bundesrat) comprises representatives from the governments of the federal states (*Länder*). In Germany, states with larger populations have more seats in the upper house than the smaller ones, but equal representation for each federal unit is more common. For example, in the USA, small states have equal representation in the upper chamber with very large states. Some cantons (administrative regions) in Switzerland, certain states in Australia, and the provinces of post-apartheid South Africa all operate such a system.

The two chambers are often elected at a different time and on a different basis from each other. This increases their ability to check and balance each other. Thus, in the USA, while the House of Representatives (the lower house) is re-elected in its entirety every two years, members of the Senate (the upper house) are elected for six years, with approximately one-third of their number retiring every two years.

In most countries, one chamber (usually the lower) is more important than the other, with the second chamber often confining itself to checking and revising the laws passed by the other. The clearest example of this division of responsibility is the United Kingdom, in which members of the upper chamber (House of Lords) are not democratically elected but are either appointed or inherit their membership; their ability to overturn or delay legislation passed by the lower chamber (House of Commons) is restricted by legal provisions.

Second chambers can also help to protect constitutional safeguards and citizens' rights against powerful executives. Yet this expectation that two-chamber parliaments provide more democratic checks and balances has in some cases been undermined by the development of disciplined party-political systems that seek to place legislatures under unified executive control by a governing party.

Presidential Forms of Government. Some countries, such as Brazil, France, and the USA, have directly elected presidents, who head the

A Congressional Hearing in Washington, DC *In many countries, much of the business of government is conducted in committees. In the USA, matters of national concern are often investigated by Congress in special hearings.* ▼

executive branches of their governments. Such systems of government can run into difficulties when the president supports a different party from the majority party in the legislature. Indeed, in the USA, even if the president is from the same party as the legislative majority, he cannot necessarily rely on their support for his programme. The president has to earn support by a mixture of pressure, persuasion, and bargaining.

The French Fifth Republic was created in 1958 with the clear intention of giving greatly increased powers to the president, in order to end the weak and divided government that characterized the Fourth Republic. The president appointed the prime minister and the government, could dissolve the parliament (National Assembly), and appeal directly to the people by calling a referendum. The Fifth Republic's arrangements were tested in 1986 when, for the first time in its history, a socialist president – François Mitterrand – was faced with the election of a parliament with a right-wing majority, led by the Gaullist politician Jacques Chirac. The experiment in **cohabitation** that followed demonstrated the adaptability of the French constitution. As a result, it was argued that the French system should properly be termed 'semi-presidential,' in contrast to the fully presidential system to be found in the USA, since it was able to accommodate a popularly elected president co-existing with a prime minister and cabinet responsible to a legislature that had also been popularly elected. In the USA, the cabinet is appointed by the president and has no independent political standing.

The most difficult problem in a presidential system of government is in drafting safeguards against its constitutional basis being undermined by a president who falls victim to debilitating illness or who abuses power. The issue of ill health arose in the USA when Woodrow Wilson (president 1913–21) suffered a stroke that prevented him carrying out his duties; this led to his wife taking many decisions on his behalf. However, it was not until 1967 that the US Constitution was amended to include a formal procedure that was to be implemented in such cases.

Corrupt or criminal behaviour on the part of a president is even more difficult to legislate against, as the president can use power and influence to inhibit investigation of his behaviour. The US Constitution contains a provision for the removal of the president through a process known as **_impeachment_**. Andrew Johnson (president 1865–69) survived impeachment by one vote in 1868, the process being invoked by Johnson's Republican opponents in an attempt to remove him from office. Impeachment proceedings were started against President Richard Nixon in 1974 over evidence that he had authorized bugging of the campaign headquarters of his Democrat opponents at the Watergate building in Washington, DC. With impeachment imminent, Nixon became the first US president to resign from office.

In Brazil, President Fernando Collor de Mello was suspended from office in September 1992 after the Chamber of Deputies had voted to impeach him on corruption charges amid widespread popular demonstrations of support for their action. In December 1992, Collor resigned only minutes after his impeachment trial began; he was banned from holding public office for eight years. These two examples illustrate the way in which starting legal proceedings may be sufficient to remove from office a president accused of wrongdoing, sparing a country the disruption and damage to international standing that would ensue from a lengthy impeachment trial.

In some countries, such as South Africa and the USA, the president combines the roles of **head of state** and **head of government**. By contrast, in the United Kingdom and Spain the head of state is the monarch. Some republics – e.g. Austria, Germany, and Italy – separate the roles of head of government and head of state. When these two roles are brought together, they can provide a powerful combination,

cohabitation A situation in which a directly elected president has to work with a government formed by a parliamentary majority from a different political party.

President Fernando Collor de Mello of Brazil _The disgraced president, impeached on charges of corruption, is shown leaving the presidential palace in Brasília with his wife and aides after suspension of his powers._ ▼

head of state The president or monarch of a country, who carries out ceremonial duties, such as welcoming heads of state from other countries. The heads of state of some countries, such as Italy, may play an important role when a new government is formed, or in a political crisis. The head of state is often seen as the guardian of the constitution. Monarchs who function in this way are referred to as *constitutional monarchs*.

head of government The political head of a government, often referred to as a 'prime minister,' although in Germany the holder of the office is called the 'chancellor' (Bundeskanzler). He or she is responsible for the overall direction of the work of the government.

enabling the president to use his or her position as head of state to boost personal popularity. However, because so much political attention is focused on one person, and so much is expected of him or her, the president often becomes a deeply unpopular figure while in office. Only in retrospect may a president's reputation be reassessed in a favourable light, as was the case with US president Harry S. Truman (president 1945–53).

However, not all democratically elected presidents or leaders can be checked by constitutional means. For example, Adolf Hitler (1889–1945) initially rose to power by means of the democratic process. His popular acclaim diminished as his abuse of power and repressive regime became too powerful to be restrained internally. Only after Germany's expansionist territorial demands became unacceptable to the rest of the world, and it had been defeated in a World War that cost millions of lives, could Hitler be removed from power.

Presidential governments are only separated from potential dictatorships by effective restraints that can be brought into play before the president has become too powerful to stop.

Joint Cabinet Responsibilities. A safer, if sometimes less dynamic, form of government is government by committee. A cabinet is a committee made up of the ministerial heads of major government departments, which meets together at regular intervals to take decisions about government policy. An important principle of cabinet government is that the members accept collective responsibility. This means that once a decision has been taken, all the members of the cabinet must either support it, regardless of their personal feelings, or resign.

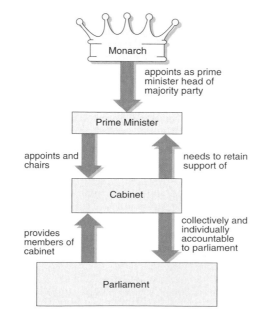

Diagram of a Cabinet System of Government *Based on the example of the United Kingdom, this diagram shows the reporting lines between the various divisions of government.*

Cabinet government is a central feature of most parliamentary systems of government, with the members of the cabinet being collectively and individually accountable to the legislature for their actions. It developed first in the United Kingdom, and is most common in Commonwealth states (countries that are, or once were, ruled by Great Britain) and postwar west European countries.

In the systems of multiparty government that operate in a number of European countries, such as Italy, the authority of the cabinet tends to be diminished, with many important issues ultimately being decided by agreements between the parties. The coalition government formed in the Republic of Ireland in 1993 was bound by the terms of a formal coalition pact known as the 'programme for government.' In such countries as Germany, ministers have more freedom of individual action, and the cabinet is less important than it is in the UK. Although cabinets exist in such presidential systems of government as the USA, they play a less central part in the business of government. It is clear, therefore, that government by cabinet can take various forms, ranging from the virtually leaderless committee to the rubber-stamping committee of the strong presidential leader.

As the workload of modern democratic cabinets has increased, greater reliance has been placed on a network of cabinet committees, each dealing with a particular issue. Some of these may be permanent committees concerned, for example, with defence or foreign affairs. Others may be set up on a temporary basis to deal with a particular policy problem and will be dissolved once legislation has been drafted or other action has been taken.

In countries that have traditional forms of cabinet government concern has been expressed that authority of the cabinet has been undermined by the growing concentration of power in the hands of the prime minister. It is debatable whether this development is simply part of a more general trend towards centralization of power in all the Western democracies. Nevertheless, the cabinet remains the place where a binding decision is finally taken on major matters of policy.

Separation of Powers

The idea of the separation of powers between a number of branches of government as a safeguard against tyranny can be traced back to Greek political thought (see INTRODUCTION). In the modern period, John Locke (1632–1704) developed the idea at the end of the 17th century, although he proposed a twofold division between executive and legislative powers. The most important work on the **separation of**

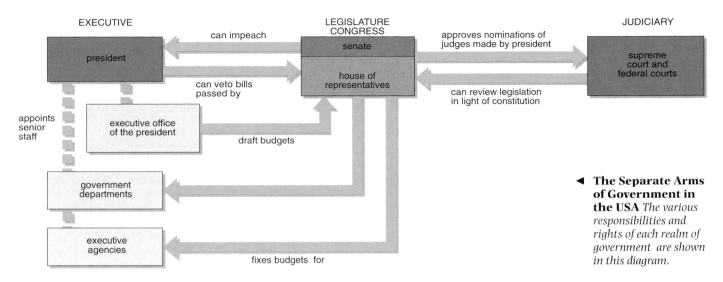

EXECUTIVE

LEGISLATURE CONGRESS

JUDICIARY

president

can impeach

senate

house of representatives

approves nominations of judges made by president

supreme court and federal courts

can veto bills passed by

appoints senior staff

executive office of the president

draft budgets

can review legislation in light of constitution

government departments

executive agencies

fixes budgets for

◄ **The Separate Arms of Government in the USA** *The various responsibilities and rights of each realm of government are shown in this diagram.*

powers was, however, that by Baron Charles de Montesquieu (1689–1755) in the middle of the 18th century. Montesquieu advocated a tripartite division of powers into *executive*, *legislative*, and *judicial* branches; he expressed concern that if any two of the three powers coalesced with one another, tyranny could be the result. The most radical separation of powers is to be found in the American constitution, although the idea also influenced the compilation of many other later constitutions.

In the USA, the three branches of government are staffed by different individuals. This contrasts with some cabinet systems of government, in which the heads of executive government departments are often members of parliament as well as members of the cabinet. The links between the different branches of

government in the USA take the form of a series of checks and balances. Thus, for example, the president can veto legislation passed by the Congress, although that veto can be overridden by a vote of both houses; the Congress can impeach the president; federal judges are nominated by the president and approved by the Congress. The only exception to this strict separation is the role of the vice-president as presiding officer of the Senate, although in practice he fulfills that role only rarely.

The Work of the Legislative Branch of Government. The principal formal role of a legislature is to make laws, but in most modern systems of government, with disciplined party systems, proposals brought forward by the executive become law with relatively little amendment. The leading exception is the USA, where much of the legislative initiative

MONTESQUIEU AND THE SEPARATION OF POWERS

In his work *De l'Esprit des Lois* (*Spirit of the Laws*; 1748), Montesquieu formulated the fundamental doctrine of the separation of powers. He considered it a safeguard against an elected government becoming a despotic regime that ceased to be answerable to the people's elected representatives. He recognized that in separating the executive from both the legislature and the judiciary there was a risk of ineffective government. He believed, however, that the risk was worth taking in the interest of preserving liberty. With separated powers, the laws are made by the legislature, put into effect by the executive, and enforced by the judiciary – each body consisting of different sets of people. Montesquieu's theory later came to influence the revolutions in his native France and in Britain's American colonies.

CAROLUS de SECONDAT BARON of MONTESQUIEU.

The accumulation of all powers, legislative, executive, and judiciary, in the same hands, whether of one, a few, or many, and whether hereditary, self-appointed, or elective, may be justly pronounced the very definition of tyranny.

James Madison,
The Federalist Papers
(No. 47), 1787–88

remains in the hands of individual members of Congress, and the form in which any piece of proposed legislation is eventually passed is highly unpredictable.

Legislatures have, however, developed new roles in response to the scope and complexity of modern government. In particular, they scrutinize the activities of the executive by means of committee hearings, which are often televised. Ministers and heads of departments are called on to explain their policies, while bureaucrats are expected to justify their actions. In this way, major scandals in the conduct of government are often exposed or avoided, while new policy ideas can be subjected to a thorough analysis in debate.

Legislatures also play an important role in the selection of the executive. In some countries, such as Japan, the legislature may be the body that actually elects the prime minister. In Germany, by contrast, the chancellor can only be removed by a constructive vote of no confidence that names a successor – a deliberate constitutional device to avoid the instability that characterized Germany during the Weimar Republic, before World War II. Even when the legislature does not have formal constitutional power to elect the prime minister, this power may, in practice, be vested in the members of the governing party in parliament. For example, if the leader of a ruling party loses the support of his or her party, that party will be obliged to elect a new leader, who may automatically become the new prime minister.

In countries with a parliamentary system of government, the reputation and future careers of members of the legislature may be strongly influenced by their performance in front of committees and on the floor of the chamber. The activities of the modern legislature are therefore very much directed towards scrutinizing the performance of the executive in terms of the record of its individual members and the success and failure of its policies.

The Work of the Executive Branch of Government. The executive branch of government is made up of a variety of government departments and agencies. Government departments are usually headed by ministerial members of the government; executive agencies may be headed by individuals appointed from outside government, or even by career bureaucrats. The US government has, since the 19th century, included a number of largely autonomous agencies whose number grew considerably under the New Deal programme of social relief legislation instituted by President Franklin D. Roosevelt (president 1933–45):see NORTH AMERICA (VOL. 5). Although generally funded by, and answerable to, Congress, these bodies lay outside the traditional government departments. However, other countries (e.g. the United Kingdom) have increasingly resorted to the use of autonomous agencies to handle particular government functions, such as the payment of social security benefits or the issue of passports. These agencies are often headed by chief executives recruited from the private sector, which has led to complaints that the proliferation of **quangos** has undermined democratic accountability through parliament.

The boundaries of modern government are very difficult to define. For example, Italy and Spain have made extensive use of state holding companies: these are umbrella organizations in public ownership that own shares in a number of other companies – however, they may be only minority shareholders in these companies. There is an increasing reliance in many countries on public–private partnerships in such areas as economic development or the provision of infrastructure (e.g. roads, bridges, and airports). Similarly, the European Union devolves much of its work to consultants or experts hired for a particular contract.

The executive may be less clearly delineated than in the past, but it cannot be disputed that its power has increased, as the modern state has extended its areas of responsibility; to the traditional realms of law and order, foreign affairs, and defence must now be added

The New Deal *Young men setting off for work camps in California in the 1930s under President Roosevelt's New Deal Programme. Several major construction projects were undertaken by New Deal agencies, such as the Tennessee River Authority (TVA) and the Works Progress Administration (WPA).* ▼

education, health, and social welfare. Even more recently, environmental regulation has become a responsibility of government. Moves in the direction of privatization and deregulation represent only a partial reverse of this general trend.

Many day-to-day decisions in the running of government are taken by the executive without reference to the legislature, for example through the use of delegated legislative powers. Many aspects of economic policy, such as decisions about the exchange rate against foreign currencies, are controlled by the executive in conjunction with such bodies as central banks, rather than in conjunction with the legislature. Putting laws into effect is the job of the executive; there can, however, be a considerable difference between the stated intentions of legislation and what happens when the law is implemented by the executive. The executive is thus the core of modern government.

The Work of the Judicial Branch of Government. As the powers of the executive have grown, so the judiciary has assumed a growing importance as a means of forestalling the abuse of power. Even in countries that do not have an administrative law tradition, the courts have shown an increasing willingness to investigate areas that would previously have been regarded as purely political domains. Within the European Union, the European Court of Justice in Luxembourg is evolving into an important decision-making institution. The Court is responsible for interpreting and enforcing European Union legislation, and has been used to ensure that reluctant national governments implement legislation on such matters as the quality of drinking water and equal pay for men and women.

Countries that have no written constitution are now the exception. Where a written constitution does exist, a supreme national court has often been instituted to interpret its meaning. This is the case in Germany, with the Federal Constitutional Court. In many Latin American countries, issues tried in lower courts may be referred to the supreme court for final judgment if they are thought to raise sufficiently important issues about the interpretation of the law. Interpretation is not limited to abstract points of political procedure, but may relate to central and highly charged political issues, such as whether the constitution permits or prohibits abortion. The longest established court with wide-ranging powers of constitutional review is the US Supreme Court. Among the many decisions of crucial importance that it has taken is that which brought about the end of racially segregated education and that which recognized that

women had a constitutional right to abortion in the early stages of their pregnancy.

Concern about the need to provide additional judicial protection for human rights led to the establishment of the European Convention on Human Rights by the Council of Europe in 1950. Signatory countries are obliged to implement judgments of the European Court of Human Rights which has had an increasing influence on domestic law.

National Constitutions

Most countries now have a written constitution that sets out the various institutions of government and their methods of establishment, functions, and responsibilities; the rules governing relationships between them; and usually a Bill of Rights, such as the Charter of Rights and Freedoms incorporated in the new Canadian constitution of 1982. Countries that do not have a written constitution include the United Kingdom, Israel, New Zealand, and Saudi Arabia.

Constitutions vary considerably in their length and the amount of detail they embody. The USA's constitution of 1789 is much shorter than most of the constitutions drafted for former British colonies that gained their independence in the years following World War II. Very long constitutions may reflect a lack of trust between different groups in society and an attempt to regulate their conduct by means of written rules.

However, a constitution is no protection against a military takeover of government, while elaborate rules designed to share power between competing communal groups cannot prevent civil war. This latter point is illustrated by the case of the former Yugoslavia after the death of Marshal Tito (1892–1980); here, the ingenious but ultimately unsuccessful device was implemented of a rotating presidency among the states that made up the federation. It was

▲ **Justices of the US Supreme Court (1990)** *The Supreme Court's decisions can have a profound effect on some fundamental aspects of life in the USA. Especially under the chief justiceship of Earl Warren, in the period 1953–69, the Supreme Court was renowned for its pioneering judgments on civil liberties issues.*

quango (*quasi-autonomous national government* [or, in US, *non-governmental*] *organization*) Authorities established by government as independent bodies but ultimately dependent upon government for subvention, etc. Replacement of direct state control by these unelected bodies (often for ideological reasons) raises serious problems concerning their lack of democratic accountability.

The Constitution of the United States ▶
This document was drafted in Philadelphia in 1788 and contains the fundamental principles of the federal system of government operating in the country. A large majority of countries have a written constitution.

the constitution. Denmark and Sweden are examples of unitary states. The United Kingdom is a less clear-cut example, because there is substantial administrative devolution to Scotland, Wales, and Northern Ireland. The separate government departments for the regions of the United Kingdom are extensively represented in cabinet and other official committees, giving them opportunities to represent their special problems. Hence, the United Kingdom is referred to as a **union state** rather than a unitary state, reflecting its establishment through the Act of Union of 1801.

Federal systems of government vary considerably in the extent to which they are centrally controlled, ranging from the relatively decentralized (e.g. Australia and Canada) to more centralized forms of government (e.g. Austria). Mexico provides another example of a centralized federal system in which the ruling Institutional Revolutionary Party – the PRI – controlled both the central state and, until 1992, all state governorships. There is also a distinctive type of federalism in which responsibility for implementing national legislation is given to the state governments (e.g. Germany and Switzerland).

Even within one federal system of government, there may be significant differences in the relationship between central and regional governments. In Canada, for example, relations between the Atlantic provinces, such as Newfoundland and Nova Scotia, and the central government are conditioned by the reliance of these poorer provinces on substantial transfers of money from the federal government. The province of Quebec, on the other hand, with its

union state A state that is not a federal state but differs from a unitary state because there is administrative or legislative devolution of government work to some, but not to all, parts of the national territory.

Serbia's refusal to allow Croatia to take its turn in the chair of the federal presidency that precipitated a final constitutional crisis in the spring of 1991. In other cases, long constitutions may reflect the inclusion of disguised pieces of legislation rather than mere procedural rules.

Unitary and Federal Forms of Government. A basic distinction in constitutions is between unitary and federal forms of government. A unitary state is one in which there are no subordinate territorial units that have a protected status or special jurisdiction within

An Independence Rally in Lithuania (1989) *Protestors in the Lithuanian capital Vilnius display banners in their own language, in Russian, and in English calling for the withdrawal of Soviet forces. The Baltic republics (Lithuania, Latvia, and Estonia) finally gained their independence after the break-up of the Soviet Union in 1991.*

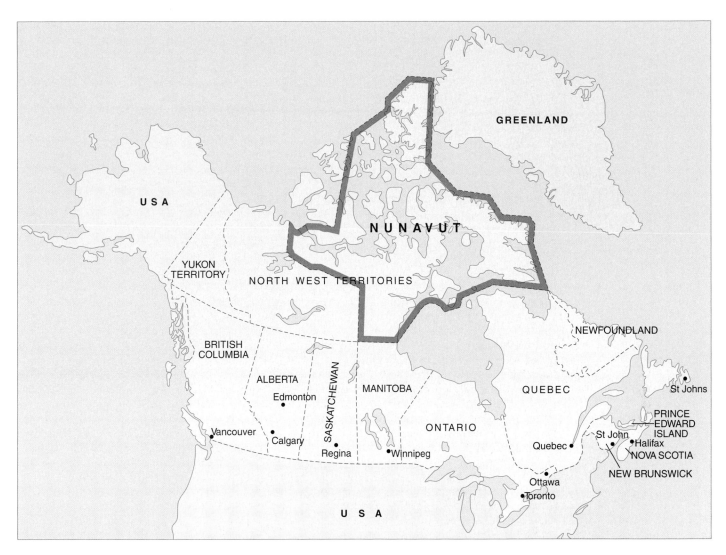

sounder economy and distinctive culture based on the French language, can credibly threaten to secede from Canada. This has led the federal government to make substantial constitutional and policy concessions to forestall the threat of secession.

In general, federal governments are usually unwilling to allow regional governments to secede; the result of secession attempts in the past has sometimes been brutal civil war leading to defeat for the secessionists. Examples of such defeats include the American Civil War (1861–65), when the southern states attempted to secede, and the Nigerian civil war between **Biafra** and the federal government. In the former Yugoslavia, Slovenia managed to secede, after a relatively limited military engagement with federal troops, and Croatia managed to establish itself as an independent state at the price of considerable destruction, severe loss of life, and the loss of control of one-third of its territory. After the collapse of the Soviet Union in 1990, Russia used economic and military pressure to re-establish control over what it calls the 'near abroad,' reincorporating

Georgia into the Commonwealth of Independent States (CIS). Federal states can, however, break up into their component parts peacefully; an example of such a peaceful demerger, the so-called 'velvet divorce,' occurred with the division of Czechoslovakia into the Czech Republic and Slovakia, which came into effect on 1 January 1993.

Federalism. Existing federal states in the 20th century are, in general, old-established countries in which separate groups have come together for their mutual benefit. In most of these countries the significance of old ethnic and religious divisions have faded into obscurity – long regarded as irrelevant or inappropriate compared to the advantages offered by federation.

In some of these countries, however, the federal model has succumbed – usually because it has failed to live up to the expectations of one or more of its ethnic or religious minorities. The former Soviet Union, Yugoslavia, and Czechoslovakia are examples. However, as some old federations break, new ones are being created. The most far-reaching of these is the European Union.

▲ **Canadian Administrative Districts**
The provinces and territories of this federal parliamentary state are shown, including the proposed province of Nunavut ('Our Land'), the territory of the indigenous Inuit people of Canada, to be instituted by the year 2000.

Biafra

The eastern region of Biafra, home of the Ibo people, seceded from the Federal Republic of Nigeria in 1967. After three years of civil war and famine, the new state capitulated in January 1970.

subsidiarity A term coined to designate the right of member states of the European Union to take those decisions that are more appropriately taken at a national rather than European level. However, there is still much debate about precisely which decisions these are.

Bosnian Serb Forces in Bosnia-Herzegovina ▶
Civil war and ethnic conflict resulted from the collapse of the Yugoslav federation.

Within the European Union, the label ***federalist*** has been applied to supporters of rapid progress towards economic and political integration. Although it is evolving in the direction of a federation, the European Union in the mid-1990s can more accurately be described as a confederation, or a union of still-independent member states. True federation remains an aspiration of some of its politicians; for others, the ideal of federalism is counterbalanced by the principle of **subsidiarity**.

Federations face a dual challenge at the end of the 20th century. On the one hand, there is the trend towards centralization represented by the increasing powers of central state executives, who are themselves seeking to respond to trends towards the globalization of economic and political power. On the other hand, the resurgence of ethnic and religious identities in some federal countries raises the spectre of secession, the threat of civil unrest, or even murderous civil wars, and the consequent dissolution of federal governments.

In a mature federation, such as the USA, much of the vitality of the federal idea is maintained by using the state governments as training grounds for national politicians. Presidents may serve as state governors prior to assuming national office. Similarly, many members of Congress began their political careers in state legislatures. The states have an independent financial base through their income and sales taxes, but they also depend on federal funds for major projects. This has created an enduring interdependence between the two levels of government. The federal government has also permitted policy innovations developed at state level to be

EXAMPLES OF FEDERAL SYSTEMS OF GOVERNMENT

Country	Federal units	Upper chamber
Australia	6 states 2 territories	Senate – 76 members, comprising 12 members directly elected from each state and 2 from each of the two territories, Australian Capital Territory and Northern Territory
Belgium	3 regions	Not applicable (no upper chamber)
Brazil	26 states 1 federal district	Senate – 3 directly elected members per state or federal district; senate renewed every 4 years, alternately by one-third and two-thirds of its members
Canada	10 provinces 2 territories	Senate – nominated by prime minister. Specified variable number for each province
Germany	16 *Länder*	Bundesrat – at least 3 members from each *Land* appointed by government of *Land*
India	25 states 7 union territories	Council of states – elected by legislature of each state; numbers vary by population
United States of America	50 states 1 capital territory	Senate – 2 per state (no representatives from capital)

applied nationally, so the states can decide whether to apply, for example, federal air-quality regulations or the more stringent regulations devised by the state of California. Federalism in the USA has shown a resilience and vitality that would not have been anticipated even as recently as the 1960s. It perhaps suggests that other, more fragile, federal systems of government may survive the test of time to emerge in renewed forms.

The Administration Of Government

Laws based on party programmes have to be converted into action by the executive branch of government. Budgets have to be formulated and funds found; staff has to be recruited or retrained; new administrative structures have to be set up; and new rule books must be written before a programme can start to work. Government is thus a major employer in all countries, even those that claim to adhere to a principle of limited government. Many of the tasks carried out by government, such as the payment of pensions and benefits, are of a routine nature and do not raise major political issues. From a political point of view, the most important parts of a civil service are the very highest levels that advise ministers and draft new policies.

Ministries and their Political Leaders. The way in which the tasks of government are divided between ministries varies from one country to another. For example, in some countries tourism will be the sole responsibility of a particular government department, whereas in others it will be grouped with several other government functions, while in yet others, it will be the responsibility of a separate public agency outside the main government structure. Nevertheless, some general trends in the organization of government departments are apparent. As governments have acquired more functions, the number of ministries has tended to increase. For example, separate departments of energy proliferated in response to the world oil crisis in 1973, while environmental departments and agencies have been established in response to greater public concern about global pollution.

Despite this general increase in the overall number of ministries, there is a considerable degree of variation among countries. Former communist countries tended to have a large number of ministries, because they were so deeply involved in the running of the centrally planned economy. By contrast, many Latin American countries have fewer government departments than is customary. On the other hand, certain government departments are almost universal; examples include a foreign affairs department, a defence ministry, a ministry of the interior, a treasury or

▲ **A Customs Post in Pakistan**
The monitoring of goods entering a country is a vital part of a nation's governmental administration.

finance ministry, an education ministry, and a health ministry.

Permanent and Politically Affiliated Civil Servants. All countries have a permanent civil service that plays an important part in the government of the country, although some countries make more use of short-term political appointees in the higher levels of the civil service than others. The style of each civil service tends to vary from one country to another, a fact that has sometimes made it difficult to reconcile different approaches in international bodies. For example, the European Commission has had to take account of the French emphasis on formal diplomacy, the German preference for a legally trained civil service observing formal legal rights and procedures, and the emphasis by the United Kingdom on the art of pragmatic compromise.

The higher levels of permanent civil services are customarily recruited from relatively narrow backgrounds. Until recently, recruits to the higher levels of civil services have generally been male, from middle- or upper-class backgrounds, and from majority or dominant ethnic groups. Above all, the tendency has been to recruit from a limited number of elite higher education institutions, for instance Tokyo and Osaka universities in Japan or the specialized **grandes écoles** in France, which prepare their graduates for senior administrative positions.

The civil service career structure is that of a series of grades. Civil services vary in the extent to which their members receive experience of life outside the government bureaucracy. In France, it has been common for senior civil servants to hold posts outside government for part of their careers. For example, they might work in a state-run industry. In Japan, it is customary for all civil servants to retire at the age of 55, a practice known as

Grandes Écoles

Institutions of higher education in France that prepare their graduates for entry to the higher ranks of the civil service. The *Ecole Polytechnique*, founded in 1794, prepares its students for technical positions. The *Ecole Nationale d'Administration* is a largely postgraduate institution set up in 1945 to train recruits for the higher levels of the general civil service, such as the Prefectoral Corps and the Diplomatic Corps.

amakudari or 'descent from heaven.' They then take up posts in the private sector or in business associations.

Many civil service traditions emphasize the political neutrality of civil servants and their ability to serve governments drawn from any political party. Even when a government changes, they remain in office. In the approach to an election, these civil servants prepare separate sets of files for each party that might be elected to government. Other countries (e.g. France and Italy) provide for a number of temporary political appointments in the civil service through ministerial teams of advisors, or *cabinets*. This system of having a small personal staff appointed by the minister has been adopted by the European Commission, where each commissioner has a *cabinet*, drawn largely from nationals of his or her own country.

The most extensive system of temporary civil service appointments is found in the USA, where senior civil servants are replaced by a new president and a new administration: thousands of posts in the bureaucracy have to be appointed by the incoming president. One drawback of this system is that filling these posts can take a considerable amount of time. This is due in part to a lack of suitable candidates (because pay is much lower than in the private sector), and in part to the fact that candidates for the more senior posts undergo a rigorous procedure of scrutiny by confirming committees in the Senate. Hence, more than a year may elapse after the new president has been elected before all the posts are filled; this seriously disrupts the conduct of the business of government.

The increased complexity of modern society places a premium on expertise, often concentrated in the bureaucracy. Civil services employ a wide range of experts, including economists, doctors, architects, and marine biologists. Perhaps the greatest field of expertise in the civil service, however, lies in the knowledge of the procedural rules and mechanisms of government.

The growth of political patronage in the bureaucracy of some countries and the attendant danger of partisanship have raised serious concerns about the undermining of accountable government. One response, albeit of limited effectiveness, has been to create new channels for individual citizens to air grievances against the bureaucracy. These mechanisms may take the form of 'citizens' charters,' special quasi-judicial tribunals that can reverse or alter administrative decisions, or adoption of the office of **ombudsman**.

Changes in the broader political system can sometimes lead to a new challenge to the power of the bureaucracy. After the Japanese

Ombudsman

An ombudsman is appointed by a government or a large financial institution to investigate complaints from citizens or customers. The post originated as a political appointment in Scandinavia (Sweden 1809, Denmark 1954, Norway 1962). Outside this region, the first ombudsman appeared in New Zealand in 1962, followed by the UK in 1967 (where the officer is called a *parliamentary commissioner*). Several countries have appointed ombudsmen to investigate maladministration by institutions, such as local government and the police. Some banks, insurance companies, etc., also use ombudsmen to investigate complaints by customers.

▲ **Japanese General Election (1993)** *Following this election, the Liberal Democratic Party was ejected from office by a 17-party coalition. The loss of power by a party that had been in government from 1955 had major implications for a civil service accustomed to serving governments of the same political complexion for over 30 years.*

Liberal Democratic Party lost power in 1993 – for the first time in the postwar period – civil servants found that decisions that had once gone unchallenged were now being questioned by politicians of the new coalition government.

Local and Civic Government

Local and civic government must be distinguished from the constituent regional governments of a federal state whose existence and functions enjoy some constitutional protection. The structure of local government may be specified in a state constitution, but it is not generally granted the share in the sovereign power of the state that is possessed by federal units. Indeed, in countries without written constitutions, local government may be accorded very little protection against the erosion of its powers, or even the abolition of whole authorities.

Each national system of local government has its own distinctive features, but there are a number of broad patterns. In northern European states, such as Denmark, Sweden, and the United Kingdom, local authorities have a wide range of functions; there is also a relatively clear division of responsibility between central and local government. Local government is not permitted to exceed its statutory powers, although it has a fair amount of discretion within those powers. In southern European countries, such as France, Italy, and Spain, local government absorbs a much smaller proportion of total government expenditure. France in particular has a relatively centralized system of local government, although there has been less supervision from the centre in recent years. In southern Europe, there is much greater reliance on detailed central government approval for the actions of local government.

The tasks carried out by local government vary from one country to another. Local government may often act as a field agent for central government, providing services according to standards laid down by central government, which meets all or most of the cost; education is one such important service, usually provided by local governments throughout the world. In some countries, (e.g. the USA), this process is so well advanced that central government has little direct influence over the education service. Rather, education in the USA is provided by school districts that vary greatly in the funds available to them, depending on whether they serve rich or poor areas.

While some countries are characterized by multipurpose authorities, with one or two tiers of local government in any one area, others are characterized by the territorial and functional overlapping of large numbers of multipurpose and special-purpose local authorities. This is the case in the USA: in California, parts of some counties have been incorporated into cities, whereas other parts have not, and the whole nature of the relationship between the cities and counties varies from place to place. Primary and secondary education is provided by special-purpose authorities, known as 'school districts,' while other special-purpose authorities deal with public transport or air-quality management.

Countries display a wide variation in the ways in which local authorities exert influence on central government. In northern Europe, the usual pattern is to have well-resourced interest groups at the national level representing particular types of local authority and bargaining with the central government for more funds and other objectives. By contrast, in southern Europe there is a greater stress on local elite groups, who represent the interests of the cities directly to the national elites controlling the central government.

In the USA, the mayors of leading cities are treated as major figures, even though their power within their own areas may be limited by the need to bargain both with their own councils and with a wide range of specialized authorities delivering key services. Mayors are regarded as being closest to local opinion and potentially able to defuse major urban flashpoints. As a result, even presidents are willing to listen to their advice.

In a period during which central government finances have been under great pressure, a common response to public expenditure problems has been to divert unpopular responsibilities onto local government, to cut central government assistance to local government, or frequently to do both. A local government unit is rarely able to fund its own expenditure, even when borrowing for capital projects is taken into account. Thus, local government is usually dependent on central government for a large proportion of its funds. Local governments rely on property taxes levied on homes and commercial premises as a principal source of revenue. Because revisions of the rateable value of property occur rarely, this source of revenue often fails to keep pace with inflation and the expansion of local government activity.

One further problem for local government is the reorganization of territorial boundaries in order to keep pace with the rapid progress of urbanization throughout the world. Local authority boundaries may be so obsolete as to reflect the size of a city 30 or even 50 years ago; hence, many of the people who currently work in a city may live outside its boundaries. Moreover, as affluent citizens move to the suburbs, the city becomes populated with low-income or even destitute residents; the problem is compounded by the loss of tax revenue from the wealthier commuters. Because they have lower taxes, suburbs are reluctant to be absorbed into cities. It has therefore been extremely difficult to develop effective metropolitan government for the world's major cities.

> **Local Government**
>
> Key areas of responsibility for the local government tier throughout the world are as follows:
> - Education (not Higher)
> - Fire services
> - Refuse collection
> - Recreational facilities
> - Bus services
> - Planning decisions
> - Social services
> - Local housing

Mayoral Elections in New York *Election victories in 1993 by White Republican mayors in cities, such as Los Angeles and New York, that had previously been led by Black Democrats were treated as a major national political development.* ▼

International Politics

Politics in the absence of government • The basis of international order • Foreign policy • Power • International organizations • Maintaining peace • The United Nations

International politics is concerned with the relationships between states, each of which has its own **sovereignty**. These links may manifest themselves as direct relations between states or, indirectly, through the actions of international organizations that consist of individual states, such as the United Nations, the Organization of American States, or the Arab League. These organizations are sometimes referred to as ***intergovernmental organizations*** (IGOs), to distinguish them from ***international nongovernmental organizations*** (INGOs or, more commonly, NGOs). Since other groups, such as multinational businesses and unofficial bodies (e.g. terrorist organizations), have the potential to exert influence on the foreign policies of states, they may also be said to play a role in international politics.

Politics in the Absence of Government

The fundamental characteristic of international relationships is that they take place in the absence of a single government to lay down and implement the rules of the relationships. In other political contexts a government is always present, and – at least in theory – it possesses both the authority to rule and the power to exercise that authority. The job of government is to provide a secure and well-regulated framework within which individuals and groups can conduct their everyday lives.

Internationally, however, there is no such government. The world's territory is divided into **sovereign states**, and each state acts, within its own territory, as the supreme authority. Of course, other states may influence its policies in a number of areas. However, in formal terms each state is at liberty to determine its own policies. Thus the security and prosperity of the state is ultimately dependent on its independent efforts. There is no world government to come to the rescue of a state that finds itself in trouble, or who considers that it is being unfairly treated by other states.

Independent Nations

On 1 April 1994 the number of sovereign states, grouped according to geopolitical region, was as follows:

Africa:	53
The Americas:	35
Asia:	47
Europe:	43
Oceania:	13
Total:	191

SOVEREIGNTY AND SOVEREIGN STATES

The most general meaning of the term 'sovereignty' refers to the degree of legal and political freedom that a state has in carrying out its foreign policy.

In international relations, sovereignty is the quality that a state – as a territorial entity – must possess in order to be eligible to participate in international politics. Sovereignty, in this sense, consists of having a constitution that is not subordinate to any other constitution. A colony, therefore, is not in a position of being sovereign since it is constitutionally subordinate to the colonial power controlling it. When such links are severed, the colony becomes a sovereign state.

The dismantling of the colonial empires of various west European countries since World War II has greatly increased the number of sovereign states. The fragmentation of the former Soviet Union and some east European states has also contributed to this process. Occasionally the number of sovereign states decreases, as a result of the union of two countries, such as the reunification of East and West Germany in October 1990.

▲ **Citizens of Belize Celebrating Independence** *The small country of Belize, on the Central American isthmus, gained its independence from the United Kingdom in 1981.*

This means that politics at the international level is strongly competitive. Each state is trying to secure the best deal for its citizens, to advance and defend their interests in an environment that is frequently hostile. Sometimes this may lead to physical conflict, in the shape of war. More commonly, however, it produces conflict of an economic or psychological kind. However, in spite of the dangers inherent in international relations, there is also a vast amount of cooperation between countries, for it has long been recognized and adopted as a principle of statesmanship that this offers the best way for states to achieve their goals. The terms and conditions for cooperation have to be defined and agreed between the participants, usually as a result of a process of tough bargaining.

The Basis of International Order

The basic task of the government of a state is the maintenance of order. Internationally, the lack of a 'world government' might lead to the assumption that international politics is disorderly. This, however, is a common misconception. In fact, relations between states are on the whole orderly, since states can predict, with a fair degree of accuracy, what other states will do, or refrain from doing. This element of predictability reflects the existence of three factors at an international level.

The first is the system of **diplomacy**. This is the means through which states are able to engage in official communication with each other. In order to do this, states appoint representatives to speak on their behalf – diplomats,

▲ **Government Buildings in Manila, the Philippines**
In great administrative buildings in the world's capital cities, matters of foreign policy are enacted, concerning the country's relations with other nations and its interests abroad.

who act on the basis of the instructions they receive from their governments. By means of this system states are able to convey to each other their views on the issues that concern them. Indeed, international politics to a large extent comprises such discussions between nations. In the light of the knowledge acquired in this way, states decide on their best course of action.

Secondly, there is a large body of **international law** (see LAW: INTERNATIONAL LAW AND HUMAN RIGHTS). This sets out the obligations, or promises, that states have given to each other on a great variety of topics. These undertakings cover such matters as defensive alliances, permission for one state to fly its aircraft through the airspace of another state, and arrangements to ensure that people based in one state but working in another do not have the same items of income taxed twice. It is generally true to say that states make strenuous efforts to abide by the terms of international law.

Finally, there are wider considerations of prudence in maintaining international order. States have no other option than to coexist with each other. Accordingly, most states take the view that it is sensible to avoid giving unnecessary offence, even if such a course might not be unlawful. Thus other states' views are taken into account, whenever such a course of action is possible or reasonable. One good reason for this is to encourage those states to behave in the same way when the situation is reversed; reciprocity is the keynote of international politics.

Foreign Policy

All states employ a body of specialized officials whose responsibility it is to advise the government minister at the head of their office on how the state should behave in the international arena. Customarily, these officials divide

---

DIPLOMACY

When two states have agreed to talk to each other through accredited representatives, they are said to have established **diplomatic relations.** If the extent of their mutual interests justifies it, they will open embassies in each other's capital cities. An embassy is headed by an ambassador, and includes a number of more junior diplomats. To enable them to carry out their duties effectively, diplomats are given certain legal and other privileges (known as **diplomatic immunity**). For example, an embassy may not legally be entered by the officials of the 'host' state, and diplomats cannot be made to appear before its courts. The permanent missions that states often establish close to the headquarters of important international organizations, such as the United Nations, are loosely referred to as embassies and their heads have the status of ambassadors.

International Law

As there is no international government, there is also no international legislature. Instead, states have to agree between themselves the rules that apply to their conduct with each other. It takes two forms. *International custom* comprises practices that have grown up among states and that have become accepted as legally binding. *International treaties*, made between states, establish legally binding rules on specific matters. These agreements may be made between any number of states, but bind only the signatories.

their time between serving as civil servants at home in the state's external affairs ministry (its precise name will vary from state to state) and as diplomats in the state's embassies and permanent missions in foreign cities.

A state's foreign policy is the product of two main political forces. In the first place, internal influences come into play: when formulating policy, a country's government must not only take account of domestic public opinion, but also of the views of legislators, officials, members of the government, and particular pressure groups. The exact balance between these various groups will reflect the procedures and politics of the state concerned. In some countries, e.g. the USA, the legislature will play a more influential role in this respect than in others. Everywhere, however, the formulation and execution of foreign policy may provoke intense discussion, indicating the important link between domestic and international politics.

Secondly, external pressures are invariably brought to bear in international politics. A state may, when formulating policy, be able to play off the interests of one outside state or group of states against those of others. However, the number of options for action that are open to a state are frequently limited. The weight of international opinion may be so overwhelming on a particular issue as to effectively restrict the choices available to the policy makers. Alternatively, so great is the imbalance of power in the world that a smaller state may be coerced by pressure, for instance the threat of economic sanctions, to fall into line with international opinion.

Withdrawal of Soviet Troops from Afghanistan in 1989 *As the USA had discovered from its defeat in the Vietnam War, military strength alone is unable to sustain a superpower's client regime.*▼

Power

The two major constituents of a state's power are its military capacity and its economic strength. Two less influential factors are its political or ideological charisma and the skill of its diplomats. The former group of elements can be quantified, whereas the latter group cannot. In practice, however, political outcomes on the world stage are frequently not predetermined by simple calculations of relative power. There are two reasons for this.

The first is that a state may be unable to bring its superior power to bear effectively in a particular conflict. Despite its overwhelming military superiority (especially in the areas of air power), the USA was unable to subdue its opponents in the Vietnam War, and was forced by a combination of circumstances to withdraw in disarray in 1975. Similarly the Soviet Union was unsuccessful in its attempt to impose its political will through armed intervention in Afghanistan in the 1980s. Secondly, the political relationship that exists between states may preclude the use of certain elements of power. Thus the west European states are not directly influenced by the military superiority of the USA. The use that can be made of military power depends to a large extent on the context.

International politics, therefore, is not simply an arena in which events are determined by the unrestrained exercise of military power. If it were, the world would not have its present political configuration. There are huge disparities between sovereign states, in terms of population, area, wealth, and military strength. Nonetheless, small states survive, and in appropriate conditions, can thrive. Switzerland is a prime example of a small state that has played an important part in world politics, being chosen as the headquarters of many UN agencies and other international organizations because of its neutrality.

International Organizations

States establish or join an international organization when they feel that their cooperation on a particular issue needs to be undertaken in an organizational framework. The essential characteristics of such a framework are that it establishes regular meetings and that it is serviced by a permanent secretariat. The resultant organizations range from very small bodies to ones that are virtually universal in membership. Their terms of reference are equally varied, from local to global, and may be either specialized or general.

There are about 300 such organizations. Among these, the most famous are the larger organizations, such as the European Union (EU), the Organization of African Unity (OAU),

◄ **UN Peacekeeping Troops in Nicaragua**
Troops from several Latin American countries were drafted in under UN auspices to oversee the Nicaraguan presidential elections in 1990 and to demobilize armed groups. Here, Colombian soldiers of ONUCA (United Nations Observer Group in Central America) arrive to set up the first of five security zones.

the Association of Southeast Asian Nations (ASEAN), and, largest of all, the United Nations (see **THE UNITED NATIONS**).

Maintaining Peace

The UN originally consisted of the victorious Allied powers in World War II, prominent among them the Soviet Union and the USA. Despite the initial hope that they would remain united, and use their combined strength to maintain world peace, rifts soon appeared– giving rise to the period of tension, lasting for over 40 years, commonly referred to as the **Cold War**. Thus, apart from one exceptional case when a permanent member of the Security Council was unable to use its veto (the decision to give military assistance to South Korea in June 1950, which the Soviet Union was unable to block, as it was boycotting the Security Council at the time), partisan interests made it impossible to agree on firm enforcement action in the name of the UN.

However, the political circumstances of some conflicts have enabled the UN to perform a peacekeeping role. Peacekeeping consists of the use of military personnel (drawn from member states) in untypical roles; they are instructed to take an impartial and nonthreatening stance in order to help disputants maintain peace. Such action depends on the willingness of the conflicting parties to coexist without violence, at least for an interim period while negotiations for an equitable settlement proceed, and to accept the UN's help in mediation. The UN's peacekeeping soldiers or military observers, who have come to be known as the 'Blue Berets' are not introduced into conflict zones to enforce the peace but to engage in such tasks as patrolling a ceasefire line or a buffer zone. Where extreme mistrust has existed between the warring factions, this kind of action is most valuable.

Apart from its response to the Iraqi invasion of Kuwait in 1990, the Security Council has neither taken nor authorized the strong enforcement action it was envisaged that it could take when it was established in 1945. Instead, it has found that the best way of proceeding is to instigate operations of a peacekeeping nature. However, there are important qualifications to this. First, a much higher proportion of recent peacekeeping operations have taken place within the area of a single state's jurisdiction rather than at the border between two states. Secondly, it has become the rule rather than the exception, for civilians, such as police or election monitors, to play an operational role. Finally, the Security Council has shown that it is willing in exceptional circumstances to authorize its peacekeepers to take tough action against those who obstruct its work.

Important instances of recent peacekeeping operations are those that helped the former non-self-governing territory of Namibia towards sovereign statehood (1989–90), and those that contributed to a reconciliation process in Cambodia by acting as a transitional authority (1992–93). At the end of February 1994, a total of 70 601 military personnel and 1215 civilian police were serving in UN peacekeeping operations.

The UN does not have a monopoly of peacekeeping activity; a number of this type of operation have been set up under other auspices. One such non-UN peacekeeping operation is the Multinational Force and Observers (MFO), which was established in 1982 to assist in the implementation of the 1979 peace treaty between Egypt and Israel.

UN Secretaries-General
1946–52 Trygve Lie (Norway)
1953–61 Dag Hammarskjöld (Sweden)
1962–72 U Thant (Burma)
1972–81 Kurt Waldheim (Austria)
1982–91 Javier Pérez de Cuéllar (Peru)
1992–97 Boutros Boutros-Ghali (Egypt)
1997– Kofi Annan (Ghana)

THE UNITED NATIONS

THE UNITED NATIONS was established at the end of World War II, as a successor to the largely ineffectual League of Nations.

MEMBER COUNTRIES OF THE UN

By 1997, the UN's original membership of 51 states had grown to 185; the only significant nations not represented are Taiwan (expelled in 1971 on the entry of communist China to the UN) and Switzerland (which considers its strict neutrality would be compromised by membership). Almost every member state has established a permanent mission to the UN, headed by a senior diplomat. In addition to the public debates in the UN's two main decision-making organs – the General Assembly and the Security Council – much private diplomacy is conducted. In the General Assembly each member state has a seat and, irrespective of its size, a single vote. UN resolutions, although not legally binding, are seen as strong expressions of international opinion. Since the early 1960s the many states that gained independence from European colonialism – especially in Africa – have collectively ensured that UN resolutions reflect their views.

THE SECURITY COUNCIL

The Security Council is composed of five permanent members (China, France, Russia, the UK and the USA), and ten nonpermanent members, each of which serves for two years. Each permanent member can veto the passage of any resolution. Security Council resolutions carry greater legal and political

The UN Building *The UN headquarters, in New York, comprises the high-rise Secretariat and the General Assembly building.*

weight than those of the Assembly, since the Security Council was designed as a vehicle to deter and if necessary repulse aggression.

However, the Cold War that ensued immediately after World War II between Western states (led by the USA) and the former Soviet bloc prevented the Council from operating as originally intended. Only since the end of the Cold War in the late 1980s has the Security Council been able to play an effective part in efforts to maintain international peace.

Under the UN Charter, all member states agree to accept and enact decisions of the Security Council.

UN SPECIALIZED AGENCIES

The 17 specialized agencies are:

FAO (Food and Agriculture Organization; *above*)

IBRD (International Bank for Reconstruction and Development)

ICAO (International Civil Aviation Organization)

IDA (International Development Association)

IFAD (International Fund for Agricultural Development)

IFC (International Finance Corporation)

ILO (International Labour Organisation)

IMF (International Monetary Fund)

IMO (International Maritime Organization)

ITU (International Telecommunications Union)

MIGA (Multilateral Investment Guarantee Agency)

UNESCO (UN Educational, Scientific and Cultural Organization)

UNIDO (UN Industrial Development Organization)

UPU (Universal Postal Union)

WHO (World Health Organization; *below*)

WIPO (World Intellectual Property Organization)

WMO (World Meteorological Organization)

STRUCTURE OF THE UN

The UN's various organizations and agencies are shown in this diagram. The Secretariat is the main administrative body.

The budget of the UN, which is set every two years, is funded mainly from the contributions of the member states. Expenditure in a typical two-year period is around US$2.3 billion.

Six official languages are used in the UN: Arabic, Chinese, English, French, Russian, and Spanish.

International Trusteeship Council

General Assembly

Secretariat/ Secretary-General

International Court of Justice

Economic and Social Council

Security Council

IAEA (International Atomic Energy Agency)

GATT (General Agreement on Tariffs and Trade)

Subsidiary Organizations including:
UNICEF (UN Children's Fund)
UNHCR (UN High Commissioner for Refugees)

Specialized Agencies

FAO
ICAO
IFAD
ILO
IMF
IMO

ITU
UNESCO
UNIDO
UPU
WHO
WIPO

WMO
[*World Bank* comprising the following agencies]:
IBRD
IDA
IFC
MIGA

Peacekeeping Organizations including:
UNTSO (UN Truce Supervision Organization)
UNIFIL (UN Interim Force in Lebanon)

Legal Systems and Their Origins

*Human laws and scientific laws • Hierarchy of rules • Natural law and positive law •
Legal families • The civil-law tradition • The spread of European civil law •
The common-law tradition • Islamic law*

Laws are rules that are devised by human societies for the regulation of relations between their members. As such they vary greatly in their nature. Modern industrial societies, for example, require detailed and complex rules regulating such matters as taxation, social welfare, the formation and management of companies, and court procedures. On the other hand, relatively simple rules – such as the Biblical Ten Commandments – may govern less economically or politically complex societies.

Laws are not the only rules that regulate societies. Social behaviour is also influenced by religious or moral precepts, and these may – sometimes to a considerable extent – shape the nature and content of a community's laws. Thus in Islamic communities, Islamic Law is observed precisely because it is believed to be the expression of the will of Allah (God).

Human Laws and Scientific Laws

Laws designed to regulate human societies differ from scientific laws. Scientific laws are predictions, based on observation and experiment, of how the physical universe will behave under particular conditions. Thus, the 'law of gravity' predicts that a one-kilogram block of metal *will* drop to earth with a specific uniform acceleration if it is dropped from the top of a skyscraper.

Although human laws can be stated in very similar terms – 'If a person commits murder he will be punished' – they are not laws in the same sense as scientific laws. Human laws are not predictions of what *will* happen, given certain conditions, but rather they are statements of what *ought* to happen in such conditions. A law stating that a person who commits murder will be punished is really saying that this is what *should* happen. If a person who commits

◄ **The Ten
Commandments**
*In this woodcut from
the Nuremberg Bible
(c.1500), Moses is
seen receiving from
God the Ten
Commandments –
divine laws imparted
directly to mankind.
Moses then brought the
Commandments to his
people, the Israelites
(right), who adopted
them as the law of their
society. Divine edicts
still form the basis of
much legislation in
some societies, e.g.
Islamic countries.*

Human law is law only by virtue of its accordance with right reason, and by this means it is clear that it flows from Eternal Law. In so far as it deviates from right reason, it is called an unjust law, and in such a case, it is no law at all, but rather an assertion of violence.

St Thomas Aquinas
(1225–74), Italian philosopher, *Summa Theologiae*

Justinian I
The Eastern Roman (or Byzantine) emperor Justinian I (reigned 527–565 AD) is shown (centre) with his retinue in this 6th-century mosaic. Justinian was responsible for sponsoring codification of Roman law into the Corpus Juris Civilis *(Body of Civil Law), which formed the basis of Western civil law.* ▼

murder is not punished (e.g. because the murder goes undetected, or because there is insufficient evidence to convict the suspect) this does not invalidate the law against murder.

Hierarchy of Rules
Laws may sometimes be deemed wrong, in the sense of being unjust. A law sanctioning racial discrimination would, for example, be widely regarded as violating fundamental principles of equality. Human beings perceive a need to test the appropriateness of laws by reference to some form of superior law.

In some modern systems this can be done by comparing ordinary laws with the terms of the Constitution. The Constitution is regarded as the paramount law of a society. Some legal systems, such as that of the USA, even allow the highest court to declare invalid any law that contradicts the US Constitution.

Similarly, a country's domestic laws may be measured against the rules of international law. If a country is party to an international agreement forbidding the use of the death penalty, and yet the death penalty is still provided for within its domestic law, the imposition of a death sentence could be contested on the ground that the domestic law must cede to the rule of international law.

Natural Law and Positive Law
Even in the absence of a hierarchy of legal rules, it is not uncommon to find the conception of a higher order of justice, against which domestic legislation is measured. Appeals are made to 'natural law,' 'divine law,' or 'morality.' Various conclusions have been drawn from such comparisons. Some writers have argued that if a human law fails to comply with the requirements of a higher moral precept, then the individual is entitled or even obliged to disregard the human law in favour of the more fundamental principle.

This ideal conception of the law stands in marked contrast to a view of the law as positive law, i.e. law laid down by a state or other human institution. The positivist approach states simply that a law that complies with the formal requirements for the making of law within a society *is* a law – and should be obeyed. It does not engage in speculation on whether a law accords with a supreme system of justice ordained by a higher power.

Legal Families
Lawyers concerned with the comparison of systems of law have long adopted the practice of grouping the world's various legal systems together into 'legal families.' This is achieved by identifying features that are shared by systems and that serve to distinguish them from others. One such systematic grouping of legal systems (formulated in 1985) proposes the following divisions: the Romano-Germanic family; the common-law family; socialist law; religious and other conceptions of law and the social order (e.g. Islamic law, Indian law); laws of the Far East; and laws of Africa.

Although such classifications are useful, their limitations must be recognized. First, the basis of the classification must be made clear; namely, whether the systems are being classified according to their historical relationship to each other, by virtue of sharing a common political ideology, or because they are based on religion, or for some other reason.

Second, since many legal systems have been influenced by others, the allocation of a system to one particular legal family may depend upon the area of the law in question. In this regard, there has been a tendency to concentrate on the private law and to ignore other important branches (e.g. constitutional law, trade law, or criminal law). For instance, the commercial law in many countries that otherwise are categorized within the Islamic system owes much to the legal systems of western Europe.

Finally, much depends upon when the classification was made. Thus, in the broad classification above, the category 'socialist law' is now wholly inapplicable to the legal systems of many states in eastern Europe or the former USSR since the demise of state socialism there in 1990–91.

The following three major groupings of legal systems emerge as distinct categories: the civil-law tradition, the common-law tradition, and Islamic law. The first two of these groups deserve particular attention because of the influence that they have had in the development of legal systems throughout the world. The third group is noteworthy as the most extensive system of law based on religion in the modern world.

THE PRUSSIAN CIVIL CODE

The Prussian Civil Code, or *Allgemeines Landrecht*, sprang from the Enlightenment reforms instigated by Frederick the Great (1740–86), but was not promulgated until 1794. In the 19th century, it was adopted by many other German states.

A major characteristic of the Code was its extraordinary degree of detail. It extended to 17 000 paragraphs and purported to make provision for many matters not normally covered by legislation. Thus, the Code required that healthy women should suckle their own children, and that a husband was empowered to decide how long his wife should continue to do this.

The Prussian Civil Code outlawed torture and restricted capital punishment, but also enshrined the rigid censorship that was to become a hallmark of the Prussian state.

The Civil-Law Tradition

The civil-law group comprises those systems that derive from Roman law as it was received and adapted in western Europe from the 13th century onwards. The civil law thus transmitted later provided the foundation for the major codifications of the law that occurred in Germany, Austria, and France during the 18th and 19th centuries. The most influential of these was the French codification beginning with the *Code civil* (or Napoleonic Code) of 1804. Within this group, a distinction may be made between the **Romano-Germanic** tradition and the **French civilian** tradition.

Roman Law. Roman law indirectly provided the foundation for much of the private law of most of the legal systems of western Europe, as well as that of Central and South America. This is largely due to the systematic attempts at **codification** of the law made in the later years of the Roman Empire. This codified law later became the subject of study in the universities that were founded in Europe from the medieval period onwards, and was adopted by emergent European nation-states.

Romano-Germanic Law. Prior to the mid-15th century, Roman law had little impact on the territories that ultimately combined to form Germany. When it did arrive, via lawyers employed in the Church and in administrative roles in the cities and principalities, it was adopted more comprehensively than elsewhere in Europe. This was due in part to the fact that German territories had no body of law equivalent to the English common law and no corresponding centralized system of courts administering royal justice (the *Reichskammergericht* was not established until

1495). Moreover, many of the local laws were thought inappropriate for the changing social and economic needs of the later Middle Ages.

In the 18th century, under the influence of Enlightenment thought, the study of law, including Roman law, was developed to a high level in the German law schools. The conviction that law could be expressed as a rational orderly system inspired a movement towards codification of laws, which found support among various German princes. The first such code was the *Codex Maximilianus Bavaricus Civilis*, written for Maximilian of Bavaria in 1756. Although an Austrian civil code was commissioned by the Empress Maria Theresa in 1753, it only came to fruition in the General Civil Code for Austria in 1811. The most influential German code of this period was the **Prussian Civil Code** of 1794.

A civil code for the whole of Germany did not arise until 1900, when the German Civil Code (*Bürgerliches Gesetzbuch*, or *BGB*) was adopted. This was largely due to the predominance in the early 19th century of the **Historical school**, whose chief exponent was the conservative jurist Friedrich Karl von Savigny (1779–1861). Savigny regarded law as reflecting the 'spirit' of a particular culture and therefore resisted the adoption of a general German code as unrepresentative of the traditions and attitudes of the German people. He was also opposed to the liberal and egalitarian principles associated with other codes (e.g. the French *Code civil*).

In other areas of the law, codification progressed more rapidly. The demands of commerce led to the adoption in 1861 of a General German Commercial Code. Following the creation of the German Empire in 1871, work began on a General Civil Code in 1873. After various drafts in the late 19th century, the code was adopted on 1 January 1900 and (with amendments) still remains in force.

French Civil Law. Before the French Revolution, France was divided into two legislative territories, or **pays**. In the north there was the **pays de droit coutumier** (customary law) and in the south the **pays de droit écrit** (written law). In both territories the law was administered through local courts known as **Parlements**, but there was no central judicial body with authority over the whole country.

Whereas in the pays de droit coutumier there was a diverse range of local customary laws, the principal influence on the law in the pays de droit écrit was Roman law. In the north, particular local customs were frequently matters of dispute. Gradually, however, the unwritten customary laws of the north were condensed into a written form. Since the Paris Parlement exercised jurisdiction over most of the north of France, with the exceptions of

▲ **Friedrich Karl von Savigny**
This influential German jurist opposed formal legislation, claiming instead that the law "is first developed by custom and popular faith...not by the arbitrary will of the lawgiver."

codification The process of collecting into one systematically organized body all the principles of a system of law.

▲ The Declaration of the Rights of Man and the Citizen (1789)
This manifesto of the French Revolution formed the basis of the major codification of the law that took place in France from the end of the 18th century onward. This process culminated in the promulgation of the Code civil *under Napoleon in 1804, which remains the basis of French law.*

Normandy and Brittany, the **Coutume de Paris** was widely applied to supplement local customs and to resolve conflicts between them. This helped to ensure both that the influence of Roman law was restricted to the pays de droit écrit and that customary laws would ultimately play an important role in the formulation of the French civil code.

During the 17th and 18th centuries, a number of Royal Ordinances (*Ordonnances*) were issued, dealing with such matters as criminal law and procedure, civil law, commercial law, and maritime law. These in turn influenced the form and content of the codes drawn up in the 19th century. A highly influential legal writer in the period prior to codification was Robert Joseph Pothier (1699–1772).

Following the French Revolution, which began in 1789, most of the legal structures and rules of the Ancien Régime were swept aside in favour of revolutionary egalitarian principles. However, all attempts to codify the law definitively in the 1790s foundered on the sheer complexity of the undertaking.

In 1799 Napoleon Bonaparte took power, initially as first consul of a three-member Consulate. In 1800 the Consulate appointed a commission to draft a civil code, which was produced in draft form within four months. Napoleon then delayed the procedure for enacting the code until 1803. The *Code civil des Français* was finally promulgated in 1804, renamed the *Code Napoléon* in 1807, and still remains in force.

The Spread of European Civil Law

Codified systems of civil law spread throughout the world by a number of routes. The Napoleonic Code spread first to other European countries, as a result of French imperialist expansion, and later to Africa and Asia with colonization by various countries. The civil law spread to Central and South America through Spanish and Portuguese expansion, and it has also been adopted by countries that were not subject to colonial rule.

The German Civil Code of 1900 was influential in central and southeastern Europe (e.g. the former Czechoslovakia and the former Yugoslavia), and especially in Greece. It also spread to Asia, being substantially adopted in the kingdom of Siam (modern Thailand) from the 1920s onwards, and in Japan.

A common feature of all civil-law systems is codification. However, it should be remembered that the principal features of the civil-law systems were developed before the movement for codification emerged. Furthermore, codification is not unique to these systems. Many countries subject to common law have codified large parts of their law. The essential difference between the civil-law and the common-law systems lies in the fact that the civil-law tradition recognizes codified law as the pre-eminent source of the law. In particular, the decisions of the courts on the interpretation of the law are not regarded as binding precedents in the way that they are in common-law systems.

The Common-Law Tradition

The common-law group includes those legal systems derived predominantly from English common law. In marked contrast to civil-law systems, the common law was hardly affected by Roman law or the codification movement.

England. The most significant event in the development of English common law was the victory of William of Normandy over the Saxons in 1066. William's consolidation of monarchical power gave rise to a centralized judicial system that gradually came to supersede the former system of local customs.

The scope of royal intervention in legal disputes – once restricted to constitutional affairs – was gradually extended as a result of growing interest by William and his immediate successors in land and the revenues it generated.

Kings also had an interest in serious criminal matters affecting the peace and security of the realm. By the end of the 13th century there had been established in London three permanent courts – the Court of Exchequer (dealing with matters of taxation), the Court of Common Pleas (covering a broad range of disputes between private individuals), and the Court of King's Bench (concerned with matters of special political importance). In addition, travelling judges were sent into the rest of the country to administer royal justice.

The effect of these developments was that the royal courts slowly supplanted the courts of local jurisdiction. More importantly, a body of law common to the entire kingdom developed. This came to be known as the 'common law.'

A significant feature in the development of English law was the separation of the common law from *equity*. By the end of the 14th century, the system of justice administered by the royal courts had become excessively formalistic. Dissatisfied litigants thus circumvented the courts by petitioning the king directly to order the other party in the dispute to agree to a just and equitable settlement, even if that result was not required by the strict rules of the common law. These petitions were dealt with by the king's chancellor, the head of the country's administrative system. In answering petitions, successive chancellors applied a body of principles that developed into a separate body of law known as 'equity,' administered latterly by separate courts called Chancery Courts. This parallel system of courts existed in England and Wales until the late 19th century. Now all judges are empowered to administer both law and equity.

The training of English lawyers has always been significantly different to that of their European counterparts. Whereas in other European countries lawyers received their training in the universities, where Roman law formed the bulk of their study, English lawyers were traditionally apprenticed to lawyers in practice before the courts. (This was a necessity, given the complexity of early English procedures, which could only be learned by daily experience of their operation.) For the aspiring lawyer who sought a training in Roman law, study at the great university centres of learning in Europe was often impossible because of the frequency with which England was involved in hostilities with its European neighbours. (This contrasts with the experience of Scottish lawyers, who, until the Union of Scotland with England in 1707, often trained abroad in the universities of the Low Countries and France.)

The English common law spread to many parts of the world through British colonization. Countries practising common law are: England and Wales (but not Scotland, whose legal system is derived in part from the civil-law tradition and in part from indigenous common-law principles); Australia; Canada (excluding the province of Quebec, whose law retains a substantial civil-law content); New Zealand; and other former British colonies, including the USA.

The USA. The USA adopted the common law on gaining independence in 1776. Despite great antagonism towards the former colonial power, the English system of law was felt by the founders of the new state (many of whom were practising lawyers) to be accessible and adaptable to new circumstances.

Due to its origins in individual colonial settlements, the USA was founded as a federation of states. Consequently, the most striking difference between its legal system and English law is that each of the 50 states of the union, and the federal government in Washington DC, has its own separate judicial system (as well as a separate legislature and executive). As most settlers had come from England, the common-law model was adopted by almost all states; the major exception is Louisiana, where the influence of French colonists produced a hybrid of civil-law and common-law systems.

Common law consolidated its position in the early decades of the USA's history through the influence of three seminal legal texts.

> Every law is a contract between the king and the people and therefore to be kept.
>
> **John Selden** (1584–1654), English historian

◄ **The King's Bench (England)**
This illustration from a 15th-century manuscript shows the court of the King's Bench. In the foreground, the accused await sentencing, while in the background, the judges preside over the proceedings. The King's Bench was of great significance in the development of the English common law, and was only abolished by the major reforms of the English legal system that were undertaken in the 1870s.

Judicial Review

Some countries allow the judiciary to review the validity of decisions made by *legislatures*, elected bodies that pass, amend, or repeal legislation. The US Supreme Court may declare Acts of Congress or laws passed by individual states to be unconstitutional. Most notable were its repeated challenges to President Roosevelt's radical 'New Deal' social legislation in the 1930s.

Commentaries on the Laws of England, by the English jurist Sir William Blackstone (1723–80) influenced both legal procedure and legal education. In the 1830s, two US jurists – James Kent and Joseph Story – wrote important commentaries on common law.

From a relatively early period, the US legal system has tended to rely less than English law on the practice of the courts in handing down precedents (*case law*). Rather, legal guidance has been sought from state and federal government legislation (*statute law*).

In matters of constitutional law, the USA recognizes the doctrine of **judicial review**. Although the country's written constitution does not expressly confer this power on any judicial body, from the beginning of the 19th century, the US Supreme Court (the country's highest court) asserted the right to pass judgment on the constitutionality of legislation.

Another distinctive feature of the US legal system, especially since the 1950s, has been its enactment of civil-rights legislation, most notably on questions of racial discrimination.

Islamic Law

Islamic law (or *sharia*; 'path') differs from civil- or common-law systems in claiming to derive its authority not from the state, but from divine inspiration. Islamic law is to be obeyed because it is the will of God. A number of important consequences flow from this. First, Islamic law cannot be changed by human practice, in contrast to laws that are based on human choice or practice. Human society must act in accordance with the law, rather than the law be adapted to meet the changing needs of society. Secondly, since Islamic law is ultimately derived from the word of God as revealed in the Koran, it is necessarily independent of all other legal systems. Any resemblance between the solutions adopted by Islamic law and non-Islamic systems must, according to Islamic law, be purely coincidental. Thirdly, since Islamic law is a reflection of the will of God, rather than of a human lawmaker, it affects the totality of the Muslim believer's life. Therefore, Islamic law touches on matters that would be considered outside the domain of the law in Western secular societies (e.g. the giving of alms to the poor).

The primary source of Islamic law is the Koran. Much of the Koran, being concerned with general codes of ethical behaviour, cannot be directly applied to individual cases. In this sense, it lacks the kind of precision necessary for legal rules. The Koran is therefore supplemented by reference to other sources.

The most important of these is the **Sunna**, ('rules of life') – the sayings and acts that tradition attributes to Mohammed and his first four successors. Collectively, these traditions are called **Hadith**; they are revered sources of religious and moral authority that were compiled during the 9th century. Although many modern Islamic scholars accept that much hadith is not based in historical fact but results from the conscious framing of the law by early writers, the Sunna remains a vital source of Islamic law, second only to the Koran.

The third source of Islamic law is the **ijma**, or unanimous consensus of the community (including lawyers) on matters relating to the duties of Muslims. The ijma offers legal solutions when they cannot be found in either the Koran or the Sunna. Islamic law adopted the principle that a proposition could be accepted as a rule of law if at any time the living legal scholars of the schools of Islamic law were all agreed upon it.

The final source is found in the *qiyas* – the application by analogy of rules recognized in the Koran or Sunna to new but similar cases.

As an integral part of Islamic religious belief, Islamic law has spread to many parts of the world. In many countries, however, traditional Islamic law functions alongside rules and principles adopted from other systems. Many states apply Islamic law in relation to such matters as the family, marriage, and succession, while applying Western-based concepts in such fields as commercial law, especially when this has an international dimension. In principle, however, when Western concepts have been adopted, they must be shown to be compatible with the ethical and legal foundations laid down by the Koran and the Sunna.

Shiite Muslims ▶

This manuscript illustration shows Ali (600–61), son-in-law of Mohammed, and his followers. The split that occurred in Islam after Ali's murder centred on who were regarded as authentic interpreters of the Sunna. *Shiites believe in the authority of five books of* Hadith *based on the teachings of Ali and the imams who succeeded him. Sunni Muslims, however, hold to interpretations offered by lawgivers – notably al Bukhari (810–70) – and collected in six books of* Hadith *known as the* Sihah Satta.

Criminal Law

The range of offences • Classification of crimes • General principles of criminal law •
General defences to crime

Criminal law is a branch of **public law**. More specifically, it is the branch of the law that determines whether, and under what conditions, a person should be punished by the state for what he or she has done – or, in some cases, for what he or she has failed to do. It is distinct from those rules of law that regulate relations between individuals – broadly described as **private law** – and also from those rules. such as administrative law or constitutional law, that govern other aspects of the individual's relation with the state or other public bodies.

This definition concentrates on the legal consequences of a person's conduct, rather than the conduct itself. The main reason for this is that since certain acts may be both a crime and a civil wrong, the crime cannot be distinguished from the civil wrong except by reference to the consequences. Thus, if one person assaults another, or deliberately damages another's property, most systems will see the victim as entitled, as a matter of private law, to compensation from the wrongdoer. Yet such an attack is generally regarded not merely as a private matter between the parties involved, but also as a crime in which society at large has an interest. It may be contrary to the interests of society to allow certain forms of wrongdoing to go unpunished, either because they are serious in themselves or because they may lead to greater harm. Consequently, the state may punish an act as a crime whether or not the victim is willing, or able, to seek any redress in private law from the wrongdoer.

In many cases the victim is not a private individual. If someone steals or damages property belonging to a local government body, such as a city council, that body is clearly a victim. In other instances, the offence may affect the public interest. For example, a person deliberately giving false testimony during legal proceedings is committing a criminal act, since attempts to pervert a fair system of justice affect the community as a whole.

There are cases, however, in which it is difficult to identify a victim. For example,

although it is a crime to be in possession of certain types of drugs, no individual is identifiable as the victim. (It is straining the concept of victimization to claim that the willing drug user is a victim.) Similar arguments can be made regarding the criminalization of obscene literature. If this is supplied only to adults willing to purchase such material, the question of whether or not there is a victim is not easily answered. Again, in such cases, it is common to resort to arguments based on protection of the public interest or protection of the moral standards of the community.

===SEE ALSO===
This section:
• Legal Systems and their Origins
• International Law
Social Sciences:
• Origins of Sociology
• Populations and Families

Police Arresting a Crime Suspect *US police officers take a man into custody. Throughout the world, the police enforce the law and investigate crime. Once a suspected felon has been detained, evidence is forwarded to the prosecuting authorities, which decide whether a case should be brought to trial.*

▲ **Alfred Dreyfus** *(1859–1935) In a celebrated case of treason, the French army officer Alfred Dreyfus (centre) was accused, in 1894, of selling military secrets to Germany. Dreyfus was found guilty and sentenced to life imprisonment. However, evidence emerged that the course of justice had been corrupted by anti-Semitic elements to secure a conviction against Dreyfus, a Jew. After 12 years, Dreyfus was cleared and reinstated with honours.*

In most systems, a strong link exists between a society's moral values and the content of the criminal law. It has often been argued that serious transgressions of the moral standards of a society should be regarded as criminal acts. Others maintain that the criminal law should be restricted to punishing conduct that positively harms another, or presents a serious threat to the orderly functioning of society.

The Range of Offences
In practice, legal systems throughout the world have found it expedient to protect a wide range of interests through the criminal law, typically these include the following.

Crimes against the State. The most serious of these offences is the crime of treason, which involves a deliberate attempt to overthrow the legitimate order or to assist an enemy state. Offences of espionage are also directed towards protecting the state as a whole, by punishing those who reveal state or official secrets to a foreign government or its agents (whether or not that state or government is

public law The area of the law that deals with the structure and functions of central and local government, and with the relationship between individuals and the state. In addition to criminal law, public law encompasses tax law, administrative law, and constitional law.

hostile). It may also, in some communities, take the form of slandering or defaming the state, or important institutions of the state, such as the head of state or the government.

Crimes against Individuals. The deliberate taking of human life is the most serious form of crime in this category, which also includes other forms of homicide and injuries that do not result in death. Offences, such as rape, that are directed towards protecting the sexual integrity of the victim are an important subcategory. An issue of special concern in many systems is the protection of children from physical and sexual abuse.

In some systems, the criminal law also protects the victim's reputation, so that certain forms of defamation, especially where the imputation is one of dishonesty or immorality, may be punished by the state. In other systems, however, such accusations may be regarded as a private dispute between the parties. Invoking the criminal law against defamation may violate constitutionally guaranteed liberties.

Crimes against Property. These offences may involve stealing, destroying, or damaging property; or fraudulently inducing the victim to part with property. Those who knowingly receive stolen goods may be punished as severely as the thief. Since many property offences were developed at a time when the only legally recognized form of property was corporeal property (i.e. items with a physical form, such as money, buildings, or animals), the law has had to be adapted to cover forms of property that have no physical existence although they can have great commercial value, such as copyright or commercially valuable information. Is it, for example, theft to misappropriate to one's own use confidential information belonging to another? Is a person who wilfully corrupts or amends information held in electronic form guilty of criminal damage? Questions of this kind have prompted many legal systems to enact new property laws.

In some instances – e.g. robbery – it is not easy to decide whether an offence is directed towards protection of the person or protection of property. Many systems regard breaking into homes as a particularly serious offence, entitling the occupier to use considerable force to resist or apprehend the offender, whether the purpose of the entry is to steal or to harm persons in the building.

Public Order Offences. Such crimes as riot, unlawful assembly, and breach of public peace not only endanger life and property, but may also threaten the stability of the community. Yet attempts to limit such disturbances may compromise the legitimate rights of public assembly and protest, which are regarded as essential freedoms in many societies.

Crimes against the System of Justice.
Such crimes are often regarded as particularly grave, since they can interfere with the fair and effective administration of the law. The more serious offences include perjury (giving false testimony in legal proceedings), attempting to pervert the course of justice (e.g. by intimidating or bribing witnesses or members of the court or by bringing false accusations of crime), and escaping from justice (including breaking out of prison and assisting offenders to escape or to evade arrest). Less serious offences in this category include obstructing police officers in the execution of their duty or wasting the time of the police.

In some legal systems the court has the power to punish individuals for contempt of court. This may take the form of showing disrespect for the court or of disrupting the proper functioning of the court. In some systems, refusal by a witness to testify, or prevarication by a witness, may be punished as contempt.

Crimes against Religion and Morality.
Offences against religion are, naturally, most frequently encountered in legal systems based on the teachings of a particular religious tradition. The clearest example of this is the crime of blasphemy. This crime varies according to local religious tenets; in its most extreme form it may consist simply in denying the beliefs of the religion and especially in denying the divinity of its god. Islamic law recognizes the offence of apostasy – the rejection of the Islamic faith by a Muslim. Even in secular systems, laws against blasphemy may exist as measures intended to protect public order, recognizing that attacks on religion may themselves be disorderly or that they may be likely to provoke a violent reaction from believers.

Many secular laws originate in religious teachings; in modern Western systems, laws against incest (sexual relations between persons who are regarded as too closely related to each other to marry) and sodomy (sexual relations between persons of the same sex or 'unnatural' sexual relations between men and women) both have, at least historically, a biblical origin. The prohibition of suicide in some systems also has a religious foundation.

In some legal systems, such as that in the USA, constitutional guarantees of religious freedom and diversity may prohibit the punishment by the state of blasphemy. To punish individuals for offending or attacking any religion would be to give a specially protected status to that religion, which is forbidden by the First Amendment to the Constitution.

Crimes against International Law.
Certain crimes are now regarded as so significant to the world community that they are looked upon as crimes against international

law. These include crimes against peace, war crimes, and crimes against humanity, including genocide and certain 'grave breaches' of the Geneva Conventions of 1949.

Classification of Crimes
Crimes vary in their gravity – homicide is universally regarded as more serious than stealing an apple from a fruit stall. This variation is often the basis for classifying crimes into different categories, according to their seriousness. The classification may determine the range of punishments that can be imposed, determine the form of trial of the offender, or influence other aspects of criminal procedure. Offences in a lower category may be tried less formally and attract a lower range of penalties than more serious offences. For example, Article 111-1 of the French penal code (Nouveau Code Pénal, 1994) provides that criminal offences are classified, according to their seriousness, as *crimes*, *délits*, and *contraventions*; crimes, as the most serious category, can only be tried before a bench of three judges and a jury in the *cour d'assises* (assize court).

Similarly, in English law, offences are classified according to the type of trial that can be adopted to try each offence. Some minor offences, known as ***summary offences***, may only be tried in the lowest level of the court system, before a bench of magistrates (who are not usually legally qualified). At the other end of the scale of seriousness are offences, called ***indictable offences***, which may only be tried in the Crown Court, before a judge and a

> ### Capital Punishment
> Capital punishment –the death penalty – is still retained by a majority of jurisdictions. Most of the countries that have abolished capital punishment are in Europe and Latin America.
> The People's Republic of China retains the death penalty for a wide range of offences, including rape and robbery with violence.
> In the USA, the death penalty depends on state law. About two-thirds of states have chosen to make provision for the legal execution of murderers.

◄ **Protests at *The Satanic Verses***
(1988) Muslim demonstrators in Beirut in the Lebanon display an effigy of Salman Rushdie, whose book The Satanic Verses *was held to be blasphemous against Islam, for the way it portrays a character intended to be the prophet Mohammed.*

213

▲ **An Electric Chair** *This instrument of judicial execution is in a US prison. The death penalty is still in force in some states of the USA and in other countries around the world (e.g. China, Saudi Arabia), and is mainly reserved for the crime of murder.*

The Elements of Guilt

A criminal offence consists of two distinct elements – the state of mind that lies behind the criminal act, or *mens rea* (Latin: 'a guilty mind'), and the act itself, which is referred to as *actus reus* ('a guilty act').
In order to secure a conviction, the prosecution must be able to establish that the two coincided at the time the alleged criminal offence was committed.

---

jury of twelve members of the public. This category of offences includes murder and rape.

In the USA, a distinction is drawn between *felonies* and *misdemeanours*, a classification derived from English common law. According to the Model Penal Code, a felony is any crime so designated by the Code, or for which a person may be sentenced to death, or sentenced to imprisonment for a period in excess of one year. Misdemeanours are offences described as such by the Code or any subsequent legislation. The distinction between a felony and a misdemeanour may affect such procedural matters as arrest. In general, a police officer may arrest without a warrant in the case of a felony, if he has reasonable grounds for suspecting that a felony has been committed. In the case of a misdemeanour, however, an officer may only arrest without a warrant if the misdemeanour is committed in his presence. The distinction may also be important for other areas of the law. So, for example, in many states in the USA, even a nonintentional killing committed in the course of a felony is murder, while a similar killing, committed in the course of a misdemeanour, would amount only to manslaughter. However, the distinction between a felony and a misdemeanour has no effect, in general, on the mode of trial in the USA, since the Constitution guarantees the right to a trial by jury; see JUDICIAL PROCESSES AND ADMINISTRATION.

General Principles of Criminal Law

Although the definition of particular crimes, such as murder or theft, is determined by the law of particular states, some principles that govern the liability for a crime are more or less universally recognized. The most important of these principles are as follows:

The Principle of Legality. The principle of legality, sometimes expressed in the Latin maxims *nullum crimen sine lege; nulla poena sine lege* ('no crime without law; no penalty without law'), contains three elements. The first of these is that a person cannot be held guilty of a criminal offence on account of conduct that did not constitute an offence at the time it was committed. This principle, found in many national constitutions, is today regarded as a basic human right and is enshrined in Article 11(2) of the Universal Declaration of Human Rights, the International Covenant on Civil and Political Rights (Article 15), and all of the major regional human rights conventions.

Criminal Conduct and Criminal Intent. Criminal offences generally comprise two elements: the **conduct** that is prohibited and the **criminal intent** necessary for the crime in question. Both of these elements must be proved before an individual can be found guilty of the crime. Thus, if a legal system defines murder as the intentional killing of another human being, before a person can be found guilty of murder it must be proved that he or she killed another human being, and that he or she intended to do so. According to this definition, if the accused were to strike the victim, intending to injure but not to kill him or her, this would not be murder, even if death were to result from that injury. By the same token, even if the accused has intended to commit murder, but has failed to do so, he or she will not be guilty of the offence. However, the accused may be guilty of attempting to commit the offence, depending on how far he or she went towards committing the offence. If the accused only thought about committing it, then no offence has been committed. If, however, the accused actually carries out an attack on the victim, which proves unsuccessful, this may be a case of attempted murder.

Acts and Omissions. While most criminal offences are defined in terms of the accused committing an act, some crimes may be committed in which the accused has failed to act; this is a crime by omission.

The offence may consist simply in failing to do something that the law requires a person to do, such as making an income tax return. Moreover, some legal systems impose a general duty on members of the public to aid, or to seek assistance for, persons in danger, if this can be done without risk to one's own safety. Other systems reject such a general duty, except in particular cases and then only when failure to act results in harm to the victim.

In other cases, the crime consists not in a simple failure to act but in a failure to act in circumstances that cause a result prohibited by the criminal law to occur. If, for example, a parent neglects to provide food and medical care for a child, and that child dies as a result, the parent may be held criminally responsible for the child's death.

The Requirement of Voluntary Conduct. Criminal liability is based on the understanding that the conduct in question – whether it is an act or an omission – is voluntary. This difficult concept is best explained by giving examples of involuntary conduct. Involuntary conduct can be defined as conduct (including the results of conduct) over which the accused had no control at the time. For example, if the accused is charged with colliding with another vehicle while driving a car, it would be a defence to show that the steering mechanism in the car had suddenly failed causing loss of control of the vehicle. Similar arguments have been used to defend those who apparently committed offences but who were unconscious or sleepwalking at the time.

General Defences to Crime

A number of general defences to crime can be identified, although not all systems recognize all these defences. Moreover, the limits of any defence are defined by the rules of the particular system.

Mental Abnormality. This is widely recognized as a defence to a criminal charge. If persons are suffering from such severe mental disorder, whether this is through mental illness, injury, or inherent defect, that they cannot control their conduct, or do not appreciate what it is that they have done, it is generally regarded as inappropriate to hold them criminally responsible. This does not always mean that such a person who commits what would otherwise be a crime will be allowed to remain at liberty. Persons with a mental abnormality who present a risk to others or to themselves may be subject to compulsory detention.

The difficulty in determining what criteria should be used in judging a person's sanity is illustrated by attempts at legal reform undertaken in the USA. Since existing legal definitions of insanity as a defence against a criminal charge did not reflect modern medical views on mental illness, a new test of insanity was devised there in the 1970s. This took account not only of the defendant's appreciation of the wrongfulness of the act, but also of whether they could control themselves. However, following the case of John Hinckley – who tried to kill US President Ronald Reagan in 1981, but was acquitted on the grounds that he acted involuntarily – US federal law dropped the test's volitional element.

Duress and Necessity. If a person is compelled, by force of circumstances or by the

◄ **Burglary** *In this reconstruction of a burglary, a criminal is shown attempting to force entry into a house. Throughout the world, such crimes against property are more common than crimes against the person.*

unlawful threats of a third party, to commit a crime, this may be a defence. There is considerable reluctance to recognize such pleas as general defences to crime, and they may be subjected to strict conditions, or excluded altogether as defences in certain categories of crime. Duress, for example, may be limited to threats of death or serious bodily harm to the accused or to a family member, and will normally be excluded if the accused could reasonably have been expected to take steps to avoid the threat (e.g. by alerting the authorities and seeking their protection). Both necessity and duress are often subject to the rule that they are only available as a defence if the harm resulting from the accused's act is less than the harm that would have resulted had the threat been carried out. For example, it may be a defence to a charge of robbery that the accused was threatened with death if he or she did not commit the act, but it would not be a defence to a murder charge.

NECESSITY AS A DEFENCE

The case of *United States* v. *Holmes* that was brought to trial in the mid-19th century established necessity as a permissible defence to a criminal charge in the US legal system.

In 1842, the shipwreck in a storm of a US commercial vessel resulted in a number of surviving passengers and crew being cast adrift in a lifeboat. Because the boat was overcrowded and in danger of being swamped by the waves, some crew members decided to throw a number of passengers overboard, whereupon these passengers perished.

In the subsequent trial of one of the crew members, the court recognized that the dire circumstances in which the survivors of the shipwreck found themselves necessitated such drastic action as that taken. This acknowledgment set the precedent that necessity could constitute a defence to a charge of criminal homicide. However, because those who were sacrificed were not in this case chosen fairly (e.g. by all the survivors drawing lots), the court found the defendant guilty of manslaughter.

Punishment is not for revenge, but to lessen crime and reform the criminal.

Elizabeth Fry (1780–1845), British prison reformer

FORENSIC SCIENCES

The forensic sciences are concerned with discovering and interpreting scientific evidence that may be of significance in legal inquiries. Its commonest application by far is in criminal investigations, where ballistic analysis of weapons that may have been used in assaults can provide vital evidence.

Forensic medicine specializes in such matters as fingerprinting, investigating the cause of death, and in tracing sexual assailants by various methods, for example **genetic fingerprinting**, which identifies suspects through examination of DNA molecules; see BIOTECHNOLOGY (VOL. 3): GENETIC ENGINEERING. Forensic psychiatry studies alleged criminals' states of mind, especially with a view to establishing the presence of mental abnormality in a defendant.

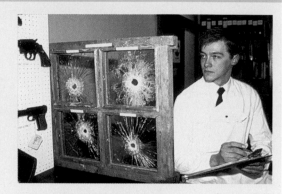

▲ **A Ballistics Expert** *Forensic investigation takes many forms. One of the most widely employed sciences is ballistics, which examines firearms and bullets in order to ascertain from where, or with what weapon, particular shots were fired. Here, a ballistics expert examines the effects of bullets on glass.*

Memorials at the Berlin Wall
Many people died attempting to escape from East Germany across the Berlin Wall. In 1991, following the collapse of communism and the reunification of Germany, two former East German border guards were tried for killing an escapee. Defence on the grounds that they were obeying superior orders was rejected and they were convicted of manslaughter. ▼

Infancy. Children and young persons are often subject to special rules in relation to the criminal law. Not only may they be dealt with by special courts or tribunals, but the penalties that may be imposed on them are likely to differ significantly from those for adult offenders. In particular, deprivation of liberty is generally regarded as a punishment of last resort; where it is imposed on a child it is now considered inappropriate for children to be imprisoned with adults; see **THE RIGHTS OF CHILDREN**.

Below a certain age, which varies according to the legal system, a child may be held to be incapable of committing a crime. This means that, even if the child has done something that would be a crime if committed by an adult, he or she cannot be held legally responsible for it.

Self-defence and the Prevention of Crime. People may use reasonable force to protect themselves from an attack by another, and it would therefore be a defence to a charge of injuring (or even killing) another person that the injuries were inflicted in self-defence. Self-defence in such cases may be extended to include defence of a third party, and, in some legal systems, a person may use reasonable force to prevent any crime, not only crimes of violence against the person. How much force is 'reasonable' may depend upon the particular circumstances of the case, such as the nature of the attack and whether it could be avoided. Some systems do not require that a person should attempt to flee if they are attacked in their own home, so that it would not be an offence if he or she stood their ground and inflicted injuries on the intruder.

Superior Orders. In certain circumstances it may be a defence for a person to maintain that he or she was ordered to commit the acts that constituted the crime. This is not a defence likely to be upheld beyond the case of military personnel acting on the orders of a superior, and even then the defence is only accepted reluctantly. The general rule is that the defence is not available if the order was clearly unlawful.

Where the crime in question is regarded as a war crime or a related offence, obedience to superior orders is categorically ruled out as a permissible defence (e.g. in the trials of war criminals after World War II; see INTERNATIONAL LAW). This principle has been followed in drawing up the principles of law to be applied by the United Nations War Crimes Tribunals in considering cases arising out of the conflicts in the former Yugoslavia and Rwanda.

Civil Law

The law of tort • Property law • Intellectual property • Family law • The law of contract • Employment law • Bankruptcy

Civil law, or **private law**, is the branch of the law that is predominantly concerned with relations between private individuals. In this context, these include **juristic persons** as well as natural persons.

In many legal systems the rules of law that apply between private individuals are not the same as those that apply between a private individual and a state entity (e.g. a government department or a local authority). For example, if a person is injured in a road accident, different principles of law will apply depending upon whether the injuries were inflicted by a vehicle driven by another private party or a refuse truck belonging to a local authority driven by one of its employees. This difference is stressed particularly by civil-law systems, in which issues of this kind may be dealt with by entirely separate administrative courts.

Likewise, the rules of law applicable to transactions between private individuals may differ from those that apply to transactions between private individuals and persons engaged in commerce. Thus, many systems accord special protection to consumers of goods and services when transacting with those who supply them. Civil-law systems distinguish between ordinary contracts and commercial contracts; in France, for example, most commercial transactions are governed by the *Code de commerce* rather than the *Code civil*. Although common-law systems also extend special protection to consumers, in general they do not distinguish between various kinds of contract.

The Law of Tort

If a person deliberately or negligently causes injury to another person or their property, it is generally accepted that the injured person is entitled to compensation. This obligation to compensate is usually regarded as independent of any other liability the wrongdoer might incur, such as criminal responsibility (which may result in prosecution by the state). This area of the law is known in common-law systems as the **law of tort** (from French *tort*, meaning 'wrong'). In civil-law systems, it is referred to as **delictual liability** (from Latin *delictum*, meaning 'fault').

Application of this basic principle of compensation varies between systems; nevertheless, some general rules can be identified.

The Requirement of 'Fault.' This is a very basic requirement. The most obvious examples of fault would be the deliberate causing of harm, for example by assaulting a person or by deliberately damaging their property. In practice, however, most examples of fault turn on the question of negligence. Thus, Article 1383 of the French Civil Code states that a person is responsible for the loss they cause not only through their intentional wrongdoing, but also through their negligence or carelessness. This principle has been established in French law since the code was promulgated, in 1804. In English law, however, the general principle of liability for harm caused negligently was only accepted in the 1930s.

Causation. Another basic principle of liability is that the wrongdoer 'caused' the harm. Lawyers often refer to the 'chain of causation' between the alleged wrongful act and the harm suffered by the 'victim' and insist that this chain must be unbroken, if liability is to be established. If, for example, A drives his car in such a careless manner as to knock B down and kill him, it is clear that A's driving is the cause of B's death. But if A merely injures B, and B suffers further catastrophic injuries due to the negligence of the doctors treating him, with the result that he dies, A could argue that B's death is due not to his bad driving, but to the incompetence of the doctors.

===SEE ALSO===

This section:
- Legal Systems and their Origins
- International Law

Business and Finance:
- Company Structure and Finance
- International Finance and Investment

Communications and Media:
- Print Media

juristic person An entity (e.g. a corporation) that is deemed to have a legal personality, i.e. it can enjoy, and be subject to, legal rights and duties. It is contrasted with a human being, who is referred to in law as a 'natural person.'

A Road Accident *In such cases of injury to people or property, establishing liability – through the principle of causation – is a prime legal concern.* ▶

CANON LAW

Canon law – the law concerning the organization and discipline of the Christian Church – arose from decrees issued by the councils of the early Church. It became the universal law of the Western Roman Catholic Church from the 12th century onwards, governing such matters as regulation of the clergy, administration of ecclesiastical courts, and questions of liturgy and doctrine.

Canon law played an important role in the spread of Roman law throughout western Europe in the Middle Ages. Moreover, popes were sometimes called upon to adjudicate in international disputes during this period; consequently, canon law became a major source of international law. In later centuries, canon-law legislation on such matters as marriage, property, and succession, was highly influential in the development of secular civil law, especially in countries with Roman Catholicism as the state religion.

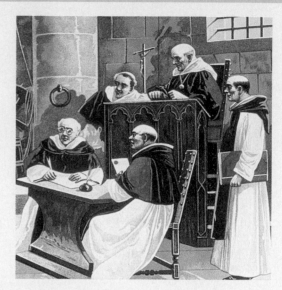

▲ **A Church Court** *Members of a 16th-century French ecclesiastical court hear a deposition.*

Contributory Fault

Where an alleged victim of negligence has contributed to his or her own injury, this may result in a lower award of compensation than would otherwise have been the case. If a motorist fails to comply with a legal requirement to wear a seat belt while driving and is more severely injured as a result, the damages received may be reduced. Some systems even refuse compensation on the ground that the victim accepted all the risks involved in a particular course of action (e.g. accepting a lift in a car driven by an obviously drunk person).

Loss or Damage. Loss or damage need not be significant in financial terms; in some legal systems, defamatory statements (i.e. untrue statements attacking a person's character) may call for compensation even though they have not caused the victim financial loss.

While the general principle governing the award of damages in this area is that the victim should receive fair compensation, rather than that the wrongdoer should be punished, awards of 'punitive' damages are not uncommon in some systems (e.g. in the USA). Such damages are frequently granted where the wrongdoer has been shown to have calculated that it is less costly to pay damages than to take steps to avoid the harm in the first place.

Strict Liability. It is generally thought unfair to impose liability on a person for causing harm when that person was not at fault in doing so. Where this is done, it is known as imposing ***strict liability***; article 1384 of the French civil code holds a person responsible not only for damage caused by their own act, but also for the damage caused by things in their care (*"responsabilité du fait des choses"*). Imposing liability without fault is regarded by some jurists as counterproductive. A main purpose in imposing liability for harm caused is to encourage persons engaged in activities that present risks to others to minimize those risks by taking reasonable care to avoid harm; liability without fault acts as a disincentive.

An alternative view is that to insist that the injured party proves that someone was at fault before he or she can be compensated is unfair on the injured party. He or she may not be able to prove that anyone was at fault, but that does not in any sense lessen the damage suffered.

One solution to this problem, adopted in some systems (e.g. New Zealand) is the principle of 'no fault' liability. According to this approach, a person who suffers injury in an accident need not establish whose fault caused the injuries. Instead, as a measure of social-welfare law, the state compensates the victim. The level of compensation is normally lower than damages, but at the same time the victim is sure of receiving the compensation and does not have to undergo the rigours of a court case. Moreover, since the system is not based on fault, compensation is not reduced even if the victim contributed to the accident.

Property Law

The law of property is concerned with the classification and acquisition of property, and with the transference of ownership from one person to another (during their lifetimes; transfer of property on death is governed by the ***law of succession***.) The law of property is also concerned with various questions of shared ownership of property.

Types of Property. Before anything can be described as 'property,' it must be something that is capable of being owned. So, for example, a living human being cannot be treated as property. Slavery, which involved the ownership of human beings as property, is universally outlawed.

Property may be categorized in several ways. One of the most obvious of these relates to the physical characteristics of the property. For instance, a distinction is made between **movable and immovable property** (or personal and real property in common-law systems). Another important distinction is between corporeal and incorporeal property. Corporeal property has a physical form, while incorporeal property has no physical existence (but does have a legal existence). An example of this would be a debt owed by A to B. As part of B's property, the debt is an item of incorporeal property.

The legal classification of property does not always correspond to its physical qualities. Thus, property that may be movable will in certain circumstances be treated as immovable; a door knocker is clearly an item of movable property, but, if fixed to the door of a building, is treated as part of the building, and hence as immovable property. This principle is common to most systems.

The transfer of certain types of immovable property – for example, land, houses, and other buildings – is accompanied by important formalities. In many systems this can only be done by means of a written contract or other document conveying the ownership of the property from the seller to the buyer. In some systems such contracts can only be drawn up by a legal official known as a *notary*, and frequently the contract and the property details must be registered in a central record of landholding.

Acquiring Ownership of Property. In a society in which commerce is widespread, the most common way of acquiring property is by buying it, or by exchanging one item of property for another. However, there are other widely recognized ways of acquiring the ownership of property. One of these is by taking possession of property that has not previously been owned, such as capturing a wild animal. Another way of acquiring property is to create it. Thus, a sculptor who makes a statue out of a block of stone becomes the owner of the statue (unless, of course, he was commissioned to create the statue).

One way in which it is generally accepted one cannot become the owner of property is by stealing it. Furthermore, it is a general principle that a person who has stolen property cannot pass ownership of that property to someone else, even if that person acquires it from the thief in good faith.

Sharing Property. Property need not be owned entirely by one person, nor need the owner be the only person who has any interest in the property. So, for example, in some systems a block of apartments may be jointly owned by all the persons who own one or more of the flats. While owning their own apartment absolutely, they may have a common share in the roof, the stairways, and

other elements of the building (and thus a shared obligation to ensure that these parts of the building are properly maintained). In some systems the ownership of property by married persons is made subject to a *matrimonial property regime*, in which property regarded as 'matrimonial' property is treated as if it belonged to both spouses, irrespective of who acquired it.

Persons may have an interest in property even though they are not its owner. For example, the owner of a building may rent it out to a tenant, who is entitled under the rental agreement to exclude the owner from their own building. Similarly, a person who owns and occupies land may be obliged to allow others to exercise rights over it. In England, a farmer may find that the general public have a right to cross his land on traditionally recognized paths known as 'rights of way.' Likewise, a householder may not be entitled to demolish a wall because a neighbouring house relies on it for support.

Intellectual Property
Intellectual property is not a form of tangible physical property, but a collective term for the rights that a person has over the product of his or her own intellectual efforts. The main forms of intellectual property are:

Copyright. Copyright is the right granted to the originator of certain types of literary or artistic work, under which he or she enjoys the sole and exclusive right to reproduce the work by copying it. Copyright was originally a domestic legal issue, but is increasingly subject to regulation by international agreement. It is accorded for only a limited period, and may relate to literary works, musical works (including both words and music), dramatic works, choreography, sculptures, paintings

---

Movable or Immovable Property

In some systems, movable property is regarded as immovable even though it is not incorporated in the immovable property. Article 524 of the French civil code treats certain items of movable property as immovable if the owner provided them for the benefit and use of the immovable property. These items include pigeons in dovecotes, rabbits in rabbit warrens, and beehives.

An Author at a Book Signing
The Chilean writer Isabel Allende is shown signing copies of one of her works. In order to protect the intellectual property of authors and artists, international accords have ensured that copyright granted in one state is respected worldwide. ▼

Destroying Counterfeit Goods ▶
A road roller destroys fake watches. Around the world, patent or copyright laws are broken by the sale of counterfeit goods bearing the trademarks of famous manufacturers. An alarming modern development has been the trade in potentially lethal counterfeit spare parts for passenger aircraft.

Trademarks

A trademark is a distinctive symbol that identifies the products of a manufacturer. The symbol may consist of a logo, or name, or both and is protected by intellectual property laws. Registration of a trademark entitles the manufacturer to its exclusive use.

---

and other graphic works, motion pictures, sound recordings, and computer programs. Copyright protects the right of reproduction but is not intended to restrict access to such matters as the ideas that may have inspired a work. Indeed, it is possible to have copyright in publications whose production may not have required much intellectual effort (e.g. a telephone directory). As with other forms of property, copyright can be transferred to another person; in the case of successful literary or artistic works, this may carry a high price.

Patents. A patent is a right granted to the inventor of an object or process to exclude others from making, selling, or using his or her invention without a licence to do so. A patent is granted for a limited period, at the end of which the patentee agrees to make the invention freely available for general exploitation. A patent can only be granted to something new and original. It may also be necessary to demonstrate that the alleged invention is useful and nonobvious. Patents are often granted to new types of toy or items designed purely for entertainment. A subject of great contemporary controversy is the patenting of the products of genetic experimentation, particularly cross-species genetic engineering.

Family Law
Family law is concerned with relations within the family unit, including the formation and dissolution of marriage and the custody and upbringing of children. Moreover, with the steady decline of the institution of marriage in Western society, family law also covers the rights and duties of cohabiting couples.

Marriage. The right to marry and found a family is regarded as a fundamental human right. It is protected by most international human rights agreements, many of which also recognize that the family, as a central unit in society, deserves special protection and support from the state.

In Western societies, largely under the influence of Christian teaching, marriage is regarded as an arrangement between the parties that is both monogamous (i.e. the parties cannot, during the marriage, marry anyone else) and that is at least intended to be permanent. In some non-Western societies, especially those governed by Islamic law, a man may have more than one wife, although this is often subject to the requirement that he must be in a position to support all of his wives, and must not discriminate between them.

Marriage is based on the consent of the parties. This does not preclude arranged marriages, provided both parties have given their consent; indeed, arranged marriages are the norm in some communities.

Parents and Children. Family law is also concerned with the relationship between parents and their children. That relationship is generally based on the view that the parent is responsible (at least until the child has reached a certain age) for its care, and for taking various decisions on its behalf. These decisions may relate to the child's education, its religious upbringing (if any), or where the child lives. In some systems parental rights remain in force until the child reaches the age of majority, or acquires an existence independent of its parents (e.g. by leaving the family home). In other systems, the rights of the parents diminish as the child gets older, even though it still remains a minor. In line with the

---

DIVORCE

Marriage may be terminated in some systems by a legal process known as divorce. The grounds on which a marriage may be ended by divorce vary from system to system, but the following reasons are commonly encountered:
- *adultery* (i.e. one of the parties has engaged in sexual relations with another person);
- *desertion* (usually a prescribed minimum period of absence must have elapsed before this ground can be invoked);
- *cruel or unreasonable behaviour* (i.e. behaviour that has caused an irretrievable breakdown of the marriage).

Since marriage is based on consent, it might be expected that the parties might simply agree to bring their marriage to an end. However, marriage often involves the rights and interests of others (principally, any children the couple may have); hence there has been a reluctance in many systems to recognize divorce by mutual consent. Even in some systems that do recognize such an agreement, some important restrictions are imposed, such as that the parties have ceased to live together for a specified time, or that they undergo counselling to ascertain whether their marriage can be saved.

increased recognition of the rights of children, in many systems the power of parents over children is becoming less absolute.

Cohabitation. In Western societies individuals may choose to live together and have children outside marriage. If they do so, they are free to regulate their relationship by agreement, and are not in general subject to rules of the kind that regulate marriage. There are no formalities required either for entering into such a relationship or for leaving it. In many Western states where cohabitation is common, cohabiting couples are treated, with regard to certain points of law, as equivalent to married couples. Thus, a cohabiting woman may seek the same legal protection against physical violence by her partner as a wife.

The Law of Contract
The Requirement of Agreement. Contracts are legally binding agreements entered into voluntarily by two or more parties and with the intention on both sides to be bound by the agreement. Ordinarily, the rights and obligations of the contract only apply to these parties, so that a third party cannot be bound by the terms of a contract or obtain any benefit from it. This is known, in common-law systems, as the *doctrine of privity of contract*. In some systems, however, it is possible for a third party to obtain the benefit of a contract to which he or she is not a party, if it is shown that the parties to the contract intended the third party to receive this benefit.

Contracts are commonly formed by a process of offer by one party and acceptance by the other. The essential feature of a contract is agreement; if an offer is made, and it is met not by acceptance, but by qualified acceptance or by a counteroffer, there is no contract. Sometimes contracts are invalidated by the fact that one party entered into the agreement while under a misapprehension. The precise effect of such a mistake depends upon the legal system. In some systems the contract is unaffected, while others distinguish between misapprehension and misrepresentation. In the former case the mistake is ignored, while in the latter the party who has been misled has the right to withdraw from the contract.

Freedom of Contract. According to this principle, the parties to a contract are free to enter into an agreement on whatever terms they choose, subject only to a limited number of constraints (e.g. the rule that a contract entered into for an illegal purpose will not be enforced). This was the basis of 19th-century laissez-faire commercial contracts. However, in the 20th century there has been an increasing tendency to limit this principle, in recognition of the fact that in certain situations there is a considerable inequality of bargaining power between the parties. This is particularly prevalent in the area of legislation known as **consumer protection**.

Contracts Contrary to Public Policy. Most legal systems regard as invalid a contract entered into for a purpose that is illegal, immoral, or contrary to public policy. For example, if A contracts with B to carry out a murder for him, this would be a contract for an illegal purpose and could therefore not be enforced.

Capacity to Enter into Contracts. A person can only effectively enter into a contract if he or she has the legal capacity to do so. Thus, children and young persons may be regarded as not competent to enter into contracts, as may persons who are mentally deficient. The purpose of this rule is to ensure that an unfair advantage is not taken of such persons.

Unilateral Promise. In some systems, a person may unilaterally undertake an obligation that can be enforced by others, and from which he or she cannot withdraw without their agreement. For example, a businessman's promise to make a donation to a school for orphans could be enforced by the school, even though they had not induced the promise or done anything in return. Since, however, there is a presumption in law against the making of gifts or gratuitous promises, a person relying on such a promise may need to prove that it was made.

> **Consumer Protection**
>
> Legislation exists in many countries to protect the consumer from unfair trading practices or unsafe products. Many rules restrict the right of a supplier to limit liability for defects in the goods or services provided; a term in a contract of sale may prevent a supplier from disclaiming liability for injury or death arising from defective goods. Consumers are also protected from unscrupulous sales methods.

A Child 'Divorces' his Parent *In a family-law case in the USA in 1992, 12-year-old Gregory Kingsley was granted leave to sue his biological mother for neglect and seek adoption by his foster parents (with whom he had lived for most of his life). This set an important precedent, in denying the parental rights of a natural mother over a minor. While some saw the case as strengthening childrens' rights, others deplored its overturning of natural 'family values.'*

Breach of Contract. Where a party to a contract fails to perform his part of the bargain without a legally acceptable excuse, he or she is said to be in breach of contract. The remedies available to the other party in such a case vary from system to system. In civil-law systems, the main redress for breach of contract is an order for the party in breach to carry out his part of the bargain. By contrast, in common-law systems, the typical remedy is monetary compensation (***damages***). In practice, however, the two systems converge. Civil-law systems have found that it is often counterproductive to order a person to perform a contract, since their reluctance will probably lead them to perform it unsatisfactorily. On the other hand, courts in common-law jurisdictions have shown a growing tendency to order that contracts be performed, in preference to awarding damages. However, certain contracts do not lend themselves to this approach. Thus it is not normally possible to obtain an order for a person to perform an employment contract. Such an order would effectively force a person to work for another, which – as a form of enforced servitude – is widely regarded as unacceptable.

Frustration of Contract. A person is only in breach of contract if he or she has failed to perform their part of the bargain without good cause. In some circumstances, however, the person allegedly in breach may be able to show that they are unable to meet their contractual obligations for reasons beyond their control. Thus, if A agrees to deliver 10 000 tonnes of steel to B by ship, and A's country declares war on that of B before the consignment can be delivered, the ship will return to its home port and the contract is said to have been frustrated. In such a case, A is not liable to pay damages to B.

Coal Miners at Work *Miners at the Donetsk coalfield in the Ukraine report for work. In many countries in the course of the 20th century, legislation has been enacted limiting the hours a person may be required to work and regulating health and safety standards in the workplace.* ▼

Employment Law

The contract of employment is one of the most important forms of contract, since it is the means by which most people are able to support themselves and their families. The contract of employment typically states the rights and duties of both parties, including the hours of work and the rate of payment. Whereas such conditions were once agreed between the employer and the employee, in the 20th century the contract of employment has been subjected to governmental regulation regarding such matters as hours of work, health and safety in the workplace, and the rights of the worker to sick pay or to compensation for redundancy. Another overriding principle imposed on the contract of work in Western legal systems is that of nondiscrimination by the employer. Thus, it is unlawful for an employer, when recruiting or dismissing staff, to discriminate between them on the grounds of race or gender. A mainstay of employment law, which is central to the law of the European Union, is that men and women are entitled to equal pay for work of equal value.

Bankruptcy

When a person engages in commercial activities, there is always the risk that they may fail (see BUSINESS AND FINANCE: COMPANY STRUCTURE AND FINANCE). In extreme cases the debts of the failed business may far outweigh its assets, and the firm's creditors may not all be able to recover the money they are owed. In many Western systems, it was once common practice to imprison debtors. This was impractical, since an imprisoned debtor was in no position to repay debts. Consequently, an alternative solution – bankruptcy – was adopted. In this process, once the debtor has been declared bankrupt, he or she is prevented from managing their own affairs. Another person is appointed to administer the debtor's affairs and to gather in all of their assets. These are then distributed among the creditors as evenly as possible. Certain creditors are, however, entitled to preferential treatment. For example, the unpaid wages of employees may take precedence over other debts, as may the fees of professional advisers. Bankruptcy lasts until the person administering the bankrupt's affairs – or in some cases the court – determines that the bankrupt may resume control. Once bankruptcy is terminated, the bankrupt is discharged and is free of all of the debts accrued prior to the declaration of bankruptcy. Since bankruptcy can be seen as a way of avoiding the obligation to pay off one's debts, it is important that the procedure is not abused. Thus, criminal sanctions may be applied if the debtor has concealed or deliberately disposed of assets in order to defraud creditors.

Judicial Processes and Administration

Court structures • Inquisitorial and adversarial procedures • The judiciary •
Lay participation in the judicial process • Legal professions in civil-law systems •
Legal professions in common-law systems • Legal ethics • Jurisdiction

In most modern legal systems the primary source of law is **legislation**; this takes two forms in many states, especially those whose legal system is based on the civil-law tradition. On the one hand, there are broadly based codes covering such areas as civil law and procedure, criminal law and procedure, commercial law, and administrative law. On the other hand, there are less general pieces of legislation that deal with particular topics or issues. In principle, codes in these systems are intended to be authoritative statements of the general principles of the law. In practice, however, they are subject to a degree of interpretation by the courts when they are applied. In the civil-law systems, judicial decisions do not create rules of law that are intended to be applied to any case other than the one in which the decision was handed down. Nor do the decisions of one judge on the interpretation of the law require other judges to follow that interpretation.

By contrast, in all common-law systems the law is developed on a case-by-case basis by the courts, either developing principles that derive purely from earlier judicial decisions, or interpreting legislation. In such systems, the decisions of the higher courts on questions of law can generate rules of law that are of general application, and are not limited to the case in which the decision is handed down. Where court judgments create rules of law they are known as **judicial precedents**.

Nevertheless, the difference between the two traditions is not as marked as this overview might suggest. First, there are areas of law in many civil-law systems that are effectively made by judges. For example, the original provisions of the French civil code covering the law of tort are a mixture of very specific provisions and a few general principles; see CIVIL LAW. Yet the code was silent on many matters regarding civil liability for causing harm. Consequently, the French courts have developed an extensive body of case law (*la jurisprudence*), upon which the bulk of the French law of tort is based.

Second, although many common-law systems operate a fairly strict doctrine of precedent, courts in such jurisdictions have recently shown themselves to be far more flexible on the question of precedents, overruling decisions made in earlier cases when they are considered inappropriate to modern conditions.

===SEE ALSO===
This section:
• Legal Systems and
  their Origins
• International Law
Politics and Government:
• Introduction
• How Countries
  are Governed

A Symbol of Justice *Situated on the dome of the Central Criminal Court in London, England, this statue symbolizes the process of criminal justice. In one hand, the figure holds a set of scales, indicating the weighing up of arguments in deciding a defendant's innocence or guilt. In the other, she holds a sword, which stands for punishment in the event of a guilty verdict.* ▶

Key Terms

legislation All or part of the written law of a country. A country's elected assembly, with the power to make law, is called a *legislature*.

judicial precedents Decisions handed down by courts of law and used as a basis for reaching the same decisions in cases thereafter. Judicial precedents are the authoritative source of law in common-law systems.

Court Structures

In many modern legal systems, the courts are arranged according to the types of business that are brought before them. There is often a broad division of functions between, on the one hand, the criminal courts, and on the other, civil courts. This is especially true at the lower level of the legal system.

However, it is equally common to find systems in which the courts have a general range of powers and deal with both civil and criminal matters. This is the case in the **courts of first instance** in civil-law systems. In such systems the significant distinction is not between civil and criminal courts, but between courts of ordinary or general jurisdiction, and courts of special jurisdiction. The general courts deal with a wide range of matters, such as questions of contract or tort or succession, while other areas are covered by more specialized courts.

In Germany, for example, in addition to the courts of general jurisdiction at both local and regional level, there are specialized courts dealing with such matters as administrative law (*Verwaltungsgerichte*), taxation (*Finanzgerichte*), labour relations (*Arbeitsgerichte*), and social-security matters (*Sozialgerichte*). The structure of these courts and the law they apply is quite different from the courts of general jurisdiction. Moreover, countries with a federal structure, such as Germany and the USA, allocate matters of federal law to special federal courts separate from the courts in the individual states.

First-instance and Appellate Courts. Most judicial systems operate on two levels – courts of first instance and appellate courts. The latter hear appeals against the decisions made by the former. Indeed, the right of a person convicted of a criminal offence to have his or her case reviewed by a higher court is now regarded as a fundamental human right, except in the case of minor offences.

First-instance courts are chiefly concerned with the factual basis of the dispute between the parties. The judge may have to determine some questions of law in deciding the case; however, such issues are rare in most trials.

The function of appeal courts differs from system to system. In civil-law systems, an appeal takes the form of a re-examination of all the evidence before a higher court. This is rarely the case in common-law systems, in which an appeal is in the form of a review of the case by a higher court, to ensure either that the law was properly applied and interpreted by the lower court, or that there was adequate evidence for the lower court to reach its decision. The power of the appeal court to interfere with decisions taken on the facts by the lower court is extremely limited, and in some systems appeals in certain types of cases may only be brought on questions of law. In other words, there can be no re-examination of the *facts* at appellate level.

This difference of approach arises mainly from the different way in which evidence is gathered and presented at trial. In civil-law systems, far less emphasis is normally placed on the hearing of evidence at the trial. The judges have before them a dossier containing the evidence, and the trial may be limited to a review of that evidence with the witnesses before the court. In common-law systems, there is a far greater focus on the trial, during which evidence is given orally – often in great detail.

Another significant difference between civil-law and common-law systems is the number of appeal courts in each. In common-law countries there is customarily only one central court of appeal, although this may be administratively split into different divisions or panels of judges. In civil-law systems it is not unusual to find several appeal courts operating at a regional level. In France, for example, there are 34 courts of appeal. This plurality of courts may produce divergent (or even conflicting) interpretations of the law. This is less problematic at the first-instance level, as there is always the possibility of remedy at appellate level. However, even at this level, disagreement may still emerge.

As a result, many civil-law countries have established a higher court above the appeal courts. In every case it reviews, the sole concern of this court is to ascertain whether the lower court interpreted and applied the law correctly. If the higher court thinks that the court of appeal made a mistake, it will strike down the lower court's judgment. This procedure is known as cassation (from French *casser*, 'to break').

A Court of Appeal
The German Federal Constitutional Court is a specialized appellate court that is empowered to review only constitutional questions. Appellate courts more typically have a wider jurisdiction, correcting the errors of lower civil and criminal courts. ▼

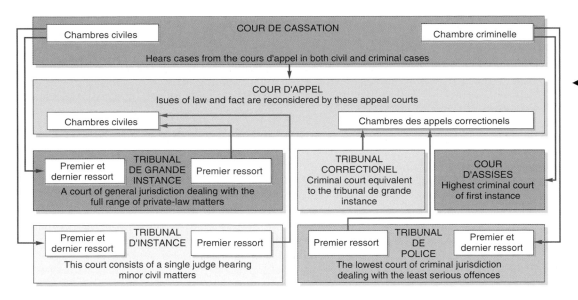

◄ **The French Ordinary Court Hierarchy** *The main courts in the French judicial system are shown in this diagram. These deal with the majority of cases; however, there is also a separate system of administrative courts, as well as various specialized courts established under different codes (e.g. the Code de commerce).*

Inquisitorial and Adversarial Procedures

A fundamental distinction can be drawn between those systems that adopt an inquisitorial approach to the legal process and those that adopt an adversarial approach. This is particularly important in relation to criminal cases. Once more, this distinction broadly reflects the division between civil-law systems and common-law systems.

The two approaches reveal a basic difference of philosophy on the purpose of the judicial process. The inquisitorial method rests on the view that it is the duty of the judge to seek out the objective truth about the issue before the court. In the adversarial approach, the court's function is not to seek out the truth, but to ensure that the evidence adduced by both sides is properly presented, accordig to the rules governing the admissibility of evidence and the conduct of the trials.

These two divergent philosophies have given rise to different rules of procedure. In an inquisitorial system, responsibility for investigating the facts of the case rests with a judge (sometimes called an ***examining magistrate***) who examines witnesses and obtains other evidence. He or she may, for example, require that reports be drawn up by expert witnesses, or may order the interception of telephone communications (although this means of obtaining evidence is not sanctioned in all systems). The results of these investigations are collected in a dossier, which is transferred to the trial court. Trial proceedings are typically confined to questioning the witnesses in order to clarify matters that are contained in the dossier. In some systems, however, the trial court has the power to call for additional evidence. The main responsibility for the examination of the witnesses and the evidence as a whole rests with the court. There is no lengthy process of examination and cross-examination of witnesses, which forms the basis of adversarial procedures. This makes the trial stage in civil-law systems, even in the case of serious crimes, considerably shorter than in common-law jurisdictions. Moreover, the principle of the free evaluation of evidence operates; thus, with some important exceptions (e.g. the nonadmissibility of evidence that has been illegally obtained), the judge is free to base a decision on any evidence that has been discovered.

In an adversarial system, there is no examining magistrate. The responsibility for gathering evidence and ensuring presentation to the court lies with the parties (in the case of a criminal prosecution, the police and the prosecutor on one side and the defence on the other). No dossier exists; evidence is brought together for the first time at the trial. The trial judge has no power to call witnesses and must confine questioning of witnesses to points of doubt that require clarification. In this system, there is a large body of rules governing the admissibility of evidence. Not all evidence that may have relevance to the case will be allowed; for example, **hearsay evidence** is usually inadmissible.

The Judiciary

The theory of the separation of powers (see POLITICS AND GOVERNMENT: HOW COUNTRIES ARE GOVERNED) that underpins many states' constitutions designates the judiciary as the arm of the state that may be required to impose checks and balances on the power of the other two arms (the executive and the legislature). An independent and impartial judiciary is therefore considered an essential feature of a healthy political system.

How judges are selected and appointed is a matter on which legal systems take different

hearsay evidence
Evidence about an event that is not experienced directly by witnesses, but recounted to them by a third party. Common-law systems customarily exclude such evidence, fearing that the jury in criminal cases, as nonlawyers, might be more easily swayed by second-hand evidence.

The Law in Japan

The Japanese legal system has been influenced by both the German Civil Code and the law of the USA. However, many disputes are resolved by nonlegal means, through conciliation between the parties. This traditional avoidance of litigation is based in Confucianism's mistrust of law as a means of social organization. As a result, the Japanese legal profession is relatively small.

approaches. Whereas the civil-law practice is to appoint judges from a corps of professionally trained judges, in the common law judges are appointed from the ranks of the practising legal professions.

In civil-law countries, judges follow the same initial stage of training as practising lawyers – a university education in law. This is followed by a period of professional training, often (e.g. in Spain and France) in a special school for judges. Judges are initially appointed to a position as a junior or trainee judge at the lowest level of the court system. Promotion is governed by a specially appointed committee, typically composed of senior judges, but possibly also including members of the executive.

In common-law systems there is no separate system of training for judges. Judges at all levels (except for lay magistrates) begin their careers as practising lawyers.

Irrespective of the way in which judges are appointed, most systems ensure their independence by making it difficult to remove a judge from office. However, in some systems – notably many states in the USA – judges are appointed by popular election. One consequence of this is to impair the fundamental principle of judicial independence.

Public Prosecutors. Responsibility for the prosecution of criminal offences rests with the state, and in most systems officers known as public prosecutors are appointed to discharge this function. An important feature of civil-law systems is that the public prosecutor is generally a member of the judiciary. Yet to preserve the impartiality of the office of judge, the

public prosecutor's functions at trial are limited to presenting the case on behalf of the public interest. Although a judge, the public prosecutor takes no part in the decision-making process in criminal proceedings.

In other jurisdictions, however, the public prosecutor is not regarded as a member of the judicial service, being either an elected public official (e.g. in the USA) or a lawyer employed by the civil service (e.g. in the UK).

Lay Participation in the Judicial Process
Another major distinction between civil-law systems and common-law systems is the extent to which the latter rely on lay people (i.e. people who are not qualified lawyers) in the judicial process. The main reason for this is that the participation of nonlawyers democratizes the legal system, ensuring that the courts reflect the attitudes of the wider community. Economic considerations also play a major part; lay people are not paid for their services. The principal countries where lay judges are employed are England, the USA, and Russia. Lay people also participate in the judicial process through service on **juries**.

Lay Participation in Civil-Law Systems.
Lay participation is not exclusive to common-law systems. The jury is used, albeit rarely, in civil-law codes. It was introduced into the French legal system in the period following the Revolution, since it was felt to be especially in keeping with the democratic spirit of the age. However its use is now confined to the highest criminal court, the *Cour d'assises*. In contrast to common-law systems, the jury in France

JURIES

A jury is a group of ordinary people (usually 12), whose function is to decide the facts of a case and give a verdict. The jury is a long-established institution in the common-law world. It is most widely used in the USA, where over 120 000 jury trials occur each year; this figure represents over 90% of all jury trials in the world.

Juries may either be chosen randomly from the ***electoral register*** (the list of those entitled to vote in public elections), or assembled through a lengthy selection process. Most juries were once required to reach unanimous verdicts, but many jurisdictions now allow majority verdicts (usually 10:2). When the prescribed number of jurors cannot agree (a ***hung jury***), different principles apply in different jurisdictions. In the USA, the judge declares a mistrial, and the case must be tried again, while elsewhere, unless two-thirds of jurors reach a guilty verdict, the accused must be acquitted.

Although France adopted the jury system for major trials after the Revolution and established it throughout Europe as a result of Napoleonic conquest, most states had abandoned juries by the end of World War II.

▲ **A Jury** *This fictional jury is from the US film* The Verdict *(1982). Most jurisdictions prohibit the photographing of real jurors, lest they be subjected to threats of violence or bribery in an attempt to influence their decision.*

does not retire on its own to consider its verdict, but reaches its decision in consultation with the presiding judges.

In Germany, there is extensive lay participation in courts above the lowest tier. All but the most minor criminal proceedings – including hearings at the appellate level – take place before a court consisting of a judge and two lay members. This system also operates in Russia, where lay judges, who are known as assessors, always sit with professional judges.

Legal Professions in Civil-law Systems

In respect of the legal professions, France – the archetype of codified systems – and Germany may be taken as representative of all jurisdictions based on Romano-Germanic law.

France. In France, the advocate (***avocat***) provides the fullest range of legal services to the public. The office of advocate existed before the Revolution. Although it was abolished during the Revolutionary period, it was restored during the Consulate (1799–1804). The structure and functions of this branch of the legal profession remained virtually unchanged thereafter until the reforms of the profession that culminated in the creation of the ***nouvelle profession d'avocat*** in December 1971. This merged the former profession of *avocat* with two other legal professions – those of the *avoué* and the *agréé*. The functions of the advocate were thus extended to include the right of audience before the *tribunal de grande instance* and the *tribunal de commerce*, duties previously discharged by the *avoué* and the *agréé*, respectively.

Further reforms to the profession were undertaken by a law of 31 December 1990, which merged the former professions of *avocat* and *conseil juridique*. Advocacy in contemporary France is thus an example of the widespread phenomenon of the **fused legal profession**, combining the dispensing of legal advice and assistance with representation of a client in court proceedings. However, a French advocate does not have the right to appear before the *Conseil d'État* or the *Cour de Cassation*.

All French advocates are members of the *barreau*, an organization that consists of all the advocates working in a particular locality. That locality is defined by the jurisdiction of the local court of first instance, the *tribunal de grande instance*. Each local *barreau* forms an order, administered by the Council of the Order, which in its turn is elected by the General Assembly of the Order. In addition to its administrative role, the Council has disciplinary powers to censure professional misconduct by its members.

In relation to his or her provision of legal advice and assistance, the advocate is entitled to practise throughout France; that is, not simply

◄ **English Appeal Court Judges**
Judges in common-law systems, such as England, first train and gain experience as legal practitioners (most commonly as advocates). By contrast, in civil-law jurisdictions, such as Spain or France, a person must enter an entirely separate system of training in order to become a judge.

in the jurisdiction of the court to which his or her *barreau* is attached. Until recently, the advocate's rights of audience in the courts were restricted; however, firms of advocates may now establish offices in the jurisdiction of another court.

Traditionally the advocate practised either as an individual or as part of a small partnership, and was always self-employed. Reforms introduced by the legislation of December 1990 mean that in future an advocate may practise either as a self-employed person or as a salaried employee.

An intending advocate must first obtain the degree of *maîtrise-en-droit*. This is then followed by a one-year course of professional training known as the *certificat d'aptitude pour la profession d'avocat* (CAPA) at one of the regional centres for professional training, plus two years' practical experience, known as a *stage*. This practical training may take place in the office of an advocate, but need not do so. The trainee advocate may, for instance, complete the *stage* in the office of a public prosecutor, or a notary, or an accountant.

Legal services of different kinds in France are provided by other types of practitioner. The notary (***notaire***) is second only to the advocate in importance and differs from the latter in several respects. Notaries are not members of an independent profession, but instead are appointed by the Minister of Justice (*Garde des*

The Fused Legal Profession

In most countries, a single legal practitioner combines both advocacy and advice to clients. The merging of functions occurred early in Germany (16th–18th centuries), and is widespread in Latin America. Similarly, in the USA, an attorney is entitled to undertake all forms of legal work.

▲ A French *Avocat*
A French advocate is shown delivering an address to a court. The profession of advocate is the principal one in the French legal system.

bar (the) Collectively, all persons qualified and authorized to conduct the trial of legal cases. The term originates from the bar or rail that enclosed a judge in a court. In France, the professional body of those who are entitled to represent a client in court is known as the ***barreau***, while those engaged in advocacy in England are called ***barristers***.

Sceaux). The position of notary, which may be retained for life, entitles its holder to a monopoly of certain types of legal service, e.g. conveyancing (the transfer of immovable property), marriage settlements, and succession. In addition, notaries are involved in a wide range of legal transactions, in which their main function is to draft legal documents. In being drafted and authenticated by a notary, such documents are accorded a special legal status, and may be challenged only on the ground that they have been falsely drawn up and are forgeries.

A person wishing to pursue a career as a notary may do so by completing his or her high school education and then undertaking an extensive period of professional training. Alternatively, a prospective notary may complete the university degree of *maîtrise-en-droit*, followed by a course of professional training at a university or regional training centre. Successful completion of this course entitles the candidate to enter a two-year programme of practical professional experience. Only on completion of this final stage is the trainee entitled to become an assistant notary.

At one time, the ***avoué*** performed important functions of representation before the lower courts. When the profession of *avoué* before these courts was combined with that of the

avocat, there remained the role of *avoué* before the Court of Appeal (*avoué près la Cour d'appel*). At appeal, the *avoué*'s function is to draw up the documents necessary for presenting the client's submission and to represent the client before the Court of Appeal. However, the *avoué*'s representation does not extend to presenting oral argument on behalf of the client, a function exclusive to the advocate. The *avoué* has the important responsibility of preparing the relevant procedural papers.

The French legal system recognizes a number of other legal professionals who have distinct areas of competence in the legal process. These include: *huissiers de justice*, whose functions include the service of writs and other legal documents on parties on behalf of the court and also on behalf of parties; and *greffiers*, whose role is to assist the court by, among other things, maintaining the minutes of court proceedings, recording decisions taken, and maintaining an official record of the action taken by the court in every case.

Germany. The German *Rechtsanwalt* is broadly equivalent to the French *avocat*. This branch of the German legal profession is organized in local **bars**, to which all advocates must belong. In order to practise before a court, the *Rechtsanwalt* must first be admitted to do so; in general the right of audience of German advocates is limited to the court to which admittance was first granted. Yet no such restriction exists on the right to engage in other forms of legal practice, and a *Rechtsanwalt* may provide such services nationwide. While German lawyers customarily practise in small partnerships of up to four or five lawyers, some larger firms of around 50 partners are now found in the major cities.

In Germany, the *Notar* equates to the French *notaire*. Certain types of legal transaction require authentication by a *Notar*, such as the sale of houses and other immovable property or the sale of shares in a company. Many other transactions are executed by a notary, even though this is not strictly required by law.

Intending lawyers in Germany must first undergo a university education in law, followed by two sets of examinations – the first and second state examinations. Following the first state examination students proceed to a period of professional training, during which they are paid by the state to undertake a number of different tasks, including work in the courts, in private practice, and with public authorities. During this time they also attend further classes in law. The second state examination is taken after this period of professional training. If the student is successful in this examination, he or she is then qualified to enter private practice or to seek employment as a member of the judiciary.

Legal Professions in Common-law Systems

Within the common-law legal family, there are pronounced differences in the structure of the legal professions. Despite the fact that the substantive law throughout most of the USA still resembles its original source – English law – the structure of the legal professions in the two jurisdictions is quite different.

England and Wales. In England and Wales the legal profession is divided into two branches – **barristers** and **solicitors**. Barristers are advocates who appear in court to represent clients. Although certain solicitors (known as solicitor-advocates) are now permitted to appear before the higher courts, most work in these courts is still done by barristers. Barristers are easily identified by the distinctive wig and gown they are required to wear when appearing in court.

Barristers are not allowed to receive instructions directly from members of the public. They may only be instructed to act on behalf of someone by that person's solicitor. Thus, an individual seeking legal representation must employ the services of two lawyers, a solicitor and a barrister. Senior barristers are referred to as 'Queen's Counsel' (often abbreviated to QC). Barristers are grouped professionally into organizations known as **Inns of Court**, of which there are four: Gray's Inn, Lincoln's Inn, Inner Temple, and Middle Temple. These are ancient institutions whose original purpose was the training of their members for practice at the bar. Although the Inns retain a residual training role, their function is now largely ceremonial and social.

Barristers are not allowed to form partnerships or work in association with other lawyers. However, they are permitted to form **chambers** – groups of barristers who share office premises and the services of a clerk. The clerk performs a central role in the chambers, acting as the main link between the members of the chambers and the firms of solicitors from whom instructions to act on behalf of clients are received.

Solicitors. Although solicitors have the right to appear in the lower courts, and may now apply for the right to appear in the higher courts, the majority of a solicitor's work is done in the office, advising clients on a wide range of legal matters. Solicitors are responsible for most day-to-day legal transactions, such as the buying and selling of houses and other properties, and the drafting of wills and other legal documents. Solicitors are also responsible for preparing the initial stages of cases that are going to be heard in court.

Legal Education and Training. In England and Wales the typical route into either branch of the legal profession begins with the completion of a three-year law degree at a university law school, or the completion of a three-year degree in another subject, followed by a one-year intensive law course at a university law school. For the next stage, the two branches follow different routes. Intending solicitors follow a course of professional training (the Legal Practice Course) at a university or a professional law school. There then follows a two-year period of training in a solicitor's office, at the end of which the trainee may be admitted to practice. He or she may not, however, practise alone or as a partner in a firm for the first two years after admission as a solicitor. Trainee barristers also follow a course of professional training in a law college, followed by a period of apprenticeship with a barrister, known as **pupillage**, which lasts a minimum of 12 months.

The USA. Professional control over legal practice and the training of lawyers is exercised by each of the 50 states of the union (and, for federal appointments, by the District of Columbia). After completing a university law degree (Juris Doctor, or JD), the prospective lawyer is required by most states to pass state bar examinations. This qualifies a person as an **attorney**, who is authorized to undertake all forms of legal work.

The growth of large business organizations in the USA since the late 19th century has been accompanied by an increase in the number of attorneys who never practise advocacy but specialize in commercial law, working either directly for commercial or financial corporations or for large law firms. In addition, many lawyers in the USA are employed by state or federal government.

Legal Ethics

The legal professions in most countries operate within a legal framework established by the state. In addition, however, lawyers are subject to codes of practice governing the manner in

▲ **John Marshall** *(1775–1835) Chief justice of the US Supreme Court from 1801 to 1835, Marshall had a great influence on the development of constitutional law. He was instrumental in establishing the principle of judicial review in the USA.*

The Palace of Justice, Peru *The Peruvian Supreme Court is housed in this building, which is situated in the capital, Lima. The Supreme Court hears appeals against decisions made by lower courts.* ▼

Advertising Legal Services

A general principle of professional legal ethics that once applied absolutely was that lawyers should not advertise their services. However, since 1977, lawyers in the USA have been permitted to advertise basic information about fees and services. In particular, the growth of litigation to secure payment of damages has led to the unethical practice of 'ambulance chasing' – attempts by lawyers to encourage accident victims to file lucrative lawsuits.

Hijacking *In June 1985, Shiite Muslim gunmen hijacked Jordanian and US airliners to Beirut in the Lebanon, in order to secure the release of fellow militants from prison. The principle of universal jurisdiction applies to such crimes as hijacking that affect the international community.* ▼

which they engage in the practice of law. These codes of professional practice – referred to as legal ethics – are established by the professions themselves and usually enforced by their professional organizations. The content of these ethical codes varies from system to system. One rule that is very commonly encountered, however, is that of professional secrecy or confidentiality. Lawyers are under an obligation to maintain strict confidentiality in respect of information communicated to them by their clients in the course of their professional relationship. If, for example, a client were to admit to the lawyer to having committed a criminal offence, the lawyer would be obliged to keep that statement secret. In some systems, lawyers cannot be compelled to disclose this information, even by a court. Moreover, in many jurisdictions, if a client were to confess to a lawyer that he had committed the offence with which he is charged, and yet still insist that the lawyer present a plea of not guilty to the court, the lawyer's code of professional ethics might oblige him or her to withdraw from the case, for fear of misleading the court.

Jurisdiction

Jurisdiction is the legal right to exercise judicial power over an issue. For example, all legal systems take the view that they are entitled to exercise criminal jurisdiction over offences that take place on their territory (including their territorial waters and ships and planes registered in their territory). This is known as the 'territorial principle.' The civil-law systems also generally take the view that they are entitled to exercise criminal jurisdiction over offences committed by their nationals, irrespective of where those offences may have been committed. This is known as the 'principle of active personality.' It is also generally

recognized as being acceptable for a state to exercise jurisdiction over criminal offences that affect vital state interests, irrespective of where these are committed or the nationality of the offender. A clear example of this is the exercise of jurisdiction over a person who has committed an act of treason against the state. A ground of jurisdiction with increasingly wide application is ***universal jurisdiction***. According to this theory, certain types of offence are of such gravity, affecting the international community as a whole as opposed to the particular interests of an individual state, that any state that is able to do so may exercise jurisdiction over an offender. The doctrine was originally formulated to deal with the problem of piracy – pirates being regarded as 'the enemies of all mankind' (*hostes humani generis*) – and was subsequently applied in the case of slave traders. It is now frequently found in international agreements dealing with such matters as hostage-taking, hijacking, and other offences against aircraft. The last ground of criminal jurisdiction that may on occasions be invoked is the nationality of the victim (the 'principle of passive personality'). While this is relied upon by some legal systems, it is not a ground of jurisdiction that is widely accepted by other countries.

In certain circumstances, individuals may be exempt from the jurisdiction of the courts of the state in which they are living. For example, international agreements concerning the status of diplomatic personnel embody the principle of ***diplomatic immunity***, according to which the courts of the country in which persons recognized as having diplomatic status cannot (without the consent of their own state) be brought before the local courts – even for serious offences. International agreements concerning the stationing of troops on foreign territory (such as the agreements between NATO countries) often provide for the exercise of jurisdiction over offences committed by visiting troops by the courts of the country in which they are stationed (the territorial principle) or the courts of the country from which they come.

Special courts and procedures are commonly established to deal with matters of military law, and in the enforcement of that law the ordinary courts have no jurisdiction. If an offence is committed that is an offence against both military law and civil law, then, depending upon national rules, the case may be dealt with before the ordinary courts or before the military courts (known as ***courts-martial***). Military courts are usually made up of officers of the relevant armed service, who will not necessarily have any legal training, although the court may be presided over by a legally trained officer.

International Law

*Public international law • International and domestic law • International treaties •
Customary international law • Other sources • Enforcing international law •
Human rights • Private international law • The rights of children*

The term 'international law' is most commonly used to refer to the body of law known as public international law, but it may also denote a significant area of the law known as private international law.

Public International Law

The traditional view of public international law as the body of law regulating the relations between states is now only partially valid. Any modern definition must take account of two important developments that have occurred since World War II. The first of these is the establishment of a large number of international organizations that are recognized in international law and that enter into relations with each other and with individual states. These organizations include such global bodies as the United Nations, the World Health Organization, the International Labour Organisation, and a number of regional groupings, such as the Organization of African Unity and the Organization of American States.

The second significant development has been the change in the status of the individual in international law. Traditionally the individual was not regarded as a subject of international law. For example, individuals could not be held personally liable for violations of international law; responsibility for these violations could only be borne by a state. Increasingly, however, international law has become concerned with protecting the individual. This has come about largely through the development of a body of international human-rights law that not only sets down the rights that are to be protected, but frequently establishes international mechanisms to enable individuals to take action to enforce those rights. International law has also come to recognize the principle of individual responsibility for the commission of certain crimes (e.g. war crimes) against international law.

Modern public international law deals with such issues as: the creation and international recognition of states; the rights of states, including the right to control their territory and their natural resources; state responsibility for the acts of their organs, officials, and representatives; the law of the sea, including the definition of territorial waters and the use of the high seas and the deep sea bed; economic and political cooperation between states; diplomatic and consular relations; the protection of individuals and groups; the law of treaties; the law relating to international organizations; the responsibility of individuals for crimes against international law; the peaceful settlement of international disputes; and the laws of war.

=SEE ALSO=
This section:
• Legal Systems and Their Origins
• Criminal Law
Politics and Government:
• International Politics
Business and Finance:
• International Finance and Investment

Salvaging a Ship
Under maritime law – an important aspect of international law – a person who has saved a ship from danger at sea is entitled to retain the cargo until salvage payment has been made. Maritime law also guarantees freedom of the high seas; piracy and slave trading are illegal under customary international law. ▼

treaty As defined in the 1969 Vienna Convention, an agreement between states that must be in written form and must be governed by international law (i.e. not the law of any one of the parties to the treaty). A treaty may be embodied in one or more related documents, but need not be expressly described in any of these as a 'treaty.'

Signing an International Treaty *President Bill Clinton of the USA (centre) signs as a witness to a peace treaty concluded in October 1994 between the Middle Eastern countries of Israel and Jordan. This treaty formally brought to an end the state of war that had existed between these two countries for more than 40 years. Treaties such as this are an increasingly common embodiment of international law.* ▼

International and Domestic Law

The relationship between international law and domestic law (i.e. the internal laws of a state) can be complex. For example, it may be necessary in a given case to ascertain whether the principles of international law contained in a **treaty** governing human rights form part of the domestic laws of the countries that are parties to the treaty. Moreover, a conflict may arise between the principles of international law and the rules of domestic law.

There are two broad approaches to the question of compatibility. Some states accept that international law and domestic law are both parts of a single system of law. This is known as the *monist* approach. Such an approach gives precedence to international law in cases in which it conflicts with domestic law.

The second approach, known as the *dualist* approach, treats the two systems as separate and gives precedence to domestic law.

Some states adopt a compromise position, according to which customary international law is taken as forming part of the domestic law, while international law based on treaty requires incorporation before it can be applied at the domestic level.

International Treaties

International treaties now form the primary source of international obligations binding upon states. There are several reasons for this. First, since states voluntarily undertake to be bound by any treaty to which they are signatories, no party can reject the terms of such a treaty on the ground that it had no choice in its adoption. Furthermore, since treaties must be in written form, there are likely to be fewer disputes about the limits of a rule

established by treaty than about the limits of a rule established by international custom.

There are also historical and political reasons why treaties have come to enjoy a paramount position in the development of international law. For instance, many of the new states that gained their independence through the process of decolonization understandably viewed with suspicion any system of international law based on custom. After all, many areas of Africa had suffered colonial annexation precisely as a result of European powers reaching informal agreements about how best to divide the continent among themselves, most notably at the Berlin Conference on West Africa in 1884–85. Customary international law was therefore regarded by newly independent states as intrinsically imperialistic and capitalistic, being formulated solely by powerful Western interests.

A further reason for the increased reliance on treaties is that customary law is inapplicable to new fields of human interest and activity that have been opened up by modern science. For example, the rapid expansion of international civil aviation in the middle of the 20th century created a need to regulate the use of airspace; an early agreement was the Chicago Convention on International Civil Aviation (1944). New technologies have also given humans access to extraterrestrial space and the deep sea bed, which were never previously the subject of legal regulation. In response to this development, a treaty was signed in 1967 on the Principles Governing the Activities of States in the Exploration and Use of Outer Space, Including the Moon and other Celestial Bodies. Consensus on the use and exploitation of the deep sea bed has been

THE ORIGINS OF PUBLIC INTERNATIONAL LAW

▲ **Hugo Grotius** *Grotius's influential treatise* On the Law of War and Peace *('De Jure Belli ac Pacis')* *was published in 1625.*

The modern system of public international law originates in early modern Europe. In the Middle Ages, the dominance of the Holy Roman Empire in Europe and the feudal structure of society had restricted the growth of nation-states. During the 15th and 16th centuries, however, a number of independent sovereign states emerged. In drafting rules to govern the relationship between these states, jurists often adapted principles of Roman law, canon law, theological doctrines, and the idea of the 'law of nature.' A body of rules and principles was devised, known as the 'Law of Nations.'

Prominent early writers on international law were the Spaniard Francisco de Vitoria (c. 1486–1546), and the Italian Alberico Gentili (1552–1608). However, the writer generally regarded as having the greatest influence in the early development of the Law of Nations is the Dutch jurist Hugo Grotius (Hugo de Groot; 1583–1645).

Key Terms

convention
A multilateral agreement between states.

protocol An addendum to a convention or treaty, dealing with points of interpretation or qualifications to the original agreement.

more problematic; it was not until 1994 that a provision attached to the United Nations Convention on the Law of the Sea relating to this area came into force.

Treaties between states are in many ways similar to contracts between individuals. They must be entered into voluntarily, by parties that have the legal authority to bind themselves in this way, and they are not binding on any state that is not a party to the treaty. Treaties may take the form of an agreement between two states – a **bilateral treaty** – or they may be adopted by any state wishing to accept its obligations; such treaties are known as **multilateral treaties**.

Occasionally, international treaties adopt, declare, or confirm a rule of international law already considered to be in existence before the treaty was drawn up. The United Nations Convention on the Prevention and Punishment of the Crime of Genocide (1948), which was drafted in the immediate aftermath of the Nazi Holocaust, is one such treaty. As well as confirming that genocide was a crime, the Genocide Convention provided for the first time an agreed definition of the term, and established an international framework for the prosecution and punishment of genocide.

Many treaties attempt to restate or codify existing rules and principles of international law and to bring them into line with contemporary needs. For example, the **Hague Conventions** of 1907 adapted and extended the existing principles of international law governing the conduct of war, in order to take

account of the advent of far more destructive modern weaponry. Similarly, after World War I, the 1925 Geneva Protocol prohibited the use in war of chemical and biological weapons. Further Geneva **conventions** and **protocols** in 1949 and 1977 provided for the protection of the victims of international and noninternational armed conflicts.

In many instances a state may wish to accede to a treaty to which it was not an original signatory. For a state to 'join' in this way may require the unanimous consent of all existing signatories; this is the case, for example, for any state wishing to accede to the treaties establishing the European Community (1957) and the European Union (1993).

While accepting the generality of a treaty, states may wish to excuse themselves from some aspects of its obligations. Treaties therefore frequently provide that a state may make 'reservations.' Such reservations are not permitted if they are expressly prohibited by the treaty, or if the reservation is of a kind that does not fall within a limited category of reservations permitted by the treaty, or if the reservation is incompatible with the object and purpose of the treaty.

Treaties are designed to govern relations between the parties to them in the future; therefore, a treaty provision will not generally bind a party in relation to anything that took place before the treaty entered into force with respect to that party.

Although treaties as such are only binding on the parties to them, the rules and principles

Ratification

A treaty may require that a process known as *ratification* be conducted before a state can be held to have accepted the terms of the treaty. What is needed for ratification depends on the requirements of the law in the particular state. In some states, ratification requires approval of the treaty by the state legislature; the state cannot consent to be bound by the treaty without such approval.

◀ **Chemical Warfare Protection** *French soldiers wear protective clothing against the possible deployment of chemical weapons by Iraqi forces in the Gulf War of 1990–91. Although the use of such weapons was outlawed by the Geneva Protocol of 1925, manufacturing and stockpiling them was not.*

binding upon them. It is not enough to show that states have consistently acted in a particular manner, but that this has arisen from a belief on their part that they are under an international obligation to do so.

A customary rule of international law may be superseded by the development of a contrary or conflicting rule of international law. Moreover, rules of customary international law may be supplanted by the adoption of treaty-based rules.

Other Sources
Two other sources of international law are judicial decisions and the opinions of jurists.

Judicial Decisions. Judicial decisions are recognized by the **International Court of Justice** as a subsidiary source of international law. The Court may refer to the decisions of international tribunals (including, of course, its own) as well as those decisions of national courts that it considers relevant to the matter in hand. At the international level there is no equivalent to the doctrine of binding precedents found in many common-law legal systems (see LEGAL SYSTEMS AND THEIR ORIGINS). International law is, therefore, much closer to legal systems that derive from the modern civil law of continental Europe. In practice, however, the International Court of Justice does tend to follow the principles established by its own previous decisions, as well as those made by other international tribunals.

The Opinions of Jurists. The opinions of writers on international law of established reputation may also be used in formulating the rules of international law, The opinions of jurists have traditionally played an important role in international law. However, for every legal opinion favouring one point of view it is often possible to find a contrary opinion of equal weight. What is usually being sought is a view that is generally and consistently held by legal writers. Writers' opinions tend to carry less weight than judicial decisions.

Enforcing International Law
In some respects, the enforcement of international law differs fundamentally from the domestic law of states. For example, there is no international equivalent of national police forces, whose function it is to enforce the criminal law within states. International courts do exist, but in general states are under no

set out in the treaty may come to be accepted as universally applicable. One such example of customary international law deriving originally from treaties is to be found in the attitude that international law adopts to the official use of **torture** by states. Torture is expressly prohibited by several human-rights conventions. Even though certain states may not be signatories to such treaties, the condemnation of torture is so widespread that it is now generally accepted that the practice contravenes general international law and must not be used by a state.

Good Faith. The fundamental principle of the law of treaties is that every treaty in force is binding upon the parties to it and must be observed by them in good faith. This principle, also known as *pacta sunt servanda* (Latin: 'treaties are to be observed'), is enshrined in the 1969 Vienna Convention on the Law of Treaties, which governs treaties concluded between individual states. Good faith is central to the operation of the law of treaties; states that are parties to a treaty are bound to ensure that their actions truly promote its purposes and that they do not merely apply the letter of the law without enacting its spirit.

Customary International Law
Despite the growing importance of treaties, custom continues to play an important role in international law and international relations. Two preconditions must be satisfied before an alleged custom can be established as a rule of customary international law. First, it must be shown that the custom has actually been a consistent practice by the states concerned. Evidence of consistent practice can be obtained from a diversity of sources (e.g. states' statements of policy, diplomatic correspondence, etc.). Secondly, it must be demonstrated that states have accepted this practice as

Torture
Torture is employed against political dissidents by repressive authoritarian regimes in an attempt to stifle opposition. It may be exercised through various kinds of physical assault, or through psychological torment of the individual (e.g. sleep deprivation). Although expressly forbidden by the Universal Declaration of Human Rights, it is estimated that torture is still used in over 100 countries. This and other human-rights abuses are monitored by the impartial pressure group *Amnesty International.*

THE INTERNATIONAL COURT OF JUSTICE

The only tribunal that has a truly global role in the enforcement of international law is the International Court of Justice, established under the UN Charter.

Each member of the UN undertakes to comply with the decision of the Court in any case to which it is a party. In cases of non-compliance, the other party may refer the matter to the UN Security Council, which may take steps to enforce the judgment. The Court consists of 15 members elected by the General Assembly and the Security Council. Its judges are independent and elected regardless of nationality. In order to be eligible for appointment to the Court, an individual must possess the necessary qualifications in his or her native country for attaining the highest judicial office. Judges are elected for a period of nine years and may be re-elected thereafter.

obligation either to recognize the competence of these courts or to submit disputes to these courts for resolution. Furthermore, these courts are limited in the types of cases they can deal with. Thus the International Court of Justice established under the United Nations Charter does not have universal jurisdiction to determine disputes between members of the UN. Nor do international tribunals have compulsory jurisdiction. Whereas an individual who is summoned to appear before a domestic court cannot avoid judgment by refusing to recognize the authority of the court, an international tribunal has no mandate to deal with a case unless the state or states in question have recognized its competence. Recognition of authority is frequently limited by the principle of **reciprocity**, i.e. the jurisdiction of the court is acknowledged as compulsory by a state only if the other party to the dispute has also recognized the competence of the court.

The absence of compulsory mechanisms of enforcement should not obscure the fact that, like municipal law, international law is generally observed without having to resort to enforcement measures. In their day-to-day intercourse, states attempt to abide by the rules of international law, if only because this is to their mutual advantage.

Human Rights

One of the most significant features of international law since 1945 has been the development of a body of law designed to safeguard human rights. This important development involves a significant departure from classical theories of international law. Traditionally, absolute respect for the sovereignty of states meant that concern at the way in which one state chose to treat its own citizens was generally regarded as unwarranted interference in that state's internal affairs. This extreme isolationist position began to break down towards the end of the 19th century, but it was not until the end of the World War II that concern for the rights of the individual was placed at the centre of the international legal regime.

Prompted by the massive violations of human rights that had occurred under totalitarian regimes in Europe and Asia, and by the claims of peoples subject to colonial rule, the UN General Assembly adopted, in 1948, the **Universal Declaration of Human Rights**. That declaration set out a broad statement of the rights that all human beings were entitled to enjoy irrespective of their racial or national origin, skin colour, sex, language, religion, or political opinion. These rights include the right to life, liberty and security of the individual, the right not to be held in slavery or servitude, and the right not to be subjected to torture or to cruel, inhuman, or degrading treatment. The Declaration also proclaimed a number of important social and economic rights, such as the right to work, the right to receive social security support, and the right to form and join trade unions.

Practical Protection of Human Rights.

Despite being an influential statement of human rights, the Universal Declaration was never intended to lay down binding rules of international law. It therefore has no enforcement mechanism, and cannot be regarded as an instrument for providing direct and effective protection of human rights. Since 1948 the protection of human rights worldwide has proceeded by a number of other routes.

> To develop friendly relations among nations based on respect for the principles of equal rights and self-determination of peoples... to achieve international cooperation in solving international problems of an economic, social, cultural, or humanitarian character, and in promoting respect for human rights and for fundamental freedoms for all without distinction as to race, sex, language, or religion.
>
> Aims of the UN, as stated in **Article I of the UN Charter**, drafted June 1945

A Sitting of the International Court of Justice
This war crimes tribunal of the International Court was convened in 1993 to deal with atrocities arising from conflict in the former Yugoslavia. ▼

Kurdish Refugees ▶
(1991) The Kurdish people of the Middle East have long been the victims of repression by various regimes in the region. Iraq devastated Kurdish areas in 1988 and 1991, creating a refugee crisis. The UN Commission on Human Rights has identified the situation in Iraq as one of several worldwide requiring constant review.

Refugees

The legal status of refugees is defined in a UN Convention of 1951 and its 1967 protocol. These contain provisions against **refoulement** – the forcible return of a person to his or her country of origin, where persecution is likely. Other rights accorded to refugees include freedom of employment and public education in their country of resettlement, on an equal footing with nationals of that country.

We look forward to a world founded upon four essential human freedoms. The first is freedom of speech and expression – everywhere in the world. The second is freedom of every person to worship God in his own way – everywhere in the world. The third is freedom from want... everywhere in the world. The fourth is freedom from fear... anywhere in the world.

US President **Franklin D. Roosevelt** (1882–1945), in a speech delivered to Congress, 6 Jan 1941

Globally, the UN has promoted a number of human rights instruments, the two most important of which are the International Covenant on Civil and Political Rights and the International Covenant on Economic, Social and Cultural Rights (both adopted in 1966). Although they both list a comprehensive range of rights, only the covenant on civil and political rights has an enforcement mechanism under which individuals may bring allegations of violations before an international body (the UN Commission on Human Rights).

The UN has also sponsored several more specialized conventions catering for particular abuses of human rights or for groups that are thought to require special protection. These conventions include the International Convention on the Elimination of all Forms of Racial Discrimination (1965), the International Convention on the Suppression and Punishment of the Crime of Apartheid (1973), and Convention on the Elimination of all Forms of Discrimination against Women (1979). In order to protect vulnerable groups the UN has adopted the Convention Relating to the Status of **Refugees** (1951) and a Convention on the Rights of the Child (1989; see **THE RIGHTS OF CHILDREN**).

Regional Human Rights Initiatives. In 1950, the Council of Europe adopted the European Convention on Human Rights. The Convention established two international bodies to ensure observance of the obligations set out in the Convention. The first of these bodies – the European Commission on Human Rights – was intended to resolve complaints of human rights violations through discussion between the individual and the state, or by unilaterally reaching a decision on the matter. The second body – the European Court of Human Rights – was given the power to make

a binding judgment in respect of cases referred to it. However, individuals do not have direct access to the Court, and a matter can only be referred to the Court for a binding ruling by the Commission, by the state that was the subject of the complaint, or by a state whose national presented the complaint.

The case law developed by the Commission and the Court represents the most detailed body of human rights law in the world. Nevertheless, some defects in the procedure have come to light, one of the most serious of which is the problem of delay. It can take several years for a case to make its way through the Convention procedures from initial complaint to final disposal by the court. Such lengthy delays can diminish the effectiveness of any remedy that may result from the process of bringing a complaint. The proposed remedy is to establish a single European Court of Human Rights. All parties to the Convention will be required to recognize the compulsory jurisdiction of this Court, and individuals will have direct access to the Court for the first time.

The structure of the European Convention on Human Rights, including its enforcement model, was followed by the Organization of American States (OAS) in 1969 when it adopted the American Convention on Human Rights (which came into force in 1978). Under this Convention the Inter-American Commission on Human Rights performs broadly the same role as that of the European Commission; in practice, however, the Inter-American Commission has taken a more active role in protecting human rights than its European counterpart. Other important differences exist between the two conventions. In particular, the right of individual application is compulsory in the American Convention, while interstate complaint is optional. Also, while under the European system only a person claiming to be the victim of a violation of human rights may bring a complaint, the inter-American procedures extend this right to any person, including nationals of states not party to the Convention.

The Organization of African Unity (OAU) has promoted the African Charter of Human and Peoples' Rights. This differs from other regional charters in two important respects. First, it contains a number of rights not included in the European and American conventions, and secondly it seeks to promote a different approach to the resolution of human rights cases, principally by avoiding resort to adjudication by a human rights court.

The African Charter refers extensively to 'people's rights,' stating that "all peoples shall be equal; they shall enjoy the same respect and shall have the same rights. Nothing shall justify the domination of a people by another." Elsewhere, it requires that "colonized or oppressed peoples shall have the right to free themselves from the bonds of domination by resorting to any means recognized by the international community." These provisions are clearly a legacy of colonial rule in Africa.

Private International Law

Private international law refers to those principles of national law that govern the relationships between individuals in cases in which those individuals, or the relationship between them, may raise questions of law under more than one legal system. For example, a French woman may marry a Polish man in England. They go to live in Texas in the USA, where the woman gives birth to a daughter. Shortly thereafter, the man goes to Mexico, where he obtains a divorce from his wife and is granted custody of their daughter. Various questions of private international law arise from this hypothetical situation (similar instances of which are encountered in practice throughout the world). Will the marriage be recognized as valid, and under what conditions? Will the divorce and the custody order be recognized as effective? Such questions are increasingly made the subject of international multilateral agreements, according to which states agree to apply common principles to resolve questions of private international law.

A similar approach has been taken to the great increase in commercial activity at a global level, which has highlighted the inconveniences that may arise from the differences in national legal systems. The trend today is, therefore, towards the harmonization of the principles of domestic private law, through the use of international agreements to that effect. Notable examples of this trend include the Hague Convention on the Civil Aspects of International Child Abduction (1980), the Hague Convention on the Law Applicable to Contracts for the International Sale of Goods (1986), and the Convention on Jurisdiction and the Enforcement of Judgments in Civil and Commercial Matters (1988).

Extradition

An extradition treaty is an agreement between states to return fugitives from domestic justice to face criminal charges, or to serve a sentence imposed by a court, in the state that is seeking extradition. Extradition can normally only be sought on the basis of such a treaty, and may be refused in the case of political offences (although, increasingly, states refuse to treat terrorism and other crimes of violence as political offences). Extradition may also be refused if the fugitive is likely to be persecuted in the requesting state.

WAR CRIMES TRIBUNALS

During World War II, the Allied powers (the USA, the USSR, and Britain) declared their intention to bring to justice the leaders of the Axis powers (Nazi Germany and Imperial Japan) for the initiation of the war and the atrocities committed by their forces and officials in the conduct of the war and in the persecution of the Jewish people and other civilian populations.

Accordingly, at the end of the war, International Military Tribunals were convened at Nuremberg and Tokyo. Surviving Axis leaders were charged with three types of crime:

• **Crimes Against Peace** The planning, preparation, or waging of a war of aggression, or a war in violation of international treaties or agreements, or participation in a common plan or conspiracy to accomplish any of these.

• **War Crimes** Violations of the laws or customs of war, e.g. murder or enslavement of civilians; murder or ill-treatment of prisoners of war; killing of hostages; wanton devastation of cities, towns, or villages.

▲ **Defendants at the Nuremberg Trials** *Many Nazi war criminals were found guilty at Nuremberg and executed.*

• **Crimes Against Humanity** Murder, extermination, enslavement, deportation, and other inhumane acts committed against any civilian populations, before or during the war, or persecutions on political, racial, or religious grounds.

As well as establishing that such acts constituted crimes against international law, the Nuremberg and Tokyo tribunals established the principle of individual responsibility for such crimes. Moreover, the tribunals expressly stated that it was to be no defence to the charges that the accused acted on behalf of the state or on the orders of a superior.

The principles established at Nuremberg and Tokyo were subsequently adopted by the UN and have been applied to similar crimes arising out of the conflicts in the former Yugoslavia and Rwanda.

THE RIGHTS OF CHILDREN

EARLY MOVES TO ESTABLISH children's rights saw the enactment of legislation on child labour by some industrialized countries in the first decades of the 20th century. However, international acknowledgment of the principle that children are entitled to the full range of human rights accorded to adults is comparatively recent.

DEVELOPING COUNTRIES
In developing economies, the continuing extensive use of child labour must be understood in context; extreme poverty and debt forces many families in these countries to employ young children alongside adult family members in subsistence farming or to send them out to seek work. Yet some basic rights are beyond dispute, such as freedom from sexual exploitation, or the right not to be exposed to dangerous or heavy work.

UN Protection of Children's Rights
In pamphlets such as this, governments of countries that have acceded to the United Nations Convention on the Rights of the Child (1989) set forth its provisions. By the mid-1990s, over 120 countries had signed the Convention.

THE UN CONVENTION
Full legal recognition of children's rights was achieved with the adoption of the UN Convention on the Rights of the Child in 1989. This international agreement sets out all the rights that should be enjoyed by every child and young person below the age of majority – the age at which a person is legally recognized as an adult. The keystone of the Convention is its declaration that the family is the natural environment for nurturing children.

PROVISIONS OF THE CONVENTION
As well as making extensive recommendations on the employment of children, the UN Convention also provides for the following areas: the right of all children to a name at birth and to be a citizen of a particular country; safety from violence and cruel punishment; access to proper daily childcare; the right to personal privacy; and the entitlement to free education, at least up to primary-school level. Moreover, if children break the law, the Convention requires that they be punished appropriately (i.e. trial and imprisonment only as a last resort).

Child Street Vendors *Kurdish children sell pastries in the city of Diyarbakir, Turkey. The UN aims to ensure the healthy normal development of children worldwide, especially those from disadvantaged ethnic minorities.*

CHILD LABOUR
The exploitation of children became widespread in countries that industrialized rapidly in the 18th and 19th centuries. The employment of children for very low wages in factories and mines was for the most part unregulated, and deaths and injuries were commonplace.
In some developing countries, children are still widely employed in agriculture and in labour-intensive industries (e.g. carpet weaving). According to estimates by UNICEF (the UN Children's Fund), children comprise over 10% of the workforce in some Middle Eastern countries and between 2 and 10% in parts of Asia and Latin America. In India, around 175 million children are engaged in service and cottage industries, or in farming.

Children in Mining *In the 19th century, many children were forced to work in strenuous and dangerous jobs.*

Economic Systems

*Market systems • Command systems • Real world economies •
Postwar developments • Changes in eastern Europe*

Economics is concerned with scarcity and choice. Specifically, the quantity of resources available at any time are finite, while human desires are usually assumed to be infinite. Thus, decisions have to be made as to the best way of allocating the limited resources available among all the competing needs that exist within society.

A major area of debate within economics literature is the role that governments should play in this process of allocating resources. At one extreme, the government has a very limited role, its responsibilities being confined to maintaining an appropriate supply of public goods, such as adequate armed defence against external attack and a legal system to protect individuals and property. In such a system land and capital is owned by individuals, while the allocation of resources is guided by prices that emerge naturally in markets inside and outside the economy. If all resources are allocated by means of the market mechanism, the system is called ***pure capitalism***.

At the other end of the spectrum is ***pure socialism***, which operates as a command system without the intervention of market forces. In socialism, land and capital are owned by the state. Decisions regarding the allocation of resources are made administratively, initially at a national level, and are subsequently implemented at regional and local levels. Although this system is frequently associated with the theories of Karl Marx (1818–83), such a viable mechanism for allocating resources was first devised by Walter Rathenau (1867–1922), who organized Germany's production during World War I.

Market Economy *Supply and demand dominates a* ▶
market economy, the most common system in the modern world. The government plays a minor role, creating a framework of rules within which the business sector can operate, controlling the money supply, and providing public goods (for example, defence). Consumers express their choices by the prices they are willing to pay for goods and services, creating demand in the market; the business sector supplies the goods and services demanded by consumers.

Market Systems

A **market** is formed when the buyers and sellers of a commodity are free to interact with each other. Markets can emerge for the buying and selling of almost anything, including the products householders buy at the supermarket, factors of production (land, labour, and capital), and financial assets. Although many people think of markets as identifiable geographical entities, such as a local vegetable market, many markets are not observable in this traditional sense. In some cases, advances in telecommunications and computer technology have made it possible for buyers and sellers to be in contact with each other without meeting or even being on the same continent. For example, long-distance trading takes place on foreign-currency exchanges.

In a market-based economy, it is the complex interaction between individual markets that determines how resources are ultimately allocated. In a profit-motivated pure capitalist system, no judgment is made regarding the

═══SEE ALSO═══
This section:
• Economic Resources
• Goals of Economic
  Policy
Politics and Government
• How Countries are
  Governed
Business and Finance:
• Goods and Services
• Company Structure
  and Finance
• International Trade
• International Finance
  and Investment

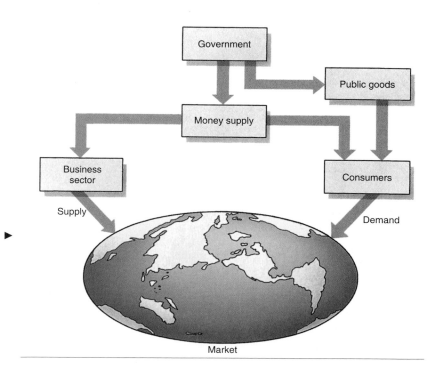

Currency Dealing Room ► *The foreign-exchange market is international and does not have one particular location. Dealers here, in Amsterdam, may be trading with their counterparts in Tokyo, Buenos Aires, or New York. Communication is by telephone and fax – prices are displayed worldwide on computer screens.*

market The activity of trading in which goods or services are exchanged, either for other goods or services but more often for money. In free markets, the price at which the exchange takes place is determined by interaction between buyer and seller on the basis of supply and demand (see PRICE MECHANISM). The activity can take place in a physical arena, also called a market (or an exchange). Alternatively, sophisticated financial markets can exist with no physical location; in these traders contact each other by telephone, fax, etc., and price variations are recorded on computer screens.

desirability or morality of the way in which goods and services are traded; nor is there any attempt to control the distribution of income between individuals within the economy.

Command Systems

Under a command system resources are allocated by administrative decision. Plans made at a central level dictate not only *what* goods and services should be produced but also *how* they should be produced. Prices of raw materials and labour used in the production process, as well as the price of the products, are also determined centrally. Thus, unlike the market system, the distribution of income between different groups within the economy is controlled at the discretion of the planning committees. For example, until the reforms that took place in the early 1990s throughout eastern European countries, the prices of most staple products in these countries were held down by government subsidies. In theory, in a command system, decisions made at a central level reflect the planners' views regarding the sectors of the economy that should be expanded or contracted; these views should reflect specific needs at regional, national, and international levels, although in practice this is not easily achieved. The result is that the average individual has little opportunity to express any preference about what is available in the shops.

Experience has demonstrated that a number of interlinked problems occur in planned economies. These relate to product quality, diseconomies of scale, and excessive bureaucracy.

Product Quality. Success within a planned economy is measured by the extent to which targets are met or exceeded; if they are exceeded the workers are rewarded by the payment of bonuses. However, if an enterprise is set too high a target by ambitious politicians, the race to achieve the target may well result in a reduction in quality. Conversely, should a target be achieved too easily, a higher target will be set in the future, which would make bonuses more difficult to obtain. Thus, the system has an in-built inertia that can promote a deterioration of quality and penalize a desire to exceed a target by too much. Moreover, in the market system inefficient firms and firms whose products do not satisfy their customers may be forced out of an industry. On the other hand an inefficient enterprise in the planned system is afforded a measure of state protection that saps any incentive to innovate or to rectify problems.

Diseconomies of Scale. A feature of planned economies has been the belief that it is better to have a few large-scale operations producing each product, rather than a more complex network of smaller firms. This was not only a feature of heavy industry and manufacturing but also of agriculture in eastern Europe. In terms of planning, the need to deal with a small number of large enterprises simplifies administration. Furthermore, large-scale production can often result in a cheaper product than smaller-scale production as a result of **economies of scale**. Average costs may fall as units of capital are fully used, an efficient division of labour is employed, and distribution systems are better coordinated. These economies may also be increased if the product is highly standardized, which is a feature of many products in centrally planned economies. However, while economies of scale can be achieved as output increases, eventually a point is reached below which average costs cannot fall; thereafter diseconomies of scale can set in as an enterprise becomes too large to organize effectively and too inflexible to respond effectively to change. Some production units in eastern Europe became so large that the advantages of large-scale production were lost and average costs rose.

Excessive Bureaucracy. Some enterprises can grow to such an extent that they become impossible to manage efficiently; others simply have too many layers of bureaucracy that are protected by vested interests. Once a bureaucratic network has been established it becomes self-perpetuating – more concerned with its own survival than with the effectiveness of its function. Several large government organizations in mixed economies, as well as in command economies, have become so inflexible as a result of over-management that governments desperate to restore momentum have removed whole layers of bureaucrats. A further point is that, even in market economies, those industries with only a few firms operating within them are less competitive than industries with a larger number of small and medium-sized firms. One of the effects of lack of competition is that the incentives to innovate are reduced.

A feature of market economies is that firms need to trade with each other in order to obtain supplies of the raw materials they need. If these raw materials are too expensive, of poor quality, or delivered late, the purchaser has the option of finding an alternative supplier. By contrast, enterprises within a planned system receive their raw materials from a distribution network. If the distribution network breaks down for any reason, the problems will knock on throughout the system. As a result, the extent to which one manager can meet a particular target will in part determine the ability of other managers to meet theirs. Because managers cannot resort to an alternative supplier in such cases, industrial output can be very uncertain. This is an example of the inflexibility of a bureaucratic system.

Real World Economies
No country can be said to use a pure form of either of these extreme systems for allocating resources; the vast majority of countries throughout the world fall somewhere between market and command systems. Yet it is possible to identify Japan and Singapore as countries that have many of the characteristics of pure capitalist economies, while China and the former Soviet Union have emerged as countries that attempted to utilize more comprehensive systems of planning.

In the majority of countries the allocation of resources has evolved with, to varying degrees, an interplay between market and central control systems. For example, although Sweden has what is essentially a market-based system, the state plays an extremely significant role in providing a highly developed welfare service, which corrects many of the potential failures of an unbridled market system (such as environmental pollution, inequality of access to welfare services, and an inequitable distribution of income).

Similarly, since World War II, such countries as France, South Korea, and Kenya have at times employed a less stringent form of planning known as ***indicative planning***. In this system, the government not only plans its future levels of expenditure but also predicts how it expects the economy to perform in the future in the light of this expenditure. If the private sector is convinced of the validity of these predictions, it will invest accordingly. Thus private-sector investment and general economic behaviour is influenced, rather than commanded, by the official plan.

An alternative approach is that adopted at various times in such countries as India and Turkey. In these countries direct controls have

economies of scale A reduction in the average cost of producing something, when the quantity produced is increased.

Command Economy
The government sets up planning committees to decide what shall be produced and to direct the production of all goods and services. Prices are determined by the planning committees, which may subsidize the cost of production. The efficiency of the system depends on how accurately the committees have forecast the requirements of consumers and how skilfully resources have been allocated between the producers of goods and services and public goods, such as defence. ▼

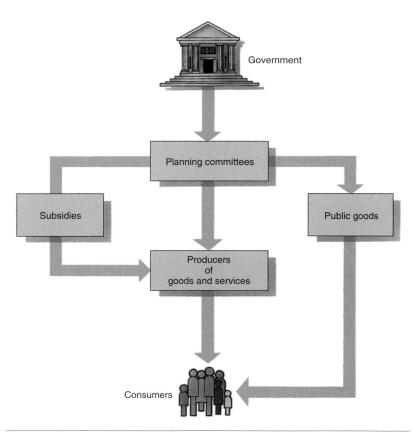

Crowding Out

There are two ways in which an increase in government expenditure can cause an economic effect known as crowding out. First, public-sector spending can absorb resources that could have been more effectively used by the private sector. Secondly, borrowing to finance public-sector expenditure drives up interest rates, making money more expensive to borrow for the private sector. This inhibits private investment. Keynes believed that this effect was limited. More recent economists think crowding out may be complete, i.e. for every additional unit spent by a government there is an equal fall in private investment.

been imposed on particular sectors of the economy, predominantly heavy industry, in order to promote economic progress. Although direct controls may also be placed upon private enterprise, the market still plays an important role in determining which goods and services should be produced. Economists use the general term **mixed economy** to refer to a country in which resources are allocated by means of a combination of the state and the market mechanism. The mixed economy is the most widely adopted system throughout the world.

Postwar Developments

After 1945, there was a tendency in Europe for governments to favour greater involvement in the allocation of resources than in the prewar period. In western Europe, this reflected the general need to promote a coordinated process of reconstruction after the war, together with the influence of John Maynard Keynes (1883–1946), whose prewar writings had identified the role of government spending in smoothing out the effects of the **trade cycle** (see GOALS OF ECONOMIC POLICY). Keynesian economists took the view that the supply of money to an economy does not directly influence consumer spending. In their view, consumer spending was largely controlled by levels of income and contractual commitments to save.

Later economists, led by the American Milton Friedman (1912–), held that increasing the money supply does directly result in increased spending and is therefore a cause of inflation. Friedman's view, known as **monetarism**, is that increased money supply encourages people to hold larger cash balances than they need, which they reduce by increased spending. This leads to a rise in prices and thus the inflationary tendency begins. Once inflation expectations enter into wage negotiations, the inflationary spiral is fuelled. In spite of differences of opinion on the way to control inflation – and in spite of persistent inflationary problems in the postwar years – the market system continued to dominate the noncommunist world.

However, during this postwar period in eastern Europe the Soviet Union seized the opportunity of increasing its sphere of influence by forcing its neighbours to adopt highly socialized systems of planning, in which market forces were allowed to play only a limited role.

To a large measure, therefore, economies throughout the world had features of one or other of these two opposing systems. Over the last two decades, however, opinion has changed in both camps as to the function of the state in the resource-allocation process.

The market-based economies of western Europe are typified by events in the United Kingdom, which is a classic example of a mixed

SIMPLIFIED MODEL OF A MIXED ECONOMY

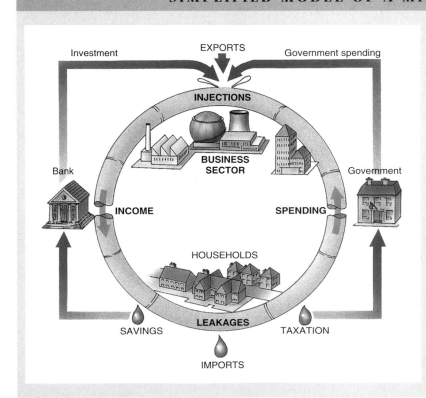

The model illustrated here assumes that all the income generated by the business sector goes to households – who either spend their income, save it, or use it to pay taxation. The proportion spent goes back to the business sector, but savings and taxation constitute a leakage from the system. Investment and government spending is regarded as an injection into the cycle. If planned injection equals planned leakage there is said to be **income equilibrium**. If planned leakages exceed planned injections, less spending money is available and surplus goods accumulate. This in turn has the effect of forcing businesses to reduce output, employment, and prices. Reduced spending and reduced saving by households continue until equilibrium has been re-established. Imports may also be considered a form of leakage, as the money spent on imported goods by households goes to foreign firms and is therefore lost to the cycle. Exports, on the other hand, constitute an injection. Goods that are sold abroad bring fresh money into the cycle from foreign buyers.

ADVANTAGES

Economies of scale

Greater R&D facilities

Division of labour

Cheaper finance, materials, etc

Greater influence on market, government, etc

Greater access to high-level managers

Small
is beautiful

SIZE OF
BUSINESS

Large is powerful

Greater flexibility

Quicker decisions

Less bureaucracy

Friendlier environment

◄ Size of Business
*The advantages and
disadvantages of size
are summarized in this
diagram. In a mixed
economy small firms
have to compete in the
market with very large
firms. Often the small
firms fill a niche in the
market, whereas large
firms offer a broad
range of products.*

DISADVANTAGES

Bureaucratic

Internal politics

No personal contact with customers

Smaller markets

Lack of finance

Inability to spread risks

economy. In 1979 a Conservative government was elected with an election promise to "roll back the frontiers of the state." This promise reflected a growing opinion that the UK economy was generally over-regulated, i.e. that too many rules prevented competition from taking place. Not only in the UK, but elsewhere in the free world, it was felt that in the postwar period the public sector had proved to be an inefficient provider of goods and services and was guilty of a process known to economists as **crowding out**. A further problem that arose was the familiar stifling effect of an expanding bureaucracy; because the public sector was largely protected from direct competition, inefficiency began to develop. As a result, the UK government adopted a long-term programme of increasing the role of market forces within the economy by reducing the extent of the public sector, a process frequently referred to as **privatization**.

In many Western countries there was an increasing tendency to follow the US model of allowing the private sector to provide many of the services (e.g. railways and energy) that had formerly been run by the public sector. This new way of thinking promoted free competition as a more desirable attribute of an economic system than pride in the corporate ownership of the fragments of the infrastructure. Individualism was more highly prized than the supportive attitudes fostered by postwar mixed-economy socialism in the European welfare states.

However, monetarist policies were applied most radically by the military junta in Chile, which restored the free market system after the overthrow of the Marxist government of Salvador Allende in 1973.

The decline of the manufacturing sector in many postwar Western economies has been matched by the rise of some economies in southeast Asia and the Pacific Rim. Low labour costs in labour-intensive industries, such as clothing manufacture, allowed Hong Kong and Singapore to capture large shares of a market traditionally dominated by European and North American producers. This first became apparent in motor vehicle production and electronics, where Japan began to make serious inroads into world markets in the 1970s. However, Japanese dominance is itself being challenged by new high-technology expertise in South Korea and Taiwan.

Changes in Eastern Europe
Equally dramatic are the changes that took place in eastern Europe with the collapse of communism in 1989–90, where countries with highly developed systems of socialization and central planning adopted more market-based structures. This not only includes the states that used to be part of the former Soviet Union, such as Russia, Ukraine, and Belarus, but also its former satellite countries (e.g. Czechoslovakia, Hungary, and Poland). Eastern Europe became a major recipient of Western aid and provided an opportunity for private investors in the West.

When a country moves from a command economy to one in which the market plays a much more dominant role, a significant amount of change must take place to its legal system. Most significant is the creation of ***property rights***. The establishment of property rights requires the creation of a legal system capable of protecting each individual's interests, whether it be the right to own a house, to engage in some sort of manufacturing activity, or not to be subjected to adverse effects arising from the activities of others. The exact nature of a particular property right depends on what the legal system sanctions. For example, in many countries the right to

privatization The sale of public-sector enterprises to the private sector. Privatization of organizations providing both goods and services has occurred in several countries. The usual method is to offer shares in the enterprise to the general public, sometimes giving preference to employees. The advantages claimed for this method of privatization is that in addition to increasing competition and providing the motivation of profit, it also increases the number of individuals in the community who own shares, i.e. it broadens the concept of a property-owning democratic system.

Free Enterprise in Moscow *In 1992 a US fast-food chain opened a branch in Moscow. More than any disarmament treaty this signalled an end to the Cold War.* ▶

property rights Legally enforceable rights conferred on individuals or groups of individuals enabling them to own and use resources and commodities. These rights are taken for granted in a property-owning democratic system based on a market economy.

opportunity cost The benefits lost by producing or consuming one thing in preference to producing or consuming something else. For example, if a man has a computing system that he could lease out for £10,000 per year, the opportunity cost of using it himself, rather than leasing it, is £10,000.

produce and sell a particular good or service is subject to the health, safety, and environmental regulations of that country.

In addition to the establishment of property rights, the introduction of a market-based economy requires the creation of a financial system enabling transactions for the purchase and sale of property to be carried out in an orderly manner. This financial system must earn the confidence of economic agents both inside and outside the country. Much of this development has been modelled so as to be consistent with practice elsewhere in Europe.

The process of transferring assets from a former state-owned enterprise to the private sector also involves the introduction of a new body of law relating to companies; in addition, it requires a fundamental change in people's attitudes. The sheer size of the privatization programmes meant that governments were unable to rely upon the experience of the West. One of the immediate results of the rationalization process has been the creation of high levels of unemployment and inflation together with a general increase in poverty as subsidies have been removed from staple products.

The mechanics of the privatization process has varied from country to country. In some cases, vouchers have been issued, providing company workers with the opportunity to own shares in newly privatized firms. However, this approach conceals the true market value of particular enterprises and does not generate revenue for the government. In other cases, entire firms have been sold off to buyers both outside and inside the country

concerned. Where size has proved to be an obstacle, firms have been broken down into more manageable units, with shares in each component being made available for purchase. However, the privatization of these large enterprises, formerly under the control of ministries or administrative districts, is less likely to be as important as the growth of the medium and small business sectors. In many cases, 40 years of politically motivated decision-making has resulted in the existence of an obsolete capital stock, an underdeveloped service sector, and a neglected infrastructure.

Prior to the reforms within eastern Europe, the centrally planned economies tended to trade mainly with each other. It was an explicit goal of Soviet economic policy to severely restrict economic dependence on the West. Furthermore, the size and political might of the former Soviet Union guaranteed it a dominant role within the system that evolved. Trade tended to be in raw materials, energy, and unsophisticated manufactured goods; prices were not related directly to scarcity and **opportunity cost** but were determined by political factors. In the early to mid-1990s several former Eastern-bloc countries attempted to cultivate new trading relationships, which look to the West and therefore have to recognize the economic reality of Western market systems.

Exactly how and with which countries this trade will evolve in the long term is a question of major significance. In 1992, Association Agreements were signed by the Czech Republic, Slovakia, Hungary, and Poland with countries of the European Community (now European Union, EU) and EFTA. A similar agreement was later signed by Russia and others will follow. Association Agreements have meant that whereas the EU has opened up the markets for its nonsensitive products almost immediately to eastern European firms, these firms have ten years before they must reciprocate. Furthermore, the agreements also represent an attempt to impose the EU's commercial framework upon the eastern European economies.

The main problem eastern European firms face is their lack of technical, managerial, and marketing skills, making it difficult for them to take full advantage of the potentially lucrative markets in the West. Nevertheless, there is little doubt that because east European domestic markets are small, weak, and unstable, Western markets represent the best opportunity to enable these countries to accomplish their transition from central planning to a more market-oriented system. Only in this way will eastern Europe become integrated into an international economic order that is based on the market system.

The Price Mechanism

Supply and demand • Market equilibrium • The price mechanism in operation •
An optimum allocation of resources • Market failure • Externalities •
Monopoly • Public goods and merit goods

All societies are faced with the same fundamental economic problem: a scarcity of economic resources that compels the society to make choices about how such resources should best be deployed. One way in which this problem is dealt with is by means of the **price mechanism**.

The price mechanism is a system of communications between sellers of goods and services (producers) and buyers of goods and services (consumers) that enables them to arrive at a price for a transaction to take place on the basis of supply and demand. Producers and consumers are guided in their production and consumption decisions by changes in relative prices. In economic terms, producers are said to supply output and consumers to demand output. When government does not intervene in the economy, resources are allocated entirely by means of the price mechanism in accordance with the decisions of buyers and sellers. Such systems are known as ***laissez-faire*** or ***free-market economies***. In these economies the role of the government is restricted to creating a framework of rules for the conduct of trade between buyers and sellers. Thus, there might be rules to protect investors against fraud or rules that restrict the use of harmful substances in the production of

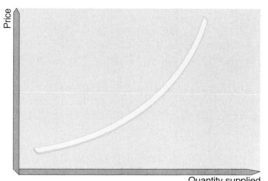

◀ **Supply Curve**
A typical supply curve shows a direct relationship between the price of a good and the quantity supplied.

food. However, the government would not intervene in the economy to influence the pattern of production or consumption that resulted from the operation of the price mechanism.

Supply and Demand

In order to understand the operation of the price mechanism, it is necessary to understand the market forces of supply and demand.

Supply. To economists, supply has a specific meaning: it is the amount that firms are willing to make available for consumption at a given price over a particular period of time. Economic theory indicates that the price of the

---

ADAM SMITH AND THE LAISSEZ-FAIRE ECONOMY

The term 'laissez faire' – which may be translated as 'let people act as they see fit' – was coined in an economic context by the French merchant J. Gourlay (1712–59). However, the most famous exponent of the theory of market forces conditioning mercantile activity was the Scottish moral philosopher and political economist Adam Smith (1723–90). In his major work, *An Inquiry into the Nature and Causes of the Wealth of Nations* (1776), Adam Smith outlined the noninterventionist approach that he believed would ensure a country's prosperity: "Little else is requisite to carry a state to the highest degree of opulence from the lowest barbarism, but peace, easy taxes, and tolerable administration of justice; all the rest being brought about by the natural course of things."

===SEE ALSO===
This section:
• Economic Systems
• Economic Resources
Business and Finance:
• Goods and Services
• Marketing
• International Trade
Ecology (vol. 3):
• Human Ecology and Conservation

Demand Curve ▶

A typical demand curve shows an inverse relationship between the price of a good and the quantity demanded.

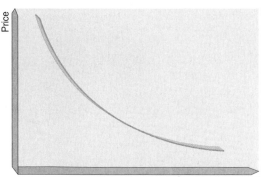

market clearing price
The only price at which the level of supply and demand balance; in other words, there is neither a surplus nor a shortage of a product at this price.

product and market supply vary directly, so that as the price of the product rises the amount supplied rises. There are two main reasons for this:

• As the price of a product rises the profit per unit produced also rises. This provides an incentive for firms to increase output. Firms in the private sector must make a profit to survive. It is assumed also that firms try to maximize their profits. A reduction in price will have exactly the opposite effect.

• Firms vary in the level of efficiency with which they operate. The lower the efficiency of a firm, the higher its cost of producing a given level of output. However, as the market price rises, less efficient firms will be able to make a profit and will therefore be able to compete in the market. As the price rises, the supply will be increased by the entry of less efficient producers. Again a reduction in price has exactly the opposite effect.

A typical graphic representation of price against supply is known as the **supply curve**.

Demand. To economists, demand also has a specific meaning; it implies a willingness and ability on the part of consumers to pay for the product. The price of a good and the amount demanded vary inversely; if the price falls the amount demanded increases. Again there are two main reasons for this relationship:

• If the price of one good falls while the prices of all other goods, as well as consumer incomes, remain unchanged, consumers will be able to buy more of that good without

buying less of something else. A rise in price will have exactly the opposite effect.

• As in many cases consumers can choose from a number of very similar products, it is reasonable to assume that as the price of one good falls, consumers will choose more of that good in preference to more expensive competitors. Again, a rise in price will have exactly the opposite effect.

The relationship between the price and the amount demanded is illustrated in the typical **demand curve**.

Market Equilibrium

In markets that are free of government intervention, supply and demand interact to determine both the price of the product and the amount that will be supplied and demanded. This is shown in the diagram of the market equilibrium.

In this diagram, the supply curve of a particular good intersects the demand curve for that good. The coordinates of this point of intersection, P and Q, give the equilibrium price (also referred to as the **market clearing price**) and the equilibrium amount supplied and demanded. If the price is above P, the amount supplied will exceed the amount demanded and there will be a market surplus. In order to be able to dispose of this surplus of supplies, prices will have to be reduced. As price falls, the demand expands along the demand curve and the supply contracts along the supply curve.

Conversely, if the price is below P, the amount demanded will exceed the amount supplied and there will be a market shortage. Whenever there is a shortage, in a market free of government regulations, price is inevitably forced upwards. As the price rises, the demand contracts along the demand curve and the supply expands along the supply curve. It is the existence of a shortage that forces the price upwards. Only when the price remains stable at P is there neither a surplus nor a shortage; there is, then, no tendency for price to change. P is the **equilibrium price** and Q is the **equilibrium quantity** supplied and demanded.

The Price Mechanism in Operation

The diagram illustrating market equilibrium makes it clear that once equilibrium is established it can only be disturbed if there is a change in the demand curve or a change in the supply curve. Economists describe these events as a change in the **conditions of demand** or a change in the **conditions of supply**. A change in the conditions of demand is illustrated in the diagram below.

In this diagram, *SS* and *DD* are the original supply and demand curves for a particular good. The initial equilibrium price is therefore

Market Equilibrium ▶

The equilibrium price in a market is given by the intersection of the supply curve and the demand curve. If the price rises above the equilibrium price P, there will be a market surplus. If it falls below P, there will be a shortage.

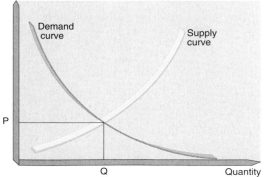

◀ **Free Markets**
The price mechanism enables this market stall, in a European country, to sell melons from Spain, grapefruit from Israel, and oranges from South Africa at prices that the buyer can afford.

P. If this good becomes more popular for any reason, other than a change in its price (e.g. the prices of other goods have increased), this implies a movement of the demand curve for this product from DD to D_1D_1. The effect of this is to pull the equilibrium price up to P_1 and to increase the equilibrium quantity supplied and demanded to Q_1.

In this case, the price increase resulted from increased consumer preference for the product. This led to a higher price; as the price rose, producers increased their output to benefit from the higher profits available from production. To be able to increase output, producers must attract resources away from alternatives. Again, it is the higher price that facilitates this, because it offers higher rewards to be earned.

This is the price mechanism in action. Consumer demand for a product increases and as a result its price rises. This signals to producers that consumers demand more of that product and at the same time provides the incentive and the means for producers to increase the supply. As a result, resources are taken away from alternatives that society values less highly. It is sometimes said that the 'consumer is sovereign,' when resources are allocated through the price mechanism, because producers are concerned to respond to consumer demands.

A change in the conditions of supply is also illustrated. Again SS and DD are the original supply and demand curves for a particular good. The initial equilibrium price is therefore P. If for some reason (perhaps an increase in wage rates without any corresponding increase in the output produced per worker) the

cost of producing this good rises, at any given price, producers will experience a cut in their profit per unit. As a result, less efficient firms will be forced out of the industry. This implies a movement of the supply curve for this product from SS to S_1S_1. As output falls, the price is forced upwards and, as a result, some consumers drop out of the market. Resources are thus released and are available for the production of other goods and services. The new equilibrium is reached when the price has risen to P_1 and the equilibrium quantity supplied and demanded has fallen to Q_1.

An Optimum Allocation of Resources

It is sometimes claimed that, when resources are allocated by means of the price mechanism, there is an *optimum* allocation of resources. Resources are deemed to have been allocated in an optimum way when it is impossible to make one member of society better off by reallocating resources, without simultaneously making another member of society

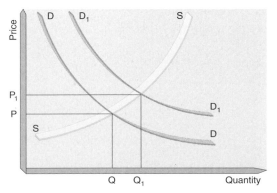

◀ **Conditions of Demand Change**
The effect of a change in demand from DD to D_1D_1 on the equilibrium price (from P to P_1) and quantity (from Q to Q_1).

Conditions of Supply Change ▶
The effect of a change in the conditions of supply (from S to S₁) on the equilibrium price (from P to P₁) and quantity (from Q to Q₁).

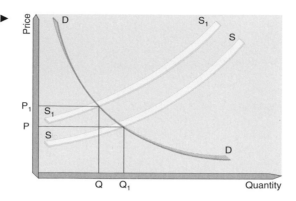

worse off. In other words, an optimum allocation of resources exists when it is impossible to improve society's welfare by a reallocation of resources.

An optimum allocation of resources is achieved when the price consumers pay for the last unit they consume exactly equals the cost of attracting resources away from alternatives. The price paid for the last unit consumed measures the value society places on that unit, while the cost of attracting resources away from alternatives measures the value society places on these alternatives. When the price of a good exceeds the cost of attracting resources away from alternatives, then society clearly prefers more of this good than the alternatives that might otherwise be produced. In these circumstances a reallocation of resources away from alternatives in favour of the good with the relatively high price would improve society's welfare.

Conversely, when the price of a particular good is less than the cost of attracting resources away from alternatives, then it is clear that society prefers the alternatives that these resources can produce. In these circumstances a reallocation of resources away from the good with the relatively low price in favour of alternatives would improve the welfare of society. Only when the price paid for the last unit consumed is exactly equal to the cost of attracting resources away from alternatives is it impossible to improve society's welfare by a reallocation of resources.

Negative Externalities ▶
The effect on the equilibrium price and quantity when the supply curve is based only on private cost and when the supply curve is based on private costs and negative externalities.

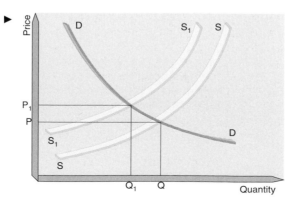

Market Failure

This analysis implies that society's welfare would be maximized if resources were allocated through the price mechanism. In fact, this is unlikely to be the case and economists refer to failure of the price mechanism to deliver an optimum allocation of resources as ***market failure***. There are many causes of market failure but its existence is used to justify government intervention in the economy. Important causes of market failure are **externalities**, **monopolies**, **public goods**, and **merit goods**.

Externalities

Free markets achieve an optimum allocation of resources, in which price measures the value consumers place on the last unit consumed and cost measures the value society places on the resources used to produce that unit. In fact, in their assessment of value and cost, consumers and producers might have incomplete information and in such cases price might not always measure the full cost to society of producing a good or the full value to society of consuming a good. This is because production and consumption often have side effects that affect parties other than the producer or the consumer. These side effects of production and consumption are known as externalities; in the modern world they are an important cause of market failure because their value or cost is not always reflected in market prices.

Economists distinguish between *negative externalities*, those that adversely affect society, and *positive externalities*, those that are beneficial to society. Probably the most widely quoted example of a positive externality arising from consumption is the case of an individual who is vaccinated against a contagious disease. This not only eliminates the risk that the individual will contract the disease but it also eliminates the possibility of the individual passing the disease on to other members of society. Thus an individual who is vaccinated against a particular disease passes on benefits to other members of society.

An example of a negative externality arises when a power station generates electricity by burning fossil fuels, and discharges carbon dioxide (CO_2) into the atmosphere. Large amounts of carbon dioxide in the atmosphere are a major cause of global warming, which has implications for society as a whole rather than being confined to those who produce or consume the power station's electricity.

To understand the relationship between externalities and market failure, consider the case of a chemical factory that discharges toxic waste into a nearby river, formerly used by anglers. Because the waste is untreated, the chemical firm's costs of production are lower than they otherwise would be; if this is reflected in lower prices, the consumers of the chemicals stand to gain. If the saving is not passed on to consumers, the shareholders in the chemical firm will gain as a result of increased profits. However, in either case there will be a cost to society because the toxic waste will kill the fish and angling will no longer be possible. Part of the cost of producing the chemicals is therefore borne by society. If the firm was compelled to internalize this cost and treat its toxic waste before dumping it into the river, its costs of production would increase and society would consume less of the firm's output. This is shown on the diagram giving the general case of a negative externality arising from production. In this diagram *SS* and *DD* are the supply and demand curves for a product based on **private costs** and **private benefits**, i.e. externalities are completely ignored. In this case the equilibrium price would be *P* and the equilibrium quantity supplied and demanded would be *Q*. However, when the cost is internalized, the appropriate supply curve to consider is S_1S_1. The equilibrium price would now rise to P_1 and the equilibrium quantity would fall to Q_1. When society is compelled to pay the full cost of production, including the cost of externalities, it therefore chooses to consume less of this product. The implication is that by ignoring externalities more of this product is consumed than society would desire; this is because, when the cost of externalities is taken into account, society chooses a different allocation of resources involving less of this product and more of the alternatives. Since firms would not choose willingly to internalize the cost of externalities, it follows that when negative externalities exist, allocating resources through the price mechanism leads to a **sub-optimum** allocation of resources.

This example describes market failure in terms of negative externalities; it is, however, equally easy to show that market failure will

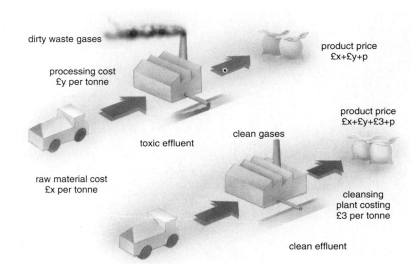

occur whenever externalities exist, whether they are positive or negative or whether they occur in production or in consumption. Whatever the cause, the result of externalities that are not internalized is always over-consumption or under-consumption of a good in relation to the optimum level.

There are several options open to governments to correct market failure that arises from externalities. In the case of negative externalities in production, one approach is to legislate to prevent the offending activity. For example, when a firm pollutes the environment, as when toxic waste is dumped into the river, the authorities could impose regulations to prevent it. A different approach is to tax the consumption of goods that impose negative externalities on society and to subsidize the consumption of those goods that confer positive externalities on society. The choice of which approach to take to control externalities depends upon the priorities of the government in question.

Many economists prefer the use of taxes and subsidies because a tax on a negative externality will have the same effect as an across-the-board increase in firms' costs of production. The end result is that price will be forced upwards and production and consumption will fall. Resources will then be reallocated to the production of other goods and services. Conversely, a subsidy will have the same effect as an across-the-board reduction in firms' costs of production. In this case the price will fall and the amount produced and consumed will increase. In other words, resources will be removed from alternatives that society values less highly.

Monopoly

Market failure might also be caused by the existence of monopoly. Strictly, a monopoly exists when there is a sole supplier of a good or

▲ **External Diseconomies**
If society is subjected to toxic effluents and dirty waste gases by a chemical factory, the factory can sell more of its product because it can offer it at a lower price for the same profit (p). If society does not accept this pollution, the factory will have the extra expense of cleansing its effluents and will therefore have to increase its prices, and consequently sell less. It is sometimes argued that governments should internalize external diseconomies, such as pollution, by means of taxation.

EXTERNALITIES

As an example of externalities, when a derelict house is purchased by a person who renovates the property, other householders on the same street are likely to experience a rise in the value of their own properties. In other words they experience a **positive externality**. On the other hand, if the house owner allows the property to fall into disrepair, other householders will experience a decline in their property values – a **negative externality**.

A Public Good ▶
National defence is a pure public good, and like other public goods will be undersupplied by the market. The ratio of the cost to the benefit for an individual does not take into account the public need for it. This provides the justification for governments to intervene in the operation of the free market.

service. In this case, market failure would arise because a monopolist would restrict supply, thus forcing the price up to achieve maximum profit. Markets would fail because the price consumers are willing to pay for additional units of the monopolist's output would exceed the cost of attracting those resources away from the alternatives. Consumers cannot bring about an optimum allocation of resources if the monopolist restricts supply.

Again there is some justification for government intervention to influence the allocation of resources; there are, however, other problems with monopoly. It is sometimes claimed that the essence of monopoly power is the ability to restrict the entry of new firms into an industry and in this way preserve the monopoly position. This might be undesirable for several reasons. It could be argued that by creating and preserving barriers to entry, monopoly implies a waste of economic resources. In addition, to the extent that monopolies restrict supply, in order to drive up the price of their product, monopolies exploit their market power to the detriment of consumers. For governments wishing to hold down pressure on prices this is clearly a cause for concern.

However, the case against monopoly is ambiguous; monopolies can benefit society in some ways. For example, because monopolies are large-scale producers, they often operate with a lower cost per unit than smaller firms. A prime reason for this is that because they buy inputs in bulk they can negotiate more favourable discounts than smaller firms. Monopolists may also have greater incentive than firms operating in a competitive environment to increase their efficiency. Firms in a competitive environment may find that any new techniques or products they develop are quickly copied by competitors. Innovations and inventions therefore offer only the prospect of a limited return. However, the absence of competition in a monopolistic market ensures that the gains from new techniques or products accrue exclusively to the monopolist.

CARTELS

Cartels, which may be national or international, arise when independent companies that trade in the same product or service group together to form an association, with the aim of regulating market conditions. The main purpose of the businesses in doing so is to enjoy some of the advantage of monopoly power over their market in two principal ways:

• **Price fixing** What may begin as an attempt by the association members to establish an equitable selling price for their product, by agreeing not to indulge in cutthroat competition, may end in a restriction of output in order to stimulate demand and so force an inflated price on the market. This adversely affects resource allocation.

• **Suppressing competition** Established businesses operating within the same market may wish to forestall the possibility of being undercut by newcomers offering discounted prices to customers. By controlling all recognized outlets for the product, or offering retailers disincentives to trade with the new company, cartel members can effectively stifle competition. In doing so, they stabilize their existing market shares.

Many governments have enacted legislation outlawing cartels, on the grounds that they are monopolies that work against the public interest, since they violate the principle that free competition drives down prices. However, especially in the case of international cartels, the charge of price fixing is notoriously difficult to prove.

Not all cartels are disadvantageous to the consumer. The International Air Transport Association (IATA) fixes flight prices worldwide, yet this is regarded as acceptable, as a price war between companies in this particular industry could have the wholly unacceptable result of compromising passenger safety.

In practice, monopolies are rare, although the problems associated with monopoly can occur in markets dominated by a single firm, or a small group of firms that collude. In dealing with the problem of monopoly, it must first be decided what level of market domination constitutes a monopoly. This varies from country to country; moreover, countries adopt different policies in dealing with the problem of monopolies. One approach, as in the USA, is an outright ban on the existence of monopolies. This approach is based on the belief that the possible abuses of monopoly outweigh any gains to society. In such cases, once a firm grows beyond a certain size it is compelled to divest itself of some of its assets so that its overall share of a particular market falls within the limit specified.

A different approach is to assess each case on its merits and decide whether a particular monopoly operates against the public interest. Such an approach operates in several countries. This approach is fraught with difficulties, not least because it is extremely difficult to define what is meant by the 'public interest.' A balanced assessment of the costs and benefits associated with each particular monopoly requires a time-consuming investigation, culminating in the production of a detailed report, which is presented to a government department for consideration. After studying the report, ministers must decide what action, if any, to take against the monopoly.

Public Goods and Merit Goods

Market failure also occurs when certain goods that confer benefits on society are either not produced at all or are underconsumed in relation to the optimum level. The former situation occurs in the case of **public goods**, the latter in the case of **merit goods**.

Pure public goods possess two characteristics. They are **nonrival in consumption** and they are **nonexcludable**. If a good is nonrival in consumption this means that consumption by one person does not diminish the amount available for other consumers. This contrasts markedly with private goods, in which one person's consumption of a good necessarily precludes anyone else from consuming the same good. It is the fact that public goods are nonrival in consumption that ensures that the price mechanism could never achieve an optimum allocation of resources. This is because an additional unit of consumption provides a benefit to the consumer but at no additional cost to the supplier. It is not necessary to take resources away from alternatives and there is therefore no way of achieving an optimum level of consumption.

A good is nonexcludable if the producer is unable to prevent anyone from consuming it.

It is this characteristic that ensures that private markets cannot function, since a producer would be unable to restrict consumption of the good to those who paid for it. Since the good could be obtained without payment, no rational person would ever pay for it.

Public goods cannot therefore be allocated through the market and the provision of public goods is a matter of collective choice. If they are provided at all, they are provided by governments and financed out of taxation. Payment is therefore spread over the whole community. An alternative would be for all the members of a community to make a voluntary agreement to provide the good and to pay for it. The problem with this approach is that some members of the community might seek to avoid payment. In effect, they would become nonparticipating passengers. This happens in neighbourhoods that hire private security firms to patrol the streets. However, because payment of taxation is compulsory, the passenger problem does not arise when public goods are provided by governments.

A lighthouse is an example of a public good. Its use by one ship as a warning against a dangerous reef does not diminish its usefulness to other ships. It is therefore clearly nonrival in consumption. It is also nonexcludable; the captain of a ship, or its owner, cannot be compelled to pay for using the lighthouse.

Merit goods are so called because they confer positive externalities on society. Merit goods do not possess the same characteristics as public goods and could easily be provided through the market. Indeed in some cases this is how they are provided. However, if the provision of merit goods is left entirely to the market they tend to be underconsumed in relation to the optimum level of consumption. The most widely quoted examples of merit goods are education and health care.

A Merit Good
Although there is no universally accepted criterion for a merit good, most people would accept that educational facilities constitute a merit good. However, because not all citizens accept the benefits of education, like most merit goods, education tends to be undersupplied in a free-market economy. This provides a need for government intervention. ▼

Measuring Economic Activity

The circular flow of income • Calculating GDP • The expenditure method •
The income and output methods • GDP, GNP, and NNP •
GNP per capita • International comparisons

The main measure of a country's economic activity is its national income or national product. This is the value of output produced over a given period, such as a year or a quarter. There are many ways of defining and calculating national income. The chief official measure of national income is the ***gross national product (GNP)***, although economists and policymakers sometimes use an alternative measure, e.g. ***gross domestic product (GDP)*** and ***net national product (NNP)***.

The Circular Flow of Income

For any economy the value of income, output, and expenditure are exactly equal. For example, when a product costing $100 is sold to a consumer, the $100 is subsequently distributed among the factors of production involved in producing and distributing it. Thus income and expenditure are different ways of looking at the same concept; the value of the output produced must be equal to the rewards paid to the factors of production creating the output. This simplified analysis ignores many of the complexities of modern economies, such as the role of international trade or the payment of taxes. Nevertheless, once allowance has been made for these complicating factors, the following basic identity remains true:
EXPENDITURE ≡ INCOME ≡ OUTPUT

This identity shows that there are three ways of measuring national income: as a flow of expenditure, as a flow of factor incomes, and as a flow of output. Each method can be used to calculate the gross domestic product.

Calculating GDP

Gross domestic product is a measure of the output an economy produces over a given period. The word 'domestic' indicates that the quantity being measured is the value of output produced within a nation's frontiers, regardless of who owns the resources used to produce that output. Some resources may be owned by one country's nationals but located in another country. This is the case with foreign subsidiaries of large corporations.

All economies produce a great variety of goods and services. To produce a figure for the value of the output of an economy it is necessary to add together the values of all the goods and services produced and assume that the price consumers are willing to pay for a product or service is a measure of its value.

National Income ►
The total national product of an economy is made up of the sum of the values of all the goods and services it produces. This diagram illustrates the conversion of trees into chairs. The tree grower sells the lumber for $30 after making a profit of $10. At all subsequent stages, payment must be made for the raw material (e.g. $60 for timber by the carpenter) and wages paid to each firm's employees. The total wage bill plus each firm's profit gives the output value of the product.

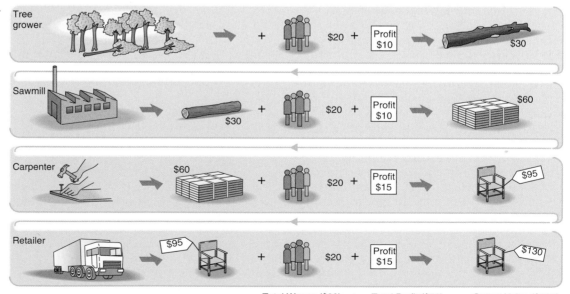

Total Wages ($80) + Total Profit ($50) = Output Value ($130)

EXPENDITURE METHOD	INCOME METHOD	OUTPUT METHOD
Personal consumption	Income from employment and self employment	Total Domestic Product
+ Gross private investment	+ Interest	= **Gross Domestic Product**
+ Government expenditure	+ Rents	+ Net Property Income
+ Exports	+ Profits	= **Gross National Product**
− Imports and transfer payments		− Depreciation
= **Gross Domestic Product**	= **Gross Domestic Product**	= **Net National Product**

Adding together the values of all of the output an economy produces over a given period may appear straightforward; however, there are several problems confronting statisticians who compile GDP statistics. There are three main ways in which GDP can be calculated: the expenditure method, the income method, and the output method.

The Expenditure Method
To calculate GDP using the expenditure method it is necessary to add together the value of total spending on **_final output_**. This is not the same as the output of each firm in the economy. Many firms produce intermediate products; i.e. output used as an **input** of some other product. If the value of intermediate output and final output are included, clearly intermediate output will then be counted twice. This is known as **_double counting_**. For example, if the GDP is calculated using both the output of the steel industry and the output of the automobile industry, then steel used in the production of automobiles will have been counted twice.

Four different types of expenditure must be added together to obtain GDP.

Personal Consumption Expenditure. This consists of spending by households on durable goods, nondurable goods, and services. It therefore includes such items of expenditure as the purchase of a new television set, a loaf of bread, and the cost of a visit to the dentist.

Gross Private Domestic Investment. This consists of all investment expenditure undertaken by private-sector firms. To economists, investment is the creation of physical output, the sole purpose of which is the production of other output. Investment therefore includes all purchases of tools, equipment, and machinery together with all construction expenditure; expenditure on the construction of residential property is included because it can be rented out. Gross investment also takes account of the change in the stocks held by all

firms. When levels of stocks increase, the amount by which their value has risen must be included because GDP measures the value of final output in the year in which it is produced, regardless of when it is sold. On the other hand, when stock levels fall, the amount of the decrease must be subtracted from the GDP because this relates to expenditure on output in an earlier accounting period.

Government Expenditure on Goods and Services. This category includes all public-sector expenditure on final output; i.e. expenditure undertaken by both central and local government. It therefore includes expenditure on such items as defence and education. However, it excludes expenditure on **_transfer payments_**, such as social security or welfare cheques given to the unemployed, because these are not expenditure on final output.

Net Exports. This is the amount spent by other nations on domestic output less the amount spent by domestic residents on foreign output. Expenditure on exports is included because exported goods and services generate incomes in the domestic economy. Conversely expenditure on imports must be excluded from calculations of national income, because imported goods and services generate incomes abroad.

The Income and Output Methods
GDP can also be calculated by adding the value of incomes received as a result of production. However, it is important to use gross incomes generated from production before deducting any tax payments. It is also important to distinguish between income generated by a productive activity and incomes derived from such state benefits as pensions or grants. These transfer payments within the community are financed by taxation. They therefore constitute a redistribution of income – payments from one section of the community to another section. Transfer payments must be excluded from the calculation of GDP because

▲ Ways of Calculating National Income
The three methods shown here – the expenditure method, the income method, and the output method – indicate the various elements that combine to give a calculation of national income. Note that GNP includes net property income from abroad, while NNP is calculated by deducting depreciation from GNP.

Measuring National Wealth

A country's wealth is not the same as its national product (however this is calculated). National wealth is estimated by conducting an audit of all the country's assets, be they physical capital or net claims on other countries. These assets are very difficult to calculate; the United Nations System of National Accounts, devised in 1968, lays down guidelines for compiling an inventory of physical capital.

newly industrializing countries (NICs)
Countries that have experienced rapid export-led economic growth since the 1970s. East Asian and Pacific Rim countries are prominent in this group. Other NICs are Brazil and Mexico.

Per Capita GNP in Latin America
Brazil and Mexico – as newly industrializing countries (NICs) – have a higher GNP per capita than some other countries on the continent. Venezuela's relative wealth is attributable to its large oil revenue. These figures are based on national statistics and relate to the early 1990s. ▼

Under *US*$500

US$500–*US*$1499

US$1500–*US*$2499

US$2500–*US*$3500

they are not made in respect of a productive activity. Four sources of income are eligible for inclusion in the GDP.

Income from Employment. This is the sum of all wages and salaries paid to employees over the course of a year. However, other benefits earned by an employee and paid by the employer must be included, such as contributions to a pension fund for the employee's benefit or health insurance payments.

Income from Self-Employment. This comprises income from unincorporated businesses. The proprietors of such businesses normally pay themselves a wage, but it is the total earnings of the business that represents its contribution to GDP.

Interest. Interest paid on loans to private-sector organizations must be included in the calculation of GDP. When money is lent to a business it is used to finance further production; interest is therefore a return to lenders on their investments. However, interest on loans to public-sector organizations is excluded from GDP calculations because public-sector organizations finance these payments from tax revenues or by further borrowing. Interest payments made by public-sector organizations are therefore a transfer payment.

Rent. In the compilation of GDP statistics, rent is regarded as a payment for the use of such assets as private homes, factories, and land.

Profits. It is necessary to include the gross trading profits of corporations as well as the gross trading surpluses of public corporations and other public-sector organizations.

A third way of calculating GDP is by adding up the output of all the sectors of the economy. Again the statisticians must take great care to avoid double counting.

GDP, GNP, and NNP

Gross domestic product is the value of the output produced within a nation's frontiers in a fixed accounting period. However, residents of one country also derive incomes by owning resources abroad. For example, people may invest abroad or own property abroad that they rent to others. The gross national product therefore refers to incomes derived from resources irrespective of where they are located.

The difference between the flows of income paid and received from abroad is referred to as ***net property income from abroad***; adding this figure to gross domestic product gives the gross national product. When the net property income from abroad is negative, the GDP is greater than GNP, whereas when net property income from abroad is positive, the GDP is less than GNP. Whether net property income from abroad is positive or negative is important because it affects the amount the residents of a nation can consume, in relation to what they produce. When net property income from abroad is positive a nation's residents can consume or invest more than they produce, because they can spend their net earnings from abroad on output produced abroad. The necessary result of this is that when net property income from abroad is negative, consumption or investment must be less than the amount currently produced. This has major implications for the standard of living.

Net National Product. During the course of a year (or any other accounting period), the value of the existing assets in an economy will depreciate. In particular, machinery will need to be replaced to take advantage of the latest technology. This implies that a portion of current output will be used to replace assets that have depreciated. In this sense the total amount an economy produces during the course of a year is less than the amount available for consumption during that year. In order to measure national income accurately, therefore, account must be taken of depreciation. Deducting depreciation from GNP yields the net national product.

Although net national product is clearly the superior measure of national income, gross national product is the most widely quoted official statistic. This is because it is impossible to measure depreciation with any accuracy. The figure used by statisticians is supplied by businesses, which owes more to tax laws than to economic logic. However, since depreciation is unlikely to change much from one period to the next, measuring national income gross rather than net is unlikely to cause serious inaccuracies.

The value of a country's output is measured in its units of currency, such as dollars or pesetas. However, the value of output changes when there is a change in the volume of production or a change in prices. When measuring changes in GNP it is only changes in the volume of production that are important. Therefore to measure changes in the volume of output from one period to another, GNP must be measured at constant prices.

▲ **Children in Mozambique** *After years of guerrilla war and drought, this southern African country, which gained its independence from Portugal in 1975, ranks among the world's poorest nations.*

GNP Per Capita

One of the major purposes for which national-income statistics are used is to provide a means of assessing changes in the standard of living in a country and for comparing its standard of living to that in other countries. The standard of living includes many variables that are difficult, if not impossible, to quantify. It is, therefore, a somewhat vague concept. For example, the extent to which the citizens of a country enjoy political freedom is an important element in their standard of living, but this is not easily measured. Economists therefore rely on ***per capita income*** to monitor and measure changes in the standard of living and to make international comparisons of living standards.

Per capita income is the GNP per head of population; the rationale for using this statistic as a standard-of-living indicator is that a major factor influencing living standards is the quantity of goods and services available for consumption. It is in this sense that GNP per capita provides a means of assessing material welfare. Despite this, economists are aware that it is a crude statistic. Changes in GNP per capita might seriously misrepresent changes in actual living standards in a particular country. The reasons for this are as follows:

The Distribution of Income. When income is distributed equally throughout a population, per capita income will be a more accurate measure of material welfare than when there is inequality in the distribution of income. It is possible for GNP per capita to remain constant between two periods but for there to be considerable change in the standard of living for most people in this period. This could be the result of a change in the distribution of income. In many developed countries during the 1980s and 1990s, income has become more

THE GNP DEFLATOR

One way of taking price changes into account is to construct an index of prices. This measures the change in price of a representative basket of goods over a period of time and using this as an average measure of price changes for the entire economy. Suppose such a basket consists of three goods, A, B, and C; between year 1 and year 2 the price of A changes from $5 to $5.50, the price of B changes from $10 to $9, and the price of C changes from $4 to $5. The table shows how the index of prices is calculated.

In Year 1, the index of prices is 300/3 = 100. In Year 2, the index of prices is 325/3 = 108.3. The implication is that between years 1 and 2 prices have, on average, increased by 8.3%. This factor can be used to measure

GNP at constant prices between years 1 and 2. Thus, GNP in Year 2 at constant Year 1 prices is given by multiplying the nominal income in Year 2 by the ratio in which prices have increased, that is, by 100/108.3. This factor is called the ***GNP deflator***.

	Year 1		*Year 2*	
	Price	*Index no.*	*Price*	*Index no.*
A	5.00	100	5.50	110
B	10.00	100	9.00	90
C	4.00	100	5.00	125

unevenly distributed; as a result, in spite of increases in real GNP, the standard of living for many people has actually fallen.

Leisure Time. Another important reason for changes in GNP per capita misrepresenting changes in the standard of living in a country is that there might have been changes in the availability of leisure time over the period. The availability of leisure time has an important bearing on the standard of living. As income rises, people often choose to work fewer hours; they may work a shorter week or they may take longer or more frequent holidays. Economists then say that they choose to consume more leisure. Measures of GNP per capita neglect the influence of leisure time on the standard of living; that is, they take no account of the hours people have to work to generate a particular level of GNP.

Environmental Considerations. Changes in the environment also have an influence on the standard of living. In the course of producing output, firms often generate ***externalities***. These are the side-effects of production that affect society generally, rather than the producers or consumers of a particular product. Society might benefit from externalities but more often they have an adverse effect. An often quoted example of an externality is acid rain, which is caused by burning fossil fuels, for example by power stations or domestic households. Acid rain results in deforestation and dead lakes as well as the erosion of buildings; this may occur in countries that burn little fossil fuel, because the sulphur that causes

Defence Spending (1994) *One example of the way in which GDP figures can be broken down into different areas of national expenditure is defence. The amount of various countries' wealth that is devoted to national security and the arms industry is shown in this chart, compiled from NATO statistics. Countries in the highly volatile region of the Middle East spend by far the greatest proportion of income on arms: Saudi Arabia has huge oil revenues, while Israel receives large amounts of aid from the USA.* ▼

PURCHASING POWER PARITIES

For purposes of international comparison it is necessary to convert GNP per capita expressed in a local currency into a common currency. The most widely used currency for this purpose is the dollar. However, exchange rates quoted on the foreign exchanges are not entirely suitable for this purpose because they are influenced by many factors, such as speculation and sentiment, which can cause quite large fluctuations; these fluctuations could undermine the value of international comparisons based on market exchange rates. When making international comparisons, economists therefore prefer to use ***purchasing power parities (PPPs)*** to calculate exchange rates. As their name suggests, PPPs attempt to measure the quantity of currency in each country required to buy a specified range of goods and services. For example, if a basket of specified foods cost $20 in the USA and 80 francs in France, then the PPP exchange rate would be $1=4 francs.

the damage is emitted during the combustion of fossil fuels and subsequently carried to other countries by clouds. Such externalities clearly have a negative effect on the standard of living; for example, because it is impossible to fish in dead lakes. Again, measures of per capita income neglect the influence of such factors on the standard of living.

International Comparisons
It is important to compare the standard of living in different countries to enable some assessment to be made of the countries in greatest need of aid or to provide a means of calculating the contribution different countries should make to international organizations, such as the International Monetary Fund. Per capita income converted into dollars by **purchasing power parities** is the most reliable technique available but it is not entirely satisfactory for several reasons.

Calculating GNP. Different countries might compile their GNP statistics according to different procedures, i.e. what is included in the GNP statistics of one country might be omitted from another. However, a more serious problem is that there might be substantial differences in the accuracy with which GNP is computed. For example, in some of the world's poorer countries a great deal of output is unrecorded, especially in rural areas where imprecise records are kept. Additionally, the

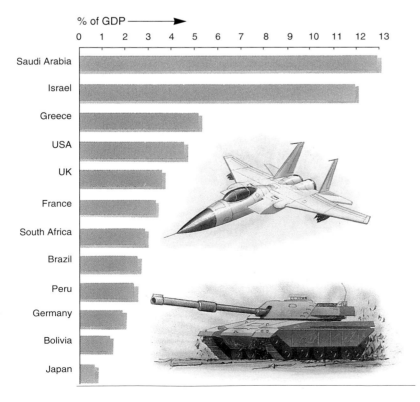

% of GDP ➡️

	0	1	2	3	4	5	6	7	8	9	10	11	12	13

Saudi Arabia
Israel
Greece
USA
UK
France
South Africa
Brazil
Peru
Germany
Bolivia
Japan

existence of an **underground economy** can make comparisons of GNP per capita an imprecise guide to relative living standards. In an underground economy transactions are carried out in cash to avoid payment of taxes. By its nature, the size of the underground economy is difficult to estimate but in many developing countries it can be as large as the legitimate economy. Even in the developed countries the underground economy can be sizeable; for example, it is thought to account for around 15% of GNP in both Italy and Sweden. The larger the underground economy, the less accurate is per capita income as a guide to living standards.

Differences in the distribution of income between countries can also reduce the accuracy of GNP per capita as a measure of relative living standards. In some countries there is considerable inequality in the distribution of income compared to others. For example, in many OPEC countries a disproportionate amount of income goes to a relatively small number of individuals. As per capita income is always a measure of average GNP, it can take no account of the actual income received by individuals.

Countries with a similar GNP per capita might have considerable differences in actual living standards as a result of differences in the range of goods and services they produce. For example, in the former Soviet Union a high proportion of GNP was spent on armaments. These resources devoted to armaments were not available for the production of other goods and services that could be consumed by the population and could have had a direct effect on the standard of living.

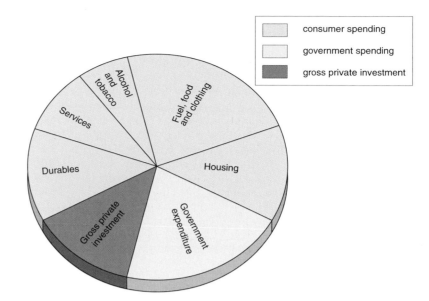

consumer spending

government spending

gross private investment

Another factor that may cause comparisons of living standards between countries to be misleading is that some countries have climatic advantages over others. For example, in certain countries fewer resources have to be devoted to heating and lighting than in those countries that cannot rely on the sun to provide these goods. Where heating and lighting are available in natural abundance the resources saved are therefore available to produce other goods and services that can add considerably to the standard of living. As a consequence two countries with a similar per capita income might have a different standard of living because one country must produce goods that are naturally available in the other country.

▲ GDP Calculated by Expenditure
The GDP of a country can be broken down as shown in this pie chart. As the average income of a country's population rises, so the proportion of the GDP spent on the basic essentials (e.g. fuel, food, and clothing) falls.

MEASURING ECONOMIC DEVELOPMENT

The world's poorest countries are often referred to as **less developed countries (LDCs)**. 'Development' is often measured in terms of the welfare of the population, often expressed in terms of its GNP per capita. However, using per capita income has serious limitations, as it focuses attention entirely on material welfare. Other factors can have a bearing on the standard of living. For example, most people would agree that the degree of political freedom of a population is important in determining its standard of living. So too are the level of crime experienced, the availability of medical care, and life expectancy. The importance of these factors suggests that the standard of living can only be measured by a social indicator that takes account of noneconomic factors as well as economic factors.

Although this idea of factoring in other considerations is by no means a new conception, it has so far proved impossible to devise such a social indicator. Apart from the problems of measuring economic welfare, it is impossible to provide an objective measure of the other variables that would need to be included in such an indicator. For example, how could the value of a reduction in the different types of crime experienced by society be assessed? How would an increase in the availability of leisure time be valued? The difficulty in measuring these factors does not diminish their importance. Economists, therefore, frequently refer to life expectancy or the number of television sets per household as measures to supplement per capita income statistics when comparing relative living standards.

Economic Forecasting

Predicting the future requirements of a country's economy is increasingly employed by governments to capitalize on a boom, or to anticipate (and forestall the worst effects of) a recession. Multinational corporations are also vitally concerned to gear company strategy to developments in the world economy. They do this by considering various outcomes in **scenario planning**.

Economic Resources

*Land • Labour • Capital • Entrepreneurship • Entrepreneurs in corporations •
Economic growth • The costs of growth*

**The Ford Motor
Works at Highland
Park, Detroit, USA**
*Henry Ford
revolutionized
industrial
manufacturing practice
by assigning each
worker on an assembly
line a specific and
limited task. Ford
adopted this practice
from Chicago meat-
packing plants. This
extreme division
of labour greatly
accelerated the
producton process
and cut costs. Here,
Model T cars are
being assembled.*

> The man who places a
> part does not fasten it;
> the man who puts in a
> bolt does not put on a
> nut; the man who puts
> on the nut does not
> tighten it.
>
> **Henry Ford** (1863-1947),
> explaining his assembly-line
> procedure

The purpose of all economic activity is to satisfy human desires. Production embraces all activities for which consumers are prepared to pay and includes the output of goods and services. However, as all goods and services are created from resources, which are in restricted supply, there is an upper limit to the amount that can be produced. Economists group resources in one of four categories, which are referred to as the ***factors of production***. These factors are land, labour, capital, and the entrepreneur.

Land

Economists define land not simply as an area of the surface of the planet; rather, it comprises all those natural resources over which land owners have control and which may be used to generate an income. The term therefore includes land used for agriculture, building, and recreational purposes. Moreover, as land is conceived of as encompassing natural resources that can produce an income, forests and lakes as well as deposits of ore and minerals must be included.

One of the principal characteristics of land is that the total supply is strictly limited. In the case of certain countries, such as the Netherlands, major reclamation and drainage projects have increased the quantity of land available, but these cannot bring about an infinite increase in the total supply of land.

Labour

Labour includes all human effort that goes into the production of goods and services, both skilled and nonskilled. It is the services of labour that are hired since firms cannot buy and sell labour in the same way as they can buy and sell capital.

The supply of labour to an economy depends on several factors; it is not only the sum total of the people available for work in an economy. It also depends on the number of hours worked. Nevertheless, the absolute size of the population of a nation is a crucial determinant of the supply of labour and sets the upper limit on its availability. If all other things are equal, the larger the population, the larger the supply of labour. The age structure of the population is also important because it is only people in certain age groups that are economically active. The minimum school-leaving age and the age of retirement set the limits on the size of the working population, although the size of the working population is also influenced by other factors. In developed countries, for example, many people remain in full-time

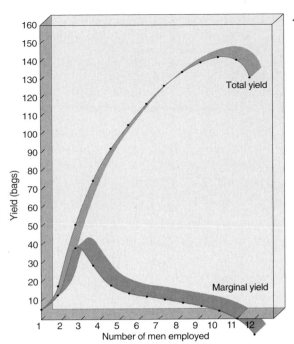

education beyond the minimum school-leaving age, while others retire early. In many countries women are not encouraged to engage in paid employment.

The number of hours worked is also important in determining the supply of labour. If 100 people work a total of 50 hours per week this is exactly equivalent in terms of labour input to 50 people working 100 hours per week. In many countries the length of the working week is regulated by the state. However, all other things being equal, the longer the working week the greater the supply of labour. In addition, the number of statutory holidays also affects the supply of labour. Here again the greater the number of statutory holidays the lower the supply of labour.

The relationship between the remuneration for employment and the quantity of labour supplied is not simple. On the one hand, it is usually argued that when rates of pay increase the supply of labour increases. However, above a certain level of pay it is possible, indeed even likely, that some sections of the population will value additional leisure more highly than additional income. If this is the case, the supply of labour will fall when incomes rise above that level.

In addition to the supply of labour, economists are also interested in the efficiency of labour. Efficiency is measured in terms of the amount produced per unit of input; here again several factors influence the efficiency of labour. One such factor is training. Developed

The Law of Diminishing Returns *The law of diminishing returns states that, as more of a variable factor of production is applied, the returns yielded by each additional unit of the variable factor will eventually decrease. In this graph, an increase in labour enables a greater crop yield to be obtained from a fixed unit of land. The marginal yield is the additional yield obtained when the labour force is increased by one. This increases sharply with extra workers, but falls as workers get in each other's way.*

economies require highly skilled workers to take advantage of the latest technologies. However, less developed countries also require a highly skilled labour force if they are to achieve developed status. Indeed, lack of adequate training is often a major obstacle to development.

One of the major factors that influence the efficiency of labour is the efficiency of the other factors of production, in particular capital. When firms use their capital to install the latest technologies, output per worker will be greater than when the workers are forced to use antiquated production techniques.

In many developed countries increasing attention has been given to the motivation of the workforce, since a highly motivated workforce will be more efficient than one that is poorly motivated. One way of increasing motivation is to encourage the workforce to have a stake in the ownership of the organization that employs them (e.g. through share issues). Another method is to offer profit-sharing schemes as part of the remuneration.

An important feature of modern production is the **division of labour**, i.e. the process of dividing the manufacturing process into a series of repetitive tasks. Many **consumer durables** are made by a process that is broken down into several hundred different operations. The main advantage of a division-of-labour policy is that it enables a massive increase in productivity to be attained, compared with what can be achieved by a single person or small group of people carrying out all of the tasks involved in producing a product. Division of labour has created a higher standard of living than would

THE DIVISION OF LABOUR

The earliest recorded exposition of the theory of the division of labour occurs in the economist and philosopher Adam Smith's book, *An Inquiry into the Nature and Causes of the Wealth of Nations* (1776). Here he describes the effect of division of labour on pin (nail) making. "But the way in which this business is now carried on... it is divided into a number of branches... .One man draws out the wire, another straightens it, a third cuts it, a fourth points, a fifth grinds it at the top for receiving the head; to make the head requires two or three distinct operations; to put it on is a peculiar business, to whiten the pins is another; it is even a trade by itself to put them into the paper." Smith noted that when a single person carried out all of the operations in pin-making, a worker might produce an average of about twenty pins per day. However, when the process was broken down in the way described, average production rose to a total of about 4800 pins per day!

consumer durables
Products whose useful life extends over a relatively long period. Such consumer goods are cars, washing machimes, etc. *Consumer nondurables* are goods that are exhausted shortly after purchase.

otherwise have been possible. There are many reasons why the division of labour increases productivity:

- People specializing in a single task or small group of tasks become highly proficient, which leads to increases in productivity;
- It is not necessary for workers to move from one machine to another or to break from production to fetch tools or spare parts;
- When production is broken down into a small number of tasks it is possible to design the most efficient machinery and equipment to carry out production. For example, it is impossible to design a machine that could produce a complete automobile, but it is easy to design a series of machines that could be used in the production of a motor car. The increased use of machinery is undoubtedly the main reason for the division of labour leading to an increase in productivity.

Capital

Capital is any aid to production that has been created from scarce resources. It therefore includes machinery, factory buildings, and tools. Capital goods are distinguished from consumer goods by the purpose for which they are used. For example, an automobile that is used by a family for social and domestic purposes is regarded as a consumer good, whereas an automobile used by a commercial traveller to sell and promote his product is considered a capital good. Large capital assets owned by a nation constitute **social capital**.

Capital Accumulation. It is important to distinguish between capital and investment. Investment is the rate at which the capital stock is changing. Since a nation has only a limited amount of resources at any time, an increase in investment is only possible if an economy produces less than the potential maximum amount for consumption. Economists regard capital accumulation (investment) as being dependent on abstention from current consumption, i.e. that resources used for one purpose cannot simultaneously be used for another purpose. Another way of stating this is to say that investment has an opportunity cost. If society produces more capital goods, it foregoes the opportunity of producing more consumer goods. This has implications for the standard of living. When more resources are devoted to the production of capital goods, if there are no unemployed resources in the economy, fewer consumer goods can be produced. Since, by definition, the output of consumer goods adds directly to current living standards, any reduction in the output of consumer goods will adversely affect these standards. However, since capital is an aid to production, an increase in the rate of investment will make it possible to produce more consumer goods in the future.

Capital Consumption. Just as it is possible for nations to accumulate capital by investment, so it is possible to reduce the capital stock by disinvestment. As capital depreciates over time, disinvestment occurs when a nation fails to invest sufficient resources to maintain its existing capital stock. Again, this has implications for the future standard of living, because as the capital stock falls a nation will be able to produce fewer and fewer consumer goods.

> **social capital** Major capital assets, such as a country's road and rail network, sewerage system, electricity grid, stock of schools and hospitals, and so on. These assets are often referred to as a nation's *infrastructure*.

THE PRODUCTION POSSIBILITY FRONTIER

When there are unemployed resources in an economy, actual output is below potential output. The production possibility frontier describes the optimal use of resources. Certain kinds of resources are more efficient at producing one type of good than another type. So, as more of one type is produced, society draws increasingly on resources that are less suited to the production of this type in favour of the other. If society currently produces OA consumer goods and OB capital goods, the economy will be located at point X. If the output of capital goods is increased to OC, the maximum amount of consumer goods that can be produced is OD, when the economy will be located at point Y.

Therefore, if a society is using resources optimally, production of one type of good cannot be increased without decreasing production of the other.

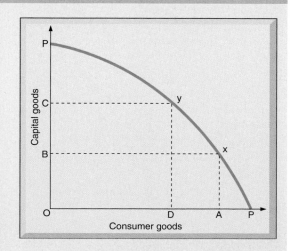

▲ **The Production Possibility Frontier**
The curve PP shows the production possibilities open to a society given existing resources and technology.

Entrepreneurship

The fourth factor of production, entrepreneurship, adds risk-taking and organizational dimensions to the production process. Traditionally these are the functions of the entrepreneur; however, it might be argued that since the functions of entrepreneurs are performed by human beings, they should not be distinguished from labour as a factor of production. Most economists would now agree that entrepreneurs have a special role that distinguishes them from labour. Nevertheless, as the predictions of mainstream economic theory can be derived without reference to the entrepreneur as a factor of production, the entrepreneur has received relatively little attention in economic theory.

The Functions of the Entrepreneur. Economists have identified a risk-taking role for the entrepreneur. In the earliest definitions it was argued that the entrepreneur is motivated by profit and is identified as a person who has the foresight and willingness to take risks in order to achieve these profits. Conventionally, it was argued that entrepreneurs take risks by using their own funds, supplemented as necessary by borrowing, to finance production. They do so with the intention of making a profit but are aware that there is an element of uncertainty in their operations, which includes the real risk that they will make a loss.

This approach is limited because it does not specify the nature of the risks that an entrepreneur undertakes. A more modern view distinguishes between insurable risks and noninsurable uncertainty. If it is possible to calculate the probability of a certain event occurring it is, in general, possible to insure against it. Thus, the insurance markets provide the entrepreneur with the opportunity of transferring certain risks onto another party (the insurer). These risks include those arising as a result of fire or theft, the probability of which can be calculated. However, some risks, by their nature, are so uncertain that it is not possible to measure the probability that they will occur. In particular, there are so many factors that might lead to business success or failure, including an element of luck, that it is impossible to predict with any degree of certainty whether or not a business venture will succeed.

Many of the noninsurable uncertainties to which the entrepreneur is exposed arise as a result of the time lags in production; this means that decisions taken in the present refer to the output of goods in the future. Risk arises because of unforeseen changes that can occur in the interim. For example, there may be changes in household circumstances, costs of production, or business confidence (perhaps because of political change or the threat of war). It is part of the entrepreneur's function to bear these uninsurable risks. In a successful business the entrepreneur is rewarded with profit; in an unsuccessful business the entrepreneur is left to stand the resulting losses.

This approach is important because it distinguishes between entrepreneurship and management. However, later economists have also emphasized the importance of the entrepreneur as an innovator in addition to his role as a risk-taker. This aspect of the entrepreneur's function sees the entrepreneur as one who overturns established approaches and introduces new techniques or new technologies so that established products can be produced in new ways. The entrepreneur may also use new techniques or technologies to introduce new products, to open up a new source of supply, or to establish a new outlet.

The implication is that the most talented entrepreneurs are the pioneers of innovation, creating by their success a following of less talented entrepreneurs. This creates a wave of innovation and encourages economic progress. While it is true that the less talented entrepreneurs bear less risk than the most talented, risk-bearing is still an important part of their function.

Entrepreneurs in Corporations

Whatever criteria are used, it is easy to identify the person or persons who perform the role of the entrepreneur in a sole proprietorship or a partnership. However, in a modern corporation where the owners of the company are the shareholders, who take little part in the day-to-day running of the corporation, it is hard to identify the entrepreneur because day-to-day control is in the hands of salaried managers. There is therefore a divorce between ownership and control of the organization. The shareholders, as owners, risk losing the value of their investment in the event of business failure. However, decisions about production and marketing are taken by people who often have no stake in the ownership of the organization and who are paid for taking decisions. In large organizations, therefore, the entrepreneurial function is split between different groups.

Economic Growth

Economic growth is defined as an increase in the gross national product (GNP) of a country at constant prices that is not directly attributable to a reduction in employment. When a country experiences economic growth it has the potential to increase the volume of output available to the population. However, in practice it is difficult to measure economic growth on the basis of this definition; economic growth is often taken to mean an increase in

▲ **Alfred Krupp**
(1812–87) A leading entrepreneur of the 19th century, Krupp expanded the iron and steel business created by his father into a huge industrial empire. The rise of the firm began with the construction of railways in Prussia. The profit and technology generated by making rails and wheels enabled Krupp to move into the production of armaments, for which the company became renowned; Alfred Krupp became known as 'The Cannon King.'

Entrepreneurs in Decline

Many families that prospered through a forebear's boldness and flair for innovation become too cautious with their accumulated wealth to sustain the entrepreneurial spirit. As a result, many descendents of 19th-century entrepreneurs ended up as politicians or academics. Another danger for successful entrepreneurs is that competitors may surpass the technology they pioneered. Innovators are often vulnerable to those who follow their lead.

This company – an electronics firm – is one of many maquiladoras, *enterprises set up in Mexico by foreign-owned businesses that profit from duty-free components and low labour costs. These factories boomed in the 1980s, introducing more modern technologies and manufacturing processes to Mexico, and helping to develop Mexican managerial and entrepreneurial talent.*

Production Sectors

Economic theory distinguishes between three sectors of production.

• *Primary production* describes such economic activities as agriculture, mining, forestry, etc.

• *Secondary production* is the manufacture of goods, buildings, etc, from raw materials.

• *Tertiary production* defines the services provided by financial institutions, transport companies, and the professions.

GNP at constant prices. This has major implications for the standard of living and is therefore an important objective of economic policy.

Causes. There are many factors that can cause an increase in economic growth. Clearly, it would increase in a community if there was an increase in the number of talented entrepreneurs. However, the particular talents required by an entrepreneur are not easy to develop. In some countries governments have initiated enterprise schemes, which aim to train individuals in opening and running small businesses. In other countries grants are provided to reduce the risk of starting a business. However, there is no standard procedure for promoting entrepreneurship. Five other factors are important in stimulating economic growth.

Increased Training. The skills of the labour force are an important factor influencing economic growth. A skilled labour force is a more productive labour force for several reasons. In particular, it enables firms to take full advantage of the latest technological advances.

Size of the Market. A large and expanding market enables firms to grow and exploit economies of scale. Economies of scale reduce the cost of producing a given output; i.e. the average cost falls as output expands. There might be several reasons for this. For example, firms might be able to buy inputs in bulk or make better use of the division of labour. Whatever the reason, if the average cost is falling, output per unit of input (i.e. productivity) is rising.

Investment. Capital can be many times more efficient than labour in increasing output and therefore increased investment might provide an important stimulus to economic growth. However, the effect of increased investment on economic growth depends on the type of investment made. In any particular

economy an increase in certain types of social capital, such as schools and hospitals, is unlikely to have a significant effect on economic growth. On the other hand, increased investment in road and rail networks or new machinery might very well encourage greater economic growth. Clearly a country's infrastructure is an important element in its ability to expand its economy.

Technological Advances. A major factor influencing economic growth is the rate of technological advance. New technologies are invariably superior to older technologies; they embrace improvements to existing machinery, the design of new machinery, and more efficient organization of production, as well as better marketing. To some extent technological progress depends on investment, although increased investment does not always guarantee that it will take place.

Resource Reallocation. Economic growth can be increased if resources can be transferred from low-productivity sectors to high-productivity sectors. Historically, relatively rapid rates of economic growth have been achieved when countries industrialized and transferred resources from the agricultural sector to the manufacturing and tertiary sectors. The economies of eastern Europe can be expected to achieve economic growth over the next few decades if they can transfer resources from low-growth sectors to high-growth sectors. However, once resources have been transferred to high-growth sectors their importance as a source of future growth disappears. In other words, a transfer of this kind is not a long-term source of economic growth.

The Costs of Growth

While economic growth is an important objective of economic policy, economists sometimes focus their attention on the costs of this growth. Increased investment can sometimes be a source of economic growth; however, there is an opportunity cost associated with this source of economic growth because increased investment involves a cut in current consumption. To many this might seem an acceptable situation, but for the older members of a community, who might not live long enough to reap the benefits of increased investment, a different view might be expected.

In spite of this aspect, the main costs associated with economic growth are undoubtedly the environmental costs. Economic growth involves increased exploitation of natural resources, which might result in environmental degradation. Clearly, externalities are sometimes generated as a result of production. Greater economic growth might well lead to an increase in the incidence of externalities, such as the pollution caused by the dumping

◄ **Destruction of the Rainforest** *Despoiling of the environment, such as the large-scale deforestation of the Amazonian rainforest to create grazing land, is one of the costs of economic growth that is coming under greater scrutiny as the earth's resources dwindle.*

of waste materials or loss of the countryside as natural resources are exploited. During the 1970s and 1980s, rainforests disappeared at an alarming rate. This has resulted in soil erosion and seriously reduced the productivity of the surrounding countryside.

In some cases externalities might have other serious consequences. With the disintegration of the former Soviet Union and its eastern European client states at the beginning of the 1990s, it emerged that dangerous procedures had been adopted in the disposal of toxic waste. This was motivated by the need to reduce costs in order to increase growth. Pollution had been allowed to spread unchecked in areas with a high concentration of heavy industry, such as Copsa Mica in Romania and

Bitterfeld in East Germany. Nor were these the only countries that were guilty of inflicting environmental damage in their quest for growth. Modern farming techniques in developed countries have led to vast increases in the productivity of land but have had a disastrous effect on wildlife. The growing number of vehicles has created increased road congestion. Yet it has also produced or aggravated a number of severe environmental problems, including pollution by lead compounds, dangers to the ozone layer from increased emissions of carbon dioxide, and the ravages caused by acid rain. Nevertheless, while economic growth clearly has its advantages and its drawbacks, it does usually enable the adverse consequences of growth to be held in check or even reversed.

Country	1988	1989	1990	1991	1992	1993
Argentina	-1.9	-6.2	0.1	8.9	8.7	6.0
Brazil	—	3.3	-4.4	0.9	-0.9	5.0
Czechoslovakia	2.3	0.7	-3.5	-20.2	-9.0	—
France	4.5	4.3	2.5	0.7	1.2	-1.1
Japan	6.2	4.8	4.8	4.1	1.5	0.4
Spain	5.2	4.7	3.7	2.3	1.0	-1.1
Sweden	2.3	2.4	1.4	-1.7	-1.7	-3.0
United Kingdom	4.9	2.1	0.6	-2.3	-0.4	1.8
USA	3.9	2.5	0.8	-0.7	2.6	2.6

◄ **Economic Growth in Selected Countries** *Percentage increases in real GDP are given in these International Monetary Fund (IMF) figures.*

Goals of Economic Policy

Instruments of policy • Macroeconomic objectives • Inflation • The balance of payments • The rate of exchange • Postwar economics • The new international order • The influence of GATT • Multinational enterprises • Overseas aid

---

The Objectives of Macroeconomic Policy

To maintain:
• low unemployment
• low inflation
• satisfactory economic growth
• a viable balance of payments
• desirable currency exchange rates
• an acceptable income distribution

In a market economy there is no guarantee that the actions of economic agents either inside or outside an economy will combine to produce an economically, politically, and socially acceptable outcome. As a result governments are required to adopt policies that exert a measure of control over their respective economies. In broad terms these may be divided into **microeconomic policies** and **macroeconomic policies**. Whereas the microeconomic policies are concerned with specific groups of society or specific industries, macroeconomic policies aim to influence the whole sweep of the economy.

Instruments of Policy

There are four main **instruments** at the disposal of governments seeking to impose macroeconomic policies: fiscal policy, monetary policy, exchange-rate policy, and supply-side policy (plus two minor instruments). There is, however, some doubt as to what constitutes a policy objective and a policy instrument. For example, in the postwar era governments have sometimes set a particular rate of exchange for their currency as a policy objective. Yet on other occasions they manipulated the exchange rate as a policy instrument in order to achieve some other objective, such as control of the balance of payments.

The relationship between policy instruments and the objectives they are intended to achieve is complicated not only by the uncertainty that characterizes all economic relationships but also by several economic, political, and institutional constraints. Economic constraints

emerge when two variables have opposing effects. For example, an increase in the money supply may encourage economic activity at home in the short term, while in the longer term it creates an inflationary spiral that could make it harder for a country to compete abroad. Moreover, political considerations rather than economic foresight often play a determining role in formulating government policies. Institutional constraints can also influence a government's decisions. Many countries are bound by international agreements, ranging from the European Union (EU) to more global organizations, such as the General Agreement on Tariffs and Trade (GATT).

A decisive occurrence that demonstrated the need for governments to play an active role in managing their economies was the rapid growth in world unemployment during the late 1920s and 1930s, an era known as the Great Depression. The response of many governments was to pursue protectionist policies, such as the erection of trade barriers, which led to a massive decline in world trade. Ironically, these policies exacerbated the

---

THE INSTRUMENTS OF MACROECONOMIC POLICY

Fiscal Policy The use of government spending and taxation to control the level of aggregate demand.

Monetary Policy The management of interest rates and the rate of growth of the money supply to control economic activity.

Exchange-Rate Policy Intervention in the money markets to influence currency exchange rates and hence the balance of payments.

Supply-Side Policy Measures to increase output and efficiency in the economy, including curbs on restrictive trade-union activities, a reduction in the real value of welfare payments, and the provision of investment grants, training grants, and tax incentives.

Prices and Incomes Policy The use of statutory and/or voluntary measures to restrain increases in both prices and incomes.

Import Controls Restrictions on imports by means of tariffs and quotas.

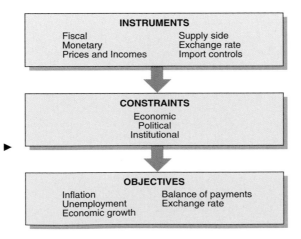

INSTRUMENTS
Fiscal	Supply side
Monetary	Exchange rate
Prices and Incomes	Import controls

CONSTRAINTS
Economic
Political
Institutional

OBJECTIVES
Inflation	Balance of payments
Unemployment	Exchange rate
Economic growth	

Factors in Macroeconomics
Instruments of government policy are subject to various constraints in achieving objectives.

JOHN MAYNARD KEYNES

After World War I, Keynes became one of the advisers to the UK government during the Versailles peace conference. Feeling that the Treaty of Versailles placed too much emphasis upon German reparations and too little on the need for European reconstruction, he resigned and returned to Cambridge University. Keynes's controversial book *The Economic Consequences of the Peace* (1919) assured him an international reputation.

In the 1920s Keynes advocated the need for governments to manage a **budget deficit** to provide the funds to create employment. This view opposed official thinking, which emphasized the role of free markets and the need for balanced budgets. However, during the early 1930s, Western governments attempted to alleviate unemployment through public works programmes, such as President Roosevelt's New Deal in the USA. Keynes's book *The General Theory of Employment, Interest and Money* (1936) provided the theoretical basis for these programmes.

Keynes was not a socialist. He attempted to provide a remedy for the shortcomings of capitalism, rather than to destroy it.

▲ **John Maynard Keynes** *Keynes's work had a considerable influence on the economic policies of many governments.*

> **budget deficit** A situation in which government expenditure exceeds government income (e.g. through taxation). Keynes argued that governments should use deficits in times of recession in order to stimulate demand and combat unemployment.

unemployment problem they were intended to alleviate. For two and a half decades after World War II, macroeconomic policymaking in most industrialized countries reflected the work of the British economist **John Maynard Keynes** (1883–1946). Both before and during the Great Depression, he had advocated expansionary government spending to pull an economy out of recession. To a large extent, his recommendations were ignored in Europe, but President Roosevelt's New Deal was based on them; indeed Keynes became Roosevelt's principal adviser.

By the end of World War II, however, many other Western governments had become convinced that explicit intervention could play a significant role in postwar reconstruction. Memories of the problems that had emerged during the interwar period encouraged governments to pursue the macroeconomic objective of trying to ensure that the economy was operating at full employment. At the same time most governments accepted the need to promote international trade. The key instrument in this process was fiscal policy.

Inflation at this time was not perceived as a significant problem, though by the early 1960s it clearly needed corrective action. Although governments continued to pursue their own domestic objectives, during the postwar period they also made determined efforts to encourage global cooperation with the goal of promoting worldwide economic growth. Examples of this cooperation include a unified system of international currency exchange, the gradual removal of tariff barriers, more formalized systems of economic integration (such as the European Union), and the promotion of growth and development in Third World economies through the World Bank.

Macroeconomic Objectives

Of the six main **objectives of macroeconomic policy**, perhaps the most important is the maintenance of low unemployment through the creation of jobs.

Unemployment. The existence of a certain amount of unemployment in a country is inevitable as people change jobs and as resources are allocated from declining sectors of an economy to expanding sectors. This is known as the ***natural rate of unemployment***. Unemployment emerges as a serious economic problem when it is caused by a general downswing in economic activity or as the result of a declining industry. Unemployment imposes a number of economic costs upon an economy and its population. First, if a country's labour force is not fully employed productively, it is foregoing output that could be sold abroad to earn foreign exchange. Furthermore, the unemployed part of the labour

> The important thing for government is not to do things which individuals are doing already, and to do them a little better or a little worse; but to do those things which at present are not done at all.
>
> **John Maynard Keynes,** *The End of Laissez-Faire* (1926)

International
Inflation Figures
*In this table, compiled
from figures issued by
the International
Monetary Fund (IMF),
the huge fluctuation in
inflation that can affect
a country is illustrated.
Newly developing
countries, such as
Brazil, are particularly
prone to inflation rises,
due to heavy
international borrowing
to finance economic
expansion. All figures
are given in percentages.*

Country	1988	1989	1990	1991	1992	1993
Argentina	343.0	3079.0	2314.0	171.0	25.0	11.0
Brazil	682.0	1287.0	2937.0	440.0	1008.0	2000.0
Czechoslovakia	0.1	1.4	10.0	57.8	12.0	—
France	2.7	3.6	3.4	3.2	2.4	2.1
Japan	0.7	2.2	3.1	3.3	1.8	1.2
Spain	4.8	6.8	6.7	5.9	5.9	4.5
Sweden	5.8	6.4	10.5	9.4	2.2	4.7
United Kingdom	4.9	7.8	9.5	5.9	3.7	1.9
USA	4.1	4.8	5.4	4.2	3.0	3.0

force is unable to buy the goods and services produced by those domestic industries that create employment. Secondly, the government loses the tax revenues paid by those in work while it has to make welfare payments to the unemployed and their families. This may curtail public spending in other areas and increase taxation of those in employment. Moreover, many firms invest heavily in training their employees. If they are laid off, their knowledge is likely to depreciate when it is left unused. Not only do firms lose the value of their investment in training but as depreciation increases, unemployed labour will find it increasingly difficult to find work.

The experiences of many countries during the interwar years convinced governments that combating unemployment should be given the highest priority after World War II.

From 1945 until the early 1970s governments, largely in accordance with the work of Keynes, intervened actively in their economies in an attempt to maintain unemployment at an acceptable level. Specifically, when economic activity was thought to be insufficient to prevent unemployment from rising, governments increased their spending and reduced taxes to stimulate economic activity. The objective was to generate extra jobs, raise incomes, and reduce the payment of unemployment benefits. However, from the late 1960s, governments began to turn away from attempts to stimulate the economy in this way as they were faced with the new threats posed by increasing and persistent inflation.

Inflation
Inflation is the rise in prices that reduces the purchasing power of a nominal sum of money. The inflation figures reported in newspapers or on the television are usually based on the change in the price of a selected number of goods and services, over a specified period – often one year. More specialized inflation figures that relate to specific groups of products, such as construction materials or medical items, also exist although these are reported less widely. The composition and relative weighting of the items in a basket can vary from country to country, yet this does not stop international comparisons being made. The variation in inflation rates between countries over the same period can be extremely wide.

When analysing inflation, economists often make a distinction between **anticipated inflation** and **unanticipated inflation**. If all inflation is anticipated then markets can still function, since economic agents can build future price changes into their dealings.

**Unemployed
Workers in Detroit,
Michigan, USA
(1982)** *During the
1970s and 1980s,
unemployment rose in
many countries,
approaching levels not
experienced since the
Great Depression of the
1930s.* ▼

Conversely, if a large proportion of inflation is unanticipated, the market mechanism may not operate effectively because price signals become inconsistent. This is not to say that anticipated inflation does not matter. Inflation, whatever its source, imposes costs upon individuals since it reduces the purchasing power of a fixed sum of money over a particular period. For example, an inflation rate of 5% will mean that a sum of $100 at the beginning of a year will buy roughly $95 worth of goods and services at the end of it. Some of this loss may be avoided by using an interest-bearing bank account or even by some form of speculation. However, the need to have a certain amount of cash available to finance day-to-day transactions means that everyone will incur losses in an inflationary period. If inflation rates are high, firms or households may need to engage in transactions or renegotiate contracts more frequently, which is another cost imposed by an inflationary environment.

Inflation can also affect the ability of countries to trade abroad. Economies experiencing high rates of inflation are likely to find themselves at a disadvantage when trading with countries with low inflation rates. Unless a high-inflation country can produce superior products, it will find that the number of markets in which it can compete will diminish; this will reduce its income from exports. Thus, high-inflation economies are more likely to experience balance-of-payments difficulties as exports fall and imports rise, unless remedial action is taken. One option in these circumstances is to allow the home currency to depreciate in value against that of its competitors, so that exports are cheaper to buy abroad. However, this solution does not solve the underlying cause of the problem, particularly if the home industry is dependent upon

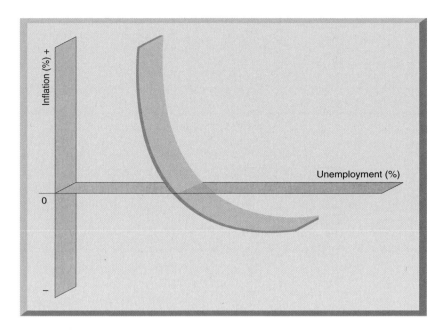

▲ **Phillips Curve**
The work of A. W. H. Phillips led to the conclusion that when inflation was running at a high rate, unemployment tended to be low, and vice versa. This relationship, seen in this generalized graph, was later shown not to be valid.

imports, which will now have risen in price. Moreover, a lack of confidence in depreciated currencies on the part of currency-market dealers may cause further depreciation.

Until the 1960s, inflation was not a significant international problem. Prompted by the empirical research of A. W. H. Phillips (1914–75) in the late 1950s, which postulated an inverse link between inflation and unemployment, it was believed that an increase in inflation was a direct result of governments seeking to maintain low levels of unemployment. This relationship was subsequently expressed in the ***Phillips curve*** (see illustration). Governments had a choice: to confront the increase in inflation at the expense of higher unemployment or to promote high employment and allow inflation to increase. In countries with strong economies, such as West Germany and the USA, emphasis was given to the control of inflation, whereas countries with weaker economies, such as the UK, tried to promote employment, at the same time using a prices and incomes policy to suppress the resulting inflationary pressures.

However, during the 1960s and early 1970s, inflation had emerged as a significant problem for many industrialized economies. It soon became clear that it was not possible to attribute this increase to any single factor. By 1968, other economists, such as **Milton Friedman** (1912–   ), were arguing persuasively that the Phillips curve relationship had broken down. In their view, any attempt to hold unemployment below its natural rate would create ever accelerating rates of inflation. With Keynesian policies appearing unable to avert an increase in unemployment and the containment of inflation emerging as the major international problem, this new

THE CAUSES OF INFLATION

Demand-pull inflation arises from variables that create an increase in aggregate demand, principally:
• an increase in the money supply
• an increase in spending by households, firms, and government. Demand-pull inflation can be summarized as 'too much money chasing too few goods'
Cost-push inflation arises when there are increases in the costs of production that do not reflect changes in demand conditions, principally:
• increases in wages brought about by trade unions
• increases in import prices, such as the rise in oil prices by OPEC (1973–74)

Inflation in the 1980s

In the 1980s, inflation was a major problem in many parts of the world. In Israel, a car costing 4.5 million shekels in September 1984 cost over 6 million by early November.
The price of flour in Bolivia rose by over 50 000% between late 1982 and early 1985. During the same period, the cost of a visit to the doctor rose by some 150 000%.

MILTON FRIEDMAN

Friedman's defence of the classical principles of free markets stands in opposition to the interventionist measures of John Maynard Keynes. Professor of Economics at the University of Chicago, Friedman was awarded the Nobel Prize for Economics in 1976.

Friedman was responsible for resurrecting the Quantity Theory of Money, which identifies a causal link between the growth of the money supply and the rate of inflation. Macroeconomic policy in many Western countries in the 1960s was guided by Keynesian principles and a belief in the Phillips curve. Friedman suggested that although governments may be able to increase spending and reduce unemployment in the short term, this policy would have no long-term impact on unemployment but would add to inflationary pressure by increasing the supply of money in the economy.

With a breakdown in the Phillips-curve relationship in the 1970s, there was a move away from Keynesian economics and greater emphasis on the control of inflation and the need to allow markets to operate more flexibly. Friedman's stress on reducing government expenditure and promoting individual responsibility was highly influential.

Milton Friedman *Despite his criticism of the welfare state, Friedman is an advocate of the concept of a minimum income.* ▶

approach became increasingly attractive. Known as ***monetarism***, it stressed the need to control the rate of growth of the money supply and to reduce government spending.

The theory that underpins much of present-day thinking on inflation is known as the ***Quantity Theory of Money***, usually credited to the US political economist Irving Fisher (1867–1947). The theory identifies a direct causal relationship between the growth of money supply and the rate at which prices increase; in its purest form the theory predicts that a doubling of the money supply will bring about a doubling of the price level. Despite its relatively long history, the theory has only become a popular basis for macroeconomic policy since its reformulation by Milton Friedman in the 1950s and 1960s. Friedman noted that periods of rising inflation in the US economy seemed to be linked to expansions of the money supply. Indeed, this relationship has been a feature of other high-inflation economies. Thus, according to Friedman and his followers, the policy instruments intended to control inflation should include a strategy to contain the growth of the money supply. This approach has been the basis of the macroeconomic policies pursued by many industrialized countries since the mid-1970s.

The Balance of Payments

A country's balance-of-payments account records all the transactions it undertakes in a given period with the rest of the world. The value of exported goods and services, dividend payments from abroad, and inward investment by foreigners are credited to the account, as each of these items involves a flow of currency into a country. Conversely, the value of imported goods and services, dividend payments made to foreigners, and outward investment by home investors in other countries are debited to the account, as they cause a flow of currency out of the country.

Inflation in Germany (1923) ▶ *Massive inflation occurred when the German mark collapsed under the strain of war reparations. So extreme was the problem that people had to pay huge sums for basic commodities.*

Balance-of-payments accounts are usually presented under a number of headings. The major division is between the **current account** and the **capital account**. The current account has two subdivisions: the **visible account** documents the trade in physical goods, while the **invisible account** identifies trade in the service sector, such as tourism, banking, and insurance. On the other hand, the capital account identifies any transactions involving a flow of investments. For example, investment by a Japanese multinational firm in Brazil is included on the credit side of Brazil's capital account but as a debit in Japan's capital account. Similarly, a foreigner choosing to deposit funds in a Brazilian bank emerges as a credit item for Brazil's capital account, whereas investment by Brazilians in a foreign bank account is a debit. Clearly, where money is invested will usually depend on the relative rates of interest in the world economy. If interest rates are high in Spain, relative to those elsewhere in the world, investors might choose to invest in Spanish banks. Thus, by controlling interest rates, a government can manipulate investment flows entering and leaving the country.

If a country's overall credits exceed its overall debits, its balance of payments is said to be in **surplus**, whereas if the opposite is true, it is said to be in **deficit**. A country can be in credit for certain items in its balance-of-payments account (e.g. its visible balance), but have a deficit on another item (e.g. part of its capital

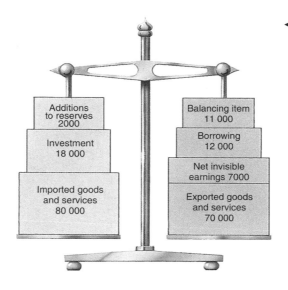

◀ **Balance of Payments** *The debit side of a country's balance-of-payments account is on the left-hand side of the scales, the credit side on the right.*

account). If a person spends more than he or she earns, savings are drawn upon; when capital is exhausted debts are incurred. A balance-of-payments deficit can have similar effects; national currency reserves are reduced and international debts accumulated. For this reason, a long-term balance-of-payments deficit is not regarded as an acceptable outcome of macroeconomic policy.

The Rate of Exchange

Currencies are traded in international markets like any other good or service. All currency markets are interrelated: dollars to sterling,

◀ **The Port of Hamburg, Germany** *Throughout the world, exports of physical goods are shipped from major ports such as this.*

Exchange Rate Graphs *Graph* **A** *assumes that currency-exchange rates are determined by market forces (known as a **freely floating system**). Graph* **B** *assumes that the government intervenes in the market to maintain a **fixed rate of exchange**.*

▶

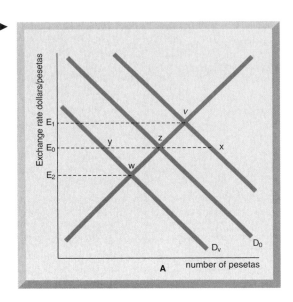

dollars to francs, francs to lire, lire to dollars, yen to dollars, yen to francs, and so on. In a free market, the value at which one currency can be sold for another therefore depends upon the demand for and supply of each currency. Persistent fluctuations in the exchange rate can cause uncertainty and discourage firms from taking risks in the international market. For example, if a Spanish firm wishes to quote for building a power station in Chile, it will need to have some confidence in the stability of the relationship between the Spanish peseta and the Chilean peso. Many of those it employs to construct the power station will be locals, who will need to be paid in Chilean pesos. In preparing a quotation for the work,

the Spanish firm must be sure that it can buy the pesos at a known rate. If the exchange rate is expected to fluctuate widely, the Spanish construction firm will either regard the project as too great a financial risk, or it will need to buy pesos on the forward-exchange market.

In a market known to fluctuate, this will be very expensive. In either case the instability of the exchange rate acts as a disincentive to the normal flow of international trade. Many governments therefore intervene in currency markets in an attempt to stabilize exchange-rate fluctuations. Sometimes this intervention is part of a formal agreement, such as the system that emerged from the Bretton Woods Agreement, which operated from the end of World War II until 1973. Alternatively, governments may intervene autonomously in the market in order to iron out any fluctuations that might otherwise occur.

Determining Exchange Rates. The exchange rate is the price at which one currency is exchanged for another. For example, it might be assumed that 100 Spanish pesetas can be exchanged for 0.8 US dollars. On this assumption, if a bottle of sherry costs 500 pesetas in Spain, it would cost $4 in the USA. However, if the value of the peseta falls against the dollar so that 100 pesetas only buys $0.50, the dollar price of sherry would fall, to a price of $2.50. Similarly, if the value of the peseta rises so that 100 pesetas buy $1, the same bottle of sherry would cost $5. If the cost of Spanish sherry falls in the USA, one would expect, everything held constant, that more sherry would be bought by Americans, which would create a greater demand for pesetas to buy the larger supplies.

This describes only one side of the market. However, just as Americans are able to buy goods and services from Spain, so Spaniards also buy goods and services from the USA. If

Currency Exchange Rates *A board in a bureau de change – usually situated in a bank or the office of a travel agent – gives the rates at which foreign currency is bought and sold.*

▶

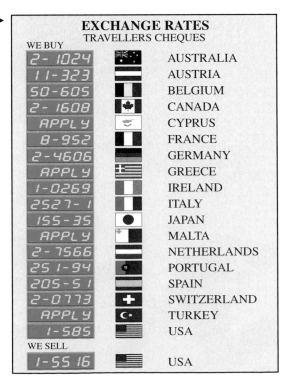

the value of the peseta is high, relative to the dollar, American goods will be relatively cheap and in greater demand. Similarly, if the value of the peseta falls relative to the dollar, US goods and services will become more expensive and Spaniards will reduce their demand for US products and, therefore, for dollars.

This situation is shown on two graphs (see diagram). In both graphs, the demand curve X_0 denotes the initial demand for pesetas by Americans wishing to buy Spanish goods. Conversely, the supply curve S_0 depicts the initial supply of pesetas determined by Spaniards purchasing American goods.

If exchange rates are allowed to float freely, as in graph **A**, the equilibrium exchange rate (E_0) is determined by the intersection of these two curves. If more Spanish sherry is bought at a particular price in the USA, the demand curve will shift to the right from D_0 to D_1. Thus, the change in tastes of the US public leads to an increase in the value of the Spanish peseta. On the other hand, if there is an increase in the demand for American goods by the Spanish public, this will cause a shift in the supply curve of pesetas to the right from S_0 to S_1. If the demand curve remains unaltered, this will cause the exchange rate to fall from E_0 to E_2.

However, if the Spanish government intervenes in the currency market to maintain its rate of exchange with the dollar at E_0, the situation is shown on graph **B**. If, again, Americans buy more sherry, there will be a

shift to the right in the demand curve. Under a freely floating system, there would be a new equilibrium exchange rate at E_1. However, at the predetermined rate of exchange of E_0, there is an excess demand for pesetas equal to the distance ZX. In order to preserve the rate of exchange E_0, the additional pesetas will need to be printed and these will be sold for dollars at E_0. These dollars then become part of the foreign reserves held by the Spanish central bank. If the demand for Spanish goods falls on the US market, the demand curve for pesetas would shift to the left from D_0 to D_2. This time there is a market pressure for a fall in the exchange rate from E_0 to E_2. In these circumstances the Spanish government has to defend the peseta, to make up the excess demand ZY, which it must do by selling some of its dollar reserves at the exchange rate E_0. If the demand curve D_2 becomes permanent, the government may be unable to uphold the exchange rate E_0 for long, since it will exhaust its foreign currency reserves. In this situation, it may choose to devalue its currency (i.e. fix a new lower rate, at which it will guarantee convertability for its currency) or allow its currency to float to its true market value.

Postwar Economics
When victory in World War II was assured, Allied governments acted to restore orderly international economic relations. A prime concern was to avoid the kind of slump that

Economics is the science which studies human behaviour as a relationship between ends and scarce means which have alternative uses.

Lord Robbins (1898–1984), British economist

POSTWAR ECONOMIC DEVELOPMENT

In the aftermath of World War II, the need for economies to grow quickly was widely accepted. Governments intervened actively in their economies to promote their macroeconomic objectives, especially low unemployment. In doing so, they attempted to provide their business sectors with an environment that encouraged entrepreneurial risk-taking. With hindsight, the mid-1950s may be seen as marking the end of postwar reconstruction and the emergence of a worldwide period of boom. Between 1960 and 1973, world production grew at an unprecedented rate, averaging 5.5% per annum. However, the extent to which this can be attributed to the successful application of Keynesian policies should not be overstated. This was also a period of cheap energy, rapid technological advances, and optimistic expectations;

▲ **Oil Production (Mexico)** *Oil prices are a vital factor in the world economy.*

together, these factors provided the conditions that stimulated world growth. Its subsequent decline had several causes: the inflationary pressures emerging in most of the

world's economies, a rapid rise in oil prices (prompted largely by the West's support of Israel during the 1973 Arab-Israeli War; see THE ISLAMIC WORLD (VOL. 5): OIL AND THE MIDDLE EAST), and the breakdown of the Bretton Woods system of currency exchange. In addition, opportunities for maintaining a high rate of growth were diminishing. By 1974, the world economy was growing at 3% per annum. Monetarist policies were adopted, which were intended to suppress the inflationary pressures that had emerged. These monetarist policies, together with another significant rise in oil prices in 1979, drove the world economy into recession by the early 1980s. Dynamic economies, such as that of Japan, were able to withstand the slump, whereas it was not until the end of the 1980s that Europe began to show signs of recovery.

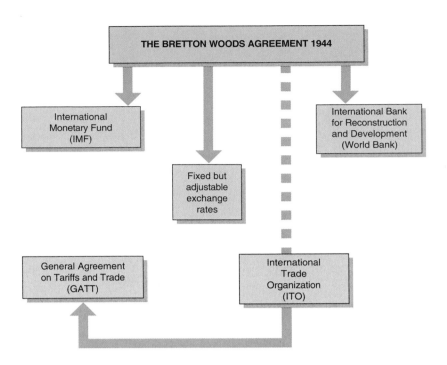

THE BRETTON WOODS AGREEMENT 1944

International Monetary Fund (IMF)

Fixed but adjustable exchange rates

International Bank for Reconstruction and Development (World Bank)

General Agreement on Tariffs and Trade (GATT)

International Trade Organization (ITO)

▲ **The Institutions Arising from the Bretton Woods Conference** *Held in New Hampshire in the USA, the Bretton Woods Conference – involving the USA, UK, Canada, and 42 other countries – established a system of international financial rules. The system lasted until 1971, when the USA suspended convertibility from dollars to gold, and finally collapsed in 1973. It was hoped that rationalization of trade would be effected by the creation of the ITO; this body never came into being, though GATT assumed part of its envisaged role.*

resulted in the 1930s from rising unemployment, the collapse of the international capital market, and the emergence of international protectionism. Thus in 1944, the representatives of the USA, UK, and 42 other countries met at Bretton Woods in the US state of New Hampshire. Although the Soviet Union participated in the conference, it opted ultimately for continued economic isolation, using its military strength to maintain an extensive power-base in central and eastern Europe. Trade was fostered within the Soviet bloc, together with other communist countries, such as Cuba, Mongolia, and Vietnam, through the Council for Mutual Economic Assistance (CMEA), popularly known as COMECON. However, East–West relations deteriorated so badly that real economic cooperation between them did not occur for another four decades.

The Bretton Woods Conference produced a new system of foreign exchange (often referred to as the Bretton Woods system), together with two supporting institutions: the International Bank for Reconstruction and Development (IBRD), known as the World Bank, and the International Monetary Fund (IMF), which began operations in June 1946 and March 1947, respectively.

Under the Bretton Woods system, member countries were required to maintain their currency within a band of ± 1% of their currency's value against the US dollar (which, in turn, was linked to gold). If the value of a currency fell towards the bottom of its agreed band, member governments were expected to buy that currency and sell their holdings of other currencies (mainly US dollars) to prevent the weak currency from falling below its

± 1% band. Similarly, when a currency was likely to break through the agreed upper limit, participating governments were required to sell their holdings of the strong currency and replenish their reserves of other currencies. In reality, the onus of intervention fell on governments with weaker currencies. Currency devaluations were only allowed to take place in the face of severe balance-of-payments problems and after negotiation with the IMF.

The system worked reasonably well for many years, with a growing level of international transactions financed by US dollars; in this period the industrialized countries enjoyed high levels of economic prosperity. By the mid-1960s, significant differences between the economic performance of countries had begun to emerge. This, combined with the pressure placed upon the US dollar by the Vietnam War, created instability within the Bretton Woods system. Attempts to rectify the problems only provided a temporary respite and the system finally collapsed in 1973.

The New International Order
No universal exchange-rate system has emerged to replace the Bretton Woods system. The value of most currencies has since been determined by supply and demand in the international money markets, subject to government intervention where it has been deemed necessary. This type of market is called a 'managed float.' Within Europe, there have been two attempts to revive an organized system of fixed (but flexible) exchange rates. The *snake* was adopted in 1973 by EC countries after the demise of the Bretton Woods system. This allowed exchange rates to 'snake' (i.e. fluctuate) within a tunnel, which imposed a limit to fluctuations of 2.25% for participating currencies but which floated freely against nonparticipating currencies. However, the snake collapsed when three EC members (Eire, France, and the UK) were unable to keep their currency within the accepted bands. In 1979 it was replaced by the *Exchange Rate Mechanism* (ERM) which, after some stability in the 1980s, experienced tensions in 1992–93.

The International Monetary Fund (IMF) was originally established at Bretton Woods to encourage international monetary cooperation, to stabilize exchange rates, and to facilitate a multilateral payments system between member countries. According to wealth, each member country was required to subscribe to a quota, made up of 25% gold and 75% of its own currency.

Since the 1950s, the IMF has lent money to countries experiencing balance-of-payments difficulties, providing resources to encourage adjustment to take place rather than a hasty reaction based on a mix of deflationary

TRADE PROTECTION

Artificial measures used by governments to influence trade patterns fall into two broad categories: tariff barriers and nontariff barriers. GATT negotiations have reduced tariff barriers; however, countries still regulate trade with the use of nontariff barriers.

Tariff barriers include:
• Lump sum (or specific) – a tariff imposed on each unit of an imported product.
• Ad Valorem – a tariff levied as a percentage of the unit value of the affected import.
• Compound – a combination of a lump sum tariff and an ad valorem tariff.

Non-tariff barriers include:
• Quota – a limit on the amount of a good that can be imported in a given period. An example is the Multi-Fibre Arrangement between exporters of low-cost textiles from developing nations and importing countries.

• Voluntary Export Restraint (or VER) – a limit set by an exporter of a commodity to discourage an importing country from imposing its own quota. Japan has used VERs in its trading relationship with the EC and the USA, particularly in relation to cars.
• Health and Safety Standards – regulations imposed in the knowledge that imported goods will not be able to meet the new requirements.
• Border Bureaucracy – excessive paperwork and invoice requirements to slow down the progress of imports into a country.
• Public-Sector Contracts – governments traditionally give preference to domestic firms when tenders are submitted for public works.
• Subsidy – home producers are given government assistance, which lowers the price of their goods.

Supply-Side Economics

In the 1980s various governments attempted to promote economic growth by using supply-side strategies. Impediments to entrepreneurial activity were removed, such as restrictive labour practices and high welfare payments. This was combined with a radical review of the public sector. Many countries, including left-of-centre democracies, such as Australia and Spain, implemented such policies.

policies, increased trade barriers, and currency devaluations. Added to this there has been a greater need to lend to developing countries experiencing problems arising from a downward pressure on the prices of the primary commodities they produce at the same time as the price of imported products, such as oil, have risen. Beyond a certain level, IMF lending can be subject to conditions set by IMF officials. These conditions usually involve reforms of domestic policies to improve the country's economic position. This has often led to criticism of the IMF, particularly when these conditions compromise a country's autonomy in policy-making – and especially when government spending has had to be curtailed. Nevertheless, the IMF has survived the Bretton Woods exchange-rate system and still attempts to provide the facilities promoting a steady growth in world trade.

The other institution to emerge from the Bretton Woods Agreement that remains in the 1990s is the International Bank for Reconstruction and Development (IBRD), or World Bank. It was established to provide cheap loans (i.e. below market interest rates) to finance postwar reconstruction, a role overtaken by the USA's own European Recovery Programme – the Marshall Plan; see THE WORLD IN THE 20TH CENTURY (VOL. 5): POSTWAR EUROPE. Its aim now is to promote economic growth in developing countries through high-priority projects, rather than to underwrite balance-of-payments difficulties. IBRD membership involves a country buying stock in the Bank. The Bank now has over 150 members, the major stockholder being the USA, with about one-third of the total stock. This stock

gives the Bank the collateral that enables it to raise money through the sale of bonds. As World Bank activities have increased, three other institutions have emerged.

In 1956 the International Finance Corporation (IFC) was formed to provide assistance to private businesses in developing countries. The International Development Association (IDA), which began its operations in 1960, provides soft loans for development projects (usually to enhance a country's infrastructure) offering more generous terms than the World Bank would normally allow. The IDA gives repayment periods for loans extending up to 50 years; indeed, there is no guarantee that these loans will ever be repaid by the borrowing country. In 1988 the Multilateral Investment Guarantee Agency (MIGA) was es-

Delegates at the G-7 Summit in Naples, Italy (1994)
This conference – of the Group of Seven most powerful industrial nations in the world – is held regularly, and in 1994 included President Boris Yeltsin of Russia. ▼

Problems Created by Multinationals

- Their transactions can significantly affect the balance of payments of their host countries
- By choosing the countries in which they will make their largest profits they can manipulate their tax liabilities
- They can demand special treatment from a government as a condition for opening new factories
- They can manipulate foreign exchanges by large credit transfers.

Protests Against the GATT Agreement *In late 1992 French farmers held demonstrations against the impending trade deal between the European Union and the USA. The farmers feared that the removal of protectionist trade barriers, especially subsidies, would threaten their livelihood.* ▼

tablished to facilitate the flow of private investment to developing member countries. Over 70 countries are members of MIGA.

The final aim of the Bretton Woods Conference was to establish an organization to promote the reduction and eventual elimination of the tariffs and other restrictions that had brought about the decline in world trade during the 1930s. This organization was to be known as the International Trade Organization (ITO). However, the ITO failed to come into operation, as a result of two interrelated problems. First, the impact of the code of practice would have been too radical for many governments; secondly, the ITO would have encroached too far on nations' own trade policies. Although the USA promoted the ITO, the US Congress, together with the governments of many other countries, failed to ratify the charter negotiated in Havana in 1947.

The Influence of GATT

After the failure of the ITO, the only machinery left in place for rationalizing international trade was the General Agreement on Tariffs and Trade (GATT). This resulted from a conference held in Geneva (1947), at which 23 countries negotiated a series of bilateral agreements to reduce trade protection. Thus, by default, GATT assumed part of the role envisaged for the ITO. Although the main catalysts for the boom in world trade between 1955 and 1973 were the rapid advances in technology combined with an abundant supply of cheap energy, this boom was undoubtedly facilitated by the gradual removal of barriers to world trade promoted by GATT.

Membership of GATT grew from 23 members in 1947 to 111 members in the early 1990s. In addition, there are some 30 associate (mainly developing) countries that follow GATT rules and to whom the benefits of

membership are extended. GATT now exerts a major influence on world trade, as over 90% of world trade is conducted between member nations. The main problem compromising the ability of GATT to function effectively is that it has no power to enforce its rules, other than through the will of its members. The most significant obligation of GATT members is that they must abide by the ***most favoured nation*** rule. This requires that any trade concession or the removal of a trade barrier between two member countries must apply uniformly to all other member countries.

There are three exceptions to this rule. First, members of free trade areas and customs unions can employ preferential tariffs and quotas to each other but exclude nonmember countries from their benefits. Secondly, less developed countries are permitted to use tariffs and other discriminatory measures in order to give themselves temporary protection from balance-of-payments difficulties or to provide a temporary respite for industries being undermined by significant increases in imports. Thirdly, countries may protect their agricultural industries through price-support mechanisms backed up by discriminatory measures. Attempts to dismantle agricultural protection have resulted in disputes, particularly between the USA and its followers (who wish to liberalize trade in agricultural products) and the European Union (for whom vested interests in its Common Agricultural Policy act as a barrier to significant reform).

When problems do emerge, members submit their grievances to GATT panels. However, the panels offer a conciliation service rather than an arbitration service and, as a result, many panel decisions have been flouted.

Since its inception, GATT has sponsored a number of conferences to promote reductions in trade protection. These conferences, known as 'rounds,' have been held over the last 50 years at various places throughout the world (see INTERNATIONAL TRADE). Initially, it was relatively easy for agreements concerning tariff reductions to be made; they mainly affected manufactured goods, with the USA, in particular, making significant concessions. However, from the Kennedy round onwards, the negotiations have become progressively more complex, involving an ever longer list of commodities (embracing services, agriculture, intellectual-property rights, and public procurement, as well as manufactured goods and textiles). The need to address an increasingly sophisticated list of protectionist measures adopted by countries (in particular, there has been a growth in nontariff barriers) and to satisfy the interests of an expanding number of participating countries have added to the problems. After the difficulties of reaching

agreement at the Uruguay round, there may be a move towards more piecemeal exercises, involving specific aspects of world trade and fewer participating countries (which will, in theory, pass on any resulting benefits to non-negotiating countries).

The Uruguay round took seven years of difficult negotiation before an agreement was signed in 1993. According to the figures produced by GATT, tariff reductions – and the expanded trade that results – should generate world income gains of $235 million a year by 2005. Since this figure excludes concessions affecting service goods, the ultimate welfare increases may be even higher. However, as with previous GATT rounds, the largest share of these gains will be enjoyed by industrialized rather than developing countries.

The process of managing world trade now seems to have retraced its steps. An organization called the World Trade Organization (WTO) was launched on 1 January 1995. The WTO resembles the ill-fated ITO.

Multinational Enterprises

A particular feature of postwar world trade has been the increase in activity of multinational enterprises. A multinational enterprise is a company that owns or controls production or service facilities outside its country of origin. Its activities extend beyond merely trading abroad or purchasing share capital in an overseas company. Instead it functions as an entrepreneur abroad, building new productive facilities outside its country of origin, often acquiring total or part control of existing foreign firms and their brand names. Currently, there are some 10 000 firms that fall into this category. Of this total, around one-third are in the field of manufacturing goods, a further one-third is oil-related, and a quarter are service industries. The rest are mining companies.

INTERNATIONAL ECONOMIC INTEGRATION

Various measures have been used to encourage integration in international trade. These measures include:
- **Preferential Trading Agreements** – countries agree to lower trade barriers between themselves. An example was the Imperial (later Commonwealth) Preference between the UK and its empire (Commonwealth).
- **Free Trade Area** – trade barriers between participating nations eliminated completely; tariffs between each country and non-members of the agreement determined separately. The most recent example (1993) is the North American Free Trade Agreement (NAFTA). See BUSINESS AND FINANCE: INTERNATIONAL TRADE.
- **Customs Union** – a common external tariff is imposed against nonmembers, while trade barriers are completely eliminated between members.
- **Common Market** – in addition to a common external tariff, a common market also allows free mobility of factors of production (e.g. labour) between states.
- **Monetary Union** – a common market in which there is a common currency and a unified monetary policy.
- **Full Economic Union** – the most complete form of economic integration, with a unified economic policy that includes transfer payments and fiscal policy.

Because of the risks involved – e.g. the need to establish trading relationships with other firms in the foreign country and the complexities arising from different government regulations and legal systems – a company is only likely to acquire multinational interests when all the profit-making opportunities have been exploited in its home country.

A multinational firm may set up a subsidiary company to produce similar goods to home-produced ones. This is known as **horizontal investment**. Yet the foreign subsidiary may produce inputs for the company's products or market and sell the company's products abroad. This is called **vertical investment**.

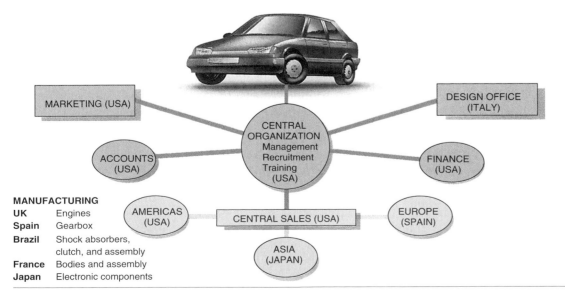

MARKETING (USA)

ACCOUNTS (USA)

CENTRAL ORGANIZATION
Management
Recruitment
Training
(USA)

DESIGN OFFICE (ITALY)

FINANCE (USA)

MANUFACTURING
UK	Engines
Spain	Gearbox
Brazil	Shock absorbers, clutch, and assembly
France	Bodies and assembly
Japan	Electronic components

AMERICAS (USA)

CENTRAL SALES (USA)

EUROPE (SPAIN)

ASIA (JAPAN)

◄ **The Structure of a Multinational**
This organizational plan of a US car manufacturer shows how vehicle parts may be manufactured in various countries and sold through a network of sales offices spread throughout the world. The advantages that are lost by having one local manufacturing centre are compensated for by having a worldwide organization that is able to take advantage of low-cost expertise wherever it occurs.

▲ Itaipú Dam
The Itaipú Dam, the world's largest hydroelectric project, was built jointly by Paraguay and Brazil between 1975 and 1982. It is typical of the large-scale prestigious economic projects undertaken by newly industrializing countries in this period.

We at Ford Motor Company look at a world map without any boundaries. We don't consider ourselves basically an American company. We are a multinational company. And when we approach a government that doesn't like the US, we always say: "Who do you like? Britain? Germany? We carry a lot of flags. We export from a lot of countries."

Robert Stevens, Executive Vice-President, Ford International Operations

The economic power of the USA after World War II made it the main source of multinational enterprises, with Canada, Europe, and Latin America the major destinations. Since the mid-1960s, the role of the USA in multinational activity has declined in favour of other industrialized countries (e.g. Canada, Germany, Japan, and the UK), and developing economies (e.g. Brazil, Mexico, Singapore, and Taiwan) have become destinations. The growing influence of multinationals in the international economy raises many ethical issues.

Although advanced capitalist economies have a complex regulatory framework that can exert a strong influence on the ways in which a multinational is permitted to behave, negotiations often have to take place between a company and a prospective host government. These negotiations involve the scope of the activities to be undertaken by the new firm; for example, whether or not training will be offered to local workers or whether the new factory will carry out research and development in addition to manufacturing.

Further complications can arise when companies from advanced capitalist economies expand their operations into less developed economies. This may result in a variety of unethical practices, ranging from exploitation of local workers in the host country (either by paying low wages or providing inadequate health and safety conditions) to pollution of the environment at a higher level than would be acceptable in the company's home country.

On the positive side, the activities of multinationals do provide the opportunity for investment to exceed domestic savings, thus providing an impetus to economic growth; the opportunity to earn more foreign exchange; and additional government revenue, which can be channelled into development projects.

Overseas Aid

Overseas aid involves the transfer of resources from one country to another without the expectation of an equivalent payment in return. This aid can take various forms, including cash donations, subsidized loans, food supplies, and such technical assistance as the provision of machinery or knowledge. If the donor country expects no repayment, of any kind, the assistance is said to be **pure aid**. Aid may take two basic forms: bilateral aid, which is given directly by one country to another or multilateral aid, which originates from international organizations.

For countries with a very low per-capita GNP, particularly those least able to borrow money on a commercial basis or to qualify for World Bank loans, foreign aid is an important source of funds. The source of most foreign aid (about four-fifths of the total) is the developed Western economies. The remainder comes mostly from Middle Eastern OPEC countries (mainly to other Arab countries). There are two main factors that prompt countries to provide foreign aid. The first is ethical, reflecting the belief that the present distribution of income is unfair and at least partly results from past exploitation of poorer countries. The second motivation is overtly political: the USA and the former Soviet Union, as well as many Western industrialized countries, tended to be guided by politics in their giving. Thus the former USSR directed its aid towards other communist countries, for example Afghanistan, Cuba, and Mongolia, whereas the USA tended to focus its benevolence on such countries as Israel, Turkey, and other developing countries it wished to favour. Since 1990 the USA has provided aid to the transitional economies in central and eastern Europe, which is likely to have repercussions for the poorer nations elsewhere in the world.

More aid is now being channelled through official organizations. In addition to the World Bank, there is a variety of development organizations that have an active role in promoting economic development: the African Development Bank, the Arab Fund, the Inter-American Development Bank, the Islamic Fund for Economic Development, and – since 1990 – the European Bank for Reconstruction and Development. Multilateral aid is largely free of the political overtones that are often part of bilateral aid. It can also be more efficient, since it cuts out the duplication resulting from a country receiving funds from a number of sources. Moreover, in bilateral aid, recipient countries may be forced to buy goods and services from the donor country, often at an artificially high cost. When aid is tied in this way, a large part of its value may be lost; it also acts as a general barrier to free trade.

BUSINESS AND FINANCE

Goods and Services

*Types of production • Importance of organization •
A production process • Automation of production •
Quality assurance • Purchasing*

It is generally agreed that people have three essential needs for survival: food, shelter, and clothing. Once these have been satisfied, and a society becomes more affluent, needs develop into wants. These wants, depending upon the wealth of the society and the availability of resources to satisfy them, tend to become limitless: people, as they have more money to spend, want better computers, bigger cars, or more exotic holidays.

Needs and wants can be conveniently classified as either **goods** or **services**. Goods are tangible objects, such as motor vehicles, television sets, and articles of clothing. Services are often referred to as intangible because no solid object is involved. Examples include banking, insurance, holidays, and education. As societies become more affluent so the demand for services tends to grow.

In order to satisfy their wants people usually have to rely upon the skills or know-how of others. Few of us will build our own cars or produce our own food – although we may work for an organization that is able to do so. It is perhaps ironical that what are referred to as 'advanced societies' are largely made up of individuals who are less and less able to satisfy their own wants. Instead, these wants are supplied by businesses and organizations special-

izing in making particular products or providing particular services. These businesses range from small local firms to large international companies. What they have in common, irrespective of size, is the need to be well organized and to be accurately focused in what they do.

Types of Production
The difference between goods and services can be further clarified by an understanding of the three main types of production. These are known as primary production, secondary production, and tertiary production: each type is characterized by the people who work in it (see table).

Primary Production. Primary production is concerned with the harvesting of goods provided by nature: above and below ground or in the seas. Farming is concerned with the use of the land and animals to produce food, timber, wool, cotton, etc. Mining produces such raw materials as oil, natural gas, coal, and mineral ores. Fishing produces both food and many products that provide the raw materials of secondary production.

Secondary Production. Manufacturing and construction are the main areas of secondary production. Both take raw materials derived from primary production and use

═══SEE ALSO═══
This section:
• Conducting Business
• Company Structure
  and Finance
• Marketing
Economics:
• The Price Mechanism
• Economic Resources

**Distribution of
Goods** *Before primary
products reach the
consumers, they pass
through many hands.* ▼

PRIMARY
PRODUCERS

Commodity
and food markets

SECONDARY
PRODUCTION

Wholesalers

Retailers

Consumers

TYPES OF PRODUCTION			
Primary Production	*Secondary Production*	*Tertiary Production*	
The production of naturally occurring goods	The production of goods using materials derived from primary products	The production of services	
		Commercial	Personal
fisherman	builder	wholesaler	teacher
miner	carpenter	retailer	doctor
farmer	shipbuilder	accountant	entertainer
oil driller	engineer	pilot	author

Retailing

The sale of goods for personal or household use. The functions of retail establishments include:

- storage and display of goods
- supplying information concerning their capabilities and use
- ensuring that the goods are fresh or fit for their purpose
- providing a choice of different manufacturers' goods
- continuous updating or replacement of stock
- arranging or giving credit for large-value purchases
- providing for the transfer of title or ownership

specialized skills and know-how to transform them into useful end products. Examples include housing, vehicles, computers, furniture, and clothing.

Tertiary Production. Tertiary production is usually regarded as including the immensely diverse range of both commercial and personal services. In the case of retailing (cars, clothes, food, etc.) the results of primary or secondary production are presented to the end-user (customer) for purchase. Both the wholesaler and the retailer provide commercial services and specialized know-how but do not actually produce anything. The author, who writes a book or play, or the banker, who looks after or lends money, provide personal services.

Importance of Organization

Whether goods or services are being produced, the need for an efficient organization and structure is essential. A farmer plants his seeds at the correct time of year, tends them, harvests the crop when it is ready, and finally sends it to market, a food processor, or retailer as quickly as possible. There is a natural progression to this cycle of operations. If the farmer gets any part of it wrong or neglects any of the essential steps, the product will suffer and the farmer will be likely to lose profit. His produce, inferior to that of his competitors, will have to be sold for a lower price or may not be sold at all.

WHOLESALING

Most wholesalers provide a very valuable link between the manufacturer and the retailer. Usually their activities are restricted to specialization in one product area (e.g. food, hardware, electrical goods, etc.). They simplify distribution, reducing enormously the number of outlets that a manufacturer has to service.

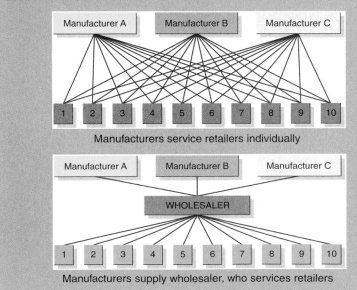

Manufacturers service retailers individually

Manufacturers supply wholesaler, who services retailers

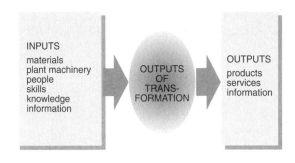

▲ **Diagram of a Production Process**
Various diverse inputs are required in order to produce a finished product.

This basic commercial model applies to all types of production and to all types of business. While there is unlikely to be only one correct way to provide a product or service, each production cycle for goods and services is likely to follow a similar sequence or method.

A Production Process

Whether the production process involves growing corn or building a motor vehicle, a series of transformations will be required. A range of inputs, including raw materials, skills, and knowledge, must be manipulated in a particular way to produce a useful output. This output is presented to the customer as the product or service. The customers' response to the product or service (whether he is satisfied or dissatisfied) may then provide information as an input when the process is repeated. Thus, if customers complain about some aspect of quality, this will have to be taken into consideration by the producer. The customers' response then becomes an input that modifies or changes the process.

It is possible to look at the process of transformation in a more detailed way. A sweet manufacturer, for example, probably manufactures a range of many different products. For each product there will be a series of steps in the process of transformation. This principle is shown in the diagram illustrating the process of making chocolate-covered toffees.

The logic to this sequence of procedures is clear. For instance there is no need to have the bags available at the beginning of the process. Nor can the manufacturer wrap the caramel until the chocolate is dry: if he does, it will stick to the wrapping and will not be in the condition expected by the customer. This example is straightforward. However, the process of manufacture becomes far more complex in the case of a products such as cars or aircraft, with thousands of different components and many different stages in the transformation process. In all cases the need for good organization, planning, and control is critical.

Automation of Production

The last decade has seen a dramatic increase in the use of robots, computer-controlled processes, and automated production. This has been made possible by advances in computer technology and the skills of individuals and organizations in taking advantage of the opportunities presented by this new technology.

Robots. These are automatic machines, programmed by computer, that are capable of doing a particular job without human intervention: for example, welding car bodies in many different places. In the past these welds would have been made by expert welders. The robot, however, brings a degree of consistency and quality to the work that could not always previously be guaranteed. Subject to the necessary maintenance and repair it can work indefinitely without becoming tired or bored. In addition, it can be reprogrammed to do a different task when production requirements demand it. One week it might be welding a product in 15 separate places, the next week it can be used to weld another product in 30 different places.

These are obvious benefits. There is, of course, another side to the use of automation. Fewer people may be needed by the company to carry out the production process. Every major step in technological progress has had its human cost, either in redundancies or the need to retrain workers.

An Automated Production Line *Robots welding car bodies on the assembly lines of the Mazda car plant in Hiroshima, Japan.* ▼

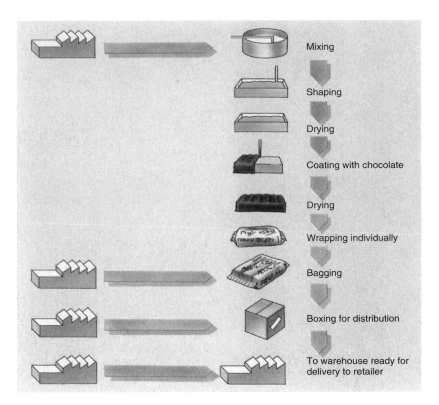

Mixing

Shaping

Drying

Coating with chocolate

Drying

Wrapping individually

Bagging

Boxing for distribution

To warehouse ready for delivery to retailer

▲ **Production of Chocolate-covered Toffees** *This flow diagram shows the many stages involved in making a manufactured product.*

Automatic Handling Systems. These are computerized systems used for handling materials and products within a company. There are three main types:

• automatic material handling – the use of conveyor belts, tubes, and trolleys to bring raw materials and components into a factory without the need for human handling;

• automatic transport between work areas – the use of computer-controlled vehicles to take part-finished products from one work station to the next;

• automatic warehousing – the use of conveyor belts to take finished products directly into a warehouse to await transport to retailers or customers.

Computer-Aided Design. The use of computers that employ sophisticated **software** to design all kinds of products – from cars to fashion items – is now well established. The computer gives the designer an opportunity to experiment, to explore different **'what if?'** options and then to produce the detailed drawings or designs chosen for the final product. It also has the ability to calculate the important engineering parameters associated with a particular design. These will tell the designer whether or not a particular shape, structure, or product will meet the standards required.

Computer-Aided Manufacturing. Computers may also be used to plan and control the production process. This may include deciding on the best way to carry out a particular job, programming the machines, and monitoring the quality of a particular process.

software The programmes used to enable computers to carry out many different functions.

'what if?' A process for considering alternative ways of doing things or different outcomes to situations.

▲ Computer-aided Manufacturing
In this control room of a fully automated steel rolling mill, one operator can regulate and monitor production. Like many manufacturing industries, steel production has become far less labour-intensive in the latter half of the 20th century.

Computer-Integrated Manufacturing. In this, the whole production process is totally controlled by computers. Human input (once the system is set up) and day-to-day involvement is limited to seeing that the computers are working as they should. The advantage of this approach is that many boring, repetitive, or dangerous jobs can be transferred to machines. The disadvantage is that fewer people will be needed to carry out the process.

Quality Assurance

The maintenance of quality to a designated standard is important throughout an organization, whether the end product is goods or services. The International Standards Organization (ISO), Standard 9000 sets down the methods by which a system can be implemented to achieve this objective throughout a company. For a manufacturing process the key word is consistency. This applies especially to:
• materials
• plant and machinery
• procedures
However many products are manufactured, whether they be cars or chocolate bars, each must be produced to an identical specification in an identical way. Only when the production process has been brought under strict control can consistent quality (to the established standard) be assured.

Purchasing

All manufacturers of goods need to purchase raw materials. Depending upon the product, this might involve as few as six different items or as many as six thousand. Raw materials might include very basic items (such as iron ore, bauxite, or crude oil) or sophisticated components (such as a motor-car engine) to

be used in the finished product with many other components.

Purchasing is a very important function in the manufacturing process; mistakes can prove very costly. There are six key areas that must be taken into consideration each time an order is placed for raw materials or components:
• Quality – the materials purchased must meet a minimum standard;
• Quantity – the quantity purchased must be sufficient for the firm's needs, if possible taking advantage of large-order discounts without over-stocking;
• Price – the person responsible for purchasing must know where to acquire the right quality materials at the lowest price. If a commodity (e.g. rubber, cocoa, coffee, etc.) that fluctuates in price is used in large quantities in the process, a forward purchasing policy must be employed that provides a hedge against price rises or falls;
• Place – the materials must be delivered to the correct address – this is a vitally important factor if the firm operates at a number of different sites;
• Time – the materials must arrive at the right time, not too early and never too late;
• Terms – the purchase contracts with the supplier must include a strict specification as to quality, quantity, price, place, delivery date, insurance terms in transit, and payment terms.

The 'Just-in-Time' Approach. Because holding stock (whether of raw materials or finished goods) is expensive in terms of tying up cash, businesses attempt to keep stocks to an absolute minimum.

The key to the success of this approach in manufacturing is efficient production planning and a good relationship with suppliers. Optimally, suppliers and manufacturers cooperate closely, sharing information and adjusting to each other's requirements. Rather than keeping days' or weeks' supplies of raw materials and components, the manufacturer may rely upon frequent deliveries from suppliers, on a daily or even an hourly basis. Each production run is carefully planned and all the material requirements identified in advance. Delays, breakdowns, or other interruptions are immediately conveyed to all parties and appropriate adjustments made.

When a retailer becomes part of this special relationship, goods (such as cars) can be produced to the customer's exact specification. This may preclude immediate delivery, but the short delay involved ensures that the customer receives exactly what has been ordered. For the manufacturer and retailer the benefit is in the reduction in the amount of money they have tied up in stock.

Conducting Business

Private sector businesses • Public sector businesses • Cooperatives • Planning

The main aim of any organization should be to maximize the **return** from its investment. In commercial concerns, that return is measured in terms of **profit**. In non-profit-making organizations (such as hospitals or schools) the return may be measured in other ways, such as throughput of patients or exam results. In both types, however, there is an implicit need for the efficient use of all the resources employed. This rule applies to the small one-person business as well as to the largest international company.

National laws differ both in the ways that businesses are structured and in the legal protection that is accorded to **shareholders**, **creditors**, and employees. In most countries, however, there are usually three distinct types of business.

Private Sector Businesses

Privately owned companies fall into three categories: the sole trader, partnerships, and limited liability companies.

Sole Trader. As the title suggests, the term refers to individuals carrying on a business on their own. This does not mean that they may not employ other people. From a legal point of view, however, they are solely responsible for the business. They are entitled to any profits made, but equally they bear any losses.

Normally their legal responsibility extends to the full limit of their personal **assets**. This means that if the business fails, creditors can pursue the owner personally for payment of any monies owed. If the owner is unable to

pay, then it is likely that he or she will be declared **bankrupt**.

Partnership. A business association between two or more persons (normally up to a maximum of 20) conducting a business with the intention of making a profit. It usually comes into being for two main reasons:

(a) a sole trader, wishing to expand a business, joins with others;

(b) individuals, who alone would not or could not operate as sole traders, come together to pool their resources and expertise.

Partners share profits and losses in the proportions agreed between them as set out in the Partnership Agreements. Like the sole trader, each partner is liable for business debts to the full extent of personal wealth. In some circumstances, it is possible for there to be a limited partner within a partnership. This arises, for instance, if an individual has money to invest but does not wish to take an active part in the day-to-day running of the business. In the event of the business failing, limited partners are only liable to lose the money they have invested. In any partnership with a limited partner, there must be at least one general partner, i.e. someone who will assume unlimited liability for the activities of the business.

Limited Liability Companies. Except in cases in which a business is on a small scale or carries few financial risks, it is usual to form a limited liability company. In law, this is deemed to be a legal entity in its own right, distinct from its owners. The most important characteristic of a limited liability company is that

═══SEE ALSO═══
This section:
• Marketing
• Company Finance
Law:
• Civil Law
Economics:
• Economic Resources

Key Terms

return The gain or benefit from an investment.

profit The excess of the income of a business over the expenditure in a particular period.

shareholder A person owning shares in a limited company.

creditor A person or organization to whom money is owed.

asset Any possession that has a monetary value.

bankrupt A person recognized by a court as being unable to pay his or her debts in full.

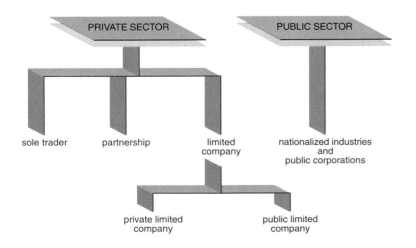

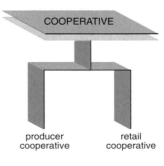

◄ **Different Business Structures** *According to whether a particular company is privately, publicly, or cooperatively owned, it is differently structured.*

audit An official examination of the annual accounts of a company to verify their accuracy. An *external audit* is conducted by a qualified accountant not employed by the company; *internal audits* are carried out by the company itself, and may relate not only to financial matters.

budget A detailed statement of expected future income and expenditure of an organization for a particular period prepared before that period begins. It will give estimates of production and sales, as well as overhead costs, etc.

cash flow The flow of cash into and out of a business, week by week or month by month. The *cash-flow projection* sets out all the expected payments and receipts on this basis. It enables the managers to arrange for employees and creditors to be paid at the appropriate time.

the owners of the company (the shareholders) are liable for any losses only to the extent of the capital they have invested by buying its shares. Limited liability companies fall into the two following main categories:

(a) *Private limited company*

Most limited companies are private; in most countries they have:

• at least one director;
• a company secretary;
• at least one shareholder;
• a registered office (where all legal documents can be sent);
• a word or abbreviation in their title to indicate that they are a limited company.

In addition, the company's stationery must show:

• the full company name;
• the registered office address.

From these features it is clear that the requirements for formation are quite straightforward. In addition, suppliers and customers often prefer to deal with a limited company, because it is a registered entity, the ownership of which can be easily discovered.

(b) *Public limited company*

A public limited company is usually regarded as being more important than a private company, although this may not always be the case. Usually a public limited company is required to have:

• at least two directors;
• at least two shareholders;
• a company secretary from a recognized professional body (e.g. an accountant or solicitor);
• a minimum and normally quite substantial share capital.

Unlike the private limited company, where the sale or transfer of shares is strictly controlled, there are no restrictions on transfer of shares in a public limited company, which can usually be bought and sold freely on a stock exchange.

Limited Company Documents. When a limited company is formed, its structure and the way in which it is to be run are set down formally in writing. As a result, two documents come into existence:

(a) memorandum of association – primarily setting out the objects for which the company was formed, a statement that the liability of members (shareholders) is limited, the share capital of the company, and the form that share capital will take;

(b) articles of association – setting out the rules by which the company is run, including such matters as the issue and transfer of shares, the powers of directors, and the calling and conduct of meetings.

Before a limited company can begin to trade, these documents have to be submitted to a registering authority that oversees and monitors business practice (in most countries). Acceptance brings the company legally into existence and allows it to commence its activities.

In addition, there are three further requirements that distinguish a limited liability company from a sole trader or a partnership:

(a) it must have a registered office – an 'official' address where all legal or statutory documents can be sent (this may be the same as or different from its main trading address);

(b) it must have an annual **audit** of its accounts, carried out by an independent authorized auditor;

(c) it must make an annual return of information relating to such items as share ownership and directors.

All documents on file with the registering authority are open to public scrutiny in most countries. However, in the case of sole traders and partnerships, no such information is publicly available.

Public Sector Businesses

These are organizations controlled by the government on behalf of the entire country. The reasons for having the organization publicly owned (as opposed to being a private sector company) may include the following:

• keeping a natural monopoly, such as water, in public ownership;
• providing services essential to the general public's welfare;
• protecting the national interest, or for reasons of national security;
• to standardize equipment and avoid duplication of services;
• to promote high-cost projects deemed beneficial to the nation;

SHARE CAPITAL

Share capital is that part of the funding of a company that is provided by shareholders. Every company must have some such capital – a minimum of two shares – when it begins trading. Shares fall into two basic categories: ***ordinary shares***, which yield a dividend that represents a proportion of the company's profits for that year; and ***preference shares***, which pay a fixed rate of interest.

Because of the growth in the capital of a company over the long term, ordinary shares bring higher rewards; however, this is offset by the greater risk in this kind of investment; if the company is forced into liquidation, the preferential shareholders are paid back first, ordinary shareholders owning anything left over.

• to protect essential but unprofitable industries and the associated jobs.

Since the early 1980s, in economies around the world, there has been a move away from public-sector companies, with a transfer of their ownership to the private sector. This change has affected public utilities, such as gas, electricity, water, telecommunications, and steel production. Some formerly state-owned railway networks have also been transferred to the private sector.

The arguments in favour of changing these organizations from public to private ownership include the following:
• the benefits of competition (such as greater efficiency, lower prices, and greater choice for the consumer);
• freedom of managers to manage without government interference;
• greater public participation (through share-holding in the new privatized companies).

Cooperatives

This form of organization is owned by a group of employees or consumers and exists for the benefit of its members. Cooperatives can trace their origins to the beginnings of organized labour movements in the 19th century. They fall into two categories:

Producer Cooperatives. The core of the producer cooperative is mutual self-help, although aims of equity and equality may also play a part. By cooperating with others, individual manufacturers or farmers are likely to have access to more capital, machinery, better marketing, and the benefits of bulk purchasing of supplies and raw materials. Each member shares in the profits and a proportion of these is reinvested in the cooperative as a whole. Producer cooperatives are quite common in several European countries.

Retail Cooperatives. As with producer cooperatives, retail cooperatives exist for the benefit of members – in this case, wishing to buy goods rather than produce them. Each member shares in the profits of the cooperative by being paid interest on the shares owned and benefiting from lower prices in the shops as a result of profits being reinvested.

Planning

Once established, all organizations, irrespective of their size or type, need to plan ahead. The act of planning sets clear objectives, identifies key issues, reduces uncertainty, and provides a guide to the way forward for that organization. Without such a plan, opportunities are missed, problems appear without warning, and the chances for growth or even survival are diminished.

In a business, three clear stages of planning can be identified:

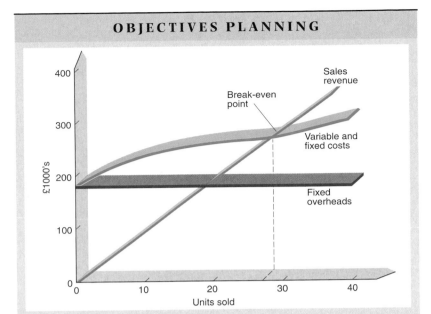

OBJECTIVES PLANNING

The break-even chart provides a quick way of visualizing anticipated changes in costs of production, fixed overhead costs, and sales revenue. The ***break-even point*** (see COMPANY STRUCTURE AND FINANCE) defines the number of units of a product that must be sold in order to cover the costs of production and overheads. Beyond this point, profit is made.

• Mission
• Objectives
• Strategies

Mission is a broad statement of intent or long-term goals, which reflects the vision of the future as seen by the management of the organization.

Objectives are more specific goals, set for a given period and relating to particular operating units, departments, or even products.

Strategies provide the means and the structure to achieve the objectives, within the guidelines of the overall mission statement of the business. At an operational level, this will include areas such as **budgets** and **cash flow**.

There is no one correct way to carry through the planning process. Uncertainty and rapidly changing environment will, for example, make a highly structured and scientific system difficult to justify. Nevertheless, a rational approach ought to be at least the starting point for any good planning process. An analysis of the firm and the environment in which it operates is often undertaken, using techniques such as ***SWOT charts***. This acronym stands for Strengths, Weaknesses, Opportunities, and Threats and the chart is based around a cruciform format.

The process involves a consideration under the four headings of all factors relating to the company, its products or services, and the market in which it operates. It offers the opportunity for a detailed analysis of all these

Scenario Planning

One of the ways for formulating a company strategy. Recognizing that uncertainty can never be eliminated, this technique is intended to reduce the impact of outside events by examining different scenarios. Each provides a different view of the future and subsequently the most appropriate response. In this way, managers are prepared for a range of changes that may occur. The process was initially used by several oil companies before being adopted by other industries.

SWOT Analysis *This form of analysis is used by companies to assess the internal strengths and weaknesses of the business, and the external opportunities and threats facing it. SWOT analysis also plays a central role in a company's audit of its managerial positions.* ▶

elements and not simply those that are the most obvious or apparent. Once the detailed examination has been undertaken, the management of the firm must prioritize each item on the basis of its likely impact on or benefit to the business.

It is important to understand that for any set of circumstances or to achieve any given objective, there is likely to be more than one choice of strategy. In selecting what is believed to be the most appropriate strategy or strategies, management will be keen to exploit strengths and opportunities and deal with weaknesses and threats.

Once this background has been established, the detailed or operational implications need to be addressed. These are likely to centre around the development of marketing and financial plans, including budgets and the all-important cash-flow projection.

Personnel. A vital element of any company's planning concerns the recruitment and retention of staff. In order to ensure that the company appoints the most suitable people to maximize its efficiency, careful attention is given to appropriate methods of employee selection. In larger companies, this task is performed by a Personnel (or Human Resources) Department; before the successful candidate is appointed to the post, a ***job description*** is written in conjunction with the line management of the relevant division, setting out the essential qualifications and experience required for the person who will occupy the vacant position, and interviews are held. For more senior positions involving greater responsibility, the interview procedure may be exhaustive, involving multiple interviews and ***psychometric tests*** (designed to assess personality traits). The demand for increased flexibility has placed a premium on job satisfaction: individual motivation is enhanced by regular appraisals and training.

COMPANY DESIGNATIONS

Country	Private Limited Company (Ltd)		Public Limited Company (plc)	
Argentina		*Sociedad de Responsabilidad Limitada*	SA	*Sociedad Anonima*
Ecuador		*Sociedad Limitada*	SA	*Sociedad Anonima*
France	SARL	*Société à Responsabilité Limitée*	SA	*Société Anonyme*
Germany	GmbH	*Gesellschaft mit beschränkter Haftung*	AG	*Aktiengesellschaft*
Italy	Srl	*Società a responsabilità limitata*	SpA	*Società per azioni*
Mexico	SRL	*Sociedad de Responsabilidad Limitada*	SA	*Sociedad Anonima*
Netherlands	BV	*Besloten Vennootschap*	NV	*Naamlose Vennootschap*
Portugal	Limitada	*Sociedade por Quotas*	CSA	*Sociedade Anonima de Responsibilidade Limitada*
Spain		*Sociedad Limitada*	SA	*Sociedad Anonima*

Marketing

The marketing mix • Product • Promotion • Price • Place • Market segmentation

In its broadest sense, marketing is concerned with all the necessary operations involved in selling goods or services to customers. To achieve its purpose, it has to bring together a number of different activities. Marketing's first task is to find out what its potential customers expect from a product or service (**market research**); this information is also needed by a firm to enable it to develop new products or services (**product development**); finally, the firm has to formulate an appropriate plan (**marketing strategy**) that will bring the product or service to the attention of potential customers and offer it to them at a price they are prepared to pay.

The Marketing Mix

The marketing strategy selected by a firm is often referred to as the **marketing mix**. It is a 'mix' that has four key elements; the strategy decides the best way to manipulate and combine these elements. The clear implication of such an approach is that there is no single correct 'recipe,' but rather that different marketing recipes are required by different products, markets, and customers. The four key elements are generally referred to as the **four Ps**, namely:

- Product
- Price
- Promotion
- Place

Product

The word 'product' is often used very loosely to include products, services, and even ideas. A product is much more than the item being offered for sale, with all its obvious features. It also includes those aspects of quality, design, and packaging that combine with its **brand name** (see panel), if it has one, and the

========SEE ALSO========
This section:
- Goods and Services
- Conducting Business
Law:
- Civil Law
Communications and Media:
- Print Media
- Electronic Media

BRANDING

Branding helps to distinguish a product from similar products offered by competitors. A **brand name** may either be specific to one particular product or applied to a range of a manufacturer's products. The objective of branding is to create a specific image for a product, make customers aware of it, and promote **brand loyalty**. Brand loyalty (ensuring that customers continue to buy a particular product rather than a rival one) is an important part of a marketing strategy. In addition to a brand name, a logo or trademark is often used to reinforce the buyer's image of the product.

guarantees associated with it, to give the product its own identity. Some customers, for example, may buy a particular make of television because it has a longer guarantee than competing sets. Other customers may make their purchasing decision primarily on the strength of the brand name – either because they have first-hand experience of that particular brand or because advertising and promotion have influenced them.

Product Life Cycle. All products move through an identifiable life cycle. Some take many years to make the 'journey,' while others (such as high-tech products) move through the process rapidly. Whatever the product, knowing where it stands in its own individual life cycle is important to the marketing process.

In companies that market a range of products, each product is likely to be at a different stage in its cycle. Once a product reaches

> **marketing strategy** The course of action chosen and the resources necessary to sell a product at an acceptable price on a target market.

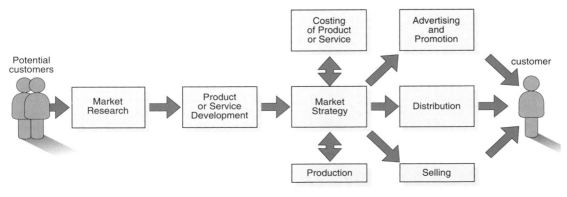

◄ **Diagram of the Marketing Process**
All inputs are shown that combine to launch a new product on the market.

Product Life Cycle ▶
The various stages through which a product passes during its exposure on the market.

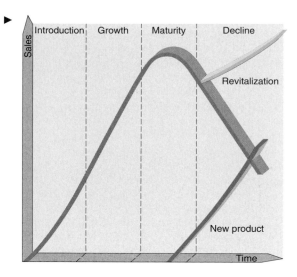

market share The percentage of the total market achieved by a particular product.

target market The group of prospective customers for a particular product or range of products focused upon by a firm.

maturity or begins to lose popularity, the company has to make a decision: either to find ways of revitalizing the product, or to prepare it for withdrawal from the market. Revitalization may simply mean repackaging the original product and launching a new promotion campaign. On the other hand, it may involve significant re-engineering or a change in its specification to take account of technology changes. If the decision is taken to withdraw it from the market, it may be advisable to plan a replacement product and even to launch it before the old product is withdrawn (see diagram).

For a company operating in a number of different businesses or markets, the status of its products can be assessed in ways other than their stage within the product life cycle. One alternative technique is ***portfolio analysis.*** Developed by the Boston Consulting Group, this offers the managers of a company a method for plotting the position of a product, by referring to its **market share** and market growth rate.

Products are placed, depending upon their performance, in one of four categories:

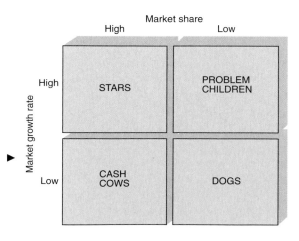

Portfolio Analysis ▶
This diagram shows the basic matrix, according to which products are categorized in marketing terms.

stars	high growth, high market-share products that may attract increased competition and therefore require cash to sustain their position and support further growth.
cash cows	high market share but low market-growth rate, providing a relatively large and stable income.
problem children	low market share in a high growth market, these products need a large investment if they are to succeed.
dogs	products in decline, possibly near the end of their life.

Using this kind of analysis, the marketing department of a company can decide which products require further investment and which products should be withdrawn.

Promotion
Promotion is concerned with making potential customers aware of a particular product's existence and its merits. The most obvious method is through advertising but this is only one among many areas. Sales promotion, personal selling, and publicity are also potentially important marketing tools.

Advertising. In deciding to advertise a product or service, a company must make decisions in three key areas: message, media, and cost.

The ***message*** should provide information to the customer about the product, persuade the customer to buy the company's product rather than a competitor's product, and serve as a general reminder that the product exists to all potential customers. The choice of ***media*** (television, radio, cinema, newspapers, magazines, or posters) will depend upon the nature of the product, where the **target market** is likely to be found, and the advertising budget. Finally, the ***cost*** of advertising will depend on the type of advertising required and the media chosen. It is important at the outset of a campaign for the advertising budget to be set. The size of this budget will depend first on whether ***consumer advertising*** or ***trade advertising*** is needed. For example, consumer advertising attempts to reach potential customers direct (such as advertising a book in the national press or on television), while trade advertising is aimed at retailers (advertising a book to booksellers in a trade magazine). Clearly, consumer advertising requires a large budget.

Having made a decision, the company must then evaluate how effective its advertising campaign has been. Sales are the principal measure of effectiveness; however, other factors are also important, such as changes in

market share and in customer awareness about the product.

Sales Promotion. Sales promotion includes a wide variety of activities aimed at creating customer awareness and therefore in increasing sales. Typical promotions include money-back offers, competitions, free samples, and in-store demonstrations.

Personal Selling. Personal selling is particularly important in selling industrial or high-value goods and in selling such services as insurance and pensions, i.e. where there is a need to develop a close and lasting relationship between the supplier and the buyer. Employing a sales force is, however, expensive. Manufacturers may be able to limit costs if they sell through wholesalers or retailers (see CONDUCTING BUSINESS). Particularly in selling services, sales overheads can be limited by linking the remuneration to the sales achieved. The salesperson may be paid a basic salary plus **commission** (a bonus based on the retail price of the product sold) on sales, while in other trades it is normal for the sales force to be paid only on commission.

Direct selling has become an important means of promotion in a number of markets and has given rise to such variants as **multi-level marketing**.

Publicity. Publicity is a potentially important form of promotion; it may be achieved by using the media directly or by employing a public relations agency. Its objective is to associate a product or service with a well-known individual, institution, good cause, or other newsworthy event. For example, associating particular sportswear with a successful sporting personality, sponsorship of a public event or competition, or donation of part of the profits generated by a product to a charitable cause are all popular ways of achieving publicity. All these methods are likely to keep the company and its product in the public eye,

◀ **Personal Selling** *In selling a high-cost product, such as a car, the sales force aims to build and foster personal contact with the customer, offering incentives, including test drives, discounts for part exchange, etc.*

with the objective of influencing sales and market share.

Price

The price at which a product will be sold is ultimately determined by its total production cost (including distribution and marketing) and the profit it is expected to make. However, in setting the final selling price a number of different factors have to be taken into account, chief among which are the following:

competition – the price of competing products;

current economic climate – including such factors as inflation, unemployment, people's disposable income, and currency exchange rates (for imported or exported products);

strategic objectives – a company may, if it is trying to increase its market share, accept temporarily a lower profit margin than usual;

availability – if demand for a product is high or availability limited, a company may temporarily be able to increase the price of a product;

company size – large companies may be able to arrange more flexible selling prices than smaller firms, at least in the short term.

direct selling Selling without the need for wholesalers or retailers — by direct mail, media advertising, or face-to-face presentations.

Multi-level Marketing

Sometimes referred to as 'network selling,' multi-level marketing is a method of selling goods directly to consumers in their homes or workplaces. The sales force generally needs little or no capital to become established and may work part time or full time, on a self-employed basis. Individuals are encouraged to build networks, by recruiting friends and colleagues to join the sales force. Rewards (commission) for the individual salesperson are based both on personal sales and on sales made by other members of the network.

◀ **Market Research** *Collecting public feedback on purchasing preferences in the intended target group is a vital element in determining the viability of an existing or future product.*

Niche Market

A discrete specialized market sector. This may be part of a much larger market, or a small market of its own. Niche markets have very clear characteristics and are targeted at specific customers. They may arise as a result of new markets emerging from new technological developments or because a company takes a decision to concentrate on one particular aspect of a much larger market.

marketing stimuli The marketing mix aimed at provoking a positive response.

Channels of Distribution *These describe the route a product takes between its point of production and consumption. Here, a car may reach a customer directly (top), or via various forms of middlemen.*

Clearly there is no simple formula for setting the selling price of a product. However, because the decision on price setting is the one that ultimately generates a company's income and profit, it is of paramount importance.

Place

The place in which a sale is made is the fourth element in any marketing strategy. Buying a product from a shop is an obvious method, but *channels of distribution* are more varied than this, as the diagram below illustrates.

In three of the four routes illustrated, the producer apparently has no contact with the customer. However, in practice this is often not the case. For example, producers of food and household goods usually use routes 2 or 3 to bring their products to their customers. The most convenient route is either to sell these in bulk to wholesalers or directly to large supermarket chains. But in the case of most fast-moving consumer goods (e.g. drinks, soap powders, etc.), it will still be the producers who do most or all of the national advertising. They will also initiate most of the special promotions and generally keep potential customers informed of any technical changes in the product. The link between producer and customer remains, therefore, very strong.

The main factor in choosing a marketing channel is to ensure that the product or service reaches the customer in the most effective manner at the lowest cost to the producer.

Market Segmentation

Some markets for goods or services are small and well-defined; these are often referred to as **niche markets**. However, many are large and widespread, both geographically and with respect to the variety of potential customers. In general, sellers will attempt to break down large markets into easily recognized and targetable categories. Market segmentation on these lines may also involve product differen-

tiation, as both elements are designed to target the requirements of specific customers.

Examples of market segments include those defined by geographical location, age, income, social class, and life-style. The belief is that people within a specific segment will respond more positively to a specific set of **marketing stimuli**. The market for package holidays provides an example of how segmentation operates. There are clearly several options available, including:

• Time of year
• Destination
• Price range
• Age range
• Hotel or self-catering
• Active or passive
• Package or exclusive

Large travel organizations may cater for most of these preferences, while small companies may concentrate on a niche market.

The key questions on segmentation are: can the segment be clearly identified; is it large enough to be profitable; can it be reached successfully with the marketing budget available; and is the company capable of serving it? If the answer to all of these is positive, one particular market segment, or a small number of market segments, can be very profitable. One possible drawback is that the growth potential of a niche market may be limited, precisely because of its small size. One further concept relating to segmentation and product differentiation should be mentioned – the *unique selling proposition* (USP). Advertising agencies in the past have been keen to identify a USP for a product or brand, believing that it helps to distinguish it from its competitors. Thus, claims are made that the product is 'preferred by' certain groups, because they believe that it 'washes whiter,' 'lasts longer,' 'gives better value,' or is 'probably the best in the world.'

Sales. A company optimizes its sales by knowing its market, its products, and its customers, and by maintaining a balance between these three aspects. Effective marketing relies on having the right product, in the right place, at the right time, at the right price – a restatement of the 'four Ps' that go to make up the marketing mix.

Most companies seek growth by increasing their market share; this is achieved by increasing sales. Generally, low-value and essential products can be sold with a minimum element of personal selling. Good examples are the thousands of products on sale in a supermarket, which rely on advertising and general promotional activities. On the other hand, a new motor car, a piece of industrial machinery, or a pension, will generally demand a personal one-to-one relationship for a sale to be achieved. This will usually involve establishing

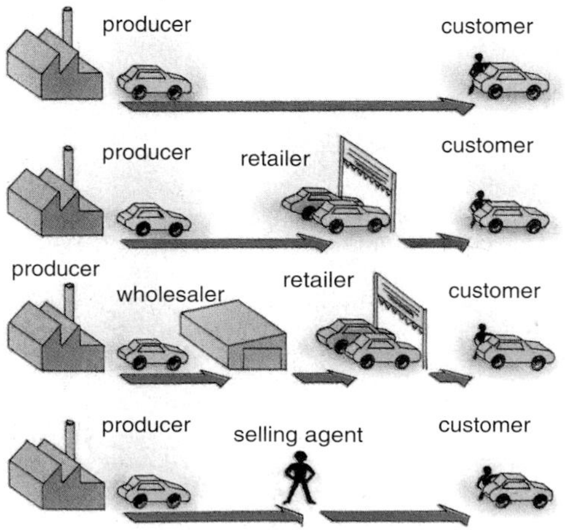

SETTING SALES TARGETS

Past and current sales performance, when coupled with systematic market research, will provide essential data for setting future sales targets. Types of information that are collected and analysed include the following:

- Sales performance figures (analysed by product, geographical area, industrial sector, etc.)
- Feedback from the sales force
- Customer comments
- Independent industry analyses
- Economic predictions or indicators
- Analysis of competitors

a relationship that builds up the customer's confidence in the seller, enabling information to be given to the buyer, doubts to be discounted, and negotiations to be carried out in a trusting environment.

Setting Targets. Setting targets and meeting them is central to the success of achieving sales objectives. These are usually established in the marketing plan, the purpose of which is to express clearly a company's strategic objectives. Company strategy (often summarized in a mission statement; see CONDUCTING BUSINESS) should be geared to match a company's strengths (products, know-how, after-sales service, etc.) to its market opportunities. The processes of portfolio analysis, segmentation, and differentiation all form important parts of the marketing exercise. For setting future sales targets, it is essential to gather and analyse current sales data, not only with respect to quantities but also with respect to the environment in which the sales have been made and the cost of making the sales (in terms of discounts, commissions, etc.).

Sales targets should not, of course, rely solely on these items. Other factors must be taken into account, which can greatly influence the sales of a particular product or service. For example, in selling goods that have a high cost (such as television sets, music systems, cookers, or cars), such incentives as favourable payment terms (including low-interest and even zero-interest loans) and apparently generous part-exchange offers can stimulate sales.

Similarly, particularly when selling services, the use of free gifts can greatly enhance a sales promotion. A gift valued at just 2–5% of the value of a purchase can often be the deciding factor in persuading an indecisive purchaser to make a positive decision.

Product Differentiation

The tactic of making a product appear to be different from competing products. This may be achieved by actually making the product unique or by influencing the way in which it is perceived by customers (for example, by giving it a unique packaging or by using advertising to create the impression that it is unique).

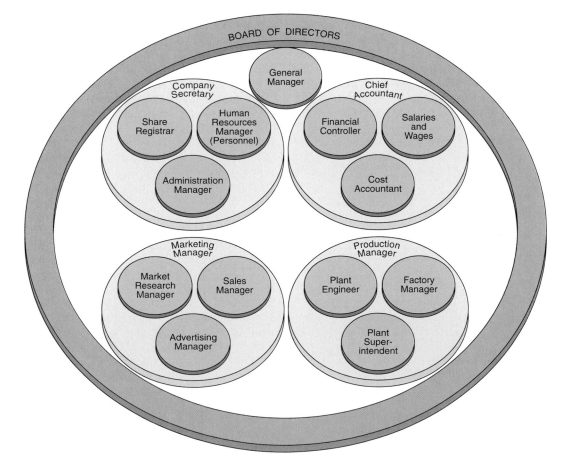

◄ **Marketing within a Company Structure**
This chart shows one possible corporate structure for a large manufacturing firm. Within this organizational structure, the marketing department is of equal importance to the production department.

Company Structure and Finance

Company management • Costing • Methods of costing • Budgeting • Financing a business • Company failure • Principles of accounting

===SEE ALSO===
This section:
• Conducting Business
• Marketing
• International Trade
Economics:
• The Price Mechanism
• Economic Resources

Organizational Structure *A chart illustrating one possible structure for a manufacturing organization. The brown side of the chart is known as the **line management**, responsible for the main activities of the company, i.e. making and selling the product. The yellow side, known as the **staff management**, provide essential support services.* ▼

No business can function properly unless it has a well-defined structure in which tasks are divided among groups, each group headed by a person in whom authority has been vested.

While it is not possible to lay down a structure that is universally applicable, it is reasonable to summarize some of the qualities that a good working business structure will have:

• **clear objectives.** The organization as a whole and the groups into which the structure is broken down must have clearly stated achievable objectives. All parties involved must be kept fully informed of these objectives.

• **responsibility.** The person or persons at the summit of the organizational structure must be aware of the extent and the limitations of their responsibilities, as well as the extent and the limitations of those to whom they have delegated responsibilty. Responsibility that has been delegated must be accompanied by sufficient authority to enable the responsibility to be exercised.

• **flexibility.** Any business structure must be flexible enough to enable it to adopt any modification arising from policy or market changes, government regulations, etc.

Company Management

The principal function of the managers of a company are to formulate its policies and to state them in the form of clear objectives. This, in many large companies, is the function of the **board of directors**. The directors of a company may be full-time employees of the company, who function as executive members of its staff in addition to being members of the board. Alternatively, they may be part-time directors who have been invited to join the board for any of a variety of reasons, including their seniority in the organization or the industry, their contacts outside (political or commercial), or their expert knowledge of one or more aspects of the company's work. Directors may or may not be shareholders in the company; they may have been invited to join the board because of their large and influential shareholding, or they may have been entitled to acquire a holding in the shares as a consequence of being appointed to the board. The **chairman of the board of directors** is nominally the head of the company, although in some countries and in some companies this office may be given to a person to honour their

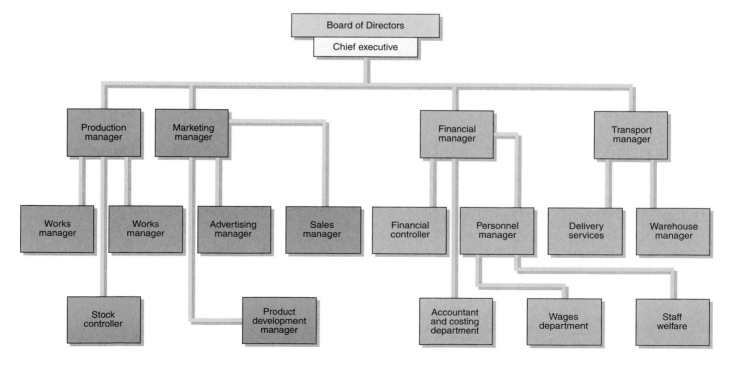

past services, rather than to give them real executive power.

The person charged with overall management of a company is usually called the ***chief executive*** or the ***managing director***. However, in large organizations the chief executive of a subsidiary company may not necessarily be a member of the main board of the holding company that owns it.

Costing

However efficient the structure of a company, it can only operate successfully if it has proper control and understanding of its finances. How much does it cost to make its products or provide its services? Does the organization keep proper financial records? Does it set financial objectives and does it achieve them? Is it profitable? Where does the capital for the business come from? Every organization, whether profit-making or not, incurs costs that have to be met from income. In a profit-making business the excess of income over costs is equal to the profit. In a non-profit-making organization, such as a charity or university, the excess of income over costs would be an operating surplus. Measuring and controlling costs is, therefore, critical to the success of all organizations, irrespective of size or purpose.

Costs arise at every stage of a business's activities. Some depend upon the volume of business (***direct*** or ***variable costs***), while others, such as rent, tend to remain static, irrespective of the activity level (***overhead*** or ***fixed costs***). The logical breakdown of costs will, of course, depend upon the type of business involved. The diagram entitled 'Elements of a Product Cost' illustrates a typical breakdown of costs for a manufacturing company.

There are several types of direct costs. ***Direct costs of raw materials*** are the costs of the raw materials used for a particular job or production batch. ***Direct labour costs*** are the costs of labour (skilled and unskilled) directly attributable to the production of a particular job or batch. Other ***direct expenses*** are additional direct costs, such as packaging, power, etc., incurred for a particular job or batch.

Overheads, both those incurred in manufacturing and the general overheads (such as the cost of marketing, new-product development, and accountancy), are costs not directly related to the production of a particular product but incurred as a result of the organization of the business. They need to be recovered in the selling price and therefore have to be included in the calculation of total cost. Various methods exist to cover the cost of overheads. In a multi-product business the calculation can be quite complex. However, for a manufacturer of a single product, say office desks, the

calculation is simple. If the manufacturer makes 3000 units per year and overheads for the year are estimated at £50,000, the overhead component for each desk produced will be £50,000 ÷ 3000 = £16.67 per desk. This component has to be recovered in the selling price of the desk, together with its direct cost and the profit element.

Methods of Costing

There are three main costing methods:
- ***Job*** or ***contract costing***: this is typically used when a specific order is costed as an independent unit. Examples could include repairing a motor car or building a ship.
- ***Batch costing***: this is most useful when there are a number of uniform products or if the items produced are small and cheap.

▲ **A Board Meeting in a Company** *Vital decisions affecting the long-term strategy of companies are taken at meetings such as this.*

Elements of a Product Cost *The various factors that come into play in determining the cost of a product are shown.* ▼

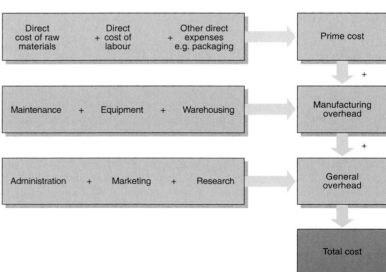

Standard Factory Cost ▶ *The methods by which a manufacturing company arrives at the ex-factory cost of a product.*

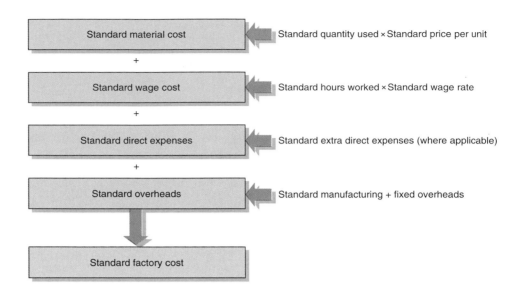

Standard material cost	◀ Standard quantity used × Standard price per unit
+	
Standard wage cost	◀ Standard hours worked × Standard wage rate
+	
Standard direct expenses	◀ Standard extra direct expenses (where applicable)
+	
Standard overheads	◀ Standard manufacturing + fixed overheads
↓	
Standard factory cost	

variance analysis An analysis of the way in which the standard cost, revenue, or profit differs from the actual figures. Variances can be analysed into their causes, e.g. price variances, quantity variances, efficiency variances, etc.

• ***Process costing***: this is applicable if the result of one process becomes the raw material of another, i.e. if a series of processes are involved before the product finally becomes saleable. Food manufacturing and the chemical industry are examples in which process costing is appropriate.

Irrespective of the method of costing, the breakdown of costs into component parts remains the same. Moreover, it is equally important for those providing services as for manufacturers. The discipline of ***cost accounting*** is concerned with analysis of the costs of running an organization. Two particular forms of costing are recognized: ***standard costing*** and ***marginal costing.***

Standard Costing. In standard costing, the term 'standard' is used in the sense of 'planned,' i.e. standard costing involves determining costs in advance. It enables the manufacturer to know what the cost of a unit of production will be – or should be. In practice there will sometimes be inevitable variations in the planned cost. These have to be monitored and, where necessary, incorporated into the costing. The diagram above shows how a standard factory cost for a particular product might be arrived at. **Variance analysis** is the method then used to check that the actual costs are equal to the planned or standard costs. Variations might turn out to be justified (say, as the result of a miscalculation when the standard was set or an unexpected change in the cost of a raw material), in which case the standard cost would have to be modified. If, however, variations are found to be unjustified (perhaps because there has been an overuse of materials), this will have to be rectified before the next production run.

Marginal Costing. This method of costing a product or service takes account of only the direct costs of producing it, rather than allocating all the costs (direct and overhead), as under a standard costing system. The basis of this method of costing is that at any particular moment certain costs are fixed (rent, administration, etc.), irrespective of the quantity of the product or the extent of the service. Therefore, the decision whether to produce X or Y units should be preceded by a consideration of the marginal costs of each. This decision should be taken on the basis of the excess of revenue over **marginal costs** for each of the alternatives. The difference between the revenue and marginal cost is known as the ***contribution*** the item makes towards the overheads and the profit.

Profitability. It is important to be able to predict at what level of activity revenue from sales will at least cover the costs of a business. The point at which sales revenue of a business equals the total costs is called the ***break-even point***. Beyond this point the business begins to make a profit. This is represented visually in the profitability charts: the first graph highlights the profit zone; the second presents the same information in such a way that the contribution to the overheads and the profit can be clearly seen.

Budgeting

Budgeting is an essential short-term expression of a management's intentions for a future period of trading (usually a year). These intentions set the targets that need to be met in order to satisfy the objectives of an organization.

The major targets likely to be set in the budget are:
• sales revenue (and volume)
• direct costs
• overheads
• profit (gross and net)

These main areas will, in turn, be broken

down by department, by activity, and perhaps by product. In the case of a business that is located in more than one place, each location will have its own detailed budget, forming part of the overall budget for the organization.

For the budgeting process to be accurate and achievable, it is important that all key personnel are involved in its development. Budgets prepared by a small group at a head office, with minimal reference to local managers, are often unreliable. There are two reasons for this:

• It is unlikely that such a small group could have all the relevant information for such a detailed exercise.
• The management and staff who have to implement a budget are likely to be more dedicated to achieving its objectives if they have been involved in its development.

Successful budgeting is usually a team effort. The first step in the process is to determine the key factors or constraints that will have a direct influence on the budget. These factors or constraints would include:

• lack of capital
• lack of production capacity
• restricted factory or retail space
• shortage of trained personnel
• a declining or static market for the product

Once any constraining factors have been identified, the most important question to be answered is 'How much can be sold during the budget period?' The answer to this question will then set the upper limit of the budget. Constraints of the type listed may then reduce this upper limit, so that a balance has to be struck between what can be sold and what can be produced. The budgetary process generally starts, therefore, with a forecast of sales (see MARKETING) for the period under review.

Complete accuracy in the sales forecast is essential. An overestimate of sales may lead to

unnecessary expenditure of capital and revenue; on the other hand, a pessimistic approach may not only affect immediate profits but may also depress the company's long-term market share. When the sales forecast has been established, it is possible to prepare a ***sales budget***.

This sales forecast and the sales budget produced from it enable the following important factors to be set:

• total forecast sales revenue
• quarterly production requirements
• levels of stock required per quarter
• materials and personnel requirements.

The process of budgeting then has to be followed through in the various cost areas. The steps involved may include:

• sales budget (as shown)
• production budget
• materials budget
• direct labour budget
• selling and distribution budget
• administration cost budget
• overhead cost budget

These individual budgets can then be amalgamated to produce the master budget, which, once approved by the directors, will form the basis for the coming year's activities. There are also likely to be two additional very important budgets: the **capital-expenditure budget** and the ***cash-flow projection*** (sometimes called the ***cash budget***).

Capital-expenditure budgeting is essentially a long-term activity; although conducted annually, it is usually part of a much larger and longer process. In drawing up a capital-expenditure budget, the following factors need to be considered:

• plant utilization and possible future shortfall in capacity
• replacement of old plant and machinery and the need for additional capacity

> **marginal cost** The extra cost of increasing the output of a production run by one unit; this extra cost consists entirely of direct costs. In conditions of perfect competition, the marginal cost would be equal to the market price.

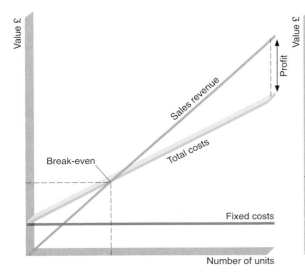

◀ **Profitability Charts**
First a unit selling price is set, enabling the sales revenue line to be drawn on the basis of predicted sales. In the first diagram, the costs are calculated on the basis of fixed costs being independent of the number of articles produced. In the second diagram, the concept of the contribution is illustrated. Both diagrams show the same break-even point and profit.

capital The money or other assets invested in a business by its owners in order to make it function. The **working capital** is the part of a company's capital that is available for use in its day-to-day trading. **Capital expenditure** is the money spent by a business to acquire **fixed assets** (assets that will usually serve the business for a long period), such as buildings or machinery.

- vehicle requirements (replacement and additions)
- fixtures, fittings, and office machinery (replacements and additions)
- land and buildings (renovations, extensions, and new construction)

Before any investment is made, it is not enough to identify the need or potential need. It is also necessary to quantify the benefits likely to result from the investment. Obviously, the larger the investment, the more important it is to make the right decision. For this reason companies use a number of techniques to predict the benefits resulting from capital investment. One of the most commonly used is the **discounted cash flow** technique (see panel).

Once a decision has been reached to make a capital expenditure, the appropriate provision has to be made for it in the cash-flow projection (see CONDUCTING BUSINESS), which is influenced by all the separate budgets and is therefore usually the last to be prepared. The cash-flow projection is the vital document that predicts the flow of cash into and out of the business during the period under review. (It is not concerned with non-cash costs, such as depreciation.) It consists of estimates of all cash receipts and payments resulting from the activities and expenditure detailed in the various budgets. Its purpose is to highlight cash deficits and surpluses, enabling management to take the appropriate action. Because fluctuations can take place within a fairly short space of time, cash-flow projections are prepared on a monthly basis (sometimes even weekly) for the period ahead and are constantly reviewed. The steps required to prepare a cash-flow projection for a given period are quite straightforward:

- establish the cash balance at the start of the period
- add income expected
- deduct payments to be made

DISCOUNTED CASH FLOW (DCF)

It is better to receive £1 today rather than in one year's time unless the delay is rewarded by interest being added to the original sum. Thus if £1 is invested today at a rate of interest of 10%, the investment will be worth £1.10 in one year's time. It follows that £1.10 received a year from now is only worth £1 at present values, because of the effects of inflation.

This simple but true concept is the basis of DCF. By predicting the benefit (income) arising over a number of years as the result of a capital investment, and then adjusting it to present values, a business can judge whether or not an investment is worthwhile.

Thus, a person considering making an investment in a business venture will calculate the future receipts he or she may expect to gain by the investment and discount them to present values. The investor will also take account of the interest that might have been earned on the investment over the relevant number of years. This will enable the investor to calculate the so-called **net present value** of the investment, i.e. its economic value calculated by deducting discounted future revenues from discounted costs.

- establish closing balance (which becomes the opening balance for the next period)

A simple cash-flow projection is shown opposite. In the preparation of a cash-flow projection, there are two important requirements to ensure its accuracy:

- Sales forecasts need to be accurate. Any shortfall will seriously affect the budget. Until production and stocks can be reduced

Sales Budget *An example of the sales budget of a company producing three products, X, Y, and Z, which sell at £8, £9, and £10, respectively.* ▶

Forecast	Quarter 1	Quarter 2	Quarter 3	Quarter 4	Total for year
No. of Units					
Product X	3,000	3,000	2,500	3,000	11,500
Product Y	2,000	2,000	2,000	2,250	8,250
Product Z	1,000	1,250	1,500	1,500	5,250
Sales Value					
Product X @ £8	24,000	24,000	20,000	24,000	92,000
Product Y @ £9	18,000	18,000	18,000	20,250	74,250
Product Z @ £10	10,000	12,500	15,000	15,000	52,500
	52,000	54,500	53,000	59,250	218,750

	Month 1	Month 2	Month 3	Month 4
Opening Balance	+3,000	+4,000	+2,000	−1,000
Receipts	7,000	6,000	7,000	8,000
Total Cash Available	10,000	10,000	9,000	7,000
Payments	6,000	8,000	10,000	6,000
Closing Balance	+4,000	+2,000	−1,000	+1,000

◄ **Cash-flow Projection (Cash Budget)** *This balance sheet shows the monthly balance of a company's accounts.*

to the appropriate level, cash flowing out will remain at the original estimated level while cash from debtors (sales) will be lower than estimated.

• It is essential that good **credit control** is maintained and that receipts from debtors arrive within the agreed credit period. This will have been the major factor in determining monthly receipts within the budget. These estimates should be realistic, rather than optimistic.

Budgetary Control. It is no use preparing detailed budgets and then trusting that they will be adhered to. They must be used as standards against which actual performance is measured. Any deviation must be carefully analysed and corrected as quickly as possible. Budgets, however, cannot be totally inflexible.

From time to time unforeseen costs may arise and are accepted by the management as necessary. If these can be shown to have a beneficial effect on the company, particularly if they are likely to add to its profitability, they should be considered, even though they did not appear in the original budget.

Financing a Business
Most businesses come into existence as a result of individuals risking their own savings or pledging their assets to a bank in return for a loan or overdraft. As the business grows so the need for funding is also likely to increase. When this happens, the business will have not only to identify the exact extent of its requirements, but also to consider which of the various options for raising money are available to

Credit Control

Many businesses sell their goods or services to customers but do not expect immediate payment. Typically, there might be a 30-day delay between the customer receiving the goods or service and being required to pay for them. This delay will, of course, be taken into account in preparing the cash-flow projection. If, however, credit is given, it is essential that the supplying company has an effective system to ensure that payment arrives in accordance with the agreed credit terms. Effective credit control may involve the use of reminder letters, telephone calls, and the suspension of further supplies.

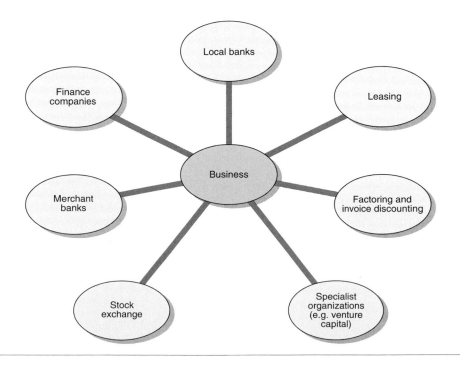

◄ **External Sources of Funding** *A company can employ various means to raise funds. The management need to quantify their requirements and approach the most appropriate source or sources.*

STOCK EXCHANGES

Stock exchanges are markets for the buying and selling of *securities* (documents issued by a company or institution, in exchange for a sum of money, that entitle the holder to interest payments or property rights). Common forms of security are bonds (usually securities for a loan issued by governments, local authorities, and companies that pay a fixed rate of interest), or share certificates (equities) that give to their owners a part ownership in the companies that issue them and a right to share in the profits in the form of **dividends**.

In order to become listed on the stock exchange (a process referred to as *flotation*), a company must first have offered a certain proportion of its shares to public ownership. It must also fulfil other conditions, which vary from country to country. The advantage to a company of having its share price publicly quoted in this way is that it can raise funds to finance its expansion. However, there are also dangers in 'going public': a company may run the risk of exposing itself to attempts by rival institutions to buy the company, by persuading the shareholders of the target company that a change of ownership would increase profits and returns to investors (**takeover bids**).

Stock exchanges exist in most of the world's capital cities or major financial centres. The largest are in New York (Wall Street), London, Tokyo, and Paris (*La Bourse*).

Since the 1980s, the character of stock exchanges worldwide has been undergoing considerable change. Despite some much-publicized flotations of formerly state-owned enterprises and the purchase of a proportion of their shares by small investors, individual private investors have become less important than large-scale investors, such as insurance companies and pension funds. Since such institutions can deploy huge sums of money amassed from their participating investors, they can cause greater fluctuations in markets than was previously possible.

Factoring

This practice provides a manufacturer or trader with funds by the purchase of his or her trade debts for cash. Thus, if a manufacturer is short of the cash required to buy new materials but is owed money by his customers, he can approach a *factor*. This is an individual or firm who – for a percentage of the invoice value – will pay an agreed percentage of the invoice (usually up to 90%) immediately and the balance after collecting the debt from the customer. The cost of the service depends on whether or not the factor assumes the credit risk (if the customer's business should fail or if he does not pay foor some other reason). Many banks provide this factoring service.

it. It then has to select the most appropriate of these options.

Under ideal circumstances a company will be generating sufficient profit to meet its financial needs. In reality, this is rarely the case. Often it will need to rely upon one or more external sources to meet its need for additional funding. The principal sources of funding are:

- *local banks* – for short-term funding (overdrafts and loans) and the provision of day-to-day banking facilities
- *finance companies* – provide funds for purchasing assets (cars, machinery, etc.), which are repaid in instalments
- *leasing* – hiring machinery or equipment without purchasing it
- *merchant banks* – provide specialist banking services, usually for larger companies requiring financing for international trade or for raising capital
- *factoring* – provides companies with a means of turning debts due to them from customers into cash
- *stock exchanges* – provide facilities for trading in shares in publicly quoted companies and for raising new capital (see panel)
- *venture capital* – funds provided by specialist organizations to help companies grow or develop new products or technologies (see panel).

Not all the sources of external funding listed above will be appropriate for or available to all businesses in all countries. However, all small businesses are likely to have a bank account.

Subject to their financial status this will give them access to bank loans and overdraft facilities. Borrowings are usually available in three forms:

- short term (day to day or up to 3 years)
- medium term (3–10 years)
- long term (10 years or over)

Selecting the right type of borrowing may be critical for a business as different types of lending usually involve different repayment conditions and different rates of interest, some of which may be prohibitively high for a small business. In practice, companies that are trying to raise investment capital often aim to put together a package of funding that is particularly tailored to their individual needs. Ideally, it should be one that minimizes cost and risk and maximizes the independence or freedom of the business.

Company Failure

It is an inevitable fact of business life throughout the world that some companies will cease trading, because they have been financially mismanaged, because of fraudulent dealing on the part of the owners, or simply because the market for their product has shrunk to a smaller than viable size. Indeed, a whole host of reasons may attend the collapse of a business. New small businesses or companies are particularly vulnerable, as they have to establish themselves in the market, often in the face of fierce competition from established firms aiming to maintain their accustomed market

◀ **The Trading Floor of the Stock Exchange in New York** *Increased computerization, which took place in the 1980s, has meant that markets across the world are now heavily dependent on each other.*

share. It has been shown that most small businesses fail within the first two years; generally speaking, if a company survives for five years, it has a far greater chance of surviving for a long period into the future.

When a firm becomes **insolvent** (i.e. its liabilities are greater than its assets – excluding assets in the form of share capital), it may seek to be declared bankrupt: its finances are placed in the hands of an official appointed by a law court, who distributes its assets to the benefit of the various creditors of the company. World recession has had the effect in many countries of replacing large-scale employment by large concerns with smaller enterprises and self employment; bankruptcies have also increased dramatically. See LAW: CIVIL LAW.

Alternatively, the insolvent company, rather than petition for bankruptcy, may seek a new injection of capital. This sometimes takes the form of a **management buy-out**. Because the management of a company has proven ability in running the business, and is well-acquainted with existing clients and the market, those in a position to offer financial support may consider this an acceptable risk.

VENTURE CAPITAL

The term 'venture capital' describes capital invested in a business in which the investor understands that there is a substantial element of risk. It is not a loan; it usually involves the purchase of part of the equity (share capital) of the business. Venture capital is often required when a new business is set up or when an existing company requires new funds in order to expand.

Venture capital may be provided by private business persons, who have spare money they wish to invest in a new enterprise. If such a person purchases a substantial part of the equity of a new business, he or she may wish to be involved in running it, for example by becoming a member of its board of directors. Merchant banks may also be willing to put up venture capital in a new or existing business, either in place of making a loan or in addition to doing so.

In some cases a supplier to an existing company may be willing to provide venture capital to finance an expansion, often because it believes that in this way it will increase its sales to the company. Similarly, a customer of an enterprise may be willing to provide venture capital to its supplier because it is doing well by selling its products and is anxious to obtain more of them. Large chains of retailers, for example, sometimes buy into their smaller suppliers in this way in order to obtain some measure of control over them.

dividend A payment made to a shareholder of a company from its profits. The value of a dividend is often given on the face value of a share. Shareholders are usually more interested in the return on their investment, which is related to the market value of the share, rather than its face value. This is often expressed as the **dividend yield** of a share, i.e. a percentage of the market price.

PRINCIPLES OF ACCOUNTING

EVERY BUSINESS NEEDS to keep records of all the transactions it enters into. In many countries, this is a legal requirement. Normally the keeping of records is achieved by means of a system of double-entry bookkeeping.

The accounts that are kept of the transactions of a business and its inward and outward flow of goods or services, as well as its cash flow, are of interest to two sets of people:
1. Those inside the company who wish to know the state of the business in order to control it; this is management accounting.
2. Those outside the company who wish to know the state of the business, because they might wish to invest in it, make a loan to it, or assess it for taxation purposes; this is called financial accounting.

The document summarizing the assets, capital, and liabilities of a business is known as a balance sheet because both sides of the account have to balance in accordance with the balance-sheet equation.

DEBTORS AND CREDITORS
Debtors are people or firms that owe money; for example, some regular customers may have an account at a shop, which enables them to make purchases and defer payment for them until the end of the month. Creditors are people or firms to whom money is owed; for example, a firm supplying stock to a trader on the understanding that he will not have to pay for his purchases for 60 days is the trader's creditor.

A more complicated analysis of a business divides assets into fixed assets, which remain unchanged for a long time, and current assets, which change regularly.

Liabilities are also customarily divided into deferred liabilities, which do not have to be repaid for more than 12 months, and current liabilities, which have to be settled within a period not exceeding 12 months.

As an illustrative example, imagine a small business consisting of a single carpenter. In this example, it is assumed that the carpenter had an initial stock of wood worth $6000, and has sold bookcases during the year for $20,000, having reduced the value of the stock to $2000. On the face of it, the carpenter has used $4000 worth of wood, made sales of $20,000, and therefore made a gross profit of $16,000. A salary of $12,000 has been taken during the course of the year for living expenses. Because the profits belong to those who have invested in the business (which may include the carpenter), profits are added to the capital, while the salary is deducted from profits.

THE BALANCE SHEET

Every commercial organization has things that it owns (e.g. its buildings and machinery). These are referred to as its

ASSETS.

On the other hand, all commercial organizations have certain financial obligations to those who have invested in it. These people are the owners of the organization (shareholders) and the money invested by the owners is called its

CAPITAL.

Further financial obligations are represented by the sums of money that the organization owes to people other than its owners. Examples include loans extended by banke to finance the business or payments due t suppliers. Collectively, these obligations a known as its

LIABILITIES.

In order to have acquired an asset, an organization must have taken money from existing capital, or have borrowed funds fr someone else, thus creating a liability. It therefore follows from this that

ASSETS = CAPITAL + LIABILITIES.

This statement is called the balance-sheet

BALANCE SHEET FOR A CARPENTER

	$			$	
FIXED ASSETS			**CAPITAL**		
Workshop	10,000		Owners' investments	6,000	
Tools	2,000		Gross profit	16,000	
		12,000			22,000
			Salary	(12,000)	
					10,000
CURRENT ASSETS			**LIABILITIES**		
Stock	2,000		**Deferred liabilities**		
Debtors	4,000		Loan	6,000	
Cash	2,000		**Current liabilities**		
		8,000	Creditors	4,000	10,000
		$20,000			$20,000

The balance sheet illustrated provides a simple but comprehensive summary of the assets, capital, and liabilities relating to the carpenter's business at the balance-sheet date.

DEPRECIATION

Many of the fixed assets of businesses wear out, become obsolete, are depleted, or lose value simply as a result of the passage of time. If an asset, say a delivery van, was purchased for $10,000 and sold three years later for $7000, its depreciation over the three-year period will have been $3000; it can therefore be said to have suffered an annual depreciation of $1000. However, it is necessary to take the depreciation of an asset into account even if it has not been sold and if there is no intention of selling it. Otherwise the balance sheet would have to show the assets at its original cost; this would have the effect of giving too favourable an impression of the company's total assets.

There are various ways of calculating depreciation; each method starts from the historical cost of the asset. It is then necessary to make an estimate of the length of the asset's remaining useful life and residual value at the end of this useful life.

Depreciation is deducted from the cost of a fixed asset in the balance sheet of a company; it also appears in the profit and loss account as an expense of the business.

INTERNATIONAL ACCOUNTING PRACTICES

National laws and codes of practice relating to taxation may require that different procedures be adopted in certain countries.

A further problem results from the effects of inflation. This has given rise to the practice of inflation accounting, in which the values of fixed assets and investments, for example, are adjusted at the end of each financial year, in accordance with price indexes (which are compiled by governments' financial advisers). Depreciation is also calculated on the values of assets after inflation adjustments.

The major advantage of inflation accounting is that it gives a far more accurate picture of a company's true financial position, since it ensures that assets are not overvalued.

THE DOUBLE-ENTRY BOOK-KEEPING SYSTEM

The basis of this system is that every transaction leads to two entries in the records: a credit and a debit.
The simple but strict rule of double-entry book-keeping is that the giver must be credited and the receiver debited. Thus, if a company buys stock on credit, it will make a credit entry in favour of the supplier and a debit entry in its stock or asset records.

PROFIT AND LOSS ACCOUNT

The profit and loss account enables the profit (or loss) of a business to be calculated, usually for one year. It consists of three separate statements:
1. The trading account is used to calculate the difference between the income received from trading and the direct costs arising from trading; this gives the gross profit

SALE OF GOODS − COST OF GOODS = GROSS PROFIT.

The direct costs include the cost of materials required. In order to find the real cost of goods sold, it is essential to take into account the value of the stock of goods or raw materials at the start and finish of the accounting period, as well as purchases of raw materials:

OPENING STOCK + PURCHASES IN PERIOD − CLOSING STOCK = COST OF GOODS SOLD.

Thus a small manufacturing company might have a trading account as shown.
2. The profit and loss account is used to adjust the gross profit from the trading account for nontrading income and the expenses. In the example of the manufacturer, part of the premises is let to another company, generating an annual income of $5000. On the debit side, the plant and machinery has depreciated by $8600. If the expenses (including depreciation) are $54,600, the profit and loss account would be as shown.
3. The appropriation account indicates what happens to the net profit. In general, a proportion of the profit will be paid out in taxation or dividends to shareholders. Appropriations of the net profit also customarily include transfers of funds to reserves. The balance of the net profit will be retained in the company in order to finance growth.

TRADING ACCOUNT OF A MANUFACTURER

	$	
Total sales		140,000
Deduct cost of goods sold		
Opening stock	20,000	
Purchases	80,000	
	100,000	
Less closing stock	24,000	
		76,000
GROSS PROFIT		$64,000

PROFIT AND LOSS ACCOUNT OF A MANUFACTURER

		$	
Gross profit			64,000
Rental income from letting			5,000
			69,000
Deduct expenses			
Wages and salaries		40,000	
Overheads (electricity, water, etc.)		6,000	
Depreciation on plant		8,600	54,600
NET PROFIT			$ 14,400

International Trade

Visibles and invisibles • Balance of trade • Trade restrictions •
Changes in patterns of trade

===SEE ALSO===
This section:
• Regional Trading Blocs
Economics:
• Measuring Economic Activity
• Goals of Economic Policy

Few people would disagree with the proposition that trade between nations is desirable. One nation sells goods to another because it is producing something that the other needs at a price it can afford to pay. This may be because it has the benefit of natural deposits (e.g. oil, iron ore, or diamonds) or climate (e.g. to grow tropical fruits or hardwood), or because it can produce a commodity more efficiently than other countries. This is sometimes referred to as the principle of **comparative advantage**.

Japanese car and motorcycle manufacturers, for example, excelled at providing vehicles to customers in international markets at prices below those of many of their competitors during the 1970s and 1980s. At the same time they managed to sustain and improve quality, making it very difficult for other manufacturers to compete. Manufacturers in other countries had either to produce comparable products at comparable prices or go out of business. Those that remained either matched or improved on the products of their Japanese competitors. Western volume car producers are an example of this, some of whom went into partnership with Japanese manufacturers. Thus, it is not the quality of the product that is the only criterion of success: poor management and over-powerful trade unions can destroy a country's competitiveness.

Visibles and Invisibles

The selling of goods and services to foreign countries is usually referred to as *foreign trade*. All countries seek to make this a two-way process. On the one hand a country imports the range of goods and services it needs; on the other, it exports its own goods and services in order to pay for the imports. As with any business or household, countries hope to achieve a situation in which exports will at least equal imports.

Ideally, the inflow of funds from exports should be greater than the outflow to pay for

Comparative Advantage

In the theory of international trade comparative advantage is sometimes also referred to as the *comparative cost principle.*

Underlying this principle is the idea that international trade in goods and services will be maximized if each nation concentrates on producing those things for which it has a comparative advantage over other countries. Thus, while a country might be capable of manufacturing products X, Y, and Z, it might make most economic sense for it to concentrate on producing X and Y, export its surplus, and import what it needs of Z.

THE ORIGINS OF FOREIGN TRADE

Trade between countries has been conducted since ancient times. One of the earliest examples of international commerce is the **Silk Road** (see below), along which the civilizations of the Mediterranean and China traded goods from the 1st century BC onwards. Silk and porcelain were brought from East to West in exchange for precious metals and gemstones. Improvements in marine navigation eventually made this hazardous overland route redundant.

The principal early seaborne traders of the Mediterranean were the Phoenicians. From their base (in modern Syria and Lebanon) they established an extensive mercantile empire after 1000 BC.

Salt – a precious seasoning and preservative – opened up trade routes between North and West Africa in the 7th century AD. Transported across the Sahara Desert by Berber tribes, it was bartered in the kingdoms of Ghana and Mali.

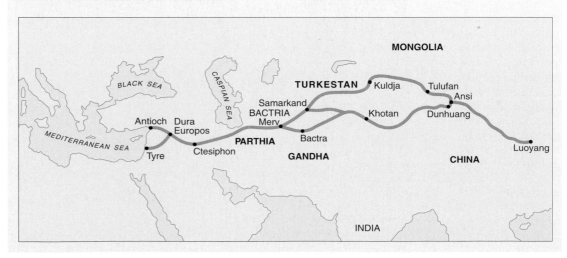

LLOYD'S OF LONDON

A 17th-century coffee shop in the City of London was the starting point for what has become the centre of the world's insurance industry. Initially concerned solely with the insurance of ships and their cargoes, Lloyd's has diversified into many other forms of insurance. Wherever there is a risk of loss, insurance can almost always be obtained from Lloyd's. The insurance businesses that make up Lloyd's are called syndicates. These are groups of individuals (known as 'names') who provide the capital to pay out claims. The names do not underwrite the business themselves, but do so through syndicate **underwriters**, whom insurance brokers representing companies or individuals approach for a quote for insuring against a particular risk. In return, the underwriter charges a premium. If a claim arises (say, a ship sinking), the underwriters and the syndicates they represent must cover the loss. If the premiums collected over a year cannot satisfy the claims, the names are obliged to meet the shortfall from their personal resources.

The Trading Floor of Lloyd's Building ▶

underwriter A person skilled in insurance business who is prepared to accept a risk and quote a premium for doing so. In addition, the underwriter fixes the terms and conditions for insurance contracts.

imports. This is referred to as a **balance of trade surplus**. In practice, however, some countries import more than they export, which creates a **balance of trade deficit**. For the majority of nations, foreign trade consists of income and expenditure in two categories: **visibles** and **invisibles**. Visible trade is concerned with the import and export of goods, i.e. such commodites as food, raw materials, and machinery. Invisible trade, on the other hand, covers less tangible imports and exports: i.e. such services as tourism, banking, and insurance.

Insurance provides a good example of invisible trade, as well as being an essential ingredient of the trading process (especially foreign trade). Whenever a risk is involved the responsible trader is bound by duty to his customers, employees, and shareholders to insure against loss or the possibility of loss. A clear instance of this occurs in the oil industry. At every stage in the process of creating a range of products from crude mineral oil, a risk is involved: in extraction, transportation, refining, and retailing. If a supertanker, perhaps carrying 250 000 tonnes of oil from the production source to the refinery, were to be involved in an accident, the losses and associated costs could be enormous, not only for the ship and its cargo, but for possible claims resulting from widespread environmental pollution. By

insuring against these risks (marine risks) the oil companies protect themselves. The premium or fee that is charged for taking on this responsibility (underwriting the risk) will be based upon the level of risk as perceived by the underwriter. **Lloyd's of London** is the world's leading insurance market, providing cover against the risks that arise in international trade.

Wreck of the Supertanker *Amoco Cadiz*
Huge insurance claims arise from disasters such as this in 1978. ▼

▲ A Container Port
The 1970s and 1980s saw a sharp increase in the amount of manufactured goods exported from Japan.

exchange rate The amount of one country's currency that is needed to purchase the basic unit of another country's currency at a particular time. This may change hourly. Two rates are usually given, the *buying rate* and the *selling rate*. The difference between the two represents the profit taken by the organization carrying out the exchange. The *spot rate* is for an immediate exchange of currencies. The *forward rate* is for an exchange at some fixed date in the future.

Balance of Trade

There are two important measurements arising out of a country's imports and exports: the *balance of trade* and the *current balance*, or current account. The balance of trade is the difference between the value of visible imports and the value of visible exports. The current balance is arrived at after including invisibles. If a country has a consistent current balance deficit, either the country's reserves of foreign currency will be depleted or it will incur increasing international debt as a result of borrowing. In the short-term, this situation may be necessary and acceptable. For example, when a country is emerging from recession, it may need to build up its stocks of imported raw materials in order to be able to create goods to export. In the long-term, however, it is not sustainable and a serious balance of payments deficit may occur. If this happens the country will be forced to take steps to bring the deficit under control.

The aim of any country faced with a long-term balance of payments deficit will be to reduce home demand (particularly for imported products) while trying to stimulate exports. The various options required to implement these policies are unlikely to be popular: they include increasing personal taxes (both to reduce consumer spending power and to boost government revenue), lower government spending, higher interest rates, and a managed **exchange-rate** policy. No single option is likely to be successful on its own. However, when a number of these measures are introduced at the same time there is a danger of overkill, i.e. they may create new problems if,

by achieving a major reduction in demand, a new recession is created. This is likely to lead to higher levels of unemployment and the failure of businesses. If some of these businesses happen to be exporters, the deficit problem can be magnified. Clearly, great care has to be taken when selecting the measures to be used in correcting a deficit.

Trade Restrictions

Another option to correct a balance of trade deficit is for a country to create trade barriers to restrict imports and possibly also to protect its own producers from foreign competition. This course can, however, rebound, resulting in retaliatory action from other countries. For many years international trading opinion has been concerned to restrict this option and instead actively to encourage free trade. Various regional trading blocs have been dedicated to the principle of free trade; internationally the **General Agreement on Tariffs and Trade (GATT)** has sought to encourage reduction in trade barriers.

In addition to correcting a balance of payments deficit, trade restrictions may be used to protect home producers (especially in the case of new or apparently vulnerable industries), to safeguard jobs, or to combat the practice of dumping (overseas producers selling at below market prices). The measures that are most frequently used to achieve these restrictions are:

• *Quotas*: a limit on the quantity of a product permitted to enter a country during a specified period;
• *Tariffs*: a special tax on foreign products to make them more expensive;

GENERAL AGREEMENT ON TARIFFS AND TRADE (GATT)

GATT, a specialized agency of the United Nations, provides a framework for the liberalization of international trade. It is the only multilateral instrument that establishes agreed rules for international trade; principal objectives of the agreement are to reduce barriers to trade, prevent new barriers being established, promote consultation between trading nations, and encourage multinational trade links.

GATT has been in force since 1 January 1948, and there are now over 100 nations taking part in the negotiations and discussions. Together, the participating countries account for almost 90% of world trade. A further 29 countries apply GATT on a de facto basis.

The major series of meetings are referred to as 'rounds,' named after the cities in which they took place. Since its formation, there have been eight GATT rounds:

Geneva	1947
Annecy	1948
Torquay	1950
Geneva	1956
Dillon	1960–61
Kennedy	1964–67
Tokyo	1973–79
Montevideo	1986–94

Agreement is often reached only after years of complex discussions. The most recent round (in Uruguay) was probably the most difficult so far. They did, however, produce the largest tariff cuts in the history of GATT. The result will be freer trade in manufactured goods, services, textiles, and agricultural products. In 10 years the agreement is expected to add £250 billion a year to world output. In addition, a new World Trade Organization to monitor international trade was created.

- **Embargoes**: a ban on trade with a particular country or in particular goods;
- **Exchange controls**: a restriction on the availability of foreign currency to importers making it difficult to pay for imports;
- **Subsidies**: a payment made or tax concession given to certain industries or producers. A country may also make it difficult for traders to import foreign goods by imposing strict rules and procedures (e.g. requiring that all goods of a certain kind be imported through one border crossing). This type of restriction, which aims to deter imports rather than openly ban them, is referred to as a **non-tariff barrier**.

As the gap between rich and poor countries becomes greater, there is an ever more urgent need to help poorer countries develop their economies. This problem has been addressed, at least in part, by the recent GATT rounds, the conclusion of the **North American Free Trade Agreement (NAFTA)**, and the United Nations Conference on Trade and Development (UNCTAD). Established in 1964, UNCTAD meets every four years, and is generally concerned with encouraging and monitoring international trade. The conference has a specific interest in helping developing countries to increase their export earnings and to protect the value of certain primary commodities when world prices for these products are low. Thus, while the general thrust in world trade is to reduce protectionism and interference and to make trading as free as possible, especially by reducing barriers, it is recognized that in some instances support is necessary.

Changes in Patterns of Trade

Trading patterns between countries and even geographical areas are subject to change from time to time. Traditional import–export relationships are modified, added to, diminished, or perhaps disappear. This may happen for political reasons or, more commonly, because new trading nations or groups of nations emerge. For example, postwar trading relationships for many European nations changed radically as their colonial trading partners were replaced by other member countries of the European Union. Similar changes have occurred in other trading blocs.

North American Free Trade Agreement (NAFTA)

In a further move towards trade liberalization, the USA, Canada, and Mexico concluded NAFTA in December 1992. This agreement created a free-trade zone between the three countries and provided for the phasing out of tariffs on almost all goods traded between the USA and Mexico. NAFTA covers a wide range of goods and services, plus telecommunications and patenting.

Anti-NAFTA Protestors in the USA *Fears were raised in the USA at the time of the NAFTA agreement that lower production costs in Mexico would cause the loss of domestic jobs.* ▼

International Finance and Investment

International monetary systems • The Bretton Woods conference • Foreign investments • International payments • Internationalization of business • Breaking into foreign markets

=====SEE ALSO=====
This section:
• International Trade
• Regional Trading Blocs
Economics:
• Goals of Economic Policy

floating exchange rate
A rate of exchange achieved when currency is freely traded and allowed to find its own level against other currencies.

The Wall Street Crash *Speculators crowding the streets after the New York Stock Exchange crashed in 1929. A casualty of the world recession was the Gold Standard.* ▼

Money is central to all economic activity. In whatever form it takes it is a measurement of value (see ECONOMICS: ECONOMIC SYSTEMS). However, each country has its own form of money – *currency* – which cannot be used in any other country. As trading between nations increased, so the need to match the value of different currencies became more important.

International Monetary Systems

Gold came to be used as the international standard. Either coins were minted in gold or the currencies of the various countries were convertible into gold at a fixed price. Effectively gold became a currency in its own right. This *Gold Standard*, as it was called, was the mechanism by which imbalances in international trade were automatically corrected. A country with a balance of trade deficit would pay out more gold than it received. The central bank would then need to contract the money supply in order to cover its liabilities to the holders of currency. In classical economic theory this would cause prices to fall, which would increase exports by making them more competitive; it would also have the effect of driving wage settlements down, which in turn would reduce the demand for imports. Increased exports and reduced imports would correct the imbalance. This arrangement was widely used in the 19th century and the early years of the 20th century. However, during World War I, when gold could no longer travel across international boundaries, the system was abandoned. Some countries returned to a modified form of the Gold Standard after the war, but the economic upheaval of the 1920s and 1930s ended its effective use.

KEY DATES IN 20TH-CENTURY MONETARY CONTROL	
1900–14	The Gold Standard was used for converting currencies and settling debts. It was abandoned during World War I owing to the impossibility of shipping gold.
1920s	A modified system of Gold Standard in operation.
1929–32	The Great Depression effectively ended the Gold Standard.
1932–39	A mixture of **floating exchange rates** and partial use of the Gold Standard.
1945–71	The Bretton Woods Conference sets up the IMF and IBRD. Steps were also taken towards freer currency movements and the reduction of **exchange controls**, while at the same time maintaining the value of currencies within 1% of a fixed gold value.
1973	Attempts to continue this level of cooperation and control, which had begun to break down in 1971, finally collapsed. Most countries opted for a **dirty float** of currencies.

EUROPEAN BANK FOR RECONSTRUCTION AND DEVELOPMENT (EBRD)

Founded in 1991, the EBRD has a set of statutes, the first article of which states its objective to be: "to contribute to the progress and reconstruction of the countries of central and eastern Europe which undertake to respect and put into practice the principle of multiparty democracy and a market economy, and to promote private initiative and the spirit of enterprise." It is able to offer unsecured loans at low rates of interest and encourages the privatization of formerly state-controlled enterprises.

The Bretton Woods Conference

The upheaval of World War II made it necessary for a new international system of monetary control to be established. In 1944 a conference attended by the USA, Canada, and the UK was held in the New Hampshire (USA) town of Bretton Woods in order to set up a postwar system. This conference created two new institutions: The International Monetary Fund (IMF) and the International Bank for Reconstruction and Development (IBRD), which is usually known as the 'World Bank.'

International Monetary Fund (IMF). The IMF was established to oversee the ***International Monetary System*** and encourage monetary cooperation between countries on the following lines:

- Member countries deposit funds with IMF, the amount in part determined by the size of their economies;
- Member countries with temporary balance-of-payments difficulties can borrow from the fund set up;
- The greater the loans from the fund given to a particular country, the more the IMF will seek to influence its economic policies;
- The IMF attempts to rebuild confidence in currencies that are in temporary difficulties.

World Bank. This organization aims to promote economic development in poorer countries. It has three component parts:

- ***The International Development Association (IDA)***, which makes interest-free loans to the poorest countries.
- ***The International Finance Corporation (IFC)***, which provides funding for private-sector ventures in developing countries.
- ***The Multilateral Investment Guarantee Agency (MIGA)***, which insures investments against risk or loss in developing countries.

A more recent initiative was the founding of the ***European Bank for Reconstruction and Development (EBRD)***.

Foreign Investments

The need for an international system of monetary control arises not only as a result of international trade but also for those wishing to make foreign investments. In the 19th century, many industrial countries acquired assets abroad, often in less developed countries, the income from which made substantial contributions to their balances of payments. After World War II and the decolonization of developing countries, many of those assets were sold to local interests. However, foreign investments are now a much more widely practised facet of international business as well as making much more frequent appearances in personal investment portfolios. Clearly all foreign investments, whether they are in productive enterprises or financial instruments (shares in foreign companies, foreign bonds, foreign currency, etc.), rely on a stable rate of exchange between the investor's own currency and the currency of the country in which he or she is investing.

The countries that receive foreign investment often have an ambivalent reaction to it – on the one hand it can be seen as creating jobs and wealth; on the other, there may be resentment that foreigners are buying into the control of local assets. Nevertheless, in the economy of the modern world foreign investment is of increasing importance.

---

exchange controls
Restriction on the outward flow of a country's currency. An importer needs government permission to buy a foreign currency or to export its own currency. Exchange controls are often used to protect a currency by restricting availability.

Dirty Float
Currency is freely traded, but each country's central bank attempts to influence its currency's value, either by intervening in the currency markets or by manipulation of interest rates. When there is no such intervention, the mechanism is referred to as a ***clean float***.

◀ **The European Bank for Reconstruction and Development in London** *The EBRD was established in 1991 to help finance projects for economic regeneration in depressed areas of eastern Europe that had formerly been part of the Soviet bloc.*

Anti-trust Legislation

The basis for such legislation is to protect consumers by encouraging competition and preventing monopoly by companies with a dominant market position. In particular, it aims to stop prices being fixed by any means other than fair competition. In addition, anti-trust laws often seek to control takeovers and mergers to prevent situations arising that lead to a dominant market position being obtained. Most industrial countries now have some form of anti-trust legislation.

Bill of Exchange *An order drawn by a creditor (the exporter, John Smith of New York) on a debtor (the importer, Manuel da Costa of Santiago, Chile) to pay a stated sum on a certain date. The bill has no value until it has been accepted by the person on whom it is drawn (the drawee). An accepted bill (as shown) becomes a negotiable instrument.* ▼

International Payments

As soon as a business decides to sell its products or services abroad it incurs new risks, which need to be understood. These risks are:
• failure of the importer (buyer) to pay;
• failure of the importer to obtain the necessary foreign exchange to pay;
• losses incurred as a result of fluctuating exchange rates.

The risk of non-payment can often be covered by insurance through government organizations that seek to promote exports. The operation of foreign-exchange transactions is normally conducted through a bank, which has the necessary expertise in this area. The bank will advise exporters which countries have exchange controls in force and whether or not the importer needs to apply for an import licence in order to obtain the foreign exchange. The methods of collecting payment for goods sold abroad are well established and include the following:

Bills of Exchange. These are documents telling an importer to pay a specific sum to an exporter, either, on demand or at some specified future date. Because a bill is transferable and negotiable, the exporter may sell it to a financial institution at a discount (i.e. for less than the sum stated on the bill) in order to secure the money before the due date. The institution buying the bill then assumes any risk attached to it.

Letters of Credit. These are documents from the importer's bank stating that the bank will pay to the exporter money due for goods when the terms of delivery have been complied with. There are various types of letter, the 'confirmed irrevocable letter of credit' offering the greatest security. It is interesting that on a shipment of goods from one country to another on a contract in which the exporter pays the freight charge and the insurance (i.e. a cost, insurance, and freight contract), the exporter is paid on presentation of the correct documents called for in the letter of credit (often a bill of lading, insurance policy, invoice, etc.), even if the ship carrying the goods sank during the voyage. Thus, the transaction is in documents, rather than goods.

Bank Draft. A cheque drawn by a bank on itself or its agent for a specific sum. The importer buys the draft from a bank and sends it to the exporter. If it is correctly made out it cannot be dishonoured unless the bank fails.

Electronic Transfer. A rapid means of transferring funds, from bank to bank, using fax or telex.

Internationalization of Business

While the development of international trade has its roots in a company in one country selling its goods to a company in another, significant changes have taken place in the growth of international trade in recent years. The most notable of these has been the increased dominance of multinational corporations – businesses with operations in more than one country. Many multinational corporations have passed through a number of different stages in their growth from a home-based exporter to a true international:

• ***First, introductory, stage***: a company's products become known in a foreign country – either by chance or deliberate policy – and they begin to export.
• ***Second, colonization, stage***: the company establishes a firm foothold in a foreign market, often using distributors at first and then developing its own subsidiary companies.
• ***Third, centralization, stage***: foreign businesses are controlled from a central Head Office in the home country, which initiates all objectives, plans, and development systems.
• ***Fourth, review, stage***: when sales are static or falling, some subsidiaries may be closed and others reorganized.
• ***Fifth, globalization, stage***: the company ceases to regard foreign markets in single-country or regional terms and instead produces products aimed at a global market.

The power and influence of the largest of these multinational companies is enormous. Their investment in a particular country and the transfer of funds or production from one location to another can have a marked impact. They are also often able to swamp competition and control prices. For this reason many countries have **anti-trust legislation** in an attempt to control undesirable activities of companies that dominate a market.

Breaking into Foreign Markets

There are a number of means by which companies may attempt to secure new markets

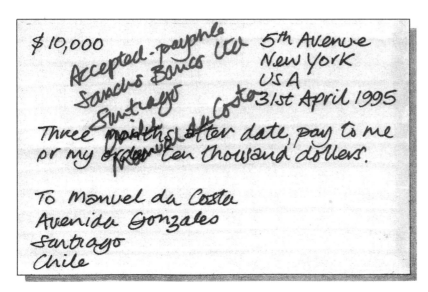

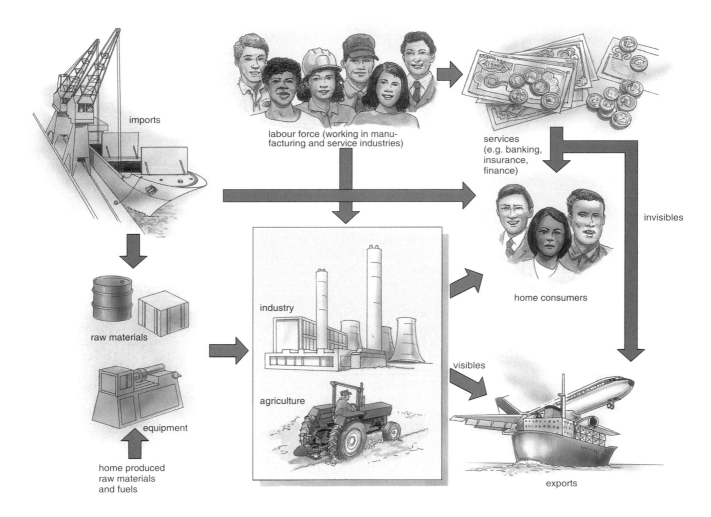

imports

labour force (working in manufacturing and service industries)

services
(e.g. banking,
insurance,
finance)

invisibles

raw materials

industry

home consumers

agriculture

visibles

equipment

home produced
raw materials
and fuels

exports

▲ **A Country's
Trade** *Imports are raw
materials required by
industry, or finished
products. The labour
force is deployed in
providing services or in
industry or agriculture.
Exports are either
visibles (goods) or
invisibles (services).*

abroad for their products or services, other than the obvious route of setting up their own companies to market or even to manufacture abroad. There may be a number of reasons for pursuing one or more of these alternative routes. Among these, the most common are the high costs of setting up a new organization abroad, and the restrictions or barriers to entry in certain foreign markets, which may limit other means of access. Alternatively, the company may be too small to enable it to set up as a truly international enterprise. The options in such a case are as follows:

Agents. These are individuals or firms that represent companies in foreign markets and attempt to obtain orders for their products or services. Agents do not usually carry stock and are unlikely to undertake any obvious form of marketing. Their task is to find potential buyers, negotiate with them, and secure a contract upon which they will earn a **commission**. They will normally have the authority to bind an exporter legally when agreeing the contractual terms with the buyer, but they will not be principals to the contracts.

Normally they do not guarantee the buyer's solvency. However, a ***del credere*** (Italian: 'of trust') agent does guarantee to pay for goods if his customer fails to do so. For this service the agent charges an extra commission.

Distributors. When a company cannot justify the cost of setting up a subsidiary company in a foreign country and yet still wishes to sell into that market, one of its options is to sell through distributors. Distributors buy goods from the exporter and sell them on through the appropriate distribution channels, usually at prices they themselves set. In many instances they will handle a number of similar products from different manufacturers. Their interest will, therefore, be in selling a range of goods rather than marketing a specific product in a focused way.

Joint Marketing Arrangements. A seller of goods can sometimes enter a foreign market by making an arrangement with a foreign manufacturer of a similar product, who wishes to extend the range or choice on offer to customers. The exporter benefits from the likelihood that the product will be marketed

commission A payment made to an agent, usually an agreed percentage of the value of orders obtained. An agent, who acts as an intermediary rather than a principal and who receives his remuneration as a commission, is known as a ***commission agent.***

patents Legal rights acquired by an inventor or developer of a product, machine, or process. These rights prevent anyone else from manufacturing or selling the product or using the process without the authority of the person holding the patent (the **patentee**). The patentee will normally require a percentage of the revenue (known as a **royalty**) from such authorized use of the product or process.

better than it would be through a distributor, while the foreign manufacturer expects to increase sales and achieve a larger market share as a result of adding this product to his range.

Licensing. Rather than manufacture its products abroad, a manufacturer can license a firm in the foreign country to do so. The rights are given by one company (the **licensor**) to the other company (the **licensee**); these rights may be to manufacture, assemble, or use **patents** relating to the licensor's product or products. In return, the licensee will normally pay an initial fee plus an annual royalty or commission to the licensor for as long as the licence is in force.

Franchising. This is a special form of licensing, with strict conditions applying to quality standards, promotional activities, etc. The licensor makes available considerable marketing and product know-how. The licensee will be required to provide capital and other resources to establish the new franchised business. Many successful businesses choose this route for expansion, in both home and overseas markets. Some of the best known are in the fast-food and beverage sectors. The licensee usually pays fees to the licensor, based on a percentage of sales or turnover.

Joint Venture. For large projects abroad a joint venture with a foreign company may be beneficial. Often, the organizations pool their know-how and resources to achieve an objective that individually they would find difficult or impossible to finance and manage. Such relationships may be open-ended or limited to a fixed period or to achieving a particular goal.

Management Contracts. Another means of establishing a presence in a foreign country is to negotiate a management contract with a firm. This contract may cover running a business or supplying the senior management to do so. Most commercial sectors can benefit from such an arrangement.

Turnkey Contracts. In some cases, the foreign company may have a suitable workforce and management but lack the expertise to design and build sufficiently high-tech premises (say, a chemical plant). In such instances a 'turnkey contract' may be appropriate: the plant will be handed over in such a state of readiness that the new owners only have to 'turn a key.' As markets become more competitive and modern communications and technology diminish the size of the world in trading terms, so the need for businesses to explore all options for growth increases.

METHODS OF SELLING GOODS ABROAD

Methods of Selling Abroad	Requirements	Disadvantages	Advantages
Set up own subsidiary	Find suitable staff and premises.	High initial cost; possible barriers to entering foreign market.	Complete control over price, conditions of sale, etc.
Appoint Selling Agent	Find suitable local representative.	No stock held locally; no exlusive marketing of product; commision has to be paid.	No initial costs.
Use Distributors	Find suitable operation selling similar goods.	No exclusive selling – goods part of range. No control of selling price.	No initial costs.
Joint Marketing	Find suitable manufacturer of similar goods wishing to extend range.	No exclusive selling – goods part of range.	No initial costs; better marketing of product than agent or distributor.
Licensing and Franchising	Find suitable local manufacturer to produce goods.	Receive only advance and royalty.	No initial or ongoing costs.
Management Contractors	Find suitable local firm to benefit from producers management.	Receive only a percentage of value of goods.	Low initial costs.
Turnkey Contracts	Find suitable local firm to run factory.	High initial cost; receive only a percentage of value of goods.	Local firm has responsibility for running factory and producing goods.

Regional Trading Blocs

Types of trading bloc • The impact of competition

As countries develop economically, they devise ways of cooperating or forging links with each other to facilitate or expand trade between them. When these relationships have reached a formal stage the countries involved may sign trade agreements with each other. These agreements may sanction **bilateral trade** or **multilateral trade**. Increasingly, such arrangements have a strong geographical or regional emphasis; for example, the trading blocs may be based in the Caribbean, or Europe, or the Pacific rim. While, on one level, these close regional groupings are effective in promoting trade and breaking down barriers between the member nations, on another level there is a risk that the new groupings will simply reproduce national protectionism on a multinational scale, i.e. that new barriers will be erected between groups of countries rather than between individual nations. The result would be the re-emergence of traditional impediments to free trade; this protectionist attitude is often referred to as a 'fortress mentality.'

Types of Trading Bloc

Common Markets. In order to establish a common market and ultimately to achieve harmonious economic policies among the member countries, the following principles are important:

• the elimination of customs duties, quotas, import restrictions, or any other barriers to trade;
• an even-handed policy on government sub-sidies to ensure that producers in the different countries compete on equal terms;
• a common policy towards trade with non-member countries;
• policies to encourage competition;
• free movement of people, capital, and services between member countries;
• common transport policies;
• procedures to coordinate the economic policies of member countries and rectify any imbalances in the balance of payments.

While this may seem a reasonable blueprint to allow countries within a region to secure greater economic success and establish a world presence in trading terms, it is not without its disadvantages. To achieve these aims may require a considerable loss of sovereignty on the part of member states. It might even be argued that these objectives can only be successfully attained by effectively creating a full economic and political union of member countries, with a common currency, unified foreign policy, and a strong central government. A limited example of such a development is the Southern Cone Common Market (*Mercosur*) in South America, initiated in 1991 between Argentina, Brazil, Paraguay, and Uruguay. This has established a council comprising foreign ministers of the member countries who are expressly empowered to discuss political questions. Indeed, some of the outstanding political difficulties between member countries have hindered progress. A far more comprehensive system of integration is envisaged by the Maastricht Treaty of the

=====SEE ALSO=====
This section:
• International Trade
• International Finance and Investment
Economics:
• Goals of Economic Policy

bilateral trade Trade between two countries that have agreed to balance the import and export trade they do with each other.

A US-owned Factory in Mexico ►
Under the terms of the North American Free Trade Agreement (NAFTA), which was ratified in 1993, all tariffs will disappear in trade between the countries. During the 1980s and early 1990s, many large US companies had already established operations in Mexico, attracted by the lower labour costs there.

multilateral trade Free trade between more than two participating countries with no barriers or controls of any kind.

Referendum in Switzerland *In December 1992, Swiss voters elected to prolong their nation's traditional isolation; they narrowly rejected a plan to involve their country in a new free trade zone – the European Economic Area – comprising EFTA members (including Switzerland) and European Community countries. The EEA came into effect in January 1994.*

▶

customs union Two or more countries agreeing to trade freely with each other, abolishing tariffs and other barriers to trade. They also agree to impose common customs duties on imports from external countries.

European Union, signed in 1992 and ratified the following year, which provides for a sophisticated degree of political, economic, and monetary union between member states (see panel). In a fully integrated single market, national policies and governments would become subsidiary to the administration of the 'united states' as a whole. The creation of a single market is therefore politically contentious and likely to encounter resistance in any area of the world where it is attempted.

Free-Trade Areas or Associations. A free-trade area or association, which does not require common policies of member countries towards nonmembers, is far easier to implement than a fully integrated common market. It certainly poses less of a threat to the independence and sovereignty of individual mem-

ber countries. On the other hand, fewer long-term benefits may accrue from this system. The chief area of influence for a free-trade association is in the removal of trade barriers, such as tariffs, between countries. Policy decisions within these associations are usually required to be unanimous; by contrast, in single-market systems, provision is usually made for decisions to be reached without the need for unanimous agreement.

The Impact of Competition

Internal Competition. A **customs union** brings with it not only freer trade between the participating countries, but also greater competition. While potential customers for a particular product or service are likely to increase (as the size of the market to which member countries have access increases), there is also a likely increase in suppliers. The outcome of this is invariably greater competition, with less efficient companies or industries suffering at the hands of the more efficient. Additionally, with a larger market potential, new entrants may be attracted into an industry if they perceive 'gaps' or opportunities.

Because any customs union is liable to erect barriers against 'foreign' suppliers, it is usual for major nonresident international companies to consider establishing production facilities within one or more of the member-countries, in order to circumvent prohibitively high tariffs and import quotas. By doing so, these companies inject capital and technical know-how into the countries in which they choose to site their operations. This is beneficial in that it creates jobs and enhances the resources, especially the skills, available to the country's economy.

THE GROWTH OF THE EUROPEAN COMMUNITY/UNION

Original members (1957):	**New member (1981):**
Belgium	Greece
France	**New members (1986):**
Italy	Portugal
Luxembourg	Spain
Netherlands	**New members (1995):**
West Germany	Austria
New members (1973):	Finland
Denmark	Sweden
Great Britain	
Republic of Ireland	

Norwegian voters rejected membership of the European Union in a referendum held in November 1994.

External Competition. In addition to the internal competition generated by the creation of trading blocs, competition from outside is a persistent factor. This can be both an incentive for closer cooperation between countries as well as a perceived threat. In terms of an incentive, a customs union will lead to a sharing of skills, research and development facilities, etc., to combat the external threat. On the other hand, the 'fortress mentality' may prevail, leading to greater protectionism without addressing the problems or weaknesses.

In the 1970s and 1980s, Japan's expertise in high technology products and general manufacturing allowed it to break into, and in some cases dominate, various markets throughout the world. In the final decade of the 20th century, new competition is arising from countries of the Pacific rim and former communist countries of eastern and central Europe. Because of their ability to offer high-quality goods produced with low labour costs, they provide an attractive investment opportunity for foreign entrepreneurs; they also open up new markets for consumer goods. Consequently, large international companies may opt to invest and expand in these areas in the future rather than in established trading blocs.

SOME REGIONAL TRADING BLOCS

Although world trade is dominated by North America, the European Union, and Japan many other groupings exist. These include:
- ASEAN – Association of Southeast Asian Nations
- CACM – Central American Common Market
- CARICOM – Caribbean Community and Common Market
- ECOWAS – Economic Community of West African States
- EFTA – European Free Trade Association
- LAIA – Latin American Integration Association
- Mercosur – Southern Cone Common Market (South America)
- ACS – Association of Caribbean States (CARICOM plus other countries in the region, including Cuba, Mexico, and Haiti)

Moreover, the potential of the Indian subcontinent and China to take a more dominant role in world trade is still to be realized.

Examples of Major Trading Blocs
Several regional organizations around the globe are shown (for 1994). The most recent of these is NAFTA, agreement on which was concluded between Mexico, the USA, and Canada in December 1992. NAFTA is the world's wealthiest trading bloc. ▼

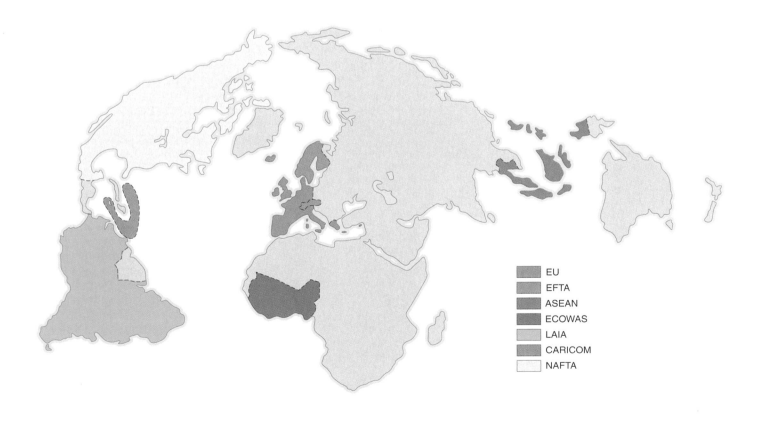

▨	EU
▨	EFTA
▨	ASEAN
▨	ECOWAS
▨	LAIA
▨	CARICOM
▨	NAFTA

COMMUNICATIONS AND MEDIA

Print Media

Origins of the written word • The printed word • The rise of newspapers • The spread of newspapers • Modern newspaper publishing • News gathering • Desktop publishing

SEE ALSO
Technology (vol. 2):
- Communications

Introduction (vol. 5):
- The Study of History
- The Beginnings of History

When people communicate, they do so by exchanging information. This information is usually received in one of two ways – visually or aurally – or simultaneously in both of these ways.

Information about current events, i.e. news, needs to be transmitted to a large audience in a short time. This has been made possible by the development of the ***mass media***. In order to be able to gather news efficiently, all the media of mass communication, whether print-based or electronic, rely not only on their own resources, but also on ***news agencies***. These enterprises, whose bureaus are located in most countries, collect news reports for wider distribution to the world's press.

A Detail from Gutenberg's 42-line Bible *This was the first printed work in the western hemisphere, produced by Johann Gutenberg in Mainz, Germany in 1455.* ▼

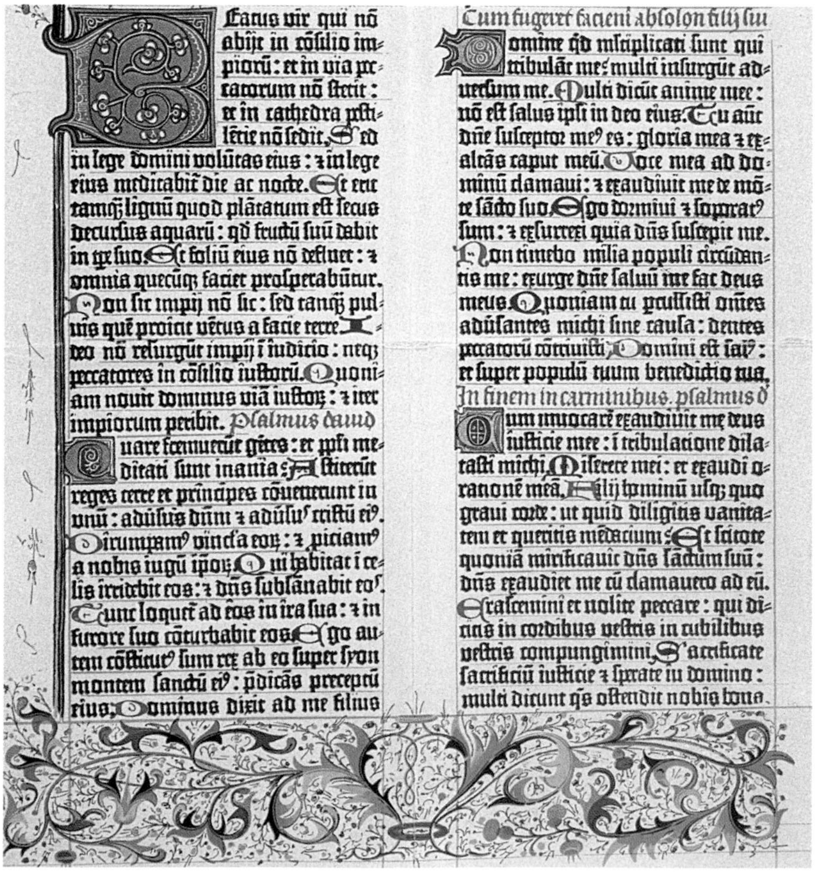

Origins of the Written Word

Although handwritten books were a mode of communication even in the ancient world, the book only became a form of mass communication following the development of the printing press in Europe in the 15th century.

The very earliest writing was in the form of ***pictograms***, symbols or pictures that were usually drawn on clay by priests. Pictograms gave way to alphabets and to writing in the modern sense of the term. The preservation and storage of this writing was made easier by the introduction of papyrus. Papyrus, which – unlike clay – was a portable and durable medium, made possible the collection of written materials and, thus, the establishment of libraries. The greatest library in the ancient world was established by King Ptolemy II (308–246 BC) at Alexandria in Egypt. This library is thought to have contained around a half a million volumes. There was also a public library in Rome during the reign (31 BC–14 AD) of the emperor Augustus .

In Ancient Greece, great importance was placed on the maintenance of library stocks, because such materials as papyrus degenerated over time (consequently, Chronos, the god of time, came to be identified as the enemy of knowledge). The first misgivings were voiced in Ancient Greece about the effect of the written word as a medium of communication. Socrates, for instance, raised the objection that, while teachers in oral preliterate cultures had had the freedom to select "a soul of the right type" to whom they could impart their wisdom, the advent of writing made ideas accessible to "those who have no business with it." Socrates was also concerned about the effect of writing on the human memory, anticipating that people would now "call...things to remembrance no longer from within themselves, but by means of external marks."

In medieval Europe, much writing was done by monks. Most of the work of these ***scribes***, as they were known, involved copying manuscripts. This performed the dual function of supplying readers and of salvaging the

◀ **Johann Gutenberg**
Gutenberg is shown in this engraving with his assistants in his printing room in Mainz, Germany.

contents of the original manuscript before it decayed. As schools and universities grew, from the 12th century onwards, the work of the scribes was taken over first by lay stationers and, from the 15th century, by printers.

The Printed Word

The printing press, developed independently in the mid-1400s by the German Johann Gutenberg (c. 1398–c. 1468) and the Englishman William Caxton (c. 1422–91), effectively combined in one process the skills of woodcutting, **illumination**, and engraving. This new technology met the increasing demand for books. While it was appropriate to the small-scale private enterprises of Europe, it was far less suited to the societies of the East, where the more diverse nature of languages made use of the invention too expensive.

From its inception, when the printed word was used to spread the ideas of the religious reformer Martin Luther (1483–1546), printing became associated with religious and political dissent. A community of writers, printers, booksellers, and intellectuals – often referred to as the 'commonwealth of learning' or the 'republic of letters' – operated throughout Europe, in such cities as Paris, Amsterdam, Antwerp, Frankfurt, Basel, and Rotterdam.

Between the late 15th and late 18th centuries, the governments of Catholic countries sought to curb the production of printed tracts by licensing only certain printers and issuing bans on reading. For example, despite the support of the English King Henry VIII (reigned 1497–1547) for the ideas of the Protestant Reformation, an Act of 1543 banned the reading of the Bible by men of middling or lower social status and by all women "other than those of noble or gentle rank." Moreover, in France between 1690 and 1790, the works of all the most popular French authors were published outside the country; within France, publishing was fiercely persecuted – between 1600 and 1756, over 800 authors, printers, and booksellers were imprisoned in the Bastille in Paris.

In the long term, however, printing could not be suppressed, since the prosperity of printers was bound up with the rise of the middle class of merchants and traders. This wealthy and increasingly influential section of society formed a significant proportion of the reading public. Printing houses grew in number – for example, while there were only 60 in London in the 1660s, there were over 150 by the 1750s. By the late 18th century, novels were selling in large quantities: *Rob Roy*, by the Scottish writer Sir Walter Scott (1771–1832), then the most popular novelist in the world, sold 10 000 copies in only two weeks.

In the early 19th century, only about half the male population of most European countries was literate. Those in power feared that the promotion of greater literacy among the working classes would create unrest. Working-class people tended to read broadsheets rather than books. These cheap publications had topical themes, such as murders or famous court cases; the description of a notorious trial could sell half a million copies.

Book publishing expanded rapidly in the late 19th and early 20th centuries. In the 20th century, one of the most significant developments in the production of books has been the emergence of the paperback. Because of their relatively low production cost, the number of paperbacks has grown considerably as publishing costs have risen.

illumination Decoration of manuscripts and printed works with designs, frequently using gold leaf to highlight an initial capital letter or to adorn the margin. This highly skilled craft was first practised by monks, who developed it into an elaborate art form.

▲ **Christophe Plantin** *(1520–89)*
Plantin, one of the leading figures of early printing, established a highly successful printing house at Antwerp in Belgium. He was the first to use copper engravings for book illustration.

A Newspaper Seller ►
This print, from the 1870s, shows a vendor of newspapers attracting the attention of passers-by. Independent journalism on a wide scale first developed in England and spread throughout Europe in the course of the 19th century.

Acta Diurna

This daily newssheet recording social news and official business was published in imperial Rome from 59 BC. Scribes made around 2000 copies of each issue and copies were posted in public places.

All the news that's fit to print.

Motto of the quality daily paper, the *New York Times*, coined by **Adolph Simon Ochs** (1858–1935), US newspaper publisher

The Rise of Newspapers

The growth of the middle classes and the steady advance of literacy also explain the emergence and expansion of newspapers.

The forerunners of the modern newspaper were newsletters. These occasional publications were usually of an exclusively commercial nature; they were produced by merchant houses in Europe (especially Germany and the Low Countries) to convey information on the price of commodities.

Early European newspapers – containing a wide range of news items – included the Austrian *Wiener Zeitung* (founded 1703) and the weekly *Post-och inrikes tidningar* (1645) from Sweden. In England, the first newspaper – the *Oxford Gazette* – was produced by the government in 1665. A commercial press began to flourish in England after the lifting of licensing restrictions in 1695, and the first independent daily, *The Daily Courant*, appeared in 1702.

Throughout Europe, early newspapers catered chiefly for the rising mercantile class, providing news of home and foreign affairs and of commerce: stocks, shares, and bankruptcies. These papers, which included the London daily *The Times* (founded in 1785 as *The Daily Universal Register*) and the Swiss *Neue Zürcher Zeitung* (1780), laid the foundation for the **quality press**, or **broadsheet press**.

In the USA, publication of newspapers was first centred on Boston, a hotbed of radicalism and opposition to British colonial government.

In 1690, *Publick Occurrences* was banned, after only one issue, for its critical stance. The *Boston Gazette* supported the secessionist cause during the Revolutionary War (1775–83). Publication of newspapers increased greatly after independence; papers at this time included the *Philadelphia Aurora* (1790) and the *Gazette of the United States* (1789).

The Popular Press. Growing commercialism and the dependence of newspapers on advertising gave rise to a third type of newspaper in the mid-19th century – the popular press. This form of journalism dealt with topics that had a widespread appeal, such as crime and sport, and was aimed at the lower middle classes. The first such newspaper – the British *News of the World* – was founded in 1843; this had achieved a circulation of 100 000 by 1855. The daily popular press expanded greatly around the turn of the century. Modern mass-circulation daily newspapers (sometimes called the **tabloid press** from their small format) include the *New York Daily News* in the USA, the British *The Sun*, and the German *Bild-Zeitung*. These newspapers are characterized by their mixture of sport, crime, celebrity gossip, and their emphasis on pictures. They are also hallmarked by their tendency to sensationalize issues and cover major news stories superficially rather than offering analysis.

The highly successful formula for popular newspaper publishing originated in the USA. The USA was the first country to detach the press from the machinery of government; the First Amendment to the US Constitution, included in the Bill of Rights (1791), guaranteed freedom of the press. US newspapers were also the first to adopt the practice of mingling news, entertainment, and advertising. A cheap daily press was established by the middle of the 19th century, beginning with the New York *Sun* in 1833. By 1850, there were over 200 daily papers in the USA. Reflecting the society of the time, the majority of them had a large working-class readership ("cent newspapers for the common man") and many were aimed at immigrants. In New York there were popular newspapers in Yiddish and in German. In 1850 the city had four German-language daily newspapers – more than even Berlin – and the German-language *New Yorker Staats Zeitung* (founded in 1880) had a larger circulation than most German dailies. There was also a significant Swedish-language press in rural areas of the USA.

The Spread of Newspapers

Across Europe in the 19th century, many newspapers arose with the growth of liberalism and the resulting relaxation of restrictions on the freedom of expression. In France, the newspaper *La Presse*, launched in 1836, quickly attained a circulation of 20 000. Other newspapers to emerge at this time were the French *Le Figaro* (1854) and the Italian *Corriere della Sera* (1876), published in Milan. The German press, despite its long history, was still made up of mainly small local newspapers at the end of the 19th century. The *Berliner Morgenpost* had the highest circulation: about 250 000, a little ahead of the *Berliner Lokalanzeiger*.

Elsewhere in the world, the establishment of empires by several European countries throughout the 18th and 19th centuries had a clear effect on the development of newspapers in the territories that they colonized, and to which they subsequently granted independence. The influence of the British in their colonial territories was especially great. Newspapers in the older parts of the British Empire – Canada, South Africa, Australia, and New Zealand – tended to serve the large urban populations created by large-scale settlement from the mother country. Canada and Australia both followed the approach adopted in the USA of unfettered commercialism. For example, in 1850, there were more newspapers in Australia than in England. There was also a substantial Afrikaans press for settlers of Dutch origin in South Africa, and a French language press in Quebec, the Canadian province where the majority of the population speaks French.

The British also established newspapers in India, initially for the expatriate community of settlers, businessmen, teachers, and colonial officials. By 1870, there were 22 newspapers in Bombay alone. English-language dailies still dominate Bombay and the other urban centres of Madras, Calcutta, and Delhi. The *Times of India*, modelled on *The Times* of London, is widely regarded as the premier Indian newspaper. The other leading paper in India is the *Navbharat Times*, which is written in Hindi, the dominant indigenous language of the country. In total, there are 11 major languages in India (each with 10 million or more speakers); by the 1970s there were more than 700 daily newspapers in India. Sales of newspapers in the subcontinent are double that of the entire African continent.

In the countries of Africa then ruled by the British, Black Africans began to develop their own newspapers in the 1930s, supporting the cause of independence, and by the 1950s White British newspaper interests had set up several of their own nationalist papers in Africa; the largest of these was the *Daily Times*, published in the Nigerian capital, Lagos.

In the colonial era, African nationalist newspapers were subject to fines, suspensions, and the occasional arrest of their editors. After independence, government control still tended to be strict. However, in some one-party states, such as Kenya, private ownership of the press was tolerated. As in India, papers generally do not reach the rural population; newspapers are too expensive for village dwellers, who have neither access to consumer goods, nor

▲ **William Randolph Hearst** *(1863–1951) Hearst, a US newspaper proprietor, built up a vast press empire. His publications were sensationalist and popular in tone. Hearst diversified into magazines and films and amassed a huge personal fortune.*

MAGAZINES

The first popular magazine, *Le Mercure Galant*, appeared in France in 1672; it contained a mixture of news and literary contributions. Periodicals with the emphasis on entertainment helped develop a mass market for magazines in the 19th century in Europe and North America. This growth was aided by the increasing use of illustrations in magazines from the 1850s onwards, supplanted by photographs towards the end of the century.

Many modern magazines cater for special interests, e.g. in sports and hobbies. Women have come to form a particularly lucrative market sector. Women's magazines typically contain features on careers, fashion, and women's health. In the 1930s, supermarkets began distributing free homemaking magazines (e.g. *Family Circle*). Advertising, which started to become a vital source of revenue for magazines from the early years of the 20th century, is especially important in the women's magazine sector, since women are major purchasers of consumer goods. In general, advertising has tended to lead the design of magazines; once colour printing techniques had been perfected, editors emulated the increased visual appeal of advertisements in their own illustrations and layouts.

▲ **A Newsstand** *A selection of popular magazine titles are displayed on this newsstand in Mexico City.*

News magazines sell well in countries with no tradition of national newspapers (e.g. *Der Spiegel* in Germany, *Time* and *Newsweek* in the USA, and *L'Express* in France). Such general-interest magazines have the largest circulations.

propaganda
The systematic manipulation of public opinion in order to promote or denigrate a particular cause, movement, or political party. The term originates from the *Sacra Congregatio de Propaganda Fide* (Sacred Congregation for Propagation of the Faith), a Roman Catholic body established in the 17th century to promote missionary work.

the means to buy them. This deters advertisers, making an affordable selling price even less achievable.

Extensive colonization also fostered newspaper publishing in the Middle East. In this region, newspapers arose in three principal languages: Arabic and the two main colonial languages, French and English. In Egypt, for example, there were 24 foreign-language daily papers (covering French, English, Armenian, and Greek), as well as 26 in Arabic, by 1948. Egyptian papers tended to be strongly political and were taken into official control by the governing party in the 1950s. The small commercial press was aimed at the expatriate European community. The leading newspapers are *Al Ahram* and *Al Akhbar*.

In many Middle Eastern countries, a number of factors – e.g. the inhospitable terrain, and widespread illiteracy – make newspapers a largely urban phenomenon. Egyptian papers are confined to the big cities of Cairo and Alexandria. Iranian newspapers sell mostly in the capital, Tehran. Authoritarian Islamic regimes have inhibited the growth of newspapers in some countries: in Saudi Arabia, daily papers have only been permitted since 1952.

The polarization between rural poor and affluent urban populations is also present in Latin American societies. With high illiteracy rates in some countries – especially Peru, Brazil, and Mexico – consumption of print media is a mainly urban phenomenon.

A Wall Newspaper ▶ *In the People's Republic of China, citizens are pictured reading of the day's events from a newspaper posted on a wall. Although most well-known as a Chinese phenomenon, the wall newspaper also exists in other countries (e.g. Bangladesh, Russia).*

The Latin American newspaper press dates from the end of the 19th century. A cheap newspaper called *El Imparcial* was launched in 1896 in Mexico City by the country's first press tycoon, Reyes Spindola, and Mexico's first daily paper appeared in 1905. US influence was strong: Americans owned many newspapers in South America and supplied new technology, such as linotype machines. Some countries (e.g. Argentina) developed an effective press later in the century: the main Argentine daily papers, *La Prensa* and *La Nacion*, were established in 1869–70. By the late 1930s, Argentina had over 380 daily newspapers and more than 1000 magazines (magazines – a media form imported from the USA – are very popular in Latin America). Apart from the principal colonial languages – Spanish and Portuguese – newspapers are also printed in English and Italian (the latter in Argentina, where there was substantial Italian immigration in the late 19th century).

Newspapers were first introduced to China (and subsequently to Japan) by the Americans and the British and other west Europeans; they initially took the form of missionary papers and newssheets. Early Chinese newspapers were in English – notably the *China Mail*, founded in 1845, and two other daily papers set up in Shanghai in the 1870s. The first major Chinese-language paper, *Shun Pao*, was also founded in Shanghai in the same decade, by a British merchant called Frederick Major. By 1930 there were around 1000 Chinese dailies. After the communist takeover in 1949 the press provided an efficient method of communicating with rural areas in this vast country. Extensive use was made by the Chinese Communist Party of the communal newspaper, pasted up on a public wall.

In the former Soviet Union, the press was under the control of the Communist Party. This situation was an extension of that existing in Russia prior to the revolution of 1917, when newspapers were controlled by the tsar's ministers. There were two principal papers in the Soviet Union: *Pravda* (the party newspaper) and *Izvestia* (the government newspaper); these formed the top of a pyramid, down which accepted political views were channelled to newspapers in individual republics and to local and factory papers. Print runs of Soviet newspapers were high, irrespective of consumer demand. Since the break-up of the Soviet Union in 1991, an independent press has developed. In Russia, however, it is still subject to government interference.

In communist systems, the press (and indeed all the mass media) assumed great importance in spreading official views to the masses. This raises the question of **propaganda**; in modern times it has generally been supposed that propaganda is an exclusive characteristic of totalitarian states, such as communist or fascist regimes and military dictatorships. Certainly, governments of this type have created efficient propaganda machines, most notoriously the Ministry of Enlightenment and Propaganda in Nazi Germany, headed by Joseph Goebbels (1897–1945). However, even democratic governments employ propaganda, in the form of 'public information.' Especially at times of national crisis the media may be obliged to accept military censorship in the interests of national security. Moreover, they are expected to reflect the mood of the patriotic majority. In Britain during World War II, and in both Argentina and Britain during the Falklands War in 1982, newspapers tended to give accounts of the military engagements that reflected what their readers expected to hear.

By the early 1990s there were some 10 000 newspapers in the world, selling about 420 million copies per day. These were not evenly distributed, however: over 80% were in North America, Europe, or Japan. Japan has more than 100 principal daily newspapers, many of which have high circulation figures. By contrast, ten Black African nations had no daily newspaper and the number of papers in this region fell by 40% between 1965 and 1980. Brazil, despite having a population of over 150 million, has no tradition of newspaper readership and hence no national papers.

Modern Newspaper Publishing

Many changes have taken place in newspaper publishing since World War II. Primarily, electronic innovations have transformed the production of newspapers from a labour-intensive industry into a high-tech business.

Mechanical typesetting processes, which had developed from single letter movable type to more sophisticated methods of composition (e.g. Linotype, Monotype) by the late 19th century, have been replaced by a far more efficient system, in which the journalist writing the story can input material directly into the production process. Computer technology has allowed the individual reporter or subeditor to compose an article or page on screen and download the finished piece into the central computer controlling the printing presses. See TECHNOLOGY (VOL. 2): COMMUNICATIONS.

Moreover, from the mid-1980s onwards, in a technique pioneered by the US financial paper, the *Wall Street Journal*, electronic and satellite technology has enabled editions of the same newspaper to be printed simultaneously in different parts of the world. In the same period, newspapers began to use full colour to an increasing extent, especially for cover pictures.

Hand-in-hand with the technological advancements in newspaper production, great

changes have occurred in the industry's working and management practices. A major effect of the advent of direct input of copy was to break the power of the trade unions, which formerly had exerted great influence in newspaper typesetting and printing. The postwar period has also witnessed the rise of the media mogul. Continuing in the tradition of such early press barons as William Randolph Hearst, the Australian-born magnate Rupert Murdoch (1931–   ) and the Italian entrepreneur Silvio Berlusconi (1936–   ) epitomize the modern multinational media proprietor. Their control of large holding companies that engage in diverse activities has allowed Murdoch and Berlusconi not only to acquire a great variety of newspaper and magazine titles, but also to diversify into many

▲ **Printing a Modern Newspaper**
A printer at the premises of the Parisian daily Le Monde *prepares an edition of the paper. Mechanical methods of printing have been superseded from the 1980s onwards by computer technology and fully automated systems.*

THE FINANCE OF NEWSPAPERS

As a commercial business, a newspaper must generate sufficient revenue if it is to survive. For the majority of papers, this means sustaining or increasing circulation figures in a highly competitive environment. Circulation wars occasionally break out between newspapers competing for the same sector of the market, with each title lowering its cover price, or offering its readers other incentives, in order to undercut the competition.

Advertising is an important source of income. This method of funding began as long ago as 1785, when the New York *Daily Advertiser* was established; newspapers in the USA now gain most of their revenue from selling advertising space. Advertising is especially significant in the high-circulation tabloid press. When the *Star* was launched in the USA by Rupert Murdoch in 1974, it had the largest advertising budget of any US newspaper hitherto.

Free newspapers – or ***freesheets*** – are financed entirely by advertising. This form of newspaper arose in the 1970s and 1980s, and is delivered door-to-door in a particular locality.

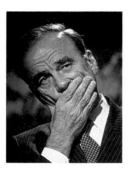

▲ Rupert Murdoch
Australian-born Rupert Murdoch is the world's most powerful media tycoon in the 1990s. Apart from owning many newspapers, he controls a number of television networks and publishing concerns.

other areas of the mass media (see ELECTRONIC MEDIA). Murdoch's huge News Corporation concern – the world's largest publisher of English-language newspapers – has extensive interests worldwide; newspapers controlled by this group include the *Star* in the USA, *The Australian*, and titles at both ends of the newspaper market in Britain – the tabloid *The Sun* and the broadsheet *The Times*.

A characteristic of these and lesser modern newspaper proprietors has been their uncompromising attitude towards the print unions. The efficiency of such owners in changing outmoded practices and increasing newspaper circulation is offset by widespread concern about the concentration of ownership of the press in too few hands. In order to secure his considerable media holdings in the USA, Rupert Murdoch took US citizenship in the late 1980s, thereby complying with laws forbidding the ownership of US newspapers by foreign nationals.

In addition to reporting the news, newspapers can play a role in influencing public opinion. While it is unusual, in those parts of the world that have a free press, for organs of the press to be owned by political parties, the political preference of proprietors can dictate the editorial content of some newspapers. This may even take the form of urging the readership to vote for a particular party in a general election. However, whether direct influence can be exerted is open to debate; for example, millions of readers of a right-wing tabloid may well be attracted by its sports coverage or features on celebrities and remain unaffected in their political choice by its stance on current affairs. Newspapers may also instigate

campaigns among their readership to lobby politicians for changes in legislation. The extreme vividness of **photojournalism** has led to it being credited with the ability to alter public attitudes, especially towards armed conflicts. Alarmingly, one measure of the general perception of the power of the press to sway opinion is the growing number of instances of violence or intimidation against journalists reporting from areas of political or military unrest.

News Gathering

Major newspapers, especially those of the quality press, keep permanent correspondents in many countries around the world. Correspondents are based in the capital city of countries where most major news stories are likely to occur. However, because not all parts of the world can be covered, and since smaller newspapers cannot afford any foreign correspondents, much of the world's news is supplied by news agencies. Newspapers – along with numerous other media, governments, international organizations, and private companies – receive news items syndicated from one or other of four major agencies: Reuters (based in the United Kingdom), Agence France-Presse (AFP), or the two US agencies Associated Press (AP) and United Press International (UPI). These agencies also supply news to the various regional and national news agencies, of which there are more than 100. Together, the agencies employ over 10 000 people.

News services date back to the Middle Ages and have the same origins as newspapers – the newsletters sent by European merchant houses to their clients, reporting the latest significant events.

The first news agency, Agence Havas, was set up in France in 1835 and bore the name of its founder, Charles-Louis Havas. Havas had representatives in all European capitals and supplied information to the press and to the French government. This information was transmitted by various means: mail coach, courier, carrier pigeon, and (later) telegraph services. Two of Havas's employees, the Germans Bernhard Wolff and **Paul Julius Reuter**, set up rival agencies; Reuter moved his operation to London in 1851.

While the European agencies were commercial enterprises separate from newspapers, news agencies in the USA were established by newspaper proprietors, who were anxious to cut their own news-gathering costs and were prepared to pool their resources to do so. AP, founded in 1848, was cooperatively funded. UPI was established in 1907.

In 1870, the three European agencies formed a cartel, agreeing to divide the world outside of the USA into three spheres of

---

PHOTOJOURNALISM

From the very earliest days of photography, the medium's potential for illustrating news items was realized. The world's first illustrated weeklies – the *Illustrated London News* and *L'Illustration* – appeared in Britain and France in 1842 and 1843 respectively. In the 1850s, during the Crimean War, and the 1860s, in the US Civil War, photography began to be used to document military conflicts. Improved portability of photographic equipment and greater clarity of reproduction led to the spread of photojournalism in the 1920s and 1930s. The current affairs photo magazine *Life* was founded in 1936 in the USA; this was the first publication to put photography at the centre of the news story, by building text around pictures. Despite the rise of electronic news broadcasts – first through the cinema newsreel and later through television – still photography continues to play a vital role in journalism. Many striking images by photographers of atrocities in the Vietnam War helped to turn US public opinion against the war. The reliance of the tabloid press on topical pictures of celebrities has led to the rise of so-called **paparazzi** – freelance photographers notorious for their readiness to invade the subject's privacy to obtain a candid picture.

operation: Reuters took Britain, the British Empire, China, and Japan; Havas was given France, French colonies, southern Europe, and Latin America; Continental-Wolff supplied news to Germany, Russia, and Scandinavia. This cartel lasted until after World War I, when it was challenged by the US agencies and by national news agencies – notably TASS (the news agency of the former Soviet Union) and the Japanese Kokusai Tsushin-sha – which wanted to sell news abroad. Competition thus grew, although foreign agencies only entered the US market in the late 1960s.

Agence Havas was closed down by the German occupation forces during World War II, but ex-Havas members of the French Resistance movement replaced it with Agence France-Presse in 1944.

In the postwar world, the US news agencies have been dominant, although, for financial reasons, they have cut back their operations in Europe, Africa, and the Middle East. Their main markets are the Far East, Latin America, and the US home market. Reuters, which became a public company in the mid-1980s, is as well known in commercial circles for its financial news service, which is an extremely profitable business, as for its general news division, which is not.

In the early 1980s, Reuters and AFP distributed news in around 150 countries; AP in 110; and UPI in 92. Reuters had around 5000 media subscribers, while AP and UPI had some 16 000: the US agencies have a much larger number of clients because of the large American market. The news service varies according to region: some news goes to all parts of the world, while other news is only distributed to certain areas. The daily output of one of the major agencies is between 25 000 and 80 000 words, depending on the region. A client agency in a developed country might receive more than 600 000 words of news in a single day.

During the 1970s concerns began to be expressed about the flow of news from the developed world to developing nations. These concerns grew out of the many successful postwar independence movements in these countries and, more specifically, out of the work of the United Nations Educational, Scientific, and Cultural Organization (UNESCO). UNESCO had been campaigning since the 1950s to alter the flow of international news from its persistently vertical direction (i.e. from north to south) to a horizontal one (i.e. south to south). Moves to bring this about were instigated after an important UNESCO conference that was held in San José, Costa Rica, in 1976, and a subsequent report to UNESCO by the MacBride Commission in 1980. This report, entitled *Many Voices, One World*, called

◀ ▲ **Photojournalists Covering Wars**
Gathering photographic documentation for news reports of conflicts began in the Crimean War (above), where the British photographic pioneer Roger Fenton travelled with a mobile darkroom to develop his pictures. On the left, a photographer is shown taking pictures during the Gulf War in 1991.

for a new order of information and communication in the world, according to which newly independent countries would have their own news-gathering organizations and rely less on agencies in the northern industrialized world. These new organizations, while cooperating with established agencies from the old cartel, would nonetheless reflect the cultures of their region and provide news from the perspectives of developing nations.

Initially, there was strong opposition to these proposals from the industrialized world. The USA withdrew from UNESCO in 1984, followed by the United Kingdom in 1985. These countries took the view that calls for a new information order were merely a front for growing state censorship of media in these new countries. This was the prevailing view among Western governments during the Cold War between the USA and the Soviet Union, and their respective client states.

With the demise of the Cold War following the collapse of communism in eastern Europe and the Soviet Union from 1989 to 1991, the picture is changing throughout the world. Moreover, independent organizations for the collection and dissemination of news have grown up in developing nations. Many of these organizations are supported by UNESCO and/or have strong links with the Non-Aligned Movement (NAM) of countries outside of the eastern and western power blocs. There are three international bodies: the Non-Aligned News Agencies Pool (NANAP), which

---

**Paul Julius Reuter
(1816–99)**

Reuter was born Israel Beer Josephat to a Jewish family in Kassel, Germany, and changed his name on conversion to Christianity. After setting up a pigeon-post service between Aachen and Brussels in 1849, Reuter established a telegraph office in London. This developed, by the 1870s, into an international concern.

▲ A Major News Agency *The Paris office of Reuters is shown here. Reuters is one of the major news agencies, which form a vital link in news gathering worldwide*

was established in 1975 and now includes the national news agencies of over 100 non-aligned countries, Broadcasting Organizations of the Non-Aligned Countries (BONAC), and Inter Press Service (IPS).

In addition, there are several important regional organizations. These include: the Caribbean News Agency (CANA), based in Barbados and set up in 1976; the Pan African News Agency (PANA), established in Dakar in Senegal in 1979; the Pacific News Exchange (PACNEWS), a cooperative news exchange in Fiji, dating from 1985 and run by public radio in the 13 independent island countries of the Pacific region; and Asia-Pacific Broadcasting Television News Exchange (ASIAVISION), founded in 1984. ASIAVISION divides the continent of Asia into two zones: Zone A, with its centre in Tokyo; and Zone B, centred on Kuala Lumpur, Malaysia.

These new 'news exchange mechanisms' have been credited with having improved the coverage of issues concerning developing nations in important organs of the print media in the industrialized world, such as the British *The Guardian*, the French newspaper *Le Monde*, and the *Washington Post* in the USA.

Desktop Publishing

The revolution that has taken place in information technology (i.e. using computer systems to generate, store, and communicate information) has led to the growing use of electronic methods for producing the printed word; see COMPUTERS (VOL. 2): APPLICATIONS PROGRAMS. Every stage in the production of printed matter has been transformed by the advent of the computer. Although large computers were first used in the 1960s to run typesetting systems, it is only the application of relatively cheap but powerful microcomputers to publishing systems, from the mid-1980s onwards, that has allowed pages to be composed (including text, graphics, and photographic reproduction) in a fully integrated manner. Such integrated systems are collectively referred to as desktop publishing, or DTP. As the name indicates, the limited environment required by one operator to produce finished pages – typically a microcomputer with appropriate software and a laser printer – has enabled even small organizations to perform many of the tasks formerly the preserve of specialist typesetters and printers. A key feature of DTP systems is the use of increasingly cheap computing power to simulate accurately the format of each page on the computer's monitor screen (a feature known as WYSIWYG, an acronym for 'what you see is what you get'), and to provide facilities that enable both layout and content to be changed easily. The most popular computer software packages developed for such operations were originally devised for magazine production, where speed and flexibility of page composition was at a premium. However, their application has extended to books, especially those with a high level of illustration.

Another key development is the increased flexibility in the methods of printing a page. A DTP software package can produce the same output on such varied devices as laser printers, colour printers, and high-resolution imagesetters. This allows the publisher close control over the trade-off between quality and price of output at all stages of a project. For example, a book might be proofed on a low-quality but cheap laser printer, then typeset on a high-resolution imagesetter; on the other hand, for a newsletter or political election leaflet, using a laser printer for the final output might well be acceptable.

In many cases, the text is not generated in-house, but is originated at an earlier stage in the electronic chain. Authors prepare material on their own microcomputer on a straightforward wordprocessing package, and send a disk of their work to the publisher, who makes the data stored on it compatible with the DTP system being used.

Electronic Media

Radio broadcasting • Television broadcasting • Satellite and cable television •
Influence of the electronic media • Radio and television in education

The dissemination of news to a mass audience was once extremely slow. As a result of the development of the electronic media, with their **broadcasting** and satellite technology, information can be transmitted around the entire globe in only a matter of seconds. In many societies a whole generation has taken this development for granted: for example, on 19 July 1969 the first landing on the moon, by US astronauts, was watched on television in 47 countries by 723 million people, more than one-fifth of the world's population. Mass communications have made the world a smaller place, or, in the words of the Canadian sociologist and communications theorist Marshall McLuhan (1911–80), a "global village."

Radio Broadcasting

Radio was developed early in the 20th century by the Italian engineer Guglielmo Marconi (1874–1937) and the Russian physicist Aleksandr Popov (1859–1905). Marconi had laid the technological basis for the development of radio, establishing the Marconi Wireless and Telegraph Company in 1900, which was concerned with Morse code signals sent by wireless from ships to shore, or between ships at sea.

THE INFLUENCE OF THE BBC

The BBC (British Broadcasting Corporation) is a public radio and TV broadcasting authority. It is politically independent, answerable to parliament, and funded by the fees charged for the licences that all television owners in Britain must hold.

Its operations began in 1922. During World War II, the radio news broadcasts of the World Service of the BBC were the only way that millions of listeners in Nazi-occupied Europe could hear an accurate account of world events.

The World Service broadcasts a third of its programmes in English, while the rest of its output is in some 40 languages.

An Early Radio Set *By the 1920s, use of the first plastic – Bakelite – had made radio receivers affordable and attractive. Millions of listeners tuned in to news, sports, and light entertainment programmes.*

Commercial radio – broadcasting services sponsored or paid for by an advertiser – was inaugurated in the USA. The first commercial radio station – KDKA – was established in Pittsburgh in 1920, and the medium flourished in the following decade under such companies as the Radio Corporation of America (RCA) and Westinghouse. In Europe, regular commercial radio broadcasts began in the Netherlands in 1919.

Advertisers soon realized that radio provided an ideal medium for promoting products, as sponsors were able instantaneously to reach a huge market. Advertising revenue quickly became the main source of funding for radio; the number of commercial stations far outweighs government-sponsored networks.

Radio spread rapidly throughout the world in the 1920s and 1930s. In Latin America, broadcasting was pioneered in Mexico and Argentina. In Asia, All India Radio (AIR) was set

=====SEE ALSO=====
Technology (vol. 2):
• Communications
Cinema (vol. 4)
The World in the 20th Century (vol. 5):
• The New Economic Powers

broadcasting The transmission of radio and television signals for reception by a general mass audience. *Narrowcasting* describes transmissions targeted at a selected audience.

▲ **Guglielmo Marconi** *Marconi's patenting of the radio receiver in 1896 laid the foundations of electronic mass communication. Because it was able to convert electromagnetic waves into electrical signals without the wires that were used by the telegraph, his invention was called the 'wireless.'*

ORSON WELLES'S *WAR OF THE WORLDS*

"Those strange beings who landed in the Jersey farmlands tonight are the vanguard of an invading army from the planet Mars." In October 1938, the US actor and director Orson Welles (1915–85) presented a radio adaptation of the science-fiction story *War of the Worlds*, by the British writer H. G. Wells (1866–1946). No introduction was given to the programme, and so vividly realistic was Welles's description of a Martian invasion of earth that many listeners thought it was a real news item. In the state of widespread panic that ensued, traffic jams occurred as thousands of people attempted to escape from New York City.

The dramatic effect of this programme was not confined to the USA. In 1949, in Quito, Ecuador, a mob attacked a radio station after a translated version of Welles's broadcast had caused general alarm.

◄ **Orson Welles** *Welles is shown rehearsing his famous science-fiction broadcast* War of the Worlds *in the studios of CBS.*

Radio Pioneers

The first transmission of the human voice occurred on 24 December 1906. Reginald Aubrey Fossenden (1866–1932), a Canadian electrical engineer, read a passage from the Bible to ships' radio operators off the coast of New England, USA.

In 1910, the US physicist Lee de Forest (1873–1961) made the first live transmission, a concert given by the Italian tenor Enrico Caruso (1873–1921) at the Metropolitan Opera House in New York.

up by the BBC in 1935, with the intention of promoting a national Indian culture while respecting the ethnic plurality of the subcontinent. Its daily news bulletins were broadcast in about 70 different languages and dialects.

Programming in the early days of radio reflected a wide range of interests, including comedy, drama, adventure stories, dance music, and sports commentaries. Each station was conceived as a magazine of the air waves, from which listeners could sample the items that particularly appealed to them. Radio stimulated the growth of new art forms, such as the radio play and the documentary, which were specifically devised for the medium. From the early days of radio, newscasts have formed a vital element of programming. The vividness with which radio could convey the drama of an event as it unfolded was brought home to listeners around the world in 1937. A radio reporter, who was present as the German airship *Hindenburg* attempted to dock at Lakehurst, New Jersey (in the USA) described the horrific scene as the craft exploded.

While diversity continues to be fostered by many broadcasters around the world, specialization has been the guiding spirit behind the huge growth in the number of stations that have come on air. Since the advent of stations devoted to popular music in general in the 1960s, smaller stations have arisen to cater solely for particular genres within this market (e.g. soul, reggae, or 'rap' music). A large

number of radio stations in the USA broadcast nothing but country music.

The news and talk format for radio programmes has also experienced a great increase in popularity, especially during the 1980s and 1990s. Listeners are invited to air their views on 'phone-in' programmes, in which issues of topical concern are discussed. Such programmes are frequently hosted by radio personalities who cultivate an abrasive attitude towards callers in order to incite controversy. These so-called 'shock jocks' (i.e. disc jockeys who aim to shock) have been heavily criticized by the regulatory bodies that scrutinize broadcasting standards, but they have also achieved immense *ratings* (figures based on a statistical sample showing what proportion of the total audience have tuned in to a particular programme or network). Talk radio is popular with the controllers of networks, as it is a far cheaper format than, say, original radio drama, where a writer has to be commissioned and actors paid, or even than music broadcasts, where fees are payable to artists whose records appear on the playlist. In the USA, there were, by the mid-1990s, more than 1000 radio stations offering either exclusively talk programmes, or a mixture of talk and news.

In many countries, a proportion of programming on radio and television is devoted to educational broadcasts for schools (see **RADIO AND TELEVISION IN EDUCATION**).

POPULAR EARLY TELEVISION PROGRAMMES

In the USA, which led the field in the development of popular programming and the export of television culture around the globe, certain shows established themselves as early favourites with audiences. The comedian Milton Berle was popular in the early 1950s with his slapstick show for children on NBC's 'Texaco Star Theater.' Another extremely successful light entertainment show was the CBS situation comedy *I Love Lucy*, starring Lucille Ball, which began in 1951. One of the longest-running shows on US television was *The Tonight Show*, hosted by Johnny Carson, which first came on air in 1953.

Television Broadcasting

Although some experiments in forming pictures from a cathode-ray tube were undertaken by a Russian, Boris Rosing, in the early years of the 20th century, the invention of television is generally credited to the Scottish engineer John Logie Baird (1888–1946), who gave the first public demonstration of the new medium in 1926. In the USA, at around the same time, Vladimir Zworykin (1899–1982), a pupil of Rosing, developed an electronic method of transmitting images, a more reliable system than Baird's mechanical devices. However, due to problems with patenting the invention, regular broadcasting did not begin until late in the 1930s. Russia, France, and the Netherlands had broadcast experimental programmes in the 1930s. The first regular public television service was provided by the British Broadcasting Corporation, from 1936 onwards. These broadcasts reached only the small minority of people who owned sets, were of poor quality, and (due to lack of transmitter power) could only be received around London. Broadcasts ceased when war was declared.

In all these countries, television only began to develop on a large scale after World War II. In the USA, commercial television grew in the immediate postwar years. In 1950 the USA had over 10 million TV sets, while the rest of the world combined had less than one million. By 1959, there were over 500 stations serving over 46 million homes across the country.

Other countries, such as Australia (in 1956), chose television systems with both public-service and commercial channels. Television came to most of the Middle East during the 1950s and early 1960s. By the mid-1960s, Israel was the only country in the region without a TV service. Saudi Arabia acquired television in the mid-1950s, a service that initially catered to US soldiers and expatriate oil workers. Television began in Iraq in 1957, in Iran in 1958, in Lebanon in 1959, and in Egypt in 1960.

Many Latin American and Caribbean countries also established television services in the 1950s – notably Cuba, Venezuela, the Dominican Republic, Mexico, and Argentina. Television began in Brazil with TV Tupi in 1950, and by 1953 there were four channels, all in either Rio de Janeiro or São Paulo. Programming was heavily dependent upon sponsorship. In the late 1950s, President Juscelino Kubitschek promoted the spread of television in Brazil, a process that was hastened in the 1960s with the advent of cheaper TV sets and the widespread availability of videotape.

Although countries throughout the world adopted the medium of television during this period, many of them lacked the resources to produce their own programmes and relied instead on imports, which usually came from the USA. By the mid-1950s, around one-third of programmes made by the three major US networks – ABC (American Broadcasting Company), CBS (Columbia Broadcasting System), and NBC (National Broadcasting Company) – were being produced in Hollywood, and were aimed at the export market. In the 1960s, countries throughout the world were importing many US television programmes. By the early 1970s, this trade generated business worth annually around $100 million for the US television companies.

In many countries, US influence was extremely pervasive. American entrepreneurs owned many TV stations outside the USA, and

> **The Launch of TV in the USA**
>
> Television was launched in the USA at the opening of the World's Fair in New York City on 30 April 1939. A public demonstration of the new medium was given by NBC. Included in the telecast of the day's events were interviews with the mayor of New York, Fiorello La Guardia (1882–1947), and with President Franklin D. Roosevelt (1882–1945).

◄ **Cartoon Satirizing Television**
This cartoon of 1935 makes fun of the disadvantages of the new medium of television, by showing families in a block of flats, all mindlessly enthralled by their television sets.

soap opera A serialized domestic drama broadcast on radio or TV. Events try to mimic real-life situations, but are treated with considerable sentimentality and sensationalism. The name derives from the US soap-powder manufacturers who were the original sponsors of such programmes.

countries in its immediate vicinity, such as Canada and Mexico, were able to receive domestic American television. The influence of US popular culture was particularly strong in Latin America. US advertising agencies had established a presence there from the 1920s onwards and the three major US television networks began to export technology, programmes, and broadcasting philosophies to the region on an increasing scale from the 1960s. Moreover, in their own programmes, many national television services adopted US-style formats. For example, the **soap opera** became extremely popular in such countries as Australia and the United Kingdom.

Two technological advances helped improve the efficiency, quality, and appeal of television. First, in the mid- to late 1960s, colour transmission (experimented with from as early as 1929) began on a regular basis in the USA and parts of Europe. Secondly, the use of videotape became widespread in television in the 1970s; this gave TV producers the ability to make instant high-quality recordings of programmes and play them back immediately. Moreover, video recordings have allowed live-action sports broadcasts to be interspersed with 'instant replays' of important moments, often enhanced by the use of special techniques, such as slow motion, stop action, or reverse-angle camera shots.

The growing trend in television programming in the 1980s and 1990s has been away from information and 'high' culture and towards popular entertainment. Misgivings about declining standards and the rise of 'tabloid television' are offset by the existence of 'open-access' television in some countries, where ordinary people are given the opportunity to record their own video footage for broadcast on topics that concern them.

Satellite and Cable Television

As television signals can only be broadcast in straight lines close to the surface of the earth, to transmit these signals around the curved surface of the earth requires a satellite in geo-stationary orbit. See ASTRONOMY (VOL. 2): SPACE EXPLORATION.

Satellite broadcasting was discussed as a possibility shortly after World War II. One of the first to envisage it was the science-fiction writer Arthur C. Clarke (1917–   ). In common with others who pioneered the idea, Clarke knew that a satellite hovering 37 000 kilometres above the earth and reflecting radio signals from one country to another would create considerable problems for individual national governments, especially those that were concerned to guard their frontiers against external influence. This prediction has been borne out in the development of the medium, especially since the application of the technology in a domestic setting, where government restriction is harder to implement.

A Television Satellite Dish in Indonesia

Satellite television has experienced rapid growth throughout east and southeast Asia. However, political restrictions have hampered expansion of the potentially huge market in the People's Republic of China. ▼

Video

The invention, in the 1970s, of video recorders that could be used with domestic television sets revolutionized home entertainment. Apart from allowing recording and playing back of television programmes, video technology was exploited by film distributors, who released movies on videotape for home viewing. Films on video are usually rented. *Camcorders* (combined video recorders and cameras) have enabled people to make home movies for TV.

Satellite communication was well established by the 1970s, by which time more than 170 countries were involved in it. The dishes that received satellite signals were, however, far too large for domestic use. Only after the development of compact dishes in the following decade did the promotion of direct broadcasting by satellite (DBS) begin.

This innovation in satellite television was pioneered by Rupert Murdoch (see PRINT MEDIA). In 1983 Murdoch launched a $20 million campaign to bring satellite TV to 30 million homes in the USA. However, both this and a similar campaign in Europe met with only limited success, owing to viewers' loyalty to programmes produced nationally by the established terrestrial networks.

Faced with consumer resistance in the USA and Europe, satellite TV concerns directed their attention in the 1990s to the markets of the Far East and Middle East. In 1993 Murdoch acquired a two-thirds share of the satellite television company STAR (Satellite Television Asia Region) TV, the principal satellite broadcaster in the Far East, based in Hong Kong. Yet these markets have also presented difficulties for satellite television entrepreneurs. In China, for example, any company wishing to establish a satellite network must deal with the Chinese government, which, although reformist in economic matters, is still restrictive in social affairs and the selection of programmes. Satellite stations retransmitting news broadcasts from the Western media are looked upon with suspicion by the authorities. In late 1994, the Beijing government banned ownership of satellite dishes receiving the STAR TV service. TV censorship in the region is not confined to China; in Malaysia in the same year, the Ministry of Information, concerned that images of dissolute behaviour would corrupt youth, banned from television advertisements promoting rock concerts.

Restrictions on satellite TV are even more severe in the Middle East, where political prohibition is often backed by religious doctrine. In Iran, for example, conservatives and modernizers have had to reach a compromise over satellite TV. Around half a million homes in the capital, Tehran, are equipped with locally produced satellite dishes, and hundreds of mini-cartels have been formed among the less well-off to buy communal dishes. Conservative Muslim clergy have called for a complete ban on satellite, but this has met with opposition, especially from the powerful bazaari merchant community. Consequently, satellite television is permitted but strictly censored. Iranian audiences received pictures of the 1994 football World Cup from the USA; however, shots of the crowd in Western summer clothing of shorts and T-shirts were deemed

▲ **Still from a CNN News Broadcast**
During the Gulf War of 1991, CNN broadcast live from the Iraqi capital, Baghdad, reaching a huge audience worldwide.

too revealing and were substituted by film of another – fully dressed – crowd.

In Saudi Arabia, there are an estimated 150 000 satellite dishes and an audience of around 1 million viewers. Viewing was at its height during the Gulf War of 1991 against Iraq. However, in 1994, the Saudi government ordered all domestic satellite dishes to be dismantled and re-exported, and planned to introduce its own satellite TV service in 1995.

Cable television has also grown rapidly throughout the 1980s and 1990s. An earlier invention than satellite television, it transmits TV pictures into the homes of viewers through an underground cable rather than by means of an aerial, and was originally devised in the late 1940s to bring TV to areas experiencing poor reception by conventional methods. However, it is only since deregulation of the industry in the mid-1980s in the USA – by far the largest market for cable – that the medium has boomed. Cable TV is also expanding rapidly in China, where it is mainly supplied by a company based in Hong Kong – TVB – which has the world's largest archive of Chinese-language programmes.

As with satellite TV, cable networks gain a large part of their revenue from viewer subscriptions; a monthly fee is paid for a basic service, with an additional fee for specialized networks. Moreover, most satellite TV customers in the USA receive their programmes through the established cable networks.

One of the principal success stories of cable television has been the Cable News Network (CNN). Founded in 1980 in Atlanta, Georgia, by the US media entrepreneur Ted Turner (1938–   ), CNN is an all-news channel that runs current affairs programmes around the clock. It gained huge audiences – estimated at over 80 million people worldwide – for its

Television brought the brutality of war into the comfort of the living room. Vietnam was lost in the living rooms of America – not on the battlefields of Vietnam.

Marshall McLuhan

MTV

A highly successful venture of the late 1980s was the introduction of the cable channel Music Television (MTV) in the USA. MTV quickly attracted a large audience of young people both in the USA and, through satellite, worldwide with its broadcasts of rock music concerts and promotional videos for groups. MTV is part of the huge US media company Viacom.

▲ **Silvio Berlusconi**
This Italian media mogul used his control of several television channels and newspapers to promote his own successful political campaign for the state presidency in 1993.

coverage of the Gulf War. Turner has since founded his own communications empire, Turner Broadcasting.

The success of CNN has helped raise the profile of news broadcasting in general. Other all-news stations have been established in the USA, while the French cable service *La chaîne d'information* emulates the CNN format.

Influence of the Electronic Media

Throughout their history, the media have aroused political controversy. The debate about the influence of the media was especially sensitive in the USA between the two world wars and into the 1950s. Those who believed in 'media effects' appeared to be supported by the astonishing degree of hysteria evoked by Orson Welles's 1938 adaptation of *War of the Worlds*. More importantly, since the media in the USA were predominantly commercial, advertisers and sponsors wanted reassurances that they were not associating themselves with harmful influences.

As a consequence, much of the early scientific media research was funded by the media companies themselves and carried out by academics, such as the sociologist Paul Lazarsfeld (1901–76) of Columbia University. One of the most significant studies – Lazarsfeld's *The People's Choice*, published in 1948 – studied the effect of the media on voting. The study concluded that a "two-step flow" was in operation, whereby information was passed to the public via "opinion leaders," who were far more influential than the media.

Most subsequent research does not bear out the 'effects' hypothesis, concluding instead that the media are part of society and that their effects cannot be considered in isolation.

Many of those who were concerned about the effects of the media were also specifically concerned that the newer electronic means of communication would cheapen the quality of life and of thought in Western societies. One of the chief exponents of this argument was the British academic and literary critic F. R. Leavis (1895–1978). While Leavis thought that great literature, or even radio, had the power to excite a person's imagination, he was adamant that film and television did not.

Electronic Publishing

A publishing revolution that began in the early 1990s was the production of books designed not to be printed but to be viewed on computer screens. Such electronic publications as encyclopedias have some distinct advantages over printed resources. For example, the use of *multimedia* can help enliven an encyclopedia entry – with computer animations, or (with the addition of sound reproduction facilities to a microcomputer) excerpts of speech or music. Electronic books are usually distributed by means of a *CD-ROM* (compact disc read-only memory).

THE TELE-NOVELA IN LATIN AMERICA

In Latin America (especially Brazil) a highly popular indigenous television product has developed, known as the *tele-novela*. Unlike the soap opera, the tele-novela is a complete self-contained story, albeit extremely long-running. For example, in 1964–65 in Brazil, TV Tupi's *The Right to be Born*, about a poor wet nurse and her relationship with a wealthy family, ran for eight months, while *Redemption*, which was begun in 1966 by TV Excelsior (also in Brazil), ran daily for 596 episodes. When *The Right to be Born* ended, the cast appeared before a crowd of 25 000 in the Maracaná Stadium in Rio de Janeiro. In general, however, a series runs for around 300 episodes. By 1989 TV Globo had produced 155 novelas, comprising a total of 22 000 episodes. On average, three novelas are shown nightly in prime time, six days a week for a duration of six months. Each episode is usually an hour long.

An episode costs around $10 000 dollars, but generates over twice that amount in advertising and export revenue: Brazilian novelas have been sold to over 45 countries, including Iceland, Kuwait, and Australia.

In prime time, the audience for a tele-novela is 50–60 million people. The dramas deal with popular themes, such as scandal, social mobility, love, and class conflict. Their popularity has helped promote commercial and social objectives. For example, the 1960s

▲ **Star of the Novela** *Escrava Isaura This popular series told the story of a White slave's efforts in 19th-century Brazil to gain her freedom.*

Mexican novela *Simplemente Maria*, the story of a slum girl who rises from seamstress to top fashion designer, boosted the sales of Singer sewing machines (the programme's sponsor) in Latin America. This novela was shown throughout the continent.

In terms of social influence, another Mexican novela, *Ven Conmigo*, successfully promoted adult literacy.

Critics of novelas argue that they depoliticize important issues and offer simple solutions to complex problems.

Many early critics of the electronic media criticized the USA's dominant influence and especially the way its media products threatened to obliterate other national cultures. This argument is often advanced against satellite broadcasting nowadays. Both right-wing and communist regimes fought for decades to keep out the 'decadent' Western media from their countries. Indeed, in 1989, the fact that the majority of East Germans were able to receive objective West German TV reports of the brutal repression of dissent in communist China helped fuel their dissatisfaction with their own regime. Satellite TV is thought to have been a factor in the downfall of other eastern European socialist regimes in 1989–91.

Whether or not their influence is seen as beneficial or malign, the fact that the media are often inextricably bound up in the world of politics cannot be denied. In democratic systems, politicians have learned to exploit the electronic media to their own advantage; the **sound bite** has become a significant element in modern political campaigning. In undemocratic circumstances, such as military coups, both rebels and government forces accord great importance to control of the airwaves. For example, in the attempted coups that took place in Russia in 1991 and 1993, the *Ostankino* state broadcaster was the scene of fierce battles.

The electronic media have come to play a major role in elections. Much air time is devoted to interviewing candidates, monitoring the popularity of parties, and projecting results from opinion polls. A prominent feature of the presidential election that is held every four years in the USA is the series of televised debates between the main contenders. Performance in these has been shown to have a marked effect on a candidate's chances.

Concerns have been raised about concentration of ownership of the mass media in too few hands. It has been claimed that the heads of the major multinational multimedia conglomerates exert far too great an influence in the transmission of information and hence in the formation of public opinion. In particular, misgivings have been expressed in the USA, the United Kingdom, and Australia about the extensive holdings of Rupert Murdoch's vast News Corporation concern, which owns book publishers, newspapers, film studios, radio stations, and both terrestrial and satellite TV channels in these and other countries.

A powerful media mogul in Latin America is the Brazilian Roberto Marinho, who runs one of the world's largest media monopolies. Marinho's company, Globo, controls most of the book and magazine publishing, radio, and terrestrial and cable television in Brazil. TV Globo began in 1966, with financial and technical support from the US publishing concern Time-Life. Although its programming is varied and based on detailed audience research, TV Globo reflects the views of its founder and proprietor. Its nightly half-hour news programme *Journal Nacional*, which is watched by around three-quarters of the Brazilian population, is a mixture of facts and opinions. Globo's principal rivals are Radio/TV Bandeirantes, TV Manchete, and TV Record, all of which are commercial companies. Although there is a public channel, and the state decrees two hours of educational television per day, there is little tradition of public-service broadcasting in Brazil; television is heavily dependent on advertising, and is consequently highly vulnerable to political pressure.

Likewise, in 1993, the Italian entrepreneur Silvio Berlusconi (1936–) used the resources of his massive holding company Fininvest to found a new coalition of right-wing political parties – Forza Italia – and his media holdings to promote his own successful campaign for the Italian presidency. His power had its limits, however: he was obliged to resign in 1994 and was arraigned on charges of corruption.

▲ **African Tribesmen Watching TV**
The Mursi, a tribe in southern Ethiopia, are seen watching a television programme made about their culture by a Western TV crew. Although television has benefited many people through its use in education, many would argue that it also undermines traditional ways of life.

sound bite A short pithy sentence or phrase extracted by radio or TV editors from a politician's speech or interview.

327

RADIO AND TV IN EDUCATION

BROADCASTING IS MOST commonly used for entertainment. However, in many countries around the world, a proportion of radio and television air time is given over to educational programmes.

TYPES OF EDUCATIONAL BROADCAST
Programmes for learning cover the full spectrum of educational instruction, from basic literacy classes to university degree courses. In some cases, they form part of distance education – teaching in which the tutor and student are separated from one another. In other instances, they are designed to supplement traditional classroom teaching.

TV in Rural Africa *Children and adults in Niger, West Africa watch a TV set run on solar power. Many new TV technologies can now transmit programmes – especially of an educational nature – to remote regions.*

PROVIDERS OF PROGRAMMES
Most educational broadcasting is the result of government initiatives. For example, in Britain the BBC transmits television and radio courses for the state-sponsored Open University, an adult higher learning project that has around 90 000 students enrolled. The Japanese NHK national network has the world's largest output of educational programmes. In some areas – e.g. Latin America – religious bodies are at the forefront of educational broadcasting.

OLD AND NEW TECHNOLOGIES
Radio remains a vital medium for educational broadcasts, since it can reach some remote areas (e.g. the Andean highlands of South America) that have no mains electricity.

Terrestrial television also plays a role in instruction: in Côte d' Ivoire in West Africa, the *Télé pour Tous* project, begun in 1973, broadcasts once a week on health-care and agricultural matters.

Satellite television is increasingly being used to reach remote learners. The University of the South Pacific, based in Fiji, beams university courses in English to surrounding Polynesian island groups (e.g. Tuvalu and Kiribati).

For adult learners, use of the electronic media has proved highly successful. However, UN education agencies have questioned the value of distance education in teaching children, since children require interaction with a teacher if they are to learn effectively.

Sesame Street *One of the most successful educational programmes for young children is the US series Sesame Street, first broadcast in 1969. The show is based around a cast of cartoon and puppet characters, such as 'Big Bird' (right), and aims to teach 3- to 5-year-olds basic reading, counting, and social skills. Sesame Street has been exported to over 60 countries.*

EDUCATIONAL BROADCASTING IN LATIN AMERICA
In many parts of Latin America, radio and television has been used for a wide range of educational purposes. These include schools broadcasts to supplement the work of teachers, programmes to help combat illiteracy, and transmissions aimed specifically at those engaged in farming, giving instruction in more effective agricultural methods.

Although much distance education is provided by individual states, the Roman Catholic Church has been a prime mover in establishing media networks to spread information on social and practical matters (e.g. health education). Stations run by the Church include Acción Cultural Popular in Colombia and Rede Nacional de Emissôras Católicas in Brazil.

Education by Satellite *Pupils in Jurvena, Mato Grosso, Brazil outside a school equipped with a satellite dish to receive educational programmes.*

Index

Combined Index

References in **bold capitals** *are to volumes, which appear in the following order:*

> **W:** stands for The World (Volume 1)
> **S:** stands for General Science (Volume 2)
> ⎫ Book 1

> **B:** stands for Biological Science (Volume 3)
> **A:** stands for The Arts (Volume 4)
> ⎫ Book 2

> **H:** stands for World History (Volume 5)
> **P:** stands for People/Society (Volume 6)
> ⎫ Book 3

Within each volume, references in SMALL CAPITALS *are to sections or supersections in that volume:*

In The World (**W:**)—CLIM: stands for Climate and Vegetation of the World, PEOP: for Peoples of the World, LANG: for Languages of the World, EU: for Europe, AS: for Asia, AF: for Africa, AM: for The Americas, OC: for Oceania and Australasia, PR: for Polar Regions, EAR: for Earth Sciences, and AST: for Astronomy.

In General Science (**S:**)—MA: stands for Mathematics, PH: for Physics, CH: for Chemistry, TE: for Technology, and CO: for Computers.

In Biological Science (**B:**)—CBG: stands for Cell Biology and Genetics, BCH: for Biochemistry, AAP: for Animal Anatomy and Physiology, PAP: for Plant Anatomy and Physiology, CP: for The Creationist Perspective, HF: for The Human Family MB: for Microbiology, PL: for Plants and Plant Allies, AK: for The Animal Kingdom, ECO: for Ecology, MED: for Medicine and Health Care, AG: for Agriculture, and BTEC: for Biotechnology.

In The Arts (**A:**)—VIS: stands for The Visual Arts, MUS: for Music, PER: for The Performing Arts, and LIT: for The Literary Arts.

In World History (**H:**)—INT: stands for Introduction to History, EU: for Europe and the Middle East, AM: for The Americas, AS: for Asia and Oceania, AF: for Sub-Saharan Africa, and TWC: for The World in the 20th Century.

In People/Society (**P:**)—SOC: stands for Social Sciences, PHIL: for Philosophy, REL: for Religion, POL: for Politics and Government, LAW: for Law, ECON: for Economics, BUS: for Business and Finance, and COM: for Communications and Media.

Within all volumes:

—Numbers refer to page numbers.

—Normal type is used to show references to the main text of the articles.

—For important references, such as main chapter headings and subheadings, the page number is printed in **bold** type.

—*Italic* type for the page number indicates a reference to a relevant illustration – in this case the term will be found in the caption.

—The symbol □ indicates that the reference is to a tinted definition box, margin text box, or feature panel on the page given. In references to Life Sciences (**B:**), the symbol * indicates that the reference is to a classification panel.

Photograph Acknowledgements

All illustrations reproduced in this encyclopedia are protected by copyright. The publishers gratefully acknowledge permission to reproduce illustrations supplied by the bodies listed below.

Archiv für Kunst und Geschichte, 11, 61, 68, 95 (top), 101, 207, 233, 312; Bridgeman Art Library, London, vii, ix (bottom), 21, 27 (bottom, top right), 53, 70, 73, 74, 79 (bottom), 83, 84, 87, 89, 94, 205, 208, 218; British Library, 132; Camera Press/Peter Abbey, 82; Sue Cunningham Photographic, 328 (bottom); Derby Museums and Art Gallery, 104; E T Archive, 90, 158 (all), 175 (top), 182, 209, 321, 323; Mary Evans Picture Library, 152 (bottom), 153, 212, 238 (bottom), 313 (top and bottom), 314; Faber and Faber/MSI, 23; Werner Forman Archive, 107, 142, 143, 151 (top and bottom), 152 (top), 154, 155, 156, 157; Globo International, 326 (bottom); Sonia Halliday Photographs, 111, 128, 131, 206; Harvard University, Department of Philosophy, 96; Michael Holford, 210; Hulton Deutsch, 3, 7, 8, 9, 10, 20, 27 (centre), 36, 66, 76, 77, 95 (bottom), 98, 99, 112 (top), 125, 161, 162, 163, 164, 166, 169, 173, 191, 192, 245, 261, 268 (top), 304, 315 (top), 319 (top right), 322 (top left); Hutchison Library, 19, 24, 25, 28, 38, 108, 109, 135, 137 (top), 144, 145, 146, 149, 262, 316, 327; The Image Bank, 63, 291; Israel Museum, Jerusalem, 112 (bottom); Koninklijke Bibliotheek, The Hague, 75; Magnum/Abbas, x (top), 26, 130, 319 (top); Magnum/Bruno Barbey, 137 (bottom); Magnum/René Burri, 51, 88; Magnum/David Hurn, 216 (bottom); Magnum/Constantine Manos, 45; Magnum/Susan Meiselas, 35, 203; Magnum/Mayer, 250; Magnum/James Nachtwey, 18 (bottom), 48; Magnum/Michael Nichols, 47; Magnum/Raghu Rai, 22, 140, 287 (top); Magnum/Marc Riboud, 228; Magnum/F. Scianna, 326 (top); Magnum/Stone, 16; Magnum/Alex Webb, ix (top), 271, 309; The Mansell Collection, 150; Martin Marix Evans, 247; Eleanor Muir, 81; National Gallery, London, 154 (top); Novosti, 67; Panos Pictures, 238 (centre), 315 (bottom), 324; Diana Phillips, 269; Photostage, 100; Popperfoto, 266; Range Pictures, 86, 175 (top right), 226, 229 (top), 237, 258, 265, 268 (bottom), 322 (top); Reuters, 320; Rex Features/Assignments, 231; Rex Features/P. Beney, 18 (top); Rex Features/E. Boloizsar, 227; Rex Features/Borich, 214; Rex Features/Boutin, 39; Rex Features/Peter Brooker, 59, 186 (bottom), 287 (bottom), 301 (top); Rex Features/

A. Brutman, 114; Rex Features/Angelo Cavalli, 2; Rex Features/Chamussy, 4; Rex Features/Carla Conway, 102; Rex Features/Clive Dixon, 103, 223; Rex Features/B. Jones, 305; Rex Features/Nils Jorgensen, 58, 216 (top); Rex Features/James Kelly, 219; Rex Features/Esko Keski-Oja, 43; Rex Features/F. Monaco, 15; Rex Features/News International, 176; Rex Features/Joe Partridge, 215; Rex Features/J. Passow, 172; Rex Features/Photo Press Service, 196; Rex Features/Photoreporters, 188; Rex Features/Elmars Rudzitis, 5; Rex Features/SIPA, 12, 54, 110, 113, 116, 122, 123, 124, 134, 170, 174, 175 (inset), 177, 179, 180, 189, 193, 194 (bottom), 197, 198, 199, 200, 211, 217, 221, 230, 297, 301 (bottom), 302, 303; Rex Features/SIPA/Al Jawad, 325; Rex Features/SIPA/Aral, 236; Rex Features/SIPA/ASL, 310; Rex Features/SIPA/Ricardo Azoury, 263; Rex Features/SIPA/Chan, 273; Rex Features/SIPA/Chesnot, 220, 274; Rex Features/SIPA/Frilet, 55; Rex Features/SIPA/Thomas Haley, 317; Rex Features/SIPA/Stefan Husch, 224; Rex Features/SIPA/Lena Kara, 213 ; Rex Features/SIPA/Laski, 178, 244; Rex Features/SIPA/Yoav Lemmer, 232; Rex Features/SIPA/Ludwig, 175 (centre); Rex Features/SIPA/Frederico Mendes, 276; Rex Features/SIPA/Maria Muinos, vi, 50; Rex Features/SIPA/Nicolas, 234; Rex Features/SIPA/Mark Peters, 255; Rex Features/SIPA/Renaudeau, 185; Rex Features/SIPA/Johan Roos, 186 (top); Rex Features/SIPA/Schneider, 202; Rex Features/SIPA/Shone, 222; Rex Features/SIPA/Torregano, 175 (bottom); Rex Features/R. Sowersby, 69; Rex Features/Hans Steinmeier, 240; Rex Features/J. Stephen, 138; Rex Features/Strong, viii (bottom), 181; Rex Features/Today, 318; Rex Features/Ian Turner 46; Rex Features USA, 119; Rex Features/Paul Vreeker, 235; Royal Anthropological Institute, London, 29; Scala, 117, 121, 160; Science and Society Picture Library, 93; Science Photo Library, x (bottom), 44, 279, 280; Scope Features, 328 (top); Scottish National Portrait Gallery, 80 (bottom); South American Pictures/Tony Morrison, 187, 229 (bottom); Still Pictures/Mark Edwards, 328 (centre); Sharada Sugirtharajah, 136, 147, 148; Telegraph Colour Library, 1, 159; John Timbers, 80; Trinity College, Dublin, 118; Trustees of the Chester Beatty Library, Dublin, 129; University College, London, 85; Warburg Institute, 78; Whitworth Art Gallery, University of Manchester, 105; Zefa Pictures, viii (top), 6, 52, 65, 71, 106, 126, 165, 168, 194 (top), 201, 204.

Contributors

Professor John Armstrong; Dr Elaine Baldwin; Michael Bird; Professor Brian Bocking; Dr James L. Cox; Dr Hayley Davis; Keith Faulks; Professor Christopher Gane; Professor Wyn Grant; Barry Harrison; Professor G. Ainsworth Harrison; Philip Hodgkiss; Professor Alan James; Dr Hugh Lawson-Tancred; Dr Jeremy MacClancy; Dr Jonathan Magonet; Dr David Mitchell; Dr Andrew Reeve; Professor Philip T. Smith; Kenneth Starling; Dr Tom Stoneham; Sharada Sugirtharajah; Dr Richard Tames; Professor Leonard Tivey; Stephen Wagg; Dr Alan Ware; Dr Robert Youngson

MANAGING EDITORS: John Daintith PhD, Elizabeth Martin MA
EDITORIAL ASSISTANTS: Jonathan Law, Fran Alexander, Giles Wilkes
DESIGN: Bob Gordon, Shelagh Ormiston
ARTWORK DIRECTION: Lynn Williams
ILLUSTRATORS: Hélène Burrow, David Woodroff, Eugene Fleury, Evi Antoniou, Simon Tegg, Richard Tibbitts, Karen Hiscock, Kevin Maddison
COMPUTER GRAPHICS: Aitch Em Ltd, Hardlines Ltd, Micromap Ltd
PICTURE RESEARCH: Diana Phillips, Adrian Bentley, Linda Wells
PRODUCTION: Ann Furtado, Anne Stibbs
COMPUTERIZATION: Edmund Wright, Anne Owen